Corporate Governance in Context

were chosen as an example of fairly new structures replacing restraints by government and trust among the players. Subsidies are a way of creating as well as distorting markets, with their predominant feature probably being the distortion of markets. However, governments everywhere are inclined to use them for political ends. In contrast to this, regulatory activities in the form of anti-trust legislation are indispensable for reining in private economic might – especially of recently privatized former state monopolies (part IV).

As government withdraws from the market – at least in terms of governance – intermediaries such as banks and accountants face growing tasks and, correspondingly, growing responsibilities. These are addressed in the fifth section. There is a persistent need to develop a pervasive theory of information, with its central role as a prerequisite for a functioning market and as a tool for policing it. For the provision and use of information, banks face multiple tasks – some old, others new. One essential function has shifted to accountants: the growing responsibility to ensure that the corporate players in the market are playing by the rules by shedding light on any wrongful and deceitful practices (part V).

This book goes back to an international and interdisciplinary conference held in Berlin from the 9th to the 11th of September 2004, jointly organized by the Hamburg Max Planck Institute for Foreign Private and Private International Law and the Japanese German Center Berlin. This in turn was – in a loose way – a follow-up to several other conferences: the 1995 symposium held in Berlin (H Baum [ed] *Japan: Economic Success and Legal System* [1997]); the 1997 symposium held in Hamburg (KJ Hopt, H Kanda, M Roe, E Wymeersch, S Prigge [eds] *Comparative Corporate Governance: The State of the Art and Emerging Research* [OUP 1998]); the 2000 symposium held in Siena (KJ Hopt, E Wymeersch [eds] *Capital Markets and Company Law* [OUP 2003]); and the 2003 symposium held in Syracuse (G Ferrarini, KJ Hopt, J Winter, E Wymeersch [eds] *Reforming Company and Takeover Law in Europe* [OUP 2004]). The aim of this book is to forward the previous discussions by broadening the perspective and putting corporate governance in the context of the more general change of governance addressed at the beginning,

Special thanks are due to *Wolf-Georg Ringe* and to *Ingeborg Stahl*, both at the Hamburg Max Planck Institute, for successfully coping with the challenge of converting the multitude of varying manuscripts into a coherent print-ready format. As always, *Kristen Zetzsche* of Winchester Bay, Oregon, took care of language issues.

The conference was supported by *Nishimura & Partners,* Attorneys at Law, Tokyo; the *Society of the Friends of the JDZB*, Berlin; *Bayerische Motoren Werke (BMW)*, Munich; and *All Nippon Airways (ANA)*, Tokyo. We are very grateful for their generous assistance – the project would not have been feasible without it.

August 2005

KJ Hopt & *H Baum*, Hamburg
H Kanda, Tokyo
E Wymeersch, Ghent

Contents

Abbreviations

A2d	Atlantic Reporter 2nd Series
AC	Law Reports Appeal Cases
ADR	American Despositary Receipt
AG	Aktiengesellschaft (German stock corporation)
AJCL	American Journal of Comparative Law
All ER	All England Law Reports
AMF	Autorité des Marchés Financiers
Anh	Anhang
ANSA	Association Nationale des Sociétés par Actions
Art	Article
BaFin	Bundesanstalt für Finanzdienstleistungsaufsicht (German Financial Regulatory Authority)
BBC	British Broadcasting Corporation
BCCI	Bank of Credit and Commerce International
BCLC	Butterworth's Company Law Cases
BGB	Bürgerliches Gesetzbuch (German Civil Code)
BGHZ	Entscheidungen des Bundesgerichtshofs in Zivilsachen
CA	Court of Appeal
CA 1985	Companies Act 1985
CAC-40	Compagnie des Agents de Change-40 Index
CCBE	Council of the Bars and Law Societies of the European Union
CEO	Chief executive officer
CESR	Committee of European Securities Regulators
cf	compare
CFI	Court of First Instance
CFO	Chief Financial Officer
ch	chapter
Ch App	Law Reports: Chancery Appeal
CMEs	coordinated market economies
COB	Commission des opérations de bourse
col	column
Cong	Congress
CPA	Certified Public Accountant
DAI	Deutsches Aktieninstitut
DAV	Deutscher Anwaltsverein (German Lawyers' Association)
DAX	Deutscher Aktien-Index (German Stock Index)
DC Cir	US Court of Appeals for the District of Columbia Circuit
Del	Delaware
Del Ch	Delaware Court of Chancery
Del S Ct	Delaware Supreme Court
DG Comp	Directorate-General for Competition
DoJ	Department of Justice
DTA	Deferred Tax Asset
DTI	Department of Trade and Industry (UK)
EC	European Community

ECB	European Central Bank
ECGI	European Corporate Governance Institute
ECHR	European Convention of Human Rights
ECJ	European Court of Justice
ECR	European Court Reports
ed / eds	editor / editors
edn	edition
EEA	European Economic Area
EEC	European Economic Community
eg	exempli gratia (for example)
ERI	Economic Research Institute
EU	European Union
EUI	European University Institute
Eur	European
f / ff	following
F2d	Federal Reporter 2nd Edition
F3d	Federal Reporter - US Circuit Courts of Appeals cases
FASB	Financial Accounting Standards Board
FRC	Financial Reporting Council
FSA	Financial Services Authority
FSMA 2000	Financial Services and Markets Act 2000
F Supp	Federal Supplement
FT	Financial Times
FTC	Fair Trade Commission (Japan)
FTSE	Financial Times Stock Exchange
FY	Fiscal Year
GAAP	Generally Accepted Accounting Principles
GAC	Committee on Governmental Affairs
GAO	General Accounting Office
GATS	General Agreement on Trade in Services
GATT	General Agreement on Trade and Tariffs
GDP	Gross Domestic Product
GmbH	Gesellschaft mit beschränkter Haftung
GNE	Gross National Expenditure
HL	House of Lords
HM	Her Majesty
IAS	International Accounting Standards
IASB	International Accounting Standards Board
ICLQ	International and Comparative Law Quarterly
ibid	ibidem (at the same place)
ie	id est (that is)
IFRS	International Financial Reporting Standards
IMF	International Monetary Fund
inc	incorporated
intl	international
IOSCO	International Organization of Securities Commissions
IOU	I owe you
IPO	Initial Public Offering
IRB	internal rating-based

J	Journal
JDB	Japan Development Bank
JFEO	Japan Federation of Economic Organisations
JFTC	Japanese Fair Trade Commission
JICPA	Japan Institute of Certified Public Accountants
L	Law
LBO	Leveraged Buy-Out
LC	Lord Chancellor
LDP	Liberal Democratic Party (Japan)
LJ	Lord Justice
LLC	Limited Liability Corporation
LLP	Limited Liability Partnership
LME	liberal market economies
Ltd	Limited
MBA	Master of Business Administration
MBO	Management Buy-Out
MEDEF	Mouvement des Entreprises de France
METI	Ministry of Economy, Trade and Industry (Japan)
MIT	Massachusetts Institute of Technology
MP	Member of Parliament
n	note
NED	non-executive director
NYSE	New York Stock Exchange
no	number
NASDAQ	National Association of Securities Dealers Automatic Quotation
NBFI	non-banking financial intermediary
NGO	Non-Governmental Organisation
NIE	New Institutional Economics
NTT	Nippon Telegraph and Telephone
OECD	Organisation for Economic Co-operation and Development
OFR	operating and financial review
OFT	Office of Fair Trading
OJ	Official Journal of the EU
OJLS	Oxford Journal of Legal Studies
OPEC	Organisation of the Petroleum Exporting Countries
OSE	Osaka Stock Exchange
OUP	Oxford University Press
p / pp	page / pages
para / paras	paragraph / paragraphs
PC	Privy Council
PCAOB	Public Company Accounting Oversight Board
PECL	Principles of European Contract Law
PhD	Philosophiae Doctor (Doctor of Philosophy)
POBA	Professional Oversight Board for Accountancy (UK)
plc	public limited company
PSI	Permanent Subcommittee on Investigations
pt	part
Q	Quarterly
QB	Queen's Bench

Rev	Review
R&D	Research and Development
SA	société anonyme
sch	schedule
Sct	Supreme Court
SE	Societas Europaea, European Company
s / ss	section / sections
SEC	Securities and Exchange Commission
SI	Statutory Instruments
SLIM	Simpler Legislation for the Internal Market
SME	smaller and medium enterprises
SOA / SOX	Sarbanes-Oxley Act
SPE	special purpose entity
SSR	sector-specific regulation
TSE	Tokyo Stock Exchange
U	University
UCC	Uniform Commercial Code
UK	United Kingdom
UKLA	United Kingdom Listing Authority
UMAG	Gesetz zur Unternehmensintegrität und Modernisierung des Anfechtungsrechts (German Act Regarding Integrity of Companies and Modernization of Stock Corporation Law)
UNCITRAL	United Nations Commission on International trade Law
URN	Unique reference number
US	United States
USC	United States Code
USSC	United States Sentencing Commission
vol	volume
WpÜG	Wertpapiererwerbs- und Übernahmegesetz (German takeover law)
WS	Written Statement
WTO	World Trade Organisation

The Contributors

Harald Baum

Harald Baum is Senior Research Fellow and Head of the Japan Law Department at the Max Planck Institute for Foreign Private Law and Private International Law, Hamburg, Germany; Privatdozent at the University of Hamburg; Research Associate at the European Corporate Governance Institute, Brussels; Vice-president of the German-Japanese Association of Jurists. He graduated from Freiburg University (1977), worked as AvH/JSPS Research Fellow at Kyoto University (1990/91), and served as Visiting Professor at the University of Tokyo (2005). PD Dr Baum is the Founding and Executive Editor of the *Journal of Japanese Law / Zeitschrift für Japanisches Recht* (since 1996) and has authored numerous books and articles on business law, corporate governance, takeovers, and capital markets regulation in Germany, the EU, Japan, and the US.

Gary M. Brown

Gary M. Brown is Chairman of the Corporate Department at Baker, Donelson, Bearman, Caldwell & Berkowitz, pc. He graduated from Vanderbilt University: JD (Order of the Coif) – 1980; Special Projects Editor, *Vanderbilt Law Review*; BA (*magna cum laude*) Economics – 1977; Minor in Business Administration. Practice: Securities; Corporate Governance and Compliance; Government Investigations; since 1994 listed in *Best Lawyers in America*. Government employment: Special Counsel – United States Senate Committee on Governmental Affairs; (Minority) – *Enron* investigation (2002). Teaching experience: *Adjunct Professor of Law* – Vanderbilt University School of Law (corporate and securities law); *Chairman and Faculty Member* – Practising Law Institute (securities law programs). Recent publications: 'Ethics: It's Not Just For Lawyers Anymore' (2005) 2 The Corporate Compliance & Regulatory Newsletter no 8; 'Resisting Temptation – New Sentencing Guidelines Prod Companies to Take Ethics More Seriously' *Legal Times* (15 November 2004).

John C. Coffee Jr

Professor John C. Coffee Jr is the Adolf A. Berle Professor of Law at Columbia University Law School and Director of its Center on Corporate Governance. He is a Fellow at the American Academy of Arts and Sciences, and for the last six years he has been listed by the National Law Journal as among its '100 Most Influential Lawyers in America'. His specialties include complex litigation, corporate governance, securities regulation, and 'white collar crime'. Professor Coffee has been a member of the Legal Advisory Board to the New York Stock Exchange, the Legal Advisory Board of the NASD, the Market Regulation Committee of the NASD, and is currently a member of the Economic Advisory Board to Nasdaq. He served as a Reporter to the American Law Institute for its Principles of Corporate Governance: Analysis and Recommendations, was a member of the SEC's Advisory Committee on the Capital Formation and Regulatory Processes, and served as chairperson of the Section on Business Associations of the Association of American Law Schools. He is the author or editor of several widely used casebooks on corporations, securities regulation, takeovers, and business organization and finance, including Coffee and Seligman, Cases and Materials on Securities Regulation (9th edn 2000) and Klein and Coffee, Business Organization and Finance (8th edn 2000). Professor Coffee has also been a visiting Professor of Law at Harvard, Stanford, Michigan and Virginia law schools and at several foreign law schools and began his teaching career at Georgetown University Law Center. Before entering academia, he practiced corporate law as an associate with the firm of Cravath, Swaine & Moore in New York City. He is a graduate of the Yale Law School and Amherst College.

Paul L. Davies

Paul L. Davies is Cassel Professor of Commercial Law at the London School of Economics and Political Science. He is a graduate of the University of Oxford (1966) and holds Masters' degrees from the London School of Economics (1968) and Yale Law School (1969). After a short initial teaching spell at the University of Warwick, he joined the Law Faculty of the University of Oxford and eventually became Professor of the Law of the Enterprise. He took up his present post at LSE in 1998. He has held visiting positions at Yale and the universities of Bordeaux, Paris, Bonn and a number of universities in South Africa. He is a Fellow of the British Academy. He is the author of *Introduction to Company Law* (2002) and the editor of the 6th and 7th edition of *Gower's Principles of Modern Company Law* and one of the editors of *Palmer's Company Law*. He was a member of the Steering Group of Company Law Review carried out under the auspices of the Department of Trade and Industry in the UK between 1998 and 2001.

Guido A. Ferrarini

Guido Ferrarini graduated from the Genoa Law School in 1972, and obtained an LLM from Yale Law School in 1978. He is Professor of Business Law at the University of Genoa and Director of the Centre for Law and Finance. He is Lead Independent Director of Telecom Italia SpA; Independent Director of Autostrade SpA, and Chairman of TLX (an Italian MTF and investment exchange). He is Vice-Chairman of the European Corporate Governance Institute, Brussels, and Independent Director of Assogestioni (the Italian Asset Managers Association). He was a member of the Board of Trustees of the International Accounting Standards Committee (IASC), London, from 2000 to 2004. He is the author of various books and articles in the fields of financial law, corporate law, and business law. He was a Visiting Professor at Bonn University, Columbia Law School, Hamburg University and University College London. He is presently a Visiting Professor at NYU Law School.

Thomas B. Ginsburg

Tom Ginsburg is Professor of Law and Political Science at the University of Illinois, Urbana-Champaign, where he directs the Program on Asian Law, Politics and Society. He has spent several years working on law and democracy programs in Asia, taught law at Kyushu University in Japan, and clerked at the Iran-US Claims Tribunal in The Hague. Professor Ginsburg has lectured at universities in Asia and Europe, and authored the book Judicial Review in New Democracies, winner of the 2004 C. Herman Pritchett award from the American Political Science Association.

Stefan Grundmann

Professor Dr Dr Stefan Grundmann, LLM (Berkeley), has been Professor at Humboldt-University, Berlin, for German, European and International Private and Business Law since 2004. He heads the Institute for banking and capital market law, and is currently the deputy of the faculty for the creation of the European Law School. He was professor for the same subjects in Erlangen (2001-2004), where he also headed the interdisciplinary Institute for European Business Law, and at the Martin-Luther-University in Halle-Wittenberg (1995-2001), where he founded their Institute for Business Law and the related study course in Business Law. His main publications include (besides more than 100 articles and contributions) a large monograph on 'Relationships of "Trust"', several commentaries on contract and banking law and an overall commentary or textbook on European Contract Law (1999) and on European Company and Capital Market Law (2004). He is co-founder and president of the Society of European Contract Law since 2001.

John O. Haley

John O. Haley is the Wiley B. Rutledge Professor of Law and Director of the Whitney R. Harris Institute for Global Legal Studies at the Washington University School of Law in St. Louis. Before joining the Washington University faculty, Professor Haley was the Garvey, Schubert & Barer Professor of Law, Professor of International Studies and Director of the Asian Law program at the University of Washington, where he taught from 1974. Considered a leading American authority on Japanese law, he has authored numerous books and articles on Japanese and comparative law including the award-winning *Authority without Power: Law and the Japanese Paradox* (OUP 1991), *The Spirit of*

Japanese Law (University of Georgia Press 1998), and, most recently, *Antitrust in Germany and Japan: The First Fifty Years, 1947-1998* (University of Washington Press 2001). He is also the co-author with John Henry Merryman and David S. Clark of *The Civil Law Tradition: Europe, Latin America and East Asia* (Michie).

Hans-Jürgen Hellwig

Hans-Jürgen Hellwig is partner of the law firm Hengeler Mueller. He was born in 1940. Legal Studies in Germany and Switzerland; Dr iur, Bonn University (1967); admitted to the Bar of Frankfurt am Main, Germany (1969). His main areas of practice are German and European Company Law and Capital Markets Law. He is a Honorary Professor for European Company Law at Heidelberg University, a Member of the European Corporate Governance Institute, Brussels, and holds the Chair at the Company Law Committee of the Council of the Bars and Law Societies of Europe (CCBE), Brussels.

Martin F. Hellwig

Martin Hellwig was born in 1949 in Düsseldorf, Germany. He holds a diploma in economics from the University of Heidelberg (1970) and a doctorate in economics from the Massachusetts Institute of Technology (1973). Following a postdoctoral year at Stanford University, he held academic positions at Princeton University, the University of Bonn , the University of Basle and the University of Mannheim, before moving to the Max Planck Institute for Research on Collective Goods in Bonn in 2004. He also held visiting positions at the Université Catholique de Louvain, the London School of Economics, Hebrew University, Jerusalem, and Harvard University. He has written extensively on the economics of information and innovation, on financial markets, financial institutions, financial regulation, and corporate governance, and on the theoretical foundations of public economics. Martin Hellwig is a Fellow of the Econometric Society, a former President of the European Economic Association and of the German Economic Association (Verein für Socialpolitik), an Honorary Member of the American Economic Association, and an Inaugural Fellow of the European Corporate Governance Institute.

Gérard Hertig

Gérard Hertig is Professor of Law at the Swiss Federal Institute of Technology (ETH Zurich), where he is responsible professor for the post-graduate program 'Intellectual Property.' He was previously Professor of Administrative Law and Director of the Centre d'Etudes Juridiques Européennes at the University of Geneva Law School (1987-1995). He served as Visiting Professor at various universities, including the University of Tokyo (1996 and 2005) and practiced law as a member of the Geneva bar. Recent publications include: *The Anatomy of Corporate Law, A Comparative and Functional Approach*, with Reinier Kraakman and others (OUP 2004) and 'Four Predictions about the Future of EU Securities Regulation' with Ruben Lee, (2003) 3 Journal of Corporate Law Studies 359.

Klaus J. Hopt

Klaus J. Hopt is Professor of Law and Director at the Max Planck Institute for Foreign Private Law and Private International Law, Hamburg/Germany. 1974-1995 he was Professor of Law in Tübingen, Florence, Bern, and Munich. – *Professional:* Judge Court of Appeals Stuttgart 1981-85; member of the German Takeover Commission 1995-2001, of the High Level Group of Company Law Experts, European Commission 2001-2002, of the Takeover Advisory Board 2002-, of the Stock Exchange Experts Commission 2002-; vice-president of the German Research Foundation (Deutsche Forschungsgemeinschaft) 2002-; chairman of the Scientific Council of the Max-Planck-Society 2003-; member of the supervisory board of the Deutsche Börse AG 2003-2005; member of the board of the European Corporate Governance Institute (ECGI) 2005-; expert for the German Parliament, various Ministries, Central Bank and Constitutional Court, the European Commission, the Bank for International Settlements, Bulgaria and World Bank; arbitrator, national and international. – *Visiting Professor:* University of Pennsylvania 1979, EUI Florence 1981, 1983, Paris I (Sorbonne) 1987, Kyoto University 1988, Université Libre de Bruxelles 1990, Geneva 1991, Tokyo University 1991, University of Chicago 1994, NYU 1999, Harvard 2002, Tilburg 2003, Paris II (Panthéon-Assas) 2003-2005. – *Recent publications:* Baumbach-Hopt, Handelsgesetzbuch 32nd edn 2005 (together with Merkt); The Anatomy of Corporate Law (with Kraakmann and others) 2004 (OUP). *(Co-)Editor*: Comparative Corporate Governance 1998, Capital Markets and Company Law 2003, Reforming Company and Takeover Law in Europe 2004 (all OUP); RabelsZ, Zeitschrift für Unternehmens- und Gesellschaftsrecht (ZGR), European Company and Financial Law Review (ECFR), International and Comparative Corporate Law Journal. *Honors:* Dr iur hc mult (Université Libre de Bruxelles 1997, U. Catholique de Louvain 1997, Université de Paris V René Descartes 2000).

Hideki Kanda

Hideki Kanda is Professor of Law at the University of Tokyo. His main areas of specialisation include commercial law, corporate law, banking regulation and securities regulation. Mr Kanda served as Visiting Professor of Law at the University of Chicago Law School in 1989, 1991 and 1993, and Visiting Professor at Harvard Law School in 1996. Mr Kanda's recent publications include 'Corporate Law' (in Japanese) (6th edn Kobundo 2005); Reinier Kraakman and others 'The Anatomy of Corporate Law' (OUP 2004). He also wrote many articles in English in the areas of commercial law, corporate law, banking regulation and securities regulation.

Christian Kirchner

Professor Dr Dr Christian Kirchner, LLM (Harvard), is Professor for German, European and International Civil Law and Business Law and Institutional Economics at Humboldt University School of Law and at Humboldt University School of Business and Economics in Berlin since 1993. He graduated from Johann Wolfgang Goethe-University, Frankfurt (Main). He was Professor at University of Hanover Law School (1984-1993). Visiting professorships at the universities of Hanover (1980), Berlin (Free University) (1982), Heidelberg (1982/83), Kiel (1983), Bochum (1983/84), Tulane Law School (US), fall 1996 and spring 1997, George Mason University School of Law, Arlington, Virginia (US), fall 1998, University of Illinois at Urbana/Champaign, January 2003 and January 2004, and Fudan University, Shanghai, March 2003. He served as Legal Advisor to PR China and to various Countries of Central and Eastern Europe (since 1992) and as Legal Advisor to the World Bank (1996/1997). His fields of research are: National and international civil law and business law, namely anti-trust law and regulation, corporate law, accounting law; US law, Japanese law, Chinese law; European Community law; law and economics, new institutional economics; constitutional economics.

Christoph Kumpan

Christoph Kumpan, LLM, is a Senior Research Fellow at the Max Planck Institute for Foreign Private Law and Private International Law, Hamburg, Germany. After graduating from the University of Heidelberg in 2000 he joined the Max Planck Institute. In 2002 he obtained a masters degree (LLM) from the University of Chicago Law School. He was awarded a scholarship of the Bucerius Foundation and the Studienstiftung des Deutschen Volkes. In 2004 he passed his Second State Examination in Hamburg. In 2005, he was a special adviser to the German Federal Ministry of Finance in the field of capital markets law. He is completing his PhD on the regulation of Alternative Trading Systems and is a member of the working committee of the Stock Exchange Expert Commission at the German Federal Ministry of Finance.

Jonathan R. Macey

Jonathan R. Macey is Sam Harris Professor of Corporate Law, Corporate Finance and Securities Law at Yale University. Professor Macey received a BA (cum laude) from Harvard in 1977, a JD from Yale Law School in 1982, and a PhD *honoris causa* from the Stockholm School of Economics in 1996. Professor Macey was law clerk to Judge Henry J. Friendly on the US Court of Appeals for the Second Circuit. His research interests include corporate governance, banking, public choice and law and economics. Professor Jonathan Macey is a member of the Legal Advisory Committee to the Board of Directors of the New York Stock Exchange and a member of the Board of Editors of Thompson*West Publishing Company. He has written over 150 scholarly articles and several books.

Joseph A. McCahery

Joseph A. McCahery is Professor of Corporate Governance at the University of Amsterdam Faculty of Economics and Econometrics and Professor of International Business Law at Tilburg University Faculty of Law. He is also Goldschmidt Visiting Professor of Corporate Governance at the Solvay Business School (Brussels). He teaches banking and securities regulation and corporate law and has written widely on corporate governance, corporate law, the political economy of federalism, and taxation and has published in a wide range of academic journals.

Ernst-Joachim Mestmäcker

Professor Dr Dr hc Ernst-Joachim Mestmäcker is Director Emeritus of the Max Planck Institute for Foreign Private Law and International Private Law in Hamburg and Professor of Law at Hamburg University. – *Academic career:* He was Professor of Civil Law, Commercial Law and Economic Law at the University of Saarbrücken (1959-1963), University of Münster in Westphalen (1963-1969), at the University of Bielefeld (1969-1978); Director of the Max-Planck-Institute for Foreign Private Law and International Private Law in Hamburg from 1978-1994. From 1984 to 1990 he served as Vice President of the Max Planck Society. – *Visiting Professor*: Law School of Georgetown University Washington DC (1959); Law School University of Michigan at Ann Arbor (1965, 1967, 1975, 1991). – *Memberships and Functions:* Scientific Council of the German Ministry of Economics (Since 1962); Special Advisor of the EC Commission on Competition Policy and Harmonisation of Laws (1962-1970); Founding President University of Bielefeld (1967-1969); First Chairman of the German Monopolies Commission (1974-1978); Member and Chairman of the Commission on Concentration in the Media in Germany (1997–2003).– *Honours and Awards:* Ludwig Erhard Preis für Wirtschaftspublizistik (1980); Honorary PhD at the Faculty of Economics and Social Sciences of the University of Cologne (1980); Honorary Senator of the University of Bielefeld (1983); Ernst Hellmut Vits Preis University of Münster (1988); Honorary Senator of the Max Planck Society (1994); Member, Order pour le Mérite for Academic Sciences and Art (Mitglied, Orden pour le mérite für Wissenschaft und Künste) (1994); Hanns Martin Schleyer Preis (1997); Great Cross of Merit with Star of the Federal Republic of Germany (Großes Verdienstkreuz mit Stern des Verdienstordens der Bundesrepublik Deutschland (1997). – *Recent Publications:* Europäisches Wettbewerbsrecht, 2. Auflage, 2004 (Together with Heike Schweitzer); Wirtschaft und Verfassung in der Europäischen Union (Collection of Essays) 2003.

Curtis J. Milhaupt

Curtis J. Milhaupt is the Fuyo Professor and Director of the Center for Japanese Legal Studies at Columbia Law School. He also serves as Chair of the Transactional Study Program. Professor Milhaupt's research interests include Japanese law, comparative corporate governance, and the relationship between legal systems and market institutions. He is the co-author or editor of four books, including Law and Capitalism with Katharina Pistor (forthcoming, University of Chicago Press) and Economic Organizations and Corporate Governance in Japan: The Impact of Formal and Informal Rules with Mark West (OUP 2004).

Yoshiro Miwa

Yoshiro Miwa is Professor of Economics at the University of Tokyo. Professor Miwa has written widely on economic issues, most recently on corporate finance, corporate governance, and government regulation. Inter alia, he is the author of Firms and Industrial Organization in Japan (Macmillan, 1996) and State Competence and Economic Growth in Japan (RoutledgeCurzon, 2004). Professor Miwa has collaborated with Mark Ramseyer on a series of books and articles that explore the ties between corporate governance and corporate finance. Their latest book, *The Fable of the Keiretsu*, will be forthcoming from the University of Chicago Press in 2005.

Luke Nottage

Dr Luke Nottage is senior lecturer at the University of Sydney Faculty of Law, and a founding co-director of the Australian Network for Japanese Law (ANJeL). He studied at Kyoto University and Victoria University of Wellington, and first taught at the latter and Kyushu University Law Faculty. His book on *Product Safety and Liability in Japan: From Minamatato Mad Cows* was published by Routledge Curzon in 2004. He has also co-authored one book, co-edited another, and written over 60 major book chapters or articles, in English and Japanese. These focus on contract law, product liability, civil dispute resolution (especially arbitration), corporate governance, cyber-law, and legal education, mostly comparing developments in Japan or transnationally. Dr Nottage is also a contributing editor for Japan in the CCH 'Doing Business in Asia' looseleaf/CDROM service.

Hiroshi Oda

Professor Hiroshi Oda (LLB, LLD Tokyo University) is the Sir Ernest Satow Professor of Japanese Law at the University of London (UCL) and professor at the College d'Europe (Brugge). He held the chair of Russian law at the Faculty of Law of the University of Tokyo before moving to London. He has also held various visiting positions, including a visiting professorship at Cornell Law School (1989-1998). He is a qualified attorney in Japan and practices Japanese and Russian law in London and Tokyo. Professor Oda represents Japan in the ICC Court of Arbitration in Paris and is the author of *Russian Commercial Law* (Kluwer 2002) and *Japanese Law* (2nd edn OUP 1999). He is also the chairman of the Russo-Japanese Lawyers' Association.

Anthony I. Ogus

Anthony Ogus holds a Chair of Law at the University of Manchester (where he was Dean of the School of Law from 1990 to 1992), having previously held appointments at the Universities of Leicester, Oxford and Newcastle upon Tyne. He is also a Research Professor at the University of Maastricht. He has had visiting academic appointments in Belgium, Canada, France, Germany, Norway and the US. He has written books on the law of damages, social security law and regulation. His research interests focus on the economic analysis of law. He was joint founding editor of the International Review for Law and Economics. He was awarded the CBE in 2002.

Katharina Pistor

Katharina Pistor is Professor of Law at Columbia Law School. Before joining the faculty of Columbia Law School in 2001, she taught at the Kennedy School of Government, and worked at the Max Planck Institute for Foreign Private Law and International Private Law in Hamburg. Her main research interests are comparative law, comparative corporate governance, and the development of legal institutions with special emphasis on the evolution of law in transitional and emerging economies. Recent publications include George Bermann and Katharina Pistor (eds) *Law and Governance in an Enlarged European Union*, (Hart Publishing); Katharina Pistor and Chenggang Xu 'Incomplete Law' (2003) 35 NYU Journal of International Law and Politics 931; Dan Berkowitz Katharina Pistor and Jean-Francois Richard 'Economic Development, Legality, and the Transplant Effect' (2003) 47 European Economic Review 165; Katharina Pistor Yoram Keinan and others 'The Evolution of Corporate Law' (2002) 23 University of Pennsylvania Journal of International Economic Law 791.

J. Mark Ramseyer

J. Mark Ramseyer is Mitsubishi Professor of Japanese Legal Studies at Harvard University. He has written widely on the intersection of law and economics in Japan – most recently in litigation, judicial structure, and corporate governance. Professor Ramseyer has collaborated with Yoshiro Miwa on a series of books and articles that explore the ties between corporate governance and corporate finance. Their latest book, *The Fable of the Keiretsu*, will be forthcoming from the University of Chicago Press in 2005.

Kahei Rokumoto

Kahei Rokumoto studied law and political science at the University of Tokyo, Faculty of Law. He spent two years at UC Berkeley and its Law and Society Center on Fulbright Scholarship before obtaining his PhD from UT and joining its Law Faculty in 1970, where he hold the Chair for the Sociology of Law for thirty years till he became Emeritus. He is author of comprehensive textbooks on law and society and numerous empirical researches on legal culture, dispute processes, medical malpractice litigation, the legal profession and its reform, etc. His Western language publications include: 'Chotei (Schlichtung): eine Japanische Alternative zum Recht' in *Jahrbuch fur Rechtssoziologie und Rechtstheorie* (1980), *Sociological Theories of Law* (editor 1994), 'Law and Culture in Transition,' in *AJCL* (2002).

Reinhard H. Schmidt

Reinhard H. Schmidt is the Wilhelm Merton Professor of International Banking and Finance at the Johann Wolfgang Goethe-University in Frankfurt (Main). Before that, he held chairs for international business at the same university (1991-1998), and for finance at the University of Trier (1983-1991), and was an associate professor in Göttingen, and an assistant professor at the University of Frankfurt. He has been a visiting professor at Stanford University, Georgetown University, the Wharton School, Université Paris-Dauphine and Bocconi University. Reinhard Schmidt has published 18 books and more than 120 academic articles in journals and chapters in books. His research interests include the economic analysis of institutions and of financial systems in industrialised as well as developing and transition countries.

Heike Schweitzer

Dr Heike Schweitzer, LLM (Yale), has joined the Institute for Law and Economics at the Hamburg University as an assistant professor in 2004, where she is teaching classes in contract, tort and European corporate law in the Erasmus Mundus Program for Law & Economics. Before, she was a research fellow at the Max Planck Institute for Foreign Private Law and Private International Law. There, she has worked and published in the field of EU law, competition law and telecommunications law. Currently, she has a position as a research fellow at the Columbia University, New York. Her main research interests are in the field of EU law, competition law, corporate law and M&A.

Fumio Sensui

Fumio Sensui, LL.M., is Professor of Competition Law at Graduate School of Law, Kobe University (2000-). He graduated from Kyoto University, was Associate Professor, Faculty of Law, Osaka City University (1993-1999) and Professor, Faculty of Law, Kobe University (1999-2000). He was visiting scholar at the Max Planck Institute for Foreign Private Law and International Private Law in Hamburg and has been working with the Japan Fair Trade Commission as the Head Visiting Fellow in the JFTC's Competition Policy Research Center since 2003. His works include a comprehensive textbook on the Japan's Antimonopoly Law ('Dokusen Kinshi Ho', Kobundo, 2004, co-authored with T Kanai & N Kawahama) and numerous articles on the topics of Competition Law, Commercial Law and Intellectual Property Law.

Horst Siebert

Professor Dr Dr hc Horst Siebert is President-Emeritus of the Kiel Institute for World Economics at Kiel and AGIP Professor in International Economics at the Johns Hopkins University at Bologna. He was Professor of Economics at the University of Mannheim (1969-1984) and at the University of Konstanz, Germany (1984-1989), and President of the Institute of World Economics (1989-2003). – *Visiting Professor:* Massachusetts Institute of Technology, Cambridge (1986), Rijksuniversiteit Ghent (1990/91), Robert-Schumann-Centre of the European University Institute of Florence (1995), Conservatoire National des Arts et des Metiers (2003). – *Memberships:* Scientific Council at the Ministry of Economics (1985-), Council of Economic Advisors of German (1990-2003), Advisory Board for the Global Competitiveness Report of the World Economic Forum (1996-), Board of Trustees Fritz Thyssen Foundation (1998-), Aspen Institute Italia (1999-), 'Group of Economic Analysis (GEA)' of the European Commission (2001-), 'Group of Economic Analysis (GEA)', advising President Romano Prodi of the European Commission (2001-2004), Advisory Committee of the Claremont-Bologna International Economic Policy Forum (2004-), Eminent Persons Group (EPG) of the Van Lennep Subsidies Initiative (2004-), 'Group of Economic Policy Analysis (GEPA)', advising President Barroso of the European Commission (2005-). – *Honors and Awards:* Honorary Doctorate of the University Ghent (2000); Karl-Bräuer-Prize (German Taxpayer's Association) and Ludwig-Erhard-Prize für Wirtschaftspublizistik (1999); Bundesverdienstkreuz of the Federal Republic of Germany (2003). – *Main Areas of Research:* International trade, labour market and employment, economy of the environment, general economic policies. – *Selected recent publications*: The World Economy (2nd edn 2002), Economics of the Environment. Theory and Policy (6th rev edn 2004), The German Economy: Beyond the Social Market (2005).

Gerald Spindler

Professor Dr Gerald Spindler, holder of a diploma in economy, studied Law and Economy in Frankfurt (Main), Hagen, Geneva and Lausanne. He completed both State Exams. He received his PhD for Civil Law, Commercial and Economic Law, International Private Law, Comparative Law and Labour Law. After teaching as an associate professor in Bielefeld and Dresden, he joined the University of Göttingen in 1997. Up to date Professor Spindler is the Head of the Chair of Civil Law, Commercial and Economic Law, Comparative Law, Multimedia- and Telecommunication Law at the University of Göttingen. He has published various books, more than 100 articles in law reviews, as well as expert legal opinions and is editor of one of the most renowned German law reviews covering the whole area of cyberspace law and telecommunication law. Professor Spindler was the national and European reporter for E-Commerce during the XVIth International Conference of the International Academy of Comparative Law in Brisbane/Australia, 2002. He also acted as a speaker at the IST-Conference of the EEC on new developments in Information Society in Nice, 2000, and had been Vice-Chairman of the German Society of Law and Information Science for several years. He has advised the German, as well as the European legislator regarding various questions concerning the information society.

Misao Tatsuta

Mr Tatsuta taught corporation law, securities regulation and other areas of business law at the Faculty of Law, Kyoto University for about 40 years, 1956 through 1997. He retired there due to age, and having taught at the Faculty of Law, Kobe-Gakuin University for five years, he has been teaching at Doshisha University Law School since April 2002. He also taught as Visiting Professor at law schools in the United States, Canada, Australia and Germany. In addition to his academic activities, Mr Tatsuta played an important role in advisory committees for the national government with regard to revising corporation law and other branches of law. He joined the bar in 1997, and practices law at Oh-ebashi LPC & Partners in Osaka.

Marcel Tyrell

Dr Tyrell received his degrees from the University of Applied Sciences in Wiesbaden, Goethe-University in Frankfurt and the University of Trier. Currently, he is a part-time lecturer in the finance departments at the latter two universities. He is also involved as researcher in projects of the Center of Financial Studies, a non-profit research institution in Frankfurt, and of the Deutsche Bundesbank in Frankfurt. His research interests include financial system architecture, the role of information in capital markets and banks, relationship lending, and macro finance. Publications appeared amongst others in the *Journal of Financial Inter-*

mediation, *Journal of Institutional and Theoretical Economics*, *European Financial Management*, and *Corporate Governance: An International Review*.

Erik P.M. Vermeulen

Erik P.M. Vermeulen is Professor of Law and Management at Tilburg University Faculty of Law and Legal Counsel at Philips International NV. He teaches corporate law and international business transactions and has written widely on topics in corporate law, corporate governance, partnership law, securities regulation and venture capital. He is author of *The Evolution of Legal Business Forms in Europe and the US* (Kluwer 2003).

Eddy Wymeersch

At present, Chairman of the Banking Finance and Insurance Commission, Belgium; co-chair of the CESR-ECB, working on clearing and settlement; member of the Committees of European Securities Regulators (CESR). Part time Professor of Commercial Law, University of Ghent where he is teaching company law, securities regulation and banking law. Formerly Consultant to EC Commission, World Bank and IFC; member of the corporate governance commission of the Brussels Stock Exchange and chairman of the SLIM working party (Simpler Legislation for the Internal Market) on the 1st and 2nd directive. He also acted as adviser to the Belgian Government, inter alia as member of the Legislative Branch of the Council of State. He was a member of the board of the National Bank of Belgium and the Belgian Corporate Governance Commission. He was Chairman of the Board of Brussels International Airport Company (BIAC) and adviser on governance issues to several listed Belgian companies. He has published extensively on securities regulation, companies law, especially groups of companies, and corporate governance in the Belgian, European and comparative perspective.

Part 1:

Change of Governance in Historic Perspective: From State to Market – Pathways of Change in the 20th Century

Change of Governance in Historic Perspective: The German Experience

HARALD BAUM*

I. Introduction

It is well known that Germany, the inventor of the Maastricht Treaty's stability criteria, violated these same criteria at least three times in a row between 2002 and 2004. It may be less well known that the average economic growth in 2003 of all countries in the Euro zone would increase by a full percentage point if one excluded the zone's largest economy and worst laggard: Germany. In 2003 the German GNP per capita was some 25 percent lower than the American. These figures are a far cry from the country's superior postwar performance that attracted worldwide admiration – as long as it lasted. However, the figures do correspond with the findings of the 2004 'Economic Freedom Report' published by the Canadian Fraser Institute that show – once again – a strong correlation between prosperity and economic freedom defined by low taxes, freedom of contract, protection of property rights, monetary stability, et al.[1] In the report's overall ranking of 123 countries, Germany has, at least in relative terms, fallen to the 22nd position behind Hong Kong, Singapore, the US, Britain, New Zealand, Switzerland, Canada, Australia, and others. With respect to government influence on the economy, the country holds a dismal 107th place due to excessive income transfers and subsidies. Regarding freedom of banking, it scores only 84th because of heavy regulation of the financial industry. These are but a few disturbing examples. Other international comparative studies come to similar dismal evaluations.[2] The worsening has not taken place in absolute but rather in relative terms,

* I am grateful to Patrick C. Leyens and Markus Roth for comments.

1 Cf <http://www.fraserinstitute.ca> (28 June 2005).

2 The World Bank's report 'Doing Business in 2005: Removing Obstacles to Growth' does not list the country among the top 20 economies for ease of doing business; cf <http://rru.

cont. ...

so the findings show that some other countries obviously have been significantly swifter than Germany in adapting their governance systems from state to market; put differently, the road ahead may be a longer or a rockier one for Germany.

As of now there is still a general apprehension toward regulatory shock therapies among the German public and hence with its political class – a German Maggie Thatcher or Ronald Reagan has yet to enter the stage.[3] However, in the last years a plethora of legislative reforms actually have taken place and many more are underway – some quite courageous and others rather cautious.[4] With the recent blessing of the Constitutional Court, shops may now even stay open on Saturday evenings until 8 p.m. – though, of course, not (yet) 24 hours a day or on Sundays.[5] The debate over opening hours of shops has distracted political minds for several years and is a telling example of the difficulties that attempts to achieve change are (still) likely to meet in Germany.

The following analysis is composed of four parts. To frame the discussion, it begins with a historical overview of the changing perceptions about the role of the state and the proper scope of government in Germany (Part II). From a bird's eye view, it then tries to point out essential structures of the corporatist German governance model and discusses a possible (cautious) shift toward a more market-based regime (Part III). The following section shows how the formation of an independent capital markets (securities) regulation, the new takeover law, and the development of company law mirror these developments; in these areas we observe a 'reform in permanence' taking place, as one legislator has aptly put it[6] (Part IV). Part V summarizes the findings.

worldbank.org> (28 June 2005). 'The 2005 Index of Economic Freedom' prepared by The Heritage Foundation puts Germany at an unsatisfactory 18th rank; cf <www.heritage.org> (28 June 2005). A biannual study on the international ranking of the 21 leading economies undertaken by the German Bertelsmann Foundation shows that between 1994 and 2004, Germany fell back by eight ranks to the 16th position; during the same time Japan lost seven ranks and now occupies the 11th position; cf Bertelsmann Stiftung (ed) *Internationales Standort-Ranking 2004* (Bertelsmann Gütersloh 2004).

[3] But at least popular books anguishing over the country's decline are starting to appear on bestseller lists, cf eg G Steingart *Deutschland: Der Abstieg eines Superstars* ['Germany: Decline of a Super Star'] (Piper Munich 2004).

[4] A harsh critique of the government policies over the past decade – often camouflaged as 'reforms' – and the resulting loss in economic growth can be found with W Hamm 'Staatlich verschuldete Wachstumsstörungen' (2004) 55 ORDO. Jahrbuch für die Ordnung von Wirtschaft und Gesellschaft 153.

[5] Bundesverfassungsgericht, decision of 9 June 2004, published in [2004] Neue Juristische Wochenschrift 2363.

[6] U Seibert 'Aktienrechtsreform in Permanenz?' [2002] Die Aktiengesellschaft 417, 420.

II. Three Stages of Development

In the classical understanding, state and society are seen as two different social entities, although this distinction is sometimes – mistakenly – regarded as obsolete in the omnipresence of today's welfare state.[7] The state is usually defined as the unity of three constituent elements – population, territory, and governmental authority – with the state's institutions having the monopoly on the use of force. The term 'society' describes all non-state areas and organizational forms of social existence.[8] It is common to distinguish between three general stages in the development of the modern conception about the role and tasks the state has to fulfill or – put differently – the proper scope of government, ie the shifting balance between state and society, and the corresponding development of regulation:[9] first, the age of liberalism; second, the birth and expansion of the welfare state; and third, its growing crisis.[10]

1. The Liberal Project

The 'first' German – ie Prussian – welfare state developed under the absolute monarchy in the 18th century. But in the first half of the 19th century – based on the ideas of Immanuel Kant and Wilhelm von Humboldt and strongly influenced by the liberal British tradition and the work of Adam Smith – we see the liberal idea and movement successfully fighting for political and economic freedom against the feudal and mercantilist state. Protection of freedom and realization of law as the liberal state's central and primary tasks gradually replaced the former absolutist public welfare orientation. State intervention was now only accepted as a means to guarantee safety and equality of opportunity; responsibility for welfare was delegated to society. Central to the liberal concept were acknowledgement and protection of civil rights. Modern codifications of civil and commercial law were written. The German Civil Code that went into force on January 1, 1900 – after twenty years of preparation – is probably one of the most prominent examples of a code shaped by the liberal concept of law.[11] A watershed in the attitude

[7] Cf the contribution by EJ Mestmäcker in this volume.

[8] L Mader 'Regulierung, Deregulierung, Selbstregulierung: Anmerkungen aus legistischer Sicht' [2004] Zeitschrift für Schweizerisches Recht 5, 18.

[9] Cf eg A Ogus *Regulation. Legal Form and Economic Theory* (Clarendon Press Oxford 1994) 6 ff; Mader (n 8) 19 ff; K Günther 'Der Wandel der Staatsaufgaben und die Krise des regulativen Rechts' in D Grimm (ed) Wachsende Staatsaufgaben – sinkende Steuerungsfähigkeit des Rechts (Nomos Baden-Baden 1990) 51 ff; also H Willke *Supervision des Staates* (Suhrkamp Frankfurt 1997) 11 ff.

[10] A complementary study focused on a four stage model of development in Italian corporate governance is G Ferrarini's contribution in this volume.

[11] [1896] Reichsgesetzblatt 195 as amended.

toward the freedom of enterprise was the law of 11 June 1870, the so-called *Aktiennovelle*, that finally abolished the long-disputed requirement to obtain a state concession before establishing a stock corporation.[12]

However, these developments notwithstanding, in the last three decades of the 19th century liberal ideas began to lose influence rapidly as the liberal project came under severe attack from two sides: the socialists as well as the conservatives. The latter especially, in the form of Bismarck's so-called *Staatssozialismus*, proved deadly for German liberalism, with dire long-term consequences for the country.[13]

2. Birth of the Modern Welfare State

From the 1870s onward, the thinking of the so-called Historical School or *Kathedersozialisten* began to dominate the political economy in Germany. The leading figure was the economist Gustav Schmoller. The Historical School became highly influential, dominating academic positions in most (especially Prussian) universities well into the 20th century. This new line of reasoning was highly critical of the laissez-faire concept based on Adam Smith's idea of a market economy that governs itself, disparaging it as 'Manchester capitalism.' Instead, the school's representatives advocated a decisive role of the state in social policy. Although opinions differed in detail, the core concept shared by most was to overcome the liberal understanding of the state as a necessary evil and replace it with a view of the state as the highest ethical institution for educating mankind. Not the individual but the national community and its noble embodiment in the nation state – in this case, the newly founded German Reich – should be regarded as the righteous center of economic and social life. Accordingly, the bureaucracy was supposed to play a very active role in the economy as in other areas of social life. In other words, in this view the scope of government

[12] Gesetz, betreffend die Kommanditgesellschaften auf Aktien und die Aktiengesellschaften [1870] Bundesgesetzblatt Norddeutscher Bund 375; KJ Hopt 'Ideelle und wirtschaftliche Grundlagen der Aktien-, Bank- und Börsenrechtsentwicklung im 19. Jahrhundert' in H Coing and W Wilhelm (eds) *Wissenschaft und Kodifikation des Privatrechts im 19. Jahrhundert* (Klostermann Frankfurt 1980) 128, 167; for an extensive analysis of the system of state concession and its overcoming, see C Schubel *Verbandssouveränität und Binnenorganisation der Handelsgesellschaften* (Mohr Siebeck Tübingen 2003) 87 ff, 280 ff.

[13] A seminal study about the political defeat of German liberalism in the late 19th century can be found with R Raico *Die Partei der Freiheit. Studien zur Geschichte des deutschen Liberalismus* (Lucius & Lucius Stuttgart 1999); the classical treatise on liberalism is von L v Mises *Liberalismus* (Fischer Jena 1927, reprint Academia Sankt Augustin 1993); cf H Vorländer 'The Liberal Tradition in Germany' in J Meadowcroft (ed) The Liberal Tradition Revisited (Cheltenham 1997); P Manow 'The Uneasy Compromise of Liberalism and Corporatism in Postwar Germany' (Center for German and European Studies Working Paper Berkeley 1999).

was to be conceived as broadly as possible. The logical consequence of the adoration of the state was a disdain for the civil (*bourgeois*) society. The notion of a strong state extended well into politics, where the Historical School strongly supported the armament of the Reich and its imperialistic foreign policy.

These lines of thinking corresponded well with the Reich's first chancellor's (and his successor's) policies. In the 1880s, Bismarck initiated a comprehensive social program – namely a social insurance system – based on a paternalistic understanding of an active state's role in social life. Actually, already existing and functioning private insurers and cooperative social insurance institutions were forcefully integrated into the new mandatory state system.[14] While officially fighting against the socialists, his conservative government was de facto promoting their ideas by ruthlessly denigrating economic liberalism and the concept of a free market economy while constantly expanding the scope of government and its interventions in the market.[15] His official policy of helping the working class notwithstanding, Bismarck raised steep tariffs on imports of corn and steel – thus burdening private households with higher costs of living – for protecting the special interests of the influential national farmers and industry to win their consent for his expensive armament program. The development of cartels and associations was allowed and sometimes even promoted. Basically, we already see the well-known pattern of a government doling out all kinds of favors to special interest groups while hiding the costs that have to be borne by society at large. The increase of tasks claimed by the government led not only to more regulation but also to the formation of state monopolies and public enterprises. This resulted in increasing economic activities of the state in public infrastructure projects such as railways or in the postal and telecommunications sector. The nationalization of the various private railways by the state at the end of the 19th century was an important further step in the gradual shift from the liberal, laissez-faire attitude to the welfare state.[16]

One of the liberal opposition's main concerns about Bismarck's welfare policy was that it would create growing expectations which the state could never fulfill in the long run.[17] This criticism prophetically describes the situation with which the system finds itself confronted one hundred years later at the beginning of the 21st century. However, liberal criticism was not restricted to the expanding state intervention in the market; it was much more fundamental. The opposition perceived the change in policy during the 1880s and 1890s as a disguised return

[14] Manow (n 13) 5.

[15] This principle-based critique was voiced by Ludwig Bamberger, one of the leaders of the liberal opposition, in a speech at the German parliament (the *Reichstag*) on 1 April 1881; the speech is (partially) reprinted in S Tamm (ed) *Kleines Lesebuch der liberalen Sozialpolitik* (Academia Sankt Augustin 2004) 35 ff.

[16] JA Kämmerer *Privatisierung* (Mohr Siebeck Tübingen 2001) 64 ff.

[17] Cf Raico (n 13) 170 ff.

to the discredited 18th-century state paternalism and mercantilism and a betrayal of what they regarded as the most important achievement of the 19th century: the liberation of the citizens and creation of an open society. In their view, Bismarck's aim was not to address actual social shortcomings in the reality of liberalism *within* its framework, but rather to *change* that frame.[18] They observed that by making people dependent on transfers from the state and by the idealization of the nation state, a mentality of blind obedience and trust in government was created. Indeed, it was the deliberate aim of the conservative government's policy not to enable the working class to build up resources of their own to secure their well-being in an independent way, but rather to keep them dependent on the state rents and benevolence to assure their identification with the state and their acceptance of its actions. In the case of the German *Reich*, this meant a notorious support for a nationalist and increasingly militarized state. But undeniably, at least in the short run, the interventionist welfare-oriented policy produced measurable improvements of life that made opposition against it difficult; however, as the liberals had warned in vain time and again, the price for the paradigmatic shift was to be paid later.[19]

The late 19th-century renunciation of the liberal project in favor of an idealized notion of the state has been presented here in some detail because it is not simply history. It has created a lasting and unfortunate legacy that is highly relevant for today's problems: the persistent and deeply ingrained present-day German belief in a perceived unlimited competence of the state that prompts people to call for the government's helping hand whenever a social problem arises, a belief which has its roots in the willful discreditation of liberalism a century ago.[20] The director of a leading German economic think tank identified the general public's deeply ingrained skepticism – if not outright rejection – of the market mechanism as the greatest single obstacle obstructing urgent reforms in 21st-century Germany. In his view, no reform of the labor market, the social system, and public finance, however well designed, will ever be successful until the historical misunderstanding of a perceived superiority of governmental and/or collective-corporatist strategies over market-based solutions is corrected and a broader understanding – and general acceptance – of the free market economy as an indispensable correlate of the open society enshrined in our Constitution of 1949 is reached.[21]

[18] Raico (n 13) 172 ff.

[19] A pointed criticism of interventionist welfare-oriented policy and its disastrous long-term consequences can be found with FA von Hayek *The Fatal Conceit* (University of Chicago Press Chicago London 1988).

[20] C Watrin 'Klassischer Liberalismus in Deutschland' in Raico (n 13) XI; F Böhm 'Die Idee des Ordo im Denken Walter Euckens' in EJ Mestmäcker (ed) *Franz Böhm. Freiheit und Ordnung in der Marktwirtschaft* (Nomos Baden-Baden 1980) 11, 43 ff.

[21] M Hüther 'Deutsche Mythen' *Frankfurter Allgemeine Zeitung* (Frankfurt Germany 7 August 2004) 11; the contribution by H Siebert to this volume seems to voice similar

cont. ...

3. Crisis of the Welfare State

By the turn of the 19th century, responsibility for public welfare had essentially shifted back from society to the state, and the 'second' – the modern – German welfare state was established. The war economy from 1914 to 1918, the economic crisis after the lost war, hyperinflation and the Great Depression, and finally the re-armament under the Nazi regime and then World War II all led to a constant increase of state intervention and growth of regulation. After 1945, at least for a short while, the trust in the authoritative state's guiding hand seemed to have been somewhat shaken. The chance was taken by economists and jurists in the ordo-liberal tradition to create a specific economic and legal order, the 'social market economy.' Some call it a 'complex historical compromise between liberalism and two competing countervailing forces, social democracy and social Catholicism; between traditionalism and two opposed versions of modernism, liberalism and socialism; and of course between capital and labor.'[22] But actually, for some time at least, the liberal element was probably the decisive aspect of this compromise. Among other reforms, the first large-scale privatization of state enterprises since the early 19th century was initiated.[23] However, even then the foundations of the welfare state were not changed. For example, the mandatory public social insurance system based on (inter-generational) shared financing was not replaced by a private scheme based on accumulation of capital.[24]

In any case, after the economic crisis of 1966/67 and the ensuing formation of the 'great coalition' between conservatives and social democrats, priorities shifted again and the old mistrust in free enterprise and market solutions raised its voice once more, this time louder then ever. The slogan of the day was to 'test' the economy's ability to shoulder social burdens in the form of ever higher taxes, social duties, and all kinds of restrictive regulations for the sake of promoting the public good.[25] By the mid-1990s, continuous expansion of the scope of government had driven the ratio of public spending to the GNP to more than 50 percent in Germany, and social transfers amounting to 1,000 billion German marks per

skepticism; cf also H Siebert *The German Economy Beyond the Social Market* (Princeton University Press Princeton 2005); RK Sprenger *Der dressierte Bürger* (Campus Verlag Frankfurt 2005); fifty years earlier Franz Böhm had articulated similar worries (n 20).

[22] W Streeck and K Yamamura 'Introduction: Convergence or Diversity? Stability and Change in German and Japanese Capitalism' in K Yamamura and W Streeck (eds) *The End of Diversity? Prospects for German and Japanese Capitalism* (Cornell University Press Ithaca 2003) 11.

[23] Cf Kämmerer (n 16) 74 ff.

[24] For an extensive analysis of the postwar developments of the German political economy see Siebert (n 21).

[25] This has been criticized as market socialism by stealth, cf A Schüller 'Soziale Marktwirtschaft und Dritte Wege' (2000) 51 ORDO. Jahrbuch für die Ordnung von Wirtschaft und Gesellschaft 169, 180 ff.

year equaled the sum of annual exports.[26] Four decades of social and economic policy based on the erroneous assumption that in an open society the repercussions of change for the individual citizen can be neutralized by government intervention have created a 'welfare state bubble' that is no longer sustainable.[27] The financial overburdening of the state has become increasingly visible, and the collapse of social security systems has become a real threat in the face of an aging society and persistent long-term unemployment at historical heights. Especially the latter is undermining the specific social cohesion that the institutions of the German political economy had been designed to ensure.[28]

Another consequence of the welfare state in Germany and elsewhere has been a steady and in some areas dramatic increase in regulation, especially in social regulation during most of the last century. Most of it has been restrictive regulation, meaning any kind of restriction decreed or enforced by the state on people's possibilities of action.[29] A corresponding phenomenon has been the increase in people employed in the public sector. From 1950 to 1985 their number more than doubled, while the German population only rose by some 20 percent. This group of the working population is also vastly over-represented in parliament: presently they hold about two-thirds of the seats. Whether – and if so, when – regulatory intensity reached its peak in Germany is difficult to say. Certainly this was not as early as in the United Kingdom, where the increase seemed to have peaked in the mid-1970s and a drive for deregulation had already started by the late 1970s.[30] In Germany, an intensification of the discussion and ensuing deregulatory measures did not start before the 1990s, and then mostly in the context of the privatization of public utilities as required by EC law.[31] In areas such as consumer or investor protection, the surge of new regulation does not seem to have significantly ebbed. In general, things have been delayed by the fact that the decade of the 1990s was partly lost for reforms as attention was focused on the historic task of coping with the (economic and other) consequences of the German unification.[32]

[26] W Möschel *Den Staat an die Kette legen – Gegen die Aushöhlung des Wettbewerbs durch den Staat* (Frankfurter Institut Bad Homburg 1995); annual transfers from the West to the East German states, the *neue Bundesländer*, accounted 'only' for some 10 to 15 percent of that amount.

[27] Hüther (n 21); cf also Hamm (n 4) 164 ff.

[28] Streeck and Yamamura (n 22) 13.

[29] For a concept of regulation, cf J Basedow 'Economic Regulation in Market Economies' in J Basedow and others (eds) *Economic Regulation and Competition* (Kluwer Law International The Hague 2002) 1 ff.

[30] Cf Ogus (n 9) 8 ff.

[31] See below at 4.

[32] This actually is reminiscent of Japan, where – though for other reasons – the 1990s are called the 'lost decade' because of missed chances for reform; cf H Baum 'Der japanische "Big Bang" 2001 und das tradierte Regulierungsmodell – Ein regulatorischer Paradigmenwechsel?' (2000) 64 Rabels Zeitschrift für ausländisches und internationales Privatrecht 633.

Along with the difficulties of financial sustainability and stifling over-regulation (over-patronization), the modern welfare state sees itself confronted with another fundamental problem: a growing discrepancy between public expectations and the state's ability to act.[33] The state has shouldered an ever greater responsibility, and by now its tasks encompass a comprehensive responsibility for maintenance and development of society in almost every aspect: social, economic, and cultural. In other words, the state's task is no longer restricted to the defense of the given social order against disturbances; instead, this order itself has become the object of design and transformation by the state.[34] However, the powers of government have not grown in proportion to its expanded tasks. Thus it has increasingly become necessary to involve non-public institutions such as associations in implementing policies by delegating tasks to them and relying on their regulations, or to enter into public-private partnerships. Where traditional imperative regulatory tools are not suited for new tasks, other indirect means and soft instruments are used to implement policies such as financial incentives and disincentives or recommendations.[35] As these devices are non-binding, implementation depends on the cooperation of the ones addressed. This results in the development of a regime characterized as a 'cooperative administrative state.'[36] At the same time, the use of individual freedom has become increasingly dependent on the prior provision of substantial or organizational means by the state. The pertinent decisions about these are often taken on a very general level in the form of planning and allocative decisions addressed to groups and not to the individual citizen. With the classical instruments of judicial control, protection by the courts is difficult to obtain if the courts are not taking the position of the planning agency, which in turn would undermine the separation between justice and administration.[37]

4. Signs of Change?

Although the attitude of the general public is (still) skeptical if not outright hostile to fundamental systemic changes,[38] the situation has become so critical that at

[33] D Grimm 'Der Wandel der Staatsaufgaben und die Krise des Rechtsstaates' in Grimm (n 9) 291, 296 ff.; Günther (n 9); H Wilke *Entzauberung des Staates* (Athenäum Königstein 1983); Wilke (n 9); cf also the contributions to the 18th International Seminar on New Institutional Economics – The Proper Scope of Government in (2001) 157 J of Institutional and Theoretical Economics.

[34] Grimm (n 33) 297.

[35] Cf Mader (n 8) 21 ff.

[36] Kämmerer (n 16) 57.

[37] Grimm (n 33) 300.

[38] And the political parties are correspondingly reluctant to initiate such fundamental changes, Hamm (n 4) 154.

least a partial retreat of the welfare state seems unavoidable. Two developments during the last years stick out, both of which can best be interpreted in accordance with this volume's topic: from state to market.

A first turning point was the previously mentioned large-scale privatization of public utilities from postal and telecommunication systems, railways, airlines, airports, et al., that began in the 1990s and was mostly initiated by EC law.[39] The most prominent example is probably the functional and organizational split of the former Bundespost into three separate entities – at the first stage still subject to public law – each responsible for one of its former services: telecommunication, postal services, and banking (*Postreform I* of 1989). In a second step, those three Bundespost business entities were formally privatized in the *Postreform II* of 1994.[40] As a result, on January 1, 1995, Deutsche Telekom AG, Deutsche Post AG, and Deutsche Postbank AG became private corporations subject to the German Stock Corporation Law (*Aktiengesetz*). All of their shares were initially held by the government but were earmarked to be sold to the investing public.[41] In a third step, one year later Deutsche Telekom AG went public – the largest-ever initial public offering by a European company. After an extensive promotion campaign, the government successfully sold a stake of 25 percent. Some 40 percent of the total issue was placed with German retail investors. Nearly two million Germans subscribed to the offering; some 400,000 of those had never owned shares before.[42] A second tranche of shares was sold to the public in another offering in 2001. Though Deutsche Telekom AG as a listed company is financially independent and accountable for its results, its business activities are regulated under a sector-specific law, the German Telecommunications Act of 1996,[43] and are supervised by a special independent agency set up in 1998. This is an example of how the *qualitative* de-regulation of an industry actually results in more *quantitative* regulation in the form of sector-specific re-regulation, the so-called 'new regulatory mix.'[44] The difficult question of whether privatized public utilities as former monopolies should be regulated in this way, ie by sector-

[39] Cf eg Deregulierungskommission *Marktöffnung und Wettbewerb* (Poeschel Stuttgart 1991); KF Kreuzer (ed) *Privatisierung von Unternehmen* (Nomos Baden-Baden 1995); Kämmerer (n 16) 85 ff.

[40] For details, see Kämmerer (n 16) 297 ff.

[41] The government plans to have sold more or less all its shares by the end of 2006; cf report *Frankfurter Allgemeine Zeitung* (Frankfurt Germany 3 January 2005) 11.

[42] For a comprehensive analysis of the privatization of Telekom, see JN Gordon 'Convergence on Shareholder Capitalism' in CJ Milhaupt (ed) *Global Markets, Domestic Institutions* (Columbia University Press New York 2003) 214, 226-242.

[43] The Act has been replaced by the new *Telekommunikationsgesetz* [2004] Bundesgesetzblatt I 1190, in force since 26 June 2004; cf J Scheer 'Das neue Telekommunikationsgesetz [2004] Neue Juristische Wochenschrift 3001.

[44] Basedow (n 29) 15 ff.; Mader (n 8) 43.

specific laws, or whether by general competition law is still debated. However, in any case, this discussion is about the *market* regulation.

Even though Deutsche Telekom AG still has a dominant market position in different areas, the privatization was a success: in the year 2000, more than 250 players were offering telecommunication services in Germany; tariffs, especially for long-distance and international calls, dropped significantly by over 90 percent compared to those before liberalization.[45] Less happy were those investors who bought shares in the secondary public offering at a high issue price only to see the share price collapse soon afterward. Between 2001 and summer 2003 (the beginning of limitation), some 15,000 aggrieved shareholders filed damages claims against Deutsche Telekom AG that since then have choked the District Court of Frankfurt.[46] Among other considerations, this in turn prompted the government to present a draft of a new law in 2004, the so-called 'Draft Act Regulating Exemplary Investor Suits.'[47] The law has the following aims: to handle mass claims more efficiently, to make it easier and less financially risky for retail investors to pursue their interests, thus promoting private law enforcement of capital market regulation, which in turn should improve Germany's position in the international regulatory competition as a financial market with a modern and efficient legal framework. Obviously, the discussion is once more about *market* regulation.

What had started at the federal level driven mostly by the implications of the evolution toward a Single European Market and corresponding EC laws has developed a momentum of its own, mostly – especially at the local level – driven by fiscal motives. We now see on all three levels of government all kinds of 'privatizations,' formal as well as substantial ones, delegation of tasks (contracting out), public-private partnerships, and other forms of de-administration.[48] For example, in the spring of 2004, the city of Hamburg held a plebiscite about a possible privatization of the city's public hospitals. A majority voted against it, but the city's government nevertheless sold a large chunk of those to a private

[45] Cf KD Scheurle 'Statement on the Regulation of Telecommunications Services' in J Basedow and others (eds) *Economic Regulation and Competition* (Kluwer Law International The Hague 2002) 265 ff.

[46] Another 17,000 have filed for mediation proceedings (*Güteverfahren*) at a special institution, the *Öffentliche Rechtsauskunft- und Vergleichsstelle Hamburg (ÖRA)*, to suspend the passage of time for purposes of limitation; they are free to join the ordinary proceedings later on.

[47] *Regierungsentwurf eines Gesetzes zur Einführung von Kapitalanleger-Musterverfahren* of 17 November 2004, published in Neue Zeitschrift für Gesellschaftsrecht, Special Supplement to issue 11/2004; for a comment, see F Reuschle 'Ein neuer Weg zur Bündelung und Durchsetzung gleichgerichteter Ansprüche' [2004] Wertpapier-Mitteilungen 2334; B Hess 'Der Regierungsentwurf für ein Kapitalanlegermusterverfahrensgesetz – eine kritische Bestandsaufnahme' [2004] Wertpapier-Mitteilungen 2329.

[48] Cf U Immenga 'Privatisierung im Zielkonflikt – Ein Vergleich der Konzeptionen' in KJ Kreuzer (ed) *Privatisierung von Unternehmen* (Nomos Baden-Baden 1995) 9, 44 ff.

company in August. Obviously, the state is gradually retreating from some of its – extensive – former economic activities.[49]

The second turning point may have been the admission that a supplementary private pillar in the public pension system is the only way out of the welfare crisis. The admittance of private provision in 2001 is regarded as a paradigmatic shift in the welfare system that was formerly designed as comprehensive state-organized protection and as the beginning of a 'privatization' of welfare arrangements and the rise of 'welfare markets.'[50] If the development of liberal law was characterized by the shift from status to contract, and the development of the law of the welfare state by the further shift from contract to social role and social capacities, we now possibly see the beginning of a return from there to contract as a consequence of the privatization of welfare. Private law institutions, especially contracts, will regain some of their former relevance as instruments of individual social security.[51] Thus, one might add, by shifting welfare at least partly back to private ordering, the challenge is to solve social problems this time *within* the framework of the liberal model of a contract-based market economy – a chance that was missed in the late 19th century as discussed above. However, success probably depends to a large degree on whether it will be possible to change the general skepticism toward a free market economy that was created during that time. The main task will be to bridge the information asymmetry between the average citizen as an investor in and a consumer of various kinds of financial products by proper – legislative or judicial – regulation of disclosure and other information duties. Again, we are predominantly speaking about regulation that addresses market behavior.

We now turn from the etatist or welfare side of the German role model to its other characteristic: the specifically corporatist and consensus-based structure of its political economy that also has shaped the country's enterprise landscape so far.

[49] In December 2004 the Social Democratic Party fraction of parliament (!) announced a plan to initiate a new law to substantially facilitate public-private partnerships in 2005 as a functioning alternative to state financing for a broad range of public projects; cf report *Frankfurter Allgemeine Zeitung* (Frankfurt Germany 28 December 2004) 11.

[50] M Bäuerle 'The Retreat of the Welfare State: Challenges to the German Welfare Regime and the Role of Law' (2003) Annual of German and Eur L 43, 56 ff; the author gives a profound analysis of these developments with extensive further references; the pertinent law is the Federal Law Concerning the Certification of Private Pension Contracts of 16 June 2001 (*Gesetz über die Zertifizierung von Altersvorsorgeverträgen* [2001] Bundesgesetzblatt I 1310, 1322). The necessity of improving private pensions as supplementary pillar to the public pension system was one of the main topics of the 65th German Lawyers Meeting ('65. Deutscher Juristentag') in Bonn in 2004; for a discussion see M Roth 'Private und betriebliche Altersvorsorge zwischen Sicherheit und Selbstverantwortung' [2004] Zeitschrift für Rechtspolitik 154.

[51] Bäuerle (n 50) 45, 57 ff.

III. Moving Toward a Market-Based Regime and Shareholder Capitalism?

1. Corporatism and Consensus-Based Interest Balancing

Not only the welfare state and its interventions substitute markets, but the same is true for corporatism, which can be described as an intermediate layer of decision making located between markets and the political process. As Professor Siebert analyzes in great detail in his contribution to this volume, the German system of governance is characterized by such a corporatist approach where decision making is delegated to a significant degree to social groups in various areas.[52] As mentioned above, up to a certain degree this is a consequence of the extended welfare state that uses cooperative means instead of mandatory measures, either because of lack of power or as a way to reduce resistance. However, the extent to which corporatist governance prevails in the German economy is not a necessary result of the redistributive aims of the welfare state, let alone the social-market economy as such. Instead, it has historical roots that date back to the 19th century. By sharing power with special interest associations – which usually then profit at the expense of the general public or other groups in society – the government secures the assistance of the players it obviously regards as important for its policies. The most prominent example is the privilege of the unions and business associations to negotiate wages for their members, which are then extended de facto to all those employed, as well as – indirectly – to the unemployed, for legal rules and courts do not allow deviations from the terms agreed upon in the collective wage contract. This setting favors those who are employed at the expense of the unemployed, who may legally not accept lower wages as a trade-off for a job.[53]

The corporatist setting is supplemented by mandatory enterprise co-determination as part of the German corporate governance structure. It was introduced in 1976 and is widely seen as one of the hallmarks of German corporatism.[54] Under

[52] For an in-depth analysis, see H Siebert in this volume; also Siebert (n 21).

[53] H Siebert, in this volume.

[54] A recent critical analysis can be found, eg, with JJ du Plessis and O Sandrock 'The Rise and Fall of Supervisory Codetermination in Germany?' (2005) 16 Intl Company and Commercial Law Review 67; M Schiessl 'Leitungs- und Kontrollstrukturen im internationalen Wettbewerb' (2003) 167 Zeitschrift für das gesamte Handelsrecht und Wirtschaftsrecht 235. A recent study found that companies with equal representation of employees and shareholders on the supervisory board trade at a 31 percent stock market discount as compared with companies where employees representatives fill only one third of the supervisory board seats, see G Gorton and FA Schmid 'Capital, Labor, and the Firm: A Study of German Codetermination' (2004) 2 Journal of the European Economic Association 863. The problems caused by trying to adjust the German concept of co-determination to the *Societas Europaea* are discussed by M Roth 'Die unternehmerische Mitbestimmung in der monistischen SE' (2004) 35 Zeitschrift für Arbeitsrecht 431.

this regime, half of the supervisory board seats of large companies (more then 2,000 employees) are filled by labor representatives. As at least two seats are reserved for representatives of trade unions, their continuous influence is stabilized in spite of a shrinking membership base. This gives labor control rights over corporate decisions and leads to a kind of negotiated management where – in the terms of Hirschman – labor has voice as an alternative to exit. The result is a willingness for long-term commitment.[55]

A further aspect has been patient capital generated by high savings and distributed to the firms by bank credit, with the banks usually holding seats on the boards – at least with good customers. Bank loans constituted some 80 percent of long-term external funding to German business in the 1990s.[56] Here, too, relations were obviously rather long term. With committed labor and patient capital, management could take the long view based on stable bargains with and between all those involved.[57] Thus quality-competitive production based on collectively negotiated cooperation could substitute for price competition that was no option for German firms because of the high costs of socially regulated labor markets and status protection for various social groups.[58]

The banks' role in corporate governance as so-called 'house banks' was enhanced not only by supplying capital and seats on the supervisory boards but also by their voting power – whether because of holding shares of their own or because of depository voting on behalf of mostly disinterested public shareholders (*Depotstimmrecht*).[59] Personal relationships also played a role. Insiders control the supervisory boards when – as is still frequently the case – the former CEO (chairperson of the managing board) changes positions after stepping down from that board by becoming the chairperson of the supervisory board.[60]

Two important additional elements of the corporatist approach to corporate governance should be mentioned. The first is blockholding. As recently as 1996, 64 percent of the voting rights of listed German companies were held by control-

[55] W Streeck and K Yamamura 'Introduction: Convergence or Diversity? Stability and Change in German and Japanese Capitalism' in K Yamamura and W Streeck (eds) *The End of Diversity? Prospects for German and Japanese Capitalism* (Cornell University Press Ithaca 2003) 13.

[56] RH Schmidt 'Corporate Governance in Germany: An Economic Perspective' in JP Krahnen and RH Schmidt (eds) *The German Financial System* (OUP Oxford 2004) 386, 395.

[57] Streeck and Yamamura (n 55) 13.

[58] ibid 12.

[59] An extensive analysis of the various elements of corporate governance in Germany and their factual settings can be found with S Prigge 'A Survey of German Corporate Governance' in KJ Hopt and others (eds) *Comparative Corporate Governance* (OUP Oxford 1998) 943.

[60] In summer 2004 this was (still) true for more than half of the incumbent chairpersons of the supervisory boards of the Dax-30 companies – a recommendation of the German Corporate Governance Code of 2002 to the contrary notwithstanding; cf report *Frankfurter Allgemeine Zeitung* (Frankfurt Germany 23 August 2004) 14.

ling shareholders whose shares in the company amounted to more than 50 percent of the capital; a further 17 percent of the companies had at least one shareholder who controlled more than 25 percent of the voting rights.[61] A large number of listed companies are part of enterprise groups (combined companies) with only a minority of their shares listed. Blockholders are mostly other business enterprises, wealthy families, and banks.[62] This pattern results in a complex web of cross-shareholdings in which two institutions traditionally have played a predominant role: *Deutsche Bank*, the country's biggest bank; and the giant insurer, *Allianz AG*. The web of cross-shareholdings is supplemented by reciprocal seats on supervisory boards. This setting has been somewhat critically labeled *'Deutschland AG'* or 'Germany, Inc.'[63]

The ownership pattern was reflected in an underdeveloped market for corporate control. Hostile takeovers were a rare exception. Hostile sales of blocks did happen, but again were much less frequent than, eg, hostile takeovers in the UK or the US.[64]

This corporatist corporate governance regime is generally classified as the standard example of an insider-controlled and stakeholder-oriented system as opposed to a 'modern' capital-marked-based and outsider-controlled system. However, as has recently been stressed, it has been a system with an inner logic, with complementary and consistent features – in other words, a system that worked.[65] Moreover, it has shown surprising stability for more than three decades. This was interrupted, however, by the successful takeover of Mannesmann AG by Vodafone AirTouch plc in 1999/2000, the biggest of all hostile takeovers so far in Europe. Might this represent the writing on the wall of Germany's corporatist setting?

2. Signs of Change?

Whether a paradigmatic change is underway remains to be seen. Dominant groups with vested interest in the given system – such as the trade unions, for

[61] F Barca and M Becht (eds) *The Control of Corporate Europe* (OUP Oxford 2001) 319; see also J McCahery and others 'The Economics of the Proposed European Takeover Directive' in G Ferrarini and others (eds) *Reforming Company and Takeover Law in Europe* (OUP Oxford 2004) 575, 584 ff; Prigge (n 59) 972 ff.

[62] RH Schmidt (n 56) 394.

[63] For a pointed critical analysis, cf J Beyer 'Deutschland AG a.D.: Deutsche Bank, Allianz und das Verflechtungszentrum des deutschen Kapitalismus' in W Streeck and M Höpner (eds) *Alle Macht dem Markt? Fallstudien zur Abwicklung der Deutschland AG* (Campus Verlag Frankfurt 2003) 118 ff.

[64] Cf T Jenkinson and A Ljungqvist 'The Role of Hostile Stakes in German Corporate Governance' (2001) 7 J of Corporate Finance 397 ff.

[65] Schmidt (n 56) 397 ff.

example – will not easily surrender their power. However, various threads of the rough picture sketched above are obviously unraveling. Just a few of those aspects follow:[66] The industrial strategy of broad incremental innovation allowed under the consensus system has ceased to generate sufficient advantages in non-price-competitive markets.[67] Capital has ceased to be patient; instead, it has become mobile and cosmopolitan in the pursuit of faster and higher profit.[68] Banks are increasingly giving up their role as *Hausbanken* and disposing of their shareholding, turning into Anglo-American-style investment banks.[69] Thus begins the dissolution of the web of cross-shareholding. Furthermore, *Deutsche Bank*, for example, seems to be actively reducing its role in corporate governance. It has given up board seats and has advised its top managers to avoid chairmanships on supervisory boards of other companies.[70]

On the other hand, certain elements typically associated with outsider- or market-based systems seem to be increasing. In particular, the privatization and going public of *Deutsche Telekom* described above has been a major boost for shareholder capitalism in Germany, ie public ownership and a strong equity market.[71] Since the mid-1990s the number of stock corporations has more or less quadrupled;[72] there has also been a rise in listings and of market capitalization;[73] and the number of Germans owning shares (directly or indirectly via funds) has nearly doubled.[74] The (initial) success of the *Neuer Markt*, established by the *Deutsche Börse* in 1997 as a Nasdaq competitor for launching initial public offerings of high tech companies, can also be seen in this way.

[66] For a comprehensive analysis, see eg Gordon (n 42); Streeck and Yamamura (n 55); Streeck and Höpner (n 63); and, controversially, Schmidt (n 56).

[67] Streeck and Yamamura (n 55) 14.

[68] ibid 15. A telling example of capital no longer being patient was the spectacular failure of the leading German exchange, Deutsche Börse AG, to takeover the London Stock Exchange (LSE) early in 2005. The management of Deutsche Börse was forced to withdraw its bid because of resistance by its own shareholders to the proposed takeover; cf report *Frankfurter Allgemeine Zeitung* (Frankfurt Germany 10 March 2005) 23.

[69] Beyer (n 63) 126 ff.

[70] Schmidt (n 56) 416.

[71] Cf Gordon (n 42) 226 ff.

[72] Cf Deutsches Aktieninstitut *DAI-Factbook 2003* (DAI Frankfurt 2004) 01-1. However, the total number of roughly 15,000 stock corporations still seems modest in an international comparison, and it compares with about one million limited liability companies registered in Germany.

[73] The market capitalization of shares of domestic companies listed at Deutsche Börse has nearly tripled between 1993 and 2003; cf World Federation of Exchanges *Statistics* <http://www.fibv.com> (28 June 2005).

[74] From 5.6 million in 1997 to 10.4 million in 2004; cf DAI-Kurzstudie 1/2005, reprinted in [2005] Die Aktiengesellschaft R67, R68; but, again, the total number of 833 listed companies (as of 2003) seems modest in an international comparison.

In addition, a cautious discussion about the advantages and disadvantages of collective bargaining and co-determination has at least begun;[75] both were absolute non-topics until very recently. The same is true for the insider control of supervisory boards by former CEOs mentioned above.

So a gradual and partial de-bundling of the corporatist '*Deutschland AG*' appears to be somewhat probable. However, it is yet another question whether this partial shift toward an outsider- and market-oriented governance model – which may result in a breakdown of the traditional system without having the new one already in place and functioning – will bring an advantage. Possibly, we might end up in the worst of both worlds, at least for some time.[76]

IV. Legislative Reactions: Change of Regulatory Model?

The structural developments are accompanied by regulatory changes that seem even more explicit. For many decades, German law basically distinguished only between corporate laws, banking, and exchange regulation – none of it with any specific reference to markets. By now this situation has fundamentally changed.

1. Financial Market Regulation

Although a market-based regulation of financial services in its own right became part of the German legal system only fairly recently, today such an independent and extensive body of financial market regulation is firmly established in addition to the exchange and banking laws.[77] Furthermore, exchange regulation itself has been developed into a modern market-based set of rules. The formation of this regulatory regime shall be briefly summarized.

Not until the early 1990s did the gradual change from bank-based to market-oriented finance and the necessity to implement EC regulation such as the insider trading rules lead to the formation of a specific securities regulation in the Anglo-American sense. An additional reason was the fear of an imminent loss of reputation for the *Finanzplatz Deutschland* (Germany as a financial center) because of

[75] Cf eg the report of a joint commission established in 2004 by the Federation of German Industries (BDI) and the Confederation of German Employers' Associations (BDA): BDA and BDI 'Mitbestimmung modernisieren. Bericht der Kommission Mitbestimmung' (November 2004) at <www.bdi-online.de> (28 June 2005); in October 2004 the liberal faction (FDP) filed a motion in Parliament to reform co-determination: Konzernmitbestimmung neu ordnen – Aufsichtsräte und Eigentümerrechte stärken, BT-Drs. 15/4039; cf also du Plessis and Sandrock (n 54) or Schiessl (n 54).

[76] This is the expressive warning of Schmidt (n 56) 419.

[77] The first German treatise dealing with that subject was KJ Hopt *Der Kapitalanlegerschutz im Recht der Banken* (CH Beck Munich 1975), which initiated the German discussion.

inferior or non-existent securities regulation. The push for modernization was therefore mainly induced from abroad.

To begin with, the Stock Exchange Act of 1896 (*Börsengesetz*) was amended several times in the last two decades. In 2002 the Act was completely revised as part of the so-called 'Fourth Financial Market Promotion Act.'[78] In an incremental, path-dependent, stop-and-go progress, the law is slowly developing into a modern market-based regulation of exchanges services to replace the former regulation of a quasi-public monopoly.[79] Today we see a mix of (mostly) state-of-the-art regulations such as §§ 58 – 60 of the Act dealing with alternative trading systems[80] standing beside (some) remaining anachronistic provisions.[81]

The decisive reform, however, was the enactment of the Securities Trading Act of 1994 (*Wertpapierhandelsgesetz*, hereinafter *WpHG*). This Act was part of the Second Financial Market Promotion Act[82] and has been described as the 'basic law' for the German capital market.[83] It transformed the Insider Directive,[84] the Transparency Directive,[85] and (partly) the Investment Services Direc-

[78] Law of 21 June 2002, [2002] Bundesgesetzblatt I 2010; the revision of the Exchange Law went into force 1 July 2002, except §§ 58 I, 59, and 60 which went into force 1 February 2003. An overview can be found with A Möller 'Das Vierte Finanzmarktförderungsgesetz' [2001] Wertpapier-Mitteilungen 2405. As the name of the Act indicates, it is the fourth in a series of Financial Market Promotion Acts starting with the First Act in 1990 ([1990] Bundesgesetzblatt I 266), followed by the Second Act in 1994 ([1994] Bundesgesetzblatt I 1760), and the Third Act in 1998 ([1998] Bundesgesetzblatt I 529).

[79] See H Baum 'Changes in Ownership, Governance, and Regulation of Stock Exchanges in Germany: Path Dependent Progress and an Unfinished Agenda' (2004) 5 Eur Business Organization L Rev 677; H Merkt 'Empfiehlt es sich, im Interesse des Anlegerschutzes und zur Förderung des Finanzplatzes Deutschland das Kapitalmarkt- und Börsenrecht neu zu regeln? Börsenrechtliches Teilgutachten. Gutachten G' in Deutscher Juristentag (ed) *Gutachten F + G zum 64. Deutschen Juristentag Berlin 2002* (CH Beck Munich 2002) G1-G143; cf also G Ferrarini 'Exchange Governance and Regulation: An Overview' in G Ferrarini (ed) *European Securities Markets: The Investment Services Directive and Beyond* (Kluwer Law International The Hague 1998) 245 ff; J Köndgen 'Ownership and Corporate Governance of Stock Exchanges' (1998) 154 J of Institutional and Theoretical Economics 324 ff; a comprehensive analysis can be found with KJ Hopt and others *Börsenreform. Eine ökonomische rechtsvergleichende und rechtspolitische Untersuchung* (Poeschel Stuttgart 1997).

[80] Also called (in EU parlance) multilateral-trading systems or (elsewhere) electronic communication networks.

[81] A prime example for this is § 1 of the Act. The provision stipulates that a competent state authority must approve the formation of an exchange instead of reserving the pure business decision for the applicant (and the market). When deciding, the state authority – a bureaucracy(!) – has to check whether the market for exchange services 'needs' the intended new exchange.

[82] [1994] Bundesgesetzblatt I 1794 / [1998] Bundesgesetzblatt I 2708.

[83] Cf KJ Hopt 'Grundsatz- und Praxisprobleme nach dem Wertpapierhandelsgesetz' (1995) 159 Zeitschrift für das gesamte Handelsrecht und Wirtschaftsrecht 135, 163.

[84] Directive 89/592/EEC [1989] OJ L334/30.

tive[86] into German law. The law introduced a new era of ordering to the German capital markets because it is not aimed at regulating a special product or participant but the market *as such*. Prior to this, the perspective of regulation could be described as having focused on the institutions and their legal form and, accordingly, the emphasis had been on the law of the stock corporation, exchanges, and banks.

Since its enactment, the WpHG has been repeatedly amended and its scope of application has been broadened. Further reforms are pending as new directives have to be implemented in German law.[87] The WpHG is independent of the Stock Exchange Act and does not regulate exchanges. Whether that distinction makes sense in the age of electronic securities trading on all different types of platforms seems at least questionable.

Along with the enactment of the WpHG, a new supervisory agency, the Federal Securities Trading Supervisory Agency (*Bundesaufsichtsamt für den Wertpapierhandel*), was established. In 2002 it was merged together with the former Federal Banking Supervisory Agency and the Federal Insurance Supervisory Agency into the Federal Financial Services Supervisory Authority (*Bundesanstalt für Finanzdienstleistungsaufsicht*, hereinafter *BaFin*).[88] The BaFin is an independent federal administrative agency under the supervision of the Ministry of Finance and thus a governmental authority rather than a self-regulatory body. Its staff consists of public employees.

With the WpHG and the BaFin, the cornerstones of a modern market-based regulatory and supervisory regime are in place. A third feature is presently in the making: private law enforcement in the form of damages suits filed by investors.

This kind of private law enforcement begins to supplement the traditional forms of public enforcement by means and sanctions of administrative and criminal law. In this regard three current legislative projects are of specific interest:[89] The 'Draft Act Regulating Exemplary Investor Suits' of November 2004 has already been mentioned.[90] In October 2004 the 'Act on Improved Investor Protection' went into force.[91] Among other changes, the law predominantly

[85] Directive 88/627/EEC [1988] OJ L348/62.

[86] Directive 93/22/EEC [1993] OJ L141/27.

[87] See below.

[88] An overview of organization and tasks of the new agency can be found with HO Hagemeister 'Die neue Bundesanstalt für Finanzdienstleistungsaufsicht' [2002] Wertpapier-Mitteilungen 1773 ff.

[89] For a more extensive English overview, see U Noack and D Zetzsche 'Corporate Governance Reform in Germany: The Second Decade' (Center for Business & Corporate Law Research Paper Series no 10 June 2005) 19 ff (<http://ssrn.com/abstract=646761> (28 June 2005).

[90] Cf n 47 and accompanying text.

[91] *Anlegerschutzverbesserungsgesetz* of 29 October 2004 [2004] Bundesgesetzblatt I 2630.

amends the WpHG by reforming the regulations of insider trading and market manipulation and extending the liability for untrue financial statements.[92] The third (and highly controversial) project is the 'Draft Act on Liability for Capital Market Information' of October 2004.[93] This law stipulates a personal liability of board members who deceive the capital markets by supplying false information.[94] Recent decisions by the Federal Supreme Court (BGH) dealing with tort liability of board members for inaccurate ad-hoc publicity (disclosure) follow the same venue.[95]

Among other considerations, the legislators justify all the reforms in these areas by the need to create an attractive legal framework so that the German financial market will become or stay attractive for foreign as well as domestic investors. This means that the legislators have (finally) accepted the fact that an international regulatory competition does exist.[96] The more recent reforms are part of the implementation of a ten-point agenda for strengthening corporate integrity and investor protection that the German government presented on 23 February 2003. If one includes the pending reforms, the emphasis is clearly on the regulation of information: enhanced disclosure duties, stricter liability for insufficient or misleading information, and more efficient means of private enforcement of mandatory disclosure rules by damages suits. The overriding principle is disclose or abstain. Regulation of disclosure is basically market regulation. Here, German legislators are obviously adapting the regulatory model of the capital-market-based and outsider-oriented system.[97] Of course, to a significant degree – but by no means exclusively – reforms are prompted by EU legislation. Whether the regulatory density caused by the accumulation of the various legislative measures is really necessary for – and actually capable of – deterring criminal behavior on the market is yet another question.[98] Given that the heavy

[92] Parts of the Act are transforming recent EU legislation. For an overview, see the contributions by G Dreyling, A Cahn, S Simon, C Kirschhöfer and M Erkens, in [2005] Der Konzern 1, 5, 13, 22 and 29 respectively.

[93] *Entwurf eines Gesetzes zur Verbesserung der Haftung für falsche Kapitalmarktinformation* of 7 October 2004.

[94] A critical analysis can be found with G Spindler 'Persönliche Haftung der Organmitglieder für Falschinformation des Kapitalmarktes' [2004] Wertpapier-Mitteilungen 2089.

[95] These are the so-called 'Informatic' decisions of 19 July 2004, published in [2004] Neue Zeitschrift für Gesellschaftsrecht 811; a comment can be found with H Fleischer 'Zur deliktsrechtlichen Haftung der Vorstandsmitglieder für falsche Ad-hoc-Mitteilungen' [2004] Der Betrieb 2031.

[96] Cf the explanatory comments to Fourth Financial Market Promotion Act by Möller (n 78).

[97] Cf text accompanying n 65.

[98] At least in Germany, (so far) there are next to no major scandals involving large established firms. More or less all the outrageous scandals concerned small, young firms and were caused by owners and/or managers with a surprising amount of criminal energy.

costs of compliance burden all firms, the overwhelming majority of which are not prone to criminal activities, a rather skeptical view may be appropriate.[99]

Furthermore, different concepts sometimes are difficult to accommodate: Early in 2005 the BaFin published draft-guidelines aimed at enhancing ad-hoc publicity (disclosure) for listed companies.[100] According to the draft, in case of a multi-step decision process, as a rule, already the first decision should be made public if it qualifies as martial information.[101] This means if the managing board of a listed company takes such a decision it has to make it public immediately afterwards, rather then to wait for advice and, where necessary, approval of the supervisory board first. A supervisory board faced with an already publicly known decision of the managing board will think twice before openly disapproving it. Thus in effect its corporate governance functions are seriously undermined by the proposed disclosure rule – despite the fact that the proposed rule as such does make perfect sense form the perspective of disclosure based capital markets regulation.

2. Market-Oriented Regulatory Approach in Company Law?

As mentioned at the beginning, a 'reform in permanence' is taking place, especially in company law.[102] The latest major reform proposal is the 'Draft Act on Corporate Integrity and Modernization on Actions to Set Aside Resolutions of the Shareholder Meeting.'[103] This Act deals with a variety of issues, namely liability of corporate managers, facilitation of shareholder activism, procedural questions of shareholder meetings, and curbing of abusive shareholder suits. As with earlier

[99] Noack and Zetzsche (n 89) 30.

[100] *Entwurf eines Emittentenleitfadens*, draft of 3 January 2005, at <www.bafin.de./sonstiges/emittenten.pdf> (28 June 2005).

[101] ibid V.2.2.5.1.

[102] U Seibert 'Aktienrechtsreform in Permanenz?' [2002] Die Aktiengesellschaft 417, with a short overview of the various reforms till 2002; for a concise in-depth analysis of the development of company law, see eg KJ Hopt 'Corporate Governance in Germany: Recent Developments in Company Law and Corporate Governance Code' in KJ Hopt and others (eds) *European Corporate Governance in Company Law and Codes* (Report The Hague 2004) 23; also KJ Hopt 'Gesellschaftsrecht im Wandel' in R Wank and others (eds) *Festschrift für Herbert Wiedemann zum 70. Geburtstag* (CH Beck Munich 2002) 1013.

[103] *Regierungsentwurf eines Gesetzes zur Unternehmensintegrität und zur Modernisierung des Anfechtunsgrechts* of 17 November 2004, published at <http://www.bmj.bund.de/media/archive/362.pdf> (28 June 2005); explanatory comments can be found eg with U Seibert 'UMAG und Hauptversammlung' [2005] Wertpapier-Mitteilungen 157; U Seibert and C Schütz 'Der Referentenentwurf eines Gesetzes zur Unternehmensintegrität und zur Modernisierung des Anfechtunsgrechts' [2004] Zeitschrift für Wirtschaftsrecht 252; H Fleischer 'Die "Business Judgement Rule"' [2004] Zeitschrift für Wirtschaftsrecht 685; M Roth 'Das unternehmerische Ermessen des Vorstands' [2004] Betriebs-Berater 1066.

reforms of company law, it is safe to assume that the German legislators are once again trying to improve the traditional tools of corporate governance rather then replacing these with a purely market-based-system of corporate control. In other words, and seen in context with the new securities regulations described above, the legislators are obviously continuing to pursue a 'dual purpose strategy' in a kind of 'hybrid approach,' relying on the one hand on the traditional governance devices, and on the other hand enhancing corporate governance through a strengthening of market forces.[104]

However, it cannot be overlooked that even company law as such becomes to some extent market-oriented as we see a growing differentiation between rules for listed and non-listed companies tentatively labeled '*Börsengesellschaftsrecht*' (listed companies' law).[105] Thus a specific body of law for listed companies is developing within company law and refers to (passive) investor-shareholders without an entrepreneurial interest in the company.[106] A prime example for this differentiation is the German Corporate Governance Code of 2002.[107] The Code itself is a piece of non-mandatory self-regulation. It is based on the modern principle of 'comply or explain.'[108] But listed companies – and only those – have to explain annually whether or not they adhere to the Code's recommendations.[109]

The 'comply or explain' principle is rather new to the traditional German concept of stock corporation law. From a functional perspective, it corresponds with the overriding 'disclose-or-abstain' principle of securities regulation and thus correlates with market regulation. From a different perspective, it can also be viewed as part of the trend to replace strict mandatory law with more flexible rules that focus on behavior of corporate managers.[110]

[104] Noack and Zetzsche (n 89) 10.

[105] H Fleischer 'Börseneinführung von Tochtergesellschaften' (2001) 165 Zeitschrift für das gesamte Handelsrecht und Wirtschaftsrecht 513, 514 ff.

[106] For a basic discussion of the relationship between company law and capital markets regulation, see S Kalss *Der Anleger im Handlungsdreieck von Vertrag, Verband und Markt* (Springer Vienna 2001); PO Mülbert *Aktiengesellschaft, Unternehmensgruppe und Kapitalmarkt* (2nd edn CH Beck Munich 1996).

[107] *Corporate Governance Kodex*; the current version can be found at <www.corporate-governance-code.de> (28 June 2005); for the background of the Code, see T Baums (ed) *Bericht der Regierungskommission Corporate Governance* (Otto Schmidt Verlag Cologne 2001); P Hommelhoff and others (eds) *Corporate Governance* (Verlag Recht und Wirtschaft Heidelberg 2002).

[108] A standard commentary is P Hommelhoff KJ Hopt and A von Werder (eds) *Handbuch Corporate Governance* (Otto Schmidt Verlag Cologne 2003).

[109] This duty to explain is made mandatory by § 161 of the German Stock Corporation Act (AktG).

[110] Cf L Timmerman 'Das Gesellschaftsrecht im 21. Jahrhundert' in P Doralt and S Kalss (eds) *Franz Klein – Vorreiter des modernen Aktien- und GmbH-Rechts* (Manz Vienna 2004) 161, 164.

The principle fits with the current general discussion to replace mandatory substantive company law with disclosure regulation. The pertinent claim is to exchange paternalistic and so-called 'merit regulation' – based on fair, just, and equitable standards – for disclosure rules.[111] Under the heading of adapting German company law to the needs of modern capital markets and making it fit for international regulatory competition, calls to deregulate the mostly mandatory stock corporation law have been raised for some time.[112] All this can be qualified as a market-oriented approach to company law.

3. The New Takeover Law

One additional recent legal development with significant relevance for the governance regime deserves attention: the new Takeover Act, the *Gesetz zur Regelung von öffentlichen Angeboten zum Erwerb von Wertpapieren und von Unternehmensübernahmen* (hereinafter *WpÜG*)[113] that went into force on January 1, 2002. Once more we see a new piece of legislation that at least predominantly qualifies as market regulation being located at the intersection of capital markets regulation and company law as a form of organizational law. The enactment of the WpÜG was triggered in part by the hostile takeover of Mannesmann AG by Vodafone AirTouch plc in 1999/2000. The legislators obviously accepted that in Germany as elsewhere, a market for corporate control as a means of external corporate governance existed, and it needed effective regulation to work properly.

[111] For a fundamental analysis, see H Merkt 'European Company Law Reform: Struggling for a More Liberal Approach' (2004) 1 Eur Company and Financial L Rev 3.

[112] Cf especially C Escher-Weingart *Reform durch Deregulierung im Kapitalgesellschaftsrecht* (Mohr Siebeck Tübingen 2001); H Hirte 'Die aktienrechtliche Satzungsstrenge: Kapitalmarkt und sonstige Legitimationen versus Gestaltungsfreiheit' in M Lutter and H Wiedemann (eds) *Gestaltungsfreiheit im Gesellschaftsrecht* (de Gruyter Berlin 1998) 61; G Spindler 'Deregulierung des Aktienrechts?' [1998] Die Aktiengesellschaft 53; HJ Mertens 'Satzungs- und Organisationsautonomie im Aktien- und Konzernrecht' [1994] Zeitschrift für Unternehmens- und Gesellschaftsrecht 426. On the tendency toward greater structural flexibility on board level in Europe KJ Hopt and PC Leyens 'Board Models in Europe – Recent Developments of Internal Corporate Governance Structures in Germany, the United Kingdom, France, and Italy' (2004) 1 Eur Company and Financial L Rev 135, 162 ff, and with a comparison of the German Aufsichtsrat to the US-board model PC Leyens 'Deutscher Aufsichtsrat und US-Board: ein- oder zweistufiges Verwaltungssystem?' (2003) 67 Rabels Zeitschrift für ausländisches und internationales Privatrecht 57 ff, especially 96 ff.

[113] Law of 20 December 2001 [2001] Bundesgesetzblatt I 3822; the law was accompanied by four ordinances dating from 27 December 2001 [2001] Bundesgesetzblatt I 4263 ff; a comprehensive legal analysis can be found with KJ Hopt 'Grundsatz und Praxisprobleme nach dem Wertpapiererwerbs- und Übernahmegesetz' (2002) 166 Zeitschrift für das gesamte Handelsrecht und Wirtschaftsrecht 383 ff; for an economic evaluation, see H Schmidt and S Prigge 'Übernahmekonzeptionen und Übernahmegesetz' (2002) 62 Die Betriebswirtschaft 225 ff.

Whether they succeeded in achieving that goal is not as clear as it might appear at first sight, however.

The WpÜG was the end of the German self-regulatory takeover regime based on the Takeover Codex of 1995.[114] The Codex mainly failed because it was not accepted by a sufficient number of listed companies. In substance, though not in form and structure, the WpÜG is modeled after the British City Code. A core element is the mandatory offer a bidder has to make if he has gained control of the target company.[115] The relevant threshold is 30 percent of the voting rights. The law thus aims at a protection of minority shareholders by granting an exit in the case of a change of control.

However, not only the mandatory bid but all 'public' offers for shares of a listed company are regulated by the law. If an offer stays below the control threshold (and the bidder owns no shares already), the procedural regulations concerning information and an equal opportunity for selling shares apply. The same is true if the bidder already has control. These kinds of offers are regulated in a manner that is somewhat similar to the US concept in the Williams Act that (only) focuses on procedural regulations for all tender offers regardless of whether a change of control is involved.[116] As a result, the WpÜG may be the most coherently structured – and most comprehensive – takeover law so far. It clearly regulates market behavior and is – apart from the mandatory bid rule – predominantly focused on disclosure of information.[117]

Based on the price regulation of the bid – the average share price or a higher price paid by the bidder during the previous three months[118] – minority shareholders participate in a possible control premium. To secure this outcome, the WpÜG – like the City Code – is necessarily characterized by a high regulatory intensity. In this regard it interferes to a much higher degree in the market process than do the alternative US or Japanese models of takeover regulation which 'only' try to guarantee a fair and equal treatment of shareholders with respect to information, proceeding, and the chance to sell in case of a partial bid. Strangely enough, the alternative model was not even discussed as viable during the reform debate in Germany, although the mandatory bid appears to be a somewhat alien

[114] *Übernahmekodex der Börsensachverständigenkommission beim Bundesministerium der Finanzen* of 14 July 1995, amended 1 January 1998.

[115] § 35 WpÜG.

[116] Law of 29 July 1968, codified as part of the Securities and Exchange Act of 1934; 15 USC §§78m(d)-(e), 78n(d)-(f).

[117] Cf especially §§ 10, 11, 14, 23, and 27 WpÜG stipulate various disclosure duties with respect to the decision to make an offer, form and terms of the offer, its publication, acquisitions of shares in the wake of the offer, and the duty of the target's board to publicly comment on the offer.

[118] § 31 WpÜG, §§ 3 – 7 WpÜG-Angebotsverordnung (Ordinance of 27 December 2001 [2001] Bundesgesetzblatt I 4263).

concept in the country's corporate law setting. The only discussion was on whether the existing law of combines in the Stock Corporation Act (*Aktienkonzernrecht*) was a functional alternative to the bid. The pull of the British model – helped by the (various) drafts of the Takeover Directive that all contained a mandatory bid as an integral part – was obviously irresistible.

However, the British model was actually not imported as a whole. In fact, only one part, the mandatory bid, was copied without the 'checks and balances' inherent to that model.[119] These are, first, a strict neutrality rule for the target's management, and second, a high degree of procedural flexibility made possible by the self-regulatory nature of the City Code. Both are a kind of 'functional counterbalance' to the regulatory costs associated with the mandatory bid. Unfortunately, the WpÜG only has a kind of watered-down neutrality rule as a result of active lobbying by parts of the industry and the unions,[120] and, being statutory law, it lacks the flexibility of the City Code. Despite its structural quality, the new takeover regime may thus result in a sub-optimal economic outcome. There is a risk that hostile takeovers as a means of corporate governance could be blocked, and friendly takeovers would not be concluded because of high costs.[121]

V. Theses

1. As elsewhere, in Germany the balance between state and society – seen as two different entities – and the responsibility for public welfare has shifted over time. During the last decades of the 19th century, a gradual shift occurred from the liberal, laissez-faire attitude to the welfare state. The accompanying renunciation of the liberal project in favor of an idealized notion of the state has created a lasting and unfortunate legacy: the persistent and deeply ingrained present-day German belief in a perceived unlimited competence of the state, and a deeply ingrained skepticism toward the market mechanism by the general public that has turned out to be the greatest single obstacle obstructing urgent reforms in 21st-century Germany.

2. Today, the financial overburdening of the welfare state has become increasingly visible, and the collapse of social security systems has become a real threat.

[119] A critical analysis can be found with H Baum 'Funktionale Elemente und Komplementaritäten des britischen Übernahmerechts' [2003] Recht der Internationalen Wirtschaft 421 ff.

[120] Cf the instructive criticism from an American perspective with JN Gordon 'Das neue deutsche 'Anti'-Übernahmegesetz aus amerikanischer Perspektive' [2002] Die Aktiengesellschaft 670 ff.

[121] There is already anecdotal evidence that planned takeovers as a means of restructuring had to be cancelled because of the rigid price rules of the WpÜG, cf report *Frankfurter Allgemeine Zeitung* (Frankfurt Germany 16 September 2002) 13.

Furthermore, the modern welfare state sees itself confronted with another fundamental problem: a growing discrepancy between public expectations and the state's ability to act. A third dismal consequence of the welfare state has been a steady and in some areas dramatic increase in regulation. At least a partial retreat of the welfare state seems unavoidable. Two developments may be indicators of a such a change: the large-scale privatization of public utilities during the 1990s in Germany and the very recent admission that a supplementary private pillar in the public pension system is the only way out of the welfare crisis. The latter can possibly be viewed as the beginning of a privatization of welfare arrangements.

3. The German system of governance is characterized by a specifically corporatist-based structure of its political economy. A corporatist approach has also been characteristic of corporate governance in Germany. Committed labor and patient capital management resulted in a willingness for long-term commitment. This regime is generally classified as the standard example of an insider-controlled and stakeholder-oriented governance system as opposed to a 'modern' capital-marked-based and outsider-controlled system. But it has been a functioning system with an inner logic, with complementary and consistent features.

4. However, various threads of this insider system have started to unravel, and certain elements typically associated with outsider systems seem to be increasing. Thus a gradual and partial de-bundling of the corporatist '*Deutschland AG*' appears to be somewhat probable. This raises the question of whether a partial shift toward an outsider- and market-oriented governance model may result in a breakdown of the traditional system without having the new one already in place and functioning.

5. The structural changes are accompanied by regulatory ones. Although most reforms of company law are aimed at modernizing the traditional system of corporate control rather then replacing it with a new one, other legislative reforms are clearly improving corporate governance through strengthening the impact of market forces and are obviously inspired by a regulatory approach typical for an outsider- and market-oriented governance model. The current general discussion is to what extent mandatory substantive company law can be replaced by disclosure regulation.

6. Since the mid-1990s, an independent and extensive body of financial market regulation in its own right has been built up in addition to the existing exchange and banking laws. The Securities Trading Act of 1994 introduced a new era of ordering to the German capital markets aimed not at regulating a special product or participant but at the market *as such*.

7. The emphasis of various recent reforms has been on the regulation of information: enhanced disclosure duties, stricter liability for insufficient or misleading information, and more efficient means of private enforcement of mandatory disclosure rules by damages suits. The overriding principle is disclose or abstain. In addition, the German Corporate Governance Code of 2002 is based on the

modern principle of 'comply or explain' that is rather new to the traditional German concept of company law. The new Takeover Act also predominantly qualifies as market regulation.

8. In summary, as market regulation is the cornerstone of a functional outsider- and market-oriented governance model, recent legislative developments may anticipate a change of the traditional governance model rather than a mere supplementation.

Corporate Governance Changes in the 20th Century: A View from Italy

GUIDO A. FERRARINI

I. Introduction

This paper comments on Harald Baum's paper[1] by briefly analysing the Italian experience in the same period of time. Whilst the individual developments in corporate governance and regulation are no doubt different in Germany and Italy, reflecting as they do profound differences in the economic, legal, and political settings, a broad view of the 20th century's evolution shows substantial similarities. First of all, at least three stages of development can be identified, as argued by Professor Baum: liberalism, the welfare state, and the welfare state's crisis. However, in this paper, I consider four stages of Italian development following a similar classification proposed by an Italian scholar:[2] liberalism, the mixed economy (characterised by the mounting role of the state in the economy), the welfare state (the origins of which, however, date back to the beginning of the century), and the new economic constitution. Each stage will be analysed by one of the following sections. The fourth stage basically coincides with that defined by Professor Baum as the crisis of the welfare state and includes changes in governance and regulation broadly converging with those found in other European states. Many of these changes were determined by the European Union either directly (through legal harmonisation) or indirectly. European developments, in turn, are often a reflection of global changes making pressure towards convergence.

Nonetheless, convergence is not sufficient to characterise the German and Italian experiences in the last two decades of the 20th century. As shown by Baum's paper, path dependency also played a role in German legal reform.

[1] See the contribution by H Baum in this volume.

[2] S Cassese *La nuova costituzione economica* (Laterza Roma Bari 2001) 7 ff.

Similar comments can be made for Italy, as the present paper will conclude. On balance, the German and Italian experiences, despite offering good examples of convergence towards global standards, do not support the 'strong convergence' theory advanced by some law and economics scholars.[3] These experiences are better explained by the rival scholarly position which sees political forces and path dependency as shaping and constraining economic evolution.[4] As I argue below, the political theories of corporate governance and financial development significantly contribute to the analysis of the Italian experience.

II. Liberalism and the Commercial Codes

In this section, I consider the formation of two consecutive commercial codes after Italy's unification in the age of liberalism. This age extends for about forty years in the second half of the 19th century and is characterised by the very limited role of the state in the economy. The state intervened mainly in the field of public infrastructures, while economic activities were private and subject to self-regulation by the newly instituted chambers of commerce.[5] Industrialisation was limited to some areas of the country, which was still mainly rural. The liberal state was confronted with industrialisation only at the turn of the century, when the Italian economy joined the second industrial revolution led by the US and Germany. Early industrialisation was accompanied by the creation of a number of public undertakings mainly in the area of public services, insurance, and banking.[6] Railways, which were privately operated under public franchises, were nationalised in 1905 and became part of the government administration.

1. The Commercial Codes' Rules on Companies

One of the main themes of discussion surrounding company law reform in the new Italian kingdom was whether limited liability companies should be subject to

[3] The strong convergence thesis is best exemplified by F Easterbrook and D Fischel *The Economic Structure of Corporate Law* (Harvard University Press Harvard 1991) 212 ff and, more recently, by H Hansmann and R Kraakman 'The End of History for Corporate Law' (2001) 89 Georgetown L J 439. See J Coffee 'The Future as History: The Prospects for Global Convergence in Corporate Governance and its Implications' (1999) 93 Northwestern U L Rev 641, 646 ff, for an enlightening overview of the main strands of thought in this area.

[4] See L Bebchuk and M Roe 'A Theory of Path Dependence in Corporate Governance and Ownership' (1999) 52 Stanford L Rev 127. J Coffee (n 3) 650 agrees that formal convergence faces too many obstacles to be predicted; he argues, however, that functional convergence can occur through the international securities markets.

[5] See Cassese (n 2) 8 ff.

[6] ibid 12 ff.

governmental authorisation, as provided by the pre-unification commercial codes[7] along the French model.[8] In a report written by Tommaso Corsi, a member of the House of Representatives who worked on a company law reform project in 1862, a proposal was made to abolish the authorisation regime as incapable of preventing frauds and excessively limiting freedom of trade.[9] In lieu of the companies' public surveillance, it was recommended to better regulate the relationships between shareholders and directors, as well as those amongst shareholders. However, this proposal was fiercely opposed in the wake of financial fraud cases and was later rejected by Parliament when adopting the first Italian Commercial Code in 1865. This Code largely followed the *Codice Albertino* model[10] and reinforced the public surveillance regime by instituting a new Control Office (*Ufficio di sindacato*), both to authorise new companies and to monitor existing ones.[11]

It was only with the second Commercial Code, adopted in 1882, that a more liberal attitude was taken and governmental authorisation was abolished, as had already been done in France in 1867. Consequently, the conditions as to company

[7] Despite the elaboration of numerous draft commercial codes in the states into which Italy was divided before its unification, Napoleon made the *Code de commerce* applicable to the Italian regions annexed to the French Empire (including Liguria, Piedmont, and Tuscany), to the *Regno Italico* (of which Milan was the capital) and to the Kingdom of Naples. See AP Schioppa *Saggi di storia del diritto commerciale* (Edizioni Universitarie di Lettere Economia Diritto Milan 1992) 137 ff. After the Restoration, the *Code de commerce* was kept in force in several regions, such as the Lombard-Venetian Kingdom and the Grand Dukedom of Tuscany and Genoa, while other states (such as Piedmont and the Pontifical State) adopted their own commercial codes, which, however, closely followed the French model (ibid 141 ff). The Kingdom of Sardinia proceeded to a new codification of all its laws in the 1830s, which led to the adoption of a new commercial Code in 1842, still modelled on the French Code but with some differences.

[8] The *Code de commerce* which was adopted by Napoleon in 1807 included a few Articles on the limited liability company (*société anonyme*). This company ceased to be subject to the special privilege of incorporation and was regulated in a general, though concise, way by the law. See G Ripert *Aspects juridiques du capitalisme moderne* (2nd ed Librairie Générale de Droit et de Jurisprudence Paris 1951) 51. However, the introduction of a general incorporation regime did not mean freedom to set up limited liability companies. Less liberal than the New York Law of 1811, which also abolished the special charter privileges, the *Code de commerce* introduced an administrative authorisation regime for the formation of the *société anonyme* (art 37). This regime was officially justified with reference to private law arguments, such as the protection of subscribers and third parties from speculation and frauds; however, it also reflected more fundamental public policy concerns, as the centralism of the Empire did not tolerate independent social powers. See P Ungari *Profilo storico del diritto delle anonime in Italia* (Rome 1974) 30 ff.

[9] See A Marghieri *I motivi del nuovo Codice di Commercio italiano* (Naples 1885-1886) app 193 ff.

[10] See n 7.

[11] See Schioppa (n 7) 213 ff.

formation were specified by the Code, and the Civil Tribunal was empowered to ascertain these conditions before the company's registration.

The Code was the result of drafting efforts which extended over more than a decade with the participation of some of Italy's finest scholars.[12] This was reflected by the high technical quality of the Code which was in line with its homologues in Europe, such as the English Law of 1861, the French Law of 1867, the German Commercial Code of 1861 (*ADHGB*) and the Law of 1870, and the Belgian Law of 1873, all widely considered throughout the legislative work.[13] The convergence of national company law rules reflected the internalisation of the economy in the 19th century. As argued by Professor H. James, at the end of that century international integration was similar, if not more advanced, than that found in the last part of the 20th century.[14] The Italian Code included, for those times, advanced regulation of limited liability companies (*società anonime*). Amongst the novelties was the introduction of a board of auditors to monitor the company's management and accounts on behalf of shareholders and creditors, along the model of English Law, and, as a counterbalance, the abolition of the administrative surveillance regime.[15] On the whole, the Code followed 'the first systematic approach to companies. The general meeting and its functioning, the directors and their responsibility, corporate control and the protection of minorities, the regulation of accounts, liquidation and mergers found in these texts [ie the Code and its previous drafts] a modern treatment'.[16]

2. Industrialisation and Financial Development

All this helps to understand why the Commercial Code and its rules on companies, in particular, remained in force, with minor modifications, for sixty years.

[12] ibid 157 ff.

[13] ibid 226.

[14] See H James *The End of Globalisation. Lessons from the Great Depression* (Harvard University Press Cambridge 2000), arguing: 'At the end of the nineteenth century, the world was highly integrated economically, through mobility of capital, information, goods, and people. Capital moved freely between states and continents' (p 10). The author provides some measures of integration with reference to the size of net capital movements and the levels of trade: 'For most countries, despite all the intervening improvements in the means of transportation, the levels of trade of the prewar world were not reached again until the 1980s' (p 12).

[15] See PE Bensa 'I sindaci della società per azioni, cenni storici e comparativi' [1883] Rassegna di diritto commerciale 1.

[16] See G Cottino and G Minervini 'La società per azioni a cento anni dal codice di commercio' in *1882-1982 Cento anni dal Codice di Commercio* (Giuffrè Milan 1984) 112. On the role of the 1882 Code in Italian legal history, see S Rodota 'Le libertà e i diritti' in R Romanelli (ed) *Storia dello Stato Italiano dall'Unità a oggi* (Donzelli Editore Rome 1995) 317.

However, the economic development that occurred throughout this period of time exerted considerable strain on the Code's regulation of limited companies. New problems were created with which the Commercial Code was ill-equipped to cope: the formation of company groups, cross-shareholdings, voting limitations and multiple voting shares, controlling minorities, and the separation of ownership and control.[17] In fact, at the time of the Code's adoption, Italy was still a rural country, despite some notable examples of industrialisation, particularly in the northern regions and in the fields of mechanical and textile industries. But in the first decade of the 20th century, Italy joined the small group of industrialised nations: 'To be true, the industrial takeoff was completed only at the end of the First World War; in addition, a significant part of the country was cut off from economic development. Nonetheless, from the beginning of the century the industrial structure of our country was consolidated and a modern society started to emerge, characterised by substantial urbanisation and fast growth of national income'.[18] This was also a reflection of the second industrial revolution occurring in other countries, particularly the United States and Germany.[19] New companies were formed in Italy to produce electricity, steel, automobiles, tyres, trains, typewriters, etc, with the financing on the part of a few large banks and the support of the state.[20]

The beginning of the 20th century was generally characterised in Europe by 'very high levels of financial development, higher than what we have seen as recently as 1980'.[21] Rajan and Zingales consider three different indicators of financial development in 1913 and 1980 for a number of developed countries (including Italy). Firstly, the ratio of deposits to GDP dropped by 20% between 1913 and 1980, suggesting that banks played a relatively bigger role in intermedi-

[17] See G Ferri 'La disciplina delle società nel Codice di commercio del 1882' in *1882-1982 Cento anni dal Codice di Commercio* (n 16) 105. For an economic analysis of the relevant governance structures, see F Amatori 'La grande impresa' in F Amatori and others (eds) *Storia d'Italia. Annali* vol 15: l'industria (Einaudi Turin 1999) 691 ff.

[18] See V Castronovo *L'industria italiana dall'ottocento a oggi* (Mondadori Milan 1990) 71.

[19] See AD Chandler F Amatori and T Hikino (eds) *Big Business and the Wealth of Nations* (Cambridge Cambridge University Press 1997), for a comparative analysis of several countries' industrial development in the period in question.

[20] See N Crepax *Storia dell'industria in Italia: uomini, imprese e prodotti* (Il Mulino Bologna 2002) 37 ff, noting that this was the American century, the age of 'Fordism', mass production, and standardisation of products (p 40).

[21] RG Rajan and L Zingales *Saving Capitalism from the Capitalists* (Random House Business Books London 2003) 191. For a more detailed analysis, see RG Rajan and L Zingales 'The Great Reversals: The Politics of Financial Development in the 20th Century' (2003) 69 J of Financial Economics 5. For an explanation of the 'great reversal' phenomenon, see E Perotti and E von Thadden 'The Political Economy of Dominant Investors' (Working Paper June 2004), arguing that some financially developed countries moved towards bank or state control as a financially weakened middle class became concerned about income risk.

ating funds at the beginning of the century.[22] Secondly, the ratio of stock market capitalisation to GDP dropped by more than 50%, indicating that equity markets were more developed at the beginning of the century.[23] Thirdly, the fraction of investments financed through equity issues dropped from 13% to 2% over the period, suggesting that equity issues were a more important source of investment funding in 1913 than in 1980.[24] There was, however, diversity amongst the countries considered: for instance, 'the equity market in 1913 was much more important in England, Belgium and France than in the United States'.[25] Moreover, Italy's level of financial development was relatively low in 1913, particularly with reference to the second and third indicators (even though both indicators dropped for Italy as well from 1913 to 1980).

Putting the Italian scenario in perspective, between 1900 and 1907 the number of companies listed at the Milan Bourse increased from 59 to 169, with the bulk of new listings concentrated in the last three years, a record figure in the whole century.[26] The stock exchanges' capitalisation amounted in 1907 to 70% of Italian equity.[27] Nonetheless, stock exchange trading was dominated by speculation, which was financed by the large banks, concurrently operating as providers of equity and loans to industry.[28] In 1907, the stock markets started declining, as a result of an international liquidity crisis which caused a credit restriction, and continued to do so until 1920, with a drop of 80% in capitalisation in real terms. This crisis caused significant problems to the banking system and is considered a landmark in the history of Italian capital markets, which subsequently ceased to develop in relative terms and remained thin and inadequate for financing economic development.[29] In the meantime, public ownership started to grow as an alternative mode of enterprise financing: railways, which had previously been run by private companies, some of which were listed, were nationalised in 1905; new banks were created as public entities to finance either public works or specific sectors of the industry; and a public insurance undertaking was formed to offer life insurance as a monopolist.[30]

[22] Rajan and Zingales (n 21) 192.

[23] ibid 193.

[24] ibid 194.

[25] ibid.

[26] See G Siciliano *Cento anni di borsa in Italia* (Il Mulino Bologna 2001) 17 ff.

[27] ibid.

[28] ibid.

[29] ibid, quoting AM Biscaini and P Ciocca, 'Le strutture finanziarie: aspetti quantitativi di lungo periodo (1870-1970)' in F Vicarelli (ed) *Capitale industriale e capitale finanziario: il caso italiano* (Il Mulino Bologna 1979).

[30] S Cassese *La nuova costituzione economica* (Laterza Roma Bari, 2001) 13.

III. The 'Mixed Economy' and the Civil Code

The period defined as 'mixed economy' covers approximately thirty years extending from Fascism to the new Republican Constitution (1948). It is characterised by state dirigisme and an increasing role for public ownership of enterprises.[31] In 1942 the Civil Code and its rules on companies were enacted following numerous attempts at company law reform throughout the whole period. As argued by Professor Cassese, economic dirigisme found three expressions in this period.[32] Firstly, whole sectors of the economy such as shipping lines and telephone services (1922), air transport (1923), mining and broadcasting (1927), and water (1933) became public monopolies. Secondly, access to almost all economic activities (banking, commerce, industry, insurance, export trade) was subjected to authorisation by the government, while the authorisation regimes were often exploited by the incumbents to protect their rents. Thirdly, plans were adopted in areas such as banking, urban development, art, and monuments.

1. The Great Crisis

In the 1930s, a severe crisis occurred as a result of the world economic recession and led to an impressive rescue operation concerning the large universal banks and almost half of the large industrial companies.[33] This operation led to the creation by the government of the *Istituto per la Ricostruzione Industriale* (IRI) which became the controlling shareholder of several industrial conglomerates (including a number of listed companies) and of the main Italian banks. In addition, a state bank was created under the name of *Istituto Mobiliare Italiano* (IMI) to extend medium and long-term loans to the industry. At the same time, a new banking law was adopted to introduce a tighter system of surveillance and sever the residual links between bank and industry at the ownership level (with the exception of IRI).[34] Public ownership of business was originally intended as a temporary measure, but it subsequently became a stable solution, characterising our system as a 'mixed economy'.[35] Not only several industrial conglomerates, but the prevailing part of our banking system, including all the large banks, were owned by the state until the wave of privatisations in the 1990s.

[31] ibid 14 ff.

[32] ibid 15 ff.

[33] See, also for references, P Bianchi *La rincorsa frenata. L'industria italiana dall'unità nazionale all'unificazione europea* (Il Mulino Bologna 2002) 38 ff.

[34] See G Conti 'Le banche e il finanziamento industriale' in Amatori (n 17) 483 ff.

[35] See F Barca and S Trento 'La parabola delle partecipazioni statali: una missione tradita' in F Barca (ed) *Storia del capitalismo italiano dal dopoguerra a oggi* (Donzelli Roma 1997) 186 ff.

Capital markets suffered both from the wide role of the state in the economy and from the Fascist government's policy aimed at reducing the stock exchanges' importance in the financial system.[36] Fascist ideology was uncomfortable with securities markets: centralised government (including tight regulation of banking), the role of the state in the economy, and the isolationism pursued at the international level militated against the formation of vibrant capital markets. Nonetheless, leading industrial figures enjoyed strong connections with the government while their firms prospered under the protection of the same.[37] Controlling private monopolies and coalescing amongst entrepreneurs were keys to economic success in Fascist Italy. As argued by Rajan and Zingales, Italian industrialists benefited from the use of public money in the wake of the Great Depression.[38] The bailouts of industrial firms and banks occurred at enormous cost to the taxpayers. However, many of the acquired enterprises remained listed at the Italian stock exchanges, while the state did not interfere with their management: 'Not only did the managers keep their jobs, but also many of the board members, who represented the interest of the previous owners, retained their seats. Public ownership and control was a façade for a much more complex intertwining of the private and the public spheres.'[39]

2. The Civil Code of 1942

These comments help to put in historical context the reformulation of company law rules in the Civil Code of 1942, which replaced both the Civil Code of 1865 and the Commercial Code of 1882 by unifying private law.[40] The Code's rules were the results of several reform projects which had been elaborated over more than forty years, as the industrial takeoff of the country and the diffusion of joint stock companies highlighted the limits of the Commercial Code in this area. The main projects were published in the first quarter of the last century and reflected either the need for improved protection of minority shareholders, widely shared by public opinion in the light of financial crisis and scandals (*Vivante* Project,

[36] See Siciliano (n 26) 32 ff.

[37] See, for example, S Romano *Giuseppe Volpi. Industria e finanza tra Giolitti e Mussolini* (Bompiani Milan 1979).

[38] Rajan and Zingales (n 21) 212 ff. Following G Toniolo 'Crisi economica e smobilizzo pubblico delle banche miste (1930-1934)' in G Toniolo (ed) *Industria e banca nella grande crisi 1929-1934* (Etas Libri Milan 1978) 331, they argue that many of the companies taken over by the government were in capital-intensive sectors and not very attractive economically. Therefore, the private sector continued to obtain the essential inputs needed, without suffering the losses affecting the relevant businesses.

[39] ibid 214, making reference also to Mediobanca, the investment bank which, despite being state-owned, had an essential role in protecting principal Italian capitalists.

[40] See, for all, R Nicolò 'Diritto Civile' XII Enciclopedia del Diritto (Giuffrè Milan 1964).

1922), or the industrialists' wish for the maintenance of the *status quo* under which they enjoyed large freedom of action (*Confindustria*'s Proposals, 1925).[41] A third initiative tried to mediate between the two opposing camps by adopting only the innovations which were thought to be needed to foster the country's economic development (*D'Amelio* Project, 1925).[42]

However, fifteen years had to elapse before the reform activity was resumed, a long delay which can be explained by reference to the conflicting views on company law reform and to the pressure exercised by industrial circles on the Fascist government. In addition, the public ownership of a large part of the industrial and financial sectors and a hostile policy towards the stock exchanges combined to play down the need for company law reform. This negatively affected the outline of such a reform, which almost ignored the connection between joint stock companies and securities markets, and avoided some of the main issues of modern corporate governance, including the separation between ownership and control in listed companies.[43] On a more general level, '[the] direct intervention of the state as entrepreneur largely replaced and crowded out the role of the private sector in the accumulation of capital. This is at odds with what happened in the United States, where the government faced similar challenges but chose to intervene as regulator of capital markets rather than as their substitute'.[44]

As a result, the Civil Code's rules on limited liability companies, despite making a distinction between private companies (*società a responsabilità limitata*) and joint stock companies (*società per azioni*) so as to better allocate the regulatory burdens depending on the size and importance of the business venture, dedicate an incomplete regulation to the latter type of companies. The limits of the Civil Code were clearly shown, almost fifty years ago, by one of the leading corporate jurists, Tullio Ascarelli, in his inaugural study on the *Rivista delle società*, where he highlighted the wide existence of 'controlling minorities' in listed companies and the ensuing separation of ownership and control.[45] This required, in the author's opinion (explicitly inspired by the Anglo-American experience), improving the internal governance structure of joint stock companies, reinforcing the shareholders' powers, and introducing a public regulator to

[41] See Schioppa (n 7) 226 ff.

[42] ibid 240 ff.

[43] See R Teti 'Imprese, imprenditori e diritto' in Amatori (n 17)1274 ff, illustrating the lukewarm reception of protection of minorities' principles in the Civil Code, which maintained a corporate governance structure similar to that foreseen by the Commercial Code, despite widespread criticism of the board of statutory auditors (*collegio sindacale*) and proposals to replace it with external auditors.

[44] See A Aganin and P Volpin 'History of corporate ownership in Italy' (ECGI Finance Working Paper no 17/2003 March 2003) 2.

[45] T Ascarelli 'I problemi delle società anonime per azioni' [1956] Rivista delle società 3 ff.

protect investors in listed companies – measures which were not taken by the Italian legislators until the last quarter of the last century, as will be shown below.

The Civil Code's fate was similar to that of the Commercial Code, to the extent that not many years after the Code's adoption, Italy went through a phase of extraordinary economic development, known as the 'economic miracle'.[46] Industrial productivity increased substantially, also as a consequence of the Common Market's liberalisation policy, and this was reflected by the stock market's exceptional performance in the postwar period.[47] However, despite the stock market's significant contribution to the financing of industry, the former's structural conditions (as measured, for instance, by the number of listed companies) were left substantially unchanged.[48]

IV. The Welfare State and the Rise of Securities Regulation

The period of time stretching from the middle of the 20th century to the 1970s is characterised by the creation of the welfare state and the completion of the public enterprise system.[49] The welfare state concerns areas such as education, social security, and employment. Its importance from a corporate governance perspective was shown, also with respect to Italy, by Professor Roe in his book on the political determinants of corporate governance.[50] The Italian welfare state no doubt contributed to keep the ownership of companies concentrated and the securities markets relatively underdeveloped for reasons which are common to social democracies. As argued by Roe:

> Social democracies demeaned shareholder primacy, pushing firms to stabilize employment, to expand whether or not expansion was profitable for shareholders, and to avoid change that would disrupt the quality of the work place. . . . Social democratic pressures increased managerial agency costs for shareholders and thus decreased the firm's value to diffuse shareholders. Owners presumably sought alternatives that reduced those agency costs, such as close ownership.[51]

Moreover, the increased role of public ownership reduced the number of enterprises that could assume a diffuse ownership structure as well as the interest in a modern listed companies' regulation. In the following two paragraphs, I analyse the company law reform adopted at the end of the period in question to modernise

[46] See, instead of many, Bianchi (n 33) 117 ff.

[47] See Siciliano (n 26) 35 ff.

[48] ibid 38.

[49] Cassese (n 30) 19 ff.

[50] M Roe *Political determinants of corporate governance. Political Context, Corporate Impact* (OUP Oxford 2003) 162 ff.

[51] ibid 27.

both the law concerning listed companies and that regulating stock exchanges; I also try to understand the Italian developments examined in this and the previous sections from the viewpoint of the international discussion on corporate governance and financial development.

1. The 1974 Reform

The renovated industrial successes of the country in the 1950s and 1960s threw new light on the inadequacy of the Civil Code's rules on joint stock companies and led to the formulation of several reform projects.[52] However, T. Ascarelli's proposal[53] of shareholders' empowerment as a means for investor protection was generally rejected. The emphasis was put instead on the distinction between two shareholders' groups in listed companies: those who are interested in the management of the company's enterprise ('shareholders-entrepreneurs', as the controllers or block-holders used to be defined) and those who are only interested in investing ('shareholders-investors').[54] In particular, it was argued that the shareholders-investors would never be active in corporate governance and would rather vote with their feet, by selling their shares in underperforming companies.[55] As a consequence, the legislators should mainly protect their position as investors by introducing mandatory rules, improving disclosure, and caring for the investors' rights to dividends. Moreover, a public regulator should be created with competencies on corporate disclosure and, under some proposals, on the legality of corporate actions.[56]

It was under the influence of these ideas that a reform of company law and stock exchange law took place in 1974. In lieu of focussing on the internal governance of listed companies, this 'small reform' (*miniriforma,* as it was dubbed by the first commentators) sought to implement the investor protection principle through a number of regulatory innovations.[57] On the one hand, convertible bonds and saving shares (ie non-voting preferred shares) were specifically regulated to offer small investors, rather than controlling shareholders, financial instruments which were better suited to their investing goals (an assumption which was proven to be wrong by later developments concerning saving shares). On the other hand, a securities commission (*Consob*) was created

[52] See, for references, Teti (n 43) 1284 ff.

[53] n 45.

[54] See G Ferri 'La tutela dell'azionista in una prospettiva di riforma' [1961] Rivista delle società 177.

[55] ibid 185 ff.

[56] See Teti (n 43) 1289 ff, also for references to the reform projects of the '60s.

[57] See P Marchetti 'Diritto societario e disciplina della concorrenza' in F Barca (ed) *Storia del capitalismo italiano dal dopoguerra a oggi* (Donzelli Roma 1997) 489 ff.

with competencies on corporate disclosure and stock exchange trading. In addition, information duties were placed on listed companies and companies making recourse to the capital markets. Furthermore, listed companies were required to appoint outside auditors to certify their financial statements, while maintaining a board of statutory auditors as foreseen by general company law.

Therefore, the reform laid the foundations of a securities regulation system.[58] However, its limits were quite clear, even leaving apart the total neglect of internal governance issues. First of all, disclosure regulation was still in its infancy: prospectuses were unknown, as were consolidated balance sheets. Consob needed some time to take off and even more time to become a securities regulator deserving of this name. Private enforcement was ignored by the 1974 law and also by subsequent laws adding new layers of public regulation. The emphasis on public regulation and surveillance was a reflection of ideologies (both Catholic and socialist) not entirely at ease with free market mechanisms. Disclosure regulation was willingly accepted because it foresaw 'public controls', while merit regulation frequently surfaced in the discussions leading to the 1974 and subsequent reforms as an alternative way to protect investors. In any case, the architecture of the securities markets was left substantially unmodified: Consob replaced the various institutions governing the stock exchanges, which kept their public nature. Access to the exchanges remained barred to banks and to investment companies, while stockbrokers were forbidden to operate in corporate form and to trade as dealers.

On the whole, the mini-reform of 1974 was not directed towards promoting the securities markets. The introduction of saving shares satisfied the interests of controlling minorities more than those of investors, who were placed at the mercy of dominant shareholders and their managers as repeated abuses in practice would subsequently prove. Higher dividends were paid to saving shares because investors were not entitled to vote; however, when interest rates came down those dividends became too onerous for issuers and saving shares were generally converted into ordinary shares and almost disappeared. Moreover, corporate governance remained poor: the boards of directors of listed companies were interlocked and ineffective, whilst statutory auditors devoted little time to their duties and generally lacked independence. In addition, outside auditors were formally regulated by the law and subject to Consob's surveillance; however, the relevant regulation was clearly deficient and public surveillance was too light and sporadic, as subsequently shown by several financial scandals (including Parmalat's unprecedented financial fraud).

[58] See G Rossi *Trasparenze e vergogna. Le società e la borsa* (Il Saggiatore Milan 1982) 113 ff.

2. Law and Finance vs Political Theories

The 'law and finance' theory explains the underdevelopment of Italian capital markets throughout most of the 20th century as a result of poor investor protection.[59] Whilst the 1882 Commercial Code may have contributed to the extraordinary financial development enjoyed by the country at the turn of the century, its inadequacy in terms of investor protection could help to understand why the stock market did not recover from its 1907 crisis and remained underdeveloped. The Civil Code of 1942 was also totally inadequate with respect to listed companies, and the 1974 law reform introducing Consob was clearly insufficient to introduce a US-type securities regulation. All this would confirm the 'law and finance' view of the civil law systems as inferior to the common law ones in creating the conditions for securities markets' development.

However, a similar explanation would be only partial. First of all, the 'law matters' argument, which is almost undisputable when establishing a correlation between law and financial development, does not necessarily mean that investor protection is necessary for securities markets to arise. As argued by Professor Coffee, the cause and effect sequence is often backwards: legal developments tend to follow, rather than precede, economic change.[60] US legal and financial history shows that securities markets preceded investor protection legislation, also suggesting that securities markets need to develop before a constituency (the dispersed public shareholders) can arise and ask for protection, thus becoming an instrument for legal change.[61] In Italy, securities regulation, despite being introduced in the 1970s, was mainly completed in the 1990s when the securities market resumed development, also as a result of the liberalisation of capital flows and integration in European economies, as will be shown below.

The political theory of financial development offers a more comprehensive explanation without necessarily conflicting with the 'law and finance' perspective. In particular, the 'political economy' view predicts a negative relationship between stock market development and state ownership of companies. Analysing the evolution of stock market development and public ownership of traded companies over time, Aganin and Volpin found that stagnation of the Italian stock market lasted until the 1980s: 'Only in 1985 did the number of companies on the stock market get past the level it had reached in 1930. . . . While the stock market stagnated, the role of government increased. From 1950 to 1980, between

[59] On this theory in general, see R La Porta and others 'Law and Finance' (1998) 106 J Political Economy 1113; R La Porta and others 'Corporate Ownership Around the World' (1999) 54 J of Finance 471.

[60] J Coffee 'The Rise of Dispersed Ownership: The Role of Law and the State in the Separation of Ownership and Control' (2001) 111 Yale L J 1, 7.

[61] ibid.

15 and 20% of traded companies in Italy were controlled by the government…'[62] The situation subsequently changed: the number of listed companies increased (despite remaining relatively low), while the share of publicly owned companies was reduced. This was also the result of privatisations mainly accomplished throughout the 1990s, at a time when the government made serious efforts to promote capital markets in Italy.

Italy's features also display key aspects of Mark Roe's political theory of corporate governance.[63] Under this theory, 'strong social democracies pressed firms to favour employees over invested capital, but shareholders resisted this, and their best way to resist was often to build or to keep concentrated, and often private, ownership'.[64] Even though Italy does not entirely fit the model of a social democracy, stakeholder pressures are high in this country and can affect shareholder interests in large firms, particularly those with diffuse ownership.[65] This helps to explain not only the absence of diffuse ownership companies, but also the limited development of Italian capital markets. Only in the 1990s did anti-market ideologies soften and the economy liberalised enough that it became plausible to think about encouraging securities markets, listed firms, and ownership dispersion.[66]

To conclude on the Italian developments up to the 1970s, the economic dirigisme characterising the welfare state and the increasing role of public ownership of enterprises militated against the securities markets and muted any claim for investor protection. Stock exchanges and listed companies still played a role; however, the markets were thin and dominated by speculation, whilst the capitalists (ie the few families controlling the largest quoted groups, often through pyramids and the like) resisted change, fearing that the development of vibrant capital markets could threaten their rents. All this was possible because national markets in Europe were still relatively closed and regulatory barriers existed to the circulation of capital (including rigid currency controls). As argued by Rajan and Zingales, incumbents find financial development less useful when an economy becomes open to the entry of foreign goods and capital.[67] First of all, there are fewer profits to protect in the system. Consequently, both the incentive to keep restraints in place and the ability to pay politicians for support diminish.[68]

62 Aganin and Volpin (n 44) 10.

63 See Roe (n 50).

64 ibid 14.

65 ibid 24.

66 ibid 83.

67 RG Rajan and L Zingales *Saving Capitalism from the Capitalists* (Random House Business Books London 2003) 182 f.

68 ibid 183.

Furthermore, even established incumbents find that the high costs of domestic finance hurt, and so become supporters of financial development.[69]

V. The New Economic Constitution and Company Law reform

Better conditions for financial development matured in Italy throughout the last two decades of the 20th century under the 'new economic constitution'.[70] This concept includes the main legal developments which occurred both in the EU and Italy during the relevant time. First of all, the internal market was completed through implementation of the fundamental freedoms foreseen by the EC Treaty. In addition, a rigorous competition policy was developed by the Union as a means for the integration of markets. Specific liberalisation measures were adopted for banks, financial intermediaries, insurance undertakings, and public utilities in order to enhance competition and harmonise regulation so as to allow the formation of a single market. This led to the formation of new regulatory structures in the member states along the US model of independent regulatory commissions and to the re-organisation of existing ones. In this paragraph, I will consider the main changes that occurred in Italy during the relevant period with respect to securities regulation and corporate governance reform, and also as a reflection of European developments.

1. Improving Securities Regulation

Liberalisation of capital movements by the European Community in the 1980s was clearly instrumental in eliminating resistance to the development of securities markets, as the Italian market was integrated into the single European market and subject to harmonised rules. In addition, the privatisation program led by the Italian government throughout the 1990s widened the shareholders' base in large companies and enhanced the stock market's liquidity. Privatisations were also motivated by developments occurring at the EU level, such as the criteria laid down in the Maastricht Treaty for qualifying for the Monetary Union and the EU prohibition of government subsidies to enterprises, including state-owned companies.[71] More recently, the introduction of the Euro gave further impetus to the integration of European securities markets and motivated new harmonisation initiatives at the EU level such as those included in the Financial Services Action Plan.

[69] ibid.

[70] See Cassese (n 30) 283 ff.

[71] Rajan and Zingales (n 67) 216.

As a result of these and similar developments, Italian securities regulation was radically transformed. The main changes took place in the 1990s. In 1991, insider trading was forbidden in compliance with the relevant EC Directive. In the same year, investment companies (*società di intermediazione mobiliare*) were introduced into our legal system to operate as multifunctional intermediaries replacing individual stockbrokers (*agenti di cambio*), who could only act in a broking capacity. At the same time, the conditions were laid down for a re-organisation of the regional stock exchanges through their merger into a national stock exchange (in fact, the Milan bourse, which was already dominant, became the Italian Stock Exchange). In 1992, takeovers were regulated and a mandatory bid rule was introduced to protect minority shareholders, albeit in a rather confused and incomplete manner.

In 1996, another important reform took place when the Investment Services Directive was implemented. Not only were the ISD rules received into our law, but other rules were introduced to allow the Italian market to better sustain the impact of liberalisation. The organisation of stock exchanges was radically reformed and privatisation of the existing exchanges was envisaged. Exchanges came to be treated as enterprises offering trading services, whilst exchange trading became subject to these enterprises' regulation (not necessarily 'self-regulation', as the exchange owners could be different from either the market intermediaries or the financial instruments' issuers). As a result, both the Italian Exchange and MTS (the sovereign bonds market) became for-profit companies and were sold to investors, mainly banks and investment firms operating in the relevant markets.[72]

2. The Draghi Law

The 1996 rules on investment intermediaries and markets were almost transplanted into the Financial Markets Consolidated Act of 1998, also known as the Draghi Law after its drafting committee's chairman. This law also included new rules as to listed companies' disclosure and governance. In fact, the emphasis placed on corporate governance at the international level, both in practice and academia, made the 1974 reform appear inadequate, as it undervalued the internal governance of listed companies by focussing on disclosure and public regulation. While these two aspects still deserved consideration and improvement, the corporate governance structure of listed companies also needed upgrading. The Draghi Law handled the matter from within a broader framework of capital market law consolidation. First of all, the law strengthened the board of statutory auditors' (*collegio sindacale*) powers and responsibilities, so as to enhance its monitoring

[72] See, also for references, G Ferrarini 'La riforma dei mercati finanziari e il testo unico' in G Ferrarini and P Marchetti (eds) *La riforma dei mercati finanziari* (Edibank Milan 1998) 25 ff.

over the company's management by the executive directors and the board of directors.[73] This part of the reform echoed the Anglo-American discussion on the role of non-executive directors, audit committees, and internal controls. However, convergence was functional rather than formal.[74] Instead of replacing the traditional board of statutory auditors with an audit committee made up of non-executive directors, the Draghi Law made the former institution appear similar to the latter from a functional perspective. Moreover, the law reinforced minority shareholders' powers, introducing, *inter alia*, the right of a qualified minority (5%) to sue the directors for damages caused to the company. In addition, the Draghi Law aimed to promote corporate control contestability in listed companies by attributing members of shareholders' agreements the right to withdraw from the same in case of a takeover bid, so as to tender their shares to the bidder. This provision, together with other rules on takeovers, reflected the Draghi Law's additional concern for the external governance of listed companies and marked an important change in the Italian system, which had traditionally favoured corporate control stability over contestability.[75]

The changes effected by the Draghi Law are particularly significant if the index of shareholder protection used by La Porta and others is considered.[76] While in 1994 Italy was still ranked amongst the industrialised countries with the lowest legal protection for investors (anti-director rights scored a meagre 1 out of 6), the impact of the 1998 reform was an improvement in shareholder protection from 1 to 5.[77] However, as noted by Professor Coffee, 'the specific 'anti-director' rights that they [La Porta and others] identify as the central factors . . . strike many legal commentators as only tangentially related to effective legal protection for minority shareholders'.[78] Moreover, recent work by La Porta and others on investor protection in 49 countries attributes to Italy (and to other 'French legal origin' countries) low scores on the private and public enforcement of securities

[73] Italian governance structure consists of a board of directors and a board of statutory auditors, despite the fact that in listed companies accounting audits are performed by external auditors.

[74] On the two types of convergence, see R Gilson 'Globalizing Corporate Governance: Convergence of Form or Function' (2001) 49 AJCL 329.

[75] For an analysis of the philosophy of the Draghi Law see P Marchetti, 'Osservazioni sui profili societari della bozza di TU dei mercati finanziari' [1998] Rivista delle società 140.

[76] See La Porta and others (n 59).

[77] Aganin and Volpin (n 44) 7.

[78] Coffee (n 60) 8, where the author critically analyses the anti-director rights selected by R La Porta and others to assess minorities' protection and concludes: 'By no means is it here implied that these rights are unimportant, but they seem to supply only partial and sometimes easily outflanked safeguards, which have little to do with the protection of control and the entitlement to a control premium'.

laws.[79] Whilst the criteria used by these authors may once again be only partial and disputable, the overall assessment of securities law enforcement in Italy more or less coincides with a widely shared opinion amongst practitioners, particularly after the recent financial scandals (see para V.4. below). Furthermore, strong indicia as to the low impact of the Draghi Law on the development of the Italian capital market could be found in the modest increases, after enactment of the same, of the number of listed companies (which went from 239 in 1997 to 279 in 2003, including the 41 companies listed on the New Market for technology stocks) and of the ratio of stock market capitalisation to GDP (which moved from 30.7% in 1997 to 37.6% in 2003, after reaching 70.3% at the heights of the world equity markets in 2000).[80]

3. The Recent Company Law Reform

By reforming the corporate governance of listed companies, the Draghi Law widened the regulatory differences between listed and unlisted companies and added arguments to the criticism of traditional company law. An extensive overhaul of the limited liability company rules was then conducted on the basis of a 2001 law empowering the Italian government to adopt a reform whose principles were loosely fixed by the same law.[81] Among these principles is a clearer distinction between private companies (*società a responsabilità limitata*) and joint stock companies (*società per azioni*). As to the former, the regime previously in force was deregulated to the extent necessary to simplify the formation of these companies and allow more freedom in their organisation, so as to reflect their nature of closed companies. As to joint stock companies, the relevant rules were reformulated on the assumption that these companies can make recourse to the equity markets, while stricter rules are applicable to the same companies if they actually do so, thus becoming 'public companies'. The joint stock companies' regime has also been deregulated and simplified, at least in part. Moreover, three new governance structures are now available: one reflecting the structure presently in

[79] R La Porta and others 'What Works in Securities Laws?' (Tuck School of Business at Dartmouth Working Paper no 03-22, 16 July 2003).

[80] For the data, see Borsa Italiana *Fatti e cifre 2003* (Milan 2004) 81. For an assessment similar to that given above in the text, see B Bortolotti and D Siniscalco 'Importare la *corporate governance*?' in Centro Nazionale di Prevenzione e Difesa Sociale *Le nuove funzioni degli organi societari: verso la corporate governance?* (Giuffrè Milan 2002) 120 ff.

[81] See, in particular, the Legislative Decree no 6/2003, carrying the substantive company law reform and amending the relevant Civil Code provisions; for a commentary in English, see G Ferrarini and others 'Company Law Reform in Italy: Real Progress?', paper presented at a Conference on Company Law Reform in Europe organised by the Society of Friends of Max Planck Institute for International and Comparative Private Law, Hamburg, June 2004 (forthcoming) in (2005) 69 Rabels Zeitschrift für ausländisches und internationales Privatrecht).

force, which consists of a board of directors and a board of statutory auditors (in addition to external auditors auditing the company's accounts); another reflecting the German two-tier structure, adapted to the Italian context; and a third one inspired by the Anglo-Saxon unitary board, with a majority of independent directors and a mandatory audit committee. The possibility to choose between these three different systems is intended as a substitute for regulatory competition, as the choice, for example, of the unitary board might work functionally as a (partial) equivalent to the choice of UK law.

It is difficult to assess the impact of the new law on Italian corporate governance so short a time after its adoption. However, an assessment recently made from the perspective of global and European trends in company law reform concluded that, at least with regard to public companies, the Italian legislators did not generally follow these trends and in some cases adopted solutions designed to relax rather than reinforce minority shareholders' protection.[82] Examples would be offered *inter alia* by the transfer of powers from the shareholders' meeting to the board of directors (for instance, as to issuance of bonds), by the limitations introduced on the possibility for minorities to plead for the annulment of shareholders' resolutions, and by the options introduced for the choice between governance systems (which could result in a relaxation of internal controls if the unitary model were chosen in preference over the traditional Italian model). These innovations would be directed, according to the study in question, to reinforce the controlling shareholders, whilst other novelties of the reform, such as the greater reliance on private autonomy and the narrower scope for mandatory provisions, would be based on an excessive faith in the equity markets, also considering the limited development of the Italian stock market.[83] Nonetheless, some aspects of the reform – such as the deregulation of shares, bonds, and hybrids – deserve approval, even though the impact of liberalisation should not be exaggerated as there are limits to financial innovation whilst market practices tend to be uniform internationally.[84] Therefore, de-regulation should help to integrate the Italian capital market into the global markets, but no radical transformation is to be expected, considering also that 'one share-one vote' is the benchmark of today's corporate governance. Moreover, the de-regulation of bonds might cause problems as fraudulent issuers could exploit it to avoid creditors' monitoring, as shown by the Parmalat scandal.[85]

[82] See G Rossi and A Stabilini 'Virtù del mercato e scetticismo delle regole: appunti a margine della riforma del diritto societario' [2003] Rivista delle Società 1.

[83] ibid 27 ff.

[84] See Ferrarini and others (n 81) s II.1.

[85] On the use of bonds to elude the monitoring of banks and creditors in general, see G Ferrarini and P Giudici 'The Parmalat Scandal: Gatekeepers and the Role of Private Enforcement' (ECGI Law Working Paper, forthcoming).

As to corporate governance, some diversity could be introduced if joint stock companies adopted either the one-tier or the two-tier model in lieu of the traditional Italian system. However, the differences amongst the three systems as defined by the Italian reform are very limited, so it is difficult to envisage a widespread recourse to either of the two new models. On the contrary, path dependency could favour adherence to the traditional system which is intertwined with other features of the Italian tradition, such as a powerful accounting profession dominating the statutory boards of auditors.[86] In any case, the 'softening' of directors' fiduciary duties and of their liability for violation of these duties might launch the wrong signal to both the national and international business community if it were interpreted as a relaxation of the relevant rules despite the recent financial scandals.

4. Financial Scandals and the Need for Further Reforms

While the company law reform was being enacted, serious financial frauds – including those concerning Parmalat's false accounts and the ensuing record losses to investors in this company's shares and bonds[87] – were brought to light and widely investigated. This was clearly a blow to the company law reform, which had been conceived of with reference to a different scenario, assuming that listed companies and their disclosure to investors were sufficiently regulated, whilst other companies needed a legislative upgrading of the rules concerning shareholders' protection along the model of the Draghi Law. The recent scandals showed that corporate governance and disclosure rules, despite their convergence towards international best practices, were insufficiently enforced. Poor enforcement resulted in macroscopic failures of internal controls and in gatekeepers' failures of the kind experienced either by Parmalat's auditors or by first-class banks placing securities issued by companies on the verge of bankruptcy (such as Cirio and once again Parmalat). The scandals also made clear that Italian regulation of auditors is inadequate to the extent that Consob, the public regulator, almost blindly relies on the work done by auditing companies with respect to audited issuers, rather than periodically controlling the quality of the audit work. In fact, inspections of auditing companies and other surveillance activities generally react to irregularities after they are found, rather than being directed to the timely discovery of the same (not surprisingly, Parmalat's accounting and auditing frauds went undetected for years). The Italian Parliament is now considering a

[86] See Ferrarini and others (n 81) s II.2.

[87] See Ferrarini and Giudici (n 85).

draft law on investor protection which should deal with some of the problems illuminated by the recent scandals.[88]

VI. Conclusions

The 1882 Commercial Code carried remarkable regulatory novelties and liberalised the companies' formation by suppressing the administrative controls foreseen by previous legislation. Liberalisation was no doubt instrumental to rapid economic development at the turn of the century, when Italy joined the second industrial revolution. In general, market openness favoured economic and financial development in the first part of the 20th century, and Italy was no exception to international trends. However, the diffusion of limited liability companies and the listing of their shares on the stock exchanges created problems which the Commercial Code was inadequate to cope with. These problems also depended on the governance structures of Italian companies, which were already dominated by minority shareholders through cross-holdings, voting pacts, and pyramidal groups, while small shareholders were largely passive. In addition, German-type universal banks concurred to the control of companies either directly or as proxies of their clients.[89]

An important feature of Italian corporate governance was the role played by the state in economic development. Initially this role was limited to supporting industrial growth through protectionism, subsidies, and the supply of goods and services to the state by private firms. At a later stage, the same role was extended through the acquisition of banks and industrial companies by the state. This had an influence on company law reform and its repeated postponements, because public ownership of large sectors of the economy, as well as the equity markets' limited role in the financing of industry, made company law modernisation less important from a policy perspective. In addition, the incumbent capitalists benefited from the state's occupation of large sectors of the economy and also from the limited role of securities markets, as shown by Rajan and Zingales and the other scholars cited above. As a result, the rules on joint stock companies, which were included in the Civil Code of 1942 following private law unification, were very mild in protecting minorities and largely ignored the joint stock companies' role in the capital markets. More than thirty years elapsed before the introduction of disclosure rules for listed companies and of a securities regulator.

88 For a critical perspective on the original draft, see G Ferrarini 'Informazione societaria: quale riforma dopo gli scandali?' [2004] Banca, Impresa, Società 411.

89 While banking law reform in the 1930s operated to sever the links between banks and industries, other corporate governance features that first appeared at the beginning of the last century were carried over to the present times: see M Bianchi M Bianco and L Enriques 'Pyramidal Groups and the Separation between Ownership and Control in Italy' in F Barca and M Becht (eds) *The Control of Corporate Europe* (OUP Oxford 2001) 154 ff.

Corporate governance reform was delayed until the end of the 1990s, while a general reform of company law was enacted in 2003. This is also a reflection of a new stage of financial development started in the 1990s as a consequence of trade liberalisation both in the EC and worldwide. In fact, the Italian legal developments found their equivalents in other EU member states and were also the outcome of European harmonisation and liberalisation policies. The Draghi Law, in particular, took care of the listed companies' internal governance by enhancing the board of auditors' role in the quasi-two-tier structure typical of Italian joint stock companies and by reinforcing minority shareholders' powers. The external governance of listed companies was also dealt with by the Draghi Law, aiming to lower barriers to corporate control contestability and improve the role of the corporate control market. On the whole, this law tried to modernise the listed companies' rules, taking into account the traditional aspects of Italian corporate governance such as ownership concentration, pyramidal groups, and shareholders' coalitions through voting agreements. In the new century, general company law reform revised the joint stock companies' rules along the lines of the Draghi Law as well as for aspects not covered by the latter, while a new regime was adopted for private companies to meet the needs of small and medium enterprises, which still represent the backbone of the Italian economy.

However, astounding financial scandals showed that even the recent reforms are based on shaky foundations, to the extent that both public and private enforcement are weak, particularly with respect to listed companies, and were not touched upon by either the Draghi Law or the new company legislation. This is proof of path dependency, as the weakness of private enforcement largely depends on the notorious dysfunctions of the Italian judicial system, which appear very difficult to cure, not least due to the resistance of powerful interest groups (including the judiciary). What is more, the limits of public regulation and surveillance which were uncovered by the recent scandals are well rooted in the Italian tradition and are likely symptoms of difficulties in transplanting the US model of regulatory agencies into a Continental European context.

Historical Pathways of Reform: Foreign Law Transplants and Japanese Corporate Governance

CURTIS J. MILHAUPT*

I. Introduction

This section of the conference volume seeks to understand corporate governance changes in historical perspective, and I have been assigned the formidable task of discussing a century of changes in Japanese corporate governance. Even if I were so qualified, I could not do justice to such a huge topic in a short essay. In contrast to Professors Miwa and Ramseyer in the companion essay, I do believe that in the postwar period Japan had a distinctive set of corporate governance institutions called *keiretsu* and the main bank system, and that these institutions are undergoing significant change. So there is much to debate, but readers can turn elsewhere to see my response to their position on these issues.[1]

The subtitle of this section of the conference volume is 'Pathways of Reform.' Rather than discussing historical reforms in detail, I wish to focus on one important pathway of change in Japanese corporate law: the transplantation of foreign corporate laws and corporate governance institutions into the Japanese system. Japanese law, particularly the legal rules governing economic organization, is a prime example of the transplant phenomenon. Japan imported its original Commercial Code (including legal rules on business corporations) from Germany in

* Portions of this article draw extensively on co-authored works with Hideki Kanda and Ronald Gilson. See H Kanda and CJ Milhaupt 'Re-examining Legal Transplants: The Directors' Fiduciary Duty in Japanese Corporate Law' (2003) 51 AJCL 887; R Gilson and CJ Milhaupt 'Choice as Regulatory Reform: The Case of Japanese Corporate Governance' AJCL (forthcoming 2005). Milhaupt thanks his co-authors for their generous permission to borrow from this earlier work.

[1] For my views on this topic, see CJ Milhaupt 'On the (Fleeting) Existence of the Main Bank System and Other Japanese Economic Institutions' (2002) 27 Law and Social Inquiry 425.

1898 as part of a fundamental reform of its legal system, and made large-scale amendments to the corporate law in the immediate postwar period by importing many specific legal rules from the United States. Indeed, Japan is widely viewed as a rare example of a 'successful legal transplant,' yet there is very little analysis of what this means, beyond the fact that subsequent to Japan's enactment of a European code system, it developed into a highly prosperous and politically stable nation.

This topic has also taken on considerable significance recently with the rise of an influential body of empirical scholarship linking legal origin to a host of outcomes, such as the size of a country's capital markets and even to economic growth.[2] Some scholars assert that adaptation of legal transplants may be the key to legal development.[3] Deeper analysis of Japan's experience with corporate law transplants may shed light on legal transplantation and adaptation while simultaneously illuminating some features of its historical corporate law development.

In this essay, I will focus on three foreign transplants related to the Japanese board of directors: the duty of loyalty governing Japanese directors [*chûjitsu gimu*] (transplanted from US corporate law in 1950), the executive officer system [*shikkô yaku*] (begun as an informal practice by influential Japanese firms in the late 1990s and formally recognized in the corporate law in 2002), and the option to adopt a US-style board committee structure featuring independent directors [*iinkai-tô setchi gaisha*] (effective 2003). Of the three transplants, I will devote the most attention to the last, because the committee system option is the most recent transplant example, and as such, offers a possible glimpse of future developments. I readily admit that the choice of these particular transplants – and indeed the decision to focus on transplants at all – is somewhat idiosyncratic. I find them interesting and important,[4] but there are certainly more systematic ways of surveying Japanese corporate governance changes in the 20th century. Yet they do facilitate an analysis of how foreign corporate laws and institutions have affected Japanese corporate governance during two distinct periods: postwar high growth and the ongoing period of transition in a time of economic distress. They

[2] Eg R La Porta and others 'Legal Determinants of External Finance' (1997) 52 Journal of Finance 1131; P Mahoney 'The Common Law and Economic Growth: Hayek Might be Right' (2001) 30 J of Legal Studies 503.

[3] D Berkowitz K Pistor and JF Richard 'The Transplant Effect' (2003) 51 AJCL163.

[4] Colleagues who apply law and economics analysis more aggressively than I typically ask why transplants are special – ie, deserving of analysis as such. After all, they argue, transplants are ubiquitous. What difference does it make to the operation of a rule that it is of foreign origin? If it is an efficient rule, rational corporate actors and law makers would ultimately adopt it in any event. I believe that transplants are interesting precisely *because* they are a ubiquitous form of legal development. And there are many reasons (including most basically a lack of familiarity with the rule by the local community charged with interpreting and enforcing it) to expect that a transplanted rule may 'behave' differently than a locally developed rule.

also invite broader thinking about the relationship between legal and economic change, a fascinating but elusive topic.

The essay proceeds as follows: Part I provides some historical and legal background for the ensuing analysis, focusing on how the political economy interacted with the corporate law in the postwar period. Part II describes the three transplants in the context of postwar Japanese economic history and analyzes how the transplants have – and have not – been utilized in Japanese corporate governance. Part III concludes with some observations on the future of Japanese corporate governance and some general comments on the transplant phenomenon.

II. A Sketch of Postwar Japanese Political Economy and Corporate Law

Not long ago, it was academically fashionable to dismiss corporate law as 'trivial'.[5] Today, a cottage industry has sprung up to discuss all the reasons why the origin and specific features of a country's corporate law are key to the size of its capital markets, corporate shareholding structures, and GDP growth.[6] This intellectual path by corporate scholars might be written off as a fad. But a nation's corporate law, like other central components of its regulatory infrastructure such as antitrust laws, banking regulations, and intellectual property regime, are deeply interwoven into the domestic political economy. As a nation's political and economic circumstances change, so too might the importance of specific components of its legal infrastructure. At the risk of caricature, Japanese corporate law took on greater importance in the period of economic difficulty in the 1990s and early 2000s than it had in the postwar high growth period. Japanese corporate law may never have been 'trivial', and it is probably not the central legal support for economic reform and performance today – if there is such a thing. But the increased relevance of the corporate law – at least as measured by the frequency of its amendment and strategic use by shareholders and managers – is palpable. As we will see, foreign practices and institutions have been near the center of this action.

As is well known, Japan's corporate law is a German transplant, dating to the *Meiji* legal reforms. Its basic structure and characteristics – the prescription of detailed capital requirements and strong shareholder control rights over corporate decisions – reflect this German origin. The corporate law was amended in 1950 under American occupation influence, principally to strengthen perceived weaknesses in minority shareholder rights and 'corporate democracy', but these amendments arguably added to, rather than relaxed, the code's rigidities. Thus, commentators have noted the 'surprisingly paternalistic, archaic and impractical

[5] B Black 'Is Corporate Law Trivial?: A Political and Economic Analysis' (1990) 84 Northwestern U L Rev 542.

[6] Eg La Porta (n 2); Mahoney (n 2).

concepts'[7] reflected in Japan's postwar corporate law, particularly in relation to corporate finance and organizational structures. To cite just a few examples, until recently, corporate stock repurchases were prohibited except in narrowly defined circumstances, limitations were placed on the type of equity a company could issue, and holding companies were banned. These constraints were designed to protect creditors or were installed in the post-World War II period to prevent the re-emergence of the *zaibatsu* conglomerates that dominated the pre-war economy. Yet they lent a highly formalistic and rigid cast to the corporate law. Its most severe critics called the Code's pervasive restrictions 'senseless.'[8]

Whether senseless or not, however, these restrictions had little impact on Japanese economic activity for most of the postwar period. Because bank lending and retained earnings were the dominant mode of corporate finance in the heyday of postwar Japanese corporate governance, the Code's strict restrictions on equity finance techniques and its emphasis on technical creditor protections posed little obstacle to firms. Some scholars have even argued that a relatively mechanical, ex ante rule-oriented approach to corporate law complemented Japan's small judiciary and accounting profession in the immediate postwar period.[9, 10]

Moreover, during the high economic growth period – when industrial organization was framed by the bank-centered *keiretsu* groups and the main bank system was thought to constrain managerial conduct, at least in poor financial states – little attention was paid to how well prosaic corporate actors such as boards, auditors, and shareholders were responding to agency problems within the firm because, in Aoki's J-form governance, these actors had little role to play in the governance structure. Japanese corporate law at the time certainly did not stand in the way of, and at the margins may actually have facilitated, the extra-

[7] K Osugi and A Zaloom 'Recent Amendments to Japan's Company Law: Drastic Overhaul or Just Tinkering?' (unpublished manuscript, 2002).

[8] JM Ramseyer and M Nakazato *Japanese Law: An Economic Approach* (University of Chicago Press Chicago 1999); see also Osugi and Zaloom (n 7).

[9] H Kanda and T Fujita 'Kabushiki kaisha-hô no tokushitsu, tayôsei, henka' [Features, Variety and Evolution of Stock Corporation Statutes] in Y Miwa and others (eds) *Kaisha-hô no keizaigaku* (1998).

[10] By contrast, characteristics of US corporate law (see, eg, WB III Chandler and LE Strine Jr 'The New Federalism of the American Corporate Governance System: Preliminary Reflections of Two Residents of One Small State' (2003) 152 U of Pennsylvania L Rev 953) – flexible and permissive corporate laws empowering boards to engage in any lawful activity, subject only to the constraints of fiduciary standards applied ex post by courts to police selfish or grossly inattentive managerial behavior – complement a fairly robust financial disclosure regime and an expansive legal system, featuring a large legal profession, a judiciary comfortable with the application of broad standards as opposed to narrow rules, and a procedural environment replete with procedural mechanisms to promote private litigation as a tool of enforcement.

legal monitoring mechanisms that characterized Japanese corporate governance in its heyday.[11]

The irrelevance of the corporate law (at worst) or the complementary fit between the corporate law and related enforcement institutions of postwar Japanese corporate governance (at best) came to an end in the 1990s. For many large firms, bank lending by that time had been replaced by the external capital market or by internally generated funding. At the same time, serious non-performing loan problems in the banking sector disabled the central mechanisms of the main bank system of monitoring. The contribution of Silicon Valley to US economic success in the 1990s, fuelled by stock options and innovative organization and contractual mechanisms not available under Japanese law, confronted the Japanese with a stark indication of the rigidities of their own legal system. Perhaps most importantly, as the Japanese economy's swoon continued and the main banks' monitoring role retreated, the corporate law's constraints on organizational form and corporate finance, latent in the main bank era but now patent in restricting an internal response to the governance vacuum, placed a serious drag on desperately needed corporate restructuring.

As corporate managers became increasingly conscious of the organizational straightjacket imposed by the corporate law, particularly in comparison to US firms, the political economy of corporate law reform changed significantly. Or to put it differently, the market for the production of corporate law in Japan became much more competitive. Throughout the postwar period, Commercial Code reform was the province of a small coterie of legal scholars and Ministry of Justice officials, who convened a Legislative Reform Council to study – often for years – the propriety of potential corporate law amendments. Under this process, the law changed slowly and seldom in response to the exigencies of the market. In the words of one scholar, much Japanese corporate law reform over the past century was 'policy pushed,' rather than 'demand pulled'.[12]

Beginning with a 1997 Commercial Code amendment to permit the issuance of stock options, however, the corporate law reform process changed significantly. Jump-starting Japan's highly underdeveloped venture capital industry, among other exigencies, precluded resort to the traditional amendment process to relax restrictions on stock options. The stock option amendment was initiated by politicians acting at the behest of the business community, rather than by bureaucrats working through the traditional, ponderous amendment process. Since then, the business community, working through their political allies in the ruling Liberal Democratic Party, has had a much larger voice in the corporate law

[11] CJ Milhaupt 'A Relational Theory of Japanese Corporate Governance: Contract, Culture, and the Rule of Law' (1996) 37 Harvard Intl L J 3.

[12] Z Shishido 'Reform in Japanese Corporate Law and Corporate Governance: Current Changes in Historical Perspective' (1999) 49 AJCL 653.

reform process.[13] Other examples of direct business and political input in the production of corporate law include a 2001 amendment permitting firms to limit the personal liability of directors, and withdrawal of a Ministry of Justice draft amendment requiring the appointment of at least one outside director to the board of large corporations.

In addition to politicians and business groups, the Ministry of Economy, Trade and Industry (METI, the successor to the Ministry of International Trade and Industry, or MITI) has also become actively involved in corporate governance reform. Concern about the international competitiveness of Japanese firms and frustration over the failure of monetary and fiscal policy to restore the country's economic health motivated the ministry to turn its focus to corporate governance. It has supported a variety of market-oriented, flexibility-enhancing institutional changes in recent years. Thus, in effect, the traditional Legislative Reform Council now has active competitors in the corporate law reform process: politicians working closely with business interests, and METI. One result of this competitive pressure is more 'demand-driven' corporate law amendments, made at an accelerated pace.

As we will see in the next section, transplants of foreign laws and institutions are deeply, if ambiguously, intertwined with these changes in the postwar political economy of corporate lawmaking and corporate governance.

III. Foreign Transplants and Their Reception

Since the transplants discussed in this essay relate to the directors of Japanese firms, we begin with a bit of background on the board of directors and a related corporate governance organ, the board of statutory audit. Fittingly, both of these corporate organs were themselves foreign transplants. The board of directors was introduced in the American-influenced 1950 amendments to the Commercial Code. Legally, the Japanese board of directors, like its US counterpart, is charged with monitoring corporate activity and vested with authority to make important managerial decisions.[14] In fact, however, Japanese boards have not traditionally emphasized their monitoring role. Widely shared beliefs about board membership created boards ill-suited to perform this role. Throughout the postwar period, Japanese boards have been comprised almost exclusively of senior managers who have served the corporation throughout their careers – typically one director from

[13] For example, in public comments the chairman of the Liberal Democratic Party's Subcommittee on Commercial Law, Seiichi Ota, leaves no doubt that his subcommittee placed priority on ensuring that the business community's views were reflected in recent Commercial Code amendments. See S Ota '"Sentakusei" saiyô ga kansayaku seido wo tsuyoku suru' [Adoption of the 'Elective System' Will Strengthen the Statutory Auditor System] (2002) 95 Torishimariyaku no Hômu 4.

[14] Commercial Code art 260.

each of the firm's major divisions. As such, board members were viewed as representing employees, or perhaps the division from which they were appointed. Since board membership was viewed as a status position – the ultimate reward for loyal service to the firm – boards tended to be very large and virtually devoid of independent members. Moreover, it was commonly understood that a few senior directors, acting informally as a management committee, or a single 'representative' director, would have the ultimate decision-making authority, rather than the board as a whole. These discrepancies between the formal role contemplated for the board in the corporate law and the role actually played in practice led a blue ribbon corporate governance panel to conclude in the 1990s that '[i]t is questionable whether the Japanese board of directors actually complies with the Commercial Code's stipulation that it function[ ] as the body which decides on corporate will and exercises corporate oversight'.[15] As the ensuing discussion indicates, the board and related institutions have been a common subject of corporate law reform.

Reflecting German influence on Japanese corporate law, a basic component of the traditional corporate governance structure is the statutory auditor [*kansayaku*]. Unlike its German counterpart, the supervisory board [*Aufsichtsrat*], however, the Japanese statutory auditor lacks the power to appoint or remove directors, and does not necessarily represent shareholder or employee interests, since auditors are nominated by the board. The sole functions of the statutory auditor are to monitor the board's compliance with law and to provide an internal audit of the financial statements. Dissatisfaction with the auditor system is longstanding, and it has been a frequent target of corporate law reforms. Over the past decade, several attempts were made to strengthen the auditor system. Amendments in 1993 extended the auditor's term of office and mandated that large companies have at least three auditors, rather than a minimum of one, and that they function as a board of audit. One member of the board of audit must be an outside auditor.[16] In 2001, amendments sought to further strengthen the auditor regime by extending the term of office and responsibilities of auditors, while increasing the required number and qualifications of outside auditors.[17] Effective in 2005, at least half of the board of audit must be comprised of outside auditors.

With this background, we now turn to the foreign transplants that are the focus of this study.

[15] Corporate Governance Committee Corporate Governance Forum of Japan *Corporate Governance Principles –A Japanese View* (1998) 41-42.

[16] Law for Special Exceptions to Commercial Code Concerning Audit etc (Special Exception Law) arts 18(1), 18-2(1).

[17] Special Exception Law art 18(1) (at least half the audit board must be comprised of outside auditors); Commercial Code art 260-3(1) (requiring auditors to attend meetings of the board); art 273(1) (four-year term).

1. The Duty of Loyalty

Like the board of directors, Article 254-3 of the Commercial Code, which provides that directors owe a duty of loyalty to the company, was imported from the US in 1950. The duty of loyalty plays a large role in US corporate law. It is the key doctrinal desideratum of many of the most well-known Delaware cases, governing conflict-of-interest transactions, corporate opportunity, controlling shareholder problems, and sale of control cases. As a broad, elastic standard that can be applied to unforeseen circumstances, it is also seen as a key facilitator of the ongoing development of US corporate law.

The exact process by which Article 254-3 was transplanted into Japanese law is not entirely clear from the historical record, but the US occupation authorities in charge of corporate law reform sought inclusion of this provision as part of a package of reforms designed to improve minority shareholders' rights. The occupation authorities were apparently not satisfied that the pre-existing provisions on the duties of directors were adequate, and perhaps since the duty of loyalty was considered to be one of the most important provisions in US corporate law, a decision was made to codify it in the Japanese Code.[18] There is no evidence that the inclusion of this provision was controversial or even widely debated at the time of its transplantation.

Subsequent to the introduction of Article 254-3 into the Code, the provision generated a large amount of doctrinal discussion concerning whether a director's duty of loyalty in Article 254-3 [*chûjitsu gimu*] is different from the duty of care under Article 254(3) [*zenkan chûi gimu*], a longstanding provision in the Code. A famous Supreme Court decision of 24 June 1970 adopted the view that Article 254-3 clarifies and restates the duty of care – it does not constitute a separate or higher duty for corporate directors. Until a new trend appeared in the late 1980s (discussed immediately below), the Japanese courts never separately applied the duty of loyalty in Art. 254-3. In each case where it was cited, the court simultaneously cited the duty of care provision, so the meaning of Article 245-3 was not clear and its application had no practical significance. In 1989, for the first time a Japanese court gave separate application to Article 254-3 and awarded damages to the aggrieved company. In that case, a director resigned to set up his own business, and persuaded several employees of the firm to join him. The Tokyo High Court ruled that poaching employees is a violation of the duty of loyalty, and held the director liable for damages. In subsequent cases, Japanese courts have followed the High Court's lead, finding directors liable for breach of the general duty of loyalty standard in Article 254-3.

Why was Article 254-3 dormant for almost forty years after it was transplanted? And why did it suddenly begin to be used in the late 1980s? There is no evidence that the Japanese judiciary suddenly became more activist, and it is

[18] M Hamada *Shinpan chûshaku kaisha-hô* [New Annotated Corporate Law] (1987).

highly unlikely that directors suddenly became more 'greedy.' Rather, it seems plausible that the changes in political economy described above contributed to the initial non-use and subsequent use of the transplant.

At the time of the transplant in 1950, the connection between Article 254-3 and the existing legal infrastructure – what Professor Hideki Kanda and I call 'micro-fit'[19] – was not close. The duty of loyalty provision is an open-ended and vague standard, which places high demands on the legal infrastructure. At a minimum, it requires a viable derivative suit mechanism and attorney incentives to bring such suits, judges and attorneys familiar with broad legal standards as opposed to narrowly tailored rules, and courts capable of detecting and fashioning remedies for self-dealing in the absence of explicit statutory guidance. But in the postwar period, that infrastructure was not highly developed. The connection between the legal rule and the larger political economy – what Professor Kanda and I call 'macro-fit'[20] – was even more tenuous. The duty of loyalty was orphaned by lifetime employment practices and high economic growth, which helped prevent the taking of corporate opportunities and other self-dealing by directors. Both micro-fit and macro-fit were also affected by the existence of partial substitutes for the duty of loyalty standard. The Commercial Code contained detailed ex ante procedural rules covering at least a subset of conduct addressed by the Article 254-3 standard. Moreover, efficient private substitutes for some corporate law rules may have existed outside the legal system, weakening the macro-fit.

Over time, however, micro- and macro-fit between the duty of loyalty and other Japanese institutions became closer, and substitutes diminished. At a micro-level, the legal community became more comfortable with the use of a standard such as Article 254-3. The derivative suit mechanism was reformed to lower the cost of filing suit. And the existence of a growing body of case law highlighted the distinctness of the duty of loyalty from the duty of care, motivating legal professionals to use the transplanted provision more extensively and in new situations. At a macro level, high growth was followed by prolonged recession and the extralegal infrastructure for Japanese corporate governance weakened, changing the incentives of managers and shareholders, and increasing the demand for corporate law.

Thus, a foreign legal transplant lay dormant for many years before it became engaged in the governance of firms. Even today, the duty of loyalty plays a far less central role in Japanese corporate law than in the United States, the country from which it was adopted, due to remaining differences in institutional settings and practices between the two countries.

[19] H Kanda and CJ Milhaupt 'Re-examining Legal Transplants: The Directors' Fiduciary Duty in Japanese Corporate Law' (2003) 51 AJCL 887.

[20] Kanda and Milhaupt (n 19).

2. Executive Officers

In the midst of the post-bubble recession, Japanese firms began to experiment informally with several reforms based loosely on the US model in an effort to enhance the effectiveness of the board as a monitoring device. In the late 1990s, Sony reduced the size of its board and began to include outside directors on the board. Sony's innovations were quickly copied by others. By May 2001, almost 40% of first-section Tokyo Stock Exchange firms had added outside directors to their boards.[21] For reasons we will discuss below, it is safe to assume that some of these new outside directors are not truly independent of the firms on whose boards they serve. Nonetheless, the move to open the board to members other than career-long employees of the firm is potentially a significant step for Japanese firms.

Until a 2002 amendment, Japanese corporate law did not contemplate a distinction between the positions of officer and director, because, as noted above, virtually all directors were in fact actively involved in management. In concert with reductions in board size, Sony informally added a new, US-inspired corporate organ – the executive officer [*shikkô yakuin*]. Two years later, the position had become a fixture at over 200 firms.[22]

The separation of board members and officers, by allowing the lodging of discretion in executive officers and casting the board of directors as monitors, is an attempt to separate monitoring and decision-making functions and thereby strengthen the supervisory – monitoring – role of the board. What is interesting about this innovation is that it began at the market level – in contrast to the typical pattern of top-down corporate lawmaking in Japan – and was codified into the corporate law only after the practice had taken root. A 2002 reform of the Commercial Code creates the board-appointed position of executive officer [*shikkô yaku*], bringing formal law into line with the existing practice at many firms.[23]

3. Committee Structure Option

As part of the same Commercial Code reform in 2002, Japanese companies were given the option, effective in 2003, to choose features of a US-/UK-style govern-

[21] 'Shagai torishimari-yaku 38% ga sennin' [38 Percent of Firms Choose Outside Directors] *Nihon Keizai Shinbun* (Tokyo Japan 16 June 2001) 1. Of the firms reducing the size of their boards, 80% scaled back to fewer than 10 directors. Tokyo Stock Exchange 'Results of Corporate Governance Survey' 30 November 2000.

[22] CJ Milhaupt 'Creative Norm Destruction: The Evolution of Nonlegal Rules in Japanese Corporate Governance' (2001) 149 U of Pennsylvania L Rev 2083.

[23] Special Exception Law arts 21-5(1). Although some corporations that do not opt into the committee structure (see item 3 in text immediately below) must still make decisions via the full board.

ance structure, centered on a board of directors and committee structure, or to adhere to their traditional, statutory auditor structure. Adopting firms abolish the board of statutory audit and establish committees of the board for audit, nomination, and compensation. Each committee must have at least three members, a majority of whom are 'outside' directors.[24] Adopting firms must appoint executive officers, including at least one 'representative officer' with authority to act for the firm – essentially a CEO. The board is to monitor the business and affairs of the company, as executed by the officers. The term of office for both directors and officers is set at one year. Firms that do not opt into the new committee system continue to operate under essentially the same governance structure as before: they retain the statutory auditor system (subject to various amendments designed to bolster its effectiveness) and may, but are not required to, have outside directors on the board.[25]

The adoption of an enabling approach to board structure in Japan is a major departure from the comparatively rigid, mandatory structure of the Code discussed in the preceding section. The new political dynamics we have just described help account for this development, as groups with newfound influence in the corporate law process failed to reach consensus on the direction of board reform. While, as we have shown, the board and statutory auditor system were a focal point for reform in the 1990s, no single model of reform gained ascendance. The Ministry of Justice was a proponent of 'US-style' board reform.[26] Its initial proposal would have permitted firms to replace the auditor system with three mandatory committees of the board, and required that all large firms have at least one outside director. This proposal met with substantial resistance from the business community on two grounds: Some objected to the idea that any particular board structure should be legislatively mandated; rather, firms should be allowed to establish only those committees they desired. More widespread criticism focused on the proposed requirement that all large firms have outside directors. Common charges against such a requirement are that outside directors are not well suited to perform a useful role in highly relational Japanese corporate affairs, and that finding suitable outside directors will be extremely difficult given the

[24] However, as discussed in more detail below, the Commercial Code's definition of outside director is broad enough to include employees of a parent company and sibling firms under a common parent.

[25] Certain firms retaining the statutory auditor system are eligible to adopt one structural innovation: Firms with boards larger than 10 members, at least one of whom is an outside director, may establish an 'Important Asset Committee' to handle a subset of issues that would otherwise be decided by the board. Until the 2002 reform, Japanese corporate law prohibited boards from delegating 'important' matters.

[26] See M Nakahigashi 'Corporate Governance in Japan: Financial Information and Auditing System' (unpublished manuscript 2002) 15-16 (describing the Ministry of Justice as 'pursuing a 'full American model'' in corporate governance reform).

lack of experience with the practice. Reflecting these sentiments, the Ministry of Finance spoke out against any imposition of the US model on Japanese firms.[27]

Resistance to the Ministry of Justice initiative partially took the form of counterproposals, backed by the political allies of Keidanren, the big business lobby, to reinforce the statutory auditor system. Preservation of this system, even at the cost of its invigoration, was tacitly understood as the best way to parry the thrust toward convergence with the US model, and especially the appointment of outside directors to the board.[28] METI and others promoted the conceptual advantages of allowing firms to adopt the governance structure best suited to their individual needs rather than imposing a uniform structure – an approach whose attractiveness increased following the Enron and WorldCom scandals in the United States. Thus, the final version of the 2002 reform contains something for everyone: no requirement that all firms appoint outside directors, amendments to buttress the statutory auditor system (thereby possibly diminishing the prospects of its elimination in the future), and a strong endorsement of the concept of choice, including the option of abandoning traditional Japanese institutions in favor of the US-style board structure. The approach is distinctive, but that distinctiveness owes much to the need to cabin the scope of reform within prevailing political and social limitations.

In total, seventy-one firms adopted the committee system in the first round.[29] Of these, forty-five are listed companies. The total represents only a tiny fraction of eligible firms. Yet it is important to evaluate this number in context. The adopting firms, of course, reflect simply the first round of adoptions in a process that will continue indefinitely; additional firms can be expected to follow the early adopters.[30] Moreover, the number of adopting firms, though small, substantially exceeded expectations. Just a few months prior to the 2003 annual shareholder season, commentators predicted that only three or four firms would adopt the committee system.[31] Thus, from the Japanese perspective, the number of adoptions presents something of a surprise on the high side. Finally, recall the timing of this reform: The 2002 amendment to the Commercial Code that enabled

[27] B Jopson and D Pilling 'US Corporate Governance not Suited to Japan, Says Ministry' *Financial Times* (21 June 2003).

[28] Even more pressing for the business community was securing shelter from the explosion of derivative litigation that followed from a 1993 amendment reducing the filing fees for shareholder suits. They achieved this goal in the 2001 reforms, which allow shareholders to limit director liability to a multiple of annual compensation ranging from two to six times, depending on the director's relationship to the firm.

[29] Actually, the total number of adoptions was slightly higher; mergers of several adopting firms within the Nomura group left 71 firms with the board committee structure as of 31 March 2004.

[30] As of the end of 2004, a total of about 100 firms have adopted the committee system.

[31] M Suzuki 'Experts Doubt Many Firms to Follow Sony and Adopt US-Style Structure' *Agence France Presse* (Paris France 29 January 2003).

choice in the selection of board structure occurred in the midst of worldwide fallout from the US scandals. Ironically, at the precise moment Japanese firms were given the option of adopting 'US-style' corporate governance (and that is how the new system is commonly, if controversially, referred to in Japan), the United States was undergoing its most serious corporate governance crisis in at least a generation. This, together with uncertainty about the stability of the political balance reflected in the 2002 amendment, may have slowed the migration to the new governance structure.

Several interesting characteristics of the adopting firms are evident. First, although we noted above that the number of adoptions was surprisingly large to Japanese observers, the aggregate number of adoptions is somewhat misleading. The total of seventy-one firms includes the Nomura financial holding company and thirteen privately held subsidiaries, as well as Hitachi Ltd. and twenty-one of its affiliates. Excluding these related-firm overlaps, the number of adoptions falls by about half.

Second, the absence of companies affiliated with bank-centered *keiretsu*, the dominant feature of postwar Japanese industrial organization in its heyday, is striking. Indeed, adopting firms are largely characterized by their independence from traditional patterns of Japanese industrial organization. Adopting firms Sony and Orix, for example, are widely perceived as mavericks in the Japanese business community. Others, such as Nojima and Gakkyusha, are relatively new start-ups, at least by Japanese standards. The Hitachi companies obviously form an industrial group, but there is no main bank at its center, and the individual companies in the group are affiliated with several different bank-centered *keiretsu*. The cluster of Nomura affiliates is the result of recent reforms permitting holding companies in the financial industry. As such, the Nomura group does not constitute a traditional *keiretsu*.

Third, adoptions are concentrated in several industries. Controlling for related firm overlaps, by sector, the largest number of adoptions is in the electronics sector. This group includes global players Sony, Toshiba, and Mitsubishi Electric. There are also clusters of adoptions in the finance and retail industries, two troubled sectors of the economy. Particularly noteworthy is the adoption by Resona, a troubled bank that was recapitalized with public funds.

Many adopting firms have substantial foreign ownership. Nineteen of the adopting firms (56% of the firms that are not subsidiaries of Toshiba or Nomura) have foreign ownership in excess of 18%. These include distressed companies that attracted foreign owners, global players whose stock has attracted a substantial following among foreign portfolio investors, and Japanese firms acquired by foreign corporations as part of a global expansion strategy.

Another noteworthy feature of the adopting firms is that cross-listing of securities on US securities exchanges does not appear to be highly predictive of the decision to switch to the board/committee system. Only four of thirty-three

(13%) Japanese firms with American Depositary Receipts (ADRs) listed on the NYSE or the NASDQ have adopted the committee system.[32] This is surprising, because one would expect that firms seeking a following among US shareholders would be most likely to adopt US-style governance mechanisms. Ironically, the US Sarbanes-Oxley Act[33] – which requires all firms listed on US stock exchanges and NASDAQ to have an audit committee composed entirely of independent directors – may actually have reduced the incentives for cross-listed Japanese firms to adopt the committee system. This is because the implementing regulations to Sarbanes-Oxley grandfather in foreign issuers operating under a legal system, such as Japan's, that provides a substitute for an audit committee. The result is that cross-listed Japanese firms may prefer to remain with the statutory auditor system (which only requires a majority of independent auditors) rather than switching to the committee system (which, under US law, requires an audit committee made up entirely of outside directors).

Finally, as would be expected given that at least two outside directors are needed to serve on the required committees, adopting firms tend to have significantly more outside directors than listed companies in general. Outside directors comprise between one-third and two-thirds of the boards of adopting firms. By contrast, only one-quarter of all Tokyo Stock Exchange-listed firms have outside directors on their boards. Of these, half have just one outside director, and outside directors comprise less than 20% of the total number of directors.[34] However, caution is warranted in discussing outside directors on Japanese boards. Under Japanese corporate law, an 'outside' director – instructively, the term 'independent' is not used – can be affiliated with a major shareholder, parent company, or another subsidiary of the parent company.[35] Thus, virtually all of the 'outside directors' of the Hitachi group companies are affiliated with Hitachi Ltd., and most of the outside directors of the Nomura subsidiaries are affiliated with Nomura Holdings or Nomura Securities.[36]

The results thus far – although admittedly very preliminary – suggest that several, non-exclusive strategies may have driven the choices of firms opting into

[32] All four are NYSE listed firms: Hitachi, Ltd., Nomura Holdings, Orix, and Sony. For a list of Japanese firms listed on NYSE, see <http://www.nyse.com/listed/7.html> (21 April 2005). For a list of Japanese firms listed on NASDAQ, see <http://www.nasdaq.com/asp/NonUsOutput.asp?page=J&> (21 April 2005).

[33] See annex 3 in this volume.

[34] NikkeiNet Interactive 'More Listed Companies Inviting Outside Directors on Board' (13 October 2003), available at <http://www.nni.nikkei.co.jp> (21 April 2005).

[35] See Commercial Code art 188 (defining outside director as a 'director who is not involved in the management of the company, nor is currently or at any time has been an executive director, manager or employee of the firm or any of its subsidiaries').

[36] Y Yamada 'Iinkai-tô setchi gaisha no unyô jitsumu' [Operation of Companies Adopting the Committee System] (2003) 28 Kansayaku 478. Responses were received from 29 group companies and 13 non-group companies.

the board/committee system. These range from signaling of adherence to 'good' governance practices, and selection of endogenously determined structures optimal to a specific firm's production technology and competitive market, to tightening parent company control over affiliates within a group. The absence of a single, clear strategy pursued by adopting firms – and the overall absence of significant stock market reaction to firms' adoption of the committee system (see below) – reflects the ambiguous underlying dynamics that led to the enabling approach over the imposition of mandatory board reforms. Simply put, providing Japanese firms with the opportunity to choose a US-style board was the product of compromise, not overwhelming consensus on (or empirical support for) the advisability of that particular US corporate governance structure. Consistent with this ambivalence among affected constituencies, board composition of adopting firms appears to be bifurcated between group-oriented firms, which lack truly independent directors, and non-group firms, which appear to have appointed more independent directors to their boards.

In an effort to distinguish which among these strategies was operative in the first round of adoptions following the 2002 reform, Gilson and Milhaupt[37] performed an event study to gauge market reaction to the adoption of the new committee structure. This study showed no statistically significant stock market reaction to the announcement by all public firms (excluding the Hitachi subsidiaries) for which we had complete data of their intention to switch to the US-style board committee system. In fact, the market reacted significantly to the announcement by only three individual firms – negatively in the case of two relatively small, domestically oriented firms and positively in the case of *Resona Holdings*, a troubled bank temporarily nationalized by the Japanese government. The results are consistent with the hypothesis that the actual reforms in fact may be innocuous. Thus, independent of whether a meaningful committee system is in the abstract superior to traditional Japanese governance structures, the alternative offered by the 2002 reform, requiring only outside rather than independent directors, may be too watered-down a version of the committee system to affect company value. The results are also consistent with the results of prior empirical tests of the valuation effects of independent directors. Other than in systems dominated by controlling shareholders, independent directors are not associated with statistically significant valuation effects. At least for the first round of adoptions, the results do not reflect gains from constraining managerial strategies harmful to shareholders interests.

This analysis, together with the first round adoption data presented above, suggests that adoption of the committee system performs at best a very weak signaling and bonding function, consistent with the absence of any systematic price movement on announcement. It could well be that other institutional

[37] R Gilson and CJ Milhaupt 'Choice as Regulatory Reform: The Case of Japanese Corporate Governance' AJCL (forthcoming 2005).

constraints, working in tandem with the committee structure, will emerge to form a complementary new governance structure.[38] But those complementarities are not apparent at this stage, and even if they emerge in the future, they are likely to look quite different than those currently at work in the United States. In a sense, this is unsurprising, because as the discussion of the political dynamics leading to the 2002 reform indicates, adoption of the committee enabling approach was the result of only a selective and skeptical transplant of the US corporate governance model.

IV. Evaluation

Japan's recent corporate governance reform is a striking example of formal but not functional convergence.[39] Japan transplanted some visible components of a US-style board committee structure, but not the complementary institutions that exponentially increase the functionality of the committee system in the host country. In the United States, the judicial system serves as a crucial complement to the committee structure. The Delaware courts are willing to grant deference to the decisions of directors in settings that pose significant risks of expropriation of minority shareholder wealth, if those decisions are made by an *independent* committee of the board in circumstances that replicate, as nearly as possible, arms' length negotiations.[40] These cases, in turn, have created significant incentives for boards to utilize independent committees to structure and negotiate conflicting interest transactions. Recent cases such as the *Oracle*[41] decision highlight the role of the Delaware Chancery Court in policing directorial independence as a prerequisite to granting deference toward business decisions where potential

[38] It is also possible that the most significant consequence of the introduction of the committee system option will be its influence on firms that retain the statutory auditor system. There is preliminary evidence, for example, that the introduction of the committee system has encouraged non-adopting firms to shorten the terms of their directors to one year (which is required for committee system firms). See 'Heisei 15 nen 6 gatsu sôkai – fugi gian no kisai naiyô' [Contents of Measures Taken at June 2003 Shareholders Meetings], in: (2003) 233 Shiroban Shôji Hômu 26, 32 (reporting that during the 2003 summer shareholder meeting season, 210 firms – 1.6 times more than in the previous year – shortened the term of their directors to one year). More broadly, if amorphously, the debate about board performance and directors' roles engendered by the 2002 reform may have useful spillover effects on Japanese corporate governance in general.

[39] RJ Gilson 'Globalization of Corporate Governance: Convergence of Form or Function' (2001) 49 AJCL 329.

[40] See, eg, *Weinberger v UOP Inc* 457 A2d 701 (Del S Ct 1983); see also RJ Gilson and JN Gordon 'Controlling Controlling Shareholders' (2003) 152 U of Pennsylvania L Rev 785.

[41] In *re Oracle Derivative Litig*, 824 A2d 917 (Del Ch 2003) (finding special litigation committee members affiliated with Stanford University lacked independence, where several defendant directors had personal or professional ties to Stanford).

conflicts of interest are present, and the expansive view of what independence entails. For the Delaware courts, independence is compromised not only by financial interest in the subject matter, but by personal and other relationships to the interested party.

Japan lacks the body of judicial doctrine necessary to complement the committee structure in this way. Japanese courts are generally unaccustomed to applying flexible, ex post fiduciary standards in conflict of interest settings, relying instead on bright line procedural rules in the Commercial Code that are unlikely to be helpful in addressing board conflicts. Indeed, this was one reason why the duty of loyalty transplant did not take root initially.[42] The development of such doctrine may actually be foreclosed by the 2002 reform, absent uncharacteristically bold judicial activism on the part of the Japanese courts. Given that the definition of outside director in the Code does not contemplate anything like complete independence, it is difficult to imagine Japanese courts finding that a committee decision is not entitled to deference because the *outside* members of the committee were not truly *independent*. Rather, the opposite result seems more likely: the fact that a committee comprised substantially of 'outside' directors endorsed a decision will lend extra credibility to the action in the eyes of the courts. Thus, without the complement of exacting ex post judicial review, the new committee system – in tandem with the Code's expansive definition of outside director – could actually become a potent new governance technology for managerial entrenchment and pursuit of non-shareholder interests that destroy firm value.[43]

Ultimately, perhaps what is most interesting about Japan's new approach to corporate governance reform is the characteristically distinctive way it underscores what we already know: The transmission of ideas from one system to another is highly complex, and thus despite outward appearances of convergence of purpose in corporate governance reform around the world, the trajectory and end point of reform in any given system will be shaped by intensely local

[42] H Kanda and CJ Milhaupt 'Re-examining Legal Transplants: The Directors' Fiduciary Duty in Japanese Corporate Law' (2003) 51 AJCL 887.

[43] This is not a farfetched concern. Keidanren, which represents the interests of major Japanese corporations, recently proposed that the Commercial Code be amended to permit the establishment of special litigation committees to respond to shareholder derivative suits. The proposal approvingly cites the US ALI Principles of Corporate Governance and implicitly suggests that, as in the United States, Japanese courts should 'respect' a decision of the special litigation committee not to pursue the litigation. Nippon Keidanren 'Proposal for Revision of the Corporations Law' 16 October 2003. But the proposal lacks any acknowledgement of the institutional differences that separate the US and Japan, and at least to the extent a comparison with US law is implicit, it misrepresents the degree of deference that the Delaware courts grant to special litigation committee decisions not to pursue a derivative suit. See *Zapata v Maldanado*, 430 A2d 779 (Del S Ct 1981).

forces.[44] Although the end point of Japan's experiment with an enabling approach to corporate governance is far from clear, little in the path of reform to date suggests that proving firms with the choice of a US board structure implies convergence, either with the US model – or even on a single new J-Form corporate governance.

But this rather skeptical assessment of the impact of the recent corporate reforms should be tempered by the lessons from the duty of loyalty transplant. In that case, the use or non-use of the legal transplant (arguably, a useful definition of a transplant's 'success' or 'failure') varied over time, and was determined largely by the degree to which the transplant fit the prevailing legal and non-legal infrastructure of which it was a part. Thus, measuring the success or failure of a legal transplant may take decades of observation. Japan's experience with the duty of loyalty shows that even an ill-fitting legal transplant may become a core rule in the host country over time, as the legal infrastructure and political economy change. This occurs as the legal and non-legal developments alter the mix of substitutes available and affect the motivation of the legal professionals who interpret and enforce the transplant. It is quite plausible that the new committee system option, though not yet widely adopted and not well matched initially to surrounding institutional structures of Japanese corporate governance, will gradually come to play a larger role as changes in the political economy and institutional structures create a closer fit between outside directors and the role they are expected to play in monitoring and making strategic decisions on behalf of the firm.

A glimpse of this potential change may be found in the recent bidding contest for UFJ Holdings, the holding company for a large Japanese bank. After UFJ signed a memorandum of agreement to sell its crown jewel, its trust business, to Sumitomo Mitsui Financial Group, UFJ entered into talks with Mitsubishi Tokyo Financial Group for a transaction to acquire UFJ. Sumitomo sued to enjoin the transaction, but ultimately lost in a case that went to the Supreme Court. When the injunction was denied, Mitsubishi entered into a merger agreement with UFJ, but Sumitomo quickly countered with its own bid. At the time of this writing, UFJ has publicly endorsed the Mitsubishi bid and plans for the merger are proceeding, though Sumitomo has not ended its pursuit of the target. The case has obvious parallels to sharp-elbowed US takeover practices, and the factual setting is reminiscent of the famous *Revlon* case in the Delaware courts. The UFJ bidding contest has invited considerable speculation that Japanese business tactics are changing – for example, Sumitomo's strategic use of litigation and fairly aggressive approach to bidding are big departures from the norm. Moreover, the

[44] GF Davis and D McAdam 'Corporations, Classes, and Social Movements After Managerialism' (2000) 22 Research in Organizational Behavior 195; GF Davis and TA Thompson 'A Social Movement Perspective on Corporate Control' (1994) 39 Administrative Science Q 141.

presence of institutional and foreign shareholders appears to have influenced the managements of both the target and bidder firms. If the actions in the UFJ case become trends, it is very possible that outside directors could come to play a pivotal role in structuring and negotiating major corporate transactions in Japan, and the new committee system could provide the institutional technology for that development. As with the duty of loyalty, changes in the surrounding legal and political-economy environments may engage a transplant that initially appeared to have little impact on Japanese corporate governance.

Ultimately, the analysis offered here suggests that, contrary to the approach of most scholars to date, it is virtually impossible to discuss the 'success' or 'failure' of wholesale transplants of entire bodies of law (such as Japan's transplantation of the European codes in the late 19th century), or to extrapolate meaningfully from a single rule or institution to the feasibility of transplants in general. Each legal rule or institution must be painstakingly examined on an individual basis, and assessments of the overall feasibility of legal transplants as a pathway of legal change require a more rigorous theoretical base than existing literature has provided.

Japan's experience with foreign legal transplants also provides an interesting perspective on the recent empirical literature suggesting that the origin of a country's legal system dictates crucial facets of its economic institutions and growth trajectory. If anything, Japan suggests that 'legal origin' is a thorny classification problem, and the causal linkage between laws and economic institutions and growth is vastly more complex than the recent economics literature implies. But Japan does support the conclusion that how a country *adapts* its laws to current needs is far more important than how and from whom it inherits them.

V. Conclusion

From its inception, foreign transplants have been a central pathway of change in Japanese corporate law. This chapter has examined the role of three foreign legal transplants in postwar Japan. The impact of these transplants on corporate governance is rather ambiguous, although the executive officer system and committee structure option are too new to evaluate meaningfully. Predictions from limited data are risky, but one seems safe: foreign laws and institutions will continue to play an important role in Japanese corporate governance – though the precise scope and nature of their impact will continue to puzzle and fascinate observers well into the 21st century.

Asking the Wrong Question: Changes of Governance in Historical Perspective?

YOSHIRO MIWA and J. MARK RAMSEYER*

I. Introduction

Conference organizers often choose topics that reflect the state of the art. In this conference on Japanese corporate governance, they ask authors to discuss 'change of governance in historical perspective'. Many scholars in the field believe Japanese investors, managers, and employees are changing the way they govern their firms, and the organizers quite properly ask us to address the issue.

The hypothesis that firms might be changing their governance is plausible enough. After all, the governance structure that maximizes a firm's value should depend on the constraints the firm faces. As such, it should vary by industry. It should vary by regulatory structure. And as industries and regulations change over time, the firms that survive should be the firms that most effectively meet these new changed constraints.

The organizers do more. Again reflecting the state of the literature, they suggest that the change in Japan has constituted a shift 'from state to market'. Japanese firms have abandoned a governance regime dominated by the state (and banks), they suggest, for one more closely tuned to the marketplace. In truth, few themes in Japanese studies do trace a stronger lineage than the proposition that the state guided and directed post-war firms. Concomitantly, few phenomena more strongly dominate accounts of current Japanese political economy than that of purportedly widespread deregulation.

For analytic convenience, we restate the hypotheses reflected in the conference title:

(a) Over the past century, Japanese firms have significantly changed the way they govern themselves.

* We received generous financial assistance from the Center for International Research on the Japanese Economy at the University of Tokyo and the John M. Olin Program in Law, Economics & Business and the East Asian Legal Studies Program at Harvard University.

(b) From a governance regime where the state (and banks) played a major role, Japanese firms have shifted to one more closely tied to the market.

To these two hypotheses, we add a third. The claim need not follow from the conference title, but we raise it because it so pervades the literature on Japan:

(c) In part because of the way the state intervened in the Japanese economy, Japanese firms long maintained (and still maintain) a variety of badly inefficient governance mechanisms.

All three of these hypotheses are factually false, and in the essay below we discuss why. We proceed through a series of seven propositions. Together, the propositions explain how, over the past century, Japanese firms created the vibrant and wealthy economy that exists today. To facilitate that growth, the government did little more than define and enforce the property rights necessary in any competitive market economy. In this world, firms used the corporate form to generate the funds they needed, and large firms heavily raised those funds through equity. They faced relentlessly competitive capital, product, service, and labor markets. And because they did, the firms that survived overwhelmingly maintained governance regimes that fit the vagaries of those markets.

II. Economic Growth in Japan

Proposition 1: Over the last 130 years, Japan has enjoyed spectacular economic growth.

The conference organizers suggest a historical focus. We could not be more pleased, for few hypotheses are less plausible than the notion that badly governed firms could have generated the economic growth that Japan enjoyed over the past 130 years. Accordingly, we begin with the obvious: the Japanese economy has grown spectacularly.

Indexed at 1934-36 prices, the Japanese net domestic product rose from 3.9 billion yen in 1885 to 16.3 in 1935 – a quadrupling in 50 years. After a disastrous drop during World War II, it again rebounded. In 1970 prices, the gross national expenditure climbed from 16.8 billion yen in 1955 to 40.9 billion in 1965 and 92.0 in 1975 – quintupling in 20 years. From 1975 to 2000, real wages climbed by nearly a third yet again.[1] In 1870, per capita real GDP in Japan was 85% of the world average. By 1998, that figure had climbed to 358%– behind the US (479%) but beyond France (343%), Germany (312%), and the UK (328%)[2].

[1] Somucho *Nihon choki tokei soran* [Historical Statistics of Japan] (Nihon tokei kyoku Tokyo 1988) v 3, tab 13-3, 13-10, and general sources.

[2] R Sylla 'Financial Systems and Economic Modernization' (2002) 62 J of Economic History 277.

Proposition 2: The rapid economic growth in Japan took place in the private sector

Japan was not the Soviet Union, and Japanese economic growth did not occur in the public sector. To be sure, the government's military misadventures in the 1930s and early '40s badly distorted the economy. Fundamentally, however, the growth that took place during the last century took place in the private sector.

In 1905, the Japanese government accounted for 7% of gross national expenditure. In 1925 the public-sector still represented only 8% of Japanese GNE. By 1935 the war in China had pushed it to 16% (military expenses ran 47% of the government budget that year[3]). Despite the lack of a major military force, in 1955 the public sector remained at 17%. By 1975, it had once again fallen to 9% of GNE.

Since the late 1980s, journalists and academics have made a cottage industry out of complaints about the waste in the Japanese public sector,[4] but in this context the complaints mislead. We would be the last to justify the elaborate city halls that so many municipal governments seem to have built in the 1980s and early 1990s. But to belabor the waste potentially exaggerates what the various Japanese governments spend. Notwithstanding their sometimes flagrant waste, they still consume a smaller fraction of GDP in Japan than in most comparably wealthy societies.

Proposition 3: The post-war national government only minimally intervened in the Japanese economy

Through their subtitle, the conference organizers imply that Japanese firm governance might be shifting 'from state to market'. In doing so, they rightly note that modern Japanese firms maintain market-based governance regimes. Crucially, however, these current regimes do not reflect a switch. Instead, successful Japanese firms have always maintained market-based governance.

Never in the last century except at the depths of the war and the early years of the occupation did the Japanese government intervene heavily in the economy. Not even during the putative interventionist heyday of the 1960s did it try to guide it. It did not ration credit; instead, the credit market cleared at market rates.[5] It did not use loans or subsidies to spur growth in targeted sectors; instead, it

[3] T Ito and T Momose *Showa senzenki no Nihon* [Pre-War Showa Japan] (Yoshikawa kobun kan Tokyo 1990) 181.

[4] eg K van Wolferen *The Enigma of Japanese Power* (Vantage New York 1989); U Schaede 'The "Old Boy" Network and Government-Business Relationship in Japan' (1995) 21 J of Japanese Studies 293; B Woodall *Japan Under Construction: Corruption, Politics, and Public Works* (University of California Press Berkeley 1996).

[5] Y Miwa and JM Ramseyer 'Directed Credit? The Loan Market in High-Growth Japan' (2004) 13 J of Economics & Management Strategy 171.

loaned and gave primarily to a few obviously low-growth sectors and in amounts that seldom affected production decisions on the margin.[6] It did not use controls over foreign exchange to enforce its views; instead, by the 1960s it had abandoned any serious controls over foreign exchange.[7] It did not guide firms through 'administrative guidance'; instead, when firms ignored its guidance it usually backed down, and when it did try to force firms to comply the courts refused to let it.[8]

Because we discuss these issues more fully in our companion article in this volume, we will not repeat them here.[9] Suffice it to say that the tale of government guidance in post-war Japan is sheer fiction. Scholars (both American and Japanese) repeat it only because they want so badly to believe it. The tale does not reflect the role of the state in the Japanese economy, and never did. It reflects instead the political wish-list of the Japanese and American professoriate.

III. Corporate Governance in Japan

Meld propositions 1 through 3, and the claim that Japanese firms could be egregiously misgoverned looks increasingly implausible. After all, these are the firms that took a country in 130 years from the ranks of the undeveloped to one of the richest in the world. They took a land of poor farmers, and transformed it into a society of wealthy consumers. They took a country with little wealth to spare, and earned investors spectacular returns.

To be sure, the firms did not avoid all agency slack. Transactions costs within a firm are not zero in Japan, any more than they are zero anywhere else. Information is costly, and investors, managers, and employees each have divergent incentives. Like firms everywhere else, Japanese firms have their agency slack, their mismanagement, their waste.

Meld propositions 1 through 3, however, and the point emerges that between 1870 and 2000 Japanese firms generated economic growth virtually unparalleled in history. That they could have done so with systematically bad governance strikes us as implausible on its face. To explore the governance they did use, turn to Propositions 4 through 7.

[6] Y Miwa and JM Ramseyer 'Capitalist Politicians, Socialist Bureaucrats? Legends of Government Planning from Japan' (2003) 48 Antitrust Bulletin 595; Miwa and Ramseyer (n 5).

[7] ibid.

[8] JM Ramseyer 'Rethinking Administrative Guidance' in M Aoki and G Saxonhouse (eds) *Finance, Development and Competition in Japan: Essays in Honor of Hugh Patrick* (OUP Oxford 2000). Neither did the wartime government guide firms. See Y Miwa *State Competence and Economic Growth in Japan* (Routledge Curzon London 2004).

[9] Cf Y Miwa and JM Ramseyer in this volume p 527 ff.

Proposition 4: From the outset, large Japanese firms used the limited liability form to raise the funds they needed through equity claims

The Japanese government began offering firms a corporate-like option on an *ad hoc* basis after 1877, and entrepreneurs chose it almost immediately. From 27 in 1877, by 1889 the number of such firms had climbed to 4,456. Limited liability became more generally available in 1893 when the corporate law section of the 1890 Commercial Code took effect.[10] By 1925 20,700 firms chose this corporate form, and by 1945 the number had climbed to 64,800.[11]

The largest of these firms (particularly the railroads) also took advantage of the stock exchanges. By 1900 113 firms chose to list their shares on the Tokyo Stock Exchange (TSE). By 1910 142 firms listed their shares, and by 1920 569. In 1900 50 firms listed their shares on the Osaka Stock Exchange (OSE). Ten years later 64 firms listed their stock, and by 1920 206. By 1920, the two exchanges collectively traded stocks worth 8.13 billion yen. As a fraction of GDP, that came to 51.1%. Even in 1990, stock turnover in the US was only 31.5% of GDP, 28.6% in the UK, and 22.1% in Germany.[12]

Cotton spinning firms epitomized the modern sector in pre-war Japan – and they overwhelmingly used stock. They were large, they were profitable, and they out-competed their international rivals. By the 1920s Japanese spinning firms consumed more raw cotton than the British. By the 1930s they produced a quarter of all domestic manufactured goods and employed 40% of all factory workers. For their funds, these spinning firms used stock: organized as corporations, they sold their stock broadly and borrowed only relatively small amounts from banks.[13]

Through their equity claims, the firms raised large amounts. In Table 1, we give bank-debt/asset and bank-debt/total-capital ratios for the largest Japanese firms during the pre-war period. In Table 2, we similarly give flow of funds measures for the large firms. We describe the data by which we constructed the tables in Miwa & Ramseyer.[14]

[10] M Hamada 'Kaisha to no deai' [Meeting the Firm] in M Hamada (ed) *Nihon keisha ho no rekishiteki kenkai* [The Historical Development of Japanese Corporate Law] (Shoji homu Tokyo 1999) 2.

[11] Somucho (n 1) v 4 tab 15-1.

[12] Y Miwa and JM Ramseyer 'Banks and Economic Growth: Implications from Japanese History' (2002) 45 J of L & Economics 127, 140.

[13] Y Miwa and JM Ramseyer 'The Value of Prominent Directors: Corporate Governance and Bank Access in Transitional Japan' (2002) 31 J of Legal Studies 273; Y Miwa JM Ramseyer 'Corporate Governance in Transitional Economies: Lessons from the Prewar Japanese Cotton Textile Industry' (2000) 29 J of Legal Studies 171.

[14] Miwa and Ramseyer (n 12) 135-139.

Table 1: Mean Bank-Debt/Asset and Bank-Debt/Total-Capital Ratios for Large Firms in Selected Industries, 1919-41

	1919	1926	1931	1936	1941
Food & paper					
Bank-debt/Assets (%)	6.18	7.50	12.63	4.78	5.64
Bank-debt/TC (%)	8.51	12.70	51.90	8.23	8.38
Chemicals					
Bank-debt/Assets (%)	4.75	4.70	6.99	2.12	14.29
Bank-debt/TC (%)	7.06	6.97	16.89	4.12	25.22
Steel machinery					
Bank-debt/Assets (%)	4.17	11.98	12.46	4.94	12.98
Bank-debt/TC (%)	8.68	60.95	27.40	7.30	33.96
Mining					
Bank-debt/Assets (%)	2.17	4.07	7.53	8.27	14.22
Bank-debt/TC (%)	3.03	5.12	11.43	10.20	29.78
Sugar					
Bank-debt/Assets (%)	0.19	1.75	8.12	7.98	1.64
Bank-debt/TC (%)	0.30	4.93	27.54	20.64	3.73
Number firms	57	61	52	67	104

Table 2: Source of Additional Funds for Large Firms, 1911-36

	1911-19	1919-26	1926-31	1931-36
Equity (%)	34.4	48.8	39.4	53.6
Earnings (%)	33.4	4.8	-2.0	28.6
Bond Issues (%)	4.5	26.4	44.1	9.1
Bank Loans (%)	4.6	6.4	14.6	-1.7
Trade Credit (%)	6.3	11.4	-3.6	-2.6
Other Loans (%)	16.9	2.2	7.5	13.3
Total Net Increase (in million yen)	2,292	4,394	2,601	2,676
Number firms	123	111	134	155

By either measure, firms relied heavily on stock. In only a few industries did they borrow more than half their equity capital, and then only during the depressed late 1920s and early 1930s. Generally, they borrowed less than a tenth of their equity from banks (Table 1). When they raised additional funds, again only in the late '20s did they borrow more than 10% from banks. During other times, they raised over half their additional funds through equity (Table 2).[15]

[15] Smaller firms did not use the stock exchanges, but they did not heavily borrow from banks either. Instead, they tapped trade credit for their funds. See Y Miwa and JM Ramseyer cont. ...

This reliance on equity continued after the war. Despite the many claims that Japanese firms rely less on equity than American firms, the typical claims mislead. According to finance scholar Stuart Myers,[16] the apparently lower American debt-equity ratios instead reflect 'differences in accounting'. Adjusted for those accounting differences, US firms in 1991 maintained book-debt/capital ratios of 33% where Japanese firms maintained 37%; US firms had a market-debt/capital ratio of 23% where Japanese firms had 17%.

Nor is this cross-national similarity a recent phenomenon. Instead, scholars like Myers simply bring to English-language readers what Iwao Kuroda and Yoshiharu Oritani[17] showed Japanese readers over two decades ago. Examining mid-1970s firms, they estimated equity/asset ratios of 33.0% for US firms and 47.4% for Japanese firms. They calculated intermediated financing ratios of 50.4% for large US firms and only 46.7% for their Japanese counterparts.

Lest anyone think these points reflect some peculiarly Japanese conglomerate form, we add two points. First, of the firms in Tables 1 and 2, less than a fifth were affiliated with any of the *zaibatsu* conglomerates.[18] Second, the occupation dismantled the *zaibatsu* in the late 1940s. As we explain in our companion article in this volume, the notion that those firms then regrouped as the *keiretsu* is again sheer fiction.[19]

Proposition 5: Firms consistently faced the discipline of the stock market

Western scholars seem wedded to the notion that the Japanese stock market does not work. It is too small, they write. Its prices do not reflect firm value. Firms sabotage its disciplinary effect by swapping large blocks of stock. And firms cannot (and did not) raise needed funds there.

In fact, the Japanese stock market is huge. Even before the 1980s climb in stock prices, the TSE ranked among the largest in the world. In 1983, it listed 1,451 domestic firms capitalized at $546 billion, and the OSE listed 1,013 capitalized at $468 billion. The US had twice the population, but the NYSE listed only 1,550 firms capitalized at $1,522 billion and the American Stock Exchange only 774 firms capitalized at $58 billion. The Paris exchange listed fewer than

'Who Appoints Them, What Do They Do? Evidence on Outside Directors From Japan' (2005) 14 J of Economics & Management Strategy 299.

[16] SC Myers 'Capital Structure' (2001) 15 J of Economic Perspectives 81, 83; see also RG Rajan and L Zingales 'What Do We Know about Capital Structure? Some Evidence from International Data' (1995) 50 Journal of Finance 1421.

[17] I Kuroda and Y Oritani 'Waga kuni no "kin'yu kozo tokucho" no saikento' [A Reexamination of "The Peculiarity of Financial Structure" in Our Country] (1979) 2 [Nichigin] Kin'yu kenkyu shiryo 1.

[18] Miwa and Ramseyer (n 12) 149 tab 9.

[19] Y Miwa and JM Ramseyer 'The Fable of the Keiretsu' (2002) 11 Journal of Economics & Management Strategy 169 and their contribution in this volume p 527 ff.

700 firms, the Amsterdam exchange listed fewer than 500, the exchanges in Madrid, Brussels, and Frankfurt listed fewer than 400, and those in Luxembourg, Zurich, and Milan listed fewer than 300 (all capitalized at less than $80 billion).[20] By 1989, both the TSE and the OSE had eclipsed even the NYSE: the TSE firms were capitalized at $4.3 trillion, the OSE firms at $3.6 billion, but the NYSE firms at only $2.9 trillion.[21] At these firms, cross-shareholding arrangements had been trivial even during the 1960s.[22]

To explore the extent to which the stock market pushes firms toward efficient arrangements, we elsewhere ask whether firms were able to maintain sub-optimal ownership patterns.[23] Observers in the Berle & Means tradition routinely assert that stock ownership (whether Western markets or Japanese) is too dispersed to protect shareholders. Because thousands of investors each own but miniscule shares of the firm, they explain, no one finds it cost-effective to monitor management. As a result, incumbent managers routinely shirk and expropriate firm wealth for themselves.

Such a story depends on stock markets that do not discipline. As Demsetz & Lehn pointed out in 1985, if a firm's ownership concentration lets managers systematically divert shareholder wealth, the firm should find it hard to raise capital.[24] Compared to rivals with ownership patterns that more effectively protect shareholders, it should face a higher cost of capital. Over time, it should either switch to an ownership structure that more effectively protects investors – or disappear.

If Demsetz & Lehn are right, then the 1947 *zaibatsu* dissolution by the occupation offers a natural experiment. Before the dissolution, both *zaibatsu* and non-*zaibatsu* firms would have (given competitive market pressures) maintained firm-specifically optimal ownership structures. To that equilibrium, the *zaibatsu* dissolution would have constituted an exogenous shock. It would have left the non-*zaibatsu* firms with their equilibrium ownership structure, but pushed the ex-*zaibatsu* firms to a sub-optimal structure.

If the Japanese market does not discipline firms, then post-1947 the ex-*zaibatsu* firms would not have faced pressure to restructure their ownership. By contrast, if (as Demsetz & Lehn posit) the market does discipline firms, then the

[20] Tokyo shoken torihiki jo *Shoken tokei nempo* [Securities Statistics Annual] (Tokyo shoken torihiki jo Tokyo 1984) 304-305.

[21] Tokyo shoken torihiki jo *Shoken tokei nempo* [Securities Statistics Annual] (Tokyo shoken torihiki jo Tokyo 1990) 362-363.

[22] Miwa and Ramseyer (n 19).

[23] Y Miwa and JM Ramseyer 'Does Ownership Matter? Evidence from the Zaibatsu Dissolution Program' (2003) 12 J of Economics & Management Strategy 67.

[24] H Demsetz and K Lehn 'The Structure of Corporate Ownership' (1985) 93 J of Political Economy 1155.

ex-*zaibatsu* firms would indeed have realigned those structures. And realign they did.

Using data on firm performance and ownership in the 1950s, we ask whether the ex-*zaibatsu* firms restructured their ownership patterns – and find that they did. Immediately after the dissolution, the ex-*zaibatsu* firms performed at a discount relative to the non-*zaibatsu* firms. During the next several years, the ex-*zaibatsu* firms realigned their ownership patterns. As they did, their performance returned to that of their non-*zaibatsu* competitors. Exactly as Demsetz & Lehn posit, the Japanese market does indeed push firms to adopt firm-specifically optimal ownership structures.

Proposition 6: That market prevents Japanese firms from maintaining systematically inappropriate governance structures.

Public intellectuals routinely decry the governance structure of Japanese firms. As part of their lament, they regularly urge firms to appoint more outside directors. Directors monitor senior managers for shareholders, they explain. Unless independent from those managers, they will not aggressively monitor. Unless they take the job from a career beyond the firm, they will not be independent.

And yet, one should wonder. Exactly the same market forces that drive firms to adopt firm-specifically appropriate ownership concentration patterns should drive them to adopt appropriate governance arrangements as well. Those firms that maintain inappropriate governance structures (like boards) will (necessarily) earn their investors sub-maximal returns. They will face higher capital costs, and those costs should increase the cost of the goods and services they sell. Given competitive product and service markets, over time they should tend to restructure their governance arrangements – or disappear.

If this logic of market discipline applies to Japanese boards, then board composition should bear no observable relation to a firm's performance. After all, firms with inefficient structures will fail and drop out of the sample. A firm for which a given structure promotes shareholder returns will tend to persist, while one for which it generates a loss will tend to disappear. Although a particular structure may well lower shareholder returns at *most* firms, that point will not appear in the data since only the firms at which it increases returns will tend to survive.

Alternatively, if (as public intellectuals routinely claim) the market does not discipline firms in Japan, then many firms may indeed maintain sub-optimal governance structures (like inefficiently few outside directors). If so, then when we regress firm performance on selected governance structures we should generate significant results: those firms with inappropriate governance structures should underperform their rivals. If we focus on the number of outside directors, for example, firms with fewer outside directors should underperform those with more.

Again, to explore the extent to which the market disciplines Japanese firms, we test the connection between governance and performance among TSE-listed non-financial firms.[25] Using a variety of financial and board composition data, we regress several indices of firm performance on the number and type of outside directors at the firms. Holding constant industry affiliation and a variety of financial variables, we find no evidence that firms maintain observably inefficient government structures. Instead, the results confirm the Demsetz-Lehn logic of market discipline. Exactly as that logic implies, firms with fewer outside directors do not underperform those with more.

To test whether the same principles govern banks, we run a separate but analogous set of regressions on the banking industry.[26] Given the industry differences, we use slightly different financial variables and focus on the regional banks. Again, we find no evidence that outside directors improve performance. Instead, exactly as Demsetz-Lehn imply, firm performance bears no observable relation to board structure.

Proposition 7: The 1990s recession did not result from a governance gap created by the 1980s deregulation

We do not claim to explain the 1990s Japanese recession, but we do know that the usual explanations do not work. Typically, those explanations take one of two lines. By one account, the 1980s deregulation let the best firms abandon their banks. Left without the borrowers they needed, banks turned to high-risk borrowers that then failed. By the second, the deregulation freed firms from the monitoring and disciplining by their main banks, and let them gamble in a speculative 'bubble'. When the 'bubble' burst, the banks found themselves left with uncollectible loans.

For two reasons, the explanations fail. First, the 1980s deregulation could not have caused the 1990s recession – for the government had no substantial regulatory program to dismantle.[27] As we explain in our companion article, the 1980s changes involved little more than the liberalization of the bond market and the elimination of caps on deposit interest rates.[28] Second, a decline in main-bank governance could not have caused the malaise either – for main banks never seriously governed the firms.[29]

[25] Miwa and Ramseyer (n 15).

[26] Miwa and Ramseyer (n 23).

[27] Y Miwa and JM Ramseyer 'Capitalist Politicians, Socialist Bureaucrats? Legends of Government Planning from Japan' (2003) 48 Antitrust Bulletin 595; Y Miwa and JM Ramseyer 'Directed Credit? The Loan Market in High-Growth Japan' (2004) 13 J of Economics & Management Strategy 171.

[28] Cf Y Miwa and JM Ramseyer in this volume p 527 ff.

[29] Y Miwa and JM Ramseyer 'The Fable of the Keiretsu' (2002) 11 Journal of Economics & Management Strategy 169; Y Miwa and JM Ramseyer 'Conflicts of Interest in Japanese

cont. ...

Consider, however, whether the best firms did abandon their banks during the 1980s, and whether the firms that failed in the 1990s were the ones that had expanded aggressively in the 1980s.[30] First, the banks did not lose good customers. During the 1980s, they did cut their loans to firms in weaker sectors like oil, non-ferrous metals, and steel. Those firms were retrenching, and many of them reduced their equity capital as well. From 1983 to 1989, banks reduced their loans to manufacturing firms by only 6.6 trillion yen; however, they increased their total loans by 174 trillion yen. Banks did not lend to real estate loans because they lost traditional customers. They lent because they amassed large amounts of loanable funds.

Second, the firms that failed in the 1990s were not the firms that had aggressively expanded in the 1980s. Rather, the firms that expanded aggressively in the 1980s were the firms least likely to fail in the '90s. The tale is mundane. The best firms in the 1980s had good projects. With projects to fund, they expanded. As they entered the 1990s, they continued to have the best projects. With good places to put funds, they contracted less than their rivals.

Table 3 illustrates the phenomenon. To create the table, we partition the non-financial TSE-listed firms by quartile according to the growth rate in their asset base during the late 1980s. In the first panel, we then give their growth during three periods; in the second, we give their profit rates (in operating income/total assets). For example, take the firms that grew most slowly during 1986-90. During that half decade they grew by 11.5% and earned profits of 3.6%. During the next half decade they grew 10.8% and earned profits of 3.3%.

Table 3: Growth and Profitability Data, by 1986-90 Growth Quartiles[31]

	Growth			Profitability		
	1980-85	1986-90	1990-94	1980-85	1986-90	1990-94
Very Low	19.493	11.463	10.848	.058	.036	.033
Low	25.203	39.043	17.017	.066	.052	.042
High	30.096	63.656	18.827	.072	.053	.042
Very High	33.346	157.153	30.379	.084	.071	.052

The firms that grew fastest in the late 1980s continued to grow the fastest in the early 1990s. During the late 1980s, they grew 157%. During the early 1990s, they grew more slowly – but at 30.4% still more rapidly than any other quartile. By

Insolvencies: The Problem of Bank Rescues. Theoretical Inquiries in Law' (forthcoming) and their contribution in this volume p 527 ff.

[30] Y Miwa and JM Ramseyer 'Does Relationship Banking Matter? Japanese Bank-Borrower Ties in Good Times and Bad' J of Empirical Legal Studies (forthcoming).

[31] ibid.

contrast, the firms that grew most slowly during the late 1980s grew only 10.8% in the early 1990s.

The fastest growing firms in the 1980s also earned the highest profits in the 1990s. They had earned profits at a 7.1% rate during the late 1980s, and continued to earn 5.2% in the early 1990s. Those in the slowest growing quartile had earned only 3.6% in the late 1980s. During the early 1990s, they earned only 3.3%.

Fundamentally, the firms that flirted with failure in the 1990s were not the firms that had gambled aggressively in the 1980s. Instead, the firms closest to insolvency were the firms that had been the least profitable and expanded the least in the 1980s. They had had the fewest good projects then, and were much more likely to fail during the 1990s recession.

IV. Conclusion

Over the past century, Japanese firms did well. They grew rapidly. They developed new products. They revolutionized industries. And they earned their investors spectacular returns.

Japanese firms did this without the government. Late in the 19th century, the Japanese government hired an honest corps of judges, enacted a standard set of capitalist legislation, and assigned its judges the job of enforcing the property rights that the statutes established. More than that, it rarely did.

Through this institutional framework, the government set the stage for a fiercely competitive economy. For most of the 20th century, the economy remained competitive. Other than the closing years of the war and the opening years of the occupation, firms bought, sold, lent, and borrowed on competitive markets. Some firms thrived, some failed, and most just survived.

Within this world, firms quickly adopted the limited liability form. The largest firms (particularly railroads) raised funds on the stock market. Smaller firms (which were most firms, and which produced the lion's share of GDP) raised some equity from family members, neighbors, and acquaintances, used retained earnings when they had them, and borrowed the rest from banks and trading partners.

By basic logic, the firms that weathered this competitive economy should not have retained serious governance problems. Yet so public intellectuals continue to assert. We doubt they can assert the point plausibly, and in our own studies we find no evidence of systematic mismanagement. But if public intellectuals hope to show that economy-wide bad governance, we suggest they focus on two tasks:

a) Identify clearly what they think those governance problems entail, and
b) Offer a coherent, incentive-compatible account of how those governance problems could have survived in a competitive market economy.

To date, they have tried the first; they have failed entirely in the second.

Politics on Wall Street: The Implications of Eliot Spitzer on State-Federal Relations in the Regulation of Public Corporations and Capital Markets in the United States

JONATHAN R. MACEY*

I. Introduction

Whatever the long-run economic consequences of the waves of corporate, securities, and accounting scandals that have rocked Wall Street and Main Street, one thing is clear: the scandals have created a fertile climate for new regulatory initiatives and for regulatory entrepreneurship by ambitious politician-bureaucrats. And we have observed both in abundance. Regulation has come in the form of the Sarbanes-Oxley Act[1] and the new corporate governance rules recently adopted by both the New York Stock Exchange and Nasdaq.[2] Regulatory entrepreneurship has come in the form of efforts of state attorneys general, especially New York's Eliot Spitzer, to achieve fame and political support by aggressively entering the regulatory vacuum created by the SEC's failure to vigorously pursue the various scandals.[3] This passivity on the part of the SEC was likely caused by the agency's capture by the very special interests it was ostensibly regulating.[4]

* A similar version of this paper was published in the Brooklyn Law Review ('Wall Street in Turmoil: State-Federal Relations Post-Eliot Spitzer' (2004) 70 Brooklyn L Rev 117). Reprinted by permission.

1 Sarbanes-Oxley Act of 2002, Pub L no 107-204, 116 Stat 745 (to be codified in scattered sections of Titles 11, 15, 18, 28, and 29 of the United States Code), see annex 3 in this volume,.

2 See NASD and NYSE Rulemaking: Relating to Corporate Governance, 68 Fed Reg 64, 154 (12 November 2003).

3 For a glimpse of how the attorney general views his role as securities regulator, see his website <http://www.oag.state.ny.us/investors/investors.html> (10 July 2005).

4 JC Coffee Jr 'A Course of Inaction' [2004] Legal Affairs 46, 49 (discussing the SEC's passivity with regard to the mutual fund crisis); JR Macey 'Administrative Agency Obsoles-

cont. ...

This article looks at the current regulatory crisis in the US capital market from the allied perspectives of political theory and federalism in order to make two points about the current regulatory environment. First, I observe that the recent history of scandals, followed closely by new regulation, illustrates the importance of utilizing opportunities created by crisis. Crisis, in this case manifested in the sudden collapse of Enron Corporation, followed closely by WorldCom and a spate of other highly salient corporate frauds (Symbol Technologies, Adelphia, Global Crossing), created the 'policy window' through which political entrepreneurs could launch their initiatives. Second, the various governmental responses to the crises reflect the nature of the ongoing jurisdictional competition between and among state regulators and federal regulators in the US federal system. State regulators have moved decisively to claim what they see as a regulatory vacuum created by the SEC. The SEC has been forced to respond to this new competition. The long-run consequences of this competition, however, are far from clear.

Part II describes the relationship between crisis and regulation. I argue that public policy crises, whether real or imagined, provide an opportunity for entrepreneurial politicians and regulators to break the typical log-jams that make it difficult to pass new rules during times of ordinary politics. In Part III, I describe the four stages of New York Attorney General Eliot Spitzer's response to this crisis. As this article is written, I contend that we are in the third and penultimate stage of the post-Enron relationship between the SEC and Eliot Spitzer, who has been the most successful of what might best be described as the emerging generation of 'Enronian policy entrepreneurs', who see the collapse of Enron as presenting the opportunity caused by the event which opened what political scientists might describe as a 'policy window', a window in time in which the political environment is unusually welcoming of new regulations and policy proposals. The emergent nation of post-Enron policy entrepreneurs, including Eliot Spitzer, consists primarily of lawyers, policymakers, lobbyists – and, of course, their clients, constituents, and potential clients – all of whom have used the collapse of Enron and the spate of other corporate scandals to provide a pretext for enhancing their own political power in ways that would not have been possible absent the opportunities created by the corporate scandals. In concluding, I make various predictions about the legacy of this competition between state and federal regulators for the future of US capital market regulation.

II. Crisis and the Growth of Government

If we assume that bureaucrats, like other people, want to lead interesting and relevant lives, then it stands to reason that crisis is good for bureaucrats. In

cence and Interest Group Formation: A Case Study of the SEC at Sixty' (1994) 15 Cardozo L Rev 909.

particular, it is quite natural for people to desire to live 'important' lives. One way to do this is to be involved in the quest to deal with the major crises of one's time. Crisis not only provides a justification for administrators to lay claim to more power and larger budgets; crisis also provides a basic rationale for the continued existence of an agency whose relevance might otherwise be questioned. For example, due to the recent spate of corporate scandals, it would now be unimaginable to think of reducing the size and power of the SEC. Today's policy debates are framed not in terms of whether the agency is relevant, but in terms of how much larger its budget needs to be in order for it to improve its effectiveness in ferreting out fraud and improving the quality of corporate financial reporting.

The SEC received a cool $100 million budget increase in fiscal year 2003, and, although the SEC was not the only agency to receive budget increases during this period, the SEC was the only federal agency to receive substantial budget increases in both 2003 and 2004.[5] Testifying before the House Commerce–Justice–State Appropriations Subcommittee, SEC Chair William Donaldson said President Bush's request for $841.5 million in fiscal 2004 'recognizes that the Commission's needs are growing and ongoing'. That funding, which was provided to SEC under the recent omnibus appropriation, 'will enable us to meet the remaining fast-approaching deadlines of the Sarbanes-Oxley Act, hire over 800 new staff [and] advance initial start-up funds to the Public Company Accounting Oversight Board'.[6] The 2005 budget request of $893 million for the SEC, an increase of $81 million, was 10% above the 2004 level.[7] The President's FY 2004 budget included $842 million for the SEC – the largest increase in the history of the agency. The 2005 budget request would nearly double the SEC budget over FY 2002 levels. According to the White House, the agency plans to use the additional money to hire new accountants, lawyers, and examiners 'to protect investors and combat corporate wrongdoing'.[8] From an economic perspective, these gigantic budget increases seem odd. Firms that are subject to market forces at best shrink and sometimes shrivel and die when they under-perform. In other words,

[5] S Dudley and M Warren 'Regulatory Spending Soars: An Analysis of the US Budget for Fiscal Years 2003 and 2004' 14-19 (July 2003) available at <http://wc.wustl.edu/Reg_Budget_final.pdf> (10 July 2005).

[6] WH Donaldson 'Testimony Concerning Appropriations for Fiscal 2004' <http://www.sec.gov/news/testimony/040803tswhd.htm> (10 July 2005).

[7] Actually, the Securities and Exchange Commission's FY 2005 budget request to Congress totaled $913 million and was 12.5% above the amount authorized for the SEC in fiscal 2004. The amount consisted of $893 million in new budget authority and $20 million in anticipated balances from the prior year. This budget request – the first crafted by Chairman Donaldson since his arrival in February 2003 – permitted the Commission to hire 106 new employees. Press Release, SEC, SEC Releases FY 2005 Budget Information, available at <http://www.sec.gov/news/press/2004-11.htm> (10 July 2005).

[8] Press Release, Office of the Press Secretary 'Restoring Economic Confidence and Tackling Corporate Fraud' (11 January 2003) at <http://www.whitehouse.gov/news/releases/2003/01/20030111-1.html> (10 July 2005).

the market punishes rather than rewards failure in the private sector. The recent spate of scandals, particularly among mutual funds and market analysts, can hardly be viewed as a success story for the Securities and Exchange Commission. In case it were needed, this recent wave of scandals can be viewed as additional evidence that administrative agencies are not subject to the same Darwinian pressures as firms in the private sector. As New York Attorney General Eliot Spitzer observed, 'heads should roll' at the SEC for failure to detect and act upon abuses in the mutual fund industry.[9] And while heads (or at least one head) did roll with the token firing of long-time SEC staffer Juan Marcelino, head of the Commission's Boston office,[10] the crisis of confidence in US capital markets was clearly beneficial to the SEC in general.

Luckily for the SEC, the situation did not devolve into a 'competitive situation between regulators'. Rather, SEC Chief William Donaldson summed up the situation aptly when he said that '[t]he spectacle of one regulatory agency criticizing another is not healthy'.[11] Clearly he is correct; from the perspective of the regulatory agencies, competition is not healthy. Indeed, collusion is the one area where regulatory agencies resemble firms in that collusion is generally a much better strategy than competition. And, happily for administrative agencies (if not for the public), unlike private firms, there are no antitrust laws that seek to constrain collusion among agencies.

Nevertheless, competition is a hard thing to quash, particularly in a federalist system. Institutions, including administrative agencies, are composed of people. People are ambitious. Over time, the private incentives of the people who work in agencies will tend to replace the public objectives articulated when the agencies were founded.[12] If one agency departs from a policy space, a rival bureaucrat is likely to emerge to attempt to fill that space. This, in my view, explains what might be described as the 'Spitzer phenomenon'. Eliot Spitzer, the attorney general of the state of New York, is ambitious. He wants to be governor. And suing (and settling cases with) securities firms is a much better strategy for obtaining this objective than suing a used car dealership in Utica, where he soon will be shaking hands on his quest for new lodging in the governor's mansion.[13]

[9] National Accounting News, Texas Society of Certified Public Accountants (Accounting Web Inc, Indianapolis, 7 November 2003) at <http://www.tscpa.org/welcome/AcctWeb/acctweb110703.asp#3> (10 July 2005).

[10] 'Need to Know: Global Business Briefing' *The Times* (London UK 4 November 2003) available at <http://www.timesonline.co.uk/article/0,,5-880041,00.html> (10 July 2005).

[11] <http://pub47.bravenet.com/forum/3986114185/fetch/202376/> (10 July 2005), see also The Corporate Reform Weekly vol II #41 3 November 2003.

[12] See A Downs *Inside Bureaucracy* (Little Brown Boston 1967) 13.

[13] See D Gross and E Spitzer at <http://slate.msn.com/id/2100951/> (10 July 2005). See also Interview by G Pressman with E Spitzer (NY Attorney General) of 17 December 2003 at <http://www.wnbc.com/news/2711555/detail.html> (10 July 2005).

Spitzer's strategy has already achieved a certain amount of success. His name is probably more widely recognized than any New York attorney general since Robert Kennedy. *Time* magazine dubbed Spitzer 'crusader of the year' in 2002, and in that same year then-presidential candidate Wesley Clark mentioned him as a possible running-mate.[14]

My purpose is not to lampoon Attorney General Spitzer's efforts to police the securities markets. Rather, my purpose is to provide a richer description of the nature of those efforts. In particular, I create a four-part taxonomy to describe Spitzer's legacy. Of particular interest, of course, are the implications for the future of Mr. Spitzer's capital markets crusade. In particular, like the world of private markets, regulatory initiatives – particularly bold, entrepreneurial initiatives such as Mr. Spitzer's – do not take place in a vacuum. These initiatives inevitably upset settled equilibria and distributions of power among regulators; in this case, the relationship between the SEC and state securities regulators has been jarred. The question is how the SEC and its friends, allies, and competitors are likely to respond to Spitzer's actions.

In my view, there are only three possible outcomes of Mr. Spitzer's efforts. We know that Mr. Spitzer will not remain the attorney general forever, regardless of whether he succeeds in attaining higher political office. We also know that the SEC will survive. Despite the quality of its performance, it appears that the Commission will thrive, at least from a budgetary perspective. One clear possibility, then, is that Mr. Spitzer's efforts will re-energize and revitalize the SEC, causing it to become not only a richer, but also a more effective administrative agency.

A second possibility is that Mr. Spitzer will fill the power and policy spaces once occupied by the SEC and cause the venerable federal agency to suffer by weakening its prestige, its moral authority, the morale of its employees. and its capacity to recruit bright and able staff.

A final possibility is that Mr. Spitzer's legacy will invigorate the SEC – not in a benign, positive way, by providing its staff with incentives to do better work policing the securities industry; but in a political way, by inducing the staff and the Commission to forge new interest group allies who will support the SEC in turf wars against the insurgent state bureaucrats led by Mr. Spitzer. Under this view (recognized by Mr. Spitzer as the likeliest possibility), once a new attorney general is in place, the SEC and its industry supporters will galvanize into an effective political coalition to lobby Congress to preempt state law in the securities area. If such preemption occurs, it is likely that nothing will stop the agency and its agenda from suffering from internal atrophy and external capture by powerful interests. Data on turnover of SEC's personnel can be useful in evaluating these alternatives, and on determining what is actually going on within the agency. As the following chart indicates, the turnover of personnel at the

[14] See interview (n 13).

SEC, while not high, is higher than that in other branches of government, reflecting both the ability of SEC employees, particularly professionals, to move in the private sector, and dissatisfaction with the SEC as a career:[15]

SEC and Government-Wide Turnover Rates

SEC Turnover Rate, 1994-2001

Fiscal Year	Permanent Employees	Attorneys	Accountants	Securities Compliance Examiners	GS-14s	GS-15s
1994	9.59%	13.90%	6.91%	5.51%	11.27%	11.45%
1995	11.39%	15.15%	9.38%	14.29%	9.61%	12.98%
1996	9.52%	11.32%	8.96%	10.31%	10.50%	9.59%
1997	11.94%	16.01%	12.13%	10.78%	14.82%	15.83%
1998	12.46%	15.19%	12.87%	10.48%	14.77%	11.36%
1999	13.72%	13.50%	13.72%	14.92%	14.35%	14.43%
2000	13.83%	17.47%	13.76%	13.93%	14.75%	11.48%
2001	8.48%	9.86%	7.00%	9.34%	8.73%	10.96%

Government-Wide Turnover Rate, 1994-2001

Fiscal Year	Permanent Employees	Attorneys	Accountants	Financial Institution Examiners*	GS-14s	GS-15s
1994	7.83%	6.51%	6.44%	8.31%	6.93%	8.63%
1995	12.33%	11.95%	8.11%	7.05%	7.84%	8.64%
1996	7.03%	6.66%	6.61%	13.77%	5.60%	7.02%
1997	7.62%	7.41%	7.14%	8.05%	6.21%	7.95%
1998	7.07%	7.05%	8.01%	5.56%	5.59%	7.02%
1999	7.08%	6.78%	6.62%	5.58%	6.08%	7.59%
2000	6.82%	8.18%	7.68%	6.12%	5.89%	7.19%
2001	6.42%	6.61%	5.80%	5.15%	5.54%	6.61%

[15] The SEC is the only government agency that uses Securities Compliance Examiners. Financial Institution Examiners in other agencies perform similar work to Securities Compliance Examiners. ibid.

III. Spitzer's Legacy: A Tale in Four Parts

1. 'New Deal' Stage

While difficult to quantify with precision, significant differences exist among regulatory agencies with respect to the amount of prestige that they enjoy. The SEC, one of the more prestigious federal agencies, provides a complete set of governmental functions for the securities industry, exercising not only executive power, but also legislative (rulemaking) power and judicial power.[16] The SEC is an 'independent' agency comprised of five members appointed by the president and confirmed by the Senate for staggered five-year terms.

Former SEC chairmen and Commission members have been chosen from the ranks of the most distinguished, high-profile lawyers in the United States. They include Joseph P. Kennedy (1934-1935), James M. Landis (1935-1937), William O. Douglas (1937-1939), William L. Cary (1961-1964), Manuel F. Cohen (1964-1969), A. A. Sommer, Jr. (1973-1976), Irving M. Pollock (1974-1980), and Harvey Pitt (2001-2003).

The SEC has outlasted many of its fellow New Deal agencies. Staff positions at the SEC, particularly in the Division of Enforcement, have long been viewed as an excellent path to successful careers in the private securities bar. The SEC Historical Society, founded in 1999, cultivates the SEC's traditions and makes sure that the 'new generation of SEC and industry staff' is aware of the 'unique history and meaning of the work of the SEC and the securities industry'.[17]

The SEC has never faced a major corruption scandal. The staff enjoys a high reputation for professionalism as well as integrity. Although the Commission has been criticized recently for responding too slowly to recent corporate, accounting firm, and investment banking scandals, these criticisms have had more to do with agency capture by powerful interest groups than with agency incompetence. Indeed, nobody would seriously argue that Eliot Spitzer, whose staff has been far more aggressive in filing complaints against the securities industry, is more of an *expert* in securities law and capital markets than his counterpart at the SEC. Rather, the intensity of Spitzer's efforts can in some measure be attributed to the fact that the New York attorney general's office enjoys more distance from, and is therefore less susceptible to capture by, the very entities it is charged with regulating.[18]

[16] See generally L Loss and J Seligman *Fundamentals of Securities Regulation* (5th edn Aspen New York 2004).

[17] SEC Historical Society Website at <http://www.sechistorical.org/> (10 July 2005).

[18] See AWA Boot and JR Macey 'Monitoring Corporate Performance: The Role of Objectivity, Proximity and Adaptability in Corporate Governance' (2004) 89 Cornell L Rev 356 (pointing out trade-off between proximity and objectivity).

Thus, when Eliot Spitzer began to move into the SEC's regulatory turf, he was moving into the regulatory turf of a venerable, prestigious New Deal agency whose authority, competence, and integrity are long-standing and unquestioned. The SEC probably reached the apogee of its power and prestige in relation to state regulators in 1996, with the passage of the National Securities Markets Improvement Act (NSMIA). The Act explicitly preempted vast areas of securities law previously regulated by the states.[19]

The Conference Committee from which NSMIA emerged used adjectives like 'duplicative', 'unnecessary', 'redundant', 'costly', and 'ineffective' to describe overlapping state and federal securities regulation, and expressed a clear preference for the New Deal administrative agency solution to this problem: federal preemption of antiquated state law.[20] The purpose of NSMIA was to firmly ensconce the SEC as 'the exclusive regulator of national offerings of securities'.[21]

Indeed, as SEC officials have observed in the wake of Spitzer's blitzkrieg into the SEC's traditional territory, the creation of the SEC in 1934 and the passage of the New Deal Securities Acts in 1933 and 1934 was to respond to 'widespread demand for the federal government to assume a rule in policing the markets' due to the failure of state laws in the period prior to their passage.[22]

Initially, Spitzer was viewed as a maverick and an opportunist, moving inexplicably into territory where he was unneeded and unwanted. This phase of his crusade can be labeled the 'New Deal' phase. The phase began in 2002 with the attorney general's investigation of investment banks' financial analysts. It culminated with the 21 May 2002 settlement agreement between Merrill Lynch, Pierce, Fenner & Smith and the attorney general of the state of New York, followed later in the year with settlements against ten other major investment banks. With these successes, Eliot Spitzer and the office of the New York attorney general, once known for regulating 'auto repair shops, nursing homes and crooked landlords', became known as the 'Sheriff of Wall Street'.[23]

[19] Remarks of SM Cutler, Director, Division of Enforcement, US Securities and Exchange Commission, at F Hodge O'Neal Corporate and Securities Law Symposium (2003) 81 Washington U L Q 545, 548; KA Jones 'The National Securities Markets Improvement Act of 1996: A New Model for Efficient Capital Formation' (2000) 53 Arkansas L Rev 153, 154.

[20] Joint Explanatory Statement of the Committee of Conference, Conference Report, National Securities Markets Improvement Act of 1996, HR 3005, HR Conf Rep no 104-864 (1996).

[21] National Securities Markets Improvement Act of 1996, HR Rep no 104-622 at 16 (1996).

[22] Cutler (n 19) 547.

[23] 'The Sheriff of Wall Street' *CBSNews.com* (25 May 2003) at <www.cbsnews.com/stories/2003/05/23/60minutes/printable555310.shtml> (10 July 2005).

2. The 'Federalism' Stage

The core characteristic of the 'New Deal' stage of the Spitzer era was a recognition that the SEC lacked motivation to pursue fraud, and that the highly publicized enforcement efforts of Eliot Spitzer not only were accomplishing useful results in and of themselves, they were motivating the Commission itself. As SEC Enforcement Chief Stephen M. Cutler has acknowledged:

> … a visible and aggressive *state* enforcement machine may motivate federal regulators, like me, to respond more quickly to potential securities-related misconduct. Of course, if we in the federal government want to be the dominant securities enforcement authority, we must be vigilant in protecting the investing public. And I think that I can safely say that (SEC) Chairman Donaldson, as well as the Commission and its staff are single-minded in our determination to do just that.
>
> Such competition among regulators to be first on the scene, if tempered by the other principles I've just identified (regulatory consistency and protection of investors), will help ensure that investors' needs are addressed promptly. As public servants, we must admit to ourselves, however, the possibility that a contest to be the most responsive regulator could easily become a contest to become the most *popular* but most *irresponsible* regulator. This in turn can have untold costs – to investors, to issuers, to financial institutions, to the capital markets, to the justice system, and ultimately, to our credibility as regulators. Federal and state securities agencies must bear this in mind at all times and exercise our judgment and discretion accordingly.[24]

During the 'federalism' stage of the Spitzer era, people stopped asking the question that was asked during the 'New Deal' phase of the Spitzer era. That question was, according to Spitzer himself, '"Well, what's the state attorney general's office in New York doing, going after this problem (cases involving stock analysts and improper allocations of shares in Initial Public Offerings). Shouldn't this be the SEC?" And my response was, "Yes, but they haven't. And if they haven't, and there are investors being ripped off, we will do it."'[25]

In the federalist stage of the Spitzer era, the attorney general's office stopped being viewed by so many people either as a 'meddler, poking around in things that were none of his business' or as an 'opportunist, grandstanding to the masses to advance his own political career'[26] as he was viewed during the New Deal stage. Instead, he came to be viewed as someone who produces real reform.

The turning point came when people started asking 'the most obvious and embarrassing question: "Where has the Securities and Exchange Commission been while all of this (the mutual fund scandals and the IPO allocation scandals) was going on? In the past 10 years, the SEC has failed to bring a single case involving stock analysis or IPO allocations."'[27]

[24] Cutler (n 19) 551-552.

[25] The Sheriff of Wall Street (n 23).

[26] ibid.

[27] ibid.

3. The 'Hostile Takeover' Stage

Up to this point, the story has been simple: in a deft display of political entrepreneurship, Eliot Spitzer moved in to fill the vacuum created by the lack of initiative at the SEC. The SEC was fully acclimated to existing market practices, and saw no urgent need to change them. The SEC staff identified with the market participants they were ostensibly regulating, and, predictably, found it difficult to visualize these people as 'evil-doers'. But very quickly things moved beyond the mere pursuit of fraudulent conduct within the jurisdictional boundaries of the state of New York, the realm within which the SEC would like to relegate state regulatory action.[28] Spitzer soon moved to usurp the SEC's core regulatory function: dictating general regulatory policy for the capital markets. Attorney General Spitzer moved from being just another policeman on the beat into a new role, that of 'the most feared, most hated and most powerful man on Wall Street'.[29] In this new role, a period I characterize as the 'hostile takeover' phase of Spitzer's career as attorney general, he began to engage in what is known as 'rulemaking by enforcement' rather than rulemaking through the appropriate procedures required by due administrative process. The ineluctable reality is that an enforcement proceeding can, in fact, realign an industry standard, where parties 'agree to change or restrict their future conduct in significant and far-reaching ways' in order to resolve the enforcement action.[30]

It is preferable, not to mention more consistent with the rule of law, for administrative agencies to clarify their positions by formal rulemaking or by an interpretive release that parties can use to guide their future behavior. However, the office of the New York attorney general, unlike the SEC, does not have the power to engage in formal rulemaking or the authority to issue interpretive releases. Its only option, if it wants to engage in rulemaking or to otherwise affect basic conduct or structure within the securities industry, is to do so through an enforcement mechanism.

Clearly, this is not an ideal strategy for rulemaking. It lacks the usual notice and comment period associated with the promulgation of rules. It does not permit participation by all, or even most, affected parties. Perhaps most disturbingly, when rulemaking takes place in the context of an enforcement action, the regulator has such a power advantage over the regulated entity that unjust results are likely to occur. Moreover, as SEC officials have stressed, in adopting the securities laws – including the New Deal legislation, the National Market System legislation of 1985, and NSMIA – Congress clearly intended 'that the *federal* government, not the states, establish the rules and policies governing the securi-

[28] Cutler (n 19) 551.

[29] W Hanley 'What Makes Spitzer Run' *Financial Post* (Don Mills Canada 30 December 2003).

[30] Cutler (n 19) 552.

ties markets, and that it do so on a national rather than a piecemeal (state-by-state) basis'.[31]

Thus it seems that when Eliot Spitzer and other state attorneys general and securities regulators engage in enforcement actions, they are acting properly. But when they engage in policy-making, which is precisely what Eliot Spitzer has been doing, they are threatening to 'destroy the balance Congress struck in its effort to strengthen and streamline our national market system'.[32]

Perhaps the point of greatest tension between the SEC and the New York attorney general was in connection with the separate settlements in the Alliance Capital case. On 18 December 2003, the Securities and Exchange Commission announced a settled enforcement action against Alliance Capital Management L.P. (Alliance Capital) for defrauding mutual fund investors by allowing market timing in certain of its mutual funds in exchange for fee-generating investments in other Alliance Capital investment vehicles. The Commission ordered Alliance Capital to pay $250 million, consisting of $150 million in disgorgement and $100 million in penalties. Under the settlement agreement, all of the money was distributed to the Alliance shareholders who were harmed by the firm's market timing arrangements.[33] The Commission also ordered Alliance Capital to undertake a variety of compliance and fund governance reforms designed to prevent a recurrence of the kind of conduct described in the Commission's order. The changes enhanced the independence of the mutual fund companies' boards and strengthened Alliance Capital's internal compliance and oversight functions with respect to federal securities laws.[34]

The Commission's enforcement order found that Alliance Capital entered into arrangements permitting market timing (trading to exploit short-term pricing inefficiencies) in certain of its mutual funds. In exchange, Alliance Capital solicited from these market timers' long-term investments. By virtue of these arrangements, Alliance Capital earned additional management fees, but allegedly exposed its mutual funds to what some thought to be potential adverse effects of market timers, thereby purportedly breaching its fiduciary duty to both the funds and those who invested in them.[35]

The Commission's order made the following specific factual findings:

– At their height in 2003, Alliance Capital arranged over $600 million in market timing in its mutual funds. Its single biggest market timer, Daniel Calugar, owner of Security Brokerage in Las Vegas, Nevada, peaked at

[31] ibid 552-53.

[32] ibid.

[33] The information about the Alliance Capital settlement with the SEC is drawn from the SEC website, at <http://www.sec.gov/news/press/2003-176.htm> (10 July 2005).

[34] ibid.

[35] ibid.

$220 million of timing capacity in certain mutual funds. In exchange, Mr. Calugar invested in hedge funds run by some of the same portfolio managers overseeing the mutual funds. For example, Alliance Capital granted Calugar $150 million timing capacity (the right to make multiple roundtrip trades up to $150 million each) in the AllianceBernstein Technology Fund in return for a $30 million investment – a 5:1 ratio – in a hedge fund managed by the same portfolio managers.

- Alliance Capital solicited shareholder approval, by means of a misleading proxy, to lift a restriction on futures trading in one of the funds. Alliance Capital failed to disclose that one reason for seeking to lift the restriction was to enable the portfolio manager to better manage the cash flows resulting from market timers.
- Alliance Capital provided confidential information about the portfolio holdings of certain mutual funds to one of the timers, Canary Investment Management. The disclosure enabled Canary to profit from market timing in declining markets.[36]

In accepting the settlement, the Securities and Exchange Commission considered Alliance Capital's cooperation in its investigation. This cooperation included the fact that the firm promptly reported its discovery of possible misconduct to the Commission, conducted a thorough and independent internal investigation, shared the results of that investigation with the SEC staff, obtained the resignations of certain supervisory personnel and other employees, and implemented remedial action.

The SEC's investigation and enforcement action were coordinated with the New York attorney general's office. However, unlike the SEC's settlement, the New York attorney general reached a settlement that required Alliance Capital to offer fee discounts to its mutual fund customers. In an unusual statement attached to the Alliance settlement announcement, all five of the SEC's commissioners stated that there was 'no legitimate basis' for a regulator to act as a 'rate setter'. The Commission issued a separate statement that discussed at length why the relief demanded of Alliance by Eliot Spitzer's office 'would not serve (its) law enforcement objectives':

> Today we announce our settled enforcement action against Alliance Capital Management, L.P. ('Alliance Capital') in connection with its illegal market timing arrangements. The Commission's settlement requires Alliance Capital to pay a total of $250 million (including a penalty of $100 million), all of which is to be returned to investors harmed by the violations. This amount will provide those investors with full compensation for fund losses due to the illegal market timing arrangements. In addition, we are requiring Alliance Capital and its mutual fund boards to adopt significant governance and compliance reforms. These reforms are designed to prevent a recurrence of the kind of conduct described in our order.

[36] ibid.

> The Commission's settlement does not require Alliance Capital to offer fee discounts to its mutual fund customers. We determined – unanimously – that such relief would not serve our law enforcement objectives in this case. There were no allegations that Alliance Capital's mutual fund fees were illegally high. This is a case about illegal market timing, not fees. Therefore, we see no legitimate basis for the Commission to act as a 'rate-setter' and determine how much mutual fund customers should pay for the services they receive in the future from Alliance Capital. This decision is better left to informed consumers, independent and vigorous mutual fund boards, and the free market. Mandatory fee discounts would (i) require that customers do business with Alliance in order to receive the benefits of the discounts, and (ii) provide monetary relief to customers who were not harmed by the violations set forth in the order. That is why our efforts focused on providing full compensation to harmed investors and a significant upfront penalty.
>
> Issues surrounding mutual fund fees are critically important. As part of our broad and unique rulemaking powers, we plan to take up these issues in the period ahead. We firmly believe that rules uniformly applicable to the entire industry are more desirable than a piecemeal approach that fragments the marketplace. The rulemaking process – with its attendant protections of notice and public comment – is a better way to address fee issues than the imposition of arbitrary discounts in individual enforcement actions about market timing. While we can all applaud fair and reasonable fees, we think the best way to ensure them is a marketplace of vigorous, independent, and diligent mutual fund boards coupled with fully-informed investors who are armed with complete, easy-to-digest disclosure about the fees paid and the services rendered.[37]

The SEC clearly thought that in requiring Alliance to cut its fees, Spitzer had exceeded his authority and engaged in inappropriate rulemaking through enforcement action. The New York attorney general is not reticent about this subject, or subtle. For example, with regard to the complaint his office filed against Merrill Lynch for publishing false and misleading analyst reports, he was clear that '[w]hat we are seeking here is to reform the system and restore integrity. …'[38] Mr. Spitzer appears to be of the view that the SEC routinely tolerated pervasive wrongdoing, and that 'nobody believed that anybody was going to put a stop to it'.[39] In other words, Mr. Spitzer has not been content to share power with the SEC. He certainly has not been content to follow the SEC's lead, or to let the SEC set the regulatory agenda. Clearly, the SEC has been far more influenced by Eliot Spitzer than Eliot Spitzer has by the SEC. Eliot Spitzer is driven by the spirit of political entrepreneurship. The SEC is being driven by a sense of rivalry with Mr. Spitzer. In a real sense, Mr. Spitzer has engineered a successful 'hostile takeover' of the SEC, hijacking its agenda and forcing the Commission to pursue Mr. Spitzer's preferred approaches to capital market regulation, or else risk

[37] ibid.

[38] The Sheriff of Wall Street (n 23) 2.

[39] ibid.

appearing slow and indifferent, and suffering a major public relations defeat at the hands of Mr. Spitzer. Mr. Spitzer has replaced the SEC as 'policy czar'.[40]

For example, Spitzer upstaged the joint investigation by state and federal regulators of market timing by mutual funds, analyst conflicts of interest, and, more recently, market manipulation by hedge funds. It appears that the SEC has been 'embarrassed' and 'upstaged' by Spitzer, not only by his ability to 'extract a whopping $1.4 billion in penalties (from Wall Street's largest broker-dealer firms), bigger than any ever won by the SEC', but also by making the Commission 'look inept'.[41] Apparently, the pace and vigor of even relatively small investigations, such as insider trading by a single individual, is influenced by the Spitzer-SEC rivalry because 'they don't want the New York Attorney General's office to make them look like Keystone Kops again'.[42]

4. The Once and Future SEC: Securities Regulation Post-Spitzer

Having moved through the initial phase of suspicion in the 'New Deal' phase of his tenure about his motives and ability, to the subsequent acceptance of his competence and professionalism in the 'federalist' stage, Mr. Spitzer has now successfully engineered a de facto hostile take over the SEC, controlling its agenda and seemingly even its personnel.[43] The important question is what will come next for capital markets regulation in the United States. In my view, there are three and only three possible 'post-Spitzer scenarios':

Scenario 1: The SEC will experience real institutional reform and be more agile and aggressive after Mr. Spitzer leaves office, filling the vacuum left by Mr. Spitzer.

Scenario 2: The SEC will be weakened and demoralized after Mr. Spitzer moves on, and oversight of the securities markets and regulatory enforcement of the securities laws will be diminished over the long run as the SEC loses stature and prestige as an institution.

Scenario 3: The SEC will continue roughly unchanged, but a political coalition will emerge to extend the partial preemption of state securities laws accomplished by the 1996 NSMIA legislation, so as to bar state attorneys general such as Mr. Spitzer from encroaching on the SEC's regulatory turf in the future.

[40] M Langley 'The Enforcer: As His Ambitions Expand, Spitzer Draws Controversy' Wall Street Journal (New York United States 11 December 2003) A1.

[41] P Tharp 'SEC's Eliot Envy' New York Post (New York United States 27 January 2003) 33.

[42] ibid.

[43] See discussion of Juan Marcelino's dismissal from the SEC, n 10 and 11 and accompanying text.

The nature of Mr. Spitzer's legacy will depend on which of these scenarios occurs in the wake of his inevitable departure from office. As for the first scenario, there is no evidence or even any indication that Mr. Spitzer's initiatives have strengthened the SEC. There is not even an extant theory in political science or the theory of federalism to support the belief that the SEC will emerge a better, stronger institution in the long run as a result of the competition Mr. Spitzer posed in the short run.

Rather, it seems more likely that the SEC 'identity crisis' will cause the agency to be more susceptible to capture by special interest groups as it seeks to curry favor with new constituencies and strengthen ties with old constituencies in the wake of its recent loss of prestige.

Two recent policy initiatives by the SEC seem consistent with this view. Both the SEC's shareholder access initiative and its ruling regarding mutual fund boards of directors represent a clear change in its institutional direction and focus. It seems impossible to avoid the conclusion that the competitive pressures exerted by the New York attorney general are at least partially responsible for this dramatic change. Having lost its original core constituency of small investors in US capital markets to Eliot Spitzer, the SEC is in search of a new one.

a. SEC Shareholder Access Proposal

Under long-standing law and corporate practice, corporations controlled the election of corporate directors through control of access to the corporate ballot box. When it came time to elect directors at the annual meeting, a company's board of directors would typically nominate the slate of candidates generated by the (generally management-controlled) nominating committee of the board of directors. If a shareholder were unhappy with the slate of candidates nominated by the board and management, she would be obliged to mount a proxy contest at considerable expense and risk, and in full compliance with applicable state and federal securities laws. The insurgent group would also exclusively shoulder the fees and expenses for the election campaign of this alternative slate of candidates.

In late 2003, reeling from pressure mounted by Eliot Spitzer and desperate to be seen as capable of making a meaningful, or at least politically salient, regulatory initiative, the SEC proposed Rule 14a-11. Under this proposed rule, some outside shareholders (though not all),[44] would be able to require that the corporation place its nominee on the corporation's proxy card and publish that nominee's

[44] Only shareholders who meet four criteria will have access to the company's proxy materials. The four criteria are: (a) beneficial ownership of more than 5% of the company's voting stock, held continuously for at least two years; (b) declaration of intent to continue owning the requisite number of securities through the date of the relevant shareholders' meeting; (c) eligibility to report their holdings on Schedule 13G rather than 13D; and (d) have filed a Schedule 13G before their nomination is submitted to the corporation.

supporting statement if one of the following two triggering events were to occur: (a) a shareholder proposal to authorize shareholder nominations is placed on the ballot under SEC Rule 14a-8 and a majority of the outstanding shareholders approves this proposal; or (b) shareholders representing at least 35% of the total votes in a corporate election for directors withhold proxy authority from the incumbent board of directors

If there are 35% 'withholds' at one meeting, or if a majority of the outstanding shares votes to approve a shareholder proposal under Rule 14a-8, then at the *following* annual meeting at which directors are to be elected, shareholder nominees must be included in the company's ballot and accompanying proxy statement.[45] This initiative reflects the SEC's 'desperate attempt to regain control of the regulatory agenda'[46] in the field of capital markets regulation.

Interestingly, this move by the SEC represents a clear incursion into the director nomination process, an area traditionally reserved for state law under the US federalist system, which has long granted states a position of primacy in the promulgation of rules related to the internal corporate governance of corporations.[47]

Oddly, the SEC has long dragged its heels in efforts to assist shareholders in improving the quality of corporate elections. In particular, the SEC has withheld vigorous support of the shareholder rights bylaw, which would allow investors to enact corporate bylaws requiring directors to permit shareholders to vote on the issue of whether a company should nullify anti-takeover devices such as the poison pill, when a company receives a fully funded cash takeover bid for all of its outstanding shares at a substantial premium to market.[48] The political pressures imposed by Eliot Spitzer provide the only reasonable explanation for its newfound interest in reforming the corporate election process.

In addition, the SEC's proposed new rule represents a radical departure from the past in terms of the constituencies that the SEC addresses. Traditionally, the SEC has appealed to shareholders, securities firms, lawyers, and other capital markets 'insiders'. This proposal is the SEC's barely disguised attempt to link itself to a new constituency: public interest pension funds and other 'activist' shareholder groups, whose preferences and agendas are unlikely to reflect the profit-maximization motive that is embraced by the average investor.

[45] 'Security Holder Director Nominations' Exchange Act Release no 48626 (proposed 14 October 2003), available at <http://www.sec.gov/rules/proposed/34-48626.htm> (10 July 2005).

[46] JR Macey 'Securities and Exchange Nanny' *Wall Street Journal* (New York United States 30 December 2003) A10.

[47] *Bus Roundtable v SEC* 905 F2d 406, 412-13 (DC Cir 1990).

[48] See JR Macey 'The Legality and Utility of the Shareholder Rights Bylaw' (1998) 26 Hofstra L Rev 835, 837.

b. SEC Mutual Fund Board Chairman Independence Rule

On 23 June 2004, by a vote of three to two, the SEC voted to require that the chairs of mutual funds' boards of directors be independent of the advisors of such funds. There is no empirical or theoretical basis for this rule. Indeed, the rule appears to be simply a political public relations ploy, which, if anything, will harm rather than benefit mutual fund investors. Commissioner Cynthia Glassman commented on the lack of bases for this proposal:

> It is a fact that many of the top-rated funds today based on high performance and low fees have inside chairs. Why should we tell shareholders they can no longer have the form of governance that produced this high level of performance? And further, why should we require them to pay for it? There can be no doubt that this requirement will add to fund expenses. An independent chair cannot be expected to have – and in most cases, will not have – hands-on knowledge about fund operations. Therefore, to be effective, the chair would have to hire a staff. Shareholders will bear that expense as well as the likely additional cost of the independent chairman. In sum, the benefits are illusory, but the costs are real.[49]

She also noted that there is no empirical evidence that mutual funds with independent chairs have either higher returns or lower overhead and administrative costs than mutual funds chaired by insiders.[50]

As with the SEC's proposed shareholder ballot-access rule, it appears that in promulgating this rule, the Commission is clearly less concerned with shareholder welfare and the quality of US capital markets than it has been in the past. The public interest concern with the quality of US investors and capital markets appears to have been replaced by a regulatory agenda that includes rulemaking oriented toward special-interest groups.

It is in this way that the recent spate of corporate scandals, combined with Eliot Spitzer's bureaucratic turf-grabbing, has influenced the SEC's behavior. Whether this is a short-term phenomenon or not will depend on what happens after Mr. Spitzer leaves his post as attorney general of the state of New York.

IV. Conclusion

The SEC's success in procuring more resources, in the form of higher budget allocations, does not necessarily mean that the SEC's power and prestige has increased in the wake of the corporate scandals that have rocked Wall Street. Also, the SEC's budget increases do not reflect heightened public recognition of

[49] Commissioner CA Glassman 'Statement by SEC Commissioner Regarding Investment Company Governance' Proposal Address at US Securities and Exchange Commission Open Meeting (23 June 2004), at <http://www.sec.gov/news/speech/spch062304cag.htm> (10 July 2005).

[50] ibid.

the SEC's relevance or effectiveness. Rather, the SEC's success in the budgetary process reflects the need for federal officials to appear to be 'doing something' in the wake of the crises that have emerged on Main Street (Enron, Global Crossing, Adelphia, Tyco, Waste Management, Sunbeam) and in the wake of the scandals that Eliot Spitzer has uncovered on Wall Street (financial analysts, market timers at mutual funds).

To date, these results suggest that the first scenario presented will not materialize: the SEC will not experience meaningful institutional reform. It will not emerge from the Spitzer-era a more agile and aggressive regulatory agency.

The second possibility is that the SEC will be weakened and demoralized after Mr. Spitzer moves on, and that oversight of the securities markets and regulatory enforcement of the securities laws will consequently be diminished. The SEC's apparent resilience in the budgetary process, coupled with steadily rising pay for SEC staffers, suggests that this is unlikely to happen. In 2004, the SEC obtained 'pay parity' with banking regulatory agencies, allowing it to pay its professionals at the highest pay scale allowed in government.[51]

As long as the SEC continues to serve as a training ground for high-paying jobs in the nation's top law firms, it will continue to attract bright, talented, ambitious, hard-working people, if only for relatively short periods of time. Thus the SEC will continue to attract high-quality professionals and find success in obtaining funding. The SEC is not going anywhere for a very long time, particularly in light of its recent efforts to cultivate support with new constituencies. Nobody is calling for the dismantling of the SEC despite its arguably poor performance in anticipating and responding to scandals in the capital markets.

The final scenario appears highly likely: the SEC will continue roughly unchanged, but a political coalition will emerge to enlarge and extend the partial preemption of state securities laws accomplished by the 1996 NSMIA legislation. I expect that this legislation will bar future state attorneys general who would seek to emulate Eliot Spitzer from encroaching on the SEC's regulatory turf. This

[51] Public Law 107-123, the Investor and Capital Markets Fee Relief Act ('Pay Parity Act'), requires the Securities and Exchange Commission ('SEC' or 'Commission') to submit a report to the Committee on Governmental Affairs and the Committee on Banking, Housing, and Urban Affairs of the Senate, the Committee on Government Reform and the Committee on Financial Services of the House of Representatives, and the Office of Personnel Management ('OPM') describing the Commission's plan to implement Section 4802 of Title 5 of the US Code.

This provision of law provides the Commission with the authority to appoint and fix the compensation of such officers, attorneys, economists, examiners, and other employees as may be necessary for carrying out its functions under the securities laws as defined under Section 3 of the Securities Exchange Act of 1934 (15 USC 78c). The statute 'places the SEC on equal footing with its sister federal financial regulatory agencies'. The SEC 'worked closely with Congress and the Administration throughout this process of resolving the agency's ongoing staffing crisis and appreciates greatly the support that it has received'. SEC 'Pay Parity Implementation Plan and Report' (6 March 2002) at <http://www.sec.gov/news/studies/payparity.htm> (10 July 2005).

sort of preemptive legislation would attract the support of a powerful farrago of interest groups. Deregulatory Republicans would join with anti-federalists to support this legislation. The deregulatory Republicans would likely support preemption because they prefer that the state attorneys general be stripped of power and be prevented from interfering with the operation of the markets; the anti-federalists would support it because they would like to see federal administrative agencies gain power at the expense of state governments. To the extent that corporate and special interests have captured the SEC, these groups similarly will favor preemption, since they have more control over the SEC than they do over a world in which the SEC and the states are locked in competition for headlines, political support, and relevant targets to prosecute.

Scandals, Regulation, and Supervisory Agencies: The European Perspective

GERALD SPINDLER

I. Introduction

The interesting story of New York attorney general Eliot Spitzer's hostile takeover of the SEC seems for the European observer – at first glance – to be one of the US-specific battles in the political scene: starring a state attorney ambitious enough to present himself for presidential elections, on the other side is a governmental agency that has grown old and suffers from capture by interest groups, with the whole conflict embedded in a general struggle between state and federal interests regulating capital markets.

Macey draws two conclusions out of this story: first, that crises facilitate new regulations; and second, that leaving a regulatory vacuum provokes other players to enter the match, thus creating new regulations. From the perspective of a European commentator, these conclusions shall be discussed under four aspects:

1. Crisis as a driving force for new regulations (II.)
2. The European parallels that can be observed in capital market regulation by the European Commission (III.2.)
3. The national perspective presenting a different model of state prosecutors (attorney general) acting in concert with Securities Exchange authorities (III.3.)
4. The parallels of the conflict between state and federal agencies on one side and the struggle on the international level between national states and international agencies or regulating bodies on the other side (III.4)

Finally, this comment will close with some observations about lessons which could be learned from a European point of view concerning regulation and agencies in a worldwide capital market.

II. Crisis as the Motor of New Regulations

The relationship between scandals and the call for regulations and new agencies cannot be denied. In the light of spectacular bankruptcies of large firms, a general deregulation of corporate and securities law is not *en vogue*. It seems obvious to the public (or the published) opinion that markets have failed and new rules are necessary to repair what could be qualified as market failures. What is true for the US and the story of Eliot Spitzer seems to be valid also for other countries, namely Germany or Europe, in particular in corporate and securities law. To name just a few examples, we observe hectic regulation on mandatory transparency of board of directors' income once the plea for self-regulation by means of a corporate governance codex has failed to convince corporations (and capital markets) to publish the income of their directors,[1] or we hear calls for a new legal framework for outside directors in boards. Regulations on prospectus obligations were modified just six months after the first act passed parliament.[2] Even regulations on the personal liability for directors having misled investors by publishing wrong information can be qualified (more or less)[3] as an immediate reaction to a crisis on capital markets, such as the breakdown of the 'New Market' for technology shares in Germany in 2001/2002.[4]

Hence, obviously the steady development of regulation by political bodies has been replaced by way of more discontinuously reacting upon sudden needs proclaimed by the public after scandals. Even in continental Europe – in general characterized by its long tradition of codified law – the careful and long-debated

[1] Draft Vorstandsvergütungs-Offenlegungsgesetz (VorstOG) of 18 May 2005, available at <http://www.bmj.de/media/archive/936.pdf> (8 June 2005).

[2] Draft Wertpapierprospektgesetz (WpPG), BR-Drucks. 85/05, available at <http://www3.bundesrat.de/Site/Inhalt/Drucksachen/2005/0085-05,property=Dokument.pdf>; Anlegerschutzverbesserungsgesetz (AnSVG), available at <http://217.160.60.235/BGBL/bgbl1f/bgbl104s2630.pdf>; Wertpapier-Verkaufsprospektgesetz, available at <http://www. bafin.de/gesetze/vkprospg.htm> (all 8 June 2005).

[3] This debate, however, goes back to 2002: H Fleischer *Gutachten zum 64. Deutschen Juristentag* (Munich Beck 2002) F 101 ff; see also J Semler and S Gittermann 'Persönliche Haftung der Organmitglieder für Fehlinformationen des Kapitalmarktes – Zeigt das KapInHaG den richtigen Weg?' [2004] Neue Zeitschrift für Gesellschaftsrecht 1081; H Fleischer 'Die persönliche Haftung der Organmitglieder für kapitalmarktbezogene Falschinformationen – Bestandsaufnahme und Perspektiven' [2003] Zeitschrift für Bank- und Kapitalmarktrecht 608; M Casper 'Persönliche Außenhaftung der Organe bei fehlerhafter Information des Kapitalmarkts?' [2005] Zeitschrift für Bank- und Kapitalmarktrecht 83; BP Paal 'Die persönliche Haftung – ein wirksames Mittel zur Verbesserung der Kontrolltätigkeit des Aufsichtsrats bei kapitalmarktorientierten Unternehmen? (Teil I)' [2005] Deutsches Steuerrecht 382.

[4] For example: BGH NJW 2004, 2664; BGH NJW 2004, 2668; BGH NJW 2004, 2971 – 'Infomatec'; BGH NJW 2005, 445 – 'EM.TV'; OLG München BKR 2004, 29 – 'ComRoad'; OLG Düsseldorf NZG 2002, 685.

preparation of civil and corporate legal regulations destined to last for a long time, even for a century, is on the way of vanishing.

However, the story seems to be much more complex than at first glance, due to the different German political system which is not so prone to reacting to sudden changes of public opinion and to lobbying influences as is obviously the case in the US History shows several different trends which may be reduced to two layers (or ways) of developing a regulation: one referring to fundamental codes, acts, or regulations (and deregulations), taking more than a decade or more to be designed; and one concerning the immediate (re-)action of regulators after scandals. This can be illustrated by two examples:

– The preparations for a (new) German code for stock corporations had already begun around 1927, long before the worldwide economic crisis of the early thirties reached Germany[5] and led in the US to the enacting of the Securities Exchange Act. Certainly, this project was greatly enhanced and propelled by the breakdowns of several major German corporations which also led to immediate regulations[6] such as the introducing of control by auditors. Nevertheless, this immediate reaction did not fundamentally change the great outlines of the later Stock Corporation Act of 1937.
– Even today, in a period of hectic regulations after the decline of stock exchanges, another regulatory body – the EU – often passes a general (master) plan which is followed by the passage of several directives. In such a manner, the EU has adopted the action plan to renew European corporate governance based on the elaborate report of the High Level Expert Group. The same procedure can be observed in securities law where the Commission sticks to the Finance Plan as well as to the adopted procedure of preparing regulation by means of the so-called Lamfalussy process.[7]

Hence, to draw a (very) preliminary conclusion, it is not always a crisis that triggers a new regulatory movement, but also a long-felt need for reforms. It is true that a crisis may enhance and accelerate these long-lasting movements or even create new regulations. However, changes in legal framework may not always be induced by a short-term policy of just reacting to some news and scandals. Moreover, some of these crisis-related regulations are more or less of an appellative character, at best just re-forming and reformulating an old rule into a

[5] G Spindler *Recht und Konzern* (Mohr Siebeck Tübingen 1993) 52 ff; HD Assmann in KJ Hopt (ed) *Großkommentar zum Aktiengesetz* (4th edn de Gruyter Berlin New York 1992) Introduction para 136; KW Nörr 'Zur Entwicklung des Aktien- und Konzernrechts während der Weimarer Republik' (1986) 150 Zeitschrift für das gesamte Handelsrecht und Wirtschaftsrecht 155, 165; see also P Doralt in B Kropff and J Semler (eds) *Münchener Kommentar zum Aktiengesetz* (2nd edn CH Beck Munich 2000) Introduction para 245.

[6] NotVO of 19 September 1931, published 21 September 1931, RGBl. 1931 part I p 493; see in particular Assmann (n 5) para 145 ff.

[7] See below III.2.

new section of a corporate act or, worse, turning the old rules into bad new acts, eg the proposed reform of the manager's liability in Germany.[8] Regulations induced by a crisis obviously have a more pointillist character than large reforms of acts. Thus, crisis as a factor in the legal process may be qualified more as a catalyst which enhances and triggers an already ongoing development rather than starting it.

Finally, we have to take into account that the American system tends to correct failures of regulations by means of common law in combination with the traditional restrictive attitude of common courts towards statutes and acts of governmental agencies. As Hovenkamp has shown for the American Supreme Court in the 19th and 20th centuries, we can also observe a certain long wave of regulating policy stemming from a general bias of the Court and political attitude.[9]

Hence, what is needed is a complex theory of regulation and public choice which takes into account crisis as a decisive factor as well as counterbalancing elements of the political system, including different ways of how public opinion, mass media, and governmental bodies are working.

III. Competition Between Regulators

1. General Lessons

Concerning the competition between regulators and agencies, Macey forecasts in particular the pre-emption of states (and Spitzer, the attorney general) in order to interdict their intermingling with competences of the SEC. This struggle between states and the federal government (and their agencies like the SEC) reminds the European spectator of the old hare and hog tales of the early 20th century when states like New Jersey and Delaware competed for the most liberal corporate law, whereas antitrust federal agencies strove to ban new conglomerates and mergers from forming under corporate laws of N.J. or Delaware.[10] The regulatory field

[8] Casper (n 3); R Veil 'Die Haftung des Emittenten für fehlerhafte Information des Kapitalmarkts nach dem geplanten KapInHaG' [2005] Zeitschrift für Bank- und Kapitalmarktrecht 91; Semler and Gittermann (n 3); O Gerber 'Die Haftung für unrichtige Kapitalmarktinformationen – Zugleich eine Besprechung der BGH-Entscheidungen vom 19.7.2004 'Infomatec' [2004] Deutsches Steuerrecht 1793; BP Paal 'Die persönliche Haftung – ein wirksames Mittel zur Verbesserung der Kontrolltätigkeit des Aufsichtsrats bei kapitalmarktorientierten Unternehmen? (Teil II)' [2005] Deutsches Steuerrecht 426; M Körner 'Infomatec und die Haftung von Vorstandsmitgliedern für falsche ad hoc-Mitteilungen' [2004] Neue Juristische Wochenschrift 3386.

[9] H Hovenkamp *Enterprise and American Law 1836 – 1937* (Harvard University Press Cambridge 1991), review by G Spindler (1994) 42 AJCL 811.

[10] Spindler (n 5) 235 ff.

was certainly not the same as in the case of Spitzer and the SEC; nevertheless, it seems that the story of Spitzer & Co. had its many predecessors in American history as corporations benefited from regulatory vacuums caused deliberately by interest-captured (state) regulators. Even more, the Delaware system of corporate law obviously benefits from a well-balanced system of capturing interests, following the insights of Roberta Romano.[11]

However, there is a fundamental difference from the story told by Macey: corporate law systems and states are still engaged in a competition for efficient corporate legal frameworks, whereas the SEC is only checked by political institutions such as Congress or mass media – and by Spitzer's activities. Hence, in principle there is no competition on the same grounds as in the case of states concerning corporate law, but a competition in the political system such as reputation, influence, budget allocations, etc. Therefore, agencies can more easily be captured by interest groups. Interestingly enough, Macey does not envisage a state-based system of capital market surveillance. If we take the results of the studies of Roberta Romano and Macey for granted, then the question is obvious why we should not open the competition for agencies in capital markets to compete for the most effective monitoring of markets. On the other hand, capital markets and in particular stock exchanges tend to form natural monopolies due to the network effects so that different agencies may be not appropriate.[12] Then, however, we should look for mechanisms to check the danger that agencies are being captured by interest groups.

2. European Perspective

If we change the perspective and analyze the European landscape, we are confronted with a different scenario.

a. Regulation Level

The European Union still ignores a pendant to the American Securities Exchange Commission as well as an attorney general who could act on a European level. Moreover, the European Commission as the principal regulatory body is not as prone as American agencies or governments to public opinion, because control of European Parliament or other public constituencies is rather weak. In contrast,

[11] See R Romano *The Genius of American Corporate Law* (AEI Press Washington DC 1993), in particular p 37, 59.

[12] See B Rudolph 'Zur Diskussion um die Börsenreform' [1999] Wertpapiermitteilungen 371, 371; S Kümpel B*ank- und Kapitalmarktrecht* (3rd edn Verlag Dr Otto Schmidt Cologne 2004) para 18.20 ff.

member states and the Council seem to control, steer, and monitor the Commission's activities the most. The complex mechanisms of necessary majorities inside the Council act as a filter for nervous actions or regulations on behalf of the Commission, thus resulting in a somehow crisis-immune procedure of enacting new regulations.

Hence, the risk of reacting to a crisis is even weaker than in the case of the SEC. Moreover, most of the staff of the European Commission stem from national governmental agencies, and not from law firms, industrial associations, etc. Though we lack empirical studies, there is little evidence that the EU Commission experiences a similar turnover of employees as industry or consulting agencies – also due to the different labour market in Europe and the special status of civil officers in the EU. For at least some countries it is still true that promising civil officers do not choose the European ladder for their career because their engagement will not be awarded by their ministries when returning home.

Nevertheless, there are some recent developments which indicate that industrial representatives and interest groups are gaining more influence upon regulation than before. Due to the insight that the Commission fails to regulate all details itself, in particular concerning some legal areas where changes take place rapidly or are too complex for the restricted resources of the Commission, Europe has adopted a so-called comitology approach.[13] Similar to product safety regulations, the EU adopted its 'new policy' in capital market regulation in order to accelerate the passing of capital market regulations on a European level. The general idea is that the EU just passes general rules (though complex as they are) and leaves numerous details to the Commission, assisted by CESR and its committees (the so-called Lamfalussy process), often consisting not only of supervising authority members but also of industrial/bank representatives. Moreover, the bulk of the members that as part of high level expert groups (a part of CESR and its working groups) shall help the Commission to identify and formulate new policies in capital market regulation are delegated by industry (banks, assurances, etc). Only a few governmental agents, researchers, or representatives of nonprofit organizations appear on their panel – and are able to participate without their own resources at these meetings and to devote their time to new regulations. Regulations in other policy areas go even one step beyond, in particular product safety directives. This acknowledges explicitly that private rules are adequate to

[13] C Mensching 'Der neue Komitologie-Beschluss des Rates' [2000] Europäische Zeitschrift für Wirtschaftsrecht 268, 270; R Streinz *Europarecht* (6th edn Müller Heidelberg 2003) para 457 ff; C Joerges ''Good Governance' im Europäischen Binnenmarkt: Über die Spannungen zwischen zwei rechtswissenschaftlichen Integrationskonzepten und deren Aufhebung' [2002] Europarecht 17; M Axmann *Genese Europäischer Rechtsetzungsverfahren* (Peter Lang Frankfurt 2001) 263, 269.

match and substantiate the requirements of the directives, thus handing the substance of formulating safety requirements over to private committees.[14]

b. Execution and Monitoring

Concerning the enforcement of securities regulation, the EU still lacks a Europe-wide agency supervising capital markets, as mentioned before. Hence, we would expect something similar to the US experience because the vacuum left by the EC Commission should be occupied by a political institution more aggressive than the EU Commission, at least at the national level (as at the state level in the case of Spitzer). In reality, the opposite has happened: agencies in Europe obviously seek cooperation inside the body of CESR as they have quickly realized over the past years that they cannot effectively regulate and supervise capital markets and actors in that playing field on a stand-alone basis. Moreover, there is little evidence that national regulators, state attorneys, or other political institutions strive to occupy the 'vacuum' left by the EU.

However, we have to admit that up to now there have been few studies that examine the work of CESR, in particular how the decision procedure is handled in practice and how pressure groups act upon CESR. This fact may be partly due to the so-called principle of country of origin which is realised in most of the European capital market regulations. If an agency suspects a bank (or broker, etc) of wrongdoing, the agency is obliged to pass the affair to the agency which is located at the seat of the bank. However, some regulations refer to the agency where the market is located in which the wrongdoing occurred, eg insider trading or market manipulation. Another, perhaps decisive, factor is that there is no (or a weak) European 'market' for politicians eager to head for an important role in the EU. The typical European political career does not start at a European level but at the national level, so there are few incentives for political players to occupy 'vacuums' left by the Commission. Moreover, if they were to move in such a way, it is highly probable that they would be checked by the other member states.

Hence, in sum we are confronted with a complex system where the incentives for an agency (or a political institution) to seek domination of other agencies are weak. Given the US experience of the SEC as a federal agency being captured by interest groups, this may serve also as an argument against a Europe-wide agency.

[14] G Spindler *Unternehmensorganisationspflichten* (Heymanns Cologne 2001) 159 ff; 186; T von Danwitz 'Europarechtliche Beurteilung der Umweltnormung: Kompetenzen – Legitimation – Binnenmarkt' in HW Rengeling (ed) Umweltnormung (Carl Heymann Cologne 1998) 187, 193 ff; A Roßnagel 'Europäische Techniknormen im Lichte des Gemeinschaftsvertragsrechts' [1996] Deutsches Verwaltungsblatt 1181, 1181; J Falke 'Techniksteuerung durch Normung im europäischen Rechtsvergleich' in K Vieweg (ed) *Techniksteuerung und Recht* (Heymanns Cologne 2000) 177, 185.

3. National Perspective

If we consider the German experience, organizational and political differences are again responsible for the differences.

a. Regulation Level

For Germany, corporate law was dominant for a long time, whereas capital markets were only partially (if at all) regulated. Regulation in the sense of passing laws and ordinances was always assigned to the federal government; *Länder* (states) never had the competence to regulate capital markets or corporate law by enacting new statutes.

Crises and scandals certainly played a major role in triggering and passing new acts such as those addressed to supervising banks and insurances. Long before the EU harmonized the control over banks and insurance companies, Germany had passed several acts after the world economic crisis in 1934. Nevertheless, until recent decades, changes in corporate law were prepared over a long period of time and parliaments were reluctant to change much. However, this situation changed during recent years when legislators began to reform corporate law 'in permanence',[15] even though these reforms had been prepared by a governmental commission with high expertise on board.[16] In contrast, the government (and the commission) declared that they were relying heavily on self-regulating mechanisms of capital markets by establishing a corporate codex and the principle of 'comply or explain', afterwards implemented in sec. 161 of the Stock Corporation Act. However, if markets and corporations obviously do not follow all the wishes of codex makers (and the government), federal government speakers have already announced a return in some areas to mandatory rules, such as the remuneration of directors in response to heavy attacks in the media concerning excessively high salaries of directors.[17] How this mandatory re-regulation is consistent with the opted self-regulation approach remains an open issue. Alas, capital markets seem to be insensible to different corporate governance approaches of corporations as a recent empirical study shows.[18]

[15] U Seibert 'Aktienrechtsreform in Permanenz' [2002] Die Aktiengesellschaft 417; see also G Spindler 'Kapitalmarktreform in Permanenz – Das Anlegerschutzverbesserungsgesetz' [2004] Neue Juristische Wochenschrift 3449.

[16] See final report 'Baums-Kommission' (10 July 2001), published T Baums *Wirtschaftsprüfung-Sonderheft 2001*, 6.

[17] Draft Vorstandsvergütungs-Offenlegungsgesetz (VorstOG) (n 1).

[18] E Nowak and others 'Wer den Kodex nicht einhält, den bestraft der Kapitalmarkt?: Eine empirische Analyse der Selbstregulierung und Kapitalmarktrelevanz des Deutschen Corporate Governance Kodex' [2005] Zeitschrift für Unternehmens- und Gesellschaftsrecht 252 ff.

In sum, the relationship between 'normal' regulation activity and crisis-driven acts is not easily established. Today it seems that we have left the traditional path of long-term preparation of new acts. Furthermore, a new phenomenon has arisen out of the need of ministries and agencies for personal support in spite of their restricted financial resources. Some lawyers highly paid by their law firms or other institutions work inside the ministerial agencies to prepare new acts. Thus, there seems to be some tendency of convergence concerning the intermingling of agencies with the private sector as Macey has shown for the SEC.

b. Enforcement Level

Even more, monitoring agencies were created just for banks and insurance companies due to the world economic crisis in the early 1930s. Until the 1980s , Germany had felt no need to establish a separate agency dealing with the supervision of securities at large. However, the *Länder* (states) still supervise the stock exchanges – which are not entities belonging to the private sector but are established as governmental or state-owned bodies – which is rather rare in the world. Thus, conflicts have arisen basically between the federal government and states because the latter want to conserve their competences in supervising stock exchanges whereas the federal government is trying to establish a federal stock exchange. This situation is complicated even more by the creation of the super-agency Bundesanstalt für Finanzdienstleistungen (BaFin) which incorporates the former supervising agency of banks and of insurance companies as well as the federal agency for supervising securities (not concerning stock exchanges). However, the *Länder* do take into account the network effects of capital markets and trading platforms by creating a CESR-like group which encompasses all state agencies acting as monitoring authorities of stock exchanges.[19] Moreover, the federal government has some representatives in this body as well as the BaFin so that regulatory activities are discussed and largely agreed upon in this body.

How conflicts between states and this federal agency will be settled in future remains to be seen. However, neither agency seems to be much captured by interest groups yet, perhaps with the particular but very important exception of the German Stock Exchange located in Frankfurt. In contrast, they both suffer from the problem of recruiting trained professionals. Hence, the BaFin could be the starter of an institution in Germany which corresponds to the SEC but does not face the same type of competition with other regulators except on the European level.

One of the most important reasons for the fundamental difference is the position of the state prosecutor (attorney general), who is not elected and acts as a normal civil officer. In addition, the probability for the state prosecutor to engage

[19] Kümpel (n 12) para 18.1 ff.

in a political career is very low and rare in Germany. Hence, he is not likely to be influenced by public opinion. However, we have to admit that some prosecutor offices have a tendency towards self-promotion. Nevertheless, these promotions are low in comparison to US experience. Other factors add to that, such as regulations of how to cooperate. Hence, conflicts such as between the SEC and an attorney general are not likely to occur in Germany.

Finally, concerning academic research on the behaviour and actions of the BaFin, we still lack empirical and political studies that will deepen our understanding of public choice mechanisms of real institutions acting on the capital market.

4. The International Level

Let's have a short look at the international level. The IOSCO acts as an institution that harmonizes regulatory approaches in the different member states. Nevertheless, there seems to be some competition between capital market regulators, in particular between the US and the EC. The tendencies of the SEC to apply US rules extraterritorially are well known; only recently the EC reacted by inserting in their directives some clauses directed to non-EC countries demanding a similar treatment as in the EC.[20] Even more, there are some diplomatic reactions to US acts like the Sarbanes-Oxley Act[21] on behalf of the EU trying to convince the US side that there should be exemptions for European corporations due to their different structure, such as German corporations with their two-tier model.[22]

Can we also talk on the international level about a competition between authorities/agencies such as the SEC? Whereas for stock exchanges this seems to be sometimes true, eg the requirement of audit committees, I have doubts concerning securities exchange agencies. They obviously serve essentially their domestic needs and the demand of local investors, but at first glance are not seeking to attract foreign investors or financial institutions. However, once again

[20] Comparable to the extraterritorial scope of EC competition law, see B Beck 'Extraterritoriale Anwendung des EG-Kartellrechts' [1990] Recht der Internationalen Wirtschaft 91; HW Knebel 'Die Extraterritorialität des Europäischen Kartellrechts' [1991] Europäische Zeitschrift für Wirtschaftsrecht 265; J Schwarze 'Die extraterritoriale Anwendbarkeit des EG-Wettbewerbsrechts – Vom Durchführungsprinzip zum Prinzip der qualifizierten Auswirkung' [2001] Wirtschaft und Wettbewerb 1190.

[21] See annex 3 in this volume.

[22] See FP Regelin and R Fisher 'Zum Stand der Umsetzung des Sarbanes-Oxley Act aus deutscher Sicht' [2003] Internationales Steuerrecht 276, 280; U Block 'Neue Regelungen zur Corporate Governance gemäß Sarbanes-Oxley Act' [2003] Zeitschrift für Bank- und Kapitalmarktrecht 774, 781; K Wolf 'Qualitative Verbesserung der Finanzberichterstattung – Spezifische Anforderungen des Sarbanes-Oxley Act' [2003] Bilanzbuchhalter und Controller 268, 269.

empirical evidence or studies concerning the international implications and public choice mechanisms are still needed.

IV. Conclusions

If we push Macey's analysis further, regulatory competition between a federal agency and an attorney general seems to result in the short-term victory of a more active attorney general, but it ends up in an extension of the competences of the federal agency. Hence, the effect is just to lift the agency to a higher level of power without changing much in its basic structure and without strengthening control over it. Furthermore, if legislation is triggered by crisis, it is likely that the results will tend to be negative and populist.

Putting that in contrast to the European and German experience, we have seen that their systems are characterized by a highly complex architecture of checks and balances, which are however not always transparent and mostly immune to interest captures. Independent agencies are welcome but expensive, and private enforcement is often ineffective due to lack of knowledge and sanctions. A competition between agencies to regulate seems too ineffective as long as capital markets produce network effects, thus tending to also produce uniform rules. In other words, concentration of markets apparently enhances concentration of supervisory agencies.

On the European level, the Lamfalussy process has no alternative but to be made more transparent and more geared towards mid- and long-term solutions instead of reacting to daily needs and demands for regulation. The creation of CESR seems to be such a cornerstone of the European building of a European homologue to the SEC.

However, we still do need more insight in the mechanisms of competing regulatory bodies and agencies, eg career paths of leading civil officers, and the influence of interest groups in different regulatory bodies. This is true in particular for the international level and the different reactions of governmental players in the game of regulating capital markets.

V. Theses

1. Regulation induced by scandals and crises tends to be inefficient in the long run. However, it can overcome path-dependent structures.
2. European regulation needs to be scrutinized with regard to being captured by interest groups, in particular concerning the consultation process in accordance with the Lamfalussy approach. Results such as the directives on product safety should be avoided (here industry is largely regulating itself by European standardization).

3. Network effects of capital markets tend to trigger concentration (or coordination) tendencies among supervising agencies. In the long run, competition between agencies is not likely to occur.
4. There is a need for more empirical research not only regarding capital markets but also concerning securities exchange agencies and their behaviour, in particular on the international level.

Part 2:

Corporations – Changing Models of Corporate Governance

European Company Law and Corporate Governance: Where Does the Action Plan of the European Commission Lead?

KLAUS J. HOPT

I. Introduction

Company law reform in the European Union[1] and European corporate governance[2] is a fascinating area which is acutely relevant for companies and company

[1] See first R Kraakman and others *The Anatomy of Corporate Law, A Comparative and Functional Approach* (OUP Oxford 2004), and the review article by DA Skeel Jr 'Corporate Anatomy Lessons' (2004) 113 Yale L J 1519-1577. On European company law, see S Grundmann *Europäisches Gesellschaftsrecht* (CF Müller Heidelberg 2004) and M Habersack *Europäisches Gesellschaftsrecht* (2nd edn CH Beck Munich 2003). The most recent German article is by KJ Hopt 'Europäisches Gesellschaftsrecht und deutsche Unternehmensverfassung – Aktionsplan und Interdependenzen' [2005] Zeitschrift für Wirtschaftsrecht [ZIP] 461 with further references. For texts and cases, see KJ Hopt and E Wymeersch (eds) *European Company and Financial Law, Texts and Leading Cases* (3rd edn OUP Oxford 2004).

[2] Cf the list of references in KJ Hopt and others (eds) *Comparative Corporate Governance, The State of the Art and Emerging Research* (OUP Oxford 1998) 1201-1210; more recently T Clarke (ed) *Corporate Governance* 5 vols (Routledge London New York 2005). As to Europe, see KJ Hopt and others *European Corporate Governance in Company Law and Codes* Report prepared for the European Corporate Governance Conference of 18 October 2004, The Hague; see also KJ Hopt 'Common Principles of Corporate Governance in Europe?' in JA McCahery and others (eds) *Corporate Governance Regimes, Convergence and Diversity* (OUP Oxford 2002) 175. As to German corporate governance, see P Hommelhoff and others (eds) *Corporate Governance* Common symposium organized by the two leading German law reviews in the field ZHR/ZGR (Verlag Recht und Wirtschaft Heidelberg 2002) with general report by KJ Hopt 27-67; and P Hommelhoff KJ Hopt and A von Werder (eds) *Handbuch Corporate Governance, Leitung und Überwachung börsennotierter Unternehmen in der Rechts- und Wirtschaftspraxis* (Verlag Otto Schmidt Cologne Stuttgart 2003).

law practice throughout Europe. After the voting down of the draft European Constitution in France and the Netherlands, there were some dire predictions about the future of the European Union in general and its law reform plans in particular. I think this is greatly exaggerated. The economic core of the Union, ie the internal market, is untouched. Economic policy-making and legal harmonization will go on, though maybe for some time at a somewhat lower speed. This is particularly true for European company law as well as securities, auditing, and takeover regulation, and even more so for the whole area of banking and financial market regulation.

The EU Company Law Action Plan of 21 May 2003,[3] and its impact on company law and in particular on corporate governance, seems to be suitable for this conference for three reasons. First, it is highly topical to know *what* the European Commission intends to regulate and what it does not intend to regulate within the next five to ten years, and *how* it is going about it, namely by aiming at a distinctively European, more flexible route as compared with the post-Enron US approach. Second, this plan, while purporting to be aimed at mere framework regulation, cuts considerably into member state company law and company practice (the well-known federal-state issue) and is already controversial for this, quite apart from specific rules. Third, I carry a certain responsibility for it because I belonged to the seven-member High Level Group of Company Law Experts chaired by Jaap Winter. This group prepared the report for the European Commission that was the basis for the Action Plan and which the Action Plan followed closely. This report of 4 November 2002 will be referred to in brief as the High Level Group Report.[4] But it must be kept in mind that the group had prepared another report for the European Commission half a year earlier,[5] thereby

[3] European Commission *Communication to the Council and the European Parliament: Modernising Company Law and Enhancing Corporate Governance in the European Union – A Plan to Move Forward* Brussels 21 May 2003, COM(2003) 284 fin (see annex 1 in this volume). Short survey by K van Hulle and S Maul 'Aktionsplan zur Modernisierung des Gesellchaftsrechts und Stärkung der Corporate Governance' [2004] Zeitschrift für Unternehmens- und Gesellschaftsrecht 484. Economic critique ('strength of diversity') for example by K Lannoo and A Khachaturyan 'Reform of Corporate Governance in the EU' (2004) 5 Eur Business Organization L Rev 37.

[4] *A Modern Regulatory Framework for Company Law in Europe – Report of the High Level Group of Company Law Experts* (European Commission Brussels 4 November 2002) 161 p, reprinted in G Ferrarini and others (eds) *Reforming Company and Takeover Law in Europe* (OUP Oxford 2004) 925 ff (annex 3). See also previously KJ Hopt 'Modern Company and Capital Market Problems: Improving European Corporate Governance after Enron' (2003) 3 J of Corporate L Studies 221.

[5] *Report on Issues Related to Takeover Bids – Report of the High Level Group of Company Law Experts* (European Commission Brussels 10 January 2002) 96 p, reprinted in Ferrarini and others ibid 825 ff (annex 2). The volume contains many articles that deal directly or indirectly with the two reports and in a certain manner may be considered the first comprehensive book on them. If necessary the two reports are distinguished in this article as High Level Group Report I and II.

helping the European Commission to again set afloat the 13th directive on take-overs after the European Parliament had voted down the proposal in a stalemate vote of 273 to 273.

Although our American and Japanese audience may be less or not at all informed about the Action Plan, since it has been discussed widely in Europe it seems best to take a middle path: instead of describing the content of the Action Plan in its many details, I shall give a background picture of why the High Level Group proposed certain actions, the problems inherent in them, and what major critiques have been brought forward in the meantime. This will be done in three parts: preparing the stage with setting the Action Plan in perspective (I), looking at the list of planned actions on topics other than corporate governance (II), and going into the corporate governance part of the Action Plan in more detail (III).

II. The Company Law Action Plan of 2003: Setting the Stage

1. The Company Law Action Plan of 21 May 2003: Its History and Background, in Particular the Report of the High Level Group of 4 November 2002

With the official List of Actions at hand, one can very quickly rush through the European Commission's plans for the next years in a first overview:[6]

The first thing to see in the list is a clear prioritization: short term, 2003-2005; middle term, 2006-2008; and long term, 2009 onward. However, the thrust is clearly on short and middle term.

In a bird's-eye view, six broad areas are covered: 1) corporate governance; 2) raising and maintenance of legal capital; 3) groups of companies; 4) restructuring; 5) new European company forms such as the European private company as well as other enterprise and foundation forms; and 6) transparency of national legal forms. The main concern of the Commission is certainly corporate governance, and this will be the focus of this article. But the other areas are also important and not less controversial.

The objectives of the Action Plan are twofold. The first goal is to strengthen shareholders' rights and the protection for employees, creditors, and other parties with which companies deal. This is meant mainly to create and maintain confidence in companies within the European Union. The second aim is closely interrelated with the first. The Commission intends to foster the efficiency and competitiveness of business, with special attention to some specific cross-border issues. The one cannot be reached without the other; they are two sides of the same coin. As Internal Market Commissioner Frits Bolkestein said,

[6] See annex 1 in this volume.

> Company law and corporate governance are right at the heart of the political agenda, on both sides of the Atlantic. That's because economies only work if companies are run efficiently and transparently. We have seen vividly what happens if they are not: investment and jobs will be lost; and in the worst cases, of which there are too many, shareholders, employees, creditors and the public are ripped off. Prompt action is needed to ensure sustainable public confidence in financial markets.[7]

This is not only a political statement. Our High Level Group is of the same opinion. Indeed, investor confidence is a key concept of European financial and company law,[8] just as it was at the origin of the American securities regulation in the 1930s. The problem with 'confidence' is that it is a rather loose concept. Taken as a legal idea, it is highly general and open to legal construction, while economically it is difficult to make it an operational concept to work with empirically, and the European Commission has done neither of both. As we all know, of course, there is certain support for the relevance of investor protection by the empirical work of LaPorta and colleagues who pretend to have proven the relationship between good, reliable company law and the financial development of countries. Yet the critique is well known as well, ie the inversion of the causal relationship, as Jack Coffee and others see it. Whatever position one takes in this debate, a replication of these American studies in Europe would be welcome, though certainly with more neutral criteria and better knowledge of the European legal and factual situation. Until then, the Commission was right to proceed and act as it did, even in the face of uncertainty and based on mere plausibilities.

The Action Plan thus positions us in the middle of European company law harmonization. This is a long and quite painful political process. There is no need to recapitulate the history of the ups and downs of company law harmonization. Nor must the many company law directives and draft directives be enumerated here once again. Quite apart from the mere drafts that have their own momentum already, there are no less than 22 original, modified, and supplementary directives in this field. One can get an idea of the sheer mass of European rules in company law and related fields by looking at a recently edited textbook, *European Company and Financial Law*,[9] which comprises the legal texts and makes reference to case law dealing with them. Besides company law it contains banking law, consumer law related to financial transactions, insurance law, and securities regula-

[7] On the history of the High Level Group Reports, see KJ Hopt 'Kapitalmarktorientierte Gesellschaftsrechtsentwicklung in Europa – Zur Arbeit der High Level Group of Company Law Experts' in P Nobel (ed) *Internationales Gesellschaftsrecht einschliesslich internationales Kapitalmarktrecht* (Stämpfli Bern 2004) 73. See also J Winter 'EU Company Law at the Cross-Roads' in G Ferrarini and others (n 4) 3.

[8] See N Moloney 'The Regulation of Investment Services in the Single Market: The Emergence of a New Regulatory Landscape' (2002) 3 Eur Business Organization L Rev 293, 297 ff.

[9] Hopt and Wymeersch (n 1).

tion. This book contains 158 legal instruments (directives, regulations, and recommendations) in 1,371 pages.

At the end of this section, a short word on the smaller and medium enterprises (SMEs): the European Commission is well aware of their different needs and intends to adapt appropriate company law and corporate governance rules for them in the form of lighter and more flexible framework rules.[10] This has been recognized in the UK and other European countries as being highly desirable in view of the overwhelming overall importance of SMEs in Europe. The European Commission is right in following this trend under European law. On the other hand, the Commission definitely plans to come up with more demanding rules for listed companies, ie companies with securities traded at a stock exchange or on a regulated market. Again, this seems to follow a trend in a number of member states to have two legal company regimes depending on stock exchange trading.

For regulatory purposes, the High Level Group has proposed making a distinction between three categories of companies instead of two, ie listed companies, open companies, and closed companies.[11] The reason for having the middle category, ie open companies, is the following: in Germany and some other countries, relatively few companies are listed.[12] As of August 2004, we had 15,835 stock corporations (AG and KGaA). As of September 2004, only 666 of the German stock corporations were listed (compare this to the UK with 2,409 listed companies, to NASDQ with 2,907, and the New York Stock Exchange with 1,823). From a European regulatory point of view, it is unsatisfactory to treat all the approximately 15,000 non-listed German stock corporations just like closed companies – or else it is difficult to really deregulate the regime for closed companies. But this is an open question.

2. The Company Law Action Plan and Its Connections with Securities, Auditing, and Takeover Regulation

The Company Law Action Plan is an ambitious program, but it does not show the true extent of European regulatory involvement in the field. There are at least two areas that are not covered in it even though they are or might be crucial for corporate governance, namely better auditing and market questions (the financial market, and in particular the market for corporate control, ie the 13th directive). This needs two words of explanation, one general and one more specific.

[10] Company Law Action Plan (n 3) 2.1.

[11] High Level Group Report I (n 4) ch II.4.

[12] For the following figures, see Deutsches Aktieninstitut *DAI-Factbook 2004* (DAI Frankfurt 2004) table 01-1-a.

In general, there is a close connection between the Financial Markets Action Plan of 1999[13] and the Company Law Action Plan of 21 May 2003. Mr. Bolkestein was highly successful with the former, but company law harmonization was unsuccessful for decades. Bolkestein's ingenious idea was to link both fields and both regulatory schemes by using the experience with and the political success of the Financial Markets Action Plan for progress in company law. This was politically very skilful and has also worked out well legally and economically, at least as far as we can see up to now.

This strategy was also used for the two specific fields mentioned previously. First, better auditing: this has long been a concern of the Commission and of separate groups within and outside the Commission that are working on it. Therefore, it was not included in the terms of reference of the High Level Group. The Commission was nevertheless very active in this field. Let me just mention the recommendation of 16 May 2002 on the independence of the statutory auditors – basic principles; the ten-point action plan on statutory audit of 21 May 2003, published on the same date as the Company Law Action Plan; the recent draft directive modernizing the 8th directive, the latter dating back to 16 March 1994; and the draft directive of 27 October 2004 on modifying the 4th and 7th directives on accounting and on group accounting.[14] Further European measures are underway. Whether the Commission should step in by regulating auditors' liability toward third parties is still an open question. The various national schemes are highly divergent and many of them are closely interwoven with general civil law liability concepts. Yet in some member states such as Germany, there is a definite trend toward establishing auditors' third-party liability, though only limited to cases of gross negligence and subject to a cap.

As to European securities regulation[15] and more specifically the market for corporate control, there is now finally the 13th directive of 21 April 2004 on takeover bids,[16] even though it is a heavily watered-down version of the Council compromise reached in December 2003. This directive has had its own path,

[13] European Commission *Financial Services Action Plan* COM(1999) 232 with progress reports. See Moloney (n 8); N Moloney 'New frontiers in EC capital markets law: From market construction to market regulation' (2003) Common Market L Rev 809.

[14] See European Commission 'Proposal for a Directive of the European Parliament and of the Council amending Council Directives 78/660/EEC and 83/349/EEC concerning the annual accounts of certain types of companies and consolidated accounts' COM(2004) 725. More generally, see T Richter *Jahresabschlußprüfung und Prüfungsanforderungen in der Europäischen Union* (Nomos Baden-Baden 2003).

[15] See N Moloney *EC Securities Regulation* (OUP Oxford 2002), and more recently E Ferran *Building an EU Securities Market* (Cambridge University Press Cambridge 2004); from a German perspective, see Stock Exchange Experts Commission at the German Federal Ministry of Finance *EU financial market integration: Achievements, deficits and proposed actions* (Frankfurt 21 September 2004).

[16] [2004] OJ L142/12.

problems, and critiques. This is not the place to take up the economic discussion as to the wisdom or misconception of the idea of a level playing field, the anti-frustration rule including the new breakthrough rule, and the mandatory bid rule.[17] Let me just make two remarks. First, I think that as far as corporate governance is concerned, having European framework rules for takeovers does not simply amount to more regulation; instead, it helps to break up artificial barriers between member states, promotes competition, and contributes to a certain degree to the development of a market for corporate control in those member states where in practice no such market has existed.[18]

Second, it seems important to see that the European takeover regime is part of corporate governance, ie external corporate governance via the market for corporate control.[19] The traditional theory is that takeovers may (but do not always) have a disciplinary effect on the management of the target. Modern empirical findings are mixed, however. While there are findings in the UK that there is little or no such disciplinary effect, other pieces of research find that corporate markets indeed act as a 'court of last resort', as an external source of discipline when internal control mechanisms are relatively weak or ineffective.[20] In Germany an intensive discussion has begun on what changes in our takeover statute will be necessary in order to comply with the directive. At a closer look these changes are quite substantial despite the optional regime of Art. 9 to 12 of the directive on neutrality of the target's board and on breakthrough.[21]

3. The Impact of the Company Law Action Plan in Brussels and in the Member States

The European Commission has already started carrying out the Action Plan. A draft 10th directive on cross-border mergers of companies with share capital has been on the table since 11 November 2003.

[17] See for example A McCahery and others 'The Economics of the Proposed European Takeover Directive' and M Burkart and F Panunzi 'Mandatory Bids, Squeeze-Outs and Similar Transactions' both in Ferrarini and others (n 4) 575 and 737 as well as other contributions contained therein; E Berglöf and M Burkart 'European Takeover Regulation' (2003) 36 Economic Policy 173.

[18] Cf P Davies and KJ Hopt 'Control Transactions' in Kraakman and others (n 1) 157.

[19] As to the distinction between internal and external corporate governance, see KJ Hopt 'Corporate Governance in Germany' in KJ Hopt and E Wymeersch (eds) *Capital Markets and Company Law* (OUP Oxford 2003) 289, 299 ff, 313 f.

[20] See for example O Kini W Kracaw and S Mian 'The Nature of Discipline by Corporate Takeovers' (2004) 59 J of Finance 1511, 1550.

[21] KJ Hopt PO Mülbert and C Kumpan 'Reformbedarf im Übernahmerecht' [2005] Die Aktiengesellschaft 109.

A pre-draft of the 14th directive on the cross-border change of seat of a company is circulating; officially only the public consultation document is available, the consultation having closed in April 2004. The pre-draft is upsetting the German trade unions who fear for their national sacred cow, the German species of labor co-determination in the company board.

A Commission recommendation fostering an appropriate regime for the remuneration of directors of listed companies was issued on 14 December 2004.[22] On 15 February 2005, the Commission came up with a further recommendation on the role of non-executive or supervisory directors of listed companies and on the committees of the (supervisory) board.[23]

Likewise, consultation on board responsibilities and improving financial and corporate governance information has taken place. The draft directive of 27 October 2004, amending the 4th and 7th directives concerning the annual accounts of certain types of companies and consolidated accounts, deals in its Section 10A with 'responsibility and liability for the annual accounts and the annual report'.[24]

Finally there is the second consultation document of 13 May 2005 on 'Fostering an appropriate regime for shareholders' rights'.

The momentum of the Action Plan as well as of its forerunner, the High Level Group report, is conspicuous. It has been discussed in all member states by the legal profession, in the political arena, and in the financial press. In general the reaction has been positive, though there has also been criticism. The criticism reaches from fundamental opposition under the subsidiarity principle and the economic concept of regulatory competition to more specific critiques of the single actions proposed. The Commission is not impressed by the fundamental critique, however, and is proceeding with various instruments concerning the different actions. I shall come to some of these later on.

After having set the stage, I would now like to highlight some of the major problems of the corporate governance actions listed in the Action Plan. I do this not just for the sake of reporting them, but in view of our conference topic: Are these measures part of a change of governance, and is such a change a transition from more state and regulation to more market and flexible solutions such as self-regulation and others?

22 See in more detail IV.4.

23 See in more detail IV.3.

24 European Commission (n 14).

III. A Glance at the List of Planned Actions: Topics Other than Corporate Governance

1. Capital Maintenance (Short Term, Medium Term, Long Term)

The legal capital issue, which is currently under the tight regime of the 2nd directive, is under intense attack by economists, comparative law experts, and the English community. At the same time, a coalition in Germany of more traditional company lawyers and federal judges is defending the status quo. The European Commission is following a careful step-by-step approach. First it wants to simplify the 2nd directive on the basis of the recommendations of the SLIM group as supplemented by the High Level Group (the so-called SLIM-Plus directive).[25] A draft directive has been issued,[26] and interestingly enough it contains provisions for a general squeeze-out as well as a sell-out right.[27] In the medium term it intends to mandate a study on the feasibility of an alternative to the capital maintenance regime.[28] Depending on the outcome of this study, such an alternative regime might be introduced in the 2nd directive. France has already reacted to these planned changes by creating a new form of limited liability company with a minimum capital of 1 euro, thus making it obvious that legal capital and capital maintenance are no longer an indispensable counterpart to limited liability. In Germany the Ministry of Justice came out with a pre-draft of a reform act on the limited liability company (GmbH), lowering the legal capital from 50.000 € down to 10.000 € and introducing stronger personal liability of the directors as a substitute, a bit along the lines of the English wrongful trading. Yet the outcry by German academics and judges made the Ministry lose courage, and the pre-draft is considerably less far-reaching. The topic is so controversial in Germany that not only are there already a considerable number of law review articles both pro

[25] *SLIM (Simpler Legislation for the Internal Market) Report of the European Commission* 4 February 2000 COM (2000) 56 fin – annex 1 Recommendations Company Law; reprinted in more detail and with reasons in [1999] Zeitschrift für Wirtschaftsrecht [ZIP] 1944; cf T Drygala 'Die Vorschläge der SLIM-Arbeitsgruppe zur Vereinfachung des Europäischen Gesellschaftsrechts' 2001 Die Aktiengesellschaft 291, 292 ff.

[26] European Commission 'Proposal for a Directive of the European Parliament and of the Council amending Council Directive 77/91/EEC, as regards the formation of public limited liability companies and the maintenance and alteration of their capital' (29 October 2004) COM(2004) 730.

[27] Art. 39a of the draft directive as amended. These squeeze-out and sell-out rights are to be distinguished from those that are following a successful public takeover and are contained in the 13th directive.

[28] High Level Group Report II (n 5) ch IV: Capital Formation and Maintenance. Cf from an economic perspective L Enriques and J Macey 'Creditors versus Capital Formation: The Case Against the European Legal Capital Rules' (2001) 86 Cornell L Rev 1166.

and con, but three major conferences are expected.[29] Furthermore, there is a large group of academics and practitioners steered by Marcus Lutter, who many years ago wrote his habilitation on legal capital.[30] Their forthcoming report is expected to try to counterbalance the report by the British Rickford group.[31]

2. Groups of Companies (Short Term and Medium Term), Pyramids (Medium Term)

Groups of companies is a famous battlefield; as early as 1998, the Forum Europaeum on Group Law proposed more focused framework regulation as a middle ground between the German Konzernrecht and the muddle-through-by-piecemeal and ad hoc interventions of some other countries.[32] Bits and pieces of the draft 5th directive and even of the abortive 9th directive on groups of companies[33] can be recognized in the Action Plan. However, in these early drafts the approach was completely different insofar as they tried the old way of full or at least maximum harmonization, with the German Konzernrecht as a model. This was doomed to fail, as legal comparativists predicted quite early, because it was legally too complicated and economically too burdensome and inflexible. The High Level Group[34] – as the Forum Europaeum before it – took a fresh look at this and chose a new approach, looking for a mere framework harmonization and picking out a few strategic problems, in particular certain rules of the game. In choosing these, the Group had its eye more on facilitating cross-border and other economic activities and less on laying down specific legal fairness rules; predictably, this was not met with praise in Germany.

[29] One in December 2005 organized by H Eidenmüller and W Schön, another in January 2006 organized by the company law review ZGR as its biannual symposium, and a third in September 2006 by the German Lawyers Association (Deutscher Juristentag) in its section on business law.

[30] M Lutter *Kapital, Sicherung der Kapitalaufbringung und Kapitalerhaltung in den Aktien- und GmbH-Rechten der EWG* (CF Müller Karlsruhe 1964).

[31] J Rickford 'Reforming Capital – Report of the Interdisciplinary Group of Capital Maintenance' (2004) 14 Eur Business L Rev 919-1027. Cf before for example E Ferran 'Legal Capital Rules and Modern Securities Markets – the Case for Reform, as Illustrated by the U.K. Equity Markets' in Hopt and Wymeersch (n 19) 115.

[32] Forum Europaeum Konzernrecht 'Konzernrecht für Europa' [1998] Zeitschrift für Unternehmens- und Gesellschaftsrecht 672, 698 ff, 704 ff.

[33] There was only a pre-draft which was circulated unofficially in December 1984.

[34] High Level Group Report II (n 5) ch V.2: Transparency of Group Structure and Relations, ch V.3: Problems for the Creation and Functioning of Groups of Companies, and ch V.4: Pyramids; as to the following discussion, see KJ Hopt 'Konzernrecht für Europa – Zur Diskussion um die Vorschläge des Forum Europaeum Konzernrecht' in J Basedow and others (eds) *Aufbruch nach Europa, 75 Jahre Max-Planck-Institut für Privatrecht* (Mohr Siebeck Tübingen 2000) 17, 23 ff.

The Action Plan followed the Group in this. The program includes 1) more disclosure on group structure and group relations, both financial and non-financial; 2) framework rules for groups allowing the adoption at subsidiary level of a coordinated group policy; and 3) prohibition of stock exchange listing for abusive pyramids. The draft directive of 10 October 2004, amending the 4th and 7th directives,[35] already contains rules on increased transparency of related party transactions and off-balance sheet arrangements, including the use of special purpose entities and offshore centers. These rules will probably be minimum harmonization, ie Germany will remain free to stick to its old, stricter group law provisions. Of course, this will come at a price in the international competition for attracting foreign companies or keeping the national ones in the country and for establishing or maintaining company headquarters in one of the EU member states. In any case, as a consequence of the Action Plan, Karel van Hulle from the European Commission declared the 5th and in particular the 9th directives to be dead.

3. Restructuring (Short Term and Medium Term)

Restructuring beyond national frontiers is an obvious economic necessity, but it is severely hampered by German boardroom labor co-determination. European progress in this respect has been blocked for decades by a baneful German coalition of trade union lobbyists and political opportunists. Yet there are signals from Brussels that a compromise might be forced on Germany, hopefully not along the example of the European company which keeps the most far-reaching (German) co-determination model as a fall-back solution and thereby hampers German enterprises considerably and unreasonably in international competition. As mentioned before, there is a draft 10th directive on cross-border mergers of companies with share capital dating from 11 November 2003,[36] and an unofficial pre-draft of the 14th directive on the cross-border change of seat of a company.[37] Furthermore, the European Commission is considering simplifying the 3rd directive concerning legal mergers and the 6th directive concerning legal division.

[35] European Commission (n 14).

[36] COM(2003) 703 as of 18.11.2003, Common Standpoint of the Council as of 15.11.2004. Cf P Wiesner 'Die grenzüberschreitende Verschmelzung und der neue Mitbestimmungs-kompromiss' [2005] Der Betrieb 91.

[37] Pre-draft as of 20 April 1997, reprinted in German in [1997] Zeitschrift für Wirt-schaftsrecht [ZIP] 1721 ff and [1999] Zeitschrift für Unternehmens- und Gesellschaftsrecht 157. Cf Grundmann (n 1) § 24; S Leible 'Niederlassungsfreiheit und Sitzverlegungsrichtlinie' [2004] Zeitschrift für Unternehmens- und Gesellschaftsrecht 531.

4. The European Private Company (Short Term and Medium Term)

The European private company is a younger sister of the European company (Societas Europaea). While the latter is a European stock corporation, the former would be a kind of European limited liability company. A model statute of the European private company has been developed through close cooperation between the University of Heidelberg and the Chamber of Commerce of Paris (there: CREDA).[38] The European Commission intends to mandate a feasibility study in order to assess the practical needs for – and problems of – such a European private company, and it envisages a possible proposal for a Statute for a European Private Company (depending on the outcome of the feasibility study). The High Level Group had taken a similarly careful approach,[39] not because it called into doubt the usefulness of the work done in Heidelberg and Paris, but because it saw the clear need for prioritization of action. After all, legislative work is a scarce resource.

5. EU Legal Forms (Short Term and Medium Term)

The European Commission intends to seek active progress on current proposals as to the European association and to assess the need for the creation of other EU legal forms, eg the European foundation.[40] The Statute of the European Mutual Society as well as the directive concerning labor co-determination were already enacted on 18 August 2003.[41]

6. Transparency of National Legal Forms (Medium Term)

Finally the European Commission intends to introduce basic disclosure rules for all legal entities with limited liability, subject to further examination.[42]

[38] J Boucourechliev and P Hommelhoff (eds) *Vorschläge für eine Europäische Privatgesellschaft* (Otto Schmidt Verlag Cologne 1999); P Hommelhoff and D Helms (eds) *Neue Wege in die Europäische Privatgesellschaft* (Otto Schmidt Verlag Cologne 2001).

[39] High Level Group Report II (n 5) ch IX: medium term.

[40] Cf KJ Hopt and others (eds) *The European Foundation – A New Legal Instrument* (Cambridge University Press Cambridge forthcoming).

[41] [2003] OJ L207/1 and L207/25.

[42] High Level Group Report II (n 5) ch VIII.2: General Rules for Enterprises (transparency for all legal persons with limited liability).

IV. Corporate Governance in Particular

1. Better Disclosure by an Annual Corporate Governance Statement

According to the Action Plan, listed companies should be required by the member states to include in their annual documents or annex to them a coherent and descriptive statement covering the key elements of their corporate governance structures and practices. Such a statement should give the investors and the market a true and fair view of the corporate governance situation of the individual company, thus enabling them to make a better and more competitive choice. It has been left open whether auditors shall have a function concerning the corporate governance statement. Disclosure, recommended by the High Level Group to the Commission as the preferable approach, is generally the least intrusive means of regulation; if effective, it may be the best way of regulating companies.[43] The draft directive of 10 October 2004, amending the 4th and 7th directives,[44] contains new articles concerning the disclosure about corporate governance practices by issuers that have their securities traded on a regulated market.

Though such a measure seems rather flexible and unobtrusive, it has been met with sharp criticism in some member states. In Germany, for example, the German Lawyers Association (DAV) has objected that such a statement is superfluous because much of the information to be included is already available from other – though divergent – sources. It is considered to stretch disclosure too far, in particular regarding the concept of related parties. But most of all, the criticism is levied against having such a statement in the annual report or otherwise belonging to it, since in this case it needs to be audited. With the latter critique the DAV may have a point, though information without a certain certification is of doubtful value.

2. Helping Shareholders Exercise Their Rights

The Action Plan seeks to promote shareholder activity, for example, by asking questions, tabling resolutions, voting in absentia, participating in general meetings via electronic means, and so on. These facilities should be offered to shareholders across the EU. Specific problems related to cross-border voting should be solved as soon as possible. These problems concern particularly cross-border institutional investors and those from outside the EU. Enhancing shareholders' rights by mandatory law fits into a governance system that is more market-oriented because it strengthens self-help by shareholders and investors. A second

[43] ibid ch II.3: Disclosure of Information as a Regulatory Tool; also already the High Level Group Report I (n 4) ch I.3: General Application of Guiding Principles, Duty to Disclose.

[44] European Commission (n 14).

consultation on 'Fostering an appropriate regime for shareholders' rights' concluded on 15 July 2005. How far this whole approach will lead remains to be seen, in particular whether institutional investors may be convinced to become more active in the general assembly instead of just following the old Wall Street rule by voting with their feet, ie walking out and selling their block of shares. The private investors themselves will hardly move, at least not the normal ones, since the possible gains and the necessary efforts are just not commensurate. Rational apathy will remain as the general rule. Whether hedge funds will jump in more often – as they already occasionally do – is quite doubtful. This is a rewarding strategy for them only if the company has reserves it does not use or intends to use as takeover currency, and if there is a chance for the hedge funds to force the company to pay out instead, as was done in the case of the German Stock Exchange (Deutsche Börse) in the spring of 2005 after its conditional takeover bid targeted against the London Stock Exchange.

3. Promoting the Role of Independent Non-executive or Supervisory Directors

The Action Plan envisages that minimum standards on the creation, composition, and role of the nomination, remuneration, and audit committees should be defined at the EU level and enforced by the member states, at least on a 'comply-and-explain' basis (some practitioners sob: 'comply-and-complain'). As mentioned before, the European Commission has already come forward with a recommendation on the role of non-executive or supervisory directors of listed companies. This recommendation of 15 February 2005,[45] provides that at least a majority of the members of the three key board committees (nomination, remuneration, and audit) should be composed of independent non-executive or supervisory directors. It goes very far in defining the requirements of 'independence'. In its annex II, the profile of independent non-executive or supervisory directors is described. The annex contains not less than nine categories of case situations which should be considered in determining lack of independence. Among them are the following:

a) not being an executive or managing director of the company or an associated company, and not having been in such a position for the previous five years;
b) not being an employee of the company or an associate company, and not having been in such a position for the previous three years;
c) not to receive, or have received, significant additional remuneration from the company or an associated company (including any participation in a share option or any other performance-related pay scheme);

[45] Recommendation [2005] OJ L52/51.

d) not being or representing in any way the controlling shareholder (control being defined as in the 7th directive);

e) not having, or having had within the last year, a significant business relationship with the company or an associated company. Business relationships include the situation of a significant supplier of goods or services (including financial, legal, advisory, or consulting services), of a significant customer, and of organizations that receive significant contributions from the company or its group.

All this has met with great concern in Germany. It was felt that, if this rule were binding, it would mean the end of both German group dominance via the supervisory boards of subsidiaries and labor co-determination in these boards. Furthermore, the DAV objected that no binding rules for committees are needed. The recommendation has taken a more careful approach than the original draft. This has been considered a victory of German lobbying in Brussels. Not only is the measure a mere recommendation, as it was always planned to be, but it is up to the board to ultimately determine what constitutes independence. Furthermore, there is an exemption for non-senior management labor members in the board under 'a system of workers' representation recognized by law and providing for adequate protection against abusive dismissal and other forms of unfair treatment'. But it seems that the German press and even many public officials and professionals are not fully aware of what such a European recommendation means. Of course, it is not legally binding. But it is well known that the European Commission practices a kind of 'salami tactic', ie getting its way by first issuing a recommendation and later enacting a directive if the recommendation is not complied with. Yet there is more to it. The recommendation lays down a good corporate governance standard on independent directors that follows closely the Anglo-American regulatory pattern and is becoming standard international practice. This means: If German boards do not follow this recommendation, they might be blamed for not living up to international good corporate governance standards. Even worse, if foreign stock exchanges incorporate this recommendation as some already do, foreign listing may become difficult for German companies.

4. Directors' Remuneration

There is no need to mention the many scandals that have come up in many of our countries and have been denounced at length in the financial press. For the US, the abuses have been described recently in a comprehensive book, *Pay Without Performance*.[46] In Europe the problem is urgently felt too.[47] For Germany, the 30

[46] L Bebchuk and J Fried *Pay without Performance, The Unfulfilled Promise of Executive Compensation* (Harvard University Press Cambridge 2005).

million DM/15 million € premium (the whole payment sum was 65 million DM/32 million €) that the remuneration committee of the supervisory board of Mannesmann granted to the outgoing chairman of the management board, Klaus Esser, after the takeover by Vodafone was cleared, continues to stir up public concern and envy. In total, 111 million DM/55 million € were handed out generously to the outgoing management. Because there is no way for single shareholders to attack this payment via a derivative action under present German company law, the case was denounced to the public prosecutor, and a criminal proceeding was started at the court of lower instance (*Landgericht*) Düsseldorf against the remuneration committee members for embezzlement of company assets. The court dismissed the claim,[48] but the public prosecutor has lodged an appeal to the *Bundesgerichtshof*. Most recently, the attorney general at the Bundesgerichtshof came up with its opinion, according to which the directors concerned committed a criminal offense. It remains to be seen how the court will decide in the end. The decision of the lower court might be reversed and the case might be sent back for decision under new instructions by the Bundesgerichtshof.[49]

The fine irony in this is that not only did the chairman of the committee benefit personally from related committee decisions, which is of course unacceptable, but the chairman of the management of the Deutsche Bank, Josef Ackermann, and the (former) chairman of the German Trade Union Association, Klaus Zwickel, were both members of this committee and are now jointly accused of embezzlement – what a nice instance of full harmony between capital and labor! But to speak less sarcastically and more seriously, the fact that the trade unions consented to the severance payment sheds serious doubts on the proclaimed monitoring quality of labor co-determination in company boards (beyond the usual pursuit of mere self-interest of labor).

Although it has been observed with some justification that German society is an envy society – in stark contrast to American society and much more than people in many other countries – the fact remains that such payments might not undermine the confidence of the shareholders and their willingness to invest in domestic and foreign companies. Accordingly, the High Level Group recommended European rules on management remuneration for listed companies. These rules comprise disclosure of the remuneration of individual directors, a shareholders' vote on remuneration policy, and accounting of remuneration including

[47] G Ferrarini and N Moloney 'Executive Remuneration and Corporate Governance in the EU: Convergence, Divergence, and Reform Perspectives' [2004] Eur Company and Financial L Rev 251; G Ferrarini N Moloney and C Vespro 'Executive Pay: Convergence in Law and Practice Across the EU Corporate Governance Faultline' (2004) 4 J of Corporate L Studies 243.

[48] Landgericht Düsseldorf, decision of 22 July 2004, reported in [2004] Zeitschrift für Wirtschaftsrecht [ZIP] 2044.

[49] Oral hearings are scheduled for October 2005.

remuneration by stock options.[50] In the meantime, the European Commission has come up with its recommendation of 14 December 2004.[51] It has taken up the first two recommendations of the High Level Group. Accounting for stock options in the balance sheet need not be dealt with in this Commission recommendation. But the IAS/IFRS have been changed recently to include such an accounting principle, and the EU accounting law will follow IAS/IFRS accounting. In the meantime, Germany has also taken action. Since I have dealt with these issues elsewhere in more detail,[52] I shall add here just a few words.

a) First as to *disclosure:* Full faithful and audited disclosure is useful, both as a basis for shareholder decision-making and as a conduit for information to the stock market, which may react to it in one way or another. The British Directors' Remuneration Report Regulations 2002 give an example of what kind of information to publish. In principle there is agreement on the usefulness of such disclosure rules. What is highly controversial is mandatory individual disclosure. The arguments that individual disclosure is not relevant for the shareholders and may even be harmful because it causes envy and tends to level up the payment habits of companies in general do have some weight, but in balance they are not convincing. Full individual disclosure, including any severance payments, is provided for in the recommendation of the European Commission. In Germany as in some other member states, the legislators went further and prescribed mandatory individual disclosure since the comply-and-explain provision in the German Corporate Governance Code as revised in the spring of 2003 was not a success. While it was expected that companies would feel uneasy and fear reactions at the stock exchange and by foreign investors if they did not follow the code – a fact which they must publish – a considerable part of the DAX 30 companies chose to explain that they did not want to follow this code recommendation. As a result, a recent German act as of July 2005 makes individual disclosure a mandatory reporting requirement. Exemption from this requirement is possible by a two-thirds majority in the general meeting.

In addition, a very recent decision of the German Federal Court found quite unexpectedly that already under the present corporate law, stock options for supervisory board members are illegal.[53] Whether the court will also extend this prohibition to phantom stock is not self-evident and must be seen. An obiter dictum in the decision and an explanation given by the chairman of the Second Senate of the Court that made the decision, *Volker Röhricht,* leads in this direc-

[50] High Level Group Report II (n 5) ch III.4.2: The remuneration of directors.

[51] Recommendation [2004] OJ L385/55.

[52] KJ Hopt 'Modern Company and Capital Market Problems: Improving European Corporate Governance after Enron' (2003) 3 J of Corporate L Studies 221, 233 ff with further references.

[53] Bundesgerichtshof [2004] Zeitschrift für Wirtschaftsrecht [ZIP] 613.

tion. The latter has illustrated the rationale of his decisions by an often-quoted slogan: 'The management board and the supervisory board shall not drink from the same fountain.' In other words, the controlled and the controller should not sit in the same boat. Yet this slogan also shows that the court may have gone too far. Quite independently of this court decision, the German government is planning new rules with specific prohibitions, and company law practice is already beginning to react to the uncertainties created by the court and the legislative measures it fears to come. Some companies have even decided to abolish their stock option plans completely for board members, ie also for management board members. Most recently, the well-known Zurich economist Bruno Frey and others have contended more generally that stock options are the wrong way of remunerating directors.

b) *Shareholder decision-making:* Board remuneration is a matter best left to the audit committee, provided that non-executive directors have at least the majority. Yet an annual vote on the principles and limits of board (and senior officers') remuneration might be beneficial in acting as a brake, even if shareholders rarely dissent from what is proposed. This is the solution that has been enacted in the UK, though there the vote is not for approval but only of an advisory nature (and, if I am not mistaken, further reforms are underway). This was also the position taken by the High Level Group. The recommendation of the European Commission followed it and settled for an advisory vote on the remuneration statement.

c) *Mandatory accounting:* The traditional accounting standards, US GAAP and IAS/IFRS, have tolerated the common practice of just mentioning the fact that share options for directors are outstanding in a mere note to the balance sheet. Since the IAS/IFRS have become stricter[54] and since the EU has decided to follow the IFRS regime, at least as a matter of principle and after reexamination for possibly appropriate European law deviations, stock options will have to be treated as a cost on the balance sheet. The hard question is how to determine this cost.[55] One route would be to account for stock options at 'fair value' and to try to specify how this should be determined in the revised accounting standards. Yet this will be settled by IFRS as it stands now and as it will be developed further after there is practical experience with the new rules. Of course, accounting for stock options as a cost will have the effect of diminishing distributable profits.

[54] The IFRS 2 as of February 2004 require that from 2005 on stock options have to be accounted for under a current fair value method.

[55] Cf K Crook 'Accounting for Share-Based Remuneration' in Ferrarini and others (n 4) 347.

Yet for this very reason, cost accounting might be the only brake on exorbitant stock options that really makes itself felt.[56]

5. Responsibility of Board Members for Financial Statements

The European Commission plans to confirm at the EU level the collective responsibility of board members for financial statements.[57] In this context, it must be seen that the Commission has supplemented the already-mentioned action of enhancing corporate governance disclosure[58] by the addendum 'including confirmation of collective responsibility of board members for key non-financial statements'. This responsibility is meant to be personal liability as a means of improving financial statements and corporate governance disclosure. The Action Plan leaves open under what conditions such liability should arise (gross negligence?), whether there may be a cap, and in particular to whom this liability should be – the company or the investors at large (internal or external liability). The relevant article of the draft directive of 10 October 2004, amending the 4th and 7th directives,[59] reads as follows:

> Member States shall ensure that the members of the administrative, management and supervisory bodies of the company are collectively responsible towards the company for ensuring that the annual accounts and the annual report are drawn up and published in accordance with the requirements of this Directive.

In Germany a draft law[60] provides for external liability (ie liability toward shareholders) for written as well as certain oral financial statements, but only in cases of gross negligence. All this is highly controversial and may lead to a host of damage suits. As an example, it must be remembered that even under the present German system – ie rather restrictive internal liability – in May 2004, 13,000 lawsuits concerning the Telekom placement were pending, and another 17,000 complaints were still under mediation. If there is a change of government in autumn of 2005, it is improbable that this draft law will still be enacted.

[56] High Level Group Report II (n 5) ch III.4.2.4.

[57] Cf the comprehensive comparative law study by KJ Hopt and HC Voigt (eds) *Prospekt- und Kapitalmarktinformationshaftung – Recht und Reform in der Europäischen Union, der Schweiz und den USA* – (Mohr Siebeck Tübingen 2005); summary in KJ Hopt and HC Voigt 'Prospekt- und Kapitalmarktinformationshaftung' [2004] Wertpapier-Mitteilungen 1801.

[58] Annual corporate governance statement, see IV.1.

[59] See already n 14.

[60] The so-called KapInHG, one of these terrible modern acronyms for new laws. For details, see Hopt and Voigt (n 57).

6. Institutional Investors, Choice Between the One-Tier and the Two-Tier Board, and More Shareholder Democracy

a) The Action Plan contains a number of other corporate governance measures.[61] One is achieving better information on the role played by institutional investors in corporate governance. Institutional investors should be obliged to disclose their investment and voting policies. The High Level Group[62] discussed whether one should go even further and oblige institutional investors to vote. But in the end, it declined recommending this, not only because of the difficulty of defining who is an institutional investor, but primarily because such an obligation could turn out to be counterproductive in leading to even more votes for the management, as German share voting by the banks indicates. But even the rather timid disclosure proposal of the High Level Group and the Action Plan has met with criticism from the DAV, for example.

In any case, it is clear that institutional investors play a major role. This is naturally true in countries such as the UK with a high percentage of shares held by institutional investors. But institutional shareholder activity is also starting to get stronger in other countries with a relatively small percentage of institutional shareholding, such as Germany. A good example can be found in the 2004 Daimler Chrysler general assembly, where a mutual fund of the Deutsche Bank criticized Jürgen Schrempp and indirectly Hilmar Kopper, the chairman of the supervisory board and former Deutsche Bank chief. The subsequent acid exchange of critiques by Hilmar Kopper and Christian Strenger from the mutual fund were telling. In late July 2005, Jürgen Schrempp had to step down before the end of his contract in 2008 without severance pay and without moving over into the supervisory board.

A problem for itself are the hedge funds and their recent activism in the general meetings. The first thunderous case was the general meeting of the German Stock Exchange (Deutsche Börse) on 25 May 2005. The German government is considering regulating these activities, though only by way of mandatory disclosure rules. More far-reaching proposals include double or multiple voting rights for long-term shareholders as in France. Yet this is a doubtful proposal, both in terms of its effectiveness as well as its compatibility with European law. Making such rules effective is highly difficult in view of the domicile of many of these funds in exotic places such as the Cayman Islands. Even enforcing the making of a mandatory bid by hedge funds acting in concerted action in another EU member state is a difficult task for a national supervisory agency in view of gathering the proofs and actually forcing the foreign hedge funds to comply. On

[61] Company Law Action Plan (n 3) 3.1.1: Information about the role played by institutional investors.

[62] High Level Group Report II (n 5) ch III.3.3: Responsibilities of institutional investors.

the other hand, the European Commission views multiple voting rights with suspicion. Their abolition is right on the agenda of the Company Law Action Plan.

b) Another measure to be mentioned is offering to listed companies the choice between the one-tier and two-tier board structures, a choice that already exists in France and Italy, for example, and which is also advocated in Austria and Germany.[63] In Germany this proposal has met with sympathy, not only from academics but also in practice, for example from the DAV. In Germany such a choice appeared unthinkable until very recently. This is due in part to the traditional – though disputed – opinion that stock corporation law must in principle be mandatory law. But a more important reason was German labor co-determination, which was felt to be incompatible with a one-tier board system. Yet the enactment of the statute of the European company (*Societas Europaea*, SE), which clears the way for shareholder choice between the two systems, has changed the mood. Germany is about to transform this statute by giving labor the same quasi-parity status in an SE one-tier board as it has now in the two-tier boards. If, as may be expected, this amounts to having no major German one-tier-board SEs, there may even be a case against Germany in the European Court of Justice for failing to transform the SE statute correctly.

c) Last but not least, the Action Plan notes that it is intended to give further effect to the principle of proportionality between capital and control. Furthermore, the Commission states that there is a strong medium to long-term case for aiming to establish a real shareholder democracy, and that the Commission intends to undertake a study on the consequences of such an approach.[64] Economically this is rather controversial. This controversy became apparent when the High Level Commission recommended breaking through double and multiple voting shares in case of public takeovers,[65] which without such special rights would otherwise be successful. Institutional investors are usually in favor of one share, one vote. This has just been shown dramatically in Sweden where, as in the other Scandinavian countries, multiple voting shares are common. As in other companies belonging to the Wallenberg empire, in Ericsson AB, Stockholm, one A-share carried one thousand votes. On 31 August, the general assembly voted to change to a system in which A-shares carry only ten votes (though with the proviso that the A-shareholders will receive compensation in kind).

[63] Cf KJ Hopt and PC Leyens 'Board Models in Europe' [2004] Eur Company and Financial Law Rev 135, 156 ff, 163 ff.

[64] Company Law Action Plan (n 3) 3.1.2: Shareholder democracy.

[65] See High Level Group Report I (n 4).

V. Outlook

There are many other pressing problems with the Action Plan and European company law reform, among them the so-called technicalities. Technicalities are often treated as less important, but actually they are often decisive as to whether certain rules are law in action or remain law in the book. I cannot do more here than to list some of them:

What are the right instruments: for example, regulation, directive, recommendation, code of conduct, study, and, instead of binding law or law at all, non-binding instruments such as recommendations and even mere studies?

A careful look at the available sanctions and their use is indispensable, for example, liability, fines, disqualification, special investigation, concepts as wrongful trading, and last not least tax (levy of tax, but also tax incentives).

The right instruments and appropriate sanctions are useless without enforcement. Relevant questions concern the force of disclosure, the choice between self-regulation and enforcement and state enforcement, and the use of class actions as they exist already in some member states, while in others consumer, investor, and other associations may bring an action under certain circumstances. In Germany an act of June 2005 provides for a *Musterklage*, ie not a class action or an association action but a 'sample' action in which certain elements common to different lawsuits by different shareholders are to be established and decided upon with binding force beyond inter partes. Finally, effective international cooperation of the national securities and exchange commissions instead of a European SEC is a hot topic.

Where does the Action Plan finally lead? Well, the European law-making process is going on rather quickly – maybe even too quickly, because following all these consultation documents, checking out what they would mean for the national companies and national company law, and coming up with good arguments and counterproposals is not easy. The stress is felt not only by the German Ministry of Justice, which is understaffed, but also by German companies.

Maybe subsidiarity, as laid down in Art. 5 EC, should be taken more seriously in company law as well as in harmonization and European rule-making more generally. Basically, it maintains that the Community may be active only and insofar as the member states cannot do it as well. Of course, this is a very general formula which in a way is more political than legal. It is controversial, indeed, as to what degree this concept is fully legal and, in particular, scrutinizable by the European Court of Justice. This is true despite the spectacular tobacco advertisement decision of the European Court which struck down a European rule in prohibition of such advertising.

An economic mirroring of subsidiarity is regulatory competition (ie competition of legislators and rule-makers). This is a topic of its own and could easily fill the whole conference.[66] Let me confine myself to two brief remarks. Europe now has its own broad political and economic discussion on this topic, with the same battle lines we're familiar with from the US and the 'genius of American law', ie the race to the bottom or the race to the top or, if you will, William Cary v Ralph Winter, Roberta Romano, and others. In contrast to the US, the European battle lines are in general still drawn between the economists and the lawyers, though this is slowly changing, as evidenced by an initiative of the European Corporate Governance Institute and the American Law Institute. Their new 'Transatlantic Corporate Governance Dialogue' was opened with a one-day panel discussion round in Brussels on 12 July 2004, entitled 'Regulatory Competition and Subsidiarity in Corporate Governance in a Transatlantic Perspective'. This controversy is naturally relevant for the subject of our conference, ie the governance systems being more state- or more market-oriented. Yet one must be aware that not having European regulation does not automatically mean less state and less regulation, since the member states may have even more regulation in the field and a regulatory competition process may be less likely to arise than in the US because of many specifically European barriers such as language, culture, history, and politics.

Finally, a word on case law is appropriate. The famous triad of leading cases of the European Court of Justice concerning the freedoms under the EC Treaty is well known:[67] *Centros*, *Überseering*, and *Inspire Art* (some also count the new French case, *Hughes de Lasteyrie du Saillant* of 11 March 2004, among this group of cases; this case dealt with taxing outgoing companies, a kind of tax *Daily Mail* situation). Though it is still disputed in Germany, the clear legal consequence of these cases is that the traditional protective seat theory is no longer applicable to member state companies.

Furthermore, one should mention the five golden share cases,[68] with more to follow, including possibly the Volkswagen case. This second group of cases sets clear limits to schemes by which member states tried to uphold their say in privatized companies by means of golden shares. While the legal details of both lines of case law belong to the most broadly discussed topics in today's European law, the overall trend is clear: these decisions break down traditional legal barriers between member states, invoke individual freedoms and private ini-

[66] As to competition and information in European company law, see S Grundmann 'Die Struktur des Europäischen Gesellschaftsrechts von der Krise zum Boom' [2004] Zeitschrift für Wirtschaftsrecht [ZIP] 2401, 2405 ff.

[67] K Schmidt 'Verlust der Mitte durch "Inspire Art"? – Verwerfungen im Unternehmensrecht durch Schreckreaktionen der Literatur' (2004) 168 Zeitschrift für das gesamte Handelsrecht und Wirtschaftsrecht 493 reports that there is a three-digit number of contributions on *Centros* and *Überseering* alone and already 60 on *Inspire Art* (as of August 2004).

[68] S Grundmann and F Möslein 'Golden Shares – State Control in Privatised Companies: Comparative Law, European Law and Policy Aspects' (2001-02) 3 Euredia 623.

tiative, and thus have the effect of strengthening competition and reducing the need for and importance of framework harmonization.

Yet this case law needs supplementation by European framework rules for company law, as illustrated by the 13th directive on takeovers. Such framework rules do not simply amount to more regulation; instead, they might help to break up artificial barriers between member states, promote competition, and contribute to a certain degree to the development of a market for corporate control in those member states where in practice no such market has existed.

In sum, I think in company law and related areas we are overall on the right track. The momentum of the Action Plan is conspicuous. It has been discussed in all the member states and, despite some criticism, the European Commission is proceeding steadily with various instruments concerning the different actions. Some of them have been discussed in more detail in this presentation. As I said at the beginning, I am not fearful for our common European future.

Changing Models in Corporate Governance – Implications of the US Sarbanes-Oxley Act

GARY M. BROWN

I. The Impetus for the Bill

On 30 July 2002, President George W. Bush signed into law the Sarbanes-Oxley Act of 2002.[1] Many observers and commentators would say that the Sarbanes-Oxley Act is the single most important piece of legislation affecting corporate governance, financial disclosure, and the practice of public accounting since the US securities laws of the early 1930s. The United States Senate passed the legislation on a vote of 97-0. The United States House of Representatives adopted it by a vote of 423-3. This was a surprising show of bipartisanship in such a politically charged environment as Washington, D.C.: What allowed this to happen?

There now is a daunting amount of verbiage written about Sarbanes-Oxley. Little has been written, however, nor has much been said in 'corporate governance' circles about two sections of the Act that, with the regulations they have spawned, offer the greatest potential implications for true 'change' in corporate governance. Those sections are sections 805 and 1104, captioned respectively, 'Review of Federal Sentencing Guidelines for Obstruction of Justice and Extensive Criminal Fraud' and 'Amendment to the Federal Sentencing Guidelines'. Pursuant to these mandates, the United States Sentencing Commission ('USSC') has passed revisions to the US Sentencing Guidelines (the 'Guidelines') that, among other things, require organizations to 'promote an organizational culture that encourages ethical behavior and a commitment to compliance with law'.[2]

[1] Public Law 107-204 (HR 3763), 107th Cong., 2nd Session (30 July 2002). See annex 3 in this volume.

[2] *Amendments to US Sentencing Guidelines* (10 May 2004).

For directors struggling in today's post-Sarbanes-Oxley world for something 'new', the proposed amendments to the Guidelines offer that. These amendments took effect on 1 November 2004. In the words of the USSC, the focus on ethical corporate behavior 'reflects a shift in the legal landscape since the promulgation of the original organizational guidelines in 1991'.

This paper examines the historical context of the conditions that led to the passage of the Sarbanes-Oxley Act. The paper then discusses the rationale for various sections of the Sarbanes-Oxley Act that deal with corporate governance and suggests that these provisions offer few long-term implications for corporate governance. Indeed, the most effective corporate governance 'reform' that could occur is to cause companies and their executives to address basic ethical and fiduciary principles. This is not to say that Sarbanes-Oxley will not be helpful as a 'reminder'; however, we all have read about or seen past 'reminders' that soon were forgotten, with an attendant return to 'business as usual'.

So, what did allow Sarbanes-Oxley to be enacted by an almost unanimous United States Congress? What allowed this to happen is what many would refer to as a 'perfect storm'. After years of rumblings about 'accounting reform', a catalyst occurred in the fall of 2001. In an eight-week period, Enron Corp. went from the eighth-largest corporation in the world to a bankrupt, scandal-ridden symbol of all that was wrong with the corporate excesses of the 1990s.

Enron, once a high-flying energy operation that achieved its status through acquisition and 'innovation', triggered a 'reform' movement on a number of fronts. Its spectacular collapse caused a public outcry in the United States. By early 2002, 'accounting reform' proposals were introduced in both the United States Senate and United States House of Representatives. The United States Securities and Exchange Commission ('SEC') proposed its own version of 'accounting reform'.

Against this backdrop, in early 2002 the United States Senate's Committee on Governmental Affairs ('GAC') (and its Permanent Subcommittee on Investigations ['PSI']) launched a wide-ranging investigation that began with a hearing entitled 'The Fall of Enron: How Could It Have Happened?'[3] In the ensuing months, no group was spared scrutiny or criticism. In short order, Senate hearings were held or reports released focusing on the causes of the Enron debacle. Among those whose conduct was highlighted for the public were:

– securities analysts who continued to recommend that the public buy the securities of various companies (including Enron) until just prior to their collapse;[4]

[3] *The Fall Of Enron: How Could It Have Happened?: Hearing Before the Senate Committee on Governmental Affairs* 107th Cong, 2nd Session (24 January 2002).

[4] *The Watchdogs Didn't Bark: Enron and the Wall Street Analysts: Hearing Before the Senate Committee on Governmental Affairs* 107th Cong, 2nd Session (27 February 2002).

- credit rating agencies that continued to rate Enron as an investment grade credit until days before its bankruptcy;[5]
- Enron's board of directors;[6]
- financial institutions that structured and executed transactions used by Enron to manipulate its financial results;[7] and
- government agencies charged with oversight of Enron, such as the SEC, the CFTC, and the Federal Energy Regulatory Commission.[8]

As we all know, however, memories always begin to fade. Despite the almost daily revelations from the ongoing Enron investigation under the glare of the spotlight of Congressional hearings, the calls for 'accounting reform' began to subside. There was much discussion of the fact that perhaps Enron was just 'one bad egg'. By early May 2002, many, including former SEC chairman Arthur Levitt, predicted that accounting reform would not become law. The press lamented the 'shelving' of the Sarbanes accounting reform bill.[9] New Jersey Senator Jon Corzine remarked that it was 'unlikely that we will get strong reform unless there is a new event that captures the [public's] imagination'.

Well, they got it. The 'one bad egg' argument began to fall on deaf ears as, one after another, high-profile accounting scandals emerged. Nowhere was this more apparent than in the 'Washington Daily Update', a daily newsletter sent

[5] *Rating the Raters: Enron and the Credit Rating Agencies: Hearing Before the Senate Committee on Governmental Affairs* 107th Cong, 2nd Session (20 March 2002).

[6] *The Role of the Board of Directors in Enron's Collapse: Hearing Before the Permanent Subcommittee on Investigations of the Senate Committee on Governmental Affairs* 107th Cong, 2nd Session (7 May 2002); *The Role of the Board of Directors in Enron's Collapse, Report Prepared By the Permanent Subcommittee on Investigations of the Senate Committee on Governmental Affairs* S Prt 107-70 (8 July 2002).

[7] *The Role of the Financial Institutions in Enron's Collapse: Hearing Before the Permanent Subcommittee on Investigations of the Senate Committee on Governmental Affairs* 107th Cong, 2nd Session (23 and 30 July 2002); *Oversight of Investment Banks' Response to the Lessons of Enron: Hearing Before the Permanent Subcommittee on Investigations of the Senate Committee on Governmental Affairs* 107th Cong, 2nd Session (11 December 2002); *Fishtail, Bachus, Sundance and Slapshot: Four Enron Transactions Funded and Facilitated by US Financial Institutions, Report Prepared By the Permanent Subcommittee on Investigations of the Senate Committee on Governmental Affairs* S Prt 107-82 (2 January 2003).

[8] *Financial Oversight of Enron: The SEC and Private-Sector Watchdogs, Report Prepared By the Staff of the Senate Committee on Governmental Affairs* S Prt 107-75 (7 October 2002); *Asleep at the Switch FERC's Oversight of Enron Corporation: Hearing Before the Senate Committee on Governmental Affairs* 107th Cong, 2nd Sess (12 November 2002).

[9] While the bill was in the Senate, it bore simply the name of Maryland Senator Paul Sarbanes, then the Chairman of the US Senate Banking Committee. After it passed the Senate, it was sent to conference committee to resolve differences between the House and Senate versions of 'accounting reform'. Upon adoption of the Senate version of the legislation in the conference committee, Representative Mike Oxley's (Chairman of the House Financial Services Committee) name was appended to the bill.

each day to GAC and other Senate staff that described newsworthy items that could affect investigations or legislation pending before Congress. In early 2002, one section each day was titled 'Enron News'. During May, the header changed to 'Corporate Scandal News', reflecting the growing number of corporate improprieties (eg Adelphia, Tyco, ImClone).

These events provided the impetus for the Sarbanes bill to be reported out of the Senate Banking Committee in late June on a 17–4 bipartisan vote. Majority Leader Tom Daschle initially indicated that the earliest the Sarbanes bill could go to the Senate floor was September. The usual result of such a delay is the death or, at minimum, substantial weakening of legislation. On 25 June 2002, it was reported 'the only thing that's going to get this ball [accounting reform] moving again is another major accounting scandal'.

Again, they got it. The very next day, as if on cue, front pages of every major newspaper reported that WorldCom had misstated billions of dollars of expenses in what might be one of the largest accounting deceptions ever. Senator Daschle accelerated the timetable, calling for a July vote on the bill. The final Senate vote on the bill took place on 15 July 2002. The vote was 97–0, a rare show of unanimity in an extraordinarily short time period on what has been termed the most sweeping changes to US securities laws since the passage of the Securities Act of 1933[10] and the Securities Exchange Act of 1934.[11]

II. History Repeats Itself

No description of legislation said to be as sweeping and far ranging as the Sarbanes-Oxley Act of 2002 is complete without the thoughts of the US president. Consider the following excerpts from a presidential speech:

> [R]ulers of the exchange of mankind's goods have failed through their own stubbornness and their own incompetence, have admitted their failure, and have abdicated. Practices of the unscrupulous money changers stand indicted in the court of public opinion, rejected by the hearts and minds of men.
>
> The money changers have fled from their high seats in the temple of our civilization. We may now restore that temple to the ancient truths. The measure of the restoration lies in the extent to which we apply social values more noble than mere monetary profit.
>
> [T]here must be an end to a conduct in banking and in business which too often has given to a sacred trust the likeness of callous and selfish wrongdoing. Small wonder that confidence languishes, for it thrives only on honesty, on honor, on the sacredness of obligations, on faithful protection, on unselfish performance; without them, it cannot live. Restoration calls, however, not for changes in ethics alone. This nation asks for action, and action now.

[10] 15 USC §§ 77a – 77qq.

[11] 15 USC §§ 78a – 78mm.

> [I]n our progress … we require … safeguards against a return of the evils of the old order: there must be a strict supervision of all banking and credits and investments, so that there will be an end to speculation with other people's money… .

These excerpts, however, are not President Bush's call for passage of accounting reform or his comments on the corporate and investment banking scandals of recent years. They are from President Franklin D. Roosevelt's inaugural speech in 1933 that focused on a major issue of the 1932 US presidential race – the sanctity of the US capital markets. The 1933 US Congress took up the challenge, quickly passing the two cornerstone acts of US federal securities laws – the Securities Act of 1933 and the Securities Exchange Act of 1934. Several other laws[12] were passed in the ensuing six years, each addressing particular problems or issues revealed in Congressional investigations.

Indeed, the problems that led to the passage of the Sarbanes-Oxley Act and the US securities laws of the 1930s are not new. They are as old as mankind and probably will be with us as long as mankind exists. Given the burst US stock market 'bubble' of the 1990s, it is ironic that one early English legislative enactment relating to joint stock companies was popularly called the Bubble Act of 1720. Late 17th- and early 18th-century promoters of English companies, both incorporated and unincorporated, foisted doubtful schemes upon the investing public. Trading in shares led to widespread speculation and wild fluctuations in securities trading markets, resulting in alternating booms and panics. For example, more than one thousand persons subscribed in a single day for shares of a company formed 'for carrying on an undertaking of great importance, but nobody to know what it is'.[13]

Led possibly by the plan of the South Sea Company to acquire the entire English national debt, the Bubble Act was passed when the speculative enterprises had reached their apex. With an 'official' name of 'An Act to Restrain the Extravagant and Unwarranted Practice of Raising Money by Voluntary Subscriptions for Carrying On Projects Dangerous to the Trade and Subjects of this Kingdom', the Bubble Act did little other than restrain the growth of corporations. Ways were found to circumvent its vague provisions, however, and by the time of its repeal in 1825, the Bubble Act had become ineffectual for its intended purposes.[14]

Early American law carried forward some of the principles of the Bubble Act, which precluded incorporated joint stock companies. Throughout the early 1800s,

[12] Public Utility Holding Company Act of 1935, 15 USC §§ 79 – 79z; Trust Indenture Act of 1939, 15 USC §§ 74aaa – 77bbb; Investment Company Act of 1940, 15 USC §§ 80a-1 – 80a-64; Investment Advisers Act of 1940, 15 USC §§ 80b-1 – 80b-21.

[13] W Holdsworth *History of English Law* (7th edn Methuen Sweet & Maxwell London 1956-65) vol 8, 214, 215.

[14] See JW Hurst *The Legitimacy of the Business Corporation in the Law of the United States* (The University Press of Virginia Charlottesville 1970) 3.

however, primarily through legislative fiat, corporations flourished. In the mid- to late 1800s, state involvement waned and corporations continued to flourish as a means to the growth of several burgeoning industries, primarily the US railroads. These industries had large capital requirements, which resulted in the development of a variety of financial instruments. Another round of abuses, however, led to the creation of the Interstate Commerce Commission in 1887 and passage of the Sherman Antitrust Act in 1890. On the private front, the shareholder suit was developing as a means to curb corporate fraud and abuse.[15]

At some time in the late 19th or early 20th century, the American corporation became the dominant institution of modern social and economic organization. Large portions of American industrial wealth were changed from individual ownership to the management of large publicly owned corporations. States, eager for the revenue to be derived from corporate activities, removed restrictions and safeguards from their corporate statutes and advertised their 'wares' – ie their corporate laws – like products. Companies were formed where the cost was lowest and the laws the least restrictive. In Justice Brandeis' words, 'The race was one not of diligence but of laxity.' One of the first 'races to the bottom' in corporate governance was underway; however, it was not to be the last.

III. Corporate Governance Continues Its Race to the Bottom: 1985 – 1995

Indeed, when asked to identify the causes of failures such as Enron, US Federal Reserve Chairman Alan Greenspan, who coined the phrase 'irrational exuberance' for the booming stock market of the 1990s, remarked, 'The historical guardians of financial information were overwhelmed.' One of the groups of guardians to which he referred was the supposedly independent directors of the fallen companies. Other 'guardians', while perhaps not 'overwhelmed', nevertheless were remiss in their responsibilities. These included auditors, Wall Street securities analysts, investment banks, and lawyers.

'Did anyone do their job?' That was the question posed early in GAC's *Enron* investigation by Senator Susan Collins (R-Maine), then the ranking member of PSI and now the chair of GAC. The answer: 'No.' As it turned out, many of the guardians not only had failed to do their jobs – they had failed to grasp basic principles of both the law and right and wrong.

Had corporate directors been overwhelmed, or had they simply *allowed* themselves to become overwhelmed? When Enron imploded, the law as it then stood was protective of directors, a perhaps unintended result of 1985's *Smith v Van Gorkom*.[16] In that case, Delaware's Supreme Court overturned a lower court

[15] An excellent history of state incorporation laws in the United States can be found in Justice Brandeis' dissenting opinion in *Liggett Co v Lee* 288 US 517, 541 (1933).

[16] 488 A2d 858 (Del 1985).

ruling that a board's action deserved business judgment rule protection and held the board members of Trans Union, a Chicago diversified holding company, liable for gross negligence after they signed off on an agreement to sell the company to Chicago's billionaire Pritzker family without displaying much curiosity about the details of the proposed sale. The board did not look for other buyers, for instance, hire an investment bank to put a fair price on Trans Union, or even recognize the role of chairman Jerome Van Gorkom in proposing the transaction. He had negotiated the deal without the knowledge of the board and had ignored the advice of key management about the true value of the company. In the words of the court, 'the directors ... breached their fiduciary duty ... by their failure to inform themselves of all information reasonably available to them'. In simple terms, the Trans Union directors failed to do their job.

The case introduced a new verb to the language of corporate lawyers – to 'Van Gorkomize' a board meant to make sure it was fully informed of the facts and its duties and responsibilities. Indeed, much as Enron and Sarbanes-Oxley would do 17 years later, the case made directors very sensitive to their potential liabilities and had similar fallout. Directors' and officers' insurance coverage became more expensive, for example, and pundits warned that public companies would find it difficult to recruit qualified directors.

And the politicians moved in; not at the federal level but at the state level, which continues even today to be where the bulk of true 'corporate governance' principles resides. In the post-*Van Gorkom* world, however, rather than set stricter rules for boards, various new laws went beyond then-existing provisions for indemnification and allowed for the *exculpation* of corporate directors. The legislatures of a number of states, led by Delaware,[17] permitted companies to amend their charters to add provisions providing that directors would have no liability for breaches of their duty of care. It is analogous to setting the speed limit at 70, but saying that you have no liability if you exceed it. This would appear to be a curious way to address a 'problem'; however, it's probably fair to say that most companies adopted such provisions. These statutes and resulting corporate charter provisions pose the fundamental question of the role that personal liability plays in a system of corporate governance; however, some see them simply as another example of the 'race to the bottom' mentality of state corporate law.

Still another post-*Van Gorkom* effect appears to have been the extent to which directors relied on consultants (eg accountants, investment bankers, lawyers) in the satisfaction of the directors' duties. A director's basic duty of care is to act in the interests of the corporation and its shareholders with the care of an ordinarily prudent person in a like position. After *Van Gorkom*, however, directors appear to have focused more on their own liabilities as directors than on their duties to act in the best interest of shareholders. Directors sought and perhaps relied more

[17] See eg Delaware General Corporation Law § 102(b)(7).

upon the advice of consultants – not necessarily to support a good decision for the shareholders, but to better insulate the directors from personal liability.

These professional consultants then began to routinely become targets of lawsuits filed by the securities plaintiffs' bar following 'surprise' announcements that often were accompanied by earnings restatements. These suits typically claimed that these consultants had 'aided and abetted' alleged securities fraud. In 1994, however, the US Supreme Court essentially put an end to these suits, ruling in *Central Bank*[18] that such 'secondary actors' could not be held liable for securities fraud in private civil litigation. The Private Securities Litigation Reform Act of 1995[19] ('PSLRA') established additional hurdles for plaintiffs seeking to recover in private securities class action litigation.

The lessening of potential liability for secondary actors brought on by *Central Bank* and the PSLRA undoubtedly emboldened these players. With Enron, for example, major investment banks stand accused of structuring transactions (known as 'prepays') that the investment banks knew were being used by Enron to manipulate its financial statements and present a false picture to the investing public. One banker's e-mail said, 'Enron loves these deals as they are able to hide funded debt from their equity analysts because they (at the very least) book it as deferred [revenue] or (better yet) bury it in their trading liabilities.' As Enron began to unwind in late 2001, one e-mail expressed alarm at the previously unknown (even to the banks who were providing the financing) extent of the manipulative deals: 'Five [billion] in prepays!!!' (15 exclamation points in original). The reply? 'Shut up and delete this email.'

Another investment bank had done its own internal analysis of Enron and concluded that there were billions more in debt structures than was reflected on Enron's books or known by credit rating agencies. This particular financial institution was marketing securities, with proceeds going in part to reduce the credit exposure of its commercial banking affiliate to Enron. Presentation materials for these transactions prepared by the bank touted their 'black box' characteristics and the fact that no disclosure of details about the underlying transactions would have to be made to credit-rating agencies.

When asked about these matters and whether additional disclosure in the securities prospectus was warranted, the banker indicated, 'No – our analysis indicated that even after adding that on, Enron was still an investment-grade company.' The bankers seemed oblivious that the translation of that comment was, 'You don't have to tell investors the truth as long as you think it's a good deal.' They had overlooked (or chosen to ignore) a basic precept of securities disclosure.

Representatives of a third investment bank appeared at Congressional hearings to defend, among other things, the 'Nigerian barge deal'. Enron had

[18] *Central Bank of Denver NA v First Interstate Bank of Denver, NA* 511 US 164 (1994).

[19] Public Law 104-67 (HR 1058) 104th Cong, 1st Session (22 December 1995).

pressured the bank at the end of 1999 to purchase an interest in three Nigerian power barges from an Enron subsidiary for a price that allowed Enron to record $28 million in revenue and $12 million in pretax profits. Despite the bank's denials, documents indicated there was an understanding that Enron would arrange for the barges to be repurchased from the bank within six months at a specified rate of return, all of which occurred as scheduled. This made the substance of the transaction at best a bridge loan because ownership of the barges did not pass to the bank. This, in turn, made Enron's recording of the revenue and profit improper because the transaction was not a true sale.

The bank was alleged to have entered into the Nigerian barge transaction solely to ingratiate itself with Enron in order to garner a larger portion of the enormous investment banking fees that Enron generated. Significantly, when reviewing whether to enter into the transaction in late 1999, one of the executives involved wrote this about the transaction: '... reputational risk (aid/abet Enron income stmt [statement] manipulation. ...'

Obviously, the risk was not great enough – the transaction was executed as planned.

Each of the investment banks involved in assisting Enron in the manipulation of its financial statements has paid substantial fines to the SEC.[20] Each still faces continuing legal exposure in claims by Enron security holders.[21] To put it gently, *Central Bank* had allowed professional advisers to be less diligent than they should have been in adhering to securities laws. With each settlement, the SEC promises that 'the Commission's investigation into Enron is ongoing'.

IV. What Got Us Here This Time?

By 2000-2001, the stage was set for the 'perfect storm' of corporate governance lapses. We have abdication of duties by directors such as Enron's, who

- authorized high-risk accounting, extensive off-the-books transactions, conflict-of-interest transactions, and excessive compensation plans.
- failed to monitor conflict-of-interest waivers that allowed executives, such as CFO Andrew Fastow, to reap tens of millions of dollars in profits.
- were unaware that Enron paid its executives bonuses of $750 million in 2001, a year in which the company's entire net income was $975 million.

[20] To settle Enron-related matters with the SEC, CitiGroup paid $120 million, JP Morgan Chase paid $135 million, and Merrill Lynch paid $80 million.

[21] To date, their efforts to be dismissed as 'aiders and abettors' under *Central Bank* have failed. In fact, in 2005, CitiGroup and JP Morgan Chase collectively paide over $4.5 *billion* to settle these Enron related securities fraud actions. Earlier in the year, several Enron and Merrill Lynch executives also were convicted of criminal securities fraud in connection with the Nigerian barge deal.

– didn't know then-CEO Kenneth Lay sold some $77 million of Enron stock back to the company over a 12-month period, while touting the shares to employees for their 401(k) plans.

As we now know, however, directors weren't the only ones who were derelict. Others were derelict, at best, and sometimes worse. Consider the investment bankers.

Many times when confronted with troubling situations or facts, witnesses responded, 'It was in accordance with GAAP [generally accepted accounting principles],'[22] or 'The lawyers said it was not illegal.' Technical compliance seemed to be stressed over all else (although many times there was not even technical compliance). No one ever seemed to ask, 'Does this work?' or 'Is this appropriate?' When concerns were raised (such as when one bank mentioned above-raised 'reputational risk'), they were quickly dispensed with, many times with the 'almighty dollar' being the determining point. Greed and self-interest appeared the overriding governing principles.

It reminds one of a skit on National Broadcasting Company's hit show *Saturday Night Live* that featured an investment advisor informing a group of investors that he had gotten out of the stock market 'three years ago (1999) and had not followed the market since'. The time is late 2002:

> *Advisor:* You see, around that time, we at Global Century became convinced that stocks were headed for a crash and bonds were the safer bet. We were right. My own bond portfolio is up nearly 30 percent.
>
> *Investor:* But, if you were moving out of stocks and into bonds three years ago, why were your brokers telling people like me to do the exact opposite?
>
> *Advisor:* Well, if you think as we did that stocks are headed down and you want to unload them before a crash, you have to convince someone out there to buy them; that's just common sense.

The skit concluded with the advisor telling the audience:

> We like to be completely upfront with our clients – that's why in our prospectus we clearly state that our investment advice is often self-interested or deceitful and may work to a client's disadvantage. We think you deserve to know that.

Sound funny? Let's go to 23 July 2003, day one of a two-day hearing before the PSI. After hours of testimony about transactions that had been structured and executed by various financial institutions that were designed to allow Enron to manipulate its financial statements, the following exchange took place between Senator Carl Levin (D-Michigan) and David C. Bushnell, managing director, Global Risk Management, Citigroup/Salomon Smith Barney:

[22] It has long been settled law that mere compliance with generally accepted accounting principles does not, alone, mean that the information presented is not otherwise materially misleading. See eg *United States v Simon* 425 F2d 796,798 (2nd Cir 1969) *cert denied* 397 US 1006 (1970).

> *Sen. Levin*: But would you agree that you have a responsibility not to participate in a deception?
>
> *Mr Bushnell*: – it depends on what the definition of deception is.

As we now know all too well, fraud and corruption have not been limited to corporations issuing securities. Wall Street itself has been tainted with revelation after revelation of wrongdoing. Consider the following quote from Richard Strong, founder of Strong Financial Corporation and now barred for life from the mutual fund industry:

> I frequently traded the shares of the Strong funds, at the same time that the advice which we gave our investors was to do the opposite and to hold their shares for the long term. My personal behavior in this regard was wrong and at odds with the obligations I owed my shareholders, and for this I am deeply sorry.[23]

Given Mr. Bushnell's and Mr. Strong's comments, has reality been all that different from the *Saturday Night Live* skit? Will investor confidence return if this continues to be the prevailing attitude of business and on Wall Street? What, if anything, will Sarbanes-Oxley do to address the root cause of the periodic booms and busts of the 'business cycle'?
Consider the following:

- Americans have become suspicious of banking practices that, in the public view, have undermined the prosperity of the past decade.
- US Congressional investigations have exposed cases of double-dealing in the securities business. Self-dealing and outright fraud (not the least of which involved a gigantic, rapidly growing energy operation) have become associated with erosion of the US stock market.
- US Senate hearings have revealed financial irregularities of large New York banks, their executives, affiliated securities companies, and Wall Street investment bankers.
- Leading Wall Street investment banks are under fire for their lending and investing practices, including transactions designed to allow companies to misstate their financial results. Private side deals and tax avoidance have evoked much criticism of executives and their corporate activities in banking and commerce.

The problem – all of the above that appear to be headlines of 2002 actually are the findings of a 1932 US Senate committee that investigated the 1929 US stock market crash, which triggered a worldwide depression. The energy company was not Enron; it was Insull. The bankers were not J.P. Morgan Chase or Citigroup, but their direct corporate predecessors. Obviously, the age-old saying – those who forget history are doomed to repeat it – still applies. Indeed, the following quote from the *Atlantic Monthly* says it all:

[23] *Wall Street Journal* (New York United States) 21 May 2004.

> For years, the rules of conservative corporate practices were disregarded; careful accounting methods were forgotten; the canons of business ethics and moral precepts were trampled upon; and sometimes even the broad boundaries of legal tolerance were overstepped.[24]

So – we have seen it before. Over the ages, extensive legislation and regulations have been passed to address it. Accordingly, it is an entirely appropriate question to ask, 'What will Sarbanes-Oxley do about it?' In fact, perhaps more importantly, what is '*IT*'? It's not their MBA; it's their DNA. *IT* is the moral and ethical laxity that has come to permeate society. If we have an overall ethically poisoned society, how can we expect business executives to act any differently than society in general? Think about sports and sportsmanship.

In 1940 (when Ivy League football still mattered), Cornell played Dartmouth. Cornell, undefeated in three seasons, was well on its way to a final #1 ranking. With less than a minute to play, however, underdog Dartmouth was ahead 3-0, with Cornell on Dartmouth's 6-yard line. Dartmouth held; however, the referees mistakenly awarded Cornell an extra down. Cornell scored on the extra down and 'won' the game.

Not having the benefit of today's instant replays, not until the game films were developed the next day was the mistake verified. League rules, however, provided that it was too late to reverse the score. Cornell was the 'winner'. Then a curious thing happened – Cornell's coach sent a telegram to Dartmouth stating:

> We congratulate you on the victory of your fine team. The Cornell touchdown was scored on a fifth down, and we relinquish claim to victory and extend congratulations to Dartmouth.[25]

One can not imagine such a thing happening today – because it wouldn't. Consider the recent Athens Summer Olympics. Was Paul Hamm the 'winner' of the men's all-around gymnastics competition? Clearly, he was not; however, he steadfastly refused to give up the gold medal. Perhaps there is a reason that he may not be included on the front of the 'Wheaties' cereal box. Perhaps someone, somewhere thinks that it would be inappropriate to put the company's imprimatur on something so clearly 'wrong'.

During the 1980s, Americans were warned about a group that undoubtedly included persons such as Hamm and some of the corporate leaders of the 1990s. They were called the IDIs – standing for I Deserve It. We were warned that a great deal was at stake in the next decade (the '90s) as IDIs gained positions of authority and power. The IDIs were poised before society like an invading army

[24] NR Danielian 'From Insult to Injury' *The Atlantic Monthly* (Boston United States no 15-4 April 1993) 308.

[25] R Horick 'Remember Sportsmanship' *The Nashville Scene* (Nashville United States August 2004).

with values and habits likely to make matters much worse.[26] Whether they were to serve as bus drivers, building inspectors, airline or auto mechanics, engineers, bankers, accountants, teachers, journalists, business executives, or politicians, it was predicted that their ethical laxity would cause significant future harm.

Some statistics from that time indicated that among American high school graduates, 33% had shoplifted, 16% had lied on a job application or resume, and 61% had cheated on an exam. Among American college graduates, 16% had shoplifted, 29% would lie to get a job and 18% had, 21% would falsify a report to keep a job, 39% had lied to their boss, 35% had lied to a customer, 32% had cheated on an exam, and 12% had inflated expense claims, lied on a loan application, lied to an insurance company, or borrowed money with no intent to repay. When asked about 'ethics', you might expect a reply such as – 'Ethics? What's that? Our world is a fast-paced, survival-of-the-fittest working zoo where the fast on their feet survive while the "ethical" perish.'

This makes it harder to believe that Ken Lay, Jeff Skilling, and Andy Fastow and the accounting and other business scandals are isolated examples of the 'ends justifying the means'. They, like our athletes, perhaps are merely polluted products of a poisoned culture.

As to the subject of culture, some commentators have expressed seeming astonishment at the education level of some of those involved in the corporate scandals: 'How could a Harvard MBA behave so unethically?' The answer is painfully simple: it's not their M.B.A; it's their DNA. That is the reason that SEC Chairman William Donaldson made these comments when addressing the Economic Club of New York in 2003:

> In my mind, the most important thing that a Board of Directors should do is determine the elements that must be embedded in the company's moral DNA....It should be the foundation on which the Board builds *a corporate culture based on a philosophy of high ethical standards and accountability*. This culture should penetrate every level of the organization and influence all of the board's decisions including the selection of a CEO and the senior management team who will ultimately ensure that the company's operations reflect its philosophy.[27]

V. What Did Sarbanes-Oxley do About Corporate Governance?

The Sarbanes-Oxley Act is thirty pages long and is divided into 11 titles and 69 individual sections. The Act is intended to strengthen the independence of audit-

[26] The 1980s had its own series of ethical challenges, such as the defense contractor scandals and the insider trading scandals that made household names of Michael Milken and Ivan Boesky.

[27] William Donaldson, SEC Chairman – Remarks made to the Economic Club of New York, 8 May 2003.

ing firms,[28] improve transparency of financial statements and disclosure,[29] improve objectivity of analyst research, and strengthen enforcement of the securities laws.[30] The final objective is to enhance corporate governance – but how?

One title (Title VI) deals with appropriations for the SEC. Another (Title X) provides simply that it is the 'sense of the Senate that the Federal income tax return of a corporation should be signed by the chief executive officer of such corporation'. Two (Titles I and II) provide for the overhaul and the regulation of the accounting profession.[31] One section out of these two titles, section 202, arguably addresses what many would refer to as a matter of 'corporate governance'. That section requires that the services provided by the company's auditor be pre-approved by the company's audit committee.

Two titles (Titles V and VII) address other actors in the spectacular corporate failures of the early century, mandating studies of securities analysts, accounting firms, credit rating agencies, and investment banks. Three other titles (Titles VIII, IX, and XI) address criminal penalties. The only 'corporate governance' provision in those titles arguably is Section 906, which requires financial certifications by a company's CEO and CFO.

The remaining two titles (Title III captioned 'Corporate Responsibility' and Title IV captioned 'Enhanced Financial Disclosures') contain 17 out of the 69 sections of the Act. Of those, ten[32] really do not address items that most would view as matters of 'corporate governance'. Included in these ten is the requirement in section 404 of the Act that internal control reports be attested to by the company's auditor. While this has been perhaps the most controversial provision of the Act due to the cost that companies have incurred and are incurring, it certainly is not a matter of 'corporate governance'.[33]

[28] Eg establishment of the Public Company Accounting Oversight Board ('PCAOB'), redefining the relationship between auditors and clients, requiring audit partner rotation, and placing direct auditor relationship responsibility on each company's audit committee.

[29] Eg CEO/CFO certifications, bonus forfeiture provisions, disclosure control and internal control effectiveness, accelerating section 16 reporting deadlines, and 'real time' disclosure.

[30] Eg increasing criminal penalties.

[31] These titles create the PCAOB and set out basic standards for auditor independence.

[32] These ten are sections 303 (amended rules adopted pursuant to the Foreign Corrupt Practices Act), 305 (lowering the standard for officer and director bars), 306 (benefit plan blackouts), 308 (fair funds for investors), 401 (rules on disclosures of off-balance sheet arrangements and pro-forma financial information), 403 (acceleration of section 16 reports), 404 (attestation of internal controls), 405 (exemption for investment companies), 408 (SEC to review issuers more frequently) and 409 ('real time' disclosure).

[33] Indeed, the controls that must be attested to were mandated by the Foreign Corrupt Practices Act of 1977. The Sarbanes-Oxley Act mandated no new controls; only that the controls be documented and attested to. It would appear that the major issue is a significant underinvestment during the past dozen or so years and, as a result, there is a large 'catch up' in costs. It is analogous to the company that has not invested in plant or technology for years and then suddenly realizes that there is both lost time and underinvestment to recover. At the same

cont. ...

This leaves seven[34] sections (eight, if one adds section 202 pre-approval requirements) that arguably address 'corporate governance' issues. Here, it is instructive to think back to Alan Greenspan's comments about the failure of the 'guardians' (ie independent directors) and review how Sarbanes-Oxley's provisions address these failures of corporate governance. Sarbanes-Oxley only indirectly addresses these failures through focusing on the independence, power, and authority of audit committees, and then primarily through exchange listing standards. Otherwise, the Act provides direct regulation over certain actions of corporate officers over whom directors had failed to exercise appropriate oversight.

In these discrete areas, the Act 'federalized' and some would argue 'intruded' upon what generally were state law concerns: namely, corporate governance and other matters that traditionally had been matters of board discretion. Many, if not all, of these 'intrusions' can be traced directly to the perceived failings of the boards of directors of Enron and other corporations that experienced high-profile failures. Consider:

– Conflicts of interest, lack of independence, and inattention to detail by boards and audit committees, as well as audit committees' failure to interact appropriately with auditors and to have effective mechanisms for 'whistleblowers' (ie Enron's Sherron Watkins) led to Section 301's requirements that the stock exchanges require listed companies to have independent audit committees, with broad powers and responsibilities in respect to the audit function and engagement and oversight of auditors, the ability to engage outside advisors, and the responsibility to institute internal complaint procedures and to Section 407's requirements for the identification of 'audit committee financial experts'.
– Jeffrey Skilling's statement that he was 'simply' the CEO and not responsible for Enron's financial statements begged the question why corporate directors already were not holding their senior financial officers responsible for the company's financial statements, which led to Sections 302's and 906's requirements for certifications of the financial reports by the company's CEO and CFO.
– The perceived inattention by boards and audit committees to excessive compensation linked to short-term stock price appreciation (that in turn was linked to 'high-risk' accounting practices and extensive off-the-books transactions) and other financial measures, and the perceived failure by Enron's board and audit committee to understand (or attempt to understand) Enron's

time, because auditing firms were not checking internal controls each year, companies benefited from artificially low audit fees over this period that now also are in a 'catch up' mode.

[34] These are sections 301 (audit committee requirements), 302 (CEO/CFO certifications), 304 (bonus forfeitures), 307 (SEC attorney professional conduct rules), 402 (loan prohibitions), 406 (codes of ethics for senior financial officers), and 407 (audit committee financial experts).

complex financial structure, contributed to the Act's requirement that CEOs and CFOs personally certify the company's financial statements and public reports and attest to the effectiveness of their internal controls, Section 304's bonus forfeiture requirements, and Section 407's disclosure requirements concerning whether a company has a 'financial expert' on its audit committee.

- The perceived shortcomings of the lawyers handling failed or deceptive transactions, as well as lack of independence in certain investigative roles, led to Section 307's requirement for 'up-the-ladder' reporting as well as the SEC pronouncement that the organization, rather than management, is the attorney's client to which the attorney's loyalties are owed.
- Excessive loans to executives (eg, Ken Lay's $4 million [increased to $7.5 million] line of credit extended him by Enron in and used in what was termed an 'ATM approach,' repeatedly drawing down the line and repaying it with Enron stock [$77 million sold to the company during a 12-month period], with board members disavowing monitoring responsibilities) led to Section 402's ban on personal loans from public corporations to their executives. Here, the theory is that if boards are incapable of exercising discretion in any meaningful way in approving loans, Congress chose to simply ban them.
- The Enron audit committee's perceived failures in its waivers of conflicts of interest that allowed corporate officers to reap multi-million-dollar windfalls led to Section 406's disclosure requirements concerning codes of conduct for senior financial officers and waivers of those codes.

The message is clear: Congress expects more of independent directors and audit committees.

VI. What is New and has Sarbanes-Oxley Addressed 'It'?

Upon signing the Sarbanes-Oxley Act, President Bush stated:

> This new law sends very clear messages that all concerned must heed. This law says to every dishonest corporate leader: you will be exposed and punished; the era of low standards and false profits is over; no boardroom in America is above or beyond the law.

Consider further the following comments:

> The anxieties created by the … Act – among men and women of utmost good faith – have been … without equal. This consternation can be attributed, in significant part, to the spectre which some commentators have raised of exposure to [SEC] enforcement action, and perhaps criminal liability, as a result of technical and insignificant errors in corporate records or weaknesses in corporate internal controls.'

> The existence of a pattern of questionable [activities] by prominent American corporations … – often in bold headlines – shook faith and trust in the integrity of the corporate sector. This reaction became part of a rising tide of public skepticism and served to

> further undermine the traditional American consensus that business conducts itself and reasonably pursues its own economic interests in a manner consistent with the standards and expectations of the larger society.
>
> Statute or no, these are, of course, inherent obligations of the stewardship of a public corporation. The standards embodied in the Act's … provisions are, in effect, the cardinal principles of managing a business enterprise. Among many members of the business community, few would dispute that acceptable management cannot be achieved absent such records and controls. In that sense, this is hardly the stuff of radical legislation.

These comments, however, are not in reference to the Sarbanes-Oxley Act of 2002; they are in reference to the accounting provisions of the Foreign Corrupt Practices Act of 1977, a major post-Watergate piece of legislation passed in the wake of disclosures of 'off-the-books' 'slush funds' and foreign bribery. What engendered those provisions? What was termed 'the most devastating disclosure', 'the fact that, and the extent to which, some companies have falsified entries in their own books and records'? These comments in the SEC's Statement of Policy Regarding the Foreign Corrupt Practices Act of 1977 were accompanied by a statement acknowledging certain developments then being made in corporate accountability. The SEC's policy statement indicated that these developments, rather than the provisions of the FCPA, were the 'most effective antidote' to the conditions that led to the questionable practices that, in turn, led to passage of the FCPA. The two leading 'antidotes':

- Increase in the number and responsibility of independent directors; and
- Effective audit committees composed of independent directors.

Remember 'it' – ethical laxity? If directors are wringing their hands over 'new' requirements or if people are wondering if Sarbanes-Oxley has 'fixed' the problem, they need look no further than two infrequently referenced sections of the Act, sections 805 and 1104. Those sections are captioned respectively, 'Review of Federal Sentencing Guidelines for Obstruction of Justice and Extensive Criminal Fraud' and 'Amendment to the Federal Sentencing Guidelines'. Pursuant to these mandates, the USSC has passed revisions to the Guidelines that, among other things, require organizations to 'promote an organizational culture that encourages *ethical behavior and a commitment to compliance with law'*. The amendments offer incentives to an organization to self-police its own conduct through an effective compliance and ethics program and thereby mitigate and substantially reduce any potential punishment of the organization.

An effective compliance program has been a fundamental component of the Guidelines since they were first promulgated in 1991. The Guidelines apply to every 'organization' – corporations (public and private, profit and not-for-profit), partnerships, joint stock companies, unions, trusts, and pension funds. Many organizations already have compliance programs in effect. These organizations are advised to review their existing programs and to make the changes necessary to meet the expanded standards set forth in the amendments. While these changes are not likely to be burdensome, the amendments do place additional responsibility on the board of directors and 'high-level personnel' within the organization.

The amendments also place an increased emphasis on training of the board and personnel, and on auditing and monitoring the effectiveness of the program. Those organizations that do not currently have an effective program in place are encouraged to implement one now.

An effective compliance program, in addition to meeting the purposes of the Guidelines, offers other ancillary benefits. From a corporate governance/director liability standpoint, it can be a shield to personal liability for directors. In the *Caremark*[35] decision, the Delaware Chancery Court opined that 'by establishing and maintaining an effective compliance program, board members can protect themselves from personal liability suits'. Caremark had pled guilty to mail fraud and to paying kickbacks to physicians for patient referrals, and paid fines of $250 million. In response, shareholders brought suit alleging Caremark directors bore personal responsibility for failure to supervise. Although the Caremark directors were relieved of personal liability because they had established such a program, the court noted that the failure to have such a program may 'render a director liable for losses caused by non-compliance'.

Compliance programs that met the 'seven elements of effectiveness' of the Guidelines quickly became the norm for compliance programs that also met the *Caremark* test. In addition to the benefits to directors, the programs offered other salutary purposes:

- They might detect and/or prevent criminal and other improper activity (ie they might work).
- They might prevent loss of business (eg suspension, debarment).
- They might avoid/mitigate the effects of a federal criminal prosecution (the 'Thompson memo'[36]).

As if in response to SEC Chairman Donaldson's call for a focus on a culture of ethics and 'moral DNA', the USSC requires that in order to have an effective compliance and ethics program, an organization is required by the amendments to exercise due diligence to prevent and detect criminal conduct and to promote a culture that 'encourages ethical conduct and a commitment to compliance with the law'. The amendments expressly impose responsibility for the compliance and ethics program on an organization's 'governing authority' (ie the board of directors) and its executives. The amendments require that the board of directors be knowledgeable about the content and operation of the compliance program and exercise reasonable oversight over the program.

Additionally, 'high-level personnel' of the organization are responsible for ensuring that the organization's program is effective and a specific individual within 'high-level personnel' is to be assigned 'overall responsibility' for the program. An individual with substantial control over the organization or who has a substantial

[35] *In re Caremark International Inc Derivative Litigation* 698 A2d 959 (Del Ch 1996).

[36] See 'Principles of Federal Prosecution of Business Organizations,' at <http://www.usdoj.gov/dag/cftf/corporate_guidelines.htm>.

role in making policy for the organization falls within the meaning of 'high-level personnel' (eg a director, an executive officer, an individual in charge of a major business or functional unit of the organization, such as sales, administration, or finance, and an individual with a substantial ownership interest). Furthermore, the amendments require that the organization assign to an individual day-to-day operational responsibility for the program and provide adequate resources and appropriate authority in order for that person to carry out such responsibility. This individual is also required to report periodically to the board of directors and to 'high-level personnel' regarding the effectiveness of the program.

Training in ethics and compliance now is mandated by the amendments. This requirement is extended to training 'high-level personnel' and the board of directors, in addition to all other employees in the organization. Training of agents of the organization may also be required when appropriate. An organization's training obligation is ongoing, and 'periodic updates' are required.

The new amendments require that organizations use auditing and monitoring systems that are intended to detect criminal conduct. Organizations also must periodically evaluate the effectiveness of their compliance and ethics program. A reporting system must permit reporting of potential or actual criminal conduct without fear of retaliation, including anonymous or confidential submissions.

Organizations must take reasonable steps to respond to and prevent misconduct. For example, organizations are required to use reasonable efforts to ensure that employees with 'substantial authority' within the organization have not engaged in illegal activities or other conduct inconsistent with an effective ethics and compliance program. Individuals with 'substantial authority' are those who exercise substantial discretion on behalf of an organization, such as 'high-level personnel', a plant manager, or a sales manager. Organizations are required to take appropriate disciplinary action involving any employee who violates the compliance and ethics program. Further, compliance is to be encouraged by providing appropriate incentives to employees.

In implementing a program, an organization must periodically assess the risk of criminal conduct. The factors that should be addressed when considering the relevant risks include: (i) the nature and seriousness of potential criminal conduct; (ii) the likelihood that certain criminal conduct may occur because of the nature of the organization's business; and (iii) the prior history of the organization. Following such an assessment, an organization must revise its program to reduce the risks identified during such assessment.

VII. The Lesson

The Sarbanes-Oxley Act clearly has resulted in a shift in the balance of power between boards and management. While it could be argued that a number of the accounting scandals of recent years resulted from failures of corporate governance and boards, much has changed.[37] Nevertheless, as we have seen, much has changed before without 'true' change. Indeed, skepticism remains today, with some saying that '[i]t is far from certain, however, how much better public companies govern themselves than they did before the reforms'.[38]

This shift in power should embolden directors to 'seize the moment'. SEC Chairman Donaldson recently indicated that the public trust in the financial markets will not return so long as executives use legal limits as the test of right and wrong. 'Compliance with GAAP', as was so vividly demonstrated during the *Enron* investigation, does not mean that financial statements and other corporate disclosures are not misleading. Donaldson called on corporate America to put honesty and integrity at the heart of every business decision. Neither the Securities Act of 1933 nor any of the other statutes of the '30s (eg the Securities Exchange Act of 1934, the Trust Indenture Act, the Investment Company Act, and the Investment Advisors Act) eliminated fraud and wrongdoing. Neither did later statutes, such as the Foreign Corrupt Practices Act. Neither did earlier statutes, such as the Bubble Act.

Likewise, neither Sarbanes-Oxley nor any of the host of rules promulgated following its passage will eliminate fraud or corporate wrongdoing. The HealthSouth scandal was the first proof positive of that. Indeed, corporate scandals have continued to occur and now have spread to Europe with Royal Ahold, Parmalat, Vivendi, Royal Dutch/Shell Group, and China Life. New and enhanced civil and criminal penalties, however, have raised the stakes for those who participate in corporate wrongdoing. More transparent accounting and more vigilant directors may eliminate some opportunities, but if the past is any indication, greed and self-interest will rise to the occasion. Perhaps now, however, with the stakes higher, people will think twice before succumbing to temptation.

Indeed, when one examines the stacks of new laws and regulations that have been adopted over the last year, most, if not all, can be summarized in a very simple principle: Do the right thing. When one examines the Enron collapse and the host of other recent corporate scandals, it is easy to conclude that no one adhered to this simple principle. Directors must insist on a higher standard of personal conduct from corporate executives, and those executives must be prepared to 'take the fall' for errors, particularly those in judgment or integrity. This standard will not be met by technical compliance (ie a 'check-the-box' approach) within a corporate environment that does not otherwise foster integrity. Directors and senior management must make clear what is expected, then reward those who conform and perform and hold accountable those who do not. Only then can we avoid the failures of the past.

[37] Audit committees have taken charge of the audit relationship, codes of conduct and committee charters have been adopted, and corporate disclosures have been both expanded and accelerated.

[38] C Hymowitz and J Lublin *Scandals Prompted Changes, But Critics Say More Are Needed to Prevent Another Enron* Wall Street Journal (New York United States 22 July 2003).

Enron and Corporate Law Reform in the UK and the European Community

PAUL L. DAVIES

I. Introduction

1. Why were there European Responses?

The collapse of Enron and of a number of other companies[1] in the United States over the period between late 2001 and the middle of 2002 has had a striking impact on the process of corporate law reform. That these events should have had an impact in the United States itself, notably in the shape of the enactment of the Sarbanes-Oxley Act of 2002[2] and the reforms of the rules of the New York Stock Exchange and the NASDAQ, is not surprising, though the speed of the reaction and its location at the federal level rather than with the states, which have traditionally carried the main burden of corporate law legislation, are notable aspects of the US reforms.[3] However, the reach of Enron in terms of its impetus to corporate law reform has extended beyond the borders of the United States, and this paper explores the European impact, notably in the United Kingdom and at the level of the European Community.

A visitor to the company law website of the Department of Trade and Industry (DTI),[4] the department of the British Government with responsibility for the state

[1] Notably WorldCom, Global Crossing, Tyco. Unfairly, but inevitably, the name 'Enron' has become a shorthand to refer to all these US corporate collapses and will be so used, where the context requires, in this paper.

[2] Public Company Accounting Reform and Investor Protection Act of 2002, 15 USC § 7201 ff (see annex 3 in this volume).

[3] WB Chandler III and LE Strine Jr 'The New Federalism of the American Corporate Governance System: Preliminary Reflections of Two Residents of One Small State' (2003) 152 U of Pennsylvania L Rev 953. It is no accident that the authors of this article are respectively Chancellor and Vice-Chancellor of the Delaware Court of Chancery.

[4] <http://www.dti.gov.uk/cld/> (25 May 2005).

of domestic company law, currently[5] sees 'post-Enron initiatives' listed in red as one of nine main areas with which the department is and has recently been concerned, and two further areas[6] are either wholly or mainly concerned with this topic. These initiatives produced a number of significant reports dealing with the regulation of audits and auditors, audit committees, and the role of non-executive directors,[7] and, just as significant, the enquiries which led to the reports were put in train by the Secretary of State at the Department (Patricia Hewitt) in February 2002, ie very soon after the Enron collapse and well before the full extent of the problems in the United States had become clear.

The British reaction was by no means an isolated one. An equally speedy and wide-ranging response can be seen on the part of the European Commission. As early as April 2002, in the Commission's note for the informal Ecofin Council meeting held in Oviedo and entitled 'A first EU Response to Enron related policy issues',[8] one finds not only auditors and auditing, but also board structure and composition, executive remuneration, reporting by financial analysts, and the operation of credit rating agencies identified as matters of concern. This note and the Council's decision on it led, amongst many other things, to an expansion of the remit of the High Level Group of Company Law Experts so as to embrace additional corporate governance issues, including the role of non-executive directors and supervisory boards, management remuneration, and the responsibility of management for financial statements. The report of that group[9] dealt with these matters as, in turn, did the Commission's response to the High Level Group's report in its Company Law Communication of 2003.[10] However, the Commission's response to Enron was by no means channelled wholly through the High Level Group. As we shall see, an equally, if not more, important part of the Commission's response lay in the area of accounting and auditing, where the

[5] As of December 2004.

[6] 'Review of Non-executive Directors', which is intimately linked to the initiatives specifically labelled as 'Post-Enron', and the 'Companies (Audit, Investigations and Community Enterprise) Act 2004', one of the main purposes of that Act being to make the legal changes necessary to implement the recommendations resulting from the 'post-Enron' initiatives.

[7] For an initial analysis see P Davies 'Post-Enron Developments in the United Kingdom' in G Ferrarini and others (eds) *Reforming Company and Takeover Law in Europe* (OUP Oxford 2004) 185.

[8] Available on <http://europa.eu.int/comm/internal_market/company/docs/enron/ecofin_2004_04_enron_en.pdf> (25 May 2005). Despite the misleading numbers contained in the URL for this website it is clear that the document emanated in 2002, not 2004.

[9] *A Modern Regulatory Framework for Company Law in Europe* (4 November 2002) available on <http://europa.eu.int/comm/internal_market/en/company/company/modern/consult/report_en.pdf> (25 May 2005).

[10] Communication from the Commission to the Council and the European Parliament *Modernising Company Law and Enhancing Corporate Governance in the European Union – A Plan to Move Forward* COM(2003) 284 final (21 May 2003) (see annex 1 in this volume).

Commission was already active on its own part. Its post-Enron reflections in that area were encapsulated in its communication on the statutory audit,[11] published at the same time as the company law communication.

Responses to Enron from member states other than the UK can also be found.[12] Should we be surprised at the speed and scope of the response in Europe? In one respect it is certainly surprising. Although an immensely newsworthy scandal, the collapse of Enron had relatively little economic impact outside the US The European assets of Enron (and the other US companies) passed into new hands with very little economic disruption. If one thinks of job losses, slimming down by continuing US corporations, such as the carmakers Ford and GM, has had a much bigger impact over the past two years on jobs in Europe than the collapse of Enron.[13] Nor, at the time that these early British and Community initiatives were launched, had there occurred any European equivalents to Enron. It seems to have been the case that fear on the part of governments of other countries that similar events could occur in their jurisdictions was sufficient to drive law reform.

It is an indication of the interconnectedness of the world economy and, more precisely, of the commonality of approaches to corporate governance across the developed world that Enron produced impetuses for law reform even in jurisdictions where the collapses caused no economic damage. Some people in Europe, of course, took the view that Enron-type scandals were a unique feature of the US system of corporate governance. However, the initial reaction that 'it could not happen here' did not long survive examination – a wise analysis in the light of subsequent European collapses such as that of Parmalat in Italy. What needs to be emphasised, however, is that even before Parmalat and Ahold, the process of reform in reaction to Enron had been set in train at both the Community and the member state level. Thus, if Enron confirms the old adage that there is nothing like a good scandal to produce company law reform, it is novel, perhaps unique, in being a foreign scandal producing law reform in Europe.

2. The Nature of the European Responses

However, it is worth pausing for a moment to analyse the nature of the reforms which have eventuated in Europe in the wake of Enron. At the opposite end of the

[11] Communication from the Commission to the Council and the European Parliament *Reinforcing the statutory audit in the EU* COM (2003) 286 final [2003] OJ C236/2.

[12] For example, in France Loi n° 2003-706 du 1er août 2003 de sécurité financière *Journal officiel de la République française du 2 août 2003* p 13220.

[13] See for example 'GM cuts 10,000 jobs in Germany' *BBC News, World Edition* (9 December 2004) available on <http://news.bbc.co.uk/2/hi/business/4083159.stm> (25 May 2005).

spectrum from those who took the view that 'Enron could not happen here' were those who analysed Enron as challenging existing corporate law rules in a fundamental way, in particular the modern emphasis on shareholder value. This was as difficult an analysis to sustain as the one which propounded the view that there was no need for a European response to Enron. The shareholders of Enron – unless connected with the management of the company or lucky enough to bail out before disaster struck – were surely one of the victims of that collapse. They lost their investment in the company which meant, for those shareholders who were also ordinary employees of the company, that their pensions disappeared with their jobs. Fortunately, the more extreme reactions in Europe to the Enron debacle did not find their way into legislation. For example, some way-out proposals emerged from the partially inaccurate perception that the creation of subsidiaries had been central to the financial obfuscation which the US companies had engaged in. Some therefore suggested going back on the principle which was at the heart of the Gladstonian reforms of the 1840s, ie the entitlement of private parties to create a company by going through a simple bureaucratic procedure. Thus, it was said, either state approval for the creation of new companies should be reintroduced or, at least, a waiting period of six months between creation and commencement of business should be introduced.[14] This is a bit like saying that because pens can be used to commit forgeries, all potential users of pens should be required to obtain state permission to own and use one.

In fact, the striking feature of the post-Enron reforms in Europe is that they do not break the mould of the traditional legal strategies used to regulate problems in the area of corporate governance, but simply modernise and extend those legal strategies so as to deal with new factual circumstances. To that extent, the post-Enron wave of reforms has been less significant than some would have wished. In order to understand why traditional legal strategies have been deployed post-Enron, it is necessary to identify the generally accepted analysis of the governance failures in the US and subsequent European scandals. This analysis is based around conflicts of interest. To take the Enron case itself, the management of the company had a self-interest in presenting the company's financial position in a more attractive light than the facts warranted, especially in view of the important role which stock options played in the make-up of their remuneration package; the auditors had an interest in not investigating the company's accounting arrangements too closely or disagreeing too vigorously with management's proposed accounting treatments of the company's transactions, in order to preserve their much more valuable non-audit work with the company; and the non-executive directors had an interest in a quiet life and not rocking the boat.[15]

[14] KJ Hopt 'Modern Company and Capital Markets Problems: Improving European Corporate Governance after Enron' ECGI Law Working Paper no 05/2002 pp 2-3.

[15] Davies (n 7) 186. There were also conflicts of interest at the level of the analysts (putting out more favourable buy recommendations that the facts warranted) and the investment banks (which participated in, sometimes even proposed, the sophisticated transactions whose proper

cont. ...

However, these are examples of the standard agency problems, the regulation of which lies at the heart of company law and always has done so since modern company law emerged in the middle of the nineteenth century. Therefore, company law has developed tried and tested techniques for addressing these problems and it is perhaps not surprising that the legislative response to Enron has consisted in a further strengthening of those techniques. Legislative reform has focussed, therefore, on matters such as strengthening the position of non-executive directors, further regulation of the independence of auditors and of supervision of auditors, and greater controls over directors' remuneration packages. None of these was an area of non-regulation before the recent reforms and none became an area where entirely novel regulatory elements were introduced post-Enron; but they are all areas where a significant ratcheting up of the applicable rules has taken place.

a. Putting New Items on the Reform Agenda

However, 'ratcheting up' should not be dismissed as a trivial type of law reform. In fact, Enron seems to have had three main impacts on the process of company law reform in Europe. First, and undoubtedly the most significant, Enron put onto European reform agendas proposals for which previously there was not sufficient support, even though minority elements within Europe were attempting to promote such changes. Both British and Community examples can be given. Between 1998 and 2001 in the UK, ie ending before Enron, there was a comprehensive, Government-inspired, but independent review of British company law, imaginatively entitled the Company Law Review.[16] It is clear from one of the many consultation documents put out by the Steering Group that both the group itself and those it consulted were conscious of the threats to auditor independence arising from the increasing importance to accounting firms of the supply of non-audit work to audit clients, and were doubtful about the adequacy of the existing rules to remove or sufficiently reduce those threats.[17] However, the Steering Group made only very limited proposals to deal with the issue, because, as it was doing its work, the Government was separately doing a deal with the accountancy professions, largely to perpetuate professional control of auditing. The Steering

treatment for accounting purposes was later controversial), but these conflicts are not dealt with in this paper.

[16] The author should disclose that he was a member of its Steering Group.

[17] 'There is a question therefore, given the centrality of the auditors' independence as a check and balance in the system, whether the existing statutory requirement for auditor independence combined with a self regulatory system of rules and discipline is adequate. There is, moreover, a danger after a long period of economic recovery and market buoyancy that the risks of abuse of this conflict are currently being under estimated.' (Company Law Review *Developing the Framework* March 2000 para 5.136.

Group thus concluded, in the civil service language of these reports, that in the circumstances it would be 'not helpful' for it to go further.[18] Post-Enron, however, in the UK and throughout the EU, professional self-regulation has given or is about to give way to independent regulation of the audit, in terms of auditing standards, the monitoring of audit quality, disciplinary action against failing auditors, and ethical guidance for auditors; and the rules on auditor independence have been substantially strengthened. Thus, in the UK the 2004 Act[19] makes the necessary changes to implement the British reforms as adopted post-Enron. Moreover, whilst the 2004 Act has put on the statute book the necessary legal changes to accommodate the regulatory reforms of auditing, the earlier but more wide-ranging proposals of the Company Law Review proceed at a much more leisurely pace through the policy-making procedures of the department and are unlikely to reach the statute book before 2006.[20]

A somewhat similar story can be told at the Community level. In 1998 the Commission issued its communication on the statutory audit.[21] In the section dealing with the action it proposed to take on the basis of the communication, the Commission was extremely cautious. Subsidiarity and proportionality were referred to; new or amended legislation 'is not necessarily envisaged'; only in response to the urgings of the European Parliament did the Commission confirm that it would not hesitate to propose legislation where necessary. Indeed, the document contained no proposals for legislation, but rather the Commission's aims were to be pursued with and through the member states and the professional bodies.[22] Post-Enron, however, the Commission was able to move, first in 2002, to a Commission Recommendation on the independence of the statutory auditor[23] and then in early 2004 to a proposal for a Community Directive[24] on the duties of

[18] ibid paras 5.137 – 138.

[19] Above n 6. See in particular its Part I. The overall reform proposals are contained in the Final Report of the Co-ordinating Group on Audit and Accounting Issues (URN 03/567) January 2003, but since many of these reform are to be implemented by standard setters, gathered together under the auspices of the Financial Reporting Council, the 2004 Act is as much concerned with conferring powers on the relevant bodies as creating regulatory structures or making substantive rules. The precise role for legislation is discussed in DTI *Review of the Regulatory Regime for the Accountancy Profession* URN 03/589 January 2003.

[20] See now DTI *Company Law Reform* Cm 6456 (March 2005).

[21] Communication from the Commission *The Statutory Audit in the European Union: the Way Forward* [1998] OJ C143/12.

[22] ibid para 3.1.

[23] Commission Recommendation on the Statutory Auditors' Independence in the EU: A Set of Fundamental Principles [2002] OJ L191/22.

[24] Proposal for a Directive on statutory audit of annual accounts and consolidated accounts, COM(2004) 177 final (16 March 2004). Recital 15 of the Commission Recommendation had suggested that the Commission would not review the operation of the, admittedly narrower, Recommendation until three years after its adoption.

auditors, their independence and ethical standards, external quality assurance, and public oversight of the audit. Thus, even if the British Government had not acted of its own motion, the rules on the independence and supervision of auditors would be about to change in any event as a result of Community legislation.[25] Moreover, in a further proposed Directive of October 2004, to amend the existing Fourth and Seventh Directives, the Commission aimed to deal, inter alia, with a matter thought to be at the heart of Enron, namely, off-balance sheet and related-party transactions.[26]

A somewhat similar but less dramatic story can be told in relation to the additional items placed on the agenda of the High Level Group as a result of Enron.[27] The result of these additions was to expand the Community's interest in corporate governance issues. However, since the group in general took a sceptical view of the benefits to be gained from giving a strong role to the Community in the area of corporate governance,[28] some of these particular additional corporate governance items fell subject to the same approach. Thus, in relation to both non-executive/supervisory board directors and management remuneration, the group recommended Community action only in the form of non-binding Commission Recommendations.[29] However, in relation to management responsibility for financial statements, the group accepted[30] that this was an area where the Community already had legislative standing through the Fourth and Seventh Directives on accounts, and so this matter, too, is dealt with in the proposed Directive

[25] In consequence, the UK Government takes a reasonably relaxed view of the Commission's proposals, except in the few areas where they both depart from the recent domestic reforms and cut across some issue which the Government regards as a matter of principle. An example is the proposal's requirement for an audit committee and its specification of the duties of the committee, matters which are dealt with in the UK on a 'comply-or-explain' basis under the Combined Code. See DTI *Proposal by the European Commission for a Directive on the Statutory Audit of Annual and Consolidated Accounts: Consultation Document* (September 2004).

[26] Proposal for a Directive amending Council Directives 78/660/EEC and 83/349/EEC concerning the annual accounts of certain types of companies and consolidated accounts (text available on <http://europa.eu.int/eur-lex/lex/LexUriServ/site/en/com/2004/com2004_0725 en01.pdf> (25 May 2005). For the British Government's response to this proposal see DTI *European Company Law and Corporate Governance Action Plan* March 2005 (URN 05/544).

[27] See text attached to notes 8 – 11 above.

[28] In particular, it rejected the notion of a Community Corporate Governance Code: High Level Group (n 9) 72.

[29] See the Final Report of the Group (n 9) 61, 67. The Recommendations have now eventuated: Commission Recommendation of 15 February 2005 on the role of non-executive or supervisory directors of listed companies and on committees of the (supervisory) board [2005] OJ L52/51; Commission Recommendation of 14 December 2004 on fostering an appropriate regime for the remuneration of directors of listed companies [2004] OJ L385/55.

[30] High Level Group (n 9) 68.

to amend those Directives.[31] The tension between pure corporate governance matters, where previously the Community has not legislated and where the group was unwilling to recommend general legislative powers, and matters of accounts and audit, where the Community has exercised legislative powers since the late 1970s, is neatly illustrated by the Commission's provisions on companies' audit committees. The group recommended that these be dealt with as part of the Commission's non-binding recommendation on non-executive directors,[32] and indeed such a provision appears in the Commission's Recommendation.[33] However, audit committees and their functions are proposed to be mandated by the Directive on the statutory audit, and this is, as we have seen, one of few provisions of that proposal to which the British Government has voiced serious objection.[34]

b. Acceleration and Re-characterisation

A second impact of Enron, falling short of putting items on the European legislative agenda which were not previously there, was the giving of an extra impetus to items already proposed. Thus, the Commission made use of its Note for the Ecofin Council[35] to stress the importance in the new post-Enron context of the adoption of its already proposed Regulation requiring the use of International Accounting Standards,[36] of its proposed Recommendation on auditor independence,[37] and of the proposed Directive on Market Abuse.[38] From here it is only a short step to a third 'effect' of Enron on European reform, which is the presentation of items recently enacted as presciently aimed at solving a problem whose significance was subsequently underlined by Enron. Thus, the reforms made to the British Companies Act in the middle of 2002,[39] to require greater disclosure of the policy behind

[31] Above n 26.

[32] High Level Group (n 9) 71.

[33] European Commission (n 23) section II.

[34] DTI (n 25). The British Government states in its Consultation Document that 'it is neither appropriate nor desirable for the proposed Directive to deal with audit committees and related corporate governance matters' (at para 12.9).

[35] European Commission (n 8).

[36] Ultimately adopted as Regulation (EC) no 1606/2002 of the European Parliament and of the Council of 19 July 2002 on the application of international accounting standards [2002] OJ L243/1.

[37] European Commission (n 23).

[38] Later adopted as Directive 2003/6/EC on insider dealing and market manipulation [2003] OJ L96/16.

[39] By SI 2002 no 1986, introducing new ss 234B and C and new sch 7A into the Companies Act 1985.

directors' remuneration arrangements and a shareholder advisory vote on the directors' remuneration report, can be seen as part of a response to the perverse incentives generated by directors' share option schemes, one of the central conflicts of interest identified in Enron. In fact, however, these reforms were driven by long-running domestic concerns about 'fat cat' pay, but their appropriateness as part of the solution to the post-Enron issues cannot be denied.

The rest of this paper is devoted to trying to make some assessment of the significance of the reforms whose implementation has been aided, in one or another of the ways identified above, by Enron. As far as core company law is concerned, the three main conflicts of interest that were identified as contributing to the scandals which occurred were those involving the executive directors/management of the company, its non-executive directors, and its auditors. We will look at each in turn, beginning with the executive directors, whose relevant conflict of interest was perceived largely to be one arising out of the process by which their remuneration was set.

II. Directors' Remuneration

In my view, the path to wisdom in relation to remuneration begins with acceptance of the proposition that allowing executive directors to play a substantial role in the setting of their own remuneration puts them in a very unusual and privileged position and generates a very high-powered conflict of interest situation. Money constitutes a very important part – though of course not the whole – of what people expect to get out of work; and a large income stream and periodic large capital gains generated by share option schemes or in other ways give those in receipt of them a freedom of action and a level of security which is denied to those who do not have access to them. So, to allow any group who receive remuneration in exchange for work to decide on what that remuneration should be is likely to produce high levels of opportunism, or worse, on the part of the remuneration setters – unless of course, as may be the case in a partnership or small company, the employers and the workers are largely the same people, so that no real transfer of resources is involved and the only substantial issue is one of creditor protection.

So much was clear to the company law judges of the Victorian era, who refused to give the board sole authority to decide remuneration issues by application of the general principle that the company was entitled to the unbiased advice of all its directors.[40] If that was not available, because one or more of them was involved in the transaction, any resulting contract would be voidable and sums paid to the directors would be recoverable by the company, unless the contract

[40] *Imperial Mercantile Credit Association v Coleman* (1871) LR6 Ch App 558, *per* Hatherley LC.

had been approved by the company, meaning in this context, not approval by the non-conflicted members of the board, but the shareholders in general meeting. In this way the shareholders were given a veto right over directors' remuneration.

Even today, one still finds that rule in the model set of articles with regard to the setting of directors' fees,[41] but it did not survive very long in relation to the setting of directors' remuneration as executives. By use of the semi-fiction that the articles constitute an agreement between the shareholders for the time being and the company, it became doctrinally possible to shift decision-making on this issue back to the conflicted board of directors, by appropriate provisions in the articles. The articles constituted, it was argued, the expression of the shareholders' consent to the decision on remuneration being taken by conflicted agents, and the courts accepted the argument.[42] That is the position one finds today in all large companies.[43]

No doubt there were some good practical reasons, in terms of speed of decision-making, for giving this task to the board; otherwise, the hiring process for executive talent would be subject to an increased level of uncertainty. However, we should not be surprised at the potential for manipulation of payments systems which is created by such an arrangement whereby directors can have a substantial influence over their own remuneration. That remark applies as much to the design of so-called performance-related remuneration schemes as much as it does to the setting of basic remuneration – in fact, perhaps it applies even more strongly to performance-related pay whose structure is inevitably more complex than basic salary and which provides correspondingly greater opportunities for distortion, notably in the setting of the performance criteria by which the payments are assessed.[44]

One question which might thus be asked is this: How far have the 2002 amendments to the Companies Act moved us back towards acceptance of the Victorian position that remuneration decisions should involve the shareholders in a meaningful way?

[41] Thus Article 82 of Table A: 'The directors shall be entitled to such remuneration as the company may by ordinary resolution determine…'

[42] *Costa Rica Railway Co Ltd v Forward* [1901] 1 Ch 746, CA; LCB Gower and PL Davies *Principles of Modern Company Law* (7th ed Sweet & Maxwell London 2003) 394-395. The development was a general one about conflicted transactions between a company and its directors and was not confined to remuneration decisions. The underlying equitable law rule and its stringent remedies revive if remuneration is awarded without shareholder sanction and otherwise than in accordance with the provisions of the articles: *Guinness plc v Saunders* [1990] 2 AC 663, HL.

[43] As reflected in Articles 84 and 85 of Table A. Article 94 prohibits the interested director from voting, but companies sometimes disapply even that provision and, in any event, the voting restriction does nothing to prevent 'mutual back-scratching'.

[44] For an overarching critique see L Bebchuk and J Fried *Pay without Performance*. (Harvard University Press Cambridge 2004).

1. Weak Shareholder Involvement

It is suggested that there is a strong and a weak way of involving shareholders in decisions over directors' remuneration. The weak way is simply to require the company to disclose to the shareholders information about remuneration decisions taken by the board and to leave the shareholders to react adversely, if they wish to do so. Formally, the remuneration decision remains with the board, but it is capable of being overturned by subsequent shareholder action. To have any chance of success, such a strategy requires a sophisticated set of rules about disclosure of directors' remuneration to the shareholders and a legal regime which makes it easy for shareholders to exercise their governance rights in the light of the disclosures. Of course, it is arguable that social factors alone, such as shareholder outrage (as it has been termed)[45] at excessive remuneration decisions, will be effective whether or not shareholders are able to respond legally to the disclosures, but effective governance rights for shareholders give that outrage a sharper edge.

This weak form of decision rights for shareholders was a well-established pre-Enron strategy, at least in the common-law world. Thus, the Listing Rules of the London Stock Exchange required highly detailed and, importantly, individualised disclosure of executive directors' remuneration.[46] In the UK there are also rules making it relatively easy for shareholders to convene meetings and to dismiss directors.[47] By contrast, in continental Europe individualised disclosure is still resisted in many states (for example, Germany)[48] and removal of directors before the end of their period of office is often not possible, except for cause.[49] The European Commission's Action Plan[50] proposed individualised disclosure but only via a non-binding Community Recommendation.[51]

[45] ibid 64-66.

[46] Listing Rule 12.43A, implementing the recommendations of the Greenbury Committee. After the amendments to the Companies Act in 2002 the purely disclosure aspects of the Listing Rules may be downgraded.

[47] CA 1985 ss 303 and 368.

[48] Berlin "should reveal top pay"' *Financial Times* (London UK 20 September 2004), reporting a call by the eminent German corporate lawyer, Professor Theodor Baums, for mandatory individual disclosure of directors' remuneration details on an individualised basis.

[49] Again for Germany see Aktiengesetz art 84(3) – removal of member of the management board by the supervisory board only for cause – though cause includes a vote of no-confidence in the shareholders' meeting unless passed 'for manifestly arbitrary reasons'.

[50] Communication from the Commission to the Council and the European Parliament *Modernising Company Law and Enhancing Corporate Governance in the European Union – A Plan to Move Forward* COM(2003) 284 final (21 May 2003).

[51] Commission Recommendation of 14 December 2004 on fostering an appropriate regime for the remuneration of directors of listed companies [2004] OJ L385/55 section III.

2. Strong Shareholder Involvement

The stronger version of the decision-rights strategy gives the shareholders an input into the remuneration decision itself, normally by way of a veto right over a decision previously taken by the board. The veto rights strategy is one the British legislature has deployed in relation to selected remuneration decisions for some time, particularly in end-game situations, in order to control directors' termination payments.[52] In end-game cases the departing director no longer has the prospect of a continuing relationship with the company to restrain his or her financial demands, and the other directors may be tempted to make large pay-offs in order to not to expose divisions in the ranks, not least of all to the shareholders. The risk here is of the so-called 'rewards for failure', a topic which has much occupied the British Government in recent years.[53]

Well established also are the Listing Rules requirements for shareholder approval of share option schemes,[54] a rule originally introduced by way of extension of the principle that share issues by the company should be subject to shareholder approval, in order to prevent dilution of the shareholders' cash flow or voting rights.[55] In other words, the rationale for this rule was not based originally in the need to subject directors' remuneration decisions to shareholder approval. Thus, the Listing Rule requirement of shareholder approval does not apply to annual bonus awards, which, together with the basic salary, stock options, or other long-term incentive plans and pension provisions form the fourth element in the make-up of the typical remuneration package of the directors of large companies.

Thus, particular elements of the remuneration of directors have long been subject to shareholder approval. What is interesting about the amendments made to the Companies Act in 2002 is that they cautiously extend shareholder voting to the whole of the remuneration package, at least in the case of 'quoted' compa-

[52] CA 1985 ss 312-316 and 319. None of these sections, however, effectively deals with contractual entitlements to termination payments (of the type exemplified in *Taupo Totara Timber Co v Rowe* [1978] AC 537, PC, where the director's service contract provided that he could resign within twelve months of a takeover and receive a lump-sum payment of five times his annual salary.) Nor does the Combined Code deal explicitly with them.

[53] DTI *Rewards for Failure' Directors' Remuneration – Contracts, Performance and Severance* June 2003. It seems likely, however, that this initiative will not lead to further legislation but rather, at least for the time being, to reliance on self-regulation, notably in the shape of the Joint Statement by the Association of British Insurers and the National Association of Pension Funds, 'Best Practice on Executive Contracts and Severance' December 2004. See also Ministerial Statement, Trade and Industry *Hansard* 25 January 2005 (Commons).

[54] Listing Rule 13.13. The obligation now extends to approval of most long-term incentive schemes as well.

[55] The current debate over the expensing of share options for reporting purposes continues the dilution discussion in a new form.

nies.[56] At the same time the quality of the information disclosure to shareholders has been improved. No longer is it necessary just to reveal information about what individuals receive. The board's policy on the remuneration front must be explained,[57] ie the board must attempt to provide a justification of the remuneration position rather than just simply reveal the facts and leave it to the shareholders to ask probing questions. In particular, the board must reveal its policy on whether performance conditions are used for share option schemes and other long-term incentive plans (*ltips*); on its choice of performance conditions, if such were used; and how those conditions were applied in practice.[58] It is clear that one of the British Government's main reasons for moving to a statutory requirement for a remuneration report was that, under the Listing Rules, where the matter was previously regulated, there was insufficient disclosure of the board's remuneration policies, which one may take as a coded reference to inadequate justification for that remuneration.[59]

The vote on the remuneration report, however, is only advisory. No director's contractual entitlement to remuneration is affected by an adverse vote.[60] The purpose of the advisory vote, one may say, is to make it easier for the shareholders to express an opinion on the information disclosed to them by reducing their collective action problems. The shareholders do not need to convene a meeting or secure the placing of an item on the agenda of a meeting in order to be able to express an opinion on directors' remuneration: they must be given an opportunity to vote at the shareholders' meeting at which the annual accounts are considered. The vote, if you like, can help to crystallise the investors' dissatisfaction and provide a symbol of that dissatisfaction which it is difficult for the board simply to ignore.

What can we expect from such advisory votes? It is not likely that shareholders will be interested in lowering the levels of directors' remuneration just for the sake of it, so that those who look at this issue from the point of view of distributive fairness are likely to be disappointed. However, shareholders are likely to be interested in making stronger links between directors' remuneration and the performance of the company. Certainly where large sums of money are at issue and where the pay/performance link appears to be negative, one can expect

[56] A quoted company is one incorporated under the Companies Acts whose equity share capital is officially listed in any EEA state or on the NYSE or Nasdaq: s 262(1).

[57] Sch 7A, para 3.

[58] None of these requirements applies, however, to annual bonus awards.

[59] DTI *Directors' Remuneration: A Consultative Document* December 2001 (URN 01/1400) para.2.12 pointed to inadequate disclosure of policy under the Listing Rules (as opposed to remuneration packages where there was 'an acceptable level of transparency') as a major reason for moving the rules on disclosure into the Companies Act.

[60] s 241A(8) – unless, of course, the director and the company contract for this to be the case.

adverse shareholder reaction to be expressed through the advisory vote. This seems to be the British experience to date, notably in the celebrated cases of GSK (the only case where a remuneration vote was lost) and Sainsbury (where the board withdrew a large section of its report in the face of shareholder opposition).

Research carried out for the DTI by Deloittes supports this analysis.[61] This found that after the introduction of the regulations a number of specific changes occurred in companies' remuneration practices which strengthened the pay/performance link. These were: the 'almost complete' reduction in directors' notice periods to one year; the removal in new plans of automatic vesting of share options (irrespective of performance conditions being met) upon a change of control; the removal from new plans of provisions for re-testing performance conditions if it becomes clear that the original conditions are unlikely to be met; and the introduction of graded performance conditions so that the full award is dependent upon more stringent performance conditions being met. Overall, there was much greater ex ante consultation by companies with major shareholders and a greater willingness to alter remuneration policies. However, the report also identified areas where further progress could be made in linking pay with performance and suggested ways of developing the regulations or industry guidance so as to promote this outcome. These included disclosure, at least on an historical basis, of the performance conditions for annual bonuses and greater clarity on what the regulations required by way of the disclosure of the company's policy on performance conditions in general.

Are these significant achievements in public policy terms? There are two reasons for thinking that they are. First, they help restore the link between work and pay. Pay can be a motivator of effort, but only if pay is a reward for work and not something that is received whether work is done or not. Second, insofar as the growth of executive pay in relation to the rewards of other sections of the community results from sudden, abnormal leaps in pay levels in particular cases which then become part of the norm, shareholder advisory votes may in fact do something to slow the rate of growth of executive pay – though there is no firm data to this effect currently available. Overall, large actual remuneration rewards in the fact of poor corporate performance are likely to be more difficult to push through under the new regime, whether those payments occur on severance or not. Companies are likely to become more sensitive to the question of whether they are crossing this particular line and to consult in advance with their major shareholders when they think they may be.

This still leaves the question of whether we should go back to the nineteenth century and move from an advisory vote to a veto vote for the shareholders. Should the director's contractual entitlement to remuneration be dependent upon shareholder approval? At the hiring stage, the costs to the company and therefore to the

[61] Deloitte *Report on the Impact of the Directors' Remuneration Report Regulations* November 2004. The research was confined to the FTSE 350 companies.

shareholders are likely to be high, because there may be competition for the best executive talent on a global scale, and a country which insists on shareholder approval will therefore put its companies at a competitive disadvantage in the hiring process. Boards should thus be left free to hire in line with their remuneration policy, subject to subsequent reporting to the shareholders and a shareholders' advisory vote. It is less clear, however, that companies need such flexibility in relation to subsequent remuneration decisions. One could envisage a rule in which subsequent remuneration changes would come into force as soon as decided on by the board, but they would be subject to a condition of subsequent of shareholder approval. If that approval were not forthcoming, remuneration would revert to the previous level (or some other higher level agreed by the shareholders) but none of the increase actually paid would be repayable. This would sharpen the incentive on boards to formulate remuneration decisions in such a way as to win approval and promote the process of engagement with institutional shareholders in this area, which seems to be the best available, if not perfect, mechanism for preventing conflicts of interest over remuneration decisions becoming uncontrollable, which in the recent past they have often appeared to be.

III. Auditor Independence

Although the underlying problem in Enron can be argued to have been the perverse incentives generated by the management's remuneration package, more attention focussed, both in the United States and in Europe, on the failure of Enron's auditors to reveal that the company's accounts did not reflect the economic reality of the situation in which the company found itself. In the United Kingdom a substantial reform effort was devoted to this topic, via the Co-ordinating Group on Audit and Accounting Issues, established jointly by the DTI and the Treasury, which looked generally at the regulation of auditors and auditing, whilst the Financial Reporting Council appointed a group chaired by Sir Robert Smith to report on the role of audit committees of the board.[62] The Companies (Audit, Investigation and Community Enterprise) Act 2004 put in place the legal changes necessary to effect the reforms recommended in the Final Report of the Co-ordinating Group,[63] whilst the Smith Report's recommendations were implemented via a revised version of the Combined Code on Corporate Governance produced in July 2003.[64] At the Community level the Commission produced in March 2004 a proposal[65] for a Directive to replace and considerably

[62] Financial Reporting Council *Audit Committees: Combined Code Guidance. A report and proposed guidance by an FRC-appointed group chaired by Sir Robert Smith* January 2003.

[63] URN 03/567 (29 January 2003).

[64] See annex 2 in this volume.

[65] COM(2004) 177 final (16 March 2004).

expand the existing Eighth Directive, which covered much of the same ground as the British initiatives. It is not proposed to analyse those aspects of the reform proposals which relate to the regulation in general of the accounting and auditing professions, but instead to concentrate on their approach to the specific issue of auditors' conflicts of interest. Nor is it proposed, for reasons of space, to consider auditors' liability for negligent audits. Although it is strongly arguable that such liability potentially constrains the willingness of auditors to give in to the temptation to conduct lax audits, extension of auditors' liability for negligence was part of neither the Co-ordinating Group's Report nor that of Mr Smith. On the contrary, under pressure from the accounting profession, the debate over liability has focussed subsequently on the relaxation of the constraints which currently limit the freedom of auditors to agree with the audit client company restrictions on the auditor's liability for negligence.[66]

1. The Nature of Auditors' Conflicts of Interest

The issue of the independence of auditors is hardly new. A threat to auditor independence is inherent in the fact that the auditor is paid the audit fee by the client whose financial statements the auditor is employed to verify. Although the audit is mandatory (for all but small companies), it is not mandatory for the client to engage any particular auditor and so it is potentially possible for audit firms to compete for engagements on the basis of their laxity in scrutinising the accounts. This risk is clearly accentuated where, as in Enron, the company is in a position to offer to the auditor additional non-audit work, the revenues of which for the accounting firm may be considerably greater than that provided by the audit itself.

Up until Enron, it was often argued that a non-legal constraint in the form of reputational considerations was extremely powerful in constraining auditors from giving way to temptation and that, accordingly, legal constraints played an essentially supplementary role. The argument here was that the analysis of competition on the basis of laxity misunderstood the incentives to which auditors are subject, because it was essentially a single-period analysis. Let us suppose that an audit firm obtains an engagement on the basis that it has indicated to the management of the company that it will not scrutinise the make-up of the accounts rigorously, thus permitting the management to present the financial position of the company in a more favourable way than the facts warrant. Let us assume also, as is realistic, that sooner or later, the truth of the company's financial position emerges as does the auditors' role in the earlier misstatements. At this point the audit firm suffers a reputational loss. This will cause problems for the firm above all in

[66] Currently prohibited by the Companies Act 1985 s 310. For the latest Government thinking on reform of s 310 see White Paper (n 20) para 3.5.

relation to managements who have no desire to mislead others about the true state of the company's finances and who will therefore not want to use audit firms whom shareholders, the investing public, or creditors do not fully trust. However, it will also reduce the firm's attractiveness to managements who do wish to mislead, because for such managements an essential ingredient of their strategy is that the auditors should be regarded as trustworthy by others. In short, reputational loss for an audit firm destroys its business model across the board.[67] Therefore, for an audit firm selling one's reputation to management would seem to be viable only as an end-game strategy and, even then, presumably only where the firm thinks it can make more money by ruining its reputation than by retaining it and selling the goodwill of the business to other participants in the market for the supply of audit services. Of course, in auditing, as in any other profession, there will be some firms or, more likely, individuals who, for one reason or another, prefer short-term gain to maximising their income stream over a longer period of time, and for them professional and legal regulation are necessary controls, but the thrust of the above argument is that conniving with management is not a systemic risk of the auditing process.

Enron cast considerable doubt on this comforting argument. As Professor Coffee has argued,[68] the equilibrium posited by the above argument seems to have been threatened by changes both on the supply and the demand side in the 1990s. On the one hand, the possible gains to auditors from conduct falling below professional standards increased as a result of the explosion in the value of non-audit work which accounting firms did for their clients; on the other, the reputational costs of slackness appeared in the 1990s to go down. The pursuit by audit firms of non-audit work substantially increased the potential benefits to be obtained from conniving with management over the preparation of the company's financial statements. In the United States the big accounting firms moved the proportion of their total income earned from consulting from 12% to 50% over the last quarter of the twentieth century.[69] Of course, not all this consulting income was derived from audit clients, but there is no doubt that being the company's auditor places the firm in an ideal position to sell non-audit services to the audit client, and some firms offered cash bonuses to their staff to sell non-audit services to audit clients. In particular, information technology, taxation, and

[67] The collapse of Andersons as a global practice in the wake of the conviction of some of its Texas partners for criminal activities associated with the Enron scandal is a dramatic illustration of the reputational risks that firms run.

[68] JC Coffee 'Gatekeeper Failure and Reform: The Challenge of Fashioning Relevant Reforms' Columbia Law School Center for Law and Economic Studies Working Paper no 237 (September 2003). Cf also the contribution of JC Coffee in this volume.

[69] W Ebke 'Corporate Governance and Auditor Independence' in G Ferrarini and others (eds) *Reforming Company and Takeover Law in Europe* (OUP Oxford 2004) 522-523. By 2000 audit fees constituted less than one-third of the income of the major accounting firms.

legal services all proved major areas of expansion.[70] In the UK recent figures show that the Big Four earned from their audit clients between one-and-a-half and two-and-a-half times as much fee income from the supply of non-audit services as from audit services.[71]

These developments by themselves might have been enough to increase significantly the proportion of firms – or, more likely, individuals within firms – choosing short-term gain over the preservation of reputational capital. However, there is evidence that in the 1990s the harm done to reputation through lax auditing fell because, in an exuberant market, investors and creditors attached much less value to the numbers appearing in the company's accounts and therefore to the certification of those numbers by the auditors.[72] Thus, by the beginning of the new millennium, there was much less reason to be confident that the incentive structure for accounting firms would ensure the previous level of adherence to professional standards. However, it should be noted that the demand-side aspect of this analysis probably has corrected itself. It is difficult to believe that the appetite for paying large sums of money for the securities of companies whose accounts reveal that they have not yet made any profits and are unlikely to do so for some years has survived the collapse of the dot.com bubble. Perhaps for this reason, the focus of reform has been on the supply-side, ie on regulation of the auditors' conflicts of interest rather than the gullibility of investors.

2. Legal Strategies

How radical have the reforms, implemented or likely to be implemented, turned out to be? In particular, have they broken new ground in the deployment of legal strategies for the control of the auditors' conflicts of interest, or is it the case, as with directors' remuneration, that the reform has remained within the established parameters? The most obvious radical strategy to deal with the conflict identified above would be to prohibit auditors from providing non-audit services to audit clients, contemporaneously with the audit services and within a certain period before or after supplying audit services. This strategy is open to the criticism that many non-audit services can be provided more cheaply by the auditors than anyone else because of the understanding of the business obtained through the audit. Thus, prohibiting the supply of non-audit services by the auditor will increase the costs of those services to companies, and so the question becomes whether those additional costs are outweighed by the reduction of the costs arising out of the

[70] ibid.

[71] OFT *An assessment of the implications for competition of a cap on auditors' liability* July 2004 (OFT 741) figure 5. Overall, the Big Four earned from the FTSE 100 companies some £234m in audit fees and £454m in non-audit fees in 2003 (ibid fig 4).

[72] Coffee (n 68) 36 ff.

conflict created by the supply of the non-audit services. Since no ultimately convincing data seems to be available on that issue, it is perhaps not surprising that legislatures have refrained from implementing this strategy, though the Commission proposes to study whether such a rule should be introduced.[73]

Failing a complete prohibition, a partial prohibition could be considered. This is the approach of the Sarbanes-Oxley legislation, which prohibits to auditors the provision of eight types of non-audit service.[74] European law-making in this area has always preferred principles to rules and so the Commission's Recommendation of 2002 on auditor independence[75] proposed as a general principle that auditors providing non-audit services should neither make any decision nor take part in any decision-making on behalf of the client or its management while providing a non-audit service.[76] This approach was presumably intended to leave auditors free to provide a rather wide range of non-audit services, but the recasting of the principle in Article 23 of the draft Directive[77] casts some doubt on that interpretation. Article 23, having reiterated the point of management decisions, goes on to require member states to ensure that the auditor shall not have a business relationship with the client, 'including the provision of additional services' which 'might compromise' the auditor's independence. On a strong interpretation of this Article, the provision of all but insignificant non-audit services will have to be prohibited since they 'might' compromise independence. It seems unlikely that the draft Directive is intended to have this effect.[78] If it does not, then the principles-based approach which lay behind the Commission's Recommendation and which was endorsed by the Co-ordinating Group will continue to apply.[79]

[73] DTI *Company Law Reform* Cm 6456 (March 2005) para 6.3.

[74] Plus any other service determined by the Public Company Accounting Oversight Board to be impermissible: s 10A of the Securities Exchange Act 1934, as amended.

[75] [2002] OJ L191/22.

[76] ibid art 7.

[77] Proposal for a Directive on statutory audit of annual accounts and consolidated accounts, COM(2004) 177 final (16 March 2004).

[78] See, for example, article 39(2)(d) requiring the audit committee of public interest entities to review and monitor 'in particular the provision of additional services to the audited entity'. This provision would seem to be otiose if the strong interpretation of Article 23 is correct.

[79] Above n 63 at paras 1.31-1.48. The group considered that giving effect to the provisions of the Recommendation in the UK would represent 'a significant tightening of existing requirements on the provision of non-audit services' (para 1.38), especially in the areas of internal audit, actuarial services, litigation support services, taxation services, and the design and supply of IT systems – a list not dissimilar to that found in the Securities Exchange Act 1934, but appearing not as prohibited but as regulated activities. For the working out of this recommendation see Auditing Practices Board, Ethical Standard 5, 2004.

a. Disclosure of Information

Beyond that, the legal strategies deployed to regulate auditors' conflicts of interest arising out of the provision of non-audit services become the familiar ones of disclosure of information; removing the appointment/removal decision vis-à-vis the auditor from the management of the company; and the specification of bright-line rules to deal with limited situations regarded as ones of high risk. Disclosure is tackled both from the perspective of the company and from the perspective of the auditor. The 2004 Act[80] replaced the existing section 390B of the Companies Act 1985, which already empowered the making of regulations for the annual disclosure of the aggregate amounts paid by companies to the auditors for non-audit services, with a new section 390B which places the disclosure on a disaggregated basis, according to the nature of the service provided. Article 38 of the draft Directive requires firms which carry out audits of public interest entities[81] to produce an annual transparency report, which has to list, among other things, 'financial information showing the importance of the audit firm such as the total turnover divided into fees from the statutory audit … and fees charged for other assurance services, tax advisory services and other non-audit services.' This is a somewhat awkwardly worded provision. Presumably it is not the importance *of* the audit firm which has to be shown but the importance *to* the audit firm of different classes of income. However that may be, the Co-ordinating Group in the UK[82] had recommended a similar principle, albeit one to be implemented on a voluntary basis, at least initially.

b. Decision Rights

The principle of taking decisions over the appointment and removal of auditors and fixing their remuneration away from management and vesting it in the shareholders is already well established in the Companies Act 1985.[83] It is doubtful whether these rules do much to combat the conflict of interest under consideration here. For the reasons given above, it is unlikely that those conflicts would drive management to seek the appointment of auditors who had a reputation for complaisance. The mere fact that the formal appointment is made by the shareholders is unlikely to constitute a significant control, for to outward appearances there

[80] s 7. The DTI consulted on regulations to be made under the new s 390B of the Companies Act 1985 in *Consultation on Disclosure of Auditor Remuneration* November 2004.

[81] This will include all companies with securities traded on a regulated market, banks and other financial institutions, and insurance companies: draft Directive art 2(11).

[82] Above n 63.

[83] ss 385, 391 and 390A – there are modifications to deal with private companies which have dispensed with the laying of accounts before the general meeting.

will be no basis for the shareholders to question the board's nomination. Further, the 'bribe' of substantial remuneration for non-audit services does not depend in any way upon a threat by the management to remove the auditors or to pay them large sums by way of audit fee. In fact, the attraction to dissembling management of the non-audit route to influence over the auditor lies precisely in the fact that this strategy does not require management to take any formal action which might need to be explained to the shareholders. Thus, if after appointment a 'corrupt' relationship develops between management and auditor, this will not be readily visible to the shareholders – indeed, it is important to both management and auditor that it should not be – so that it will not influence shareholders' decisions on removal or re-appointment, at least until it is too late to mater.[84]

Nevertheless, Article 35 of the draft Directive mandates what is probably the practice in most member states of shareholder appointment, but Article 36 deals with removal by stating that auditors 'may only be dismissed where there are proper grounds, divergence on accounting treatments or audit procedures shall not be a proper ground for dismissal.' This is probably a sensible rule – though again not much directed at the conflict arising out of the provision of non-audit work – if the removal decision lies in the hands of the management. If, however, as under the British Act, removal as well as appointment lie in the hands of the shareholders, it seems a positively counter-productive rule. Shareholders would no longer be able to remove the auditor on suspicion that there is something inappropriate in the auditor's relationship with the management, but would seem to have to be able to prove their suspicion.[85]

Overall, increasing the shareholders' decision rights in relation to the appointment or removal of auditors does not seem a strategy well directed at addressing the conflicts of interest arising out of the provision of non-audit work to the auditors. What is needed is a closer continuing scrutiny by a body independent of management of the development of the auditor/management relationship after the shareholders have exercised their rights of appointment, a task which the shareholders themselves, who meet only episodically, are not well placed to undertake. Thus, the main thrust of the reforms within the company to tackle auditor/management conflicts of interest has been via a further strength-

[84] Moreover, in the absence of a good reason to change, it is entirely rational for the shareholders to stay with the existing auditors. It is well established that the first audit conducted by new auditors is likely to be unchallenging because the auditor is still learning the business. See further below on auditor rotation.

[85] In relation to auditors who do resist management's blandishments, a useful reform would be a requirement on auditors who are ceasing to hold office (whether by resignation or by not seeking re-election) to report in all cases to the shareholders on the circumstances connected with this event, ie a strengthening of the current section 394 of the CA 1985 which requires such a statement only where the auditor 'considers' that circumstances exist which ought to be brought to the shareholders' attention. See Audit Quality Forum *Auditor Resignation Statements* February 2005. This proposal also goes beyond Art. 36(2) of the Draft Directive.

ening of the role of the audit committee of the board of listed companies, as recommended by the Smith Committee,[86] endorsed by the Co-ordinating Group,[87] given effect to in the UK by the revised Combined Code in July 2003,[88] and proposed at the EU level for public interest entities by Article 39 of the draft Directive. Focussing monitoring of the management/auditor relationship in a small and expert board committee, meeting relatively frequently, stands a much better chance of success than expecting the large and possibly inexpert body of shareholders, meeting only infrequently, to play an important role of this type. The Combined Code spells out the audit committee's monitoring role in considerable detail.[89] That role is by no means confined to the auditor/management relationship, but in that crucial area it requires the committee to monitor the auditor's independence, objectivity, and effectiveness and to develop and implement a policy on the provision of non-audit services to the company by the auditor. Since the committee is also to 'monitor the integrity of the financial statements of the company' and to review 'significant financial reporting judgements' contained in the company's financial statements, the auditors will also have to deal with the audit committee, and not just the management, on all important matters relating to the compilation of the company's annual accounts.

As with all schemes for using non-executive directors to control the self-interest of the executives, one must wonder whether they will be up to the task. The Combined Code says that the audit committee (of three persons or two in smaller listed companies) should consist entirely of independent non-executive directors of whom at least one must have 'recent and relevant financial experience' – but, equally, it seems that the other two may not have such experience.[90] The draft Directive is less prescriptive in one sense, not specifying the minimum number of members and requiring only one of them to be an independent NED (who must also have 'competence in accounting and/or auditing'). The Directive is more prescriptive in another, since its rules are mandatory, whilst those of the Combined Code operate on a 'comply-or-explain' basis.[91] However, it is difficult to believe that listed[92] companies will find it easy to explain to their shareholders non-compliance with the audit committee provisions of the Combined Code, and so the matter may not be very important in practice. Nevertheless, if the Com-

[86] Above n 62.

[87] Above n 63 para 1.51 ff.

[88] pp 15-17 and 43-57.

[89] Combined Code, provision C.3.2.

[90] C.3.1, worryingly suggesting that the other two may not have such knowledge.

[91] Listing Rule 12.43A.

[92] Article 39 applies to all companies with securities traded on a regulated market (n 81) and so is potentially much more wide-ranging than the Combined Code which applies only to listed companies. However, in the UK much of the force of this extension has been removed by the decision of AIM to cease to be a regulated market.

bined Code and the proposed Directive take some steps to promote independence (of management) and expertise on the audit committee, the question still remains whether the members of that committee have sufficient incentives to do a good job. The tone of the Smith Report, when describing potential problems between committee and management, was notably adversarial:[93] the committee might have to 'pit its judgement . . . perhaps on technically complex issues' against both senior management and auditors and for that reason its members would need to be 'tough, knowledgeable and independent-minded'. The lack of appropriate incentives to undertake this daunting task is perhaps showing itself in a reported reluctance of people holding top positions in companies to take on the role of chair of the audit committee in other companies, on the one hand,[94] and decisions by companies to raise the pay of non-executive directors in general and audit committee chairs in particular.[95]

c. Bright-line Rules

An alternative strategy for addressing the lack of visibility to the shareholders and the outside world in general of any lack of rigour in the relationship between the auditors and the management is the deployment of bright-line rules which do not require the exercise of discretion on the part of any person. Such rules are simple to apply, but may involve costs arising from the fact that they catch both situations where intervention is required and those where, in fact, it is not, because the rule is not capable of distinguishing between the two situations. As we have seen, uncertainty about the balance of costs and benefits has so far prevented adoption of the simple rule that auditors should not be permitted to provide non-audit services to non-audit clients. Less stringent bright-line rules have proved acceptable, however. Thus, rules have been introduced, or proposed, requiring the rotation of the lead audit personnel after the relationship with the management has lasted for a certain period of time. The thought is that the risk of too 'cosy' a relationship between management and auditors increases with the length of that relationship and that at some point a change in the personnel involved on the audit side should be imposed, without proof that the quality of the relationship has in fact deteriorated.

Article 40(c) of the proposed Directive requires member states to impose either rotation of the 'key' audit partner after five years or of the audit firm after

[93] Smith Report (n 62) pp 22-24.

[94] 'UK chiefs reluctant to take on audit role' *Financial Times* (London UK 31 January 2005).

[95] GSK is reported to pay £30,000 per annum to its NEDs, an extra £20,000 to those NEDs who chair its remuneration and appointment committees, and an extra £30,000 to the chair of the audit committee: *Financial Times* (London UK 5 October 2004).

seven. In the UK the Auditing Practices Board of the Financial Reporting Council has already moved to a five-year rotation of the audit engagement partner (from the previous seven-year rule) under pressure from the Co-ordinating Committee.[96] However, neither in the UK nor in the rest of the EU[97] has mandatory rotation of the audit firm proved a popular rule.[98] The argument against it is that it involves a complete loss of the expertise built up by the existing audit team, leaving the new team to begin from scratch, with the likely consequence that the first audit from the new team will be both more costly and less searching than the previous year's audit.[99] In other words, a continuing relationship between client and auditor generates the risk of a cosy relationship developing but also the strong likelihood that valuable expertise will be acquired by the audit team. This argument convinced the Co-ordinating Group that mandatory rotation of the firm should not be imposed,[100] and the Directive seems unlikely to prompt a re-think.[101]

IV. Non-executive Directors

The third problematic area identified by analysers of the Enron scandal concerned the failure of the non-executive directors to discover what the management was doing – a failure put down in part to their self-interest in having a quiet life and not standing up to management, who were not likely to take their interventions kindly, but also to structural weaknesses in the position of the non-executives on the board which limited what it was feasible to expect them to do. Thus, it was not surprising that, in parallel with the Smith enquiry established by the FRC into the role of the audit committee of the board, the DTI itself established a general

[96] n 63 paras 1.20-1.22. See the Auditing Practices Board, Ethical Standard 3, 2004. For a 'key' audit partner who is not the engagement or independent partner, the standard requires rotation every seven years, a position the proposed Directive would appear to change.

[97] Of the EU fifteen, only Spain and Italy have imposed it. Spain later abandoned the rule and Italy imposes it (on a nine-year rotation) only on a small number of large companies: Co-ordinating Group Report (n 63) 26.

[98] Nor does Sarbanes-Oxley require it: s 10A of the Securities Exchange Act, as amended, imposes a five-year rotation rule for the lead audit partner.

[99] Alternatively, this result might be avoided by the audit team (minus presumably the lead partner) moving to the new audit firm, a consequence which would totally undermine the initial objectives of the rule.

[100] n 63 paras 1.23-1.30.

[101] A further important specific rule to be found in the proposed Directive is the prohibition in article 40(d) that the key audit partner may not take up a 'key' management position in the audit client (where that is a public interest entity) within two years of ceasing to be the audit partner – an extension of s 27 of the CA 1989 which applies only to contemporaneous appointments, but one already recommended by the Co-ordinating Group (para 1.61) and adopted by the professions in respect of listed companies.

investigation by Mr Higgs into the functioning of non-executive directors. Both enquiries reported on the same day[102] and both were carried forward, eventually, into a single set of revisions to the Combined Code.

Despite the fact that the joint reforms are generally referred to as the 'Higgs reforms', it is arguable that those made in relation to the audit committee and discussed above were more significant than the reforms proposed in the role of the non-executive directors elsewhere.[103] If the Smith reforms were more evolutionary than revolutionary, the reforms proposed by Higgs can be regarded as purely incremental in character. They built on the foundations laid by the Cadbury Committee[104] a decade earlier, a report to which Mr Higgs gave the accolade: 'the fundamentals of corporate governance in the UK are sound, thanks to Sir Adrian Cadbury.'[105] Consequently, although there was much to welcome in the Higgs Report, its main recommendations were limited: the proportion of non-executive directors on the board should be raised from one-third (of whom under the old Code only the majority had to be independent) to one-half (all independent); and the desirability of not having the roles of CEO and chair of the board held by the same person was stated in more prescriptive language than previously.

A similar pattern can be seen at the Community level. The Community proposals on audit committees, as we have seen, have been embodied in a draft Directive, whilst the Community developments on non-executive directors have taken the form of a non-binding Recommendation.[106] Of course, the Commission was better placed to proceed with 'hard' law in relation to the audit committee, because audit was already accepted as an area for regulation by Directive (albeit within a narrow compass), whilst member states for many years had fiercely resisted Commission attempts to regulate the board structure of national companies. Nevertheless, it is probably true to say that at both the national and the Community level, the perception was that management and auditors were more to blame for the Enron scandal than the non-executive directors.[107] At any rate, the impact of Enron was not enough to overcome the traditional opposition of the member states to Community regulation of issues of board structure.

[102] D Higgs *Review of the role and effectiveness of non-executive directors* DTI, January 2003. For the Smith Report, see above n 62.

[103] The remuneration committee acquired extra significance as a result of the reforms discussed above, but they resulted from legislation, not the Higgs proposals.

[104] Report of the Committee on the Financial Aspects of Corporate Governance, 1 December 1992 (Cadbury Committee Report).

[105] n 102 p 3.

[106] [2004] OJ L385/55.

[107] Sarbanes-Oxley did not deal with board structure either – traditionally a matter for state law also in the US – but there were some changes in the rules of the NY Stock Exchange.

Despite the limited nature of the reforms proposed by Mr Higgs, the reaction of the management of British companies was initially one of fierce resistance. Higgs proposed no changes in the comply-and-explain system via the Listing Rules nor, in relation to the substantive content of the Code, was it proposed to introduce new elements but simply to strengthen the existing elements; nevertheless, opposition from management circles was especially strong, and not just on the grounds that this was the straw which breaks the camel's back. The main ground for management's opposition, in my view, was the parallel changes which Government had been promoting, independently of Enron, in the role of institutional shareholders as holders of governance rights within companies. Since non-observance of the Code carries sanctions for companies only to the extent that shareholders respond adversely to explanations of non-compliance, a more active shareholder body has the potential to impart to what seem relatively straightforward developments in the Code a qualitatively different character.

However, is the level of shareholder activism, which management so fears, a realistic prospect in the United Kingdom? Despite the potential for greater shareholder activism in portfolio companies which institutional shareholding has created, there is general agreement that the levels of such activism have been, and still are, sub-optimal. Sub-optimal in this context means that less intervention in the affairs of portfolio companies occurs than would be the case if the institutions, individually or collectively, were single-mindedly committed to the maximisation of the value of their portfolios. Both Black and Coffee and Geof Stapledon in his book, *Institutional Shareholders and Corporate Governance*, found levels of intervention to be sub-optimal, despite increasing absolute levels of intervention.[108] Partly, such sub-optimal behaviour is due to competition among the fund managers acting on behalf of institutional shareholders and the consequent temptation for any one manager to free ride on the efforts of others when it comes to forming a coalition to exercise corporate governance rights. The recent Company Law Review identified conflicts of interest as an important additional contributor to sub-optimality, again especially at the fund-management level.[109] Financial conglomerates which provide investment management services to institutions are reluctant to be active shareholders in portfolio companies if this would jeopardise their corporate finance links with the management of those companies.

The Government's interest in changing that situation was revealed most clearly with the appointment of Paul Myners to carry out a review of institutional investment, whose report was received in 2001,[110] ie before Higgs was appointed. This report accused institutional shareholders of failing to discharge their obligations to those on whose behalf they held the shares by failing to exercise

[108] See notes 7and 9 above.

[109] Company Law Review *Completing the Structure* November 2000 paras 5.2-5.12; Company Law Review *Final Report* vol 1 paras 6.19-6.40, July 2001.

[110] P Myners *Institutional Investment in the UK: A Review* (March 2001) 1-26, 147-151.

their voting power at meetings of the company and more generally by failing to exercise their governance rights so as to influence the management of portfolio companies. The Government proposed legislation, partly derived from the US model of the ERISA,[111] to require greater activism. For the time being, however, the institutional shareholders seem to have staved off that threat by adopting a voluntary code which commits them to monitoring the performance of portfolio companies, including compliance with the Combined Code; intervening where necessary, up to and including seeking to change the board; and reporting the results of their activities to their clients.[112] However, that the pressure is still on the institutions is shown by the recent Treasury review of the Myners principles in operation.[113]

The prospect of more active institutional scrutiny of areas where companies are not in compliance with the Combined Code was enough to generate on the part of management of large British companies a spirited opposition to Higgs' proposals when they were first announced. In particular, management feared that institutions would not take seriously companies' explanations of their reasons for not complying with areas of the new Code, so that the Code would become based *de facto* on compliance, rather than comply or explain. However, the Government holds the whip hand: the threat of legislation. Once the Government made it clear it supported the Higgs proposals, management had little choice but to accept them, for fear of the Government deciding to take the Combined Code system out of the Listing Rules and placing it in the Companies Act, just as it had done with the regulation of directors' remuneration.[114] Thus, in the end the Financial Reporting Council, the body responsible for the Combined Code, accepted the Higgs proposals with essentially cosmetic changes, and they came into effect in the second half of 2003.

The recent post-Enron reform of the Combined Code demonstrates two interesting features of the mechanisms which make it an important source of regulation. First, despite its non-legislative status, reform of the Code is driven by the threat of legislation or, more precisely, by the desire on the part of those affected by it to avoid direct legislation for fear, presumably, that legislation would be even less palatable than the Code. Second, the day-to-day sanction behind the Code is provided not simply by the requirement, which is legally sanctioned,[115] to disclose and justify areas of non-compliance, with possible

[111] Employee Retirement Income Security Act 1974 (29 USC 1001 ff).

[112] Institutional Shareholders' Committee *The Responsibilities of Institutional Investors and Agents – Statement of Principles* 2002.

[113] H M Treasury *Myners principles for institutional investment decision-making* December 2004 especially pp 27-29.

[114] See above text attached to n 46.

[115] Listing Rule 12.43A requires the company to state annually the extent of its compliance with the Combined Code and to explain areas of non-compliance, and breach of a Listing Rule cont. ...

reputational costs where the justification is thought to be inadequate. Rather, the ultimate sanction appears to be the fear of adverse investor reaction to disclosure of non-compliance, expressed either through the market for the company's shares or, more likely, through the exercise by shareholders of their governance rights in a way which is adverse to the interests of the incumbent management.

V. Conclusions

'Enron' opened up the path to some important corporate governance reforms in Europe which previously had not been accessible. Legislating in reaction to the latest scandal has its dangers, of course, not least the danger of overreaction, of legislating before a robust and dispassionate analysis has been established of the lessons to be learned from that scandal. On the other hand, in democracies a public scandal makes available for reformers that most precious of legal commodities, legislative time. For corporate law, not otherwise likely to be given a high political ranking, the scandal, by breaking down the stranglehold which interest groups are often able to lay upon the process of reform, may provide an important opportunity to make changes which the prior consensus had prevented (and which it is beyond the competence of the courts to achieve). Neither in the UK nor at the level of the Community can it be said that the temptation of overreaction has been much in evidence. Well before the events in the US unfolded, respected voices were criticising the European and domestic rules on auditors', managers', and non-executive directors' conflicts of interest, and the reforms proposed or enacted in the UK and at the Community level have generally eschewed the options which were likely to do more harm than good. In this respect, the fact that Enron pointed clearly to the dangers of the governance systems of large companies, as then configured, but did not inflict in Europe the scale of direct harms to the investors and employees which were suffered in the US, seems to have provided the correct blend of stimulation without panic which the political process, domestic and European, needed to produce valid results.

attracts the sanctions laid down in FSMA 2000, notably in s 91 which permits the FSA to impose penalties on the issuer and/or its directors for contravention of the Listing Rules.

Ongoing Modernization of Japanese Company Law

MISAO TATSUTA

I. Introduction

In Japan of late, company law has been amended almost every year, and more than once in some years. On each occasion of such an amendment, the drafters have to write new stipulations in the literary style of a century or more ago. This is because the substantial portion of our company law constitutes an integral part of the Commercial Code of 1899.[1] Statutory texts written in a pseudo-classical, non-spoken style have helped prevent people at large from making themselves familiar with company law.

The Legislative Council is in the last stage of drafting a new company law.[2] The cabinet is expected to submit the bill to the Diet in 2005.[3] The bill, unlike revisions thus far, is to enact a statute embracing all types of corporations independent of the Commercial Code. The bill will be written in a colloquial style.

Apart from the modernization in the form described above, modernization in the substance of company law is now in progress, and needless to say this is the more important aspect. The committee within the Legislative Council in charge of drafting the new company law is specifically called the 'modernization committee'. We should take note, however, of two points: (1) statutory amendments

[1] Shōhō (1899 Law no 48). This Code contains provisions relating to the partnership corporation (OHG), limited partnership corporation (KG), and stock corporation (AG). Separate company statutes of importance, among others, are Yūgen kaisha-hō (Limited liability corporation [GmbH] law, 1938 Law no 74) and Kabushiki kaisha no kansa-tō ni kansuru shōhō no tokurei ni kansuru hōritsu (Law concerning special measures in connection with audit of stock corporations, 1974 Law No 22 – hereinafter 'Special Audit Law'). The 1938 statute is in the same pseudo-classical style as the Commercial Code.

[2] In addition to the orthodox process of formulating company laws, ie submission to the Diet by the cabinet of a bill based upon the proposal of the Legislative Council, the business circle, impatient of the time-consuming orthodox process, resorts to a speedier method, ie having some Diet members submit their own proposals.

[3] After approved by the House of Councilors on 29 June 2005, the bill has come to be the Company Law of 2005; cf the postscript.

always aim at modernizing the regulatory rules; and (2) the 2005 Bill is to be composed of the achievements of recent reforms as well as brand-new innovations.

Part II of this paper looks back briefly at the history of Japanese company law so that we may distinguish the 2005 modernization from the rest of the revisions we experienced during the period of over a century. Part III focuses on major topics of the 2005 Bill. These observations will be made in terms of corporate governance.

II. Modernization of Company Law: Major Steps

1. What Is Modernization?

When a rule no longer fits social needs due to changes in technology, ways of life, and so on, the rule has to be modernized; in other words, it must be revised so as to meet the new environment. This feature seems to be common in most legal revisions. Thus, reforms are almost always regarded as, or at least designed for the purpose of, modernizing a social institution.

As long as society changes along the lines of evolutionary process, modernization must connote improvement in quality. When it comes to company law, improvement relates to enhanced achievement of efficiency as well as to better adjustment of interests among relevant groups of people. In order to clarify the exact goals of modernization that the 2005 Bill would imply, we had better examine the respective implications of each of the major reforms in the past.

2. The First Westernization

The Commercial Code of 1899[4] was a part of an overall modernization of Japanese legal systems, which was necessitated in order to get rid of unequal treaties agreed upon with Western powers at the time when Japan ceased its isolation policy. What was most important then was for Japan to be equipped with the same legal institutions as seen in major Western nations. Whatever was different from the counterpart in their home countries was not regarded by Westerners as civilized, and Westerners insisted on their own extraterritoriality, refusing to subject themselves to the jurisdiction of Japan. Thus 'modernization' at that time meant Westernization.

[4] This Code was popularly called the 'new Commercial Code'. The old one, drafted by a German but modeled after the French Code de commerce, was promulgated in 1890; only those provisions relating to business corporations, negotiable instruments, and bankruptcy came into force in 1893.

The Commercial Code provided for stock corporations (AG) and three other types of business corporations, all of which had been hitherto unknown in Japan.[5] The stated capital of a stock corporation was fixed by the corporate charter; thus, each issuance of additional shares needed charter amendment. A stock corporation was managed by one or more directors elected by the general meeting of shareholders. One or more corporate auditors (*kansayaku*), also elected by the shareholders, were in charge of supervising the directors, such as by approving or rejecting the director's self-dealing, but without the power to dismiss the director.

The company law basically copied that of the European continent at that time, especially the German model. The fundamental features continued until after World War II, although company law underwent some revisions to introduce Anglo-American concepts via European laws, eg preferred stock and convertible debentures.

3. GHQ Transformation

The 1950 reform was carried out on instructions of the general headquarters of the occupation forces. It transformed Japanese company law into one of Anglo-American features, with not a few exceptions that resulted from compromise.

A director of a stock corporation ceased to be a manager, and was reduced to being a member of the board consisting of three or more directors. On the other hand, one or more representative directors, appointed by the board from among the directors rather than employee officers, were in charge of managing daily business and implementing the board decisions.

The board of directors oversees their management. It has the power to dismiss representative directors, approve self-dealings and competitive transactions by the directors, propose the next slate to the general meeting, supervise the conduct of all directors, and make decisions on corporate business of importance. Corporate auditors survived, though their power was confined to account auditing.

The general meeting of shareholders ceased to be an omnipotent decision-making body: unless the corporate charter expands its power, it can decide upon only such matters as are assigned to it by the Commercial Code. The board of directors now has power to issue additional shares, as long as the resultant aggregate number of issued shares does not exceed the ceiling authorized by the charter.

In order to cover the abridged power of the general meeting, the 1950 reform created new types of rights for both individual and minority shareholders. For

[5] The three other types were the partnership corporation (OHG), limited partnership corporation (KG), and limited partnership stock corporation (KGaA). The last one had a complicated structure in that it was a mixture of a stock corporation and limited partnership corporation, and only seldom made use of. It was abolished in 1950.

instance, a shareholder may bring a derivative suit to have the directors compensate the corporation for losses incurred by their misconduct.[6] A shareholder may enjoin, including institution of an injunctive action, illegal conduct by the director that will cause irreparable harm to the corporation, or an issuance of additional shares that can give rise to disadvantage to the shareholder. Minority shareholders are entitled to inspect books and records,[7] petition the court to dismiss a director,[8] and so forth. Cumulative voting for electing directors underwent an unhappy fate in Japan.[9] Shareholders' proposal rights did not have a foothold in the Commercial Code until 1981.[10]

4. Reforms During the High-Growth Economy

Plenty of revisions have taken place since the 1950 reform. They were motivated either by demands on the part of the business circle or by the need to cope with scandals. Through these amendments, company law has become tinged with Japan-specific characteristics. Among these, two major reforms of 1974 and 1981 are worthy of mention.

[6] The shareholders' derivative suit, an important tool for corporate governance, was seldom resorted to, partly due to heavy litigation costs. Only after the 1993 revision, which fixed the fee irrespective of the amount of the damages claimed by the suit, have a considerable number of derivative suits been brought against directors and corporate auditors, though far less compared with that in the US.

[7] The 1950 reform granted the inspection right to such shareholders as had at least 10% of the outstanding shares. On the occasion of the structural initiative impediments (SII) talks in the late 1980s, the US representative complained that this right was too restrictive. Later amendments took this complaint into account, and now those shareholders who have 3% or more of the aggregate voting rights may inspect books and records. Shareholders of the same category may petition the court to appoint an inspector where gross maladministration is suspected.

[8] Where the general meeting of shareholders rejects a proposal to dismiss a director responsible for gross maladministration, shareholders with 3% or more voting rights may petition the court to dismiss him. See n 10 below.

[9] According to the 1950 version of the Commercial Code, cumulative voting was mandatory where shareholders having at least a quarter of the aggregate outstanding shares requested it, even if the corporate charter was negative as to this method. The 1974 revision made it possible for the corporate charter to discard this method, and nearly all corporations have such a provision in their charter.

[10] A shareholder of a listed corporation enjoyed a kind of counter-proposal right pursuant to the proxy regulation under the Securities and Exchange Law of 1948 for only a short while after the enactment of the statute. Since rejection by the general meeting was the prerequisite for shareholders to petition the court to dismiss a director (n 8), they had to apply to the court first for permission to convene the general meeting by themselves until the 1981 reform introduced the shareholders' proposal right.

The 1974 reform classified stock corporations into three categories according to their size. This revision was caused by a series of business failures on the part of listed corporations in the mid-1960s. It was found that these corporations had indulged in consecutive window-dressing with regard to their financial statements. Certified public accountants audited these documents pursuant to the Securities and Exchange Law, but only after these documents had been fixed by the annual meeting of shareholders. The 1974 reform mandated ex ante audit by CPAs as far as large corporations are concerned.[11] Except in small corporations, corporate auditors are empowered to audit not only accounting but also management: eg to attend meetings of the board of directors and to enjoin directors' illegal conduct.

Revisions in 1981, among others, mandated a large corporation to appoint at least two corporate auditors, and, in the case of one with 1,000 or more common shareholders, to accept voting by mail. Without regard to corporate size, the power of the board of directors was clearly defined. The statute expressly provided for shareholders to have rights to make proposals[12] and to ask questions at the general meeting, and for more stringent restrictions on corporate expenditure that benefited gangster-like professional shareholders, a practice that had distorted the function of the general meeting. Disclosure requirements were also considerably strengthened by this reform.

Preparatory works for the 1981 reform began right after the consummation of the 1974 revisions. At the outset it was designed to overhaul the entire company law so as to enact a separate statute in modernized style. The goal is just the same as that of the ongoing project for the 2005 Bill. Along this line, draft revisions were publicized one by one for public comment. When they covered such areas as shares of stock, shareholders, directors, corporate auditors, and financial statements, however, many people regarded it as desirable to amend the Commercial Code on the basis of draft revisions already completed then, rather than to wait

[11] Corporate size depends upon the amount of stated capital and that of total liabilities on the balance sheet. Annual sales and the number of employees were rejected for the test on the ground that these figures are too variable to serve as the base for the classification relating to different governance schemes.

[12] The proposal right was endowed to such shareholders as had, individually or as a group, at least 1% of the aggregate outstanding shares or 300 shares for a period of six months or longer. The 1981 reform required listed corporations to bundle shares into units, and provided shares of less than a unit with only limited sorts of rights, mainly the right to dividends. This scheme was designed to eliminate penny stock that had been an easily available weapon for gangster-like professional shareholders. Since a unit of shares worked like one share, and most corporations bundled 1000 shares into one unit, it was necessary to hold 300,000 or more shares in order for shareholders to make use of the proposal right. The 2001 reform replaced the unit share scheme with another one that bundles shares only in connection with voting rights. On the other hand, minority shareholders' rights, including proposal rights, are now granted to such shareholders as have at least a certain percentage or number of voting rights.

for the last draft revision, which, together with other ones, would cover all parts of the company law.[13]

III. Modernization Now

1. The Project and Its Prelude

The first official document regarding the current modernization project was the October 2003 Tentative Draft Revision prepared by a subcommittee of the Legislative Council.[14] Since the project aims at overhauling the whole company law, this document covers a wide range of subjects, including the corporate name and key employees as well as various types of business corporations and foreign companies. On the other hand, it is far from being a comprehensive company bill because the 2005 Bill is due to embrace not only the Modernization Tentative Draft but also the rest of company law provisions reflecting the reforms already made.

The preceding reforms to be integrated in the 2005 Bill mostly took place during the last decade of the last century and within the first couple years of this century.[15] Among the latter reforms, above all, it is worthy to note in the first place that the 2002 revision allows a large corporation to choose from two types of governance structure: (1) the traditional type with the board of directors and board of corporate auditors; and (2) the new type with executive officer(s) and three committees within the board of directors, ie the audit, nominating, and

[13] The 1981 reform was a stopping over, so to speak, and the ongoing project for the 2005 Bill may be a challenge de novo. Some of the subsequent revisions, mostly taking place after the high economic growth was over, were designed to play parts of the entire overhaul project, in addition to meeting the needs of the time: eg formation of a stock corporation (1990); corporate debentures (1993); mergers and consolidations (1997); and restructuring through corporate division and similar means (1999 and 2000).

[14] Hōsei Shingi-kai Kaisha-hō (Gendaika-kankei) Bukai (Subcommittee on corporate law [relating to modernization]), Legislative Council, Kaisha hōsei no gendaika ni kansuru yōkō shian (Tentative Draft Revision on Modernization of Corporate Legislation), 22 October 2003 – hereinafter referred to as 'Modernization Tentative Draft', Shōji Hōmu (Commercial Law Review) no 1678 at 4-35 (2003). This document, together with supplementary comments by the drafters, is available from the website of the Ministry of Justice: <http://www.moj.go.jp> (1 July 2005). The website publication was made for the purpose of inviting public comments. Following legislative developments are summarized in the postscript.

[15] As for those reforms implemented in the 1990s, see n 14. Besides those enumerated there, the statutory ban on the repurchase of shares by the issuer was almost completely lifted through a series of recent amendments. Management now enjoys broad powers to decide the amount and timing of repurchase and reissue.

compensation committees.[16] Because of this prior reform, the Modernization Tentative Draft puts less emphasis on the governance structure of large corporations compared with that of smaller ones. We shall revisit this topic later.

The second point to note among the preceding revisions relates to liabilities of directors. By virtue of the 1950 reform, directors could be released from their liability only on the condition that unanimous consent by the shareholders supports it;[17] otherwise each shareholder's right to bring a derivative action would be reduced to meaninglessness. The increase in the number of such suits after the 1993 revision[18] augmented the case for mitigating directors' liability. The 2001 revision granted this desire to some extent. It is now possible for a company to curtail the damages it claims against its directors up to a statutory minimum if the company resorts to any of these three measures: (1) a super-majority resolution by the general meeting of shareholders to reduce the amount of damages the company is definitely entitled to; (2) a decision by the board of directors to reduce the same if the board is authorized to do so by the charter; or (3) an ex ante agreement with an outside director to limit the corporate claim if the charter permits it.[19] Fundamentally the same scheme applies to executive officers and corporate auditors. The statutory minimum of damages, only beyond which exoneration is permissible, depends upon the function and remuneration of the person to be exonerated.[20]

Third, apart from amendments to the Commercial Code and related statutes administered by the Ministry of Justice (MOJ), we cannot ignore forward measures by means of special statutes applicable to a somehow limited scope of business, mostly within the jurisdiction of the Ministry of Economy, Trade and Industry (METI).[21] METI has drafted and implemented a number of such statutes

[16] A large corporation is one whose stated capital is 500 million yen or more or whose balance sheet shows 20 billion yen or more in liabilities (Special Audit Law art 1-2 para 1). Selection between two types is also available to a constructive large corporation, ie a corporation with stated capital of less than 500 million yen but over 100 million yen and with less than 20 billion yen in balance sheet liabilities, and which voluntarily has its financial statements audited by a CPA.

[17] Commercial Code art 266 para 5. A director may be released from the liability arising from his illegal self-dealing if shareholders having at least two-thirds of voting rights agree upon it (ibid art 266 para 6).

[18] See n 7.

[19] Commercial Code art 266 paras 7-23. All three measures are allowable only where the director's liability arose out of mere light negligence unrelated to specified violations such as illegal distribution, self-dealing, and competition with the company.

[20] A representative director or a representative officer – six times the annual amount of his remuneration; a director or an executive officer – four times the annual amount of his remuneration; an outside director or a corporate auditor – two times the annual amount of his remuneration. The statute provides in detail for how to calculate the amount of remuneration, in particular in the forms of stock option and retirement annuity.

[21] The former name was Ministry of International Trade and Industry (MITI).

stipulating exemptions from the regulation of the Commercial Code, Anti-Monopoly Law, tax laws, and so forth, for the purpose of promoting the business of the addressees. Lately the scope of applicability of METI statutes has broadened to transcend specified industries, and some of the exceptional easings by these statutes have gained general applicability.[22] The Modernization Tentative Draft proposes to abrogate the stated capital requirement for a stock corporation, following suit from one of the recent METI statutes.[23]

2. Types of Business Corporations: Small Businesses

The legislature must have assumed that closely held corporations would take the form of limited liability corporations (GmbH), and that all stock corporations would be of considerable size with a substantial number of shareholders.[24] In reality, however, roughly 99% of stock corporations are closely held and of small size.[25] Business people prefer the phrase 'stock corporation' to that of 'limited liability corporation', probably because they believe that the former sounds more reputable. On the other hand, some limited liability corporations, in particular subsidiaries of big businesses, are large enough in size to compare with a large corporation in the meaning of the Special Audit Law: they can dispense with auditing by a CPA.

[22] For example, exemption from the mandatory investigation by a court-appointed inspector as to contribution-in-kind or the like; dispensation of shareholders' approval to sell whole assets of the company; and repurchase of shares by the issuer beyond the usual limit or through a streamlined procedure. These privileges are available where the project has cleared the review by METI in advance.

[23] See n 45 and the accompanying text.

[24] The Limited Liability Corporation Law, art 8, sets a ceiling on the number of members at 50 as a rule. A member's interest (share) is prohibited from being represented on a negotiable certificate (ibid art 21). Its transfer to a non-member is subject to approval by the general meeting of members (ibid art 19). A company need not have a board of directors; only one director suffices (ibid art 25). The law does not provide for a term of office for a director. A company may appoint a corporate auditor, but it is not required to do so (ibid art 33). The general meeting of members can decide upon any matter unless it is violating the law. These presuppose that ownership is not separate from control and management in the case of a limited liability corporation.

[25] There are well over one million stock corporations in Japan, of which large stock corporations within the meaning of the Special Audit Law (n 1) number approximately 10,000. Only around 4,000 issuers are subject to the disclosure requirement under the Securities and Exchange Law. Corporations listed on a stock exchange, including the JASDAQ market, are still less than this figure. Most unlisted corporations restrict the transfer of shares: the 1966 reform made it possible for a stock corporation to stipulate in its charter that shares may be transferred only when approved by the board of directors (Commercial Code art 204 para 1, proviso clause). A stock corporation with such a charter provision is usually called 'closely held'.

The Modernization Tentative Draft proposes to abolish the type of limited liability corporation by fusing it with that of the closely held stock corporation. A restriction on stock transfers subjects the company to such rules as are alien to other stock corporations.[26] The 2005 Bill will create a new subcategory within the category of the closely held stock corporation. In other words, the shareholders will have a choice between the two governance structures: one having fundamentally the same structure as that of a closely held stock corporation at present, and another with a structure as similar in substance to that of a limited liability corporation.

A stock corporation, even if it is closely held, must be equipped with a board of directors comprising three or more members, and at least one corporate auditor. If the corporate charter specifically provides, however, a closely held stock corporation will be able to appoint only one director who is empowered to manage and represent the company, and to dispense with a board of directors as well as a corporate auditor. The function of corporate auditor in a small stock corporation, at present confined to account auditing, will be extended to cover oversight of management as a whole.

It is difficult, however, to find a reasonable ground for such scheme: ie a corporate auditor with full power in a company having a board of directors on one hand, and no corporate auditor in a company without a board of directors. In the former case the board of directors is in charge of monitoring as well as management, whereas the latter company absolutely lacks any monitoring body. The only explanation might be that it would be too harsh for an existing limited liability corporation to be forced to appoint a corporate auditor when the transformation will take place by force of law. It might be possible that the structure without a board of directors and a corporate auditor will be available only to a company whose charter grants an inspection right to each shareholder without regard to the number or proportion of votes he owns.[27]

[26] For instance, additional shares may be issued only by way of a rights offering unless approved by a super-majority of the general meeting, Commercial Code art 280-5-2; the company may increase the total number of issued and unissued shares by a charter amendment even beyond the usual ceiling of four times the issued shares (ibid art 347 proviso clause).

[27] The Limited Liability Corporation Law art 44-2 para 2 provides that a company whose charter grants an inspection right to each member without regard to the number or proportion of votes he owns does not have to prepare schedules of financial statements. The Modernization Tentative Draft proposes to make this provision applicable to stock corporations as well. It is important to ensure that shareholders are well informed of the effect of their decision when selecting the structure without a board. Even if the shareholders themselves are content, it is questionable to deprive creditors of an opportunity to inspect schedules, in particular audited schedules, when the shareholders enjoy limited liability.

3. Management and Monitoring: Big Businesses

The Modernization Tentative Draft does not have as many items regarding big businesses as smaller ones because it presupposes the fruits of recent reforms.[28] The dichotomy of traditional and new types of governance structure[29] will be carried over into the 2005 Bill.

The traditional type consists of a board of directors that both manages and monitors, three or more corporate auditors, and at least one account auditor. Each time a corporate scandal was revealed, the legislature responded by amending provisions on the corporate auditor. It was the easiest way to show that the government was doing its best to cope with scandals because corporate auditors did not draw much attention and it was unlikely for reforms on them to meet with stiff resistance. Some reforms affected corporate auditors of all stock corporations without regard to the size.[30] Most reforms, however, related to corporate auditors of large corporations, because it is the failures of big businesses that gave rise to social problems and made a lot of noise in the mass media.

A large corporation must appoint three or more corporate auditors. At least one of them should be an outsider. From April 2005 on, however, at least half of them should be outsiders, and the qualification of an outsider will be narrowed.[31]

The notion of the outside director dates back to the 2001 revision. The distinction between outside and inside directors at that time only had to do with the reduction of their liabilities.[32] Since the 2002 reform, it has related to the governance structure. When a company wishes to achieve quicker decision-making without opting for the new type, the board of directors may delegate a part of its power to a sort of executive committee within the board, and one of the conditions for this delegation is that one or more directors are outsiders.[33] It does not

[28] See n 14 and accompanying text.

[29] See n 16 and accompanying text.

[30] The term of office of a corporate auditor was extended from two years to three years, then to four years, in order to enhance its independence from the management.

[31] Special Audit Law art 18 para 1. At present, an outsider is such a person as was not a director, executive officer, or employee of the company or any of its subsidiaries during the period of the last five years. As of April 2005, only those who have never been in such an above-mentioned position will be qualified as an outsider. 'Old boys and girls' will all be disqualified, and the five-year waiting period will lose its meaning. In a body consisting of a small number of members like corporate auditors, 'at least one-half' differs from 'a majority' to a great extent: eg in the case of a company with four corporate auditors in total, two outsiders meet the former test, whereas under the latter test three or four must be outsiders.

[32] See n 19 and accompanying text.

[33] Special Audit Law art 1-3. Other conditions are: (1) the company is a large or constructive large corporation (n 16); (2) the company has ten or more directors. The statute calls this committee *jūyō zaisan i'in-kai*, literally meaning 'material assets committee', because delegation of power is permissible only with regard to disposal or acquisition of assets of materiality. Due to its limited scope of power delegation, this committee is not popular.

seem important to require only one outside director. When a company opts for the new type, each of the three committees is to consist of three or more directors, and a majority of committee members must be outsiders, but it is not necessary for a majority of board members to be outsiders.[34] As long as each committee maintains its independence, and the board of directors may not overrule a committee decision, there would be no problem regarding independence of the board.

Then what is an outside director? It is a director who refrains from engaging in management of the company; in the past has never been a managing director, executive officer, or employee of the company or its subsidiary; and who is not currently a managing director or executive officer of a subsidiary or an employee of the company or its subsidiary.[35] According to this definition, a director or employee of the parent company can be an outside director. Also a person who relies heavily on the business with the company or its affiliate is not disqualified to be an outside director. Not all outsiders are independent.

The 2002 reform, which introduced the new type of governance structure, came into force in April 2003. Since then more than one year has passed, but only a small number of companies have opted for the new type. One company is going to return to the traditional type after one year of experience with the new type.[36] In response to questionnaires, most top executives answered that they did not have a plan to transform their company into the new type. The strongest reason for their negative attitude seems to be their unfamiliarity with the new type. Besides, many of them feel confident that they can implement their decisions without much delay under the traditional type with some modification of their own.

4. Classes of Shares

The 2001 and 2002 reforms deregulated classes of shares to a great extent and increased the variety of such classes. For example, it was previously unknown in Japan to classify shares with regard to the election of directors or corporate auditors. If the management makes full use of classifying shares, the whole picture of

[34] Special Audit Law art 21-8 para 4.

[35] Commercial Code art 188 para 2 item 7-2. A director engaging in management or a managing director embraces two categories, both appointed by the board: (1) representative director; and (2) non-representative director designated by the board to manage the company (ibid art 260 para 3).

[36] Nihon Keizai Shinbun (7 August 2004) 10. The president of the company pointed out two reasons: (1) the new type, dispensing with a resolution of the general meeting for the distribution of profits and remuneration of officers, deprives the shareholders of their voice; and (2) former workplaces of the outside directors were in conflict of interest with the company on the occasion of M&A.

share structure will be too complicated for many shareholders to understand their exact position. Hereafter, the focus will be put upon voting rights.

Non-voting stock was first introduced by the 1938 revision based on the US model. The 1950 reform tied it to preference in the dividend payment. A company could issue such shares only up to one-fourth of the total until 1990, when the limit was loosened to one-third.[37] At any rate, all versions of our statute knew only the dichotomy between non-voting and full-voting shares. Instead, however, the 2001 reform introduced the notion of limited voting stock: ie the corporate charter may provide for a class of shares whose holders are denied voting rights as to all or a part of the items to be decided upon by the general meeting. A company may issue such shares up to one-half of the aggregate outstanding shares.[38]

The 2001 reform also changed the nature of unit bundling of shares so as to have only to do with voting rights.[39] Where shares are bundled in units, the number of units of limited voting shares may not exceed one-half of the total number of units embracing aggregate outstanding shares.[40] Apparently this looks to function as a brake against abuse by the management through controlling the company by means of a negligible amount of their investment. However, since the number of shares comprising a unit may vary from class to class,[41] the said ceiling will be reduced to meaninglessness; to wit, the management holds a small number of voting shares bundled in tiny units, whereas large amounts of limited voting shares, bundled in units by the maximum allowable number, are in the hands of non-management shareholders.

At last, the Modernization Tentative Draft proposes removing any ceiling with regard to limited voting shares. In light of the questionable function of the statutory ceiling, this proposal may well be reasonable. At the same time, however, the drafters may be said to have given up blocking abusive maneuvers on the part of management by making use of limited voting shares.

5. Minimum Amount of Stated Capital

As has been seen earlier, approximately 99% of stock corporations are small in size.[42] It was the lack of a statutory minimum amount of initial investment that

[37] Commercial Code art 242. Here we take no notice of detailed provisions on the revival of voting rights when preferred dividends were in arrears. These provisions were repealed by the 2001 revision.

[38] Commercial Code art 222 paras 4, 5.

[39] See n 12.

[40] Commercial Code art 222 para 6.

[41] Commercial Code art 221 para 3. The only restriction is that the number of shares comprising a unit may not exceed 1000 or 1/200 of the aggregate outstanding shares (ibid art 221 para 1 proviso clause).

[42] See n 25 and accompanying text.

made it possible for so many small businesses to take the form of stock corporations. Such a situation was regarded as undesirable at the time of the 1950 reform, but an attempt to introduce a threshold failed due to strong resistance on the part of small businesses.[43]

At length the 1990 reform came to require a ten million yen minimum of stated capital for a stock corporation and three million yen for a limited liability corporation.[44] This weak child soon came across a teaser and is destined to be short-lived. A METI statute enables the formation of a stock corporation with one yen of stated capital.[45] The privileged company has to increase its stated capital to ten million yen within five years of its formation, and the company may not pay dividends before such an increase in capital. The Modernization Tentative Draft proposes to generalize this exceptional regime: ie the 2005 Bill will entirely discard the statutory minimum amount of stated capital, without any time limit.

It is true that a minimum share capital requirement may not do much to protect creditors.[46] But complete elimination of such a requirement would render a stock corporation into a different type of business organization. A stock corporation with one yen of share capital means nothing but a company without a shareholder in substance. Creditors of such a company have nobody to rely on who is expected to exert constraint on the management. The company is devoid of one of the fundamental elements of corporate governance.

IV. Concluding Remarks

Each reform is designed to modernize the target institution. Modernization has various colors reflecting the backdrop of the time. About a century ago it was Westernization. In the middle of the last century it was Americanization. Then followed adjustments to fit the Japanese economy. The ongoing modernization, which started about one and a half decades ago and will be consummated in the

[43] The Limited Liability Corporation Law, while it was designed for smaller businesses, required 10,000 yen in minimum stated capital at the time of its enactment in 1938. This amount was increased to 100,000 yen by the 1950 amendments. On the other hand, prior to the 1950 reform, a stock corporation could be formed with 350 yen in initial investment: 50 yen a share and seven incorporators (initial shareholders). The 1950 reform raised the amount to 3,500 yen: 500 yen a share and seven incorporators. The 1981 revision increased it to 350,000 yen: 50,000 yen a share and seven incorporators.

[44] Commercial Code art 168-4; Limited Liability Corporation Law art 9.

[45] Shin-jigyō sōshutsu sokushin-hō (Law for facilitating the creation of new business, 1998 Law no 152) arts 10 ff. See n 22 and accompanying text. As of 30 January 2004, there were over 8000 stock corporations that had stated capital of less than the minimum amount required by the Commercial Code, of which 367 companies had 1 yen in stated capital. Nihon Keizai Shinbun (4 February 2004) 3.

[46] Eg PL Davies *Introduction to Company Law* (OUP Oxford 2002) 85.

2005 Bill, aims at improvement in style as well as an overhaul of company law in substance along the lines of globalization. The recent developments in global scale seem to have been affected by US leadership. Thus the reform movement in present-day Japan is likely to have another American tint, in that the Modernization Tentative Draft looks somehow pro-management.

V. Postscript

The modernization project referred to above[47] has been making progress as scheduled. On 8 December 2004, the Subcommittee on Corporate Law published the final version of its Draft Revision. The Legislative Council approved it on 9 February 2005.

The final version of the Draft Revision is fundamentally the same as the Tentative Draft Revision of 22 October 2003. However, some changes of importance were made:

(1) Existing limited liability corporations will be grandfathered to be subject to the current statute, while no such company may be incorporated anew.
(2) Stock corporations will enjoy broader freedom to choose their structure from among a variety of governance models.
(3) A stock corporation may appoint an accountant or tax adviser to help prepare its financial statements; this will hopefully enhance the reliability of financial statements of small businesses.
(4) The Japanese version of the LLC has been named '*gōdō kaisha*', literally meaning a collective company. Since the tax authority seems to be reluctant to grant pass-through taxation to its members, the Ministry of Economy, Trade and Industry (METI) is reportedly preparing another bill on the LLP.

The House of Councilors approved the Company Bill on 29 June 2005. Along with the prior approval by the House of Representatives on 17 May, the bill has come to be the Company Law of 2005. The effective date will be announced by a Cabinet rule: the date shall not be later than the end of the 18th month after the promulgation of the law. The general expectation is that most provisions will be effective in spring 2006, whereas the amendment relating to mergers will take effect in 2007. The latter revision will remove limitations on consideration for a merger or other restructuring: eg the absorbing corporation will be able to deliver shares in its parent in exchange for shares in the absorbed company, while under the present law consideration other than shares in the absorbing corporation and cash is not permissible. The one-year postponement of this revision is to help potential targets prepare defensive measures.

[47] See n 2, 14.

Japanese Perspectives, Autonomous Firms, and the Aesthetic Function of Law

JOHN O. HALEY

The study of corporate governance and legal reform in Japan has become something of a cottage industry, at least so it seems from what has been and continues to be written. For the most part – well represented by the papers presented at this symposium – the quality matches the quantity. Here in Berlin we have been treated to the best by the brightest. All of the authors merit commendation. I was especially pleased that few if any of the papers are guilty of a tendency to overcompensate for an early emphasis on Japanese exceptionalism that I, perhaps mistakenly, detected in their other writings. Reacting perhaps to what had already become a quarter century ago a stereotyped view of the Japanese firm, some appeared to argue in effect that Japan fits so comfortably within widely accepted patterns of corporate behavior and models of corporate governance[1] that we need not investigate further. In the works of others, I thought I detected – perhaps erroneously – a construction of Japanese patterns in terms of such models as main bank relationships, property rights regimes, and relational contracts[2] developed principally in other contexts instead of the articulation of a more inclusive theory of corporate governance incorporating the distinguishing characteristics of the Japanese experience. I was therefore especially pleased that several of the authors explicitly refer to corporate governance and legal reforms in Japan as distinctive. This proposition – concession perhaps – is significant. For it forces our attention to what in my view as a comparativist really matters – the identification of the relevant and distinguishing features of the Japanese experience and how they relate to law in the interaction with legal rules, institutions, and processes. As I argue below, one of the most distinctive features of Japanese economic life is often overlooked – the autonomous firm.

[1] See eg SN Kaplan and JM Ramseyer 'Those Japanese Firms with Disdain for Shareholders: Another Fable for the Academy' (1996) 74 Washington L Q 403, but see also JM Ramseyer 'Takeovers in Japan: Opportunism, Ideology and Corporate Control' (1987) 35 UCLA L Rev 1.

[2] See eg MJ Roe 'Some Differences in Corporate Structure in Germany, Japan and the United States' (1993) 102 Yale L J 1927 and CJ Milhaupt 'Property Rights in Firms' (1998) 84 Virginia Law Review 1145. Also compare CJ Milhaupt 'A Relational Theory of Japanese Corporate Governance: Contract, Culture and the Rule of Law' (1996) 37 Harvard Intl L Rev 3 with MM Blair and LA Stout 'A Team Production Theory of Corporate Law' (1999) 85 Virginia L Rev 247.

I also question a basic but unstated premise which I detect in the papers that deal with corporate governance and legal reform. All at least appear to assume that law matters. They present various enthymenes but each is based on the unstated premise – the lemma of the argument – that the legal structure for corporate governance is significant in terms of how Japanese corporations are actually managed and how effectively they operate. I disagree. The significance of company law resides elsewhere. To be specific, I question whether the legal rules have in any meaningful way shaped the ways in which Japanese firms are actually governed. My doubts arise from what we know of corporate governance and legal reform from the papers presented here and elsewhere. Professors Ramseyer and Miwa come close to saying that law is not relevant, but I read them to assume that the relevant legal rules will ultimately be shaped by efficiency, and thus in successful economies those rules that ultimately prevail are the ones that lead to efficient outcomes. Law thus does matter. Moreover, with profound respect and acknowledgment for the career contributions of Professor Misao Tatsuta to our understanding of Japanese company law, I wonder whether he too assumes that law matters. One can read his paper both ways. As he notes, despite the fact that for over a half century Japanese company law has provided for five separate forms of limited liability firms, one of which was expressly designed for closely held companies,[3] 99% of all Japanese companies are in fact incorporated as joint stock companies (*kabushiki kaisha*) in large part, it appears, because of the prestige the 'K.K.' form offers. As I explain below, whether Japanese legal reformers in fact designed the reforms to have any significant influence is subject to question. Instead, I suspect, they operated with an opposing premise – also assumed and unstated – that the aim of the law was more aesthetic than instrumental.

Let me begin with what is distinctive. Few knowledgeable observers need to be reminded that Japanese patterns of corporate organization differ significantly from those in other industrial societies, as well as in Asia. The features of employment in both private and public organizations are well known. For most if not all non-family-owned firms, Japanese corporate structure is characterized by an employment structure in which core employees are hired exclusively at the entry level, and all personnel are managed by a central personnel office with full responsibility for the recruitment, training, assignment, and promotion of career staff.[4] This office is itself staffed by senior career managers, who serve only temporarily for a period of years before they too are reassigned to other sections

[3] *Yūgen kaisha-hō* (Law no 74 of 1938, as amended by Law no 88 of 2004).

[4] Beginning with J Abegglen's 1958 study *The Japanese Factory* (Free Press Glencoe 1958), the prevalence of career employment for workers with a single firm in large and medium enterprises has long been noted by leading social scientists in various disciplines writing about Japan in English. See RE Cole *Work, Mobility, & Participation* (University of California Press Berkeley Los Angeles London 1979) esp 1-10, citing decades of subsequent scholarship by R Dore, H Mannari, R Marsh and T Rohlen.

or divisions of the organization. One major effect of this pattern of organization is the limited opportunity for exit that it creates. As Ronald Gilson and Mark Roe note to their credit,[5] this 'dark side' of career employment counterbalances the benefits of job security. No analysis of corporate governance or even descriptions of the firm in Japan, to my knowledge, however, point out that these features of medium- and large-scale firms in Japan are also shared by nearly all government agencies and public sector organizations.[6] Aside from universities, few if any large or even middling-sized public or private organizations depart from this organizational pattern. It is, I believe, important to keep in mind the fact that this pattern of employment is common to public as well as private institutions. Its ubiquity maximizes its effects. I know of only a handful of organizations in the United States – none private and only a few public – that replicate all of its essential features: the career military services and perhaps the Federal Bureau of Investigation (FBI). The US Forest Service shares many of the most telling,[7] but it lacks the ubiquitous central personnel office. In short, the prevalence of this organizational structure appears to be both a uniquely Japanese phenomenon and one whose pervasiveness produces consequences of major significance for Japanese society in general and corporate governance in particular.

To repeat observations I have made elsewhere,[8] the postwar prevalence of career employment has meant that most Japanese males who work in most public and nearly all medium to large private organizations begin their careers as generalists in their early twenties. Lateral hiring rarely exists except for marginal or relatively new skill-based positions in high demand, such as computer programming. Corresponding legal and social protections ensure against termination without cause. Consequently career employees know with reasonable certainty as they enter the workforce that they are likely to remain with this one employer for the duration of their careers – that is, until retirement thirty or so years hence.

[5] RJ Gilson and MJ Roe 'Lifetime Employment: Labor Peace and the Evolution of Japanese Corporate Governance' (1999) 99 Columbia L Rev 508.

[6] The practice is said, for example, to have developed in the private sector in the 1930s in response to mutual needs of both labor and management. See A Gordon *The Evolution of Labor Unions in Japan: Heavy Industry, 1853-1955* (Harvard University Press Cambridge 1985) esp 125-55. However, such explanations do not tell us how, when, or why similar patterns of employment and personnel control mechanisms also developed in the public sector. Other often quite influential studies of Japanese corporate governance suffer similar weakness. See eg Gilson and Roe (n 5).

[7] JO Haley 'Mission to Manage: The U.S. Forest Service as a Japanese Bureaucracy' in K Hayashi (ed) *The U.S.-Japanese Economic Relationship: Can It Be Improved?* (New York University Press New York 1989) 196-225.

[8] See JO Haley 'Heisei Renewal or Heisei Transformation: Are Legal Reforms Really Changing Japan?' (2005) 19 Zeitschrift für Japanisches Recht / J of Japanese L 5 (and JO Haley 'Career Employment, Corporate Governance and Japanese Exceptionalism' available as faculty working papers at <http://law.wustl.edu/Academics/Faculty/Workingpapers/index.html> (17 May 2005).

Their economic future is thus irreversibly tied to the success, however measured, of the institution within which they work.

The effects of career employment on corporate governance are buttressed by a second set of characteristics of Japan's postwar corporate structure. Within East Asia, Japan remains unique as the only country in which large publicly held corporations with diffuse shareholding and professional managerial control have developed. The contrast with the prevailing pattern of family control in other parts of East Asia is stark. A recent World Bank study found that nearly 80% of all publicly traded Japanese companies are widely held, and less than 10% of publicly traded firms are family-controlled.[9] In all other East Asian economies, virtually all privately owned firms including those that are publicly traded are family controlled.[10]

South Korea offers the most telling Asian comparison. A 1998 World Bank study[11] found that of 345 publicly traded companies in South Korea, only 14.3% were widely held (at a 10% ownership concentration cutoff) and nearly 68% were family owned or controlled. A subsequent study by a team of researchers at the Korea Development Institute[12] concluded that the World Bank data significantly understates the extent of control of the 34 *chaebol* conglomerates studied, which account for a major share of all publicly traded firms. The conglomerates in other parts of East Asia, like the *zaibatsu* of prewar Japan, are structured as a pyramid of multiple subsidiary companies with an individual or family owning the controlling interest in a holding company or parent corporation. In contrast, the *chaebol* are characterized by complex patterns of inter-firm cross-sharing akin to so-called horizontal *keiretsu* company groups that emerged in postwar Japan after

[9] S Claessens S Djankov and LHP Lang 'East Asian Corporations: Heroes or Villains?' (World Bank Discussion Paper no 409 January 2000) 9.

[10] See IC Nam Y Kang and JK Kim 'Comparative Corporate Governance Trends in Asia' in J Zhuang and others (eds) *Corporate Governance and Finance in East Asia* (Asian Development Bank Manila 2000) 85-119, analyzing data from S Claessens and others *Ownership Structure and Corporate Performance in East Asia* (Mimeo Washington DC 1998). The Claessens data shows that except for Japan and Korea less than 3% of all publicly traded corporations are widely held. In every country except Japan (13.1%) and the Philippines (41.3%), more than 50% of these were family-controlled (with a 10% shareholding cutoff). Excluding state-controlled corporations and those with at least a 10% equity stake by widely held financial institutions or other widely held corporations, nearly all publicly traded corporations are family owned or controlled. Nam and his co-authors believe, however, that the Claessens study actually understates the extent of family control. For example, their data does not disaggregate corporate shareholding in family-controlled pyramidal conglomerates.

[11] S Claessens and others *Ownership Structure and Corporate Performance in East Asia,* cited in Nam and others (n 10) 94 table 3-2.

[12] IC Nam and others 'Corporate Governance in Korea' in J Zhuang and others (eds) *Corporate Governance and Finance in East Asia* (Asian Development Bank Manila 2000) 155-208.

the occupation dissolution of the *zaibatsu*.[13] Although more complex and less transparent, the effect of cross-shareholding is the same as pyramidal shareholding. Having controlling interest in only one or two key companies enables effective control over the entire conglomerate. Hence, as noted by Nam and his colleagues at the Korea Development Institute, a single shareholder with personal holdings of only 4% of the total shares of group companies is able to control one of Korea's largest *chaebol,* the Samsung group, through effective control of more than 46% of group company shares.[14]

But, one might ask, what about Japan's industrial peers, the United States and Europe? Once again, the contrast with the United States is telling. In Japan the percentage of publicly traded shares held by individuals steadily decreased from 1949 to 1985, bottoming out at approximately 20% of the total stock of all publicly traded companies.[15] Shareholding by foreign corporate and individual investors, never more than 5% prior to 1980, rose and fell in the early 1980s but increased from 1990 to 2000, stabilizing also at around 20% of total shareholdings. Unlike the United States, no appreciable percentage of shares is now or has ever been held by institutions on behalf of individual investors, such as mutual funds and pension funds. Their closest Japanese equivalents, investment and annuity trusts, in combination account at current levels – the highest ever – for less than 10% of all shares held. Although the percentages fell in the late 1990s, financial institutions (banks and insurance companies) and other corporations still hold over 50% of all shares of publicly listed firms. Other papers included in this volume show that this pattern of shareholding would not be considered as unusual in Europe as it is in the United States. Indeed, they confirm the conventional wisdom that in all countries in continental Europe, individuals (families) control the vast majority of all firms. But recall that 80% of all publicly traded Japanese companies are widely held – a figure not reached in any part of Europe. Based on these figures and very rough corresponding estimates, it appears that somewhere between a plurality to an overwhelming majority of all publicly traded Japanese firms are controlled in fact by other corporations and banks, with the remaining firms closely held or at least controlled by a small number of individual Japanese shareholders or corporate and individual foreign shareholders. These patterns of ownership differ from both the United States and Europe (including the United Kingdom). A recent OECD study of selected

[13] See EM Hadley *Antitrust in Japan* (Princeton University Press Princeton 1970).

[14] Nam and others (n 12) 167.

[15] For statistics on declining individual ownership of shares from 1949 through 1981, see L Repeta 'Declining Public Ownership of Japanese Industry: A Case of Regulatory Failure?' (1984) 17 Law in Japan: An Annual 153, 159, reprinted in JO Haley (ed) *Law and Society on Contemporary Japan* (Kendall/Hunt Dubuque 1988) 113-138, 117. For further reference, see <http://www.tse.or.jp/english/data/factbook/fact_book_2005.pdf> (19 May 2005).

OECD countries[16] indicates that Japanese patterns of shareholding differ in the paucity of shareholding by investment funds (0%) and the relatively small percentage of shareholding by financial institutions other than banks and insurance companies (15%). The patterns for Germany resemble the Japanese ratios with 22% of shareholding by banks and insurance companies and pension funds (27% for Japan) and 42% by non-financial enterprises (27% Japan).

Professor Reinhardt Schmidt describes in his paper the characteristics of 'insider' control systems. Given these patterns of shareholding, Japan fits well within the ambit of this category. However, one feature separates the Japanese pattern from other 'insider' systems. In Japan the insider in widely held corporations is the career employee, not the capitalist. Assuming that Japan's financial institutions and firms not only share organizational characteristics and collective cultures, their control of even a plurality of publicly traded companies to social and economic consequences is surely significant. As equally highly interdependent communities of career employees whose interests, concerns, and values are similar if not identical to those in the firms whose shares they control, we surely must presume that these financial and corporate shareholders will act accordingly as they exercise the right of controlling shareholders. Professional managers without opportunities for lateral movement are hardly likely to exercise shareholder rights to reduce the managerial control of their peers. In a world of common interest and reciprocity, professional managers in one firm are likely to vote the shares they control in ways that preserve the status quo. At least, we can hardly expect them to take advantage of legal rules designed to foster 'shareholder democracy' in ways that maximize short-term institutional economic gains but jeopardize their long-term individualized self-interest. Finally, shareholding patterns – and their dynamics – in Japan have also tended to be relatively stable. Thus despite increases in foreign holdings, shareholding patterns in Japan continue to buttress existing patterns of corporate organizations and governance.

To be sure, in the private sector shareholders in Japan as elsewhere remain the residual claimants. Theirs is, however, a purely *de jure* claim that can be effectively postponed to ensure the perpetual life of the enterprise by actions of the controlling managerial employees if necessary in cooperation with other stakeholders – and sometimes the government. For shareholders, their day of reckoning as residual claimants never comes. In effect they become higher-risk lenders whose returns are based primarily on stock market performance and capital gains and only secondarily on dividends. Take, for example, the story of Yoshiaki Murakami as told by *The Wall Street Journal* in a rare glimpse at the efforts company executives who have risen through career employee ranks take to maintain

[16] S Nester and JK Thompson 'Corporate Governance in OECD Economies: Is Convergence Under Way?' (OECD Paper 1 January 2001) 4 <http://www.oecd.org/dataoecd/7/10/1931460.pdf> (17 May 2005).

control.[17] Murakami owned outright or controlled 11.9% of the shares of Tokyo Style Company, a medium-sized clothing manufacturer with less than US$500 million in annual sales. Foreign investors owned an additional 30 or so percent. Since 1970 the firm paid its shareholders a fixed dividend of 12.5 yen (US$.10) per share despite large earnings. In an effort to force the firm to return a portion to its shareholders, he made two formal proposals for consideration at a February 2002 shareholders' meeting. The first was to require the firm to issue a special dividend of 500 yen ($3.91) per share, and the second to reacquire a third of its outstanding shares. Murakami failed. Tokyo Style's various banks and suppliers, holding in aggregate about 40% of its shares, were persuaded by the company president, a career employee who had worked for the firm for five decades since the age 18, to outvote Murakami and his foreign backers. The shareholders may have had legal rights as owners and residual claimants, but from the perspective of those who had spent decades of hard work to make Tokyo Style a success, allowing those with paper stock market gains to walk away with those gains surely seemed unjust. And they found responsive supporters among similarly situated career employees in the firms with the controlling shares. The episode also illustrates quite well Ronald Gilson's observations on the effects of repeated interaction among career managers in separate firms.[18] In Gilson's words, '[R]epeated dealings with cohorts in other companies… result in an individual's developing a substantial stake in his own reputation for cooperative behavior.'[19]

Experiences such as these help to explain the consistent dearth of mergers and acquisitions in Japan. For a half century, even through the troubled decade of the 1990s, the number of mergers and acquisitions in Japan in comparison with the United States and Europe has been extraordinarily low as well as extraordinarily constant.[20]

In short, because of career employment, widely held Japanese firms during the past half century have increasingly taken on the characteristics of the Tokugawa village as a largely immobile community whose residents found ways to ensure autonomy from outside control.[21] The strategies for autonomy of the contemporary firm include various strategies to protect against outside intrusion –

[17] P Landers 'Rare Proxy Battle Aims to Redress Japanese Capitalism' *The Wall Street Journal* (New York United States 15 May 2002) A1, A12-A13.

[18] RJ Gilson 'Value Creation by Business Lawyers: Legal Skills and Asset Pricing' (1984) 94 Yale Law Journal 239.

[19] ibid 309-10.

[20] See eg JO Haley *Antitrust in Germany and Japan: The First Fifty Years, 1947-1998* (University of Washington Press Seattle 2001) 89.

[21] For more on the Tokugawa village as a paradigm for social ordering in Japan, see JO Haley *Authority Without Power: Law and the Japanese Paradox* (OUP Oxford 1991) 58-65.

by shareholders or by banks – not the least of which is the protection offered by 'safe' corporate shareholders and a marked emphasis on retained earnings.[22]

To the extent that employee-controlled Japanese firms face significant domestic and international rivals, they have been able to achieve a remarkable degree of both autonomy and effective internal monitoring. In competitive markets, employee control – what I prefer to call 'firm autonomy' – can be provided as effective monitoring on managerial competence as either shareholder or creditor control. In an early piece, Professor Ramseyer persuasively argued that career employment provided an effective monitoring function of career employees. Analyzing corporate control in the context of takeovers in Japan, he concluded that the two markets that most effectively monitor and discipline firms are the internal labor market and the external market for the firm's products or services.[23] In a rivalrous marketplace, the quality of a firm's product and the efficiency of its production determine success. To the extent a firm is subject to competitive pressures, career employees have sufficient incentive to take innovative risks and, as a consequence of their acquired knowledge of the industry and their firm, also have the capacity to make informed and carefully calibrated decisions. I would thus add these early insights to the more recent observations now offered by Professor Ramseyer and Professor Miwa.

The key factor is firm rivalry. Where the firm can rest on its laurels without the demands of customers or the public it serves to provide continuous pressure and challenge, then career managers are apt to take fewer risks, to choose options that seem safe and undemanding. Without the external pressure of competition, the effects of job security are more likely to take hold and managers and the firm become even more risk averse, less innovative, and increasingly stagnant. The postwar financial services industry, I submit, illustrates this tendency. As market competition and firm rivalry increase, however, the dangers of inaction begin to outweigh those of taking risks to promote innovation and efficiency. Thus the pressures that foster stagnation begin to work in the opposite fashion to produce a powerful force for change. Even within hierarchically structured organizations – including those where pay is based on seniority and rank – internal labor markets operate in tandem to ensure that those employees who contribute most to the quality of the product and the efficiency of its production are rewarded. They receive the best assignments, promotions, and ultimately pay. (I argue else-

[22] The extent of retained earnings as a source of capital for future growth as a distinctive characteristic of Japanese firms has not generally received the attention it deserves. Professor Gérard Hellwig to his credit noted this phenomenon during discussion.

[23] JM Ramseyer 'Takeovers in Japan: Opportunism, Ideology and Corporate Control' (1987) 35 UCLA L Rev 1, 48-49.

where[24] that Professor's Ramseyer's subsequent research on judges illustrates the accuracy of his insights here.)

We are still left with the lawyer's question: Does law matter? Despite the intrusion of American corporate law rules during the last months of the Allied Occupation,[25] as summarized so well by Professor Tatsuta and predicted by early observers,[26] the new rules did not transform the system. Little if any change can be detected in either the patterns of shareholding (except the continuing decrease of the individual shareholder) or governance. Professors Ramseyer and Miwa add another dimension. They note the success of the system. Here too law seems to matter little. They offer no evidence that law mattered at all – either positively or negatively – in over a century of legal reform.

In the context of the history of corporate law reform as described by Professor Tatsuta, the two presumptively 'distinctive features' of Japanese corporate organization lead me to question what meaningful effect law has on corporate governance. Insofar as I have been able to determine, during the past half century, neither the patterns of employment nor shareholding trends have changed significantly if at all.

As to the first, career employment for core managerial employees remains a fundamental aspect of Japanese government and business organizations. Again, to repeat what I have noted in previous writings: Studies and statistics on Japanese labor and corporate restructuring indicate that despite marginal change, no fundamental transformation is taking place.[27] Public and private organizations continue to recruit new core managerial employees from the pool of recent university graduates. Lateral entry remains rare, generally limited to marginal positions or persons with especially needed skills. Central personnel offices continue to have broad control over all core employee hiring, assignments, and promotions. Japanese firms may have actually solidified their central personnel

[24] 'Career Employment, Corporate Governance and Japanese Exceptionalism', available as faculty working papers at <http://law.wustl.edu/Academics/Faculty/Workingpapers/index.html> (17 May 2005).

[25] See LN Salwin 'The New Commercial Code of Japan: Symbol of Gradual Progress Toward Democratic Goals' (1962) 50 Georgetown L J 478. Salwin was the author of the reforms.

[26] TL Blakemore and M Yazawa 'Japanese Commercial Code Revisions Concerning Corporations' (1953) 2 AJCL 12.

[27] See, eg, K Ariga and others *Internal Labor Markets in Japan* (Cambridge University Press Cambridge 2000) esp ch 5 pp 121-68; H Sato 'Human Resource Management Systems in Large Firms' in M Sako and H Sato (eds) *Japanese Labour and Management in Transition: Diversity, Flexibility and participation* (Routledge London 1997) 104-29; A Holzhausen 'Japanese Employment Practices in Transition: Promotion Policy and Compensation Systems in the 1990s' (2000) 3 Social Science Japan Journal 221-35; D Kruger and I Fuyumo 'Job Flexibility in Japan' *Far Eastern Economic Review* (Hong Kong 8 February 2001) 66. Nor do the most recent statistics from Japan's Labor Ministry show any appreciable change. See <http://www.mhlw.go.jp/english/database/db-hw/index.htm> (17 May 2005).

offices and may be taking measures to reassure the job security of beleaguered mid-career employees. Political and economic pressures may have led agencies and enterprises to reduce the number of entry-level recruits, to assign more employees to affiliated agencies or firms, and to increase the number of early retirements, but except perhaps for foreign-affiliated or controlled enterprises, involuntary terminations on economic grounds[28] remain low in number. Business enterprises have also responded to economic pressures and pleas for structural change in various ways. Many have increased the number of temporary workers – that is, reducing each year's cohort of core career employees – as well as experimenting with more flexible pay schemes. Apparently, however, recent experiments with new merit-based approaches have not fared well. In any event, however, neither an increase in the number of temporary workers nor the elimination of rigid seniority pay and promotion patterns alters the basic structure of career employment. I am unaware of any evidence of meaningful change in inter-agency and inter-firm mobility, which has been notoriously low throughout the postwar era. In short, the markets for experienced workers remain undeveloped. Thus all of the consequences attributable to this pattern of organization are equally likely to persist. It appears to be an enduring institutional feature of Japanese society, and thus one of the underlying factors in explaining elements of continuity in Japan both today and tomorrow.

Among the papers presented here, Professors Schmidt and Tatsuta ultimately provide, in my view, the most apt explanatory views of the Japanese firm and the role of law. Professor Schmidt correctly understands Japan as an example of insider control. As detailed above, this is hardly contestable. On the other hand, Professor Tatsuta has traced over a century of corporate law reform as a never-ending process of 'modernization,' in which lawmakers strove continuously to ensure that the nation has the most modern, up-to-date set of legal rules. Although not without effect and consequence, these reforms appear neither to have made nor to have been fully designed to make any significant change in the fundamental patterns of corporate governance and control. We are left, I suggest, with an aesthetic explanation of law reform. All of us have friends or relatives or both who, like the Japanese law-makers described here, are continuously in the market for the newest, most highly touted, or appraised gadget, apparel, music, work of art, whatever. No matter the cost, no matter what the instrumental value or use, no matter whatever – except its essential aesthetic appeal as the newest, most highly touted, or appraised – in other words, the most modern.

[28] Business necessity is generally viewed as a 'just ground' for involuntary termination. See K Sugeno *Japanese Labor Law* (University of Washington Press and The University of Tokyo Press Seattle and Tokyo 1992) 402-403.

Corporate Governance Crises and Related Party Transactions: A Post-Parmalat Agenda

JOSEPH A. McCAHERY and ERIK P.M. VERMEULEN

I. Introduction

The fallout from the collapses at Enron and WorldCom and the accounting, fraud, and governance failures in the United States (US) and Europe has again focused public debate about how to govern publicly listed companies. The political response to the instability caused by the governance failures was rapid and widespread, prompting lawmakers on both sides of the Atlantic to propose measures to protect a corporation's shareholders from fraud and poor board performance. These most notably included board certification of accounts, the regulation of audits and auditors, the imposition of independent audit committees, and enhancing the role of non-executive directors.

Subsequently the US Congress promulgated the Sarbanes-Oxley Act of 2002, which is designed to create improvements in governance by inducing increased oversight and monitoring of companies. The SEC has followed from Congress, drafting new regulations needed to interpret and enforce the Act. There is no question that the recent scandals in the US caused EU regulators to react by devising a set of legal strategies to constrain diversions by officers, board members, and controlling shareholders of publicly listed companies.[1] The European Commission (EC) launched, for example, a number of initiatives that were announced in its May 2003 Communication on the statutory audit.[2] Moreover, the EC, in its Action Plan on modernizing company law and enhancing corporate

[1] PL Davies 'Enron and Corporate Law Reform in the UK and the European Community in Armour' in J Armour and JA McCahery (eds) *After Enron: Improving Corporate Law and Modernising Securities Regulation in Europe and the US* (Hart Publishing Oxford 2005).

[2] Communication from the Commission to the Council and the European Parliament, *Reinforcing the statutory audit in the EU* COM(2003) 286 final [2003] OJ C236/2.

governance,[3] announced plans to increase transparency of intra-group relations and transactions with related parties and to improve disclosures about corporate practices.[4] Attention quickly turned to accounting and audit reforms when Parmalat collapsed with debt of €14.5 billion in December 2003. The debacle, which shattered any illusions that accounting and boardroom scandals were uniquely an American phenomenon, led regulators – who were already active on the implementation of the International Accounting Standard (IAS)[5] – to propose additional measures concerning transactions involving related parties of a company, including family controlling shareholders and key managers, and special purpose entities (SPEs).[6] At the same time, the Commission has promulgated a recommendation on the independence of the statutory auditor and also a directive on the duties of auditors.

Like the Enron case,[7] Parmalat's underlying problems were due to the massive fraud that was facilitated by the prevalence of special purpose entities (SPEs) and offshore subsidiaries that were used by the managers and officers to carry out

[3] Communication from the Commission to the Council and European Parliament, *Modernising Company Law and Enhancing Corporate Governance in the European Union – A Plan to Move Forward* COM(2003) 284 final 21 May 2003 (see annex 1 in this volume).

[4] Communication from the Commission to the Council and European Parliament, *On Preventing and Combating Corporate and Financial Malpractice* COM(2004) 611 final 27 September 2004.

[5] Report on the proposal for a European Parliament and Council regulation on the application of international accounting standards (COM(2001) 80 – C5-0061/2001 –2001/0044 (COD)); Proposal for a Directive of the European Parliament and of the Council amending Council Directives 78/660/EEC, 83/349/EEC and 91/674/EEC on the annual and consolidated accounts of a certain type of companies and insurance undertakings COM(2002) 259 final 2002/0112 (COD).

[6] Proposal for a Directive of the European Parliament and of the Council amending Council Directives 78/660/EEC and 83/349/EEC concerning the annual accounts of certain types of companies and consolidated accounts, available at <http://europa.eu.int/eur-lex/lex/LexUriServ/site/en/com/2004/com2004_0725en01.pdf> (30 June 2005).

[7] Enron exploited accounting benefits that would not have been available in arm's length transactions with third parties. For example, since independent parties would not provide economic hedges for its merchant investments, Enron engaged in hedging transactions with related entities that in theory allowed Enron to accomplish its temporary accounting objectives of not reporting any decline in the value of the investments. Since the hedges lacked economic substance, the temporary accounting results were unsustainable and eventually required the reporting of significant losses that surprised the marketplace. FASB, Consolidation of Certain Special Purpose Entities: An Interpretation of ARB No. 51 (proposed 1 July 2002). The proposal deals with SPEs and would have caused the consolidation of Enron's LJM 1 and 2. It also increases the outside equity requirement to 10% for a residual class of SPEs that would have included those in question. A second initiative addresses disclosures of guarantees, on the grounds that the present rules lack clarity. FASB, Interpretation No. 45, Guarantor's Accounting Disclosure Requirements for Guarantees, Including Indirect Guarantees of Indebtedness of Others (25 November 2002).

illicit related party transactions.[8] But, unlike Enron, it was Parmalat's family-controlled management and advisors that structured the group's various financial arrangements to enrich members of the Tanzi family at the expense of the shareholders and creditors.[9] While extreme, the Parmalat case is hardly unique. A number of similar cases, employing complex and opaque strategies, have emerged within continental Europe exploiting regulatory weaknesses at both the member state and the European Union (EU) level. There are both industry and market reasons that explain the appearance of this form of financial transaction and complex fraud. Evidence suggests that private benefits extraction is higher in European groups of companies, particularly those organized in a pyramid structure.[10] Inefficient controlling shareholders have given rise to a huge variety of sophisticated techniques to tunnel assets, profits, and corporate opportunities. The investigations into the Parmalat scandal showed that management used a virtual hydra head of offshore subsidiaries and special purpose entities to cover up their losses and prop up the financial situation of the group.[11]

Attempts to locate effective solutions to the arrangements that led to the collapse of Parmalat have run up against interest group pressures in Italy. Despite these barriers, the need is apparent and urgent for new mechanisms to address the regulatory problems triggered by the Parmalat scandal. Leaving aside the question as well as the possibility of there being no efficient regulatory option to control such transactions, there continue to be various conventional legal strategies available to curtail management's capacity to carry out self-dealing trans-

[8] WW Bratton 'Does Corporate Law Protect the Interests of Shareholders and Other Stakeholders: Enron and the Dark Side of Shareholder Value' (2002) 76 Tulane L Rev 1275; S Schwarcz 'Lessons from Enron: The Use and Abuse of Special Purpose Entities in Corporate Structures' Working Paper Duke University Global Capital Markets Center 2002; JC Coffee 'A Theory of Corporate Scandals: Why the US and Europe Differ' (2005) 21 Oxford Rev of Economic Policy 198.

[9] G Ferrarini and P Giudici 'Financial Scandals and the Role of Private Enforcement: The Parmalat Case' in Armour and McCahery (n 1).

[10] La Porta and others 'Ownership Around the World' (1999) 54 J of Finance 471; M Bertrand and others 'Ferreting Out Tunneling: An Application to Indian Business Groups' (2002) 117 Quarterly J of Economics 121; M Holmén and P Högfeldt 'Pyramidal Discounts: Tunneling or Agency Costs?' ECGI Working Paper in Finance no 73/2005. E Friedman S Johnson and T Mitton 'Propping and Tunneling' (2003) 31 J of Comparative Economics 732 advance the view that a firm controlled by a pyramid structure makes propping easier.

[11] *Securities and Exchange Commission v Parmalat Finanziaria SpA* Case no 03 CV 10266 (PKC) Complaint, United States District Court (SDNY) 29 December 2003, available at <http://www.sec.gov/litigation/complaints/comp18527.htm> (30 June 2005); *Enrico Bondi, Extraordinary Commissioner of Parmalat Finanziaria Spa, Parmalat Spa and Other Affiliated Entities in Extraordinary Administration v Citigroup Inc, Citibank NA, Vialattea LLC, Buconero LLC and Eureka Plc* no BER-L-10902-04 (NJ Super Ct Law Div) (unpublished decision on motion to dismiss).

actions.[12] The post-scandal debate reveals significant differences of opinion regarding the extent to which mandatory disclosure, director's fiduciary duties, and audit control can prove effective in discouraging these value-decreasing transactions.[13]

In many jurisdictions, lawmakers have strengthened regulation in the core areas of audit and auditors, non-executive directors, and board structure. Yet legal protections and organizational change are not the whole story. Perhaps the most important change lies on the enforcement side, where the private and public institutions are notably weak compared to the US. In circumstances where legal regulation would otherwise be justified, market mechanisms can be of considerable practical significance in imposing costs on managerial self-dealing. This is not to say that market mechanisms are the most important factor in curtailing self-dealing. [14] There is much to be said for a regulatory framework that would employ a diversity of legal rules and standards to govern related party transactions.

This chapter focuses on the regulation of related party transactions by corporate managers and transactions by controlling shareholders which conflict with the interests of minority shareholders. We will consider the Community-level and national legal frameworks that are designed to deter related party transactions by controlling shareholders and directors and officers. Attention will be given to the Commission's proposed regulation of related party transactions and the variety of devices for dealing with these issues at the member state level.[15]

The purpose of the chapter is fourfold. First, it critically evaluates the proposed EU framework designed to regulate related party transactions. Second, it reviews current legal strategies in the European Union that address the problem of related party transactions and off-balance sheet arrangements involving special purpose vehicles. It then considers recent proposed changes to legislation and evaluates the implications of the reforms that may have a significant impact on commercial practice within the EU. We attempt to assess to what extent and through which channels information on related party transactions is provided to the company, shareholders, and the market. It is widely recognized that a lack of transparency contributes to tunneling by concealing related party transactions.

[12] R Kraakman and others *The Anatomy of Corporate Law: A Comparative and Functional Approach* (OUP Oxford 2004).

[13] WW Bratton 'Rules, Principles, and the Accounting Crisis in the United States' (2004) 5 Eur Business Organization L Rev 7; cf the contribution of JC Coffee in this volume.

[14] M Klausner 'Limitations of Corporate Law in Promoting Good Corporate Governance' Stanford Law and Economics Olin Working Paper no 300 (2004).

[15] Since this paper addresses the optimal regulatory design of conflicted transactions in a controlling shareholder regime, we leave aside discussions of conflicted transactions in a widely dispersed corporate governance system which focus on managerial opportunism and the various mechanisms designed to overcome shareholder collective action problems.

Our central observation is that while most European jurisdictions provide similar legal techniques to regulate related party transactions, we observe that the newly proposed EU accounting regulation is far-reaching and probably well-designed to redress the causes of the Parmalat crisis. We caution, however, that these measures could be counter-productive, rooting out usually efficient related party transactions.

The paper is divided into six parts. The next part analyzes the significance of diverse patterns of ownership and control for regulating the conflicts between majority and minority shareholders. This part also discusses the Parmalat scandal and explores the mechanisms employed by the family-controlling shareholder to extract private benefits at the expense of minority shareholders and creditors. Part III explores the arguments for and against the regulation of related party transactions. Part IV examines legal mechanisms designed by EU lawmakers to regulate these transactions. Part V evaluates the variety of strategies that have been developed by member states to regulate conflicted transactions. Many of the provisions, which are based on the comply-and-explain approach, leave firms with sufficient discretion to tailor their own governance structure. However, while making no judgments about which institutional arrangements work best in any particular country, it is argued that codes of conduct principles tend to have the same effect as hard law provisions. Lawmakers should thus take a balanced view of the potential merits of related party transactions before devising legal – hard or soft – techniques. Part VI concludes by offering an alternative technique to regulate these transactions.

II. Prevailing Ownership and Control Structures

Generally, continental European jurisdictions have developed their own corporate governance and ownership structures that differ significantly from those of the United Kingdom and the United States. There are also major divergences across the EU member states. The most important variation between the US and EU is that while the US has achieved complete separation of ownership and control, the separation has not fully occurred in most EU member states due to the presence of controlling shareholders. In blockholder systems, information and collective action problems typically prevent close monitoring of management performance by widely dispersed shareholder owners holding small stakes.[16] These infirmities give rise to different forms of opportunism on the part of controlling shareholders

[16] Clearly, there are controlling shareholder regimes in jurisdictions in Europe where the rule of law is strong and minority shareholders are better positioned to monitor their investments and limit the extraction of private benefits by the company's management or blockholders through asset sales or purchases, transfer prices, or related party transactions (A Dyck and L Zingales 'Private Benefits of Control: An International Comparison' (2004) 59 J of Finance 537).

and management insiders, which can lead to significant levels of private benefit extraction if the regulation of accounting, disclosure, and corporate governance allows it.

1. Controlling Shareholdings in Europe

Ownership concentration in continental Europe is very high.[17] In French, German, Austrian, Belgian, and Italian companies, a single shareholder (or a shareholder group) usually owns an absolute majority of shares. This stands in sharp contrast with the US and the UK where the largest shareholder owns an average stake of respectively 22.8% and 14%.[18] Whereas a coalition of the three largest shareholdings gives a cumulative share stake of more than 60% in continental Europe (up to a super-majority of 75% in France and Austria), a similar coalition can vote a mere 30% of the shares in Anglo-American countries. Furthermore, not only is there a striking difference between ownership concentration in the EU and US, but the main categories of owners and the instruments of ownership vary significantly as well. Unlike the US, ownership in continental Europe is highly concentrated in the hands of families and the corporate sector through pyramids and ownership cascades.

We now turn to analyze the trade-offs between concentrated ownership and share dispersion and then focus on the mechanisms that allow controlling shareholders to obtain a greater premium for their shares. Much of the recent commentary on the impact of concentrated ownership on shareholder behavior indicates that increases in ownership levels limit free rider problems, ie closer proximity lessens the information asymmetry problem.[19] They show that the coalescence of voting power in a small number of hands means earlier, cheaper intervention in the case of management failure. The system's other primary benefit stems from the blockholder's ability to access information about operations. This lessened information asymmetry permits blockholders to invest more patiently. The longer shareholder time-horizon in turn frees management to invest for the long term and creates a more secure environment for firm-specific investments of human capital by the firm's managers.

These studies show that there is a trade-off between liquidity and control. Trading markets in blockholder countries tend to be thinner and less transparent

[17] F Barca and M Becht *The Control of Corporate Europe* (OUP Oxford 2001).

[18] JA McCahery and others 'The Economics of the Proposed European Takeover Directive' in Ferrarini and others Reforming Company and Takeover Law in Europe (OUP Oxford 2004) 575.

[19] M Burkart D Gromb and F Panunzi 'Why Higher Takeover Premia Protect Minority Shareholders' (1998) 106 J of Political Economy 172; P Bolton and EL von Thadden 'Blocks, Liquidity and Corporate Control' (1998) 53 J of Finance 1.

than in market system countries, and firms in search of financing encounter a more restricted range of alternatives. Meanwhile, the blockholders themselves give up the benefits of diversification and, given thin trading markets, liquidity and the possibility of easy exit through sale. Finally, there is a shortage of loyalty. Blockholders, having sacrificed diversification and liquidity, extract a return in the form of private benefits yielded through self-dealing or insider trading.[20]

European company law regimes have traditionally included a number of mechanisms that constrain blockholders from extracting resources from enterprises they control. Such disparity between ownership and control is characteristic of countries that permit the exploitation of corporate opportunities. These include: (1) distributions of cash and property to confer benefits on shareholders; (2) dilutive share issues; (3) interested transactions; (4) allocation of corporate opportunities; (5) allocation of business activities; and (6) selective disclosure of non-public information. Figure 1 depicts two instances in which the majority shareholder has voting control.

Figure 1. Voting control within the firm

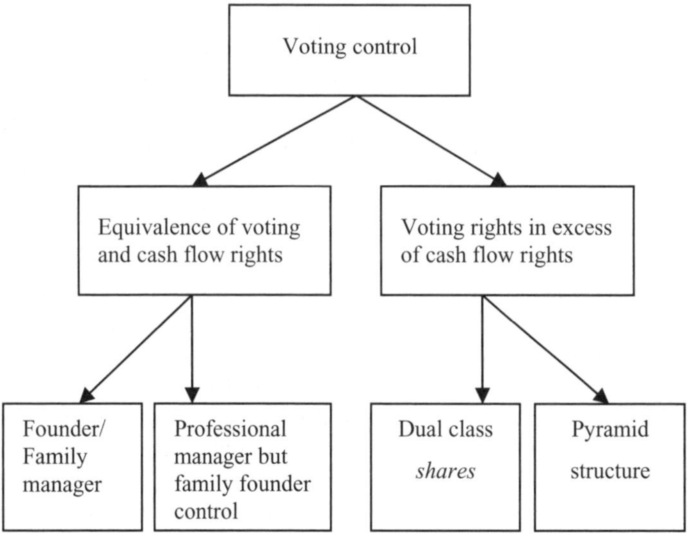

Source: P Halpern 'Systematic Perspectives on Corporate Governance Systems' Working Paper University of Toronto 1999.

[20] WW Bratton and JA McCahery 'Comparative Corporate Governance and the Theory of the Firm: the Case Against Global Cross Reference' (1999) 38 Columbia J of Transnational L 213.

The most widely used mechanism to accumulate control power with a limited investment is ownership pyramids or cascades which can enable a shareholder to maintain control throughout multiple layers of ownership while at the same time sharing the investment with other (minority) shareholders at each intermediate ownership tier. Some European countries have traditionally allowed companies to design a pyramidal structure, which is one of the mechanisms that reduces the liquidity constraints of large shareholders while it allows those shareholders to retain substantial voting power.

In a similar vein, the issuance of dual-class voting shares to separate ownership and control allows a large shareholder to transfer resources from the company. The private benefits of control are non-transferable benefits beyond the financial return on investment. The large shareholder is usually allowed a seat on the board of directors and will thus receive non-public information on the firm's cost structure or on supply contracts of the competitors. The large shareholder could, for example, after obtaining such strategic information, renew negotiations about the subcontractor's price. Consequently, such transactions can lead to the creation of an agency conflict, namely the oppression of minority shareholders' rights.

Dual-class shares are frequently used in Scandinavia, France, Spain, Italy, and the US but are not present in the UK. Dual-class shares are commonly employed by European firms, but with large differences across EU member states. Faccio and Lang document 5,232 firms in 13 western European countries.[21] For instance, in Finland, Italy, Denmark, Switzerland, and Sweden, the proportion of firms with outstanding dual-class stocks ranges from around 35% to 65%. For Norway, Germany, UK, Austria, and Ireland, the range varies from 13% to 24%. In Portugal and Spain, the proportions are almost negligible.

The negative effect of concentrated ownership is reflected in the size of the control premium. This is the difference between the market value of shares, and how much someone is willing to pay for those shares if they confer (or maintain) control over a company. The existence of a control premium reflects the gains that majority shareholders can make at the expense of outside, minority shareholders. The size of the control premium depends on a number of factors, including the competition in the market for corporate control, the size of the block sold, the distribution of shares in the target firm, the inequality of voting power, the nationality of the buyer, and the financial condition of the firm involved.[22] The existence of large private benefits of control suggests that blockholders may be able to obtain a large share of the rents. In some European countries, the size of private benefits appears to be significant.

[21] M Faccio and L Lang 'The Ultimative Ownership of Western European Companies' (2002) 65 J of Financial Economics 365.

[22] E Berglöf and M Burkart 'EU Takeover Policy' (2003) 18 Economic Policy 173.

Almost invariably, the existence of large private benefits of control suggests that blockholders may be able to obtain a large share of the rents.[23] The control premium is lower in Anglo-American market-based corporate governance systems that have widely dispersed ownership structures and provide a high level of legal protection for minority shareholders. For example, the mean premium in Austria, Italy, and Portugal was 38%, 37%, and 20% respectively.[24] At the same time, there are some European countries that show a mean premium below 10%, suggesting there are significant variations in levels of extraction of private benefits. Economists studying private benefits of control warn that estimating the value of control premium is complicated. In trying to explain the size of private benefits, economists have pointed to a number of factors, including the competition in the market for corporate control, the size of the block sold, the nationality of the buyer, the inequality of voting power, and the financial condition of the firm involved.

Goergen and Renneboog[25] show why the levels of control are so different in two countries with strongly varying corporate governance regimes, Germany (a bank- and blockholder-based governance system) and the UK (a market-based regime). A first reason for shareholders to hold larger voting stakes in German firms is found in the differences in the regulatory and legal environment. A detailed analysis of the regulation of the German and UK stock exchanges, of the rules on minority shareholder protection, of informational transparency, and of the takeover codes shows that there is lower shareholder protection in Germany. The voting practice at annual meetings, the composition of the board of directors, and their fiduciary duties further reinforce this relative weakness of shareholder rights in Germany. As a consequence, control is more valuable to shareholders of German firms, either to avoid expropriation of their investments or to take advantage of the higher levels of private benefits. Furthermore, holding large control stakes is less expensive in Germany relative to the UK because ownership pyramids, the possibility of issuing non-voting stock, and the possibility to nominate one's representatives to the board of directors ensure that control can be maintained with relatively low levels of cash-flow rights.

Recent studies have attempted to show more directly the influence of controlling shareholders' non pro rata distributions on the shares of the company. Claessens and others[26] study the implication of greater control rights versus

[23] LA Bebchuk 'A Rent-Protection Theory of Corporate Ownership and Control' Harvard Law and Economics Discussion Paper no 260/1999.

[24] Dyck and Zingales (n 16).

[25] M Goergen and L Renneboog 'Why are the Levels of Control (so) Different in German and UK companies? Evidence from Initial Public Offerings' (2003) 19 J of L, Economics and Organization 141.

[26] S Claessens and others 'Disentangling the Incentive and Entrenchment Effects of Large Shareholdings' University of Amsterdam Working Paper 2003.

greater cash-flow rights on firm value. It is assumed that the lower the cash-flow rights of controlling shareholders, the greater the incentive for dominant insiders to divert firms assets for their own benefit. Evidently, these studies support calls for new legal rules and other reform strategies that offer a better chance to limit the effects of managerial self-dealing and transactions involving controlling shareholders. In response to the weaknesses of established company law frameworks, policymakers have attempted to address these agency problems by providing more effective courts, better mechanisms to enforce shareholders' rights, and increased transparency. Certainly, in some continental European jurisdictions with poor quality law, the question is what combination of measures will suffice. More particularly, if self-dealing is the mainstay of blockholder returns, then the introduction of a tougher reform package may be necessary to constrain self-dealing transactions. The experience in other jurisdictions has shown that strong legal rules and institutions can place constraints on the potential for insiders to tunnel resources out of firms.[27] Unsurprisingly, controlling shareholders operating in weak legal environments in the EU will systematically resist reforms that affect both private benefits of control and managerial agency costs.[28] That said, it is suggested that weak legal environments should avoid transplanting regulations that are in place in stronger legal systems. It may turn out that, by devising their own legal strategies to prevent detrimental outcomes associated with self-dealing and related party transactions, these 'weaker' legal environments are better placed to create more efficient mechanisms to limit the risks associated with illicit related party transactions in their own jurisdictions. Not only will these reforms take into account regulatory structures and enforcement strategies in place, but experience suggest that they are likely to be more effective when implemented with other rules developed to regulate problems in the area. Moreover, this gives these countries the necessary discretion to legislate related party transactions without hampering their beneficial aspects. But, as the next example from Italy shows, if exogenous pressures are present, for example, due to a scandal, inertia still plays a pivotal role in the evolution of regulatory reform.

[27] Friedman and others (n 10).

[28] Ferrarini and Giudici (n 9). The recent experience of the protracted conflict over the Takeover Directive illustrates this point. An organized coalition of interest groups was able to minimize the chances that lawmakers would pass legislation that would affect the private benefits of blockholders and managers. These groups maintained an effective coalition over time and consequently obtained a legislative compromise that allows member states to opt out of Article 9 and 11 of the Directive on Takeovers (G Hertig and JA McCahery 'Company and Takeover Law Reforms in Europe: Misguided Harmonization or Regulatory Competition' (2003) 4 Eur Business Organization L Rev 179).

2. Parmalat

As highlighted above, good corporate governance can make it hard for controlling shareholders – that are organized in pyramids – to arrange to use, without risk of punishment, a variety of illicit related party transactions and other financial transactions for their own benefit.[29] Often described as the European Enron, the collapse of the Parmalat Group drew attention to the urgent requests by many governments and the Commission to respond to the cause of these problems.[30]

The Parmalat Group raised more than €13.2 billion in debt and equity from investors in Europe and the US Even though the company was highly successful in raising new sources of funding, the Parmalat Group was forced, due to its loss-making operations, to divert many of its proceeds from these issues to cover expiring bonds. As it turns out, Calisto Tanzi, Parmalat's chairman and CEO, employed a range of fraudulent schemes to enrich family members and private companies controlled by the family trust. Not only were the company's top directors and family-controlled managers involved in perpetuating the scheme, but the gatekeepers and lawyers allegedly facilitated the fraud by manipulating balance sheets and financial disclosures to regulators. The deceit was pursued successfully over a number of years until the group's eventual collapse in December 2003. It is hard to imagine a more devastating critique of the controlling shareholder system of governance in Europe. For these reasons, the basic element of the fraud is discussed below.

Until its collapse, the Parmalat Group was one of the world's largest leading dairy and food products groups with operations in more than 30 countries worldwide. The company, which was controlled by the Tanzi family and operated out of Collecchio, Parma, was formed in the 1960s as a classic food trading concern. The family-controlled business was rapidly transformed, as a consequence of innovations in the processing of milk (UHT), into a dairy company, and thereafter quickly extended its operations into foreign and food-related markets. By the 1980s, the group had diversified into non-food-related markets. However, these ventures were unsuccessful, which eventually led to financial problems. In order to redress these financial problems, Coloniale restructured the group, and Parmlat Finanziaria, the listed holding company, emerged.

In the 1990s, Parmalat continued its expansion of its dairy and food services and diversified into tourism and the professional sports sector through the sponsorship of a number of domestic Italian and foreign football teams. For Parmalat, most of these investments were loss making from their inception. Having extended its reach to North and South America to more than fifty companies by the end of the decade, Parmalat derived most of its income

[29] Friedman and others (n 10); S Johnson and others 'Tunneling' (2000) 90 American Economic Rev (Papers and Proceedings) 22.

[30] Communication from the Commission to the Council and European Parliament (n 4).

internationally. Parmalat financed its ambitious growth expansion strategy by a combination of national and international debt issues and equity

In 2001, Parmalat suffered financial difficulties with its operations in Latin America, which, if known to the market, would have led to higher costs of capital. In order to appear investor-friendly, Parmalat artificially enhanced its consolidated income statements and balance sheets while taking actions to conceal its ever-increasing debt mountain. This led top management and officers, in turn, to undertake a series of paper trail transactions designed to systematically mislead investors regarding certain assets and liabilities. For example, Parmalat's management created false documentation and bank accounts to improve their cash position. As part of this effort, a letter from the Bank of America was created confirming a €3.9 billion bank account of Bonlat Financing Corporation, a Parmalat subsidiary incorporated in the Cayman Islands.[31] This false confirmation letter was used by Bonlat's auditors to certify its 2002 financial statement. Moreover, as part of its fraudulent effort, Parmalat supported its 2003 offerings of unsecured notes to US investors by disclosing Bonalat's 2002 certification and its 2002 audited financial statement, which included references to a non-existent bank account.[32]

During the years 2002 and 2003, the Parmalat Group encountered questions from supervisory authorities and gatekeepers about the quality of its financial statements and disclosures. For example, a February 2003 bond issue was cancelled due to concerns over debt sustainability and accounting problems. Subsequently the placement of private bonds in July 2003 led to regulatory pressures from Consob, the Italian financial regulator, when Parmalat Finanziaria's statutory auditor, Deloitte, cast doubt on financial statements. On 8 December 2003, the Parmalat Group was unable to make payment on a bond expiry, which led Standard and Poors to downgrade its debt to junk status. Meanwhile, Tanzi resigned as CEO on 15 December after acknowledging that company records were false, which the Bank of America confirmed on 19 December 2003. The company filed for bankruptcy on 23 December and was declared insolvent on 27 December 2003.

In the end, between 1990 and 2003, the Parmalat Group increased its total debt by €13.2 billion, while generating €1 billion from operations. But it spent €5.4 billion for unproductive acquisitions, €5.3 billion in bank charges and commissions, and €2.3 billion in financial diversions. From this perspective, then, the behavior of the Parmalat Group is immediately apparent. The expansion strategy was a costly failure that led to huge losses. The financial structure of the group needed to be expanded in order to support significant diversions of private

[31] *In re Parmalat Securities Litigation*: Master Docket 04 Civ 0030 (LAK) ECF Case, First Amended Consolidated Class Action Complaint for Violation of the Federal Securities Laws, United States District Court (SDNY).

[32] *SEC v Parmalat Finanziaria SpA* Complaint p 4.

benefits, the rapidly deteriorating balance sheet, and the costly arranging and borrowing fees. The architects of the fraud had anticipated that their strategy of foreign expansion and corresponding exploitation of weak foreign and Italian governance systems would allow them to exploit minority shareholders and creditors for a reasonably long period. If nothing else, the detailed investigations into Parmalat's collapse revealed the extent to which the same gatekeepers who did a poor job with Enron were prone to a sobering list of failures in their role of securing investors against fraud and improper disclosure.[33] In several important areas, the gatekeepers provided little monitoring help and, in some cases, may have made accurate certification of the financials more difficult. In an environment with these characteristics, crises will persist unless regulators have an incentive to alter the governance structure.

The sudden financial collapse at Parmalat quickly shattered any illusions that the accounting fraud and boardroom scandals were uniquely an American phenomenon. The Parmalat scandal not only drew attention once again to the susceptibility of European companies to internal fraud, but revealed that fraud is not concentrated in any one geographic region, industry, or size of company.

In retrospect, it was naïve to think that Europe would be shielded from the management practices and regulatory and social environment that gave rise to Parmalat's corporate culture, much less that it could achieve its corporate governance goals without building the institutions to support standards and procedures that protect investors and provide timely and high-quality company disclosure. Admittedly, the EU has supported the adoption of US-style corporate governance and securities law rules, and created a Financial Services Action Plan (FSAP) that calls attention to the need to regulate financial analysts, the accounting profession, audit quality, and off-balance sheet treatment of special purpose entities (SPEs).

However, the level of public and private securities law enforcement needed to encourage good corporate governance practices and disclosure – to prevent multiple crises – remains underdeveloped. Moreover, national-level reform efforts have run up against special interest group pressures.[34] The configuration of interests that retards efforts to enact strict oversight and effective control measures at the national level casts doubts on the effectiveness of legislative solutions introduced and implemented by the EU. And the problem is growing more severe with the enlargement of the EU and the political difficulties encountered by national governments to introduce far-reaching reforms. To further complicate matters, the presence of controlling shareholders in many eastern European member states questions the extent to which directors' fiduciary duties, mandatory disclosure, and voting can prove effective in discouraging

[33] Ferrarini and Giudici (n 9).

[34] 'Move to toughen Italy's law on false accounting fails' *Financial Times* 4 March 2005.

value-decreasing transactions.[35] Finally, the problem is complicated by the fact that neither the EU nor other national-level securities authorities have sufficient staff and expertise needed to root out the causes of opportunism and fraud.

III. Related Party Transactions

The Enron and Parmalat scandals illustrate the difficulty that auditors and regulators face in identifying related party relationships and transactions that are motivated by fraud or illicit earnings management. While there is widespread agreement on the need to regulate related party transactions, there is much less convergence on what transactions should be subject to deterrent regulation.

1. Why Should One Care About Related Party Transactions?

The received wisdom is that related party transactions play an important and legitimate role in a market economy. For firms, trade and foreign investment is often facilitated by inter-company financing transactions. Lower costs of capital and tax savings provide a strong incentive for engaging in these transactions. Indeed, there are many examples of related party transactions that yield benefits for companies. By far the most popular transactions include (1) inter-company loans or guarantees from parent to foreign subsidiary; (2) the sale of receivables to a special purpose entity; and (3) a leasing or licensing agreement between a parent and a foreign subsidiary. A key concern about related party transactions is that they might not be undertaken at market prices but can be influenced by the relationship between the two sides of a transaction: there is a conflict of interest for some person in the company. For both controlling shareholders and insiders such as management, related party transactions can be the mechanism for extracting private benefits of control at the cost of other shareholders. There are a broad array of legal strategies to regulate disclosure of related party transactions and conflicts of interests. Before proceeding, we will begin in the next section with a summary of the competing strategies for dealing with these transactions. The US debate provides a good summary of the lack of consensus around conflicted transactions.

[35] E Berglöf and S Claessens 'Enforcement and Corporate Governance' World Bank Policy Research Working Paper no 3409 (Septermber 2004).

2. Understanding the Competing Regulatory Visions

A large body of literature has considered these issues by referring to the American experience with conflicted transactions by management and controlling shareholders. It is important to recognize that US law once prohibited interested transactions involving managers and directors.[36] But the strategy for prohibiting self-dealing transactions underscores a particular political-legal tradition rather than a credible means to protect private investors and foster a more equitable distribution of wealth in society. Accordingly, the prohibition strategy failed to deter reallocations of wealth. In fact, aside from providing little protection against a single undetected transaction, the prohibition of self-dealing may have left many companies worse off as a consequence of preventing many efficient transactions.

This prompted the need for regulators to allow companies to pursue certain related party transactions not leading to conflicts of interest. The shift in self-dealing rules reflected the view that some non-abusive transactions are valuable and that parties should have incentives to pursue these transactions. US company law rules provide that self-dealing transactions are permitted subject to legal controls.[37] To protect outside investors from abusive transactions, state and federal laws regulate self-dealing, corporate opportunities, insider trading, and the compensation agreements with executives.

However, there are suggestions that the modern regulation of self-dealing transactions is misguided.[38] Thus, where managerial value diversion does not raise fairness and distributional concerns, there is no obvious need to protect shareholders against expropriation. Moreover, to the extent that value diversion is an alternative form of compensation, it probably makes little sense to subject conflicted transactions to restrictive legal rules.

Another approach, inspired in part by these views, stresses that the benign view of value diversion is misleading.[39] Managerial value diversion creates significant agency costs by eviscerating the incentive effects of performance-based pay. To be sure, there is evidence that extra-legal mechanisms, such as trust and loss of reputation, can lessen but not eliminate the inefficient subtraction of firm earnings. Notwithstanding these constraints, if the gains of opportunism are very large, legal standards may be insufficient to limit management from engaging in opportunistic behavior. This is an argument for encouraging more protec-

[36] R Clark *Corporate Law* (Little & Brown Boston 1986) 160-66.

[37] W Klein J Ramseyer and S Bainbridge *Business Associations* (Foundation New York: 2003).

[38] FH Easterbrook and DR Fischel *The Economic Structure of Corporate Law* (Harvard University Press Cambridge 1991).

[39] LA Bebchuk and C Jolls 'Managerial Value Diversion and Shareholder Wealth' (1999) 15 J of L, Economics and Organization 487, 488.

tive measures of minority investors, increased transparency, and stronger shareholder involvement in decisions involving transactions that could implicate a conflict of interest with management or a controlling shareholder.

While there is little agreement on the rationale to regulate related party transactions, there is even much less consensus on what transactions should be subject to deterrent regulation. To be sure, the nature of the problem varies: in companies with controlling shareholders and with corporate groups, the measures need to be different from those situations where ownership is spread and where the board and management is effectively entrenched.

3. Identifying Related Party Transactions

Various terminology and definitions are employed to define related parties and related party transactions across jurisdictions. In the US, the Financial Accounting Standards Board's (FASB) Statement no 57[40] provides that related party transactions involve transactions between a parent company and subsidiary; subsidiaries of a common parent; an enterprise and trusts for the benefit of employees; an enterprise and its principal owners, management, or members of their immediate families; and affiliates.[41] It is unlikely, however, that there is a simple definition that is sufficient for identifying all the transactions with related parties. A second ground for eliminating this approach is that certain complex transactions, which fail to meet the relevant criteria, may be too easily excluded on these grounds. Ruling out this approach is an important step for developing a basis to identify these transactions.

Seen in this light, the attempt to identify related party transactions raises complex issues. That said, the nature of related party transactions is best highlighted by general principles such as those of the International Accounting Standards Board rather than listing categories of people and entities. According to IAS 24, parties are considered to be related if one party has the ability to control the other party or exercise significant influence over the other party in making financial and operating decisions. Related party transactions are defined as a transfer of resources or obligations between related parties, regardless of whether or not a market price is charged. The OECD Principles take a similar approach and state that related parties can include entities that control or are under common control with the company, board members, and significant shareholders, including members of families and key management personnel.

[40] FASB Statement no 57 *Related Party Disclosures*.

[41] See also the revised version of IAS 24 9 (2003).

Transactions involving major shareholders or their close family either directly or indirectly are potentially the most difficult types of transactions to identify.[42] Again, the Enron and Parmalat scandals illustrate the difficulty that regulators face identifying related party relationships and transactions that are motivated by fraud. The complications arise not only from the complexity of many of these transactions, but also involve auditors' problems of detecting material misstatements in financial statements due to a related party transaction.

There is no question that the American Institute of Certified Public Accountants' (AICPA) Statement of Auditing Standard no 45, AU Sec 334 (2001) has supplied a feasible approach for identifying material transactions, such as interest-free borrowing, asset sales that diverge from appraisal value, in-kind transactions, and loans made without scheduled terms. Other indicators can be used as well to detect potential opportunism. One possibility is to have auditors obtain information about management responsibilities to run the company, controls over management activities, and management arrangements with various components of the entity. At the same time, AU Sec 334 can be used to identify the existence of related party transactions. Company auditors can employ a range of audit procedures, from the review of non-recurring transactions to the invoices of regular services, to evaluate conflicted transactions.

That said, there are countless other procedures that could be used to identify the existence of conflicted transactions. Ultimately, policymakers must employ a practice-sensitive approach in establishing the appropriate regulatory strategies. There can be little doubt that we should not underestimate the ability of managers and other participants to respond to regulators' strategies to restrict their activities. Given the significant transaction costs in developing new regulatory techniques and the incentives of insiders to create more opaque and effective means to transfer assets, lawmakers should, in the absence of a complete restructuring of the legal system, be encouraged to consider other mechanisms besides the company law and securities regulation to monitor and enforce these agreements. Critically, market mechanisms can also be used in conjunction with mandatory regulation because they take into account the role of reputation effects to stem the abusive practices of management and controlling shareholders and their affiliates.

IV. Regulation of Related Party Transactions

As noted above, the Commission and member states have undertaken steps to tackle the weaknesses in the governance system as revealed by the Parmalat scandal. EC regulators have recommended collective board responsibility for financial disclosure, and mandated fuller disclosure of related party transactions

[42] IAS 24.9 provides 'that a related party transaction is a transfer of resources, services, or obligations between related parties, regardless of whether a price is charged.'

and of off-balance sheet transactions including SPEs. In the next section, we assess the measures designed to regulate related party transactions.

1. Information Rights

Minority shareholders must have means to detect opportunistic behavior by the controlling shareholders. Minority shareholders may gather public information and private information. The main source of public information is the periodic publication of the company's financial disclosures and audited annual report. In Europe, public companies are obliged to publish their annual reports under law. The Fourth Directive contains detailed requirements for the preparation of balance sheets, profit and loss statements, and annual reports. Although the directive demands that the accounts give a true and fair view of the assets, liabilities, financial position, and results of the company, the information is not always accurate. While annual accounts must be adopted by the shareholders in many jurisdictions within five months following the end of the financial year, some companies may extend this period to 13 months, which will obviously diminish the reliability of the disclosed information. Moreover, annual reports do not fully disclose information about the possible expropriation of the company's benefits. Direct and indirect transactions between the company and controlling shareholder can affect the accuracy of the annual reports.

2. Disclosure of Related Party Transactions: EU Regulation

There is satisfactory transparency regarding such transactions for all listed companies with the European Union under IAS 24 and under the national codes.

In terms of disclosure of related party transactions, regardless of whether there have been transactions between a parent and a subsidiary, an entity must disclose the name of its parent and, if different, the ultimate controlling party. If neither the entity's parent nor the ultimate controlling party produces financial statements available for public use, the name of the next most senior parent that does so must also be disclosed (see IAS 24.12). Furthermore, IAS 24 mandates that for each category of related parties, companies should disclose the nature of the related party relationship as well as information about the transactions and outstanding balances necessary for an understanding of the potential effect of the relationship on the financial statements (see IAS 17-18). Such disclosure should include the amount of the transactions, the amount of outstanding balances, provisions for doubtful debts related to the amount of outstanding balances, and expenses recognized during the period in respect of bad or doubtful debts due from related parties.

Recently, the EU proposed extending the disclosure of related party transactions for non-listed companies beyond affiliated undertaking in order to restore public confidence in companies' financial statements and contribute to integrated capital markets.[43] EC regulators defend the requirement on the grounds that (1) related party transactions are very often material for non-listed companies; and (2) disclosure would not be too cumbersome, as these firms usually do not have complicated off-balance sheet arrangements.

Nevertheless, there are numerous techniques that parties use to avoid the IAS 24. As we have seen earlier, the controlling shareholder is able to obtain non-public information and use it for personal financial benefit or tip other family members – who might then make an investment decision on the basis of the information. The inaccuracy of public information is less pressing if a minority shareholder is also a director in a company. In that case, he will be able to

Table IAS 24 (after the December 2003 revision)

Objective: ensuring that a firm discloses the existence of related parties and related party transactions, which may affect its financial position.	
Related Parties IAS 24.9	A party is related to an entity if: (a) directly, or indirectly through one or more intermediaries, the party: (i) controls, is controlled by, or is under common control with, the entity (this includes parents, subsidiaries, and fellow subsidiaries); (ii) has an interest in the entity that gives it significant influence over the entity; or (iii) has joint control over the entity; (b) the party is an associate (as defined in IAS 28 Investments in Associates) of the entity; (c) the party is a joint venture in which the entity is a venturer (see IAS 31 Interests in Joint Ventures); (d) the party is a member of the key management personnel of the entity or its parent; (e) the party is a close member of the family of any individual referred to in (a) or (d); (f) the party is an entity that is controlled, jointly controlled, or significantly influenced by or for which significant voting power in such entity resides with, directly or indirectly, any individual referred to in (d) or (e); or (g) the party is a post-employment benefit plan for the benefit

[43] European Commission 'Proposal for a Directive of the European Parliament and of the Council amending Council Directives 78/660/EEC and 83/349/EEC concerning the annual accounts of certain types of companies and consolidated accounts' (n 6).

	of employees of the entity, or of any entity that is a related party of the entity.
IAS 24.11	Not related are: • two enterprises simply because they have a director or key manager in common; • two venturers who share joint control over a joint venture; • providers of finance, trade unions, public utilities, government departments, and agencies in the course of their normal dealings with an enterprise; • a single customer, supplier, franchiser, distributor, or general agent with whom an enterprise transacts a significant volume of business merely by virtue of the resulting economic dependence.
Related Party Transaction	
IAS 24.9	A related party transaction is a transfer of resources, services, or obligations between related parties, regardless of whether a price is charged.
Disclosure	
IAS 24.12	Relationships between parents and subsidiaries (irrespective of transactions)
IAS 24.16	Key management compensation
IAS 24.17-18	Related party transactions: • the amount of the transactions; • the amount of outstanding balances, including terms and conditions and guarantees; • provisions for doubtful debts related to the amount of outstanding balances; • expense recognized during the period in respect of bad and doubtful debts due from related parties
IAS 24.21	The firm must provide proof if it states that related party transactions were made on terms that are common in arm's length transactions.

Source: Deloitte. IASPLUS <http://www.iasplus.com> (3 July 2005).

influence and monitor management decisions directly. Legally requiring shareholder approval may have the same effect. However, if minority shareholders are not in a managerial capacity or involved in the decision-making process, they are unlikely to gather the information without relying on a legal mandate.

Thus, even though enhanced financial statement transparency should be encouraged, regulators must not underestimate the higher costs of disclosure for those non-listed companies. If the idea is to increase the accountability of non-listed companies, the EC may need to subject disclosure of related party transactions on an aggregate basis.

3. Transparency of Special Purpose Entities

Typically, SPEs are employed by financial intermediaries and companies to facilitate arm's length financial transfers. As noted above, Parmalat and former CEO Fausto Tonna used an array of off-balance sheet arrangements in pursuit of this scheme to artificially inflate assets on the group's consolidated balance sheet and preserve its access to external funding, particularly in the US. The preferred method was to transfer assets, falsely, from Parmalat to an SPE in exchange for consideration, which the SPEs would raise from loans from Parmalat. Subsequently, management of Parmalat would remove the asset from its own books and then record the loan as an asset. Since these off-balance sheet arrangements played a central role in the Parmalat fraud and accounting scandal, the Commission has attempted to improve disclosure by proposing an amendment to the Seventh Directive, mandating that companies must disclose all off-balance sheet arrangements that have a material impact on the company.

The new SPE rules are arguably likely to improve the source of information to investors. The complex and obscure transactions designed by Parmalat's executive and professional advisors ensured that investors would have little accurate and timely information to assess the company's performance. To the extent the rules are likely to have an impact on companies, it should be clear that the new measures will likely cause the most difficulties for groups of companies, such as Parmalat, that have been able to successfully prevent disclosure of these type of conflicts.[44]

4. Internal Governance Structure

Since the fallout from the audit scandals, the need for strong board oversight has been a dominant theme in corporate governance discussions. The role of independent, non-executive directors, in particular, has resurfaced as a key issue in the policy debate. Outside directors are claimed to be an indispensable part of any good corporate governance system. In the US, for example, the Sarbanes-Oxley Act of 2002 includes important provisions on directors' independence only for audit committee purposes. Measures relating to audit committees are to be implemented through a self-regulatory process of stock market listing standards.

[44] Department of Trade and Industry (UK) *European Company Law and Corporate Governance, Directive Proposals on Company Reporting, Capital Maintenance and Transfer of the Registered Office of a Company, A Consultative Document* (DTI London 2005).

Second, the Sarbanes-Oxley Act proposes only two criteria for purposes of independence of audit committee members: (1) the acceptance of compensatory fees from the company or any subsidiary (other than for services as a director); and (2) whether or not the director is an 'affiliated person' of the company. The NYSE and NASDAQ also offer similar definitions and criteria of independence.

In continental Europe, the creation of independent boards is problematic. In most member states, controlling shareholders retain the power to appoint and dismiss both the board and the management of the company. Thus, the effectiveness of adopting US-style board independence rules to ensure independent audit committees – where the board remains exposed to controlling shareholder influence – is likely to yield few benefits.[45] Clearly there are no simple solutions.

Yet economic evidence suggests that one way to constrain controlling shareholder opportunism is to strengthen the independence of the board and the role of non-executive and supervisory directors in key areas of conflicts of interest.[46] Overall, decisions in the areas of executive remuneration and audit supervision should be made exclusively by non-executive directors, a majority of whom are independent. Recently, the Commission has proposed a set of non-binding minimum standards for independence and requires enhanced identification of conflicts of interest.[47] Crucially, because of the diversity of legal systems in the EU, the Commission did not recommend a precise number of independent supervisory members on the board. Moreover, the Commission proposed that audit members be composed exclusively of non-executive or supervisory directors, a majority of which are independent.

To be sure, the evidence is mixed concerning whether director independence actually curbs agency problems and increases efficiency of board decision-making.[48] In general, the thrust of the empirical literature does not seem to support the common perception that board independence increases decision-making capacities of the board and the value of the firm. Independence is a matter of objective judgment rather than definition. Second, nagging questions remain about the value of audit committee independence. Nevertheless, the Commission, to the extent that it has taken steps to establish rules that are consistent with the diversity of governance regimes in Europe, has provided measures that are likely to promote, as we have seen elsewhere, better internal governance in a controlling shareholder system of governance.

[45] JC Coffee (n 8).

[46] BS Black H Jang and W Kim 'Does Corporate Governance Predict Firms' Market Value? Evidence From Korea' Stanford Law and Economics Working paper no 237/2003.

[47] European Commission, Recommendation on the Role of (Independent) Non-executive or Supervisory Directors and on the Committees of the (Supervisory) Board, available at: <http://europa.eu.int/comm/internal_market/company/docs/independence/2004-recommendation_en.pdf>.

[48] R Romano 'The Sarbanes-Oxley Act and the Making of Quack Corporate Governance' (2004) 114 Yale L J 1521.

V. National-Level Reforms

The purpose of this section is to analyze the evolution of corporate governance mechanisms governing related party transactions at the member state level. In contrast with the US, where the evolution has been well publicized, developments in European jurisdictions are less easily accessible due to inherent differences in doctrine and language. Moreover, in Europe corporate governance reforms are too diverse, making it difficult to speak of genuine European developments. For instance, the differences in ownership structures, as noted earlier, tend to be relevant in shaping corporate governance reforms. While some EU member states have a blockholder system (Germany, France, and Italy), others can be characterized by a dispersed equity system (eg United Kingdom). In addition, some jurisdictions have established a hybrid system (eg the Netherlands). Consequently, and because what matters here are corporate governance reforms in practice, this comparative survey needs to be selective. Accordingly, this section confines itself to controlling shareholder-oriented jurisdictions in which corporate governance reforms have recently attracted the attention of law reformers, such as Germany and the Netherlands.

It appears that reform-oriented jurisdictions in the EU attempt to discourage abusive related party transactions not only via changes in their company laws – which focus merely on improving transparency – but also through the promulgation of more enabling corporate governance codes.[49] Nevertheless, the mandatory and enabling legal mechanisms that could discipline the behavior and provide minority shareholders with greater protections are unlikely, as we will show, to be found sufficient.

1. Germany

The modernization of corporate governance codes is arguably focused on increasing the competitiveness of indigenous firms and fostering confidence in the management of these firms. Based on these principles, the Government Commission on the German Corporate Governance Code addressed amendments in several important corporate governance areas, such as the establishment of an auditing committee and the conflicts of interests in the supervisory board. The supervisory board consists merely of outside and independent directors and has

[49] OECD Steering Group on Corporate Governance *Survey of Corporate Governance Developments in OECD Countries* (2003). Since tunnelling is an important problem in Italy, the Italian legislature has also promulgated rules that deal with the definition and control of conflicts of interests and the role of independent directors (L Enriques 'Bad Apples, Bad Oranges' A Comment from Old Europe on Post-Enron Corporate Governance Reforms' (2003) 38 Wake Forest L Rev 911).

the task to appoint and supervise management.[50] Germany has a two-tier board system; that is, publicly held companies – and large close companies – have a mandatory separation between a management board and a supervisory board. The supervisory board plays a pivotal role in the event that conflicts of interests appear at the level of the management board. The German corporate governance code, which follows a 'comply-or-explain' approach,[51] states that 'all members of the management board shall disclose conflicts of interest to the supervisory board without delay'.[52] Substantial transactions also require the approval of the supervisory board. This corresponds to §112 of the German Stock Company Act, which states that the supervisory board represents the company in deals with self-interested members of the management board. Disregarding the procedures related to self-dealing and abusive related party transactions will render the members of the management board and supervisory board personally liable.[53] Willful and deliberate actions can entail criminal charges against the defaulting members.

Members of the supervisory board who have a personal interest in a transaction with the company must inform the supervisory board.[54] Subsequently, the

[50] German law attempts to guarantee the independence of the members of the supervisory board. See T Baums and K Scott 'Taking Shareholder Protection Seriously? Corporate Governance in the United States and Germany' University of Frankfurt Working Paper no 119/2003: 'German law seeks to guarantee the independence of the supervisory board members from the management board. First, the members of the management board are appointed by the supervisory board (§ 84 Stock Corporation Act), and second, the management board's influence on the selection of the members of the supervisory board is limited because in companies with more than 2,000 employees, only half of the supervisory board is appointed by the shareholders and the other half is elected by the employees (in corporations with between 500 and 2,000 employees, the employees appoint one-third of the supervisory board). The management board's ability to influence the selection of the shareholders' representatives seated on the supervisory board will depend on whether the company is a publicly held company with a widely dispersed free float or a corporation with one or more dominant shareholders. In a company with a majority shareholder both organs will be dominated by this shareholder, whereas in companies with widely dispersed ownership the management board and in particular its chairman will often have a decisive say in who will become a management board or a supervisory board member, insofar as the latter are elected by the shareholders.'

[51] On 26 July 2002, an amendment to the German Stock Corporation Act took effect. The amendment provided a statutory basis for the German corporate governance code and obliged publicly held corporations to publish on a yearly basis a statement in which they declare compliance with the code or explain any deviations from it.

[52] § 4.3.4 of the German Corporate Governance Code also states that members of the management board must inform the other members of the management board of any conflicts of interests. The code does not include related party transaction with persons connected with the members of the board of management. See Baums and Scott (n 50).

[53] See § 93 and §116 of the German Stock Corporation Act.

[54] See § 5.5 of the German Corporate Governance Code. The personal interests may result from a consultant or directorship function with clients, suppliers, lenders, or other business partners.

supervisory board must disclose any conflicts of interests to the general meeting of shareholders in their annual report.[55] Material conflicts of interests and those which are not merely temporary can result in the termination of the member's mandate.[56] The company will be represented by the entire board of management and supervisory board in transactions with an interested member of the supervisory board.[57]

While the German corporate governance code addresses merely related party transactions involving members of the board of management and supervisory board, German law has primarily focused on conflicts between controlling shareholders and minority shareholders. The German law on groups of companies (*Konzernrecht*) provides for the disclosure of transactions between the company and its affiliated companies in an annual report that must be controlled and verified by an independent auditor. Disclosure to the supervisory board should ensure that the transactions have taken place at arm's length prices.[58] Controlling shareholders also owe duties of loyalty to the minority shareholders.[59]

In order for the duty of loyalty to operate effectively, shareholders must have means to detect opportunistic behavior by controlling shareholders and managers. To this end, the German government drafted and published a plan[60] that emphasizes the importance of information, transparency, and disclosure. It is, among other things, proposed that shareholders holding the greater of 1% of the total share capital or shares with a value of €100,000 may appoint a special auditor to investigate fraud and offenses by controlling firm participants. However, if shareholders initiate investigations based on false pretenses and lies, they will bear the costs of the auditor's appointment and investigations.[61]

This raises the question of how minority shareholders can enforce legal rules and duties and bring an action against alleged offenders. While German law posed significant hurdles for shareholders to bring actions for breach of fiduciary duties, the German government's plan, which aims at strengthening business' integrity and shareholder protection,[62] also contains elaborated provisions to enforce shareholders' rights.[63] One of the issues the government addressed in its

[55] See § 5.5.3 of the German Corporate Governance Code.

[56] See § 5.5.3 of the German Corporate Governance Code.

[57] See § 114 of the German Stock Corporation Act.

[58] See Baums and Scott (n 50, arguing that the fact that the report is presented only to the supervisory board – and not the shareholders – presents an enforcement issue).

[59] J Dine *The Governance of Corporate Groups* (Cambridge University Press Cambridge 2000) 58.

[60] Bundesregierung *Maßnahmenkatalog der Bundesregierung zur Stärkung der Unternehmensintegrität und des Anlegerschutzes* (Berlin 2003).

[61] See the contribution of K Pistor in this volume.

[62] Bundesregierung (n 60).

[63] See the contribution by H Baum in this volume.

plan seeks to broaden the possibility of shareholders to bring a derivative suit against directors and supervisory board members. §147 of the German Stock Company Act, which facilitates derivative suits, must be amended by lowering the threshold for bringing these actions to shareholdings of 1% of the share capital or a quotation or market value of €100,000. In order to prevent misapplication of derivative actions, the government proposes to introduce and clarify the business judgment rule in § 93 of the German Stock Company Act. Moreover, the report stresses that courts should endeavor to employ principles when determining whether a derivative action should be allowed to proceed.

The supervisory board is allowed to pursue direct actions against a member of the board of management who is liable to the company.[64] However, since a breach of duty by a director also implies a failure of the supervisory board to supervise the policy of management and the general course of affairs of the company, a board, in practice, will be reluctant to bring these actions. As a consequence, the German legislature has given shareholders the right to demand that the company initiate an action against members of the management board or supervisory board. In such a case, it is obvious that the board of management or the supervisory board are likely to represent the company, depending on the defendant in question.[65] Although Germany has recently published plans to clarify the position of shareholders, more needs to be done to align Germany with prevailing corporate governance practices around the world. Among other things, German academics have recommended clarifying the standard for liability and simplifying the procedure used to enforce liability. For instance, they argue that German law should provide for US-like class actions, which give affected shareholders a better incentive to bring an action against opportunists within the company.[66]

2. The Netherlands

The Netherlands has a reputation for a business-friendly environment. However, its reputation for corporate integrity was recently tarnished by the Ahold accounting scandal. In order to shore up investor confidence, Dutch policymakers appointed a special committee of businessmen and experts to draft a new code of corporate governance. On 9 December 2003, the Tabaksblat Committee released

[64] Cf § 112 of the German Stock Corporation Act.

[65] See § 147 of the German Stock Corporation Act (provision granting a special right to the general meeting of shareholders to appoint a representative. In most cases this will be granted to a corporate body, such as the board of management or the supervisory board).

[66] Baums and Scott (n 50).

its report on corporate governance.[67] In line with international developments, the code relies on the 'comply-or-explain' rule.[68] The code is based on two pillars: 'Good entrepreneurship, including integrity and transparency of decision-making by the management board, and proper supervision thereof, including accountability for such supervision, are essential if the stakeholders are to have confidence in the management board and the supervision.'

As for related party transactions, the code recommends that, besides disclosure to the chairman of the supervisory board, board members – and/or the company – need the approval of the supervisory board to enter into transactions in which they have a material interest.[69] The code states that a conflict of interests exists, in any event, if the company intends to enter into a transaction with a legal entity (i) in which a management board member personally has a material financial interest; (ii) which has a management board member who has a relationship under family law with a management board member of the company, or (iii) in which a management board member of the company has a management or supervisory position. The same procedure applies to members of the supervisory board and persons who own at least 10% of the shares in the company. Thus, transactions involving conflicts of interests need supervisory board approval. Moreover, such transactions must also be included in the company's annual report. Additionally, Dutch case law appears to be moving in the direction of requiring management board members to notify shareholders of material decisions that impact their interests.

It is worth noting that the code requires the independence of supervisory board members. Yet forcing companies to explain why individual non-executive directors are qualified to serve on the board in their particular role is a requirement that is past its prime. Moreover, by increasing the role of independent supervisory board members, the Tabaksblat Committee implicitly acknowledges a trade-off between the restriction of any potential conflicts of interest on the one hand, and the incompatibility of the independent board members on the other hand.[70] To be sure, the Tabaksblat Committee attempts to resolve this difficulty by introducing an induction program that is designed to expose directors to the

[67] The Corporate Governance Committee drew up this corporate governance code at the request of Euronext Amsterdam, the Netherlands Centre of Executive and Supervisory Directors (NCD), the Foundation for Corporate Governance Research for Pension Funds (SCGOP), the Association of Stockholders (VEB), the Association of Securities-Issuing Companies (VEUO), and the Confederation of Netherlands Industry and Employers (VNO-NCW) at the invitation of the Minister of Finance and the Minister for Economic Affairs.

[68] J Rickford 'Codes and Codification of Corporate Governance – The UK Perspective and Europe' Working Paper prepared for the CEPS Roundtable Conference on Corporate Governance Reform in the European Union (2004).

[69] See principle II.3 of the Dutch Corporate Governance Code.

[70] KJ Hopt 'Modern Company and Capital Market Problems Improving European Corporate Governance after Enron' (2002) 3 J of Corporate L Studies 221.

legal and financial affairs of the company, and any unique or specific features of the company along with its regulations covering the conduct of supervisory board members.

Finally, the Dutch corporate governance code recognizes the importance of whistleblowers in detecting and disclosing abusive related party transactions and illegal acts. Since it is often difficult to define and monitor related party transactions, particularly in complex and international groups, the corporate system of checks and balances has a high propensity to fail to prevent opportunistic behavior by insiders. In these cases, whistleblowers play a pivotal role in unfolding scandals and protecting firm participants, such as shareholders, investors, and creditors, from harm resulting from opportunism. Still, whistleblowers run the risk of employers wreaking havoc on the employee's career. Current law fails to adequately protect whistleblowers from employer retaliation when they come forward with crucial information. In order to improve and clarify the rights of whistleblowers, the Tabaksblat Committee imposes an obligation on the management board to ensure that employees have the possibility of reporting irregularities without having a ruinous effect on their reputation and career.[71] It remains to be seen whether this arrangement is sufficient. Still, legislative and statutory safe harbor provisions, which clearly articulate whistleblowers' rights rather than leaving this protection up to the determination by the company's board of management and the courts *ex post*, arguably provide a better mechanism for encouraging whistleblowers and punishing those who retaliate against them.[72]

3. The Stickiness of Corporate Governance Codes

As we have seen, both Germany and the Netherlands have, both through their company law statutes and corporate governance codes, attempted to create an environment in which there is limited space for abusive related party transactions. Given the difficulties of identifying and curbing the effects of illicit related party transactions, it might be argued that a 'comply-or-explain' strategy is the preferred mechanism for lawmakers. The function of corporate governance codes is to offer firms and other stakeholders with a set of flexible principles that represent 'best practice' norms, and hence help to mitigate opportunism and enhance business performance. These codes have many benefits. Bar associations and other private interest groups can draw on their own resources when participating in the drafting process. Even though there are significant costs associated with participation in the corporate governance reform project, people tend to place

[71] See § II.1.6 of the Dutch Corporate Governance Code.

[72] See § 806 of the Sarbanes-Oxley Act, which prohibits retaliation against whistleblowers, and § 1107 which poses criminal penalties on retaliators (see annex 3 in this volume).

high value on being part of reform committees, party because of the reputational benefits associated with the creation of such a code.

Compared to statutory law, corporate governance codes may rely on a greater variety of legal techniques. First, these codes are for the most part drafted by disinterested lawmakers and experts, whose main concerns are reputational benefits and updating their legal expertise. Second, the code drafting process, which relies on technical input from experts rather than interest groups, is more likely to produce a coherent set of rules that may in the long run reduce opportunistic behavior of majority shareholders. In contrast, statutory lawmaking, which relies on politically oriented decision-makers to reach substantive compromises, more closely tracks a political model of decision-making. As a consequence, the legal rules produced will tend to reflect the interest group compromises overall. Third, since drafters of corporate governance codes are often motivated by considerations of reputation, they will be less inclined to create value-decreasing statutes. Fourth, corporate governance codes facilitate the optimal production of best practice principles that meet the needs of distinct firms on the one hand, while introducing norms that reflect the ever-changing needs of the business environment in which firms operate on the other hand. In general, codes serve to limit the effects of 'lock-in' obsolescence when the corporate governance groups and committees are engaged in the continuous revision of the codes against the background of changing market conditions.

However, since the success of the corporate governance codes depends on their adoption by firms without amendment, reform committees have little incentive to instigate radical changes that firms are unlikely to adopt. In other words, it is a better strategy for committee members to distil the common denominator of the various business practices and to leave aside the controversial subjects. In fact, as corporate governance committees put pressure on firms to adopt the principles, it is obvious that interest groups have high-powered incentives to lobby the reform committees. Interest groups run the risk of being stuck with a corporate governance code that may be disadvantageous to them. The 'stickiness' of promulgated corporate governance principles reinforces their incentives.[73] Thus, if interest groups are successful in their influence activities, their efforts may have widespread effect.

As discussed earlier, special interest groups have taken political actions, on behalf of their constituencies, to defeat reforms that threaten to alter the status quo. Even if lawmakers can surmount the influence activities of organized special interests by promulgating new legislation, the outcome may be suboptimal due its cumbersome nature. To be sure, the voluntary and flexible aspects of the corporate governance codes – which implicitly acknowledge that 'one size does not fit all' and thus takes into account the diversity of national company law

[73] EPM Vermeulen *The Evolution of Legal Business Forms in Europe and the United States* (Kluwer Law International The Hague 2003).

regimes – would provide firms with the necessary leeway for entering into beneficial related party transactions without facing costly and burdensome regulatory measures.

However, it is submitted that firms tend to adopt and comply with boilerplate and standardized provisions of the codes rather than explain such non-compliance – even though it might be more optimal.[74] In fact, it might be argued that the 'comply-or-explain' approach contributes significantly to the 'lock-in' effect in the context of the rules and norms of corporate governance. This inflexibility often leads to inefficiency, as the codes' provisions and mechanisms fail to respond to changes in the underlying social and economic conditions. In our view, the attempts to determine detailed 'best practice' codes could entail a costly and 'sticky' mechanism, which turns the corporate governance codes into little more than blueprints for box-tickers.

VI. Conclusion

This chapter has argued that the influence of the relative weight of different factors in a given corporate governance system will affect the choice of the appropriate rule for regulating conflicted transactions. We began with a description of the contrasting ownership structures in Europe and argued that the problems created by majority and minority shareholder relationships are complex and that, given the variety of circumstances in which problems can arise, the balance of strategies needed to provide an effective regulatory framework will be determined by different factors in each system and policy debate in each jurisdiction. The marked differences in systems of ownership and finance in continental European countries affect corporate performance in several ways and, therefore, influence the choice of strategies available for dealing with the agency problems of controlling shareholders. The Parmalat scandal was used to exemplify the importance of a variety of legal techniques to curb related party transactions.

We then turned to asking whether regulators should be concerned with related party transactions. We pointed out that, in some cases, related party transactions can play a positive role for firms. But to the extent that illicit related party transactions are detrimental to firm performance, we argued that they can be identified and prevented by a range of non-legal mechanisms, such as market reputation. It is submitted when private benefits from self-dealing transactions are high, such non-legal norms will be less effective in curbing fraud and abuse by controlling shareholders. In this regard, we pointed at the newly proposed audit and board reforms introduced by the EU, which are designed to restore and enhance investor confidence through increased disclosure and transparency of

[74] M Kahan and M Klausner 'Standardization and Innovation in Corporate Contracting (or "The Economics of Boilerplate")' (1997) 83 Virginia L Rev 713.

related party transactions and SPEs. Moreover, it appears that the appointment of independent directors, in firms with controlling shareholders, tends to increase firm performance and enhance minority protection.

Finally, we have seen that the member states are inclined to support the Commission's recent corporate governance action plan by promulgating 'comply--or-explain' based codes rather than hard law rules. By offering firms the much-needed flexibility to contract around a particular corporate governance best practice principle, the member states seem to acknowledge the fact that many related party transactions are neither inefficient nor illegal. However, we concluded by showing that the reform drive toward best practice solutions has the danger of firms adopting and complying with the boilerplate and standardized provisions of the codes, rather than explain such non-compliance – even though it may be more optimal. Thus, the 'comply-or-explain' approach may contribute significantly to the 'lock-in' effect in the context of the rules and norms of corporate governance.

Although this chapter emphasized the importance of clear and simple company law rules, it is argued that one legal framework suitable for companies across the board would be difficult to achieve. It is therefore suggested that company rules need to be as flexible as possible to enable these companies to contract into the desired transactions. In order to help participants to organize and manage their business in the most effective manner, optional guidelines could be implemented to supplement the existing legal frameworks. Such guidelines do not enshrine principles and norms that are a 'must' for adoption by all firms. These guidelines should be in the form of advice. In that respect, they serve three purposes: (1) they provide the business participants with recommended solutions to complement the contractual flexibility of the company law rules; (2) they provide focal point solutions to corporate governance problems among business participants; and (3) they are meant to assist business participants in the interpretation and implementation of good governance practices. These guidelines should arguably contain recommendations on the different ownership and control structures of companies, the composition of the board of directors, and the best practice regarding related party transactions.

Part 3:

Bureaucracy and Regulations

Legal Ground Rules in Coordinated and Liberal Market Economies

KATHARINA PISTOR*

I. Introduction

This contribution seeks to explain the affinity between the nature of economic systems – coordinated market economies (CMEs) and liberal market economies (LMEs) on the one hand, and legal origin (civil vs common law systems) on the other. The paper starts with the simple observation that LMEs tend to be common law jurisdictions, and CMEs civil law jurisdictions. It proposes that the affinity between economic and legal system offers important insights into the foundations of different types of market economies and, in particular, differences in the scope of the state vs the powers of the individual. The main argument is that the legal system serves as a coordination device for social preferences. At the most basic level, these social preferences are reflected in the allocation of rights and responsibilities either to individuals or away from them – to the collective or the state. These social preferences are reflected in legal ground rules stipulating who has the power to determine the meaning and contents of private contracts and who may seek outside help – judicial recourse – to settle disputes: the individual(s) or the collective.

This paper uses examples drawn from contract and corporate law to illustrate this point, but consciously refrains from making any value judgments. Moreover, each system produces its own costs and benefits in economic, social, and political terms, and the relative costs and benefits may change over time. Each system is

* I would like to thank participants at the Berlin Conference of September 2004 on 'Changes of Governance in Japan, Europe, and the US', as well as Harald Baum, Jeffrey Gordon, and participants in the seminar on 'Advanced Readings in Corporate Law' at Columbia Law School for insightful comments and suggestions. Any remaining errors are those of the author.

highly path dependent.[1] By implication, changes in a subset of rules that realise ground rules of the legal system, such as the relaxation of mandatory provisions governing workers' participation in corporate governance (co-determination) in countries that follow a stakeholder model, or, conversely, the introduction of constituency statutes in systems that adhere to the shareholder value model, will not fundamentally alter the basic nature of the respective legal or economic system.

II. Types of Market Economies

Recent years have seen a renewed interest in comparing different types of market economies, or capitalist systems. Hall's and Soskice's publication of 'Varieties of Capitalism'[2] is only the culmination of a voluminous body of literature in political sciences on this issue. In economics, the collapse of the socialist system has precipitated substantial interest in comparing different types of capitalist systems.[3]

Observers of European economies have long noted differences across economic systems that are all built on principles of market economies, yet applied quite differently in practice. Much of this literature has focused on the distinction between corporatist and market systems. Indicators for corporatist systems have varied substantially across the literature, and attempts to standardise them have not been entirely satisfying. Indeed, there is often little correlation between what different scholars have proclaimed to be the core characteristics of corporatist systems.[4]

More recently, it has been proposed to simplify the classification and distinguish only between coordinated and liberal market economies.[5] A major reason for this reclassification has been the difficulty of identifying basic characteristics

[1] On the concept of path dependency, see DC North *Institutions, Institutional Change, and Economic Performance* (Cambridge University Press Cambridge 1990) 11.

[2] PA Hall and D Soskice *Varieties of Capitalism* (OUP Oxford 2001).

[3] S Djankov and others 'The New Comparative Economics' (2003) 31 J of Comparative Economics 595-619. To be sure, there has been a substantial and growing literature on the new institutional economics, which predates the collapse of the socialist system. See only DC North *Structure and Change in Economic History* (Norton New York 1981); North (n 1); and OE Williamson *The Economic Institutions of Capitalism: Firms, Markets, Relational Contracting* (Free Press New York 1985).

[4] For a comprehensive analysis of indicators of corporatism and their interaction, see L Kenworthy 'Quantitative Indicators of Corporatism: A Survey and Assessment Max-Planck-Institut für Gesellschaftsforschung' Discussion Paper 2000/4 <http://www.mpi-fg-koeln.mpg.de/pu/mpifg_dp/dp00-4.pdf> (6 May 2005).

[5] D Soskice 'Reinterpreting Corporatism and Explaining Unemployment: Coordinated and Non-coordinated Market Economies: The Case for an Extended Perspective' in R Brunetta and C Dell'Ariga *Labour Relations and Economic Performance* (Macmillan London 1990) 170-214.

of corporatism in all countries for which a broad consensus exists that they are certainly *not* pure market economies. Japan is the most glaring example. While there is widespread agreement that in Japan the government plays an important coordinating function, it is equally clear that labour unions are not nearly as strong as in the European corporatist economies. Moreover, the size and reach of welfare programs as well as processes of policy formation differ markedly from European corporatist systems.[6]

Following Hall and Soskice,[7] I define *liberal market economies* (LMEs) as economies in which 'firms coordinate their activities primarily via hierarchies and competitive market arrangements' and where 'the equilibrium outcomes of firm behaviour are usually given by demand and supply conditions'. *Coordinated market economies* (CMEs), by contrast, are economies in which 'firms depend more heavily on non-market relationships to coordinate their endeavours with other actors to construct their core competencies'. Hall and Soskice refrain from developing a detailed list of indicators to distinguish between the two types of economies, but highlight some core characteristics, such as formal contracting vs relational contracting, competition vs coordination, and different institutions for exchanging information, monitoring behaviour, and sanctioning defection.[8] Based on these general characteristics, they classify 17 leading OECD countries as follows (Table 1).

Table 1: Liberal and coordinated market economies

LME	CME
Australia	Austria
Canada	Belgium
Ireland	Denmark
New Zealand	Finland
United Kingdom	Iceland
United States	Germany
	Japan
	Netherlands
	Norway
	Sweden
	Switzerland

Source: PA Hall and D Soskice *Varieties of Capitalism* (OUP Oxford 2001)

[6] A Siaroff 'Corporatism in 24 Industrial Democracies: Meaning and Measurement' (1999) 36 European J of Policy Research 175-205.

[7] Hall and Soskice (n 2) 8.

[8] ibid p 10 following Ostrom's classification of core functions of institutions. See E Ostrom *Governing the Commons – The Evolution of Institutions for Collective Action* (Cambridge University Press Cambridge 1990).

Comparative law scholars and readers familiar with the new comparative economics literature (which emphasises the importance of legal families)[9] will note that all LMEs are common law countries, and that all CMEs are civil law countries.[10] This relation could be spurious. However, as I will argue below, there is a strong affinity between economic and legal institutions. The link between the type of legal system and the type of market economy, I suggest, constitutes the ground rules that allocate basic control rights. These ground rules do not necessarily originate in law, but they reveal social preferences, which have become deeply rooted in law and complementary legal institutions.

III. Legal Ground Rules and the Scope of the State

None of the characteristics that are commonly attributed to LMEs or CMEs – ie arm's-length vs relations contracting, competition vs coordination – directly refer to the role of the state. However, an important role of the state is implied in both types of market economies. In the ideal type of LMEs where formal contracting is said to prevail, disputes are resolved and contracts enforced by a 'neutral arbiter'. Typically this neutral arbiter is a state court. In this case the state provides a public good in the form of law and legal institutions in whose shadow parties can negotiate and re-negotiate private contracts, and on which they can rely for enforcing their contractual rights and obligations.[11] The state also plays an important role in safeguarding competition by way of antitrust regulation.[12] In CMEs, a more expansive role of the state is typically assumed. This role can take

[9] The basic paper is R La Porta and others 'Law and Finance' (1998) 106 J of Political Economy 1113-1155.

[10] Comparative law scholars subdivide the civil law family into the French, the German, and the Scandinavian legal families – all of which are represented in this sample.

[11] There is extensive literature on non-legal sanctions. See only AT Konman 'Contract Law and the State of Nature' (1985) 1 J of Law, Economics, & Organization 5-32 and D Charny 'Nonlegal Sanctions in Commercial Relationships' (1990) 104 Harvard L Rev 375-467.

[12] For a thorough treatment of antitrust law and corporate control in the US, compare N Fligstein *The Transformation of Corporate Control* (Harvard University Press Cambridge 1990). For a more critical assessment of the need for state intervention and the efficacy of the antitrust regime that has evolved, see H Demsetz *100 Years of Antitrust: Should We Celebrate?* (George Mason University School of Law: Law and Economics Center 1991). The nature of antitrust regulation in LMEs and CMEs has changed considerably over time. The US was a major advocate of antitrust law since the late 19th century and in fact transplanted this law to many CMEs (Germany and Japan after the Second World War). Prior to this, Germany actively fostered cartels and thereby created an environment based on extensive bargaining. G Spindler *Recht und Konzern – Interdependenzen der Rechts- und Unternehmensentwicklung in Deutschland und den USA* (Mohr Siebeck Tübingen 1993). In recent years, however, antitrust authorities have retreated from intervening more aggressively in market forces. By contrast, the EU has taken a more aggressive role.

the form of coordinating bargains among social partners (labour and employers), or may amount to increasing interventionism.[13]

The major difference in ground rules between CMEs and LMEs is the extent to which individuals vs collectives or the state are vested with important control rights. Ground rules in this context refer to how a legal system allocates the power to determine the meaning and contents of agreements among private parties (substantive ground rule); and to initiate judicial review (procedural ground rule). This argument differs from standard arguments that view the major differences between the two systems in more extensive codification in the civil law system as opposed to the common law system.[14] Along this dimension there is arguably a substantial degree of convergence, as common law jurisdictions have made increasing use of statutory law,[15] and civil law jurisdictions have witnessed the growth of case law to interpret and apply their codes to ever new circumstances.[16] The comparative law literature has taken a broader view, noting that major differences between legal families lie in 'legal styles' (*Rechtsstile*).[17] Elements that form a legal style are said to include the prevailing method of legal thought, particular legal institutions characteristic of that style, the sources of law, ideological factors, the nature of the legal profession, and ultimate history.[18] These elements are helpful for identifying differences across legal systems, but the analysis remains very much at a descriptive level.

This paper seeks to take the analysis a step further by identifying basic constraints that have shaped the evolution of different legal systems in a path-dependent fashion. Analytically, this approach is close to the new institutional economics, in particular to North's work on institutions and institutional change.[19] North argues that institutions are the basic rules of the game, be they formal and informal. They constrain human action by shaping the expectation of

[13] See H Siebert in this volume.

[14] See, for example, La Porta and others (n 9) with further references. See also K Pistor and others 'The Evolution of Corporate Law' (2002) 23 U of Pennsylvania J of Intl Economic L 791, who compare the evolution of corporate law across countries and find that civil law countries are somewhat less flexible than common law countries.

[15] The Companies Act of 1844 codified UK corporate law. In the US, the 1811 New York corporate law marked the beginning of a trend of codifying this law at the state level. In addition, the 1933 Securities Act and the 1934 Securities and Exchange Act codified the law that governed investor protection.

[16] The best evidence for this is the sheer length of standard commentaries to s 242 of the German Civil Code. For a theoretical treatment of the impact of socioeconomic and technological change on law, compare K Pistor and C Xu 'Incomplete Law' (2003) 35 J of Intl L and Politics 931-1013.

[17] See K Zweigert and H Kötz *Einführung in die Rechtsvergleichung auf dem Gebiet des Privatrechts* (2nd edn Mohr Siebeck Tübingen 1984) 78.

[18] ibid 79.

[19] North (n 1).

individual actors about the behaviour of others.[20] Institutional change is path dependent because expectations change slowly and existing constraints therefore influence actions not only today, but also in the future.[21] Not every rule constrains human action in a path-dependent fashion. Moreover, not only formal law, but also social habits do change over time, and often radically.[22] The task therefore is to identify basic norms, or ground rules, that are 'sticky' and therefore shape the style of a legal and economic system.

The claim is that the basic allocation of substantive and procedural powers to either individuals or the collective/state constitutes such ground rules. Whatever their historical origins – and this paper does not make any claims about how they have come about[23] – social expectations about how and by whom conflicts are resolved influence bargaining choices at the contracting stage. Moreover, the interplay between substantive and procedural ground rules may facilitate private contracting and judicial review, or else create conditions under which relational contracting or collective decision making prevails.

1. Substantive Ground Rules

Substantive ground rules determine the extent to which private relations are either contractible or are governed by mandatory law. The most prominent example is the mandatory nature of corporate law in Germany, and its extensive contractibility in Delaware.[24] Substantive ground rules also establish to what extent

[20] See also M Aoki *Toward a Comparative Institutional Analysis* (MIT Press Cambridge 2001) 11, who defines institutions as 'sustainable systems of shared beliefs.'

[21] On evolution and change in legal systems, see MJ Roe 'Chaos and Evolution in Law and Economics' (1996) 109 Harvard L Rev 641. For a related argument on the path dependency of corporate law, compare also L Bebchuk and M Roe 'A Theory of Path Dependence in Corporate Governance and Ownership' (1999) 52 Stanford L Rev 127 as well as the edited volume by J Gordon and M Roe *Convergence and Persistence in Corporate Governance* (Cambridge University Press Cambridge 2004).

[22] Kahn-Freund suggested long ago that areas which were often thought to be not amenable to fundamental change or legal convergence, such as family and inheritance law, have indeed converged substantially in the 20th century. See O Kahn-Freund 'On Uses and Misuses of Comparative Law' (1974) 37 The Modern L Rev 1.

[23] For a (problematic) attempt to trace the origins of legal systems back to the 11th century, see EL Glaeser and A Shleifer 'Legal Origins' (2002) 117 The Quarterly J of Economics 1193. Economic historians and economic sociologists, by contrast, regard the confrontation with industrialisation and emerging capitalism as the formative period for today's economies. See Gerschenkron for basic argument: A Gerschenkron 'Economic Backwardness in Historical Perspective' in A Gerschenkron (ed) *Economic backwardness in historical perspective: a book of essays* (Harvard University Press Cambridge 1962) 5 and more recently N Fligstein *The Architecture of Markets* (Princeton University Press Princeton 2001).

[24] On the debate about the extent of mandatory vs enabling corporate law in the US and the desirability of more mandatory standards, compare JN Gordon 'The Mandatory Structure of

cont. ...

issues that are contractible in principle are still subject to overriding social norms. Every society knows fundamental norms that cannot be contracted out of. Such norms are recognised, for example, in international conventions that allow countries to refuse abidance by the norms set out therein if their enforcement violates their *ordre public* (or public policy).[25] I exclude these fundamental norms from this analysis. Instead, the paper focuses on the more subtle guidance of contractual relations, as expressed in norms that require contracting 'in good faith' or similar general clauses, which allow for review of private transactions on the basis of social or collective norms, not only individual aspirations.[26] The distinction between contractible vs non-contractible on the one hand and unconstrained vs socially conditioned freedom of contract is depicted in Table 2 below.

Table 2: Substantive Ground Rules

	Contractible	Non-contractible
Individual preferences	Unlimited contractual freedom Judicial enforcement of contractual rights dominates	Bright-line rules limit freedom of contract Judicial enforcement of contractual rights
Social norm conditionality	Standardised contracts with social norm conditionality Limited judicial enforcement	Mandatory regulation of socially sensitive issues without opt out Little judicial enforcement

The cells inside the matrix make predictions about the kind of contracts parties will enter into and the nature of governance mechanisms they will employ in light of the substantive ground rule. The upper left and the lower right-hand corners give the two extremes – highly individualised contracts with extensive judicial review on the one hand, and mandatory regulation of socially sensitive issues on the other. In the latter case, judicial enforcement mechanisms may exist, but their primary function is to enforce the mandatory rules, not to resolve a dispute between parties with (assumed) equal bargaining power. In the real world we are

Corporate Law' (1989) 89 Columbia L Rev 1549; R Romano 'Answering the Wrong Question: The Tenuous Case for Mandatory Corporate Law' (1989) 89 Columbia L Rev 1599; JC Coffee Jr 'The Mandatory/Enabling Balance in Corporate Law: An Essay on the Judicial Role' (1989) 89 Columbia L Rev 1618.

[25] See most prominently the 1958 New York Convention on the International Sales of Goods, art V.2.

[26] On the 'good faith' principle in continental European contract law and its 'transplantation' into UK law, see G Teubner 'Legal Irritants: How Unifying Law Ends up in New Divergences' in Hall and Soskice (n 2) 417-441 and the further discussion below, n 31 and accompanying text.

likely to observe mixed responses to these constraints. Put differently, the argument is not that freedom of contract absent social norm conditions means that parties will *always* revert to judicial enforcement of their rights, but that they will be more likely to seek judicial review when they have reached an impasse than parties contracting in a system with extensive social norm conditionality. There are two possible explanations for this. In the absence of well-established social norms that might help resolve a dispute, parties may be in greater need of third-party intervention.[27] Alternatively, they might be less fearful of social norm conditions imposed on them in the process of litigation.[28]

2. Procedural Ground Rules

Procedural ground rules determine the extent to which individuals have access to judicial review for resolving disputes. A procedural ground rule can take different forms. It may grant universal justiciability, where in principle any dispute may be brought to court, or delegated justiciability, where only those issues that are explicitly mentioned by law may be subject to judicial law enforcement. Moreover, the law may allocate the initiation right to individuals, the collective, a state agent, or a combination of the above (see Table 3 below).

Table 3: Procedural Default Rule

	Universal	Selective
Individual	Wide use of judicial enforcement	Moderate use of judicial enforcement
	Extensive formal contracting	Mix of formal and relational contracting
Collective	Relational contracting dominates	Relational contracting dominates
	Moderate judicial review	Limited judicial review

The nature of procedural ground rules determines the extent of formal vs relational contracting and the use of formal judicial review. Where the ground rule stipulates that collectives (the shareholder meeting) rather than individuals have the initiation right, litigation is less likely. The reason is that collectives typically

[27] The predictability of the outcome of a case seems to create incentives for parties to settle voluntarily and thus save litigation costs. See GL Priest and B Klein 'The Selection of Disputes for Litigation' (1984) 13 J of Legal Studies 1.

[28] These propositions are only suggestive. While it is possible to document differences in substantive ground rules, the incidence of judicial enforcement of contracts is difficult, if not impossible, to verify in the absence of comprehensive data on contracts, including relational contracts, which by definition are difficult to verify and record.

face substantial 'collective action costs'[29] in making a decision. They may have access to alternative governance devices, and mutual monitoring and reputation bonds, including political bonding devices, or may simply concede power to those who exercise de facto control rights. By contrast, if the initiation right is firmly vested with individuals, it is likely to be used more frequently. The downside for this allocation of control rights is that individuals may hold up transactions that might be beneficial for others. This outcome, however, can be avoided by switching from property to liability rules.[30]

The nature of procedural ground rules determines the extent of formal vs relational contracting and the use of formal judicial review. Where the ground rule stipulates that collectives (the shareholder meeting) rather than individuals have the initiation right, litigation is less likely. The reason is that collectives typically face substantial 'collective action costs'[31] in making a decision. They may have access to alternative governance devices, and mutual monitoring and reputation bonds, including political bonding devices, or may simply concede power to those who exercise de facto control rights. By contrast, if the initiation right is firmly vested with individuals, it is likely to be used more frequently. The downside for this allocation of control rights is that individuals may hold up transactions that might be beneficial for others. This outcome, however, can be avoided by switching from property to liability rules.[32]

The above argument notwithstanding, procedural ground rules are not the only determinants of the level of litigation one might observe in a given jurisdiction. Other factors, such as the cost of litigation, the independence, impartiality, and efficacy of the judiciary, and the availability of alternative dispute settlement and enforcement mechanisms will also play a role. Still, ground rules will effect the parties' bargaining strategy ex ante and influence the kind of monitoring systems they will establish. I would therefore posit that the scope of relational vs arm's-length contracting is, to a large extent, a function of the procedural ground rule. Where individuals may initiate litigation as a default, they

[29] M Olson *The Logic of Collective Action: Public Goods and the Theory of Groups* (Harvard University Press Cambridge 1971).

[30] For the conceptual distinction between property and liability rules in the law, see G Calabresi and D Melamed 'Property Rules, Liability Rules, and Inalienability: One View of the Cathedral' (1972) 85 Harvard L Rev 1089. For an analysis of conflict-of-interest rules in corporate law from this perspective, compare Z Goshen 'The Efficiency of Corporate Self-Dealing: Theory meets Reality' (2003) 91 California L Rev 393.

[31] M Olson *The Logic of Collective Action: Public Goods and the Theory of Groups* (Harvard University Press Cambridge 1971).

[32] For the conceptual distinction between property and liability rules in the law, see G Calabresi and D Melamed 'Property Rules, Liability Rules, and Inalienability: One View of the Cathedral' (1972) 85 Harvard L Rev 1089. For an analysis of conflict-of-interest rules in corporate law from this perspective, compare Z Goshen 'The Efficiency of Corporate Self-Dealing: Theory meets Reality' (2003) 91 California L Rev 393.

may be less inclined to safeguard their contracts by alternative mechanisms. By contrast, where the right to take recourse to the courts (and the formal legal system) is restricted, either because the law allows judicial recourse only when it explicitly says so, or because a collective rather than an individual holds the initiation right, the propensity to use non-legal mechanisms increases.

3. Ground Rules in LMEs vs CMEs

Applying this analytical framework to CMEs and LMEs, preliminary evidence suggests a fairly consistent pattern with respect to the allocation of substantive review and procedural initiation powers.[33] LMEs tend to rely on extensive contractibility that is not socially conditioned *and* on individual/universal enforcement rights. By contrast, CMEs condition freedom of contract on compliance with broadly accepted social norms and re-enforce this condition by limiting individual access to judicial review.[34]

Table 4: Ground rules in LMEs and CMEs

	LME/Common Law	CME/Civil Law
Substantive Default Rule	Contractibility/ Primacy of individual preferences	Contractibility is socially conditioned and/or limited by mandatory law
Procedural Default Rule	Universal justiciability/ Individual initiation rights	Selective justiciability/ Collective initiation rights

Ground rules embedded in formal law also influence the scope of state monitoring of private economic activities and the nature of judicial review, ie whether its purpose is primarily the enforcement of individual rights, or of justice understood as a social good. Law and legal institutions are important determinants of state involvement in the economy. This is most explicit in the case of specific rules designed to enforce these norms and can be most easily found in the areas of labour and social law. This should, however, not distract from the fact that the law functions as a coordination device for enforcing social preferences across the legal system. In the absence of specific legislation, the interpretation and enforcement of these norms is typically left to the courts which monitor private contracts and subject them to social norm conditions.

[33] This conclusion is drawn from the analysis of the US and the German system that follows. More extensive research would be needed to substantiate the conclusion for other countries.

[34] This proposition is based on a limited review of CMEs and LMEs – primarily in Germany on the one hand and the UK as well as the US on the other.

IV. Substantive Ground Rules in Private Law

This section seeks to substantiate the above propositions with examples drawn from contract law and corporate law primarily in two jurisdictions: Germany and the US. The areas of the law were selected to highlight the propensity of ground rules that may influence adjudication across different areas of the law and to demonstrate that they are not limited to the regulation of co-determination or labour law, areas that are most commonly selected to illustrate differences between LMEs and CMEs. Legal ground rules in areas of the law not typically targeted by legislation designed to re-enforce the choice of a particular, and perhaps temporary, economic model give greater credence to the argument that law serves as a coordination device between widely held social preferences and economic outcomes. An important implication of this argument is that altering specific legal realisations of such ground rules will not alter the social preferences on which a legal system rests. A moderate amount of judicial activism may ensure maintenance of the status quo, as judges may use general clauses (ie the good faith principle in contract law, or notions of the 'interest of the corporation') to re-enforce social preferences, even after specific legal incarnations of such principles have been abolished.

1. Ground Rules in Contract Law

The most prominent example of a substantive ground rule in contract law is the 'good faith principle' in most continental European legal systems – which incidentally are CMEs and civil law countries. In Germany, the provision can be found in section 242 of the Civil Code (Bürgerliches Gesetzbuch).[35] The principle has been incorporated into a European directive,[36] and as such has made its way into the UK legal system – an LME and common law country. In analysing the likely impact of the directive on the UK legal system, Gunther Teubner characterises the *bona fide* principle as 'clearly one of the unique expressions of continental legal culture'.[37] He notes that the principle has been used to infuse communitarian principles into contract law, or as 'contract law's recourse to social morality'.[38] The principle has been used as an overriding social condition for private contracts, which in principle

[35] 'Der Schuldner ist verpflichtet, die Leistung so zu bewirken, wie Treu und Glauben mit Rücksicht auf die Verkehrssitte es erfordern.' (The obligor must perform in a manner consistent with good faith taking into account accepted practice.)

[36] Regulation 4 of the Unfair Terms in Consumer Contracts, SI 1994 no 3159, implementing Council Directive 93/13/EEC of 5 April 1993 on Unfair Terms in Consumer Contracts [1993] OJ L95/29.

[37] Teubner (n 26) 427.

[38] ibid 431 quoting Esser and Wieacker.

are governed by the 'freedom of contract'. It is less clear whether the drafters of the civil code anticipated this development or had even meant this provision to serve this purpose. Arguably to the contrary, the framers of the German code had sought to limit the extent to which contractual parties could escape their obligations because of their limitations in adequately forecasting future events or anticipating all future contingencies. The overriding principle established by the German Civil Code of 1900 – which was deplored by Otto von Giercke as lacking even a drop of social oil – was that '*pacta sunt servanda*'.[39] It explicitly rejected a widely accepted legal principle known prior to the codification of the civil code, according to which each contract was based on implicit assumptions, ie the 'foundation of the transaction' (*Geschäftsgrundlage*), and that serious deviations from this foundation would justify an escape from contractual obligations.[40] This older principle was revived only in the wake of hyperinflation in the 1920s. The rigid enforcement of the principle *pacta sunt servanda* (without indexing for inflation) resulted in an 'endogenous legal boom'[41] that almost brought the judicial system to its knees, as the failure to account for galloping inflation resulted in a flood of cases brought by creditors who rushed to the courts to contain losses that grew larger by the day. In the inter-war period, the principle was primarily used to adjust prices to take account of inflation. However, in the postwar era, the principle was more extensively used in cases where imbalances in the original contract resulted from the 'discovery of unknown facts or the occurrence of unexpected events'[42] in cases where parties had not made provisions for such events, nor had they allocated the risk for unanticipated events among themselves. This practice has found widespread acceptance, and as a result has been incorporated in a recent revision of the Civil Code.[43]

By contrast, a general principle of good faith is not part of the common law tradition.[44] Courts invoke general principles of reasonableness, fairness, and good faith, or rather the absence of bad faith, but they are likely to interpret them in the context of a specific case and give much credence to the parties' intent. These

[39] See JP Dawson 'Judicial Revision of Frustrated Contracts: Germany' (1983) 63 Boston U L Rev 1039 for an excellent English-language survey of the developments that led to a change of this doctrine in subsequent case law.

[40] The relevant principle is the so-called *clausula rebus sic stantibus*. Ibid 1040.

[41] HC Wolf 'Endogenous Legal Booms' (1993) 9 The J of L, Economics, and Organization 181-187.

[42] See Dawson (n 39) 1075. German courts have, by way of case law, created different groups of cases that may qualify for adjustment of the original contract. See R Zimmermann and S Whittaker (eds) *Good faith in European Contract Law* (Cambridge University Press Cambridge 2000) 22 for a discussion of the proliferation of case law under BGB s 242.

[43] See the new provision s 313 in the BGB as enacted 1 January 2002 (Bundesgesetzblatt I 3138).

[44] See also Zimmermann and Whittaker (n 42) 39.

principles are not abstract doctrines that could be invoked to condition private contracts on the basis of social norms. Moreover, the doctrine of frustration, which is closest to the 'foundation of contracts' doctrine in the German tradition, is used to discharge both parties of their duties when performance of a contract becomes impossible. It is not, however, an invitation to courts to adjust contracts consistent with some overriding principles of justice or fairness.[45]

Against this background, Teubner predicted that the 'transplantation' of the bona fide principle will cause irritation in the UK legal system. As Teubner pointed out, it was, however, unlikely that the introduction of this principle would radically transform UK contract law. Instead, it was more likely that the principle's meaning and contents will be transformed when courts apply it to specific cases. This is so, because the UK legal and economic system is based on a different set of principles which are unlikely to be affected by the selective incorporation of foreign legal principles.[46] The latter is characterised by the principles of arm's-length contracting in a market-based system and case-by-case review of judicial disputes. Teubner's predictions about the limited impact of the good faith principle in UK contract law are supported by subsequent case law, and more explicitly by a review of this case law by the Lando Commission charged with developing the Principles of European Contract Law (PECL).[47] The Commission explicitly criticises English courts for failing to use the good faith principle to contradict or overrule express contractual terms.

A recent study by Zimmermann and Whittaker[48] suggests that there are more commonalities between continental European jurisdictions and English common law when it comes to good faith principles than is typically acknowledged. They survey the general principles of the law as well as a series of typical case studies and find that in most instances, English law reaches the same conclusions as civil law jurisdictions of continental Europe.[49] The argument put forward in this contribution is not necessarily at odds with their findings. This contribution focuses on frustration of contracts, not on other aspects of good faith. More importantly, we are less concerned with the question of whether broadly defined good faith principles can be found in English law, but in the allocation of decision-making powers and their use to either re-enforce the parties' will or impose social conditions on private contracts. From this vantage point, it appears that German law is more inclined to impose social conditionality, whereas English law is much more wedded to principles such as *caveat emptor* (buyer

[45] On the development of the frustration doctrine primarily in US case law, see JP Dawson 'Judicial Revision of Frustrated Contracts: The United States' (1984) 64 Boston U L Rev 1.

[46] Teubner (n 26) 426.

[47] O Lando and H Beale *Principles of European Contract Law Parts I and II Combined and Revised* (Kluwer Law International The Hague/Boston 2000) 117-118.

[48] Zimmermann and Whittaker (n 42).

[49] ibid 12, 653.

beware) and individual parties' risk taking.[50] Moreover, judges in Germany are more likely to overrule and actively adapt a contract than judges in the UK. The same does not necessarily hold for all civil law jurisdictions, however. In comparison with German law, French law appears to be more formalistic and less open to judicial intervention.[51]

Another counter argument against the suggestion that the good faith principle in contracts is alien to the common law system is that this principle can also be found in the US Uniform Commercial Code (UCC).[52] This general principle, which resembles continental European (as well as PECL) notions of good faith has, however, been enforced in a manner that is more consistent with UK practices than civil law practices, with Germany being the most prominent case. In fact, the official comment to the relevant UCC provision stresses that the good faith doctrine 'merely directs a court towards interpreting contracts within the commercial context in which they are created, performed, and enforced . . .'.[53] In other words, the provision is not meant to be used by courts to contradict or override express contractual terms.[54] Importantly, the UCC Permanent Editorial Board concluded after reviewing some of the case law that had emerged that section 1-203 'does *not* support a cause of action where no other basis for a cause of action exists.'[55] As Flechtner observes, while the wording of the good faith principle in the UCC might resemble those of the PECL or even the German civil code, in practice the good faith principle in the US is a weak interpretative tool. And he goes on to suggest that 'this undoubtedly reflects the traditional distrust in the English common law tradition, which is the foundation for US contract law, of the vagueness of the good faith concept, and the sense that a strong good faith principle would give judges a dangerous power to create contractual obligations to which parties had not actually agreed'.[56] This, of course, is in contrast to legal

[50] This distinction is particularly apparent in cases involving asymmetry of information between the parties and one party taking advantage of the other party's lack of information or knowledge. See their discussion of the 'Degas Case' at p 208; on English law at p 226 and p 656.

[51] See ibid 34.

[52] The relevant provision is s 1-203 (2000 edition of the UCC) and states that 'every contract or duty within this Act imposes an obligation of good faith in its performance or enforcement'.

[53] UCC 1023, cmt.

[54] See H Flechtner 'Comparing the General Good Faith Provisions of the PECL and the UCC: Appearance and Reality' (2001) 13 Pace Intl L Rev 295-337 for a detailed comparison of the UCC approach with the PECL. For a summary on good faith in US contract law, see also RS Summers 'The Conceptualisation of Good Faith in American Contract Law: A General Account' in Zimmermann and Whittaker (n 42) 118.

[55] Quoted in Flechtner (n 54) 310.

[56] ibid, quoting A Farnsworth 'Duties of Good Faith and Fair Dealing under the UNIDROIT Principles, Relevant International Conventions, and National Laws' (1995)

cont. ...

practice in Germany, where the good faith principle – as described above – has been widely used as an independent cause of action and has allowed courts to develop extensive 'case law' beyond the specific strictures of the civil code.

The comparison of 'good faith' doctrines in common and civil law also helps refute the widely held notion that the main difference between the major legal systems is the greater 'rigidity' or formalism of law in codified systems, or the more limited power of judges in civil law as opposed to common law systems.[57] As this example demonstrates, in crucial areas civil law judges wield much more power and have much greater discretion than common law judges do. More important than this stylised comparison seems to be the extent to which judges are empowered to subject private contracts to social norm conditionality. This is where civil law judges can exert their greater powers and where common law judges are restricted to the will of the original contracting parties.

2. Default Rules in Corporate Law

Up to now the fundamental ground rule for corporate law in Germany has been first that corporate law is not contractible, and second that the interests of the corporation include the interests of all stakeholders without a single group prevailing over another. The corollary of a mandatory corporate law is limiting firms' choice over the corporate law they may wish to choose for incorporation. Not surprisingly, until recently Germany adhered to the so-called 'seat theory', which required a company to be incorporated where its headquarters were located. This theory came under attack by the European Court of Justice, which held in the famous *Überseering Decision* that a denial of legal personhood for a corporation which had been legally incorporated in another member state, simply because – under German law – this corporation had changed its seat without re-incorporating there, breached the principle of freedom of establishment under the European Union Treaty.[58] Subsequently Germany's Supreme Court has moved away from the seat theory.[59] Still, the legal implications for a German corporation

3 Tulane J of Intl and Comparative Law 55. In this article, Farnsworth reports the scepticism among common law experts in contract law about incorporating similar principles into the Convention on the International Sale of Goods.

[57] R La Porta and others 'Judicial Checks and Balances' (2004) 112 J of Political Economy 445-470; R La Porta and others 'The Guarantees of Freedom' Harvard Institute of Economic Research working paper <http://post.economics.harvard.edu/hier/2002papers/2002list.html> (9 May 2005).

[58] Preliminary Ruling of the European Court of Justice on 5 November 2002 on a referral from the *Bundesgerichtshof* (German Federal Court of Justice) in the proceedings *Überseering NV and Nordic Construction Company Baumanagment GmbH* (Case C-208/00).

[59] See Bundesgerichtshof of 13 March 2003 (VII ZR 370/98) available at <http://www.jurawelt.com/gerichtsurteile/zivilrecht/bgh/8514> (9 May 2005).

that wishes to re-incorporate elsewhere are yet to be clarified. Even here European law is likely to change the landscape in the future. The Regulation on the European Company (*Societas Europaea*) allows corporations from at least two member states to merge into one governed by the regulation and the law of the member state where the now merged company is located.[60] It has been suggested that this regulation could open the door to greater choice for the place of incorporation in Europe[61] and thus undermine each member state's 'monopoly' over regulating the affairs of corporations that are operating within its jurisdiction. The point is that while change is underway, the traditional approach to corporate law in Germany has been one that limited firms' choice and placed the governance structure of firms firmly under socially agreed-upon norms. The non-contractibility of German law is still reflected in a provision in the code that stipulates that the corporate charters may not deviate from statutes except where explicitly provided for.[62]

By contrast, the ground rule in English and American corporate law is that corporate law is contractible except where otherwise stated in the law. Most importantly, English and US corporate law have traditionally allowed corporations to choose their place of incorporation. Implicit in this choice is the power to opt out of the social consensus in the jurisdiction where the corporation is operating. This choice reflects a preference for individual choice by companies – or their management[63] – over social consensus with regard to the principles that shall govern a corporation's affairs. Consistently with this general approach, corporate law tends to be less mandatory. As is well known, the law of the state of Delaware is among the most 'enabling' of corporate statues in the common law world, with most of the statutory provisions providing opt-out or fall-back clauses

[60] Council Regulation (EC) 2157/2001 of 8 October 2001 on the Statute for a European Company (SE) [2001] OJ L294/1.

[61] L Enriques 'Silence is Golden: The European Company Statute as a Catalyst for Company Law Arbitrage' (ECGI Working Paper 2003).

[62] See s 23 para 5 Aktiengesetz (AktG). The general trend seems to be to relax the rigidity of mandatory corporate law. See H Baum 'Change of Governance in Historical Perspective: The German Experience' (ECGI Working Paper 2005) with further references. Note, however, that concurrently with this trend towards a more enabling corporate law, discussions are underway to make the voluntary corporate governance code of 2002 (available at <http://www.corporate-governance-code.de/index-e.html> [9 May 2005]) mandatory as most companies chose to opt out of it. Thus, there seem to be conflicting trends suggesting that the outcome is still unclear.

[63] The fact that management, or the law firms they choose, rather than shareholders typically determine the incorporation choice has long been recognised in the literature. See, for example R Romano 'Law as Product: Some Pieces of the Incorporation Puzzle' (1985) 1 J of Law, Economics, and Organization 225-283; R Daines 'The Incorporation Choices of IPO Firms' (2002) 77 New York U L Rev 1559-1611; M Kahan and E Kamar 'The Myth of State Competition in Corporate Law' (2002) 55 Stanford L Rev 679.

rather than mandatory law.[64] English company law provides a middle ground in that it firmly vests shareholders with basic control rights, but, in comparison to the law of Delaware, is more restrictive in allowing opt-outs or the delegation of control rights from shareholders to the board of directors.[65]

The nature of corporate law as contractible vs non-contractible (or mandatory vs enabling) has important implications for complementary institutions that have evolved over time.[66] A mandatory law relies heavily on the enforcement of these provisions ex ante when the company registrar reviews the consistency between the charter's provisions and statutory law. Since every change in the charter must be recorded, violations can be detected when they are registered. In the eyes of ex ante lawmakers, there was therefore little apparent need for ex post judicial review. It should, however, be noted that it has become increasingly obvious that everyday management decisions which do not require registration may endanger stakeholder interests just as much but largely escape judicial review, mostly because procedural ground rules limit the justiciability of corporate decision making (see below).

By contrast, when corporate law is contractible, violations of the law are harder to detect and require more extensive ex post review. The major complementary device to a contractible corporate law is therefore judicial review. With case law establishing the limits of private contracting, the need for statutory restrictions may in fact diminish over time.[67] To be sure, judicial review as the only check on free contracting is increasingly challenged, in particular by the growing influence of mandatory federal law in the US, which is intruding on the traditional territory of state corporate law.[68] This trend may suggest a shift in the ground rule in the US corporate law system from one that relied primarily on private contracting to one that is increasingly regulated by federal law. So far, however, the trend has not gone far enough to suggest a fundamental shift. The reason is that both securities regulations and corporate law in the US continue to be almost silent about the substantive norms that shall govern the corporate contract. Instead, both statutory and case law focus largely on process rather than substance. This is most apparent in the interpretation of the directors' and officers' fiduciary duties. Judicial review of the duty of care has developed into a review of procedures, except where the substance meets the threshold of 'bad

[64] On the balance between mandatory and enabling corporate law as a positive and a normative matter, see Coffee Jr (n 24) 1618-1691; Gordon (n 24) 1549-1598 and Romano (n 24) 1599-1617.

[65] English law is much more restrictive in allowing for a re-allocation of key control rights from shareholders to managers than Delaware corporate law.

[66] Pistor and others (n 14) 830 with table 5 ibid.

[67] This is the core of Coffee's argument that fiduciary duties enforced by the Chancery Courts are Delaware law's most mandatory core.

[68] See especially M Roe 'Delaware's Competition' (2003) 117 Harvard L Rev 588.

faith' or 'waste'. The doctrinal device is the business judgment rule which stipulates that judges will *not* second-guess the decision of directors or officers or try to impose their own or 'society's' values on them. Instead, they will review only whether a decision was made at all, whether the decision was informed, and whether it was below the bad faith threshold.[69] Statutory law in Delaware even allows corporate charters to eliminate directors' liability for duty of care violations except when they meet the bad faith threshold.[70] Defining the threshold as 'bad faith' rather than superimposing a 'good faith' review by the courts – as is the case for private contracts in civil law system – is crucial, because it limits the scope of judicial review and, by implication, the extent to which social norms can be invoked to limit contractibility in substance.[71]

The duty of loyalty review also focuses primarily on procedure. Transactions are not void just because they were conflicted, as long as the conflict was disclosed and the transaction was approved by disinterested directors or shareholders.[72] Even when courts apply the entire fairness test, they restrict their review to fair dealing and fair price. The first prong once again focuses on procedure; only the latter gives more room for debate over substance. Even here, much of the assessment is left to experts as judges try to avoid deciding matters beyond the strictures of the law. The Sarbanes-Oxley Act[73], which was enacted in 2002 in response to the uncovering of corporate scandals in the wake of the 'dot com bubble', follows this tradition. To the extent federal law intrudes into the realm of state law by regulating details of the corporation's governance structure, the manner of regulation remains primarily procedural, not substantive. Corporations require audit committees with independent directors;[74] corporate officers need to sign off corporate financials and stipulate that they have read them[75] and are required to create governance structures

[69] See MA Eisenberg WL Cary and MA Eisenberg *Corporations* (7th edn Foundation Press New York 1995).

[70] See Delaware General Corporate Law s 102(b)(7).

[71] The same principle can be found in tort law. Under 19th-century English law, tort liability was limited to intent, unless the particular relation among parties warranted liability for negligence or gross negligence. By contrast, Sec. 1382 of the French Civil Code and (though somewhat more restrictive) Sec. 823 of the German Civil Code establish universal liability for negligent misconduct. It was left to the courts to *restrict* this universal liability, whereas in England they had to create more extensive liability on a case-by-case basis. For a detailed analysis of comparative tort law across legal systems, see K Zweigert and H Kötz An *Introduction to Comparative Law* (3rd edn OUP Oxford 1998). The leniency of traditional common law torts has been corrected by a move toward strict liability in the area of product liability, in particular. Arguably, this 'backlash' (MJ Roe 'Backlash' (1998) 98 Columbia L Rev 217-241) was a heavy price to pay for a more lenient historical approach.

[72] See Delaware General Corporate Law s 144.

[73] See annex 3 in this volume.

[74] SOX s 301.

[75] SOX s 302.

that will help detect any misrepresentation of information at an early stage.[76] An exception to this pattern is the prohibition of credit contracts between the corporation and its management.[77] This explicit prohibition comes close to the substantive regulation of corporate affairs under German corporate law, where credit contracts between the corporation and members of the management board are prohibited, unless approved by the supervisory board.[78]

In general, German law denies directors or shareholders a voting right in the case of conflicted transactions.[79] This is true even if the others were informed about the decision. Moreover, German statutory law regulates the standard of behaviour for key corporate constituencies to a much larger extent than does US or English corporate law. Statutory law thus functions as a guideline for corporate conduct, even where it lacks specific enforcement mechanisms. Apparently, the lawmakers thought these guidelines to be largely self-enforcing.[80] An example are legal standards about executive compensation. German law provides that compensations paid to the members of the management board (ie the executives) must be 'reasonably related' to the tasks of the respective board member and to the overall situation of the corporation.[81] This provision, which was introduced into the law in 1937, had never been enforced or interpreted by a court until the Mannesmann trial of 2004. In this case, the payment of, according to German standards, a hefty 'appreciation award' in the amount of 15 million euro to the CEO of Mannesmann, Klaus Esser, resulted in a criminal investigation that gave a criminal court the opportunity to interpret this provision. Esser had been appointed CEO of Mannesmann fourteen months prior to the merger agreement. His compensation package included a fixed salary and bonuses but no stock options or a proviso for the event of a takeover or other change of control. Vodafone of UK launched a hostile tender offer for Mannesmann in November 1999. By February 2000, the virulent defence Mannesmann mounted under the leadership of Klaus Esser was crumbling. At that time, Vodafone and Mannesmann agreed to a friendly merger. The conditions favoured Mannesmann shareholders when compared with the initial offer. In particular, the value of the exchange ratio had

[76] SOX s 404.

[77] SOX s 402.

[78] Even then, they are restricted to 'specific credit transactions' and may not be granted more than three months in advance.

[79] The relevant provision is Civil Code s 34, which governs organisations with membership. The provision is applicable to corporations.

[80] For a more general argument about the nature of self-enforcing law drawing, however, on a more individualist model of (Anglo-American) corporate law, see B Black and R Kraakman 'A Self-Enforcing Model of Corporate Law' (1996) 109 Harvard L Rev 1911.

[81] See AktG s 87.

increased by 65 billion euro.[82] Two days after the merger agreement was signed, the presidium of Mannesmann's supervisory board met and agreed to pay Esser (and others) an appreciation award of 15 million.[83] The decision had the support of Vodafone (ie the acquirer) and Mannesmann's largest shareholder at the time.

Several shareholders notified the state prosecutor of a potential breach of the duty of trust (*Untreue*) under German criminal law. The relevant provision prohibits a *serious* breach of trust by someone who was charged with taking care of someone else's property or assets. A violation of the criminal law depended on whether the extra compensation violated any provisions of the corporate law. The court held that it did. It pointed out that the extra compensation was not 'reasonably related' to any 'task' the CEO, Klaus Esser, had yet to perform. In particular, the German word '*Aufgabe*' in the provision meant, according to the court, that the compensation had to be paid for future tasks. At the time the appreciation award was granted, however, all tasks related to the merger had already been performed and Esser had thus already been fully compensated for them. Neither was there a 'reasonable relation' between the extra compensation and the situation of the corporation. The court pointed out that under German law, the interests of the corporation are not limited to shareholder value. A broader assessment of the situation of the corporation at the time the appreciation award was granted should have included an assessment of the fact that Mannesmann was losing its independence as a result of the merger and that some of its subsidiaries were to be spun off. Having concluded that the payment constituted a breach of corporate law, the court nevertheless acquitted, because the breach of trust did not meet the threshold required under criminal law. In this context the court stressed that the decision had been made by the correct body, that it had been informed, and that the results of the decision had been disclosed in accordance with legal requirements.

Contrast this decision with the arguments of the Delaware courts in the context of the shareholder derivative action against Disney Corporation because of breach of fiduciary duty related to a compensation and termination package for the company's vice president, Michael Ovitz, a personal friend of the president, Michael Eisner. Ovitz had received a substantial compensation package including a fixed salary, bonuses, and stock options when he joined the corporation in the fall of 1995. The package was approved by the board, but it remains unclear how

[82] The original exchange rate offered by Vodafone was the equivalent of 240 Euro per share. The stock for stock price finally paid had a value of 360 Euro per share. Moreover, Mannesmann shareholders were given 49.5% in Vodafone, whereas the original deal had given them only 47.5% of the company's shares.

[83] Most contentious was another payment made to Mannesmann's former CEO, Joachim Funk, who was a member of the presidium and voted on his own compensation package. The issues under corporate law this case raises, however, are the same as those raised by the Esser compensation package. I will therefore limit the analysis to Esser.

well they had informed themselves prior to approving the package.[84] When he left the company less than a year later, he negotiated with Eisner a no-fault termination, which was also approved by the board. This allowed him to walk away with a total compensation of 140 million US dollars.[85]

The Delaware Supreme Court strenuously avoided any judgment of the level of compensation. Instead, the court stipulated the standard of review narrowly and in line with the procedural nature of court review of directors' action:[86]

> The inquiry here is not whether we would disdain the composition, behavior and decisions of Disney's Old Board or New Board as alleged in the Complaint if we were Disney stockholders. In the absence of a legislative mandate, that determination is not for the courts. That decision is for the stockholders to make in voting for directors, urging other stockholders to reform or oust the board, or in making individual buy-sell decisions involving Disney securities. The sole issue that this Court must determine is whether the particularized facts alleged in this Complaint provide a reason to believe that the conduct of the Old Board in 1995 and the New Board in 1996 constituted a violation of their fiduciary duties.[87]

This implied that the major issue the court had to decide was whether the directors who had approved the severance package were independent and (financially) disinterested, or whether for other reasons their business judgment may have been impaired. In the end, the analysis focused on the question of whether the board had taken its responsibilities seriously or absconded them in favour of the chief executive officer, Michael Eisner. In May 2003 the Chancery Court ruled that there was sufficient evidence that the board may have frivolously neglected its duties and that therefore Ovitz's employment contract fell outside the directors' business judgment rule.[88] It therefore allowed the case to move forward into full trial.

The major difference between the approach taken by the German court and that of the Delaware court is the extent to which the substance of the decision about the compensation package was deemed justiciable. Under Delaware law, judicial review is very much limited to procedural aspects of decision making,

[84] This was the focus of the trial at the Delaware Chancery Court in the fall of 2004. A final decision is still pending at the time of this writing (February 2005).

[85] Of which USD 101 million resulted from the fact that most of his stock options vested immediately.

[86] Supreme Court of Delaware, 746 A2d 244; 2000 Del Lexis 51. It should be noted that at this stage the major question was whether a derivative action was admissible, in particular whether a demand on the board was excused under procedural rules governing derivative action.

[87] ibid 31

[88] Court of Chancery of Delaware, in *re The Walt Disney Company Derivative Action* CA no 15452 of 28 May 2003.

and does not extend to judicial review of the level of compensation.[89] By contrast, German law not only stipulates a reasonableness standard, but also states that the interests of the corporation as a whole, not only those of shareholders, have to be taken into consideration. The court did not leave the balancing act to the relevant decision makers, but itself decided on the standard. In doing so it clearly confirmed the principle long established in German corporate law that the interests of the corporation are not limited to its shareholders, and that there is a corporate interest that can be clearly distinguished from the interest of other stakeholders. In the case at hand, the court suggested that the fact that Mannesmann was losing its independence as a result of the merger plan and that the merger also contemplated spinning off some of its subsidiaries clearly spoke against the 'corporate interests'. The case is now under appeal at the Supreme Court (BGH).

V. Procedural Ground Rules in Private Law

This section primarily addresses procedural ground rules in the context of corporate law. With regard to contract law, the ground rule in common and civil law systems is that private parties may seek judicial recourse to enforce their rights. Parties may choose arbitration over litigation, but absent a clearly expressed choice, the ground rule is litigation. In fact, comparative analysis of litigation rates across Europe suggests that Germany is quite a litigious society.[90] It has also been correctly noted that German civil procedural rules allow for a fairly adversarial procedure. Still, important differences consistent with the approach developed in this paper remain. Judges play a central role in collecting evidence, in contrast to civil procedure rules in the US that leave evidence collection primarily to the parties of the lawsuit.[91] German procedural law allocates the powers to examine witnesses primarily to the judge.[92] The parties may suggest questions to

[89] As Jill Fisch notes, these procedural requirements often bar judicial review of substance. See J Fisch 'Teaching Corporate Governance Through Shareholder Litigation' (2000) 34 Georgia L Rev 745, 760.

[90] HFP Ietswaart 'The International Comparison of Court Caseloads: The Experience of the European Working Group' (1990) 24 L and Society Rev 571.

[91] JH Langbein 'Comparative Civil Procedure and the Style of Complex Contracts' (1987) 35 AJCL 381, esp 387. Langbein's article triggered a vivid debate about the differences in civil procedural rules across legal systems, an area that has been much neglected in comparative law. For a recent summary of this literature, compare B Bryan 'Justice and the Advantage in Civil Procedure: Langbein's Conception of Comparative Law and Procedural Justice in Question' (2004) 11 Tulsa J of Comparative and Intl L 521-555.

[92] According to Civil Procedure Code (ZPO) s 273, the judge may prepare a hearing in court by requesting additional information from the parties and asking them to produce documents to verify their statement. The judge may also request information from state agencies and call expert witnesses independent of a move by one of the parties. However, with regard to ordinary witnesses, it can call only those that have been proposed by one of the parties.

the judge, but there is no cross-examination of witnesses.[93] Moreover, the judge is empowered and frequently exercises that power to call expert witnesses. Expert witnesses are required by law to give 'neutral' opinions and to use their special knowledge to help the judge – not the parties – ascertain facts.[94] Whether or not these procedural rules make for more or less efficient discovery, whether they distort or help uncover the truth, is not the primary concern in this paper. The key is that important control rights are allocated not to individual parties and their legal agents, but to an agent – the court – that is supposed to be neutral and advance the social interests of litigation, ie the discovery of the 'truth'.[95]

Litigation in the area of corporate law offers a fertile ground for comparing the allocation of litigation initiation rights across countries. In England and the US, the initiation right is firmly vested with individual shareholders. Reading through English or US corporate statutes, one looks in vain for a provision that explicitly states that shareholders have a right to sue to enforce their rights, as the right of shareholders to seek judicial recourse preceded statutory corporate law and was thus assumed.[96] Still, English and US corporate law does not offer the same tools for bringing corporate officers and directors to justice. English law has been much more reluctant to allow for derivative action, ie shareholders' rights to sue on behalf of the corporation.[97] Even direct shareholder actions are much less frequent in England than in the US This may be explained in part by the fact that English law vests key decision-making rights with shareholders and is less flexible in allowing them to delegate these rights to directors.[98] In addition, attorneys do not have the same incentives to function as 'bounty hunters', searching for suitable cases to offer their services.[99] Despite these differences, it still seems

[93] A Stadler 'The Law of Civil Procedure' in WF Ebke and MW Finkin *Introduction to German Law* (Kluwer Law International The Hague 1996) 357.

[94] ibid 367. See also German Civil Procedure Code (ZPO) s 402.

[95] The notion that litigation has both social and private costs as well as social and private benefits is based on S Shavell 'The Fundamental Divergence Between the Private and the Social Motive to Use the Legal System' (1997) 26 J Legal Studies 575.

[96] By the time the relevant statutory law had been enacted a substantial body of case law on agency, partnerships, and trust already existed. On the history of English company law prior to 1825, see PL Davies *Gower's Principles of Modern Company Law* (6th ed Sweet & Maxwell London 1997) 18-35.

[97] See *Foss v Harbottle* 2 Hare 461 (1843). For the development of shareholder action under English law, see Davies (n 96) 658. For a comprehensive analysis of English company law, see also BR Cheffins *Company Law: Theory, Structure, and Operation* (OUP Oxford 1997).

[98] See Pistor (n 14) 832 for an argument along these lines.

[99] This role of the attorney in the US system has given rise to considerable attorney agency costs. Congress has sought to limit these costs by passing two Acts over the past 10 years, the Private Securities Litigation Reform Act (PSLRA) of 1995, and the Securities Litigation Uniform Standards Act (SLUSA) of 1998. For details on this Act and its impact on securities

cont. ...

fair to say that the ground rule in both countries is that shareholders have a right to sue, at least when their own rights and interests are at stake. Class action suits are not a deviation but an extension of the principle that enforcement rights are firmly vested with the individual. Class actions allow individual shareholders to claim that they are acting on the part of other aggrieved parties, without having to organise them prior to bringing suit. Even with regard to derivative action, the key question is whether an *individual* shareholder can bring action on behalf of the corporation, or whether this should be the task of the board.[100] Not a single state in the US requires this question to be decided by the collective, ie by the shareholder meeting.

By contrast, under German corporate law this has been the ground rule up to now.[101] The shareholder meeting is to determine whether or not a special auditor shall be appointed to review managerial misconduct, or whether to bring action against the management board.[102] Alternatively, a group of minority shareholders representing at least 5% of the corporate capital may request legal action if they can credibly demonstrate that they have been shareholders for at least three months. This may be a single shareholder, but the threshold excludes shareholders holding less than 5% of the total capital or capital valuing at least 500,000 euro from initiating lawsuits on their own.[103] While this threshold is easier to reach than the previous threshold of 10%, the law still establishes a powerful deterrent against litigation by requiring the minority to compensate the corporation for the costs of litigation should the corporation lose partially or fully, at least to the extent that the corporation's costs exceed what it received as a result of the lawsuit.[104] Not surprisingly, according to German law the default mechanism for enforcing shareholder rights against management to this date is not litigation, but making use of the corporation's internal governance structure, ie the shareholder meeting, the right to elect and dismiss members of the supervisory board, and their right to appoint and dismiss (albeit only for cause prior to their usual five-

litigation, see JA Grundfest and AC Pritchard 'Statutes with Multiple Personality Disorders: The Value of Ambiguity in Statutory Design and Interpretation' (2002) 54 Stanford L Rev 627.

[100] This is the core of the 'demand rule', which requires the suing shareholder to first put his demand for legal action before the board, unless, however, such a demand is excused. See the leading decisions under Delaware law, *Aronson v Lewis* 473 A.2d 805 (Del 1984); and *Levine v Smith* 591 A 2d 194 (Del 1991).

[101] Proposed changes in this regard are discussed below at text accompanying notes 126 following.

[102] See AktG ss 142 and 147 para 1.

[103] AktG s 147.

[104] AktG s 147 para 3.

year term) members of the management board.[105] In exceptional cases, judicial review has been sought by way of criminal, not civil law.[106]

In the past, shareholder litigation rights against management have been somewhat extended by the *Holzmüller* decision of the German Supreme Court of 1982.[107] It established that shareholders have a right to bring an action with the aim of establishing the management's legal obligation to refer a decision to the shareholder meeting.[108] The decision is an excellent example for the prevailing ground rule, ie that legal actions are the exception and not the rule for upholding and enforcing shareholder rights. In its decision, the court carefully carved out a legal vacuum which justified the recognition of a right to sue, if only for a declaratory judgment rather than for damages. The court discussed selective procedural rights of shareholders found in statutory corporate law, including the right to challenge decisions of the shareholder meeting in court,[109] and the right to force the supervisory board to bring action against members of the management board after tangible harm has been done.[110] None of these provisions, however, allowed shareholders to enforce their right to vote on a major issue – in this case a capital increase in a subsidiary controlled by the parent following the transfer of assets from the parent to that subsidiary. The court concluded that in cases where a substantive shareholder right to vote on an issue is either explicitly granted in statutory law or recognised by the courts, as in the case at hand, the enforcement of this right should not fail just because the corporate law failed to specify a procedure for enforcing it.[111]

Despite all the fanfare that accompanied this decision, it did not establish a universal procedural rule, but maintained corporate law's ground rule that only in exceptional cases was judicial review of managerial actions an appropriate remedy for aggrieved shareholders. In fact, it took until April 2004, or 22 years, for the next case with a comparable fact pattern to be decided by the German Supreme Court[112] – which denied the claim on substantive grounds.[113]

[105] NR Banerjea *Die Gesellschafterklage im GmbH- und Aktienrecht* (Heymanns Cologne 2000) 16 for a review of the literature.

[106] See the discussion of the recent *Mannesmann* case below.

[107] BGH, 25 February 1982, II ZR 174/80, published in BGHZ 83, 122.

[108] The procedural device was the use of the *Feststellungsklage* in accordance with German Civil Procedure Code s 256, which allows parties to sue for confirmation that a legal obligation exists or does not exist between the parties. This lawsuit is not for remedies, however.

[109] AktG s 241.

[110] AktG ss 117, 147.

[111] 'Eine materiell begründete Rechtsverfolgung darf aber grundsätzlich nicht daran scheitern, daß die dem Aktiengesetz eigenen Rechtsbehelfe tatbestandsmäßig versagen.' BGH (n 107) 127.

[112] Decision of 26 April 2004. BGH II ZR 154/02. Available (in German) at <http://www.recht-in.de/urteile/master.php?wahl=101&u_id=111452> (30 June 2005).

An important exception to the limited rights to seek judicial review under current law are the extensive rights of shareholders to challenge decisions of the shareholder meeting.[114] Allowing individual shareholders to challenge in court the legality of decisions taken at the shareholder meeting, but limiting their powers to sue members of the management board, is consistent with the notion that relational contracting should prevail over judicial enforcement. The only disputes that are referred to the courts are disputes among shareholders, ie disputes for which there is no resolution within the corporation, such as by electing a different board. Nonetheless, the legal device has created costly hold-up problems and is at least in part responsible for the reluctance to extend shareholder litigation rights.

Further evidence for differences in the allocation of procedural control rights are claims in the context of mergers. Under Delaware law, shareholders who voted against a merger may use appraisal rights,[115] or under certain conditions, attach the merger agreement on the grounds of fiduciary duty violations.[116] The fairness of the price paid to shareholders is assessed only once such a claim is made by individual shareholders, or, in the case of fiduciary duty claims, in the form of class action suits. Thus, the allocation of control rights is firmly vested with individual shareholders. By contrast, under German law, *every* merger agreement has to be assessed by an independent agent before it is submitted to the shareholder meeting for approval.[117] This agent, the 'merger reviewer' (*Verschmelzungsprüfer*), is recommended by the management board but appointed by the court. The underlying rationale seems to be that whether or not a merger agreement is fair should not be left to a cost-benefit analysis of individual shareholders, who may in the end decide not to pursue the matter for reasons other than the unfairness of the price. In legal practice, the difference may not be substantial – in the US many firms will use independent committees and their financial advisors to assess the fairness of a merger. The difference, however, is that under German law such a mechanism is mandated by law, whereas in the US it is a quasi-voluntary arrangement aimed at avoiding an 'entire fairness' review by the

[113] A major difference to the Holzmüller decision was that this time the action was brought as a shareholder action against decisions taken by the shareholder meeting. Thus, the question about the scope of shareholders' procedural rights was not addressed.

[114] The relevant provisions are AktG ss 241, 243.

[115] See Delaware General Corporate Law s 262.

[116] See post-Weinberger case law, such as *Rabkin v Phillip A Hunt Chemical Corp* 498 A 2d 701 (Del 1985) and its prodigee.

[117] Compare Reorganisation Law (*Umwandlungsgesetz*) ss 60, 9-12. Note that s 12 explicitly requires that the reviewer states whether the exchange ratio or cash payment is appropriate (*angemessen*).

courts.[118] Companies that do not face legal challenge may thus 'get away' with less scrutiny in the US, not, however, in Germany.

Similarly, any claim for damages that may result from a merger transaction may not be brought directly by a shareholder, but only by a 'special representative' who is appointed by the court upon request from individual shareholders or creditors.[119] This special representative differs in important ways from a lead plaintiff's attorney in an American class action suit. The representative's function is to compile all claims by shareholders, creditors, or the merged company and ensure that primarily creditors of the merged companies are satisfied from the compensation payments.[120] Moreover, his or her remuneration is regulated by law and is ultimately determined by the courts. In other words, the special representative is not the agent of an aggrieved party, but a neutral agent of the court.

In light of this analysis it should not come as a surprise that under German law, investors' private rights of action are equally limited. In fact, the 1994 Securities Trading Law explicitly stated that wrongful ad hoc disclosure does not give rise to individual claims.[121] This has been recently confirmed in a decision of Germany's Supreme Court, which reiterated that ad hoc disclosure obligations of material company information had the purpose of protecting the capital market as such, but not, at least not directly, the interests of individual investors.[122] The decision also declined to give a private right of action to enforce section 88 of the Stock Exchange Law (*Börsengesetz*), which prohibits actions aimed at manipulating stock prices. The court held that the law's purpose was to ensure honesty of price formation on the market. Achieving honesty would also indirectly serve the interests of individual investors; however, the alignment of social and individual interests did not give rise to individual claims for compensation.[123] Surprisingly, the decision nevertheless held – and for the first time ever in Germany – that members of the board could be held personally liable for misrepresentation of material information. This ruling was based on a general tort provision that requires intentional misconduct in a grossly unfair manner.[124]

[118] Delaware courts will shift the burden of proof if a truly independent committee has been appointed with sufficient bargaining power so as to assure the courts that the transaction is at arms' length. See *Kahn v Lynch Communication Systems Inc* 638 A 2d 1210 (Del 1994), where such independence was, however, denied.

[119] Reorganisation Law s 26.

[120] Reorganisation Law s 26 para 3, which states that to the extent creditors of the merged company have not been satisfied, compensation payments shall be used to this end.

[121] See Securities Trading Law (*Wertpapierhandelsgesetz*) s 15 para 6. The law has meanwhile been amended to give investors some private right of action. See the discussion below.

[122] BGH II ZR 402/02 of 19 July 2004 at p 8.

[123] ibid 10.

[124] The relevant provision is BGB s 826 stipulating that whoever causes damage to someone else in a manner that violates general norms of conduct (*gute Sitten*) shall be liable for compensation.

There are signs that Germany is changing the allocation of procedural control rights. First, the securities trading law has been amended to give investors a private right of action against companies or their representatives who fail to comply with ad hoc disclosure requirements or engage in insider trading.[125] Moreover, a new draft law on the corporate integrity and the modernisation of legal claims[126] is under review by the upper house, and is expected to enter into force before the end of 2005. The explicit purpose of the law is the strengthening of shareholders' litigation rights. The threshold for appointing a special auditor to investigate wrongdoings by company insiders has been reduced to shareholders representing only 1% (rather than 10) of total shares or holding shares with a value of 100,000 euro (rather than 1,000,000 euro).[127] This change was, however, accompanied by an important change on the allocation of costs. While the previous version of section 146 AktG imposed the full cost for a court-appointed special auditor on the corporation, the suggested revision of this provision now adds a sentence stating that if the appointment was based on the initiator's intentional or grossly negligent representation of facts, he or she will have to bear the costs for the auditor and the judicial proceedings for appointing him or her.[128] This cost allocation could prove to be a powerful deterrent, especially in light of the fact that under German corporate and civil procedure rules, parties have only limited rights to discovery, thus limiting their ability to ascertain their claims.[129]

[125] Compare Securities Trading Law (*Wertpapierhandelsgesetz*) ss 37 b and 37 c as amended 15 December 2004, BGBl I 3408.

[126] The German title of the draft law is 'Entwurf eines Gesetzes zur Unternehmensintegrität und Modernisierung des Anfechtungsrechts (UMAG)'. The draft law in German language is available at <http://www.bmj.bund.de/media/archive/362.pdf> (30 June 2005).

[127] AktG s 142 in the version suggested by UMAG (n 126).

[128] AktG s 146 as amended by UMAG reads: 'Bestellt das Gericht Sonderprüfer, so trägt die Gesellschaft die Gerichtskosten und die Kosten der Prüfung. Hat der Antragsteller die Bestellung durhc vorsätzlich oder grob fahrlässig unrichtigen Vortrag erwirkt, so hat der Antragsteller der Gesellschaft die Kosten zu erstatten.'

[129] Shareholders do have a right to request information from the management board under German corporate law, but the right is limited to a request at the annual shareholder meeting. See AktG s 131. This does not preclude dissemination of information outside the shareholder meeting. However, AktG s 131 para 4 stipulates that whenever information has been made available to one shareholder outside the general shareholder meeting, the same information must be disseminated to all other shareholders, even if that information is not relevant for decision making. The implication of this provision is that specific requests of information are likely to be discouraged as the corporation entails substantial costs even when responding only to a single request. Note also that this provision is broader than Regulation FD in the US, which subjects only publicly traded corporations to the obligation to share information given to some shareholders with all other shareholders. See <http://www.sec.gov/rules/final/33-7881.htm> (effective as of 23 October 2000). Compare General Delaware Corporate Law s 220, which gives every shareholder the right to inspect the corporation's books and request information from the corporation during normal business hours, as long as this is done for a 'proper purpose', which the law defines as a purpose 'reasonably related to such person's interest as a stockholder'.

With regard to the shareholders' rights to initiate judicial review, the draft law establishes a new procedure that allows individual shareholders who represent at least 1% of the total stock of hold shares equalling 100,000 euro in value to seek judicial certification for bringing action against corporate insiders on behalf of the corporation themselves – ie without a special court appointee.[130] The court is to allow the litigation to proceed if the shareholders can substantiate a claim that they have made a demand on the corporation and that the corporation has been harmed by misconduct or major violations of law or the corporate charter.[131] The corporation has to reimburse the claimants for their costs should the claim not prevail unless the claimants obtained the right to bring litigation on the basis of intentionally or grossly negligently misrepresented facts.[132] The law seeks to limit the potential costs of litigation by also stipulating that shareholders acting together can be reimbursed only for one attorney, unless they can show that additional attorneys were indispensable for pursuing the matter.[133] At the same time, shareholders' ability to challenge decisions of the shareholder meeting shall be curtailed according to the proposed law. In the future, a decision can be challenged on the grounds that information provided to shareholders was insufficient or incorrect only if an 'objectively deciding' shareholder would regard the information as crucial for exercising his rights.[134] The provision implicitly empowers courts to dismiss claims that they deem to be abusive, as they will define how an 'objectively deciding' shareholder might act.

Finally, the Ministry of Justice is currently proposing a new law that would introduce 'model trials' for investor claims into the German system.[135] The purpose of this law is to bundle multiple lawsuits on related issues in a more efficient manner than is currently possible. In particular, the result of a model trial would be binding on other claims brought on the basis of the same fact pattern. For this legal effect to arise, however, a claim must be filed with the appellate court to hold a model trial and after such a trial has been decided, individual lawsuits will proceed for final resolution. The draft law explicitly rejects the US-style class action suit, which binds not only the named plaintiffs but other represented members of the class. The reason given in the proposal is that Germany is committed to an 'individualised' litigation system.[136] This argument is interesting from the perspective of the analysis presented in this paper, which suggests that Germany favours

[130] See the new AktG s 148 as proposed by UMAG.

[131] See AktG s 148 para (1) 1-4 as proposed by UMAG. In addition, the shareholders must show that they held the shares before the challenged incident occurred. See ibid.

[132] AktG s 148 para 5 as proposed by UMAG.

[133] ibid.

[134] Revised AktG s 243 para 4 (as proposed by UMAG).

[135] The full text of the proposal (in German) can be accessed at <http://www.bmj.bund.de/media/archive/798.pdf> (30 June 2005).

[136] See proposal (n 135) 35.

collective or state-centred approaches over individualised ones. Formally, the notion that a class action suit collectivises an individual lawsuit is correct, and in that sense German law is indeed more individualistic. Functionally, however, it allocates the entire cost of a lawsuit to that individual. If these costs are prohibitively high, it thereby effectively denies judicial recourse. Conversely, in order to allow litigation to go forward, the US system subordinates individual claims to the interests of the class with the effect that the balance of bargaining power shifts from the defendant to the lead plaintiff and/or its attorney.

As the above discussion suggests, different legal systems allocate (or at least, have allocated) the right to initiate judicial review in the context of corporate law quite differently. Whereas in the US individual shareholders and their attorney have the power to initiate lawsuits, in Germany they can only demand action from the corporation or request a special representative to be appointed by the court. The allocation of initiation powers reflects the same preference for individual over collective interests (or the reverse) that can also be found in substantive ground rules. The US, a common law jurisdiction and LME, favours universal litigation and individual initiation rights. In contrast, Germany has opted for selective litigation rights and, even when doing so, tends to vest the collective rather than the individual with the power to initiate legal action.

The changes now underway in Germany indicate an important change in the allocation of procedural ground rules. Private litigation will be given more room in the future, and its usefulness for enforcing corporate law and shareholder rights more generally is finally being acknowledged. However, whether the proposed changes will fundamentally alter the operation of the German system remains to be seen. There are reasons to caution against high expectations that shareholder and investor lawsuits will play an important role in the future. While the threshold for initiating litigation has been reduced significantly, the cost of litigation and the risk of costs that litigants bear when the case is dismissed remain substantial. Future judicial interpretation of what would amount to intentional or grossly negligent misrepresentation of facts that triggered a lawsuit will be crucial for any litigant's cost-benefit analysis prior to initiating legal actions. Absent extensive discovery rules and shareholder information rights,[137] which might reduce the risk of misrepresentation, this uncertainty alone might deter litigation. In addition, the fear of creating attorney agency problems has led the German legislature to propose a rule that limits compensation for attorneys' fees to a single attorney per case, even if the case is brought by several shareholders. In light of the staggering awards of attorney fees in the United States, the fear may be justified, but it also is likely to undermine the role of attorneys as 'private attorney generals', which has been identified as crucial for the private enforce-

[137] See n 129.

ment regime in the US[138] Finally, litigation might also be deterred by uncertainties about outcomes. As has been noted, given the traditional hostility towards shareholder litigation, there is very little case law interpreting and clarifying the *Aktiengesetz*, the German law on publicly held corporations. Case law developed for the law of limited liability corporations (GmbH), which is much more voluminous, may serve as a guideline, but clarification as to the extent to which courts will apply the same principles to publicly held corporations is still warranted. Moreover, unlike UK or Delaware corporate law, German corporate law was not written to be litigated, but more as a guideline for the corporation's stakeholders' main rights and responsibilities, subject to bargaining within the corporation rather than external judicial review. Many provisions include ambiguous terms that could give courts ample room for interpretation. The Mannesmann case is one example of how this might be done. The particular approach taken by the court of first instance in that case may have been influenced by the fact that it was a criminal rather than a civil lawsuit. Nevertheless, the case does suggest that courts may declare many of the ambiguous provisions justiciable and may interpret them in a fashion that is consistent with social preferences that value the collective good over individual interests, the greater role shareholders may now play in litigation notwithstanding.

VI. Conclusion

This paper set out to explain the apparent affinity between the type of market economy and the type of legal system operating in a given country. Among the 17 major OECD countries that have been the subject of much analysis in the debate on corporatist vs market systems, or coordinated vs liberal market economies, all LMEs are common law countries, and all CMEs are civil law countries. This paper has sought to explain this link. It argues that social preferences for individual rights vs social norms on one hand, and for the pursuit of individual enforcement of legal rights vs bargaining and other collective enforcement mechanisms on the other, are deeply embedded in legal systems. They can be found in ground rules in areas of the law well beyond labour rights and union organisations, which have typically been the focus of analysis in the debate about corporatist systems. The paper developed ideal types for the allocation of substantial and procedural ground rules and illustrated them with examples drawn from contract and corporate law in primarily two jurisdictions – Germany and the US. These jurisdictions may not be representative for all CMEs/civil law systems

[138] JC Coffee Jr 'The Unfaithful Champion: The Plaintiff as Monitor in Shareholder Litigation' (1985) 48 L & Contemporary Problems 40. For a more recent discussion on the role of the state, law, and law enforcement, especially in systems with dispersed ownership, see JC Coffee Jr 'The Rise of Dispersed Ownership: The Roles of Law and the State in the Separation of Ownership and Control' (2002) 111 Yale L J 1.

or LMEs/common law systems. More research will need to be done to establish that similar ground rules can be found in other jurisdictions and that they confirm the link between legal families and types of market economies.

Assuming that this link can be further substantiated, it has important implications for the comparative analysis of economic/legal systems. It suggests that the rules and regulations that have commonly been identified with the corporatist system (or CMEs), may only be the tail end of norms engrained in formal rules and complementary institutions that govern these economies. Their adoption was not inevitable, as societies could have 'agreed' on less far-reaching legal representation of such norms. Moreover, societies, or lawmakers as their representatives, may choose to change specific rules. Yet, such a change, at least in isolation, is unlikely to change the social preferences that prevail in these economies. Even in the absence of specific legal arrangements, the basic allocation of substantive and procedural decision-making rights will continue to influence lawmaking and adjudication.

That is not to say that more far-reaching change is impossible. Recent changes in procedural ground rules governing corporate law in Germany are a case in point. They reflect a different perception of shareholder rights, and as such may be indicative of a more general change in social preferences towards greater recognition of individual rights and procedural powers. Still, the final assessment has to await the development of a body of case law that would indicate whether the reallocation of procedural ground rules also implies a shift in substantive ground rules away from concepts that give primacy to the interests of the corporation as a community of interests, to those of shareholders. While changes in procedural ground rules could in fact trigger lasting change over time, for the time being it seems to be premature to use the still marginal changes in specific legal rules as a sign of convergence of legal and/or economic systems.[139]

Table 5: Overview

	LME/Common Law	CME/Civil Law
Substantive Default Rule	Private contracts are valid unless they violate procedural rules and are in 'bad faith'	Private contracts are governed by 'good faith'
Procedural Default Rule	Individual initiation rights	Individual litigation rights limited and frequently delegated to the collective and/or a neutral agent

[139] Despite all the fanfare about convergence as a result of globalisation (see, for example, H Hansman and R Kraakman 'The End of History for Corporate Law' (2001) 89 Georgetown L J 439), there is little empirical evidence to substantiate this claim. See Fligstein (n 23) 191.

Corporatist versus Market Approaches to Governance

HORST SIEBERT

I. Introduction

Germany has developed a system of governance in which, besides markets and the political process, non-market mechanisms to find a consensus on economic issues play an important role. In this corporatist approach, markets and the political process are partly replaced by the decision-making of social groups. Decision rights are formally assigned to social groups which are given norm-setting privileges and which can make binding decisions for their group members and for society. Social groups also participate informally in decisions, mostly in decisions of the government. Moreover, informal personal relationships may play a role in economic decisions instead of market processes. In this paper, I look at the role of corporatist decision-making or governance in Germany, the areas in which it takes place, and its impact on the economy. Germany has a restrained market economy, and this is at the root of its unemployment problems and its poor growth performance.[1]

II. Three Different Institutional Arrangements: Markets, the Political Process, and Corporatist Decision-Making

The dichotomy between markets and the political process as institutional mechanisms for economic decision is a phenomenon well known from other market

[1] For a more detailed analysis of Germany's institutional system, see H Siebert *The German Economy: Beyond the Social Market* (Princeton University Press Princeton 2005) chs 4, 8, 10 and 14.

economies. Markets are used for the allocation of private goods where the marginal willingness of individuals to pay is aggregated horizontally. Markets and competition coordinate the decisions of households and firms, stimulate technological innovations, and bring forward new solutions to problems in a decentralized way. In contrast to the allocation via markets, the political process is applied in the allocation of public goods that, by definition, are used in equal amounts by all. Here the marginal willingness to pay can only be added vertically and individuals can therefore take the free rider position; parliament, political parties, indirect or direct democracy, and federalism with the principle of fiscal equivalence serve to aggregate the preferences of individuals in a society and to secure the financing of public goods (Table 1). The dividing line between these two institutional arrangements gives rise to many debates, including the role of the state, taxation, the privatization of governmental tasks, property rights for network industries, the internalization of externalities, and other issues.

Table 1: Markets, Political Process, and Corporatist Decision-Making

I. Markets and competition
Private goods, frame of reference by competition policy, and regulation including the internalization of externalities

II. Corporatist decision making by groups
'Collective interest', norm-setting by groups, participation, informal decision-making

III. Political process
Public goods, parliaments, parties, direct and indirect democracy, federalism

Germany's corporatist approach is an intermediate layer of decision-making between markets and the political process. Here markets are substituted by delegating decisions to social groups. This means that social groups can determine or influence market prices. At the same time, social groups are given the right to define important aspects of the institutional arrangements. They set norms instead of the political process.

III. Main Areas of Corporatist Decision-Making

Germany's corporatist approach to governance pervades many areas. It includes the labor market where the social partners with the trade unions and the employers' association determine wage formation and the institutional set-up of the labor market; it comprises the capital market and corporate governance where banks, the workers, and the trade unions play an important role in the governance of firms with the German specifics of codetermination; and it also involves informal personal relationships as in the bank-based capital market with bank-intermediated instead of market products. The approach also applies to other areas as well, such as the steering of the university system not organized by competition but by governmental planning and by codetermination and the regional associations of statuary health insurance physicians in the public health system.

1. The Social Partners in the Labor Market

Trade unions and employers' associations have been granted the privilege of setting the wages for their members and determining the working conditions, including working time, holidays, fringe benefits, and other aspects of work. Wage formation is not left to the markets but determined by the social partners in a sector-wide bargaining process. The typical procedure is to start wage negotiations for a specific sector in a specific region, and then to apply the negotiated wages to all the other regions of the same sector. Normally, negotiations are started in economically strong regions. Usually, the sector-wide wage contracts are mimicked in the other sectors of the economy, including the public sector. As a result, the bargaining process is *de facto* nationwide. Usually, the larger unions begin the negotiations, either the metalworkers' union or the service sector union. About 70% of the dependently employed are covered by collective contracts. It is estimated that the contracts serve as an orientation for another additional 15% of the work force. It is a puzzle that this coverage is reached in spite of the fact that trade unions are losing members. As of 2003 only 17.4% of the total work force was organized in the DGB, the German Federation of Trade Unions, the umbrella organization of the sectoral trade unions.

The answer to this puzzle is that the unions' power is rooted to a large extent in Germany's institutional set-up. Membership is voluntary, but the result of collective bargaining is binding for the members. Thus, the negotiated wage applies to all firms that are member of the employers' association and to all workers who are members of the trade union. That means that the social partners are legally entitled to regulate labor relations as if they had parliamentary power to pass laws (*wage autonomy or Tarifautonomie*). The collective contract is defended by the courts; it even applies to the unemployed union members who can only take a job at the union wage. Whereas in principle, both workers and firms are required to be members of the respective organizations for collective bargaining to be binding, in practice the collective contract has an impact beyond membership. *De facto*, firms do not differentiate wages according to union membership of workers or non-membership. Firms apply the negotiated wage to non-union members as well; otherwise they fear motivating workers to join the unions and thus make the unions stronger. Moreover, the negotiated wages set the standard for the non-unionized firms as well. Thus, negotiated wages represent the norm for the economy, even for the unemployed.

The clue to grasping the German set-up is to know that the negotiated collective wage contract is legally protected by a number of provisions.

a. Constitutional Freedom of Coalition

Article 9 sec III of the German constitution defines the right to form a coalition. This positive freedom of coalition, the cornerstone of all other legal stipulations with respect to the labor market, finds a limit in that nobody can be forced to become a member of a coalition (negative freedom of coalition). The Constitutional Court has ruled that the social partners – although having norm-setting rights – do not have a norm-setting monopoly. Parliament may intervene in the *wage autonomy* of the social partners if other constitutional rights are violated. Reducing mass unemployment allows individuals to realize their constitutional right of the freedom of occupation (Article 12) and to develop their personality (Articles 1 and 2). Thus, Article 9 and the positive right of coalition do not imply that some limits cannot be put on *wage autonomy*.

b. Limiting the Individual's Option to Deviate

One basic legal principle, the *Günstigkeitsprinzip* (the principle of the most favorable condition, paragraph 4 Sec 3 *Tarifvertragsgesetz*), stipulates that the individual worker can as a union member deviate from the negotiated union wage contract if this is favorable for him. 'Favorable', however, is interpreted in a narrow sense by the labor courts as a wage higher than in the collective contract or as less working time. The risk of becoming unemployed or the security of the job cannot legally be part of the consideration of whether deviating from the union contract is favorable; this has been explicitly decided by the highest labor court (*Bundesarbeitsgericht*) in 1999. According to this decision, wages and working time on the one hand and the security of a job on the other hand are not allowed to be compared, whereas the three variables – wage level, working time, and job security – are strongly correlated in economic reality. Moreover, all three variables can be expected to be argument variables in the utility function of workers. Limiting the individual's choice means rigidity in the labor market; it also contributes to the low degree of wage differentiation. To stipulate that the risk of losing the job should be taken into consideration or that the individual worker should have the right to decide for himself whether he wants to deviate from the union contract meets the strong opposition of the trade unions which fear losing organizational power. The equivalent to these provisions for the employed is that the unemployed can only enter the labor market according to the rules of the collective contract, unless the social partners have introduced provisions that the unemployed can start a job below the collective pay scale.[2]

c. Limiting the Firm's Option to Deviate

Another important legal provision is equally essential in establishing the role of the collective contract and the power of the unions. It stipulates that firms cannot deviate from the union contract unless this is permitted in the contract itself (Paragraph 77, Sec 3 *Business Constitution Act or Betriebsverfassungsgesetz*). Thus, even if the workers of a firm agree by an overwhelming majority to work more hours per week or to accept a lower wage in order to make their jobs safer, this is *verboten* (forbidden). This regulation even applies to those firms that are not a member of the employers' association.[3] Labor contracts including besides the wage also the security of the job have advantages both for the workers and the firm. In that sense they are efficient contracts; they allow a higher welfare than the union contract. Moreover, they give important signals to the market. But such efficient labor contracts are legally not feasible in Germany. Admittedly, firms and workers have disregarded this legal stipulation to some extent, and trade unions have no choice but to accept an agreement reached with the workers' council as in the Siemens and the DaimlerChrysler deals in 2004. But legal battles in the courts have sustained the law that prevents efficient labor contracts. Other legal stipulations also defend the power of the unions, for instance layoff restraints. In addition, the trade unions can be tempted to rely on governmental schemes to reduce unemployment, ie to be bailed out from their responsibility by a third party, namely the state and the taxpayer. In essence, labor market rules can be interpreted as protecting the wage cartel and securing the power of the trade unions.

The protection of the collective wage contract allows unions their wage policy favoring the employed. Trade unions have not accepted what the German Council of Economic Advisers has proposed as an orientation for union wage policy in order to establish high employment and to prevent unemployment. The social partners have been given the right to set the wages, but no institutional mechanism has been established defining their responsibility for unemployment. It is naïve from the point of view of basic economics to expect a market-clearing equilibrium with a favorable employment situation under these circumstances. If

[2] For instance, in the chemical sector such a provision holds with a discount of 10% below the collective wage in the first year of employment.

[3] It thus *de facto* violates the negative 'freedom of coalition' guaranteed by the Constitution, ie that no one should be forced into a union membership.

one fixes a price in a market, demand and supply will react. There are not too many reasons why the social partners, naturally guided by their self-interest, are likely to find the market-clearing equilibrium price that brings full employment for the economy. In Germany the corporatist approach in the labor market has protected the insiders, the employed. But there is a conflict between the protection of the employed and the discrimination against the unemployed. The real political task is to appraise that conflict. The answer is: The protection of those employed should be reduced to such an extent that the discrimination against the unemployed disappears.

The solution to this problem lies in allowing a more decentralized autonomy in the collective labor contract, both for the individual worker and for the workers of a firm as a group. Germany has to move in the direction of a market solution. With respect to the individual worker, one has to allocate more decisions to him by allowing him to deviate from the collective contract if this can make his job more secure, for instance by a commitment from the firm that there will be no layoffs say in the next three years. This requires a legal redefinition of the *Günstigkeitsprinzip*, inserting a rule that the security of a job should be an aspect in the decision of whether a deviation is favorable for the individual worker. A more radical solution is that the right to decide on the deviation from the collective is given to the individual. Such a right would also apply to the unemployed, who then is allowed to enter the labor market below the collective wage. At the same time, more individual, result-oriented elements should be introduced into the work contract without a link to the collective contract.

With respect to the workers of the firm as a group, they should be granted the right to deviate from the collective contract if a majority so desires. If no majority exists, the union contract holds. If one wants to protect the collective treaty, the threshold of the necessary majority could be set high, for instance at two-thirds. This means changing paragraph 77 Sec III of the Business Constitution Act (*Betriebsverfassungsgesetz*). In the legal sense, this alteration would refer to union members only. The decision to deviate would be their decision. This follows from the positive freedom of coalition: union members cannot be forced by non-union members into a contract they do not want. Therefore, non-union members would not have a vote on the union contract. But of course they and the management would be free to enter into a non-union contract. In all these cases, the workers' councils also play a role; they could become part of a practical solution in finding a majority. It should be noted, however, that each employee is bound by law by the decisions of the workers' councils, so that wage-setting by the councils would to some extent even represent more collectivity than by the trade unions whose membership is voluntary. Therefore, workers' councils should only enter into wage formation in the form of a recommendation[4] on which then individual contracts can be made.

[4] *Betriebsabreden* instead of *Betriebsvereinbarungen*.

2. The Social Partners in the Capital Market: Codetermination in Corporate Governance

In several aspects, Germany has chosen a distinct approach to the control and the management of firms, commonly referred to as corporate governance. Important differences exist relative to other countries in the entire range of mechanisms and arrangements that shape the way in which key decisions are taken within companies. First, a special feature of German corporate law is the separation between a supervisory board (*Aufsichtsrat*) and a management board (*Vorstand*) in stock companies.[5] Second, banks play a vital role in the controlling of firms due to the dominance of intermediated products and along with the banks' position in the supervisory boards. As indicated by the term 'house banks', informal or personal relationships are relevant factors, the reason being the lack of alternatives to these mechanisms of allocation, namely market products. Third, in contrast to the system in operation in the more stock-market-based economies of the United States or the United Kingdom, blockholder representation in the supervisory boards is much more pervasive within the German system. In the following, I look at another decisive specialty, namely that employees and the trade unions represent half of the votes in the supervisory board of incorporated companies with more than 2000 employees; it is one-third of the votes in smaller incorporated companies above 500 employees.

Under the law of codetermination, introduced in 1976, employees are legally allocated control rights over all corporate decisions in the form of seats in the supervisory board. They have the same right as an owner of equity. The general idea is that the suppliers of capital and suppliers of labor steer the firm 'cooperatively'. In incorporated firms, ie in stock companies and in limited liability companies (*GmbHs*) with more than 2,000 employees, half of the seats are allocated to the capital owners, the other half to the employees (Figure 1).[6] In firms with less than 10,000 employees, there are six seats for both sides. One of the positions on the employees' side is earmarked for the managerial employees; two of six seats are reserved for the trade union representatives who do not have to be employees at the respective firm. This regulation gives trade unions a foothold in the governance of firms entirely independent of the degree of organization (or lack thereof) among the company's employees.[7] The board members representing the equity holders are elected by the shareholders' meeting, while the members of the board on the employees' side are elected by a conference of employee delegates or by direct ballot. The employee representatives have to be employees of

[5] On the discussion of the German versus the Anglo-Saxon Model, see Siebert (n 1) ch 10.

[6] A specific law of codetermination applies to the coal and steel industry (Codetermination Law of 1951), with a stricter form of participation.

[7] The number of seats increases with the size of the firm. In larger firms with ten seats for each side, ie in firms with more than 20,000 employees, the unions have three seats.

the company, with the exception of the trade union representatives. Trade unions have the right of nomination for their positions. The members of the supervisory board elect its chairman and the deputy chairman with a two-thirds majority. If this majority is not attained, the representatives of the shareholders elect the

Codetermination in German Firms

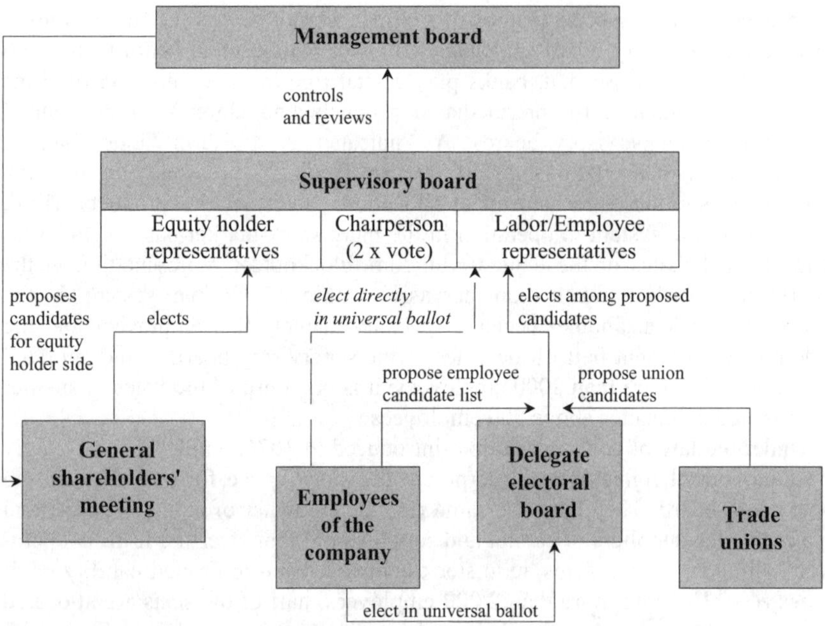

chairman, and the representatives of the employees his deputy. At a parity of votes in decisions of the supervisory board, the chairman has two votes. In incorporated companies with less than 2,000 and more than 500 employees, workers must make up a third of the members of the board according to the Business Constitution Act.

Limited liability companies (*GmbHs*), which are not generally required by law to have a supervisory board, are obliged to establish such a board in order to introduce codetermination. For them, the same thresholds and majorities of codetermination apply, ie half of the seats for companies with more than 2,000 employees go to labor (one-third of the seats for companies between 2,000 and 500 employees).

How codetermination affects the decisions of firms and their performance in an international comparison is a heavily debated issue. This issue is additional to the question of how the German two-tier system fairs relative to the Anglo-Saxon system of corporate governance. It can be argued that the advantage of this system of codetermination is the cooperation between different groups of a company so that the interests of the employees, the shareholders, and the firm are considered when important decisions are made. It is a kind of 'stakeholder value' concept that attempts to lessen conflict potential by institutionalizing consultation and by cooperative decision-making. This is expected to ensure, in addition to the participation of the workers' council, a positive motivation of the employees, and this is seen in turn as beneficial for the performance of a company.

A firm can be understood to be an implicit contract between the factors of production defining which factor carries which risk and which factor receives which expected remuneration under unknown states of the world. Traditionally, this contract is understood to guarantee a secure income for labor, an important input provided to the firm, with capital taking on the income risk. Income to labor is guaranteed only under the assumption that the firm continues to be economically viable so that labor also carries the employment risk, reduced by the legal setting; capital carries the risk of bankruptcy. With codetermination, employees can influence how this implicit contract is written *de facto* and how income is distributed among the factors within the firm. If codetermination sufficiently empowers employees, and if stockholders' rights cannot be contractually protected, then employees are able to change the risk allocation redistributing the firm's surplus towards themselves, thus increasing the *ex ante* uncertainty for capital owners. They then alter the nature of the firm. Thus, codetermination is about the allocation of risk and the very nature of the capitalist firm. It also is about the allocation of power over the distribution of income and employment opportunities under unknown states of the firm's environment and determines the weight of shareholders versus that of stakeholders in these basic issues. Both sides are likely to have different preferences on these points, especially with respect to securing jobs.

Under the existing rules of codetermination, decisions are influenced by the workers and the unions. In such an institutional set-up, one normally likes to have the consensus of all the groups involved. Thus, if the representatives of the employees will not vote for the chairman of the management board, the capital side is likely not to insist on its candidate or the candidate himself will withdraw in view of the lack of support from the employees, as happened in the election of the last chairman of BMW in 1999 and in constituting the management board of DaimlerChrysler in 2004. For trade unions, codetermination is an important source of power; it increases their political leverage and also provides positions for their members, especially their leaders. Consequently, they have a strong interest in preserving codetermination. However, there is a clear conflict of interest between the role as a trade union leader and as a member of the supervisory board. For a member of the board, the obligation is to promote and to protect the interest of the firm, whereas for a trade union leader the aim is to promote the interest of the union. The possibility of having to call a strike against the firm exists in this case; in principle, the firm would have the option to close out workers. This conflict became apparent in early 2003 when Bsirske, the leader of the service sector union Verdi and a member of the supervisory board of Lufthansa as well as its vice chairman, called a strike against this very firm. This conflict of interest exists independently of whether the trade union members of the board pass on their remuneration largely to the trade unions' foundation.

With codetermination defining the weights of the shareholders and the employees, and furthermore with the workers' councils as an institution to voice the interest of employees, it is held within the economics literature that the German system, particularly when also taking into account the role of banks and blockholders, has proved to be less able than the Anglo-Saxon system to make decisions quickly.[8] It is fair to say that in the end, structural change and plant closings were not prohibited by Germany's institutional approach.[9] If people had to be laid off, this was done predominantly via the combination of social closing plans and governmental programs of early retirement, solving labor market issues at the cost of the pension system. Together with the rigidity of wages, however, the adjustment of the German industry did not result in the creation of any new jobs. Relative to structural change, codetermination can be seen as a defensive instrument. Looking at it in a long-run view, it protected the insiders, at least temporarily; such protection always comes at the disadvantage of the outsiders.

Besides sector adjustment, another issue is innovation. In this respect, codetermination and the workers' councils seem to be appropriate in finding a consensus along the firm's established technological trajectories, marginally improving the existing production technology and modernizing established products. These approaches are, however, less apt in an environment where a new technology has to be applied, where new products have to be developed, and when leapfrogging to a new technology is the key task. These more radical changes, often viewed with suspicion as job-killers, conflict with the structurally conservative mindset epitomized by the institutions of codetermination.

Both forms of participation of employees reduce the attractiveness of Germany as a location for investors from abroad. Moreover, they affect the locational advantage when domestic investors look at options in other countries. This argument deserves more weight with the increased international mobility of capital and technology. A smaller capital inflow or even a capital outflow as a consequence of these forms of participation means that less capital would be accumulated in Germany and fewer new technologies might be attracted so that the German employee will be equipped with capital less generously, reducing his productivity and his wage-earning potential. In addition, codetermination ac-

[8] B Holmström 'Managerial Incentive Problems: A Dynamic Perspective' (1999) 66 The Review of Economic Studies 169; KJ Hopt and others (eds) *Comparative Corporate Governance: The State of the Art and Emerging Research* (OUP Oxford 1998); CP Mayer 'New Issues in Corporate Finance' (1988) 32 European Economic Review 1167.

[9] For instance, when Krupp had to close its steel plant in Rheinhausen under severe public and workers' protest in 1993, it could do so with the vote of the 'neutral man' in the supervisory board.

cording to the German set-up leads to a lower international evaluation of companies incorporated as joint stock companies. This means that Germany would become unattractive for holding companies.

Whereas in the past, raising issues of codetermination in public has virtually been a taboo – with chairmen of the boards usually stressing that these institutional approaches were a good thing and that they personally were getting along very well with their partners in the supervisory boards and the workers' council – one can now hear statements questioning the concept of codetermination, especially in light of the necessity to respond swiftly to a changed economic environment and therefore to quickly reach decisions. In any case, besides the aspect of providing power to the trade unions, it is now recognized that there is a trade-off with respect to codetermination: it is an instrument bringing about coherence of the firm, even partly allowing the implicit contract between the factors of production within the firm to be self-enforcing and sustainable, but at the same time delaying decisions, slowing down innovation in focusing the interest on marginal improvements of a given trajectory, and making Germany less attractive as a location for international investment. In a way, we meet again the basic conflict of the German approach: the dichotomy between coherence, social considerations, and equity on the one hand and dynamics and efficiency on the other.

The international conditions in which the German system of governance, including codetermination, is embedded and by which it is affected, are changing. The shareholder structure is becoming more international due to globalization and the diversification of large, institutional, and actively managed portfolios, making blockholding less likely. 'Shareholder activism', increasingly exercised by institutional investors, will work towards more profitability-oriented and value-oriented corporate policies. These international developments in the market for corporate control will leave their mark on Germany. But in addition, the German system of codetermination is becoming incongruous with the internationalization of German firms.[10] Foreign employees of German firms do not participate in the election of the workers' representatives in the supervisory board, nor are their trade unions represented. Since larger German firms meanwhile have half of their employees abroad, the legal stipulations of the codetermination law of some thirty years ago now appear as an attempt to secure representation and voting power to the German employees. It can be interpreted as an institutional arrangement in favor of a specific group of insiders. This inconsistency between the desire to secure the position of German employees and the reality of worldwide employment in German firms cannot be overcome by a worldwide approach to co-

[10] T Baums 'Unternehmensführung und Unternehmenskontrolle: Brauchen wir eine neue Konzeption für Corporate Governance?' in Kiel Institute for World Economics (ed) *Die Weltwirtschaft vor den Herausforderungen von morgen. Vortrags- und Diskussionsveranstaltung des Instituts für Weltwirtschaft am 23. Januar 2003 in Frankfurt am Main* (Kiel Institute for World Economics 2003) 31-41.

determination along German lines. On the contrary, the issue is that the actual system does not seem to be tenable under conditions of globalization.

Moreover, in the European Union the principle of non-discrimination of EU citizens prevents the continuation of the German arrangement as it now stands. To extend the German approach of codetermination to the other member states of the European Union, for instance by having an EU-wide regulation, would rightly meet the opposition of the other EU members, which have a different institutional practice with their own historic experience and their own preferences. Moreover, the concept of institutional competition and the EU's principle of mutual recognition of national institutional set-ups prevent such a harmonization. In this spirit, the European Court of Justice has allowed firms from other EU countries with a different form of incorporation and without codetermination to operate in Germany. This ruling from November 2002 has generated interest among German companies to move their legal headquarters into a neighboring country, evading codetermination while continuing their operations in Germany as before. Codetermination thus joins tax optimization as an important rationale for corporate relocation.

3. The Workers' Councils

The workers' council has a set of decision rights where its consent is mandatory according to the Business Constitution Act (*Betriebsverfassungsgesetz*). These rights of codetermination (*Mitbestimmung*) effectively limit management's directive powers, requiring the approval of either the council or a successful mediation for decisions to become effective.[11] The rights of codetermination apply to decisions of special interest to the employees, especially the conditions of work and the workplace in a business. This includes the organization of the work process, for instance group work, the arrangement of working hours in a plant per day, the length and lay-out of work shifts, and the design for working time on the weekend and overtime, unless specified by a collective contract with the unions. Codetermination also extends to vacation plans, ergonomic standards, special company benefits such as housing or daycare, remuneration schemes and means to measure and supervise the efficiency and performance of the employees – these include for instance agreements with superiors on individual annual objectives, performance-based remuneration schemes, and process performance measurement such as activity-based costing – and team-based arrangements of workflows. Agreement is needed on measures when employees lose their qualifications due to the introduction of new production processes. The workers' council

[11] In addition, the law establishes the right of collaboration in decision-making (*Mitwirkung*), requiring that the workers' council must be heard on the relevant issues; failure to do so may result in the invalidity of a decision taken by management. Furthermore, there are informative and consultative rights and the right of autonomous administration of all workers' council affairs.

also approves the hiring of new personal and staff planning, pertaining to the assignment of new responsibilities and company-internal transfers. The workers' council can thus effectively block the promotion of an employee if it believes, for example, that the pay raise involved unduly favors this employee over others. Its consent is required for layoffs and for social closing plans. In the case of regular layoffs, the workers' council can disapprove of the decision based on certain criteria (employer did not screen for social aspects in selecting employee to lay off, or continued employment would be possible given certain adjustments); this disapproval by the council gives the employee the right to sue for continued employment, delaying his dismissal until a final court ruling.

General tasks of the workers' council extend to supervising the compliance with collective bargaining results and legal stipulations in the company, among them workplace safety and environmental regulations, promoting equal rights among the workforce, as well as helping to foster and secure the conditions for employment. On all these issues, management and the workers' council, who meet at least once a month, are called upon by law to cooperate in an atmosphere of confidence, looking for solutions in the best interest of the company and its employees; accordingly the workers' council as an institution may not take part in hostile activities of collective action. Agreement of the workers' council is not explicitly needed in strictly entrepreneurial decisions, including investment and financing, product development, marketing, and public relations.

The workers' council's decisions are binding for all employees of a firm.[12] The workers' council members are elected; they are not necessarily representatives of the trade unions although the unions play a dominant role. The right to establish a workers' council refers to businesses with at least five regular employees. A council is established by election of its members through the employees. Where employees do not care to vote, firms are without a workers' council. Similar rights hold for the personnel council in the public sector, including the universities and research institutes.

The workers' council represents an institution that helps to standardize rules in firms and also allows discussion of conflicts and bringing about of consensus. At the same time, the institutional set-up assigns decision rights and thus power to an elected body, taking it away from individual employees, the management, and the owner of a firm. It allows participation of employees and trade unions, but puts restraints on the management of firms. If things go smoothly, this institutional arrangement reduces transaction costs. If, however, the issues roughen and if fronts between the two sides harden, transaction costs may actually be increased. For instance, the workers' council may use its power to refuse its consent to a management proposal if it does not get one of its projects through in return. This deal-making may imply economically inefficient solu-

[12] Unless they represent recommendations for the individual labor contract (*Regelungsabreden*).

tions. What is more important: Besides being time-consuming, a workers' council requires quite a bit of attention and energy. In larger firms, in which the personnel director manages the ongoing relationship with the workers' council, this normally does not tend to represent a problem. In smaller and medium-sized firms, however, which crucially depend on the energy of the owner-entrepreneur, the attention required by the workers' council eats up part of the available entrepreneurial energy that then no longer is available for innovation, marketing, and strategic positioning of the firm.

4. Non-Private Banks and Relationship Banking

The German banking industry is characterized by a large presence of publicly owned or government-influenced institutions. Publicly controlled savings banks including their central institutions, the state banks (*Landesbanken*), make up about 36% of the market; here important changes in the public guarantees can be expected from 2005 on due to the requirement of the single European market. Another distinguishing feature of the German banking industry is that commercial banks extent credit to firms and that credit plays an important role relative to equity capital, taking the experience in other countries as a frame of reference. Yet another feature is that commercial banks generally hold equity of firms and thus have capital locked-in in industrial holdings. Equity held by banks and insurance companies creates a network of cross holdings between the financial and the non-financial sector. Thus, the larger banks and the larger insurance companies are sitting in a delicate and complex cobweb of holdings, so that the firms of the industrial sector and of the service sector are intertwined with the financial sector. These interdependencies are even further intensified by the other financial institutions, eg the investment funds, being interrelated with banks or insurance companies as well. Banks exercise control in the supervisory board of companies where they are represented on the capital side of the supervisory board. They play a vital role in corporate governance. Banks use their presence in the boards to collect information on their creditors (relationship banking).

This approach has negative implications for the financing of new, innovative, but risky technologies. The commercial banks, savings banks, and cooperatives tend to shy away from financing large risks. They are more comfortable with incremental changes. R&D funding of the private sector typically comes from retained earnings, which is a means more plentifully available to established firms with relatively constant cash flows. Another implication of the German approach is that new market solutions such as a functioning venture capital market have more difficulty developing in an environment that is characterized by intermediated products and by personal, informal relationships.[13]

[13] The venture capital market has recently improved.

5. Other Institutional Set-Ups Outside the Market Process

Other important areas, left to the markets and competition in other countries, are assigned to the public sector without being public goods in the strict sense. An important area is the university system with nearly two million students and an annual budget of 29 billion euro for public and a few private universities. The university system is organized as a governmental system and is financed from tax revenue, except for several private universities already existing and a few that are now coming into being on the education sector's fringe. The funds are allocated by the parliaments of the federal states. The governance system is one of administrative planning in which the respective ministry of culture of the federal state is in charge of administering the university in many respects more or less directly. Recently, the ministries of several states have attempted to write contracts with the universities defining the universities' targets and providing funds for a planning period, thus granting the universities more autonomy. These principal-agent contracts are reminiscent of a central agency like GOSPLAN in the former Soviet Union writing such a contract with the firms. As a positive step, in quite a few cases a board of regents has now been introduced, endowed with the authority to decide some of the issues that previously were dealt with by the ministries. Codetermination through personnel councils applies.

As the universities are public, each student who has obtained his high school diploma (*Abitur*) has a right of access. Student fees are a taboo. As of now, student tuition fees are prohibited for any student's first degree studies by the Federal Framework Act for Universities (*Hochschulrahmengesetz* § 24 Sect 4) so that scarcity of student slots cannot be dealt with by a price mechanism. Where student slots are scarce, a nationwide allocation mechanism has been introduced that allocates the scarce slots to the student candidates in a lengthy process, in which the interest of universities in obtaining motivated and qualified students does not play a role. Thus, a bureaucratic procedure is relevant for access to the university. Some federal states now want to introduce student fees of 500 or 1,000 euro and are granting the universities the right to choose and recruit a part of their student body themselves. The approach of administrative planning used for German universities does not rely on the force of competition. Except for the intrinsic behavior of individual professors, universities and their departments are really not in competition with each other. Thus, competitive pressure is not used as a controlling device for German universities. Not being able to set fees, they cannot raise money for their operation and for investment. For instance, they cannot cater to the international market for undergraduate and graduate degrees and skim off the internationally given willingness-to-pay with receipts that could be used for investment.

Yet another example of the German approach of group-based decision-making is the associations of statuary health insurance physicians in the public health system (*Kassenärztliche Vereinigungen*). These organizations represent the physicians whose patients, about 90% of the population, are covered by the public insurers. These physicians are required by law to be members of the organization. According to the social law,[14] the role of these organizations is to negotiate the physicians' fees with the public health insurers. These organizations may be seen as the physicians' trade union, but with mandatory membership. Although they can be interpreted as a countervailing power to the public health insurers, this approach establishes at the same time a bargaining cartel that develops its own interest. Thus, individual public insurers are forbidden to negotiate their fees directly with specific physicians and hospitals so that an integrated health management system, which can be found in Switzerland and in the United States, is legally prevented. In such an integrated system, insurers offer their own medical services through a network of physicians and hospitals at a reduced insurance rate. In this way, competition between public insurers can be initiated. The associations of statuary health insurance physicians in the public health system also limit the number of doctors in any field of specialization in areas moving towards an 'excess supply' of certain physicians, such as inner-city locations. In this area, then, an implicit distrust of market forces becomes evident – market failure is assumed a priori.[15]

IV. The Informal Consensus Approach in Governmental Decision-Making

In addition to these formalized institutional approaches of group decision-making, as written into law, more informal attempts to find a consensus have been tried as well. These included the 'concerted action' between the relevant social groups, especially the trade unions and the employers' association, by the

[14] Sozialgesetzbuch V § 82.

[15] Other areas in which decision-making is allocated to groups are the chambers of agriculture, chambers of commerce, chambers of craftsmen, chambers of architects, and regional bar associations, all with mandatory membership. These organizations represent part of self-administration in Germany, dealing with issues of a common interest for those organized. This includes, for instance, administering the apprenticeship system and standardizing apprenticeship profiles and the examinations for these profiles by the chambers of commerce and craftsmen. While a case can be made for self-administration in these areas, because problems are solved in a decentralized way according to the subsidiarity principle, these approaches also drive out market solutions. For example, the fees architects and lawyers can charge are strictly regulated, and advertising is prohibited for them just as for other professions such as physicians, dentists, or pharmacists (all forming part of *Freie Berufe*) which are considered a sphere where competition is not desired. Chambers of craftsmen also may be considered an instrument of colluding on prices and controlling the access to the market by administering the exams to be a master craftsman. All chambers publicly express the joint interest of their constituents, participating as lobby groups in the political process. They represent interest groups, which get support from the state for their organization by the device of mandatory membership and the transferal of exclusive norm-setting privileges, exempting their respective sectors from the rule of market forces.

economics minister Schiller in the 1960s and Chancellor Schröder's roundtables representing different groups of society. An example was the 'Alliance for Work', a forum including the trade unions, the employers' association, German industry, and the German Chamber of Commerce, in which Schröder tried to reach some consensus in the years 1998-2000 on important questions concerning unemployment. This attempt quickly failed. The main reason was that unions were not willing to discuss the issue of wage-setting. Another example has been committees such as the 'Hartz Commission' and the 'Rürup Commission', which were created to develop blueprints for major reform steps and to secure the consent of the groups represented in these committees.

V. Implications of the Corporatist Approach: The Restrained Market Economy

Looking at the governance approach used in Germany, the social market economy is a restrained market economy. In many areas, the institutional set-up moves decisions away from the market process and from competition and assigns them to the government, to social groups, organizations, and informal relationships (Table 2, see following page).

The German consensus approach in a corporatist setting has a number of serious implications.

First, the actions of government are likely to become more unsteady and short-run-oriented. An informal consensus procedure creates an environment in which the government makes discretionary decisions. A politician who can focus such decisions into popular issues that make the headlines in the press can use this approach to put himself into the limelight. He then is like a fire fighter. If a fire breaks out, he can come to the rescue. If there is problem, he will step in and solve it. If a firm is threatened by a crisis, such as one of illiquidity or even insolvency, he will come and help. He proves his indispensability to society. This activist approach is made easier in an environment in which corporatist decision-making is the rule. Thus, the corporatist approach leads to interventionism, to adhockery, and to a short-run orientation. More fundamental restraints are likely to be put on the back burner, for instance long-run impacts of economic policy measures, issues of sustainability, and intergenerational budget constraints. In such an approach, the politician does not lead in the true sense of the word and he is not a statesman. During his first term, Chancellor Schröder used this short-run approach, for instance, when he attempted to prevent the collapse of the construction firm Holzmann in 1999 due to illiquidity, presenting the rescue in the evening news and in front of cheering workers of the ruined company. Three years later, the firm was gone. Its restructuring plan had failed despite public loan guarantees and dumping prices that hurt the already strained German construction sector.

Table 2: Cooperative Decision-Making versus Markets and Competition

Area	Cooperative Decision-Making	Markets and Competition
Employment	Wage formation and institutional setting by social partners	Labor markets determining the equilibrium wage
Governance of firms	Two-tier board system, control by the supervisory board	Strong reliance on the capital market and the threat of takeover
	Codetermination in the supervisory board	No formal restraint on the decision space
	Workers' councils	Self-interest of the firm to be attractive to its employees
Banking	Bank-intermediated products, relationship-banking	Capital market-intermediated products
	Public guarantees, protection against takeover	Market control by the threat of takeover
Universities	Governmental administrative planning of the university sector	Competition among universities
	Entitlement to free access	Scarcity prices for students
Health	Associations of statuary health insurance physicians in the public health system	Competition of integrated systems of insurers and health service providers
Steering the economy	Roundtables and committees (consensus approach)	Decentralized decisions via markets
Governance of government	Cooperative federalism	Competitive federalism
	Mix of majority and plurality voting	Majority voting

Second, this ad hoc approach is likely to lead to different answers over time, ie to time inconsistency, as it reacts to acute problems as they appear, looking at them as singular cases without any consistent line. During his two terms, Schröder has changed his positions so that laws passed on his initiative had to be undone. In 1998, the limit for firms for which the layoff restraint did not apply was lowered from more than ten to more than five employees – in 2003, the decision was reversed. In 1998, the demographic factor in the pension formula was suspended – now a similar factor has been reintroduced. In 2000, the tax allowance for commuting from home to the workplace was enlarged – in 2003, the allowance was reduced. At the end of 2000, the options provided by law for employment contracts of limited duration were reduced – in 2003, newly founded firms were exempted from the regulation in the first four years. In 2001, the Business Constitution Act was tightened under resistance from the entrepreneurs, especially from the *Mittelstand* – now we are looking for ways to intensify the investment activity of the enterprise sector. Such varying concepts of economic policy are especially relevant as the state plays a decisive role in the governance system of the German economy. They are particularly damaging in their effects on expectations of entrepreneurs and firms in Germany.

Third, parliament becomes disempowered when decision rights are given to interest groups, either informally or formally. This holds if decisions are informally taken in roundtables or if they are prepared by commissions and public pressure is built up. Parliament then often has no other choice but to accept the proposals. Parliament is also disempowered when norm-setting authority is given to interest groups such as the social partners.

Fourth, an important implication of the corporatist approach is that the decisions taken reflect the interest of organized groups and of the incumbents and the status quo dominates. Organized interest groups are endowed with bargaining power; they get a *de facto* veto right. Consequently, major changes are not accepted when important groups of society are negatively affected by them. For instance, the trade unions have so far blocked important modifications in the system of rules and regulations for the labor market. Or, as another case in point, the Riester reform of the pay-as-you-go pension system was only possible after the unions agreed in December 2000 on the pension formula. In a way, the consensus approach is an application of the Pareto criterion according to which an increase in welfare presupposes that at least one wins and no one loses. This problem, however, is that in a corporatist setting and in a static perspective a relative improvement for one group is considered a loss for the other groups. This prevailing mood becomes even more severe in a situation in which all groups must cut back their social absorption. The consensus approach implies that the status quo plays a central role and development becomes extremely path-dependent. Decisions tend to be blocked if you look for consensus on all sides, effectively handing out veto rights to groups with a vested interest in the status quo. A standstill is the most likely outcome. Institutional modernization is blocked when the conditions of the world change and demand changes.

Fifth, the institutional setting favors marginal technological changes, but it is not an institutional environment which is conducive to technological leapfrogging. Consensus translates into risk aversion, and economic dynamics are lost.

The consensus approach may have been appropriate in an environment of high GDP growth rates of 8% as in the 1950s, and over 4% in the 1960s when the German economy was catching up to the United States and welfare gains could be spread widely. In a situation in which the growth path is characterized by a growth rate of only about 1½%, as in the eight years since 1995, restraints become more binding and goal conflicts more biting. Negative external shocks then are hard to come by. This suggests that the institutional set-up for decision-making is part of the German problem of low growth performance.

Sixth, the most serious shortcoming is that such an approach does not make use of decentralized allocation through markets and competition in which changes occur more or less automatically and where market participants are expected to adjust to new economic conditions. Roundtables do not have an automatic and decentralized way of finding new technological and organizational solutions. They are concerned with formally establishing and adjusting the rules. Such a system does not make use of the problem-solving capacity of decentralized markets and of competition. Creative energy is lost because the problem-solving potential of the market and decentralized competition is not exploited. What needs to be avoided, in conclusion, is to empower interest groups by handing them the bargaining power over changes in the status quo as this institutionalizes obstacles to an evolutionary process of economic and social change given the conservative incentive structure of these incumbents.

Instead of letting decisions take place in a decentralized way in the markets and by competition, the German approach seeks to establish consensus and relies on non-market processes. Unlike in the US, German public opinion does not ask first "Where is the market solution?" when a new problem arises, but it nearly instinctively looks to the intervention of politicians for a solution. Non-market approaches get an implicit preference; there is even a deeply rooted mistrust of markets and competition, possibly more so after German unification. The non-market processes are often thought of as protecting the collective interest, including the aspect of equity, whereas it seems difficult for the public to understand that the aggregation of decentralized market decisions and competitive processes leads to efficient results for the economy and also stimulates dynamics. Thus, whereas Germany has prevailed over the extreme form of collectivism in eastern Germany, soft forms of collective decision-making continue to exist.

In any case, the corporatist approach is not a necessary element of Germany's 'social market economy', which can be interpreted as an attempt to marry the efficiency of the market system with aspects of redistribution. This mixture can be obtained by a tax-transfer mechanism, although some redistributive measures are hidden. The social market economy does not require corporatist decision-making.

It is my hypothesis that Germany has lost economic dynamics due to its institutional set-up. Its institutions favor the status quo and consequently make economic development extremely path-dependent. Given technological trajectories and long-practiced organizational approaches dominate the road to the future, allowing marginal improvements in the familiar areas of production, but the conditions are not incentive-compatible for leapfrogging. In contrast, other countries, especially the small and foreign trade-oriented economies in Europe, have changed their institutional arrangements as a response to new challenges in the world economy.

This leads to the fundamental question of whether and to what extent Germany has become immobile with respect to institutional modernization. One answer is that the institutional arrangement is the expression of political preferences of a country. Given these preferences, a trade-off exists between the wish for collective decision-making and the performance of the economy. Those who want more collective choices instead of markets and competition have to pay the price of a lower economic dynamic. This may well be the decision of a mature economy having reached a satisfactory level of income to allow itself the luxury of consensus-seeking solutions. Then, relative decline in comparison to other countries is certain to come, and absolute economic decline cannot be ruled out.

The other answer is that the institutional structures have become so rigid that institutional adjustment can no longer take place, and that vested interests have captured the institutional set-up and control it to such an extent that the political process has lost its problem-solving capacity. Then a country like Germany must rely more and more on decisions of the Constitutional Court to unblock political deadlocks. In such a scenario, Germany can indeed be compared to Japan as another mature economy.[16] In that sense, Germany may face a similar problem as Japan. Their institutional systems were appropriate for expanding economies, but no longer seem to be appropriate to solve structural issues. We then have the new category of NDCs in the world economy, the newly declining countries.

I do not believe that is the inevitable answer for Germany. The institutions are not completely captured by political groups, and with enough energy and resilience, the country can find a way out of the deadlock in which it is caught.

[16] For Japan, the reason for political immobility is seen in the relative over-representation of agricultural voting districts to the city districts; it finds its equivalent in the consensus approach in Germany.

Regulatory Paternalism: When is it Justified?

ANTHONY I. OGUS*

I. Introduction

Near the University of Manchester there is a road junction with traffic lights where pedestrians can also cross. The rotation authorised by the green light is first north and south vehicles; then east and west vehicles; and then pedestrians south, west, north, and east. Casual observation of the system in operation reveals that pedestrians do not wait for the signals in their favour but cross whenever it is safe to do so. During three hours every day (so-called 'rush hours') there is significant congestion of traffic on both south-north and east-west roads. Impressionistically, we might guess that the inclusion in rotation of authorisation for pedestrians to cross adds 90 seconds to the journey of the average vehicles (and during the rush hours, this might be in excess of five minutes). If so, is this form of traffic regulation justified?

That is a difficult question to answer because it depends on many variables, including the traffic and pedestrian flows and the benefits of accident avoidance which the system is ostensibly designed to achieve. Intuitively, I would expect the costs significantly to outweigh the benefits, and that intuition primarily rests on an assumption that, at a much lower cost, pedestrians could themselves make the decision when it would be safe to cross.[1] And the intuition is strengthened by the fact that so many pedestrians do not wait for the protected period, but cross

* I am grateful for the helpful comments of discussants and fellow participants of the Conference 'Changes of Governance in Europe, Japan, and the US: Corporations, State, Markets, and Intermediaries', Berlin 10 September 2004.

[1] Normally north-south pedestrians would cross when the red light prevented the east-west traffic flow. Of course, some of the north-south traffic will want to turn east or west, and these vehicles must be avoided.

when they think it safe to do so. If I am right, it is difficult to justify the regulatory arrangements in cost-benefit terms. How should we explain their existence? One plausible possibility[2] is a paternalist stance taken by regulatory policymakers. They might wish to deprive pedestrians of the freedom of choice of when to cross the road because there is insufficient confidence that that choice will be exercised wisely.

On the face of it, paternalism would seem to lie behind a large number of regulatory measures. These include not only specific instances such as compulsory social insurance; the compulsory wearing of seatbelts and safety helmets; and 'cooling-off periods' enabling consumers and investors to withdraw from contractual undertakings. They also include, more generally, prohibiting or controlling certain risk-generating products and services (for example, meat which may be contaminated by BSE) as an alternative to providing information on the risk and leaving it to consumers to decide whether they wish to purchase the product or service.[3]

The appropriateness or otherwise of a paternalist intervention would appear to be a particularly important issue for theoretical analysis, not the least because in modern times policymakers appear to be caught on the horns of a dilemma: in a risk-obsessed society there is an ever-increasing expectation that governments will provide citizens with protection, and yet there is also a greater degree of scepticism of the ability of governments to do this successfully.[4] Nevertheless, discussions of paternalism are not easy to find. As regards governmental policy analysis, this is, perhaps, not so surprising since politicians will not want to be heard to say that they (or bureaucrats) know better than ordinary citizens what is good for them. Moreover, much of the traditional literature on regulation and regulatory policy has been derived from neo-classical economic methodology with its basis in individual autonomy and rationality and is therefore antagonistic to paternalist ideas.[5] Within recent years, and drawing on the empirical work of social psychologists, there have been efforts to relax assumptions of the neo-classical approach,[6] but analysis of paternalism as an input in regulatory policy-making is still relatively rare.[7]

[2] Others include a general aim of adding to the delays of urban traffic, thus encouraging greater use of public transport and reduced traffic congestion.

[3] See A Ogus *Regulation: Legal Form and Economic Theory* (Clarendon Press Oxford 1994) 122-123.

[4] C Hood and others *The Government of Risk: Understanding Risk Regulation Regimes* (OUP Oxford 2001).

[5] For example, Stephen Breyer's classic monograph *Regulation and Its Reform* (Harvard University Press Cambridge 1982) has a single paragraph on the general topic (pp 33-34).

[6] See eg CR Sunstein (ed) *Behavioral Law and Economics* (Cambridge University Press Cambridge 2000).

[7] For valuable exceptions, see especially P Burrows 'Analyzing Legal Paternalism' (1995) 15 Intl Rev of L and Economics 542; E Zamir 'The Efficiency of Paternalism' (1998) 84

cont. ...

II. Economic and Paternalist Reasons for Overriding Individual Preferences

Paternalism has been defined as 'the interference with a person's liberty of action justified by reasons referring exclusively to the welfare, good happiness, needs, interests or values of the person being coerced'.[8] Many apparently interventionist measures, overriding individual preferences, can be rationalised economically without reference to paternalist arguments. Most obviously and importantly, some unwise individual decisions generate negative externalities, that is, impose costs on third parties. Regulating the individual's conduct may, then, constrain or internalise those costs. Thus, insistence that a safety helmet or an equivalent protective device be worn by those at risk may reduce the accident rate and thus also the health care costs borne by taxpayers and health insurance contributors. And in relation to measures designed to inhibit personal financial losses – for example, by doorstep selling – the analogous justification is that social security and other welfare provision might come to the rescue of the impoverished individual.

But care must be taken when invoking externality justifications. The mere infliction of third-party costs cannot, of course, by itself justify intervention. In some circumstances, for example, the benefit to third parties from the individual activity may exceed the costs. Paradoxically, this may be the case with cigarette smoking if that activity accelerates death, such that there is a net[9] saving on the medical and other costs which taxpayers bear. Admittedly this calculation does not take account of the cost to the smokers of their lives being shortened. But that cost is not an externality and for the legal intervention to be justified on this basis normally implies a paternalist approach, if the individual's preference, with adequate information on the impact on life expectancy, is to smoke.

More generally, what society gains from reducing negative externalities by a relevant legal instrument has to be compared with the costs of that intervention. That latter figure should include not only the costs of compliance of all those subject to the legal requirement, but also the administrative costs of the legal and other machinery necessary to achieve this end.

Another economic justification for overriding individual preferences may be related to information. Economists do indeed recognise that since many individuals do not have the appropriate information to form preferences, or proceed on the basis of false information, there is no reason to suppose that meeting their expressed preferences will always maximise their welfare. So if, as a cyclist, I do

Virginia L Rev 229; C Camerer and others 'Regulation for Conservatives: Behavioral Economics and the Case for "Asymmetric Paternalism"' (2003) 151 U of Pennsylvania L Rev 1211.

[8] G Dworkin 'Paternalism' in RA Wasserstrom (ed) *Morality and the Law* (Wadsworth Belmont 1971), 108. See also J Kleinig *Paternalism* (Manchester University Press Manchester 1983) ch 1.

[9] Taking account of any increase to health care and analogous costs during the abbreviated lifetime.

not have adequate information on the risk of a serious head injury and on how the wearing of a helmet might reduce that risk, then my decision whether or not to wear a helmet cannot be assumed to be an efficient one. But here again some caution in invoking the justification is necessary: the costs of requiring me to wear the helmet may outweigh the benefits; and even if they do not, a cheaper solution may be to furnish me with the relevant information, leaving the choice to me.

Mainstream economists draw a distinction between inadequate information, the consequences of which they are willing to investigate, and an individual's inability to respond rationally to adequate information. The notion of 'bounded rationality' is recognised[10] but mainly as an indicator of the parameters beyond which traditional analysis cannot go.[11] If remedial interventions are based on some anti-individualist approach to welfare, holding that society – or more particularly, certain 'experts' in society – should make decisions for individuals, that clearly cannot be reconciled with economic reasoning based on individual autonomy. However, as we shall now see, a paternalist policy does not necessarily involve abandoning an individualist approach to welfare.

We may first find acceptable the notion of rational delegation.[12] Individuals can recognise that they will be subject to temptations – for example, drug consumption or a gambling urge – which they will find difficult to resist. To succumb may generate short-term utility gains which will be substantially outweighed by the longer-term costs, of addiction, ill health, or penury. In such circumstances, the utility of individuals is enhanced if they agree ex ante to submit to an external control depriving them of the temptation.[13] It is then possible to extend this reasoning to situations where individuals can recognise ex ante that they may behave irrationally or make errors of judgement. If, in such circumstances, they would hypothetically consent to being deprived of freedom of choice, then a paternalist intervention may be legitimised on individualist grounds.

On the basis of the above arguments, the paternalist goal of increasing social welfare becomes that of meeting what it is assumed would have been the preferences of individuals if they had responded rationally to full information. And particular paternalist measures can then be justified if the benefits of the

[10] For example, in the seminal work of OE Williamson *The Economic Institutions of Capitalism* (Free Press New York 1985).

[11] DM Kreps 'Bounded Rationality' in P Newman (ed) *The New Palgrave Dictionary of Economics and the Law* (MacMillan London 1998) vol 1, 168-173.

[12] Kleinig (n 8) 55-67.

[13] For the economic basis to this reasoning, see G Loomes and R Sugden 'Regret Theory: An Alternative Theory of Rational Choice under Uncertainty' (1982) 92 Economic J 805. The same idea is present in the contention that paternalism may be justified where individuals' second-order preferences conflict with their first-order preferences: C Sunstein 'Legal Interference with Private Preferences' (1986) 53 U of Chicago L Rev 1129.

intervention exceed the costs. However, determining when individuals are likely to act irrationally and when the cost-benefit condition is met is, of course, not easy. I address both of these issues in turn.

III. Individual Decision-making and Irrationality

It is generally assumed, uncontroversially, that regulation should protect children below a certain age and individuals with a certain level of mental incapacity, on the ground that their expressed preferences may not be consistent with their long-term welfare maximisation. Difficulties obviously arise in determining to what extent the assumption of rationality should be relaxed for other individuals. But social psychologists have done much in recent years to enlarge our knowledge concerning the way people make decisions and how the latter diverge from what may be regarded as rational decision-making. From this work, we can highlight certain key phenomena which relate to situations where paternalist regulation is often found.

1. Status Quo Bias

Individuals systematically undervalue the costs, and risks, arising from choices they are accustomed to make, and undervalue the benefits to be derived from different, or new, options.[14] Others things being equal, they will therefore tend to opt for status quo outcomes. Paternalist regulation can help to counteract this bias.

Take, first, behaviour such as smoking or alcohol consumption which individuals have engaged in for a number of years apparently without significant adverse effects. This will typically distort their perception of the risks involved in continuing the activity, notwithstanding the flows of information generated by greater scientific knowledge of the risks. We might be led, in consequence, to question the familiar regulatory strategy, requiring suppliers simply to signal the dangers on the labels or packaging of the products.[15]

Status quo bias is closely related to problems of inertia. Individuals may not be prepared to incur even the trivial costs of exploring beneficial alternatives to customary choices.[16] The phenomenon is familiar to those promoting competition

[14] R Noll and JE Krier 'Some Implications of Cognitive Psychology for Risk Regulation' (1990) 19 J of Legal Studies 747, 765-767.

[15] C Scott and J Black *Cranston's Consumers and the Law* (3rd edn Butterworths London 2000) 344-345.

[16] R Korobkin 'Inertia and Preference in Contract Negotiations: The Psychological Power of Default Rules and Form Terms' (1998) 51 Vanderbilt L Rev 1583.

in hitherto monopolistic markets: a significant proportion of purchasers remain faithful to the dominant supplier, even though the price and quality offered by newcomers apparently better meet their preferences.[17] This in turn leads to a further proposition: other things being equal, individuals will typically prefer doing nothing (omission) to doing something (commission). This has implications for a wide range of paternalistically motivated measures. For example, individuals – if pressed – may recognise the advantages of insuring themselves against future contingencies but might err on the side of doing nothing.

2. Availability Heuristic

The easier a phenomenon is brought to mind, the greater the influence it will have in the formulation of preferences.[18] Advertisers and others seeking to influence purchasing behaviour exploit individuals' vulnerability in this respect by emphasising the advantages of particular products. Again, other things being equal, people will in consequence tend to overestimate the benefits and underestimate the costs of the product.

The availability heuristic applies equally to the risks of detrimental occurrences. If media coverage has given prominence to a given contingency, say an accident, individuals will attribute a greater probability to the contingency recurring than is objectively justified. Now, of course, that is likely to lead individuals to take excessive, rather than insufficient precautions, relative to how they would have behaved if responding rationally to the risk, and – as such – might lead to the exact opposite of what we observed in relation to status quo bias: detrimental action, as opposed to beneficial inaction. That might seem to preclude the possibility of paternalist intervention, but there is no theoretical reason to limit paternalism to precautionary measures, and we might envisage paternalistically forestalling the taking of excessive safety measures.

3. Excessive Discounting

Individuals often discount future costs and benefits to a greater degree than is objectively justified.[19] In other words, the shorter-term consequences of a particular choice unduly influence decision-making relative to the longer-term conse-

[17] A Fishman and R Rob 'Consumer Inertia, Firm Growth and Industry Dynamics' (2003) 109 J of Economic Theory 24.

[18] T Kuran and CR Sunstein 'Availability Cascades and Risk Regulation' (1999) 51 Stanford L Rev 683.

[19] M Eisenberg 'The Limits of Cognition and the Limits of Contract' (1995) 47 Stanford L Rev 211, 222.

quences. Not unexpectedly, individuals with addictions have a very rapid discount rate for benefits which accrue only after some time,[20] but there is evidence of the same – if less drastic – phenomenon applying in a wide range of activities including career and investment choices.[21] Among several policy consequences which may be derived from this phenomenon, mandatory retirement pension programmes constitute an obvious example.[22]

4. Selective Optimism and Control

Individuals are not always good at reasoning on the basis of representative sources of information; rather they tend to generalise from highly selective examples.[23] That can lead them to becoming excessively optimistic regarding the unlikelihood of a risk materialising,[24] The fact that they exert a degree of control over the circumstances may exacerbate the problem.[25] Thus drivers, including those whose judgement is affected by alcohol, tend to underestimate the probabilities of being involved in an accident, compared with those who are driven by others; and one study revealed that 90% of drivers thought that they drove more safely than the average driver![26]

5. Social Pressure

Choices made in purchasing and other activities are often highly imitative of those made by other individuals. This might, of course, be rational if it is reasonably to be assumed that the relevant preferences are shared with those who take the lead in decision-making and that they have better information on which

[20] NM Petry and T Casarella 'Excessive Discounting of Delayed Rewards in Substance Abusers With Gambling Problems' (1999) 56 Drug and Alcohol Dependence 25.

[21] J Myerson and L Green 'Discounting of Delayed Rewards: Models of Individual Choice' (1994) 64 J of Experimental Analysis of Behavior 263.

[22] M Feldstein 'The Optimal Level of Social Security Benefits' (1985) 100 *Q J of Economics* 303.

[23] A Tversky and D Kahneman 'Belief in the Law of Small Numbers' in D Kahneman and others (eds) *Judgement Under Uncertainty: Heuristics and Biases* (Cambridge University Press Cambridge 1982) 23-25.

[24] DM DeJoy 'The Optimisim Bias and Traffic Accident Risk Perception' (1998) 21 Accident Analysis and Prevention 333.

[25] ibid 336.

[26] O Svenson 'Are We All Less Risky and Skilful Than Our Fellow Drivers Are?' (1981) 47 Acta Psychologica 143, 146.

to make choices.[27] But individuals may come under direct or indirect pressure to make purchases which imitate the behaviour of others.[28] Although it may enable them to earn social esteem, and thus increase their welfare in this respect, the behavioural trait often distorts preferences.[29] It may also lure individuals into levels of expenditure which they are unable to sustain and to which otherwise they would not have committed themselves.

IV. The Benefits and Costs of Paternalist Inverventions

Let us assume that, with the aid of the psychological evidence described above, we can identify situations in which many, perhaps most, individual decision-makers select options which would not reflect their preferences if they had been responding rationally to the information available. The benefit of a legal intervention forcing an individual to adopt the rational choice may then be expressed as the difference between the utility she has gained from complying with the legal requirement and the utility she would have gained from her own preferred option. The social benefit of the measure would then be the aggregate of such increases in utility for all those subject to the requirement, though some deduction would have to be made for imperfect enforcement of the law.[30]

Of course, these variables cannot be quantified with any precision, but it is helpful to proceed to examine the broad profile of costs likely to be incurred and speculate on whether they are likely to be disproportionate to the benefits.[31] In doing so, we should distinguish between different forms of paternalist intervention, because some are significantly more costly than others.

We may start with administrative and institutional costs which, in the case of regulatory interventions, are largely borne by public agencies. They include the costs of acquiring relevant information, formulating relevant standards or other controls, monitoring behaviour, and enforcing compliance. Another possibility is to use principles of private law – for example, those giving rise to entitlement to damages or contractual invalidity – although account has to be taken here of the fact that the beneficiary of the entitlement might not have the means to enforce it or be competent to reap the advantages of legal invalidity.

[27] J Bjönerstadt and KH Schlag 'On the Evolution of Imitative Behaviour' (Discussion Paper no B-378 Universität Bonn 1996).

[28] T Tassier 'A Model of Fads, Fashions, and Group Formation' (2004) 9 Complexity 51.

[29] G Duffield and P Grabosky *Psychology of Fraud* (Australian Institute of Criminology 2001).

[30] For a more sophisticated model based on the same idea, see Zamir (n 7).

[31] For another approach to the assessment of the benefits and costs of paternalist intervention, see Camerer and others (n 7).

The costs may be reduced, or avoided, if the paternalist – regulatory or private law – is formulated and/or administered as a default rule, applying only to those who have manifestly not adopted the required, or some analogous but equally effective, course of conduct.[32] The device renders the law more complicated but it helps to reduce the (not trivial) 'frustration' costs of imposing controls on individuals whose behaviour does not justify paternalist intervention.[33]

Paternalist intervention controls sometimes the intended beneficiary – for example, requiring the wearing of safety equipment – but sometimes third parties, such as employers or traders who must do, or abstain from, some act, in order to protect the beneficiary. Clearly the subjects of the control, in whatever category, incur the cost of being informed as to its existence and content. What then of compliance costs? Here we can assume that if the intervention is well-targeted, in the sense of compelling a beneficiary to do what he or she would have done if responding rationally to the information available, then those costs would, in any event, have been incurred, as part of the utility-maximising behaviour. That does not apply to third parties, and their compliance costs may be substantial.

The indirect costs of paternalist intervention – for example, externalities – may also be important. Paternalism may prevent individuals learning from the consequences of their own decisions, pushing them into a vicious circle where they become more and more dependent on governments.[34] Regulation of any kind can also artificially generate demand for particular products – for example, safety equipment conforming to certain specifications which can be of advantage to the suppliers of those products, to the detriment of others supplying equally effective products but not conforming to the specifications. This not only undermines the competitiveness of markets; it also creates perverse incentives for suppliers to spend resources convincing politicians and others of the need to prescribe those particular products – a significant deadweight loss to social welfare.[35]

V. An Analytical Framework for Paternalist Regulation

The discussion above provides us with an analytical framework – albeit one which is far from precise – to explain and evaluate paternalist regulation. In relation to each such case, we need to ask three questions:

32 Cf Camerer and others (n 7) 1224-1230.

33 See Zamir (n 7) 260.

34 BJ Winick 'On Autonomy: Legal and Psychological Perspectives' (1992) 37 Villanova L Rev 1705, 1756 ff.

35 G Tullock 'The Welfare Costs of Tariffs, Monopolies and Theft' (1967) 5 Western Economic J 224.

- Are there plausible traditional justifications (externalities, information failure, inadequate competition) for the measure, operating independently of paternalism?
- If not, and taking account of the insights of social psychology, is the regulated activity one with regard to which a significant proportion of the agents make decisions that are unlikely to reflect their real preferences?
- If so, are the likely costs of the regulatory measure proportionate to the likely benefits and/or could the same outcome be reached at lower cost by an alternative instrument?

It remains to apply this framework impressionistically to some examples of paternalist regulation.

VI. Some Examples of Paternalist Regulation

1. The Pedestrian Crossing Near Manchester University

Take first the situation described in the introduction to this paper. Like any health and safety measure, there are possible externality justifications arising from the fact that some of the damage costs, should the risk materialise, fall on third parties – here the health care costs incurred by taxpayers funding the National Health Service. Nevertheless, as already indicated, we may plausibly assume that paternalist reasoning featured significantly in the policy-making decision.

In relation to the paternalist justification, we should note that children sometimes cross the road at this point; also I have a visually handicapped colleague who might occasionally benefit from the protection (and there may be others in this category). But these cases apart, I would be very surprised if evidence could be produced showing that pedestrians systematically misperceive the risks of crossing the road when 'unprotected' and in consequence fail to take optimal care. Even if I am wrong, the fact that so many of them ignore the protected period and cross when it is not lawful to do so suggests that the arrangements as currently implemented do not generate significant benefits for this group. That might change if the police were to alter their apparent non-enforcement policy; but that would of course massively increase the costs of this regulatory intervention – and not only enforcement costs but also frustration costs, those incurred by individuals who feel perfectly safe in crossing the road without protection.

We may thus rapidly (and to my personal satisfaction!) reach the conclusion that the paternalist justification can be sustained only in relation to children and visually handicapped pedestrians; and, as regards these individuals, there are almost certainly cheaper means of achieving the safety goal, for example, by enabling them to cross with the aid of fully sighted adults.

2. Other Health and Safety Measures

From the vast array of other health and safety measures for which paternalist arguments, as well as externality justifications, can be made out, I select two: seatbelts in cars, and beef possibly affected by BSE.

The wearing of seatbelts in private motor vehicles has been mandatory in many countries for a number of years, and the evidence is overwhelming that this reduces the incidence of serious injuries and fatalities resulting from road accidents.[36] It seems too that, notwithstanding this evidence which has been widely disseminated, there has been a reluctance on the part of some classes of drivers and passengers to use the belts. This may have been particularly marked when seatbelts were novel, thus displaying the status quo bias; and, insofar as it applies to drivers, reflects the selective optimism and control phenomenon. It does not seem unreasonable, therefore, to conclude that the wearing of seatbelts would represent the preferences of the large majority of car travellers, if not constrained by bounded rationality, and that there are very significant welfare gains to accrue from interventionist measures securing this outcome.

There are at least three types of intervention which have been used in this context: the manufacturers of vehicles are obliged to install seatbelts;[37] the failure to wear a seatbelt can reduce the amount of compensation payable to a road accident victim in private law;[38] and criminal sanctions are available to punish such failures even if no accident occurs.[39] The cost of the first two measures may be assumed to be rather small: it is easy to monitor compliance by car manufacturers; and although the second may give rise to additional litigation and other dispute costs, these may not be large. The third does potentially involve significant enforcement costs – behaviour must be sufficiently well monitored for the sanction regime to be an effective deterrent.[40] The measure may also be regarded by some as a non-trivial interference with liberty, and thus give rise to what we have referred to as frustration costs. But the effectiveness of the first two options to secure the desired outcome may be doubted and, impressionistically, it would seem that the costs associated with the third measure are still small, relative to the benefits to be obtained. The conclusion is, then, that this instance of paternalist regulation is justified.

[36] D Dewees D Duff and M Trebilcock *Exploring the Domain of Accident Law* (OUP Oxford 1996) 44-45.

[37] Road Vehicles (Construction and Use) Regulations 1986 SI 1986/1078 reg 47.

[38] *Froom v Butcher* [1976] QB 286.

[39] Motor Vehicles (Wearing of Seat Belts) Regulations 1993 SI 1993/176.

[40] See generally on this A Ogus 'Enforcing Regulation: Do We Need the Criminal Law?' in H Sjögren and G Skögh (eds) *New Perspectives on Economic Crime* (Edward Elgar Cheltenham 2004) 42-56.

The scenario of how BSE ('mad cow disease') was identified in certain cattle herds and was (and still is) thought by some to create the risk of humans contracting Creutzfeld Jacob Disease (CJD) is reasonably well known.[41] A number of regulatory measures were taken in consequence, notably – following a decision of the EU Veterinary Committee – the prohibition of export of British beef within the EU, and it was several years before this ban was lifted.

This measure, along with many others of the same kind, can be considered as a paternalist intervention, in that it deprives individuals of the choice of whether they wish to purchase and consume a product which carries with it an uncertain risk of harm. Now, of course, that very quality of uncertainty renders problematic appraisal of the benefits of intervention, particularly where potential fatalities are involved. Definitive conclusions on whether the measures are justifiable are therefore difficult. However, there are three features of the BSE case which merit our attention because, taken together, they suggest that the case for paternalist intervention was not as strong as it was made to appear.

First, the costs to the agriculture industry, to dependent industries, and to taxpayers as a result of the ban were colossal.[42] Care must be taken in invoking these figures because presumably a significant proportion of the costs would in any event have been incurred if there had been a non-paternalist response: if governments had simply provided information to consumers on the nature and evidence of the risk, we must assume that demand for the product would have fallen substantially. Nevertheless, the difference between the costs that did occur and those which would have occurred in this later contingency must still be very large. Second, there were groups of private interests, notably the suppliers of non-British beef, who benefited from the ban and may well have exerted their influence on the decision-makers.[43] Third, this is a case where the evidence from social psychology undermines, rather than strengthens, the arguments for paternalist intervention. The massive media coverage of the incident would, according to the availability heuristic, have led many individuals to exaggerate the risk.

3. Doorstep and Distance Selling

Doorstep selling and distance selling are two practices which are widely considered to be prejudicial to some consumers, thus justifying regulatory control.[44]

[41] Cf A Dnes 'An Economic Analysis of the BSE Scare' (1996) 43 Scottish J of Political Economy 343.

[42] See the OECD Report *The Incidence and Costs of Foodborne Disease* (OECD 2003) 56-57.

[43] This was certainly the case in France (the agricultural lobby being particularly strong there) where the ban was, in defiance of EU law, extended beyond the period required by the Veterinary Committee *The Guardian* (London UK 2 October 2002).

[44] Scott and Black (n 15) 427-433.

At the heart of this concern is the suspicion that in the given circumstances many consumers will agree to purchases which, because they may later regret them, do not reflect their longer-term preferences, or at least which are not in their long-term interests. With regard to both, there are certainly information problems: consumers will often be unable to draw inferences regarding the reputation and reliability of the trader when the transaction takes place away from business premises; and in the case of distance selling there is the additional problem of inability to inspect products being sold. Paternalist arguments would seem to be particularly plausible in relation to doorstep selling and perhaps to distance selling where this takes place by telephone. This is because of the availability heuristic: traders should have little difficulty in getting customers to focus attention on the advantages, rather than the disadvantages, of a particular transaction.

These phenomena have led to different regulatory responses in different countries. In some jurisdictions, doorstep selling is prohibited unless there is a prior request by a customer; in other jurisdictions it is allowed only with a licence authorising the practice.[45] Application of our analytical framework raises doubts as to whether these measures can be justified. Prohibiting the practice is very costly, insofar as it deprives individuals who are less mobile of the opportunity of purchasing on the doorstep; and a licensing system generates very high administrative costs. Much more cost-effective would seem to be the mandatory imposition of a cooling-off period, as now required by European law:[46] customers may without penalty cancel the agreement within seven days of entering into the transaction. There are here non-trivial costs to be considered, particularly those arising from any exercising of the right to cancel, as well as from the monitoring required to ensure that customers are being adequately notified of the right. But the benefits of the measure are likely to be secured not so much from the exercise of the right as from the chilling effect the existence of the right is likely to have on behaviour – both that of traders in not over-selling the product and that of consumers in getting to think twice about whether they really wish to purchase.[47]

[45] Netherlands is an example of the first; Italy of the second: ibid 428-429.

[46] Council Directive 85/577/EEC, implemented in the UK by the Consumer Protection (Cancellation of Contracts Concluded Away from Business Premises) Regulations 1987 SI 1987/2117. For distance selling, see Council Directive 97/7/EC, implemented in the UK by the Consumer Protection (Distance Selling) Regulations 2000 SI 2000/2334.

[47] Camerer and others (n 7) 1239. 'Those who complain about "cooling-off" provisions are not buyers fearful that their decision will be undermined, but sellers fearful that what has been extracted through virtuosity may be less captivating the following day': Kleinig (n 8) 195-196.

4. Consumer Credit

The supply of consumer credit has been for several years one of the most regulated areas of commerce.[48] Much of this can doubtless be justified on traditional market-failure grounds. Those entering into consumer credit transactions often face major information problems, particularly regarding the rate of interest that will be charged and the consequences of failing to meet their repayment obligations. So also there are assumed to be significant externalities resulting from over-indebtedness, including the costs of administering bankruptcies, welfare payments for impoverished people and, in extreme cases, increased crime and health care costs.[49] Nevertheless, paternalism appears also to have played an important role in motivating the legislation.[50]

There are several features of the circumstances surrounding the obtaining of consumer credit which suggest that the transactions might often fail to match the assumed longer-term preferences of individuals. We may note, in the first place, that consumer credit is particularly associated with socioeconomic groups of lower education attainment,[51] and that these groups may be particularly prone to errors in the discounting of future costs and benefits. So, too, there is evidence that social pressure – the 'keeping-up-with-the-Joneses' phenomenon – lures many people into unwise levels and cycles of indebtedness from which it is difficult to escape,[52] although their selective optimism may suggest otherwise.

Many of the regulatory controls on consumer credit trading are designed to enhance the information available to consumers and, as such, should not be regarded as paternalist measures. Although the licensing of consumer credit suppliers[53] might be considered to be intended primarily to overcome the inability of consumers to judge the reliability of suppliers and therefore an information measure, it is clear that the process is intended also to screen out creditors extending credit unwisely (ie to those already in bad debt) and therefore, presumably, with a paternalist motive.[54] However, the administrative costs of

[48] Scott and Black (n 15) 229-232.

[49] RP Hill 'Stalking the Poverty Consumer: A Retrospective Examination of Modern Ethical Dilemmas' (2002) 37 J of Business Ethics 209.

[50] The word 'paternalist' is, of course, absent from policy statements, but the concept is not far from the surface. See eg the speech of the UK Director General of Fair Trading on 'Credit, Consumers and Codes of Practice' (2001) available at <http://www.oft.gov.uk/nr/rdonlyres/5076b62e-0f1c-4b15-b76b-80232691c4a0/0/spe0301.pdf> (16 June 2005).

[51] I Ramsay *Access to Credit in the Alternative Consumer Credit Market* (Office of Consumer Affairs 2000) 1-3.

[52] UN Development Programme *Human Development Report 1998* ch 3.

[53] Consumer Credit Act 1974 ss 21 and 145.

[54] See the *Report of the (Crowther) Committee on Consumer Credit* (Cmnd 4596, 1971) which instigated the system, especially at 150.

operating such a system are very large and are likely to be disproportionate to any paternalist benefits,[55] given, in particular, the difficulty of identifying suppliers who exploit debtors in this way.

Among the other instruments which can be characterised as paternalist, we can highlight the imposition of cooling-off periods[56] and the control of other contractual terms. There is little to add to what was said about the former in relation to doorstep selling: the arguments for the cost-effectiveness of the measure would seem to be equally applicable here. As regards controls on other terms, some jurisdictions[57] have rendered unenforceable rates of interest exceeding the current rate by more than a certain percentage, and Canada has used the criminal law to prohibit such practice.[58] Legislative provisions of this kind might constrain the supply of credit to higher-risk borrowers, and therefore paternalistically protect some of the more vulnerable consumers, because lenders will not be able to charge rates of interest sufficient to meet the greater risk of default; and these measures are not particularly costly to administer. On the other hand, if it achieves this objective, it imposes frustration costs on those who wish to engage in higher-risk transactions and who do not need protection. It may also force some of the more vulnerable consumers to obtain loans in the black market, with even greater potential losses. The paternalist justification for such controls is, therefore, more contentious.

5. Listing of Securities

My final example is drawn from corporate law and securities regulation; it concerns controls exerted over the listing of securities on the stock exchange. Traditionally such controls have focused on disclosure requirements, ensuring thereby that potential investors have the appropriate level of information on which to make decisions. However, in some jurisdictions, there is what is sometimes called 'merit regulation', the authorities having power to exclude from the market firms which, in their view, constitute a risk of such dimensions that

[55] Cf A Ogus and CK Rowley 'The Costs and Benefits of Part III of the Fair Trading Act 1973 and Licensing under the Consumer Credit Act 1974' (unpublished study commissioned by the Office of Fair Trading 1981).

[56] Consumer Credit Act 1974 s 67: the period is 12 days, compared to the seven imposed for non-credit doorstep and distance transactions: n 46.

[57] Eg France and Germany: G Howells 'Controlling Unjust Credit Transactions' in G Howells I Crow and M Moroney (eds) *Aspects of Credit and Debt* (Sweet & Maxwell London 1993) 92-108. The British legislation enables a court to review the terms of a contract if the payment terms are 'grossly extortionate': Consumer Credit Act 1974 ss 137-140, but is apparently little used: Scott and Black (n 15) 256.

[58] Criminal Code s 347. See Ramsay (n 51) 31-33.

individuals should not be allowed to invest in them.[59] In the UK, for example, the listing authority can reject an application on the ground that 'it considers that the applicant's situation is such that admission of the securities would be detrimental to the interests of investors'.[60]

In this area, it not always easy to differentiate between disclosure regulation, responding to information asymmetry, and merit regulation involving paternalist intervention: an adverse decision on the latter basis may in fact result from insufficient information and be remedied by more information.[61] Nevertheless, some 'merit' scrutiny clearly involves substantive evaluation of risk by reference to what the regulatory agency considers to be tolerable risk. Although the agency's function in this respect can be analogised to that of a (private) financial adviser, the fact that the investor is not allowed to ignore the advice, because the investment may, following an adverse review, be withdrawn from the market, means that there is a strong paternalist content to the arrangement.

That some individual investors are unsophisticated and will make poor evaluations of risk even when they have full information is, of course, clear.[62] Nor is it difficult to relate such behaviour to the social psychological phenomena of excessive discounting and selective optimism. The availability heuristic, too, may be relevant insofar as the information supplied with public offers typically highlights positive, rather than negative, characteristics of the firm. It is also the case that many unwise investments involve sums of money which are large, relative to the individual's wealth. There are, therefore, potentially substantial benefits to be gained from interventions where investments do not conform to the preferences which individuals would have had if responding rationally to the information provided.

However, the situation is very different from the doorstep selling problem. In the first place, the proportion of the total population of investors for whom paternalist protection might be justified is much smaller. Institutional investors and experienced brokers now play such a major role in relation to the floating of the securities that to deprive them of the choice of purchasing when typically they have much greater knowledge and expertise than the regulators approaches the

[59] D Vagts 'Securities Regulation' in K Zweigert and U Drobnig (eds) *International Encyclopedia of Comparative Law* (Nijhoff Lancaster 2000) vol XIII 10-16. For an excellent, if dated, description of systems in US state, not federal, law, see ABA Subcommittee Report on State Merit Regulation of Securities Offerings, reprinted in (1986) 41 Business Lawyer 85. For Japanese law, see A Beller T Terai and RM Levine 'Looks Can be Deceiving – A Comparison of Initial Public Offering Procedures under Japanese and US Securities Law' (1992) 55 L and Contemporary Problems 77.

[60] Financial Services and Markets Act 2000 s 75(5). For further details, see Listing Rules (Financial Services and Markets Act 2000 Amendment) Instrument 2001.

[61] ABA Subcommittee Report (n 59) 823.

[62] BR Cheffins *Company Law: Theory, Structure and Operation* (OUP Oxford 1997) 134-138.

absurd, and gives rise to substantial frustration costs.[63] Indeed, the regulatory strategy may also be criticised for inhibiting one of the basic functions of public trading in shares, that of investors diversifying risk in their portfolios and thereby enabling riskier ventures to make their contribution to the productive economy.[64]

As a regulatory instrument, the ex ante imposition of minimum standards of investment risk by the agency can be classified as a form of licensing and, as such, involves very large administrative costs. In the present context, if the aims of the system are to be adequately met, those costs may be particularly high because of the complexity of the decisions that have to be made.[65] And the uncertainty, and possible inconsistency, to which such complexity gives rise, imposes costs on firms seeking to list their securities, adding to the, in any event, serious costs arising from the delay in listing. In short, in the light of very large costs and questionable benefits, it is very difficult to justify this form of paternalist regulation.

VII. Conclusions

In this paper, I have argued that paternalism is, in appropriate circumstances, a legitimate and important reason for interventionist measures and, as such, should be taken seriously by regulatory scholars and policymakers. Of course, there are risks that governments, while not admitting to adopting this stance because it is not politically correct language, will arrogate to themselves extensive powers to override individual choice, to the benefit neither of those individuals nor of society at large.

A more careful, reflective approach to paternalism requires an analytical framework based on what social psychologists have been able to tell us about commonly occurring flaws in reasoning about preferences and choices. That can help us to identify circumstances in which meeting expressed preferences may generate significant welfare losses. It does not, of course, follow that systematically replacing those preferences with others determined by third parties will alleviate those losses. We need to explore carefully the costs involved in regulating paternalistically, particularly where such intervention frustrates those who do not need the protection.

The analytical framework which I have used in this paper is by no means robust and, at best, can establish an impressionistic profile for a given paternalist-

[63] R Romano 'Empowering Investors: A Market Approach to Securities Regulation' in KJ Hopt and others (eds) *Comparative Corporate Governance: The State of the Art and Emerging Research* (OUP Oxford 1998) 163.

[64] EW Kitch 'Regulation of the Securities Market' in B Bouckaert and G de Geest (eds) *Encyclopedia of Law and Economics* (Edward Elgar Cheltenham 2000) vol III 821-822.

[65] ABA Subcommittee Report (n 59) 832-833.

ically justified measure, thereby giving some indication of whether the costs involved are likely to be disproportionate to the prospective benefits. To illustrate the approach, I have applied the framework to some familiar areas of paternalist regulation, reaching the hesitant conclusion that some (for example, cooling-off periods for doorstep trading and consumer credit transactions) are justified, while others (for example, the prohibition of sales of foodstuffs subject to uncertain and remote risks and the ex ante scrutiny for public offers listings) are probably not.

The Regulation of Regulation: Judicialization, Convergence, and Divergence in Administrative Law

THOMAS B. GINSBURG*

I. Introduction

Surveying recent developments involving regulation in advanced industrial societies, one notices two broad characteristics. First is the 'globalization' of business regulation, leading broadly speaking toward convergent ratcheting up of standards in environmental and safety regulation on the one hand, and substantial liberalization in economic regulation on the other.[1] The second feature is the apparent continuing divergence in systems of *regulating* regulation, that is, controlling the administrators and bureaucrats who often make the rules. That is, despite convergence in substantive standards (either ratcheting up or ratcheting down), there is little convergence in the *way* that regulation is made, implemented, and enforced. While corporatist democracies retain a consensual approach to regulation, American regulation remains primarily adversarial in character.[2] EU institutions have their own, increasingly important, distinct modalities of regulation. In Vogel's[3] term, there remain substantially different *styles* of

* Many thanks to Lee Fennell, Luke Nottage, Yoav Dotan and participants at the Berlin meeting for helpful comments.

[1] J Braithwaite and P Drahos *Global Business Regulation* (Cambridge University Press Cambridge 2000). The authors note that intellectual property is the one exception to the latter statement, where regulation has increased rather than decreased.

[2] R Kagan 'Introduction: Comparing National Styles of Regulation in Japan and the United States' (2000) 22 Law and Policy 225; R Kagan *Adversarial Legalism: The American Way of Law* (Harvard University Press Cambridge 2002).

[3] D Vogel *National Styles of Regulation: Environmental Policy in Great Britain and the United States* (Cornell University Press Ithaca 1986).

regulation. This is closely related to the fact that there also remain substantial differences in institutional mechanisms of controlling the modern state and its core functions of making, applying, and enforcing law.

This paper focuses on administrative law systems as sites of and barriers to convergence. It outlines the sources of convergence and divergence, and argues that, despite substantial institutional differences, there is some movement toward convergence in administrative procedure from a broad perspective. First, there is a shift toward judges as monitors of the administration in most industrial democracies and within the EU. Second, a core set of principles of administrative procedure are emerging, developed in large part by these judges. In terms of Professor Ogus' paper in this volume,[4] this means that judges are increasingly the actors who are called on to evaluate when and how paternalistic regulation is appropriate.

At the outset, it must be stated that the body of literature on comparative administrative law is small and mainly descriptive in character. There has been no general attempt to my knowledge to actually examine the extent to which systems have converged or diverged. In order to conduct this inquiry, we must start with some general appreciation of the scope of administrative law, which of necessity must proceed at a broad and abstract level. That is, rather than examine the regulation of mad-cow disease,[5] genetically modified organisms,[6] corporate law,[7] or funeral parlors,[8] to name but a few of the specific fields of regulation which have been substantially affected by global developments, this paper tries to draw some broader conclusions about systems of regulating regulation, and to provide a preliminary framework to understand dynamics of convergence and divergence. It seeks to call attention to administrative law, and administrative procedure in particular, as an important point of inquiry for understanding contemporary regulation.

II. Precis: Dynamics of Convergence and Divergence

The dynamics of convergence and divergence should be familiar to most readers, since they have constituted perhaps the central issue in comparative corporate law

[4] Cf the contribution of AI Ogus in this volume.

[5] L Nottage *Product Safety and Liability Law in Japan: From Minamata to Mad Cows* (RoutledgeCurzon London New York 2002).

[6] *Metalclad Corp v United Mexican States* Case No ARB(AF)/97/1 (30 August 2000). See generally CC Pearce and J Coe Jr 'Arbitration Under NAFTA Chapter Eleven: Some Pragmatic Reflections upon the First Case Filed Against Mexico' (2000) 23 Hastings Intl & Comparative L Rev 311.

[7] C Milhaupt (ed) *Global Markets, Domestic Institutions: Corporate Law and Governance in a New Era of Cross-Border Deals* (Columbia University Press New York 2003).

[8] *Loewen Group Inc v United States* NAFTA arbitration ICSID Case No ARB (AF)/98/3.

scholarship in recent years. Broadly speaking, there are three major forces driving systems of law to converge: mobility, ideas, and power. We take each in turn.

Mobility is the primary driving force discussed in the corporate law area. Competition for capital under conditions of mobility, it is argued, will drive jurisdictions to adopt similar, efficient rules, at least to the extent that rules affect economic performance. Each jurisdiction will seek to capture the benefits of capital by adopting rules that attract it. Liberalization will therefore push legal and regulatory change, and in particular will push things in efficient directions. The extent to which this has occurred is the subject of empirical debate.

A second source of convergence is ideas. When confronted with similar problems, different jurisdictions can converge around particular solutions because of the prestige and power of ideas. Ideational convergence may be accelerated because of common demands driven by similarities in lifestyle associated with post-industrial society. As societies are confronted with many of the same problems generated by economic change, solutions may tend to converge. While there are counterarguments, discussed below, emphasizing how ideas can be sources of resistance to convergence, it is at least plausible that mobility of capital is accompanied by a mobility in ideas that will tend to push law closer.

A third source of convergence is power. Many scholars emphasize the coercive quality of regulatory changes under the influence of international institutions and transnational capital.[9] The increasing scrutiny of regulations as barriers to trade and investment, and the development of institutions to examine them, are oft-cited evidence.[10]

Against these pressures for convergence lies a formidable set of forces. These include institutional inertia, entrenched political interests, path dependencies, and cultural preferences that render particular solutions unattractive in particular polities. Administrative law is full of these types of barriers to convergence. Many argue that public law should see less convergence than corporate or private law because it reflects values rather than interests, and hence is less likely to be shaped by short-term economic factors. Schwarze[11] catalogues the traditional arguments that administrative law expresses 'national particularities' and is therefore relatively impermeable to change.

To these value-oriented reasons for continued divergence, one can add institutional factors. Administrative law concerns the control of regulatory institu-

[9] M Hardt and A Negri *Empire* (Harvard University Press Cambridge 2000).

[10] V Been and J Beauvais 'The Global Fifth Amendment' (2003) 78 New York U L Rev 30.

[11] J Schwarze 'Enlargement, The European Constitution, and Administrative Law' (2004) 53 ICLQ 969, 971-2; see also P Lindseth '"Always Embedded" Administration: The Historical Evolution of Administrative Justice as an Aspect of Modern Governance' in C Joerges B Strath and P Wagner (eds) *The Political Construction of Modern Capitalism* (GlassHouse Press London forthcoming 2005).

tions, and regulatory institutions are difficult to establish. Once they are established, they are even harder to get rid of. In the United States, one of the very few federal regulatory agencies to be dismantled is the Interstate Commerce Commission, disbanded in 1996 under President Clinton's 'reinventing government' plan. This independent regulatory commission had been established in 1887 as the very first element of the modern administrative state. This commission had the mandate of setting railroad transportation rates to prevent the railroads from gouging customers, but over time became a paradigm case of regulatory 'capture', with the regulated entities becoming the loudest voices for regulation. Rather than serving to protect the public and consumers, the purpose of ICC regulation increasingly looked like the maintenance of barriers to entry on behalf of producers. With business dependent on regulation for rents, getting rid of an agency is a formidable feat. 'Capture', as the phenomenon is known in the American literature, is a potential cost of regulation that is not addressed in Professor Ogus' contribution to this volume, but a significant barrier to convergence in regulatory institutions.

If one cannot get rid of agencies, one might seek to control them, and administrative law becomes a natural solution. It is perhaps no surprise that all industrialized countries have developed extensive bodies of administrative law in the past century. But administrative procedures, like primary regulatory rules, also have the quality of establishing their own communities around them. The much-criticized Administrative Procedures Act in the United States has never been changed despite numerous proposals to that effect. Nor is it likely that specialized administrative courts can be disbanded without a major constitutional revolution. While we have seen the establishment of *new* administrative courts and specialized benches (ie in Korea, with similar proposals circulating in Japan), it is rare to see an administrative court merged into the ordinary court system. In short, then, inertia can make switching costs of change prohibitive and the disbanding of institutions difficult.[12] While judicial control becomes a solution to the problem of regulatory power, it itself is resistant to easy change. We should thus expect some resistance to forces for convergence within both regulation and administrative law.

III. The Scope of Administrative Law

One bit of evidence that administrative systems, no less than corporate governance systems, are subject to what might be called convergence-inhibiting path dependencies is the wide definitional variety in what is considered within the domain of administrative law in different countries. Logically, one might think

[12] M Roe *Strong Managers, Weak Owners: The Political Roots of American Corporate Finance* (Princeton University Press Princeton 1994).

that 'administrative law' would encompass all the law made by administrative agencies, including sub-legislation, regulations, decrees, and other laws made by government actors who are not directly politically accountable. This definition, however, has not been adopted in most administrative law systems in the Western tradition. Instead, the substantive rules made by bureaucrats are considered to be specialized domains subject to their own expertise, such as environmental law, labor law, and agricultural law; administrative law becomes only the procedural law regulating these areas.

One might also think of administrative law as encompassing the organization of government, that is, the organic acts establishing and empowering government agencies. Something very close to this definition constituted the entire corpus of administrative law in the Soviet Union, for example. Administrative law in this conception is not at all about constraint of government but about empowerment of government within a framework of legality. The orientation here is not about protecting citizens from the mighty power of the state, but about accountability of the state to its political masters. The emphasis is on what administrative lawyers in the common law tradition would call issues of delegation, namely ensuring that the agency has been properly granted powers from the law maker.

Another feature of socialist administrative law, quite intact in China today, concerns law enforced by administrative authorities rather than judicial authorities. There are a wide range of violations for which one is subject to administrative punishments from police or executive authorities without judicial supervision.[13] Administrative law contains the substantive rules as well as the procedures for punishment, which can include significant periods of detention of the type normally considered criminal in Western conceptual architecture. Nevertheless, if one were to adopt a definition of administrative law as all law implemented by agencies, socialist quasi-criminal law ought to come within its scope.

Setting aside these outliers, administrative law in the Western legal tradition has traditionally been seen as encompassing the internal organization of the state and the mechanisms of appeal and control to protect citizens from arbitrary state action. The latter reflects an ideology of rights. An initial concern for property rights, which after all are the rights most threatened by regulation, expanded in Europe to accommodate the postwar framework of positive rights to education, health, and welfare.[14] As the scope of the state expanded both to address social and economic rights and to regulate business, it became necessary to act through the creation of general rules. Administrative law systems have adjusted to ensure

[13] R Peerenboom 'Out of the Pan and Into the Fire: Well-Intentioned but Misguided Recommendations to Eliminate All Forms of Administrative Detention in China' (2004) 98 Northwestern U L Rev 991.

[14] Such positive rights are minimal at the American federal level. *Deshaney v Winnebago County Department of Social Services* 489 US 189 (1989). They do, however, exist at the state level in the United States.

participation in policy-making as the scope of *explicit* bureaucratic lawmaking has increased, in the form of subordinate legislation by the administration.

Administrative law affects regulatory lawmaking in two ways that can be characterized as wholesale and retail regulation of regulation (or meta-regulation). Wholesale meta-regulation employs *ex ante* controls on rule-formation, typically through requirements of public participation, notice and comment, and agency responsiveness to public input; retail meta-regulation concerns *ex post* examination of rule implementation at the level of individual cases, through rules designed to protect citizens' interests from arbitrary or abusive administrative action. The distinction between the two is not as rigid as it may seem. Even courts that only have the power to examine the application of rules, rather than the formation of rules, can have a significant impact on rule formation. After all, an agency that wishes to adopt a general course of action may be forced to modify it if the courts regularly strike applications of the policy to individuals. The difference really concerns the timing of regulating regulation rather than the fact of regulating regulation. Must meta-regulation wait until a particular party is aggrieved by a regulation or not? Or may the court (and by extension private litigants) shape the general policy at the wholesale level? If the court is restricted to retail-level review of policies, may the courts strike the regulation as a whole or only its particular application? These issues may have a great deal of impact on the relative balance of power between courts and agencies, but they are differences in degree rather than kind. They constitute an important dimension along which administrative law systems differ a good deal.

IV. Divergent Systems of Administrative Law

This section contains thumbnail descriptions of leading national administrative law systems to illustrate institutional stickiness. Readers are asked to forgive the brevity of the accounts; the intention is not to provide a comprehensive overview of the world's administrative law systems but a simple description of who carries out review and whether review is wholesale or retail.

The French tradition of administrative law, so essential as a foil to Dicey's conception of the rule of law, essentially derives from a tradition of statism and a fear of judges. It recognized early on that 'to judge the administration is still to administer',[15] but resisted the notion that judges ought to be involved. The notion of *séparation des pouvoirs* contrasted with its common law counterpart in that it saw judges as the *most* dangerous branch,[16] and hence cabined them to their own zone. Once this choice was made early, public law doctrine grew up around the conceptual framework and was unsusceptible to easy change.

[15] Lindseth (n 11) at 2.

[16] *Contra* AM Bickel *The Least Dangerous Branch: The Supreme Court at the Bar of Politics* (Harvard University Press Cambridge 1962).

French tradition has focused on a distinctive set of administrative courts, governed by distinctive procedures, and headed by the *Conseil d'Etat*. The *Conseil* consists of senior administrators and young star graduates from the *Ecole Nationale d'Administration*. It is thus composed of the elites among the elites in the statist tradition. The *Conseil* has a policy-making component, comments on legislation, and also has an administrative law section that hears appeals from administrative courts. Since France lacks a domestic constitutional court capable of supervising legislation after promulgation, the *Conseil* is the ultimate national body deciding on administrative law questions. *Conseil* rules are essentially judge-made law, developed in a case-by-case process, that nevertheless provides a clear set of general rules that constrain the administration in independent ways.[17] The *Conseil* regulates regulation at both wholesale and retail levels, without a conceptual distinction between general rules and specific applications. It has been described as the most powerful administrative court in the world.

To American eyes at least, French administrative procedure seems to share characteristics of the continental legal systems generally. The process and style is inquisitorial. Parties communicate through the judge, and the judge conducts the pre-trial investigation. Writing dominates, and lawyers are absolutely essential in administrative adjudication, indeed required before the *Conseil d'Etat*. The citizen thus must translate his or her claim into the language of the state.

The German administrative law tradition shares with the French a generalized concept of the state as a distinct actor, but emphasizes judicial control of the state to a greater extent. It has long featured a separate system of administrative courts at *Länder* and appellate levels, headed by the Supreme Administrative Court (*Bundesverwaltungsgericht*) in Leipzig. The appellate courts can examine and quash legal norms below the level of a state statute. In addition to a distinctive institutional environment, German administrative law differs dramatically from the French in the presence of a detailed administrative code. Tort liability and government contract law, however, are seen to be outside the realm of administrative law.[18] The scope of administrative law is narrower, but perhaps more precisely articulated.

In the German tradition, the central concept is that of an administrative act, a retail-level concept. An administrative act is defined broadly as every direction, decision, or measure by an authority to regulate an individual case with direct external legal effect. While it can also include general policy directions, German administrative law focuses more on individual rights-type issues than on public participation in rule-making. This is reinforced by the fact that German adminis-

[17] LN Brown and JS Bell *French Administrative Law* (5th edn Oxford University Press Oxford 1998).

[18] The scope of government liability is in fact less extensive in Germany than in France. In Germany it is covered by principles of negligence, whereas in France no-fault liability for regulations is allowed.

trative law in the postwar period has been heavily influenced by constitutional considerations. The German constitution was quite focused on limiting state power, and contains a number of provisions limiting the administration. With a distinctively powerful constitutional court as the supervisor of constitutionality, the administrative courts have an ally as well as an effective supervisor over their jurisdiction and decisions.

In the United States and the United Kingdom, for a variety of reasons, administrative law came to focus on procedural law rather than substantive law-creating agencies or the laws that they actually made. The reasons have to do with history. Strong common law courts existed in both countries prior to the development of the modern administrative state. The state itself was assumed to be subject to constraints provided by the courts as general guardians of legality, and there was no real separate concept of administrative law requiring specialized adjudication. All state action was subject to judicial control under the same principles as private action; all law was either made by judges or legislators. Bureaucracies making law and adjudicating individual claims were interfering with the prerogatives of courts. Furthermore, individual rights were threatened by the expansion of the state. The courts were thus part of the anti-regulatory forces in the United States and the United Kingdom.

Despite the eventual acquiescence of the US courts to the regulatory state under the threat of Roosevelt's court-packing plan, reliance on judicial control has remained essential to the American notion of administrative law. Initially the constitutional notion of due process was a primary vehicle. Judicial control was cemented by the adoption of the Administrative Procedures Act (APA) in 1946. The APA featured strong judicial review of agency actions at the retail level, with a more deferential standard for wholesale regulation, which was only to be overturned if it was 'arbitrary and capricious'. The initial deference with regard to rule-making was in keeping with New Deal ideology. Over time, however, courts became more active in scrutinizing rules, and essentially imported lower standards of review into the APA's 'arbitrary and capricious' standard. Judges adjusted their standards of review, sometimes requiring agencies to take a 'hard look' at inputs provided through public participation, and other times requiring deference to expert decisions in agencies. The various modulations of greater and lesser judicial review have occupied American scholars, but the overall effect has been fairly intense judicial scrutiny of rule-making, and the creation of judge-made doctrines to ensure public participation in policy-making. US administrative law today decidedly covers both wholesale and retail regulation.

English administrative law labored under Dicey's suspicion of the very concept.[19] Dicey saw virtue in control by the common law courts rather than a distinctive set of institutions, but as the modern state expanded, it became clear

[19] D Williams 'Law and Administrative Discretion' (1994) 2 Indiana J of Global Legal Studies 191; Lindseth (n 11).

that the sheer volume of appeals would overwhelm the traditionally small English judiciary. The result was the creation of independent 'tribunals', distinct from the common law courts, to hear appeals from initial decisions by administrators. These are specific and specialized, tied to individual bureaucracies such as the Health Service, Immigration, and Social Welfare bureaucracies. As regularized in the Tribunals and Inquiries Act of 1958, tribunals had an obligation to deliver independent justice, and they came to rely on notions of 'natural justice' in developing constraints on administrative discretion and procedure. British administrative law is designed to be case-level retail review and *not* wholesale policy-making. It shares with the other systems a strong reliance on quasi-judicial control.

The countries of Northeast Asia were heavily influenced by the Prussian notion of the state. Pre-war Japanese administrative law was based on a distinctive administrative court and the notion of strict reviewability of formal administrative acts. With postwar reforms under the American occupation, the administrative courts were disbanded and ordinary courts took over review. Many observers argue that Japanese courts have been deferential to the administration, but it is clear that there is some review of retail-level administrative actions that affect individual property rights.

In terms of administrative policy-making, Japan historically relied on an informal, flexible style of regulation based on broadly worded statutes. While a large amount of administrative policy-making is inevitable in any modern state since bureaucrats fill in the details of statutes, it has been especially apparent in Japan because of broad delegation to ministries. Less precise legislation requires more making of new rules by ministries. In Japan, this involved a consensual policy-making process governed by *shingikai*, deliberative councils involving the concerned parties as determined by the relevant ministry. The emphasis was on *ex ante* private participation in policy-making arenas that were structured by ministries, rather than *ex post* monitoring of application of policy, which was left to administrative law. This system provided transparency for the most interested players, and high levels of compliance once policy was adopted.[20] Thus Japanese administrative law provided some review of retail-level regulation as applied to individual cases, but virtually no challenge to wholesale level rule-making.

The 1990s will likely be seen as a major turning point in Japanese administrative law. During that decade, Japan adopted three major legal reforms that substantially impacted the Japanese administrative system: the Administrative Procedures Law (APL), the Information Disclosure Law (IDL), and a Cabinet resolution requiring public notice of administrative rule-making.[21] The first two

[20] H Kanda 'Financial Bureaucracy and the Regulation of Financial Markets. Japan: Economic Success and Legal System' in H Baum (ed) *Japan: Economic Success and Legal System* (Walter de Gruyter New York 1997) 315.

[21] Issued 23 March 1999, effective on 1 April 1999.

of these reforms are statutory in character and have received some attention abroad. The Cabinet resolution has received less attention but may prove to be equally significant, especially if it is expanded and strengthened to include provision for judicial review. (As of yet agency actions under it are not subject to judicial review, but the scope is quite broad.)

This thumbnail survey allows us to deduce certain divergences in national administrative law systems.

Obviously the conceptual architecture of administrative law varies. The boundaries of administrative law differ (where government contracts fall, for example), as does the precise mix of tort liability, judicial remedies, and other mechanisms of control. Administrative procedure calibrates the rigidity of the boundary between state and society, and reflects different conceptions of public and private. For example, continental and Japanese systems draw on a strong conceptual distinction between public and private law. In the United States the public-private distinction is less rigid, with private law regularly utilized to accomplish regulatory ends.[22] The relative mix of natural law principles and positivistic focus on proper delegations also varies across systems.

More to the point of the present chapter, systems differ dramatically in their mix of wholesale and retail regulation of regulation. In the United States and France, administrative law includes in its ambit the external control of both individual level decisions and rules of general application. In Germany and Japan, it focuses on the retail, rights-oriented element.

Institutional structures differ, too, with distinctive administrative courts in France and Germany, while the Anglo-American systems rely on the generalized notion of the rule of law to subject the state to ordinary courts, just as citizens. Japan has vacillated between these institutional models, with some now proposing a return to the distinctive specialized fora.

The systems exhibit similar divergence on the extent to which administrative law has been developed primarily through case-by-case judicial decision-making or through legislative exercises in codification; though it must be said that judicial development has played a prominent role nearly everywhere. Germany provides the paradigm example of an extensive procedural code passed by the legislature, but in response to judicially developed principles. The United States' APA is a code written in broad terms, with language sufficiently flexible to allow fairly significant shifts in the scope of judicial review; yet the United States may rank second among the countries surveyed in terms of its administrative codification. Japan's Administrative Procedures Law is written in quite general terms, and codification is very limited in France and the United Kingdom.[23] The table

[22] J Freeman 'The Private Role in Public Governance' (2000) 75 New York U L Rev 543; J Freeman 'Extending Public Law Norms Through Privatization' (2003) 116 Harvard L Rev 1285-1352.

[23] C Harlow 'Codification of EC Administrative Procedures' (1996) 2 Eur L J 3, 3-6.

below describes these general features, along with a column describing the extent of constitutionalization of administrative law.

Table 1: Features of Administrative Law Systems

	Main Form of Meta-Regulation	Level of Codification	Level of Constitutionalization
Germany	Retail	High	High
US	Retail and Wholesale	Medium	Medium
Japan	Retail	Low	Low
France	Retail and Wholesale	Low	Low
UK	Retail	Low	Low but increasing under Human Rights Act

V. Trends: Judicialization and the Search for Neutral Third Parties

Despite this wide variety of scope of administrative law systems, there are certain trends that can be discerned. I do not go so far as to assert that there is a global convergence by any means. As mentioned above, there are reasons to believe that the institutional structures of national administrative law systems are peculiarly resistant to change. Nevertheless, there are some trends that can be identified.

Lawyers and political scientists have identified the central problem of modern government as one of principal and agent. Modern government involves complexity and requires adjustment to changing conditions. We are accustomed to thinking of democratically accountable politician-lawmakers as setting the broad goals of policy, and unelected expert bureaucrats as implementing it. The problem is that implementation of generally applicable rules involves an inherent degree of making policy. Politicians may know what they wish to do, but in the scope of making generally applicable rules must leave some room for flexibility and adjustment. Therefore they delegate decision-making authority to unelected bureaucrats who have the necessary expertise to make these decisions on the basis of constantly changing conditions. But how can one be sure that the agents will follow the instructions of the principals?

In earlier work, I defined three different mechanisms for dealing with the agency problem of modern government, which I call ideology, hierarchy, and administrative law.[24] First, the principal can utilize ideology, that is, getting the

[24] T Ginsburg 'Comparative Administrative Procedure: Evidence from Northeast Asia' (2002) 13 Constitutional Political Economy 247.

agent to internalize her instructions. Second, the principal can utilize hierarchy, that is, utilizing superior levels of the bureaucracy to control inferior levels. Third, the principal can hire another agent, typically a judge, to monitor the agent and punish him for failing to obey instructions.

For a variety of reasons, the third-party, judicial solution is increasing around the globe. If one characterizes the *Conseil d'Etat* as an administrative court run by experts in the science of administration rather than as a superior administrative agency (and it seems fair to do so given its rule as locus of appeals from lower administrative courts), all major industrialized countries have some scope for judicial review of particular agency actions affecting individuals. Even within these systems, the scope of judicial supervision seems to be increasing, as Japan edges toward wholesale-level review.

We can speculate on a number of causes of this judicialization. The decline of socialist ideology, and of political parties generally,[25] means that the 'first-party' solution of internalization is no longer as easily available. While a nationalist ethos may have provided enough motivation to keep bureaucrats loyal for many decades, it is arguably declining in effectiveness as a pure substitute for external controls. The result is a turn toward third parties and police bureaucrats.

A second cause may be increasing rights ideology. Although regulation interferes with property rights, a classical 'negative liberty' of 18th-century liberalism, the state also has expanded to providing positive benefits to citizens in accordance with 'second-generation' welfare state rights. As the state expands its direct provision of services – health, education, and housing – the denial of these benefits comes under the framework of administrative law. Whether such an ideology exists is largely a matter of speculation, but it is an oft-asserted cause of judicialization.

The human rights regime has emerged as an important source of procedural convergence. In particular, the European Convention of Human Rights and its requirements in Article 6(1) of a fair and public trial[26] have led to extra-national supervision. This has also been used to expand judicial supervision over administrative action, from everything from drunk driving license revocations in Norway[27] to health regulations in France. The categorization of a particular regime as criminal or administrative does not depend on the country's nominal

[25] A process labeled 'dealignment' by political scientists. See H Wilensky *Industrial Democracies* (2002) 398-429.

[26] European Convention on Human Rights and Fundamental Freedoms, 4 November 1950, art 6(1), 213 UNTS 221 ('In the determination of his civil rights and obligations or of any criminal charge against him, everyone is entitled to a fair and public hearing within a reasonable time by an independent and impartial tribunal established by law.').

[27] TN Lockney 'A Comparison of Drinking and Driving Law in Norway and North Dakota' (2000) 76 North Dakota L Rev 33, 64; see generally A Boyle 'Administrative Justice, Judicial Review and the Right to a Fair Hearing Under the European Convention on Human Rights' [1984] PL 89.

categorization but on an independent assessment by the judicial enforcers of the Convention regime, at the national level and ultimately at the European Court of Human Rights.[28] ECHR scrutiny has entailed changes in *Conseil d'Etat* procedure[29] and a restructuring of the United Kingdom's entire court system, through the restructuring of the powers of the Lord Chancellor. The general shift toward judicial review contemplated by the adoption of the Human Rights Act was of course foreshadowed by judicial supervision of administrative action under the same principle.[30] Thus one sees some institutional convergence in Europe, and some shift toward generalist third-party monitoring as a result.

But why should *courts* emerge as the third-party monitor of choice? One can imagine a wide array of possible solutions to the monitoring problem. Yet there are reasons courts have proven attractive. First of all, since World War II, industrialized democracies have been increasingly willing to allow courts to evaluate legislation for conformity with the written constitution.[31] If a court can set aside legislation passed by a democratically elected parliament because of its nonconformity with the constitution, surely a court can also set aside actions of unelected bureaucrats for the same reason? Direct examination of administrative action for constitutionality is part of the general trend toward judicialization. The same logic leads toward expanded judicial supervision of administrative actions under delegated statutory authority. Certainly if judges can examine administrative action for conformity with the constitution, it is hardly objectionable that other judges examine the same action for conformity with the statutory dictates of the legislature itself. Now the courts are not attacking the legislature but serving it. So the expansion of constitutional review, by increasing the prestige of courts and their reputation as guardians of rights, may naturally lead toward greater supervision of administrative action.

The above discussion has focused on ideational factors that might lead to greater judicialization of administrative law. A second set of sources of judicialization are economic, and follow the logic of mobility mentioned at the outset of this paper. I refer of course to trade liberalization and integration. Liberalization and the expansion of markets mean that parties are often doing business with those far away, subject to different rules. The expansion of markets heightens the potential for regulation to serve as disguised trade barriers, and reinforces the

[28] Eg *Ozturk v Germany* Series A No 73 (1984) (holding a traffic violation to be a criminal charge although it was considered to be an administrative offense under German law).

[29] See CA Paris, 7 March 2000, [2000] Bulletin du Conseil National des Commissaires aux Comptes No 119 (holding that there was no independent tribunal because the state actors who brought the charge were also represented on the tribunal deciding the case).

[30] See eg *Equal Opportunities Commission v Secretary of State for Employment* [1994] 1 All ER 910; *Johnston v Chief Constable of the Royal Ulster Constabulary* [1987] QB 129 (1986).

[31] T Ginsburg *Judicial Review in New Democracies* (Cambridge University Press Cambridge 2003).

need for transparent third-party fora to adjudicate the disputes which follow. Liberalization also means that vital services – telecommunications, electricity, health care, working class housing, transportation systems, financial services – are increasingly provided by privately owned companies rather than government monopolies. Where government has less involvement in direct service provision, there are fewer institutions that can informally contain conflict among businesses, punish misbehavior, or forestall insolvency. This is all the more true when the businesses providing services are themselves outsiders. Freer markets generate demands for more legalistic modes of regulation, since informal, hierarchical means of control are no longer adequate.[32]

The history of EU regulation of regulation illustrates this most dramatically. As the European Court of Justice has been confronted with a steady diet of cases concerning the rules of fair competition and elimination of non-tariff barriers, it has been propelled into the realm of EU-wide policy-making. By formulating the 'direct effect' doctrine, it has invited private interests to bring cases based on EU law into member state courts, expanding their role in governance as well. This has extended its purview to include national systems of administrative law.

The Union has no general competence to harmonize public administration in the member states, which retain their own national structures and are the primary implementers of EU law. But Schwarze[33] has demonstrated that there is a nascent EU administrative law, developed by the European Court of Justice and Court of First Instance, covering both fields under direct EU regulation, such as competition law, and national administrative systems in their role as primary implementers of EU law. National systems of public procurement law and environmental law have been substantially modified in response to European-level requirements.[34] The general phenomenon that implementation of EU law shall not differ in different member states means that the European courts are now able to scrutinize national administrators when they are implementing the ever-expanding body of European law.

Over time, judicial intervention into administrative law, perhaps necessitated by the building of the common market, has been given legitimacy by the Charter of Fundamental Rights (now part of the draft Constitution) which provides for the right to good administration and to access to documents.[35] The content of European administrative law extends to individual procedural rights such as the right to be heard, to be provided with reasons and access to judicial review, the right to access to files, the protection of legitimate expectations, proportionality,

[32] S Vogel *Freer Markets, More Rules* (Cornell University Press Ithaca 1996).

[33] J Schwarze *European Administrative Law* (Sweet and Maxwell London 1992); J Schwarze 'Enlargement, The European Constitution, and Administrative Law' (2004) 53 ICLQ 969.

[34] Schwarze (n 33) 975-6.

[35] Articles 41 and 42.

and state liability for breaches of community law. Further requirements flow in the area of competition law and internal market rules, which affect public undertakings as well as private. All this has led to a discussion of the 'Europeanization' of administrative law, notwithstanding the lack of EU jurisdiction to create a general code of administrative procedure.[36] One might thus argue that Europe as a whole is moving toward a German-style model of administrative law, based on a quasi-constitutional set of norms based on 'higher law' natural justice-type principles, implemented by local authorities and enforced by courts at all levels.[37]

Transnational developments have also affected institutional structures and mechanisms for administrative law. The WTO has forced massive changes in administrative procedures related to customs matters. Article X of the GATT 1994 requires that 'Laws, regulations, judicial decisions and administrative rulings of general application [...] shall be published promptly...' and administered 'in a uniform, impartial and reasonable manner', notably by independent administrative tribunals or procedures.[38] Similar requirements for independent and transparent regulation are found in the newer agreements on services and intellectual property. It is thus clear that international commitments will affect administrative law by expanding its scope and demanding transparency.

These effects were most dramatic in the case of WTO accession by China, which committed to making WTO commitments directly challengeable by the courts.[39] China agreed to impartial and uniform implementation of its commitments and of trade-related laws; to substantial transparency and notice and comment procedures of those laws, regulations, and measures; and most dramatically, to set up and maintain impartial judicial review of all administrative action. The WTO became, in essence, an amendment to the Chinese constitution, requiring both wholesale and retail regulation of regulation. Internal forces wished to 'lock

[36] Schwarze (n 33).

[37] C Harlow 'Codification of EC Administrative Procedures' (1996) 2 Eur L J 3.Another trend within the member states is increasing focus on administrative codes, with the southern countries shifting here from the French sphere toward the German (though there is no shift toward a codification at the EU level). See Italy, Act 241/1990; Spain, Law No 30 of 1992 (26 November 1992); Greece, Act 2690/1999; Portugal, Act Decree No 442/1991 of 15 November 1991; Netherlands, General Administrative Procedural act of 4 June 1992.

[38] General Agreement on Tariffs and Trade 1994, 15 April 1994; Marrakech Agreement Establishing the World Trade Organization, Annex 1A, art X, 1867 UNTS 187, 33 ILM 1153 (1994). Note that Article X.3(c) qualifies the obligation so as not to 'require the elimination or substitution of procedures in force in the territory of a contracting party on the date of this Agreement which in fact provide for an objective and impartial review of administrative action even though such procedures are not fully or formally independent of the agencies entrusted with administrative enforcement. Any contracting party employing such procedures shall, upon request, furnish the Contracting Parties with full information thereon in order that they may determine whether such procedures conform to the requirements of this subparagraph.'

[39] Art 2 of the Protocol for Accession of China to the World Trade Organization (2003).

in' commitments before they could be whittled away at the local level, and third-party monitoring, locked in by international agreements, provided the mechanism.

Rationalist analyses of international institutions suggest that one of their primary functions is information generation. International institutions are said to provide high-quality information about performance by the parties to international treaties and about their own performance.[40] The Chinese commitment illustrates also that the international commitment device can help provide transparency *within* a country, enhancing predictability for domestic actors by constraining government. Thus WTO requirements of publication of laws and regulations; notice of new measures and provision for comment; and independent adjudication and sites of appeal will have substantial effects on administrative law systems. The WTO secretariat itself claims that transparency is especially important with respect to domestic regulations aimed at legitimate public policy objectives that might have an effect on international competition, such as public health or protection of the environment.[41] By extending the right to comment on new regulatory measures to those outside national borders, the WTO expands judicial or at least adjudicative evaluation of rule-making.

The final source of pressure for convergence we identified was power. Powerful states might wish to force less powerful states to change their administrative law systems in a manner that accrues advantage to the powerful state. It is difficult, however, to disentangle the effects of power from those of liberalization itself. The European example belies the idea that the shift toward judicialization reflects a distinctively American innovation, and suggests that it is more structural in nature. Of course, liberalization itself reflects interests of powerful states. But convergence in administrative law seems to be incidental to broader goals of economic liberalization rather than a direct goal of powerful states. Perhaps this point helps explain the continued divergence in the conceptual architecture of administrative law, even while there is some convergence with regard to the scope of administrative law and the presence of third-party monitors.

VI. Conclusion

This paper has catalogued a trend toward judicialization of regulation that is apparent in Europe, Japan, and the United States. Despite continuing doctrinal divergences and quite different institutional structures, there has been substantial convergence in the core elements of administrative law, namely a right to present one's case, to receive reasons for adverse decisions, and the right to appeal

[40] RB Mitchell 'Sources of Transparency: Information Systems in International Regimes' (1998) 42 International Studies Quarterly 109.

[41] WTO 1999, The Fundamental WTO Principles of National Treatment, Most-Favored Nation and Transparency.

administrative decisions. There is also a shift, apparent in Japan and the world trading regime, toward transparency of new generally applicable policy measures, broadly drawing on American notice and comment rule-making. The shift is toward wholesale regulation of regulation, as well as retail. This trend has its origins in convergent interests in regulatory transparency in an increasingly integrated world economy, along with convergent ideas about the proper monitors of regulators.

The problem with judicial control is that it is imperfect. Judges are by their nature generalists without expertise in the particular area of administration at issue in individual cases. This is true to a certain degree even when there are specialized administrative courts. It is the generalist nature of the judge that makes her such an attractive monitor. But comparative experience suggests that judges alone are not capable of constraining the state without substituting their own policy preferences.

We thus see at the same time as expanded judicial supervision a number of other efforts to search for neutral principles. One of the more popular is cost-benefit analysis.[42] The OECD (2000) reports that 14 of its members have some form of regulatory impact analysis, under which regulations are scrutinized typically before promulgation. While the scope of these analyses differs according to the policy agendas, they involve *ex ante* evaluation according to some external and general criteria, for example, impact on business; paperwork reduction; and the effect of proposed rules on subnational governments, the environment, or particular socioeconomic groups. The United States version, copied in Australia, requires a regulation to be justified in cost-benefit terms. But cost-benefit principles offer no panacea. Rather they tend to shift the discretion to those calculating costs and benefits, which in many cases must be delegated to precisely the same experts doing the regulating.

[42] B Morgan 'The Internationalization of Economic Review of Legislation: Non-Judicial Legalization?' in T Ginsburg and R Kagan (eds) *Institutions and Public Law: Comparative Approaches* (Peter Lang Berlin 2005).

The Proper Role of Bureaucracy in a Modern Market Economy: The Case of Japan

CHRISTIAN KIRCHNER

I. The Problem under Review

1. Markets and Their Institutional Framework

Markets do not function in an institutional vacuum but in a given institutional framework.[1] Well-defined property rights and a contract law which allows the conclusion and enforcement of private contracts are the cornerstones of that institutional framework. Two other fundamental market institutions are important: (1) competition law (in the United States: 'antitrust law'), enforced by competition authorities (antitrust authorities) and law courts, i.e. a competition policy; and (2) sector-specific regulation, enforced by regulatory agencies and law courts in certain markets where competition law as such cannot produce effective competition. Such markets are to be found in so-called network industries, also called 'natural monopolies'.[2]

2. The Regulatory Framework: Deregulation, Re-regulation, and the Proper Balance between Competition Policy and Regulation

Competition policy and (sector-specific) regulation today play a major role in all market economies. Yet three questions have to be answered: (1) What should be the substance and the scope of competition law and how should it be enforced?

[1] C Kirchner 'Market Organization: A New-Institutional Perspective' (1995) 151 J of Institutional and Theoretical Economics 260.

[2] G Knieps *Wettbewerbsökonomie – Regulierungstheorie, Industrieökonomie, Wettbewerbspolitik* (Springer Berlin and Heidelberg 2001) 21-44; W Kerber 'Wettbewerbspolitik' in D Bender and others *Vahlens Kompendium der Wirtschaftstheorie und Wirtschaftspolitik* vol 2 (8th edn Vahlen Munich 2003) 348-352.

(2) What should be the substance and the scope of sector-specific regulation and how should it be enforced? (3) What should be the balance between competition policy and (sector-specific) regulation?

The answers to these questions have differed widely in industrialised countries in the last fifty years. Due to new economic doctrines and political movements, the relative weight of competition law and regulation has changed dramatically. Starting in the United States and the United Kingdom, traditional economic regulation has been drastically reduced and reshaped under the flag of 'deregulation'. One of the main fields which was affected by this fundamental change in the regulatory framework has been the telecommunications sector.[3] A comparable development then took place in the European Community, later the European Union,[4] and in Japan.

With the ongoing deregulation process, new problems had to be solved. Eliminating traditional economic regulation of the above-mentioned 'natural monopolies' and opening up competition in markets which in the past did not exist as separate markets – e.g. telecommunications services as distinct from the telecommunications network – could either mean replacing sector-specific regulation with competition law or remodelling regulation as such. Such a 'reformed regulatory approach' would then turn away from price control to access control, so that competitors on downstream markets could enjoy non-discriminatory access to the network. The network would either remain in the hands of the former monopolist (incumbent) or be separated and run by a network owner (the common carrier approach). Price control could then be focussed on access pricing. In the other alternative, sector-specific regulation could be abolished as such and be replaced by the control of abuse of the dominant position by means of competition law. The access problem would then have to be solved by means of the so-called essential facilities doctrine. Both solutions would lead to a kind of re-regulation. Both solutions would fundamentally change the role the state played in the market economy, from state ownership and direct control of economic activities to a more indirect control by establishing a regulatory framework in which certain property rights are defined for the market players.

Re-regulation does not simply mean the abolishment of old economic regulation by modern access regulation. It has to be decided which problems should be better handled by means of sector-specific regulation and which by application of competition law. If the monopoly of the existing network were challenged by the creation of – competing – networks, access regulation could be reduced. Remaining problems could then be more adequately solved by the application of competition law. To which degree and when this substitution takes place is a matter that depends on the developments of markets, on the relative

[3] J Scherer *Telekommunikationsrecht und Telekommunikationspolitik* (Nomos Baden-Baden 1985) 205 ff.

[4] U Immenga and others *Telekommunikation im Wettbewerb* (CH Beck Munich 2001) 130 ff.

efficacy of competition law enforcement and sector-specific regulation, and on political factors. Regulators are not supposed to give up sector-specific regulation voluntarily. Politicians might be tempted to make use of sector-specific regulation in order to present the short-term success of driving down prices in downstream markets without being held responsible for potentially negative long-term effects.

3. Regulatory Reform and the 'Proper Role of Bureaucracy'

The necessity to develop new modes of regulation (including replacement of sector-specific regulation by competition law) after the deregulation and re-regulation movement has led to a demand for 'regulatory reform'.[5] The widely shared goal of such regulatory reform is to improve the general welfare of a country through growth, innovation, and international competitiveness.[6] One of the major issues of regulatory reform is to strengthen competition in free markets and find new modes of sector-specific regulation. Such reforms will affect the role of government in the economy. Deregulation has cut back direct state intervention in the market economy. Re-regulation may lead to over-regulation again and to a strengthening of the position of the state vis-à-vis the economy. On the other hand, effective enforcement mechanisms for competition law need effective control structures. One important element of regulatory reform is thus determining the 'proper role of bureaucracy' in a market economy. The given balance of competition law and sector-specific regulation as well as the mode of regulation will affect the size and the role of such parts of the bureaucracy which are in charge of making markets functions.

4. Regulatory Reform in Japan

Regulatory reform is an important issue in all countries, including industrialised countries. Thus, the OECD has been pursuing the goal of reforming the regulatory frameworks of its members for more than a decade.[7] OECD reports have investigated the specific problems of various countries and have made reform proposals,[8] amongst others for Japan.[9]

[5] OECD *OECD Review of Regulatory Reform* (OECD Paris 1999).

[6] OECD *The economic benefits of regulatory reform* (Paris 1998).

[7] OECD (n 5).

[8] OECD (n 6).

[9] OECD *Regulatory Reform in Japan: The Role of Competition Policy in Regulatory Reform* (Paris 1999); OECD *Regulatory Reform in Japan: Government Capacity to Assure High Quality Regulation* (Paris 1999); OECD *Regulatory Reform in Japan: Enhancing Market*
cont. ...

Regulatory reform appears to be an issue of major importance, especially for such countries where growth rates have been insufficient and the overall shape of the economy has been unsatisfactory. If such deficiencies can be traced back to an outmoded regulatory framework, specific proposals for regulatory reform for such countries may be formulated not only by an international organisation like the OECD[10] but also by trading partners with an interest in improved export opportunities to that country.[11]

The essence of the problem of regulatory reform in Japan seems to be to strengthen competition by (1) reforming existing competition law, (2) better enforcing competition law, (3) and opening up downstream markets in network sectors by means of sector-specific regulation. All these issues have been stressed as well by the OECD and the European Union.[12]

II. Methodological Approach

1. In Need of an Interdisciplinary Approach

When issues of regulatory reform are under review, economic, political, and legal factors have to be taken into account. Economics should illuminate how various instruments applied to reforming the regulatory framework are functioning (impact analysis) and how to decide which instruments are better suited to solve the problem. Political issues have to be tackled because regulatory reform is a political process in which political actors participate who may be winners and/or losers. Legal devices – their substance and their enforcement – play a major role because most of the instruments proposed for regulatory reform are such legal instruments.

Any uni-disciplinary approach, whether it stresses economic, political, or legal reasoning, will be unable to produce a solid positive analysis of the given state of the regulatory framework and the expected effects of possible instruments. And it cannot develop a good basis for normative proposals. Thus a multidisciplinary approach appears to be needed in order to solve the problem. Moreover, the problem may differ from country to country due to specific characteristics of the different overall institutional frameworks. This means that the methodological approach must be able to identify the characteristics of a

Openness through Regulatory Reform (Paris 1999); OECD *Regulatory Reform in Japan: Regulatory Reform in the Telecommunications Industry* (Paris 1999).

10 OECD (n 9).

11 European Commission *EU Priority Proposals for Regulatory Reform in Japan* (Brussels 2002).

12 OECD (n 5-10); EU (n 11).

national institutional framework. This is especially important because of the problem of path dependence.

Regulatory reform – viewed from these different perspectives – entails a reform of the institutional framework of an economy. Various players interact in that reform process: politicians, voters, experts, managers of business enterprises, consumers, bureaucrats in regulatory agencies, bureaucrats in competition authorities, and judges in law courts. If it is assumed that all these players follow their own interests and act rationally, the process of institution building may be analysed by a modern approach called 'new institutional economics'.

2. New Institutional Economics

New institutional economics as a modern theoretical approach of economics may be characterised as the attempt to apply the tools of economics to the development, change, and functioning of institutions. Institutions in the sense of institutional economics are taken as sets of general rules together with the enforcement mechanisms. Whereas the old institutional economics focussed on institutions but rejected the neo-classical approach of economics as such, new institutional economics rests on the foundation of neo-classical economics with some – important – modifications to that approach.

In new institutional economics, individual actors are taken as decision makers acting according to their individual preferences (methodological individualism). They interact in a world of scarce resources (assumption of scarce resources) so that they have to make choices about how to utilise and allocate resources (either within a given organisation or via the market mechanism). They follow their individual interests (assumption of self-interested, opportunistic behaviour) without purporting that they always try to maximise their individual utility. They act rationally (rationality assumption), but according to systematically incomplete information, existing information costs, and a potential individual deviance from utility maximisation, their rationality is bounded (assumption of bounded rationality). As far as the assumptions of scarce resources and self-interested rational behaviour are concerned, new institutional economics is in line with neo-classical economics. But the rationality assumption has been modified (to 'bounded rationality'). The systematic incompleteness of information and the existence of transaction costs is stressed by new institutional economics, so that economic models working with the assumption of full information and zero transaction costs (the 'nirvana approach') are rejected.

The theoretical approach of new institutional economics thus may be understood as a necessary modification of the neo-classical approach in order to be able to study phenomena of non-market allocation of resources and the functioning of legal rules, regulation, and governance structures (of business corporations as well as public bodies). The discipline is no longer confined to the 'economy' (understood as the world of material goods and market transactions), but it can be understood as that branch of social science which analyses social interactions under the assumptions outlined above. Characterising this approach as 'rational choice' might insofar be misleading because the rationality assumption used in neo-classical economics is modified; furthermore, there are other important assumptions that are introduced besides the assumption of – bounded – rationality. In a world of scarce resources and systematically incomplete information, individual actors try to develop institutional arrangements which seem to be preferable compared to the given institutional framework. Interactions between individuals take place on two levels: (1) interactions within given institutions, and (2) interactions aimed at changing given institutions (decisions within rules and decisions on rules). Institutional economics focuses on interactions of the second type.

The new institutional economics approach as outlined above has much in common with approaches to the sociology of law which study the origin of legal rules, causes of changes of legal rules, and the (real or expected) impact of legal rules. But the new institutional economics approach is closer to mainstream economics. And it works with a clear and precise set of assumptions.

As far as normative proposals are concerned, in new institutional economics their foundation is a positive comparative analysis of alternative institutional solutions. Only in the light of expected outcomes of alternative solutions does the choice between such options make sense. This means a turnaround of the means-and-ends approach as used not only by conventional welfare economics but by many scholars in the fields of legal policy as well. Whereas in the means-and-ends approach it is necessary to assume that the choice of given means does not affect the chosen goal (which in most cases is not possible), in the new institutional economics approach the underlying positive comparative analysis leads to refutable hypotheses which are the foundation of each normative proposal. Good arguments for the – normative – choice have to be brought forward. It is not enough that an abstract goal is to be attained, nor is it sufficient that the general welfare – as such – is improved. It is necessary that those individuals who choose the new institutional arrangement and who have to live with it have a reason to prefer the new institutional solution. Under the assumption of self-interested behaviour they are supposed to choose the new solution only if they can expect to be better off, if there are 'benefits of co-operation'.

3. Competition Policy in a New Institutional Economics Perspective

In a new institutional economics perspective, *competition policy* may be understood as the design of an *institutional framework (competition law)* together with the *enforcement of such legal rules*.[13]

Competition law in a new institutional economics perspective provides generally applicable rules which function as constraints on competitors when they take strategic decisions on how to maintain or improve their position in a particular market.

Competition policy in this new institutional economics perspective may be understood as a game between lawmakers, administrators, law courts, and private actors. All actors in this game are understood to pursue their own interests; they act in a world of incomplete information and positive transaction costs. Their rationality is bounded.

According to the institutional economics approach, there is no pre-defined public interest.[14] Neither administrative authorities nor law courts are assumed to pursue *the* public interest. Rather, individual actors on all levels are presumed to pursue their own objectives.

A new institutional economics approach necessarily makes a clear-cut distinction between a *positive* and a *normative approach*. Whereas the former analyses the given effect of alternative institutional arrangements and/or the creation and evolution of such institutional arrangements, the latter produces arguments for choosing between competing institutional solutions.[15]

This institutional economics approach may be applied to regulation as well. Most elements of the institutional approach are the same whether applied to competition policy or regulation. But there are some specific features of an institutional economics approach to regulation which have to be discussed below.

[13] C Kirchner 'Competition policy vs. regulation: Administration vs. judiciary' in M Neumann and J Weigand (eds) *The International Handbook of Competition* (Edward Elgar Cheltenham 2004) 306, 310-312.

[14] C Kirchner 'Gemeinwohl aus institutionenökonomischer Perspektive' in GF Schuppert and F Neidhardt (eds) *Gemeinwohl – Auf der Suche nach Substanz* (WZB-Jahrbuch Berlin 2002) 157-177.

[15] I Pies *Normative Institutionenoekonomik. Zur Rationalisierung des politischen Liberalismus* (Mohr Tübingen 1993); I Pies 'Institutionenökonomik als Ordnungstheorie' in H Leipold and I Pies (eds) *Ordnungstheorie und Ordnungspolitik – Konzeption und Entwicklungsperspektiven* (Stuttgart 2000); K Homann 'Die Legitimation von Institutionen' in Korff and others (eds) *Handbuch der Wirtschaftsethik* vol 2 (Gütersloher Verlagshaus Gütersloh 1999) 50-95.

4. Regulation in a New Institutional Economics Perspective

Applying the new institutional economics approach to regulation means first of all clearly distinguishing between a *positive theory of regulation* – which explains why and how existing regulatory structures have been developed[16] and how the existing regulatory instruments work in practice[17] – and a *normative theory of regulation* which discusses the justification of regulation[18] and/or the merits of competing regulatory regimes and/or the rationale of a choice between regulation and the application of competition law.[19]

As argued above, the assumption of self-interested (bounded) rational behaviour is combined with that of systematically incomplete information and positive transaction costs. As in competition policy, there is no pre-defined public interest in a new institutional economics approach.

Regulation in an institutional economics perspective might be seen as an activity in which lawmakers, administrators, and – to a certain degree – judges are engaged in *public control of business activities*. Market forces are totally or at least partially replaced by an administrative decision process.

Lawmakers, administrators, and judges – as agents – have to justify their (costly) activities vis-à-vis the citizens, i.e. the principals, in the light of a positive balance between social benefits and social costs. Such a calculation has to take into account the cost of regulation as well. If regulation is justified by an appeal to existing 'market failures', the problem arises that one cannot compare the existing market imperfections with perfect markets. These perfect markets would be a good benchmark, but they do not exist. Such a comparison would thus lead to a nirvana approach. And it has to be taken into account that there are imperfections in state activities as well which may produce high – often invisible – costs. A cost-benefit analysis of the pros and cons of regulation in a specific market has to weigh costs and benefits not just in a static model; instead, it must take into account the impact of regulation on innovation as a driving force of future benefits as well. It must be remembered that all the relevant decisions – at the level of lawmaking, administration, and application of law by the law courts – take place in a world of systematically incomplete information.

Such an institutional economics approach to regulation is a far cry from the conventional welfare economics approaches to regulation which focus on the efficiency implications of regulation and sometimes confuse the positive and normative approaches. On the other hand, an institutional economics approach cannot be reduced to a simple positive analysis of the relevant factors of existing regulatory structures. A normative analysis of alternative institutional devices is

[16] S Voigt *Institutionenökonomik* (Wilhelm Fink Verlag Munich 2002) 179-243.

[17] ibid 61-177.

[18] I Pies *Normative Institutionenökonomik* (n 15); Voigt (n 16) 245-299.

[19] Kirchner (n 13).

necessary in which regulation and competition policy are analysed in a comparative setting. This type of normative comparative institutional approach then may serve as a basis for choosing between competition policy and regulation in given market situations.

III. Regulatory Reform in Japan: The Outside Perspective

1. OECD Perspective

In 1999 the OECD undertook an in-depth investigation of the Japanese regulatory framework. This has resulted in a number of reports: (1) OECD Review of Regulatory Reform, Regulatory Reform in Japan; (2) OECD, Regulatory Reform in Japan: The Role of Competition Policy in Regulatory Reform; (3) OECD, Regulatory Reform in Japan: Government Capacity to Assure High Quality Regulation; (4) OECD, Regulatory Reform in Japan: Enhancing Market Openness through Regulatory Reform; (5) OECD, Regulatory Reform in Japan: Regulatory Reform in the Telecommunications Industry.[20]

The coverage of these reports has been extremely wide,[21] starting with a general evaluation of 'market openness and regulation in the policy environment of Japan' and a discussion of principles of 'efficient regulation' (transparency, non-discrimination, avoidance of unnecessary trade restrictions, use of internationally harmonised measures, mutual recognition of regulatory measures, and application of competition principles from an international perspective). The reports cover the following selected sectors: automobiles and components, telecommunications services, telecommunications equipment, and electricity.

As far as competition policy is concerned, the OECD stresses the policy option of strengthening competition policy enforcement, reinforcing the role of the Japanese Fair Trade Commission (JFTC), and applying competition policy more effectively to private anti-competitive practices.[22] Policy recommendations for the telecommunications sector include steps to better grant access to existing

[20] OECD *OECD Review of Regulatory Reform, Regulatory Reform in Japan* (Paris 1999); OECD *Regulatory Reform in Japan: The Role of Competition Policy in Regulatory Reform* (Paris 1999); OECD *Regulatory Reform in Japan: Government Capacity to Assure High Quality Regulation* (Paris 1999); OECD *Regulatory Reform in Japan: Enhancing Market Openness through Regulatory Reform* (Paris 1999); OECD *Regulatory Reform in Japan: Regulatory Reform in the Telecommunications Industry* (Paris 1999).

[21] OECD *OECD Review of Regulatory Reform, Regulatory Reform in Japan* (Paris 1999); OECD *Regulatory Reform in Japan: Enhancing Market Openness through Regulatory Reform* (Paris 1999).

[22] OECD *Regulatory Reform in Japan: Enhancing Market Openness through Regulatory Reform* (Paris 1999) 44-47.

networks and supplementing sector-specific regulation by enforcement of competition law.[23]

In 2004 the OECD pointed out that Japan has achieved progress in implementing regulatory reform.[24] The report states that Japan has introduced a number of measures to enhance regulatory quality and promote regulatory reform, competition policy, and market openness. But the report calls for efforts to improve regulatory tools and institutions.[25]

In the field of competition policy, the OECD acknowledges progress achieved. The competition authority has been strengthened, the quality of competition law has been improved, and the powers and the capacity of the Fair Trade Commission have been strengthened.[26] Nevertheless, competition law enforcement remains on the agenda as well as further deregulation of the telecommunications sector.[27]

On 6 May 2004, two OECD experts published an in-depth study on 'Product Market Competition and Economic Performance in Japan'.[28] They point to certain deficiencies in the traditional Japanese regulatory framework. Policies promoting product market competition have long been compromised by ministerial guidance (*gyōsei shidō*) and explicit exemptions from the competition law.[29] The authors criticise that enforcement of competition law is not strong enough.[30] The provisions of the Antimonopoly Act (AMA) are too wide and too vague, thus inducing the Fair Trade Commission to be very cautious and to rely on self-regulation and administrative guidance (*gyōsei shidō*). This is especially true when it comes to the application of competition law in the newly deregulated industries. While the authors point to the success of liberalising and deregulating the telecommunications sector, they nevertheless call for improvements of access regulation.[31]

[23] OECD *Regulatory Reform in Japan: Regulatory Reform in the Telecommunications Industry* (Paris 1999) 41-43.

[24] OECD *Japan: Progress in Implementing Regulatory Reform* (Paris 2004).

[25] ibid 1.

[26] ibid 2.

[27] OECD *OECD Reviews of Regulatory Reform – Japan: Progress in Implementing Regulatory Reform* (19 July 2004) <http://www.oecd.org/document/60/0,2340,en_2649_37421_32979132_1_1_1_37421,00.html> (4 August 2005).

[28] J Høj and M Wise 'Product Market Competition and Economic Performance in Japan' OECD Economics Department Working Papers no 287/2004.

[29] ibid 5, 17-19.

[30] ibid 17-20.

[31] ibid 32, 33.

2. The Perspective of the European Union

Part of the ongoing dialogue between Japan and the European Union on regulatory reform[32] includes the 'EU Priority Proposal for Regulatory Reform in Japan'.[33] Amongst many other problems, competition policy is also addressed. The European Commission acknowledges recent progress in substantial Japanese competition law as well as in enforcement of competition law.[34] But amongst the priority reform proposals put forward by the European Commission are strengthening the resources (staff and budget) of the Fair Trade Commission and enhancing the investigative powers of the Commission.[35]

3. Need for Reform: Essential Issues

The main problems of regulatory reform in the field of competition policy and sector-specific regulation identified by the OECD and the European Union are the following: (1) an insufficient legal foundation for competition policy, (2) weak enforcement of competition law due to lack of resources and powers of the FTC, and (3) weak regulation of network industries (e.g. telecommunications).

IV. A New Institutional Economics Approach to Regulatory Reform in Japan

1. Competition Policy

Translated into a new institutional economics perspective, these three weaknesses indicate deficiencies (1) of the law-making process and (2) of public governance structures.

The broad and vague language of the Japanese Antimonopoly Act (AMA) may be explained by the fact that the act was formulated at a time when the objective of that act was not to improve competition in open markets but to regain full sovereignty by meeting the conditions of the victors after World War II in the field of antitrust law.

The broad and vague formulation of the provisions of the AMA – together with a host of exceptions – allowed Japan to develop its own specific institutional

[32] Cf eg <http://www.mofa.go.jp/region/europe/eu/overview/dereg0503.html> (4 August 2005).

[33] European Commission *EU Priority Proposals for Regulatory Reform in Japan* (Brussels 2002).

[34] ibid 15, 16.

[35] ibid 16.

framework for markets. This national institutional framework borrows its flexibility from a system of administrative guidance (*gyōsei shidō*). Such a national system works better with a powerful bureaucracy in ministries and weak antitrust authorities. Broad and vague provisions of the AMA and numerous exceptions from antitrust provisions are helpful devices for such an institutional framework.

What has been characterised as 'deficiencies of public governance structures' today (by the OECD) has for a long time been viewed as an important comparative advantage of Japanese governance structures, namely the informal and flexible institutional arrangement between government and business, working with the instrument of *gyōsei shidō*.

This system appears to be quite effective in a period of dynamic economic growth when the success of the export industries renders the relatively low productivity and the slow innovation of domestic sectors barely visible; however, in a recession period such weaknesses become evident and the informal institutional arrangement loses much of its glamour. In order to improve the given weak governance structures, structural reforms appear to be necessary.

Such structural reforms that are necessary to overcome the inherent weaknesses of Japanese competition policy have to be radical reforms of public governance in the field of competition policy, and not just a re-allocation of resources to enforcement agencies in the field of competition policy.

Proposals for regulatory reforms which ask for stricter rules and a more powerful enforcement mechanism lead in the right direction. But they are only scratching the surface.

Allocating more resources to the FTC, improving enforcement devices, and clarifying the language of the AMA are helpful steps. But as long as such 'reforms' do not remove the informal links between ministerial bureaucracies and business enterprises and the interdependencies between factions of political parties, ministerial bureaucracies, and business elites, such reforms will be futile. Such interdependencies have the consequence that agents in political parties, in government, and in bureaucracy can act more or less independently and have no sufficient incentive to act on the behalf of the interests of the principals, i.e. the citizens.

Regulatory reform then means the reshaping of the structure of governance in the field of public governance. The 'proper role of bureaucracy' is not a matter that can be defined in quantitative terms, e.g. financial and personal resources for public agencies. The 'proper role of bureaucracy' then becomes a matter of effective public governance structures.

2. Regulation

When it comes to sector-specific regulation, the OECD proposals are in line with conventional wisdom of regulation of network industries in Europe. Such proposals focus on strong regulatory agencies with ex-ante regulation powers in order to break up existing monopolistic positions and enable the entrance of new competitors. Such proposals do not take into account the long-term effects of sector-specific regulation, which is more interested in access to existing networks than in infrastructure-based competition that leads to competition between business enterprises within their own infrastructure. Just directing sector-specific regulation towards non-discriminatory access to existing networks is a short-term option which may cause more harm in the future than expected.

It may well be understood that OECD proposals for regulatory reform in the field of regulation of network industries are leading in the direction of stressing access to existing networks. This strategy will be a device to open up markets more quickly than a strategy based on infrastructure-based competition in network industries. But it is questionable whether such proposals of the OECD are in accordance with the long-term interests of Japanese citizens.

When it comes to the proper role of bureaucracy in a market economy, in the field of sector-specific regulation another problem has to be discussed: sector-specific regulation goes hand in hand with the establishment of regulatory agencies with rich financial and personal resources. If sector-specific regulation is successful and the markets become more competitive, the need for sector-specific regulation becomes less important; sector-specific regulation should be replaced by competition policy. But there will be stiff resistance to reducing sector-specific regulation in the light of difficulties in reducing the staff of existing regulatory agencies. Thus over-regulation will be the expected outcome of starting sector-specific regulation without a clear phase-out concept (sunset regulation). Such provisions for a phase-out of sector-specific regulation have not been taken into account in the proposals of the OECD studies, thus automatically leading to over-regulation in the future if the proposals of such studies are introduced. The proper role of bureaucracy will not be met if such mechanical and constructivist proposals are put into effect.

V. Concluding Remarks

Determining the proper role of bureaucracy in a market economy has turned out to be a problem which should not be solved by simply applying universally the tools of neo-classical economic analysis. It has been demonstrated that meaningful proposals require an in-depth analysis of the institutional framework of the country under review. A new institutional economics approach is helpful in identifying the crucial issues of regulatory reform.

In the case of Japan, it has been demonstrated that regulatory reform is more than enhancing the efficiency of existing mechanisms. A structural reform of the political system appears to be a necessary step in order to reach the goals of regulatory reforms.

The Role of Bureaucracy in Deregulation – The Case of Justice System Reform in Japan

KAHEI ROKUMOTO

I. Introduction

To the theme of the role of bureaucracy in the market economy, I would like to present as material for discussion a case from Japan of the role played by a top bureaucrat in bringing about a major reform in public governance, namely the justice system reform (JSR).

The justice system reform is an umbrella name for a comprehensive package of reform programs comprising a series of structural changes in the judicial system and the legal profession that started in the latter part of the 1990s and is still continuing at the time of this writing. (Figure 1 summarizes the chronology of the reform process.)

Figure 1: Chronological Summary: Justice System Reform

1947	Legal Training and Research Institute (LTRI) established
1962	Investigating Committee of the Judicial System
1967	Five-Year Plan for Undergraduate Legal Education (University of Tokyo)
	End of the Cold War, start of economic globalization and depression
1987-1981	Reforms of legal education
	(Quota system and increase of passes)
	(Legal Professions Consensus Formula)
	Reforms of governance systems (political, administrative, decentralization)
1991-1995	Shift of weight to graduate schools
1996	LDP sets up Special Research Committee on Judicial Reform
	(demands a radical expansion of the legal profession and other measures)
1999 (June)	Justice System Reform Council established
	(Political Choice Formula)
2001 (June)	JSRC Final Opinion
2003 (Autumn)	First law schools (about 65) authorized
2004 (Spring)	First law schools start to operate
2004	National universities become 'independent administrative agencies'

This comprehensive reform of the justice system of Japan in turn constitutes an essential component of the larger reform efforts to restructure the nation's system of governance as a whole in the general direction of 'deregulation', as well as to equip the society with institutional capabilities to cope with the consequences of regulation.

It is commonly accepted that in Japan there is an unusually large gap between the law in books and the law in action, even though there have been lively controversies among academic scholars as to its causes as well as to its policy implications. However, in the domestic context of the recent policy discussions, it has come to be accepted that in order to prepare the nation for a deregulated society which we are becoming whether we like it or not, we must make our legal system more efficient and more easily accessible to its users, whether individuals or corporations. In these discussions, deregulation was characterized as transformation from a society of the 'advance-control type' into one of the 'post-check type'. In other words, the traditional top-down control and protection by governmental bureaucracy over private actors will no longer be the mainstay of social order. Instead, private individuals and corporations, liberated from governmental control and protection, will be acting as freely choosing and responsibility accepting agencies, subject to review, ultimately entrusted to the court, according to the rules and procedures of law.

Therefore, reforms to be achieved through the Judicial System Reform implied a power shift from bureaucracy to courts and lawyers. However, when we look at the processes by which the institutional settings for the JSR were established, we observe that it could only be realized by a strong and far-sighted initiative on the part of bureaucracy, the very target of the reform plans as a whole.

It is important to note here that regulation is not simply a matter of formal legal arrangements conferring the national or local government power to oversee and give or deny permission to private citizens and enterprises to engage in certain conduct on certain conditions. Regulation is often also a matter of 'living law', the informal practice patterns founded in tradition and culture or even those simply maintained by inertia and vested interests of the parties concerned. The term 'deregulation' that often appears in the context of political argumentations advocating and defending the reform agenda is meant to cover both of those two aspects indiscriminately.

II. The Case: The Role Played by Bureaucracy in the Justice System Reform

We have no space here to go far into the background of the reform: why it was needed, what was to be changed, how difficult the task was, and so on. Nevertheless, a minimum summary review will be in order.

1. Problem

We should first be reminded that the present Japanese legal system was originally created by the government during the formative era of the modern state following the westernizing revolution called the Meiji Restoration of 1868.[1] It was cast in a mould, so to speak, which has been exerting a lasting influence on the judicial system as well as the legal profession of Japan. I think we can say this despite the various institutional modifications that were made in the subsequent decades, particularly the far-reaching democratizing reforms made following the end of World War II. The latter reforms brought about significant changes including, for example, the US-inspired system of conferring on all the courts the power of declaring any law or governmental act unconstitutional and void ('judicial review'), and the uniform qualifying examination coupled with the practical training at the Institute for Research and Training for all aspiring lawyers, common to future judges, prosecutors, and attorneys.

In the subsequent five decades these changes had the effect of gradually establishing the court's authority as the ultimate arbitrator of legal issues, and enhancing the position of a 'private branch' of lawyers (attorneys) vis-à-vis the 'official branch' (judges and prosecutors) both in quality and quantity. Nevertheless, the tradition of the relative unimportance of the judiciary within the structure of governance as well as the weak position of private lawyers within the divided legal profession persisted.

The Japanese justice system was characterized by the following features.

(1) a divided legal profession;
(2) the judiciary bureaucratically organized with career judges (constituting a characteristically deviant version of the continental German model);
(3) private attorneys occupying a subdominant rather than dominant position vis-à-vis the official branches in prestige if not in quality; and
(4) the legal education oriented primarily to educating state officials and lawyers in government who legislate, interpret, and apply the law and only secondarily to training professional lawyers for private practice.

Over the century, this structure undoubtedly allowed the institutionalization of a legitimate legal order characterized by a stable and honest, albeit passive, judiciary in the overall structure of governance that relied heavily on the state bureaucracy in policymaking and maintenance of social order. This pattern had a good fit with a society characterized by homogeneity, symbolically epitomized in the extremely low crime rate, and undoubtedly corresponded to the numerous other sets of social conditions favourable to economic development and growth.

[1] See K Rokumoto 'Law and Culture in Transition' (2001) 49 American Journal of Comparative Law 545; K Rokumoto 'The Historical Roots of Stasis and Change in Japanese Legal Education' in A Rosett and others (eds) *East Asian Law – Universal Norms and Local Cultures* (Routledge Curzon London 2003) 156.

On the other hand, the weak development of the private sector of the legal profession coupled with a scarcity of practicing attorneys both reflected and entailed inadequate provision of legal services for business corporations and above all legal services to protect and promote the legal rights of individuals, particularly in regions other than large metropolitan centres.

Criticisms had already started to be raised against this regime in rather early periods following the post-war democratizing reforms. Legal academics have always been virtually unanimous in their critical stance toward the state of the legal examination as well as the legal profession. Many proposals were put forward and many attempts were made to improve the situation, but all these efforts failed on the whole in the face of tenacious resistance put up by the legal profession, especially the bar.

2. Political Background of Reform

Why then did a large-scale reform scheme such as the justice system reform suddenly come to be perceived as an urgent political requirement and as a realizable goal? In the background, there was a turn in the current of public opinion that began a little before 1990, when the present era of Heisei Emperor started and the exultation of 'Japan as number one' began to sound hollow and superficial. Around this time the view started to spread that the Japanese system of organizing and governing society was facing a deep crisis, a total systemic crisis or even a national crisis. This sentiment was triggered by the events, indicative of failure in the economy, which became revealed one after another: banks and securities companies went bankrupt, occurrences which were unheard of before; enormous amounts of public money had to be spent to cover up slack or corrupt operation of business corporations at a time when the future security of individual citizens was threatened by perpetual financial deficits of the government; and a long series of political scandals were brought to light involving leading politicians, high governmental officials, and corporate executives. These events exposed the 'iron triangle' of Japan to the public eye, and made it clear that 'Japan Incorporated' led by bright bureaucrats was no longer working. In addition, all of this coincided with the end of the Cold War and the onset of globalization of the economy, making it more imperative that Japan open up its economic system more to the outside world and make its decision-making processes more efficient, fair, and transparent.

There was a general consensus in this among the thinking elite of Japan. This was reflected in the fact that the conservative business elite, organized in such powerful pressure groups as the Keidanren (now renamed as Nippon Keidanren) and Keizai Dōyūkai [Federation of Economic Organization, and Japan Committee for Economic Development], began around the year 1990 to advocate radical restructuring of the legal profession as well as of the governmental structures along the broad ideological lines of neo-liberalism.

The sense of crisis came to be shared by reform-minded politicians as well as by the media. The so-called 'political reforms' were attempted in order to make the parliamentary system function more effectively, and the administrative reforms were started to make administrative processes more transparent and fair. These represented fundamental restructuring of the relationship between the government and the citizen to make the latter more autonomous and independent from the former. The justice system reform followed as the third component of this series of efforts to transform the system of governance as a whole. It was against this background that the Justice System Reform Council coined the catch-phrase that its reform proposals were for changing the 'shape of this nation'.[2]

The task of the JSRC of 1999-2001 was to alter these basic features of the Japanese justice system by buttressing with major reconstructions the main body that threatened to crumble under the growing social demands. This is why its final report contains far-reaching and wide-ranging reform proposals. At the centre of its agenda, in my view, is the plan to triple the number of new entrants to the bar within fifteen years, coupled with the introduction of the graduate school of law and concomitant reforms of the legal examination. But it contains many other important proposals. For example, concerning the judiciary, the Council did not endorse a wholesale shift to the 'unitary system' of recruiting judges, but proposed vigorously promoting the appointment of judges from among attorneys as well as from among other groups of lawyers, which would enhance the status of the bar. It also proposed establishing an independent committee to advise the Supreme Court on the nomination of candidates to be appointed judges as well as on their subsequent promotions. In addition, the JSRC proposed as a measure of broadening the popular basis of the judicial authority a new system of lay judges in which randomly selected members of the public sit on the bench together with professional judges to decide serious criminal cases.

3. Institutional Setting for the Reform

How could a reform plan of this magnitude be put in place? The process by which the legal mechanisms for achieving the justice system reform were set up can be summarized as follows.

In July 1999 the Justice System Reform Council was established directly in the cabinet led by the prime minister. Equipped with a special secretarial staff, the council was given exceptionally high status and authority. The thirteen members of the council included five academics representing two national universities and

[2] Shihō Seido Kaikaku Shingi-kai [The Justice System Reform Council] *Shihō Seido Kaikaku Shingi-kai Ikensho* [Opinion or the Final Report of the JRC] 2001 (an English translation of this document is available under <http://www.moj.go.jp> (11 June 2005).

three private universities. It was presided over by an eminent constitutional law professor, and had only three members appointed from the legal profession, with only one representing the bar. The other five members representing the general public were drawn from associations of business, labour, and housewives. Two years later, in June 2001, the council duly submitted its final opinion, a bulky booklet, to the prime minister, thus formally launching the long and elaborate processes of the justice system reform. The government promptly reacted by legislating the basic legal basis for the reform (Law for Promotion of Justice System Reform of December 2001), and by setting up the Headquarters for Promotion of Justice System Reform in the cabinet, under which more than ten study groups were formed to discuss and propose concrete measures to realize the reform plans in so many sub-areas. Both the Supreme Court and the Japan Federation of Lawyer's Associations issued outlines of their own reform plans following the reform guidelines set by the legislation.

III. Behind the Scene

Now the stage is set for us to go into more informal aspects of the initial phase of the reform, the actual processes that went on behind the scenes. For this fascinating excursion, I am entirely indebted to the admirably candid report made public by the former *kanbo-fukuchōkan* (deputy chief cabinet secretary), Mr Teijiro Furukawa,[3] now retired, who was in office at the time when the whole of the above processes were played out. He himself was a career bureaucrat and his last position was the very top of the entire state bureaucracy, for the cabinet is at the top of the administrative structure headed by the prime minister, having all the ministries under its aegis. (Incidentally, the chief cabinet secretary is a post for a politician.) During his eight years in this office, Mr. Furukawa served four or five consecutive prime ministers. His report made it possible for me to try to reconstruct the wiring diagram hidden beneath the surface of the formal processes just described.

The first move was made in the early summer of 1998 by the undersecretary of the justice ministry. Originally a prosecutor, he was a member of the legal profession and had been posted in the justice ministry for many years. This person, together with a practicing attorney, appeared before the deputy chief cabinet secretary. The undersecretary confided to the latter with a facial expression of dismay that a justice system reform was necessary, but was beyond the capacities of the justice ministry alone, insinuating that some form of engagement on the part of the cabinet might be helpful. The deputy chief responded on the

[3] T Furukawa *Shihō seido kaikaku ni tsuite* [On the Justice System Reform]; *Shihō kaikaku chōsashitsu-hō* [edited and published by The Judicial Reform Research Room of The Japan Federation of Attorneys] no 3 (2004) 2-24.

spot with a suggestion of setting up in the cabinet itself a consultative meeting of the persons of knowledge and experience in the matter. He added: 'Let us make it an all-Japan affair.' For him this was an inevitable course of action because the matter in question concerned the jurisdictions of not just one ministry, but of many other ministries as well. (For example, setting up a totally new institution of a law school is a matter that comes under the jurisdiction of the education ministry, to say nothing of the necessity of cooperation of the finance ministry for financing such a large-scale institutional change.) On top of that, however, he had his own personal conviction that major reforms along the lines described above were indeed necessary. For the undersecretary of the justice ministry, this quick response was a pleasing surprise. 'Would you do this?', was his first reaction.

Somewhat later on the very same day, the deputy chief received a phone call from an LDP politician who was in charge of the party's Special Research Committee on the Judicial System, and who would himself be appointed justice minister two years later. Over the phone, the LDP committee chairman first asked the deputy chief about the news that the cabinet would be taking up the matter. Having received confirmation, he expressed gratitude in authentic sounding words to the deputy chief.

The Justice System Reform Committee was prepared and created in this way in close cooperation between the cabinet and the representatives of the justice ministry as well as the other ministries concerned. It was the deputy chief himself who persuaded the Kyoto University professor to accept an appointment to the chair of the JSRC. Subsequently, the deputy chief was present, together with the justice minister, at most, if not all, of the 43 council meetings. When the council issued its final opinion in June 2001 and was abolished with its mission completed, the Headquarters for the Promotion of the Justice System was set up immediately to implement the council recommendations. A governmental statement was issued on the cabinet's decision, declaring that the government would take the responsibilities of implementing the justice system reform on its own shoulders. Further, a senior advisory meeting representing the original positions of JSRC was established to look over the implementing processes. The deputy chief was involved in all these processes, even though he or the cabinet did not make any specific proposal concerning the content or outcome of the discussions of the JSRC. He was convinced that the reform was a great matter of national interest, but he did not go beyond preparing the political channels for it to be realized.

IV. Analysis: The Role of Bureaucracy in Deregulation

Thus, a most crucial step toward realization of the deregulating reform of the Japanese government and bureaucracy was taken by the person who was sitting at the top of the entire national bureaucracy. This seems to present a little paradoxical picture of the working of government structure in a parliamentary democracy.

For an observer like me who resides inside the political system in question, this is not exactly a familiar pattern, but certainly a readily understandable one. However, I am not sure if this represents a uniquely Japanese phenomenon or if under similar conditions similar responses will be found in other polities as well. Therefore, it may be worthwhile to attempt to depict certain elements that made up the process in this particular case.

The Role of Bureaucracy in JSR

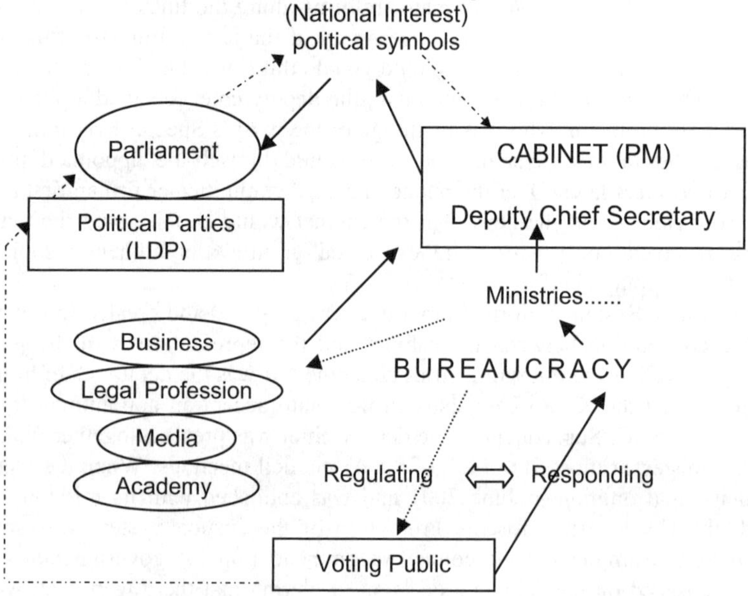

Figure 2 summarizes the analysis, depicting the major players in this political arena. The dotted arrows indicate the direction of political signals or influences assumed in a conventional concept of 'regulation'. The arrows originating in the wishes and preferences of the voting public are transmitted through political parties to parliament; the resulting legislation then forms the basis for the regulating activities of ministerial bureaucracies directed toward the individuals and organizations in society. In contrast, the case we have seen suggests a flow of (solid) arrows going in opposite directions. Let us follow the counter-clockwise movement of those solid arrows starting from the voting public.

1) In our present case, the will of the people, where the ultimate legitimacy of political decisions resides, cannot be appealed to directly by political parties because the issue of justice system reform is too remote for the voters. No vote or parliamentary seat is at stake on this issue from the point of view of the ordinary politicians. Certainly it is important for citizens to have a good judicial system and a good supply of legal services, for legal issues and problems constitute

important affairs for citizens once those occur in their lives. However, from the point of view of ordinary citizens, legal problems occur only occasionally, probably to only a small minority of citizens and then only once in their lifetime. Therefore, even if the issue of the justice system were put on the election campaign, most ordinary voters would have virtually no experience on which to base their political choice in voting, even though their long-term interests in aggregate are clearly involved. Only a few enlightened people would respond to such an issue.

2) On the other hand, in the eyes of an enlightened statesman or a bureaucrat, the issue clearly carries important national interest. The welfare of individual citizens is at stake, and therefore the catchword 'widening of access to justice' became the word of the day and circulated as a valid currency bearing the stamp of political legitimacy. There is also clearly a national interest component that directly affects the interests of the business community. The business community ordinarily has in its command a strong means of realizing its own will in the political arena. But in our present case, it turned out that the political channels they could rely on were not effective. Even the politicians of the dominant political party (LDP) were finding it difficult to persuade the party's policy-forming centre to go along with the reform plans.

3) Undoubtedly, the difficult nature of this issue lay to a large extent in the fact that the reform plans directly affected powerful vested interests, namely that of the legal profession and especially of the bar, which has consistently and successfully resisted any attempt at a radical increase in the number of its new recruits. Therefore, a device was needed to overcome the traditional 'consensus method', which had been employed for a long time and which had even been enshrined in a formal decision attached to one of the past pieces of judicial reform legislation. The consensus method meant that all the parties whose interests were directly affected by a legislative reform proposal, ie the three branches of the legal profession, were not merely to be consulted but also to consent. It was necessary to break up this path, and that formidable task was cleverly lapped up in the deputy chief's 'all-Japan' approach. This all-Japan approach was reflected in the composition of the JSRC that was subsequently set up, as mentioned above.

4) In this situation, it was the bureaucracy that played a decisive role, not the political parties or any citizen movement. It was necessary to rely on the initiative and political ingenuity of the public-minded top official, who could act as a self-appointed, well-meaning champion of the national interest, to persuade various ministries and to work out an effective mechanism to pave the way for its realization. The bureaucrats who were involved in setting up the platform for the reform with the cooperation of the academics were acting on behalf of the people's will that was not voiced at all, even though it was clear for many what their voice ought to say.

The Transatlantic Financial Markets Regulatory Dialogue

HANS-JÜRGEN HELLWIG

Until rather recently, only a few insiders knew of the Transatlantic Financial Markets Regulatory Dialogue and what it is about. This dialogue became more widely known only when Alexander Schaub, Director General, DG Internal Market of the European Commission, testified on 13 May 2004 before the Committee on Financial Services of the US House of Representatives.[1] Two days later I invited Alexander Schaub to address the Plenary Session of the Council of the Bars and Law Societies of the European Union (CCBE) on the very same topic.[2] In the following I shall give a brief overview of what the Transatlantic Financial Markets Regulatory Dialogue is and how it works. In doing so I will also rely on various personal discussions that I was fortunate to have with both Alexander Schaub and Commissioner Frits Bolkestein, who has been responsible for this dialogue within the EU Commission. In addition I am indebted to Meyer Eisenberg, Deputy General Counsel of the US Securities and Exchange Commission. My discussions with him and his colleagues in the SEC have shown that the US partners in the dialogue have the same perception as the European participants.

I. The Problem of Extraterritorial Regulatory Spillover Effects

We are all familiar with the fact that in particular in trade, commerce, and all the other areas of business, national laws quite often produce extraterritorial regulatory effects. The importance of this phenomenon is continuously increasing, due

[1] <http://europa.eu.int/comm/internal_market/finances/docs/general/2004-05-13-testimony_en.pdf> (6 May 2005).

[2] Unpublished.

to the ongoing globalisation of almost all business activities. The tools to deal with these extraterritorial effects that have been in use so far have turned out to be inadequate. The possibilities of litigation are limited. While the International Court of Justice at The Hague/Netherlands is of hardly any relevance in this context, the World Trade Organisation (WTO) in Geneva does have the authority to decide regulatory conflicts;[3] however, its jurisdiction is limited to trade matters only. In any case, litigation has one considerable drawback: It comes too late, namely after the regulatory effect in question has come into being. Another possibility for dealing with extraterritorial regulatory effects is by treaty between the nations concerned. Yet this possibility as well can bring remedy only after the event. Apart from that, a treaty with all its formalities is time consuming and usually is practicable only if there are extraterritorial effects on both sides. What is really needed is a process that, if ever possible, comes before the extraterritorial effects commence, and that in any case is informal and flexible.

II. The Genesis of the Dialogue: The US Sarbanes-Oxley Act

The reaction of the US legislature to Enron, Andersen, and the many other scandals in the US financial markets was the Sarbanes-Oxley Act of 2002[4], the extraterritorial effects of which are widely known. The scope of territorial applicability is not specified in a general provision of the Act but rather depends on the nature and addressees of the individual sections. Most provisions address issuers,[5] a term that includes in particular all US or foreign companies listed on a US Stock Exchange. Many provisions of the Act have extraterritorial effects, eg the provisions on the audit committee or the independence of directors, and in particular the provisions on auditors which provide for mandatory registration with the new Public Company Accounting Oversight Board (PCAOB)[6] and also for far-reaching restrictions on non-audit services.[7] These extraterritorial effects were already severely criticised during the legislative process (January to July 2002) by various European parties, in particular the EU Commission. Commissioner Bolkestein made his views known in many personal meetings as well as in public speeches

[3] The Helms-Burton Act of 1996 and the Iran-Libya Sanctions Act of 1996 are two examples where the EU Commission sued the US before the WTO for (intentional) extraterritorial effects. This litigation apparently was so embarrassing to the US that in a memorandum of understanding of 11 May 1998 they agreed not to apply both Acts to EU companies and individuals, provided the EU Commission would suspend the litigation. It took several years of difficult negotiations before this extraterritorial conflict was finally resolved.

[4] See annex 3 in this volume.

[5] Sarbanes-Oxley Act s 2(7).

[6] Sarbanes-Oxley Act s 102.

[7] Sarbanes-Oxley Act s 201.

and interviews in the US Some voices in Europe totally denied the right of the US to give its legislation extraterritorial effect, and went so far as to speak of 'regulatory imperialism'. The EU Commission took a different position, remembering that in cases like Boeing/McDonnall Douglas and General Electric/Honeywell it had itself claimed extraterritorial application of the EU merger regulation, provided that a foreign merger would have effects in Europe. The Commission therefore argued that the extraterritorial effects of the various provisions of the proposed Act were unnecessary and not proportionate in view of the state of regulation in Europe. However, the Commission soon realised that this argument was not convincing enough to prevent the extraterritorial effects of the forthcoming US legislation.

Starting from there, the Commission was concerned that European companies that need the US financial markets for financing would come under total US regulation. Such a regulatory dependence could be avoided only by entering into a dialogue with the US The individual member states of the EU would not be powerful enough for such a dialogue, and even the EU Commission would have sufficient power only if it could truly speak from a pan-European financial markets position. This means that the EU Financial Services Action Plan of 1999 (as well as the EU Company Law Action Plan of 2003 which covers the area of corporate governance, among others) are gaining an additional dimension: At stake is not only the European single financial market but also whether the EU Commission is a sufficiently powerful partner in the dialogue with the US There might, however, be areas where it would not be sufficient that the EU Commission is speaking on behalf of a single EU financial market, but where in addition it is required that the level of regulation in Europe is about comparable to the level of regulation in the US In other words, there might be a need for Europe to deploy new 'regulatory arms' in order to get to a 'regulatory armament level' comparable to the US, ie to introduce in Europe new regulatory provisions with extraterritorial effects into the US Thereafter a mutual 'regulatory disarmament' might be possible by both sides taking back their extraterritorial effects. In a nutshell, this is the core concept of the Transatlantic Financial Markets Regulatory Dialogue.

III. The Dialogue and How It Works

Many provisions with extraterritorial effects of the Sarbanes-Oxley Act, which was signed into law by President Bush on 30 July 2002, call for further implementation by the US Securities and Exchange Commission (SEC) and the new US Public Company Accounting Oversight Board (PCAOB). On the other hand, the EU Commission and the European member states were also proposing legislative and regulatory measures to deal with the various problems that had come to light through the various scandals in the financial markets first in the US and then in Europe. As a result, regulatory measures were underway on both sides of the

Atlantic. It is before this background that the EU/US Financial Markets Regulatory Dialogue has taken place ever since summer 2002, involving the EU Commission on the one hand and the US Treasury Department, the US Federal Reserve Board, and the SEC on the other hand. The EU member states participate in this dialogue not directly but indirectly, namely through the parallel dialogue between the EU Commission and the national regulatory and supervisory authorities in charge of the financial markets of the 25 EU member states.

The Transatlantic Dialogue does not have precisely defined goals. The true purpose is the dialogue, not the result. If goals are set by the participants, they are very general in nature.

The decision about whether a particular topic is agreed to be discussed in the dialogue is based solely on the merits of the issue, without any regard to systematics of regulation. This conclusion at first sight appears surprising, given the many systematic differences that exist between the two sides of the Atlantic and within Europe; however, it is being confirmed by participants from both sides in the dialogue.

The dialogue includes discussion of how the dialogue can be improved. This has led to the fact that certain dialogue topics are dealt with by specialised bodies at a lower level, on the European side in particular by the International Accounting Standards Board (IASB) and on the American side by the Financial Accounting Standards Board (FASB) and the PCAOB.

There is an annual 'summit' at which both sides agree upon which topics are to be discussed in the forthcoming year and how they shall be handled procedurally. The last such summit between the EU Commission, US Treasury, US Federal Reserve Board, and US SEC took place in June 2004. The following is an excerpt from the press communiqué[8] issued thereafter:

> The US-EU Financial Markets Regulatory Dialogue is entering its third year with a demonstrated record of contributing to improved understanding and resolution of complex financial and regulatory issues on both sides of the Atlantic.
>
> – The European Union has moved rapidly forward with its Financial Services Action Plan, aimed at achieving a uniform legal framework for an integrated EU-wide capital market. It has also proposed legislation introducing important corporate governance, company law, accounting and audit reforms. The United States strongly welcomes the FSAP and recent reforms intended to create an integrated European capital market.
> – The United States is moving forward with essential measures to strengthen investor confidence, pursuant to the President's 10-point plan and the Sarbanes-Oxley legislation. The EU agrees with the underlying objectives of these US efforts, many of which are reflected in current EU legislation.
>
> The United States and the European Union have different legal, cultural and historical traditions in the financial sphere. Thus, actions by each can have unintended spillover

[8] <http://europa.eu.int/comm/internal_market/finances/docs/general/eu-us-dialogue-report_en.pdf> (6 May 2005).

effect for the other. The Dialogue is an important component in the effective management of these spillover effects.

- European concerns over the Sarbanes-Oxley legislation have been taken into account through strong engagement, while the letter and spirit of the law have been fully met.
- US concerns that European legislation might not allow for full US participation in European capital markets are being substantially addressed.

The United States and the EU will intensify their cooperation through the Dialogue and have agreed procedural steps to be taken over the coming year to take this forward. Together, both sides will encourage work; maintain the highest standards of investor protection; promote international convergence of accounting standards, including their consistent application, implementation and enforcement; strengthen corporate governance on each side of the Atlantic; and lower transaction costs of cross-border business. In doing so, participants in the Dialogue intend to consult with and encourage more input from the private and academic sectors.

The dialogue has four structural elements as follows:

1. Mutual Understanding of Existing Regulation

The dialogue can function only if both sides have an optimal understanding of each other's regulations, including both general purpose and approach as well as detailed provisions of regulation. This process of mutual understanding includes comparing each other's regulation, with the question in mind of whether regulatory differences are needed and how they could be reduced or removed.

2. Information and Transparency of New Regulations

Proper information and transparency is given whenever new regulatory provisions, and in particular new regulatory goals and approaches, are to be introduced by either side. This includes new regulatory measures by lower-level authorities or bodies or by member states. In that regard, each side in the dialogue must ensure that it is internally properly informed of such developments so that it can perform its function as an information and transparency link. When I discussed with SEC staff members the regulatory proposals made in Europe by the EU Commission and the various member states, I was impressed to see how well this element of information and transparency of new regulations works in practice.

3. Convergence of Regulations

The two dialogue elements mentioned so far eliminate regulatory surprises; however, they do not prevent extraterritorial effects, since those are a problem of regulatory content. The third dialogue element therefore consists of both sides aiming for some degree of convergence of new regulations, regarding both goals and approaches. This is made possible by the first two elements, namely mutual understanding of existing regulations and information and transparency of new regulations.

4. Equivalence of Regulations

The aim of convergence does not mean identity in all details. Such an aim would be neither realistic nor necessary. The ultimate purpose of the dialogue is to avoid or to eliminate unnecessary extraterritorial effects of regulation (so-called spill-over effects). To that end, functional equivalence is sufficient. Equivalence in systematic approach or in provisions of detail is not required.

It is interesting to note that this concept of functional equivalence is the same as the principle pursued today in the harmonisation of national laws of EU member states. At the beginning, the European Community aimed at more or less full harmonisation, ie identity of national norms. This aim has long been given up because it has been realised that full harmonisation is neither politically achievable nor necessary, and that it is sufficient if national laws in Europe converge to each other to the point of functional equivalence. I was impressed to see that SEC staff members in their discussions with me drew a parallel between the element of functional equivalence in the Transatlantic Dialogue and the aim of functional equivalence in the harmonisation of national laws in Europe.

The element of equivalence applies not only to the content but also to the enforcement of regulation. The enforcement aspect is of particular importance to the US participants. They have made it known that they are prepared to accept the EU Commission as a dialogue partner for Europe only if the authority of the Commission is not limited to the content of regulation; instead, the Commission, in the absence of a European-level oversight system, has sufficient authority vis-à-vis the supervisory and enforcement authorities of the EU member states.

IV. Concrete Examples of Topics in the Regulatory Dialogue

1. SEC Standards of Professional Conduct of Attorneys

After the sharp criticism from Europe that the legislative process for the Sarbanes-Oxley Act did not give due regard to foreign issuers, auditors, etc, the SEC took great pains to include foreign lawyers when drafting the 'Implementation of Standards of Professional Conduct for Attorneys' that was required by Section 307 Sarbanes-Oxley Act to be issued by 26 January 2003. In early November 2002, when the detailed drafting had not yet been completed, the SEC published some points of substance of the contemplated rule, according to which any (US or foreign) attorney 'appearing and practising before the Commission' – a term that was given a very broad definition – would be under an obligation for internal reporting 'up the ladder' in case of certain violations by the client company; if there was no appropriate response to such reporting, the attorney had an obligation for external reporting to the SEC ('noisy withdrawal'). Shortly thereafter an emissary of the SEC discussed the contemplated rule with the EU Commission and with the CCBE, and on 17 December 2002 the SEC organised a round table with representatives of international and foreign bar associations and law firms to discuss the text of the draft rule that had been published on 21 November 2002. Many of the observations so received were taken up in the final rule adopted by the SEC at the end of January 2003. Most foreign lawyers are now exempted from the rule because they fall under the newly created definition of 'non-appearing foreign attorney'. The circumstances triggering the reporting obligation have been made more objective. Attorneys practising outside the US are not required to comply with the rule to the extent that such compliance is prohibited by applicable foreign law. The obligation for noisy withdrawal that had been objected to by both foreign and US lawyers and bar associations was not put into effect; instead, the rule provides that in case the internal reporting up the ladder finds no adequate reaction, the lawyer is obliged to withdraw from the matter, and it is the company (and not the lawyer) that is obliged to notify such withdrawal to the SEC ('silent withdrawal').

Thus, the first two elements of the Transatlantic Dialogue (mutual understanding and information/transparency) were effectively implemented when the SEC 'Standards of Professional Conduct of Attorneys' was adopted. Elements 3 and 4 (convergence and equivalence) were not applicable because in Europe comparable regulatory provisions are neither in existence nor intended. Therefore, the SEC has unilaterally eliminated those extraterritorial effects that were unacceptable to the European side. This concession, as has been confirmed by SEC staff members, was largely due to the written comments of the EU Commission on the proposed rule.

2. Auditors' Independence

The development was quite different in the area of auditors' independence. Section 102 Sarbanes-Oxley Act, as already mentioned, requires auditors to register with the PCAOB, and Sections 201 ff contain detailed provisions for the protection of auditors' independence (far-reaching restrictions on non-audit services, audit partner rotation, auditor reports to audit committees, and a cooling-off period of one year if an issuer company wants to employ an employee of an audit firm who has participated in the audit of the issuer company for defined leading positions). These provisions were refined and supplemented by the SEC rule 'Strengthening the Commission's Requirements regarding Auditors' Independence' of 18 March 2003. The new rule is applicable also to foreign auditors. This extraterritorial effect was already provided for in the draft rule of early December 2002. This draft, of course, met with sharp criticism from Europe, in particular from the EU Commission and the auditing profession. However, for those following developments closely, the draft rule of early December 2002 had made it sufficiently clear that the SEC was unimpressed by the criticism from Europe regarding sections 201 ff Sarbanes-Oxley Act that had commenced during the legislative process beginning January 2002 and had continued ever thereafter. The SEC was not prepared to mitigate the extraterritorial effects of auditors' regulations by and on the basis of the Sarbanes-Oxley Act. The development in Europe must be seen before that background.

On 16 March 2004, ie two days before the SEC Auditors' Independence Rule, the EU Commission published a proposal for an EU Directive on Auditors, the main content of which may in brief be summarised as follows.

Article 21 on professional ethics addresses the overall responsibility of auditors to the public, their integrity and objectivity, and their professional competence and due care. Article 22 covers confidentiality and professional secrecy which, however, shall not impede enforcement of accounting standards by national authorities or the exchange of information with authorities of other member states.

Article 23 calls for independence and objectivity of the auditor, who shall not in any way be involved in management decisions of the audited entity and who shall not carry out a statutory audit if there is any financial, business, employment, or other relationship, including the provision of additional services, with the audited entity that might compromise independence. Thus, Article 23 is a provision of principle, whereas sections 201 ff Sarbanes-Oxley Act and the SEC Auditors' Independence Rule contain very detailed provisions. Article 23 of the proposed Directive leaves the drafting of details to the EU member states.

The principles of public oversight are dealt with in Article 31, and Article 32 deals with the cooperation between the national public oversight systems at the Community level. Enforcement remains a domain of the member states and their oversight systems; however, Article 32 provides for the above-mentioned minimum authority of the EU Commission in this area as required from the US perspective for purposes of functional equivalence.

Articles 15 ff, according to which auditors must register at the EU member state level, according to Article 45 is applicable also to auditors from third countries if they audit accounts of foreign issuers whose securities are admitted to trading on a regulated market of an EU member state. Such foreign auditors are further subject to the system of oversight, the quality assurance system, and the systems of investigations and sanctions of such EU member state. Thus, in a nutshell, US (and other foreign) auditors are subject to European registration and to European regulation, as is the case in the US for European (and other foreign) auditors under the Sarbanes-Oxley Act and the SEC Auditors' Independence Rule. This is exactly what Commissioner Bolkestein, in public speeches in Europe and in private meetings in the US, had said the Commission would do if the SEC were to insist on the extraterritorial effect of the forthcoming Auditors' Independence Rule.

Of particular interest in the context of the Transatlantic Dialogue is Article 46 of the proposed EU Directive, according to which member states may decide not to apply to foreign auditors the requirement of European registration and European regulation as provided for in Article 45, if the foreign auditor is subject to systems of public oversight, quality assurance, and investigations and sanctions in the country of origin that meet requirements equivalent to those provided for in the Directive. This equivalence shall be assessed by the Commission in cooperation with the member states and shall be decided upon by the Commission with the assistance of an Audit Regulatory Committee composed of representatives of the member states and chaired by a representative of the Commission. Thus, there is the possibility for the Commission to make a decision to the effect that the relevant regulations in force on both sides of the Atlantic are equivalent to one another, with the consequence that US auditors can be exempted from European registration and regulation. The EU member state in question would grant such exemption only if European auditors are also exempted by the SEC from US registration and regulation: mutual exemption on the basis of mutual recognition of equivalence.

Article 47 permits the transfer of audit working papers and other auditing documents to the competent authorities of a third country if, among other considerations, such authorities meet requirements that have been declared adequate by the Commission. The assessment of adequacy shall be based on the requirements laid down in the Directive 'or essentially equivalent functional results' and shall be carried out with the assistance of the aforesaid Audit Regulatory Committee. Thus, the Directive speaks of functional equivalence not only with regard to the content of regulation but also with regard to the regulatory authorities. In both respects it is the decision-making power of the Commission which is assisted by the Audit Regulatory Committee in which the member states are represented, that, seen from the US side, ensures the necessary European-level powers in the content and enforcement of regulation.

The aforesaid brief summary shows that there are many regulatory parallels between the Sarbanes-Oxley Act and the Auditors' Independence Rule on the one hand and the proposed Directive on the other hand. These parallels are the result of almost one year of intensive discussion between the Commission and the SEC and the PCAOB. As already mentioned above, the Commission realised early on that the US side, given the present state of regulation in Europe, was not prepared to exempt European auditors from US registration and regulation. This left the Commission with one choice only, namely to bring the European level of regulation to a level that is functionally equivalent to the regulatory level in the US, both in regard to substance and enforcement of regulation. Of course, the US side had an advantage of time over the European side insofar as the Sarbanes-Oxley had been in effect since July 2002. On the other hand, the Commission and the member states in Europe had realised that after the many scandals in the US and in some European countries, there was a need for regulatory reform in Europe as well. In fact, the EU Commission had been at the problem of auditor regulation since 1996 when it published its Green Paper on 'The Role, Position and Liability of the Statutory Auditor in the EU', which was followed by the Recommendation of November 2000 on 'Quality Assurance for the Statutory Auditor in the EU' and by the Recommendation of May 2002 on 'Statutory Auditors' Independence in the EU'.

Thus, the proposed Directive in the area of regulation of auditors will mean the 'deployment of new arms' mentioned above. The next step to follow would be the regulatory 'disarmament', in the sense that the EU and the US, as partners in the regulatory dialogue, recognise the functional equivalence of each other's regulation, with the consequence that each side will not apply the extraterritorial effects of its regulation to auditors from the other side. In my discussions in Brussels and in Washington, I gained the impression that the Transatlantic Dialogue in the auditing area that has taken place so far pertained not only to the 'deployment of new arms' as provided for in the Directive proposal, but that the subsequent 'disarmament' by taking back extraterritorial effects on the basis of functional equivalence was also discussed and agreed upon in principle. There is some hint in this direction to be found in the explanatory memorandum accompanying the Directive proposal, where it is stated that 'the proposal also provides a basis for effective and balanced international regulatory cooperation with oversight bodies of third countries such as the US Public Company Accounting Oversight Board (PCAOB). This is crucial because capital markets today are globally interconnected.'

Once foreign auditors are exempted from the extraterritorial effects of regulation prevailing in the country of destination, they are subject only to regulation, in substance and in enforcement, of their country of origin. Here we have another interesting parallel to the EU single market, where ever since the European Court of Justice decision of 1979 in 'Cassis de Dijon', the country-of-origin principle has been introduced in the free movement of goods area and is now increasingly being introduced in the freedom of services area.[9]

3. Accounting Standards

The International Accounting Standards Board (IASB) and the US Financial Accounting Standards Board (FASB) were included early on in the Transatlantic Dialogue in order to deal with differences between US Generally Accepted Accounting Principles (US GAAP) and European International Accounting Standards (IAS).[10] IASB and FASB, based on a written memorandum of understanding, are now continuously working on converging the two sets of accounting

[9] cf EU Commission proposal of January 2004 on Services in the Internal Market, in particular art 16.

[10] Now referred to as International Financial Reporting Standards.

rules. The EU Commission has asked the Committee of the European Securities Regulators (CESR) to submit a report by 30 June 2005 on the issue of equivalence of accounting rules, not only in relation to the US but also in relation to Canada and Japan, whose accounting rules very much follow US GAAP. Foreign issuers listed in the EU are required by EU Directives to render their accounts based on IAS. This requirement has been criticised by the US, Canada, and Japan. The CSR report will have to deal with the question of which modifications of IAS are necessary in order to have equivalence with US GAAP, Canadian GAAP, and Japanese GAAP; on this basis, issuers from these countries listed in Europe could be exempted from the requirement of IAS-based accounting, while vice versa European companies listed in the US, Canada, or Japan could be exempted from the requirement of following local accounting rules, ie could be permitted to render their accounts based on IAS.[11]

Commissioner Bolkestein has long raised the question of whether the IASB with its present structure, and in particular with its present funding – voluntary contributions from contributors ranging from listed companies to accounting firms – is sufficiently independent. He specifically referred to the different funding system for the US FASB, under which part of the mandatory listing fee that all companies in the US have to pay goes towards funding the FASB.[12] It will be interesting to see whether the present funding system of the IASB and the conflict-of-interest potential following from it will become a topic in the Transatlantic Dialogue.

4. International Audit Standards

Commissioner Bolkestein again and again has publicly stated that the Commission considers international audit standards as important as international accounting standards. The proposed Auditors' Directive in Article 26 provides that the Commission, assisted by the Audit Regulatory Committee, shall adopt such international audit standards. This is another topic for the Transatlantic Dialogue. One of the questions in this context is to what extent the auditing profession shall be permitted to set international audit standards by self-regulation. The US PCAOB is a truly independent board and neither a governmental agency nor a self-regulatory institution. On the European side of the Atlantic, the structures presently differ from member state to member state. It is most likely that these

[11] cf <http://www.europa.eu.int/comm/internal_market/securities/cesr/index_en.htm> (6 May 2005).

[12] New Commissioner Charlie McCreevy is now firmly pushing this issue, due to the fact that the Commission in late 2004 strongly criticised the new standard on fair value reporting of financial instruments (IAS 39), which the Commission fears will lead to greater market volatility and instability. IAS 39 is now being redrafted.

structural issues will at some point in time also be discussed in the Transatlantic Dialogue.

5. Other Regulatory Topics

Basically all corporate governance activities of the EU Commission contemplated in the Company Law Action Plan of May 2003 have relevance for the Transatlantic Dialogue, eg in the area of disclosure of directors' remuneration, of board responsibilities, of improving financial and corporate governance information, of directors' independence, of shareholders' rights, etc. Additional topics are to be found in the Financial Markets Action Plan of the EU Commission. It is noteworthy that in the regulation of hedge funds the SEC is adopting European concepts, thus demonstrating that the Transatlantic Dialogue is not a one-way street.

V. Final Remarks

It is evident that it is the executive rather than the legislative branch of government that is conducting the dialogue on either side of the Atlantic, although some measures resulting from the dialogue require subsequent legislative action. It is therefore important to note that the European Parliament on the one hand and the US House of Representatives on the other hand, through their respective committees, are internally included in the Financial Markets Regulatory Dialogue.

The need for legislative action with regard to measures resulting from the dialogue is relatively small in the US, given the far-reaching law-making powers in particular of the SEC. There is greater need on the European side as is evidenced by the proposed Auditors' Directive. Of course, the European legislators can reject measures that have been proposed by the Commission and that reflect results achieved in the Transatlantic Dialogue. If this risk is for all practical purposes to be excluded, there needs to be at all times a close interface between the Commission and the European Council and European Parliament. It would not be harmful if in the legislative process, modifications were introduced to measures that were proposed by the Commission as a result of the Transatlantic Dialogue, provided that the functional equivalence is not impaired.

The Transatlantic Dialogue and its implementation present some interesting questions when viewed from the aspect of Montesquieu's traditional separation of functions doctrine. However, the real reason for these questions would not be the Transatlantic Dialogue as such but rather the speed of internationalisation and globalisation of all business activities, which is faster than the traditional legislative process. It is therefore probably correct to say that for practical purposes there is also a certain convergence of the processes of regulation.

Whether in a given area the level of regulation as a result of the dialogue goes up or down depends, among other aspects, on the balance of political and economic power. In any case, differences of regulatory levels will be reduced, and so will the anti-competitive effects resulting from them.

With regulatory differences being reduced or even removed, other aspects may be likely to gain in importance when it comes to the behaviour of companies competing internationally. Liberalisation under the old General Agreement on Trade and Tariffs (GATT) and under the present General Agreement on Trade in Services (GATS) has removed regulatory differences and has led to an increase in cross-border competition. This in turn, it is argued by some, has led to an increase in corruption, child labour, etc in certain countries, in particular developing countries. As many countries find it difficult to successfully deal with such practices of foreign companies, there is a growing need to regulate such practices at the country-of-origin level. Because many feel that governments react too slowly, non-governmental organisations (NGOs) are stepping in. Transparency International has concluded so-called 'integrity pacts' with about 100 companies operating internationally or globally.[13] 'Corporate social responsibility' is attracting more and more interest, to the point that codes of conduct have been drafted.[14] The four leading international coffee producers have signed a code of conduct in which they undertake to improve the working conditions of coffee farmers and to comply with environmental norms in developing countries.[15] Dow Jones, the world-wide index company, has created a 'sustainability index' in which companies will be included that play a leading role in ethics of management.[16] Given the fact that some large companies have more economic power than the countries in which they operate, the question is being raised in international public law whether human and fundamental rights obligations should be binding not only upon states but also (and directly) upon companies. The High Commissioner to the United Nations Commission on Human Rights is preparing a report on this issue, with the aim of introducing concrete and binding business conduct obligations for companies.[17] All of this shows that there is more and more focus on questions of the substance of business behaviour and competitive conduct. The major driving force behind this development are probably NGOs. The strength of NGOs, for example, is evidenced by the fact that the International Criminal Court in The Hague goes back to initiatives by NGOs with the United Nations.

The Transatlantic Financial Markets Regulatory Dialogue, just like any other regulatory dialogue, will lead to increased competition between companies. This

[13] Professor Dr Peter Eigen, Chairman, Transparency International, at the 21st Conference of International Law Association of 17 August 2004 in Berlin.

[14] cf CCBE 'Corporate Social Responsibility and the Role of the Legal Profession' <http://www.ccbe.org/doc/En/guidelines_csr_en.pdf> (6 May 2005).

[15] cf *Financial Times Deutschland* (Hamburg Germany 10 September 2004) 1.

[16] cf *Frankfurter Allgemeine Zeitung* (Frankfurt Germany 7 September 2004) 21.

[17] Office of the United Nations High Commissioner for Human Rights <http://www.ohchr.org/english/issues/globalization/business/reportbusiness.htm> (6 May 2005).

is a major purpose of such a dialogue, and this is first of all a positive effect. However, it should be realised that increased competition is not in all respects a value on its own, and there could be other consequences that one should not overlook, as the experience from GATT and GATS shows.

Part 4:

Markets – Creation, Risks, Safeguards

Market Discipline, Information Processing and Corporate Governance[*]

MARTIN F. HELLWIG

I. Rhetoric, Semantics, and Reality of 'Market Discipline'

This paper discusses the rhetoric, the semantics, and the reality of 'market discipline' in the 1990s. 'Market discipline' has been one of the miracle words of the last decade. In 1998, lack of market discipline was cited as a major source of the Korean crisis. Institutional changes designed to strengthen market forces and market discipline were a precondition of IMF help. Earlier in the 1990s, the resumption of capital flows to Mexico and other Latin American countries was said to be closely tied to the use of market-related financing instruments, direct investments, and portfolio investments, which were protected by 'market discipline' – unlike the bank loans of the 1970s which had to be repeatedly renegotiated in the international debt crisis of the 1980s. Questions about the effectiveness of 'market discipline' – say for the protection, following the Mexican Revolution of 1911, of direct investments and portfolio investments in the 1890s – were typically dismissed as politically incorrect.

The notion of 'market discipline' also figures prominently in discussions about bank failures and banking crises and about the prudential regulation and supervision of banks. Based on Calomiris and Kahn,[1] Calomiris has called for a system of banking regulation which exploits markets (in this case, markets for subordinated debt) and the discipline that they impose to provide regulators with

[*] I am grateful to Stefan Bechtold, Christoph Engel, and Isabel Schnabel for helpful comments and to the Deutsche Forschungsgemeinschaft for research support through Sonderforschungsbereich 504 and SonderforschungsbereichTransregio 15.

[1] CW Calomiris and CM Kahn 'The Role of Demandable Debt in Structuring Optimal Banking Arrangements' (1991) 81 American Economic Rev 497.

information about where to intervene and where not and to provide incentives for bankers to behave well.[2] The Calomiris position has not been adopted by the regulatory community, but even so, the Basel Committee on Banking Supervision lists market discipline as the 'third pillar' of risk control in banking, after capital requirements and the supervisory review process.[3] Behind these recommendations, we have the notion that the S&L crisis of the 1980s in the United States was due to a 'lack of market discipline' as deposit insurance eliminated all incentives for depositors to monitor the institutions where they were depositing their savings.

References to 'market discipline' should be seen as part of a wider debate on corporate finance and corporate governance. Elsewhere,[4] I have referred to this debate as the 'ongoing repertory play "banks versus markets"', with some scepticism as to whether this is really the right play to be performing. In previous times, performances of this repertory play enacted the myth that long-term implicit relations of nonfinancial institutions with banks were responsible for the perceived superiority of the German or the Japanese economy relative to the UK or the US economy because these long-term relations enabled the German or Japanese financial systems to mobilize funds for large-scale, long-term investments.[5] In contrast, more recent performances have stressed the ability of markets – in a suitable legal and political environment – to provide finance to people who are complete outsiders to the system, thereby preventing the kind of sclerosis that sets in when routes to the top of the social hierarchy are strictly controlled by those who already are at the top.[6] Given the downturn of Japanese banks since the early 1990s and the spectacular performance of worldwide stock markets in the second half of the 1990s, ascendance in these debates has moved from the 'pro-bank' to

[2] CW Calomiris 'Reducing Moral Hazard: Introducing Market Signals into Banking Supervision' Economic Perspectives (US Information Agency) 1998; CW Calomiris 'Market-Based Banking Supervision' (1999) 4 The Financial Regulator 33.

[3] Basel Committee on Banking Supervision *International Convergence of Capital Measurement and Capital Standards, A Revised Framework* (Bank for International Settlements Basel 2004).

[4] MF Hellwig 'On the Economics and Politics of Corporate Finance and Corporate Control' in X Vives (ed) *Corporate Governance* (Cambridge University Press Cambridge 2000) 95.

[5] A Gerschenkron *Economic Backwardness in Historical Perspective* (Harvard University Press Cambridge 1962); C Mayer 'New Issues in Corporate Finance' (1988) 32 Eur Economic Rev 1167; T Hoshi A Kashyap and D Scharfstein 'The Role of Banks in Reducing Financial Distress in Japan' (1990) 27 J of Financial Economics 67; T Hoshi A Kashyap and D Scharfstein 'Corporate Structure, Liquidity and Investment' (1991) 106 Q J of Economics 33.

[6] R La Porta and others 'Legal Determinants of External Finance' (1997) 52 J of Finance 1131; RG Rajan and L Zingales 'The Great Reversals: The Politics of Financial Development in the Twentieth Century' (2003) 69 J of Financial Economics 5; RG Rajan and L Zingales 'Banks and Markets: The Changing Character of European Finance' in V Gaspar P Hartmann and O Sleijpen (eds) *Second ECB Central Banking Conference: The Transformation of the European Financial System* (European Central Bank Frankfurt 2003) 124.

the 'pro-market' exponents. However, the analytical basis for either assessment is unclear.[7]

In this context, developments since 2000 should give us pause. Discoveries of fraud in companies such as Enron and WorldCom raise questions about the reality of 'market discipline'. Even where there was no wrongdoing, the ready availability of funds in the late 1990s to any company with a 'dotcom' in its name suggests that, at least at this time, markets did not impose much discipline. Cash was generously delivered and generously burnt. The subsequent burst of the bubble provides some indication of overvaluation. It also seems clear that there has been excessive real investment, eg in fibre glass transmission facilities in telecommunications. In current performances of the repertory play 'banks versus markets', these developments are sometimes treated as unfortunate accidents due to the misdeeds of particular persons, soon to be eliminated through the enactment of appropriate new rules.[8] I am not convinced of this assessment. One must be concerned about the possibility that the misreporting and fraud, the development of the bubble and its burst, as well as the long reluctance that the Unites States Administration and Congress have shown against corrective measures may be a reflection of systematic problems which must be encompassed by any serious debate on finance and governance.

Any assessment of 'market discipline' is impeded by the fact that the meaning of the term is unclear. Journalists nowadays use it with reference to day-to-day stock market valuations of firms and the interpretation of these valuations as a measure of corporate performance. However, for such market assessments to have a disciplinary effect, there must be a mechanism by which share prices feed into managerial incentives. In the 1980s, the literature on the market for corporate control suggested that the takeover mechanism fulfils this role (though day-to-day stock market valuations play hardly a role in that context).[9] The more recent literature on corporate governance[10] still lists the legal environment facilitating hostile takeovers as one of the preconditions for a well-functioning 'market-oriented' financial system, but given the developments of the 1990s, emphasis on the takeover mechanism has been replaced by considerations of explicit managerial incentives. Perhaps the role of 'shareholder value' rhetoric as a focus of boardroom conversation and boardroom rivalries should also be considered. How

[7] See eg the comments of F Allen 'Discussion of "Banks and Markets: The Changing Character of European Finance" by R. Rajan and L. Zingales' in Gaspar Hartmann and Sleijpen (n 6) 169; and MF Hellwig 'Discussion of "Banks and Markets: The Changing Character of European Finance" by R. Rajan and L. Zingales' ibid 173.

[8] Rajan and Zingales 'Banks and Markets' (n 6).

[9] Eg MC Jensen and RS Ruback 'The Market for Corporate Control: The Scientific Evidence' (1983) 11 J of Financial Economics 5.

[10] A Shleifer and R Vishny 'A Survey of Corporate Governance' (1997) 52 J of Finance 737; La Porta and others (n 6); R LaPorta and others 'Law and Finance' (1998) 106 J of Political Economy 1113.

else could one explain that 'shareholder value' standards have come into prominence even where shareholder powers were reduced or at least not increased?

In the context of banking and banking regulation, 'market discipline' is used in yet another sense. In Calomiris and Kahn[11] or Diamond and Rajan[12] – and in the various critical assessments of the S&L as well as other financial crises[13] – the banker is subjected to discipline by the requirement to repay deposits 'on demand'. The combination of the 'on demand' clause and the sequential-service provision in the demand deposit contract provides depositors with an incentive to monitor the banker. If they don't like what they see, they can ask for their money back, with some chance that if matters are really bad, they may be first in line at the bank. Here the disciplining mechanism is provided by an explicit contractual arrangement, though no market is involved. In Calomiris[14], in contrast, the proposal is for bankers to have relatively short-term subordinated debt outstanding, which is traded in organized markets, so the market price of this debt indicates the market's assessment of the bank's solvency. As for the question of discipline, the premium over the market rate of interest which the market requires in order to be willing to hold the bank's debt is supposed to serve as a signal for supervisory intervention. In extreme cases, the unwillingness of the market to roll over the bank's subordinated debt when it comes due would force the bank out of business, either because it fails to meet the regulatory requirement of x% subordinated debt or because the lack of the money itself creates an outright liquidity problem. In this proposal, there is an involvement of the market but, as in the corporate governance context, the disciplinary mechanism is not entirely clear. To a large extent, discipline is brought about by regulatory intervention on the basis of market signals rather than an intervention by market participants.

These observations suggest that perhaps the eminence of the term 'market discipline' is based less on the analytical rigour of the concept(s) than on the emotional appeal of any reference to the strength of 'markets'. The emotional appeal is particularly strong in the United States where 'the market' serves as a dream factory second only to Hollywood, and where financial institutions as well as the media that thrive on 'the market' seem to be in a position to determine the rules of public rhetoric.[15] Rhetorically, 'the market' tends to be identified with

[11] n 1.

[12] DW Diamond and RG Rajan 'Liquidity Risk, Liquidity Creation and Financial Fragility' (2001) 109 J of Political Economy 287.

[13] CW Calomiris and G Gorton 'The Origins of Banking Panics' in G Hubbard (ed) *Financial Markets and Financial Crises* (University of Chicago Press Chicago 1991) 109.

[14] Calomiris (n 2).

[15] One sometimes wonders to what extent the 'Washington consensus' by which such public discussion feeds into policy measures of the United States and of the International Monetary Fund may not be reflecting the particular interests of these institutions; see JE Stiglitz *Globalization and Its Discontents* (Norton New York 2002).

'the market system', which makes it difficult to express scepticism about the wonders that are to be expected from 'market discipline'. For economists, the difficulty is particularly great because the notion that markets function well is at the core of economic theory, and we all know about the wonders that can be expected if the law of demand and supply is allowed to work without extraneous intervention.

However, we should appreciate that discussions of 'market discipline' have little to do with 'the market system' or even the simple notion of a 'market' as it is analysed in economic theory. Economic theory looks at markets in the abstract, focussing on their implications for the allocation of resources, without saying anything – at least in general discussions – on the institutions that serve to implement these allocations. To the extent that we refer to this issue at all, we talk about a fictitious Walrasian auctioneer who sets prices so as to equate demands and supplies. We don't talk about this person's information, about his incentives, or even his wages – after all, he is just a fiction.

We do tell our students that, in real life, stock markets are the ones which most resemble the markets in our models, but we do *not* go on to make the policy recommendation that all markets should be organized like stock markets. When we see automobile markets characterized by close relations between producers and dealers, which enable consumers to identify a dealer with a certain brand, we do not complain about the lack of anonymity and the scope for corruption that are provided by such personalized car provision. Instead we see such vertical relations and the use of brand names as devices to handle moral hazard in relations between the producer and the distributor and to reduce the impact of information asymmetry about quality, solving problems which the Walrasian market model has not even addressed. Standard banking theory suggests a similar role for banks acting to facilitate economic transactions in the face of problems which in the theoretical models are hidden underneath the fictitious auctioneer.[16]

Thus, discussions of 'market discipline' should be freed from references – explicitly or emotionally – to 'the market system'. In all of the instances given, 'market discipline' is presented as a device to affect the behaviour of a corporate manager or a banker so as to reduce the agency costs associated with external financing of this person's operations. This has little to do with the law of demand and supply and a lot with the institutional framework which implements 'market allocations', presumably in a way which reduces the impact of moral hazard and asymmetric information to ensure that the provision of external finance is reasonably viable. In terms of the automobile example, this is like the question of what combination of brand reputation and warranty provision is appropriate or what exclusionary clauses should be stipulated in the dealership contract.

[16] MF Hellwig 'Banks, Markets, and the Allocation of Risks in an Economy' (1998) 154 J of Institutional and Theoretical Economics 328.

Given the need to descend from the lofty heights of economic systems rhetoric to the nitty-gritty of information and incentive problems, it is a bit disconcerting to see that the term 'market discipline' covers so many different examples. It is also disconcerting that the term is used in a wholesale fashion without much concern for what the alternatives are in any one instance. In the following, I will attempt to bring some structure into the discussion on both counts. I will begin with a discussion of what financial 'markets' actually do and in what sense one can speak of 'markets' as performing such functions differently from other institutions. In particular, I will discuss the specifics of information processing in different institutions and different governance structures. Finally, I will return to a discussion of 'market discipline' and corporate governance.

II. What Do Financial 'Markets' Do? What Do They Do Differently?

At a first glance, the answer to the question of what financial 'markets' do is rather obvious: They provide finance to households and firms that need extra funds, relying on the surpluses of other units of the economy. In so doing, they have an influence on what kinds of expenditures are undertaken, in particular what investment projects are selected, which in turn is a major determinant of the economy's return prospects and the economy's risks.

In cases where the investment horizons of final investors fall short of the length of life of an investment project, secondary financial 'markets' provide liquidity, enabling the initial investor to sell when he wants to even when the project is still going on. In such cases, the later returns of the investment project benefit the initial investor not because he is around to reap them, but because the prospect of these returns determines the price at which he can sell.

On a second look, however, one appreciates that the preceding account characterizes the functions of the financial system as whole rather than anything specific about financial 'markets'. In a standard account of a bank-dominated financial system, we see banks collecting funds from households and firms with surpluses and using these funds to provide finance to households and firms that need them, thereby affecting what investment projects are selected and what return prospects and risks the economy is facing. To the extent that these banks engage in maturity transformation, they also provide liquidity, eg as the 'on demand' clause enables each depositor to reap his returns whenever he wants to. At this superficial level then, there is no difference between the functions of a system of financial 'markets' and the functions of a banking system.

In terms of the mechanics of the system, two major differences between a system based on 'markets' and a system based on banks jump to the eye. First, on the financing side, 'market' finance involves multiple financiers and tends to be more anonymous, with less of an ongoing relationship and less scope for 'cronyism', than bank finance. Second, in terms of the relation between final users and final providers of funds, 'market' finance tends to involve more direct finance, ie claims that are issued by the final user of funds and that directly expose the final provider of funds to the specific risks associated with the final user. For 'market' finance, a paradigmatic example would be the issue of common stock of a firm to final investors; and for bank finance, the use of customer deposits to provide bank loans to a firm in the context of an exclusive 'main bank' relation.

However, there are many hybrids. Banks controlling access to the stock market in pre-1914 Germany and selling their customers the shares of firms with which they had a main bank relation would be an instance of banks using their dominance over the financial system to influence an operation that would ordinarily be associated with 'market' finance. The provision of bank loans to large corporations in Germany in the 1980s did not involve organized exchanges, yet was by all accounts characterized by an absence of relationship effects and a high degree of competitiveness.[17] (The same can be said about Switzerland during these years.) The existence of such hybrids indicates that one must go beyond a wholesale observation of whether or not a financing operation involves organized exchanges and whether or not final providers of funds are left to bear specific risks, and instead look at the details of the interactions between the different units that are involved: final users of funds, final providers of funds, and financial institutions from banks to stock brokers and analysts.

At this point, the discussion must turn to matters of information, incentives, and governance. As is well known, the financing relation is fraught with information and incentive problems because, in return for his money, the financier receives no more than a piece of paper with an I.O.U., the value of which is hard to assess and is indeed endogenous because it depends on the issuer's behaviour. If the issuer steals the money or mismanages it, the financier's claim is worth nothing; the same is true if the issuer is honest, but his undertaking is doomed to fail. For finance to be viable, the parties involved must find ways to reduce the impact of the information and incentive problems which thereby arise. The task is made difficult by the fact that the mere provision of external finance tends to generate moral hazard and adverse selection because (i) the mere existence of the financier's claim is likely to distort the issuer's incentives against all modes of behaviour that benefit the financier at a cost to himself, and (ii) the mere availability of finance is likely to attract 'entrepreneurs' who know that they don't have much of a chance but may as well try it anyway – at somebody else's expense.

To deal with these problems, financiers need information and control. Information should improve the selection of projects funded; it should also provide a base for monitoring whether the financing contract is being adhered to. Most importantly, information provides a base for using whatever scope for control the

[17] J Edwards and K Fischer *Banks, Finance, and Investment in Germany* (Cambridge University Press Cambridge 1994).

financier has been given. Control enables the financier to reduce moral hazard on the side of the borrower; however, control by the financier may be limited by the borrower's comparative advantage in running the venture and by the borrower's worry about moral hazard on the side of the financier using excessive powers to control as a tool to expropriate him.

The use of information and control to support a financing relation depends on the provisions of the contract(s) and on the incentives of the different parties as the contract is being carried out. Incentives of the different parties depend in important ways on how many financiers there are; this is one point where the difference between 'market' finance and bank finance matters. Two effects seem to be important. First, there is a public-goods effect by which the efforts of one financier at gathering information and exerting control over the management of the venture that is being funded benefit not just this financier, but all the other financiers as well. When there are multiple financiers, this public-goods effect gives rise to a free-rider problem because, at least in the absence of counteracting devices, each financier will tend to neglect the benefits that his effort brings for the other financiers. Relative to the efficient amount, there is then likely to be an undersupply of effort for information gathering and exertion of control. The free-rider problem is a major focus of discussion in the literature on corporate take-overs as an incentive mechanism supporting the viability of stock market finance.[18]

Second, the individual financier's effort at information gathering and exertion of control may exert negative externalities over the other financiers, serving redistributive rather than allocative purposes. This is the case, eg if the information collected by the bank depositor in a Calomiris-Kahn type of model and the liquidation induced by his withdrawal of funds have no effects on the total of funds available to depositors[19] and serve only to ensure that the informed depositor is the first to run so that he gets his money back and the others are left to see what assets of the bank are still there. A similar redistributive externality is at work in models of costly information collection for the purpose of speculation in organized markets. Thus, in the standard models of Grossman and Stiglitz[20] or

[18] HG Manne 'Mergers and the Market for Corporate Control' (1965) 73 J of Political Economy 110; SJ Grossman and OD Hart 'Takeover Bids, the Free-Rider Problem, and the Theory of the Corporation' (1980) 11 Bell J of Economics 42.

[19] Calomiris and Kahn (n 1) assume that the bank's liquidation through a run prevents worse and actually enhances the assets that are available to depositors. However, with multiple depositors, the incentive mechanism they describe does not depend on this assumption. Indeed, the redistributive externality described here has the interesting implication that the threat of premature liquidation under deposit finance may be credible and may therefore provide proper *ex ante* incentives even though *ex post* it is (collectively) inefficient to carry this threat out.

[20] SJ Grossman and JE Stiglitz 'On the Impossibility of Informationally Efficient Markets' (1980) 70 American Economic Rev 393.

Verrecchia[21], with exogenously given asset supplies and asset returns, the speculative use of information advantages comes at the expense of other market participants, in particular those who have 'real' reasons for wanting to trade and rely on secondary markets for liquidity. In the literature on market microstructure, this consideration provides one of the many arguments against the admission of insider trading.[22]

Whereas the free-rider problem suggests that a multiplicity of financiers gives rise to an underinvestment in effort for information gathering and control, the redistributive externality considered in the preceding paragraph suggests the opposite. To the extent that information and control yield individual benefits at the expense of other participants, and to the extent that effort choices neglect the negative externalities on other participants, private incentives for investing in effort for information gathering and the exertion of control will tend to be excessive.

Having both the free-rider problem as a reason for underinvestment and the redistributive externality as a reason for overinvestment in information and control, one is tempted to conclude that there must be some number of outside financiers for which the two effects cancel each other out so that one actually gets an efficient level of investment in information and control. Efficiency here would have to be understood in a suitable n^{th} best sense, as referring to that level of investment which is called for from an optimal incentive-contracting perspective *ex ante*. By this interpretation, the number of financiers would have to be determined as part of the overall contract *ex ante* with a view to its subsequent incentive implications.

The notion that the number of financiers should be determined *ex ante* with a view to its subsequent incentive implications is developed in Calomiris and Kahn.[23] However, they are less concerned with the redistributive externality[24] than with the possibility that the information collected by multiple financiers, each receiving an independent signal, may, on aggregate, be better than whatever information a single financier could obtain. The very same notion underlies the view that stock market finance involves many people collecting information, with information aggregation through market prices providing a better base for deci-

[21] RE Verrecchia 'Information Acquisition in a Noisy Rational Expectations Economy' (1982) 50 Econometrica 1415.

[22] See eg J Dennert 'Insider Trading' (1991) 44 Kyklos 181.

[23] n 1.

[24] Indeed, for the case of multiple depositors, the payoff matrix that they present is incomplete, which makes them miss the observation that the withdrawal game generated by their model exhibits the same multiplicity of equilibria, including 'sunspot' runs equilibria such as the Diamond-Dybvig liquidity provision model of deposit finance, cf DW Diamond and PH Dybvig 'Bank Runs, Deposit Insurance, and Liquidity' (1983) 91 J of Political Economy 401.

sion making than would be available to any one investor.[25] An example is provided by Allen[26], suggesting that stock prices based on aggregate information provide better guidance for the allocation of investment funds than would be available on the basis of individual information.

The view that there are benefits to having multiple sources of information stands in marked contrast to the alternative view that information generation involves scale economies in that the duplicate generation of the same piece of information is wasteful. The Calomiris-Kahn model of deposit finance of banks and the theory of information aggregation through asset prices, which underlies the assessment of Allen[27], are based on the assumption that additional pieces of information are not simply duplicating the first one, but are providing new signals in the sense that different information sources involve stochastically independent errors. We should recall, however, that the duplication-of-information view of multiple sources of information plays an important role in the theory of financial intermediation. Since Diamond[28], much of the literature on financial intermediation has associated banking with 'delegated monitoring' of loan clients, the idea being that it suffices for the monitoring costs to be spent once, by one monitoring agent, and that duplicate monitoring would involve costs without providing more information. Given this view of duplicate monitoring, much of the literature on financial intermediation has been concerned with the agency costs that arise when the task of monitoring loan clients is 'delegated' to an intermediary who collects funds from depositors and uses them to provide loans, with monitoring of loan clients. I will return to this question below, when I contrast the role of banks serving as financial intermediaries à la Diamond[29] and the role of stock market institutions (brokers, analysts, accountants, investment bankers) providing information to shareholders.

The number of external financiers for a given user of funds also affects the strategic interdependence between the contracting parties. One factor may simply be negotiation costs and transactions costs. When the number of financiers is

[25] On information aggregation through market prices, see SJ Grossman 'On the Efficiency of Competitive Stock Markets When Traders Have Diverse Information' (1976) 31 J of Finance 573; MF Hellwig 'On the Aggregation of Information in Competitive Markets' (1980) 22 J of Economic Theory 477; AS Kyle 'Informed Speculation with Imperfect Competition' (1989) 56 Rev of Economic Studies 317; on the usefulness of such information, see F Allen 'Stock Markets and Resource Allocation' in C Mayer and X Vives (eds) *Capital Markets and Financial Intermediation* (Cambridge University Press Cambridge 1993) 81; B Holmström and J Tirole 'Market Liquidity and Performance Monitoring' (1993) 101 J of Political Economy 678.

[26] n 25.

[27] ibid.

[28] D Diamond 'Financial Intermediation and Delegated Monitoring' (1984) 51 Rev of Economic Studies 193.

[29] ibid.

large, such costs may eliminate any scope for renegotiating the initial contract. Whereas in the international debt crisis of the 1980s the sovereign debts that had been incurred in the late 1970s were renegotiated throughout the 1980s with a consortium of a few hundred banks, in the international debt crisis of the 1930s the various sovereign bond issues of previous decades were not renegotiated and simply went into default.[30] From a theoretical perspective, inability to renegotiate has advantages and disadvantages. The advantage is that threats of bankruptcy are more credible – and can have beneficial incentive effects – because even renegotiation *ex post* is infeasible.[31] This is presumably a reason why adherents of 'market discipline' extol the toughness by which markets – or rather the financiers with market instruments – avoid being drawn into cosy renegotiations with errant debtors. However, the disadvantage is that, in the absence of subsequent renegotiations, it is impossible to adapt the contractual relation to changing circumstances, eg changes in international currency exchange rates, oil prices, and the like. Which of the two effects dominates depends on circumstances. However, it is interesting to note that the international loan renegotiations of the 1980s did end up providing the international banks with substantial returns.[32]

Given these abstract theoretical considerations, I return to the question of what it is that financial 'markets' do. The two simple characteristics that were mentioned above, namely a multiplicity of financiers and a prevalence of direct rather than intermediated finance, lend themselves to the view that market finance involves a regime where multiple investors fund a firm and collect information about a firm, with incentives for such information collection being provided by the fact that, through direct finance, they have a direct involvement. This view of market finance contrasts with a view of bank finance where a financial intermediary collects funds from final investors and, on his own account, invests these funds in various firms, each of which it monitors. The intermediary saves on information costs and is able to renegotiate contracts – indeed he is unable to commit not to renegotiate contracts.

These different views of market finance and bank finance involve different assumptions about information technologies. In one approach, it is advantageous to have multiple sources of information; in the other this would be wasteful. Given the differences in assumptions, it seem fatuitous to search for an unambiguous assessment as to which arrangement is likely to do better in the real

[30] On the distinction between the debt crises of the 1930s and the 1980s, see B Eichengreen and R Portes 'Debt and Default in the 1930's: Causes and Consequences' (1986) 30 Eur Economic Rev 599.

[31] In Diamond and Rajan (n 12) this is the advantage of having multiple depositors providing finance to a bank.

[32] On rates of return to international lending from the 1970s to the 1990s, see C Klingen B Weder and J Zettelmeyer 'How Private Creditors Fared in Emerging Debt Markets 1970-2000' International Monetary Fund Working Paper 04/13 (Washington 2004).

world. This must depend on circumstances favouring one set of conditions or the other.

III. Information Processing and 'Discipline' Under Market Finance

Leaving the general comparative discussion, I now turn to the details of information collection, information aggregation, and incentive provision under market finance. The notion that prices aggregate information has been formalized by Grossman.[33] In his analysis, there are *n* agents, each of whom receives a signal about a firm's returns. On the basis of his information, he buys or sells shares in the market. As the market price reflects the different traders' choices, so it will reflect their information, going up if on aggregate they want to acquire the stock and going down if on aggregate they want to divest it. In Grossman's model, remarkably, the price acts as a statistically efficient aggregator, ie once one knows the price, one knows as much about the stock return as if one knew the entire vector of individual signals.

This latter result is probably not more than a curiosum. Hellwig shows that statistical efficiency of the aggregation of information through prices disappears once there is some 'noise' in the market, ie a dependence of equilibrium prices on unknown variables other than the participants' information signals.[34] Moreover, endogenizing people's decisions to acquire information or not, Verrecchia[35], following Grossman and Stiglitz[36] for the case of homogeneous information, has shown that, if the cost of acquiring information is positive, then the statistical properties of equilibrium prices are bounded away from efficiency even if the level of 'noise' in the market is small. If there is little 'noise', there will just be very few people acquiring information, so that the effects of the information and of the 'noise' on the equilibrium price will still be commensurate with each other, and the 'noise' is strong enough to contaminate the statistical properties of the relation between prices and information. The resulting equilibrium prices provide a noisy signal of aggregate information. This signal is useful to every individual in the market, but does not supersede the information that any one individual has on his own. The equilibrium informativeness of asset prices will depend on private incentives for information acquisition; it becomes larger if the costs of information acquisition decrease, eg because of a government subsidy.

Suppose we append a real investment story to the Grossman-Hellwig-Verrecchia model. For instance, suppose that the equilibrium real investment of the firm in question is given by an increasing function of its share price. Such a

[33] Grossman (n 25).

[34] Hellwig (n 25).

[35] Verrecchia (n 21).

[36] Grossman and Stiglitz (n 20).

relation can easily be derived from a Tobin-q type of model based on the supply function of the investment goods industry. Then we find that positive information about the firm's prospects induces informed traders to buy the firm's shares; this generates a price increase. This price increase in turn motivates the firm to issue more shares and to buy additional investment goods. Alternatively, if information is negative, the firm is induced to reduce its real investment.

In this account, it is beneficial to have the information in question. By inducing the firm to have more real investment when the information about return prospects is good and the share price is high, and to have less real investment when the information about return prospects is bad, the system enables the economy to better adapt the allocation of scarce investment resources to the actual prospects that the different firms have. This enhances the efficiency of the use of these resources. Allen's view[37] of the benefits of stock market finance for resource allocation is based on essentially this story.

Within the model, information acquisition choices are not actually efficient. If the response of the firm's real investment to the stock price is highly elastic, information acquisition is inefficiently low, and a subsidy to information acquisition, financed by a lump sum tax, would raise aggregate surplus. There is a kind of free-rider problem in that each agent deciding upon the acquisition of information neglects the benefits he conveys to others when the impact of his portfolio choice on the stock price communicates some of his information to the rest of the economy, enabling them to adjust their portfolio positions as well and, most importantly, inducing the firm to adapt its real investment to the information.

In contrast, if the response of the firm's real investment to the stock price is highly inelastic, information acquisition is inefficiently high and a tax on information acquisition used to provide everybody with a lump sum subsidy would raise aggregate surplus. In this case, there is hardly any reaction of the firm's real investment to the information. There is, however, a redistributive effect by which 'liquidity traders', eg those people who want to liquidate stock for extraneous reasons that have nothing to do with the information, get less favourable terms from the market. The idea is that somebody has to make up for the costs of information acquisition of informed traders. 'Uninformed' conscious speculators will not do so because they appreciate the problem and can protect themselves, eg through the use of passive portfolio strategies. 'Liquidity traders' are the only alternative. They suffer the redistributive externality, which is at work when information acquisition takes place even though there is no or hardly any social benefit to be reaped from the information.

The proposition that information acquisition and the presence of people with private information harms those people who want to use the market for 'real' purposes is very robust to changes in the institutional setting. This proposition identifies a key problem in the analysis of market microstructure. For example, if

[37] Allen (n 25).

we consider a system based on market makers announcing buying and selling prices, the market makers must be afraid of being taken up by an informed trader who causes the market maker to sell when the information is good and to buy when the information is bad. To reduce the impact of this problem, the market makers have a spread between buying and selling prices. The spread is higher the more they are afraid of informed speculators; for infrequently traded stocks, eg in London, spreads on the order of 30% would not be unheard of. The spreads hurt liquidity traders, eg the person who wants to sell in order to buy a house. As a seller, the liquidity trader receives a lower price; as a buyer, he pays a higher price than would be the case if market makers were sure that he is not acting on private information.

Informed speculation is thus a major problem for the viability of secondary financial markets. In some of the literature on insider trading, this observation is used to argue the extreme proposition that any securities trade on the basis of private information should be banned as insider trading. This extreme position was the foundation for the US Supreme Court's position in the 1960s, for example, as well as the prosecution's stance (and some dissenting votes) in the cases of Chiarella and Dirks in the 1970s and 1980s. In these latter cases and others in the eighties, the US Supreme Court interpreted the bank on insider trading more narrowly, asking that there be some violation of fiduciary duty as well as a use and information advantage.[38] However, the notion of a ban on insider trading as a measure to protect market functioning (as opposed to protecting fiduciary relationships) is based on the harm done by informed speculation to liquidity traders as they try to rely on the market.

In the model sketched above, these considerations of the harm that informed trading does to the functioning of secondary markets must be balanced against the social benefits of having real investment depend on the information. As discussed above, the comparison depends on whether real investment depends strongly or not so strongly on the information. Only if real investment choices are strongly affected by the information contained in stock prices will the social benefits outweigh the costs of having the functioning of markets disturbed. The Allen view[39] that was reported above seems to presume that this is indeed the case.

Turning from the discussion of models to an assessment of such matters in reality, we need to ask how strongly the behaviour of the corporation depends on the price of its stock. In particular, how strong is the improvement-of-financing effect of the previous discussion in reality? What can be said about additional real effects of movements in stock prices?

Empirically, there is little doubt that asset prices do contain useful information. A particularly striking example is given by Roll's[40] analysis of the futures

[38] Dennert (n 22).

[39] Allen (n 25).

[40] R Roll 'Orange Juice and Weather' (1984) 74 American Economic Rev 861.

market for frozen-orange-concentrates. According to Roll's findings, the prices for these contracts incorporated all the information that was contained in the forecasts of the US weather service – and some additional information on top of that; the US weather service could have improved the quality of its forecasts if it had taken account of the information contained in those prices. Similarly, Flannery's[41] review of the empirical literature on information contained in bank share prices supports the policy recommendation that bank supervisors should try to exploit this information, using market assessments to shorten the lag before they intervene when an institution is in trouble.

Even so, I am highly sceptical about the practical relevance of the improvement-of-financing effect. The reason is not so much that some of the stock market finance we saw in the late 1990s was misdirected. Rather, I am not convinced that the financing role of stock markets is anywhere commensurate with the overall activity in stocks that we observe. My scepticism is based on the observation that in terms of net flows, in most economies, in terms of aggregates, equity finance through new stock issues plays a relatively minor role;[42] moreover, for most firms, equity finance through new stock issues tends to be a once-in-a-lifetime event.[43] When this event occurs it may be of crucial importance, but this is quite a different story.

Strategies of paying out cash that were pursued by American companies in the 1990s in the form of repurchasing equity and simultaneously issuing new shares may lend more weight to the improvement-of-financing effect. Here, however, I would like to have a more precise account of how the effect plays out in the context of such strategies.

Given this scepticism about the improvement-of-finance effect, I turn to incentive provision as the second main candidate for explaining social benefits of stock prices containing information. Here I see three possible channels: outright incentive schemes, takeover threats, and boardroom rivalry. Outright incentive schemes involve stocks, stock options, and other devices that make managerial pay depend directly on the stock price. Up to 1990, such schemes played a surprisingly small role;[44] since then they have become very prominent in some European countries as well as the United States. Incentive effects of takeover threats and boardroom rivalry depend on the possibility that a low share price may attract

[41] MJ Flannery 'Using Market Information in Prudential Bank Supervision: A Review of the U.S. Empirical Evidence' (1998) 30 J of Money, Credit and Banking 273.

[42] Mayer (n 5); A Hackethal and RH Schmidt 'Financing Patterns: Measurement Concepts and Empirical Results' Discussion Paper no 33, Working Paper Series Finance and Accounting (University of Frankfurt 1999).

[43] RG Rajan and L Zingales 'Financial Dependence and Growth' (1998) 88 American Economic Rev 559.

[44] MC Jensen and KJ Murphy 'Performance Pay and Top Management Incentives' (1990) 98 J of Political Economy 225.

a potential raider or motivate a boardroom rival to stage a palace revolution. Either possibility may provide strong incentives to managers to prevent the stock price from falling.

Behind the notion that market discipline has beneficial incentive effects, there is the idea that, in the absence of better information about managerial performance, reliance on the stock price can be useful because in any incentive problem it is always better to use additional information if one has it.[45] On the basis of this idea, Holmström and Tirole[46] have actually devised a model in which incentive schemes based on stock prices are useful – in spite of the existence of other sources of (partial) information about the company and in spite of the need to worry about speculators' incentives for information acquisition and the impact of informed speculation on the functioning of secondary markets.

However, there are two caveats. First, *optimal* incentive contracting conditions incentive pay on those aspects of stock price movements which fall under the control of the managers in question. To the extent that a firm's prospects are determined by overall macroeconomic conditions, and to the extent that the firm's share prices are driven by overall market movements which have nothing to do with managerial behaviour, there is no reason to have managerial pay depend on these price movements. Rewards that are paid when the overall market is going up have little to do with incentive provision. As discussed by Bebchuk and Fried[47], outright incentive schemes that were implemented in the 1990s did not make these distinctions and therefore had little to do with optimal incentive contracting.

Second, the theoretical models that have been studied have looked at effort as a single variable. In practice, managerial effort has many dimensions, eg effort to improve the firm's performance today and effort to improve the firm's prospects for the future. From the theory of multidimensional incentive provision,[48] we know that in such situations, one must worry about the distribution of effort across the different dimensions. In particular, there is a danger that strong incentives in one dimension may induce an undersupply of effort in another dimension. This danger is particularly strong if the results of taking effort in one dimension can be measured relatively precisely, and in the other dimension their measurement is subject to great uncertainty. In this case, the implementation of the opti-

[45] B Holmström 'Moral Hazard and Observability' (1979) 10 Bell J of Economics 74.

[46] Holmström and Tirole (n 25).

[47] L Bebchuk and J Fried *Pay without Performance: The Unfulfilled Promise of Executive Compensation* (Harvard University Press Cambridge 2004).

[48] Eg B Holmström and PR Milgrom 'Multitask Principal-Agent Analyses: Incentive Contracts, Asset Ownership, and Job Design' (1991) 7 J of L, Economics, and Organization suppl 24.

mal unidimensional incentive scheme for the first dimension leads to precisely the crowding out of effort in the second dimension that is to be feared.[49]

The stock price is a measure of the firm's overall return prospects, more precisely, of the risk-adjusted expected present value of returns. As such it depends on current returns as a signal of overall prospects as well as any additional information about what the firm's future prospects might be. In terms of the preceding discussion, one may therefore ask whether a stock price orientation of managerial incentives gives appropriate weight to different effort dimensions for performance today and for future prospects. If we think about cost cutting as a major element of managerial activity, we may ask whether outside investors would really be in a position to assess the relation between current cost savings and the associated diminution in output quantity or quality, especially if the latter concerns the future. Could it be that stock prices and shareholder value give too large a weight to the relatively hard information about current costs, relative to the relatively soft information about future prospects, thereby distorting incentives in the direction of excessive cost cutting? Discussions about stock-based incentive schemes as well as shareholder value have perhaps paid too little attention to the problem of effort allocation when effort is multidimensional.

To conclude this discussion of information acquisition, information processing, and 'market discipline', I note that none of the mechanisms effective today involves outright 'discipline' in the sense of market participants getting explicit powers to exert control. Incentive schemes are mutually agreed upon and, moreover, they have little to do with control. They are introduced by corporate boards, usually at the initiative of incumbent managers; this is reflected in the observation that many of these schemes appear more as mechanisms for enrichment than as optimal contracting devices.[50] Hostile takeovers have, by and large, ceased to be serious threats. The installation of anti-takeover defences in the years after 1989 has ensured that a takeover without managerial consent is hardly possible;[51] managerial consent therefore is usually bought by large severance payments.

Finally, shareholder value rhetoric as a focus of boardroom rivalry is a matter which can be abandoned without difficulty if boardroom fashions change once again. Its rise to prominence in the 1990s poses a paradox, for, interestingly, the very corporate executives who have extolled shareholder value since the early 1990s have also gone out of their way to reduce the scope for shareholder interference with their activities, introducing poison pill amendments into their corporate charters and the like.[52] The paradox is perhaps resolved by observing that the

[49] Holmström and Tirole (n 25).

[50] Bebchuk and Fried (n 47).

[51] M Useem *Executive Defense: Shareholder Power and Corporate Reorganization* (Harvard University Press Cambridge 1993).

[52] ibid.

rise of shareholder value rhetoric coincided with the increase in the use of stock-price-related pay. However, this explanation would be all the more reason for doubting the role of 'stock market discipline' as a mechanism for control.

To understand this point, it is useful to go back to the Calomiris-Kahn model of deposit finance. In that model, control is exerted by each depositor individually as he asks for his money back; if enough depositors do this, the borrower goes bankrupt and is taken out of the hands of incumbent management. In contrast, the mechanisms of 'market discipline' that are associated with stock price movements have no such immediate impact on the incumbent management's positioning of the firm. As discussed by Rochet and Vives,[53] the control mechanism associated with deposit may force inefficient liquidations. There seems to be a trade-off between the power of the disciplinary mechanism to really impose discipline and the efficiency of the ensuing resource allocation. The trade-off has to do with the greater subtlety of information aggregation through prices rather than the demand deposit mechanism. The former provides more precise information without prejudging the ensuing allocation. The latter prejudges the ensuing allocation in that it imposes bankruptcy whenever a sufficient number of depositors want their money back. The relation between information aggregation mechanisms on the one hand and disciplinary intervention modes on the other hand would seem to be an important matter for future research.

IV. Market Discipline and Corporate Governance in the 1990s

The 1990s, and especially the second half of the 1990s, saw a remarkable shift towards market finance. Most prominent was of course the burst in outright equity finance that was supported by and in turn supported the stock market boom. Whereas the economic expansion of the mid-to-late 1980s had largely been funded by debt instruments, bonds in the United States, and bank loans in continental Europe, a large part of the expansion of the late 1990s was financed by new equity, in continental Europe as well as the United States.[54] Even where loan finance was used, many of the issuing banks used securitization, in particular through credit derivatives, to shift the inherent risks from their own books into the books of third parties, In this way, in a certain sense, their role began to look like that of a broker or market maker rather than that of an intermediary who puts his own money at risk.

[53] JC Rochet and X Vives 'Coordination Failure and the Lender of the Last Resort: Was Bagehot Right After All?' Discussion Paper no 3233, Centre for Economic Policy Research (London 2002).

[54] Debt finance did become prominent in the very late stages of the expansion, around the year 2000, as telecommunications firms used bonds to continue financing their investments in network and in UMTS licences.

Expansion of equity finance in the 1990s was accompanied by an expansion of stock-price-related remuneration schemes for corporate executives as well as an expanded use of the term 'shareholder value' as the criterion by which to judge corporate managers, in the financial press as well as in boardroom infighting. At first sight, therefore, it looks as though the developments of the 1990s should be interpreted as a movement towards availing oneself of the benefits of market finance/direct finance and the associated incentive effects. Indeed, prior to the burst of the bubble in 2000, many observers interpreted the developments of the 1990s in precisely these terms, arguing that, at least at this stage of economic development, a system based on market finance is superior.[55] The fact that this system facilitated the rise of Internet and biotech firms provides some substance to the assessment. After all, these are the sectors that capture the imagination as obvious carriers of technological progress.

Even the bubble and its fallout can be seen in a positive light. A decade earlier, the economic expansion of the late 1980s in continental Europe and Japan had largely been financed by bank loans to firms and real-estate investors. In the subsequent downturn, when loans turned sour, many banks were hard hit and, in many countries, there were severe banking crises. Banking crises and banking problems in turn impaired the ability of these institutions to provide loans for new investments. In the absence of other institutions taking their place, there was a pronounced contraction in business investment, contributing further to a deepening of the recession. In some of the Scandinavian countries, for instance, the recession of the years 1991-1994 rivalled the Great Depression in severity. In contrast, the fallout from the stock market implosion from 2000 to 2003 has been comparatively mild. The reason is that, apart from certain life insurance and pension institutions with insurance policies and pension plans involving defined benefits rather than defined contributions, the financial sector itself has not been much hit.[56] In contrast to the early 1990s, we have not seen a severe banking crisis during these years. The fallout from the burst of the bubble has not severely impaired the ability of financial systems to fund new investment. To the extent that investment has lagged, this has been mainly because of a lack of demand, due to the presence of excess capacity in the aftermath of strong expansion in the late 1990s.

At this point, banking regulators might chime in and suggest that this beneficial development is precisely what they would have hoped for and what the various improvements in capital adequacy regulation of banks, in particular under

[55] See eg RG Rajan and L Zingales 'The Great Reversals: The Politics of Financial Development in the Twentieth Century' (2003) 69 J of Financial Economics 5; RG Rajan and L Zingales 'Banks and Markets: The Changing Character of European Finance' in V Gaspar P Hartmann and O Sleijpen (eds) *Second ECB Central Banking Conference: The Transformation of the European Financial System* (European Central Bank Frankfurt 2003) 124.

[56] A caution about telecommunications bonds may be in order here.

the Basel II accord, are intended to achieve – namely, shift risks, in particular securitizable risks, out of the banks' books and into somebody else's who presumably is better able to bear these risks, who is perhaps also better – or has better incentives – for monitoring the ventures that are being financed. Economists worried about moral hazard in banking and finance would tend to agree, arguing that banks themselves are financed by deposits, ie debt-like instruments, and that the use of such instruments gives rise to excessive risk-taking as the borrower's gambles benefit him in the event of success and hurt the lenders when they fail and the borrower goes bankrupt.

However, this sanguine view neglects a few observations which seem highly relevant for an appropriate descriptive assessment and a normative evaluation of what actually happened. In the first place, the fact that we have not had a major financial crisis induced by the stock market implosion does not mean that there have been no adverse effects. Adverse effects have merely been borne by parties other than banks, in particular by final consumers. As holders of stocks and mutual funds certificates or as participants of defined-contributions pension plans, final consumers have been hard hit, with the consequence that many people will have to retire later and have to do with lower retirement incomes than they could have reckoned on. Insurance and pension institutions with contracts involving defined benefits have also been hit; the fact that these institutions' liabilities have long maturities has so far made it possible to smooth over many of their difficulties, but even so there remains an open question for the future.[57] At the very least, these observations require an argument as to why it should be preferable for private consumers and retirement institutions rather than banks to be bearing the consequences of the downturn.

Second, we need to take account of the fact that the overall development was accompanied by significant instances of wrongdoing, such as fraudulent reporting of business results or the mishandling of conflicts of interest by accounting firms and financial analysts, all of which occurred on a large scale, not just in a few exceptional cases. We also need to take account of the fact that the greater reliance on stock-price-related executive compensation was initiated by corporate management itself and that the details of this compensation had little to do with incentive provision in the sense of the theoretical models. Corporate managers were rewarded for stock price increases that were recognizably due to overall market developments or even macroeconomic developments that had nothing to do with their behaviour. Finally, we need to take account of the fact that resistance from corporate managers induced the political system in the United States to refrain from imposing appropriate accounting rules for certain forms of

[57] However, for someone recalling the US S&L crisis in the 1980s, the question arises whether the attempt to smooth over the effects on these institutions of the asset depreciation that has occurred may not give rise to a sort of gambling for resurrection that may end up being more detrimental than any effects of an immediate acknowledgement of the extent of the difficulties.

managerial compensation such as stock options, so profit reports were *per se* exaggerated, and there was no clear account of the cost of such compensation to the firm.

In the accounts of Rajan and Zingales,[58] the various instances of malfunctioning and malfeasance appear as unfortunate mishaps, as does the resistance of political systems towards correcting them. These mishaps are seen as exceptions which should not lead us to question the ascendance of market finance. I disagree with this assessment. In my view, the instances of malfunctioning and malfeasance that we have seen exhibit some systematic features which, at the very least, raise doubts as to whether the ascendance of market finance in the 1990s has anything to do with 'market discipline', let alone any of the theoretical models supporting the notion of market discipline.

As a first piece of analysis, consider the roles of analysts and accountants. The models of information processing through markets that I discussed above have no room for them; they are models of independent information gathering by final investors themselves. As discussed above, such information gathering by final investors is useful because it exploits the benefits of having multiple independent sources of information. In contrast, the analyst and the accountant would seem to be somewhat closer to the notion of delegated monitoring that is the basis of Diamond's theory of financial intermediation.[59] The analyst specializes in information acquisition and communicates this information to investors. By having multiple investors rely on the information provided by an analyst, the system exploits the scale economies that are available through the avoidance of duplicate information collection.

The analogy between analysts gathering information on behalf of their clients and banks providing delegated monitoring à la Diamond[60] raises the question of how a system involving analysts deals with the incentive problems arising from delegation. In Diamond[61], this incentive problem is solved by having the bank provide financial intermediation as well as monitoring services, with debt finance of the bank ensuring that there is no incentive to misreport monitoring results or to underinvest in monitoring effort. In contrast, there is no such arrangement for stock market analysts. Given this lacuna, we should expect to see precisely what we saw in the late 1990s, namely analysts not doing their homework or, worse, issuing reports that were at odds with the information they actually had if this served their other interests.

Adherents to the doctrine of market discipline would probably interject that analysts and accountants as well as investment bankers have their reputations to take care of, so proper incentives are being provided by the fact that they want to

58 Rajan and Zingales (n 55).

59 Diamond (n 28).

60 ibid.

61 ibid.

be successful in the future as well as the present. The argument presumes that the people concerned attach a lot of weight to the future relative to the present, and moreover that stakes in the present are sufficiently small so misbehaviour does not pay very much. On both accounts, I am sceptical. If current misbehaviour provides opportunities for earning a few million dollars, one may not care very much about losing one's business thereafter, provided one expects to keep the ill-gotten gains. We must also keep in mind that detection of misbehaviour may be quite difficult. After all, the investments in question are risky, so the mere fact that things turn sour does not provide evidence that the advice was bad, let alone fraudulent. In this context, we may point to the results of empirical research on investment funds indicating that a fund's ability to acquire new clients depends most strongly on return realizations in the immediate past, without much concern for the fact that high return realizations may reflect risk-taking rather than competence; the unhappy fate of LTCM shows where such neglect may lead.

Another observation to be studied concerns the nature and governance of executive compensation schemes that were introduced. As mentioned before, these schemes had little to do with the incentive schemes studied in theoretical models.[62] First, they provided remuneration for positive returns that had nothing to do with managerial behaviour – and could be recognized as such. Second, these schemes provided ample scope for mishandling of the allocation of effort across different dimensions, eg through cutting clearly measurable costs today at the expense of immeasurable – but nonetheless real – prospects for tomorrow. To the extent that the effects of cost cutting were presented in terms of profit growth effects rather than level effects, the resulting incentive distortion was even larger. Third, these schemes provided significant management participation in upside risks, but, given the scope for the timing of the exercise of options, they provided little participation in downside risks.

As for the governance of these schemes, they had of course been introduced on the initiative of incumbent management itself and ended up providing a source of significant enrichment. Transparency about the costs of these schemes to the companies in question was impeded by inappropriate accounting rules, maintained by the US Congress at the insistence of managerial lobbies. To the extent that incumbent managements were able to manipulate profit reports and influence accountants, investment bankers, and analysts, incentive schemes may actually have generated more effort at influencing stock prices through these channels than at influencing them through an improvement in actual business activities.

[62] Bebchuk and Fried (n 47).

In earlier work,[63] I questioned the relevance of the traditional paradigm for studying corporate governance in terms of contractual relations and institutions providing final investors with sufficient information and control to make it worth their while to provide companies with money. Pointing to the observation that corporate management in market-oriented and in bank-dominated systems alike enjoys a significant degree of autonomy, I suggested that this similarity of governance structures across systems might be more important than the apparent differences. For bank-dominated systems I pointed to the fact that in a system where managements of large corporations are by and large autonomous, subject to little outside control, there is no reason to expect banks to act as 'delegated monitors' on behalf of final investors rather than as defendants of managerial interests, hoping to participate in the spoils by providing investment banking services as corporate executives with cash cows in their back yards were looking for mergers and acquisitions. At the time, I formulated this argument as a comment on the role of main banks in a bank-dominated system. The experience of the 1990s suggests that the very same argument is relevant for understanding the role of market institutions, accountants, analysts, and investment bankers in a market-oriented system. This suspicion could give us pause in thinking about market discipline. Perhaps the market – just like any other institution – is just an instrument which corporate managers can use when it suits their purposes, as it so obviously did in the second half of the 1990s. It certainly did not provide much discipline in that period.

However, we should recognize that the malfunctioning of institutions of the financial system that we have seen corresponds to what we should expect under financing structures involving significant elements of equity-like finance and securitization of risks. Thus, a defined-contributions pension plan is subject to the standard agency problem of share finance, namely the final investor bears the consequences of what the fund managers do, so in a trade-off between what contract theorists euphemistically call 'private benefits' and the interests of the fund, the fund managers may have a tendency to go for their own private benefits rather than the interests of the fund and its investors.

The increased incidence of this class of agency problems is a direct consequence of the move towards having more equity finance and more securitized financial arrangements. Finding mechanisms for keeping these problems under control is essential to the viability of such arrangements in the future. However, we must keep in mind that although a system of supervision may seem foolproof by the standards of the day, if the stakes are high enough people will look for ways to get around them, and if enough people do so, they will find such ways.

[63] MF Hellwig 'On the Economics and Politics of Corporate Finance and Corporate Control' in X Vives (ed) *Corporate Governance* (Cambridge University Press Cambridge 2000) 95; MF Hellwig 'Corporate Governance and the Financing of Investment for Structural Change' in Deutsche Bundesbank (ed) *Investing Today for the World of Tomorrow · Studies on the Investment Process in Europe* (Springer Verlag Berlin Heidelberg New York 2001) 201.

From this perspective, the instances of malfunctioning and malfeasance that we have seen should not have come as a surprise. Given the way the system evolved, they were bound to come. Moreover, if we think about modes of correction only in terms of the particular kinds of fraud and corruption that we have seen, the next round of problems is bound to come. We need to think about the problem as endemic to a system in which the final investor foots the bill.

V. Concluding Remarks

The analysis of this paper indicates that 'market discipline' is no more a panacea for the problems of information, incentives, and control in finance than the 'main bank relation'. Different arrangements have different advantages and disadvantages in terms of how they align incentives between entrepreneurs and managers, financial institutions, and final investors. The experience of the past decade has shown the pitfalls of excessive confidence in a poorly regulated regime of 'market discipline' – just as the experience of the years 1980 through 1995 taught about the pitfalls of excessive intermediated loan finance inducing the risk of a credit crunch or a banking crisis. Putting these episodes next to each other provides a wholesome warning against excessive enthusiasm about either 'system'. However, as one thinks about the implications to be drawn, one should also bear in mind that in the actual developments of the 1990s, the rise of market rhetoric – in academic as well as political discussion – seems to have merely provided the background for a development that was driven more by the people and institutions whom market discipline was supposed to be controlling than by the people and institutions for whom such control was supposed to be beneficial.

Implementation of the Corporate Governance Codes

EDDY WYMEERSCH

I. Introduction

Codes on corporate governance have by now been developed in most of the EU states.[1] This wave has been strongly supported by the recommendations of the High Level Expert Group on Company Law and by recommendations of the European Commission, and it is now increasingly anchored in specific legislative proposals of the EU Commission. Therefore, it seems useful to dwell on the way these codes fit into the overall legislative framework of the EU and of the member states.

Several issues will be touched upon: How do these codes relate to market practice? Who makes the codes and who supervises their implementation? What about the rights and liabilities of the company and its officers and directors flowing from the code's provision? These are questions that arise at the sidelines of the phenomenon, but are nonetheless of great importance as drivers in the corporate governance movement.

II. Who Is Setting the Rules?

It is important to identify with some precision who is drawing up the national corporate governance codes. This analysis may help to understand the national political and legal environment in which these codes have been issued, and the

[1] The codes can be consulted at the website of the European Corporate Governance Institute: <http://www.ecgi.org/> (18 April 2005). Luxembourg was one of the last of the original 15 states to announce the drawing up of a corporate governance code.

relationship of the self-regulatory instrument with the drive for more legislative intervention.

Generally speaking, the corporate governance codes have been drawn up by committees, usually chaired by a leading businessperson. The codes are therefore usually referred to by the name of that person. The composition of these committees and the political environment in which they have been set up is quite different and not always easy to understand from abroad.

In the earlier stages, when corporate governance was considered as a somewhat less relevant issue, the codes were drawn up by the market itself, often with the support of academics or other experts. The stock exchanges had a direct interest in developing a governance code and supporting the reputation of their marketplace, especially as some scandals had dented the reputation of some of the listed companies. Institutional investors from abroad often asked to identify the applicable code. Although at that time some of the exchanges could actually impose the code by introducing a listing condition, most refrained from doing so in order to preserve their competitive edge.

The governance rules applicable to the now defunct NASDAQ Europe (previously Easdaq) were the work of the EASD, or the European Association of Securities Dealers, assisted by academic experts. The first Belgian governance code was also based on an initiative of the Brussels stock exchange, although the committee in charge of drafting the code had a wider composition, including businessmen, academics, consultants, and so on. Stock exchanges are often linked with the business associations because this would enhance the acceptance of the codes. It is not clear whether the supporting associations also have the power to require their members to abide by the code; most of the time, their 'endorsement' has had a moral or political value, not a legal one. An example of this technique can be found in the Swiss code, which was drafted by a committee of legal experts, some of whom have high academic standing, with the support of the stock exchange. The code was explicitly endorsed by the principal business associations in Switzerland.

A second series of codes are more clearly linked to business, more precisely as the result of initiatives taken by business associations. The French Viénot and Bouton codes, which are essentially statements of good practice, are published under the aegis of the Medef, the French employers' association,[2] and the AFEP.[3] The moral authority of the business leaders involved contributed to the recognition of these statements as good practice.

A comparable but more broadly based model lies at the basis of the Cadbury Code on 'the financial aspects of corporate governance'.[4] The committee was set

[2] *Mouvement des enterprises de France.*

[3] *Association française des enterprises privées.*

[4] In its version of 1 December 1992.

up by the Financial Reporting Council,[5] the London Stock Exchange, and the accountancy profession. The committee itself was composed of a broad selection of leaders from the different professions, with responsibility in the overall functioning of the London financial world. To be noted: the DTI sent an observer, while an advisor to the Bank of England's governor was part of the committee. One of the objectives of this committee was clearly to restore confidence in the financial system after BCCI, a case to which the Cadbury Code expressly referred.

The Swedish code, which was proposed in October 2004, is described as a joint effort of the Government Commission of Business Confidence and of the Swedish business associations. It was drawn up by a panel chaired by a former minister of finance who also chairs the said Government Commission, and is further composed of representatives of the business associations.[6] The code is based on a comply-or-explain approach. The annual report has to state whether the report has been audited or not.[7]

The Dutch code was established at the invitation of the minister of finance and the minister for economic affairs. The Tabaksblat committee was composed of representatives of the main professional organisations in the Netherlands. The ministries were not part of the committee, but they played a significant role at the level of the secretariat of the committee. The code was given a statutory basis in 2004.

The public authorities seem to be paying increasing attention to the corporate governance movement without – at least up to now – officially intervening. None has taken the step to ensure enforcement by way of government measure. However, developments in corporate governance should not only be measured by looking at the implementation of the codes; one should also take into account the parallel changes in the law that have taken place. In many jurisdictions, there have been quite significant changes in company law, whereby important corporate governance changes were facilitated rather than mandated. Changes in the composition of the board were introduced in Belgium, France, Netherlands, and Italy to name but a few. In each of these cases, the existing regime has been relaxed rather than tightened.

[5] More on this infra p 416.

[6] The code seems to be quite demanding on specific points, and for SMEs, see FT, 2 December 2004.

[7] One of the members of the commission published an additional opinion, underlining the self-regulatory character of the instrument and regretting deviation from internally accepted standards.

III. The Codes Are Self-Regulatory

The corporate governance codes are essentially not mandated by the law; they are the result of self-regulation. There are different degrees of self-regulation, going from self-proclaimed rules of behaviour to rules that are rooted in the law but whose detailed compliance is not supervised by a public body.

Voluntary compliance with the codes has been generally quite satisfactory, with the exception of a few sensitive provisions – eg on disclosure of directors' remuneration. Compliance overviews have been published by academics, business consultants, and ratings organisations. These reviews are based on the disclosures in the annual reports. In fact, compliance has often taken the form of changes to articles of incorporation, leading to a stronger juridification of the recommendations of the codes.

An analysis comparing the late nineties to today would probably reveal for all jurisdictions that some of the cornerstone provisions of the codes, eg the rules on audit committees or on independent directors, have largely been complied with. In parallel, the information disclosed about internal governance has increased significantly. Whereas in the 1990s the annual reports contained almost no mention of governance matters, voluminous sections of annual reports these days are devoted to documenting and analysing governance matters. Few listed companies would dare to ignore the subject these days. Although there may be some lip service in these disclosures, there remains the greater consciousness about the overall purpose of the exercise.

Why have companies voluntarily complied with these self-regulatory instruments? It is undeniable that the codes are being implemented under the pressure of the 'markets'. From a subject that was barely mentioned in academic circles ten years ago, corporate governance has become a popular notion, used even in the wider press. The theme is not restricted to the financial markets: in all large transactions, including those that do not directly affect the securities markets, eg those relating to government-owned entities, governance is considered at the heart of the matter. Even universities have discovered the virtues of better governance.

As the securities markets have gained importance in western Europe, an astonishing sensitivity to governance issues has developed. The success of the governance codes is largely linked to a market phenomenon. This notion should be further analysed: it can be compared to a continuous voting system, whereby the management is continuously assessed and the future results predicted. By referring to the markets, one should first directly refer to price evolutions that may be measured by using event studies and statistical regressions. There is ample anecdotal evidence that governance events have affected the prices of listed securities. Also, good governance practices are widely considered to have a positive influence on the price evolution. But nothing is mathematical: some of the most successful companies simply refuse to follow the governance precepts, without negative effect on their financial results or their market valuation. Also, governance rules and especially codes – in contrast to practices – may not have the same effect; a code will have a positive effect on price formation only indirectly by offering a yardstick against which 'good governance' can be measured.[8] One understands why institutional investors generally require that there should be a governance code applicable in each jurisdiction. The EU Commission has endorsed this idea by requiring companies to refer to the 'applicable governance code'.

The phenomenon of market influence is broader than the direct impact on price formation. It also relates to opinion building through the media, as well as the ratings agencies and the financial analysts. Here also there is a remarkable difference from the late nineties: the press frequently refers to governance issues, including governance codes, especially when special events have disturbed public opinion. Academic opinion should also be mentioned: academics have contributed significantly to opinion building, generally endorsing the need for good governance and its main principles. Some comparative studies have highlighted the degree of compliance with the codes.[9] The role of consultants should not be underestimated: they play a first-line role in advising on the right governance practices to be developed. Usually they adhere to US standards and develop governance practices that are based on a dispersed ownership model. This explains why in companies with concentrated ownership, models have been proposed that are at odds with the prevailing model of concentrated ownership. One of the striking features of the European debate is why provisions adapted to one model have so readily been received in a substantially different model. To mention one example: the concept of independent directors is almost incompatible with a position of a board member who can be revoked 'ad nutum' by a controlling shareholder. Nevertheless, controlling shareholders are sometimes willing and even eager to accept independent directors on their boards because they contribute to better monitoring of the management. This sometimes results in substantial conflicts between these shareholders and the company.

IV. Ambit of the Governance Codes

To whom should the codes be applied? There is little doubt that they should apply to listed companies, here meaning companies whose securities are widely traded on organised markets. There may be some discussions about the definition of the publicly traded company, but these are borderline issues.

[8] See the plan of the FT to develop a FTSE/ISS index which aims to calculate which markets have the most well-governed companies, FT 'Special Report Corporate Governance' 15 December 2004.

[9] See for comparative studies; also progress reports are regularly published: see A von Werder, Berlin Center of Corporate Governance.

More controversial is the application of the codes to large non-listed companies. One may argue that due to the social impact of these companies, they should be held to the same principles. The interest of creditors and of employees – normally outside the scope of the governance rules – may also be served by better governance practices.

In some jurisdictions, special attention is drawn to the governance of closely held, family-owned businesses. There is undoubtedly a strong need for better governance in this field, whether in the interest of the firm or to defend the rights of the minority shareholders.

In some jurisdictions, special codes have been developed to address the unlisted family-held businesses. They serve more as a model for inspiration.

A difficult subject is that of governance of state-owned firms. A difference should be made between whether the business firm is the legal form for organising a public interest function or whether the firm is part of the competitive economy, in which case the same safeguards should apply. However, one sees that the states are unwilling to abandon their influence on the last-mentioned group of firms, sometimes until market competition brings it down. Good governance ought to be a guarantee for insuring the survival of the enterprise.

V. Enforcing the Corporate Governance Codes

As more and more corporate governance codes are being developed, and as their application attracts wider attention, questions about their enforcement have become increasingly poignant. In some jurisdictions, as principles of good governance have been blatantly violated, public opinion and politicians have questioned the value of instruments that rely entirely on the willingness of business leaders not only to adhere to the codes but also to put them into practice. Enforcement of self-regulatory instruments in an increasingly legalistic environment poses some interesting challenges: a more refined analysis, especially focusing on the gradual character of the enforcement techniques, is necessary. Indeed, between pure self-regulation, government-supported self-regulation, and full or partial government enforcement, there are numerous steps and shades that can only be captured in a detailed analysis. As they are embedded in the legal and social culture of the jurisdiction in which they are being practiced, any analysis is limited to the outsiders' view. The latter is not irrelevant as it often is also the view adopted by the markets .

1. Self-regulation

In the original approach to self-regulatory codes of corporate governance, codes were developed by business leaders as a guide for their own correct behaviour. There was no reference to any form of external monitoring, whether by a self-regulatory panel or by government. Within the firm the board was responsible, and it was the role of the chairman of the board to watch over adequate compliance. Sometimes there was a governance committee at the board level, or special meetings were devoted to governance issues. Some external monitoring of the code's implementation was based on comparative analysis, undertaken by academics, consultant firms, or even market supervisors. But these only took stock of the state of implementation, pointing to the progress achieved or to the most visible shortcomings. The entire implementation of the codes is based on disclosure and on market monitoring; if the code is insufficient, or is not sufficiently implemented, the investors will sanction the market by refusing to invest in the equities on offer.

Market monitoring is considered by some to be very weak: it is invisible, often clearly contrary to the manifest shortcomings, and in general difficult to capture. However, to the extent that most of the existing codes are based on disclosures in the annual accounts, it should be remembered that untrue or false statements in the annual reports may expose the board members to civil liabilities – towards third parties, creditors, investors relying on the information in the report in the prospectus, and so on – and that in some cases even criminal liability may not be excluded. Whether these sanctions would be applicable depends very much on the national legal regime. The European Commission has called for a stronger regime of liability for directors. Whether this includes statements in the annual accounts, even after these have been approved by shareholders, could be the subject of further analysis. The basis of liability is not the provisions of the governance code, but the false or misleading character of the disclosures in the annual report, or in other company publications.

2. Self-regulatory Monitoring

The self-regulatory code could be monitored by a self-regulatory panel, composed of business representatives originating in the same associations or interest groups that have drawn up the code. The panel's action would essentially be based on disclosure: it would identify the cases in which the code has not been adequately implemented, and invite the firm to state its reasons for not implementing the code. The panel could support the code's implementation by publishing comparative tables of implementation and exercising peer pressure on the firms that stay behind. In defined cases, the panel could even be authorised to publish its individual findings, using some technique of 'name and shame'.

The designation of a monitoring committee raises the question of what will be monitored: Will this only relate to determining whether the different items of the code have been filled in, or will the panel also look into the content of the disclosures? In the latter case, one could further distinguish between cases in which the explanation is manifestly insufficient, obscure, contradictory with other statements, and so on. Or should the monitoring also go into the substance, determining whether the factual data are true (eg does the published remuneration correspond to the internal figures) or also to the more substantive issues ('adequate control mechanisms have to be in place'), in which case a parallel system of external controls, parallel to the regular financial auditor, would be introduced? At a certain moment, the monitoring panel runs the risk of substituting itself for the board of directors. This cannot be the purpose, and therefore clear lines have to be agreed upon which limit the panel's intervention to the formal compliance with the code.

3. External Monitoring by the Company's Auditor

An alternative to external monitoring could be to extend the statutory auditor's brief to the verification of compliance with the code. There are certain advantages to this approach: it maintains the self-regulatory, internal nature of the monitoring process; and it allows the board to make necessary corrections where needed or, if no changes are needed, to adopt the explanations that are called for in the codes. The auditor is already present in the firm, is familiar with the internal functioning of the firm, and has to verify the internal control mechanisms supporting his review of the financial statements. In case of shortcomings, he would have direct access to the appropriate company bodies, such as the audit committee or the chairman of the board. Any necessary changes would be submitted to the board, which remains in charge of the implementation of the self-regulatory code.

There are some drawbacks to involving the auditors. Apart from their limited expertise in governance matters, auditors should restrict themselves to controlling financial information. Reviewing governance matters may be considered non-audit services, especially as it may lead to advising the board or the management on developing techniques to improve governance or change disclosures as called for by the code.

In certain jurisdictions, the auditor already reviews part of the annual report. His intervention is limited to very specific items, most of the time reflecting specific transactions that have been registered in the accounts (eg date on repurchases of own shares). His review does not extend to management issues or items for which there are no underlying data.

In other jurisdictions, the entire annual report is reviewed by the auditor; therefore, it would also include those items that have to be included in the report. This is the case in the Netherlands; however, it is accepted that the auditor's intervention is limited to external review of the code-mandated items, ie whether there is a statement that a code is applicable and has been complied with, and where applicable, the explanation about an item on which the firm did not comply. It would in no case include review of the substantive issues.

4. External Monitoring by the Securities Market Supervisor

Should the securities market supervisor be involved in the monitoring of the corporate governance code, and what would a possible monitoring action consist of? The issue has been raised in several states, and the answers remain far from clear.[10] Especially in the Netherlands, this matter has recently been discussed in the Parliament, leading to a rather clear delimitation. Similar tendencies exist in the other states where the subject has been officially discussed.

If there were monitoring by the securities market supervisor, one would have to determine the nature of this supervision. One could, theoretically at least, devise a whole range of different types of supervision, ranging from maximum to minimum.

The maximum hypothesis – which would be very difficult to implement – would consist of the supervisor verifying in substance whether the code's provisions have been met. This would require an in-depth analysis of the internal functioning of the company, with an outcome that would still be insecure. In other fields, such as accounting or the mandatory statement in the annual report, the supervisor would not go through the account but would rely on the statements of the board and the auditors. There is no reason to require a stricter system of supervision in a field of company law where the rules remain less restrictive than in accounting. Moreover, by so doing, the nature of the codes would be changed: from mere self-regulatory codes, they would become public policy instruments that were neither so conceived nor approved by the competent public authorities. This action would no longer be monitoring of the code, but of the governance practices themselves. It might result in subjecting the firm to a regular corporate governance review under the guidance of the public supervisor. Would this review be undertaken by a third party – eg a specialised governance consultancy – or give rise to direct monitoring of the supervisor, including on-site inspections? The risks and liabilities could be unfathomable.

As in many respects, there is no single, best, generally accepted approach. Supervisors – and regulators as well – are very unwilling to intervene in the field of enforcing the substantive rules that are contained in the governance codes.

An intermediate step could consist of the supervisor verifying whether the strictly defined legal obligations have been met. The subject is far from theoretical: corporate governance statements will – at least according to a proposed EU directive – become a mandatory part of the annual reports of listed firms. In many jurisdictions, market supervisors have some powers to review annual reports, and in case of a deficiency, to mandate additional or corrective disclosures. Hence, in

[10] See H Merkt 'Selbstkontrolle und Staatsaufsicht bei der Corporate Governance' in P Hommehoff, KJ Hopt and A von Werder (eds) *Handbuch Corporate Governance* (Otto Schmidt Verlag Cologne 2003) 715.

the future there should be a clear understanding about the extent of the supervisors' intervention.

In some jurisdictions, the legal obligations of the company include the designation by the board of a certain governance code and its review of whether the different provisions of that code have been met, in the sense that the company declares whether it is complying, where it is not complying, and its reasons for doing so. In this case, the monitoring role of the supervisor can be called 'external': he will ascertain whether the board has adhered to the applicable code and has disclosed the necessary information mandated by the code, stating the reason for which the board has diverged from complying with the code for specified items. In exceptional cases, where there is clear unwillingness on the part of the company, or where the information is manifestly inconsistent or misleading, the supervisor could require additional disclosures or changes to the proposed disclosures. In fact, this approach is not very different from the type of supervision that is already exercised today in the annual reports in some jurisdictions. It does not delve in depth into the substance of the disclosures, but points to inconsistencies or misleading information.

According to a third scheme, the supervision would intervene only by exception when specific facts have been brought to its attention, and in that case it could recommend that the company adopt the applicable standard as contained in the governance code. It would also monitor the implementation of the code by all market participants as a whole, identifying the fields in which business practice and code provisions diverge.

In each of these cases there will also be a question about which enforcement instruments can be used. In the strongest hypothesis, the supervisor would be allowed to use the stronger instruments, such as administrative fines, court injunctions, or 'name and shame'. This is the case where legal provisions have been violated, and it is already applied today. The 'name and shame' is more indicated in the second hypothesis, while 'moral suasion' through recommendations would be the approach in the third case, which relies essentially on market discipline.

5. Some Comparative Elements

As of this writing, the opinions about the different techniques of monitoring the corporate governance codes are still very much in a state of flux.

In most jurisdictions in Europe, the model followed is that of self-regulatory monitoring, relying on the market mechanism. In several cases, market pressure has proved to be quite efficient: the governance structure of Royal Dutch/Shell was radically overhauled due to criticism in the markets that led to strong pressure in the market. Other examples relate to several (esp. Dutch) cases where anti-takeover protections were abandoned under the pressure of the markets.

The Italian code is designated as a point of reference but has no binding force.[11] The Spanish code was introduced pursuant to a decision of the Spanish cabinet, and calls attention to the need for ethical behaviour, but in full respect of its self-regulatory nature. It is based on the 1997 Olivencia Report, delivered by a commission that was created by the government. The document makes three suggestions for government action: disclosure about the compliance or non-compliance with the code, general duties of care and loyalty, and rules on the functioning of the board and of the general meeting

A somewhat stronger approach has been followed in France and in Belgium. In Belgium, the code refers to the market supervisor as lending moral support to the code, while envisaging a recommendation to listed companies to implement the code. Comparative analysis will also be published from time to time, as has been the case in the past. It is important to note that in both cases, the market supervisors do not claim competence to effectively monitor the substantive provisions of the code, and hence will not make use of their statutory powers to enforce it. Only to the extent that the code's provisions would run parallel to legal obligations could use of the statutory powers – including imposition of sanctions – be envisaged.

However, at least in Belgium, the discussion about the role of the securities supervisor in the implementation of the code is not closed: the Parliament is expected to state its opinion in early 2005. In the meantime, proposals to mandate the disclosure of directors' remunerations by law have been tabled in Parliament.

The French situation is somewhat different to the extent that quite substantial changes in the governance rules have been introduced by two recent laws, the *Loi sur les nouvelles regulation économiques* in 2001, and the *Loi sur la sécurité financière* of 2003. The first introduced important changes in the company law, i.a. mandating remuneration disclosure and allowing the split between chairman of the board and leader of the management (so-called pdg-regime).[12] According to the latter law, specific duties are imposed on the chairman of the board. In a report separate from the annual report, the chairman of the board must report to the shareholders about the way the board meetings have been prepared and organised, probably including a significant part of what in other jurisdictions is referred to as corporate governance.[13] His obligation to report, in this document, on the internal control procedures is very important, and this section of his report

[11] See 'Linee Guida per la redazione della relazione annuale in materia di corporate governance' <http://www.borsaitalia.it/opsmedia/pdf/8947.pdf> (18 April 2005).

[12] G Rameix *Orientations en matière de gouvernement d'entreprise et contrôle interne et Recommendations pour l'élaboration des documents de reference 2003* (AMF 23 January 2004); AMF 'Gouvernement d'entreprise et contrôle interne, obligations de publication des émetteurs faisant appel public à l'épargne' <http://www.amf-france.org/styles/default/documents/general/5269_1.pdf> (18 April 2005).

[13] Art 117 LSF: 'des conditions de préparation de d'organisation des travaux du conseil ainsi que des procédures de contrôle interne mises en place par la société'.

is to be separately reviewed by the statutory auditors.[14] Both rules indicate that a substantial part of corporate governance rules has been rooted in the law itself.

In addition, the Autorité des Marchés Financiers are acting in support of the implementation of the rules. According to the AMF's instructions, the information about the company's governance is to be published either in the 'document of reference' or in the annual report. In the former, one will find the overview of governance practices, the internal control procedures, and the special report of the audit committee. The company will describe its governance system, and for each of the recommendations, indicate whether or not it complies, stating the reasons for any non-compliance. AMF recommends that companies follow the governance codes and guidelines, as established by the ANSA for legal matters,[15] and for internal control matters by other associations as well.[16] In addition, AMF has 'called attention to the following orientations' of the companies on a certain number of matters for which additional disclosures would be required. The AMF[17] must publish an annual report on the information thus published.[18] AMF, acting by way of recommendation, sees its role in the implementation of the governance rules as one of support, inspiration, consensus building,[19] and ensuring that the required information is made available to the market.

In Germany the Cromme Code was imposed by § 161 of the Aktiengesetz.[20] According to this provision, the management board and supervisory boards of listed companies have to annually publish that the recommendations of the 'Regierungskommission Deutscher Corporate Governance Codex',[21] as published by the ministry of justice, have been complied with, or which parts of the code have not been complied with. The declaration has to be made accessible for shareholders on a continuous basis.

In the Netherlands, probably due to the fact that the code served as a response to the important cases that shook the Dutch stock market, the debate has always had a stronger legal flavour. This resulted in writing the 'comply-or-explain'

[14] Art 120 LSF.

[15] Note du comité juridique d'Ansa no 3267 of 5 November 2003.

[16] Medef and Afep.

[17] See Recommendations pour les documents de référence 2002, applicable to 2003 as well.

[18] Art 122 LSF.

[19] See M Prada 'Intervention au colloque de l'IFA 'Contrôle interne et gouvernement d'entreprise, Point de vue du régulateur'' 13 October 2004.

[20] § 161 as modified by the law of 19 July 2002.

[21] This is the so-called Cromme Code: see <http://investors.dpwn.de/en/corporate_gov/entsprech_corporate_governance_kodex_e.pdf> (18 April 2005).

For a recent state of developments see G Cromme 'Stand und Entwicklungen Corporate Governance in Deutschland' 24 June 2004 <http://www.corporate-governance-code.de/ger/download/GC_Konferenz_Berlin_ 2004_Dr_Cromme.pdf> (18 April 2005).

principle into the law itself, and specifying that a further implementing decree would contain the details about the follow-up mechanism. The Dutch law has made it mandatory for listed companies to publish a statement about their compliance with the code. In the annual report, 'the company will report on compliance with the code's principles and its best practice rules. If the company has not complied with the principles or with the best practice rules, or does not intend to do so during the current or the forthcoming year, it will have to state its reasons in the annual report'. The companies law was changed so as to enable the minister of justice to take an implementing decree.[22] As of this writing, this decree has not yet been adopted

At the end of 2004, a discussion was launched over whether the market supervisor, the AFM ('Autoriteit Financiële Markten'), would have a role to play in the follow-up to the code. The AFM chairman, in a public speech held in November 2004, announced that it was considering the exercise of a 'marginal review' of the application of the code.[23] This was motivated by the fact that the code had been a 'legal obligation', and this by virtue of Art. 391, §§ 4 and 5, of Book 2 of the Dutch Civil Code. This statement provoked an angry reaction from a member of Parliament, who considered that the code as a self-regulatory instrument developed by the private sector should not be the subject of government supervision. The supervision of compliance with the code and of the information to be disclosed in the annual report was the task of the auditor, not of the markets' supervisor, according to the parliamentarian.[24] During the following parliamentary debate, the minister of justice clarified the role of both the AFM and of the auditor.[25] The AFM should, according to the minister, limit itself to determining whether the company has mentioned the implementation of the code in its annual report, and verifying whether that mention is consistent with the remainder of the annual report. The auditor, on the other hand, would check whether the board had mentioned in the annual report that it had complied with the code, and whether this mention was consistent with the remainder of the annual report and the financial statements.[26] It was, according to the minister, not the task of the auditor to check whether the firm had included all legally mandated information in either the annual report or in the financials.[27] In cases where the company would give

[22] Art 391, §§ 4 and 5 of the Civil Code, Book 2.

[23] See AD van Leeuwen 'Wie houdt het raam schoon?' speech 13 October 2004, see AFM website.

[24] See Financieele Dagblad, 1 December 2004.

[25] See 'Meer uitleg over rol AFM en accountant bij naleving code' 1 December 2004 <http://www.commissiecorporategovernance.nl/Nieuws/> (18 April 2005).

[26] According to two planned laws, 'wetsvoorstel toezicht accountantsorganisaties' and 'wetsvoorstel toezicht financiële verslaggeving'.

[27] See 'Meer uitleg over rol AFM en accountant bij naleving code' (n 25).

no information about its compliance with the code, the auditor could mention this in his report.[28]

Recently it was decided that the so-called Tabaksblat Code will be monitored by a 'Monitoring Commission Corporate Governance',[29] the eight members of which have been designated by the ministers of finance, justice, and economic affairs, chaired by Professor Fryns. The commission will review the usefulness of the code and its up-to-date character. It will follow up on the implementation of the code by the Dutch business world. To that purpose it will make an annual inventory of the way Dutch firms have respected the code, will follow up on international developments and business practice, and identify lacunae or insufficiently clear provisions of the code. It may make proposals to amend the code without being empowered to effectively change it. From this description, it follows that the commission has no mandate to ensure the individual follow-up of the code, nor the power to investigate whether the code has been complied with or to further impose any sanctions.

In the UK, the Financial Reporting Council will review the Combined Code and propose amendments to it.[30] In March 2004 the FRC set up a new committee to lead its work on corporate governance. The committee's terms of reference are:

– To keep under review developments in corporate governance generally, reflecting the FRC's objective of fostering high standards of corporate governance; to undertake reviews, either directly or by overseeing the work of others, and then to consider whether any actions by the FRC would be desirable; and to put proposals to the Council where appropriate.
– To monitor the operation of the Combined Code on Corporate Governance and its implementation by listed companies and by shareholders.
– Where significant doubts are raised about the appropriate interpretation of part of the Code, to consider the case for issuing a clarification, and if appropriate to do so, after any suitable consultation.

The Combined Code is annexed to the Listing Rules. Listed companies must include in their annual report a narrative statement about the way they have complied with the principles of the code, allowing shareholders to evaluate how they have lived up to the code's principles. As far as the provisions of the code are concerned, companies must make clear whether or not they have complied, and state their reasons in case of non-compliance. The FSA as a listing authority makes no judgement about the accuracy or adequacy of the compliance state-

[28] <http://www.commissiecorporategovernance.nl/Nieuws#Nieuws_413> (18 April 2005).

[29] Composed of eight members selected from business, institutional investors, academia, and the audit profession. The commission is chaired by Professor Fryns, CFO of the ABP, the largest Dutch pension fund. See 8 December 2004 'Monitoring Commissie Corporate Governance Code ingesteld' website of the Dutch corporate governance commission: <http://www.commissiecorporategovernance.nl/Nieuws/> (18 April 2005).

[30] See annex 2.

ment: it is up to the board of the company and to the shareholders to make such an evaluation. If a company fails to include a statement in the required form, the FSA has announced that it may use its powers, including its fining powers against that company. The FSA will use its compliance powers by sampling a number of annual reports on a routine basis.

VI. European Company Law Initiatives

The proposed European directive amending the 4th Company Directive on annual accounts contains a specific arrangement addressing the position to be taken with respect to the national corporate governance codes. According to the proposed new Art. 46 a of the 4th Directive, the annual report of listed companies will have to contain 'a corporate governance statement' in a separate section.[31] The content of the statement is defined in the directive: the company will have to refer to a corporate governance code that it has decided to apply. The provision makes it clear that the governance code will not necessarily be the one applicable, depending on the company's registered office. Indeed, market considerations may incite companies to adhere to stricter standards as applied on their principal place of listing: international companies may prefer to state that they are subject to the Sarbanes-Oxley Act and the NYSE governance rules. The code of its registered office will be applicable as a default option. The content of the governance statement in the annual report will conform at least with the following provisions:

- Identification of the applicable code
- Compliance statement, indicating whether and to what extent the company complies with the code
- The composition of the board and its committees
- Description of the internal controls and risk-management system
- Description of the rules on the functioning of the general meeting, its powers, and shareholders' rights
- Some of the information as required in the Takeover Directive:[32]
    - Significant direct or indirect shareholding, including through pyramid structures
    - Holders of securities with special control rights and the description of these rights
    - Restrictions on voting rights, such as limitation on the number of votes that can be cast

[31] The preamble underlines that there should not be a separate statement in the consolidated annual reports, but that risks management and internal control on a groupwide basis has to be considered.

[32] Directive 2004/25/EC of 21 April 2004 [2004] OJ L142/12.

- Rules on appointment and replacement of board members and on amending the articles of association
- The powers of board members, especially the rules on issuing or buying back shares

The comply-or-explain principle is stated in the following terms: to the extent that the company departs from the corporate governance code, it shall explain from which parts of the code it departs and the reasons for doing so.

Art. 50 b would impose collective liability for the members of the boards towards the company for ensuring that the annual report is drawn up according to the provisions of the directive.

The proposed directive contains little information about the way the codes have to be enforced: this will be left to the member states and to the overall regime of supervision on the annual report. Art. 67 of the Directive 2001/34 states that the annual reports must give a true and fair view of the assets and liabilities, the financial position and profit or loss, and, if not, that additional information must be provided. All other aspects, such as whether the data on governance will have to be audited, and the extent of this audit or of any other type of external monitoring, are left to the member states. Therefore, the directive's regime corresponds by and large to the rule that is applied today in most of the member states.

VII. The Effects of the Governance Rules: Risks and Liabilities

To what extent will corporate governance rules and principles as embodied in self-regulatory governance codes become part of the legal system? Will soft law become hard, and how is this likely to happen? Are not the efforts that are made to keep these instruments out of the legal sphere futile, as the law will sooner or later incorporate them? The issue is that of 'juridification', a phenomenon that applies to all types of soft law.

The legal system will in one way or another incorporate the essential findings stemming from the corporate governance debate, as this has crystallised in the governance codes. As with other soft law instruments, the legal system has a tendency to incorporate the standards of the codes as the normal benchmark against which conduct in a specific case will be measured. In terms of liability, of interpretation of contract clauses, and so on, it does not seem unlikely that the rules as adopted in the code will be considered the standard.

If the disclosures about governance rules or practices are false or misleading, they may lead to liability on that ground. In addition, they may offer evidence of unlawful or negligent conduct. One may imagine liability of boards resulting from violations of the duty of care if the board had not developed the risk-control mechanisms that would be considered prevalent in large groups. The same reasoning may be applied to conflicts of interest. Therefore, it is very important that the code clearly distinguish between the principles that are binding and for which no derogation would be considered acceptable, and the provisions for which 'comply or explain' applies. In the latter, liability would be much more difficult to apply because the rules, as incorporated in the code, accept that there is no single way of dealing with the matter. The designation of an audit committee may be considered such an elementary precaution against accounting fraud or violation, that the board may be considered negligent if has not constituted such a committee. In the absence of independent directors, liability for conflicts of interest may be increased.

A factor of further complexity is likely to be the differences in the liability regimes in the different European jurisdictions. This especially applies with respect to liability to third parties, where mere negligence will be held sufficient in some jurisdictions, while only qualified shortcoming will have to be proved in others.

The relationship to substantive provisions should also be mentioned. Especially in connection with related party transactions, self-dealing provisions, and the like, one may expect that the criteria used for defining independent directors will have a spillover effect in defining conflicts of interest.

The subject of external effects of corporate governance codes deserves further analysis.[33]

VIII. Conclusion

The phenomenon of the corporate governance code raises a number of new issues in company law. Some of these are related to the application of the code: Will these codes be applied on a voluntary basis or is some form of legal support necessary? The comparative overview indicates that states have already given ample attention to this question, and that up to now most have come out for a prudent approach, leaving it to the companies and the financial markets to ensure that the codes are applied. At the same time, one sees increasing legislative activism in issues that, without directly dealing with the core issues of the codes, move in parallel to them: obligation to apply a code, requirements on annual reports, mandatory statements on risk management, and so on. Is this a case of intra-regulatory competition?

[33] See P Hommelhoff and M Schwab 'Regelungsquellen und Regulungsebenen der Corporate Governance: Gesetz, Satzung, Codices, unternehmensinterne Grundsätze' and W Goette 'Haftung' in P Hommehoff KJ Hopt and A von Werder (eds) *Handbuch Corporate Governance* (Otto Schmidt Verlag Cologne 2003) 51, 749.

The Market for Corporate Control: The Legal Framework, Alternatives, and Policy Considerations

STEFAN GRUNDMANN*

I. Introduction: Competition Over Which Assets in the Market for Corporate Control?

When the concept of a market for corporate control was developed, the core idea was that a potential new management entered into competition with the existing management of a public corporation. The instrument envisaged was mergers – in US American terminology – ie takeovers[1] (as distinguished from mergers in the

* This paper was planned to supplement a paper by Joseph A McCahery on 'The Market for Corporate Control (Mainly from an Economic Perspective)' and to comment on it. This other paper, however, deals only marginally with the change of control positions, though the concept of a market for corporate control – as understood in the discussion – is in fact about these changes, mainly in takeovers. Therefore, I chose to discuss the recent developments in the legal framework of the market for corporate control independently of McCahery's and Vermeulen's paper and, in due course, only point to the few hints to be found in his paper. In the much shorter section 4 of my paper, however, quite another question is raised: the extent of the control. This question is about limitations of the management's control position – any management, old or new. McCahery's and Vermeulen's paper focuses on one aspect of this question, limits set by bans on self-dealing. Other limits are the exclusive competences of the shareholder meeting, and these seem even more related to the traditional discussion of the market for corporate control, given that one legal solution which can be found for takeover situations is that there is an exclusive competence of the shareholder meeting to decide on defensive measures.

[1] Classical JC Coffee Jr 'Regulating the Market for Corporate Control: A Critical Assessment of the Tender Offer's Role in Corporate Governance' (1984) 84 Columbia L Rev 1145; FH Easterbrook and GR Fischel 'Corporate Control Transactions' (1981/82) 91 Yale L J 698; HG Manne 'Mergers and the Market for Corporate Control' (1965) 73 J Pol Econ 110, esp cont. ...

narrow sense negotiated by the managements of two corporations and then ratified by the shareholder meetings of both). Competition in the market for corporate control is then directly about the control position as managers of a (public) corporation. On the other hand, in the descriptions and analyses, there is also an element of competition in stock markets, although the market for corporate control is seen as distinct from – and not just a sub-set of – public capital markets.[2] There is this element because the means by which new management would oust old management is the acquisition of a control position in voting stock. If, however, competition directly relates to the control position as managers of a corporation, the question arises whether alternative ways of competition for the management control position must be considered to give a balanced picture – two or more managements competing to be hired and offering their services to the prime decision makers – above all shareholders (namely control shareholders) or their representatives, for instance in supervisory boards, who are or may be responsible to the other or to all shareholders. Thus competition for the control position as managers ('corporate control') is certainly a core element of the corporate governance structure.

Therefore, in the following, primarily takeovers will be considered. The approach will be comparative in principle. Special emphasis will, however, be put

114-120; RK Winter *Government and the Corporation* (American Enterprise Institute Washington DC 1978) 16-28; today mainly FH Easterbrook and GR Fischel *The Economic Structure of Corporate Law* (2nd edn Harvard University Press Cambridge 1996) esp 124-132; SJ Grossmann and OD Hart 'One Share-One Vote and the Market for Corporate Control' (1988) 20 J of Financial Economics 175; DS Scharfstein 'The Disciplinary Role of Takeovers' (1988) 55 Rev of Economic Studies 185; J Zwiebel 'Block Investments and Partial Benefits of Corporate Control' (1995) 62 Rev of Economic Studies 161; and the contributions to KJ Hopt and others *Comparative Corporate Governance: The State of the Art and Emerging Research* (OUP Oxford 1998) 639-697; in German literature eg J Reul *Die Pflicht zur Gleichbehandlung der Aktionäre bei privaten Kontrolltransaktionen – Eine juristische und ökonomische Analyse* (Mohr Siebeck Tübingen 1991) 128-132; also P Behrens 'Corporate Governance' in J Basedow KJ Hopt and H Kötz (eds) *Festschrift for Ulrich Drobnig* (Mohr Siebeck Tübingen 1998) 491 (500).

[2] EF Fama 'Agency Problems and the Theory of the Firm' (1980) 88 J of Political Economy 288. Besides capital markets and the market for corporate control, there are at least two more markets which should have disciplining effects on management similar to those attributed to the market for corporate control: product markets or more generally markets for the offers the enterprise makes (some see this market as the one which has the strongest disciplining effect and is even largely sufficient for disciplining management; see F Allen and D Gale 'Corporate Governance and Competition' in X Vives (ed) *Corporate Governance: Theoretical and Empirical Perspectives* (Cambridge University Press Cambridge 2000) 23; and also Behrens (n 1) 500; and the labour market which, however, may be efficient only when hiring management and much less so when firing it, because this management may monopolise assets which guarantee influence, namely information; see Company Law Review Steering Group *Modern Company Law for a Competitive Economy: The Strategic Framework. A Consultation Document* (2/1999) 35; see for all this also S Grundmann 'European Company Law: From Crisis to Boom' (2004) 5 Eur Business Organization L Rev 601.

on EC law, given that this is the jurisdiction where regulation is most recent and, moreover, where all major types of takeover regulation identified can be found (see below, section II.). This section will be followed by one on the mechanisms which improve the possibility that management would be replaced within the organisational framework and normal decision making process of the company, ie without 'structural change' from outside. Here, convergence and uniformity will be seen as a major trend which makes comparative law inquiries perhaps a little less important (see below, section III.). These two sections deal with replacement of management and the disciplinary effects of such instruments, ie with full loss of the control position. Alternatively, however, it is also possible to limit the control which managers have (partial loss of control position). Therefore, in a last section (section IV), the question will be raised whether a restriction of competences and other arrangements limiting the power of management are not relevant for a 'market for corporate control' as well, because then certain powers cannot be subject to competition between managements.

II. Takeover Regulations

1. Overview

In takeover law, the focus of discussion and regulation is on two topics, only one of which is directly related to the market for corporate control. This is the mandatory bid, which may influence this market indirectly (because it may prevent some bidders from bidding). Its scope, however, is rather the equitable distribution of proceeds (the 'control premium') among shareholders, and its focus is on the relationship between majority (or dominant) and minority shareholders.[3] In this respect, there is now uniformity in principle in Europe, though not in the United States.[4]

[3] On this discussion see eg H Rau-Bredow 'Ökonomische Analyse obligatorischer Übernahmeangebote' (1999) 59 Die Betriebswirtschaft 763; SA Ravid and MI Spiegel 'Toehold Strategies, Takeover Laws and Rival Bidders' (1999) 23 J of Banking & Finance 1219 (1237 and passim); Reul (n 1) 188 ff esp 238-250; A Shleifer and R Vishny 'Value Maximisation and the Acquisition Process' (1988) 7 J of Economic Perspectives 13-15; and various contributions in KJ Hopt and E Wymeersch (eds) *European Takeovers: Law and Practice* (Butterworths London 1992); critically C Bergstrom and others 'The Regulation of Corporate Acquisitions: A Law and Economics Analysis of European Proposals for Reform' [1995] Columbia Business L Rev 495, 516-519. The same accounts, in principle, for squeeze-out and sell-out rights which, in some countries and on the EC level, are regulated in conjunction with takeover law; for a short comparative law survey, see Grundmann (n 2) para 1053.

[4] In Europe, uniformity is due to Art 5 of the Directive 2004/25/EC of the European Parliament and of the Council of 21 April 2004 on takeover bids [2004] OJ L142/12; the mandatory bid, however, existed in virtually all member states before; see short comparative law survey on the mandatory bid in various member states in Grundmann (n 2) para 1032. For

cont. ...

The second focus is of greater interest here. It is on arrangements or decisions which make takeovers more difficult or even prevent them completely (defensive measures). These measures were the reason why it took so long to adopt the EC Takeover Directive and why the compromise eventually found is often considered to be largely insufficient.[5]

The regulation in Europe[6] – but not in the US[7] – consists of prohibiting management from taking defensive measures when a takeover bid has been made (see below 2). More complex, though not necessarily more controversial, is the legal treatment of arrangements made before this phase which carry a particular risk of deterring potential bidders and thus frustrating bids even before they have been made. These must be treated differently because, here, prohibitions are even more delicate, given that the company is not only affected for a short period of time and that arrangements made by the board and based on shareholder resolutions have to be distinguished. In Europe, a new type of regulation has been introduced with the breakthrough rule (see below 3). Under the EC Directive, each member state may opt out of this regime, but ECJ case law, which is the second element of EC regulation in this area – besides (secondary) statutory law – may well strike down such state laws under fundamental freedoms (see below 2 and 3). The result of all these rules is to regulate arrangements or decisions which make takeovers more difficult or even prevent them, and to restrict the freedom of the parties to make such arrangements or to take such decisions.

the US, where only few decisions have developed a right of minority shareholders to have a share in the control premium and where the mandatory bid is virtually nonexistent, see the landmark decisions in, on the one hand *Jones v Ahmanson & Co* 460 P.2d 464 (Cal 1969); *Perlman v Feldmann* 219 F2d 173, 178 [2nd Circuit 1955]); and on the other *Zetlin v Hanson Holdings* 397 NE2d 387, 388 (NY 1979); for a description see eg SM Bainbridge *Mergers and Acquisitions* (Foundation Press New York 2003) 214-218; FA Gevurtz *Corporation Law* (West Hornbook St Paul 2000) 631-644.

[5] S Maul and D Muffat-Jeandet 'Die EU-Übernahmerichtlinie' [2004] Die Aktiengesellschaft 221, 224 ff; R Skog 'The Takeover Directive: An Endless Saga?' (2002) 13 European Business L Rev 301. The ambiguous feelings about this part of the directive are perhaps best shown by the fact that the EC commissioner responsible (Bolkestein) wanted to withdraw the proposal altogether (and was only outvoted by the majority in the EC Commission which then, however, voted against the compromise): for all this, see PM Wiesner 'Die neue Übernahmerichtlinie und die Folgen' [2004] Zeitschrift für Wirtschaftsrecht [ZIP] 343, 343-346.

[6] Directive 2004/25/EC (n 4); comparative law survey on takeover measures in various member states: V de Beaufort *Les OPA en Europe* (Economica Paris 2001); S Grundmann and F Möslein 'Die Goldene Aktie und der Markt für Unternehmenskontrolle – insbesondere Staatskontrollrechte, Höchst- und Mehrfachstimmrechte sowie Übernahmeabwehrmaßnahmen' (2003) 102 Zeitschrift für vergleichende Rechtswissenschaft [ZvglRWiss] 289, 323-334.

[7] Good comparative law survey in P Davies 'The Regulation of Defensive Tactics in the United Kingdom and the United States' in Hopt and Wymeersch (n 3) 197-215; DA DeMott 'Current Issues in Tender Offer Regulation: Lessons from the British' (1983) 58 New York U L Rev 945.

The regulation in Europe is particularly unusual in two other respects. These are rules which are distinct from regulation in the sense considered so far. These rules enhance market reactions to arrangements or decisions which make takeovers more difficult or even prevent them. One is a traditional disclosure rule. What is new, however, is that it asks for an ordered takeover arrangements statement including virtually all arrangements which are nowadays thought to have some influence on potential takeover bids (see below 4). The other new instrument may be found where member states opt out of the regime on defensive measures. In this case, each company has the right to opt in again. If they do not do so, this may have two adverse effects: they cannot invoke the regime on defensive measures when they themselves are the bidders; and the stock price may react again because a decision not to adhere to this regime must be reported by each company (see below 5).

2. Duty of Neutrality in the Takeover Situation

The first distinction needed is between measures taken against a bid which has already been made and measures taken at an earlier stage ('prophylactically'), without such concrete background. This is important because most arrangements cannot only defend management against takeovers but also have other aims as well, and therefore a complete ban would seriously affect the business of the company, perhaps even paralyse it (for this second phase, see below 3.).

a. Comparative Law Survey

For the phase when a concrete bid has been made, regulation, if there is any, is typically of one type only: the board is completely prohibited from defending itself; only the day-to-day business can be carried on. This is now the regulation also on the European level in Art 9 of the Takeover Directive. It also spells out the overriding principles in this respect in Art 3 para 1 lit c and f. According to these, while the power of the shareholders of the target company to decide on the bid takes absolute priority, the business operation of the target company may be affected only to the extent which is absolutely necessary.

This rule has been shaped basically on the model of the City Code on Takeovers and Mergers[8]. The characteristics are (1) the strict prohibition of defensive measures with (2) an exception only in two cases: for the current business operation (there are variants of this exception, see below), and in the case of an

[8] The Panel on Takeovers and Mergers *The City Code on Panel on Takeovers and Mergers* as of 1985 <www.thetakeoverpanel.org.uk> (27 June 2005).

authorisation by the shareholder meeting (not the board or parts of it).[9] A comparative law survey in Europe[10] shows those countries following the London regime in contrast with Germany, France, and also the Netherlands. The first group comprises Italy, where the regulation is to be found in Art 104 Testo Unico and where high majorities are required for the authorisation by the shareholder meeting,[11] and also Belgium and Spain.[12] In Germany, defensive measures – despite a prohibition in principle – are largely possible because of three exceptions (§ 33 para 1 (2) and 2 WpÜG):[13] the board may carry on an action already started, even if it does not constitute current business operation; the shareholder meeting can give a (blanket) authorisation for at most 18 months; and – in the German *'Sündenfall'* (Hopt) – the supervisory board can ratify the action. The prevailing view is, however, that the board, when deciding, has to take the company's, ie mainly the shareholders', interests as the sole guideline (strict duty of loyalty of the board members).[14] Whether this regime will be given up or only individual German companies will opt into the regime of the directive is by no means clear. France takes the opposite way. There is no prohibition in principle;

[9] City Code General Principle 7; see for instance Davies (n 7) 195; on the link between the directive and the City Code in more detail: M Andenas 'European Take-over Regulation and the City Code' (1996) 17 Company Lawyer 150.

[10] De Beaufort (n 6); T Baums and GF Thoma (eds) *Takeover Laws in Europe* (RWS Cologne 2002) (legislative texts); G Hertig and JA McCahery 'Company and Takeover Law Reforms in Europe: Misguided Harmonization Efforts or Regulatory Competition?' (2003) 4 Eur Business Organization L Rev 179; E Wymeersch 'The Proposal for a 13th Company Law Directive on Takeovers: A Multi-jurisdiction Survey' (1996) 3 and (1997) 4 Eur Financial Services L 301 and 2; more specifically on defensive measures and on the following: Grundmann and Möslein (n 6) 323-334; GA Ferrarini 'Le difese contro le o.p.a. ostili – analisi economica e comparazione' [2000] Rivista delle società 737, esp 764-791.

[11] 30% of the capital and two-thirds of the voting stock present (see Codice Civile Art 2368 para 2 (2)). On this M Mucciarelli 'Combinazioni aziendali e passivity rule' [2000] II Banca, Borsa e Titoli di Credito 223; more in detail also Grundmann and Möslein (n 6) 331 ff.

[12] On these countries see de Beaufort (n 6) 149-152 and 219-222; Grundmann and Möslein (n 6) 332 ff; in this sense most member states by far, see KJ Hopt 'Verhaltenspflichten des Vorstands der Zielgesellschaft bei feindlichen Übernahmen – zur aktien- und übernahmerechtlichen Rechtslage in Deutschland und Europa' in UH Schneider and others (eds) *Festschrift für Marcus Lutter* (Otto Schmidt Cologne 2000) 1361, 1372-1374.

[13] From the host of literature on defensive measures under § 33 WpÜG see only KJ Hopt 'Grundsatz- und Praxisprobleme nach dem Wertpapiererwerbs- und Übernahmegesetz' (2002) 166 Zeitschrift für das gesamte Handels- und Wirtschaftsrecht [ZHR] 375, 426 ff; and the references in S Grundmann *Europäisches Gesellschaftsrecht – eine systematische Darstellung unter Einbeziehung des Europäischen Kapitalmarktrechts* (CF Müller Heidelberg 2004) para 968.

[14] For instance Hopt (n 13) 427 ff; for members of the supervisory board in particular: H Lange 'Das Unternehmensinteresse der Zielgesellschaft und sein Einfluss auf die Rechtsstellung der die Übernahme fördernde Aufsichtsratsmitglieder' [2002] Wertpapier-Mitteilungen [WM] 1737.

however, not only the information duties are intensive, but all measures not authorised in detail by the shareholders meeting which go beyond current business operation have to be reported (to the stock exchange supervisory authority which, however, has no power to prohibit them).[15] In Dutch law, there are traditionally far-reaching possibilities for defensive measures because measures taken in advance are largely possible, though the takeover phase itself is increasingly regulated.[16]

US law is closer to this minority trend in Europe. Frustrating measures are not prohibited under federal securities law,[17] but they are scrutinised by state courts under corporate fiduciary duties. At least in Delaware, an intermediate standard of review is applied, because management decisions on these defensive measures are neither as free of conflict of interests as normal business decisions subject to the business judgment rule, nor do they entail any self-dealing transaction calling for application of the fairness test.[18] Therefore, directors are required to prove that they possessed reasonable grounds for believing a threat to corporate policy and effectiveness existed and that the defensive measure used to be reasonable in relation to the threat posed.[19]

b. Policy Considerations

The policy discussion on takeovers is complex. It is much disputed whether they are generally beneficial or whether such rules on the mandatory bid are needed to filter bids which increase overall efficiency and those which do not do so. However, what cannot be disputed is (1) the disciplinary effect which was para-

[15] Règlement n 2002-04 de la Commission des Opérations de Bourse (COB) of 22 April 2002, implementing regulation May 2002; still on the forerunner rule (which now has been supplemented by some information duties): de Beaufort (n 6) 252-333; D Carreau and H Letréguilly 'Offres publics (OPA, OPE, OPR)' (2001) Rép Sociétés Dalloz 4 esp para 224-271; C Klein and D Stucki 'Öffentliche Übernahmeangebote (OPA/OPE) in Frankreich' [2001] Recht der Internationalen Wirtschaft [RIW] 488; on the duty of loyalty highlighted there: D Schmidt *Les conflits d'interêt dans la société anonyme* (Editions Joly Paris 1999) 92 ff; more in detail also Grundmann and Möslein (n 6) 328-330.

[16] De Beaufort (n 6) 450-492; Grundmann and Möslein (n 6) 333 ff.

[17] The prohibition of material misstatements, omissions, and fraudulent practices in Section 14(e) Securities Exchange Act might, however, very well have been read to apply to defensive measures, see TL Hazen *Securities Regulation* (3rd edn West Hornbook St Paul 1996) 635 ff, 661; H Dietrich *Die Tender Offer im Bundesrecht der Vereinigten Staaten* (Metzner Frankfurt 1975) 255-259. This approach, however, was rejected by the US Supreme Court in *Schreiber v Burlington Northern Inc* 472 US 1, 105 SCt 2458, 86 LEd2d 1 (1985).

[18] More in detail: RJ Gilson and RH Kraakman 'Delaware's Intermediate Standard for Defensive Tactics: Is There Substance to Proportionality Review?' (1989) 44 Business L 247.

[19] The landmark decision is *Unocal Corp v Mesa Petroleum Co* 493 A2d 946, 954 (Del 1985).

mount in the discussion and described at the beginning of this paper, and (2) that the number of takeovers which indeed increased efficiency is not completely irrelevant. The core question therefore has to be who should be competent to decide on whether a takeover is seen as increasing efficiency. It would be sub-optimal just to allow anybody in the company to deter takeovers. In this respect, virtually all the legal measures existing and discussed only consider efficiency in the target company, although it would be appropriate to include also the potential welfare gains or losses in the bidder company and establish an overall calculus. In the bidder company, the competence of the board is still not seriously challenged.

If one concentrates indeed on the competence of the target company, the following would seem to be important: the members of the board – obviously – are subject to a massive conflict of interests; they can always be tempted to give priority to their own interests; and often other reasons to justify the steps taken can be invoked.[20] The question can therefore only be whether no more suitable decision maker can be found. Moreover, if the board is really given the power, a scrutiny as to whether the decisions taken were in the interest of the principal must necessarily follow, if one does not give up the foundations of principal agent theory altogether. Therefore, besides the risks of conflict of interests, there is intensive, unforeseeable involvement of external control (by courts), and this means that decision power is in fact shifted from the principal to a third party.

The most obvious alternative decision maker would seem to be the principal. The argument against such a competence is mainly that he lacks capacity or willingness to gather and process all material information, ie to decide rationally and in a maximizing way, and this in a sufficiently short period of time so as not to paralyse the business of the target company.[21] What is still relatively easy to arrange is calling in a forum fast enough (shareholder meeting called in at short

[20] A particularly intensive analysis can be found in PO Mülbert and M Birke 'Das übernahmerechtliche Behinderungsverbot – die angemessene Rolle der Verwaltung einer Zielgesellschaft in einer feindlichen Übernahme' [2001] WM 705 (on conflict of interests and possibilities to hide them; 709-712); and GW Schwert 'Poison or Placebo? Evidence on the Deterrence and Wealth Effects of Modern Antitakeover Measures' (1995) 39 J of Financial Economics 3; JF Weston, JA Siu and BA Johnson *Takeovers, Restructuring, & Corporate Governance* (3rd edn Prentice Hall Upper Saddle River 2001); also Ferrarini (n 10) for instance 783; opposite, because the management of European companies should not be less well equipped then that of US American companies: C Kirchner and RW Painter 'European Takeover Law – Towards a European Modified Business Judgment Rule for Takeover Law' (2000) 1 Eur Business Organization L Rev 353; before already Bergstrom and others (n 3) 510; also T Wiese and D Demisch 'Unternehmensführung bei feindlichen Übernahmeangeboten – eine Kritik des geplanten Übernahmerechts aus ökonomischer Sicht' [2001] Der Betrieb 849.

[21] H Eidenmüller 'Kapitalgesellschaften im Spiegel der ökonomischen Theorie' [2001] Juristenzeitung 1041, 1048; Ferrarini (n 10) 783; J Dean 'Directors' Duties in Response to Hostile Takeover Bids' (2003) 14 International Company and Commercial L Rev 370, 373-375; also Mülbert and Birke (n 20) 708, 718 for the prohibition of provisional resolutions by shareholder meetings [informational basis is sufficient only when the concrete bid is made].

notice). It is already more difficult to answer the question of which majority (for the principal) should decide on defensive measures: the simple majority (of the voting stock present), a qualified majority (as, for instance, in Italy, see above), or, quite to the contrary, only a minority capable of vetoing charter amendments, because the takeover would change the fundamentals of the company and this can be avoided by such a minority in other cases of structural changes. The most important question, however, would be whether typically the capacity and willingness to receive and process all material information can be expected. In this respect, it is important that in all large European capital markets in virtually all PLCs whose shares are admitted to regulated markets, there are either large shareholders having invested with an entrepreneurial intention or institutional shareholders holding substantial blocks of stock. And capital markets are already largely efficient if information is processed by the market makers[22] (and the same is true *cum grano salis* in such an outstanding situation as an extraordinary shareholder meeting deciding on takeover defensive measures).

Summarising these considerations, one can say that the prohibition of defensive measures taken by the board helps to install market solutions in this respect; the question is only whether the market – because the bidder is much better informed or because of the scattered structure of the decision maker in the target company – does not tend to fail. If considered this way, it seems evident that the first approach would be to counteract the information asymmetry and consequences of dispersed ownership, and only if all else fails to renounce market solutions. In case of a takeover bid, all this speaks in favour of the (in principle) exclusive competence of the principal.

c. The EC Law Rule (Art 9 Takeover Directive)

Today, the EC Law Rule is the prime example for such a rule. As soon as the bid has been disclosed to the board (or earlier if a member state opts for it) and until the result of the bid has been determined (or until the bid failed), the board of the target company is strictly prohibited from preventing the bid (para 2, for the two exceptions see below). Art 9 thus deals with defensive measures taken during the takeover procedure, not with measures taken before. Defensive measures during the procedure may be taken exclusively by the shareholder meeting. Therefore, the content of the rule is not a prohibition of defensive measures, but a shift of competence to the shareholder meeting. Defensive measures are not made impossible; the national legislatures are instead encouraged by EC law (it would be

[22] Behrens (n 1) 500; HH Kallfass *Kapitalmarktkoordination – die Koordinationsprozesse über Märkte für Beteiligungstitel in der Theorie und in der westdeutschen Realität* (Vandenhoeck & Ruprecht Göttingen 1992) 82-90; FH Easterbrook and GR Fischel 'Mandatory Disclosure and the Protection of Investors' (1984) 70 Virginia L Rev 669, 695.

better if were obliged) to allow the possibility of calling a shareholder meeting at short notice (para 4) – and this is the only harmonisation, ie a true cornerstone in the procedure. 'Short notice' seems to mean 'without unnecessary delay'; at the same time a minimum period of two weeks is fixed, which seems strictly necessary to properly inform the shareholders. The competence of the shareholder meeting begins as soon as there is even a risk that the bid could be prevented. The board is thus prohibited not only from preventing but also from hampering the bid – ie anything which makes its success less likely.[23] The issue of authorised capital is mentioned explicitly. While this is only one example, it nevertheless demonstrates two arrangements which are usually quite illicit. Firstly, the authorisation of a defensive measure by another part of the board, mainly the supervisory board (as in Germany, see above), and secondly an ex ante authorisation by the shareholder meeting (again important, for instance, in Germany). The latter must be able to decide in full knowledge of all the concrete facts of this individual case.[24]

The two exceptional cases in which competence is not shifted to the shareholder meeting seem plausible: the current business operation ('normal course of the company's business') typically does not have a high potential of frustrating the bid, and suspending this activity also for up to ten weeks would seriously affect target companies. National law decides on how the board may use its discretion in the exceptional cases where current business operation nevertheless hampers the bid – balancing the interests of the success of the bid with the interests of maintaining the business operation. What has not been retained in the directive is a broader version of this exception which can be found in some national laws. These laws allow the board to carry on actions already started, even if they do not constitute current business operation.[25] The second exception, looking for a rival bid, is not really an exception. Auctions may be questionable

[23] The (subjective) intention to frustrate the bid is not needed: Hopt (n 12) 1387.

[24] Prohibition of provisional resolutions, discussed mainly in German literature (because important there): KJ Hopt 'Takeover regulation in Europe: The battle for the 13th directive on takeovers' (2002) 15 Australian J of Corporate L 1, 16; B Dauner-Lieb and M Lamandini 'Der neue Kommissionsvorschlag einer EU-Übernahmerichtlinie – Stellungnahme der Gutachter des EU-Parlaments' [2003] Betriebs-Berater 265, 266; Eidenmüller (n 21) 1048; HW Neye 'Der Vorschlag 2002 einer Takeover-Richtlinie' [2002] Neue Zeitschrift für Gesellschaftsrecht 1144; C Seibt and J Heiser 'Der neue Vorschlag einer EU-Übernahmerichtlinie und das deutsche Übernahmerecht – Analyse und Umsetzungserfordernisse für den deutschen Gesetzgeber' [2002] Zeitschrift für Wirtschaftsrecht [ZIP] 2193, 2195 ff (also on the fact that § 33 para 2 WpÜG which allows them is little used because of negative effects on capital markets); different still the legislative motion of the European Parliament for a Common Standpoint of the Council with a view of adopting a Company Law Directive of the European Parliament and of the Council on takeovers [2000] OJ C232/168, 171 (re-drafting Art 9 para 1 lit a).

[25] For instance in Italy, Comunicazione Consob n DAL/99039392 of 18 May 1999 para 2.3; much more restrictive is rule 21.1 of the City Code (only if there is an obligation, at least a moral one). For Germany see above a. The directive again provides for a shift of competence to the shareholder meeting: Seibt and Heiser (n 24) 2196.

from the overall perspective of national economies.[26] In the takeover situation itself, however, the situation of the shareholders is only enhanced – on the condition, however, that the board does not further one (less advantageous) bid over the other, which is indeed prohibited under the directive.

An additional safeguard concerns information. The informational base for the decision is to be strengthened by an opinion given by an expert who is independent of the bidder, here the board of the target company (para 5). While it is true that this organ is also subject to conflicts of interest, this is clear to the shareholders and the adverse effects of it are limited given that there are now two divergent perspectives presented. One more – really neutral – expert opinion is not provided for (which differs from the regime in all other structural changes in EC law). Apparently confidence is placed in the presence of enough professional shareholders in the capital market segments affected. The content of the statement of the board of the target company is broad: all interests of the 'company' (apparently the target company) have to be taken into account and commented on – not only the desirability of the transaction as a whole, but also the interests of the single groups.

Under the EC Directive, each member state may opt out of this regime,[27] but ECJ case law – which is the second element of EC regulation in this area besides (secondary) statutory law – may well hold such state laws to violate fundamental freedoms.

d. The Relevance of ECJ Case Law

Another minefield under EC law – to be discussed very briefly here – is indeed the ECJ case law.[28] On the basis of the freedom of capital movement, the ECJ scrutinised arrangements in companies whose (voting) stock was traded on public capital markets quite intensively. It also scrutinised arrangements which did not

[26] See on the policy considerations with respect to auctions (the possibility of rival bids may lower the readiness of others to make bids in the first place): FH Easterbrook and GR Fischel 'Auctions and Sunk Costs in Tender Offers' (1982) 35 Stanford L Rev 1; more positive: LA Bebchuk 'The Case for Facilitating Competing Tender Offers' (1982) 95 Harvard L Rev 1028, 1039-1041; H Fleischer 'Konkurrenzangebote und Due Diligence – Vorüberlegungen zu einer übernahmerechtlichen Gleichbehandlung der Bieter' [2001] Zeitschrift für Wirtschaftsrecht [ZIP] 651, esp 653; RJ Gilson 'Seeking Competitive Bids versus Pure Passivity in Tender Offer Defence' (1982) 35 Stanford L Rev 51; undecided Eidenmüller (n 21) 1048; Mülbert and Birke (n 20) 712.

[27] On this regime of options see also below section 5.

[28] Mainly case C-503/99 *Commission v Belgium* [2002] ECR I-4809; case C-483/99 *Commission v France* [2002] ECR 2002 I-4781; case C-483/99 *Commission v Portugal* [2002] ECR 2002 I-4731. See more in detail, also for the following S Grundmann and F Möslein (2001-2002) 1 Euredia 623, 648-674 (with extensive further references).

completely exclude the acquisition of such shares, but which simply made the acquisition less desirable for investors willing to acquire control (so-called indirect limitation of access to shares). This includes increased voting power of existing shareholders, for instance in golden share arrangements. The fundamental criterion was whether an investor willing to acquire control could potentially be deterred. In this case, the ECJ required that the national law be justified by mandatory reasons of public good, namely that it had to be narrowly focused, quite detailed, and not based only on general economic considerations (principle of proportionality and specificity). The potentially deterrent effect of a board's competence to take defensive measures can hardly be doubted; moreover, if one considers the ECJ case law so far, it seems fair to predict that measures taken by the board will rarely prove to be justified by mandatory reasons of public good.

There is really only one question where doubts can arise as to whether the ECJ case law in fact applies: the main question is whether the ECJ will transfer these rules to arrangements in favour of private law subjects. The cases so far have dealt with arrangements in favour of public entities. Considering the ECJ case law on direct applicability of fundamental freedoms to private law subjects, it is very likely that the same rule applies at least to arrangements taken by one party only and not based on agreement by all parties concerned.

The main problem with this argument – from a policy perspective – is to be seen in one assumption the ECJ makes: it assumes that it may scrutinise such arrangements even though the market has other ways to react, namely by acquiring these shares only at a discount. This assumption is even more problematic in cases where – as in the privatisation (Golden Shares) cases – the rule in the law would make arrangements possible only for few companies. This assumption is, if anything, less problematic where a law is capable of 'closing' a whole national market for entrepreneurial investors willing to take control. Even with respect to such rules affecting a whole national market, however, the alternative of a market reaction, based on enhanced disclosure of takeover impediments, is worth discussion (see below 4 and 5).

3. Prohibition or Breakthrough Rule for Arrangements Made Prior to the Takeover Bid

Traditionally, arrangements made prior to the takeover bid have been tested under different standards. In this area, for all important potential defensive measures, it is already an important step if transparency is prescribed (see below 4.). In quite a few jurisdictions, some arrangements are moreover subject to substantive mandatory regulation. The most important divide in this respect has always been between arrangements made by the board and those based on shareholder resolution.

a. Arrangements by the Board

The above-mentioned rule in the City Code on Takeovers (duty to abstain when the bid is made) is supplemented by one for the pre-bid phase: measures taken in advance (before the publication of the bid), while not prohibited, are scrutinised under the duty of loyalty.[29] The EC Directive does not deal with this phase. As a matter of principle, however, such a duty of loyalty was accepted also in those jurisdictions reluctant to accept a duty to abstain when the bid is made – mainly Germany in the European Community,[30] and in many states in the US.[31] Formally, therefore, there is convergence in the major jurisdictions. The results of the application of this rule have, however, been far from uniform – not surprisingly, given the vagueness of the standard.[32]

The standard is, in principle, that which is also applied for self-dealing, and as such it was extensively described by McCahery/Vermeulen at this conference. The test is whether similar solutions would have been adopted in arm's length situations. For many decisions, however, this standard is of little help, for instance for the takeover of a firm which is a competitor of a potential bidder, such as Orange in the case of the Mannesmann-Vodafone Takeover. For such a takeover, solid business reasons could easily be invoked. It also had the effect, however, that a takeover of Mannesmann by a large British supplier of telecommunication services was potentially prejudiced, given that a group containing both Vodafone and Orange would have violated (EC and national) antitrust laws as applied to the United Kingdom. Both firms taken together had a dominant position on the English market.

On the other hand, even this vague standard would still exclude, quite naturally, at least those arrangements where business reasons – besides takeover deterrence – are not really plausible. It produces the best results in two situations: where there is also self-dealing in the traditional sense, namely with respect to questions of remuneration; and even more so where the results of the arrangement are conditional on the formulation or the success of a bid. The latter, while they

[29] On this aspect (in addition to those named in n 9), see eg JE Parkinson *Corporate Power and Responsibility* (OUP Oxford 1995) 143-158.

[30] S Winter and M Harbarth 'Verhaltenspflichten von Vorstand und Aufsichtsrat der Zielgesellschaft bei feindlichen Übernahmeangeboten nach dem WpÜG' [2002] Zeitschrift für Wirtschaftsrecht [ZIP] 1, 4; see also KJ Hopt 'Aktionärskreis und Vorstandsneutralität' [1993] Zeitschrift für Unternehmens- und Gesellschaftsrecht [ZGR] 534, 558-560; more specifically KJ Hopt 'Präventivmaßnahmen zur Abwehr von Übernahme- und Beteiligungsversuchen' in WM-Festgabe für Theodor Heinsius (WM-Gruppe Frankfurt 1991) 22.

[31] As a matter of principle, the same standard of review applies as for post-bid defensive measures: *Moran v Household International* 500 A2d 1346.

[32] See eg WT Allen JB Jacobs and L Strine Jr 'Function over Form: A Reassessment of Standards of Review in Delaware Corporation Law' (2001) 56 Business L 1287 (claiming inconsistency of the standards of review applied by Delaware courts).

are formally arrangements made in the pre-bid phase, are materially equivalent to arrangements made during the takeover phase proper. Thus, for instance, poison pills would violate the duty of loyalty standard,[33] and golden parachutes would at least need to be tested under the arm's length standard.[34]

b. Arrangements Based on Shareholder Resolutions (Art 11 Takeover Directive)

Traditionally, arrangements based on shareholder resolutions have often been seen as potential impediments to takeovers. One core example is multiple voting rights.[35] However, where shareholders made use of national law enabling them to introduce such arrangements, a theoretical foundation for testing such arrangements seemed much less developed than in the case of arrangements introduced by the board or board members. Scrutiny of these measures is not really discussed in Anglo-American literature nor even in German literature.[36] This is worth mentioning because quite a few other types of shareholder resolutions are put to a rather intensive judicial control.

An interesting solution is now proposed in the EC Takeover Directive, in Art 11. The rule – like the disclosure rule contained in Art 10 (below 4) – was introduced only in the last proposal in 2002, based on the recommendation of the

[33] In the United States, poison pills were mainly justified to give the management the possibility to fight so-called coercive bids, see *Moran v Household International* 500 A2d 1346 (1354 ff); Gevurtz (n 4) 694-696. Coercive bids, however, are not a problem where the bidder has to make a bid to all shareholders, as under Art 5 of the EC Takeover Directive. In the US, however, even poison pills which take effect in any case (no-hand pills), are put only to a rather weak test, see *Mentor Graphics v Quickturn Designs Sys* 728 A2d 25 (Del Ch 1998), affirmed on other grounds, 721 A2d 1281 (Del 1998). A rather strict scrutiny under the proper purposes doctrine can be found in the United Kingdom, however; see *Criterion Properties plc v Stratford UK Properties LLC* (2003) 2 BCLC 129.

[34] With respect to US law, see E Block DJ Barton and SA Radin *The Business Judgment Rule* (5th edn Law & Business Aspen 1998) 1296-1332.

[35] Seen as a potential impediment to takeovers for instance by *Report of the High Level Group of Company Law Experts on Issues related to Takeover Bids* (2002), available at <http://www.law.ugent.be/fli/WP/takeover%20bids.pdf> (27 June 2005) 21-36 and government explanation to the German KonTraG, BT-Drucks 13/9712 p 20; S Kalss *Das Höchststimmrecht als Instrument zur Wahrung des Aktionärseinflusses* (Service-Fachverlag Wien 1992); path-breaking Grossmann and Hart (n 1). Deviations from this principle are increasingly prohibited, at least for companies whose stock is traded on regulated markets, in Germany, in Italy, and under listing rules of the London Stock Exchange; France and also Sweden are still forming exceptions: see comparative law survey in Grundmann and Möslein (n 28) 634-636.

[36] H Hirte in H Hirte (ed) *Kölner Kommentar zum WpÜG* (Heymanns Cologne 2003) § 33 para 46 ff.

High Level Group.[37] All restrictions on transfer are suspended during the bidding phase, ie mainly restrictions on transferability, pre-emption rights, and penalties,[38] as far as they are based on arrangement by the parties (para 2), charter, or contract (except for contracts with third parties). Moreover, for a general meeting deciding about defensive measures, all limits to voting rights based on arrangement by the parties (para 3), charter, or contract (except for contracts with third parties) are suspended. This does not comprise limits to voting rights imposed by law, mainly those in cases of conflicts of interest and on the basis of fiduciary duties. This means mainly voting caps and all contracts binding a partner to exercise its voting rights in a prescribed manner.[39] Neither exception, however, applies to preferential stock (para 5), which is seen as being less problematic.[40] Moreover, there is a rule for a first general meeting after the success of the bid (para 4). The bidder must have the possibility to convene it at short notice, at the latest two weeks after the publication of the result. If he now disposes of the majority needed for charter amendments (under national law), restrictions to the transfer of shares and voting rights (as described in para 2 and 3) are suspended for this first meeting, as well as any nomination and removal rights of other shareholders for members of the board. Therefore, for instance, the board can be nominated anew (apparently irrespective of when their term would normally end). As the general meeting does not decide on restrictions on transfer anyway, and as these had already been suspended during the takeover procedure, the rule is meaningful only if interpreted in the sense that all specific rights mentioned are not only suspended in this meeting but can be removed by charter amendment (with the required majority) in this first meeting,[41] at least arrangements laid down in the charter which do not constitute individual rights.

[37] *High Level Group* (n 33), 29-39; worth reading PO Mülbert 'Make it or Break It: The Break-Through Rule as a Break-Through for the European Takeover Directive?' in GA Ferrarini and others (eds) *Reforming Company and Takeover Law in Europe* (OUP Oxford 2004) 711.

[38] Explanation by the EC Commission of Art 11; Neye (n 24) 1145; Seibt and Heiser (n 24) 2200; NJ Clausen and KE Sørensen 'The 2003 Proposal for a Directive on Takeover Bids – Impact on the Regulation in Scandinavia' (2003) 45 Scandinavian Studies in Law 89, 103-108; Hopt (n 24) 12, 16 ff; very critical: Hertig and McCahery (n 10) 200-203; W Knapp 'Proposed Takeover Directive: Will the break-through proposal work?' (2003) 23 The Company Lawyer 134.

[39] Explanation by the EC Commission of Art 11; Clausen and Sørensen (n 38) 106 ff; Neye (n 24) 1145.

[40] Clausen and Sørensen (n 38) 106 ff; Neye (n 24) 1145; Seibt and Heiser (n 24) 2200 (and not for the limits imposed by law to voting rights, mainly in conflict-of-interest cases). The amount of preferential stock is limited in some countries eg in Italy to 50% of the capital (Codice Civile art 2351 para 2).

[41] JA McCahery and L Renneboog *The Economics of the Proposed European Takeover Directive* (Centre for European Policy Studies Research Report in Finance and Banking no 32/2003) 55 ff.

This means that the legal situation must be clarified and changed immediately. The impact on the freedom to arrange the internal structure of the company by charter provisions is thus kept to a minimum.

c. The Relevance of ECJ Case Law

Again, each member state may opt out of this rule,[42] but once more ECJ case law may well hold such state laws to violate fundamental freedoms. The line of arguments would be the same as that referred to for the defensive measures taken by the board, but with one exception: It is at least possible that all shareholders have accepted the arrangement – by adopting it at the time of incorporation or accepting it when investing. At least in these cases, ie where no shareholder has been outvoted, all parties concerned (if one does not count potential investors among them) have created the arrangement by consensus. In these cases, a strong argument against any scrutiny under fundamental freedoms can be found in the ECJ case law. The ECJ seems to be unwilling to use the fundamental freedoms to restrict party autonomy where all parties have agreed, because in fact the aim of fundamental freedoms is extending the realm of such party autonomy – across borders – and fundamental freedoms should not be instrumentalised to avoid such party agreement.[43]

4. Transparency and the Price of Anti-Takeover Arrangements (Art 10 Takeover Directive)

Yet another rule was introduced only in the last proposal of the EC Takeover Directive and has really no precedent. It is contained in Art 10 and is a systematic disclosure rule. Its basis is clearly the efficient capital market hypothesis, according to which (in the version endorsed by the prevalent view) prices on capital markets not only reflect the information about historic price development but also at least material information publicly available.[44]

[42] On this regime of options see also below section 5.

[43] See case C-339/89 *Alsthom Atlantique* [1991] ECR I-107, 124; and for this explanation: S Grundmann 'The Structure of European Contract Law' (2001) 9 Eur Rev of Private L 505, 513 ff; more extensively S Grundmann 'Europäisches Handelsrecht – vom Handelsrecht des laissez faire im Kodex des 19. Jahrhunderts zum Handelsrecht der sozialen Verantwortung' (1999) 163 Zeitschrift für das gesamte Handels- und Wirtschaftsrecht [ZHR] 635, 656-659.

[44] Three forms of efficiency on capital markets are distinguished: it is weak if prices only reflect the knowledge of the development of prices in the past, semi-strong if they reflect (all) public information, and strong if they also reflect insider information; authors usually start from the semi-strong form. See RJ Gilson and RH Kraakman 'The Mechanisms of Market Efficiency' (1984) 70 Virginia L Rev 549; building on EF Fama 'Efficient Capital Markets: A

cont. ...

The core idea of the rule is that impediments to takeovers can be formed not only by measures taken in the takeover phase, but also by permanent arrangements. The rule is not aimed at informing shareholders of the target company about the terms of the bid,[45] not even about its chances. The elements about which disclosure is prescribed (see below) clearly show that the rule is aimed instead at systematically informing interested investors (much earlier) about the potential for preventing a takeover bid, and thus also about the chances that such a bid will occur. The disclosure is therefore aimed at potential investors evaluating two options: those seeking control and those desiring to profit from a potential control premium.

The distinction drawn with respect to the Golden Shares decisions of the ECJ between direct and indirect restrictions of access to shares is also helpful here. The most important examples of both types of restrictions have to be disclosed in the future (for the list, see below). For more systematic disclosure, arrangements which potentially impede takeovers will be even more visible – for potential bidders and even before and in particular for the market as a whole, which can reflect the decreased potential for takeovers more easily in the prices. The extent to which the relationship between the management and the shareholders is suboptimally arranged would then be reflected more directly in prices and thus would decrease the attractiveness of such arrangements. Or to put it differently: the decision on whether arrangements are suboptimal at all is left to the markets. Thus, impediments to takeovers are not regulated (away), but only the (potentially negative) reaction of the market is facilitated. An additional information tool and disciplinary instrument can be seen in the duty of the board to explain these arrangements (para 3 (2), apparently every second year). It is not clear whether this – like many disclosure duties – applies only to arrangements introduced on the basis of party autonomy or – more convincing from an investor protection perspective – also for arrangements introduced directly by the state (in Germany, for instance, the Law on VW).

Review of Theory and Empirical Work' (1970) 25 J Finance 383; today eg P Fenn A McGuire and D Prentice 'Information Imbalances and the Securities Markets' in KJ Hopt and E Wymeersch (eds) *European Insider Dealing – Law and Practice* (Butterworths London 1991) 3, 5; MJ Fishman and KM Hagerty 'Disclosure Decisions by Firms and the Competition for Price Efficiency' (1989) 44 J Finance 633; R Trigo Trinidade 'Corporate Governance – La responsabilité des conseils d'administration dans les sociétés' (2000) 8 Eur Rev of Private L 281, 284, 287; and also BR Cheffins *Company Law: Theory, Structure and Operation* (Clarendon Press Oxford 1997) 55-58; SM Keane *Efficient Markets and Financial Reporting* (Institute of Chartered Accountants of Scotland Edinburgh 1987); BG Malkiel 'The Efficient Market Hypothesis and its Critics' (2003) 17 J of Economic Perspectives 1; B Rudolph and H Röhrl 'Grundfragen der Börsenorganisation aus ökonomischer Sicht' in KJ Hopt B Rudolph H Baum (eds) *Börsenreform* (Schäffer Poeschel Stuttgart 1997) 143, 181 ff.

[45] In this sense, however, the contribution of JA McCahery and EPM Vermeulen in this volume.

The list of arrangements to be disclosed comprises the most important arrangements[46] which make the acquisition of shares (in part) impossible (direct restrictions of access to shares, lit b and g)[47] or which impinge upon the principle of 'one share one vote' and thus reduce the attractiveness of the share (indirect restrictions of access to shares, lit d, f, and h).[48] Moreover, two groups of questions are included in the list. The first group has at least a close relationship to indirect restrictions; these are traditional defensive measures which, however, materialise automatically (condition precedent) and which only for this reason do not fall under Art 9; the (typically adverse) effects the takeover has on contracts which are important to the company etc (poison pills, lit j); and (high) compensation agreements made for the case of a takeover (golden parachutes, lit k). The second additional group comprises situations in which the fact pattern in the PLC (not the legal arrangement) makes participation less attractive. Under lit a, the percentage of securities admitted to regulated markets is to be disclosed.[49] Under lit c, transparency of blockholdings is now prescribed also in regulated markets (not only in the segment of the official listing where this was already regulated in the Stock Exchange Directive).[50] The following must also be disclosed: the exercise of voting rights from shares attributed to labour by persons other than the employees (strong influence, for instance, by trade unions, lit e) and (extended) powers of the board via authorised capital and in cases of repurchases of share capital (own shares, lit i). In most cases, these are arrangements on the basis of party autonomy. Also covered are arrangements agreed on at a shareholder meeting. An arrangement on the basis of party autonomy is, however, not ex-

[46] Detailed description in High Level Group I (n 33) 25 ff; Clausen and Sørensen (n 38) 102 ff; Seibt and Heiser (n 24) 2196-2199.

[47] This refers to restrictions on transferability and rigid limits to acquisition (acquisition only of specified percentages etc). In this, lit b applies to restrictions favouring the company itself, lit g to those favouring a shareholder which have to be disclosed only if he (possibly in collaboration with others) owns a majority of the voting stock. If the restriction is in favour of third parties it is apparently not subject to any duty to disclose. See on all this Seibt and Heiser (n 24) 2197 ff.

[48] The first item refers to multiple voting rights of other persons, typically shareholders (including veto rights), the third item also, but now with respect to one particular issue, ie the nomination of the members of the board. Examples are multiple voting rights, Golden Shares, and the power to designate (some) member(s) of the board directly (as in AktG § 101 para 2); see Grundmann and Möslein (n 28) (634-640). The second item refers to the restriction of one's own voting rights, mainly voting caps.

[49] The other indications have to be disclosed already under Art 3 lit b, c, e of the 2nd Directive (in the companies' register); what is important now in this respect is that they now appear (as well) in the annual report and therefore are more visible (and more easily understood) in the larger context of indications.

[50] Seibt and Heiser (n 24) 2197 stress that now also indirect ownership has to be considered when computing the relevant thresholds (although this is reflected already in Art 85 Stock Exchange Directive as well).

plicitly required (unlike Art 11). This would then also cover the voting cap contained in § 2 of the Law on VW.

The rule has been criticised for being redundant, as quite a few identical rules can already be found in the Stock Exchange Directive of 2001.[51] Even from a technical point of view, this is not completely correct. The Stock Exchange Directive of 2001 covers only securities officially listed; the Takeover Directive was thus aimed at extending the scope of application (to regulated markets). More importantly, however, the IAS/IFRS have often been hailed for prescribing the systematic and ordered disclosure of some core parameters, whereas under the traditional EC Accounting Directives such disclosure was not prescribed: namely cash flow statement, the statement of all changes in equity, and the [business and geographical] segments' report).[52] Many elements of these statements can be found elsewhere as well. For good reasons, however, these parameters are considered to be such important indicators that they must be disclosed in a systematic and ordered way. The core question with respect to the 'market for corporate control statement' would then be whether the takeover regime is important enough to justify such a specific statement also in this respect. If typical control premiums amount to 30% of the stock price, and if in some markets up to 15% of the companies are involved in takeover situations every five years,[53] this is at least plausible.

5. Reciprocity Rules and the Price of Takeover Reluctance (Art 12 Takeover Directive)

A third mechanism would be to attach negative consequences to takeover reluctance (negative incentives). Such an arrangement can be seen in the option model adopted in Art 12 of the EC Takeover Directive, which is again unique from a comparative law perspective. Typically, this rule is seen as a compromise only, introduced initially by the Portuguese presidency.[54] However, the rule is

[51] eg JA McCahery and EPM Vermeulen in this volume.

[52] For these elements in the accounts under IAS/IFRS: D Cairns *Applying International Accounting Standards* (3rd edn Butterworths London 2002) 177-210, 915-954; BJ Epstein and AA Mirza *Interpretation and Application of International Accounting Standards* (Wiley Hoboken 2002) 124-149 and 707-721.

[53] In the British market, see for figures E Wymeersch 'A Status Report on Corporate Governance Rules and Practices in Some Continental European States' in Hopt and others (n 1) 1189, 1190-1195; see also, still more recently C van der Elst 'The Equity Markets, Ownership Structures and Control: Towards an International Harmonization?' in KJ Hopt and E Wymeersch (eds) *Capital Markets and Company Law* (OUP Oxford 2003) 3, 37-41.

[54] Unlike the High Level Group, the EC Commission had not included multiple voting rights into the regime – stating that the relevance for takeovers was not proved and that there were constitutional law problems: Explanation by the EC Commission of Art 11; harsh criticism

cont. ...

more complex. Where member states opt out of the regime described in sections 2 and 3 above and do not introduce it at least as a default rule, each company has the right to opt in again. If they are reluctant to do so there is a twofold reaction. Where companies do not opt in again, other member states may provide that the regime is not applicable to their companies where they are the subject (target) of a bid from companies reluctant to have the regime applied to themselves. Thus, two market reactions are potentially enhanced. On the one hand, companies (ie market players) themselves have to choose between the possibility of protecting themselves by defensive measures and enhanced capacity as bidders. Self-protection thus potentially leads to a decrease in strategic possibilities. On the other hand, this choice is again made public, and such a preference by the company for a defensive attitude may again affect the market price.

This mechanism leaves the decision again more to the markets than to the regulators, and, in theory, it leaves the choice to each player in the market. Founders and shareholders of companies which go public can choose a regime where their influence is also better protected in the future; however, if capital markets function, they have to pay the price for it via lower stock exchange prices. New investors in such companies receive a discount for accepting a regime where competing bids for their shares are less likely to occur. This solution is worth careful consideration, at least where arrangements, besides having adverse effects on takeovers, can have other – positive – effects.

mainly in Germany: A Arnold 'Entschädigung von Mehrstimmrechten bei Übernahmen' [2003] Betriebs-Berater 267; H Krause 'Der Kommissionsvorschlag für die Revitalisierung der EU-Übernahmerichtlinie' [2002] Betriebs-Berater 2341, 2342 ff, 2346; Neye (n 24) 1145; Wiesner (n 5) 1967, *Börsen-Zeitung* (Frankfurt Germany 4 October 2002) 1 ('zweierlei Maß'). It seemed possible to many that this move was perhaps also motivated by the desire to get countries with multiple voting rights 'on board'. See de Beaufort (n 6) 171 (Denmark), 239 (Finland) and 591 (Sweden) (voting power multiplied by ten, in Finland twenty), in France, double voting power is possible for those owning the stock for more than two years (premium for fidelity). Also Golden Shares arrangements remained untouched: Seibt and Heiser (n 24) 2199 ff. But soon all was negotiated again: *Handelsblatt* (Düsseldorf Germany 14/15 March 2003) 4. The Portuguese proposal was then adopted by the Council with minor modifications on 23 November 2003, see Wiesner (n 5) 343, 346; S Maul and D Muffat-Jeandet 'Die EU-Übernahmerichtlinie – Inhalt und Umsetzung in nationales Recht' [2004] Die Aktiengesellschaft 221, 225.

III. Alternative Forms of Replacement of Management: Within the Organisational Framework of the Company

1. Takeovers and Replacement of Management Within the Company as Alternatives

Since Hirshman distinguished 'exit and voice', both options have been seen as alternatives.[55] In the corporate governance debate, a similar distinction has often been considered to be paramount: the distinction between internal and external corporate governance.[56] In both cases, instruments have been seen as supplementing each other and by no means as mutually exclusive.[57] Were only one to be considered, one would risk cutting the regulatory organism in two. For the market for corporate control debate, this would favour the more intensive consideration of takeovers in conjunction with the existing legal framework for reactions possible within the organisation, influencing the competition for corporate control by management. Changes in management and in CEOs in particular which were due to such internal mechanisms have by no means been the exception over the last years – also and perhaps particularly in highly dynamic companies, and this long before the manager(s) reached a certain age. BMW is one of the popular examples in Germany.

The functional parallel is replacement. There is, however, an important functional difference as well. Takeovers are motivated by the potential for synergies and by increases in the efficiency of the management, ie by two types of efficiency considerations, whereas changes within the organisational framework of the company are motivated only by the latter. With this proviso, however, a comparison is worth discussing – albeit only briefly.

There is, of course, also a major factual difference. The triggering of management changes within the organisational framework of the company is only likely to happen if there is a strong decision maker within the company, ie where there

[55] AO Hirschman *Exit, Voice and Loyalty* (Harvard University Press Cambridge 1974).

[56] KJ Hopt 'Common Principles of Corporate Governance in Europe' in BS Markesinis (ed) *The Clifford Chance Millenium Lectures: The Coming Together of the Common Law and. the Civil Law* (Hart Publishing Oxford 2000) 105 (106 ff); C Teichmann 'Corporate Governance in Europe' (2001) Zeitschrift für Unternehmens- und Gesellschaftsrecht [ZGR] 645 (646 ff); segregating those member states which stress external mechanisms (apart from the Anglo-American world and, in tendency, also France) and those which definitely put more weight on internal mechanisms (all the others, esp Germany): E Wymeersch 'Unternehmensführung in Westeuropa – ein Beitrag zur Corporate Governance-Diskussion' (1995) Die Aktiengesellschaft [AG] 299, 309-315 (more intensively on Germany and – in an intermediate position – France and Belgium).

[57] For corporate governance see eg Parkinson (n 29) 178-199; WF Ebke 'Unternehmenskontrolle durch Gesellschafter und Markt' in O Sandrock and W Jaeger (eds) *Internationale Unternehmenskontrolle und Unternehmenskultur* (Mohr Siebeck Tübingen 1994) 7, 27; Teichmann (n 56) 663, 671, 675, 678 ff.

are large block holdings, and these are much more common on the Continent.[58] Institutional investors, who can increasingly be found in all countries, typically step in much less. Therefore, the full potential is reached on the Continent, and this may also decrease the importance of takeovers (which are in fact much less common here, see n 51).

2. Regulation Increasing Readiness of Decision Makers to Oust Inefficient Management

The readiness to replace management depends basically on two elements: the information decision makers have on the performance of the management and their readiness to act on such information.

With respect to the information decision makers have on the performance of the management, there may also be changes as to the information which they receive within the company. In Germany, for instance, one core aim of the reforms over the last few years was better information within the supervisory board. Much more radical – worldwide – are the changes in the framework with regard to information received from outside. Both major channels of corporate finance are affected: as of 2005, financing on capital markets has the consequence that in all EC member states, consolidated accounts must be drafted according to IAS/IFRS.[59] The consequence is that accounts can be more readily compared,[60] thus facilitating the comparison of management with management from outside. Comparability is even increased worldwide, as IAS/IFRS then apply uniformly

[58] For figures, see the studies of the 'European Corporate Governance Institute' (in particular Becht) <http://www.ecgi.org>; M Becht and A Röell 'Blockholdings in Europe: An International Comparison' (1999) 43 European Economic Rev 1049, 1052 ff; in extenso and very systematically drafted: Wymeersch (n 56) 1045, for the United Kingdom 1170-1173, in 81% of the cases, the biggest shareholders hold less than 25% of the stock. Similar to the United Kingdom are only the Netherlands where, however, defensive measures are stronger, see Wymeersch ibid 1175; majority shareholders in about 65% of the listed companies in Germany, Belgium, and Italy: Wymeersch ibid 1168 ff, 1154-1157, 1164-1166; cf the contribution of JA McCahery and EPM Vermeulen in this volume.

[59] As the group of companies is the typical form of business organisation (for figures see only Grundmann (n 2) para 1060), it is not so important that the same does not necessarily apply to the accounts of a single company.

[60] For higher comparability as an effect of IAS/IFRS, see for instance the 3rd recital of the Regulation (EC) 1606/2002 of the European Parliament and the Council of 19 July 2002 concerning the application of international accounting standards [2002] OJ L243/1; W Ballwieser 'Grenzen des Vergleichs von Rechnungslegungssystemen – dargestellt anhand von HGB, US-GAAP und IAS' in KH Forster and others (eds) *Festschrift für Bruno Kropff* (IDW Düsseldorf 1997) 371, esp 376 ff, 381 ff; Hopt (n 56) 105, 114 ff. One major reason is that all assets are activated and at fair value so that a true and fair view of the company is given with all its risks but also all its chances (and this is what matters, at least for equity capital investors).

across the EC and as they do not differ substantially from US-GAAP.[61] And moreover, techniques by which losses, ie potential problems in management, can be hidden for a certain period are much less readily available.[62] The second channel of financing is (bank) loans. Again, in this case due to the Basel II accord,[63] comparison on an individual basis for each company is increased. And again, the scope is in principle comparison on a worldwide scale.[64] The mechanism is outside the rating system (at least from a certain size on). Rating is in fact imposed on all companies because the costs of banking supervision (own funds requirements of banks) will depend on the individual risk of each borrower, and this risk is assessed by professional and independent (outside) rating firms.[65]

The second parameter is readiness of decision makers to act on such information. One core factor in this is certainly independence. The more decision makers are independent of management, the higher the likelihood that they will accept advice given from outside, even where this is negative for management, when the advice is highly professional, such as from rating firms or analysts acting on the basis of accounts which become more readily comparable. A second parameter, and in particular when decision makers are not sufficiently independent, is liability. For the first parameter, it seems fair to state that there is a trend towards increasing safeguards for material independence, at least on the part of the decision makers. Specifying this would be (and is) the scope of yet another

[61] J Baetge and T Beermann 'Vergleichende Bilanzanalyse von Abschlüssen nach IAS/US-GAAP und HGB' [2000] Betriebs-Berater 2088 passim; K Born *Rechnungslegung nach IAS, US-GAAP und HGB im Vergleich* (2nd edn Schäffer-Poeschel Stuttgart 2001) 24; FW Selchert and M Erhardt *Internationale Rechnungslegung – Der Jahresabschluss nach HGB, IAS und US-GAAP* (3rd edn Oldenbourg Munich/Vienna 2003) 5 ff; see also Financial Accounting Standards Board *The IASC-US Comparison Project: A Report on the Similarities and Differences between IASC Standards and US GAAP* (2nd edn FASB 1999).

[62] For this effect of IAS/IFRS, see eg AG Coenenberg *Jahresabschluss und Jahresabschlussanalyse – Betriebswirtschaftliche, handelsrechtliche, steuerrechtliche und internationale Grundlagen – HGB, IAS/IFRS, US-GAAP, DRS* (19th edn Schäffer-Poeschel Stuttgart 2003) 297-299; B Kremin-Buch *Internationale Rechnungslegung – Jahresabschluss nach HGB, IAS und US-GAAP – Grundlagen, Vergleich, Fallbeispiele* (3rd edn Gabler Wiesbaden 2002) 178-180 (all authors for all sets of rules).

[63] Bank for International Settlements *Basel II, International Convergence of Capital Measurement and Capital Standards: A Revised Framework* Basel Committee Publications no 107/2004, available at <http://www.bis.org/publ/bcbs107.htm> (27 June 2005).

[64] ibid Introduction para 3.

[65] For this fundamental change in approach in banking supervision see JM Netter and AB Poulsen *Operational Risk in Financial Service Providers and the Proposed Basel Capital Accord: An Overview*, Working Paper (2003) esp 6, available at <http://papers.ssrn.com/sol3/papers.cfm?abstract_id=369581> (27 June 2005).

paper.[66] Among all the factors mentioned, the liability of the decision makers (and in particular the procedural framework for imposing such liability) is probably still the area which is most nationally rooted and different from country to country. However, decision makers in companies traded on regulated markets, where they do not have control over the shares, are also subject to a market for corporate control, namely takeovers. And majority shareholders certainly have enough incentives to replace inefficient management, even if there is no considerable risk of liability for not doing so. Thus also on this level, the market for corporate control may fix the defects in liability regimes at least in part.

IV. The Content of the Control Position of Management and its Limits

Finally, in principle, even a restriction of the managerial control of the company has to do with the structure of corporate control. McCahery's and Vermeulen's paper discusses one such restriction extensively, ie the limits set on self-dealing transactions. One other important limit would be the exclusive competences of the shareholder meeting. There is one prominent instance of such an exclusive competence in the regulation of the market for corporate control: the exclusive competence to decide on defensive measures. For the one body of the law, regulation of self-dealing, Anglo-American law would seem to be paradigmatic and still more developed.[67] For the other, however – exclusive competences in important questions, namely structural changes and capital measures – only European law seems to have a consistent policy of transferring the power back to the principal.[68]

With respect to these limits on managerial control, the core question is whether such restriction of competences and other arrangements limiting the power of management are in fact relevant for a 'market for corporate control' (because then certain powers cannot be subject to competition between managements). In fact, the aims of regulation of the market for corporate control and of self-dealing regulation are similar in that both have to do with disciplining the management and combating opportunistic behaviour by the management. Exclusive competences reduce the possibility of opportunistic behaviour by the management even more directly – by transferring decision power back to the principal (which, of course, still leaves some scope to influence, for instance via the information given).

[66] For the UK, see D Higgs *Review of the Role and Effectiveness of Non-Executive Directors* Consultation Paper (June 2002), available at: <http://www.dti.gov.uk/cld/non_exec_review/pdfs/condoc.pdf> (27 June 2005).

[67] See only JA McCahery and EPM Vermeulen in this volume.

[68] See V Edwards *EC Company Law* (OUP Oxford 1999) 67, 71, 77 ff, 87, 106-109; Grundmann (n 2) para 354, 380, 383, 388 ff, 394, 397, 950 ff, 962, 1276, 1289.

The market for corporate control, however, is not only about limiting opportunistic behaviour; it serves at least two more important aims. Takeovers are also a response to inefficient management – even if not behaving opportunistically – and they can create or increase synergies (between the target company and the bidder) because they transcend the setting of one existing company (or group). Therefore, while a market for corporate control may be of even greater importance where there are no other efficient instruments against opportunistic behaviour, it remains in any case important for other reasons. And even in an efficient self-dealing regime, the problem is dealt with on a case-by-case approach and proof before the court is often difficult or impossible. Takeovers (and the threat of takeovers) are a reaction to the problem as such, and problems of proof no longer play an important role. One can phrase it differently as well: limits to managers' control of the company, even the strictest ones, always leave a large area in which management has control and where such control is the condition for a split of labour and capital. At least for this area – which is important, if not more important than the limits – the disciplinary effect of the market for corporate control is completely independent of where those limits of managerial control are set. It is a completely different question whether, to what extent, and under which conditions the effects of the market for corporate control are already produced by the product markets (see n. 2).

V. Conclusions

Taking up the theme of the conference, the market for corporate control – and namely the framework of (legal) institutions regulating it – is indeed changing. This is most evident in takeovers, given that one of the large economic blocks in the world, Europe, has recently enacted an extensive takeover regulation. The instruments here not only include a duty of neutrality and breakthrough rules for arrangements impeding takeovers. They also include rules on transparency as to all elements in the corporation's arrangement which affect takeovers, presuming that such transparency may also affect the stock price of the corporation and penalise arrangements which are too defensive, putting these corporations at a competitive disadvantage in financing.

The framework has also changed, however, with respect to alternative instruments, producing effects mainly via the (internal) organisational framework of the company. Change has occurred mainly with respect to instruments which directly serve to compare companies and thus also management performance. The further they are developed, and the more a comparison is made possible across markets, the more pressure, it is suggested, may be put on decision makers within the company, the more they may be convinced to replace management. This is true for supervisory boards or nomination committees, ie where the decision makers are relatively independent, but also for large shareholders or even institutional investors which, in turn, may put pressure on the other decision makers.

The framework has changed with the breakthrough of IAS/IFRS in Europe; also for those entities that matter in capital markets on the Continent, groups whose securities are traded in regulated markets; and with Basel II, because for the second source of financing (loans), individual rating on the basis of largely comparable standards is due to be imposed on all companies.

The question as to how far the control position reaches, ie what are the limits to managerial power and control, is rather marginal for the market for corporate control discussion, although the regulation of such limits and (regulation of) the market for corporate control may have one common goal: rebutting opportunistic behaviour by the management. At any rate, this is a goal which inspires almost all company law and most of the corporate governance debate, and moreover this is only one of many goals that are important to the market for corporate control debate.

Antitrust, State Aid, and the Governance of Public Undertakings

ERNST-JOACHIM MESTMÄCKER

I. The System of Property Ownership in the Internal Market

A market economy works best when there is a clear separation of public authorities and the system of property ownership. This separation is part of the constitutional principle of the division and limitation of governmental powers. In the liberal tradition, this principle implies a strict distinction of state and society forcefully articulated first by Adam Smith for state and economy. The reasons are twofold: According to Adam Smith, governments are notorious for their extravagance. They are always and without exception the greatest spendthrifts in the society.[1] There is, however, another probably even more important reason. It is the insatiable inclination of governments to restrict and regulate competition through privileged companies. In this way they interfere with the property every man has in his own labour. This property is the most sacred and inviolable.[2] Here we have in a nutshell the interdependence of the division of governmental powers and the division of labour based upon individual economic rights. The position of Adam Smith may be summarised in the terminology of modern economics: In the hands of governments, property rights tend to lose their function to internalise the costs of using economic resources. And as lawyers we note that individual economic rights are inseparable from that 'just liberty' that political constitutions are to preserve.

[1] A Smith *An enquiry into the nature and causes of the wealth of nations* (Oxford Edition 1976) 346.

[2] ibid 138.

The separation of state, society, and economy is frequently considered to be obsolete or irrelevant under the conditions of the modern industrial and welfare state. This view neglects the fact that the identification of state and society is the earmark of totalitarian systems, frequently combined with central economic planning and state ownership of all economic resources. In democracies, the separation of state and society including the economy is a necessary condition of individual political and economic liberties.[3]

In the context of international trade and the EU internal market, the separation of public authorities and commercial undertakings has a specific significance. All rules that forbid or limit governmental interventions are predicated on the assumption that they create new markets or new market access for private undertakings. Where the government is the undertaking or controls undertakings, it is in a position to implement protectionist policies without apparent infringement of its treaty obligations. This is the most important reason why socialist states with central economic planning are structurally incompatible with GATT and the WTO.[4]

It is worthwhile to recall that at the beginning of European integration, there was serious concern whether the substantial public sectors in France and Italy were compatible with the internal market and the system of undistorted competition. As a matter of law, the EC Treaty answers this question in the affirmative. Article 295 EC Treaty reads: 'This treaty shall in no way prejudice the rules in member states governing the system of property ownership.' Community legislation and the European courts are reading this provision as guaranteeing the equality of private and public undertakings before community law. The principle of equality is applicable only where undertakings are in a comparable position. The influence of public authorities on their undertakings and the ability of these undertakings to disregard economic considerations because of their access to public revenues justifies and demands special rules and obligations. In the words of the court:

> In that regard, it should be borne in mind that the principle of equality, to which the governments refer in connection with the relationship between public and private undertakings in general, presupposes that the two are in comparable situations. Within the limits laid down by the applicable legislation, private undertakings determine their industrial and commercial strategy by taking into account in particular requirements of profitability. Decisions of public undertakings, on the other hand, may be affected by factors of a different kind within the framework of the pursuit of the objectives of public interest by public authorities which may exercise an influence over those decisions. The economic and financial consequences of the impact of such factors lead to the establishment between those undertakings and public authorities of financial rela-

[3] See HH Rupp 'Die Unterscheidung von Staat und Gesellschaft' in J Isensee and P Kirchhoff (eds) *Handbuch des Staatsrechts* (3rd edn Müller Heidelberg 2004) vol 2 para 31.

[4] For details, see T Cottier and P Mavroidies (eds) *State trading in the 21st century* (Michigan University Press Ann Arbor 1998).

> tions of a special kind which differ from those existing between public authorities and private undertakings.[5]

The preservation and guarantee of the system of property ownership of member states does not mean that property rights as such are exempt from the rules of the treaty. It rather is the system of ownership that is beyond the jurisdiction of the community, not the exercise of rights which are derived from that system. It follows that community law accepts the tradition of member states in the organisation of public undertakings. In France, Italy, and Spain, the concept of service public informs the governance of the more important public undertakings with or without monopoly rights. In Germany as in other member states, there are no general rules that determine how governments have to organise their economic activities. Public and private corporations are used for commercial purposes. An important example in Germany and other continental member states was the organisation of communication services and postal services as departments of the government with monopoly rights. The fact that the German constitution mentioned this organisation was frequently interpreted as a constitutional guarantee of state ownership and monopolistic privileges. As far as governance structures are concerned, the only generalisation possible is the next-to-unlimited discretion enjoyed by governments in using public or private law instruments for their purposes.

It follows that it was unfeasible to base community law rules on specific types of governance for public undertakings. Proposals to exempt public undertakings as such from the rules of the treaty, forcefully presented by Italian and French scholars in the early days of European integration, are obsolete.[6]

The underlying controversy surfaced again, however, in the context of the recent so-called 'golden share' judgments of the Court of Justice. Advocate General Ruiz-Jarabo Colomer argued that the limitations of community powers flowing from Article 222 EC Treaty (now Article 295) included governmental measures for the control of public or private undertakings.[7] The court only repeated its well-settled jurisprudence that the system of property ownership in member states was not exempted from the application of basic treaty rules.[8] The court recognised, however, the right of member states to take into account in the preservation of residual control of privatised corporations the Article 86 para 2 exemption for services of general economic interests.

[5] Case C-188/90 *France, Italy and United Kingdom v Commission* [1982] ECR I-2545 para 21; see also joined cases T-228/99 and T-233/99 *Westdeutsche Landesbank Girozentrale and Land Nordrhein-Westfalen v Commission* [2003] ECR II-445 para 272.

[6] See contributions to A Benzoni (ed) *L'entreprise publique et la concurrence* (de Tempel Bruges 1969).

[7] Case C-367/98 *Commission v Portugal* [2002] ECR I-4731 para 65.

[8] Case C-483/99 *Commission v France* [2002] ECR I-4781 para 44.

As far as the development of community law is concerned, we have seen major shifts in the case law of the European courts, the attitude of the commission, and even of treaty rules. The development may be summarised as a shift from public undertakings in general, to undertakings with exclusive or special rights, to the Article 86 para 2 exemption for undertakings entrusted with services of general economic interest. The abolition or modification of exclusive and special rights dominated the liberalisation of telecommunications. The Article 86 par 2 exemption took centre stage after the court ruled that it is – contrary to the former jurisprudence – directly applicable. The Maastricht Treaty adopted a new Article 16 with the apparent purpose of strengthening the position of member states in the management of their undertakings for political purposes. The powerful lobby of public enterprises succeeded in further protecting their position in the draft constitution. Article II 36 of the Charter of Fundamental Rights of the Union reads:

> The Union recognizes and respects access to services of general economic interest as provided for in national laws and practices, in accordance with the constitution, in order to promote the social and territorial cohesion of the Union.

Heike Schweitzer's analysis of this part of the draft constitution sees it as part of a political development that may undermine the community's economic constitution that so far is based upon economic liberties constituting the internal market and the system of undistorted competition.[9] The draft constitution furthermore empowers the community to legislate in the field of services of general economic interest. The commission declares in its latest of many papers on services of general interest that it will re-examine the feasibility of and the need for a framework law for services of general interest after the entry into force of the constitutional treaty.[10] According to the Commission, it is primarily for the relevant national, regional, or local authorities to define, organise, finance, and operate services of general interest. The unusually moderate interpretation of its own role indicate the Commission's awareness of political and ideological conflicts. They are caused by the deep-seated conviction in many member states that governments ought to be free in the legal qualification of their economic activities.

More fundamentally, governments ought to reign supreme over the anonymous forces of markets and competition. Recently a member of the German constitutional court declared:

[9] H Schweitzer 'Die Daseinsvorsorge im Verfassungsentwurf des europäischen Konvents – ein europäischer service public?' in J Schwarze (ed) *Der Verfassungsentwurf des europäischen Konvents. Verfassungsrechtliche Grundstrukturen und wirtschaftsverfassungsrechtliches Konzept* (Nomos Baden-Baden 2004) 269-312.

[10] Communication from the Commission to the European Parliament, the Council of the European Economic and Social Committee and the Committee of the Regions, White Paper on Services of General Interest, Brussels, COM (2004) 374.

> The competition, as propagated by community law, lacks all considerations of the public interest (*Gemeinwohl*) and has no relation to society or state as such. Competition is independent from such considerations, neutral towards all values *vulgo*: ruthless and merciless.[11]

According to this view, it goes almost without saying that the community law for services of general economic interest (*Daseinsvorsorge*) is considered to be unconstitutional under German law.

These more general observations indicate the political stakes governments have in the development and application of community law to public undertakings. I propose to discuss first the communities' jurisdiction, and then how the application of community law to public undertakings affects their governance. There is a basic difference in this analysis compared with corporation law in general. In the law of private corporations, rules of organisation are the backbone of their governance. They are indispensable for the formation of a corporation and for its relations to members and the outside world. Under community law this approach must be reversed. The existence and organisation of public undertakings are taken for granted. Organisational rules follow, if at all, from the substantive rules of the treaty. It is from this perspective that I propose to look at the governance of public undertakings.

II. Jurisdiction: The Concept of Undertaking

The most important concept that governs the community law of public undertakings is that of 'undertaking'. This is no circular reasoning and no tautology. Here as elsewhere the terminology of community law and its interpretation are autonomous and independent from the law of member states. An undertaking, according to the jurisprudence of the European courts, is any legal or natural person engaged in an economic activity regardless of its legal status and the way it is financed.[12] An economic activity constitutes an undertaking whether or not it is intended to earn a profit. The European court added a resource-oriented definition: a collection of physical and human resources capable of taking part in the commission of an infringement of the kind covered by the rules of competition.[13] This functional definition looking to the purpose of the rules to be applied is frequently at odds with member state traditions. This approach means in particu-

[11] S Bross 'Daseinsvorsorge, Wettbewerb, Gemeinschaftsrecht' [2003] Juristenzeitung 874, 875.

[12] For details, see CW Bellamy and GD Child *Common market law of competition* (4th edn Sweet & Maxwell London 1993) para 2-005; case C-41/90 *Höfner and Elser v Macrotron* [1991] ECR I-1979; EJ Mestmäcker and H Schweitzer *Europäisches Wettbewerbsrecht* (2nd edn CH Beck Munich 2004) para 33 III 18-39.

[13] Case T-6/89 *Enichem v Commission* [1991] ECR II-1623 para 235.

lar that states as such, departments of member states, and even individual administrative units are undertakings when they engage in commerce. The court observed that for the purpose of distinguishing the exercise of public powers by the state and its economic activities, it was of no importance whether the state carried out its economic activities by way of a distinct body over which it may exercise directly or indirectly a dominant influence, or carried out the activities directly through a body forming part of the state administration.[14] It follows that undertakings need not have legal personality and that the concept of undertaking is a relative concept. The same organisation and its sub-divisions may act in their governmental function or as an undertaking.[15] This strictly functional approach supersedes organisational forms and cuts across national governance principles. In this perspective the purpose of an activity is irrelevant if it is pursued by economic means. That does not mean that community law is blind to the role an organisation has in the governmental or social fabric of member states. In the final analysis, the question to be answered is whether competition rules and the exceptions provided for in the treaty are adequate to cope with the public interest of member states and of the community.

III. Public Undertakings

In the perspective of corporate governance, public undertakings are of no special interest with respect to their market activities. They are of special interest only because of the control member states or other public authorities exercise over them. Member states have a special responsibility that their own undertakings act in harmony with and not contrary to community law. This principle is enshrined in Article 86 para 1 EC Treaty. The provision stipulates the obligation of member states not to enact or maintain with respect to public undertakings any measures contrary to competition rules and other provisions of the treaty. When the treaty or secondary legislation address public undertakings, they really address the controlling public authority. This is obvious where treaty obligations are applicable to member states as such, as are the rules on state aids and on public procurement. But it applies as well to the other rules of competition. The very broad concept of

[14] Case 118/85 *Commission v Italy* [1987] ECR 2599 para 8.

[15] Another interpretation applies where the applicability of community law procurement rules is concerned. Procurement rules cover public bodies of a non-commercial nature that are typically under political pressure to prefer national undertakings in their buying policies. The determinants of finding a contracting authority that is not the government itself follow from the political temptation and opportunity to deviate in their procurement of goods or services from normal commercial considerations. Once it is established that a buyer is a 'contracting authority', it is subject to the procurement rules for all its activities. Contrary to the concept of undertaking under competition rules, there is no limitation to procurement activities that are related to public interest activities.

'undertaking' is a necessary condition for the implementation of the principle of equal rights and equal duties for private and public undertakings. The competitive position and legal conduct of private undertakings is the yardstick to measure the conduct of public undertakings. This applies to the interpretation of Article 81, 82 as well as to the remedies once an infringement has been found.

1. Public Undertaking Defined

There are close similarities to the law of corporations and of corporate groups in the application of state aid rules to aid by public authorities to their undertakings. This is obvious where public undertakings or groups of them are organised as private law corporations. But even in these cases, the corporate law publicity is not sufficient to distinguish in their financial relations the role of the state as public authority and its role as proprietor. The starting point of this enquiry is the finding of control by public authorities of an undertaking.

The transparency directive[16] based on Article 86 para 3 defines a public undertaking as 'any undertaking over which the public authority may exercise directly or indirectly a dominant influence by virtue of their ownership of it, their financial participation therein or the rules which govern it' (Article 2, 1c).

A dominant influence shall be presumed (Article 2 para 2) when these authorities directly or indirectly in relation to an undertaking

a) hold the major part of the undertaking's subscribed capital; or
b) control the majority of the votes attaching to shares issued by the undertakings; or
c) can appoint more than half of the members of the undertaking's administrative, managerial, or supervisory body.

These are the organisational conditions that trigger the obligation of public authorities to reveal and report their financial relations with their undertakings. These obligations come close to a community law of the internal governance for public undertakings. The directive distinguishes public undertakings, undertakings with special or exclusive rights, and undertakings entrusted with services of general economic interest. With respect to public undertakings, member states have to report all funds made available to them and the use to which these funds are put (Article 1 para 1). Article 3 specifies transactions and practises that are most liable to cloak financial favours.

[16] Commission Directive 80/723/EEC of 25 June 1980 on the transparency of financial relations between Member States and public undertakings [1980] OJ L195 as amended by Commission Directive 2000/52/EC of 26 July 2000 [2000] OJ L193.

2. Market Economy Investor Test

The test by which financial investments in public undertakings are to be judged under state aid rules is the 'market economy investor principle'. The Commission will examine whether the terms on which the funds are provided go beyond those that a private investor, operating under normal market conditions, would find acceptable when providing funds to a comparable private undertaking.[17] In Alfa Romeo, the court specified that public investors are entitled to take into account a long-term view of profitability like private groups of enterprises that pursue a structural, global, or sectoral policy (para 20).

In the West LB case, the European court reviewed a Commission decision finding an infringement of Article 87 through the rather complex transfer of Wohnungsbauförderungsanstalt Nordrhein Westfalen to Westdeutsche Landesbank.[18] The court's decision reads like a textbook on the application of the market economy investor principle to transactions where a public undertaking is transferred to another public undertaking. The Federal Republic argued that in such a case, there was a special private proprietor interest (*Eigentümerinteressen*). In calculating the return on investment, such a proprietor would take into account the positive effects the acquisition would have on his controlling interest in the acquiring undertaking. It was therefore incompatible with the market economy investor principle that the commission relied on an average rate of profitability of the investment. The court held that the average rate of profitability was a legitimate instrument of analysis but was no substitute for a comprehensive examination of the individual transaction. In the words of the court:

> Since the commission must always examine all the relevant features of the transaction at issue and its context, it must take into account the question whether an informed private investor, in the place of the public investor in question, would have accepted a lower return than the average return in the sector concerned as an appropriate return because of economic considerations other than the optimisation of his return. The same observation applies to the argument alleging discrimination between public and private undertakings in as much as the specific features of the transaction at issue relating to the beneficiary undertaking must also be taken into account when the principle of the private investor is applied.[19]

This proviso turned out to be dispositive. The court ruled that the Commission's decision failed to give sufficient reason for its finding that a rate of return of twelve per cent on investment would have been an 'adequate compensation'. The Commission's reliance on its own experience and various expert opinions by investment bankers were no substitute for the explication of the essential consid-

[17] Case C-305/89 *Italy v Commission* [1991] ECR I-1603 para 19.

[18] Case T-228/99 *Westdeutsche Landesbank Girozentrale v Commission* [2003] ECR II-435 para 185-277.

[19] Case T-228/99 (n 18) para 270.

erations which led the Commission to choose the specific figure for the rate of return (para 402).

The observations of the Commission were insufficient to permit meaningful judicial review and to safeguard the rights of the parties to the case.

IV. Undertakings with Exclusive or Special Rights and Undertakings Entrusted with Services of General Economic Interest

In 2001 the transparency directive was amended in order to cover the relation of member states to undertakings with exclusive or special rights (Article 86 para 1) and undertakings entrusted with services of general economic interest. These obligations of member states are even more specific and far-reaching in terms of governance structures than those applicable to public undertakings. Article 1 para 2 of the directive refers to these undertakings as undertakings required to maintain separate accounts. The provision reads:

> Without prejudice to specific provisions laid down by the community the member states shall ensure that the financial *and organisational* structure of any undertaking required to maintain separate accounts is correctly reflected in the separate accounts, so that the following emerge clearly:
> a) the costs and revenues associated with different activities;
> b) full details of the methods by which costs and revenues are assigned or allocated to different activities.

Article 3a specifies the cost accounting principles: the internal accounts corresponding to different activities have to be separate; all costs and revenues must correctly be assigned or allocated on the basis of constantly applied and objectively justifiable cost accounting principles; and the cost accounting principles according to which separate accounts are maintained must be clearly established.

The purpose behind this regulation is the organisational separation of privileged activities from competitive activities. The directive is justified as a precautionary measure against infringements of Article 82 and of Article 87 and as a generalised additional remedy if infringements did occur.

1. Abuse through the Combination of Governmental Functions and Economic Activities (Article 82)

In several cases, the Court of Justice ruled that there may be an abuse of a dominant position if the role of the state as a public authority and as undertaking are combined in the same organisation. Examples are government monopolies administered by a public authority that simultaneously operates in the market for telecommunications equipment and has the authority to license private operators in that market. Such an organisation would be incompatible with the principle of equal opportunities for competitors.[20]

2. Cross-subsidisation

It is an abuse of a dominant position if monopoly profits are used to gain advantages in competition on neighbouring markets.

Organisational divestiture will frequently be the remedy against such a transfer of monopoly profits to competitive markets.[21] This situation occurs where monopoly rights are maintained for services in the general economic interest and the privileged undertaking offers services on neighbouring markets in competition with private operators. This structure has been the result of the abolition of exclusive rights for certain functions and the maintenance of those rights for other activities on the markets for postal services.[22]

An example is the use of profits from the monopoly for letter mail services to subsidise the activities in the parcel delivery business. The Commission found an abuse on the basis of the rules that govern predatory pricing by dominant enterprises. Deutsche Post agreed to organise its parcel service in a separate subsidiary.[23]

3. Financing Services of General Economic Interest

Member states have specific obligations with respect to undertakings entrusted with services of general economic interest within the meaning of Article 86 para 2 EC Treaty and undertakings charged with universal service within the meaning of the appropriate directives on telecommunication services, postal services, and energy services.[24] Member states are not permitted to define universal service by their legislation differently from the conditions of community law directives.[25] The preserved activities must be strictly limited in accordance with the applicable community law. Member states must by a formal act of a public authority clearly define public service obligations with respect to both the privileged public or private entity and actual or potential competitors.

[20] Case 18/88 *RTT v GB-Inno-BM* [1991] ECR 5941 para 25.

[21] For details, see Mestmäcker and Schweitzer (n 12) para 18 I 3, 34 IV 5.

[22] Case C-340/99 *TNT Traco* [2001] ECR I-4109 para 58.

[23] Commission decision 2001/354 *Deutsche Post* [2001] OJ L125.

[24] For details, see Mestmäcker and Schweitzer (n 12) ch 18 para 73 (Universaldienst in der Energie), ch 34 para 21 (Universaldienst in der Telekommunikation).

[25] Case C-240/02 *Asempre and Asociación Nacional de Empresas de Externalización y gestión de Envíos y Pequeña Paqueteria* [2004] ECR I-2461 para 25.

Services of general economic interest are regulated and privileged because they are not profitable and would not be provided by undertakings in competition. It follows that undertakings charged with such services are entitled to remuneration that covers the difference between market proceeds and the actual costs incurred. One of the more controversial issues has been whether this supplementary financing provided by a public authority is state aid in the meaning of Article 87 EC Treaty and must be notified to the Commission. The court held that the compensation for the services provided by the recipient undertakings in order to discharge public service obligations is not state aid, if the compensation covers the extra costs only and does not have the effect of putting the undertaking in a more favourable position than competitors.[26] Services of general interest can be provided by public or private undertakings. When the services are provided by an undertaking with exclusive rights, the rules on cost subsidisation apply. Where the public service is or can be provided by private undertakings as well, the procedure for their selection becomes important.

An adequate compensation without favouritism will be presumed where the undertaking has been chosen pursuant to a procurement procedure that allows for the selection of the least cost tenderer (case Altmark para 93). In all other cases, the parameters on the basis of which the compensation is calculated must be established in advance in an objective and transparent manner. The level of compensation must be determined on the basis of an analysis of the cost which a typical undertaking, well run and adequately provided with the means to be able to meet the public service requirements, would have incurred in discharging those obligations, taking into account the relevant receipts and a reasonable profit (Altmark case para 91, 93).

Consequently, there is no state aid if these requirements are met. There is a notifiable state aid if payments are made to cover losses incurred by an undertaking without prior determination of the standard of compensation. If the parameters of compensation are established in advance, payments made on that basis must not be notified. This does not exclude, however, a later commission review on whether the actual compensation provided by a public authority is cost-justified.

V. Unbundling in the Energy Industry

In most member states, the energy industry (electricity and gas) is controlled by public undertakings with or without exclusive rights. In this industry, community regulation is, however, not directed at the control relations of member states to their undertakings but at monopolistic market structures. The hardcore monopolies are the transmission and distribution networks. They are natural mono-

[26] Case C-280/00 *Altmark Trans* [2003] ECR I-7747 para 87.

polies because the long-term average costs of producing a good decrease with increasing quantities in the relevant output range.[27] In other words, the incumbent operator can always be cheaper than any additional supplier. The local or regional networks are monopolies quite independent from their public or private ownership. The traditional idea that public ownership is the most effective regulation in the interest of consumers has been thoroughly discredited. And it is impossible to inject competition into natural monopolies. Competition is possible, however, in energy generation. And consumers are always willing to consider alternative sources of supply. If the regulator wants to encourage competition in the markets for energy products, the intermediate monopolistic segments must be neutralised. One way to do this is to organise the transmission and distribution networks as common carriers with equal access for all producers of electricity or gas. The independent operation of transportation and distribution conflicts, however, with the traditional vertical integration of energy undertakings. In order to facilitate trans-border competition, the EC Commission is developing a policy of 'unbundling' of transmission and distribution functions within vertically integrated undertakings. Unbundling means the organisational separation of the different stages of energy supply without interfering with the ownership of the assets. The aim is to provide for competitive and equal access to transmission and distribution networks without favouring the supply by members of the corporate group. The implementation of this policy leads to highly complex governance structures.

According to the recent directives concerning common rules for the internal market in electricity and gas,[28] member states shall designate a transmission or distribution system operator. Where the transmission activities are under the control of a company which is involved in the generation or supply of energy, unbundling applies.[29] The concept of control that establishes vertical integration and leads to unbundling is taken over from the merger regulation. Where the network operator is part of a vertically integrated undertaking, it shall be independent at least in terms of its legal form, organisation, and decision-making from other activities not relating to transmission or distribution. The transmission and distribution activities must be organised as a subsidiary that becomes the 'network company'. It must be operated as if it were an independent corporation. The directives provide in detail for Chinese walls and other measures that are to assure the network company's independence from the parent company. Arrange-

[27] E Kantzenbach and J Kruse 'Could the Energy Mix Be Optimised Through Competition or Regulation' in EJ Mestmäcker (ed) *Natural gas in the internal market. A Review of Energy Policy* (Graham & Trotman London 1993) 59, 61.

[28] Directive 2003/54/EC of 26 June 2003 (electricity) [2003] OJ L176/37; Directive 2003/55/EC of 26 June 2003 (gas) [2003] OJ L176/57.

[29] For an overview of the unbundling regime, see note of DJ energy and transport on Directives 2003/54/EC and 2003/55/EC on the internal market in electricity and natural gas of 16 January 2004.

ments have to be made to assure management separation and independence of personnel. A comprehensive compliance programme is to provide a formal framework for ensuring that the network business as a whole, as well as individual employees and members of management, comply with the principle of non-discrimination (see Commission Note 4.4). Separate accounts for transmission and distribution activities are to be kept 'with a view to avoiding discrimination, cost subsidization, and distortion of competition'. The revenue from ownership of transmission or distribution networks shall be specified in the accounts.

All these arrangements are to be monitored and enforced by national regulatory authorities (Article 23 Electricity Directive; Article 25 Gas Directive). We know from the law of corporate groups how difficult it is to separate the economic and financial interests of the group as such from the interests of individual subsidiaries. These difficulties are compounded where corporations are asked to disregard their legally and financially preserved ownership interests in favour of customers who are frequently their competitors. The major purpose of the exercise is, of course, trans-border competition in the internal market. In order to assure effective access to transmission systems for the purpose of cross-border transactions, a special regulation has been adopted.[30] This regulation aims at setting fair rules for cross-border exchanges in electricity, thus enhancing competition within the internal electricity market, taking into account the specificities of national and regional markets. This will involve the establishment of a compensation mechanism for cross-border flows of electricity and the setting of harmonised principles on cross-border transmission charges and the allocation of available capacities of interconnection between national transmission systems (Article 1).

The EC Commission will report annually on the extent to which the unbundling and tarification requirements have been successful in ensuring fair and non-discriminating access to the community's networks. We are all looking forward to that report.

VI. Costs and Benefits

In advocating community initiatives, the EC Commission frequently relies on the hypothetical costs of 'non-Europe' in order to measure the potential benefits of Europe. There are no indicators for the measurement of costs and benefits of Europe flowing from the application of competition rules to public undertakings. We can compare, however, the legal position of public undertakings without Europe and with Europe. The legal position without Europe is the position under

[30] Regulation (EC) no 1228/2003 of 26 June 2003 on conditions for access to the network for cross-border exchanges in electricity [2003] OJ L176/1.

the law of member states before the Treaty of Rome (1958). The major benefit is that community law has pierced the veil of sovereign immunity for all economic activities of public authorities.[31] The most important effect has been a better knowledge and understanding of the real costs of doing business through factually or legally privileged public undertakings. These costs include the prevention or restriction of technical progress, favouritism towards selected monopolistic suppliers, exclusion or cartel control of competitive activities, and the legally uncontrolled financing of expansionist investments through tax money or fees. In telecommunications, the German courts including the Constitutional Court found most of these practices legal and constitutional.[32] The structural changes and the redress of national legal abuses in telecommunications brought about by community law and community policies are among the undoubted benefits of Europe. Finding the right balance of the costs of non-Europe and the benefits of Europe is an ongoing struggle. The area of social policy is a promising candidate for legally even more interesting and politically even more dramatic conflicts.

[31] Sovereign immunity from the antitrust laws for all governmental activities, including the sovereign's economic enterprises, is still the law in the United States. For details and some new developments, see DEM Sappington and JG Sidack 'Competition Law for State-Owned Enterprises' (2003) 71 Antitrust L J 479, 481.

[32] For an overview, see EJ Mestmäcker 'Fernmeldemonopol und Nachfragemacht – Wirtschaftsrechtliche und ordnungspolitische Probleme der hoheitlichen unternehmerischen Funktionen der DBP' in EJ Mestmäcker (ed) *Recht und ökonomisches Gesetz* (2nd edn Nomos Baden-Baden 1984) 764-804.

Sector-Specific Regulations and Antitrust: Corporate Governance of Public Undertakings in Japan

FUMIO SENSUI

I. Non-EU Nations where State Aid Rule does not exist and their Coping Strategies

In similar fashion to a lot of non-EU nations, the Antimonopoly Law in Japan does not have a general provision or rule that monitors state aid directly by specific regulations. Moreover, the Japanese Antimonopoly Law does not have general provisions like Article 86 of the EC Treaty that rules on the relationship between public undertakings and issues concerning the state aid rule. Nor does it provide, for instance, provisions based on the EU-specific term 'general economic interest'. However, the regulatory approach of the EU (the EU approach) does provide a good reference for those who reside outside the EU. This is chiefly because the EU approach is robust and persuasive as a regulatory mechanism that specifically aims at the correction of market failure.

As mentioned, we have no general rules on state aid in Japan. Instead, we deal with such problems (which are in fact the same problems that EU state aid rule faces) by taking advantage of a combination of sector-specific regulations (SSRs) and the Antimonopoly Law. However, the Antimonopoly Law does not unambiguously regulate state aid. The Antimonopoly Law applies to state aid only when the acts with which the entrepreneur[1] who has received state aid fulfill certain

[1] Section 2 of the Antimonopoly law provides that the term 'entrepreneur' as used in this Act shall mean a person, who carries on a commercial, industrial, financial or any other business.

requirements. Examples of this include activities which fall under the unjust low price sales or predatory pricings mechanisms (Antimonopoly Law, Section 19; Designation of Unfair Trade Practices, Section 6).

II. Control by SSRs in Japan

To a significant degree, SSRs cover the regulation of state aid in Japan. For instance, the Telecommunications Act and the Nippon Telegraph and Telephone Act (The NTT Act) apply to the NTT Group[2] (notably NTT West and NTT East) and require it to maintain accounting separation when it engages in competitive telecommunications activities in Japan. Moreover, similar regulations are imposed on public undertakings in the energy industry in Japan, with cross-subsidization restricted by SSRs.

In the case of the NTT Act, it prohibits NTT West, which dominates the local loops in the western area of Japan, from using the income obtained from the fixed telephone service (FTS) to win over customers to its ADSL services. Furthermore, NTT West and NTT East, which dominate the local loops in their respective areas, are not allowed to provide a long-distance communications service by themselves – a market in which the competition between long-distance carriers is very keen.

However, structural separation of privileged activities from core activities might be requested. Therefore, NTT West and NTT East can implement a long-distance communication service (LDCS) or a mobile phone service (MPS) only when they purposely establish a new corporation. Examples like NTT Communications for LDCS and NTT Mobile Communications Network, Inc. (NTT DoCoMo) for MPS are evidence of this. The NTT Group does, in fact, provide these services through NTT Holding Company subsidiaries rather than directly through NTT West and NTT East. The electric power companies, however, are permitted to enter the telecommunication market voluntarily without the constraints faced by NTT, a notable asymmetric regulation.

First, as noted above, the regulations based on SSRs remain insufficient, especially in respect to the energy industries, though the control over the telecommunication services sector is sufficient to a large degree. Therefore, there remain some significant problematic issues in SSRs from the viewpoint of equal footing,

[2] In 1985, the Japanese Government privatized the Telecom Public Corporation, giving birth to the Nippon Telegraph and Telephone Corporation (NTT). The Ministry of Posts and Telecommunications (MPT) and NTT reached a compromise in 1996, under which NTT agreed to restructure itself into a holding company. Under the parent holding company, two local telecommunications subsidiaries (NTT East and NTT West), one long-distance company (NTT Communications), one cellular company (NTT Docomo), and several other subsidiaries coexist. See T Takigawa 'Competition Policy toward Dominant Utility Companies: Vertical Divestiture or Access Rules?' (2002) 1 Washington U Global Studies L Rev 301, 314-317.

mainly because the SSRs are not cross-sectoral and not neutral in respect to different technologies.

Second, the notion of withdrawing SSRs and unifying the regulations under an all-encompassing Antimonopoly Law to enhance competition in the realm of public undertakings, even from the standpoint of 'general economic interest' (thus rendering SSRs superfluous), is a not widely held view in Japan. Therefore, even in cases where the Antimonopoly Law is fully applicable and hence SSRs are unnecessary, SSRs often remain in place. In this regard, I believe that the EU approach – that is, resorting to a process of effective competition review[3] in respect to telecommunication services – serves as a useful reference for non-EU nations.

In the following sections, I will introduce some cases in Japan where courts ruled on whether cross subsidies violated the Antimonopoly Law or not.

III. Controls through the Antimonopoly Law in Japan

In Japan it should be noted that the Antimonopoly Law also applies to public undertakings.

1. Public Undertakings and the Antimonopoly Law

It is the entrepreneur (*jigyōsha*) to which the Antimonopoly Law applies. The term 'the entrepreneur' has a very broad definition in Japan. It is almost the same as in EU competition law. In Japan, Article 2 (1) of the Antimonopoly Law explicitly describes that '[t]he term "entrepreneur" as used in this Act shall mean a person who carries on a commercial, industrial, financial or any other "business".' In this regard, a Supreme Court decision has defined *business* as 'economic activity that receives repeated and continuing benefits corresponding to the supply of some economic interests.'[4] Therefore, the legal form of the business entity is not the primary point. Moreover, the Antimonopoly Law applies not only to for-profit ventures but also to not-for-profit businesses. A 'natural person,' an 'artificial person,' private corporations, and public corporations are all deemed to be entrepreneurs under this law.

Even public undertakings, therefore, are not exempted from the Antimonopoly Law. For instance, the Antimonopoly Law applies even when the Japanese government owns the public undertaking or has a minority shareholder's

[3] See Directive 2002/21/EC on a Common Regulatory Framework [2002] OJ L108/33.

[4] Supreme Court decision, 14 December 1988, 43 Minshû [Supreme Court civil affairs Law Reports] 2978 (1988), available at <http://courtdomino2.courts.go.jp/schanrei.nsf/> (19 April 2005).

right for public undertakings through a subsidiary company. As in the EU, there is little deterrence in Japan's Antimonopoly Law, whether it is applied to a public corporation or a private enterprise. Moreover, we can note that it is not inquired in Japan as to whether 'the public authority exercises directly or indirectly a dominant influence by virtue of their ownership of it, their final participation therein or the rules that govern it.'[5]

As I will describe later in section VIII, the Osaka High Court ruled that the Ministry of Posts and Telecommunications (MPT) was an entrepreneur when issuing and offering mail postcards. In similar fashion, the Japanese Supreme Court also ruled that the Tokyo Shibaura Public Slaughterhouse (TPS), which was owned by the Tokyo metropolitan government at the time, was also an entrepreneur.

In the first case, the Osaka High Court decided that the Antimonopoly Law did not apply to the delivery of correspondence (*shinsho*). The reason is as follows: the MPT is not an entrepreneur in its delivery of correspondence because the Mail Law describes the delivery of posted correspondence by the MPT as a legally granted monopolistic business, and thus there should be no competition between the MPT and other entrepreneurs. The universal service obligation imposed on the MPT also helps to explain MPT's monopoly on the delivery of correspondence. However, the court ruled that the Antimonopoly Law applied to the MPT for issuing and selling pre-stamped postcards because the MPT was an entrepreneur, and because of the existence of competition between the MPT and private enterprises over the same commodity. In doing so, the court analyzed the acts of each public undertaking and found that each act did not violate Antimonopoly Law, not because they were not entrepreneurs, but because they did not fulfill the requirements of unjust low price sales as prohibited by the Antimonopoly Law.

In the second case, the Supreme Court decided that the Tokyo metropolitan government also did not violate the Antimonopoly Law. However, in this case it examined whether the Tokyo metropolitan government, the owner of the Tokyo Shibaura Public Slaughterhouse (TPS), met the requirements of the unjust low price sales regulation by charging unreasonably low slaughter fees; it concluded that it did not. At the same time, we should also be aware that the Supreme Court also prudently added that the purpose of the subsidy had a public nature, that is, to supply adequate amounts of meat to citizens at reasonable prices. The Osaka High Court gave a similar evaluation to the case involving Japan Post, chiefly because the business of the MPT (ie, the delivery of posted correspondence) has a public nature. This way of evaluating the public nature of a certain case might be seen as conceptually close to the EU's notion of 'general economic interest.'

In conclusion, the national government and the local authority are clearly viewed as entrepreneurs, insofar as they are not legally granted as monopolists.

[5] See the contribution by EJ Mestmäcker in this volume.

Under the current legal system, the national government, for instance, is a competitor or at least a potential competitor to other entrepreneurs. However, at the same time, the public nature of its acts is taken into account when evaluating the anticompetitive effects of its practices.

2. The Relationship between SSRs and the Antimonopoly Law

Both SSRs and the Antimonopoly Law can be applied to the practices of an entrepreneur simultaneously. This point can be clearly seen in the 'Guidelines for Promotion of Competition Policy in the Telecommunications Business Field,' which was drawn up jointly by the Fair Trade Commission of Japan (hereafter the JFTC) and the Ministry of Public Management, Home Affairs, Posts and Telecommunications (hereafter the MPMHAPT), and the 'Guidelines Concerning Appropriate Electric Power Dealings,' which was drawn up jointly by the JFTC and the Ministry of Economy, Trade and Industry (METI); both documents offer clear-cut guidelines that exemplify this doctrine.[6]

In Japan, there is no rule dictating that when a 'conflict of laws' situation arises, priority of application is undertaken; in such a situation, both SSRs and the Antimonopoly Law are applicable. When the practice in question fulfills the requirements of the Antimonopoly Law, the JFTC is able to state that the practice violates the Antimonopoly Law even if the MPMHAPT has already decided that it is allowable in light of SSRs. However, when the MPMHAPT decides that the acts concerned are lawful, the JFTC normally does not prohibit it, though we have had some cases where the JFTC took action. This is primarily because the MPMHAPT, the METI, and other regulatory authorities are increasingly taking into account the importance of competition policy, especially when both establishing and enforcing SSRs.

However, the JFTC has shown a tendency to apply the Antimonopoly Law aggressively in a number of cases.[7] (i) The JFTC aggressively applies the Antimonopoly Law to industries without SSRs (for example, in the absence of the interconnection and collocation rules involving ADSL services); and (ii) when the regulatory authority does not enforce competition policy enough – though the SSRs include competition-promoting regulations, in which case the JFTC also applies the Antimonopoly Law (see section VIII).

[6] See 'Guidelines for Promotion of Competition Policy in the Telecommunications Business Field' of 30 November 2001 <http://www2.jftc.go.jp/e-page/legislation/ama/telecom. pdf> (19 April 2005); 'Guidelines Concerning Appropriate Electric Power Dealings' of 25 July 2002 <http://www2.jftc.go.jp/e-page/legislation/ama/electric.pdf> (19 April 2005).

[7] A US Federal Supreme Decision may yet give us some suggestions on this issue. See *Verizon Communications Inc v Law Offices of Curtis V Trinko LLP* 124 S Ct 872 (2004).

IV. Postal Service and Predatory Pricing?

A good example of what is occurring in areas where both SSRs and the Antimonopoly Law are applied simultaneously can be found as a result of the ongoing privatization of the postal service – a key aim for Prime Minister Koizumi that has become a hot political issue in his reform agenda. Nevertheless, we should note that the postal service receives a subsidy by means of a guarantee from Japan's government and a significant tax exemption. For these reasons, many people believe that competition in both the (postal) savings deposit service market and (postal) life insurance market is therefore being distorted. Moreover, there are further criticisms of Japan Post (the JP or *Nippon Yûsei Kôsha*) involving a newly proposed parcel delivery business. Currently, the JP's parcel delivery business (named *You Pack* Delivery) has started making the Lawson Group (a national brand of a convenience store chain) a handling base, resulting in vigorous opposition from private parcel delivery businesses (such as *Yamato* Transport Co., Ltd.). In fact, *Yamato* filed a lawsuit with the Tokyo District Court against JP in September 2004. In the complaint, *Yamato* alleges that JP is engaging in unjust low price sales (or predatory pricing) and deceptive customer inducement (Antimonopoly Law, Section 19; Designation of Unfair Trade Practices, Section 9), therefore violating the Japanese Antimonopoly Law. A similar case arose in Germany when a parcel delivery business utilizing the post office infrastructure (a network specifically established for providing a public mail delivery service) was deemed to be involved in predatory pricing and in violation of Section 82 of the EC Competition Law: Abuse of the Dominant Position.[8] However, the *You Pack* Delivery case will be more complicated, because *You Pack*'s price will not fall below 'avoidable cost,' in contrast with the Deutsche Post case, in which the European Commission found that Deutsche Post's price was below the 'avoidable cost.'

V. Unbundling in the Energy Industry in Japan

In the telecommunication sector in Japan, the unbundling of local loops and collocation for ADSL is advancing steadily, as we will see in section IX. However, unbundling in the energy industry has just started. In the gas and electric power business, the SSRs have been giving the entrepreneurs regional monopolies. The entrepreneurs in the gas and electric power business have been making strong objections against the separation of infrastructure and operations (vertical divestiture) and regulatory authority, with METI supporting them in their opposition to this move. Therefore, we have no example that utilizes the approach of vertical

[8] For further details on this case involving Deutsche Post see COMP/35.141 *Deutsche Post AG* [2001] OJ L125/27.

divestiture in these businesses. Entrepreneurs remain vertically integrated, despite the regulatory authority's intention to rely on the unbundling approach in the future as a means of coping with cross subsidies and the state aid problems in this sector. Recently, SSRs were revised and entry into this industry was partly liberalized, resulting in new entrants finally entering these kinds of markets. We have thus reached a stage where the unbundling restriction of transmission and distribution of electricity and gas has started to occur. Moreover, METI has set up a relevant dispute settlement organization for the purpose of enabling new undertakings to enter into this market.

The JFTC for its part has tried to introduce a new regulation based on Essential Facilities Doctrine (EFD) within the context of the Antimonopoly Law, in addition to control under the SSRs, but without success. Therefore, ongoing monitoring for possible future cases of violations will occur through the present Antimonopoly Law. I will touch upon this interesting discussion concerning the legislation proposal based on EFD, which is closely associated with the relationship between SSRs and the Antimonopoly Law, later in section VIII.

Moreover, we can also note that the railway businesses have also been vertically integrated. In the metropolitan area (notably the Tokyo and Osaka areas) in Japan, we can see two or more private railways competing with JR (Japan Railways), in which the Japanese government is the majority stockholder. This is becoming a predominant feature of this system as JR and the airline companies are also seen competing with each other to a significant degree in regional areas.

VI. Role of Competition Law within Corporate Governance in Japan

In the following sections, I will briefly discuss several issues involving the amendment of the Antimonopoly Law in Japan, especially those issues concerning the role of the Antimonopoly Law in corporate governance in general. After that, I will return to the major issue of competition policy vis-à-vis public undertakings.

The role of competition law within corporate governance has grown considerably in Japan. It has become commonplace for major enterprises to implement competition law observance guidelines into their compliance programs since the early 1990s.

However, some companies in Japan do not necessarily consider the Antimonopoly Law to be an important matter within the overall system of compliance. For instance, the JFTC implemented formal bans on 25 antitrust cases in the fiscal year of 2003 alone. These cases included bid-rigging (25 cases), price-fixing cartels (3 cases), and unfair trade practice (9 cases). Upon the discovery of such violations, the JFTC is required to go back three years and, as a general rule, collect 6% of the sales that stemmed from the initial violation (whether it was a bid-rigging conference or a price-fixing cartel). Consequently, the JFTC imposed surcharges of about 4.3 billion yen on 507 entrepreneurs in the fiscal year 2003.[9]

This is the main underlying reason why the JFTC is now proposing large-scale amendments aimed at strengthening the Antimonopoly Law, including greatly improving the surcharge system as a sanction against entrenched cartels.

These drafts for legal revision are based on a key report completed by a JFTC study group which consisted of legal scholars, economics scholars, and representatives of economic organizations. The study group discussed revisions in the law for these issues for about two years. The report was made public in October 2003. The Study Group Report (hereafter termed the Report) consists of a review of the procedural system (Review of Enforcement Systems) and of the monopoly and oligopoly regulations (Review of Monopoly and Oligopoly Regulations), and proposes significant legal revisions in each case.

We can note, however, that the review of enforcement systems in the Report is taken up in section VII of this paper. Significantly, the Report proposes to revise the surcharge system through a series of Antimonopoly Law amendments, roughly doubling the amount of money of surcharges while introducing a leniency program of the sort already adopted in the US, EU, Canada, and other countries.[10]

The review of monopoly and oligopoly regulations in the Report, which was another important proposal, tries to introduce a so-called essential facilities doctrine into the Antimonopoly Law as legislation. Section VIII of this paper deals with this proposal briefly.

Section IX of this paper will introduce some cases within Japan involving the application of cross subsidies in public utilities, which is the central theme of Professor Mestmäcker's report. In the following section (section VII), the Report's two chief proposals mentioned above for legal revision will be discussed in more detail.[11]

VII. Review of Enforcement Systems and Corporate Governance

According to the present Antimonopoly Law, the JFTC can take several important steps against so-called hardcore cartels, especially those involved in bid-rigging, price-fixing, quantity-limitation practices, and the purposeful division of

[9] <http://www.jftc.go.jp/info/nenpou.htm> (only Japanese).

[10] The content of the JFTC's amendment bill is published at the following URL 'Main Features of the Proposal to Amend the Antimonopoly Act' of 1 April 2004 <http://www2.jftc.go.jp/e-page/pressreleases/2004/april/040401summaryamareview.pdf> (19 April 2005).

[11] On the Study Group Report and law revision see 'Tokushû: Dokkin-hô kaisei no hôkô wo yomu' [feature articles: Anticipating the direction of Antimonopoly Law amendment] (2004) 1270 Jurisuto [Jurist] 6-77.

a market. These steps include: (1) collecting 6% of sales based on violations (however, this surcharge on sales is limited to the previous three years); (2) imposing a prison term of three years or less, or a penalty of 500,000 yen or less on natural persons (while a fine of 500 million yen or less can be imposed upon corporations) and; (3) under the Antimonopoly Law, victims can directly claim compensation for damages from the violating firm.

However, we should note that these penalties are rarely imposed except in extremely serious cases. Criminal charges are only filed at a rate of about one every one to two years. In addition, a suspension of sentence of natural persons who are in violation of the Antimonopoly Law in Japan is common. To date, there is no precedent for the court to impose a sentence without a stay of execution for natural persons in violation of the Antimonopoly Law. In both the Antimonopoly Law and civil law, the amount of compensation for damages is limited to the amount of damage actually suffered. In short, there is no system of treble damages or punitive damage in Japan. In light of such a situation, surcharges are very important measures in Japan and are therefore viewed as the most effective deterrent against violators of the Antimonopoly Law.

The Study Group Report describes the overarching purpose of their key proposals as being to promote:

> '[t]he implementation of structural reforms to achieve a society and economy based on market principles and the principle of self-discipline has become an urgent topic in Japan. To realize such reforms, active enforcement of competition policy in conjunction with the pursuit of regulatory reform has taken on greater importance.'

Furthermore, we can note that in regard to the comprehensive review of enforcement systems in Part 1 of the Report, it makes the following points:

Surcharges

- Increase the surcharge calculation percentage and broaden the range of conduct subject to surcharges
- Review the surcharge system in order to ensure the effectiveness of the Antimonopoly Act's prohibition provisions
- Change the character of the surcharge system to achieve a change from a 'deprivation of unreasonable profits'-type system to a system of 'collection of surcharges based on the assessment that can construct an amount equivalent to losses accompanying conduct in violation of the Antimonopoly Act'
- Increase the fixed surcharge calculation percentage and introduce a system of additional surcharges for use when entities commit repeated violations or in other situations
- Expand the range of surcharge applications against cartels that restrict market share and customers, purchasing cartels, private monopolization

related to prices, and private monopolization which eliminates competitors.[12]

In cases warranting a reduction or exemption from surcharge, the following legal requirements need to be fulfilled:

- Introduce a leniency program into the surcharge system to provide an incentive for firms to quit cartel activities and quickly restore competition
- Self-reporting of information to the JFTC by the firm that committed violations
- A firm voluntarily terminates its unlawful conduct.

Prosecution

When reviewing criminal prosecution procedures and penal provisions, the Report proposes:

- Introducing criminal investigation processes from the standpoint of increasingly using criminal prosecutions and ensuring due process and review of penal provisions, in order to strengthen the enforcement and deterrent powers of all the Antimonopoly Act enforcement systems
- Introducing a criminal investigation process
- Increasing penalties related to indirect investigation and non-observance of decisions by referring to provisions of other statutes
- Considering the introduction of penalties to unfair trade practices such as those unlawful conducts that cause grievous injury and substantially obstruct competitive discipline from the standpoint of consumer protection, etc.

Review of hearing procedures

Review hearing and other procedures from the standpoint of assuring due process and increasing efficiency by:

- Changing procedures so that elimination measures and surcharge payment orders take effect simultaneously
- Changing recommendations to cease and desist orders, and providing opportunities for entities to submit opinions prior to issuance of orders
- Establishing a system to make entrepreneurs pay or place in escrow the full amount of surcharges that should be paid when a hearing procedure is initiated based on the complaint against surcharge payment order.

[12] The Bill of October 2004 restricted scope of private monopolization, which is the target of surcharges, to that through controlling the business activities of other enterprises which restrains the price of their goods or services or which may affect the price of their goods or services by substantially restraining the volume of their supply, market share or customers.

The JFTC attempted to submit these proposals enshrined in a bill during last year's regular session of the Diet. However, it faced substantial opposition from the business community and was forced to abandon its proposal. The JFTC faced particularly stiff opposition from the Japan Federation of Economic Organizations (the JFEO or *KEIDANREN*).[13] The JFEO's opposition to these proposals is summarized below.

First, in regard to the above-mentioned surcharges, it follows that even if the figure of 6% is levied as a surcharge, it is assumed that there are a lot of cases where the surcharge actually exceeds the amount of profit the entrepreneur attained by means of the violation. It is the JFEO's view that the figure of 6% should be maintained.

The JFEO furthermore insists that the JFTC should take into account whether a significant 'cumulative factor'[14] (in total 100% or less) or a 'mitigating factor' (in total 70% or less) exists in actuality or not. Accordingly, if there is a cumulative factor then the surcharge should be implemented. Conversely, in the case of there being a mitigating factor present, the charges should be reduced.

Based on this concept, the following have been enumerated as possible cumulative factors:

- Seriousness (for instance + 10%);
- Level of economic gain (in the case that it is proven by the JFTC that an economic gain remarkably exceeds the standard amount of surcharge (6%)) (for instance, + 20%);
- Continuance of the violations (3 years or more) (for instance + 10%);
- Repetition of an offense (for instance + 40%);
- Malignancy (for instance + 10%);
- Role played in the violations (ie, if the enterprise concerned is a major conspirator) (for instance + 10%);

[13] Two members of the study group are from economic organizations, including the JFEO. The JFTC and JFEO are negotiating continuously on law revisions since the publication of the Study Group Report, and the amendment bill was changed in some points from its original one in process of their negotiations. The latest opinion on this matter from the JFEO is 'Proposal for suitable Antimonopoly Law revision for the 21st century' of 13 July 2004 <http://www.keidanren.or.jp/japanese/policy/2004/061.html> (19 April 2005); comment on 'Outline of Antimonopoly Law amendment bill' of 25 June 2004 <http://www.keidanren.or.jp/japanese/ policy/2004/056.html> (19 April 2005). However, these opinions published on the website of JFEO are only in Japanese. An English version was made available in September 2003 before the original report was made public: 'Proposal of Nippon Keidanren regarding revision of the Antimonopoly Act enforcement systems' of 5 September 2003 <http://www.keidanren.or.jp/english/policy/2003/088.html> (19 April 2005).

[14] Cumulative factors are defined as additional circumstances/actions that on top of the initial violation result in a more severe penalty to be sought. Conversely, mitigating factors are viewed as circumstances/actions that result in more leniency being sought when penalties are being considered.

- Obstruction of the investigation (for instance + 10%);
- No approach taken on corporate compliance (for instance + 10%);
- Level of approach on corporate compliance (for instance + 10%).

Moreover, the following have been enumerated as possible mitigating factors in terms of reducing a punitive surcharge:

- Non-seriousness of the case (for instance – 10%);
- Level of economic gain (in the case where the enterprises concerned can prove that an economic gain falls significantly below the standard surcharge of 6%), (for instance – 20%);
- Non-malignancy (for instance – 10%);
- Actual role played in violations (ie, when the enterprise concerned was not a major conspirator) (for instance – 10%);
- Cooperation in the investigation (for instance – 20%);
- Whether there is an approach on compliance (for instance – 10%);
- Level of approach on compliance (for instance – 10%);
- Timing of cessation of the violations (for instance – 10%).

Second, the JFEO insists that both surcharges and criminal punishment should not be applied to a corporation under the Antimonopoly Law. That is, surcharges should target the entrepreneur, while criminal punishment should only target natural persons (ie, individuals).

Third, the JFEO insists that the leniency program in Japan should be more generous. For example, the first reporter should be exempted from the surcharge; the second reporter should receive reduced surcharges by a figure of 50%; and the third reporter should have their surcharge reduced by 30%. Even more surprising is the claim that the reduction rate when applied to the reporters in question should be divided in proportion to the number of entrepreneurs concerned, regardless of whether violators report to the JFTC collectively and/or simultaneously.

However, these criticisms from the JFEO of the JFTC's amendments to the bill in question seem to be lacking in several areas.

First, according to the JFTC's estimation and the precedents available within civil suits, an unjustified profit by either bid-rigging or a price-fixing cartel is estimated to be about 20% of sales of goods or services in question. The figure of 6% of the target sales for violations is remarkably low compared with the standard of penalties in the United States and the EU. Antimonopoly laws will not function as law if they become more lenient and the level of surcharges is decreased further – a notion that the JFEO is seen to be proposing.

Second, the reduction ratio for the second reporter is too high. Moreover, it is not persuasive that the third reporter should receive such a substantial reduction. The key point is that, when a violator reports to the JFTC collectively and/or simultaneously, the application of a leniency system in any form is unwise. Under these restrictions proposed by the JFEO, the JFTC could technically allow those running a cartel to be exempt from punitive surcharges. The proposal is therefore one that distorts the fundamental premise of a leniency program – that is, to introduce a degree of instability (a so-called prisoners' dilemma) among those involved in profiting from cartels.

Third, the JFEO insists that when calculating surcharges it should take an affirmative evaluation approach in regard to corporation compliance. If a given enterprise has an appropriate compliance program, the JFEO insists that JFTC should reduce the surcharges. However, if the enterprise had an appropriate compliance system, it would be difficult to understand how the enterprise had violated the Antimonopoly Law in the first instance. Moreover, even if violations were carried out, the compliance program should have promptly discovered the violation. Therefore, there is no reason to affirmatively evaluate (on a cumulative percentage-based system such as that noted above) a compliance system that has failed at critical two stages.

In September 2004, the industry lobby finally reached agreement with the JFTC after certain compromises from both sides. The nature of the JFTC's compromise was that the surcharge – for instance, for large-sized manufacturers – was 10% of sales (although the JFTC had initially demanded 12-15%). The Liberal Democratic Party (LDP) accepted the bill, which was submitted to the Diet following the October 15 cabinet meeting and just prior to the Diet recess.[15] The bill was consequently carried over to the next session, and it presently remains under deliberation in the ongoing Diet session as of 28 February 2005. Whether the bill will be passed is not yet clear, because the opposition party, the Democratic Party, has submitted a counter-offer to the bill which closely resembles the JFEO's earlier proposal.

VIII. Review of Monopoly and Oligopoly Regulations

In Part 2 of the Report, the central theme is 'Comprehensive Review of Monopoly and Oligopoly Regulations.' The Report proposes to introduce an Essential Facilities Doctrine (EFD) for the infrastructure of public undertakings and for computer programs (especially operating systems) into the Antimonopoly Law. The Report refers to the Act against Restraints of Competition of Germany (ARC) (*Gesetz gegen Wettbewerbsbeschränkungen,* GWB), in addition to similar precedents set in the United States and the EU. However, the JFTC abandoned legal revisions in April 2004 because there were some points where the examination proved to be insufficient. However, the general recommendations put forward within this proposal are outlined as follows:

- Prompt and effective action against conduct to prevent market entry when essential facilities exist
- Monopoly and oligopoly regulations should be focused on the elimination of such conduct to prevent market entry

[15] <http://www2.jftc.go.jp/e-page/pressreleases/2004/october/041014.html> (19 April 2005).

– Highlight 'essential facilities' as a modern monopoly problem

A definition of essential facilities is given as:

(1) Facilities possessing natural monopoly characteristics, de facto standards based on technology possessing network externalities (a result in which use value rises as the number of participants in the network increases, also further increasing the number of participants); or scarce resources for which an institution such as the central government exclusively allocates usage rights
(2) Facilities whose use is necessary and indispensable when providing goods and/or services
(3) Facilities that competitors or other entities will face extreme difficulty in constructing in order to compete with existing providers. In addition to the above basic requirements, JFTC should take into consideration (i) the influence on long-term competition at a dynamic level, such as technology development or capital investment, and (ii) the size of the market concerning use of facilities.
    – To promptly and effectively eliminate conduct to prevent market entry by entrepreneurs having an overwhelmingly advantageous competitive position as a result of owning essential facilities.

The Report defines the following conduct to prevent market entry as unlawful when conducted without reasonable cause, and enacts appropriate measures (injunction orders, supplementary measures to restore competition):

(1) Conduct by entrepreneurs that monopolize and share essential facilities (rejection of, discrimination in, or restrictions or obligations concerning the use of the facilities)
(2) Conduct to prevent the shift of customers to competitors (long-term agreements accompanied by large-sum penalties for breach of contract, etc)
(3) Conduct in parallel to prevent market entry by two or more entrepreneurs, which have been exclusively allocated usage rights for essential facilities by an institution such as the central government,
    – Direct a comprehensive review of the reporting system concerning parallel price increases
    – Abolish this system, taking into consideration changes in economic conditions, changes in corporate awareness, and administration costs
    – Also aggressively implement investigation into conduct other than price increases in oligopoly-type business segments that have been legalized in advance
    – Implement effective exposure of parallel price increases that have a cartel in the background by methods such as introduction of a leniency program.

The criticisms that have been leveled at revising this law can be outlined as followed: (1) These requirements are so broad that new regulation will unduly restrict competitive behavior of public undertakings and the creation of computer programs. Consequently the investment incentive for the infrastructure becoming insolvent could lose significance (however, it should also be noted that it was difficult for the JFTC to establish additional requirements in the short time limit required to become legislation). (2) The present Antimonopoly Law prohibits private monopolization (Section 3). It also prohibits other refusal to deal (separate from a concerted refusal to deal) as one of the prohibited unfair trade practices (Section 19; Designation of Unfair Trade Practices Section 2).

It is argued, therefore, that these existing provisions, if taken into account and executed properly, should be sufficient to deal with possible antitrust issues arising from essential facilities. The JFTC should then only propose law revision when the executions of these provisions fall short of their intention.

We should note, however, that the JFTC has since abandoned this process of legal revision. Despite this development, the JFTC is resolutely confronting these issues in the field of public undertakings and deregulated industries. Some typical cases will be described in the next section.

IX. Application of the Antimonopoly Law to Public Undertaking

In the past, there were some cases where state-level aid or at least cross-subsidization in public undertakings might have caused violations of the Antimonopoly Law. There are also civil cases in which it was assumed that the practices involved were predatory pricings that violated the Antimonopoly Law.

First, in the aforementioned case involving the Supreme Court decision on the Tokyo Shibaura Public Slaughterhouse (TPS), this was a case that came from a private action for damages alleging that the defendant (TPS) owned by the Tokyo metropolitan government violated the Antimonopoly Law by charging extremely low slaughter fees. This outcome was ostensibly only made possible by the fact that the Tokyo metropolitan government compensated losses through a system of subsidies.

The Supreme Court and the Tokyo High Court reversed the district court's decision of adopting the plaintiff's claim and denied any liability involving TPS. Both courts held that the two slaughterhouses were in competition with many competing slaughterhouses not only in the Tokyo area but also in the greater Kanto and Tohoku area. Therefore, the Supreme Court and the Tokyo High Court judged that the pricing practice of TPS was nothing more than genuine competitive pricing.[16]

The second (aforementioned) case involves the suit filed seeking damages for the bargain sale of pre-stamped postcards that were offered for sale by the Ministry of Posts and Telecommunications (today known as Japan Post). In Japan,

[16] The Tokyo High Court decision of 24 February 1986 [1986] Hanrei Jihô [Judicial Reports] no 1182 p 34.

New Year's greeting cards are exchanged on New Year's Day. The postcards that the MPT issues are used as New Year's cards. In addition, these New Year's cards issued by the MPT have a lottery number found on the bottom portion of the cards. Winning numbers are announced on TV and in newspapers with the winners bringing their cards into the post office to claim their prizes. New Year's greeting postcards are sold for the same price as a regular stamp (40 yen). Therefore, the postcard and lottery number were both sold for 0 yen. Private manufacturers claimed that MPT's selling of the New Year's greeting postcards was an act of unjustified predatory pricing. They asserted that non-government-issued postcards could not compete fairly with the MPT postcards. A number of private postcard manufacturers subsequently filed a claim for damages. In this case, the Osaka High Court judged that the practice did not fall under the category of unjustified predatory pricing on three points. First, present laws relating to postage in Japan state that the prices of government-issued cards without pictures are to be 60 yen. Second, the additional costs of pictures per card are only a few extra yen, and in such cases postcards with pictures can be priced at the discretion of the government. Third, the postal service is a public undertaking.[17]

However, we should note that the number of cases in which the Antimonopoly Laws are applied to public undertakings are becoming increasingly common. In recent years, the JFTC issued one recommendation and two warnings against Nippon Telegraph and Telephone Group (notably NTT West and NTT East) that are seen to typify this trend. In these cases, a series of acts by the NTT Group, which monopolizes the local loop, to acquire market power in the broadband market (namely ADSL and/or FTTH (fiber to the home)) became Antimonopoly Law issues. Serious issues arose over refusals and delays of collocation, discriminatory treatment on transaction terms, and price squeezing. In addition, these cases became the focus of attention because the JFTC tried applying the Antimonopoly Law to the violation of Antimonopoly Laws, even though the Ministry of Public Management, Home Affairs, Posts and Telecommunications had already taken steps against these acts under the authority of SSRs. Below, I will outline a series of recommendations that resulted from an NTT-specific case concerning price squeezing that is now in the middle of an adjudicatory hearing.

NTT East possesses high speed fiber-optic networks over eastern Japan, offers optical broadband communications services (FTTH service: fiber to the home Internet access service) to consumers, and rents unused optical fibers to other telecom carriers. It is difficult for telecom carriers to offer an FTTH service without accessing the fiber-optic networks owned by NTT East because it is hard for them to build new fiber networks on their own. NTT East rents each optical fiber

[17] The Osaka High Court decision of 14 October 1994 [1994] Hanrei Jihô [Judicial Reports] no1548 p 63; Supreme Court decision of 18 December 1998 (1998) 45 Shinketsu-shû [JFTC Rulings Reports] 467.

to other telecoms at 5,074 yen per month. NTT East offers an FTTH service named 'B-FLET'S' to consumers.

When a company publicized its entry plan into FTTH service in March 2002, NTT East considered providing a cheaper FTTH service for consumers. Because NTT East considered that it was problematic in terms of fair competition to set a user surcharge which is cheaper than the access fee for each optical fiber cable, it avoided discounting the access fee for an optical fiber cable by creating the system in which each cable is split into up to 32 consumers. Thus NTT East introduced a bargain category of 'B-FLET'S' named 'New Family Type' for detached-house consumers in June 2002 and set the surcharge (5,800 yen per month) after notification to the Minister of Public Management, Home Affairs, Posts and Telecommunications. But actually, NTT East did not practice the split system because of so little demand among consumers and used the direct cable connecting method as before. The competitor discounted its fees in December 2002 and NTT East considered discounting the user surcharge. In March 2003, NTT East notified the Minister of Public Management, Home Affairs, Posts and Telecommunications of discounting the New Family Type (4,500 yen per month) on the basis of cost down simulation per user by the split method with the intention of preventing the fees of an optical fiber from dropping in order not to let other telecoms enter into the detached houses market. But actually, the company continues providing the service by the direct cable connecting method.

As a result, the New Family Type fee (4,500 yen per month) is lower than the access fee to other telecoms (5,074 yen per month), and telecoms, except that carriers with their own fiber networks cannot enter into the detached houses market.

In this way, NTT East prevents other telecoms from starting FTTH service to detached houses. The JFTC concludes that the conduct of NTT East substantially restricts competition in the trading field of FTTH service in eastern Japan.

The JFTC recommends as follows:

- NTT East to cease the above-mentioned activities;
- NTT East to do fair and proper indications to consumers in advertising of 'New Family Type';
- NTT East to inform the other telecoms which access the optical fibers of NTT East and consumers of the measures taken according to the above and non-recurrence of the above-mentioned activities in the future;
- NTT East not to do the above-mentioned activities in the future

It is important to note that the NTT group monopolizes the local loop in Japan. This is because the JFTC only began to apply the Antimonopoly Law at an early stage of the development of ADSL services.

The market share of the Yahoo Group now rivals the market share of NTT in the broadband market (especially ADSL) in Japan. As for FTTH, the competition from entrepreneurs of the affiliated electric power companies and enterprises using unbundled NTT line is active in the market for the housing and apartment complexes. However, the fact that the Ministry of Public Management, Home

Affairs, Posts and Telecommunications has been imposing a severe unbundling obligation and connections conditions on NTT is an important additional factor to understanding the telecommunications sector in Japan today.

With regard to the broadband market, the Antimonopoly Law and sector-specific regulations (SSRs) are being used in tandem to develop this market, even though they are, at times, found to be in opposition to each other. However, discussion of the issue of unbundling obligations of the optical fiber in regard to NTT and the various electric companies that are involved in cable network activities is expected to continue into the near future.

X. Conclusion

By analyzing how regulations in Japan are coping with a system that strikingly lacks general rules on regulating public sector state aid, this paper has illustrated how SSRs and the Antimonopoly Law are key regulatory authorities – which alongside the JFTC are seen to be both *cooperating* and *competing*. However, universal service realized by cross-subsidization induces complicated regulations and distorts competition, as outlined in some of the cases this paper introduces. Unbundling and access charge regulations also create unnecessarily complex regulations, thus resulting in SSRs increasingly adopting competition law standards recently. In the medium- and long-term, the role of the Antimonopoly Law's ex post regulation will become almost the sole regulation, even in the above-mentioned areas. Meanwhile, ex ante regulations by SSRs will remain in place to cope with exceptional issues that ex post regulations from existing competition rules are unable to competently deal with.

Part 5:

Intermediaries – Functions and Responsibility

Information Theory and the Role of Intermediaries

REINHARD H. SCHMIDT and MARCEL TYRELL*

I. The Problem and Its Context

The topic of corporate governance has received a great deal of attention in recent years and has become a focus of political debate and economic and legal research. However, in much of the Anglo-Saxon literature, which dominates the political and academic debate to date, it is still regarded in largely the same way as in the writing of Adam Smith more than 200 years ago.

In their seminal book from 1932, Berle and Means[1] saw corporate governance problems similarly, and still today most American scholars, especially those with an economic background and perspective, regard corporate governance as concerning how the providers of capital, and often only the investors in corporate equity, can assure themselves of getting their money back and earning a return that is commensurate with the risks they bear, as Shleifer and Vishny state in the opening sentence of their well-known survey article[2]. Since what providers of capital, especially those of corporate equity, can expect to get back in the future depends on the decisions taken by management, their interest in corporate governance is evident – and certainly also legitimate.

From a perspective which focuses only on investors, it may be easy to appreciate the possible role of investment and pension funds in the governance of those corporations in whose shares they invest. However, it is less evident why banks should also have a governance role. Nevertheless, in view of the reality of corporate governance in Europe and many other parts of the world, one could hardly do justice to our topic if one were to exclude banks from the discussion. It

* The authors are grateful to Marco Weiss for advice and support.

[1] A Berle and G Means *The Modern Corporation and Private Property* (Macmillan New York 1932).

[2] A Shleifer and R Vishny 'A Survey of Corporate Governance' (1997) 52 Journal of Finance 737.

is a fact of life that banks and investment and pension funds play a role in corporate governance, irrespective of whether they are aware of this role and whether they like it or not. This consideration suggests that it might not be appropriate to take the narrow 'shareholders-only' view of corporate governance as the starting point. Indeed, there are other views of what constitutes 'the corporate governance problem'. A broader view, which is prevalent in Europe, holds that corporate governance encompasses the totality of institutional and organisational mechanisms that influence how (important) decisions in (large) companies are made.

For playing their respective roles, those who are in some way involved in corporate governance need to acquire, transmit, and use information. Therefore, the objective of this paper consists in discussing the specific informational aspects of corporate governance, especially in connection with the possible roles of intermediaries.

The issue of the acquisition, transfer, and use of information for corporate governance purposes is difficult because information is a good with unconventional attributes. Moreover, as we will discuss in this paper, there are different ways in which information is acquired and used in different corporate governance systems.

The second specific aspect of our topic is that of intermediaries. We will largely concentrate our discussion on financial intermediaries and mention other intermediaries only in passing. In the case of investment and pension funds, one can expect them or their managers to act on behalf of, or as agents for, the investors in these funds. The issue here is a 'simple' agency relationship, which suggests asking questions like these: Do they really act in the interests of their investors/shareholders when they play a governance role, or do they use these roles to pursue their own objectives, which may in some respects differ from those of their principals? Which governance roles do they have and which roles do they indeed play? And finally: What does this agency relation imply for the issue of information acquisition and use?

Banks are intermediaries which, in many countries, especially in continental Europe, play an even greater role in the governance of corporations than investment and pension funds. The case of banks is more difficult than that of funds since the main role of banks is that of lenders. If the governance role of banks can at all be fruitfully regarded as that of an agent, one should be careful to ask whose agents banks are when they play a governance role.

What does this suggest for the definition of our topic and the context in which it needs to be discussed? If one includes banks in the discussion, it seems almost natural to go one step further and also include other stakeholders as having a role – or at least as being relevant – in the context of corporate governance. In this broadened context, the topic of corporate governance turns out to be about more than merely aligning management behaviour with shareholder interests. It also includes asking who and what shapes the objective function of a corporation which is supposed to provide guidance for management. Depending on the answer, the conventional topic of corporate governance as an agency problem concerning the monitoring of management might also require redefinition as the monitoring that management does what it is supposed to do if it is to act in the interest of more stakeholders than merely the shareholders. This also has implications for the issue of information acquisition and use.

There is one more aspect that makes our topic complex and is largely disregarded in the recent economic and agency-theoretic literature, although it is a part of corporate governance which practitioners, including managers and also lawyers, have certainly always understood: Corporate governance also has the function of monitoring and improving the quality of management decisions irrespective of all conflicts of interest. Evidently, for this advisory and quality-control function of a governance system, information is also extremely important. This is why we cannot disregard this function in dealing with our topic.

Thus, this paper has to address (1) information as an economic good with specific characteristics, (2) intermediaries, including banks which are essentially lenders, as part of certain corporate governance systems, (3) the different types and conceptions of what corporate governance is all about, and (4) the different functions of the various institutions which are elements of a corporate governance system. As we will see, these issues are closely related, but distinguishing corporate governance systems according to the conventional dichotomy of insider- and outsider-controlled corporate governance systems will turn out to be a useful way of coping with the complexity of the topic. As a caveat, we already at this point want to note that in accordance with the task assigned to us by the organisers of the conference at which the paper was presented, our discussion will be highly stylized and theory-driven. This should help to understand just some aspects of the 'reality' of different corporate governance systems.

The paper is structured as follows. In section II, we will discuss some aspects of the economics of information to lay the groundwork for what follows later. We show why the specific features of information as an economic good can lead to incentive problems in the production and use of information and to market failure in a market for information in general. We then distinguish between internalisation and externalisation as two fundamentally different ways of dealing with information in economic systems, and thereby introduce a distinction which surfaces again when we discuss corporate governance systems and the way they use information in section III. Subsection III.1 contains the presentation of the two types of corporate governance systems, including the roles of information in these systems in general, while section III.2 extends the discussion to include the specific problems of intermediaries. Section IV concludes by summarising our argument, discussing briefly the issue of the interrelations between the prevailing corporate governance system and types of activities or industry structures supported in the respective countries, and offering some open questions concerning the possibility of combining the two types of corporate governance systems and the two ways of dealing with information.

II. Elements of the Economics of Information

1. Information as a Good and the Difficulties of Providing and Transmitting Information

A large fraction of economic activity in any advanced economy is dedicated to the production, transmission, and dissemination of information. The financial sector provides the most striking example since a considerable part of its activity consists in handling information. Given the importance of information in general as well as that of the financial sector, it does not come as a surprise that economic theory has made information one of its main topics for many years.

What is the notion of information among economists? Can information be regarded as a good, and if so, what are the specific characteristics of this good? The standard notion of information is that it is knowledge about facts as well as about regularities and relationships between classes of facts, and most often such knowledge has relevance for decision making and valuation; it is decision- and value-relevant knowledge. Economic agents typically decide and act under uncertainty. Information can reduce uncertainty and lead to better decisions and economic outcomes.[3] This is why information is valuable. In a decision-making context which only takes into account the decisions of an individual agent, ie single-person decision problems, information always has a positive value.[4] However, in a market context in which the consequences of individual agents' decisions on prices and allocations are considered, the value of information can also be negative under certain circumstances, as we will argue in more detail below.

As a good, information differs from normal goods in several respects. One of these is that information is rarely consumed and valued as such but rather used as an input into decisions about other real or financial goods or assets. Therefore, information cannot be evaluated independently of these other decisions. This leads to indivisibilities, as Arrow already showed in 1962.[5] A related finding is

[3] Strictly speaking, in modern economic theory information can broadly be defined as any device that helps to reduce uncertainty. In this context, uncertainty means that one out of several possible, mutually exclusive states of the world prevail in the present as well as in the future. Information is any device that helps economic agents either to identify the current state of the world or to forecast the future state of the world. See JJ Laffont *The Economics of Uncertainty and Information* (MIT Press Cambridge 1989) and M Brunnermeier *Asset Pricing under Asymmetric Information – Bubbles, Crashs, Technical Analysis and Herding* (OUP Oxford 2001) for surveys of this literature.

[4] This is the famous theorem of D Blackwell 'Equivalent Comparisons of Experiments' (1953) 24 Annals of Mathematical Statistics 265.

[5] K Arrow 'Economic Welfare and the Allocation of Resources for Invention' in R Nelson (ed) *The Rate and Direction of Inventive Activity* (Princeton University Press Princeton 1962) 609.

due to Radner and Stiglitz, who demonstrated that there are economies of scale in the production of information[6]; that is, the value of information increases more than proportionally if the effort to produce information is increased. Indivisibilities and increasing returns to scale are standard reasons why a market for a good under consideration may not be competitive, or why some form of market failure can be expected to materialise.

Even more importantly, information exhibits features of a public good.[7] Public goods have two characteristics: non-rivalry in consumption or use, and non-excludability. Non-rivalry means that the use of a given good by one agent does not reduce the possibility of others to use this good too. Non-rivalry not only applies to the use of information but also to its transmission. Passing on information to others does not eliminate the information for the party which has transmitted the information. The possible and even likely effect that the economic benefit from using information that has been passed on to others declines is a secondary effect which does not contradict the assessment that information is a good with the feature of non-rivalry.

Non-excludability refers to the effect that there may be technical (or economic) problems of preventing others from using a certain good. In the case of information, non-excludability results from the possibility of others observing the behaviour – or economic effects which are caused by this behaviour – of someone who is assumed to have certain information, and deducing the content of the information from the observed behaviour or its consequences. Especially in large anonymous markets, there is the definite possibility that the observable behaviour of market participants and even market prices 'reflect' the information which some market participants may possess.

Individually and even more so in combination, the two features of non-rivalry and non-excludability have an important effect: An agent who generates or buys information cannot expect to appropriate the full economic value of the information. As a consequence, the incentives to produce or buy information are weaker than would be socially optimal.

There is thus a problem of under-investment in information production.[8] However, the converse can also occur. In two very influential papers, Hirshleifer has shown that there may also be excessive incentives to generate information

[6] R Radner and J Stiglitz 'Nonconcavity in the Value of Information' in M Boyer and R Kihlstrom (eds) *Bayesian Models in Economic Theory* (North-Holland Publishing Amsterdam 1984) 33.

[7] See J Stiglitz *Whither Socialism?* (MIT Press Cambridge 1994) for a similar characterisation.

[8] See S Grossman and J Stiglitz 'Information and Competitive Price Systems' (1976) 66 American Economic Rev 222; S Grossman and J Stiglitz 'On the Impossibility of Informationally Efficient Markets' (1980) 70 American Economic Rev 393, as the standard reference and M Hellwig 'Zur Informationseffizienz des Kapitalmarktes' (1982) 102 Zeitschrift für Wirtschafts- und Sozialwissenschaften 1 for an insightful early summary.

and thus over-investment.[9] The examples for this effect discussed by Hirshleifer refer to information about facts which will become publicly known in the near future or, in other words, to uncertainty which is about to be resolved soon anyway. In this case, trading of assets based on unevenly distributed information is a zero-sum game without social value. If one adds risk aversion, the social value of trading even becomes negative. However, the possibility of a negative social value of privately valuable information production is not confined to a pure exchange economy. Even in an economy with production, in which information can be 'productive' by improving production decisions, the 'premature' generation of information can still be socially undesirable since it may preclude options to share risk.[10]

There is thus by now a long list of settings in which the social and the private value of information differ, giving rise to possible inefficiencies of a market-based determination of the optimal level of information.

In addition to indivisibilities, increasing returns to scale, and the divergence of social and private value of information, there is one more problem which can stand in the way of a functioning market for information: the problem of reliability. How can it be assured that someone who claims to have valuable information which she would like to sell, really has this information and that it really is valuable? As it seems, one possibility would be to require that the seller reveal the information for inspection before the sale. However, if this happened the potential buyer would already have the information and might be inclined to argue that the information is not valuable for him in order to avoid paying for the information which he then had already obtained.

Irrespective of this problem of inspecting information before an eventual sale, a buyer of information also has to worry that the information is not trustworthy. Even an ex post assessment of the value of information may be extremely difficult since recipients of information tend to aggregate many different pieces of information before making decisions based on the information. Thus the marginal content of a given piece of information may be impossible to determine. In general, the credibility of information in the sense of its verifiability ex post depends on the nature of the information: Is it hard information which can at least in retrospect be determined to be true or not, or soft information which when received is in some informal way integrated into the set of beliefs and expectations of the recipient?[11] Note that a great deal of economically relevant informa-

[9] J Hirshleifer 'The Private and Social Value of Information and the Reward to Inventive Activity' (1971) 61 American Economic Rev 561; J Hirshleifer 'Where Are We in the Theory of Information' (1973) 63 American Economic Rev 31.

[10] See J Dow and R Rahi 'Informed Trading, Investment, and Welfare' (Working Paper London School of Economics, London 2002); F Allen 'The Efficiency and Stability of Banks and Markets' (National Bank of Belgium Working Paper No. 52, Brussels 2004).

[11] See JC Stein 'Information Production and Capital Allocation' (2002) 51 Journal of Finance 1891 for this distinction.

tion is not about facts which are already given, but about the future. It is therefore almost always probabilistic information expressed in the form of subjective probabilities. As such, it is soft information.

Reputational mechanisms may help to alleviate problems of market transactions for information. However, especially in large anonymous markets with many market participants, the likelihood of ever running into the same trading partner again may be low. Thus it may be difficult to make a credible commitment underpinned by one's own reputation.

The problems of information as a good which may be generated under market-induced financial incentives and traded and transmitted in markets are serious and general in nature. However, they are particularly acute and particularly relevant in the financial sector, for which information has such an enormous importance.

Even this short account of some key results of the economics of information may be sufficient to demonstrate that the idea of a well-functioning market for information is not at all plausible. In other words, it is worth discussing and analysing how the production, distribution, and use of information is organised in any financial system.

2. Two Types of Information Processing: Internalisation and Externalisation

In spite of the problems which we have described, the production, distribution, and use of information must be organised somehow, even if this does not amount to a perfect solution of the problems. There are essentially two approaches or types of solutions to these problems, which differ in a fundamental way. We will characterise these two approaches in general terms in this section and discuss them again and in more depth with special reference to financial and corporate governance systems in later sections.

An efficient and effective way of dealing with information problems in such a way that a great deal of information is generated and used is extremely important for any economic system. As early as 1945, Hayek pointed out that one standard for assessing an economic system is the extent to which it can use a great deal of information for the decision of how to allocate scarce resources.[12] As is well known, Hayek's innovative idea was that the price mechanism should be conceived as a mechanism to generate, aggregate, and transmit information. If what Hayek assumed to be the normal case in a market economy really does take place – that is, if information used in economic decisions is integrated into prices and transmitted via prices and from there on used for further decision making – we have a case of information externalisation. The most prominent example is the

[12] FA von Hayek 'The Use of Knowledge in Society' (1945) 35 American Economic Rev 519.

externalisation of information through stock prices in an informationally efficient capital market in the sense of Fama.[13 14]

Externalisation of information via the price mechanism is facilitated by disclosure to the general public, and it supports the direct effects of disclosure. This is why one typically finds both disclosure and information revelation through well-functioning markets side by side.

The distribution of information is of general importance for a market economy. But it is particularly important in the context of financial relationships since these relationships span different time periods and thereby offer the opportunity of one or both sides to a financial transaction to undertake actions which hurt the interest of the other side. The problems of *adverse selection* and *moral hazard* are particularly severe in financial relationships. However, since this is known to both sides of a potential transaction, both would suffer if no way were found to curb opportunistic behaviour, and therefore both will be interested in improving disclosure and information revelation through prices. In a later section of this paper, we will discuss how this can be implemented.

We now turn to the other approach to solve or at least mitigate information problems and information-based problems of cooperation and coordination. The other approach rests on creating and maintaining proximity: proximity generates information, and it increases credibility if there is the need to transmit or exchange information since there are possibilities to sanction opportunistic behaviour which would consist in transmitting irrelevant or wrong information. Proximity permits the building-up of trust, and trust is a 'good' whose value can best be preserved by acting in a trustworthy manner.

Creating, transmitting, and using information within a close relationship or a network of such relationships constitutes what one can call 'internalisation of information'. The term reflects that the information remains internal to a closely limited circle of recipients and users and that it is also not at all – or only to a limited extent – made public by being reflected in relevant prices. The problems resulting from the public good character of information are also less acute if the information is kept within a close relationship or, more precisely, within a network of several long-lasting relationships. However, the internalisation of information has one important drawback. Its ability to aggregate different and diverse pieces of information is limited. Thus a characteristic strength which Hayek had rightly claimed for a market economy is largely suppressed if information internalisation through close and lasting relationships is used extensively in an economy. As we will see in what follows, there are advantages and disadvantages

[13] EF Fama 'Efficient Capital Markets: A Review of Theoretical and Empirical Work' (1970) 24 Journal of Finance 387.

[14] See Grossman and Stiglitz (n 8) 404, who, referring to Hayek and Fama, discuss the logical impossibility of informationally efficient markets in the sense of prices fully reflecting all available information at any time.

to the modes of information externalisation and information internalisation which are reflected in the relative strengths of two types of financial systems and corporate governance systems.

III. The Use of Information and the Difference between Corporate Governance Systems

1. Information Processing in the Insider and the Outsider Systems

a. Information and Corporate Governance System Design

The way in which information is generated, transmitted, and used is the most important determinant of how a corporate governance system functions. However, there is not one single way but rather two ways, as there are two fundamentally different types of corporate governance systems which are well known and largely understood and which seem to function more or less equally well.[15] Franks and Mayer have called them the insider control system and the outsider control system.[16] The terminology reflects the way in which information is generated, transmitted, and used in the two types of corporate governance systems or, in other words, the nature of information which makes them function.[17]

The nature of information is not the only aspect in which the two types of corporate governance systems differ and which may have inspired the terminological distinction. The other aspects include the very definition of 'the problem of corporate governance'; the objective function of the corporation and its management; the set of persons and institutions which have an active role in governance; the closeness of the relationship between those with a role in corporate governance and the corporation itself; and the relative importance of internal mechanisms such as boards and markets. Together with the nature of governance-relevant information, these other features form a system of complementary elements which is consistent both in the insider and the outsider system,

[15] See assessments such as M Blair *Ownership and Control: Rethinking Corporate Governance for the 21st Century* (Brookings Institution Washington DC 1995); Shleifer and Vishny (n 2), as well as descriptive accounts such as J Charkham *Keeping Good Company* (OUP Oxford 1994).

[16] J Franks and C Mayer 'Corporate Control: A Comparison of Insider and Outsider Systems' (Working Paper, London Business School, London 1994).

[17] Of course, one can argue that more than two different corporate governance and financial systems are possible. For instance, until 1980 the French system could be classified as being state-dominated. But the point we want to make is a different one. Understanding the logic of corporate governance systems in connection to the information processing mode suggests focusing on these two idealised systems.

but differs in a fundamental way between these systems.[18] In other words, the other differences between the two systems 'reflect' differences in the nature of the corporate governance-relevant information in the sense that they are at the same time cause and consequence of the informational features.

b. The Insider Control System

We will now first characterise the insider control system. We will do this in general terms, but will use the case of German corporate governance for illustrations. An insider control system is one in which the information used to control and support management is inside information; it is generated internally, and it is kept, transmitted, and used internally, for instance and most importantly by a board and in its deliberations and decisions. Some of the information used by those active in corporate governance typically stems from close relationships to the respective corporation, which implies that it can include soft and confidential information and can be detailed. At least at the stage of its generation, the information is unevenly distributed among the active participants, and it is used in a way which does not have the consequence that it is revealed to a broader public through disclosure or the observability of decisions and their consequences. Thus, the internal information remains largely internal, which is one reason why the incentives to contribute private information to the governance process are not mitigated as would be the case if information were made public through some process.

What is corporate governance in an insider control system? To answer this question, one should be aware of the fact that most insider control systems for large corporations go hand in hand with stakeholder orientation.[19] Stakeholder orientation means that de facto or even by law – as in the German case[20] – both the supervisory board and the management board have a strong commitment to the 'interest of the enterprise', which can be interpreted as meaning the interests of various stakeholder groups, among which shareholders are, however, the most important group.

[18] For an exposition of the concept of complementarity and its application to financial systems and corporate governance, see A Hackethal and RH Schmidt *Komplementarität und Finanzsystem* (Kredit und Kapital, Beiheft 15 'Neue finanzielle Arrangements: Märkte im Umbruch' 2000).

[19] Closely held family-owned firms also have an insider control system of governance but rarely are stakeholder-oriented.

[20] See O Rieckers and G Spindler 'Corporate Governance: Legal Aspects' in JP Krahnen and RH Schmidt (eds) *The German Financial System* (OUP Oxford 2004) 350; RH Schmidt 'Corporate Governance in Germany: An Economic Perspective' in JP Krahnen and RH Schmidt (eds) ibid 386 for details.

In such a system, a central issue of corporate governance is to assure that the corporation is run in such a way that the interests of various stakeholder groups are taken into account to such an extent that they all find it attractive to cooperate and to contribute their respective resources to the corporation – or to put them 'at stake' – and at the same time that the economic survival, stability, and growth of the corporation is highly likely.[21] This balancing out of divergent interests is a task which typically falls on both the supervisory and the management board in a German *Aktiengesellschaft*. Moreover, corporate governance is about monitoring management and supporting it in its decision making. Note that the task of monitoring the management in terms of its adherence to the 'objectives of the firm' is particularly difficult since it is anything but clear what the main objective is to which management should adhere in a stakeholder-oriented insider control system.

The central and characteristic institution and mechanism in insider control systems is a board which oversees the decisions taken by the management. The formal legal governance system of (large, publicly held, and exchange-listed and -traded and co-determined) German joint stock corporations comes to mind as an example. The fundamental stakeholder orientation of German corporate governance is most clearly reflected in the composition of the supervisory board and the definition of its role in comparison to that of top management (the management board). The (supervisory) board in an insider control system is composed of members of whom most are in some sense quite close to the corporation. They may be – or may represent – blockholders such as owner-founder families or other large corporations or financial institutions which have been blockholders for a long time; or they represent banks or other important lenders or company staff, especially of higher ranks and core employees. Because of their specific ties to the company, many board members can be expected to have information which is not publicly available and which they can use in fulfilling their governance functions. Note that the representatives of 'genuine shareholders' without close ties and specific information, who would only have an interest in dividends and share price appreciation, hardly play a role in German supervisory boards. If present at all, they are clearly in a minority position.

In a way, one can consider the various stakeholder groups which jointly determine the policy of a supervisory board as a coalition. The members of this coalition have divergent interests as well as common interests. The divergent interests result from the affiliation with different constituencies which the board members represent. The common interest is based on the fact that most of the members of this coalition are not so much concerned with the financial benefits for 'genuine shareholders' but in the stability and growth of the company. This

[21] See RH Schmidt and M Weiss 'Shareholder vs. Stakeholder: Ökonomische Fragestellungen' in P Hommelhoff and others (eds) *Handbuch Corporate Governance* (Schäffer-Poeschel Stuttgart 2003) 107 for an extended analysis of this concept.

holds evidently for board members with a special allegiance to lenders, to general staff, and to management, but also largely for those who represent blockholders or 'strategic investors'. If 'genuine shareholders' or funds which acted like genuine shareholders had a stronger role than they typically have in insider control systems, it would be very difficult to find sufficient common ground for the board to act effectively as a 'watchdog' over, and an advisor to, management. However, even if they play only a limited role, they can be useful by contributing stock market-related information and by assuring that the 'governing coalition'[22] does not go too far in pursuing goals other than those of shareholders.

This list of functions of the supervisory board, its composition, and the way in which it exercises corporate governance in a well-functioning insider control system suggests what kind of information the board members can contribute, may be willing to contribute, and are expected to contribute to their joint tasks. It is largely non-public, sometimes soft, and confidential internal or inside information which relates, for instance, to the question of what certain management decisions would imply for the respective constituencies with which board members are affiliated or how certain policies affect the commitment of the respective stakeholder group. This kind of information must come from within and from various sources, which explains why a supervisory board should be composed of members from different stakeholder constituencies that are in some way close to the company. Moreover, the information often refers to topics on which management may really need advice and information from someone whose advice it cannot easily shrug off. Thus the kind of information which an insider control system with various stakeholder groups represented on the board tends to generate and use, is in principle well suited to support both the monitoring and the advisory functions of the supervisory board at the same time.[23]

One element which is conspicuously absent from an insider control system is a public market for corporate control in the sense of a hostile takeover market. We have described in earlier papers why an active takeover market would hardly be compatible with the logic of a stakeholder-oriented insider control system.[24] If it were active, such a market would reduce the incentives for board members with an affiliation to stakeholders who are not shareholders to generate information and to contribute this information to the working of governance.

[22] See A Hackethal and others 'Corporate Governance in Germany: Transition to a Modern Capital Market-Based System?' (2003) 159 J of Institutional and Theoretical Economics 664 for more on the governing coalition in insider control systems.

[23] See EF Fama and M Jensen 'Separation of Ownership and Control' (1983) 26 Journal of Law and Economics 301 for a similar argument.

[24] See RH Schmidt and M Tyrell 'Financial Systems, Corporate Finance and Corporate Governance' (1997) 3 Eur Financial Management 159.

c. The Outsider Control System

In comparison, and in fact also in contrast, to that of an insider control system of corporate governance, the design of an outsider control system is rather simple. This is mainly due to the clear objective function which applies for the management of a corporation. In an outsider control system like the British system, management has one and only one objective, namely to act in the financial interests of shareholders. Shareholder value orientation is only limited by the inevitable 'business judgement', which might suggest certain concessions to other stakeholders in order to secure their cooperation and loyalty. In economic terms, a corporate governance system of the outsider control type is not meant to function in the genuine interests of other stakeholders besides shareholders. These other stakeholders can, and are expected to, secure their interests through clear and easily enforceable contracts and well-functioning markets for labour or credit which offer 'exit options' if there is reason for discontent. In the British corporate governance and largely also that of the United States, banks and employees do not have any board representation or other active corporate governance function which one could consider as requiring 'voice' in the sense of *Hirschman's* well-known dichotomy, since non-shareholders are not tied to the corporation by 'loyalty'.[25] Corporate governance in an outsider control system consists almost exclusively in mitigating the 'classic' Smith-Berle-Means-Shleifer-Vishny agency problem of preventing negligence and self-serving behaviour of management.

There is of course also a board of directors in an outsider control system, which includes a certain number of outside directors. But this board is more restricted in its functions than a (German) supervisory board. Its functions do not include the balancing of divergent interests since there is simply no room for 'legitimate' divergences of interest in a corporate board. Also the monitoring is easier in principle – though certainly not in practice – because what management is supposed to do is unambiguous. The only real monitoring function is to limit the extent to which management pursues its own interest at the expense of shareholders, the common agency problem. But the board can hardly be regarded as the main instrument or mechanism for monitoring. Since shareholder value is the supreme and sole objective, the advisory role of outside board members is also restricted to eventually telling managers what they think might be the reaction of the stock market to certain corporate policy decisions. This brief list of tasks indicates what the information is which outside boards are supposed to have and to contribute: It is essentially stock market-related and thus public or outside information.

[25] See AO Hirschman *Exit, Voice and Loyality* (Harvard University Press Cambridge 1970) for the roles of 'Exit, Voice, and Loyalty' in the design of organisations. In a highly inspiring comparative study of the German and the British corporate governance systems, A Mann *Corporate Governance Systeme* (Duncker & Humblot Berlin 2003) uses these concepts to characterise insider and outsider governance.

The structure and the composition of 'the board' in an outsider control system correspond to this restricted set of functions of the outside board members. First and foremost, there is typically only one board; reasons for having a dual-board structure do not apply. The outside board members are at the same time trustees of the general shareholder population and experienced advisors to the inside board members, but their expertise should mainly refer to general management issues and to how the stock market would evaluate certain policies. If one leaves aside cynical explanations of how outside board members are selected,[26] this is also the general logic which determines board compositions.

In a theoretical perspective, boards are not the main element of an outsider control system. This role is reserved for the capital market and especially one segment or aspect of this market, namely the market for corporate control. Bad management, in the sense of a management team which fails to maximise shareholder wealth, is disciplined by the capital market or the threat coming from this market. Bad management runs into difficulties if there is the need to raise external capital. It is exactly for this reason, ie to provide a control device for bad management, that in countries with an outsider control system of corporate governance bank financing is less extensive and dividend payout ratios are more generous than in countries with insider control systems.

Even more so, the market for corporate control can in principle provide discipline. It serves to replace bad management and, following Manne,[27] the threat of being replaced is what induces managers to behave in the interest of shareholders. The best policy for incumbent management of avoiding a hostile takeover and of protecting its attractive position is to drive the cost of a takeover up as much as possible. By this means they maximise the rents that can be extracted by the (minority) shareholders. And this is exactly what shareholders want management to do anyway!

For the proper functioning of the capital market as a disciplinary device, this market must be liquid and its participants must be well informed. Liquidity requires more than anything else equality of information for all market participants. Inside information is inimical to a well-functioning market. The same holds for the takeover market. Thus, ultimately it is the market which 'governs' corporations, and the typical market participants must not be close to the corporation, since closeness generates informational asymmetries and reduces liquidity. Thus the – anonymous and not really active or 'voice-based' – actors in an outsider control system are indeed 'outsiders'.

[26] See for instance B Hermalin and M Weisbach 'Board of Directors as an Endogenously Determined Institutions: A Survey of the Economic Literature' (2001) 9 Economic Policy Rev 7.

[27] H Manne 'Mergers and the Market for Corporate Control' (1965) 73 J of Political Economy 110.

Given the way in which an outsider control system is designed and functions, it follows directly what kind of information and what distribution of information is required for the functioning of the system: Again it is largely information about the capital market and for the capital market, thus public information or information which can be passed on to the general public – in other words, outside information. Outside information is the basis of markets, especially capital markets; and inversely, well-functioning or efficient markets (in the spirit of Fama[28]) contribute themselves to making information public by revealing it through publicly observable prices. Outsider control systems rely on the externalisation of information and at the same time reinforce externalisation.

d. Complementarity between Information, Governance, and Financial System

Only in passing, we want to point out an important parallel between the insider and the outsider control system. Both are systems composed of complementary and consistent elements among which the nature of governance-relevant information plays a key role, and both are embedded in the financial, legal, and economic system.

The outsider control system is composed of elements which fit together well: Outside information, strict shareholder orientation, a unitary board, and no board representation for lenders and employees form a consistent system of complementary elements, just like the converse features provide consistency to the insider control system.

In the case of the outsider control system, the surrounding financial, legal, and economic system comprises, among other things, well-functioning labour and capital markets and an efficient legal system to protect employees and lenders, less durable employment patterns, less bank lending and lending with shorter maturities and higher collateral requirements and little involvement of banks in the case of borrowers' distress, and many other features.[29] For short, we call this larger system a capital market-based financial system. The capital market-based financial system and the outsider control system are complements and are consistent, and both rely on the externalisation of information.

The converse features make up a bank-based financial system. An insider control system of corporate governance belongs to and complements this system, which also relies on the internalisation of information. Thus the nature of information is not only the key to understanding specific corporate governance systems and their differences, but also the systems at large to which they belong.

[28] Fama (n 13).

[29] For an extended analysis of the correspondence between corporate governance (as a system) and the financial and economic system at large in which the corporate governance system is embedded, see Hackethal and Schmidt (n 18).

2. Financial Intermediaries as Providers and Processors of Information

a. Introduction

This section adds the aspect of intermediaries to the line of reasoning developed so far. In order to analyse the role of financial intermediaries in corporate governance systems, we first have to clarify our notion of financial intermediaries. In doing so, we also limit the scope of our discussion. The financial sector of a country encompasses financial intermediaries, which can be subdivided into banks, non-bank financial intermediaries (NBFIs) and financial markets, and also the regulatory environment in which these institutions operate.[30] To focus our discussion, we will employ a more narrow definition of financial intermediaries as institutions which have mainly financial assets and liabilities on their balance sheets. Thus we will only discuss banks and NBFIs, which seems appropriate since only banks and NBFIs can be *active* financial intermediaries in the corporate governance systems, while capital markets are not acting themselves but are used by banks, investment funds, and other market participants. The role of markets will be discussed later in this section when we focus on the externalisation of information.

It is the purpose of this section to analyse which type or types of financial intermediary is or are the dominant player(s) in the two generic corporate governance systems, and how their specific roles relate to the specific mode of information processing which characterises the respective corporate governance system. As we will argue, especially in the case of banks it is of paramount importance that they are intermediaries and not just any kind of lenders.

b. Insider Control Systems and the Role of Banks as Financial Intermediaries

As we have argued above, there is a close correspondence between a bank-based or bank-dominated financial system and an insider control governance system.[31] In a bank-based financial system, banks play a dominant role in the process of financial intermediation, they are the main providers of external finance to companies, and they are (still) the main recipient of the households' financial funds.[32] This has important consequences for the role which banks have in an

[30] See RH Schmidt and M Tyrell 'What Constitutes a Financial System in General and the German Financial System in Particular?' in Krahnen and Schmidt (eds) (n 20) 19.

[31] This is certainly true for industrialised countries. See F Allen and D Gale *Comparing Financial Systems* (MIT Press Cambridge 2000) ch 1; and F Allen and D Gale 'Comparative Financial Systems' in A Boot and others (eds) *Financial Intermediation* (OUP Oxford 2005, forthcoming) for further details.

insider control system of corporate governance, and especially to the way in which they deal with information in fulfilling their governance role.

First of all, due to a dominant role in the intermediation process, risk sharing will be executed mainly through banks. As Allen and Gale argue in a number of important contributions, banks are specialists in handling inter-temporal risk and in implementing risk sharing among generations.[33] In a formal model, Allen and Gale show that with respect to the handling of risk, a bank-based financial system can be superior to a capital market-based financial system because banks can better allocate risk and smooth consumption inter-temporally. This can be achieved by households accumulating claims against banks. A key feature of asset accumulation as a mechanism of risk reduction is that the holders of the claims do not incur any, or only a very minor, price risk, even though the value of the assets by which their claims are ultimately secured are subject to risk. In practical terms, this requires that households hold their financial wealth mainly in the form of fixed claims on banks, ie as deposits, and that the banks can credibly commit to honour these claims in full and without delay if the depositors want their money back. Banks can offer these secure investment opportunities and therefore allow socially desirable – ie welfare-enhancing, inter-temporal risk-reduction – under two conditions. Firstly they must be sufficiently stable and profitable so that they can build up a buffer stock in good times when returns on the assets they hold are high, and reduce this buffer stock in bad times. Secondly, competition between banks and capital markets must not be all that strong, because otherwise agents – including the banks themselves – would turn to investing in the capital market when returns are high and thereby undermine the income smoothing function of banks. Only if the outside options of the agents are not 'too good' will they stick to the financial arrangement which has been agreed ex ante because of its efficiency property, namely the deposit contract with a bank which builds up and occasionally depletes a buffer.

[32] See for instance the empirical results in RH Schmidt and others 'Disintermediation and the Role of Banks in Europe: An International Comparison' (1999) 8 J of Financial Intermediation 36 and A Hackethal and RH Schmidt 'Financing Patterns: Measurement Concepts and Empirical Results' (Working Paper Series: Finance and Accounting no 125, University of Frankfurt 2004). Of course, we could also include non-bank lenders into our analysis. But in a typical bank-based financial system like that of Germany, most investment funds are owned by banks and insurance companies, and/or are often closely interlinked with banks and/or behave in ways which are largely similar to those of banks.

[33] See especially F Allen and D Gale 'A Welfare Comparison of Intermediaries and Financial Markets' (1995) 39 European Economic Review 179; F Allen and D Gale 'Financial Markets, Intermediaries and Intertemporal Smoothing' (1997) 105 J of Political Economy 523. Inter-temporal risk results, for example, from macroeconomic developments, such as the oil price shock in the early 1970s, the stock market crashes of 1987 and 2000/2001, or the dramatic fall of asset prices in Japan since the early '90s. In all of these cases there were pronounced, long-lasting, and highly correlated changes in the prices of most assets, including market-traded assets, such that investors were unable to effectively offset the resulting non-diversifiable risks.

What are the informational aspects of this arrangement, and what is their relationship to corporate governance? In contrast to cross-sectional or intra-temporal risk sharing, where risk referring to a given point of time is allocated and distributed efficiently among agents and which can be achieved via markets, efficient inter-temporal risk sharing does not require that information be symmetrically distributed between depositors and banks. Hence, the important function of banks – and more generally of a bank-based financial system – to mitigate inter-temporal fluctuations is consistent with banks holding assets which are not easily marketable in a secondary market, and with relationship lending.

In bank-based financial systems, relatively little information is made available to financial markets and is generated and transmitted by financial markets. Disclosure requirements are not as strict as in market-based systems, and the role of accounting is not so much that of making information publicly available, but to facilitate relationship-based lending, for instance, by restricting dividend payments to outside shareholders and by informing management and supervisory boards, ie the insiders.[34] Both the 'handicap' for capital markets and the privilege for banks as lenders are based on the information system, and both have the effects that bank lending is more important and especially long-lasting relationships between banks and corporations are more prevalent in bank-based financial systems.[35] In an ongoing credit relationship, banks acquire considerable information about their borrowers, more than what is released to the markets in bank-based systems. A considerable share of the accumulated information is soft information which cannot be credibly communicated from one agent to another because it is not verifiable by anyone other than those who have generated it.[36]

Much like investors in corporate equity, lenders with long-term engagements depend in a crucial way on the decisions taken by management on behalf of borrowing corporations. This is why they have a genuine interest to be involved in corporate governance: They need 'voice', since 'exit' is difficult and costly, and they contribute information which is relevant for monitoring and advising

[34] See C Leuz and J Wüstemann 'The Role of Accounting in the German Financial System' in Krahnen and Schmidt (eds) (n 20) 450 on how much information audit reports contain and who gets this information. See also L Correira da Silva and others *Dividend Policy and Corporate Governance* (OUP Oxford 2004) for an interesting comparative analysis of dividend policy in different industrialised countries.

[35] See R Elsas and JP Krahnen 'Universal Banks and Relationships with Firms' in Krahnen and Schmidt (eds) (n 20) 197 on empirical evidence concerning relationship lending in Germany.

[36] See JC Stein 'Information Production and Capital Allocation' (2002) 51 J of Finance 1891 for this definition of soft information which also refers to the tacit dimension of knowledge and A Berger and others 'Does Function Follow Organizational Form? Evidence From the Lending Practices of Large and Small Firms' (Working Paper, New York 2004) whose results support the hypothesis that relationship lending goes hand in hand with the use of soft information.

management. Thus the informational features of a bank-based system create both the need and the potential of banks as lenders to actively participate in corporate governance.

Based on accumulated soft information and also the mainly internal use of potentially hard information, borrowers are locked in; they are dependent on their bank(s). Of course, this has important advantages: Close ties between a bank and its debtor provide incentives for information production, monitoring, and advising the debtor; they enable (efficient) renegotiation of contracts; and they allow for inter-temporal transfers.[37] But this closeness also has a dark side: Over time, banks as lenders who can rightly be assumed to have more information than potential other lenders, acquire a certain degree of monopoly power, and therefore the ability to extract excessive rents from their borrower-clients. This is a potential weakness of a bank-centred internal control system, but this disadvantage can be mitigated if *multiple* constituencies, ie stakeholders, are represented on the board of the company. With the mixed composition of (supervisory) boards, not only the interests of banks and shareholders but also those of employees and sometimes even suppliers and customers have to be taken into account. These different stakeholder groups are sharing control, thereby incorporating the diverse information they have. Since the 'stakes' of all groups of stakeholders tend to be substantial, their incentives for producing and using information is also substantial. The free rider problem of large groups is not likely to apply, and the disadvantage of institutions relative to markets pointed out by Hayek, that not enough information and not sufficiently diverse information will be incorporated into an economic system when information is not disclosed through the price mechanism, is to a certain extent alleviated in an insider control system.

This description of the role of banks in an insider control system serves to show that certain aspects of the insider control system can only be explained by invoking the role of the banks which we have sketched, and the kind of information which banks can contribute and which is important for governance. But three questions are still unanswered up to this point.

First, what are the incentives of banks to fulfil their roles? Of course, they can earn rents by being relationship lenders. Being involved in governance and thereby obtaining additional information enables them to make better lending decisions. Moreover, by contributing to the control of management together with other groups which have a strong interest in stable growth rather than merely in maximising future profits irrespective of its riskiness, they have a certain

[37] See R Rajan 'Insiders and Outsiders: The Choice between Informed and Arm's-length Debt' (1992) 47 J of Finance 1367; A Boot 'Relationship Banking: What Do We Know?' (2002) 9 J of Financial Intermediation 7; and R Elsas and others 'Multiple but Asymmetric Bank Financing: The Case of Relationship Lending' (Working Paper, University of Frankfurt, Frankfurt/Main 2004) for a theoretical analysis of relationship lending and R Elsas and JP Krahnen 'Is Relationship Lending Special? Evidence from Credit-File Data in Germany' (1998) 22 J of Banking and Finance 1283; Elsas and Krahnen (n 35) for empirical support.

assurance that management decisions are not 'biased' in favour of shareholder interests and too risky from the standpoint of a lender.

But generating information and contributing to the governance of corporations is also costly for banks. What prevents them from taking a free ride on the efforts of others in this respect? As was argued first by Calomiris and Kahn[38] and later on more generally by Diamond and Rajan[39], banks are disciplined by the threat of runs. The argument goes like this. On their asset side, banks have illiquid loans whose market prices in a fire sale would be below their intrinsic values. Having to sell or to call loans prematurely would involve losses. The greater part of the activities which banks undertake – and need to undertake – to monitor their loans, which includes their active involvement in the governance of borrowing corporations, are not really observable for depositors.

At least a certain part of a bank's liability are call or sight deposits, which are by definition and by law to be paid back on demand and on a first-come first-serve basis. This rule of distribution makes depositors wary that they might be late or stand too far behind in the waiting line if a bank should encounter problems, and it makes them even aware of what little information they may have on the monitoring activity of the bank. This situation can lead to a bank run, and the danger of a run is what induces banks to do what their depositors want them to do, namely to be active delegated monitors in the spirit of Diamond[40].

According to the present state of the theory of financial intermediation,[41] this is the incentive mechanism which forces banks to be active monitors and makes an active governance role attractive for them. Thus ultimately, the role of banks in corporate governance rests on the interaction of information internalisation and the role of banks as financial intermediaries. However, the incentive mechanism of banks being exposed to the threat of a run on sight deposits also has a downside: As Diamond and Rajan show,[42] this feature leads to 'natural' instability of banking sectors and makes bank-based financial systems susceptible to crises.[43]

[38] CW Calomiris and C Kahn 'The Role of Demandable Debt in Structuring Optimal Banking Arrangements' (1991) 81 American Economic Rev 497.

[39] D Diamond and R Rajan 'A Theory of Bank Capital' (2000) 55 J of Finance 2431; D Diamond and R Rajan 'Liquidity Risk, Liquidity Creation and Financial Fragility: A Theory of Banking' (2001) 109 J of Political Economy 287.

[40] D Diamond 'Financial Intermediation and Delegated Monitoring' (1984) 51 Rev of Economic Studies 393.

[41] For a recent survey of this literature, see M Tyrell 'Kapitalmärkte und Banken – Formen der Informationsverarbeitung als konstitutives Merkmal' (Deutscher Universitäts-Verlag Wiesbaden 2003) ch C.

[42] D Diamond and R Rajan 'A Theory of Bank Capital' (2000) 55 J of Finance 2431.

[43] This incentive argument also carries over to large lenders in the interbank market. As JC Rochet and X Vives 'Coordination Failures and the Lender of Last Resort: Was Bagehot Right After All?' (2004) 2 J of Eur Economic Association 1116 recently stated, emphasis in the last years shifted from maturity transformation and liquidity insurance of small depositors to a

cont. ...

The second question is what the roles of other financial intermediaries in an insider control system are. Empirical evidence supports the assumption that pension and investment funds do not play an active role in the monitoring of companies.[44] But as long as they cannot and do not pressure too much in the direction of profit maximisation, their presence would be compatible with the logic of an insider control system. Insurance companies are in some way similar to banks and support the latter in their corporate governance functions.[45]

We conclude with a brief look at what one could call information intermediaries. Auditors provide a particularly important function in an insider control system based on information internalisation. As shown by Leuz and Wüstemann[46] for the case of Germany, a substantial amount of information is generated by auditors and communicated through non-public channels to supervisory boards. This is consistent with information internalisation.

The third question is which firm characteristics and industry structures are particularly well suited to an insider corporate governance system. We will take this question up in our concluding section.

c. Outsider Control Systems and the Role of Financial Intermediaries and Markets

In a typical capital market-based financial system, NBFIs and especially investment and pension funds play a dominant role in the accumulation of household savings and in the financing and the governance of corporations.[47] Since investment and pension funds – as those NBFIs and financial intermediaries in the narrow sense to which we confine the following discussion – invest a large share of the funds which they collect in the capital market, the intermediation process relies heavily on financial markets.[48] This is reflected in the ownership structures of most listed companies in countries with capital-market based financial systems

'modern' form of bank runs where large, well-informed investors do not renew their credit – for example, negotiable certificates of deposit – in the interbank market and thereby discipline banks.

[44] See Mann (n 25) and the references given there. Actually, in Germany and other countries with an insider control system, most investment and pension funds belong to banks or are in some other way controlled by them.

[45] For instance, in Germany there is a complex web of ownership linkages between banks and insurance companies.

[46] Leuz and Wüstemann (n 34).

[47] See Schmidt and others (n 32). Of course, in some outsider control systems, banks are also important intermediaries in terms of the quantity of funds transmitted. But as we will argue later on, most of the loans granted by these banks are not 'relational' but 'transaction-based'.

[48] In the following, the terms capital markets and financial markets will be used as synonyms.

and outsider-controlled corporate governance systems. Companies' shares are primarily held by institutions such as investment and pension funds, and by individual investors. Ownership is typically dispersed in the sense that no one institution or investor holds a large stake in a single company.[49] All in all, capital market-related NBFIs and markets are important institutions in market-based financial systems.

As Allen and Gale argue[50], financial markets are particularly well suited to achieve cross-sectional risk sharing. More risk-tolerant agents end up bearing more risk than more risk-averse agents. This presupposes that markets are largely complete, transaction costs are low and, what is particularly important in the context discussed here, information is symmetrically distributed among market participants. The way in which capital markets function is consistent with the nature of the most important group of assets held by the most important financial intermediaries in this system.

Disclosure to the general investing public is better and more strongly enforced. Furthermore, the information provision and dissemination process is supported by many financial analysts working for the NBFIs, by financial newsletters, by full-service stockbrokers, and so on. As explained in Section 2, these features of the financial system are consistent with the predominance of outside information or, in other words, the system is grounded on information externalisation.

As we have argued above, corporate governance in an (idealised) outsider control system is not 'actively' pursued by certain persons and institutions but results as a side effect of the working of financial markets. The same holds for information transmission: It is also a by-product of the way in which financial markets function, as the well-known concept of 'informationally efficient markets'[51] suggests.

These considerations have led the research literature to delve deeply into the question of whether there could be a separate but nevertheless well-functioning market for information. In view of the peculiarities of information as a good, which we discussed in Section 2, the answer to this question is not trivial. Suffice it to note here that, in principle, such a market is conceivable and may play a role in the design of a corporate governance system. But for the purpose of the present paper, another aspect of this literature is more relevant: It provides at least some foundation to discuss the question of why intermediaries such as investment and

[49] See F Barca and M Becht *The Control of Corporate Europe* (OUP Oxford 2001) for a comparison of ownership structures in different industrialised countries.

[50] F Allen and D Gale 'Financial Markets, Intermediaries and Intertemporal Smoothing' (1997) 105 J of Political Economy 523.

[51] EF Fama 'Efficient Capital Markets: A Review of Theoretical and Empirical Work' (1970) 24 Journal of Finance 387.

pension funds exist at all and what their existence implies for the relationship between information and corporate governance.

Admati and Pfleiderer[52], Allen[53] and Bhattacharya and Pfleiderer[54] have developed models which show that these intermediaries can be interpreted as institutions that mitigate the above-mentioned problems of selling information. In a nutshell, the argument goes as follows:[55] A monopolistic information owner creates a mutual fund to 'sell' his information *indirectly*. Investors purchase shares in the fund, thereby buying the information without observing it. When they buy information jointly with shares in the fund, investors are charged a fee that is a function of the shares each one of them buys. By selling the information in this way, the information owner can control and limit the effects of competition among the traders who are indirectly informed through the leakage of information via observable asset prices. This possibility to appropriate at least a certain part of the value of information mitigates the public good and free-riding problems of information production and in turn encourages agents to produce information. The incentives for information production and acquisition in capital markets are strengthened, and the extent to which market prices reflect the information of informed individuals increases.[56]

The problem of reliability in the sale of information mentioned in Section 2 can also be alleviated by creating a mutual fund: As was shown by Allen, mutual funds employ analysts to acquire information about stocks in order to achieve a reliable information transfer.[57] A fund uses the information of the financial analyst, who is the original information seller, to determine its trading positions and the resulting portfolios can be marketed truthfully to investors.[58] Through a set of portfolios and payments, the fund can correctly reveal the signal it gets from the financial analyst. Investors again buy the information by purchasing shares of the fund. As a result, the reliability problem of information transfer leads to a theory of NBFIs which is not based on transaction costs. The

[52] A Admati and P Pfleiderer 'Selling and Trading on Information in Financial Markets' (1988) 78 American Economic Review 96; A Admati and P Pfleiderer 'Direct and Indirect Sale of Information' (1990) 58 Econometrica 901.

[53] F Allen 'The Market for Information and the Origin of Financial Intermediation' (1990) 1 J of Financial Intermediation 3.

[54] S Bhattacharya and P Pfleiderer 'Delegated Portfolio Management' (1985) 36 J of Economic Theory 1.

[55] See Tyrell (n 41) ch B, for a summary of this line of research.

[56] This means the Grossman-Stiglitz problem of the impossibility of informationally efficient markets is diminished. Of course, the informational status of a capital market also depends on the existence of liquidity or noise traders who are the lubricant for an active trading mechanism; this is an issue we will not discuss here due to space limitations.

[57] Allen (n 53).

[58] See also Bhattacharya and Pfleiderer (n 54).

intermediary captures a part of the value of information since the original seller, the financial analyst, cannot obtain its full value because of the reliability problem.

In a similar vein, Biais and Germain analyse the agency relation between investors and NBFIs.[59] They derive the optimal incentive-compatible contract for the case of a financial institution that can trade on private information *and* also sell the information to investors through a managed fund. In order to give the fund an incentive to trade in the interest of its clients, the contract requires a compensation scheme for the fund that is an increasing function of the fund's profits. This contractual feature limits the aggressiveness of the total trade of the financial institution, ie the fund's trade *and* the institution's proprietary trade, thus reducing the information revelation and increasing the overall profits of the financial institution.

In summary, one can say that the somewhat esoteric literature sketched here has in common that it provides an economic explanation for the existence of NBFIs based on their pivotal role in creating a market for information. This idea can be carried one step further: There are many different funds with different management styles acting on the capital market in order to benefit from whatever information they have. Different funds can be expected to have and use and process different pieces of information. As a result a great deal of information will be aggregated and incorporated in the share prices of non-financial firms. Thus NBFIs contribute in a crucial way to the liquidity of capital markets, externalising information and supporting the functioning of the price mechanism. If this process of information production, use, and dissemination goes on according to the concepts discussed in this strand of the literature, share prices of corporations are objective and (frequently) reliable indicators of firm values which are not and in fact cannot be manipulated by individual investors and stakeholders, an outcome of market processes which has immediate and important implications for the corporate governance of quoted corporations.

In finance and legal writings on corporate governance, it is frequently argued that shareholder value maximisation is the 'natural' efficiency criterion. For instance, Jensen and Meckling have argued that corporate governance should be exclusively oriented towards promoting the interest of shareholders.[60] They view a firm as a nexus of contracts with various groups of stakeholders, of which only those with shareholders are open-ended or incomplete whereas others are complete. Thus in the analysis of these authors, only shareholders are unprotected and in need of protection through a corporate governance rule. However, this argument is overly restrictive. In a world of general contract incompleteness, one can

[59] B Biais and L Germain 'Incentive Compatible Contracts for the Sale of Information' (2002) 15 Rev of Financial Studies 987.

[60] M Jensen and W Meckling 'Theory of the Firm: Managerial Behavior, Agency Costs and Ownership Structure' (1976) 3 J of Financial Economics 305.

also argue in favour of shareholder value maximisation as long as shareholders are *relatively* less well protected than other constituencies. If, for instance, workers and creditors are not locked into a firm-specific relation and can quit at a reasonably low cost, the corporate governance rules should primarily be designed to protect shareholders' interests. However, a precondition for the functioning of an outsider control system based on shareholder value maximisation is an informative share price. Only then the set of corporate governance mechanisms, including active markets for corporate control and executive compensation packages with a high equity-based component, ensures that managers of the firm act in the interest of shareholders.

It is noteworthy that the NBFIs are not only pivotal in contributing to the externalisation of information but also in implementing the above-mentioned mechanism to discipline management in the interest of shareholders.[61] However, in contrast to the governance role which banks play in an insider control system, NBFIs do not *actively* monitor the management of the corporations in an outsider control system but rather stay passive. Consistent with the logic of an outsider control system, they put pressure on management by investing only in companies that follow certain corporate governance principles and codes, thereby supporting and strengthening the governance mechanisms.[62] In the terminology of Hirschman, NBFIs use the 'exit option' instead of 'voice'. In this way they contribute to a functioning outsider control system which ensures that agency problems and information asymmetries between investors and firms are primarily resolved via public disclosure and the price mechanism. As in the last section, at least three additional questions arise.

First, what are the incentives of NBFIs to fulfil their role? One has to consider the agency relationship between investment and pension funds, the funds' managers, and the investors. In a corporate governance system based on shareholder value maximisation, the investment funds themselves should also maximise their own value if they want to act in the interest of their investors.[63] Hence, incentive contracts between an investment fund and its management, ie the asset managers, and between an investment fund and its investors should be written in such a way that profit/value maximisation is the ultimate goal.[64] On the

[61] See Mann (n 25) for further references.

[62] CalPERS, the Californian pension fund for state employees, only invests in companies that obey certain specified corporate governance rules. See R Romano 'Less is More: Making Institutional Investor Activism a Valuable Mechanism of Corporate Governance' in JA McCahery and others (eds) *Corporate Governance Regimes – Convergence and Diversity* (OUP Oxford 2002) 507 for an analysis of investor activism.

[63] In clarifying the argument, we do not consider certain portfolio restrictions actively managed funds may have to obey.

[64] We cannot go into detail here. But see J Franks and others *Asset Management and Investor Protection* (OUP Oxford 2003) for an analysis of the asset management industry which uncovered many deficiencies in the investment business.

other hand, NBFIs should invest in such a way that they can immediately react if new investment opportunities should arise. Together these two considerations imply that NBFIs will be active participants in the capital market, thereby reacting to new information and price signals and promoting shareholder value maximisation in the corporate sector as a guideline for management decisions. Only then is there an objective measure by which NBFIs can themselves be valued. However, such a structure also has a dark side.[65] If the investors as the ultimate providers of funds are unable to observe the characteristics of the investments undertaken by the funds, a classical risk-shifting problem arises: Asset managers have incentives to take 'excessive' risk. If their investment strategies are successful, they will be rewarded by a share of return and attract new investors in the future. Typically they receive management fees in proportion to the assets under their control. Thus they are better off as a result of good performance. However, there is a limit to the downside risk that an asset manager bears in the case of being unsuccessful. He can be fired, but this is almost all, since his financial liability is a priori limited. One effect of this agency problem of excessive risk taking is that it can lead to asset-pricing bubbles.[66] Thus, the possibility of financial crisis is not only a feature of bank-based financial systems and insider control governance systems, but also of capital market-based financial systems and outsider control governance systems.

Second, what is the role of other financial intermediaries in such a system? As far as their asset allocation is concerned, life insurance firms in Anglo-Saxon countries act in largely the same manner as mutual funds.[67] They invest their funds in the capital markets and support the corporate governance mechanism based on share prices and exit opportunities. They rarely use their 'voice' to influence and monitor the management of corporations or to give advice. To a large extent, banks in these countries also grant so-called 'transaction-based' loans, secured by good collateral and with short maturities, thereby using hard information in originating the loan.[68] At least with respect to listed companies, banks are typically not interested in an active monitoring role. As convincingly argued and shown by Kroszner and Strahan, a strong shareholder regime, such as the US regime, discourages banks from playing an active role in monitoring and from acquiring information through an active role in corporate governance.[69]

[65] See F Allen and D Gale 'Bubbles and Crises' (2000) 110 Economic J 236.

[66] In a similar vein, contracts which make asset manager remuneration depend on relative performance can induce herding behaviour on the side of the manager. This, in turn, also can cause bubbles. See A Gümbel 'Herding in Delegated Portfolio Management: When is Comparative Performance Information Desirable?' (2005) 49 Eur Economic Rev 599 for an efficiency analysis of relative performance contracts in the investment industry.

[67] See Franks and others (n 64) for a survey.

[68] See Allen and Gale (n 31) for further details.

[69] R Kroszner and P Strahan 'Bankers on the Boards: Monitoring, Conflicts of Interest, and Lender Liability' (2001) 62 J of Financial Economics 415.

American and British banks rarely have privileged access to information because they are – rightly – concerned about lender liability and want to avoid conflicts of interest in the case of financial distress.[70] Instead, bank debt should be a hard, non-renegotiable claim in the capital structure of the company, serving as a device which also puts effective pressure on management to pursue shareholder interests. As a consequence, in a capital market-based system, the role of banks is also supportive of an outsider control system and consistent with a general regime of information externalisation.

So-called information intermediaries such as rating agencies, newsletters, financial analysts, and investment advisory services also play a role in contributing to the information provision process. The accounting and disclosure system, strictly enforced by public authorities and the stock exchanges, focuses on outside investors to ensure that they are reasonably and equally well informed and, hence, willing to invest in the capital markets.[71]

The third question which concerns the interrelations between an outsider control system with information externalisation and the types of activity promoted in the economy, ie the industry structures, will be taken up in the concluding section.

IV. Conclusions

Our paper argues that the mode of information processing, ie internalisation or externalisation, shapes the corporate governance system and at the same time reflects its general features. An outsider control system goes hand in hand with externalisation of information, whereas an insider system is consistent with information internalisation. Furthermore, intermediaries play crucial, but different, roles in the respective corporative governance system. In a bank-based financial system, banks build up long-term financial relations with corporations, thereby acquiring considerable amounts of information about their borrowers which they use to allocate resources. An insider control system that explicitly takes into account the interests of other constituencies besides shareholders provides incentives and offers opportunities for banks to play an active monitoring role in the corporate governance. In market-based financial systems, NBFIs typically dominate the financial sector by using capital markets to facilitate the allocation of resources. As a consequence, information is quickly reflected in stock prices and we see a great deal of information disclosure. Hence, stock prices are an important element of corporate governance, and accordingly shareholder value maximisation is the only 'game in town' in outsider control systems. This, in

[70] See Kroszner and Strahan (n 69) for a most interesting analysis of the role of banks in the US corporate governance system.

[71] See Leuz and Wüstemann (n 34) 450 for more details.

turn, reinforces the incentives for NBFIs to adopt a passive monitoring role in corporate governance. In outsider control systems, corporate governance is mainly exercised – directly or indirectly – via share price.

In sum, we have two corporate governance systems which are – at least in principle – consistent and workable. One question that immediately arises from these considerations is this: Is there a relationship between the effectiveness of a specific corporate governance system and the role of certain industries? Allen suggested that capital market-based economies with outsider control governance systems, such as that of the US, are particularly successful at developing and financing new industries, such as the computer industry after the second world war and more recently the biotechnology and Internet industries.[72] In contrast, countries like Germany and Japan with bank-based financial and corporate governance systems seem to do better in traditional lines of business such as the automotive industry, the engineering industry, or electronics in Japan. Although we cannot discuss this issue in detail here, we want to point to some aspects which are of direct relevance for our topic because of their implications regarding the prevailing types of information processing and corporate governance in the respective industries and countries.

The above observations can be explained referring to the different types of information processing in the respective systems.[73] Funding really innovative industries is difficult because there is hardly any evidence based on experience, investment is risky, and there is typically a wide diversity of opinion regarding success and success conditions. Capital-market based economies with their well-developed systems for the acquisition, aggregation, and distribution of information have advantages in financing these industries. As we argued above, for individual investors and investment funds, the costs of gathering information are kept relatively low because of the well-functioning market for information and the price mechanism, and those investors or NBFIs that anticipate high returns can provide financing for new firms. The mechanism first explained by Hayek can function under these conditions.

When the decision to finance the new industries is delegated to one or only a few banks, which is what would typically happen in a bank-based financial system, the allocation of funding would not function well. In a set-up in which internal information processing prevails, there is no easy way to account for diversity of opinion. Investors anticipating that they may disagree with the

[72] F Allen 'The Market for Information and the Origin of Financial Intermediation' (1990) 1 J of Financial Intermediation 3. See also C Mayer 'Financing the New Economy: Financial Institutions and Corporate Governance' (2002) 14 Information Economics and Policy 311 for an interesting analysis of broadly defined financial sector preconditions, ie embedding corporate governance, for the successful development of a high technology sector.

[73] The theoretical model on which this section is based is developed in F Allen and D Gale 'Diversity of Opinion and the Financing of New Technologies' (1999) 8 J of Financial Intermediation 68.

intermediary would be reluctant to provide funds for these investments without acquiring information on their own, thus in fact undermining the specific strength of a bank-based system. This is why a bank-based financial system has a comparative disadvantage in the financing of innovations. However, banks are better equipped to finance established industries. Here the advantages of an internal information process come into play because the problem of financing these industries is not so much ex ante disagreement on how – if at all – they should be managed, but the timely monitoring of management and the containment of moral hazard problems. At least in principle, banks are specialists in performing these functions.[74]

Our second concluding remark refers to the trade-off between objectivity and proximity as a central issue in the basic orientation of the corporate governance structure in different countries.[75] Outsider control systems are based on objectivity because potential monitors such as mutual funds, individual investors, outside lenders, hostile acquirers, analysts, and credit rating agencies remain 'distant' from the management and use a reasonable objective criterion to evaluate management performance. In insider control systems, various stakeholder groups monitor management more or less on a real-time basis. Their representatives are in close contact with the management and on a number of occasions also involved in important decisions.

Thus at least in principle, monitoring in an outsider system based on information externalisation is ex post and evaluative, while it is ex ante and proactive in an insider system based on information internalisation. Typically, one cannot have both objectivity and proximity at the same time, because as an insider one frequently tends to adopt the perspective of the firm. Hence, an insider control system is in principle more effective if the benefits of proximity dominate the benefits of objectivity, and vice versa. At this point the specificity of investments by the stakeholders comes into play. An insider control system with prompt correction of management failure is especially valuable when the investments made by stakeholder(s) need to be firm-specific.[76] In this case, late intervention is harmful because it leads to an irreversible loss for the stakeholders. If they anticipated this effect of ex post monitoring, they would be inclined to limit the

[74] See Mayer (n 72) for a similar analysis of the requirements for the financing of 'new economy industries'.

[75] The following reasoning follows closely A Boot and others 'Towards a new Theory of Corporate Governance: Objectivity versus Proximity' (Working Paper, University of Amsterdam, Amsterdam 2004) and RH Schmidt and M Weiss 'Shareholder vs. Stakeholder: Ökonomische Fragestellungen' in P Hommelhoff and others (eds) *Handbuch Corporate Governance* (Schäffer-Poeschel Stuttgart 2003) 107.

[76] This argument also explains why all these groups should be involved in the monitoring and advising process, and why there should be a 'balance of power' between these groups in the governance system if it is important that different stakeholder groups – ie shareholders, lenders, and employees – undertake firm-specific investments.

extent of their firm-specific investments. This implies that insider control and stakeholder orientation are expected to be dominant if specific and irreversible investments of various stakeholders are essential for firm success, and thus characterise firm assets. In contrast, if firm assets are readily marketable and investments largely reversible, the ex post correction mechanism connected with an outsider system provides better incentives. Thus again, in principle different industry structures tend to go hand in hand with different corporate governance systems.[77]

In conclusion, what does all of this suggest for the question of whether it is possible to combine the two types of corporate governance systems and their specific ways of dealing with information problems? We have no ready answer to this question. In earlier work we were sceptical since – according to our argument – institutional arrangements such as corporate governance systems or more generally financial systems characterised by complementarity need to be consistent in order to function properly, and combining important elements of both systems might destroy consistency.[78] But this view was based on an analysis of existing systems. It does not preclude the possibility of the emergence of new institutional structures which provide room for two different yet consistent and functioning governance systems for big companies. Legal developments in Europe and general economic developments seem to point in this direction.[79] Therefore we invite law scholars to discuss this possibility with us: Is it possible and also desirable, or is it simply an inevitable consequence of globalisation and European integration, that we shall in the near future have corporate governance systems which combine information internalisation and externalisation – or proximity and objectivity – and hopefully exploit their respective strengths while keeping the possible negative effects of inconsistency at bay?

[77] See W Carlin and C Mayer 'Finance, Investment and Growth' (2003) 69 J of Financial Economics 191 for first empirical results in this direction.

[78] See RH Schmidt and G Spindler 'Path Dependence and Complementarity in Corporate Governance' in J Gordon and M Roe (eds) *Convergence and Persistence in Corporate Governance* (Cambridge University Press Cambridge 2004) 114.

[79] See O Rieckers and G Spindler 'Corporate Governance: Legal Aspects' in JP Krahnen and RH Schmidt (eds) *The German Financial System* (OUP Oxford 2004) 350 for the case of corporate governance systems and JP Krahnen and RH Schmidt 'Taking Stock and Looking Ahead' in JP Krahnen and RH Schmidt (eds) ibid 487 for the more general case of financial systems.

Using Basel II to Facilitate Access to Finance: The Disclosure of Internal Credit Ratings

GÉRARD HERTIG[*]

I. Introduction

Under the revised capital adequacy framework (Basel II), banks will be allowed to calculate regulatory capital using either a standardized approach to credit risk or a more sophisticated internal rating-based (IRB) approach.[1] The IRB approach should bring capital requirements closer to credit risk profiles and all major banks can be expected to adopt it.

Basel II has generated substantial discussion about the reduction in regulatory capital it is likely to generate. However, the transparency opportunities it offers have been largely ignored. This paper suggests that it would be efficient to require all banks opting for the IRB approach to disclose their internal rating information to the public.

The externalization of internal rating information should not result in significant inconsistencies. National financial systems continue to differ due to country-specific trade-offs,[2] but there is a convergence trend. Financial intermediaries play an increasingly similar role in both market-oriented and (still) intermediary-oriented systems. Operational firms, for their part, are increasingly subject to a common regulatory framework when it comes to external finance, as exemplified

[*] I thank Thomas Bernauer, Guido Ferrarini, Martin Hellwig, Klaus J. Hopt, Reinhard H. Schmidt, Gerald Spindler, and the participants in the conference on *Changes in Governance in Europe, Japan, and the US – Corporations, State, Markets, and Intermediaries* (Japan-German Center Berlin, 9-11 September 2004) for their helpful comments.

[1] See *International Convergence of Capital Measurement and Capital Standards*, available at <http://www.bis.org> (17 May 2005).

[2] cf P Milgrom and J Roberts 'Complementarities and Systems: Understanding Japanese Economic Organization' (1994) 9 Estudios Economicos 3; RG Lipsey and K Lancaster 'The General Theory of Second-Best' (1956) 24 Revue of Economic Studies 11.

by the development of regulatory arbitrage within Europe, the convergence of venture capital contracts around the world, and the harmonization of disclosure requirements and practices.

Against this background, requiring the disclosure of internal ratings would have the advantage of reducing the cost of capital for large and small firms alike. It would provide lenders and investors with a richer data set. Moreover, disclosure should improve rating reliability, facilitate investor diversification, and decrease market uncertainty. To be sure, internal rating disclosure would also have its costs. It could increase market volatility and negatively affect intertemporal risk allocation. It also may negatively affect lender-borrower relationships, which could result in adverse selection effects or make it more difficult for lenders to obtain rating information.

This paper argues that it is possible to design a regulatory framework under which the benefits of mandatory rating disclosure clearly outweigh its costs, which in turn should minimize interest group opposition to the externalization of banks' private information. First, it would remain possible for lenders to keep internal ratings confidential by opting to continue to use the standardized approach. Second, lenders that opt for the IRB approach would not have to disclose the internal ratings themselves, but would do so through one of several (public or private) regional entities.

Third, regional entities would publicize ratings in consolidated form. Each borrower would get a rating corresponding to the average of the individual ratings it gets from its lending banks. This procedure would have several advantages. It is likely to improve rating quality (extremes will at least partly cancel each other out) and protect individual lender anonymity. It would also allow individual lenders to keep a comparative advantage (or reduce a comparative disadvantage) if their internal rating differs from the disclosed average. Admittedly, overlapping disclosure by multiple regional entities may cause some uncertainty as a given firm may get diverging average ratings. However, rating multiplicity would also reduce moral hazard effects (excessive rating reliance would be prevented) and preserve competition by non-bank rating firms (they could continue to offer uncertainty-reducing services).

Fourth, borrowers would be allowed to opt out. The availability of a non-disclosure alternative should protect borrowers against rating mistake risks. It should also minimize reductions in the information flow between borrowers and lenders because of relationship-damaging disclosure.

The remainder of the paper is structured as follows. Section II provides an overview of the internal rating approach under the Basel II agreement. Section III discusses the inconsistency risk as well as the specific costs and benefits of mandating the disclosure of internal ratings. Section IV sketches a simple regulatory framework under which this private information could be efficiently externalized with minimal interest group opposition.

II. Basel II and Internal Credit Ratings

On 26 June 2004, the central bank governors and the heads of bank supervisory authorities in G10 countries approved a revised capital adequacy framework, commonly referred to as Basel II.[3]

The revised framework, which is expected to be implemented by the end of 2007, aims at providing banks with more risk-sensitive capital requirements. Regulatory capital is to be calculated under either a standardized approach to credit risk or an approach based on banks' internal ratings (IRB). Banks that opt for the IRB approach can expect their capital requirements to become closer to their credit risk profiles. However, only banks that have robust validation procedures will be allowed to use the IRB approach – meaning that supervisory approval of IRB is likely to be restricted to sophisticated intermediaries.

Under the IRB approach, credit exposures must be categorized in five broad classes of assets: corporate, sovereign, bank, retail (which may include corporate exposures of less than €1 million), and equity. Banks will also be permitted to distinguish between exposures to small and medium-sized firms and exposures to large firms.

Banks opting for the IRB approach will have to use internal ratings for credit approval, risk management, and internal capital allocation purposes. As far as corporate exposures are concerned, the rating system must include a minimum of seven borrower grades for non-defaulted borrowers and one for those that have defaulted – with credit risk increasing from one grade to the next. A borrower's grade must not only reflect its current financial condition.[4] The grade must also indicate the borrower's ability and willingness to contractually perform despite adverse economic conditions or the occurrence of unexpected events. In other words, there is a link between credit rating and probability of default.[5]

In the past decade, risk management has become an important activity for financial intermediaries, whereas credit risk capital allocation increasingly plays a role for determining the bonuses of bank managers. Reflecting this evolution, there is widespread use of internal credit risk rating grades by major banks across developed countries.[6] Taking into account that IRB requirements have been

[3] The *International Convergence of Capital Measurement and Capital Standards* (Basel II, available ibid) are replacing a first set of standards set out by the 1988 Basel Capital Accord.

[4] Note that financial condition is influenced by financial as well as non-financial factors, such as management quality and corporate governance. See eg J Grunert L Norden and M Weber 'The Role of Non-financial Factors in Internal Credit Ratings' (2005) 29 J of Banking and Finance 509.

[5] JP Krahnen and M Weber 'Generally Accepted Rating Principles: A Primer' (2001) 25 J of Banking and Finance 3.

[6] See eg M Carey and M Hrycay 'Parameterizing Credit Risk Models with Rating Data' (2001) 21 J of Banking and Finance 197 for the US; Krahnen and Weber (n 5) for Germany.

developed on the basis of existing practices, most, if not all, of these major banks can be expected to opt for the IRB approach.

The generalization of internal ratings does not imply that there is uniformity among banks in firm grading. Empirical studies show that there can be substantial differences among internal rating systems[7] and in risk assessments.[8] These differences will not disappear under Basel II because the regulatory framework is flexible and leaves room for diversity in implementation by individual banks.

These differences, however, are unlikely to remain significant or prevent a comparative analysis of internal ratings. First, supervisory authorities will require banks using the IRB approach to establish that their ratings are consistent and meaningfully differentiate risk. This should minimize internal rating system divergence, as confirmed by the current trend toward using the Standard & Poor's 26 borrower grade scale for internal rating purposes.[9] Second, differences in rating methods and grades among the major external rating agencies (Standard and Poor's, Moody's in particular) do not prevent market participants from using and comparing them.[10]

Given the lack of competition in the external rating industry and rampant skepticism about the quality of credit ratings produced by its major players, the forthcoming availability of 'authorized' and, therefore, consistent internal ratings naturally leads to the question of whether it would be advantageous to disclose them to the public.

III. Efficient Disclosure of Internal Credit Ratings

Financial markets are generally divided in two categories: intermediary-oriented systems (basically continental European and Japanese systems) and market-oriented systems (basically Anglo-Saxon systems). The difference in regimes brings the risk that harmonization efforts will result in inconsistencies.[11] On the

[7] See WF Treacy and M Carey 'Credit Risk Rating Systems at Large US Banks' (2000) 24 J of Banking and Finance 167 for the US.

[8] See T Jacobson J Lindé and K Roszbach 'Credit Risk versus Capital Requirements under Basel II: Are SME Loans and Retail Credit Really Different?' (Working paper 2004) available at <http://www.ssrn.com> (17 May 2005) for Sweden.

[9] See also EI Altman and A Saunders 'An Analysis and Critique of the BIS Proposal on Capital Adequacy and Ratings' (2001) 25 J of Banking and Finance 25.

[10] The difference between 'internal' and 'external' ratings is that the former are attributed by lenders for their own purposes, whereas the latter are done for third-party use by specialized providers (also called rating agencies).

[11] See the contribution of RH Schmidt and M Tyrell in this volume; RH Schmidt and G Spindler 'Path Dependence, Corporate Governance and Complementarity' (2002) 5 International Finance 311; K Pistor M Raiser and S Gelfer 'Law and Finance in Transition Economies' (2000) 8 Economics of Transition 325.

other hand, we can observe a convergence toward market-oriented systems in all developed countries.[12] Differences are not only being reduced by capital markets gaining in importance across countries. Financial intermediaries also contribute to the convergence trend by playing increasingly similar roles in both market-oriented and (still) intermediary-oriented systems.[13]

Of course, differences among countries will not disappear in the near future. However, convergence significantly reduces the risk that internal ratings disclosure requirements will result in significant inconsistencies. This conclusion is reinforced when considering regulatory arbitrage developments within Europe, the global standardization of venture capital contracts, and the harmonization of disclosure requirements and practices.

1. Inconsistency Risk

Regulatory arbitrage. Three recent decisions by the European Court of Justice have made it significantly easier for new firms to incorporate in a member state other than the one they conduct business in.[14] There is some debate about whether these decisions will result in many firms engaging in regulatory arbitrage and in regulatory competition developing among member states. What cannot be disputed, however, is the increase in the number of firms choosing to be governed by UK law (a so-called outsider-controlled jurisdiction), even though they will operate in Germany (a so-called insider-controlled jurisdiction). It is also noticeable that France, Germany, and the Netherlands have recently undertaken legislative reforms in the wake of UK regulatory changes.[15]

These developments are likely to produce a three-staged outcome. First, most EU member states will face a situation where closely held firms operating on their territory will be governed by corporate laws that are enacted by another member state. Second, if early US developments have any comparative value, the cohabitation of closely held firms subject to different regimes is likely to produce converging corporate laws.[16] Third, some closely held firms will become public

[12] F Allen and D Gale *Comparing Financial Systems* (MIT Press Cambridge 2000).

[13] See RE Breuer 'The Role of Financial Intermediaries and Capital Markets' in KJ Hopt and others (eds) *Comparative Corporate Governance, The State of the Art and Emerging Research* (OUP Oxford 1998) 537.

[14] See Case C-212/97 *Centros Ltd v Erhvervs-og Selskabsstyrelsen* [1999] ECR I-1459; Case C-208/00 *Überseering BV v NCC Nordic Construction Company Baumangement* [2002] ECR I-9919; Case C-167/01 *Kamer van Koophandel en Fabrieken voor Amsterdam v Inspire Art Ltd* [2003] ECR I-10155.

[15] G Hertig and J McCahery 'Company and Takeover Law in Europe: Misguided Harmonization Efforts or Regulatory Competition' (2003) 4 Eur Business Organization L Rev 179.

[16] WJ Carney 'The Production of Corporate Law' (1998) 71 Southern California L Rev 715.

under the regulatory regime of a member state other than the one in which they operate, putting high pressure on the latter member state to adjust its own regime for publicly held firms. As a result, the European regulatory framework governing access to external finance is likely to converge further, which in turn will reduce inconsistency risks.

Venture capital contracts. Whereas the US venture capital market is large and well established, European venture capital activity was still close to non-existent in the mid-1990s.[17] In recent years, however, venture capitalists have become increasingly active in Europe, with investments averaging around €10 billion per year since 1999.[18] This favorably compares with current levels of US venture capital financing. For example, funds raised for the European market in 2003 were up to about two-thirds of those raised for the US market (€6,350 and US$11,183 billion respectively).[19] To be sure, US venture capital activity has seen a dramatic decline since 2001, but this is also true for Europe and reflects the cyclical nature of the business.[20]

Interestingly, the development of the European venture capital market has gone hand in hand with a gradual replication of US practices. A keystone of the US venture capital market is that information asymmetries, conflicts of interests, and uncertainties are dealt with through private ordering.[21] Very early European attempts to develop a venture capital market relied upon governmental financing, the usual European approach for risky projects, but were plagued by failures.[22] When experienced US venture capitalists started investing in Europe, they used the US-style contracts with which they were familiar. The available empirical evidence shows that the approach proved successful across jurisdictions, regardless of the applicable legal regime.[23]

[17] See B Black and RG Gilson 'Venture Capital and the Structure of Capital Markets: Banks versus Stock markets' (1998) 47 J of Financial Economics 243.

[18] Source: ECVA 2004 Yearbook

[19] Source: ECVA 2004 Yearbook (for Europe) and Thomson Venture Economics & National Venture Capital Association (for the US).

[20] J Lerner 'Boom and Bust in the Venture Capital Industry and the Impact on Innovation' (Working paper 2002) available at <http://www.ssrn.com> (17 May 2005).

[21] RG Gilson 'Engineering a Venture Capital Market: Lessons from the American Experience' (2003) 55 Stanford L Rev 1067.

[22] See R Becker and T Hellmann 'The Genesis of Venture Capital: Lessons from the German Experience' in C Keuschnigg and V Kanniainen (eds) *Venture Capital, Entrepreneurship, and Public Policy* (MIT Press Cambridge 2004).

[23] SN Kaplan F Martel and P Strömberg 'How Do Legal Differences and Learning Affect Financial Contracts?' (Working paper 2004) available at <http://www.ssrn.com> (17 May 2005).

This result may reflect smaller than expected divergence between the US and German poles,[24] or rapid convergence due to German banks' realization that venture capitalism was likely to foster their lending activities.[25] In any event, venture capital is a good example of the increasing similarity of financial systems and the potentially limited role of inconsistencies when it comes to external finance.

Harmonized disclosure. EU jurisdictions and Japan impose more stringent accounting and disclosure requirements on closely held firms than the US, whereas the latter regulates disclosure by public companies more heavily. Moreover, public corporations are subject to higher regulatory pressures in the US when it comes to forward-looking information.

However, market pressures have reduced the regulatory gap by forcing US closely held corporations as well as European and Japanese public corporations to disclose more data than required by applicable regulation.[26] In other words, despite claims about differences in governance regimes requiring separate modes of information processing to avoid prohibitive inconsistencies, market forces have led to *de facto* harmonization of disclosure practices.

Lawmakers are attempting to consolidate and extend the scope of convergence in disclosure. For example, the more than 7,000 EU firms traded on regulated markets have been required to comply with Anglo-Saxon-oriented accounting standards.[27] Similar policies are being implemented in Japan.[28] Here again, the harmonization path is not always smooth, and differences will remain in disclosure requirements or practices. However, those differences reflect diverging views about the costs and benefits of disclosure in a market-oriented financial system and cannot be considered a source of financial system inconsistencies.

Summing up, the dynamics of regulatory arbitrage, globalization of venture capital financing, and disclosure harmonization make it unlikely that mandating the disclosure of internal ratings will result in significant inconsistencies.

[24] See A Bascha and U Walz 'Financing Practices in the German Venture Capital Industry, An Empirical Assessment' (Working paper 2001) available at <http://www.sssrn.com> (17 May 2005).

[25] See TF Hellmann LA Lindsley and M Puri 'Building Relationships Early: Banks in Venture Capital' (Working paper 2003) available at <http://www.ssrn.com> (17 May 2005).

[26] G Hertig and H Kanda 'Creditor Protection', in R Kraakman and others *The Anatomy of Corporate Law, A Comparative and Functional Approach* (OUP Oxford 2004) 71; G Hertig R Kraakman and E Rock 'Issuers and Investor Protection' ibid 193.

[27] See Regulation on the Application of International Accounting Standards [2002] OJ L 243/1.

[28] See C Smith 'Called to Account' *Institutional Investor* (New York United States December 2002) 62.

2. Costs and Benefits of Disclosure

The above conclusion does not, however, mean that the benefits of internal rating disclosure requirements exceed their costs. It is well known that credit markets are characterized by incomplete information, which gives rise to problems of adverse selection and moral hazard.[29] Mandating internal ratings disclosure can thus be expected to reduce the cost of capital, but the strategy may also have disadvantages in terms of data reliability, risk sharing, market uncertainty, and rating providers. These potential trade-offs justify a more detailed cost-benefit analysis.

Cost of capital. Internal ratings disclosure is likely to provide investors with richer and timelier information than currently available from external rating firms. This should reduce the cost of capital for both publicly held and closely held firms.

For listed firms or initial public offerings, the disclosure of internal ratings should lead to an increase in stock prices as investors will expect lower returns following the disclosure of private information.[30] The same should be true for larger non-listed firms. Lenders' regulatory capital requirements will be lower under the IRB approach than under a standard approach, which should allow large non-listed firms to profit from improved loan pricing.[31]

Internal rating disclosure should make smaller non-listed firms more attractive for venture capitalists and private equity investors. It is indeed often difficult for smaller firms to get a reliable rating from external rating providers, either because smaller firms deem rating costs and risk not worth the reward or because there is an insufficient supply of external rating capabilities. The externalization of lenders' internal ratings information would therefore reduce venture capitalists' and private equity funds' cost of information gathering and processing. These financial intermediaries will thus be able to make better use of their information assessment capabilities, in turn facilitating smaller firms' access to finance.

Data reliability. Borrowers generally have longstanding relationships with one or several banks, giving the latter privileged access to firm-specific information. Hence, major banks can be expected to often have better solvency information than rating agencies and other providers of financial information.

On the other hand, an analysis of insolvencies throughout the twentieth century would reveal many examples of uninformed lenders. It is also probable

[29] Allen and Gale (n 12).

[30] D Easley and M O'Hara 'Information and the Cost of Capital' (2004) 59 J of Finance 1553.

[31] See also M Dietsch and J Petey 'The Credit Risk in SME Loans Portfolios: Modeling Issues, Pricing, and Capital Requirements' (2002) 26 J of Banking and Finance 303.

that current pressure to cut costs will result in some lenders lacking adequate monitoring capabilities. Remember, however, that only sophisticated lenders will get supervisory approval to use the IRB approach. Internal ratings disclosure will thus be limited to banks with validated tools and procedures.

To be sure, regulatory approval will not eliminate the risk of internal credit ratings being based on deficient information or biased because of lenders' regulatory capital interest in tampering ratings upwards.[32] Switching from the standardized to the IRB approach could also result in excessive reliance on models, which may increase systemic errors (if many lenders use similar models) and lead to the disregard of critical subjective information (such as failure to pass the 'smell test').

Nevertheless, these risks should not be overestimated. First, the race for competitive advantages and differences in corporate cultures are likely to make internal ratings vary from lender to lender, a phenomenon that can already be observed across rating agencies. This should improve supervisory authorities' capability to detect anomalies in a timely manner and prevent blind reliance on faulty models. Second, model dependence issues should not prevent internal ratings from being more reliable than currently available rating data. As indicated, lenders are generally better informed than rating agencies. Moreover, lenders should face lower reputation and liability risks when significantly downgrading a borrower than firms that sell rating data. Indeed, the move would reflect prudential rather than informational considerations, reducing the likelihood of market or judicial sanctions.

One could argue, however, that the reliability advantage of internal ratings may end up being an issue by itself. First, it may result in excessive investor reliance. However, this potential moral hazard effect should not be overestimated. Adding internal rating to external rating information can, as we shall see, be a source of stock price volatility and this should keep investor reliance within acceptable limits. In addition, it is possible to further reduce moral hazard effects by institutionalizing multiple rating sources (see Section IV).

Second, lender disclosure of low internal grades may have stigma effects, especially for listed firms with small-sized capitalization or for very small firms. External rating firms may pay limited attention to small caps, which could magnify the impact of lower internal rating disclosure. Very small firms may have only one rating, the one provided by their single lender, and downgrades could make it very difficult for them to get alternative sources of finance.

The fact that the stigma effect could increase the cost of capital for certain firms does not necessarily mean that it is a source of inefficiency. For small caps, the stigma effect is likely to merely reflect the improved and timelier nature of rating information. For very small firms, the stigma effect may remain a

[32] Carey and Hrycay (n 6).

hypothetical one to the extent they are less likely to borrow from lenders who use the IRB approach.

Risk-sharing. Disclosure could increase risk-sharing opportunities. First, the availability of major banks' internal ratings may decrease the probability that unsophisticated lenders using the 'crude' standardized approach will take uninformed lending risks.[33]

Second, internal rating disclosure should facilitate investor portfolio diversification. The number of rated firms will increase and the granularity of existing credit ratings should improve, especially given the trend toward general use of a harmonized rating scale. Moreover, rating agencies' tendency to inflate the ratings of those firms that solicit their services[34] should decrease or at least be balanced by the availability of internal ratings.

Third, internal rating information should make investors less prone to become victims of conflicts of interests. This is especially true for investors that have their assets managed by financial intermediaries which also act as corporate lenders.[35] In such situations, the disclosure of internal ratings will make it more difficult for asset managers to 'stuff' debt instruments that are unpalatable into the discretionary portfolios of unsuspecting investors.

On the other hand, internal rating disclosure may also reduce risk-sharing opportunities. Banks have a comparative advantage in handling inter-temporal risk sharing due to their ability to allocate risk and smooth consumption over time.[36] However, this advantage presupposes that households have at least part of their financial wealth in the form of deposit accounts rather than securities. If so, and should internal rating disclosure result in households transforming fixed claims against banks into securities, lenders' risk-sharing ability may decrease.

Whether the net effect of internal ratings disclosure will be an increase or a decrease of risk-sharing opportunities is ultimately an empirical question. It would, however, be rather surprising to see the potential costs in terms of inter-temporal risk sharing end up exceeding the sum of all the mentioned risk-sharing benefits.

[33] See B Rime 'The New Basel Accord: Implications of the Co-existence between the Standardized Approach and the Internal Ratings-Based Approach' (Working paper 2003) available at <http://www.szgerzensee.ch> (17 May 2005).

[34] See WPH Poon 'Are Unsolicited Credit Ratings Biased Downward?' (2003) 27 J of Banking and Finance 593.

[35] cf P Bolton X Freixas and J Shapiro 'Conflicts of Interests, Information Provision, and Competition in Banking' (Working paper 2004) available at <http://wwww.ssrn.com> (17 May 2005).

[36] See Allen and Gale (n 12); J Hirshleifer 'The Private and Social Value of Information and the Reward to Inventive Activity' (1971) 61 American Economic Rev 561.

Market uncertainty and volatility. The availability of internal ratings in addition to existing external ratings should decrease market uncertainty. As mentioned, rate inflation due to the self-selection bias inherent to external ratings will be reduced. Moreover, market participants will be able to rely on a broader rating sample and get a better picture about the extent to which there is consensus on a given firm's solvency. Finally, internal rating disclosure should improve rating methodology transparency. Very limited information is currently available about the methodology used by rating agencies. By contrast, the methodology used by lenders under the ISB approach will be known to supervisory authorities. The latter can be expected to make the main rating parameters public, so as to streamline IRB approval procedures and facilitate regulatory monitoring. The disclosure will not only benefit users of internal ratings, but also put pressure on rating agencies to provide better information about their own methodology.

Internal ratings disclosure may also lead to a decrease in stock price volatility. In particular, lenders should prove faster than other providers of solvency data in adjusting ratings to changes in circumstances.[37] Investors would thus get information that is timelier, which should permit more accurate pricing and reduce stock price volatility. However, the benefits of timeliness should not be overestimated, as it may also increase stock price volatility. This could, for example, be the case if there is significant variance in rating across banks or if there is a large increase in the frequency of rating reversals.[38]

Rating providers. Somewhat counterintuitively, rating agencies are also likely to benefit from the disclosure of lenders' internal ratings. It should reduce their liability risk when providing corporate ratings to banks using the standardized credit risk approach.[39] Credit rating agencies will be able to refer to internal ratings to either justify their call (if internal and external ratings are similar) or hedge their bets (if external and internal ratings diverge). Moreover, the availability of internal ratings as a new source of information should decrease the risk of rating agencies becoming regulated by supervisory authorities[40] or investigated

[37] See S Claessens and GCMW Embrechts 'Basel II, Sovereign Ratings and Transfer Risk, External versus Internal Rating' (Working paper 2003) available at <http://www.ssrn.com> (17 May 2005).

[38] See G Löffler 'Ratings versus Market-Based Measures of Default Risk in Portfolio Governance' (2005) 28 J of Banking and Finance (forthcoming).

[39] Basel II provides that lenders using the standardized approach must have their credit risk measurement supported by external credit assessments.

[40] Compare International Organization of Securities Commissions (IOSCO), Code of Conduct Fundamentals for Credit Ratings Agencies (December 2004, available at <http://www.iosco.org> [17 May 2005]); Committee of European Securities Regulators (CESR) 'CESR's Technical Advice to the European Commission on Possible Measures concerning Credit Rating Agencies' (Consultation Paper November 2004) available at <http://www.cesr-eu.org> (17 May

cont. ...

by competition authorities. Indeed, the availability of internal ratings will make it harder to pin the blame for market failures upon rating agencies or to establish their market dominance.

By contrast, it could be costly for lenders to disclose their internal ratings.[41] First, they could expose themselves to significant liability. Borrowers could face higher than justified costs of capital or even be made insolvent because of being rated below what they should be. Investors or creditors could suffer significant losses because they have been misled by rating mistakes or delayed updates.

Second, lenders' relationships with borrowers could suffer from disagreements over internal ratings. This could not only negatively affect the gathering of borrower information, but also subject lenders to adverse selection effects. For any given lender, underrated borrowers will look for other sources of finance, whereas overrated borrowers will stay put.

Third, free riders could take advantage of lenders that disclose their internal ratings. For example, some lenders may decide to gain a competitive advantage by relying on other lenders' internal ratings while refraining from disclosing their own. Or, to take another example, a disclosing lender's counter-party could use the rating information to asymmetrically improve its trading or bargaining position.

These disadvantages explain why lenders do not voluntarily disclose internal ratings, but do not imply that a disclosure requirement would be inefficient. As the next section will show, lender disclosure disadvantages can be minimized under an adequate regulatory framework.

Summing up, the costs of mandating the disclosure of internal ratings are unlikely to exceed its benefits. Admittedly, mandatory disclosure could increase the 'flawed model' costs of the IRB approach and negatively affect inter-temporal risk sharing. However, the link between the adoption of a disclosure requirement and the occurrence of these disadvantages seems weak, as other factors are likely to play a much more significant role. The only real objection to mandatory disclosure has to do with its potential costs for lenders, an issue that can be dealt with by the proper design of the regulatory framework.

IV. Sketching a Mandatory Disclosure Regulatory Framework

It is relatively easy to design a procedure making the disclosure of internal ratings mandatory. Major legal issues could be avoided by integrating into Basel II a provision according to which the use of the IRB approach is contingent upon the

2005). See also CA Hill 'Regulating the Rating Agencies' (Working paper 2004) available at <http://www.law.bepress.com> (17 May 2005).

[41] See also R Kirstein 'The New Basel Accord, Internal Ratings, and the Incentives of Banks' (2002) 21 Intl Rev of L and Economics 393.

public disclosure of internal ratings. The effort and time needed to achieve international harmonization would thus be significantly reduced. Constraints on lenders could also be kept low. On the one hand, banks could still avoid disclosure by opting for the standardized approach. On the other hand, compliance costs would be minimal for those banks opting for the IRB approach, as their choice makes the disclosure of ratings almost costless to them.[42]

However, market participants as well as banking supervisors can be expected to oppose this 'simple' procedure. First, lenders will argue that mandatory disclosure would leave them open to liability suits by borrowers, investors, or creditors claiming to have been damaged by erroneous or misleading ratings. Lenders will also stress that internal rating disclosure will damage their relationship with borrowers and allow other market participants to take advantage of the revealed exposures. Second, small-caps and very small borrowers are likely to object to the requirement because of its perceived stigma effects. Third, rating agencies will oppose any development that could damage their own relationship with rated firms, in particular a requirement that would force them to disclose proprietary information.[43] Fourth, supervisory authorities may object because of the potential moral hazard effect of disclosing data generated by systems they have vetted. Lenders, investors, and creditors may consider the disclosed ratings as backed by supervisors and thus reduce information-gathering and processing efforts – the perception being that 'guilty' supervisors will arrange for a bail-out in case of major borrower insolvency.

This combination of interest group opposition is most likely to prevent the adoption of a straightforward conditionality approach. The efficiency and political economy issues raised by the disclosure of internal ratings must be dealt with under a more sophisticated regulatory framework. This paper thus proposes the adoption of a three-step approach. First, internal ratings would be disclosed by a third party and as averages. Second, there would be multiple third-party disclosure. Third, borrowers would be given the right to opt out.

Third-party disclosure. Requiring disclosure through a third party rather than directly by lenders has two advantages. It puts some liability distance between lenders and disclosure. It mimics the procedure for external ratings and should thus foster competition in the rating industry. Admittedly, the designation of the disclosing third party could be an issue, because its privileged access to rating information could lead to abuses. It may be necessary, at least in a first stage, to

[42] See also L Zingales 'The Costs and Benefits of Financial Regulation' (Working paper 2004) available at <http://www.ssrn.com> (17 May 2005).

[43] See eg C Batchelor 'Rating Agencies Win Rule Victory' *Financial Times* (London UK 28 December 2004) reporting IOSCO's abandon of a proposal to require rating agencies to make public confidential information obtained from companies seeking a rating.

put a public entity in charge of disclosure – central banks being among the possible candidates, as exemplified by the Banque de France firm-scoring practice.[44]

In addition, third-party disclosure would permit the institutionalization of the publication of average ratings. As most borrowers deal with more than one major bank, the third party would be able to consolidate the various ratings a firm gets and disclose an 'average' to market participants. Individual lender's contributions would thus remain anonymous, which would further distance lenders from the process and avoid direct effects on bank-borrower relationships. Moreover, the disclosure of average ratings would allow better-informed lenders to keep a competitive advantage while giving less-informed lenders an opportunity to revise their analysis – or even reconsider the robustness of their IRB approach. The disclosure of averages could also reduce excessive subjectivity risks as well as rating biases because of the regulatory capital advantages in tampering ratings upwards or the negotiation value of imposing a below-market grade upon a recalcitrant borrower.[45]

From a methodology perspective, disclosing averages could be considered problematic. Major banks are unlikely to use uniform rating procedures and differences in the nature and importance of their relationship with individual borrowers may affect the relevance of their ratings.[46] However, supervisory approval of IRB systems should prevent differences from being significant enough to make ratings inconsistent. In addition, the existence of differences in methodology should contribute to smoothing the effect of rating biases.

To be sure, the disclosure of averages may nevertheless mislead market participants insofar as they underestimate the extent to which major banks diverge in their estimation of the credit risks associated with an individual borrower. To deal with this issue, the disclosing third party could be required to single out borrowers with significant rating divergence or even to disclose standard deviation data.

Multiple rating disclosure. Given that large borrowers have relationships with major banks around the world, disclosure could be organized so as to take place through multiple third parties. For example, US banks would report their internal ratings to a US-based third party, whereas European and Japanese banks would report theirs to a Europe-based or Japan-based third party.

[44] See S Foulcher C Gourieroux and A Tiomo 'La Structure par Termes des Défauts et Ratings' (Working paper 2004) available at <http://www.banque-france.fr> (17 May 2005).

[45] See eg A Klein 'Credit Raters' Tactics in Pursuing New Work Frustrate Companies' *Wall Street Journal Europe* (Brussels Belgium 25 November 2004) A1 (reporting that borrowers refusing to ask for an external rating for cost reasons were sanctioned by the unsolicited disclosure of low-grade ratings).

[46] R Elsas 'Empirical Determinants of Relationship Lending' (2005) 14 J of Financial Intermediation 32.

Having multiple ratings for one borrower may cause some uncertainty, but this would contribute to a reduction in liability risks and moral hazard effects. Uncertainty would make it more difficult for investors and creditors to attribute insolvency-related losses to a single third party, bank, or supervisor. It would also prevent excessive internal rating reliance by market participants and leave those best placed to monitor borrowers with an incentive to do so. In addition, having multiple rating disclosures would avoid giving excessive power to any third party and, probably, foster competition in the rating industry.

Opting out. Finally, each borrower could be given the right to avoid disclosure by instructing its banks not to provide its internal rating to the disclosing third parties. Allowing borrowers to opt out would significantly reduce the potential for stigma effects as well as the risk that disagreements over ratings end up damaging lending relationships. At the same time, the availability of such an option is unlikely to result in a significant number of borrowers opting out. Firms that opt out would have to explain to their investors or creditors why they do not want their internal ratings to be disclosed. This should limit the exercise of opt-outs to those instances where borrowers have solid reasons to oppose disclosure.

Minimizing opposition. The proposed framework should minimize opposition to mandating the disclosure of internal ratings. Investors can be expected to welcome a requirement that improves transparency, facilitates portfolio diversification, and reduces the risks related to conflicts of interests. Similarly, the majority of borrowers should be in favor of a mechanism that is likely to reduce the cost of external finance while leaving a possibility to opt out.

Rating agencies and major banks could prove less enthusiastic. However, rating agencies should be quick to realize that uncertainties inherent to the proposed framework leave them sufficient room for the provision of value-added services while reducing the risk of regulatory intervention because of rating deficiencies or insufficient competition. Major banks, for their part, could have an interest in being given an opportunity to calibrate their internal ratings against average ratings. Both rating agencies and banks may still find the *status quo* as interesting or even preferable, but it is unclear why they would engage in a major lobbying effort to oppose a reform that does not cost them much.

Finally, supervisory authorities should prove supportive of a disclosure requirement that improves transparency, allows for multiple cross-checks of internal ratings, and leaves room for enough uncertainty to avoid moral hazard effects. More importantly, supervisory authorities should be willing to implement a mechanism that is likely to improve financial stability by providing more timely warnings of industry-specific, country-specific, or a more general deterioration of the economy – especially considering that they drafted Basel II with the aim of minimizing systemic risk and its impact on financial stability.

V. Conclusion

This paper argues that the Basel II accord provides an opportunity to efficiently externalize internal rating information across jurisdictions, regardless of the orientation of their financial system.

It is thus proposed to require the disclosure of internal ratings of those banks that adopt the IRB approach for calculating capital requirements. Disclosure would occur in averaged form through multiple third parties, whereas borrowers would be allowed to opt out to prevent outsiders from having access to their internal ratings.

This framework would minimize the disadvantages of disclosure while preserving its advantages. As a consequence, one could expect interest group opposition not to prove strong enough to prevent its implementation.

The Multiple Roles of Banks? Convenient Tales from Modern Japan

YOSHIRO MIWA and J. MARK RAMSEYER*

I. Introduction

They are nothing if not enthusiasts.

Not satisfied to study firms that take deposits and lend money – even lots of it – banking theorists tell us banks do far more. They monitor their customers. They intervene in their affairs and tell them what to do. They agree to rescue them should they fall into distress. And lest they waste social resources by duplicatively monitoring the same firms, they agree among themselves which one of them will monitor which customer. Nobel laureate Merton Miller[1] once suggested banks might represent obsolete '19th-century technology'. Indeed, continued he, perhaps they embody 'disaster-prone technology' that survives only as a regulatory artifact. Not banking specialists. Apparently, they would celebrate banks as central not just to 19th-century finance but to the 21st as well.

Theory seldom convinces without a story, of course, so to motivate their theory banking specialists needed an anecdote. Enter Japan. There, claim they (or at least so they claimed before the 1990s recession), their theory fits banking practice to a tee. The tale varied a bit with the teller, but in the telling it usually went something like this. In Japan, big firms borrow from several banks, but keep one as their 'main bank'. Usually, they also join a bank-centered *keiretsu* cor-

* We received helpful comments and suggestions from participants at presentations at Columbia University, Cornell University, George Washington University, and the Japanisch-Deutsches Zentrum Berlin. We gratefully acknowledge the generous financial assistance from the Center for International Research on the Japanese Economy at the University of Tokyo and the John M. Olin Program in Law, Economics & Business and the East Asian Legal Studies Program at Harvard University. A version of this article may be forthcoming as part of an article entitled 'Japan as Urban Legend'. The hypotheses and evidence in this essay are explored more fully in the several articles cited below, and are collected in the forthcoming book Y Miwa and JM Ramseyer *The Fable of the Keiretsu: Urban Legends of Modern Japan* (draft 2004).

[1] MH Miller 'Financial Markets and Economic Growth' (1998) 11.3 J of Applied Corporate Finance 8.

porate group. They then use that group's money-center bank as their 'main bank'. From it, they borrow the lion's share of their funds.

This main bank monitors its customers, banking scholars assure us. It gives them advice, both financial and non-financial. It dominates their boards of directors. It otherwise keeps them well-run. Should a firm find itself in distress, it dispatches financial and other help. It nurses it back to health. And among the several banks from which the firm borrows, it acts as delegated monitor for the rest.

Lest the main bank shirk on these roles, the Japanese government monitors the main bank itself. Staffed by able and dedicated bureaucrats – the best and the brightest in the country – it insures that the banks keep the deals they make with their clients. Both to compensate the banks for their many services and to insure them access to the information they need from their client firms, until the late 1980s it heavily regulated the financial services industry. Effectively, it insured that even the biggest firms had little choice but to raise their funds from banks.

Unfortunately, the tale is an urban legend.[2] Like the best urban legends, scholars collectively repeat the tale only because they so badly want it to be true. In turn, they collectively want it to be true in part because it so wonderfully motivates the theory of banking they hope to propagate. They want it to be true because it ascribes such a marvelous multiplicity of roles to banks.

In the modern banking literature, scholars who write about Japan focus on this concept of a 'main bank': the notion that all (or most, in more restrained accounts) large Japanese firms maintain a specially close relationship with one bank that performs these multiple roles. That notion, however, constitutes but the most recent (and most mathematical) iteration of a myth that has thrived for nearly a half-century: the notion that large Japanese firms organize themselves around a few key banks as *keiretsu* corporate groups. And those two myths, in turn, constitute part of a larger tale that places Japanese firms within a non-market, government-dominated hothouse environment.

To unravel these inter-related urban legends, we proceed in reverse order. In Part II we explain the role the government has (and has not) played in the Japanese economy (1.). We then discuss the putative *keiretsu* corporate groups (2.) and 'main bank' relationships (3.). All three of these urban legends – for such is what they are – share a common intellectual ancestry that traces its roots to the peculiar politics of the post-war Japanese and American universities. Accordingly, we close by telling that intellectual history (Part III).

[2] We leave other aspects of the legend peculiar to the governance of the Japanese firm to our companion paper in this volume p 73 ff.

II. Three Urban Legends

1. The Legend of Government Guidance

a. Introduction

Few legends of modern Japan come with as storied a heritage as the notion that talented and industrious bureaucrats routinely manipulate substantively powerful but legally informal tools to guide the economy. At least until recent deregulatory programs, explains a recent Brookings study, Japan assigned 'high levels of discretion' to its regulators and maintained 'a high degree of informality in administrative activities'. That discretion and informality, in turn, 'extend[ed] well beyond that which is stipulated in laws'. Through the resulting web of informal regulation (area specialists call it 'administrative guidance'), 'Japanese officials actively pursued [their] industrial policies'.[3]

We begin by exploring the three cases most often cited to illustrate the ostensibly heavy hand of the bureaucracy (b.). We then outline how Japanese courts treat bureaucratic intervention (c.), and how the government regulated the financial markets (d.).

b. Three Case Studies[4]

As with so much Western scholarship on Japan, the work on government power depends heavily on anecdote. Given the massive government power observers posit, one might have expected a correspondingly massive number of anecdotes. Not so. Instead, in the English-language press the legend hinges primarily on one: the mid-1960s confrontation between MITI (the Ministry of International Trade & Industry) and Sumitomo Metals Industries. The legend appears in such classics

[3] LE Carline and MC Tilton 'Preface' in LE Carlile and MC Tilton (eds) *Is Japan Really Changing Its Ways? Regulatory Reform and the Japanese Economy* (Brookings Washington DC 1998) 9. In turn, many specialists tie this account of a highly interventionist post-war bureaucracy to the notion that wartime (and early post-war) bureaucrats successfully planned the economy in the 1930s and '40s. In fact, wartime (and early post-war) planning had been a disaster – as explained in Y Miwa *State Competence and Economic Growth in Japan* (RoutledgeCurzon London 2004) and Y Miwa and JM Ramseyer 'Keizai kisei no yūkōsei – "Keisha seisan" seisaku no shinwa' [The Effectiveness of Economic Regulation: The Myth of "Priority Production" Policy] (2004) 70 Keizaigaku Ronshū 2, 70.

[4] More fully developed in Y Miwa and JM Ramseyer *Sangyō seisaku-ron no gokai: kōdō seichō no shinjutsu* [Misunderstandings about Industrial Policy: The Truth about High Growth] (Tōyō Keizai Shinpo-sha Tokyo 2002); Y Miwa and JM Ramseyer 'Capitalist Politicians, Socialist Bureaucrats? Legends of Government Planning from Japan' (2003) 48 Antitrust Bulletin 595.

in the field as Upham[5], Caves & Uekusa[6], Johnson[7] and van Wolferen[8]. In the Japanese press, observers add two others: the disputes involving the Nisshin spinning and Idemitsu oil firms.

(i) Sumitomo Metals[9]

(a) The legend

To most Western observers, MITI used its 1965 dispute with Sumitomo Metals to show firms what it could and would do to those that flouted its will. It enjoyed more power at the time than it ever would again, they explain, because of its power over foreign exchange. The statutes governing the field delegated such broad discretion to it that it could use that power to enforce even entirely unrelated dictates. So broadly did they delegate that the ministry could, as the Japanese aphorism put it, 'take Edo's revenge in Nagasaki'.

In early 1965, observers typically begin, Japanese steel makers faced a drop in demand. To address the problem, they organized a trade association committee, and that committee reported to MITI. In turn, MITI ordered it to organize a cartel to prevent 'excess competition'.

Through the committee, MITI then coordinated production cuts. It expected firms in the industry to comply, and most planned to do just that. Sumitomo Metals, however, wanted to produce more. By the fall of 1965, it decided to act alone. The cartel, it announced, it would ignore. Instead, it would produce as it wished.

MITI was not about to suffer independent firms. If Sumitomo thought it could do as it pleased, it thought wrong. Did not Sumitomo need coking coal? Should the firm try to ignore the cartel, it – MITI – would cut the foreign exchange it needed to import that coal. Absent coal Sumitomo could not make steel, and absent foreign exchange it could not buy coal. Recognizing its hopeless position, Sumitomo caved. Duly chastised, it pledged its cooperation.

For would-be renegades, the moral was clear. Should they buck MITI's leadership, MITI could and would retaliate. Even over matters that had nothing to do with foreign exchange, the ministry could and would use its power over that exchange to enforce compliance. By making an example of Sumitomo Metals,

[5] FK Upham *Law and Social Change in Postwar Japan* (Harvard University Press Cambridge 1987).

[6] RE Caves and M Uekusa *Industrial Organization in Japan* (Brookings Washington DC 1976).

[7] C Johnson *MITI and the Japanese Miracle: The Growth of Industrial Policy, 1925-1975* (Stanford University Press Stanford 1982).

[8] K van Wolferen *The Enigma of Japanese Power* (Vintage New York 1989).

[9] This discussion draws heavily from Miwa and Ramseyer (2003 n 4).

concludes Upham,[10] the ministry showed any firm with dreams of independence that it could and would manipulate its 'abstract legal powers' to 'ensure compliance'. Vehemently, it demonstrated that it faced 'virtually no statutory restrictions on [its] regulation of foreign trade'.

(b) The history

As critical a rhetorical role as the tale of Sumitomo Metals may play, the tale is too tall by half. If MITI enjoyed any control over foreign exchange, it had not used it earlier to induce firms to accept its unrelated dictates. It did not start now. And if Sumitomo Metals faced any vulnerability, it did not show it now. Instead, it refused to back down, and within a few weeks MITI capitulated.

MITI's role: At root, the tale of Sumitomo Metals is simply false. Begin with the question of why MITI intervened. The ministry did not intervene to implement any 'industrial policy'. Instead, it intervened to enforce a private cartel.

Steel firms had cartelized their market for several years. Sumitomo Metals, however, increasingly found the quotas unsatisfactory. Having invested aggressively in new facilities, it wanted a chance to expand its market share. Domestically, it was willing to follow quotas. Overseas, it wanted none.[11] Nonetheless, in mid-1965 it agreed again to acquiesce. With the lone dissident in line, the others set the quotas for the second fiscal quarter (July-Sept., 1965): production volumes set at 90% of the amounts they had each sold during the previous fiscal year's uncartelized third quarter.

The steel producers needed to agree not just on price and quantity, but on enforcement as well. If they formed a private agreement, they faced potential criminal liability. They could avoid that risk by forming a 'depression cartel' under the Antitrust Act, but could not then enforce the cartel's terms on any dissident. To avoid criminal liability while enforcing compliance, they instead decided to ask MITI to enforce their arrangement unofficially.[12] In the process, reasoned they (wrongly, as we explain below), they would both bind recalcitrant firms and protect themselves from criminal charges.

Despite its acquiescence, Sumitomo Metals continued to press for export exclusions. When by November its competitors still refused, it simply withdrew from the cartel. Exclusions or no exclusions, it would sell as it pleased. MITI promptly ordered it to comply with the cartel, but Sumitomo indignantly replied that 'production cutbacks should be decided strictly by agreement among the

[10] Upham (n 5) 176, 179.

[11] Asahi 13 July 1965; Mainichi 16 November 1965 (references are to Japanese newspapers).

[12] Asahi 13 July 1965; 16 December 1965.

firms'.[13] Let MITI try to enforce the cartel, it declared. 'We intend immediately to file suit'.[14]

The punishment: MITI faced a defiant Sumitomo Metals, but it did not punish the firm. It did not even try. Although it threatened to punish the firm, it never did. Instead, it simply caved.

To force Sumitomo Metals to comply, MITI would have had to take measures far more drastic than it even threatened. Suppose it allowed Sumitomo only enough foreign exchange to buy the coking coal it needed for the authorized steel. Given that Sumitomo maintained a full two months' worth of coking coal in reserve and wanted to produce only 10% more than its cartel quota, it could safely have ignored the cartel for another 20 months.[15]

Even if MITI tried to exhaust its coal reserves, declared Sumitomo, it still would not comply. At that point it would just import pig iron directly.[16] After all, by the mid-1960s, it faced no limits on pig iron imports (or most other imports, as we detail in II.1.d(iv) below). Coal imports were subject to the foreign exchange limits only because of the role mining villages played in keeping the Liberal Democratic Party (LDP) in power.

The victor: Ultimately, Sumitomo – not MITI – won the dispute. Notwithstanding the many accounts to the contrary, MITI did not obtain the result it wanted. Sumitomo did.

Most basically, Sumitomo Metals wanted steel exports outside the quotas. It did not object to cartels in principle. It wanted a cartel in the domestic market, and the ability to sell as it pleased abroad. Eventually, that was exactly the framework MITI and the steel industry offered it.

MITI talked conciliation from the start. Already in early December it announced it would consider keeping the export market uncartelized.[17] In its January deal with Sumitomo, it did just that. During the third quarter (Oct.-Dec. 1965), Sumitomo had exceeded its quota by 88,000 tons, and of that excess had exported 55,000 tons. For the next quarter, MITI forgave Sumitomo the exported 55,000 tons, and docked it only by the 33,000-ton excess.[18] Less than two months after declaring defiance, Sumitomo had obtained what it wanted.

Defiance paid. Soon, Sumitomo Metals tried the ploy again. When market demand rose unexpectedly in early 1966, Sumitomo decided that even its revised quotas cut profitability. Rather than comply with the cartel to which it had just

[13] Mainichi 16 November 1965.

[14] Nikkei 28 November 1965.

[15] Nikkei 20 November 1965.

[16] Nikkei 20 November 1965.

[17] Mainichi 3 December 1965.

[18] Nikkei 12 January 1966.

agreed, it decided to go its own way. Its rivals complained, but to no avail. 'Even if the industry decides to continue the crude steel adjustments into October,' announced the Sumitomo president, 'we do not intend to comply'.[19] By their original terms, the cartel would have lasted through September. Duly chastened, MITI dropped the quotas at the end of August.[20]

(ii) Nisshin Spinning

According to some accounts of Japanese bureaucratic power, in the mid-1960s MITI not only intervened to enforce its policies on a non-compliant Sumitomo Metals, it enforced them on the Nisshin cotton-spinning firm, too. Through early 1966, 174 spinning firms had maintained a 'depression cartel' under the Anti-monopoly Act. With the cartel expiring at the end of March, MITI proposed to extend it. When Nisshin refused to cooperate, it intervened and pressured the firm to comply. Nisshin recanted, and MITI obtained its cartel.

In fact, MITI did not actively pressure Nisshin. First, the textile industry was too widely dispersed. In cotton spinning, 350 legal firms (ie excluding the black-market firms, discussed below) competed, and the top 13 produced only half the industry output.[21] Second, MITI had no obvious way to compel compliance. At least in steel it could plausibly threaten to cut Sumitomo's coking coal. In cotton spinning Nisshin had been able freely to import what it wanted since 1961. Last, on a long-run basis, MITI did not want to cartelize the industry anyway.[22] Through the 1950s, it had allocated the foreign exchange for raw cotton imports among the spinning firms according to the number of spindles they registered. In 1961 it voluntarily abandoned that power. It did not do so because it had to abandon it. It abandoned it to further the LDP's largely free-market policies.

Although the LDP relied in part on small firms for political support, it set its small-business policies within a capitalist, free-market context. Japanese voters did not want an interventionist government, and the LDP knew that. Socialist and Communist candidates regularly offered them interventionist alternatives, and they regularly rejected them. Reflecting their policy preferences, the LDP instead maintained a fundamentally non-interventionist course. As its faithful agent, so did MITI.

Nisshin opposed the planned cartel, but for the same reasons that the other big firms opposed it, too.[23] First, the cartel favored the less efficient firms. Fundamentally, the industry had too much capacity. Of the 12.8 million total spindles,

[19] Nikkei 25 August 1966.

[20] Nikkei 30 August 1966.

[21] Tsūshō Sangyō-shō Sen'i-kyoku *Nihon bōseki geppō* (May 1966) 24; 1966 figures.

[22] Nikkei 26 January 1966, 3 February 1966.

[23] Mainichi 21 January 1966; Nikkei 23 January 1966, 26 January 1966.

industry insiders estimated that only three-quarters would survive in a competitive market. The cartel mandated production cutbacks, but because it mandated them uniformly they fell on the efficient and inefficient alike. If the industry could eliminate the cartel, market competition would instead force the cutbacks on the inefficient firms – eventually driving them out of business. What the larger firms (and MITI) wanted were policies that tracked that market competition.[24]

Second, the cartel favored the black-market shops and the legal firms that had not joined the cartel. Since the 1950s, firms could legally spin cotton thread only on those spindles they registered with the government. That ban, however, the government had enforced haphazardly, if at all – resulting in an estimated 500,000 unregistered spindles by the mid-1960s.[25] Yet the cartel applied only to participating firms. The black-market firms obviously did not participate, and neither did over 170 legal firms – who probably used another half-million spindles.[26] By requiring only participating firms to cut back, the cartel effectively expanded the market into which the black-market and non-participating legal firms could sell.

At least before 1961 the black-market firms could not import raw cotton directly. Because they lacked registered spindles, MITI would not allocate them foreign exchange. Once MITI abandoned its control over cotton imports, they could freely obtain their cotton. In truth, though, even under exchange controls MITI had not stopped firms from reselling the cotton they imported. As a result, the less efficient legal firms had simply re-sold the cotton they imported to more efficient black-market firms.

Although Nisshin eventually acquiesced to the cartel, it did so only after the trade association and MITI gave it much of what it wanted. It had hoped to eliminate all controls, and the association and MITI agreed to work toward that end. Even the structure of the cartel reflected Nisshin's aims. In exchange for Nisshin's cooperation, the association and MITI specified in the cartel that firms could sell on the market only 70% of their output.[27] Because the larger firms maintained vertically integrated weaving operations, the limit left them largely untouched (none of the ten largest firms sold 70% of their output on the market[28]). It hit instead the independent smaller firms.

True to the LDP's non-interventionist policies (and consistent with its actions in the Sumitomo Metals dispute), MITI never seriously tried to sway Nisshin. When Nisshin first announced that it would not comply with a new cartel, MITI

[24] Nikkei 15 February 1966.

[25] Mainichi 21 January 1966.

[26] Tsūshō (n 21) 24.

[27] Nikkei 10 March 1966.

[28] Mainichi 4 March 1966.

talked to Nisshin. Never did the ministry do more than talk. Fundamentally, it agreed with Nisshin, but the smaller firms stood in its way. By making its compliance with the cartel contingent on market-liberalization reforms, Nisshin gave MITI the leverage it needed to pursue policies it supported anyway.

As had Sumitomo Metals, Nisshin soon put the lessons it learned to further good use. In the rayon fiber industry as well, in 1966 several firms tried to coordinate capacity cuts. Nisshin refused to cooperate, and the group dropped its proposal.[29] When they raised it again the next year, several remaining firms did agree to scrap facilities. Nisshin scrapped none.[30]

(iii) Idemitsu Kōsan

From time to time, observers also use the dispute over the Idemitsu Kōsan petroleum firm to tell the story of Japanese government power. Readers should recognize the tale: MITI ordered the industry to cut production, a nonconformist firm refused, MITI threatened to punish, and the firm complied. The story did not describe Sumitomo, did not describe Nisshin, and does not describe Idemitsu Kōsan.

Through the 1950s, MITI had used its foreign exchange powers to control crude oil imports. In October 1963, it lifted those controls and substituted the authority it gained through one of the few industry-specific post-war control statutes – the 1962 Petroleum Industry Act.[31]

The Act gave MITI dubious control over short-term production. It allowed the ministry to set five-year supply plans, to issue refining licenses, and to allocate new facility permits. It required refiners to submit annual production plans to the ministry. It authorized MITI both to recommend changes if those plans seemed excessive, and to determine non-binding standard sales prices.

Crucially, the Act authorized MITI neither to force firms to follow its production recommendations, nor to require that they follow its standard prices. The recommendations it authorized were instead just that – recommendations. To force an adamant firm to comply, MITI would have needed to use its power over new investments to penalize non-compliance. Hence the crucial issues: Could it have done so, and did it try?

For its suggested production plans, MITI sought to use quotas developed by the industry trade association, the Petroleum Federation. As in cotton-spinning, however, the trade association was split. The larger, more efficient firms wanted a looser structure that rewarded firms for new investment – if they wanted quotas at

[29] Tsūshō (n 21) 132.

[30] Tsūshō Sangyō-shō (ed) *Tsūsanshō nenpō* (Okura-shō Insatsu-kyoku Tokyo 1967) 142-43.

[31] Sekiyū gyō-hō [Petroleum Industry Act], law no 128 of 1962.

all. Many of them, like Idemitsu Kōsan, wanted none. The smaller, less efficient firms wanted a straightforward cartel. With the firms unable to agree among themselves, MITI found itself in a quandary.

For the October 1963 – March 1964 period, MITI adopted quotas that largely tracked its April-September 1963 numbers. Idemitsu Kōsan promptly refused to comply. It was the second biggest firm in the industry, and one of the most aggressive. It had just opened a new plant in February, yet the quotas ignored the plant almost entirely. We will 'produce as much as we can sell', announced company president Sazo Idemitsu. MITI's quotas 'completely ignore our special circumstances'.[32]

Idemitsu Kōsan did not just refuse the quotas. It cancelled its Federation membership, and on 29 November 1963, announced its withdrawal.[33] Repeatedly, MITI pleaded with it to rejoin and follow the quotas. Repeatedly, it refused. Declared its president, the production restraints potentially violated the Antimonopoly Act (he was right, as we note below). MITI pressure or no, he would never agree. After all, the Petroleum Industry Act gave the ministry no authority to make him comply.[34] Idemitsu 'opposed the production adjustments themselves', he explained. 'Unless those adjustments are themselves abolished, we cannot agree to any compromise'.[35]

MITI talked and pleaded, but – crucially – that was all it did. Never did it threaten to penalize Idemitsu when next it applied for approval on new facilities. Never did it threaten otherwise to penalize it for non-cooperation. Instead, it recognized that it could not force Idemitsu Kōsan to comply. As the minister himself told the press, the ministry hoped Idemitsu would compromise. If it refused, he would issue a ministerial recommendation under the Petroleum Industry Act. If it ignored the recommendation, there was nothing he could do.[36] 'Because a ministerial order carries no penalty or other legal force', explained the *Nikkei* newspaper, 'MITI believes that Idemitsu would ignore it and continue with its own production plans'.[37]

A few days later, Idemitsu Kōsan did agree to quotas – for the time being.[38] To induce it to agree, MITI promised to produce new quotas that reflected Idemitsu Kōsan's concerns and hiked its allocation from 113,000 barrels a day to 131,000.[39] Provided Idemitsu cut output during the low-demand summer months,

[32] Nikkei 6 October 1963.

[33] Nikkei 30 November 1963.

[34] Nikkei 12 December 1963.

[35] Nikkei 12 January 1964.

[36] Nikkei 14 January 1964.

[37] Nikkei 19 January 1964.

[38] Nikkei 25 January 1964.

[39] Nikkei 24 January 1964.

calculated the *Asahi* newspaper, it could now produce almost what it could with no cartel at all.[40] As a further part of the deal, Idemitsu demanded that MITI agree to abolish production restraints as soon as possible.

Yet 'as soon as possible' is not now – and the persistence of the restraints proved the deal's undoing. From the outset, MITI refused to say when it would actually abolish them.[41] Neither would Idemitsu Kōsan rejoin the Federation until it did. Instead, when sailors went on strike the next year, Idemitsu used the pretext to cancel the deal. Consumers needed their oil, it declared. With supplies now uncertain it would again produce whatever it could sell. Over the intervening year, MITI had raised its quota to 192,000 barrels a day. It would produce 240,000.[42]

MITI pleaded its case, but the company president seemed determined to kill the cartel. 'Ever since freeing crude oil imports', he complained, 'MITI has used administrative guidance to control production. Our firm left the Federation because we opposed this.... We cooperated only on the condition that MITI promise to abolish the production controls..... That promise it still has not kept'.[43]

This time MITI did keep its promise and Idemitsu cooperated. As soon as the sailors returned to work, Idemitsu agreed again to the cartel.[44] MITI abolished the price controls at the end of the month and the production restraints at the end of the next biannual period.[45] With the restraints dead at the end of September, Idemitsu Kōsan rejoined the Federation.

c. Judicial Review of Bureaucratic Intervention

(i) Introduction

According to the anecdotes recounted in b., bureaucrats used the power they had in one area to force firms to comply with their dictates in another. According to the facts, they did nothing of the sort. According to the facts, they did not even try.

Bureaucrats did not use unrelated retaliation to induce compliance for two reasons: the courts would not have let them retaliate, and they had few powers (even unrelated powers) that they could have manipulated anyway. We turn to the latter in c., and focus first on the discretion courts gave bureaucrats: on their willingness to review informal regulatory measures (ie 'administrative guidance';

[40] Asahi 26 January 1964.

[41] Nikkei 24 January 1964.

[42] Mainichi 12 January 1966.

[43] Mainichi 21 January 1966.

[44] Nikkei 1 February 1966.

[45] Nikkei 2 February 1966.

(ii)), on the legality of those informal measures ((iii) and (iv)), and on criminal liability for complying with illegal regulatory measures (v).

(ii) Justiciability of informal regulation

Despite occasional references in the literature to the contrary, when MITI regulated informally it did not do so to avoid judicial review. It regulated informally for the same reason most regulators everywhere regulate informally: informality saves costs.

MITI could not have stayed informal to avoid judicial review, because informality would not have stopped that review. If a Japanese firm wants to contest an informal instruction in court, it need simply ignore it. By doing so, it will force the government's hand. To induce it to comply, the government will then need to take more formal steps. When it does, in most cases courts will review what it does.[46]

This is not peculiar to Japan. Rather, it is as true in the US as in Japan. If an American firm wants to contest an informal government action, it must first force the government's hand. Until it does, American courts will not review the action. When it does, they generally will. The point is true in the US It is true as well in Japan.

(iii) The case law on informal regulation[47]

Nothing better illustrates the way Japanese courts handle informal regulatory measures than the travails of Musashino mayor Kihachirō Gotō. In late 1971, one Motoharu Yamada marched into Gotō's office. As a bedroom Tokyo suburb, Musashino had boomed over the last decade, and as head of the local Yamaki construction firm Yamada had played his part. He built condominium buildings. Now, however, the city wanted his money.

As Gotō explained it, the city wanted developers like Yamada to do two things: to get their neighbors' consent before they built new buildings, and to donate money for school facilities. If they potentially inconvenienced their neighbors, they should make sure those neighbors did not mind. If they packed more students into the already crowded schools, they should do their part to build more. Many Musashino voters opposed the new construction projects, and Gotō owed his position to local voters.

[46] JM Ramseyer and M Nakazato *Japanese Law: An Economic Approach* (University of Chicago Press Chicago 1998) ch 8.

[47] JM Ramseyer 'Rethinking Administrative Guidance' in M Aoki and G Saxonhouse (eds) *Finance, Development and Competition in Japan: Essays in Honor of Hugh Patrick* (OUP Oxford 2000).

Given that the Musashino government had made these demands informally, Yamada opted not to comply. He continued to build his condominiums. Although he sometimes tried modestly to placate his neighbors, he seldom gave on issues that mattered and sued those neighbors who tried to block his crew. When he did, the courts forthrightly ordered the neighbors to pay him damages.[48] Rarely did Yamada give to the city's school fund either. When the city stalled his applications in response, he sued it, too.

Yet if Yamada could play to the courts, Gotō (quintessentially a politician) could play to the cameras. When Yamada proved particularly obdurate, he went to the construction site personally. With a handful of wet cement, he plugged Yamada's water pipes. Not that it stopped Yamada. He simply marched back into court. The city had a legal duty to provide the water, he demanded, regardless of whether he paid off his neighbors or donated to the schools. The court agreed, and ordered Gotō to unplug the pipes.[49]

Alas for Gotō, the local prosecutors noticed the dispute. Rather than commend him for promoting the local welfare, they thought his behavior criminal. He had a legal duty to run water to Yamada's apartments, they reasoned, whether Yamada talked to his neighbors or not, whether he gave toward the schools or not. Forthrightly, they filed criminal charges. The Tokyo District Court convicted, and the Tokyo High Court affirmed. By 1989, so did the Supreme Court.[50] In enforcing the city's informal regulatory regime, Gotō did not just break the law. According to the Supreme Court, he committed a crime.

Yamada then sued Gotō on behalf of the city. Under Japanese law, taxpayers can sue derivatively on behalf of their community those local officials who misuse funds. When the prosecutors filed charges against Gotō, Musashino had paid his defense costs. After all, he was responsible for promoting the town's welfare, and had made his demands on the contractors to carry out that responsibility. To Yamada, however, the regulatory framework was illegal – and if Gotō broke the law in enforcing it, then the city broke the law in paying his legal fees. As a Musashino taxpayer, he filed a taxpayer derivative suit to force Gotō to refund his attorney's fees. Again Yamada won, and again the High Court and Supreme Court affirmed.[51]

[48] *Yamaki Kensetsu KK v Suzuki* 1151 Hanrei Jihō 12 (Tokyo High Court 26 March 1980).

[49] *Yamaki Kensetsu KK v Musashino* 803 Hanrei Jihō 18 (Tokyo High Court 8 December 1975).

[50] *Kuni v Gotō* 1323 Hanrei Jihō 16 (Supreme Court 7 November 1989), aff'g 1166 Hanrei Jihō 41 (Tokyo High Court 30 August 1985), aff'g 1114 Hanrei Jihō 10 (Tokyo District Court 24 February 1984).

[51] *Yamada v Gotō* 1354 Hanrei Jihō 62 (Supreme Court 23 March 1990), aff'g 1186 Hanrei Jihō 46 (Tokyo High Court 26 March 1986), aff'g 1080 Hanrei Jihō 40 (Tokyo District Court 27 May 1983).

And still Yamada continued. When Musashino tried to force the informal regulatory policies on him, argued Yamada, he incurred a variety of costs. For those damages, the city owed him damages. To the court, the case was easy. It had already held the city's actions illegal. If Yamada had lost money, the city had a duty to pay. This time, Musashino did not even bother to appeal.[52]

In all this, Musashino's policies were not unusual: city governments had adopted them the country over. Neither was the Tokyo District Court's response (declaring attempts to enforce the policies flatly illegal) unusual: courts adopted it nearly everywhere, too. One developer applied to the Tokyo government for construction permits on a couple of condominium buildings. The government cited opposition from his neighbors, and stalled. The developer sued, and in 1982 won.[53] Another developer applied to the Kyoto prefectural government for a hotel building permit. When the government told him to negotiate, he refused – and this court declared the stalling illegal, too.[54]

By 1985, the Supreme Court entered the fray and announced that developers could freely ignore the informal policies. When they did, city governments could not use their intransigence to delay their applications.[55] To be sure, it left open the possibility that a developer might act so obstreperously that a city could withhold its services after all. Over the next several years, however, the courts made it clear it was a possibility in theory only. Obnoxious developers came and went, but the courts refused to let cities stall applications.

By the early 1990s, the suits had become commonplace. When a firm applied to Tochigi prefecture for a permit on an industrial waste plant, the government told it to obtain its neighbors' consent. The developer refused, sued for its permit, and won.[56] Another developer applied to Yamanashi prefecture for a construction permit on vacation condominiums. The prefecture stalled on grounds that he had not cooperated, he sued, and he won.[57]

A developer in northern Kyūshū wanted a condominium complex in suburban Fukuoka. The city told him to reduce the complex's size. He refused, sued, and won.[58] Still others found their plans for a golf course or pinball parlor stymied by

[52] *Yamaki Kensetsu KK v Musashino* 1465 Hanrei Jihō 106 (Tokyo District Court 9 December 1992).

[53] *Fujisawa Kensetsu KK v Tokyo* 1074 Hanrei Jihō 80 (Tokyo District Court 12 November 1982).

[54] *Sankei Kanko YG v Kyoto* 1116 Hanrei Jihō 56 (Kyoto District Court 19 January 1984).

[55] *Tokyo v GG Nakaya Honten* 1168 Hanrei Jihō 45 (Supreme Court 16 July 1985).

[56] *Shiroyama Kankyō Jōka YG v Tochigi* 1385 Hanrei Jihō 42 (Utsunomiya District Court 28 February 1991).

[57] *Arakawa Kensetsu Kōgyō KK v Yamanashi* 1457 Hanrei Jihō 85 (Kōfu District Court 24 February 1992).

[58] *Tōhō Jūtaku Sangyō KK v Shime* 1438 Hanrei Jihō 118 (Fukuoka District Court 13 February 1992).

the informal policies, sued, and won.[59] The disputes continued even into the next decade – when a resort condominium developer contested a local regulatory program and in 2001 won.[60]

(iv) The case law on foreign exchange

Although plaintiffs to these disputes over informal regulatory measures most commonly sued local governments, they did not always do so. Sometimes they sued MITI, and in the 1960s at least one set of plaintiffs sued MITI over foreign exchange. Commentators routinely claim MITI could use its control over foreign exchange allocation to do as it pleased (see d. (iv) below). Yet in deciding the litigation over foreign exchange, the court did not tell MITI it could use its foreign exchange powers to punish the firm over unrelated matters. It told MITI (and we know of no cases telling it anything else) the opposite: the ministry could *not* use its power over foreign exchange to enforce unrelated policies.

The case involved 'COCOM': an informal Cold War arrangement engineered by the US to block the exports of militarily sensitive equipment into the Soviet bloc. In the 1960s, a leftist Japanese group decided to send COCOM-banned products to two Chinese trade fairs. To do so, it needed foreign exchange clearance, and applied to MITI. Rather than risk US retaliation, MITI refused.

The group sued. On the issue of MITI's authority, the court found for the group. The foreign exchange statutes gave MITI considerable discretion, reasoned the court. Yet crucially, that discretion did not extend to non-economic concerns. In refusing the foreign exchange to enforce non-statutory political concerns, MITI violated the law. If MITI wanted to enforce COCOM, it needed a statute to that effect – and a statute it did not have. Accordingly, by denying foreign exchange to enforce COCOM-related concerns, it violated the law.[61]

(v) Criminal liability for regulatory compliance

Not only did courts let firms challenge informal regulatory programs they hated, they refused to let firms use programs they liked to avoid criminal liability. Take the oil firms. Since the 1960s they had (haphazardly, given the opposition of firms like Idemitsu Kōsan) cut production and fixed prices. They had managed

[59] *KK Yasu Kōpōreeshon v Ego* 1634 Hanrei Jihō 84 (Osaka High Court 27 May 1997) (golf course); *Odaka v Funabashi* 1513 Hanrei Jihō 145 (Chiba District Court 19 November 1993) (pachinko parlor).

[60] *Daisei Kikaku v Gunma* 1757 Hanrei Jihō 81 (Tokyo High Court 16 July 2001).

[61] *Hokkyō Jōkai Nihon Kōgyō Tenran-kai v Japan* 560 Hanrei Jihō 6, 21-22 (Tokyo District Court 8 July 1969).

their deals in the Petroleum Federation, and (like the steel firms) had tried to delegate enforcement to MITI.

In turn, MITI had implemented their cartel through informal regulatory policies. The Fair Trade Commission (FTC), however, decided that the arrangement violated the antitrust statute and launched criminal prosecutions. In 1980 the trial court straightforwardly convicted the firms.[62] Never mind that MITI had told them to follow the price-fixing schedule, explained the court. Never mind either that the Petroleum Industry Act authorized it to advise them to cut output or to set resale prices. Given that they could have ignored MITI's instructions had they wanted, in using the ministry to enforce their cartel's terms they fixed prices – and price-fixing constituted a crime.

On appeal, in 1984 the Supreme Court duly affirmed.[63] Firms need not follow informal regulatory programs, it noted. Precisely because compliance is voluntary, the programs will shield no one from criminal prosecution.

d. Regulatory Powers

(i) Introduction

By most accounts, Japanese bureaucrats controlled an array of powerful measures, and enjoyed wide-ranging discretion in exercising them. Through that combination of controls and discretion, they used their power over issue X to punish a firm that ignored their instructions on issue Y. In the process, they manipulated the economy as they pleased.

In c. we addressed bureaucratic discretion – and illustrated how the courts did *not* give bureaucrats the discretion the conventional literature posits. Turn now to the measures they supposedly controlled. Typically, Japan specialists claim that bureaucrats obtained their power through two sources: their ability to ration credit in highly regulated capital markets, and their control (as noted above) over foreign exchange. We begin with the former, and turn to the latter in (iv).

[62] *Japan v Idemitsu Kōsan* 985 Hanrei Jihō 3 (Tokyo High Court 26 September 1980), affirmed in part and revised in part, 1108 Hanrei Jihō 3 (Supreme Court 24 February 1984) (two of the firms and one of the executives were acquitted on appeal); *Japan v Sekiyū Renmei* 983 Hanrei Jihō 22 (Tokyo High Court 26 September 1980) (acquitting the Petroleum Federation).

[63] *Japan v IdemitsuKōsan* 1108 Hanrei Jihō 3 (Supreme Court 24 February 1984) (other than the convictions of two of the firms and one of the executives).

(ii) Capital market regulation[64]

(a) Introduction

According to the conventional wisdom, in the 1950s and '60s, Japanese bureaucrats motivated reluctant firms by rewarding them in the credit market.[65] There, the bureaucrats could do two things: they could lavish low-interest government loans (particularly from the Japan Development Bank [JDB]) on compliant firms, and they could ensure the firms access to private bank loans.

Bureaucrats could influence private loans, reason observers, because the government had taken three crucial steps. First, it had disabled the securities markets. By strictly regulating both stock and bond markets, it had prevented firms from raising more than limited quantities in either. When firms needed funds, they had little choice but to borrow from banks.

Second, the government used its control over foreign exchange to insulate the capital market from international competition. As Henderson[66] put it, it had 'shield[ed]' the domestic market 'from international market forces'.

Last, the government capped loan interest rates. Through rigid caps, it had forced banks to lend at rates below those that would have prevailed in a competitive market.[67] Compelled to lend at rates that did not clear, banks had no choice but to ration the credit they provided. By pressuring those banks, the government could then determine which firms borrowed and which went without. As we show below, none of this is true. By the 1960s the financial markets did clear. The government did not disable the securities markets, foreign firms did invest in Japan, and the interest-rate caps did not bind. Because banks lent at market rates, the government could not have influenced the allocation of private credit.

[64] This discussion draws heavily from Y Miwa JM Ramseyer 'Directed Credit? The Loan Market in High-Growth Japan' (2004) 13 J of Economics & Management Strategy171.

[65] DM Meerschwam 'The Japanese Financial System and the Cost of Capital' in P Krugman (ed) *Trade with Japan: Has the Door Opened Wider* (University of Chicago Press Chicago 1991) 191, 206; JR Lincoln M Gerlach and C Ahmadjian 'Evolving Patterns of Keiretsu Organization and Action in Japan' (1998) 20 Research in Organizational Behavior 303, 324; KE Calder *Strategic Capitalism: Private Business and Public Purpose in Japanese Industrial Finance* (Princeton University Press Princeton 1993) 35.

[66] DF Henderson 'Access to the Japanese Market: Some Aspects of Foreign Exchange controls and Banking Law' in GR Saxonhouse and K Yamamura *Law and Trade Issues of the Japanese Economy: American and Japanese Perspectives* (University of Washington Press Seattle 1986) 131, 132.

[67] So constrained were interest rates, argue some scholars, that banks sometimes circumvented them by requiring borrowers to take more than they needed and deposit the 'compensating balance' in a low interest-bearing account at the bank. Through the ploy, they raised the effective interest rate on the loan. In fact, this largely did not happen – for the simple reason that the regulated interest rates were not sub-market rates (as we explain below).

(b) Equity issues

Despite the many references in the literature to highly regulated securities markets, the Japanese government never seriously tried to restrict equity issues. Instead, it merely imposed securities registration and corporate law requirements analogous to those in the US Facing no regulatory hurdles, firms issued stock in large amounts. Take just the TSE (Tokyo Stock Exchange)-listed firms. In 1964, they raised 531 billion yen through 533 issues. In 1970, they raised 681 billion yen through 537 issues, and by 1975 raised 1,001 billion yen through 285 issues (through 1970, $1 traded for about 360 yen, and in 1975 traded for 305 yen[68]).

Overall, Japanese firms raised about the same fraction of their capital through equity as US firms. Although scholars do claim Japanese firms raise more money through debt than US firms, they mislead. Corrected for 'differences in accounting', writes Stewart Myers[69], US firms in 1991 had a book-debt/capital ratio of 33% while Japanese firms had 37%. They had a market-debt/capital ratio of 23% while Japanese firms had 17%.

These numbers do not reflect recent cross-national convergence. Instead, they merely repeat what Japanese scholars noted years ago. As early as 1979, Kuroda & Oritani[70] observed that US firms maintained equity/asset ratios of 33.0% while Japanese firms maintained ratios of 47.4%. Large US firms had intermediated financing ratios of 50.4% while Japanese firms had ratios of 46.7%.

(c) Bond issues

Japanese firms did face more stringent limits on their ability to issue bonds, but the limits did not reflect regulatory practice. Instead, they reflected anti-competitive efforts by banks. Despite those efforts, TSE-listed firms used bonds to raise substantial amounts. In 1965, they raised 324 billion yen through 467 issues, and 509 billion yen in 1970 through 306 issues. By 1975, they raised 1,406 billion through 306 straight bond issues, 408 billion through 57 convertible issues, and another 372 billion through 52 foreign issues.[71]

What is more, those firms that could not meet the bank-mandated issuing requirements could – and did – readily circumvent them. Rather than sell bonds, they just borrowed directly from the institutional investors who would otherwise have bought their bonds. When firms issue bonds in the US, they primarily sell them to institutional investors like insurance companies. In Japan, although banks

[68] Tōkyō Shōken Torihiki-jo (ed) *Shōken tōkei nenpō* [Securities Statistics Annual] (Tōkyo Shōken Torihiki-jo Tokyo 1985) 110 tab 37.

[69] SC Myers 'Capital Structure' (2001) 15 Journal of Economic Perspectives 81, 83.

[70] I Kuroda and O Yoshiharu 'Wagakuni no "kin'yū kōzō tokuchō" no sai-kentō' [A Reexamination of "The Peculiarity of Financial Structure" in Our Country] [Nichigin] (1979) 2 Kin'yū Kenkyū Shiryō 1.

[71] Tōkyō Shōken (n 68) 111.

prevented many firms from issuing bonds, they did not prevent them from borrowing from insurance firms. Rather than sell those institutional investors bonds, the firms merely borrowed from them directly.

(d) The overseas market

To regulate firm behavior through capital market controls, the Japanese government would have needed to insulate the Japanese market from foreign investors. It did not. Although it banned foreign investment 'in principle', almost immediately it began to gut that 'principle' through a variety of exceptions. It started modestly: from 1952 to 1960, foreign entities invested only $1.01 billion in Japan, and only 16% of that as equity.

During the 1960s, foreign investment boomed. In 1961, foreigners invested $581 million. In 1963, they invested $904 million, and by 1967 $880 million. Increasingly, they used the money for equity (and thus long-term) positions. By 1971, they invested $4.3 billion, and 63% of that as equity.[72]

'In principle' the government banned foreign investment. By the 1970s, it subjected that principle to an annual $3 to $5 billion exception.

(e) Interest rate caps

Whether the government could allocate credit depends crucially on whether the credit market cleared. If banks lent at market interest rates, anything the government did to direct funds would simply have produced offsetting shifts elsewhere. Because the marginal cost of funds would generally have stayed at market levels, even loan subsidies would seldom have affected investment patterns.

During the 1960s, the government limited the maximum interest rate banks could charge their customers. Subject to a variety of exceptions, it set the limit at 8.4 to 9.2%. It applied the limit, however, only to large short-term loans: loans of more than 1 million yen, and for terms of less than 12 months.

The banking association imposed an even more stringent set of interest rate caps, again on loans of more than 1 million yen for terms of less than 12 months: during 1960-86, a maximum of 5.5 to 8.4%.[73] The caps suggest a puzzle. One might expect banks to impose a *floor* on loan interest rates. One might expect them to impose a cap on *deposit* interest rates. One would not expect them to impose a *cap* on *loan* rates.

[72] Tsūshō Sangyō-shō (ed) *Tsūshō sangyō seisaku-shi, dai-6-kan* [A History of Trade and Industry Policy, Vol. 6] (Tsūshō Sangyō Chōsa-kai Tokyo 1990) 402-410; Nihon Ginkō (ed) *Keizai tōkei nenpō* [Economic Statistics Annual] (Nihon Ginkō Tokyo 1974) 210.

[73] Zenkoku Chihō Ginkō Kyōkai (ed) *Kin'yū ginko sho-tōkei* [Statistics for Finance and Banking] (Zenkoku Chihō Ginkō Kyōkai Tokyo various years); T Nakabayashi *Shin ginko jitsumu kōza* [New Lectures on Banking Practice] vol 15 (Yūhikaku Tokyo 1968).

In fact, however, the puzzle is more apparent than real. Fundamentally, the caps – even the bank association-imposed caps – did not bind. In 1965, the large money-center banks lent money at modal rates of 8.0 to 8.4% within a range of 6.2 to 9.5%. During the same period, the smaller regional banks (with their higher-risk borrowers), lent at modal rates that ranged from 8.4 to 8.8% within a 6.2 to 9.9% range.[74]

Banks could lend at these high rates because they could so readily avoid the caps. For smaller borrowers, they could split the loans into smaller segments. For the larger borrowers, they could lend the money for terms longer than one year. After all, most loans they rolled over anyway. Rather than lend at regulated rates for a year, they could lend at market rates for 13 months. And so they did. From 1960 to 1968, the larger banks made one-third to one-half percent of their loans on terms not subject to the bank association-imposed caps. The regional banks made only one-quarter to one-half of their loans within the caps.

Because the restrictions did not bind, firms in 1960s Japan borrowed at rates that reflected the factors that routinely determine interest rates in competitive markets. They paid higher rates if they had volatile performance, for example. They paid lower rates if they had a large stock of mortgageable assets.[75]

(iii) Government loan programs[76]

Although the JDB did make subsidized loans, it lent heavily to firms in ocean shipping.[77] From 1961 to 1970, the government routed shipping firms over a third of the JDB's entire loan base (an average of 204 billion yen a year). In addition, to shipbuilding firms preparing vessels for export it routed nearly half its export-import bank loans (a loan base averaging 247 billion yen a year).

Although the loans transferred substantial wealth to the shipping firms, innovative shippers could flourish without them. Indeed, the Sankō steamship firm flourished precisely because it did refuse to take them. To Sankō, the subsidized loans came with too much government control. Take the loans, it reasoned, and it could not offer its customers the services they demanded. Accordingly, by the mid-1950s it decided to do without. Rather than take the government's subsidies and comply with its terms, it would raise its own funds and follow its own plans. While its rivals stayed within the government's orbit, it repaid its JDB loans and turned exclusively to private sources.

[74] Zenkoku (n 73).

[75] Miwa and Ramseyer (n 64).

[76] For more details on the shipping industry and Sankō's history, see the fuller account in Miwa and Ramseyer (n 64).

[77] Nihon Zōsen Kōgyō-kai (ed) *Nihon Zōsen Kōgyō-kai 30 nen-shi* [A 30-Year History of the Japan Shipbuilding Industry Association] (Nihon Zōsen Kōgyō-kai Tokyo 1980).

Sankō jettisoned government subsidies all the way to the bank. It had opened the 1950s with virtually nothing. It closed the 1960s as the most profitable firm in the industry. During the last half of the decade, it earned shareholder returns of 32% a year, and by the early 1970s 62%. Its closest rival during the late 1960s was Shōwa, but it earned only 17% and in the early 1970s only 32%. Its closest rival during the early 1970s was Japan Lines, but it earned only 50% and in the late 1960s only 9%.

By the early 1970s Sankō had grown from the sixth-ranked firm (in 1964) to the largest. From a stock market capitalization of 3.59 billion yen in 1964, it had boomed to 514 billion yen by 1973, three times its nearest rival. Despite making no government-'approved' vessels, it commanded a shipping capacity second only to Japan Lines. Despite collecting no government-subsidized loans, it serviced the third-largest debt in the industry.

To be sure, OPEC changed all this. Facing radically higher oil prices, Western firms now cut the amount of oil they consumed and shipped. Firms like Sankō that had invested heavily in tankers suffered accordingly. Although in 1985 it filed for bankruptcy, it did have good company. Government-favored firms lost heavily, too. By 1988, the government-anointed Japan Lines failed as well.

(iv) Foreign exchange controls

According to the legend of Sumitomo Metals, bureaucrats also motivated recalcitrant firms by withholding foreign exchange. Claims Johnson,[78] the foreign exchange law constituted 'the single most important instrument of industrial guidance and control that MITI ever possessed'. According to Caves & Uekusa[79], a 'major sanction until the mid-1960s was the MITI's authority over the allocation of foreign exchange for the purchase of essential inputs'. Indeed, added they, '[c]ontrols over international transactions have *often* served as a club when gentle persuasion failed'.[80]

To the best of our knowledge, before the Sumitomo Metals dispute, MITI *never* used its powers over foreign exchange and trade to enforce unrelated policies.[81] To be sure, it did eventually try the ploy once – in 1969, to enforce COCOM. It tried the ploy, and the Tokyo District Court declared it flatly illegal.

In fact, by 1969 the issue was almost entirely moot anyway. By then, the Japanese government had freed most imports, and MITI had few foreign

[78] C Johnson *MITI and the Japanese Miracle: The Growth of Industrial Policy, 1925-1975* (Stanford University Press Stanford 1982).

[79] RE Caves and M Uekusa *Industrial Organization in Japan* (Brookings Washington DC 1976).

[80] Italics added.

[81] Nikkei 20 November 1965.

exchange control powers left to wield. The shift had begun in the late 1950s, when it decided to integrate Japan more fully into the international economy. In 1960, measured by volume, 44% of all imports were unrestricted. By 1963 that fraction had reached 92%.[82] Only exceptionally (coal in the case of the LDP's core constituents, or militarily sensitive equipment in the case of the COCOM dispute) could it review foreign exchange applications at all.

2. The Legend of the Keiretsu

a. Introduction

By classic accounts, most large Japanese firms organize themselves into '*keiretsu'* corporate groups. Each group sports a major money-center bank at the center, encircled by dozens (or hundreds, or thousands, depending on the observer) of service and industrial firms. These firms then preferentially trade with each other, finance each other, invest in each other, cut each other slack – and (when necessary) rescue each other.

Most scholars put total *keiretsu* members at several hundred, but not all. The *Harvard Business Review* put it at 12,000 firms, and attributed 'virtually all business activity [to] one or another *keiretsu* or cartel'.[83] And Kensy[84] counts 15,540 firms *just in the Mitsubishi group*. The total number of 'people who are, in some way, directly associated with the Mitsubishi Keiretsu' he places at 31 million.[85]

Most scholars agree that the *keiretsu* do matter. Wrote Harvard and University of Tokyo economists Richard Caves and Masu Uekusa, for example, they constitute 'a major and conspicuous force in the Japanese economy'.[86] Yet about

[82] R Komiya 'Kōgyōhin ni kansuru NTB' [NTBs Relating to Industrial Products] in K Kojima and R Komiya (eds) *Nihon no hikansei shōheki* [Japan's Non-Tariff Barriers] (Nihon Keizai Shinbun-sha Tokyo 1972) 71 tab 2. Thus, claims that liberalization essentially began in the 1980s (eg U Schaede 'The Japanese Financial System: From Postwar to the New Millennium' Harvard Business School Case 9-700-049 [2000] 2) are simply wrong. The details of industry-specific practice are crucial – as much as Western scholars routinely miss the point. For example, statements like those by Kaplan (EJ Kaplan *Japan: The Government-Business Relationship – A Guide for the American Businessman* [Books for Business Washington 1972] 145) that '[u]ntil 1965 MITI directly controlled the importation and allocation of ... [steel] ore ... through the mechanism of foreign exchange import quotas' are flatly untrue. Instead, by 1965 steel had already been freely importable for several years.

[83] RL Cutts 'Capitalism in Japan: Cartels and Keiretsu' *Harvard Business Review* (Cambridge United States 1 July 1992) 48, 49.

[84] R Kensy *Keiretsu economy – new economy* ? (Palgrave New York 2001) 252.

[85] ibid.

[86] Caves and Uekusa (n 79) 63.

quite why the *keiretsu* might matter – on what functions they serve – scholars agree much less. Many, like Nobel laureate Paul Samuelson, consider them 'large oligopolies'.[87] Others, by contrast, attribute to them myriad efficiencies.

In any case, most scholars also consider the *keiretsu* quintessentially Japanese. According again to the *Harvard Business Review*, they reflect 'Japan's basic nature'. As such, it explained, they illustrate the way 'Japanese capitalism differs greatly' from that in the West.[88] They cooperate with other group members, wrote a Berkeley business school team, because they bind themselves to each other through a 'web of obligation'. Given those obligations, to do anything else would not be 'the Japanese way of business'.[89]

b. The Groups[90]

(i) What are they?

By most accounts, there are (or were) six of them: the Mitsui, the Mitsubishi, the Sumitomo, the Fuji, the Daiichi Kangyō, and the Sanwa. Within each group, a massive money-center bank dominated the others. Around it, dozens of industrial and service firms borrowed, built, and traded among themselves.

The firms also met regularly, the accounts continue. Every month, the presidents of the firms met for lunch. And at least the membership of these lunch clubs was clear enough. A man is either invited or not invited. Come noon on the second Thursday of each month, *keiretsu* or no *keiretsu* he must decide where he will eat his lunch.

(ii) Whom do they include?

Yet if observers agree that *keiretsu* matter, they seldom agree about whom they include. As the range of membership estimates from several hundred to 15,540 illustrates, membership is anything but straightforward. To be sure, the lunch club invitation lists themselves are clear. Yet observers seldom use them. If they had,

[87] PA Samuelson 'Japan's future financial structure' (2000) 12 Japan and the World Economy 185, 186.

[88] Cutts (n 83) 48.

[89] Lincoln Gerlach and Ahmadjian (n 65) 318.

[90] The following account draws on Y Miwa and JM Ramseyer *Nihon keizai-ron no gokai: "Keiretsu" no jubaku kara no kaihō* [Misunderstandings in the Theory of the Japanese Economy: (1) Liberation from the Spell of the "Keiretsu"] (Tōyō Keizai Shinpō-sha Tokyo 2001); Y Miwa and JM Ramseyer 'The Myth of the Main Bank: Japan and Comparative Corporate Governance' (2002) 27 Law & Social Inquiry 401; Y Miwa and JM Ramseyer 'The Fable of the Keiretsu' (2002) 11 Journal of Economics & Management Strategy 169.

no one would have paid attention. Moving the *keiretsu* from an academic sideshow to a central institution in Japanese business instead involved a crucial sleight-of-hand: coupling the accounts of regular presidential lunches with lists of hundreds (or thousands) of firms whose presidents were never invited.

For what the lunch club presidents had in common – in truth, all they had in common – was that they each ran a firm that had once been part of a pre-war *zaibatsu* group (predecessors to the putative *keiretsu*). Many of the firms were minor affairs. As of 1967 (the alleged heyday of the *keiretsu*, and the earliest date for which we have invitation lists), the lunch clubs included firms like the Hokkaidō Colliery and Steamship company (1965 market capitalization of 6.9 billion yen; at the then-current exchange rate of 360 yen/$, about $19 million). They similarly included the Toshoku trading firm (3.0 billion), Mitsubishi Steel (2.8 billion), Mitsubishi-Edogawa Chemicals (3.1 billion), Sumitomo Coal (3.2 billion), Mitsubishi Mining (3.5 billion), and Mitsubishi Plastics (3.7 billion).

The lunch clubs could not conceivably have dominated the national economy. As groups of ex-*zaibatsu* firms, many of their members competed in industries that had dominated the economy before the war but had since gone nowhere – industries like mining, ocean shipping, warehousing, and cement. In turn, they missed the firms most central to growth postwar. Again as of 1967, the *keiretsu* lunch clubs omitted Toyota (1965 market capitalization of 135 billion yen), Toshiba (91 billion), Takeda Pharmaceuticals (61 billion), Kinki Nihon Railway (43 billion), Honda (42 billion), Bridgestone Tire (42 billion), Kajima Construction (37 billion) – not to mention Matsushita Electric (Panasonic), Sharp, Sony, Kyocera, Suzuki, Cannon, and Nikon.

Even collectively, the lunch club firms remained modest. Take the number of employees in 1973 at all lunch club firms, and compare it with the number of employees at several non-Japanese firms:[91]

Mitsui	259,084	IBM	268,130
Mitsubishi	269,147	Siemens	302,000
Sumitomo	159,395	ITT	433,000
Sanwa	414,731	Philips	386,500
Fuji	345,549	GM	804,571
DKB	546,312	Ford	458,463

If one added all employees at the Mitsubishi lunch club firms, together they rivaled IBM. None of the groups even remotely approached GM.

We know of no lunch club decision that mattered. Occasionally, the lunch clubs collectively decide whether to license the old *zaibatsu* trade names and trademarks. For the 1970 Osaka World's Fair, they planned group displays. Rumors allege that the Sumitomo group once tried to stop Sumitomo Metals and

[91] Miwa and Ramseyer 'The Fable of the Keiretsu' (n 90).

Sumitomo Chemicals from expanding their aluminum refining, and that the Mitsubishi group once tried to stop Mitsubishi Petrochemicals and Mitsubishi Chemicals from expanding ethylene production. If they did, neither succeeded.[92]

As rhetorically crucial as they may be, economically the lunch clubs have always been trivial. To avoid that triviality, most writers thus couple the accounts of the meetings with much longer lists of firms. For those lists, they most commonly turn to the rosters published by the obscure Economic Research Institute (ERI) as the annual *Research on the Keiretsu (ROK) [Keiretsu no kenkyū]*.[93]

The ERI did not obtain its lists from the firms themselves. Instead, it manufactured them. In virtually all cases, it merely grouped exchange-listed firms by the source of their loans. In turn, that loan data it obtained from the disclosure statements required by the Japanese securities law.

In general (it actually provided several quite different rosters), the ERI placed in a *keiretsu* those firms that borrowed the most from the (now long-independent) banks and insurers that before the war had been part of a given *zaibatsu*. It classified as independent those that borrowed the most from any other financial institutions.[94] If the total a given firm borrowed from the Mitsubishi Bank, the Mitsubishi Trust Bank, the Tokyo Marine and Fire Insurance Co., and the Meiji Life Insurance Co., for example, exceeded the total it borrowed from any other similarly grouped set of financial institutions, the ERI placed the firm in the Mitsubishi *keiretsu*. Only if it borrowed more from a non-*keiretsu* institution (generally, a much smaller regional bank) than the sum of its debt from any of these grouped money-center financial institutions did the ERI consider it independent.

Among observers who do not read Japanese, Dodwell Marketing Consultants posed the stiffest competition to the *ROK*. Every few years since the early 1970s, it published its own *keiretsu* roster: *Industrial Groupings in Japan*.[95] Where the ERI relied on loans, Dodwell apparently (it does not clearly explain the procedure) turned to equity. Apparently, it started with the lunch club invitation lists. To those lists, it then added those firms where lunch group invitees appeared prominently among the 10 largest shareholders.

If the different *keiretsu* definitions captured otherwise real but unobservable group characteristics, the *ROK* and Dodwell's should have produced similar

[92] ibid.

[93] Keizai Chōsa-kai (ed) *Keiretsu no kenkyū* [Research on the Keiretsu] (Keizai Chōsa-kai Tokyo various years).

[94] Given that the ERI based its rosters on loans, the firms obviously (by definition) borrowed heavily from *keiretsu* financial institutions. For that reason, we do not discuss loan patterns below. For more detail on the subject, see Miwa and Ramseyer (n 91).

[95] Dodwell Marketing Consultants *Industrial Groupings in Japan* (Dodwell Marketing Consultants Tokyo various years).

rosters. Yet even the *ROK* rosters themselves vary. Because the *ROK* used several different definitions, its own Mitsui *keiretsu* ranged from 48 firms in 1965 to 82 (1965 data). Because Dodwell's uses yet another definition, its rosters vary still more. Indeed, the Mitsui group in Dodwell's has fewer than half its members in common with the principal *ROK* Mitsui roster. Only 48 to 65% of *ROK keiretsu* members appear in the Dodwell *keiretsu* roster of TSE Section-1 firms, and only 49 to 55% of the Dodwell members appear in the *ROK* lists (1975 data).

(iii) What do they do?

(a) Trades

If the *keiretsu* mattered so much, one might have thought the members would trade with each other. According to a survey by the FTC, however, manufacturing firms in 1992 in the six lunch clubs *sold* a mean 12.58% of their output within the group.[96] They made most of these intra-group sales to the trading company, which then resold the goods elsewhere. Other than sales to the trading company, they sold only 2.38% of their output within the group. The amounts ranged from 5.57% (1.49%, excluding the trading company) for the Sanwa group, to 31.67% (0.61%, excluding the trading company) for the Sumitomo.

These same manufacturing firms *bought* a mean 6.71% of their supplies within the group. Again, much of this volume they bought from the trading company, which in turn acquired them elsewhere. Other than purchases from the trading company, the firms bought only 2.24% of their supplies within the group. The amounts ranged from 3.67% (1.23%, excluding the trading company) for the Fuji to 15.87% (5.40%, excluding the trading company) for the Mitsubishi.

(b) Cross-shareholding

By most accounts, the *keiretsu* firms control each other through stock ownership. Yet most of the non-financial firms invest nothing in the other *keiretsu* firms. Although the law generally let them buy stock in each other, they rarely did. As of 1965 the 46 Mitsubishi non-financial firms could each have invested in 45 other firms – for a total of 2070 investment opportunities.[97] Of these, the firms made investments in 219, or 10.6%. They made at least 1% investments in 61, or 3.0%. In only 11 cases (0.5%) did any non-financial firm hold more than 5% of the stock of another. The Daiichi firms made 1% investments in 4.8% of the potential cases, Sumitomo firms in 3.7%, Mitsui firms in 2.6%, Sanwa firms in 2.1%, and Fuji firms in 1.8%.

[96] Kōsei Torihiki Iinkai (ed) *Kōsei Torihiki Iinkai nenji hōkoku* [Fair Trade Commission Annual Report] (Kōsei Torihiki Iinkai Tokyo 1994) 139.

[97] We take the data from the *ROK*. For shareholdings, it uses a different (and smaller) set of rosters than it uses for other purposes. See generally Miwa and Ramseyer (n 91).

Nor did the non-financial firms *collectively* own much stock of each other. In the Mitsubishi *keiretsu*, the non-financial firms together held 4.9% of all outstanding shares of the group. In the Sumitomo, they held 6.1% of the shares of member firms, in the Daiichi 4.8%, in the Mitsui 3.5%, in the Sanwa 2.1%, and in the Fuji 2.0%.

Although the financial firms did hold stock in *keiretsu* members, the point misleads. Where the law banned US banks from holding corporate stock during this period, Japanese law allowed it – and Japanese banks responded by diversifying broadly. Although they owned stock in *keiretsu* firms, they owned large amounts of stock in non-*keiretsu* firms as well. By law, until the late 1970s the financials could have held up to 10% of any other firm's stock, and had they wanted to control the firms they would have bought that 10%. They did not. Although the Mitsubishi Bank invested in 41 of the 46 non-financial group members, it held more than 5% of the stock of only 8, and more than 8% of the stock of only 2. The trust bank held more than 8% of only 3, the life insurer of only 3, and the casualty insurer of none (1965 data).

If intra-group shareholdings were rare, true *cross*-shareholding arrangements were rarer still. Equity investments seem consistently highest at the Sumitomo group, and in 1965 there were 11 pairs of cross-shareholdings involving at least 1% there. Yet among the Mitsui and Sanwa firms there were only six such pairs, among the Mitsubishi four pairs, among the Fuji three pairs, and among the Daiichi firms two.

3. The Legend of the Main Banks

a. Introduction[98]

Like the fable of the *keiretsu*, that of the 'main bank system' starts with a bank. Every large Japanese firm has a long-term relationship with a leading bank, the fable begins. Called the firm's 'main bank', that bank maintains a set of implicit contracts with the firm. Under that implicit deal, it agrees to monitor the firm (often through board appointments). It promises not just to monitor for itself, but to monitor on behalf of other creditors. It agrees to intervene in governance (again, through board appointments) as appropriate. And as necessary, it agrees to

[98] For further detail, see Miwa and Ramseyer 'The Myth of the Main Bank' (n 90); Y Miwa and JM Ramseyer 'Conflicts of Interest in Japanese Insolvencies: The Problem of Bank Rescues' (2005) 6 Theoretical Inquiries in Law (Online Edition) no 2 article 2 <http://www.bepress.com/til/default/vol6/ iss2/art2> (18 July 2005); Y Miwa and JM Ramseyer 'Does Relationship Banking Matter? Japanese Bank-Borrower Ties in Good Times and Bad' (2005) 2 J of Empirical Legal Studies 261.

loan extra funds, to subordinate its claims to those of other creditors, and to send in experts to remake the firm.

If the accounts of the main bank seem familiar, they should. At root, to tell the main bank story, theorists merely recast the *keiretsu* accounts in a form more congenial to modern economics. To do so, they first stripped the *keiretsu* stories of their culture-specific sociological gloss. They then retold them as game-theoretic and information-based accounts that illustrate aspects of current relationship-banking theory. *Keiretsu* scholars told of groups centered about the major money-center banks; main-bank scholars told of firms that use a given money-center bank as their 'main bank'. Most *keiretsu* scholars relied for their group rosters on lists the *ROK* constructed by asking where a firm borrowed the most; most main-bank scholars defined a firm's main bank as the bank from which it borrows the most. And when the main-bank scholars did not sort firms by the amount of their loans, they usually just sorted them by a *keiretsu* roster directly.

By basic logic, however, the terms to the putative main-bank arrangement should trouble. Given that a bank which commits itself to rescuing defaulting borrowers will attract the highest-risk firms, banks would seem to do best if they refused ever to become a main bank. Given that a bank that sends good money after bad usually loses both, banks that did agree to rescue troubled firms would seem to face incentives to renege after the fact. Given that a bank often does best if it quietly pulls its loans at the first sign of trouble, banks would seldom want to promise to monitor 'on behalf' of their rival – and those rivals would not trust them if they did. Given all these problems, if firms and banks did negotiate these terms, one would think they at least would do what insurance companies do with their own obligations: draft fine-print contracts about each.

Yet according to the conventional wisdom, banks and firms draft none. Indeed, according to that wisdom, they not only leave the 'main bank contract' unwritten, they leave it unspoken as well. In the language of the literature, they negotiate their terms 'implicitly' – and to say that they negotiate them implicitly, of course, is to say that they negotiate them not at all.

b. Some Examples

At the firm level, the evidence at least shows that Japanese banks never tried to save all large troubled firms. Even before the 1990s recession, they did not try to save them. And if they did not try to save the firms that did fall into distress, they could not credibly (albeit implicitly) have promised to save the rest either. Take several examples from our own work:[99]

[99] Miwa and Ramseyer 'Conflicts of Interest in Japanese Insolvencies' (n 98).

(i) Mazda

Consider Mazda. As Western observers recount the story, the firm entered the 1970s with an iron-willed, engineering-obsessed, and somewhat pig-headed CEO from the original Matsuda family.[100] Under his leadership, it invested heavily in rotary engines. Alas, when the OPEC-induced price hikes hit in the middle of the decade, consumers abandoned the rotaries for the more fuel-efficient Toyotas, Nissans, and Hondas. To turn Mazda around, the Sumitomo Bank then stepped in as main bank. It sent personnel, loaned money, repositioned the product line, enforced austerity. Through all that, it ultimately saved the firm.

Yet the way Mazda reacted to the bank belies the notion that they implicitly agreed that the bank would rescue the firm. Had they cut such a deal in advance, the bank should not have faced the resistance it did after the fact. In fact, as the two leading scholars on the event acknowledge, the firm fought the bank at every turn – with its managers referring to the new arrivals as the 'occupying army'.[101] Under pressure in December 1974, Mazda did accept several outsiders to its 30-member board. Yet the new men did not come just from the Sumitomo Bank. Instead, they came from the Sumitomo Trust Bank, two local banks, and the trading companies with which Mazda dealt as well. Although Mazda named a Sumitomo Bank representative vice president in early 1976, it was late 1977 before the outsiders could oust the pig-headed Matsuda as CEO. When they did, they did not fire him or install a banker in his stead. Instead, the firm named him chairman of the board and replaced him with its incumbent third-in-command, a long-term Mazda engineer. By 1978, Mazda still had only four bankers on its board.

To keep Mazda alive, several institutions helped. The Sumitomo Bank did lend money, but so did the Sumitomo Trust Bank. In November 1979 Ford took a 25% equity interest. The director from the Trust Bank supervised capital budgeting issues, one director from the Sumitomo Bank managed exports while another directed accounting and cost controls, the director from the C. Itoh trading firm coordinated sales, and the director from Sumitomo Trading took charge of managerial consolidation.

The legend in the West characterizes the Mazda 'turnaround' as a story of main bank rescue, but one should wonder. The Sumitomo Bank never had the stake in Mazda that would induce a bank or firm to invest much in saving it. Although it had lent more to Mazda than anyone else, it had long kept its share of Mazda's debt modest: 13.6% in October 1974 and 14.5% in October 1977. By October 1977 it was *cutting* the amount it lent Mazda: from 53.6 billion yen in October 1976 to 46.1 billion in October 1977, and by October 1980 to 26.3 billion. As of 1974 (and still in 1977) it held less than 4% of the stock. Had it

[100] RT Pascale and T Rohlen 'The Mazda Turnaround' (1983) 9 J of Japanese Studies 219.

[101] ibid 233, 236.

wanted to own more, at the time it legally could have held up to 10%. Instead, it kept its share even below that of the Nippon Life Insurance firm.

In truth, the Sumitomo Bank did *not* rescue Mazda. Instead, the institutions with the greatest stake in the firm *collectively* rescued it. None of them knew how to make cars, of course, but Mazda's problems did not lie in automotive engineering. Instead, they lay in financial management and marketing. Banks do know how to balance books, and trading companies know how to read consumer preferences and cultivate export markets. What Mazda needed, these others could contribute. They did, and Mazda survived.

(ii) Eidai Industries

Mazda still makes cars, but troubled firms do not always recover. Sometimes, banks and trading partners intervene and fail. Eidai Industries mass-produced pre-fabricated housing, and by the 1970s listed its stock on Section 1 of the Tokyo Stock Exchange. In the mid-1970s it found itself out-competed. Out-maneuvered by its competitors, in December 1975 it posted a large loss.

Eidai's banks had known of its travails already by late 1974. To resolve those problems, in the fall of 1975 the largest five creditors agreed collectively to lend it more and to excuse it from its 2 billion yen semi-annual interest payment. True to their word, they lent large amounts. From 1971 to 1977, they boosted their loans to Eidai from 7.5 billion yen to 75.3 billion.

The banks took a variety of other steps besides. They enlisted the help of two trading firms that handled Eidai accounts. They encouraged Eidai to increase its sales force. They introduced clients to Eidai branches. They placed three bankers on Eidai's eleven-member board. They replaced the Eidai president, first with a former president of a Daiwa Bank-affiliated securities firm, then with the number-four man at Daiwa itself.

But monitoring a borrower effectively is hard. If its rivals out-competed Eidai, Eidai outfoxed its banks. The second Daiwa-sent president had planned to rebuild Eidai within two years. It was not to be. Despite having had three bankers on its board and a banker in its vice presidential post even before the crisis, despite eventually accepting its president and fourteen other senior executives from the Daiwa Bank – despite all this, Eidai carried problems that went deeper than any bank knew. By 1978, one year after the ambitious second Daiwa-sent president took office, the banks petitioned the court for its reorganization. 'Banks know they're easy to fool', a senior Daiwa executive recalled. 'But they got fooled again anyway'.[102]

[102] Chūo Kōron (special management prob. issue winter 1978) 334.

(iii) Sasebo Heavy Industries

When a rescue occurs and a firm does survive, sometimes it survives only by happenstance. During the 1960s and early '70s, the Sasebo Heavy Industries (SHI) shipbuilding firm had thrived. What with the explosive economic growth and the increasing need for large tankers (from firms like Sankō), demand had boomed. Come 1977, however, the Arab oil embargo and the massive revaluation of the yen (from 290.3 yen/$ in January 1977 to 195.4 in December 1978) had turned the boom into a bust. With total industry shipbuilding capacity of 19 million tons, Japanese firms had 1977 orders of only 5 million. At least the largest shipbuilding firms had diversified their product line. Medium-sized SHI had not. By the fall of 1978, it had no orders at all.

Like most large Japanese firms, SHI had borrowed broadly. From over a dozen banks, it had borrowed (as of March 1977) more than 79.7 billion yen. Among the commercial banks, it had borrowed the most from the Daiichi Kangyō Bank (DKB): 3.3 billion. It had four major shareholders: the Kurushima dry-docks firm (25.0%), the Nippon Kōkan (NKK) steel firm (24.2%), Nippon Steel (14.1%), and the Nisshō Iwai trading firm (10.1%). Kurushima had bought its interest because its CEO Toshio Tsubouchi wanted to integrate SHI's large dock facility into Kurushima. When he had earlier tried to become president, however, NKK had blocked his move and instead engineered the appointment of its own representative.

To deal with the non-existent demand, in early 1978 SHI asked for early retirements. By April 1,600 employees had volunteered, but to finance their retirement package the firm needed 8.2 billion yen. It would also have to finance other changes, of course, and all told could expect to need about 20 billion. When it approached its banks, however, they balked. Rather than volunteer more money, they simply told it to file for bankruptcy.

The banks would agree to lend the money only if SHI's lead shareholders guaranteed the debt, but the shareholders would not guarantee. NKK controlled SHI, and Tsubouchi – bitter still about the way NKK had blocked him from becoming president – was not about to guarantee any loans suggested by its handpicked managerial team. Absent a co-guarantee from Kurushima, neither would NKK guarantee a loan. And if Tsubouchi and NKK would not guarantee, Nippon Steel and Nissho Iwai would not do so either.

In short, neither the firm's creditors nor its shareholders would invest anything more in the firm. Ordinarily, such a firm would promptly go bankrupt. It did not, but only because SHI dominated the city of Sasebo, and Prime Minister Takeo Fukuda owed the city a massive political debt. When the government's nuclear-powered ship 'Mutsu' had developed a radioactive leak in 1974, all other ports had refused to take it. With a leaking nuclear ship sitting off the Japanese coast and nowhere to send it, Fukuda faced a political disaster. He averted it, but only when Sasebo agreed to take the ship.

For that favor Fukuda now intervened personally. He struggled mightily to accomplish anything at all. Repeatedly, he urged the banks to fund SHI.

Repeatedly, they refused. They would not loan the money unsecured and unguaranteed, they declared, and the firm could not secure and the shareholders would not guarantee.

Tsubouchi eventually did gain control and SHI did survive, but it survived largely without banks and only on a reduced scale. From 79.7 billion in March 1977, by 1979 its debt had fallen to 51.1 billion, by 1981 to 38.7 billion, and by 1983 to 10.2 billion. From 6968 employees in 1977, by 1979 its workforce fell to 4223, by 1981 to 3422, and by 1983 to 2760.

(iv) Other cases

Hanasaki: Other distressed firms – even big firms –expeditiously went out of business. In the early 1970s, the venerable 40-year-old Hanasaki firm was one of the largest Japanese manufacturers of women's clothing. When it tried to expand in 1976, it found itself with enormous unsold inventory: 1.6 to 1.7 billion yen on annual sales of 18.5 billion.

'We begged it several times to come up with a consolidated rationalization plan, and a plan to rebuild', recalled one Sumitomo Bank representative.[103] 'But it wouldn't comply.' So, when in October it saw Hanasaki's winter clothes moving slowly, the bank offset 200 million yen's worth of Hanasaki liabilities against Hanasaki's deposits. Early the next year it announced that 'there are limits to a bank's assistance', and declared an end to all further loans. Hanasaki promptly went out of business.

Hayashi: Sometimes a rescue succeeds, but only after creditors manipulate the bankruptcy process to oust the incumbents. The Hayashi firm had been one of the largest wool-spinning firms in Japan. When business fell in the 1977, the founder-president resigned. As his family had earlier pledged their stock in Hayashi Spinning to the Tokai Bank in exchange for its aid, they now sued to retrieve that stock.

Soon, rumors began to circulate that the family would liquidate the firm at the February shareholder's meeting. Apparently, they planned to use their equity stake to demand concessions from their creditors. Afraid of losing control, the Tokai Bank promptly filed for reorganization under the bankruptcy laws. Through the bankruptcy proceeding, it cut the incumbent shareholders' interests to less than 10% of the firm's stock. It then reorganized and revamped the firm. The factories continued to operate with the labor force uncut – but now under bank control.

[103] Apareru sangyō 'shissoku' [Apparel Industry Nose Dives] *ShūkanTōyō Keizai* (13 May 1978) 80.

Mitsumi: And sometimes if banks try to intervene, the firms reject the banks and restructure on their own. Electrical parts maker Mitsumi had fallen on hard times in 1970 after issuing bearer securities in Germany the previous year. In 1971 the Mitsui Bank sent in one of its men as Mitsumi vice president and another as director – this in addition to the Mitsui banker already on the 10-member board. As of early 1970, the Mitsui bank as Mitsumi's fourth-largest creditor had lent Mitsumi 340 million yen. By 1972 it was its largest creditor and had 635 million outstanding.

Within a year the Mitsui officers had largely disappeared. The vice president had become an ordinary director, and the other directors had vanished. Apparently, the incumbent managers – still under the control of an autocratic CEO – had fought the bankers and pushed them out. Where Mitsumi had had 3528 employees in January 1971, three years later it was down to 2002 employees. It survived, but for several years only on a much reduced scale.

c. The Evidence

If the 'main bank system' ever functioned, the anecdotes in b. suggest it functioned haphazardly at best. Banks missed problems. Firms failed. Banks jettisoned them when they did. Broader empirical evidence, however, suggests the system never functioned at all. Indeed, the evidence suggests it never existed. Consider the approximately 1000 firms listed on Section 1 (the largest firms) of the TSE in the 1980s and early '90s, and define the main bank as the bank that lends the most to a given firm.[104]

(i) Delegated monitoring

Main-bank theorists do not just claim that the main bank monitored its debtors. After all, good banks everywhere do keep tabs on their debtors. Rather, they claim that the main bank monitored on behalf of all other banks. Rather than waste their resources duplicating each other's efforts, the banks collectively delegated monitoring to the firm's main bank.

The hypothesis has an obvious testable implication: if Japanese banks monitor through board appointments and delegate that monitoring to a firm's main bank, then virtually all banker-directors should come from the main bank. By contrast, if banks do not delegate, then banker-directors should come from a variety of banks. Given that the firm will have closer ties to its main bank than to others (after all, by definition it has borrowed the most from that bank), it may appoint

[104] We take the empirical evidence from Y Miwa and JM Ramseyer 'Does Relationship Banking Matter? Japanese Bank-Borrower Ties in Good Times and Bad' (2005) 2 J of Empirical Legal Studies 261.

more directors from the main bank than elsewhere. If – but only if – banks delegate their monitoring to the main bank, however, will all banker-directors come from the main bank.

Banker-directors do not come only from the main bank. Instead, they come from a variety of banks. As of 1985, of their retired banker-directors, firms appointed 57% from their main bank. They appointed 1.1 mean retired banker-directors in total. They appointed a mean 0.6 from their main bank.

(ii) Main bank rescues

(a) Main bank stability

According to most accounts, Japanese banks implicitly agreed to rescue those distressed clients for which they acted as main bank. Effectively, the accounts claim that main banks offered implicit insurance policies against financial or economic distress. The claim suggests several testable propositions.

First, if firms purchase implicit insurance from their main bank, then firms should switch main banks seldom and those closest to insolvency should never switch. After all, the firm (by hypothesis) has paid the premiums on its policy for years. It will not – at the very point when it can expect to start collecting on the policy – try to switch carriers.

In fact, main bank relations were anything but stable – either among the profitable or the unprofitable. During each half-decade from 1980 to 1994, over a fifth of the firms found a new main bank. Just as the more profitable firms switched, so too did the less (the differences are not statistically significant): during 1980-85, 28% of the firms in the least profitable quartile switched main banks, while 30% of the others did; during 1986-90, 23% of the least profitable switched while only 20% of the others did; and during 1990-94, 27% of the least profitable shifted while 28% of the others did.

(b) Main bank dependence

Second, if main banks offered implicit insurance against financial distress, the firms most likely to have 'collected' on the policies would have been those closest to insolvency. If so, then on average the nearly insolvent firms should have owed a larger fraction of their loans to their lead bank than the other firms owed.

The phenomenon does not occur: main banks had not loaned a larger share of a firm's debt to the least profitable firms than to the others (none of the differences are statistically significant). During 1980-85, the least profitable quartile of firms borrowed from their main bank 27.8% of their loans while the others borrowed 30.6%. During 1986-90, the least profitable quartile borrowed 32.0% from their main bank while the other firms borrowed 33.9%. During 1990-94, the least profitable quartile borrowed 34.4%, while the others borrowed 33.8%.

(c) Change in main bank dependence

If the main bank implicitly agreed to shoulder a disproportionate amount of the additional loans troubled firms needed, then as firms entered financial distress they should also have increased the fraction of the debt they borrowed from their main bank. On average, a main bank would have lent additional funds to healthy firms roughly proportional to its share in the firm's existing debt. To the financially distressed firm, however, it should have increased that share.

This did not happen: the least profitable firms did *not* increase the fraction they borrowed from their lead bank. Again, partition the TSE firms by profitability quartile in 1980-85, 1986-90, and 1990-94. Then compare a) the mean increase in the fraction of its debt a firm borrowed from its main bank at the least profitable quartile against b) the mean increase at the others. According to the standard accounts, the increase should have been larger among the distressed firms than among the others. It was not. During 1980-85 and 1986-90, the main bank increased its share of a firm's debt more at the top three quartiles than at the bottom. During 1990-94, it cut its debt share less drastically at the top three quartiles than at the bottom. Again, none of the differences are statistically significant. The point, however, is clear: main banks did not try to help unprofitable firms.

(d) Expertise

Last, main-bank theorists typically claim banks helped troubled firms by dispatching experienced officers to the firm. As the anecdotes above relate, sometimes banks did indeed send their officers to troubled firms. Yet seldom did those officers 'rescue' the firms – for fundamentally they did not know how. Bankers may be smart, but they needed more than smarts to run an industrial firm. They needed experience, and that they did not have. Some of them had successfully run financial intermediaries, but none had built cars or sold detergents. Complained one businessman:[105]

> The biggest problem with having a bank control management is that bankers can't stop thinking like bankers. Sure, they can cut personnel and inventory. But they don't seem to realize that even in the middle of all the cut-backs, you've got to plan for the future and invest in the right facilities.

As Mansaku Takeda, senior consultant to the Daiichi Kangyō Bank, put it:[106]

> Banks are places to oversee loans. There's no reason to think a banker has any talent for running a firm, and there're precious few examples of firms that did better because a banker came to run them. ... Sure, bankers may be smart. But whether they have any managerial talent is another issue.

105 'Ginkō kanri' *ShūkanTōyō Keizai* (Tokyo Japan 18 March 1978) 80, 87.

106 M Takeda 'Ginkō keiei no "genten" in kaeru toki' [Returning to the Fundamentals of Bank Management] *Shūkan Tōyō Keizai* (Tokyo Japan 11 March 1978) 40, 41.

III. Genesis

1. Introduction

Three urban legends: government leadership, *keiretsu* groups, main banks. The legends do not just share a substantive resemblance. They share a common intellectual ancestry as well. For ultimately, all three trace their origins to the peculiar politics of the post-war university: to the overwhelming dominance of Marxism within Japanese economics departments on the one hand, and the hostility of Western Japan specialists toward modern (non-Marxist) economics on the other. To trace this intellectual odyssey, we begin with the legend of a powerful bureaucracy (2.). We then turn to the fables of the *keiretsu* (3.) and the main bank (4.).

2. Bureaucratic Power

a. Japanese Production

From the chaos of the war, the right emerged discredited. The left stood poised to grab control. In England, Labour had ousted Churchill. In China, Mao had Chang on the run. In the USSR, Khrushchev had yet to disclose Stalin's terror. All across Europe, social democrats had begun to transform their governments. And in Japan, two years after the war the Socialists grabbed the cabinet. They took the major newspapers. They took the national union federation. And they took almost all university social science departments.

By the 1950s, Marxists ran the economics departments. They excluded market-oriented scholars when they could, and virtually everywhere framed the debates. They framed a bizarre set of debates indeed. Take but a few articles from a standard index of journal articles in economics for the first half of 1967: 'Lenin's Concept of Imperialism', 'Dehumanization in Marx's Concept of Class', 'The Method of Monopoly Capitalism', 'New Currents in the World of Soviet Economics', 'A Study of "The Capital Accumulation Process" in Part I Section 7 of *Das Kapital*', and 'Lenin's Critique of Rosa Luxembourg's "Theory of Capital Accumulation"'.

Within these departments, legends of government planning flourished naturally. Majority politicians everywhere take credit for bull markets that co-incide with their tenure, of course. They do in Japan as well. When in the 1960s the GDP doubled in less than a decade, they happily claimed responsibility. Had not their prime minister, they pointed out, announced his plan to do just that?

When US politicians take credit, economists yawn. Trained in a world of Friedman and Stigler, they realize economies are not so docile. The GNP does not grow just because bureaucrats tell it to grow. Scholars raised on Engels and Marx, though, saw the world differently. Given a choice between attributing growth to bureaucratic planners and uncoordinated market competition, they chose the former. Invisible hand? What invisible hand? Whatever the case in the West, reasoned they, Japan grew because planners planned.

b. Western Consumption

For Western specialists on Japan, the tales of government planning represented dreams come true. During the last decades of the 20th century, economists had steadily amassed power in Western universities. They and their allies had taken over the business and public policy schools. They had begun to dominate scholarship in political science and law. Sometimes they dominated it even in sociology. They attracted the best students. And as a corollary, the other fields (outside natural science) had lost salaries, faculty positions, and research budgets.

Overwhelmingly, Western Japan specialists stood outside this economics juggernaut. For better or for worse, Western economics departments have long ignored country-specific expertise – and consequently at any given time only a handful of Western economics professors have been able to read Japanese. Western Japan specialists instead came from other departments. Primarily, they came either from departments (like literature) that top students avoided, or from the anti-economics camps within fields (like political science) besieged by economic theory. To them, the tales of government planning promised evidence that proved their rivals wrong. Did not economists insist that market planning could never work? In Japan, planners doubled the GDP in less than a decade. If economic theory proved the folly of government planning, well, Japan proved the folly of economics.

3. *Keiretsu*

The *keiretsu* owes its genesis to much the same dynamic. To Marxists of the late 1950s and early '60s, Japan was a world of 'bourgeois capitalism'. By standard Marxist theory, the country should have been plagued with 'contradictions' and 'dominated' by 'monopoly capital'. In the 1930s, Marxists had located that 'monopoly capital' in the *zaibatsu* conglomerates. By 1960, they were stuck. Although still caught in the world of 'bourgeois capitalism', they faced ruthlessly competitive markets. Their 'monopoly capital' was nowhere to be found.

Enter the ERI. To a shrewd entrepreneur, a Marxist market niche was as good as any other. If the Marxists could not find their 'monopoly capital', the ERI would invent it for them. And so it did. It called the monopoly capital '*keiretsu*', compiled annual membership rosters, and sold university libraries the expensive subscription.

To the Marxist-inclined, the ERI had a plausible story to tell. The war had largely bankrupted the family-controlled *zaibatsu*, but just to make sure the

Americans had confiscated (actually, bought on credit and then massively inflated the currency) each family's stock. They then banned the old trade names besides.

Once the Americans left in 1952, the government lifted the ban on the old names. Given the reputational capital the firms had earlier invested in those names, almost immediately they retrieved them. Yet Marxist theory does not deal with reputational capital. It does deal with 'monopoly capital'. When the formerly *zaibatsu* firms retrieved their old names, to a good leftist the action signaled nothing so much as a resurgence of the monopoly capital that had so cruelly dominated Japan before.

To create their new monopoly capital empires, the ERI merely traced the loans from the formerly *zaibatsu* (albeit now long-independent) financial institutions. On the basis of those loans, it sorted borrower firms among the financial institutions, and christened the resulting groups '*keiretsu*'. These groups, it proclaimed in 1960, were nothing other than 'monopolistic organizations of giant firms ... that constitute trusts and industrial-capital combines'. They 'have a bank at their apex, and pursue their domination of capital through loans and their consolidation of that domination through equity'.[107]

Western scholars welcomed the legend of the *keiretsu* as greedily as they welcomed the stories of government planning. Economists posited universal models of market competition, did they? In Japan, firms did not transact in markets at all. Instead, they traded within quasi-familial *keiretsu*, and on the basis not of self-interest but of generalized reciprocity and multi-stranded ties. Rather than maximize shareholder value, they disabled the stock markets through cross-holdings and maximized group welfare. If economists posited universal models of market competition, well, they posited models that excluded Japan.

4. Main Banks

For an ambitious *non*-Marxist economist (whether in the West or, increasingly after the early 1980s, in Japan) this now-longstanding legend of the *keiretsu* posed a challenge. If those anti-economic Neanderthals in political science or sociology – the ambitious economist apparently told himself – thought economics could not explain the *keiretsu*, they thought wrong. By the 1980s, economics did not just explain market behavior. Becker had analyzed crime, racial discrimination, and marriage. Coleman was transforming theory in sociology, Riker in political science, and Posner in law. Surely, he apparently reasoned, he could do the same with Japanese firms.

To recast the *keiretsu* in rational choice terms, modern economists simply transformed them into 'main bank' groups. They first re-described bank-centered

[107] Keizai Chōsa-kai (ed) *Keiretsu no kenkyū* [Research on the Keiretsu] (Keizai Chōsa-kai Tokyo 1960) 3-4.

keiretsu as networks of firms holding sets of 'implicit contracts' with their banks. To those implicit contracts, they then ascribed the purported characteristics of the *keiretsu*. A few more minor adjustments, and they had transformed the quasi-familial culture-bound *keiretsu* into incentive-compatible culture-free relationship banking.

Main-bank theorists then would use these *keiretsu*-turned-main-bank sets of stylized facts to other ends as well. In time, they would use them to illustrate the role of information economics in banking. They would use them to show the importance of 'relationship banking' more generally. And – to return to the assigned topic of this paper – they would use them to exemplify the 'many roles' banks play in the modern economy.

Alas, the stylized *keiretsu* facts described nothing that real firms and banks actually did. Neither did the re-stylized main bank facts.

5. A Postscript

As a modest postscript, consider a further implication this intellectual odyssey poses. More particularly, consider what all this implies about the apparent contrast between the US and Japanese economies. In most conventional accounts, the US economy captures the transactional structures and market behavior described by standard micro-economic theory. The Japanese economy epitomizes the opposite: webs of inter-twined, multi-faceted, culture-bound, relationship-based ties.

And yet, from whom did we obtain these descriptions? For our accounts of the US economy, we turned to reports by armies of financial economists poring over stock price tapes from Chicago. For our accounts of Japan, we turned to reports by Western sociologists and anti-rational-choice political scientists pouring over secondary work by Japanese Marxists.

Our two accounts describe different worlds. Did we expect anything else?

IV. Conclusions

Do banks have multiple roles? They take deposits. They lend. To ensure that they obtain their money back, they sometimes take security interests and guarantees. Do they do much else? Banking scholars apparently wish they did, and in the past two decades have latched onto Japanese 'main banks' for examples of the many roles they would have banks play. Alas, the tales of the main banks are so many urban legends – part of the broader legend about powerful Japanese bureaucrats and *keiretsu* corporate groups.

The Japanese government has not dismantled any interventionist regulatory regime, for (except in a very few sectors) it had no such regime to dismantle. At least since the 1960s, regulators controlled few means by which to induce firms to comply. Firms and banks have not dismantled their *keiretsu* corporate groups, for they had no such groups to dismantle. Even in their purported heyday of the 1960s, the groups never constituted anything more than the feverish figment of an over-active Marxist imagination. Firms and banks have not dismantled their main bank arrangements, for they had no such arrangements to dismantle. Banks never dominated firm governance, secondary banks never delegated monitoring to a firm's main bank, and banks never agreed (even implicitly) to rescue firms in distress.

The economy in post-war Japan was a competitive market economy rather than a controlled one, and it grew rapidly for just that reason. The government did not heavily regulate markets, large groups of firms did not stifle competition, and banks did not control firms. Instead, firms bought and sold, borrowed and lent, and thrived or failed – on highly competitive markets.

Know thy data, Zvi Grilliches told generations of budding Harvard econometricians. Office-chair theorists would do well to learn a little data too.

Legal Explanations on Bank Behavior

HIDEKI KANDA

Banks take deposits, lend, and participate in payment systems. Where permitted, they underwrite and sell investment securities. Banks, however, act under constraints. Those constraints come from laws, regulations, and other environments. This means that those constraints affect how banks in a given country behave. In the following, I will discuss two examples where somewhat unique bank behavior is found in Japan, and attempt to offer legal explanations.

I think how banks in Japan operate is not entirely clear. The bank-customer relationship in Japan has several distinct characteristics.[1] Some of them are common in other business relationships in Japan, and others are unique to banking transactions. Banking transactions between banks and their customer firms in Japan show three unique characteristics. First, banks and their customer firms engage in a very wide range of transactions, from straightforward lending to newer types of transactions, such as swap transactions, and even to a bank's stockholding in their customer firms. Second, a company usually establishes a long-term contractual relationship with more than one, and typically several, banks. One of these banks typically serves as the 'main bank.' Third, banks obtain a strong legal position under a standard form contract known as the Banking Transactions Agreement, but they sometimes show behavior that appears quite inconsistent with their strong legal position. To take a familiar situation where a firm is in financial trouble, the traditional behavior of the main bank (which usually has a first mortgage over the firm's property securing its loans) is often to pay off other debts (which are legally subordinated to the bank's claim) and to pay off outstanding debentures or bonds.

At least in the past, these three distinct characteristics were found in many situations, including daily credit transactions, rescue actions when the customer firm is in financial distress, and in the bank's stockholding in its customer firms.

There is a vast amount of literature on the Japanese firm.[2] Most articles, however, fail to discuss the interaction between law and practice. They usually do not consider the existence of legal rules that appear to encourage different behavior from what they think they observe about public companies in Japan. The inter-

[1] The discussion that follows draws from H Kanda 'Trends in Japanese Corporate Governance' in KJ Hopt and E Wymeersch (eds) *Comparative Corporate Governance* (de Gruyter Berlin New York 1997).

[2] There are numerous recent studies by economists about Japanese firms. The key question is whether Japanese and Western firms are different. See, for example, M Aoki and R Dore (eds) *The Japanese Firm* (OUP Oxford 1994).

action between law and practice is sometimes difficult to identify, but once it is properly identified, one can better ascertain how legal rules affect corporate behavior in Japan and thus obtain a better understanding of how firms operate in Japan.

Take as an example the main bank concept. While past research is divided as to whether the main bank is the most powerful monitor of its customer firm, such research does not show how legal rules affect the main bank's (and others') behavior.[3] The focus has been on the main bank's behavior when the costumer firm is in financial distress. The conventionally observed behavior of the main bank in such situations is to 'rescue' the firm. One question is how. Another question is under what legal rules. And the most important question is why. Past literature has tried to answer the first and third questions. But failure to consider the second question can easily lead to wrong answers to the other questions.

Some scholars have an interesting theory that the main bank is a delegated monitor (of other creditors).[4] The problem is that this does not explain what we observe. Moreover, in theory, two questions must be answered. First, why do other creditors delegate monitoring to the main bank? And how can they freeride on the main bank's monitoring efforts (or otherwise contract with the main bank)? Second, why does the main bank perform such 'excessive' monitoring? And why does it agree to that? The explanation the theory offers centers upon hypothetical (or implicit) contracting between the main bank and other creditors.

It seems, however, that this ex ante approach is the source of a problem. The main bank's rescue behavior is better explained when one focuses on the bank's behavior after the customer firm gets into financial trouble. In such situations, the bank (which usually is the first mortgage holder) has a choice: to foreclose the mortgage or to rescue the customer firm (often by employing a reorganization procedure). When a bank pursues the latter path, it is beneficial for the bank to take control of the whole reorganization process (given that the bank – and the debtor – will have better information than the other creditors). At least in the past, the main bank often paid off other debts (that were legally subordinated to its claim) and always paid off outstanding bonds. By doing so, the bank could take control of the restructuring process. Other creditors could have disagreed, but the bank was armed with the threat of enforcing its first mortgage right.

I think this suggests that enforcement costs associated with claims owned by banks with respect to their customer firms are the key factor that produces different bank behavior between Japan and other countries.

[3] A notable exception is JM Ramseyer's work. See 'Explicit Reasons for Implicit Contracts: The Legal Logic to the Japanese Main Bank System' in M Aoki and H Patrick (eds) *The Japanese Main Bank System* (OUP Oxford 1994) 231.

[4] P Sheard 'The Main Bank System and Corporate Monitoring and Control in Japan' (1989) 11 Journal of Economic Behavior and Organization 399.

Take another example: the popularity of promissory notes in Japan.[5] Until recently, promissory notes were often used in business transactions in Japan. Typically, when a firm purchased widgets, it paid by writing a promissory note to the seller. The seller then went to a bank, which discounted the note. This style of financing was popular in Japan. Internationally, a more popular way of financing seems to be that banks lend to their customers by taking accounts receivable as collateral. In the above example, the buyer would not write a promissory note but simply buy the widgets on credit, which seems easier and less costly. However, this form of financing has been less popular than promissory note financing in Japan. Why?

One explanation is concerned with cost differences between promissory note financing and receivable financing. On one hand, Japanese law is not well developed in permitting the creation of a security interest for future and unspecified receivables in Japan. If that were possible, accounts receivable financing would seem less costly. On the other hand, when a promissory note is not honored (that is, if the writer of the promissory note does not pay when the note is due), not only the bank that discounted the note but all banks that participate in the exchange system of promissory notes refuse to do business with the writer, in accordance with the rules of the clearing house with which notes are processed. The court held that such a rule was not a violation of the Anti-Monopoly Act.[6] Of course, private parties have tried to circumvent this rule. For instance, when the note was dishonored, the customer then would attempt to continue the business by using the spouse or other relative's name in dealing with the bank.[7] In any event, the popularity of promissory notes in Japan, and the unique behavior of banks in Japan in that they would take promissory notes rather than accounts receivable, is noteworthy. This area may be worth exploring further as an interesting example of a situation where law may produce unique banking behavior in a given country.

In sum, a deeper and more systematic examination of the interactions between law and bank behavior would enrich our understanding of bank behavior and related matters in Japan and other countries.

[5] See generally T Matsumura and M Ryser 'Revelation of Private Information About Unpaid Notes in the Trade Credit Bill System in Japan' (1995) 24 J Legal Studies 165. See also RJ Mann 'Verification Institutions in Financing Transactions' (1999) 87 Georgetown L J 2225.

[6] Tokyo High Court Judgment of 17 November 1983, 690 Kinyu Shoji Hanrei 4.

[7] See, for example, Supreme Court Judgment of 12 December 1978, 22 Minshu 13-2963 [brother's name was used].

Redirecting Japan's Multi-level Governance

LUKE NOTTAGE*

I. Introduction

These remarks were sparked in part by two terms in the title of Professor Ogus' paper: 'levels of regulation' and 'risks'. He focuses rather on a 'goal' of regulation, namely paternalism and possible contemporary justifications for it. It is commendable and timely to revisit that, in the light of the latest (behavioralist) wave of law and economics thinking[1] – although his concern may reflect a British mood engendered by the Blair government's 'third way', and raise the hackles of some American and even Japanese theorists. However, a more specific starting point for my remarks is an example where Ogus indicates that paternalistic regulation needs closer examination: controls imposed on the production and distribution of British beef, especially after the British government admitted in 1996 that Bovine Spongiform Encephalopathy (BSE, or 'mad cow disease') could indeed be linked to variant Creuzfeldt-Jakob Disease (vCJD), fatal to humans.

* Research on comparative regulation aspects of this work is supported by the Australian Research Council (Discovery Grant A1753, 2004-6). Research on the 'mad cow disease' case study was supported by grants from the University of Sydney's Legal Scholarship Support Fund, and preliminary conclusions were published in L Nottage and M Trezise 'Mad Cows and Japanese Consumers' (2003) 14 Australian Product Liability Reporter 125. In addition to my co-author and those thanked therein, I am grateful to Harald Baum, Rainer Kulms, and Axel Metzger (Max Planck Institute for Foreign Private Law and Private International Law, Hamburg), Hunter Nottage (Advisory Centre for WTO Law), Takao Tanase (Kyoto University), and participants at the Berlin conference for stimulating discussions, particularly about developments in German, EU, Japanese, and global governance.

1 See also generally CR Sunstein *Risk and Reason: Safety, Law, and the Environment* (Cambridge University Press Cambridge 2002). For an application in international sales law, see L Nottage 'Who's Afraid of the Vienna Sales Convention (CISG)? A New Zealander's View from Australia' *Paper presented at the International Trade Law conference* (Victoria University of Wellington, 18 February 2005). Specifically on 'asymmetric paternalism', see C Cammerer and others 'Regulation for Conservatives: Behavioral Economics and the Case for "Asymmetric Paternalism"' (2003) 151 U of Pennsylvania L Rev 1211-54.

I agree that there may have been overreactions, and that certain developments at the European Union (EU) level may not have been optimal. However, as explained in Part III below, BSE epitomizes a growing number of risks in contemporary societies involving great scientific uncertainty, requiring a response from the legal world. Further, the EU response seems to have been better than regulation at the national (UK) level, or at the global level (potentially, the WTO and other international standard-setting bodies). Japan's poor regulatory response before and after its first mad cow was discovered in 2001, almost exactly three years prior to this symposium, suggests that a regional dimension there would have been even more helpful. Accordingly, and perhaps ironically as a non-European, I will end up advocating that Japan should learn from and develop EU-like regional arrangements. Adding new levels to its regulatory apparatus would build up capacity for more effective and legitimate harmonization relating to a range of other complex human and animal health risks nowadays, such as Genetically Modified Organisms.[2] It would also provide extra underpinning for other aspects of Japan's ongoing program of economic liberalization that do not directly implicate such risks or constraints, since dismantling barriers to trade and investment has been the primary force behind the EU project.[3]

[2] Cf New Zealand Law Commission 'Liability for Loss Resulting from the Development, Supply or Use of Genetically Modified Organisms' (2002) NZLC Study Paper 14, freely downloadable via <http://www.lawcom.govt.nz> (14 June 2005); with M Lee and M Burrell 'Liability for the Escape of GM Seeds: Pursuing the "Victim"?' (2002) 65 Modern L Rev 517-37; and G Shaffer and M Pollack 'Regulating Between National Fears and Global Disciplines: Agricultural Biotechnology in the EU' (2004) 10/04 Jean Monnet Working Papers <http://www.jeanmonnetprogram.org/papers/04/041001.html>; and the debate on the new EU regime versus WTO standards, eg J Scott 'European Regulation of GMOs: Thinking about "Judicial Review" in the WTO' (2004) 4/04 Jean Monnet Working Papers <http://www.jeanmonnetprogram.org/papers/04/040401.pdf> (14 June 2005).

[3] See generally C Barnard *The Substantive Law of the EU: The Four Freedoms* (OUP Oxford 2004). As observed by R Dore 'Setting Agendas' in Anglo-Japanese Academy (ed) *Proceedings for the Anglo-Japanese Academy 'Workshop for Young Social Scientists' (4-6 and 9 September 2001) and 'Conference on National, Regional and Global Transition: A Common Agenda for Anglo-Japanese Relations in the 21st Century' (7-8 September 2001)* (ICCLP University of Tokyo 2002) vii, 19-27; and G Jackson 'Corporate Governance in Germany and Japan: Liberalization Pressures and Responses' in K Yamamura and W Streeck (eds) *The End of Diversity? Prospects of German and Japanese Capitalism* (Cornell University Press Ithaca 2003), this EU liberalization agenda does seem to have generated a stronger move towards deregulation in Germany compared to Japan since the mid-1990s. Further, pushed along by the European Court of Justice in its *Cassis de Dijon* judgment as early as 1979, and especially as the EU gained 'creeping competence' over socio-legal problems, the trend has been towards less invasive forms of harmonization in advancing economic integration: see L Nottage 'Legal Harmonization' in D Clarke (ed) *International Encyclopedia of Law and the Social Sciences* (Sage New York forthcoming 2005). However, the degree and nature of regulation in Germany may have been relatively higher, and market-opening measures from the EU need not mean extensive deregulation, depending on where the new lines are drawn. Further, Germany may have had a head start over Japan in the 1990s, in a growing acceptance of the need for 'regime

cont. ...

Euro-skeptics may shudder at the idea of recreating another level of governance for Japan.[4] But Japan has long experience in developing, and (to a lesser extent) legitimizing, multi-level governance processes at least *within* its borders. Ironically, just as self-regulation and co-regulation have become the buzzwords in Europe and Australia since the 1990s, Japan is moving in the other direction – towards a more straightforward form of liberal law-making and law enforcement. Aiming at further happy convergence, Japan should now redefine and redirect its multi-level governance system, to include a new *external* dimension in the form of regional arrangements. One possibility is to add clearer provisions on regulatory harmonization, and develop new EU-like institutions – or at least processes – within Japan's recent bilateral arrangements. Those comprise even the loose trade facilitation arrangement with Australia, and especially the free trade agreements already with Singapore and Mexico, and foreseeably soon Thailand and Korea.

Japanese policy makers will take some convincing to move in this direction, especially those involved in negotiating such arrangements, who have tended to focus on economic dimensions in a narrower sense.[5] To make this proposal for multi-level governance more plausible, therefore, Part II ties it also to broader 'neo-proceduralist' models of law paralleling 're-regulation' patterns observed worldwide since the 1990s. This constellation can be contrasted with the 'regulatory state' underpinned by welfare statism, and hard-core 'deregulation' under-

change' as problems in extending its socioeconomic model to the former East Germany became apparent by the mid-1990s. See generally also H Kitschelt and W Streeck (eds) *Germany: Beyond the Stable State* (Frank Cass Publishers London 2003).

[4] Generally, for several reasons, this chapter uses the term 'governance' instead of 'regulation'. First, the traditional association of 'regulation' with direction provided by 'public' authorities still makes it difficult to extend the concept to now frequently observed overlap and blurring with 'private' norm-setting and enforcement (cf J Black 'Critical Reflections on Regulation' ESCR Centre for Analysis of Risk and Regulation Discussion Paper 4 (2002) <http://www.lse.ac.uk/collections/CARR/pdf/Disspaper4.pdf> (27 June 2005). Secondly, especially as regulation also 'goes global' (S Picciotto 'Introduction: Reconceptualizing Regulation in the Era of Globalization' (2002) 29 J of L and Society 1-11), its normative dimensions have increasingly come to the fore (Nottage [n 3]). Thirdly, more formalistically, 'governance' was the broader term framing this conference, and 'multi-level governance' has become a widely used expression to analyze contemporary developments, particularly in the EU (see eg C Joerges 'On the Legitimacy of Europeanising Europe's Private Law: Considerations on a Law of Justi(ce)-fication (justum facere) for the EU Multi-Level System' EUI Working Paper LAW 2003/2 <http://www.iue.it/PUB/law03-3.pdf> [27 June 2005]; Shaffer and Pollack [n 2]).

[5] See generally METI's 'Japan's Policy on FTAs/EPAs' (March 2005, <http://www.meti.go.jp/english/information/downloadfiles/FTAprogress200503.pdf>, especially the 'FTA Schedule' chart [27 June 2005]). But cf eg a METI-commissioned study released in 2004 on the environmental impact of a possible free trade agreement between Japan and Korea (formerly available via <http://www.meti.go.jp/english/policy/index_externaleconomicpolicy.html>; and, more generally, H-B Lee and S Okuda 'Possibilities of Realizing a Japan-Korea FTA' (2004) 18 J of East Asian Affairs 131.

pinned by neo-liberalism. Both those alternatives are problematic for Japan, making the 'neo-proceduralist' approach more viable, including my proposal in the latter vein to develop a regional level regulatory interface.

II. Contextualizing and Conceptualizing for Japan

A broader theoretical framework for regulatory intervention is set out by Ogus, with illustrations taken primarily from Europe and the US Let me therefore first sketch some background in Japan, especially major regulatory shifts (Part II.A) and models of law that explicitly or implicitly underlie them (Part II.B). This sets the stage for extending the combination of 're-regulation' and neo-proceduralism for Japan (Part II.C), to address contemporary challenges such as BSE (Part III).

1. Regulation, Deregulation, and Re-regulation

The starting point in Japan, as is widely known, has been the perception (at least) of a strong regulatory state, particularly from (at least) the 1960s through to the 1980s. The conventional wisdom held this model to involve pervasive ex ante control through public authorities, especially bureaucrats, negotiating with the business world and citizens largely unconstrained by loosely defined and enforced legal norms.

Even from the early 1980s, the fiscal costs involved did prompt some attempts at downsizing and reforming the administrative apparatus (*gyōsei kaikaku*), or 'relaxation' of regulation (*kisei kanwa*).[6] Changes in particular sectors, especially financial markets, have also been re-appraised in analyses since the 1990s. The political upheavals and then deepening economic stagnation over that 'lost decade' led to pervasive and more intense deregulatory initiatives, at least in some sectors.[7]

[6] H Otake 'From "Participatory Democracy" to "Freedom of Choice": The Transition in France and Japan, 1968-1983' (2004) 1 Kyoto J of L and Politics 79-99.

[7] H Otake (ed) *Power Shuffles and Policy Processes: Coalition Government in Japan in the 1990s* (Japan Center for International Exchange Tokyo 2000); J Basedow and others (eds) *Economic Regulation and Competition: Regulation of Services in the EU, Germany and Japan* (Kluwer Law International The Hague 2002). Increased media attention to 'reform' over the 1990s originally focused on specific problems such as the bad loans disaster, then increasingly on broader 'structural' issues: see I Kume 'Politics of Institutional Complementarity: Unbundling the Japanese Management System' (2004) 37 Kobe U L Rev 1-18. But some assert the emergence of new 'iron triangles' impeding extensive change: see eg P Maclachlan 'Post Office Politics in Modern Japan: The Postmasters, Iron Triangles and the Limits of Reform' (2004) 20 J of Japanese Studies 281-314.

Nonetheless, Japan has begun to track other advanced industrialized democracies that have joined this bandwagon, as economic globalization also gained momentum from the 1980s. 'Re-regulation' was observed and analyzed first in the US and the EU (including the UK), but similar phenomena are evident also in New Zealand and Finland, as well as countries as diverse as Australia and Mexico.[8] One commonly observed aspect involves substituting sector-specific regulation for more general rules, especially competition law.[9] A Japanese twist is the possibility of 'self-regulation' instead filling the space opened by deregulation, but developing in anti-competitive forms at least in weaker sectors, in the shadow of ongoing enforcement problems in competition law as a whole.[10] More generally, Japan is said to be undertaking 'managed globalization', with differential change depending on the competitiveness and openness of particular sectors.[11] That analysis seems overly schematic, as evidenced by the uptake so far of the more Anglo-American corporate governance option now available to large Japanese firms.[12] Where the theory does have some traction, moreover, Japan's

[8] Respectively, see eg G Majone *Deregulation or Re-Regulation?: Regulatory Reform in Europe and the United States* (Pinter London 1990); SK Vogel *Freer Markets, More Rules: Regulatory Reform in Advanced Industrial Countries* (Cornell University Press Ithaca 1996); L Nottage 'New Zealand Law through the Internet: The Commonwealth Law Tradition and Socio-Legal Experimentation' (1999) 12 Forum of Intl Development Studies [Nagoya University] 55; C Parker 'Restorative Justice in Business Regulation? The Australian Competition and Consumer Commission's Use of Enforceable Undertakings' (2004) 67 Modern L Rev 209-246; R Snyder *Politics After Neoliberalism: Reregulation in Mexico* (Cambridge University Press Cambridge 2001). More generally, see eg L Weiss *States in the Global Economy: Bringing Domestic Institutions Back In* (Cambridge University Press Cambridge 2003); and B Simmons and Z Elkins 'The Globalization of Liberalization: Policy Diffusion in the International Political Economy' (2004) 98 American Political Science Rev 171-89.

[9] Cf also J Basedow 'Economic Regulation in Market Economies' in Basedow and others (n 7) 1, 2-3; K Hopt 'Trans-Sectoral Issues of Regulation: Concluding Remarks on Banking, Capital Market, Insurance and Telecommunications Regulation' in Basedow and others (n 7) 305, 311-312.

[10] U Schaede *Cooperative Capitalism: Self-Regulation, Trade Association, and the Antimonopoly Law in Japan* (OUP Oxford 2000). See also eg M Kojo 'Kōsei Torihiki Iinkai no Dokkinhō shikō [Enforcement of the Anti-Monopoly Act by the Fair Trade Commission]' (2002) 1128 Jurisuto 101. But see JO Haley *Antitrust in Germany and Japan: The First Fifty Years, 1947-1998* (University of Washington Press Seattle 2001), highlighting 'sanctions' via the media, and growing formal enforcement powers (especially when comparing Germany, rather than just the US).

[11] U Schaede and W Grimes *Japan's Managed Globalization: Adapting to the Twenty-First Century* (M E Sharpe New York 2002).

[12] L Nottage and L Wolff 'Corporate Governance and Law Reform in Japan: From the Lost Decade to the End of History?' in R Haak and M Pudelko (eds) *Japanese Management: In Search of a New Balance between Continuity and Change* (Palgrave Macmillan New York forthcoming 2005); CJ Milhaupt in this volume.

experience seems to have much in common with patterns in other countries that have deregulated – but also re-regulated.[13]

2. Models of Law in Japan: Welfarist, Neo-liberal, Neo-proceduralist

Underpinning each of these regulatory paradigms is a different way of analyzing (and evaluating) law in Japan. Again, there are similarities to, but with some

Type of Law/ Characteristics	**Managerial law**	**Autonomous law**	**Self-ordering law**
Fundamental characteristic	Means to realize certain political ends	Generality, formality, universalism	Informality, spontaneous nature
Thinking and decision-making method	Means-end scheme	Condition-effect scheme	Consensual coordination scheme
Legal process	Administrative process	Adjudication process	Private negotiation process
Legal relationship	Vertical relationship	Triad relationship	Horizontal relationship
Response strategy for new area	Legal instrumentalism	Legalism	Informalism

variations on, conceptual frameworks developed in the US and Europe since the 1980s.[14] Professor Shigeaki Tanaka, a leading legal theorist in Japan who has

[13] H Yoshimatsu *Internationalization, Corporate Preferences and Commercial Policy in Japan* (St Martin's Press New York 2000) emphasizes the importance of Japan's more internationally competitive firms and associations in pushing along deregulation. Many studies now document Japan's more complex re-regulatory experience. See eg Basedow and others (n 7); P Drysdale and JA Amyx (eds) *Japanese Governance: Beyond Japan Inc* (Routledge Curzon London 2003); JA Amyx *Japan's Financial Crisis: Institutional Rigidity and Reluctant Change* (Princeton University Press 2004); JR Lincoln and ML Gerlach *Japan's Network Economy: Structure, Persistence, and Change* (Cambridge University Press Cambridge 2004). On the variable adaptation of 'New Public Management' within Japan's bureaucracy itself, see also M Hori 'Japanese Public Administration and Its Adaptation to New Public Management' (2003) 20 Ritsumeikan L Rev 1; M Hori 'Japanese Public Bureaucracy in the Era of Globalization' (2004) 21 Ritsumeikan L Rev 1; and compare the contribution by T Ginsburg in this volume.

[14] Cf eg G Teubner 'Substantive and Reflexive Elements in Modern Law' (1983) 17 L & Society Rev 239. A related essay, published in German the following year, has been widely read in Japanese translation: G Teubner (H Kashizawa, trans) 'Hōka – gainen, tokuchō, genkai, kaihisaku [Legalization: Concepts, Defining Features, Limits, Ways Forward]' (1990) 59 Kyūdai Hōgaku 235-292.

provided much of the intellectual firepower behind its current wave of judicial system reforms, presents the following 'model of three types of law'.[15]

A common starting point has been growing dissatisfaction, even in Japan especially since the 1990s, with 'managerial law' – or what I call 'welfarist' law, to emphasize parallels with Japan's regulatory state. Both involve increasing policy-based intervention by the legal system in social and economic ordering. In private law, for example, this emerged first through case law innovations (eg accelerating invocation of general clauses like the principle of good faith), and then specific legislation (particularly to protect consumers in narrow areas of activity).[16] Since the late 1990s, however, the move has been away again from particular measures to 'protect the weaker party', and towards more general information disclosure.[17] This tracks a more widespread perception of regulatory failure, linked to the over-ambitious agenda and relatively crude regulatory methods adopted under welfare statism. Anyway, on several key measures, Japan's welfare statism remained an odd hybrid on the spectrum with Anglo/American 'liberal market economies' at one end, and continental European 'coordinated market economies' at the other.[18]

That more long-standing ambivalence in Japan's economy and polity has made it easier for theorists like Professors Miwa and Ramseyer ('M&R') to try to take Japanese law 'back to the future'. They perceive and advocate what I view as a 'neo-liberal' model, relating to Tanaka's 'self-ordering law' paradigm, which corresponds also to a hard-core deregulation agenda. Over a decade or more, they

[15] S Tanaka 'A Perspective on the Reconstruction of the Japanese Legal Ordering in the 21st Century' (2004) 1 Kyoto J of L and Politics 9, 19. See also Editorial Board 'In Commemoration of Founding the Kyoto Journal of Law and Politics' (2004) 1 Kyoto J of L and Politics 1.

[16] N Segawa 'Minpō' (2002) 491 Shosai no mado 2.

[17] S Kozuka 'The Use of Economic Analysis in Japanese Commercial Law' *Paper presented at the ANJeL conference 'Japanese Law on Trial'* (University of Sydney, 23 February 2005) available at <http://www.law.usyd.edu.au/anjel/documents/23Feb2005Conf/Kozuka2005_EconomicAnalysis.pdf> (27 June 2005). Cf also eg V Taylor 'Consumer Contract Governance in a Deregulating Japan' (1997) 27 Victoria U of Wellington L Rev 99. For Japanese private law more generally, see Z Kitagawa 'A Reflection on the Three Law Models' in J Becker (ed) *Recht im Wandel seines sozialen und technologischen Umfeldes [Law Amidst Changes in Its Social and Technological Milieu]* (CH Beck Munich 2002) 559. Professor Kitagawa raises concerns overlapping with those presented here. He criticizes both the conventional 'Western model' (the liberal Civil Code that Japan sought to adopt in the late 19th century), and the simplistic 'Pluralist model' that gained currency during the 1990s (emphasizing and acclaiming idiosyncrasies in Japanese law and practice). He sketches an interdisciplinary 'Law Model of the Near Future', able to deal more effectively with problems such as the human genome, 'system contracts', defectively delivered information, and copyright in a thoroughly digital era.

[18] Compare PA Hall and D Soskice *Varieties of Capitalism: The Institutional Foundations of Comparative Advantage* (OUP Oxford 2001), with L Nottage 'Japanese Corporate Governance at a Crossroads: Variation in "Varieties of Capitalism"' (2001) 27 The North Carolina J of Intl L & Commercial Regulation 255, and K Pistor's contribution in this volume.

(and a few other close associates) have developed this remarkable set of propositions:

- Japanese law is already clear and predictable, as urged by other neo-liberals.[19] This is true not only for (some) everyday situations, like resolving traffic accident disputes.[20] The behavior of Japanese judges is also predictable in (some) categories of 'politically charged' cases: they will tend to rule in favor of the dominant Liberal Democratic Party (LDP) preferences.[21]
- Strict liability in product liability had been achieved anyway by private ordering, namely by manufacturers developing their own certification and insurance schemes.[22]
- 'Administrative guidance' (*gyōsei shidō*) is not powerful, because damages claims can be brought, and were quite successful against 'jawboning' bureaucrats in local governments – less under LDP sway since the late 1960s.[23]
- Relational contracting in supply chains is largely a myth, because relationship-specific investments are actually limited.[24] Because vertical integration is

[19] Cf eg RA Epstein *Simple Rules for a Complex World* (Harvard University Press Cambridge 1995); RA Epstein *Skepticism and Freedom: A Modern Case for Classical Liberalism* (University of Chicago Press Chicago 2003).

[20] JM Ramseyer and M Nakazato 'The Rational Litigant: Settlement Amounts and Verdict Rates in Japan' (1989) 18 J of Legal Studies 263. But see L Nottage 'The Present and Future of Product Liability Dispute Resolution in Japan' (2000) 27 William Mitchell L Rev 215 (pointing out eg the more complex factual scenarios in product liability dispute resolution), and L Nottage 'Form, Substance and Neo-Proceduralism in Comparative Contract Law: The Law in Books and the Law in Action in England, New Zealand, Japan and the US' (PhD in Law thesis Victoria University of Wellington 2002) (comparing fewer 'bright-line rules' in Japan's contract law). Cf also the recent literature on cognitive biases (n 1), which should anyway afflict 'rational litigants' deciding whether and how to settle claims even after traffic accidents.

[21] JM Ramseyer and E Rasmusen *Measuring Judicial Independence: The Political Economy of Judging in Japan* (University of Chicago Press Chicago 2003). But see eg JO Haley 'The Japanese Judiciary: Maintaining Integrity, Autonomy and the Public Trust' Washington University in St Louis School of Law Faculty Working Papers (2003) <http://law.wustl.edu/Academics/Faculty/Workingpapers/TheJapaneseJudiciary10_03.pdf>. For rare engagement by a Japanese legal academic, see M Usami 'Saiban rinri toshite no shihōken no dokuritsu [The Independence of the Judiciary Branch as Judicial Ethics]' [2003] Hōritsu Jihō 932.

[22] JM Ramseyer 'Products Liability through Private Ordering: Notes on a Japanese Experiment' (1996) 144 U of Pennsylvania L Rev 1823. But see L Nottage *Product Safety and Liability Law in Japan: From Minamata to Mad Cows* (Routledge Curzon London 2004) 175. The latter points out that there is no data confirming Ramseyer's claim that the industry-operated scheme had voluntarily adopted a strict liability approach to product defects; and also stresses the well-documented problem that the scheme was (and remains) virtually unknown to consumers, even those suffering injuries from certified products.

[23] JM Ramseyer 'Rethinking Administrative Guidance' in M Aoki and G Saxonhouse (eds) *Finance, Governance and Competitiveness in Japan* (OUP Oxford 2000). But see eg T Nakagawa 'Administrative Informality in Japan: Governmental Activities Outside Statutory Authorization' (2000) 52 Administrative L Rev 175.

still less common in Japan, the implication is presumably that the arm's length spot contracting beloved of neoclassical economists is pervasive, and rightly so. This also means that vertical keiretsu (corporate groups) were largely defunct, even before Carlos Ghosn ('le cost-cutter') arrived to restructure Nissan's supply chains.[25]

- The 'main bank' is a total myth, invented by some Japanese Marxists and believed by gullible foreign economists and lawyers. This also helps kill off the notion of horizontal keiretsu,[26] even before financial markets crises and reorganization from the late 1990s.
- Lifelong employment is basically a myth, too. In its heyday, it only ever applied to a limited proportion of the workforce. For them, it was forced on employers by mandatory rules developed by courts.[27]
- Correspondingly, disdain for shareholders in Japanese corporate governance is also a 'fable'.[28]

Yet, why do so many economists and lawyers – even non-Marxists – still not believe this iconoclastic ensemble? There are grains of truth in each of these assertions, and the evidence chosen to support them. However, as indicated by some of the literature cited here against key studies published by M&R, each overall proposition goes too far. For example, Professor Curtis Milhaupt has pointed out numerous problems with their (lack of) historical or comparative analysis and with other current data on horizontal corporate groups, as well as their reinterpretations of the enduring nature of ties between main banks and their

[24] Y Miwa and JM Ramseyer 'Rethinking Relationship-Specific Investments: Subcontracting in the Japanese Automobile Industry' (2000) 98 Michigan L Rev 2636. But see eg SE Masten 'Reaffirming Relationship-Specific Investments' (2000) 98 Michigan L Rev 2668.

[25] On the latter, see generally D Magee *Turnaround: How Carlos Ghosn Rescued Nissan* (Harper Business New York 2003).

[26] Y Miwa and JM Ramseyer 'The Myth of the Main Bank: Japan and Comparative Corporate Governance' (2002) 27 L and Social Inquiry 401. But see eg C Milhaupt 'On the (Fleeting) Existence of the Main Bank System and Other Japanese Economic Institutions' (2002) 27 L and Social Inquiry 425.

[27] Note, however, that this judicial development seems quite 'politically charged', and yet contrary to conservative politicians' preferences. Product liability or environmental cases seem all the more so.

[28] S Kaplan and JM Ramseyer 'Those Japanese with Their Disdain for Shareholders – Another Fable for Academy' (1996) 32 Washington U L Q 403. But see eg Z Shishido 'Reform in Japanese Corporate Law and Corporate Governance: Current Changes in Historical Perspective' (2001) 49 AJCL 653; Kume (n 7); JO Haley 'Career Employment, Corporate Governance, and Japanese Exceptionalism' Washington University in St Louis School of Law Faculty Working Papers no 04-27-04 (2004) <http://law.wustl.edu/Academics/Faculty/Workingpapers/Haley/CorporateGovernance04-27-04.pdf> (27 June 2005); and CJ Milhaupt and MD West *Economic Organizations and Corporate Governance in Japan: The Impact of Formal and Informal Rules* (OUP Oxford 2004).

clients.[29] Working through such exchanges, M&R rarely seem to come out ahead on their key generalizations, even on a 'balance of probabilities' standard – that is, it almost always seems that they are more likely wrong than right. Even when they are at their most compelling, so that the point might be conceded, it is hardly by much, and this makes it difficult still to take a leap of faith and accept the entire package.[30] Ultimately, M&R will first have to convert mainstream professional economists, and indeed other social scientists of industrial organization.[31] Then they must provide a more profound explanation to lawyers – always interested in the normative as well as the factual, the present and future as well as the past – as to why this new paradigm is most relevant.[32]

In particular, even if they can prove convincingly to everyone that main banks never in fact existed, for example, why should lawyers care? Isn't it enough that virtually everyone acted on the assumption that they did? If so, despite this lesson, collective delusion or other cognitive problems may re-surface – and even prove useful. Alternatively, even 'socially constructed' institutions or associated rules may provide helpful 'focal points' for social ordering and decision-making.[33]

Even without going that far, what lessons for the present and future should we draw from firmer conclusions generated by the tsunami of studies emanating from M&R? Assuming for example that Japanese judges until the early 1990s did

[29] Milhaupt (n 26) notes that key post-war *keiretsu* are direct descendants of pre-war *zaibatsu*; business groups are found in many other countries, even without Marxist conspiracies; and that OECD and other data reveal significant mutual shareholdings, especially given that 33.3 percent provides the crucial blocking stake under Japanese corporate law. He also criticizes M&R for not including all intra-group trading ties, or examining intra-group personnel relations. (Related especially to the latter, see also now Milhaupt's analysis in this volume, demonstrating how some firms adopting the new 'Anglo-American' option in corporate governance are in fact using it in a more German way, namely to control corporate groups.) On main banks, Milhaupt stresses how the data presented can instead be reinterpreted as indicating instead significant loyalty of the bankers, and how some further data instead suggests a link to comparatively fewer bankruptcies – especially of larger firms. Almost all these points, as well as Milhaupt's broader methodological critique, are still not addressed by M&R in their contribution to this volume.

[30] Consider an analogy with boxing – quite appropriate also in view of the increasingly pugilistic style adopted by M&R. Engaging with their work is like watching a close match where the boxers are quite evenly matched, so that when the judges add up who came out ahead over all rounds, the declared overall winner often does not seem a convincing choice.

[31] Cf eg Y Arikawa and H Miyajima 'Relationship Banking in Post-Bubble Japan' RIETI Discussion Papers 05-E-015 (2005) <http://www.rieti.go.jp/jp/publications/dp/05e015.pdf> (27 June 2005); R Haak and M Pudelko (eds) *Japanese Management: In Search of a New Balance between Continuity and Change* (Palgrave Macmillan New York forthcoming 2005).

[32] Cf generally eg D Vick 'Interdisciplinarity and the Discipline of Law' (2004) 31 J of L and Society 163.

[33] Cf generally eg T Ginsburg and R McAdams 'Adjudicating in Anarchy: An Expressive Theory of International Dispute Resolution' (2004) 45 William and Mary L Rev 1229.

tend to rule in favor of the LDP in politically charged cases, acting like good little butlers anticipating their masters' every need, then surely they will have become sensitive to the more fluid party politics since their masters fell dramatically from power in 1993.[34] M&R do not really address such questions, but it seems that they have a two-pronged dual agenda, as Milhaupt has also pointed out regarding their work on corporate groups and main banks. First, they wish to show that very conventional assumptions of economic rationality apply to adequately explain law-related behavior in Japan. This implies that if incentives generated by existing legal and social institutions are changed, other predictable outcomes will readily follow. Secondly, therefore, they wish to develop a normative agenda: introducing reforms that will generate the most economically efficient system. In particular, by asserting that Japan in fact already had operated almost as a neo-classical free market economy even after World War II – making complications like 'transaction cost economics' irrelevant – M&R imply that it will be straight-forward to perfect this model in Japan. That means complete deregulation, and the model of 'self-ordering law'.

In other words, the overarching problem remains that M&R have discovered everything in Japan that neoclassical first-wave law and economists expected (and wanted) to find in market-oriented economies like the US – except they didn't.[35] As one economics lecturer warned me years ago, when an economist pulls a rabbit out of the hat ('proving' an unusual hypothesis), the response should be to try to work out when and how he or she put the rabbit in the hat in the first place (the assumptions and data chosen to test the hypothesis). Further, social psychologists now warn us of human tendencies towards 'confirmatory bias', whereby we interpret ambiguous evidence to confirm current hypotheses about the world.[36] Secondly, taking this a step further, although M&R do profess to be conducting purely positive economic analysis,[37] their normative preference for laissez faire becomes readily apparent. Yet, as a moral philosophy – so

[34] See generally SR Reed *Japanese Electoral Politics: Creating a New Party System* (Routledge London, New York 2003). More specifically on the partial but significant upset this has caused to the old regime, see JAA Stockwin 'Electoral Pressures for Change: The Effect of Political Reform' in P Drysdale and JA Amyx (eds) *Japanese Governance: Beyond Japan Inc* (Routledge Curzon London 2003) 15; and I Kabashima and T Sugawara 'Prospects for a Two Party System' (2004) 31 Japan Echo 33.

[35] See eg the many empirical studies in the transaction-cost economics 'wave' confirming relational contracting in the US: PG Klein 'New Institutional Economics' in B Bouckaert and G de Geest (eds) *Encyclopedia of Law and Economics* (Edward Elgar Publishing Northampton 2000) 456.

[36] Cammerer and others (n 1) 1217 n 23.

[37] Indeed, M&R (n 24) profess they are 'not theorists', when digging out some data to test for relational contracting!

important for lawyers and policy makers – normative law and economics is intensely problematic.[38]

This combination sits particularly uneasily for Japan, where a rather crude but widespread critique of law and economics is that it is both 'unrealistic' and 'libertarian'.[39] Thus, to make a more pervasive and lasting impression on Japan's ongoing deregulation program, M&R somehow will have to backpedal – themselves identifying the limits to their empirical analyses of Japanese law, and becoming more transparent about their normative preferences. Even then, their work will likely remain less promising for both explaining and justifying (or criticizing) the patterns of re-regulation we are witnessing in Japan, as in other parts of the world.

Indeed, this re-regulation paradigm can develop more support from another set of contemporary perspectives on Japanese law more generally. These can be termed 'neo-proceduralist', because they go well beyond some legal positivist models insisting that law's structures and legitimacy can be derived from formal reasoning and related constitutional processes. Neo-proceduralists with significant influence in Japan come in several variants. Two influential ones are introduced here. But all imply a much more complex interaction between (even scaled-back) regulation, and economic or social phenomena, by adopting a post-instrumentalist approach.[40]

First, Tanaka himself advocates an updated version of 'autonomous law'. This remains based on applying a set of formal, general, and universal norms triggered by specific facts, primarily through court adjudication, creating a triangular relationship between individuals and the state. But his version goes beyond the narrower legalism envisaged by the drafters of Japan's Codes in the late 19th century, and even by the law reformers during and after the post-war occupation. Tanaka advocates a legal system operating as 'a forum in which people with different opinions and interests coordinate their behavior through voluntary negotiations and rational argumentation under fair procedures in accordance with

[38] See eg H Spector 'Foreword' (2004) 79 Chicago-Kent L Rev 345. Fifteen years ago, similar arguments seriously derailed the economic analysis of law in Japan: see T Uchida *Keiyaku no saisei [The Rebirth of Contract]* (Kobundo Tokyo 1990); Kozuka (n 17). More generally, see DJ Brion 'Norms and Values in Law and Economics' in B Bouckaert and G de Geest (n 35) 1041.

[39] N Kawahama '*Hō to keizaigaku no yukue [Law and Economics – Quo Vadis]*' (2003) 75 Hōritsu Jihō 43, 44.

[40] See generally K-H Ladeur 'Proceduralization and Its Use in Post-Modern Legal Theory' European University Institute Working Paper LAW no 96/5 (1996); and, especially on the work of Teubner and Habermas as applied to Japanese law, Nottage PhD thesis (n 20) ch 5. Reviewing these theories in the Japanese context, particularly for their implications for the phenomenon of 'legalization', see T Tanase 'Hōka to jiritsu ryōiki [Legalisation and Autonomous Spheres]' in T Tanase (ed) *Gendai hōshakaigaku nyūmon [Contemporary Legal Sociology: An Introduction]* (Hōritsu Bunkasha Tokyo 1994) 73.

public norms',[41] not just in courts or with unrealistically strong claims to universalibility. This is premised on inter-subjective 'dialogical rationality', rather than the narrow self-interest driving 'self-ordering law' or the equally debilitating 'state interest' driving 'managerial law'; but there remains scope to collaborate with elements of those two models, not just to oppose them, provided this variant of 'autonomous law' retains sufficient distinctiveness in its guiding principle and institutionalization. Through such 'soft legalism', Tanaka seeks to avoid 'anti-legalization', degenerating either into state-driven legal instrumentalism, or into narrowly self-interested informalism. Yet he wishes to concede – and indeed justify – some contemporary tendencies towards 'de-legalization', allowing more elements of 'non-legal' phenomena into substantive law and creating more pluralistic venues for making legal arguments. Thus, for example, he urges judicial reform in Japan that advocates both a much stronger court system, and more varied 'alternative dispute resolution' processes, all providing real scope for individuals to apply and develop their facility for rational argumentation.

Tanaka's 'soft legalism' model, influential first in academia and then in the recent judicial reform project, draws significantly on what I see as the 'supra-liberal' discourse theory of law developed by Juergen Habermas. Tanaka and other followers in Japan accept the phenomenon of increasing differentiation of social subsystems, including the legal system.[42] But they emphasize an under-

[41] Tanaka (n 15) 12.

[42] Another neo-proceduralist strand in Japanese legal and social theory, more specifically oriented towards the design of regulatory regimes, is the social systems theory laid out by Niklas Luhmann and popularized in the legal world particularly by Gunther Teubner (see eg G Teubner and Z Bankowski *Law as an Autopoietic System* (Blackwell Oxford 1993)). This theory is more thoroughly post-modern in eschewing methodological individualism. The analysis focuses on social sub-systems that evolve and differentiate from each other, generating complexity to match that of modern society as a whole. In the modern legal subsystem, based on a binary distinction between legality and illegality, a 'hyper-cycle' involving the creation and application of law generates relative autonomy. This then allows only loose 'structural coupling' with other social subsystems, like the economy (operating on a different underlying rationality). Teubner's theory thus helps identify why and where regulatory failures occur, but makes it difficult *precisely* to explain or promote re-regulatory phenomena (see eg G Teubner 'Societal Constitutionalism: Alternatives to State-Centred Constitutional Theory?' in G Teubner C Joerges and I-J Sand (eds) *Transnational Governance and Constitutionalism* (Hart Oxford 2004) 2).

Perhaps for this reason, interest in this variant of neo-proceduralism appears to have leveled off in Japan after generating considerable excitement over the 1990s (see Tanase [n 40]). However, a recent article extending a book-length study published in Japanese in 2002 develops Luhmann's systems theory to highlight the ambivalent nature of Japan's judicial reform initiatives: K Fukui 'Justice System Reform in Japan: The Connection between Conflict Management and Realization of General Rules of Law' (2004) 51 Osaka U L Rev 55. Fukui points out that there is mutual dependence, but also (often hidden) tension, between law-related communication among judges (tending towards the principle of general application of laws) and communication among parties involved in conflicts (tending towards effective conflict resolution). From this perspective, he acclaims suggestions within Japan's judicial reforms that

cont. ...

lying process still of communicative action in social life, involving discourse oriented towards inter-subjective understanding. This opens up an important role for law to mediate between facts and norms, even (or especially) in a globalizing world.[43] Further, similarly softening some more universalizing tendencies, many of Habermas' insights have been refined to rethink (re-)regulation in countries like the UK,[44] and at EU and global levels.[45] In particular, interpretations 'taking Habermas seriously' to analyze – and hopefully improve – EU and transnational multi-level governance allows more potential for such regimes to avoid two extremes. On the one hand, they become less likely to seize up, as the EU did under its welfarist mode through to the 1970s. On the other, they are less likely to confound broader legitimacy claims, by pursuing a narrow instrumentalist agenda of economic deregulation.

The prolific work of Professor Takao Tanase since the late 1980s has also shown growing dissatisfaction with the model of 'managerial law', with its affinities to welfare state dirigisme.[46] Yet he too points to a neo-proceduralist model that can help explain and guide re-regulation, without having to revert to

certain activities should be subjected to strict application of legal rules (eg for complex business transactions, claims against bureaucrats, and even tort claims from accidents), while other activities should involve more flexible rules (eg in domestic or workplace settings).

[43] J Habermas *Between Facts and Norms* trans W Rehg (MIT Press Cambridge 1996); J Habermas and M Pensky (eds) *The Postnational Constellation: Political Essays* (Polity in association with Blackwell Publishers Cambridge 2001). On the 'reception' of Habermas in Japan, see eg Tanase (n 40). Several commentators have suggested that Teubner himself develops his systems theory to reveal a more normative agenda, with parallels therefore to Habermas' approach: O Gerstenberg 'Justification (and Justifiability) of Private Law in a Polycontextual World' (2000) 9 Social & Legal Studies 419; T Vesting 'Constitutionalism or Legal Theory: Comments on Gunther Teubner' in Teubner and others (n 42) 29.

[44] eg J Black 'Proceduralizing Regulation: Part 1' (2000) 20 OJLS 597.

[45] See especially the work of Christian Joerges (eg C Joerges and F Roedl '"Social Market Economy" as Europe's Social Model?' EUI Working Paper LAW 2004/8 (2004) <http://www.iue.it/PUB/law04-8.pdf> [27 June 2005]); and, more critically, K-H Ladeur 'Discursive Ethics as Constitutional Theory: Neglecting the Creative Role of Economic Liberties?' (2000) 13 Ratio Juris 95; K-H Ladeur 'Globalisation and the Conversion of Democracy to Polycentric Networks: Can Democracy Survive the End of the Nation State?' EUI Working Paper LAW 2003/4 (2003) <http://www.iue.it/PUB/law03-4.pdf> (27 June 2005). For a very specific application of Habermasian theory to disclosure rules in corporate regulation, see J Villiers 'Disclosure Obligations in Company Law: Bringing Communicative Theory into the Field' (2001) 1 J of Corporate L Studies 182.

[46] For a widely read article in English on integrated 'management' of traffic accident dispute resolution, signaling already towards the end the instability of such regimes and therefore his 'interpretive turn' accelerating over the 1990s, see T Tanase 'The Management of Automobile Disputes: Automobile Accident Compensation in Japan' (1990) 24 L and Society Rev 651.

an extreme liberal approach to regulation and the legal world more generally.[47] Tanase claims that the liberal approach is based on a modernist epistemology sharply dividing subjects from objects, the private from the public, and goals from means.

Figure 1a: Modern liberal model

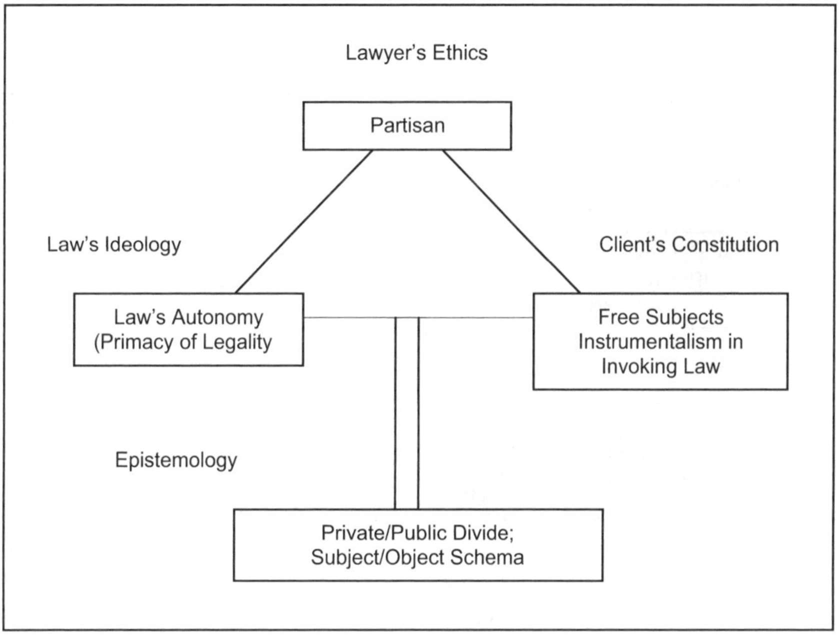

Thus, its ideology of law becomes one of its 'autonomy', giving primacy to the question of legality (whether or not something is legal or illegal), and hence eg partisanship as the guiding principle for lawyers' ethics. Instead, Tanase favors a hermeneutical approach, perceived as more in tune with the contemporary world, constructed inter-subjectively through the narratives we engage in. The corresponding ideology of law becomes one of 'appropriateness' (whether and how it

[47] Generally, see T Tanase *The Hermeneutics of Japanese Law: Community and Modernity* trans. L Nottage and L Wolff (forthcoming), and already L Nottage and L Wolff 'Translating Tanase' Berkeley Boalt Hall Working Paper special issue (forthcoming 2005). Specifically, see also eg T Tanase 'Fuhō kōi sekinin no dōtokuteki kiso [The Moral Foundations of Tort Liability]' in T Tanase (ed) *Gendai fuhō koi hō [Modern Tort Law: Ideals of Law and the Life-World]* (Yūhikaku Tokyo 1994). He criticizes both (welfarist) 'total justice' and (liberal) 'individual justice' approaches to torts, favoring instead (relationship-building) 'communitarian justice'.

may be valid to invoke the law in particular circumstances), and lawyers' ethics become directed at building a two-way interpretive relationship with clients.[48]

Figure 1b: Post-liberal narrative model

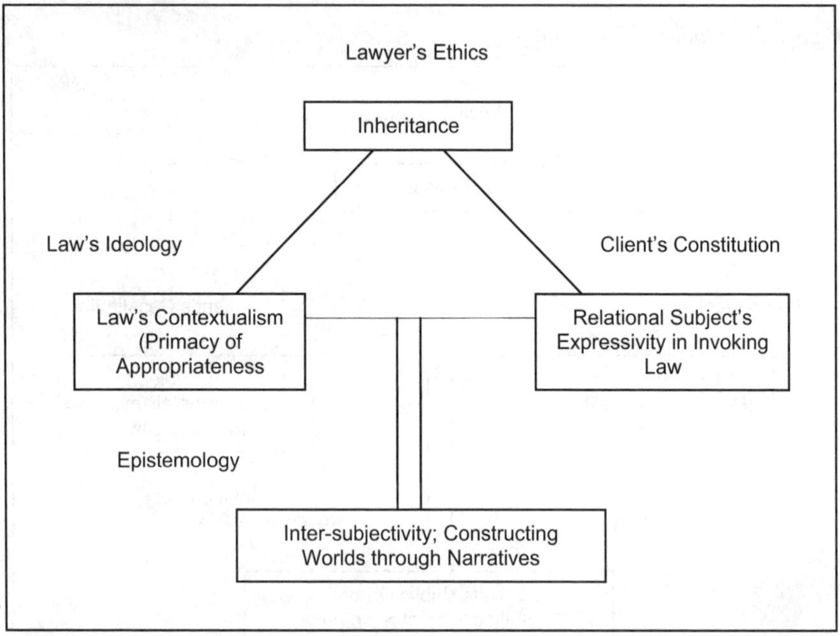

Tanase believes that this neo-communitarian (or perhaps 'post-liberal') approach remains particularly apt in Japan, with its ambivalent attitude towards (industrial, political, and legal) modernization,[49] and that it helps explain only slowly rising civil litigation rates in genuinely contested cases.[50] In constitutional law, which of

[48] T Tanase 'Katari toshite no hō enyō – Hō no monogatari to bengoshi rinri [Invoking Law as Narrative: Lawyers' Ethics and the Narrative of Law]' (1995) 111 Minshōhō Zasshi 677 and 865.

[49] T Tanase 'The Empty Space of the Modern in Japanese Law Discourse' in D Nelken and J Feest (eds) *Adapting Legal Cultures* (Hart Publishing Oxford 2001) 187. See also T Tanase 'Kindai no rinen to yuragi – Kawashima hōshakaigaku no riron to jissen [Cracks in the Ideal of Modernity: The Theory and Practice of Kawashima's Sociology of Law]' (1993) 65 Hōritsu Jihō 26. Cf also eg S Wada 'Three Cases of Non-Instrumental Rationality: Communitarian Ideals, X-Efficiency, and Ikigai' (2002) 23 Waseda J of Asian Studies 1.

[50] T Tanase 'Soshō riyō to kindaika kasetsu [Litigation Use and the Modernization Hypothesis]' in *Minji sosho-hō riron no arata na kōchiku [New Constructions in Civil Procedure Law Theory]* (Yūhikaku Tokyo 2001) 287. Cf eg T Ginsburg and G Hoetker 'The Unreluctant Litigant? An Empirical Analysis of Japan's Turn to Litigation' J of Japanese Studies, forthcoming 2006).

course sets the tone still for much regulatory activity by or involving the state, he also calls for a middle way. Community should be invoked and promoted not in a politically 'conservative' way, as still in some constitutional case law; but rather in a more 'republican' mode, focused instead on individuals engaging in a dialogue aiming at developing consensus on generally shared values. But republicanism needs to learn from structuralism, which emphasizes deep-rooted oppositions in values. Structuralism can also helpfully pull (liberal) individualism towards a focus on social structures.

Figure 2: Beyond four invocations of community in Japanese public law

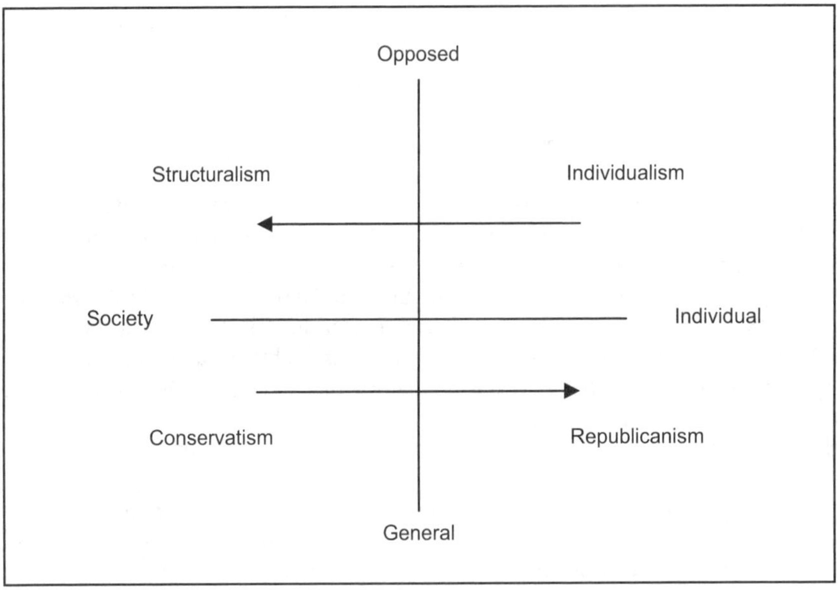

Tanase then focuses on how an extreme liberal model for self-determination rights becomes inherently unstable, and the potential for re-reading and re-directing Japanese public law towards an alternative neo-communitarian model.[51]

Whereas Tanaka still tends to value a legal core over a socio-economic periphery, Tanase perceives and prefers both to interact on a more equal footing. Thus, he finds and accepts much more diffuse notions of substantive rights in Japan, as well as advocating more ADR.[52] Tanase also remains more skeptical

[51] T Tanase 'Kyōdōtai-ron to kenpō kaishaku [Communitarianism and Constitutional Interpretation]' (2002) 1222 Jurisuto 11 and 138.

[52] On the former, see also eg T Tanase 'The Japanese Attitude Towards Judicial Reform' (2004) 1 Kyoto J of L and Politics 27. On ADR, see also eg Tanase (n 46) and Tanase (n 47) part 5 (torts).

about the key 'legal actors' that Tanaka and other judicial system reformers seek again to build up, especially judges and lawyers,[53] due to the social (power) structures that persist – for better or worse – in Japan. Nonetheless, even more so than Tanaka (assuming more directionality imparted by 'legal argumentation' processes), Tanase acknowledges that such tensions are negotiated out in much more complex processes, than assumed by narrow instrumentalist accounts. Hence, too, he would be critical of more instrumentalist tendencies that have emerged in enacting a raft of laws as part of Japan's judicial reform package in the last few years.[54] Similarly, especially during the current implementation phase, Tanase is one of very few legal theorists with a prominent public profile.[55] Finally, although more pointedly than Tanaka, he has emerged recently as a critic of economic globalization, specifically invoking the countervailing EU model of the social market economy.[56]

3. Extending Neo-proceduralism for Japan

More generally, both these neo-proceduralist approaches – refined and applied by prominent theorists in Japan, but based on careful comparative analysis of developments in the US and Germany or the EU – should continue to sit better with Japan's ongoing processes of re-regulation. They still resonate the flexible normative and institutional framework we grew to love in Japan over the 1980s, but which we now at least question – leading undoubtedly to more and harder legalization being injected into the regulatory mix. Yet that framework is and seems to remain quite inward-looking, despite the general impetus from globalization and the specific regulatory solutions it can sometimes offer.

A re-regulating Japan, underpinned by a more functional and legitimate neo-proceduralist vision of law, therefore should look at ways of improving its multi-level governance capacity, by developing and better incorporating norms from abroad. This may seem an odd proposal, for we know how diligent Japan has been in studying and transplanting law from abroad. But Japanese law remains

[53] Respectively, see Tanase (2004) (n 52); and T Tanase 'Hōsō ichigen no kōsō to gendai shihō no kōchiku [Lawyers Becoming Judges, and the Construction of the Contemporary Judicial System]' (2000) 1170 Jurisuto 56.

[54] Compare I Ozaki 'Judicial System Reform and Legalization: A Hasty Lapse from Idealism to Instrumentalism' *Paper presented at the 6th Sho Sato Japanese Law Conference* (UC Berkeley, 12 February 2005).

[55] See eg T Tanase and others 'Zadankai – Bengoshi rinri no arata na tenkai [New Developments in Lawyers' Ethics – A Colloquium]' (2002) 1080 Hanrei Taimuzu 4.

[56] T Tanase 'Gurobaru shijō to hō no shinka [Global Markets and Law's Progress]' (2003) 1528 Jurisuto 44.

surprisingly 'autistic',[57] or at least hesitant, particularly in incorporating transnational legal norms (eg from the WTO) into its legal order.[58] It has been particularly slow in developing a multi-directional flow in legal ideas and institutions within the Asia-Pacific region.[59]

Thus, taking neo-proceduralist 'multi-level governance' seriously nowadays, for Japan, suggests in particular the need to add a legal (harmonization) dimension to the (economic liberalization) agenda it is currently developing in bilateral trade agreements in its region. The EU provides an increasingly attractive model, even in its messy and evolving 'state' – indeed, partly because of the regulatory dialogue potential added by such a regime.[60] Adding such a new dimension to the

[57] H Sono 'The Multiple Worlds of "Nihon-ho"' in L Nottage T Ginsburg and H Sono (eds) *The Multiple Worlds of Japanese Law: Disjunctions and Conjunctions* (University of Victoria Victoria 2001) 47. On Japan's multi-level governance *within* its own borders, see eg Nakagawa (n 23).

[58] Y Iwasawa *International Law, Human Rights, and Japanese Law: The Impact of International Law on Japanese Law* (OUP Oxford 1998). See also M Dean 'Criminals or Asylum Seekers? Japanese Approaches to International Law on Refugees' *Paper presented at the ANJeL conference 'Japanese Law on Trial'* (University of Sydney 23 February 2005) forthcoming via <http://www.law.usyd.edu.au/anjel/content/anjel_events_conf2005.htm> (27 June 2005).

[59] L Nottage 'Japanese Law, Asian Law and Comparative Law' (2003) 15 J of Japanese L 41-61. There are also parallels with Japan's reluctance to engage in currency harmonization in the Asian region: Y Rhee 'Asian Monetary Integration: Destined to Fail?' (2004) 7 Social Sciences Japan J 83. Compare also the restrained tone of N Sopiee, Y Hara and T Tanabe 'Three Views of East Asian Integration' (2004) 31 Japan Echo 29, with the more upbeat appraisals of regional integration potential by CM Dent and DWF Huang (eds) *Northeast Asian Regionalism: Learning from the European Experience* (Routledge Curzon London 2002); A Kojima 'Seeking a Regional Framework for East Asia' (2005) 32 Japan Echo 37-41; and TJ Pempel (ed) *Remapping East Asia: The Construction of a Region* (Cornell University Press Ithaca 2005).

[60] This is a bold assertion, since many within Asia remain sensitive about such 'Western' models, emphasizing for example the region's internal diversity (TJ Pempel 'Introduction' in (n 59) 1, 5). However, nation-states in Asia have become more established, confident, and outward-looking, especially since the 1980s (TJ Pempel 'Conclusion' in Pempel (n 59) 256). Ironically, this may have been reinforced by Japan's decline as a role model over the 1990s (cf A Macintyre and B Naughton 'The Decline of a Japan-Led Model of the East Asian Economy' in Pempel (n 59) 77). Correspondingly, there have been some areas where more formal governmental policy coordination has grown – albeit less evident in the economic arena: K Tsunekawa 'Why So Many Maps There? Japan and Regional Cooperation' in Pempel (n 59) 102. More recently, the 'ASEAN + 3' evidences a broader move towards more formal top-down regionalism, not just bottom-up regionalization driven by cross-border business and NGOs: P Evans 'Between Regionalism and Regionalization: Policy Networks and the Nascent East Asian Institutional Identity' in Pempel (n 59) 195.

In parallel, the EU has also had to overcome extensive diversity amongst its members, and is further developing this capacity as its boundaries move eastwards. For more on the evolving EU governance framework, see eg C Joerges and R Dehousse (eds) *Good Governance in Europe's Integrated Market* (OUP Oxford 2002); I Pernice 'Multilevel Constitutionalism in the

cont. ...

regulatory regime, however, does not necessarily abandon regulatory potential at other levels. Nor does it guarantee that the regional solution is the best for each particular problem. Nonetheless, the rest of my remarks will suggest how it may best combine both effectiveness and legitimacy in dealing with certain remote risks such as BSE. By contrast, neither a managerial (welfarist) approach nor a self-ordering (neo-liberal) approach seems as helpful either to understand how the regulatory response has unfolded so far in countries in Japan or, more pressingly, to justify how best to proceed in the face of such increasingly common risks.

III. Dealing with Mad Cows in Japan, and Beyond

Japan reported its first case of BSE on 10 September 2001. The Japanese government's initial responses and the lead-up to the discovery bore some harrowing parallels with the inept British government reactions when mad cow disease developed into an epidemic over a decade ago in the UK, soon spreading to other parts of the EU and the rest of the world.[61] By 4 February 2005, 14 mad cows had been reported in Japan, along with its first human fatality from vCJD.[62] Disturbingly, two of these cows were 21 and 23 months old. Even after governments in the UK, Japan, and elsewhere became more realistic and cautious about mad cow disease, they have tended to follow scientific advice suggesting that BSE required a longer incubation period and to regulate accordingly, notably by excluding from the food chain or testing only slaughtered cows aged thirty months or older.

The repercussions of the outbreak for the beef industry in Japan, including Australia's multi-billion dollar export industry, have been phenomenal. Beef

European Union' (2002) 27 Eur L Rev 511; O Gerstenberg 'Governing in Europe: Effective and Democratic?' (2002) 22 OJLS 563; G de Burca 'The Constitutional Challenge of New Governance in the European Union' (2003) 28 Eur L Rev 814; M Zürn and C Joerges (eds) *Law and Governance in Postnational Europe: Compliance Beyond the Nation-State* (Cambridge University Press Cambridge 2005).

[61] This part is based on L Nottage and M Trezise 'Mad Cows and Japanese Consumers' (2003) 14 Australian Product Liability Reporter 125. Detailed citations and appendices are provided in that article, so only new reference material is added here. For a chronology of Japan's mad cow saga, its comparative regulatory response, and cases of BSE reported world-wide, see the appendices to that article.

[62] 'First Mad-Cow Related Death Reported in Japan' *Mainichi Shinbun* (4 February 2005) available via <http://mdn.mainichi.co.jp> (and on file with the author). No doubt seeking to minimize public concern, since epidemiologists at one stage estimated deaths in the tens of thousands worldwide, one official claimed that the deceased had probably caught the disease while visiting the UK. By the end of 2004, 157 deaths from vCJD had been reported worldwide, but with 147 confirmed to have caught the disease in the UK, and with four of the remaining ten having visited the UK. For updates on mad cow numbers reported in Japan and elsewhere, see <http://www.oie.int/eng/info/en_esbmonde.htm> (27 June 2005).

consumption halved (even for imported products, which should have been safer than Japanese beef), reflecting the growing 'people power' of Japanese consumers.[63] Compulsory inspections and slaughtering were implemented, followed by a massive compensation scheme for Japanese beef producers and processors. Abuses of the scheme were soon discovered, including Australian beef being relabeled as Japanese beef (to attract compensation), resulting in fines, prosecutions, and even shareholder derivative actions against Japanese firms or executives. Foreign suppliers were also hit hard. Australian beef export sales to Japan, its leading market, dropped 56 per cent in September 2001, at the height of the BSE scare in Japan. After beef consumption and imports picked up in 2002, Japan raised tariffs from 38.5 to 50 percent under 'safeguard' provisions contained in WTO rules – despite the protests of the Australian government and beef industry leaders that those rules were not intended for this situation of rapid recovery to similar levels of imports following a drastic fall.[64]

Conversely, Japan has maintained a ban on the vast trade in American beef since Canada and the US reported their first mad cows in 2003, despite intense pressure especially by US trade negotiators – especially during 2004, election year in the US.[65] In September 2004, the Japanese government's new Food Safety Commission first moved to relax requirements that all cows be tested in Japan, limiting tests to those aged 20 months or older. This was clearly aimed at resolving the impasse with the US, because it still does not test all its cows. However, further negotiations were envisaged on the age below which untested US beef might be sent to Japan, as testing in the US is limited to cows aged 30 months or older. The US also did not track birth dates precisely, and wanted to persuade Japan to accept some statistical sampling.[66] Responding to widespread public concern, in March 2005 a committee of Japan's House of Representatives urged caution in lifting the ban on American beef. But the US has redoubled diplomatic efforts, and the Food Safety Commission is expected to release its final report in April 2005, recommending the relaxation of blanket testing for BSE in Japanese cow and opening the way again to American beef imports.[67]

[63] See generally also P Maclachlan 'From Subjects to Citizens: Japan's Evolving Consumer Identity' (2004) 24 Japanese Studies 115.

[64] See further H Iwamura 'Memoir of International Trade Law: Issues of Translating WTO Safeguard Provisions into Japanese' (2004) 5 Asian Pacific L and Policy J 188.

[65] Compare also the trade friction between the US and the EU over BSE: HB Freeman 'Trade Epidemic: The Impact of the Mad Cow Crisis on E.U.-US Relations' (2002) 25 Boston College Intl and Comparative L Rev 343.

[66] L Nottage 'Comparing Product Liability and Safety in Japan: From Minamata to Mad Cows – to Mitsubishi' in D Fairgrieve (ed) *Product Liability in Comparative Perspective* (Cambridge University Press Cambridge forthcoming 2005).

[67] 'Washington to Up Pressure on Japanese Ban' *Mainichi Shinbun* (31 March 2005), available via <http://mdn.mainichi.co.jp> (and on file with the author).

The issue remains complicated by ongoing scientific controversy, not just by domestic and cross-border politics and economics.[68] Certain transmission mechanisms have been clarified during the 1990s. The simplest is when BSE infected beef is processed ('rendered') into Meat and Bone Meal ('MBM'), which is then fed to other cows (particularly dairy cows, to improve their milk yields); and when humans eat infected parts of such cows, or consume further processed products containing such parts. However, scientists remain divided about which parts are readily infectious with the (protein-like) 'prion' causing mad cow disease, and possible 'maternal' or lateral transmissions within herds. Scientists and regulators also remain concerned about the disease spreading to other animals, especially sheep. Also, once humans get infected with BSE and die of vCJD, then various mechanisms might conceivably lead to them infecting others. Perhaps most disturbingly, there is still uncertainty about how cows can get BSE in the first place, without human intervention. Much attention – and blame – has been directed to imported products (live cows, beef products, and especially MBM) as the source of BSE emerging in new countries like Japan or the US However, it remains unclear how the (first) 'index case' emerged, for example in the UK. The possibility of some spontaneous emergence in other countries, from domestic 'natural' causes (such as a genetic development), cannot be excluded. Thus, as well as being a global problem, spreading across borders and disrupting billion-dollar trade flows, BSE remains characterized by extensive scientific uncertainties.

1. Beefing Up the Regulatory Response

Such uncertainties explain why mad cow cases continue to be reported throughout the world, even in countries like the UK and Japan where regulators have imposed an increasingly strict and broad array of regulatory controls on animal husbandry and processing practices. Government and industry leaders responsible for agricultural products in Australia, with a huge beef export industry at stake, have mostly proclaimed that the country does not have mad cow disease and that measures are in place to prevent it breaking out. The recent BSE outbreaks in North America, where Canada and the US had maintained a similar stance, reinforce the need to be realistic and respectful about the continuing scientific uncertainties involved. The need for transparency, and realistic risk assessment and communication involving a broad range of stakeholders, are key lessons that emerged from the BSE Enquiry in the UK. A related point involves thinking more broadly about appropriate regulatory responses, appreciating problems of

[68] See Nottage and Trezise (n 61) and especially the special issue no (2003) 22/1 of the *Scientific and Technical Review* from the Organisation Internationale des Epizooties (available via <http://www.oie.int/eng/publicat/rt/A_rt22_1.htm>).

design and especially enforcement in varying institutional environments. The outbreak of mad cow disease in Japan has forced the government to belatedly address such problems, resulting for example in the new Food Safety Commission getting underway from July 2003. The council is decidedly less formidable than the counterpart agency established in the UK in 2000. However, Food Standards Australia-New Zealand and Australia's various policy makers in agricultural affairs may not be robust enough either to deal openly and effectively with a problem like mad cow disease.

More generally, how can and should legal systems in complex industrialized democracies address such problems of scientific uncertainty? Ironically, as science and technology achieve ever more progress, more risks can be created or we become more conscious of them.[69] Globalization exacerbates this situation.[70] So the problem of mad cow disease, unlikely to go away, seems best addressed as follows. First, in devising and enforcing regulatory measures (imposed or promoted, eg via industry 'self-regulation' by public authorities), a multi-level strategy must be considered.[71] Regulation at the global level, particularly the WTO, may play a role. However, the present regime lacks strong enforcement powers, and even that may be under challenge on legitimacy grounds – as evidenced by the collapse of broader WTO negotiations at Cancun in September 2003.[72] A fundamental problem is relatively limited normative reference points for WTO decision makers (especially the Appellate Body) in balancing international trade and health concerns. This leads towards increasing reliance on the seemingly more objective criterion of science, which ironically may not hold the answers precisely in these complex cases – and anyway distinguishes itself by adherence to a non-normative role.[73]

Regulation at the national level – and states (in a federal system like Australia's or the US) or smaller local units – involves potentially much stronger enforcement and fewer problems of legitimacy. However, it risks being 'cap-

[69] Cf generally eg U Beck *Risk Society: Towards a New Modernity* (Sage London 1992).

[70] See eg U Beck *World Risk Society* (Polity Press Malden 1999); U Beck *What Is Globalization?* (Polity Press Malden 2000); D Held and M Koenig-Archibugi *Taming Globalization: Frontiers of Governance* (Polity Cambridge 2003); Ladeur (2003) (n 45).

[71] Cf C Joerges 'Law, Science and the Management of Risks to Health at National, European and International Levels: Stories on Baby Dummies, Mad Cows and Hormones in Beef' (2001) 7 Columbia J of Eur L 1.

[72] See generally R Wilkinson 'The WTO in Crisis: Exploring the Dimensions of Institutional Inertia' (2001) 35 J of World Trade 397; A Beviglia Zampetti 'Democratic Legitimacy in the World Trade Organization: The Justice Dimension' (2003) 37 J of World Trade 105.

[73] See N McNelis 'The Role of the Judge in the EU and WTO: Lessons from the BSE and Hormones Cases' (2001) 4 J of Intl Economic L 189; J Peel 'Risk Regulation Under the WTO SPS Agreement: Science as an International Normative Yardstick?' Jean Monnet Working Papers 2/04 (2004) <http://www.jeanmonnetprogram.org/papers/04/040201.pdf> (27 June 2005).

tured' by coordinated interest groups (like the beef industry in the UK and, perhaps to a lesser extent, Japan).[74] Further, even balanced regulation may not be fully appreciated and therefore enforced by all participants (a problem highlighted by the BSE Enquiry in the UK).

Accordingly, the best potential for effective *and* legitimate regulation in this situation comes at a regional level.[75] In Europe, for example, the EU eventually was able to bring the UK into line, and yet absorb some criticisms of its own processes to bring about broader improvements in product safety regulation – and, in the shadow of compensation claims as well as broader public concern, EU governance more generally.[76] Some neo-proceduralists no doubt would value the new European Food Safety Authority, with its advisory role in risk assessment, as promoting multi-level governance in regulating food risks, perhaps 'irritating' national regimes in broader areas such as nutrition.[77] In product safety regulation more generally, since the 'new approach' to technical standard-setting, the EU also offers an intriguing experiment in hybrid public/private governance – more complex, still, at the transnational level.[78]

[74] Conversely, H Rothstein 'Precautionary Bans or Sacrificial Lambs? Participative Risk Regulation and the Reform of the UK Food Safety Regime' ESCR Centre for Analysis of Risk and Regulation Discussion Paper 15/2003 <http://www.lse.ac.uk/collections/CARR/pdf/Disspaper15.pdf> (27 June 2005) notes the suggestion that the UK's new Food Safety Agency may have been forced by more organized consumer pressure nowadays to go too far in the recent sausage casings regulation. The EU body, still more insulated, advocated a different standard.

[75] See also C van Gelderen, EJ Gimeno and AA Schudel 'Bovine Spongiform Encephalopathy in South America: A Regional Preventive Approach' (2003) 22 Rev sci tech Off int Epiz 227. Of course, this may not be enough, as recent outbreaks of mad cow disease in North America indicate (cf JA Kellar and VW Lees 'Risk Management of the Transmissible Spongiform Encephalopathies in North America' (2003) 22 Rev sci tech Off int Epiz 201).

[76] See Nottage (n 22) 30, 210. But see eg SK Fodor 'How Does the European Union Solve Crises – with Solutions or Avoidance? A Study of the "Mad Cow Disease" Crisis' (1998) 27 Georgia J of Intl and Comparative L 249.

[77] See generally G Teubner 'Legal Irritants: Good Faith in British Law and How Unifying Law Ends Up in New Divergences' (1998) 61 Modern L Rev 11. But see D Chalmers '"Food for Thought": Reconciling European Risks and Traditional Ways of Life' (2002) 66 Modern L Rev 532. He takes the more characteristically British view that the authority will have a more powerful effect, undercutting national diversity. Cf eg D Geradin and N Petit 'The Development of Agencies at EU and National Levels: Conceptual Analysis and Proposals for Reform' Jean Monnet Working Paper 1/2004 <http://www.jeanmonnetprogram.org/papers/04/040101.pdf> (27 June 2005).

[78] Compare eg GG Howells 'The Relationship between Product Liability and Product Safety – Understanding a Necessary Element in European Product Liability through a Comparison with the US Position' (2000) 39 Washburn L J 305, with Teubner and others (n 42); and A Ostrovsky 'The New Codex Alimentarius Commission Standards for Food Created with

cont. ...

2. Private Law and Governance

Relatedly, more thought should be given to using private governance, particularly product liability (PL), as complementary 'pseudo-regulation'.[79] This should add further legitimacy and perspectives on essential 'risk communication'.[80] Further, several empirical studies on product safety suggest that it is the *combination* of (more) public and (more) private law controls that generates more enduring and nuanced safety outcomes. Although the private law enforcement process has many problems, it can be an important back-up in cases of regulatory failure, as the asbestos disaster illustrates.[81]

To address problems like BSE, a threshold private law issue involves ensuring that primary agricultural products are covered by strict-liability PL regimes.[82] More importantly, the interrelationships between (public safety) regulation standards and key PL concepts like 'defectiveness' should be better clarified (and, arguably, linked); 'causation' requirements may have to be considerably liberalized; the 'development risks defense' should be limited; and time limits for bringing claims should be extended.[83] Through such reforms, courts, commentators, and businesspeople would be forced to look at risks in overlapping but

Modern Biotechnology: Implications for the EC GMO Framework's Compliance with SPS Agreement' (2004) 25 Michigan J of Intl L 813.

[79] A broader perspective on private law as itself regulation is presented eg by H Collins *Regulating Contracts* (OUP Oxford 1999). More recently, looking at potential for co-regulation in the proposed Unfair Practices Directive, see also H Collins *The Forthcoming EC Directive on Unfair Commercial Practices* (Kluwer Law International The Hague 2003).

[80] This dimension has often been overlooked by policy makers in government, and even advocates for consumer interests. See eg D McCrea 'Risk Communication of Transmissible Spongiform Encephalopathies' (2003) 22/1 Rev sci tech Off int Epiz 251-57. Cf also eg J Stapleton 'Bugs in Anglo-American Products Liability' (2002) 53 South Carolina L Rev 1225.

[81] See Nottage (n 22) ch 5. As pointed out in A Ogus 'What Legal Scholars Can Learn from Law and Economics' (2004) 79 Chicago-Kent L Rev 383, there are problems created eg by the shield of bankruptcy and courts' hindsight bias. However, M White 'Asbestos and the Future of Mass Torts' (2004) 18 J of Economic Perspectives 183, emphasizes that the vast litigation in the US grew out of regulatory capture by manufacturers, leading (ironically) to massive compensatory and punitive damages through US courts. Even today, the US has not prohibited the use of asbestos, as in the EU.

[82] This has always been the case under the 1992 amendments in Part VA of the Trade Practices Act (Cth); and was achieved in the EU by an amending Directive in 1999, to the 1985 PL Directive; but has yet to be achieved under Japan's Product Liability Law of 1994, despite recent expansive interpretations of 'manufactured or processed movables' by Japanese courts. See Nottage (n 22) 85-90.

[83] See generally, ibid, respectively, pp 95-6, 140-41, 124-31, 134-37. Cf H Schepel 'Constituting Private Governance Regimes: Standards Bodies in American Law' in Teubner and others (n 42) 161-188, on the broader difficulties US law has in dealing with private standardization bodies.

different ways, compared to regulators and others addressing risks through the lens of public law and policy.

Even some such reforms of PL would also create more constructive regulatory dialogue, perhaps forcing re-conceptualizations of these various actors' underlying preferences in regard to product safety, and the legal system's ability (as a whole) to interrelate with the world of science.[84] Even more broadly, this approach promises some new directions for Japan's ongoing debates about corporate compliance and governance.[85]

IV. Conclusions

Rethinking along these lines the balance – and potential synergies – between public and private governance approaches to BSE should also prove useful in addressing other contemporary problems of scientific uncertainty. These include Johne's disease in cattle and sheep, uncertainties about vaccines against anthrax, GMOs, and Asian bird flu.[86] In times of heightened consumer activism, in Japan as elsewhere, the legal world must think creatively about how best to address the broader phenomenon of the 'globalization of risk'.[87]

In this new environment, the old regulatory paradigm and related welfarist or managerial law no longer generates sufficient benefits, tangible (economic) or intangible (democratic legitimacy). This also exposes more clearly the downside risks of interventionism, such as misuse of the compensation schemes introduced in Japan in the wake of their BSE debacle.[88] Yet total deregulation and neo-liberal or self-ordering law, leaving 'the market' to sort out all the problems created by increased scientific uncertainty in an increasingly globalized economy and polity, cannot explain – let alone justify – attempts to resolve such problems in Japan

[84] Nottage (n 22) 208-11. See also generally C Joerges and others (eds) *Integrating Scientific Expertise into Regulatory Decision-Making: National Traditions and European Innovations* (Nomos Baden-Baden 1997).

[85] See generally T Kitagawa and L Nottage 'Globalization of Japanese Corporations and the Development of Corporate Legal Departments: Problems and Prospects' in W Alford G Chin and LA Cecere (eds) *Raising the Bar* (Harvard University Press Cambridge 2005); Milhaupt and West (n 28); and especially eg Nihon Bengoshi Rengōkai Kokusai Jinken Mondai Iinkai (ed) *Kigyō no shakaiteki sekinin to kōdō kijun: Kompuraiansu kanri – Naibu kokuhatsu hogo seido [Corporate Social Responsibility and Codes of Conduct: Compliance Management and Systems for Protecting Whistleblowers]* (Shōji Hōmu Tokyo 2003).

[86] See eg n 2 and n 78; and eg <http://www.oie.int/eng/avian_influenza/pub.htm> (27 June 2005).

[87] Cf also eg G Little 'BSE and the Regulation of Risk' (2001) 64 Modern L Rev 730.

[88] See especially the criticism by AG Mulgan *Japan's Interventionist State: The Role of the MAFF* (Routledge Curzon London 2004).

and other parts of the world.[89] Instead, the re-regulatory paradigm and neo-proceduralist models of law best help us to understand how and why almost all policy-making and even public debate in Japan, for example, has revolved around strengthened or remodeled intervention by public authorities (albeit incorporating broader stakeholder participation), rather than considering possible new interfaces with private law enforced through or in the shadow of the court system. This approach also provides readier standards for normative evaluation of such developments – no doubt more critical, on the 'soft liberalism' variant propounded by Tanaka, but less so on Tanase's neo-communitarianism variant.

Drawing then on parallel neo-proceduralist theory developed and applied more in the EU context recently, it seems particularly promising for Japan to add a new *outward-looking* facet to its multi-level governance framework, hitherto and still evident *within* Japan. Specifically, the best way forward would be for Japan to introduce bilateral or regional arrangements capable of addressing issues such as BSE through new forums. These would aim at a better combination of regulatory effectiveness and legitimacy than we have seen (and can readily foresee) at both national and global levels. But those levels could also be productively 'irritated' by the new regional arrangement, and vice versa, as some neo-proceduralists see and welcome (more) in the EU governance system. That system, nowadays, also offers important experimentation in re-thinking the interface between public regulation and private law (and norm-setting more generally). Specifically, a less invasive but significant way forward for Japan to adopt at a cross-border level the best features from the EU's new 'agencies' as well as its most effective 'committees', to address standard-setting and broader problems with systematic risks.[90] Longer term, Japan should already be thinking of more hard-core law-making and dispute-resolving institutions along EU lines.

By chance rather than design, the bilateral arrangements that the Japanese government has been negotiating since 2001, as a back-up to multilateral trade liberalization through the WTO, may be quite promising if a more refined harmonization agenda can be added and institutionalized properly. Japan involves quite different economic and legal dimensions compared to Singapore – a trader rather than a producer, and still firmly within the common law tradition. Mexico, Japan's latest free trade agreement partner, adds the interesting dimension of its own clear 're-regulatory experience', underpinned by quite an intense regional arrangement (NAFTA), which also challenges its strong civil law tradition.

[89] Even M&R have had little to say about these issues. Presumably, they would leave it to firms to develop their own mechanisms for regaining profitability and public confidence. But the BSE saga shows vividly the unlikelihood of market forces, on their own, overcoming massive coordination problems. It also shows the unacceptability of risking national and transnational disaster while experimenting in that way, even without adopting a strong version of the 'precautionary principle' (cf generally Rothstein [n 74]).

[90] See eg Geradin and Petit (n 77); C Joerges and E Vos (eds) *EU Committees: Social Regulation, Law and Politics* (Hart Oxford 1999).

Korea, with which Japan is now approaching a free trade arrangement, would stabilize an emergent system, given much closer affinities in economic patterns and legal institutions.

This proposed expansion and re-direction for Japan's multi-governance system admittedly has little chance of gaining immediate traction, especially amongst the diplomats and economists now negotiating various bilateral agreements, broader arrangements in the Asian region, and the ongoing WTO round. Still, as a provocative idea prompted in turn by Professor Ogus' thought-provoking paper, the seed may be planted. To have any chance of germinating, however, our starting point should be that Japan shares with Europe and other complex industrialized democracies a re-regulatory shift best explained and justified by neo-proceduralist models of law.

Gatekeeper Failure and Reform: The Challenge of Fashioning Relevant Reforms

JOHN C. COFFEE, JR.*

I. Introduction

Securities markets have long employed 'gatekeepers' – independent professionals who pledge their reputational capital – to protect the interests of dispersed investors who cannot easily take collective action.[1] The clearest examples of such reputational intermediaries are auditors and securities analysts, who in different ways verify or assess corporate disclosures in order to advise investors. But during the late 1990s, these protections seemingly failed, and a unique concentration of financial scandals followed, all involving the common denominator of accounting irregularities. What caused this sudden outburst of scandals, involving a seeming epidemic of accounting and related financial irregularities, that broke over the financial markets between late 2001 and mid-2002 – eg Enron, WorldCom, Global Crossing, Tyco, and others? To date, much commentary has broadly and loosely attributed these scandals to any or all of: (1) a stock market bubble;

* This submission is an update of an article titled 'Gatekeeper Failure and Reform: The Challenge of Fashioning Relevant Reforms' (2004) 84 Boston U L Rev 301.

[1] Probably, the first systematic use of this term, 'gatekeeper', was in an article by Ronald Gilson and Reinier Kraakman. See R Gilson and R Kraakman 'The Mechanisms of Market Efficiency' (1984) 70 Virginia L Rev 549, 612 (discussing role of investment bankers as gatekeepers). See also JC Coffee Jr 'Brave New World?: The Impact(s) of the Internet on Modern Securities Regulation' (1999) 52 Business Lawyer 1195, 1210-13, 1232-33. For a fuller discussion of the concept of gatekeepers as 'reputational intermediaries', see n 13-14 and accompanying text. The use of such private agents substantially predates the appearance of public regulation, either the federal securities laws or the state 'Blue Sky' laws. The New York Stock Exchange began to require the publication of financial statements certified by an independent auditor around 1900, well before the passage of the first 'Blue Sky' statute. See JC Coffee Jr 'The Rise of Dispersed Ownership: The Roles of Law and the State in the Separation of Ownership and Control' (2001) 111 Yale L J 1, 37-39.

(2) a decline in business morality; (3) weak boards of directors;[2] or (4) an increase in 'infectious greed'.[3] Without denying that any of these factors could have played some role, this article begins from the premise that explanations phrased in terms of greed and morality are unsatisfactory because they depend on subjective trends that cannot be reliably measured.

Even those explanations that focus on corporate governance have failed to account adequately for the sudden increase in financial irregularity. Take, for example, the popular explanation that boards failed. While some boards certainly did perform miserably, the problem with this explanation is that the overall independence and power of outside directors has only increased over recent years. Thus, the 2001-2002 epidemic of financial irregularity cannot be satisfactorily explained in terms of any recent decline in board performance. If board failure was the cause of Enron or WorldCom, why didn't these failures occur twenty years earlier when boards were less independent and proactive? In short, to explain an epidemic of irregularity, one must identify some force or factor that changed – either intensifying or weakening – so that its influence can account for the overall shift in behavior. Clearly, the performance of boards of directors of publicly held corporations, even if inadequate, improved over the relevant interval of the 1990s and thus cannot explain a sudden outbreak of financial irregularity.

A final oversimplified explanation is that a 'few bad apples' – ie a small group of 'rogue managers' who were corrupt – caused these scandals. This explanation overlooks the pervasiveness of the sudden surge in financial irregularities in the late 1990s. As will be seen, approximately 10% of all publicly listed US companies restated their financial statements at least once between 1997 and June

[2] For a representative such statement, see SL Gillan and JD Martin 'Financial Engineering, Corporate Governance and the Collapse of Enron' SSRN Working Paper id=350040 (2002) 3 (finding first cause of Enron's breakdown to have been 'a lack of board independence and board oversight'). In contrast, this paper doubts the adequacy of such an explanation. Admittedly, boards did fail, and even a special committee of Enron's own board has concluded that the Enron board failed to monitor officers for conflicts of interest adequately. See WC Powers Jr and others, 'Report of investigation by the special investigative committee of the board of directors of Enron Corp' (1 February 2002) 2002 WL 198018. Similarly, a Senate subcommittee has assigned the principal blame to the Enron board. See Report of the Permanent Subcommittee on Investigations of the Committee of Governmental Affairs, United States Senate 'The Role of the Board of Directors in Enron's Collapse' (Report 107-70) (8 July 2001). Nonetheless, such studies beg the larger question: Why did these boards fail now and not earlier? Although board procedure or independence may have been deficient, they were almost certainly superior to a decade ago when such scandals were rare.

[3] Federal Reserve Chairman Alan Greenspan coined this colorful phrase, saying that 'An infectious greed seemed to grip much of our business community'. See F Norris 'The Markets: Market Place: Yes, He Can Top That' *New York Times* (New York USA 17 July 2002) A-1.

2002,[4] and the annual rate of financial restatements soared during the latter half of the 1990s.[5] Such financial irregularity is, of course, characteristic of a bubble, and little doubt now exists that a large frothy bubble burst in 2000-2001. As a historical matter, bubbles tend to produce scandals and, in turn, prophylactic legislation,[6] but this loose generalization leaves unanswered the critical questions: What caused this bubble and how does the growth of a bubble relate to the apparent breakdown of our once-confident system of corporate governance?

This article will focus on an alternative explanation for the wave of accounting and financial reporting irregularities that surfaced in 2001-2002: namely, that the gatekeepers failed. That is, the professionals who serve investors by preparing, verifying, or certifying corporate disclosures to the securities markets acquiesced in managerial fraud – not in all cases, to be sure, but at a markedly higher rate than during the immediately preceding period. While the concept of gatekeeper will be discussed and refined later, this term certainly includes the auditors, securities analysts, and securities attorneys who prepare, review, or analyze disclosure documents. Part II of this article develops competing, but complementary, explanations for gatekeeper failure. The behavior of gatekeepers cannot be examined in isolation, but rather appears to have been significantly influenced by the incentives that drove corporate managers over the same period. To this extent, the recent explosion of financial irregularity was less the product of ineffable factors – such as 'infectious greed' or mass irrationality – than the natural and logical consequence of trends and forces that had been developing for some time. Ironically, the blunt truth is that both the recent accounting scandals and the broader phenomenon of earnings management were the by-products of a system of corporate governance that has indeed made corporate managers more accountable to the market. Sensitivity to the market, however, can be a mixed blessing – particularly when the market becomes euphoric and uncritical. As a result, a corporate governance system that was adequate for a world in which the agents' incentives to act opportunistically were weaker failed when these same agents – managers, gatekeepers, and financial intermediaries – responded to stronger incentives and rationally pursued their own self-interests to the detriment of shareholders.

Part II will conclude that the factor that most destabilized our contemporary corporate governance system was the sudden change in executive compensation

[4] See United States General Accounting Office, Report to the Chairman, Committee on Banking, Housing and Urban Affairs, US Senate 'Financial Statement Restatements: Trends, Market Impacts, Regulatory Responses and Remaining Challenges' (October 2002) (GAO-03-138) 4 (hereinafter 'GAO Study').

[5] See n 21-29 and accompanying text.

[6] Professor Stuart Banner has argued that, over the last 300 years, most major instances of legislation regulating the securities markets have followed a sustained price collapse on the securities market. See S Banner 'What Causes New Securities Regulation?: 300 Years of Evidence' (1997) 75 Washington U L Q 849, 850.

during the 1990s. As executive compensation shifted to being equity-based, instead of cash-based, a greatly enhanced incentive arose for managers to manipulate earnings – and to induce their gatekeepers to let them. To this extent, blaming the board is a myopic theory of causation that leads nowhere, because it does not explain the sudden surge in irregularities. In truth, in most cases, boards cannot detect earnings manipulation in the absence of warnings from their professional gatekeepers.

This focus on executive compensation as the destabilizing force that led managers to overreach gatekeepers is subject to a major qualification: gatekeepers do not have the same, identical relationship to corporate managements around the world. Outside the United States, no similar outburst of accounting irregularities or financial statement restatements occurred during 2000 to 2002, even though stock markets receded uniformly in the United States and Europe. Indeed, most of the non-US companies that did experience accounting irregularities over this same era either had significant US operations where the fraud originated or also relied on stock options to compensate senior management. Across most of the world, however, little use is made of equity compensation, because most firms have concentrated ownership, and their controlling shareholders do not need to rely on equity compensation to align shareholder interests with their own. Thus, the absence of accounting scandals in Europe over the 2000-2002 period, coupled with the limited use made in Europe of equity compensation, tends to corroborate the basic hypothesis advanced in Part II that changes in executive compensation destabilized American corporate governance.

Still, accounting scandals have recently surfaced in Europe, most notably in the case of Parmalat.[7] Part II finds that these scandals were qualitatively different than Enron and WorldCom in several respects. Thus, these scandals demonstrate that gatekeeper failure is a worldwide problem, but one that has different causes and cures depending upon the different structures of corporate governance involved.

Although Part II offers a diagnosis, it proposes no prescription, in part because effective prescriptions must be context-specific and not universal. Part III approaches the task of prescription by first mapping the range of strategies available to regulators. Basically, it groups the realistic regulatory options for dealing with conflicts of interest under four headings: (1) structural rules, which, for example, subject gatekeepers to greater public oversight; (2) prophylactic rules, which typically seek to preclude conflicts of interest; (3) 'empowerment' rules, which seek to assure greater independence or to give the gatekeeper greater leverage over the principal that it is expected to monitor; and (4) liability-enhancing rules. Seeking to curb the conflicts of interest that compromised audi-

[7] See M Landler 'Scandal Outrages Europeans; Solutions May Be Patchwork' *New York Times* (New York United States 25 December 2003) C-1 (discussing Parmalat and other recent European accounting scandals).

tors and analysts, the Sarbanes-Oxley Act of 2002,[8] passed by Congress in response to the wave of corporate scandals that crested in 2002, utilizes all these strategies – except the last. Although enhancing liability rules is probably the most obvious and traditional response to scandals, this was also the one strategy that business interests effectively resisted during the enactment of Sarbanes-Oxley. Ironically, even though Congress has not used this technique, Part III finds that courts in today's 'post-Enron' environment appear to be enhancing the risk of legal liability on their own through the creative reinterpretation of ambiguous doctrines.

But therein lies a host of problems. Although gatekeepers need to face some legal threat if they are to remain faithful to shareholders, the optimal level of deterrence is much harder to estimate. Some recent commentators have proposed a strict liability regime for gatekeepers, arguing that only strict liability provides gatekeepers with optimal incentives to prevent client misconduct.[9] Other commentators have disagreed, replying that strict liability may cause the market for gatekeepers to fail or may simply deny some law-abiding, but higher risk, issuers access to the capital markets.[10] Although the magnitude of the litigation 'threat' that is now facing gatekeepers can reasonably be debated, and probably varies with the type of gatekeeper, the increasing risk of gatekeeper insolvency in at least the US context suggests the need to consider alternative reforms that may be desirable because they can modify gatekeeper behavior by means that do not directly threaten gatekeeper solvency.

In this light, Part IV proposes alternative reforms intended to make gatekeepers more responsive to the interests of investors. Initially, Part IV proposes a modified form of strict liability for auditors that caps their maximum exposure at a multiple of their expected revenues from the client. The attraction of this combination is that it combines the superior incentives of a strict liability regime with both reduced transaction costs (as courts are spared the costly obligation of determining when gatekeepers acted with scienter or without reasonable care) and a reduced risk of gatekeeper insolvency or market failure in the market for gatekeeper services. Similarly, the prospect that law-abiding issuers might be denied access to the capital markets because of their liability risk they posed to their

[8] Technically, this statute is entitled the 'Public Company Accounting Reform and Investor Protection Act of 2002' 15 USC § 7201 et seq, 107 Public L no 204, 116 Stat 745 (see annex 3 in this volume.

[9] See eg F Partnoy 'Barbarians at the Gatekeepers? A Proposal for a Modified Strict Liability Regime' (2001) 79 Washington U L Q 491; T Hardy 'The Proper Legal Regime for 'Cyberspace'' (1994) 55 U of Pittsburgh L Rev 993 (proposing strict liability for Internet service providers).

[10] A Hamdani 'Gatekeeper Liability' (2003) 77 Southern California L Rev 53. Professor Reinier Kraakman has also warned that strict gatekeeper liability may be undesirable. See R Kraakman Gatekeepers: 'The Anatomy of a Third-Party Enforcement Strategy' (1986) 2 J L Economics and Organization 53, 76.

gatekeepers is also alleviated. Concededly, this proposal does subordinate the goal of victim compensation to that of deterrence, but gatekeepers simply lack the economic scale to be able to fund significant compensation to investors, particularly in the new era of mega-litigation. Finally, by moving closer toward a strict liability system, this proposal eliminates the incentive for auditors to rationalize or overlook fraud or irregularity and later assert on its discovery that they were deceived by management. Rather, the auditor would know that it sinks or swims with its client; hence, half-hearted or pro forma monitoring, which may be a rational strategy under a negligence or fault-based legal regime, no longer protects the gatekeeper.

Part IV recognizes, however, that all gatekeepers are not alike, that strict liability only makes sense when the gatekeeper can effectively prevent client misconduct, and that the attorney is not as well positioned as the auditor to detect client misconduct. In that light, Part IV does not propose strict liability for attorneys, but instead a structural reform: namely, imposing gatekeeper responsibilities on attorneys to monitor their corporation's disclosures, with a special emphasis on non-financial disclosures. The goal here is to empower the gatekeeper and increase its leverage with respect to its client. To achieve this goal, Part IV proposes that the attorney should be given a functionally corresponding responsibility for non-financial disclosures as the auditor now has for financial disclosures. Easy as this is to say, the devil lies in the details. Specifically, Part IV outlines a 'negative assurance' certification requirement, an enhanced independence standard for special contexts, and a due diligence obligation under which the SEC could suspend or disbar securities attorneys who failed negligence or malpractice tests. To be sure, the SEC has already begun to move modestly and tentatively in this same direction by adopting an 'up-the-ladder' internal reporting requirement under which attorneys must report evidence of certain material violations of law that they acquire in their representation of the corporation to the corporation's general counsel or, if necessary, its audit committee.[11] The SEC is also considering, and a number of academics have urged, a further reform under which the attorney would be required to make a 'noisy withdrawal' if the violation continued and threatened serious injury to the corporation.[12] Without disputing the justifications for such a broader rule, Part IV predicts that only modest benefits can be expected from such a reform, because it demands heroism on rare and isolated occasions from the attorney without resting its obligation on a broader functional foundation. In contrast, certification requirements create the broader framework within which the attorney must function on an ongoing basis as a gatekeeper.

[11] See Securities Act Release no 33-8185 ('Implementation of Standards of Professional Conduct for Attorneys') 2003 SEC LEXIS 256 (29 January 2003); see also n 167-182 and accompanying text.

[12] See Securities Act Release no 33-8186 ('Implementation of Standards of Professional Conduct for Attorneys') 2003 SEC LEXIS 266 (29 January 2003).

Of course, any claim that the attorney is, or should be, a gatekeeper, will trigger predictable responses from the bar that such a role conflicts with the other roles that attorneys perform or that it will dry up the flow of information between attorneys and clients. Part IV assesses and rejects these arguments, concluding that the principal consequence of expressly recognizing attorneys as gatekeepers will be instead to enhance their leverage with their clients. In short, the unrecognized consequence of expanded ethical or professional obligations is to empower the gatekeeper, thus responding appropriately to the phenomenon of 'gatekeeper failure'.

II. Gatekeepers: Past and Present

1. Defining the Concept

The term 'gatekeeper' has been widely used to refer to the outside professionals who serve the board or investors.[13] Broadly as the term may be sometimes used, two core elements underlie the concept of gatekeeper, and it is important to distinguish between them. First, the gatekeeper is a person who has significant reputational capital, acquired over many years and many clients, which it pledges to assure the accuracy of statements or representations that it either makes or verifies. Thus, if the gatekeeper's reputational capital exceeds its expected gain from any transaction that it certifies or approves for its client and if this capital is truly at risk, then this system becomes self-enforcing, even in the absence of effective litigation remedies.[14] Second, because the gatekeeper typically receives a far smaller payoff for its role, as an agent, in approving, certifying, or verifying information than does the principal that it serves, it also follows that the gatekeeper is easier to deter. This latter premise means that deterrence is feasible even if the gatekeeper has little or no reputational capital. These two elements – that the gatekeeper is a reputational intermediary and that it receives only a limited payoff from any involvement in misconduct – suggest a strategy for law compli-

[13] The SEC regularly uses this term. See Securities Act Release no 7870 (30 June 2000) (noting that 'the federal laws . . . make independent auditors 'gatekeepers' to the public securities markets'); see also Securities Act Release no 33-7314 (25 July 1996) (discussing 'The Role of Gatekeepers in Maintaining the Quality of Disclosure'). Professor Kraakman has defined gatekeepers as 'private parties who are able to disrupt misconduct by withholding their cooperation from wrongdoers'. See Kraakman (n 10) 53. A Hamdani uses a similarly broad definition, describing them as 'parties who sell a product or service that is necessary for clients wishing to enter a particular market or engage in particular services'. Hamdani (n 10) 58.

[14] In this sense, gatekeepers provide a 'real world' illustration of Oliver Williamson's theory of self-enforcing penalties through the exchange of hostages. See O Williamson 'Credible Commitments: Using Hostages to Support Exchange' (1983) 73 American Economic Rev 519. By pledging its reputational capital, the gatekeeper in effect gives a de facto hostage.

ance: the more the law makes the involvement of gatekeepers in sensitive transactions mandatory, the more it acquires a lever by which it can effectively discourage law violations.

To be sure, the term 'gatekeeper' has also been used more broadly to describe any person or entity who provides a necessary service or certification without which the corporation cannot accomplish a transaction.[15] This may accurately describe their organizational position, but it seems overly broad because it ignores both the deterrent capacity of the gatekeeper and whether it possesses reputational capital. Under this broader definition, Microsoft might become a 'gatekeeper' for most of the business world (on the assumption that its basic Windows technology was indispensable). Thus, this article will use the term 'gatekeeper' more narrowly to mean a reputational intermediary who provides verification or certification services to investors. Still, the focus on the gatekeeper's role in providing a necessary service or certification is useful, because it suggests a regulatory strategy on which this article will focus: by mandating gatekeepers, the law can maximize the probability of deterrence by creating a necessary actor whose compliance with the law it can more effectively influence.

Obvious examples of gatekeepers who provide such verification or certification services would include: (1) the auditor providing its certification of the issuer's financial statements; (2) the debt rating agency certifying the issuer's creditworthiness (or relative creditworthiness); (3) the security analyst providing its objective assessment of the corporation's technology, competitiveness, or earnings prospects; (4) the investment banker providing its 'fairness opinion' as to the pricing of a merger; and (5) the securities attorney for the issuer providing its opinion to the underwriters that all material information of which it is aware concerning the issuer has been properly disclosed. The underwriter in an initial public offering is probably also a gatekeeper in the sense that its reputation is implicitly pledged and it is expected to perform due diligence services. Some professions (most notably, the auditor) provide services that consist primarily of gatekeeping, whereas other professions engage in such services only as an ancillary activity (for example, as discussed later, the attorney is primarily an advocate or a transaction engineer and only sometimes a gatekeeper).

Characteristically, the professional gatekeeper essentially assesses or vouches for the corporate client's own statements about itself or a specific transaction.

[15] Professor R Kraakman originally defined 'gatekeepers' simply in terms of their blocking capacity as private parties who are able to prevent misconduct by withholding their cooperation from wrongdoers. See R Kraakman (n 10) 53; see also R Kraakman 'Corporate Liability Strategies and the Costs of Legal Controls' (1984) 93 Yale L J 857; Hamdani (n 10) 58. This definition strikes me as overly broad, at least for purposes of discussing the role of professionals. It would potentially hold liable persons who sold pencils to Al Capone's gang on the theory that one could not run a brewery and tavern business without using pencils to keep records. Ignored by this definition is whether the gatekeeper possessed the ability to monitor whether its product or service has been misused.

This duplication is desired because the market recognizes that the gatekeeper has a lesser incentive to deceive than does its client and thus regards the gatekeeper's assurance or evaluation as more credible. Unavoidably, the gatekeeper as a watchdog is compromised to a degree by the fact that it is typically paid by the party that it is to monitor. Still, the gatekeeper's relative credibility stems from the fact that it in effect pledges a reputational capital that it has built up over many years of performing similar services for numerous clients. In theory, the gatekeeper as an entity would not rationally sacrifice its reputational capital for a single client or a modest fee.

Nonetheless, here as elsewhere, logic and experience can conflict. Despite the clear logic of the gatekeeper rationale, reliance on gatekeepers can prove to have been misplaced for any of the following reasons:

(1) A sudden decline in the deterrent threat facing gatekeepers could occur, thereby increasing their willingness to take legal risks.

(2) The inducements offered to gatekeepers to breach their duties could similarly be increased, with the same likely result.

(3) The value of their reputational capital could decline, possibly because investors came to undervalue gatekeeping services in a 'bubble market'.

(4) Reputations are relative. Thus, the severity of an injury to a gatekeeper's reputational capital from involvement in a scandal depends on the likelihood of similar injury to its leading competitors. In a very concentrated market (such as the market for auditing services), it might become foreseeable that all the principal firms in the market would be involved in some roughly equivalent number of scandals. As long as each firm was confident that its rivals would behave similarly, it could acquiesce to its client, suffer some rate of scandal, but not fall behind its major competitors. So long as reputations thus became 'noisy' and investors could not distinguish meaningfully among rival firms, the firm could profitably sacrifice reputational capital.

(5) Principal/agent problems can arise within the gatekeeper firm such that agents can rationally decide to risk the firm's reputational capital to a degree that the firm as a whole would resist. This decision to risk the firm's reputational capital may be rational for the agent, but not for the firm, because the agent does not fully bear the loss.

For all these reasons, professional gatekeepers may sometimes acquiesce in managerial fraud, even though the apparent reputational losses seem to dwarf the gains to be made from the individual client.[16]

Much evidence corroborates each of the foregoing hypotheses and suggests that the 'few bad apples' theory is simply incorrect as applied to the performance of gatekeepers in the late 1990s. Still, if we shift from theory to the world of real

[16] This observation is hardly original with this author. See, for example, RA Prentice 'The Case of the Irrational Auditor: A Behavioral Insight Into Securities Fraud Litigation' (2000) 95 Northwestern U L Rev 1333.

actors, consider the facts surrounding Arthur Andersen's fall in 2002. In theory, Andersen should not have acquiesced in accounting irregularities, because it had many clients, each of whom paid a fee that was modest in proportion to the firm's overall revenues. Specifically, Arthur Andersen had approximately 2,300 audit clients.[17] On this basis, the firm seemingly had little incentive to risk its considerable reputational capital for any one client, even if that client paid a multi-million dollar fee. As will be seen however, each of the foregoing hypotheses can contribute to an explanation of gatekeeper failure.

Nonetheless, during the 1990s, many courts bought the logic that gatekeepers do not fail hook, line, and sinker. For example, in *DiLeo v Ernst & Young*,[18] Judge Easterbrook, writing for the Seventh Circuit, outlined precisely the foregoing theory:

> The complaint does not allege that [the auditor] had anything to gain from any fraud by [its client]. An accountant's greatest asset is its reputation for honesty, closely followed by its reputation for careful work. Fees for two years' audits could not approach the losses [that the auditor] would suffer from a perception that it would muffle a client's fraud .... [The auditor's] partners shared none of the gain from any fraud and were exposed to a large fraction of the loss. It would have been irrational for any of them to have joined cause with [the client].[19]

Of course, the modest fees in some of these cases (for example, the audit fee was only $90,000 in *Robin v Arthur Young & Co.*)[20] were well less than the $100 million in prospective annual fees from Enron that Arthur Andersen & Co. explicitly foresaw. But this difference in magnitude cannot really explain Arthur Andersen's collapse. Even if Arthur Andersen saw Enron as a potential $100 million client, it must be remembered that Arthur Andersen generated over $9 billion in revenues in 2001 alone (so that its expected Enron revenues would total only around 1% of its aggregate revenues).[21] Hence, a fuller explanation seems necessary.

[17] See M Mittelstadt 'A Andersen Charged With Obstruction, Vows to Fight' *Dallas Morning News* (Dallas USA 15 March 2002) 1.

[18] 901 F 2d 624 (7th Cir 1990); see also *Melder v Morris* 27 F 3d 1097, 1103 (5th Cir 1994); *Robin v Arthur Young & Co* 915 F 2d 1120, 1127 (7th Cir 1990) (a mere $90,000 annual audit fee would have been an irrational motive for fraud).

[19] See *Dileo v Ernst & Young* 901 F 2d 629.

[20] See *Robin v Arthur Young & Co* 915 F 2d 1120, 1127 (7th Cir 1990).

[21] Arthur Andersen's website reports that revenues for 2001 were $9.34 billion. Also, the $100 million figure was the expected revenue per year that Andersen partners foresaw in the future, when overall revenues would presumably also increase.

2. The Auditing Profession During the 1990s: A Study in Transition

Once among the most respected of all professional service firms (including law, accounting, and consulting firms), Andersen became involved in a series of now well-known securities frauds – eg Waste Management, Sunbeam, HBOC-McKesson, The Baptist Foundation, and Global Crossing – that culminated in its disastrous association with Enron. Those who wish to view the recent corporate scandals as simply the work of a 'few bad apples' may seek to characterize Arthur Andersen as a deviant firm, in effect an 'outlaw' that masqueraded as an honest sheriff. This theory, however, conflicts with the facts. The available evidence in fact suggests that, in terms of the percentage of accounting restatements experienced by its audit clients, Andersen was not significantly different from its peers and experienced the same (or lesser) rate of financial restatements.[22] Although it was more aggressive than its peer firms in the pursuit of consulting income from audit clients, it ultimately made no sense for Andersen to risk its reputational capital by certifying fraudulent financial statements at Enron, when Enron represented at most a projected $100 million in annual revenues to Andersen and Andersen, itself, earned over $9 billion in total annual revenues.[23] Thus, Andersen imploded over a seemingly irrational attempt to earn an additional 1% in revenues.

Indeed, this is the area where the data seems the clearest, and indicates a clear erosion in the quality of financial reporting during the late 1990s. During the 1990s, earnings restatements, long recognized as a proxy for fraud, suddenly soared. One study, conducted in 2001 by Moriarty and Livington, found that the number of earnings restatements by publicly held corporations averaged 49 per

[22] Compared to its peers within the Big Five accounting firms, Arthur Andersen appears to have been responsible for less than its proportionate share of earnings restatements. While it audited 21% of Big 5 audit clients, it was responsible for only 15% of the restatements experienced by the Big Five firms between 1997 and 2001. On this basis, it was arguably slightly more conservative than its peers. See 'A Periscope: How Arthur Andersen Begs for Business' *Newsweek* (New York USA 18 March 2002) 6. For a fuller discussion of the evidence, which reaches the same conclusion that Andersen did not differ materially from its peer firms, see T Eisenberg and JA Macey 'Was Arthur Andersen Different?: An Empirical Examination of Major Accounting Firms' Audits of Large Clients' (2004) 1 J of Empirical Legal Studies 263. In discussions with industry insiders, the only respect in which I have ever heard Andersen characterized as different from its peers in the Big Five was that it marketed itself as a firm in which the audit partner could make the final call on difficult accounting questions without having to secure approval from senior officials within the firm. Although this could translate into a weaker system of internal controls, this hypothesis seems inconsistent with Arthur Andersen's apparently below average rate of earnings restatements.

[23] Arthur Andersen's total revenues for its fiscal year ended 31 August 2001 were $9.3 billion. See M Klein 'Guilty Verdict Draws Mixed Reactions: Profession Mulls Post-Andersen Future' *Accounting Today* (8 July 2002) 1. On this basis, even the $100 million in total fees that Andersen projected from Enron would have come to only slightly over 1% of its total revenues.

year from 1990 to 1997, next increased to 91 in 1998, and then skyrocketed to 150 and 156 in 1999 and 2000, respectively.[24] A fuller study conducted by the United States General Accounting Office in October 2002 examined all financial statement restatements (not just earnings restatements) and also found a similarly sharp, discontinuous spike in 1999 that has continued through 2002.[25] The GAO Study's data shows the following trend line:[26]

Figure 1: Total Number of Restatement Announcements Identified, 1997-2002

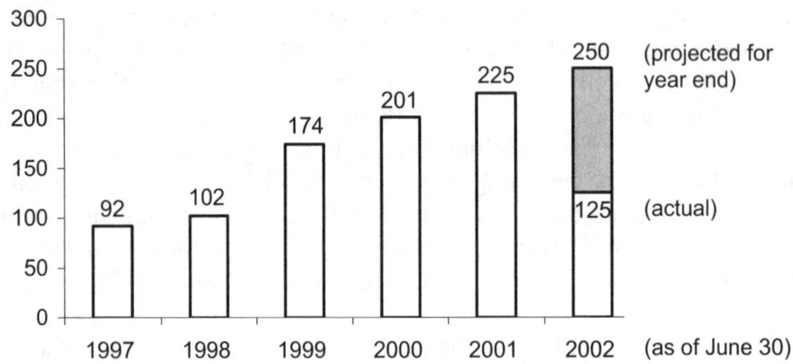

Not all restatements, however, are equal. Some may involve small, infrequently traded companies or involve only trivial changes or trigger only modest stock price reactions, while others may be on a scale with Enron or WorldCom. Some restatements actually involved increases, rather than declines, in earnings. Given the diversity of restatements, it is useful to focus more precisely on financial statement restatements by companies listed on the NYSE, Amex, and Nasdaq, thereby excluding smaller companies that trade only on regional exchanges or over the counter. Between 1997 and 2001, the proportion of listed companies on the NYSE, Amex, and Nasdaq that restated their financial statement approximately tripled, increasing from less than 0.89% in 1997 to approximately 2.5% in 2001.[27] Indeed, the GAO Study further predicted that this percentage would reach

[24] See GB Moriarty and PB Livingston 'Quantitative Measures of the Quality of Financial Reporting' (2001) 17 Financial Executive 53, 54.

[25] See GAO Study (n 4) 4-5. A more recent study by the Huron Consulting Group finds an even higher rate of restatements: 216 in 1999; 233 in 2000; 270 in 2001; and 220 in 2003. On this basis, roughly one in eight publicly held companies restated their financial statements. See Huron Consulting Group *2003 Annual Review of Financial Reporting Matters* 4. The number of restatements fell modestly to 323 in 2004, but has since risen again.

[26] See GAO Study (n 4) 15.

[27] ibid 4.

nearly 3% in 2002.[28] Overall, the GAO Study found that from January 1997 to June 2002, approximately '10 percent of all listed companies announced at least one restatement'.[29] Also noteworthy was the fact that the size (in terms of market capitalization) of the typical restating company rose rapidly over this period,[30] and in 2002, companies listed on the NYSE or Nasdaq accounted for over 85% of all restatements identified in that year.[31] Hence, restatements no longer reflected mistakes made by small, new, or inexperienced companies, but instead indicated behavioral changes and increased risk-taking at large, mature firms.

In theory, financial restatements could simply be the product of changes in regulatory rules, and an increase in frequency could signify only tighter regulation. But this premise is disproven if the market is surprised by the restatement. Also, in the real world, issuers resist restatements because they fear that stock price drops, securities class actions, and SEC investigations generally follow in the wake of financial statement restatements. In any event, the GAO Study found that restating companies over the 1997 to 2001 period suffered an immediate market-adjusted stock price decline equal to 10% on average of the restating firm's market capitalization, measured on the basis of the stock's three-day price movement from the trading day before the announcement through the trading day after the announcement.[32] Between 1997 to 2002, restating firms lost over $100 billion in market capitalization just over this three-trading-day period surrounding a restatement announcement.[33]

Given these significant and adverse stock price effects, it is implausible to read the sharp increase in restatements at the end of the 1990s as the product of any new tolerance for, or indifference to, restatements. Even if (as some audit firms have contended) some portion of the change might be attributed to a new SEC pronouncements or, more generally, to an SEC activism about 'earnings management',[34] which became an SEC enforcement priority by 1998,[35] this ex-

[28] ibid.

[29] ibid. However, this figure rises to around 12 ½% (or one in eight) if one instead relies on the Huron Consulting Group's study. See Huron Consulting Group (n 25).

[30] Specifically, the average (median) size by market capitalization of a restating company rose from $500 million ($143 million) in 1997 to $2 billion ($351 million) in 2002. See GAO Study (n 4) 4.

[31] Of the 125 actual restatements identified through mid-2002, 54 were listed on Nasdaq, and 53 were listed on the NYSE (for a total of 107 or 85%). ibid.

[32] ibid 5. The GAO Study also found a longer term market-adjusted decline of 18% over the period from 60 trading days before the announcement to 60 trading days after the announcement. ibid 29.

[33] ibid 28.

[34] Accounting firms have sometimes attempted to explain this increase in restatements on the basis that the SEC tightened the definition of materiality in the late 1990s. This explanation is not very convincing, in part because the principal SEC statement that tightened the definition of materiality – Staff Accounting Bulletin no 99 – was issued in mid-1999, after the number of

cont. ...

planation cannot carry us very far. Although SEC activism might trigger some increase in the number of restatements, it cannot explain the growth in the magnitude of restatements or the sharp stock price decline (averaging 10%) on their announcement.[36] 'Technical' restatements made simply to comply with new SEC interpretations should produce only an indifferent yawn from the stock market. But an average drop of 10% clearly shows that the market was on average surprised.

The available data shows that, during the late 1990s, the magnitude of financial restatements increased, both in absolute terms (nearly doubling) and as a percentage of the issuer's rapidly increasing market capitalization.[37] This suggests that managers became progressively willing over this period to take greater risks. Moreover, as the decade of the 1990s wore on, earnings restatements were increasingly experienced by large, mature, publicly held firms, rather than by smaller or newly public companies that might be expected to be more inexperienced or rash. Managerial behavior within the largest firms seems then to have changed over this period.

In particular, the GAO Study's data corroborates this interpretation that managerial behavior changed, because it shows a significant change in motive. Although there are many reasons why a company may restate its financial statements (eg to adjust costs or expenses or to recognize liabilities), one particular reason dominated during the period from 1997 to 2002. The GAO Study found that issues involving revenue recognition accounted for almost 39% of the 919 announced restatements that it identified over the 1997 to 2002 period.[38] In effect, attempts by management to prematurely recognize income appear to have been the most common cause of restatements. Earlier in the decade and during prior decades, earnings management was more a game of 'smoothing out' the peaks and valleys in a corporation's income flow in order to reduce the apparent

restatements had already begun to soar in 1998. Also, SAB no 99 did not truly mandate restatements, but only advised that any rule of thumb employed by auditors and issuers that assumed that amounts under 5% were inherently immaterial could not be applied reflexively.

[35] The SEC's prioritization of earnings management as a principal enforcement target can be approximately dated to SEC Chairman Arthur Levitt's now famous speech on the subject in 1998. See A Levitt 'The Numbers Game, Remarks at NYU Center for Law and Business' (28 September 1998).

[36] See text and notes supra at notes 32-33.

[37] According to Moriarty and Livingston (n 24), companies that restated earnings suffered market losses of $17.7 billion in 1998, $24.2 billion in 1999, and $31.2 billion in 2000, ibid 55. Expressed as a percentage of the overall capitalization of the market (which was ascending hyperbolically over this period), these losses for 1998 through 2000 came to 0.13%, 0.14%, and 0.19%, respectively, of market capitalization. In short, however expressed, the relative size of the losses increased over this period.

[38] See GAO Study (n 4) 5. Revenue recognition was also the leading reason for restatements in each individual year over this period.

volatility in the corporation's returns. Thus, managements characteristically attempted to hide 'excess earnings' in 'rainy day reserves' in order to use such funds later to smooth out undesired declines in the firm's earnings.

Despite this earlier preference for income-smoothing, by the end of the 1990s, these same firms were robbing future periods for earnings that could be recognized immediately. In short, 'income smoothing' gave way to more predatory behavior. Symptomatically, restatements involving revenue recognition produced disproportionately large losses.[39] The market appears to have responded more negatively to revenue recognition restatements than to any other form of restatement.[40] Seemingly, the market feared revenue-timing restatements because of the apparent signal they carried that reported earnings could not be trusted. Yet, despite the market's antipathy for them, revenue recognition restatements became the most common form of restatement. At a minimum, this suggests that the interests of management and shareholders were not aligned, and that gatekeepers became progressively unable to serve shareholders, who deeply feared revenue recognition errors.

3. Security Analysts During the 1990s

Before any attempt is made to generalize about the motivations that led managements to pressure their auditors for premature revenue recognition, it is useful to recognize that this pattern of increased acquiescence by the gatekeeper to its clients' demands during the 1990s was not limited to the auditing profession. Security analysts are probably the only other profession that has experienced equivalent (or harsher) criticism since the collapse of the high-tech bubble in 2000. Again, growing conflicts of interest appear to explain their change in behavior.

Some of the evidence relating to gatekeeper failure involving analysts is anecdotal, but striking. As late as October 2001, shortly before Enron's bankruptcy, 16 out of the 17 securities analysts covering Enron maintained 'buy' or 'strong buy' recommendations on its stock.[41] Yet, months earlier as of 31 Decem-

[39] While revenue recognition restatements accounted for 39% of restatements over the 1997 to 2002 period, they were associated with $56 billion (or roughly 56%) of the $100 billion in market capitalization that restating companies lost over this period. Ibid 28.

[40] See KL Anderson and TL Yohn 'The Effect of 10k Restatements on Firm Value, Information Asymmetries, and Investors' Reliance on Earnings' <http://ssrn.com/abstract=332380> (25 April 2005) 13.

[41] See 'Statement of Frank Torres, Legislative Counsel, Consumers Union, Before the United States Senate, Committee on Governmental Affairs, on the Collapse of Enron: The Role Analysts Played and the Conflicts They Face' (27 February 2002) 6 ('In the case of Enron, 16 out of 17 analysts had a buy or a strong buy rating, one had a hold, none had a sell – even as the company stock had lost over half its value and its CEO suddenly resigned.'). 2002 WL cont. ...

ber 2000, Enron already had a stock price that was 70 times earnings and six times its book value, and had earned an 89% return for the year (despite a 9% decrease over the same period for the S&P 500 index).[42] Such a profile should have seemingly alerted any analyst who was even half awake to the possibility that Enron was seriously overvalued. Symptomatically, however, the first brokerage firm to downgrade Enron to a 'sell' rating in 2001 was Prudential Securities, which did not then engage in investment banking activities.[43] Prudential was also believed to have the highest proportion of sell ratings among the stocks it evaluated.[44] Perhaps Prudential also woke up late, but it is still at least revealing that the least conflicted were the first to awake.

How close then are the similarities between analysts and auditors? Much like auditors, analysts are also 'reputational intermediaries', whose desire to be perceived as credible and objective may often be subordinated to their desire to retain and please investment banking clients. One statistic inevitably comes up in any assessment of analyst objectivity: namely, the curious fact that the ratio of 'buy' recommendations to 'sell' recommendations has recently been as high as 100 to 1.[45] In truth, this particular statistic may not be as compelling as it initially sounds because there are obvious reasons why 'buy' recommendations will normally outnumber 'sell' recommendations, even in the absence of conflicts of interest.[46] Yet, a related statistic may be more revealing because it underscores the apparent transition that took place in the 1990s and parallels the earlier noted increase in accounting restatements during the 1990s. According to a study by

2011028; see also testimony of F Partnoy 'Hearings before the United States Senate Committee on Governmental Affairs' 24 January 2002 (similar 16 out of 17 tabulation).

[42] See PM Healy and K Palepu 'Governance and Intermediation Problems in Capital Markets: Evidence From the Fall of Enron' Harvard NOM Research Paper no 02-27 (August 2002) 2.

[43] See L Young 'Independence Day' *Smartmoney* (1 May 2001) 28 vol XI no V, 2002 WL 2191410.

[44] ibid.

[45] A study by Thomas Financial/First Call has found that less than 1% of the 28,000 stock recommendations issued by brokerage firm analysts during late 1999 and most of 2000 were 'sell' recommendations. See Opening Statement of Congressman Paul E Kanjorski; Ranking Democratic Member, House Subcommittee on Capital Markets, Insurance, and Government Sponsored Enterprises 'Hearing on Analyzing the Analysts' 14 June 2001, 1 (citing and discussing this study).

[46] 'Sell-side' analysts are employed by brokerage firms that understandably wish to maximize brokerage transactions. In this light, a 'buy' recommendation by a sell-side analyst addresses the entire market and certainly all the firm's customers, while a 'sell' recommendation addresses only those customers who own the stock (probably well less than 1%) and those with margin accounts who are willing to sell the stock 'short'. In addition, 'sell' recommendations annoy not only the issuer company, but also institutional investors who are afraid that sell recommendations will 'spook' retail investors, causing them to panic and sell, while the institution is 'locked into' a large position that cannot easily be liquidated.

Thomson Financial, the ratio of 'buy' to 'sell' recommendations increased from 6 to 1 in 1991 to 100 to 1 by 2000.[47]

Other evidence corroborates this picture of a systematic analyst bias toward optimism. Studying security analyst career patterns over the last two decades, Hong and Kubik find that career advancement for analysts depended more on a bias toward optimism than on the overall accuracy of their forecasts.[48] Although accuracy did matter, a tendency to be more optimistic than the consensus of analysts seemed to protect analysts from downward movement within their industry's hierarchy, and this tendency was most pronounced in the case of analysts who covered stocks underwritten by their own firms.[49] More importantly, this tendency for optimism to outweigh accuracy increased during the late 1990s.[50] They interpret their findings as at least consistent with the view 'that Wall Street lost any self-discipline to produce accurate research during the recent stock market mania'.[51] Perhaps this assessment overstates, but the conclusion seems hard to escape that something happened during the 1990s that compromised the independence and objectivity of the gatekeepers on whom our private system of corporate governance depends.[52] Even before Enron, much evidence showed that the most sophisticated market participants understood the extent of these conflicts and had ceased to rely on 'sell side' analysts.[53]

4. Explaining Gatekeeper Failure

The same observation has probably occurred to many: none of the watchdogs that should have detected Enron's collapse – auditors, analysts, or debt rating agencies – awoke before the penultimate moment. This is the common denominator, not

[47] See Opening Statement of Congressman Paul E Kanjorski (n 45) 1 (citing study by First Call).

[48] See H Hong and J Kubik 'Analyzing the Analysts: Career Concerns and Biased Earnings Forecasts' (2003) 58 J of Finance 313.

[49] ibid 341.

[50] ibid 342, 346 (finding that between 1996 and 2000, a strong bias toward optimism decreased an analyst's risk of downward movement in the industry).

[51] ibid 345-46.

[52] Participants in the industry also report that its professional culture changed dramatically in the late 1990s, particularly as investment banking firms began to hire star analysts for their marketing clout. See G Morgenson 'Requiem for an Honorable Profession' *New York Times* (New York USA 5 May 2002) section 3-1 (suggesting major change dates from around 1996).

[53] Although the empirical evidence is limited, it suggests that independent analysts (ie analysts not associated with the underwriter for a particular issuer) behave differently than, and tend to outperform, analysts who are associated with the issuer's underwriter. See R Michaely and K Womack 'Conflict of Interest and the Credibility of Underwriter Analyst Recommendations' (1999) 12 Review of Financial Studies 653.

just in the case of Enron, but also in many of the other 'accounting irregularity' cases of 2001-2002. What plausible hypothesis can explain the collective failure of these gatekeepers? Here, several different, although ultimately complementary, stories can be told. Initially, this section will first review two generalized stories: the first will be called the 'general deterrence' story; and the second, the 'bubble' story. Then, it will focus on allocating responsibility among gatekeepers, managers, and investors.

a. The Deterrence Explanation: The Underdeterred Gatekeeper

The general deterrence story focuses on the decline in the expected liability costs associated with acquiescence by auditors in aggressive accounting policies favored by managements. It postulates that, during the 1990s, the risk of auditor liability declined, while the benefits of acquiescence increased. Economics 101 teaches us that when the costs go down, while the benefits associated with any activity go up, the output of the activity will increase. Here, the activity that increased was auditor acquiescence.

Prior to the 1990s, auditors faced a very real risk of civil liability, principally from class action litigation.[54] Why did the legal risks go down during the 1990s? The obvious list of reasons would include:

(a) the Supreme Court's *Lampf, Pleva* decision, which in 1991 significantly shortened the statute of limitations applicable to securities fraud;[55]

(b) the Supreme Court's *Central Bank of Denver* decision,[56] which in 1994 eliminated private 'aiding and abetting' liability in securities fraud cases;

[54] As of 1992, Congress was advised that the securities fraud litigation costs for just the six largest accounting firms (then the 'Big Six') accounted for $783 million, or more than 14% of their audit revenues. Potential exposure to loss was in the billions. See Private Litigation Under the Federal Securities Laws: Hearings Before the Subcommittee on Securities of the Senate Committee on Banking, Housing and Urban Affairs, 103rd Cong, 1st Session no103-431 (1993) (statement of JL Netterville), reprinted in Fed Sec L Rep (CCH) no 1696 (10 January 1996). One major auditing firm, Laventhol & Horwath, did fail and entered bankruptcy as a result of litigation and associated scandals growing out of the savings and loan scandals of the 1980s. See 'What Role Should CPA's Be Playing in Audit Reform?' Partner's Report for CPA Firm Owners, April 2002 (discussing experience of Laventhol & Horwath). The accounting profession's bitter experience with class litigation in the 1980s and 1990s probably explains why it became the strongest and most organized champion of the Private Securities Litigation Reform Act of 1995.

[55] *Lampf, Pleva, Lipkind & Petigrow v Gilbertston* 501 US 350, 359-61 (1991) (creating a federal rule requiring plaintiffs to file within one year of when they should have known of the violation underlying their action, but in no event more than three years after the violation). This one- to three-year period was typically shorter than the previously applicable limitations periods which were determined by analogy to state statutes and often permitted a five- or six-year delay – if that was the period within which a common law fraud action could be maintained in the particular state.

(c) the Private Securities Litigation Reform Act of 1995 ('PSLRA'), which (i) raised the pleading standards for securities class actions to a level well above that applicable to fraud actions generally; (ii) substituted proportionate liability for 'joint and several' liability; (iii) restricted the sweep of the RICO statute so that it could no longer convert securities fraud class actions for compensatory damages into actions for treble damages; and (iv) adopted a very protective safe harbor for forward-looking information;[57] and

(d) the Securities Litigation Uniform Standards Act of 1998 ('SLUSA'), which abolished state court class actions alleging securities fraud.[58]

The individual impact of each of these changes probably cannot be reliably measured, but their concurrent aggregate impact is clear: they greatly reduced the plaintiffs' incentives in securities class actions to sue secondary participants, such as auditors, analysts, and attorneys. As an SEC study noted, the number of audit-related suits filed against the then 'Big Six' accounting firms in 1990 to 1992 was 192, 172, and 141, respectively.[59] Yet, in the first year following the passage of the PSLRA (1996), the SEC found that out of the 105 securities class actions it found to have been filed in that year, accounting firms were named in only six cases, corporate counsel in no cases, and underwriters in nineteen cases.[60] It concluded: 'Secondary defendants such as accountants and lawyers, are being named less frequently in securities class actions.'[61]

[56] *Central Bank of Denver NA v First Interstate of Denver NA* (1994) 511 US 164.

[57] The relevant provisions of the PSLRA are contained in section 21D of the Securities Exchange Act of 1934, except for the 'safe harbor', which is in Section 21E of that Act.

[58] See Public L no 105-353, 112 Stat 3227 (codified in scattered sections of 15 USC). For an analysis and critique of this statute, see R Painter 'Responding to A False Alarm: Federal Preemption of State Securities Fraud Causes of Action' (1998) 84 Cornell L Rev 1.

[59] See US Securities and Exchange Commission, Office of the General Counsel *Report to the President and the Congress on the First Year of Practice under the Private Securities Litigation Reform Act of 1995* (April 1997) 22 (available on SEC website at <http://www.sec.gov/news/studies/lreform.txt> (21 April 2005)). The figures for the years 1990 to 1992 were reported to the SEC by the Big Six and include all class actions against them, which could include some non-securities class actions. Nonetheless, the number of such non-securities actions seems likely to have been small. As the above SEC study further notes: '[D]uring the period from 1991 through June 1996, accountants were defendants in 52 reported settlements (as opposed to complaints) … and law firms were defendants in 7. Thus, there seems to be a real decline in the number of lawsuits against secondary defendants.' ibid 22. This low incidence of securities class actions against auditors appears to have continued through 2001 – and then began to rise dramatically. See PriceWaterhouseCoopers *LLP 2002 Securities Litigation Study* (2003) 7 (reporting that number of securities class actions against auditors fell from 1998 to 2001).

[60] US Securities and Exchange Commission (n 59) 21-22.

[61] ibid 4. As this study expressly noted, this decline could have been caused both by the PSLRA and by the Supreme Court's decision in *Central Bank of Denver* in 1994 that ended private 'aiding and abetting' liability under Rule 10b-5. See n 56-57 and accompanying text.

Not only did the threat of private enforcement decline, but the prospect of public enforcement similarly subsided. In particular, there is reason to believe that, from some point in the 1980s until the late 1990s, the SEC shifted its enforcement focus away from actions against the Big Five accounting firms toward other priorities.[62] In any event, the point here is not that any of these changes were necessarily unjustified or excessive, but rather that their collective impact was to appreciably reduce the risk of liability. Auditors were the special beneficiaries of many of these provisions. For example, the pleading rules and the new standard of proportionate liability protected them far more than it did most corporate defendants.[63] Although auditors are still sued today, the settlement value of cases against auditors has gone way down.

Correspondingly, the benefits of acquiescence to auditors rose over this same period, as the Big Five learned during the 1990s how to cross-sell consulting services and to treat the auditing function principally as a portal of entry into a lucrative client. Prior to the mid-1990s, the provision of consulting services to audit clients was infrequent and insubstantial in the aggregate.[64] Yet, according to

[62] This point has been orally made to me by several former SEC officials, including Stanley Sporkin, the long-time former head of the Commission's Division of Enforcement. They believe that the SEC's enforcement action against Arthur Andersen, which was resolved in June 2001, was one of the very few (and perhaps the only) enforcement action brought against a Big Five accounting firm on fraud grounds during the 1990s. See *Securities and Exchange Commission v Arthur Andersen LLP* SEC Litigation Release no 17039, 2001 SEC LEXIS 1159 (19 June 2001). Although the Commission did bring charges during the 1990s against individual partners in these firms, the Commission appears to have been deterred from bringing suits against the Big Five themselves because such actions were extremely costly in manpower and expense and the defendants could be expected to resist zealously. In contrast, during the 1980s, especially during Mr. Sporkin's tenure as head of the Enforcement Division, the SEC regularly brought enforcement actions against the Big Five.

[63] At a minimum, plaintiffs today must plead with particularity facts giving rise to a 'strong inference of fraud'. See eg *Novak v Kasaks* 216 F3d 300 (2nd Cir 2000) *cert denied* 521 US 1012 (2000). At the outset of a case, it may be possible to plead such facts with respect to the management of the corporate defendant (for example, based on insider sales by such persons prior to the public disclosure of the adverse information that caused the stock drop), but it is rarely possible to plead such information with respect to the auditors (who by law cannot own stock in their client). In short, the plaintiff faces a 'Catch 22' dilemma in suing the auditor: it cannot plead fraud with particularity until it obtains discovery, and it cannot obtain discovery under the PSLRA until it pleads fraud with particularity.

[64] Consulting fees paid by audit clients exploded during the 1990s. According to the Panel on Audit Effectiveness, which was appointed in 1999 by the Public Oversight Board at the request of the SEC to study audit practices, 'audit firms' fees from consulting services for their SEC clients increased from 17% . . . of audit fees in 1990 to 67% . . . in 1999'. See the Panel on Audit Effectiveness *Report and Recommendations* (Exposure Draft 2000) 102. In 1990, the Panel found that 80% of the Big Five firms' SEC clients received no consulting services from their auditors, and only 1% of those SEC clients paid consulting fees exceeding their auditing fees to the Big Five, ibid 102. While the Panel found only marginal changes during the 1990s,

cont. ...

one recent survey, the typical large public corporation now pays its auditor for consulting services three times what it pays the same auditor for auditing services.[65] Not only did auditing firms see more profit potential in consulting than in auditing, but they also began during the 1990s to compete based on a strategy of 'low balling' under which auditing services were offered at rates that were marginal to arguably below cost. The rationale for such a strategy was that the auditing function was essentially a loss leader by which more lucrative services could be marketed.

Although this argument that the provision of consulting services eroded auditor independence has considerable explanatory power, there is an obvious reply: those who defend the propriety of consulting services by auditors respond that the growth of consulting services made little real difference, because the audit firm was already conflicted by the fact that the client paid its fees. Put as bluntly as possible, the audit partner of a major client (such as Enron) is always conflicted by the fact that such a partner has virtually a 'one-client' practice. Whoever is the gatekeeper – attorney, auditor, or analyst – a 'one client' practice compromises the agent. Should the partner lose that client for any reason, the partner will likely need to find employment elsewhere. In short, both critics and defenders of the status quo tend to agree that the individual audit partner is already inevitably compromised by his or her desire to hold the client on whom the agent's career depends. From this premise, a prophylactic rule prohibiting the firm's involvement in consulting would seemingly achieve little.

Even if true in part, this rebuttal nonetheless misses one key point: namely, the difficulty faced by the client in firing the auditor in the real world. As discussed below, there are real costs associated with firing an auditor (but, in contrast, none to speak of in firing a consultant). Given this disparity, an unintended consequence of combining consulting services with auditing services in one firm is that the union of the two enables the client to more effectively threaten the auditing firm in a 'low visibility' way. To illustrate this point, let us suppose, for example, that a client becomes dissatisfied with an auditor who refuses to endorse an aggressive accounting policy favored by its management. Today, the client cannot easily fire the auditor. Firing the auditor may result in public embarrassment, potential public disclosure of the reasons for the auditor's

later studies have found that consulting fees have become a multiple of the audit fee for large public corporations. See n 65 and accompanying text.

[65] A survey by the *Chicago Tribune* this year finds that the one hundred largest corporations in the Chicago area (determined on the basis of market capitalization) paid consulting fees to their auditors that were on average over three times the audit fee paid the same auditor. See JK Stewart and A Countryman 'Local Audit Conflicts Add Up: Consulting Deals, Hiring Practices In Question' *Chicago Tribune* (Chicago United States 24 February 2002) C-1. The extreme example in this study was Motorola, which had over a 16:1 ratio between consulting fees and audit fees.

dismissal or resignation, or a probable SEC intervention.[66] However, if the auditor also becomes a consultant to the client, the client can then easily terminate the auditor as a consultant (or reduce its use of the firm's consulting services) in retaliation for the auditor's intransigence. This low visibility response neither requires any disclosure, nor invites any SEC oversight, and yet incentivizes the audit firm to replace the intransigent audit partner. In effect, the client can bribe (or coerce) the auditor in its core professional role by raising (or reducing) its use of consulting services.

Of course, this argument that the client can discipline and threaten the auditor/consultant in ways that it could not discipline the simple auditor is based more on logic than actual case histories. But at least some data corroborates it. One recent study by academic accounting experts, based on proxy statements filed during the first half of 2001, finds that those firms that purchased more non-audit services from their auditor (as a percentage of the total fee paid to the audit firm) were more likely to fit the profile of a firm engaging in earnings management.[67]

b. The Market Bubble Story

Alternatively, Enron's and Arthur Andersen's downfalls, and the host of other sudden stock declines in 2001 to 2002, can be seen as the consequence of a classic bubble that overtook the equity markets in the late 1990s and produced a market euphoria.[68] But what exactly is the connection between a market bubble

[66] Item 4 ('Changes in Registrants Certifying Accountant') of Form 8-K requires a 'reporting' company to file a Form 8-K within five days after the resignation or dismissal of the issuer's independent accountant or that of the independent accountant for a significant subsidiary of the issuer. The Form 8-K must then provide the elaborate disclosures mandated by Item 304 of Regulation S-K relating to any dispute or disagreement between the auditor and the accountant. See 17 CFR 228.304 ('Changes in and Disagreements With Accountants on Accounting and Financial Disclosure').

[67] See R Frankel M Johnson and K Nelson 'The Relation Between Auditors' Fees for Non-Audit Services and Earnings Quality' MIT Sloan Working Paper no 4330-02 (available from Social Sciences Research Network id 296557). Firms purchasing more non-audit services were found more likely to just meet or beat analysts' forecasts, which is the standard profile of the firm playing 'the numbers game'. Since the publication of the Frankel, Johnson, and Nelson study, there have been a host of similar studies, many reaching inconsistent results, and this article will not seek to resolve this dispute.

[68] The literature on bubbles is now burgeoning. Perhaps the best-known scholar in this field was Charles Kindleberger, who viewed bubbles as 'demand determined' and the product of irrational investors. See CP Kindleberger *Mania, Panics and Crashes: A History of Financial Crises* (Wiley New York 2000) 76-78. See also RJ Shiller *Irrational Exuberance* (Princeton University Press Princeton 2001); A Shleifer *Inefficient Markets* (OUP Oxford 2000); KA Froot and M Obstfeld 'Intrinsic Bubbles: The Case of Stock Prices' (1991) 81 American Economic Rev 1189. While most of these recent accounts focus on and assign causal responsibility to

cont. ...

and gatekeeper failure? Here, a hypothesis needs to be advanced that cannot be rigorously proven, but that is consistent with modern behavioral economics: in a bubble, gatekeepers become less relevant and hence experience a decline in both their leverage over their client and the value of their reputational capital. That is, in an atmosphere of market euphoria, investors rely less on gatekeepers, and managements in turn regard them as more a formality than a necessity. Gatekeepers provide a critical service only when investors are cautious and skeptical and therefore rely on their services. Conversely, in a market bubble, caution and skepticism are by definition largely abandoned. In such an environment, auditors continue to be used more because SEC rules mandate their use (or because no individual firm wishes to call attention to itself by becoming the first to dispense with them) than because investors actually demand their use. As a result, because gatekeepers have reduced relevance in such a environment, they also have reduced leverage with their clients. Thus, if we assume that the auditor will be largely ignored by euphoric investors, the rational auditor's best competitive strategy (at least for the short term) was to become as acquiescent and low cost as possible.

Although this thesis assigns some causal responsibility to investors themselves for their own losses, it does not absolve gatekeepers from responsibility. For example, even if shareholders do not care much during a bubble about the auditor's reputation, it is still possible for an auditor to intervene effectively and prevent fraud, either by refusing to certify the issuer's financial statements, by withdrawing its certificate on a later discovery of the fraud, or by notifying the SEC.[69]

The key element in this story involves why investors ceased to care about the gatekeeper's reputation. After all, the rise of auditing as a profession was the product of investors' own concerns about fraud and irregularity, not regulatory requirements. What then caused this concern to weaken? Here, behavioral economics supplies a plausible answer. Modern economics recognizes that individuals, including investors, have 'bounded rationality' and do not pursue all information relevant to an optimal decision.[70] The Nobel Prize-winning research of

'noise traders', the account offered here focuses more on a behavioral phenomenon: 'persistence bias' and the tendency of investors to expect recent exceptional returns to continue.

[69] Securities Exchange Act of 1934 s 10A requires the auditor of a public company to notify the Commission where the auditor discovers an 'illegal act [that] has a material effect on the financial statements of the issuer' and management and the board of the issuer have not taken 'timely and appropriate remedial action' after notification by the auditor. See 15 USC §78(j)(A). Since its adoption in 1995, this provision has been seldom, if ever, employed.

[70] For overviews of behavioral economics, see C Jolis C Sunstein and R Thaler 'A Behavioral Approach to Law and Economics' (1998) 50 Stanford L Rev 1471; C Sunstein 'Behavioral Analysis of Law' (1997) 64 U Chicago L Rev 1175. The term 'bounded rationality' was coined by Herbert Simon, a Nobel prize winner, and is broadly accepted by most economists. See HA Simon 'Rationality As Process and Product of Thought' (1978) 68 American Economic Rev: Papers & Proceedings 1.

Professors Kahneman and Tversky has in particular demonstrated that individuals typically make decisions by using heuristics – that is, rules of thumb – rather than by incorporating all obtainable information. A heuristic that they find to be pervasively used by individuals and that has particular relevance to the context of securities markets is the 'availability heuristic'.[71] It asserts that individuals estimate the frequency of an event by recalling recent instances of its occurring (even if these instances are normally rare or infrequent, when viewed from a longer term perspective). Hence, if the stock market has recently experienced extraordinary returns for several years, it becomes predictable that individuals will overestimate the likelihood of such extraordinary gains continuing.[72] In effect, there is a status quo or persistence bias – what has recently occurred is expected to continue. Thus, as the market soared in the early and mid-1990s, investors, operating on heuristics, came to assume that this pattern would continue. Further aggravating this tendency is the deep-seated bias displayed by many individuals toward optimism in predicting future events.[73]

Thus, from the perspective of behavioral economics, 'bubbles' are not irrational moments of speculative excess or frenzy, but rather are the product of the predictable expectations of individuals who tend to assume that whatever has recently occurred will persist. To trigger this persistence bias, it is arguably only necessary that market returns have in fact been extraordinary for a few successive years in order to cause investors to treat this phenomenon as normal and likely to continue. Such an explanation helps us understand why bubbles have re-occurred throughout history. Their re-occurrence is explained not by the hypothesis that investors are inherently gullible, but by the explanation that a period of extraordinary returns creates an expectation that such returns are normal and will persist.

Such heuristic biases are not, of course, the whole story. For the securities analyst, a market bubble presents a different and more serious challenge: during a bubble, those who are cautious and prudent will be outperformed by those who recklessly predict extraordinary returns. Hence, in a bubble, extreme optimism for analysts becomes less a heuristic bias than a competitive necessity. Put more bluntly, it is dangerous to be sane in an insane world. As a result, the securities analyst who prudently predicted reasonable growth and stock appreciation during the 1990s was increasingly left in the dust by the investment guru who pro-

[71] See Jolis Sunstein and Thaler (n 70) 1477-78. See also A Tversky and D Kahneman 'Judgment Under Uncertainty: Heuristics and Biases' in D Kahneman P Slovic and A Tversky (eds) *Judgment under Uncertainty* (Cambridge University Press Cambridge 1982) 3.

[72] This is by no means the only way to explain bubbles without resorting to claims of mass delusion. An alternative theory is that institutional money managers have rational incentives to engage in 'herding behavior', preferring a common wrong decision to a risky correct one. See n 89 to 91 and accompanying text.

[73] See Jolis Sunstein and Thaler (n 70) 1524-25; see also ND Weinstein 'Unrealistic Optimism About Future Life Events' (1980) 39 J of Personality and Social Psychology 806.

phesized a new investment paradigm in which revenues and costs were less important than the number of 'hits' on a website.

Institutional factors compounded this problem. As the initial public offering (or 'IPO') market soared in the 1990s, securities analysts became celebrities and valuable assets to their firms;[74] indeed, they became the principal means by which investment banks competed for IPO clients, as the underwriter with the 'star' analyst could produce the greatest first-day stock price spike in an IPO. But as their salaries thus soared, analyst compensation came increasingly from the investment banking side of their firms. Hence, just as in the case of the auditor, the analyst's economic position became progressively dependent on favoring the interests of persons outside their profession (ie consultants in the case of the auditor and investment bankers in the case of the analyst) who had little reason to respect or observe the standards or professional culture within the gatekeeper's profession.[75]

One common denominator linking these examples is that, as auditors increasingly sought consulting income and as analysts became more dependent on an investment banking subsidy, these gatekeepers' normal desire to preserve their reputational capital for the long run become subordinated to their desire to obtain extraordinary returns in the short run by risking that reputational capital. Alternatively, the value of gatekeepers' reputational capital may have simply declined in a bubble, because investors in such an environment rationally reduce their reliance on gatekeeping services based on their false belief that extraordinary returns will persist. Under either story (or both together), it could have become more profitable for firms to realize the value of their reputational capital by trading on it in the short run than by preserving it forever. Indeed, during the 1990s, to the extent that auditing became a loss leader for multi-service accounting firms eager to sell more lucrative consulting services and, to the extent that securities analysts began to be subsidized by investment banking, each profession became less self-supporting and more dependent on those who wished to profit from the liquidation of their reputational capital.

[74] For the view that investment banking firms changed their competitive strategies on or around 1996 and thereafter sought the 'popular, high-profile analyst' as a means of acquiring IPO clients, see Morgenson (n 52) 3-1 (quoting chief investment officer at Trust Company of the West).

[75] This idea that professional gatekeepers became dominated by persons outside their profession is at the heart of a recent lawsuit initiated by the New York attorney general against five chief executive officers of major US corporations. See P McGeehan 'Spitzer Sues Executives of Telecom Companies Over "Ill Gotten" Gains' *New York Times* (New York United States 1 October 2002) C-1.

c. Allocating Responsibility Among Gatekeepers, Managers, and Investors

The foregoing explanations still do not fully describe the motives for why reputational capital that had been built up over decades might be willingly risked, sacrificed, or even liquidated. Because gatekeepers are agents who must compete in increasingly competitive markets to win and hold clients, changes that affect their principals will necessarily affect them as well. Whether we view the gatekeeper's principal as corporate management or as shareholders, the behavior and incentives of both changed during the 1990s, and thereby placed gatekeepers, as their agents, under increased pressure, as next described.

(1) The changing motivations of managers

The pressure on gatekeepers to acquiesce in earnings management was not constant over time, but rather accelerated during the 1990s as managerial incentives changed. Executive compensation shifted during the 1990s from being primarily cash-based to being primarily equity-based. By 2001, equity-based compensation constituted approximately two-thirds of the median annual compensation of chief executives of large public corporations, up from 8% in the 1990 and 0% in 1984.[76] Another measure of this shift is the growth in stock options. Over the last decade, stock options rose from 5% of shares outstanding at major US companies to 15% – a 300% increase.[77] The value of these options rose by an even greater percentage and over a dramatically shorter period: from $50 billion in 1997 in the case of the 2,000 largest corporations to $162 billion in 2000 – an over 300% rise in three years.[78] Stock options create an obvious and potentially perverse incentive to engage in short-run, rather than long-term, stock price maximization because executives can exercise their stock options and sell the underlying shares on the same day.[79] To illustrate the impact of this change,

[76] See BJ Hall 'Six Challenges in Designing Equity-Based Pay' (2003) 15 Accenture J of Applied Corporate Finance 21, 23 and Figure 1.

[77] See G Morgenson 'Corporate Conduct: News Analysis; Bush Failed to Stress Need to Rein in Stock Options' *New York Times* (New York United States 11 July 2002) C-1; see also G Morgenson 'Market Watch: Time For Accountability At the Corporate Candy Store' *New York Times* (New York United States 3 March 2002) 1.

[78] See Morgenson 'Corporate Conduct' (n 77) C-1 (citing study by SC Bernstein & Co). Thus, if $162 billion is the value of all options in these 2,000 companies, aggressive accounting policies that temporarily raise stock prices by as little as 10% create a potential gain for executives of over $16 billion – a substantial incentive.

[79] See Hall (n 76) 24-29 (surveying misincentives in stock options). This point has also been made by a variety of commentators who have called for minimum holding periods or other curbs on stock options. These include Henry M. Paulson Jr, chief executive of Goldman, Sachs, and Senator John McCain of Arizona. See D Leonhardt 'Corporate Conduct: Compensation:

cont. ...

assume a CEO holds options on two million shares of his company's stock and the company is trading at a price to earnings ratio of 30 to 1 (both reasonable assumptions for this era). On this basis, if the CEO can cause the 'premature' recognition of revenues that result in an increase in annual earnings by simply $1 per share, the CEO has caused a $30 price increase that should make him $60 million richer. Not a small incentive!

Obviously, when one pays the CEO with stock options, one creates incentives for short-term financial manipulation and accounting gamesmanship. Indeed, financial economists have found strong statistical correlation between higher levels of equity compensation and both earnings management and financial restatements. One recent study by Efendi, Srivastava, and Swanson utilized a control group methodology and constructed two groups of companies, each composed of 100 listed public companies.[80] The first group's members had restated their financial statements in 2001 or 2002, while the control group was composed of otherwise similar firms that had not restated. What characteristic most distinguished the two groups? The leading factor that proved most to influence the likelihood of a restatement was the presence of a substantial amount of 'in the money' stock options in the hands of the firm's CEO. The CEOs of the firms in the restating group held on average 'in the money' options of $30.9 million, while CEOs in the non-restating control group averaged only $2.3 million – a nearly 14 to 1 difference.[81] Further, if a CEO held options equaling or exceeding 20 times his or her annual salary (and this was the 80th percentile in their study – meaning that a substantial number of CEOs did exceed this level), the likelihood of a restatement increased by 55%.

Other studies have reached similar results. Denis, Hanouna, and Sarin find a significant positive relationship between a firm's use of option-based compensation and securities fraud allegations being leveled against the firm.[82] Further, they find in their study of 358 companies charged with fraud between 1993 and 2002 that the likelihood of a fraud charge is positively related to option intensity

Anger At Executives' Profits Fuels Support for Stock Curb' *New York Times* (New York United States 9 July 2002) A-1.

[80] See J Efendi A Srivastava and E Swanson 'Why Do Corporate Managers Misstate Financial Statements: The Role of Option Compensation, Corporate Governance, and Other Factors' <http://ssrn.com/abstract=547922> (8 July 2005). For an earlier similar study, see SA Johnson HE Ryan Jr and YS Tian 'Executive Compensation and Corporate Fraud' <http://ssrn.com/abstract=395960> (8 July 2005).

[81] Efendi Srivastava and Swanson (n 80) 2.

[82] See DJ Denis P Hanouna and A Sarin 'Is There a Dark Side to Incentive Compensation?' <http://ssrn.com/abstract=695583> (8 July 2005). For an earlier study finding that the greater use of option-related compensation results in greater private securities litigation, see L Peng and A Roell 'Executive Pay, Earnings Manipulation and Shareholder Litigation' AFA Philadelphia Meetings <http://ssrn.com/abstract=488148> (8 July 2005).

– ie the greater the amount of the options, the higher the likelihood.[83] Similarly, Cheng and Warfield have documented that corporate managers with high equity incentives sell more shares in subsequent periods, are more likely to report earnings that just meet or exceed analysts' forecasts, and more frequently engage in other forms of earnings management.[84] As stock options increase the managers' equity ownership, they also increase their need to diversify the high risk associated with such ownership, and this produces both more efforts to inflate earnings to prevent a stock price decline and increased sales by managers in advance of any earnings decline. In short, there is a 'dark side' to option-based compensation for senior executives: absent special controls, more options means more fraud.

The key problem here is not that stock options provide excessive compensation, but that they provide excessive liquidity.[85] This excess liquidity was, in turn, partially the product of deregulatory reform in the early 1990s, which relaxed the rules under Section 16(b) of the Securities Exchange Act of 1934 to permit officers and directors to exercise stock options and sell the underlying shares without holding the shares for the previously required six-month period.[86] Thus, if executives inflated the stock price of their company through premature revenue recognition or other classic earnings management techniques, they could quickly bail out in the short term by exercising their options and selling, leaving shareholders to bear the cost of the stock decline when the inflated stock price could not be maintained over subsequent periods. Given these incentives, it became rational for corporate executives to use lucrative consulting contracts, or other positive and negative incentives, to induce gatekeepers to engage in conduct

[83] Denis Hanouna and Sarin (n 82) 4.

[84] See Q Cheng and T Warfield 'Equity Incentives and Earnings Management' (November 2004) <http://ssrn.com/abstract=457840> (15 July 2005).

[85] See Hall (n 76) 24-29. It should be noted here that other forms of equity compensation, such as restricted stock, do not give rise to this same conflict because management must either hold the stock longer or can only sell a modest percentage of it in any given year, thus precluding the possibility of a bail-out.

[86] Rule 16b-3(d) expressly permits an officer or director otherwise subject to the 'short-swing' profit provisions of section 16(b) of the Securities Exchange Act of 1934 to exercise a qualified stock option and sell the underlying shares immediately 'if at least six months elapse from the date of the acquisition of the derivative security to the date of disposition of the … underlying equity security'. See 17 CFR 240.16b-3(d). The SEC comprehensively revised its rules under section 16(b) in 1991, in part to facilitate the use of stock options as executive compensation and to 'reduce the regulatory burden' under section 16(b). See Securities Exchange Act Release no 34-28869, 1991 SEC LEXIS 171 (8 February 1991). A premise of this reform was that 'holding derivative securities is functionally equivalent to holding the underlying equity security for purpose of Section 16', ibid 35-36. Hence, the SEC permitted the tacking of the option holding period with the stock's holding period, thereby enabling officers and directors to exercise options and sell on the same day (if the option had already been held six months).

that assisted their short-term market manipulations. The bottom line is then that the growth of stock options resulted in gatekeepers being placed under greater pressure to acquiesce in short-term-oriented financial and accounting strategies.

(2) The role of investors

Investors cannot be fairly presented as entirely innocent victims in the recent epidemic of financial irregularities. At a minimum, a bubble reflects investors' acquiescence in unrealistic valuations. More importantly, conflicts of interest on the part of gatekeepers that might alarm investors in other circumstances may be accepted (or at least repressed) during a bubble. To be sure, many investors were likely misled by biased analyst research and overstated earnings, but this does not absolve the 'buy side' of all responsibility. Particularly in the case of institutional investors, who account for over half the ownership and 75% of the trading in NYSE-listed equities,[87] financial intermediaries may again have failed. According to one estimate, at the peak of the market, 60% of Enron stock was held by large institutional investors.[88] Why didn't they see that Enron was overvalued, at least once alarm bells began to sound? A plausible explanation for the failure of institutional investors to respond to warning signals in the case of Enron starts from the premise that professional money managers are principally motivated by the desire to perform no worse than their major institutional rivals; this pressure quickly leads to herding behavior.[89] According to this analysis, fund managers attract investor funds and maximize their fees based on their 'quarterly reported performance relative to comparable funds or indices'.[90] Thus, if a fund manager discovers that Enron is overvalued and sells his firm's investment, the manager and the manager's clients do well – but only if the market agrees and Enron's stock price falls that quarter. If the market persists in overvaluing Enron or actually climbs based on biased 'sell-side' research, the manager becomes an unfortunately premature prophet, and the manager's performance relative to his rivals falls. Precisely to the extent that this manager is accountable to the market, clients' funds flow out of their manager's account to those of rival fund managers, thereby collapsing like an accordion the funds under his management,

[87] For these statistics, see JD Cox and R Thomas 'Leaving Money on the Table: Do Institutional Investors Fail to File Claims in Securities Class Actions?' (2002) 80 Washington U L Q 855 n 4.

[88] See PM Healy and K Palepu 'Governance and Intermediation Problems in Capital Markets: Evidence From the Fall of Enron' Harvard NOM Research Paper no 02-27 (August 2002) 22.

[89] The term 'herding' was coined over a decade ago by Scharfstein and Stein. See DS Scharfstein and J Stein 'Herd Behavior and Investment' (1990) 80 American Economic Rev 465; see also Healy and Palepu (n 88) 26-27.

[90] Healy and Palepu (n 88) 26.

so that this manager does not profit significantly even when Enron ultimately does collapse. In such an environment, there is little incentive to be ahead of the crowd and considerable incentive to ride the bubble to its top in order not to underperform rival investment managers. The result is 'herding' because, by following the herd, the fund manager will not underperform most of the manager's rivals. Put differently, the fund manager can survive mistakes that others also make, but will be more severely injured by correct decisions that the market only belatedly recognizes. In turn, this may explain why institutions would herd and follow 'sell-side' research that they know to be biased: that is, because they anticipated that others would follow it also, leaving them in the safe position of being part of the herd.

(3) The role of gatekeepers

This conclusion that even sophisticated investors will follow and rely on 'sell-side' research that they know to be biased brings us back to the central role of gatekeepers. To some degree, gatekeepers will be followed even when they are not trusted, because it is expected that they will influence the market. In addition, there is evidence that gatekeepers 'herd' for careerist reasons. For example, career concerns appear to motivate security analysts not to deviate far from the consensus earnings forecasts, and particularly to avoid downward deviations.[91] As a result, it becomes predictable that some degree of bias will distort analyst recommendations (and that such advice will be followed), even when the market expects inflation. Moreover, ending the most obvious conflicts of interest (as Sarbanes-Oxley and related reforms attempt to do) will not solve this problem, because the careerist motives will remain.

d. A Preliminary Evaluation

Does it matter which of the foregoing two stories – the deterrence story or the bubble story – is deemed more persuasive? Although they are complementary rather than contradictory, their relative plausibility may bear on whether particular reforms are necessary, desirable, or sufficient. To the extent one accepts the deterrence story, the logical prescription is legal change aimed at restoring an adequate legal threat. In principle, these changes could either raise the costs or lower the benefits of acquiescence to auditors (or both). To the extent one accepts

[91] See H Hong JD Kubik and A Solomon 'Security Analysts' Career Concerns and the Herding of Earnings Forecasts' (2000) 31 RAND Journal of Economics 121. See also H Hong and J Kubik 'Analyzing the Analysts: Career Concerns and Biased Earnings Forecasts' (2003) 58 J of Finance 313, 341-46 (finding systematic tendency toward overly optimistic advice based on careerist considerations).

the bubble story, the problem may be self-correcting. That is, once the bubble bursts, gatekeepers come back into fashion, as investors become skeptics who once again demand assurances that only credible reputational intermediaries can provide.[92] Alternatively, structural reforms may be desirable to enhance the independence of analysts, auditors, and other gatekeepers. Clearly, all gatekeepers are not alike. Thus, the deterrence story may work better for auditors than for analysts, while in the case of analysts, structural reforms aimed at increasing the independence of the gatekeeper may outperform litigation remedies.

e. An International Perspective

Although gatekeepers are universal and found in all systems of corporate governance, corporate governance itself varies widely around the world. In particular, the structure of share ownership is polarized between a system of dispersed ownership that prevails largely in the United States and the United Kingdom (and some other common law countries) and a system of concentrated ownership that is prevalent elsewhere.[93] In the dispersed ownership structure that characterizes the US and the UK, controlling shareholders or controlling blocks are uncommon; managers have at least relatively greater autonomy as a result;[94] and

[92] Federal Reserve Chairman Alan Greenspan has indeed suggested that market corrections will largely solve the problems uncovered in the wake of Enron. See 'Remarks by Chairman Alan Greenspan, Corporate Governance' at the Stern School of Business, New York University, New York, 26 March 2002 (available on the Federal Reserves website at <http://www.federalreserve.gov/boarddocs/speeches/2002/200203262/default.htm> (15 July 2005). In his view, earnings management came to dominate management's agenda, and as a result: 'It is not surprising that since 1998 earnings restatements have proliferated. This situation is a far cry from earlier decades when, if my recollection serves me correctly, firms competed on the basis of which one had the most conservative set of books. Short-term stock price values then seemed less of a focus than maintaining unquestioned credit worthiness', ibid 4. He goes on to predict that: 'A change in behavior, however, may already be in train', ibid 5. Specifically, he finds that 'perceptions of the reliability of firms' financial statements are increasingly reflected in yield spreads of corporate bonds' and that other signs of self-correction are discernible, ibid.

[93] For an overview of the differences between dispersed and concentrated ownership systems, see JC Coffee Jr 'The Rise of Dispersed Ownership: The Roles of Law and the State in the Separation of Ownership and Control' (2001) 111 Yale L J 1; for empirical support, see R La Porta and others 'Corporate Ownership Around the World' (1999) 54 J of Finance 471.

[94] This relative autonomy is evidenced by the enormous differential between chief executive compensation in the United States and that in other major economies. According to a study by Towers Perrin, a compensation consulting firm, chief executive compensation as a multiple of average employee compensation is 531 times greater in the United States, but the multiple is only 16 in France, 11 in Germany, 10 in Japan, and 21 in Canada. Even in Britain, which also has dispersed ownership and uses stock options, chief executive compensation is only 25 times average employee compensation. See G Morgenson 'Explaining (or Not) Why the Boss Is Paid So Much' *New York Times* (New York United States 25 January 2004) section 3-1.

dispersed shareholders must rely on indirect means, such as equity compensation, to align managers' self-interests with those of the shareholders. In contrast, in concentrated ownership systems, there is normally a controlling shareholder who can directly monitor the firm's management and who thus does not need to rely on indirect mechanisms, such as equity compensation, to incentive management. As a result, Europe has made far less use of stock options and other forms of equity compensation than has the United States and the United Kingdom.

A further reason why European corporations have less incentive to manage for short-term profit maximization is that controlling shareholders seldom, if ever, sell their control blocks into the market; rather, they sell to an incoming controlling shareholder in privately negotiated transactions at a control premium. As a result, they have less interest in the day-to-day stock price, because it does not determine the price they will receive on such a sale (whereas managers in the US and the UK do sell their shares at the market price and so are more concerned with maximizing it).

These factors probably explain why there was no corresponding wave of accounting irregularity cases in Europe when Enron, WorldCom, and their progeny exploded across the American business scene in 2001 to 2002. Because European managers were less compensated with equity and because European controlling shareholders had less reason to manage for the short term, they had far less incentive to 'cook the books'. To be sure, some accounting irregularity cases did arise in Europe, but they usually had an American dimension. Thus, Royal Ahold, the Dutch retailing firm, experienced a $1.2 billion fraud, but its accounting irregularities were largely localized within its US foodservice division.[95] Similar controversies arose at Skandia Insurance, a Swedish company, and at Vivendi Universal, a French company, but both had sought to convert themselves into American-style conglomerates that made frequent acquisitions and utilized equity compensation.[96] Most recently, problems (and whistleblowers) at the North American subsidiary of Adecco, a Swiss company and the world's largest employment services company, have triggered the latest financial scandal.[97] Given this American nexus, European commentators could continue to dismiss Enron and WorldCom as examples of American 'greed' which would never arise in Europe.[98]

[95] See M Landler 'Scandal Outrages Europeans; Solutions May Be Patchwork' *New York Times* (New York United States 25 December 2003) C-1, C-3.

[96] ibid.

[97] See F Fleck '2 Executives Resign at Adecco in Fallout Over Its Accounting' *International Herald Tribune* (Neuilly France 17 January 2004) 9; H Simonsian, 'Adecco's Problems are Shrouded in Mystery' *Financial Times* (New York United States 17 January 2004) 2.

[98] See Landler (n 95) C-3 (quoting S L'Helias, a French corporate governance expert, that 'Europeans used to say, "This could never happen here; such greed is limited to America."').

Then the Parmalat scandal broke. At least $4.8 billion in cash simply disappeared from its balance sheet, and approximately $16 billion in net debt was hidden from the market according to PriceWaterhouseCoopers.[99] Unlike American scandals, the evidence suggests that the fraud had continued for years and had been assisted by Parmalat's bankers. The principal victims were Parmalat's creditors, not its shareholders (indeed, the controlling shareholders appear chiefly responsible for the fraud). Yet, while the end goal of the fraud was different from the typical American scandal, the means used were similar and involved use of some of the same exotic financial engineering that characterized Enron's failure.[100] Attorneys, auditors, and investment bankers have similarly been implicated. In short, gatekeeper failure is now a recognized problem on both sides of the Atlantic.[101]

But it is not the same problem. While Enron, WorldCom, and similar cases appear to have been driven by managers seeking to inflate earnings and maximize the stock price, Parmalat looks more like a fraud primarily directed at creditors and intended to hide the diversion of assets to controlling shareholders.[102] While accounting irregularities in the US most commonly involve revenue recognition issues relating to the income statement, the characteristic problem in a concentrated ownership system is overstated, fictitious, or diverted assets – in effect, fraud on the balance sheet. In short, different systems of corporate governance have different vulnerabilities: in a dispersed ownership system, the typical securities fraud will be a management-engineered and intended to create a short-term stock price spike, while in concentrated ownership systems, the goal is instead to permit controlling shareholders to divert 'private benefits of control' to themselves. The common denominator is, however, that gatekeeper acquiescence is necessary for either form of fraud to be consummated.

[99] See A Galloni 'Scope of Parmalat's Problems Emerges' *The Wall Street Journal* (New York United States 27 January 2004) A-3; H Sender and M Pacelle 'Parmalat Probers Are Likely to Focus On Role of Banks' *The Wall Street Journal* (New York United States 24 December 2003) C-1.

[100] See Sender and Pacelle (n 99) C-1.

[101] See J Plender 'Problems at Ahold, Parmalat and Now Adecco Raise New Questions About How Global Accounting Firms Should Work With Multinationals and Risk of Modern Investment Management Techniques', *Financial Times* (New York United States 22 January 2004) 15.

[102] See 'Parma Splat – European Corporate Governance' *The Economist – United States Edition* (New York United States 17 January 2004) (noting that the Tanzi family held 51% of Parmalat's voting power and appears to have diverted assets to itself).

III. The Near Future of Gatekeepers: Sarbanes-Oxley and the Looming Litigation Crisis

Historically, bubbles are followed by crashes, which in turn are followed by punitive legislation.[103] The 1999-2003 era is fully consistent with this pattern, and this section will focus on the likely impact of these reforms on gatekeepers. Still, because the problem of gatekeeper failure is not uniform, either in its character or intensity, it is important initially to outline the range of strategies that regulators could follow in response to corporate scandals and conflicts of interest.

1. Typology of Conflict-of-Interest Reforms

A range of well-recognized strategies exist for responding to corporate financial scandals, each of which has well-known precedents. Although other typologies can undoubtedly be constructed, the following four categories probably capture most of the realistic regulatory options:

a. Structural Reform

A new body or agency can be created, either public or private, to monitor conflicts and assure higher quality disclosure. The Securities and Exchange Commission, created by the Securities Exchange Act of 1934 in the wake of the 1929 market crash, is probably the clearest example of such a response, but the creation of the Public Company Accounting Oversight Board ('PCAOB') by the Sarbanes-Oxley Act to monitor auditing firms is a modern example that follows in its wake.[104]

Structural reforms can also change the obligations of private actors. For example, the law can create a new gatekeeper. In the 1930s, the federal securities laws and the SEC effectively made auditors into gatekeepers for the public (and not just for the clients who retained their services), and to a limited extent Sarbanes-Oxley has imposed new gatekeeping responsibilities on attorneys and securities analysts. Part IV will suggest that these initial steps should be generalized.

[103] For a discussion of this cycle over history, see S Banner 'What Causes New Securities Regulation?: 300 Years of Evidence' (1997) 75 Washington U L Q 849.

[104] Title I of the Sarbanes-Oxley Act creates the PCAOB as a regulatory body subject to SEC oversight, and section 101(c) of the Act further directs the PCAOB to 'establish or adopt . . . auditing, quality control, ethics, independence and other standards relating to the preparation of audit reports for' publicly held issuers. See 15 USC § 7211(c).

b. Prophylactic Rules

Fiduciary law has long forbidden some forms of self-dealing between the fiduciary and the beneficiary. Thus, the trustee cannot transact business with the trust estate, because such transactions are either void or voidable. Over the course of the 20th century, American corporate law largely relaxed the prohibition on self-dealing, provided that certain procedures were followed.[105] Offsetting this trend in state law, however, the federal securities laws introduced new prophylactic prohibitions, including a prohibition on a corporate officer or director retaining the proceeds of certain forms of short-term trading in his or her company's stock.[106] Sarbanes-Oxley has now introduced similar rules, most notably including a prohibition on a public company making or arranging for loans to its executives.[107]

c. Independence and Empowerment Rules

For the gatekeeper to be an effective monitor of management on behalf of investors, it must be independent of management. Sarbanes-Oxley recognized this by transferring all responsibility for the hiring, supervision, retention, and compensation of the auditor to the audit committee, whose own independence it also enhanced.[108] Some have argued that this step does not go far enough; instead, they have proposed procedures by which persons even more independent than directors

[105] For a detailed discussion of the gradual relaxation over the last 150 years of American corporate law of the once standard prophylactic rule against self-dealing, see H Marsh Jr 'Are Directors Trustees?' (1996) 22 Business L 35. Essentially, disclosure to, and approval by, disinterested directors replaced proof of the transaction's intrinsic fairness as the necessary precondition to sustaining a self-dealing transaction's validity.

[106] Section 16(b) of the Securities Exchange Act of 1934, 15 USC § 78p(b), mandates that senior officers, directors, and 10% shareholders must return to the corporation any profits they make, or losses they avert, on purchasing and selling the corporation's stock in any sequence within six months. The provision is a federal rule intended to discourage manipulation of the corporation's stock price by insiders.

[107] Section 402 of the Sarbanes-Oxley Act, which has been codified as section 13(k) of Securities Exchange Act of 1934, forbids public companies 'directly or indirectly, ... to extend or maintain credit, to arrange for an extension of credit, or to renew an extension of credit, in the form of personal loan to or for any director or executive officer . . . of that issuer'. See 15 USC § 78m(k). This is in effect a throwback to the form of strict prophylactic rule that characterized 19th- and early 20th-century American corporate law.

[108] Section 301 of the Sarbanes-Oxley Act mandates that the audit committee 'be directly responsible for the appointment, compensation, and oversight of the work' of the independent auditor. This provision has been codified as section 10A(m)(2) of the Securities Exchange Act of 1934.

would select and hire the independent auditor.[109] Although the feasibility of these proposals is debatable, they are an example of an 'empowerment' rule that increases the independence and thus the monitoring capacity of the gatekeeper.

d. Liability Rules

The standard response to a corporate scandal is to enhance liability rules, either by increasing penalties, eliminating defenses, or creating new private causes of action. The Securities Act of 1933 is here the classic example, as it creates virtual strict liability for the corporate issuer if the issuer's registration statement contains a material misstatement or omission.[110] Yet, as discussed below, Sarbanes-Oxley basically did not follow this path, except to the extent that it increased criminal penalties and SEC powers.

2. The Sarbanes-Oxley Act: What It Did and Did Not Do

Passed almost without dissent, the Sarbanes-Oxley Act essentially addresses the problem of accounting irregularities by shifting control of the accounting profession from the profession to a new body: the Public Company Accounting Oversight Board ('PCAOB'), which is authorized to regulate the profession, establish auditing standards, and impose professional discipline.[111] Conceptually, this is not a new approach, as the PCAOB's authority largely parallels that of the National Association of Securities Dealers ('NASD') over securities brokers and dealers. What is new, however, is explicit recognition of the significance of conflicts of interest, because the Act expressly bars auditors from providing a number of categories of professional services to their audit clients and further authorizes the PCAOB to prohibit additional categories of consulting services.[112] To be sure, auditors might still be compromised by the ability of management to reduce their audit fees, or terminate them as the company's auditor, but Sarbanes-

[109] See J Ronen 'Post-Enron Reform: Financial Statement Insurance, and GAAP Revisited' (2002) 8 Stanford J of L Business and Finance 39.

[110] Section 11 of the Securities Act of 1933 creates strict liability for the issuer (but grants a variety of affirmative defenses to secondary participants) if the registration statement contains a material misstatement or omission of which the purchaser was unaware. See 15 USC § 77(k).

[111] Section 101(c) of the Act enumerates broad powers, including the authority to 'establish ... auditing, quality control, ethics, independence, and other standards relating to the preparation of audit reports for issuers ...'

[112] Section 201 of the Act, which is to be codified as section 10A(g) of the Securities Exchange Act of 1934, specifies eight types of professional services which the auditor of a public company may not perform for its audit client, and also authorizes the PCAOB to prohibit additional services if it determines that they may compromise auditor independence.

Oxley addresses these concerns by transferring all control and supervision of the auditor to the audit committee, whose independence it also enhanced.[113] Thus, to the extent that conflicts of interest compromised auditors, the Act responds with a relevant answer.

Yet, if Enron and similar cases of accounting irregularities were more caused by the principal than the agent and were the product of the increased incentive of corporate executives to 'cook the books' because of the temptations created by stock options, then Sarbanes-Oxley is less clearly responsive to these problems. Nor does it increase the deterrent threat facing gatekeepers to offset the predictably increased pressure from managements. For example, except in one minor respect, the Act does not seek to revise or reverse the PSLRA.[114] Finally, the Act never addresses stock options or executive compensation, except to the extent that it may require the forfeiture of such compensation to the corporation if the corporation later restates its earnings.[115] In short, while the potential benefits from acquiescing in accounting irregularities appear to have been reduced for auditors, the expected costs to them from such acquiescence also remain low because the level of deterrence that they once faced has not been restored.[116] Arguably then, the Sarbanes-Oxley Act represents an incomplete response – relevant in its desire to reduce agent conflicts of interest, but still not sufficient to the extent that underdeterrance remains the problem. But this assessment must be qualified to the extent that courts have begun to act on their own to fill this void.

3. The Judicial Response

Any assessment of gatekeeper liability that presupposes that their exposure to liability has remained constant is probably inaccurate. Although the Congress has

[113] Section 301 of the Sarbanes-Oxley Act gives the audit committee full responsibility for supervision and compensation of the outside auditor. See text and note at n 108. In addition, section 301 establishes minimum standards for audit committee members and bars them from accepting 'any consulting, advisory or other compensatory fee from the issuer'. See section 10A(m)(3)(B) of the Securities Exchange Act of 1934.

[114] Section 804 of the Act does extend the statute of limitation for securities fraud suits, thereby reversing a 1991 Supreme Court decision that had shortened the time period. See n 55.

[115] Section 304 of the Act requires the forfeiture of certain bonuses 'or other incentive-based or equity-based compensation' and any stock trading profits received by a chief executive officer or chief financial officer of an issuer during the 12-month period following the filing of an inflated earnings report that is later restated. This does cancel the incentive to inflate earnings and then bail out, but the enforcement methods applicable to this provision are unspecified and the provision applies only if the earnings restatement is the product of 'misconduct'. Ambiguities abound here.

[116] Prior to the 1990s, private litigation was a real (and arguably even excessive) constraining force on auditors, which required them to devote as much as 14% of their revenues to litigation costs and expenses. See n 54 and accompanying text.

been cautious about changing the balance of advantage in civil litigation involving gatekeepers, a wave of post-Enron jurisprudence is sweeping across state and federal courts and has already shifted the balance of advantage in civil litigation significantly in the plaintiff's direction. The most obvious example of this shift is the decision in late 2002 in *In re Enron Corp. Secs., Derivative & ERISA Litig.*,[117] which seemingly has outflanked the Supreme Court's decision in *Central Bank of Denver*,[118] and largely restored private 'aiding and abetting' liability under a different name. In the *Enron* case, the district court denied the motions to dismiss filed by Enron's auditors, its principal outside law firm, and six major banks, all of whom asserted that they could not be deemed primary violators and so were immune from private suit under *Central Bank*. Adopting the position urged by the SEC in an *amicus curiae* brief,[119] the court ruled that primary liability could extend to any person who contributes materially false or misleading information to persons whom it understands to be preparing or drafting a report or press release to be filed with the SEC or disseminated to the investing public, even though this peripheral defendant neither solicited sales, participated in the actual drafting of the document, nor was otherwise identified in the document so filed or released.[120] The *Enron* decision not only rejected the majority rule in the federal courts, which seems to permit a private suit against the secondary participant only when the latter makes or authorizes an 'attributed statement' that specifically identifies it and its conclusion,[121] but also went well beyond the few cases that have allowed primary liability to extend to persons who 'substantially participate' in the drafting of an SEC document.[122] Under the *Enron* ruling, most who could formerly be reached under 'aiding and abetting' liability now seemingly can be reached as a 'maker' or 'creator' of a public statement.[123]

[117] 235 F Supp 2d 549 (SD Tex 2002).

[118] *Central Bank of Denver NA v First Interstate Bank of Denver NA* 511 US 164, 177 (1994).

[119] The SEC's amicus brief was largely modeled on a similar brief filed by the SEC (and initially adopted by the Third Circuit) in *Klein v Boyd* 1998 US App LEXIS 2004 (3rd Cir 12 February 1998), *vacated and reh'q en banc granted* 1998 US App LEXIS 4121 (9 March 1998).

[120] 235 F Supp 2d 549, 582-591. Judge Harmon added that a defendant 'can be a primary violator if he or she writes misrepresentations for inclusion in a document to be given to investors, even if the idea for those misrepresentations came from someone else', ibid 693.

[121] See *Wright v Ernst & Young LLP* 152 F3d 169, 175 (2nd Circuit 1998) (requiring that 'the misrepresentation must be attributed to the specific actor at the time of public dissemination').

[122] *In re Software Toolworks Secs Litig* 50 F3d 615, 627 (9th Circuit 1994) (using 'substantial participation' test).

[123] For this common assessment, see K Eichenwald 'Ruling Leaves Most Players Exposed to Suits on Enron' *New York Times* (New York United States 21 December 2002) C3; B Schwartz and J Freedman 'Aiding and Abetting Liability and Enron' *New York Law Journal* (New York United States 23 January 2003) 5; W Gleeson and J Minier 'Financial Institutions

cont. ...

Whether the *Enron* decision is correct can be (and is being hotly) debated. But the more relevant point for this article is that the decision seemingly signals a judicial shift – whether conscious or unconscious – toward imposing greater liability on gatekeepers. Symptomatically, *Enron* is not the only recent post-scandal decision to have expanded the scope of liability for secondary participants. In a series of decisions involving Lernout & Hauspie,[124] another federal court has refused to dismiss securities fraud allegations in private class actions against a variety of secondary defendants, including the firm's outside directors, auditors, stock analysts, and others. Unlike the *Enron* court, the *Lernout & Hauspie* court did not need to focus on whether the defendant corporation's audit committee members had substantially participated in the drafting of SEC reports or press releases. Rather, because each director had signed the defendant's Form 10-K, the court found this fact alone sufficient to deem the audit committee members to have made a fraudulent statement.[125]

In an even more sweeping conclusion, the court further found that audit committee members could be held liable as 'controlling persons' under Section 20(a) of the Securities Exchange Act of 1934. Under long-established SEC rules, 'control' 'means the possession, direct or indirect, of the power to direct or cause the direction of the management and policies of a person'.[126] Although the *Lernout & Hauspie* court acknowledged that outside directors were not inherently 'control persons', it relied on an earlier decision to find that:

> [A]n outside director and audit committee member who is in a position to approve a corporation's financial statements can be presumed to have the 'power to direct or cause the direction of the management and policies of' the corporation, at least insofar as the 'management and policies' referred to relate to ensuring a measure of accuracy in the content of company reports and SEC registrations that they actually sign.[127]

Unmentioned by the *Lernout & Hauspie* decision was the Sarbanes-Oxley Act, which, of course, could not apply retroactively to the facts of *Lernout & Hauspie*; still, that statute only reinforces this mode of analysis because it greatly enhances the powers of the audit committee, thus making them look more like 'controlling

and the Enron Whiplash: The Growing Pain of Rule 10b-5 Liability' (2003) 22 Banking & Financial Services Policy Report 1; AE Davis 'Professional Responsibility – Who Should Regulate Lawyers?' *New York Law Journal* (New York United States 6 January 2003) 3.

[124] See *In re Lernout & Hauspie Sec Litig* 286 BR 33, 2002 US Dist LEXIS 22708, 2002 WL 31662595 (D Mass 18 November 2002); see also *Bomberg v SG Cowen* 2002 US Dist LEXIS 23527 (D Mass 9 December 2002) (declining to dismiss action against security analyst who covered the issuer); *In re Lernout & Hauspie Sec Litig* 236 F Supp 2d 161 (D Mass 2003).

[125] 2002 US Dist LEXIS 22708 at 11-13.

[126] See 17 CFR § 240.12b-2 (defining term 'control').

[127] 286 BR 33; 2002 US Dist LEXIS 22708 at 14 (quoting *In re Livent Inc Noteholders Sec Litig* 151 F Supp 2d 371, 437 (SDNY 2001); see also *In re Reliance Sec Litig* 135 F Supp 2d 480, 518 (D Del 2001).

persons'. As a result, audit committee members would now seem significantly more exposed to personal liability. Finally, although a plaintiff is still required to plead facts raising a strong inference of fraud, the *Lernout & Hauspie* court found this last requirement satisfied by the fact that the audit committee members all allegedly had known that their corporation lacked an adequate system of internal controls and that its outside auditor had raised specific problems with its financial reporting.[128] Again, on this basis, many audit committee members could be held liable in the near future.

The net impact of these rulings is to substantially heighten the prospective liability of audit committee members. By signing a periodic report, by helping to draft such a report, or by acquiring knowledge of adverse facts as a 'controlling person', such a person faces a non-trivial risk of personal liability. Already there are signs that the major auditing firms recognize that they face increased liability and are beginning to internalize new controls and standards in light of it.[129]

On the state level, some signs of a similar, if milder, shift toward imposing heightened responsibilities on directors are also evident in Delaware, where respected members of its judiciary have called for new legislation and an expanded meaning to be given to the critical Delaware concept of 'good faith'.[130] These comments have warned that a conflicted director may not be found to have acted in 'good faith'. 'Good faith' is a key requirement under Delaware law, because, in its absence, a Delaware corporation generally cannot indemnify an officer or director;[131] in addition, charter provisions eliminating monetary liability for breach of the duty of care (which most public companies in the US now have) are ineffective if the director did not act in 'good faith'.[132] Following in the wake of these comments have come a flurry of recent Delaware decisions that have

[128] ibid 8-10.

[129] See J Glater 'PriceWaterhouse Taking A Stand and A Big Risk' *New York Times* (New York United States 1 January 2003) C1 (noting pledge of PriceWaterhouseCoopers to resign as auditors 'in any case where we cannot resolve concerns about the quality of the information we are receiving or about the integrity of the management teams with whom we are working'.). Of course, from a distance, it is impossible to determine if such assurances are largely self-promotional or whether they reflect a real change in behavior.

[130] See WB Chandler III and LE Strine Jr 'The New Federalism of the American Corporate Governance System: Preliminary Reflections of Two Residents of One Small State' SSRN Working Paper no 367720 (2003). Mr Chandler is the Chancellor and Mr Strine a Vice Chancellor of the Delaware Chancery Court. See also T Becker 'Delaware Judge Warns Boards of Liability for Executive Pay' *The Wall Street Journal* (New York United States 6 January 2002) A-14.

[131] See Delaware General Corporation Law section 145(a) (Delaware corporation has power to indemnify person who 'acted in good faith and in a manner such person reasonably believed to be in or not opposed to the best interests of the corporation').

[132] See Delaware General Corporation Law section 102(b)(7) (permitting charter provision to eliminate due care liability if director acted in 'good faith').

declined to dismiss derivative actions and that have otherwise raised the standards both for director independence and for the duty of care.[133] Outside of Delaware, the trend has been the same, as plaintiffs have repeatedly won since Enron.[134] Although derivative actions are not the normal mechanism by which liability is asserted against gatekeepers, both the holdings and dicta in these recent cases have upgraded the level of care and attention that courts are expecting all corporate fiduciaries to exercise. In short, all the judicial straws in the wind point toward a higher risk of liability, although for the present the principal target of this new litigation appears to be directors, rather than gatekeepers.

A focus on individual cases, particularly at the lower court level, is open to criticism for relying on anecdotal evidence whose ultimate impact remains speculative. But aggregate data also indicates that the risk for gatekeepers is real and growing. Here the most telling statistic is the rising settlement value of securities litigation. According to one recent survey, which extended through mid-2003, the average value of securities class action settlement has risen steadily since the mid 1990s:[135]

Year	Average Settlement
1996-2000 (excluding *Cendant* settlement)	$14.2 million
2001	$17.7 million
2002	$19.9 million
2003 (through 8/21/03)	$25.1 million

Compounding this rising settlement value is the additional fact that the number of securities class actions also appears to be rising, if more modestly.[136]

[133] Chief among these decisions are (1) *In re Oracle Corp Derivative Litigation* 824 A 2d 917 (Del Ch 2003) (deeming directors not to be independent of an academic colleague or a university contributor); (2) *In re Walt Disney Company Derivative Litigation* 825 A 2d 275 (Del Ch 2003) (finding board's action in approving compensation and non-fault termination of Michael Ovitz, a senior officer, not to have been taken in good faith); (3) *In re Health South Corporation Shareholders Litigation* 2003 CVL 22769045 (Del Ch 24 November 2003) (refusing to dismiss or stay derivative raising insider trading claims); (4) *In re Pure Resources Inc Shareholders Litigation* 808 A 2d 421 (Del Ch 2002) (finding tender by controlling shareholder to be coercive).

[134] See eg *In re Abbott Laboratories Derivative Shareholders Litigation* 325 F 3d 795 (7th Circuit 2003); (derivative action for 'conscious inaction' in face of potentially illegal corporate activities reinstated and demand futility test simplified); *McCall v Scott* 239 F 3d 808 (6th Circuit 2001) (derivative action reinstated where plaintiffs had sufficiently alleged a sustained failure by board to exercise appropriate attention).

[135] See PriceWaterhouseCoopers LLP 2002 Securities Litigation Study at 2.

[136] Excluding very specialized 'laddering' and 'analyst' cases, some 217 securities class actions were filed in 2002, up from 207 in 1999, 201 in 2000, and 176 in 2001 (when over 300 'laddering' cases were, however, filed), but down from 1998 when 258 cases were filed, ibid 1-

cont. ...

Averages can be misleading. The real fear of the major auditing firms is one catastrophic experience that exceeds their total insurance and other reserves. Such a loss could not be offset by increasing client fees and would result in likely insolvency. Here, it is relevant that the six largest recoveries against audit firms have all occurred since 2000:[137]

Name of Case	Year	Settlement Amount	Firm
1. Cendant	2000	$335 million	Ernst & Young
2. Baptist Foundation of America	2002	$217 million	Andersen
3. Rite Aid	2002	$125 million	KPMG
4. Sunbeam	2001	$110 million	Andersen
5. Waste Management I	2000	$75 million	Andersen
6. Oxford Health	2003	$75 million	KPMG

Had Andersen not liquidated following its criminal conviction, its Enron liabilities might easily have exceeded Ernst & Young's record settlement in *Cendant.* In any event, the risk of catastrophic loss, not the increase in average settlement value, is the factor that will most cause the market for gatekeeper services to unravel.

Although auditors continue to be sued only in the minority of securities class actions, the number of securities class actions naming auditors as defendants has also recently risen, climbing to 34 cases in 2002 (up 21% over the 1998-2001 period and by 89% over 2001).[138] For the future, the most ominous fact may be

2. From 1996 to 2001, securities class actions averaged 186 cases per year, ibid 2. Hence, the recent total has been up, but only after some adjustments are made to the data.

[137] In compiling this list, I have relied on data made available to me by the firm of Milberg, Weiss, Bershad, Hynes & Lerach, for whom I served as an expert witness during the Rite Aid Litigation. The principal cases on this list are, however, a matter of public record. See *In re Cendant Corp Litig* 264 F 3d 286 (3rd Circuit 2001) (approving $335 million settlement by Ernst & Young and $2.85 billion settlement by Cendant); *In re Rite Aid Corp Secs Litig* 269 F Supp 2d 603 (ED Pa 2003) (approving $125 million settlement by KPMG); 'News in Brief: $300 Million Oxford Settlement Approved' *New York Law Journal* (New York United States 19 June 2003) 1 col 1 (noting that Oxford Health would pay $225 million and KPMG $75 million). Arthur Andersen's involvement in the *Waste Management, Sunbeam* and *Baptist Foundation of America* litigation is all concisely summarized in *In re Enron Corp Secs Litig* 235 F Supp 2d 549, 676 n 110-111 (SD Texas 2002) (noting that Andersen paid $110 million to settle in the *Sunbeam* class action in 2001 and $217 million to settle the *Baptist Foundation* litigation in 2002).

[138] See PriceWaterhouseCoopers LLP 2002 Securities Litigation Study 7-8. This represented 34 out of 217 total securities class actions filed in that year (or 16%), ibid 8. In contrast, the number of securities class actions brought against auditors declined from 1998 to 2001. See PriceWaterhouseCoopers LLP 2002 Securities Litigation Study 7. Still, the highest number of such actions against auditors over the past five years was 39 in 1998, ibid 8.

that accounting irregularities tend increasingly to be the primary focus of securities class actions.[139] The more actions filed against auditors, the greater the chance of a catastrophic judgment.

4. The Prospective Litigation Impact of Reform

Little agreement exists about the overall impact of the Sarbanes-Oxley Act on civil litigation. Some critics have viewed it as more rhetoric than serious reform;[140] others contend that it is a sweeping intrusion into the US's existing system of corporate governance. Both perspectives miss, however, what it most important: Sarbanes-Oxley ushers in and accelerates a major and probably inevitable transition, which will move us from a rules-based system of financial disclosure to a principles-based system. In contrast to Europe, the US has long relied on a rules-based system in which generally accepted accounting principles (or 'GAAP') were precise, technical, and limited. Typically, these narrow rules afforded safe harbors from liability for issuers and gatekeepers. In contrast, European accounting principles were broader, more generalized, and sometimes indefinite to the point of being ineffable. As discussed below, Europe could live with this imprecision because Europe is characterized by a relatively low rate of litigation, and thus its issuers did not need to fear American-style entrepreneurial litigation.

Precisely for this reason, however, a shift to a principles-based system exposes American issuers and their gatekeepers to a substantially heightened threat of liability. At the core of a principles-based system is the notion that the issuer must not only comply with GAAP, but must make a 'fair presentation' that provides a full, fair, and holistic picture of the issuer's financial condition and results of operations. In both Sections 302 and 906 of the Sarbanes-Oxley Act, Congress directed the chief executive officer and chief financial officer of every publicly held company to certify in every periodic report filed with the SEC 'that information contained in the periodic report *fairly presents*, in all material respects, the financial condition and results of operations of the issuer'.[141] This

[139] Over 50% of the securities class actions settled between the passage of the Private Securities Litigation Reform Act and 31 December 2002 appear to have involved accounting irregularities and over 60% involved a restatement of financials. See LE Simmons and EM Ryan 'Post-Reform Act Securities Lawsuits: Settlements Reported through December 2002' (Cornerstone Research 2003) 10.

[140] See LA Cunningham 'The Sarbanes-Oxley Yawn: Heavy Rhetoric, Light Reform (and It Might Just Work)' (2003) 35 U Connecticut L Rev 915.

[141] The quoted language is from section 906, which has been codified as 18 USC § 1350, a penal code provision (emphasis added). Section 302 of Sarbanes-Oxley Act uses slightly different language: 'the financial statements, and other financial information included in the report, fairly presents in all material respects the financial condition and results of operations of

cont. ...

concept of 'fair presentation' is not limited by any reference to GAAP, and compliance with GAAP is clearly not dispositive of whether the issuer has provided a 'fair presentation'. Instead, the standard seems to intend that the issuer provide full and fair disclosure in the form of a holistic picture of the company that reveals all material financial weaknesses, even if their disclosure were not required by GAAP.

Historically, this concept of 'fair presentation' was the standard prescribed by Judge Henry Friendly for the Second Circuit in *United States v Simon*.[142] Although *Simon* has never been reversed or even called into question, it had over recent years seemingly become a forgotten decision, honored more in the breach than in the observance.[143] Virtually overnight, however, Enron and related scandals have resuscitated *Simon's* concept of 'fair presentation'. The reason for its revival is obvious: Enron showed beyond argument that a rules-based system of financial disclosure could be gamed and distorted to the point that investors could have little confidence in it. Even if newer and tighter rules were drafted, practitioners would predictably stay one step ahead of regulators by finding new ways to game and evade narrow and specific rules. As a result, Congress and the SEC framed the Sarbanes-Oxley Act's new certification requirements in terms of the *Simon* case, and in interpreting this new requirement, the SEC has cited *Simon* for the proposition that: 'Presenting financial information in conformity with generally accepted accounting principles may not necessarily satisfy obligations under the antifraud provision of the federal securities laws.'[144]

While this shift to a principles-based system is obviously consistent with the public's post-Enron mood, it poses significant risks for issuers and gatekeepers. Cases that might have been dismissed on summary judgment now seem more likely to survive, because the claim that full and fair disclosure was not provided is hard to resolve pre-trial. More importantly, the shift to a principles-based system reduces the prospect that the auditor can truly 'audit' the more ineffable style of disclosure that such a system invites. Finally, this shift underlines the differences between the European and the American legal environment. Lacking class actions, contingent fees, or the 'American rule' that generally precludes fee-shifting against the plaintiff, Europe experiences little securities litigation and hence can tolerate abstract generality in the formulation of its accounting rules. In

the issuer as of, and for, the periods presented in the report'. No difference in scope or meaning seems intended by this slight difference in phrasing.

[142] 425 F2d 796, 807-09 (2nd Circuit 1969).

[143] No Circuit Court decision that I have found over the past twenty years appears to cite the *Simon* case in a decision upholding civil or criminal liability for securities fraud. The decision has been cited by dissenting judges who believed that a case should not have been dismissed or overturned. See eg *In re K-Tel Intl Sec Litig* 300 F3d 881, 906 (8th Circuit 2002). The last decision citing it in a decision favoring private plaintiffs or the SEC appears to have been *SEC v Seaboard Corp* 677 F2d 1301, 1313 (9th Circuit 1982).

[144] See Securities Exchange Act Release no 33-8124 (9 September 2002) 57279 para 55

contrast, US issuers are likely to encounter greater difficulty in any transition to accounting principles framed in broad brush strokes. The combination of broad disclosure obligations and a legal environment that encourages class litigation means both a higher volume of litigation and higher settlement values to claims against gatekeepers and outside directors.

Nonetheless, this transition appears inevitable, not only because of recent scandals, but because of globalization as well. Globalization necessitates a common, worldwide accounting language. Under their 'Norwalk treaty', the Financial Accounting Standards Board ('FASB') and the International Accounting Standards Board ('IASB') are committed to developing international accounting standards that both US and European regulators will accept.[145] Europe has little interest in moving toward a rule-based regime, and the FASB cannot credibly push in this direction after Enron. As a result, the development of a common global accounting language will likely finish what Enron started: namely, the demise of a rules-based system.

So where do these trends leave us? The original issue was what level of legal threat would optimize deterrence. Too high a level of liability may cause the contemporary markets for gatekeeping services to fail, and too low a level invites future Enrons. This recognition has two implications that inform Part IV. First, public policy should attempt to focus liability rules so that they incentivize gatekeepers to search diligently for fraud and irregularity, but do not employ excess deterrence that threatens gatekeeper solvency. In this light, it will next be argued that a combination of stricter liability standards with a ceiling on damages represents a sensible compromise that is superior to an existing liability regime that both (a) predicates liability upon proof of scienter, and (b) sometimes immunizes even the intentional aider and abetter. Second, to the extent that some gatekeepers lack the ability to detect frauds by their clients, strict liability is an inappropriate legal standard, and other types of legal rules – structural, prophylactic, and empowering – merit greater attention and should be blended into any overall policy response. The shift to a principles-based system aggravates this problem because it makes it more problematic whether the auditor can truly prevent fraud or irregularity as the principles of financial reporting become more open-ended and ambiguous.

[145] The two bodies – the FASB and the IASB – announced in October 2002 that they were committed to achieving convergence between their respective accounting standards by 2005 with an initial exposure draft being scheduled for late 2003. See 'Convergence of Global Accounting Standards; Regulatory Watch' *Accounting Today* (New York United States 25 January 2003) 512 (describing memorandum of understanding between the two bodies).

IV. The Future Gatekeeper: Remedies for Gatekeeper Failure

Three linked problems dominate any attempt to redefine the role or restructure the obligations and liabilities of market gatekeepers:

First, in striking an appropriate balance between excessive liability and an inadequate legal threat, public policy must recognize the peculiarly American dimensions of this problem. The market for auditing services has become increasingly concentrated in the United States (and in consequence around the world, as most global corporations are either American or follow similar norms and standards). The ironic truth is that the four global accounting firms that today remain have become 'too big to fail'. In addition, the threat of excessive liability is also uniquely an American problem because the prospect of large class actions and jury decision-making is almost unique to the American legal system.

Second, public policy must seek to minimize the perverse incentives that induce the gatekeeper not to investigate too closely. For example, in securities litigation against auditors, the defense is frequently raised by the auditors that they were deceived by corrupt managements on whom they had justifiably relied. Often, this may be true, but it can still create an incentive not to inquire too closely – lest one acquire information that should place one on notice. More generally, the Private Securities Litigation Reform Act requires a particularized pleading at the outset of the case that gives rise to a 'strong inference of fraud'.[146] In the case of accountants, this standard means that more than reckless indifference must be shown and as of the very outset of the action, when typically little is known about the accountant's involvement. As a result, the auditor who remains ignorant of the fraud, even though recklessly inattentive, probably escapes liability.

But how much can we realistically expect of the auditor? Auditors have long argued that there is an 'expectations gap' between what the public wants them to do and their actual capacity.[147] This expectations gap is greatest, they assert, when it comes to the ability of auditors to detect fraud or illegal acts.[148] Of

[146] See section 21D(b)(2) of the Securities Exchange Act of 1934, 15 USC §78u-3 (requiring complaint to 'state with particularity facts giving rise to a strong inference that the defendant acted with the required state of mind').

[147] For an overview of asserted 'expectations gap', see C Pacini MJ Martin and L Hamilton 'At the Interface of Law and Accounting: An Examination of a Trend Toward a Reduction in the Scope of Auditor Liability to Third Parties in the Common Law Countries' (2000) 37 American Business L J 171, 215-217 (discussing the 'expectations gap'); see also B Porter 'An Empirical Study of the Audit Expectation-Performance Gap' (1993) 24 Accounting and Business Research 49.

[148] Over 70% of investors questioned in one survey expected absolute assurance that material misstatements due to fraud would be detected. See M Epstein and M Geiger 'Investor Views of Audit Assurance: Recent Evidence of the Expectations Gap' (1994) 177 J Accountancy 60.

course, any profession has a collective self-interest in reducing its own risk of liability or public criticism. Still, independent observers agree that some elements of financial statements are simply 'not verifiable' and could not accurately be audited by even the most diligent and well-motivated accountant.[149] To this extent, an undiluted regime of strict liability could be counter-productive.

Third, public policy must also strike an acceptable balance between the obligation of client loyalty and the role of protecting the integrity of the market. This is the unique problem associated with asserting that securities attorneys owe gatekeeper obligations – either legal or ethical – to investors, as well as to their clients. Defenders of the traditional advocacy role of the lawyer find this conflict unbridgeable, and argue that imposing gatekeeper obligations on attorneys will simply 'dry up' the free flow of information between attorney and client, thus possibly resulting in greater illegality. This section finds this claim to be unsupportable. Rather, it concludes that the primary consequence of imposing gatekeeper obligations on attorneys will be to increase their leverage over their clients.

1. Striking the Balance on Liability

Recent commentators have divided over whether gatekeepers should be held strictly liable for client misconduct.[150] Both sides in this debate recognize the advantages of strict liability over negligence liability: (1) strict liability gives the gatekeeper greater incentive to take precautions and exercise due diligence; (2) strict liability induces the gatekeeper to limit its level of activity, for example by rejecting overly risky corporations as clients; and (3) strict liability spares both courts and regulators the need to descend into the Serbonian bog of defining precise standards of care, thereby reducing transaction costs and increasing predictability.[151] Obviously, under a strict liability system, gatekeepers would raise their fees to cover their increased liability, but even this increase can be presented as one of the attractions of this approach because it forces the client to bear a higher fee precisely to the extent that it cannot convince its auditor that it presents a low risk of fraud or irregularity. In a perfect market, the issuer would

[149] See Ronen (n 109) 41. Professor Ronen objects that Generally Accepted Accounting Principles ('GAAP') contain many elements that are 'simply not auditable', ibid. Applying an undiluted regime of strict liability to such principles would achieve little of value, but would risk market failure.

[150] Professor Partnoy has proposed such a strict liability regime for underwriters, auditors, and attorneys in light of Enron. See F Partnoy 'Barbarians at the Gatekeepers? A Proposal for a Modified Strict Liability Regime' (2001) 79 Washington U L Q 491. To the contrary, Assaf Hamdani has argued that strict liability would be excessive. See A Hamdani 'Gatekeeper Liability' (2003) 77 Southern California L Rev 53.

[151] See Hamdani (n 150) 59; Partnoy (n 150) 514.

thus bear the expected social cost of the fraud, which would in turn imply that the only issuers that could access the market would be 'those for whom the value of the public financing exceeds the harm caused by fraud'.[152] Put more simply, very high audit fees should tend to deter the fraudulent actor.

Although possibly optimal in theory, enormous problems surround implementation of any such proposal. First, as even its proponents acknowledge, the gatekeeper may not be able to distinguish *ex ante* the 'honest' client from the 'fraudulent' one. Hence, it will charge both a single common fee – but a much higher one. Predictably, this inflated fee structure would still allow the 'fraudulent' client to access the market, but it might drive many honest clients from the market.[153] Even if we relax this assumption and assume that some broad risk classifications could be made, it still remains true that, to the extent these classifications are broad and general, then some clients within each category will pay too little and others too much.

Moreover, the increase in audit fees might have to be enormous in order to enable auditors to survive under a regime of strict liability. During the collapse of the high-tech bubble in 2000 and 2001, the market value of publicly held firms audited by the then Big Five fell by over $1 trillion.[154] Under a strict liability regime, the auditor would be jointly and severally liable for this amount with the issuer, at least if a material misrepresentation or omission and loss causation were shown. To protect itself against such exposure, the auditor would need to charge a fee that funded its expected liability costs – a loss that could potentially reach multi-billion dollar sums.[155] Not only would corporate clients be unable to pay

[152] See Hamdani (n 150) 60. These observations are not original to these authors. Conventional 'law and economics' analysis sees strict liability as superior to negligence-based liability in two respects: first, strict liability gives the principal actors optimal incentives to comply with legal requirements, while freeing courts from the need to make imperfect and error-prone liability determinations; and, second, it induces the principal actors to adopt an optimal level of activity. See S Shavell *Economic Analysis of Accident Law* (Harvard University Press Cambridge 1987) 5-18.

[153] This 'adverse selection' problem can result in a 'lemons market' that causes the honest company to leave the market. See G Akerlof 'The Market for Lemons: Quality Uncertainty and the Market Mechanism' (1970) 84 Quarterly J of Economics 488.

[154] One survey of 33 public firms that restated their earnings finds that companies audited by the Big Five fell in value by roughly $1.3 trillion. See S Taub 'Big Five Gets Low Grades For Performance' <http://www.economist.com> 12 July 2002 (noting fall from $1.8 trillion to only $527 billion in market capitalization).

[155] Of course, securities class actions today settle for a fraction of their asserted losses. But this fraction will certainly rise (and steeply) if we move to a strict liability regime. Even today, neutral third parties have placed the likely settlement value of some outstanding securities class actions at $1 billion or higher. See M Peers 'Suits Cloud AOL's Optimism: Cost of Settling Holder Litigation May Hurt Effort to Cut Debt' *Wall Street Journal* (New York United States 1 May 2003) B2 (estimating settlement cost of securities class action against AOL Time Warner Inc at $1 billion).

such an amount, but they would predictably oppose such a fee increase with sufficient vigor as to make the adoption of strict liability politically infeasible.

Given the risk of being rendered insolvent by a single client, some auditors also might simply cease to offer auditing services, concentrating instead on consulting services or simply on providing bookkeeping services without the provision of any certification. If some firms were to exit, replacements might well enter. But in all likelihood, new entrants would be smaller, risk-preferring 'fly-by-night' firms that might seek to charge very high fees for the short term and then liquidate on an adverse judicial determination. Increasingly, audit firms would seek to protect their partners' assets by minimizing their capital investments in their firms and by use of limited liability organizational forms, such as the limited liability company or limited partnership. Even if auditor exit from the market were deemed a remote risk, it is a virtual certainty that heightened liability would cause existing auditors to be far more selective in the public companies that they would accept as clients. Although this might desirably result in some 'lawless' corporation being denied access to public markets, auditors lack the ability to distinguish *ex ante* the 'law-abiding' client from the 'lawless' one; hence, some 'law-abiding' firms would be denied access to the market with a resulting social loss. Some recent evidence suggests that this screening process may already have intensified[156] and that audit fees are rising dramatically.[157]

Finally, there still remains the possibility of litigation error. Even under a regime of strict liability, it would still be necessary to show that the issuer made a material misrepresentation or omission before the auditor could be held vicariously liable.[158] Given the potential of stock price drops resulting in damages in the multi-billion dollar range, this means that litigation errors could easily be bankrupting to the auditor, which in turn means that the auditor would be under

[156] In 2003, over 1,460 public companies changed auditors, which was the highest number in at least five years. Although such switches could be because the client was dissatisfied with the auditor, many were because the auditor considered the client too risky – or because the auditor raised its fees in light of that increased risk. This phenomenon of auditor switching affected over one-third of the firms in the Russell 3,000, which covers most smaller market capitalization firms. See M Krantz 'More Firms Part Way With Auditors' *USA Today* (New York United States 9 February 2004) 1B. This evidence may not prove that auditors are becoming significantly more selective with regard to clients, but it is at least consistent with such a hypothesis.

[157] Audit fees appear to have increased 'by as much as 30% or more this year …' See D Salomon and C Bryan-Low, 'Companies Complain About Cost of Corporate-Governance Rules' *The Wall Street Journal* (New York United States 10 February 2004) A-1. This increase could be because of the increased compliance costs of Sarbanes-Oxley, as this story implies, or it could also in part be attributable to the increased risk and litigation exposure faced by auditors, which they need to pass back to their clients.

[158] In addition, it would be necessary for the plaintiff to prove loss causation, as otherwise in its absence the plaintiff would receive a seeming windfall. Thus, some complex litigation issues will still remain.

great pressure to settle such litigation. Such pressure in turn exacerbates the problem of 'extortionate' or 'frivolous' litigation. Stock prices can fall for a variety of reasons that are unrelated to fraud or misrepresentation. Yet, if the stock price decline is great enough, an almost irresistible incentive arises for the plaintiff's attorney to sue, as it has now been freed from the burden of alleging, pleading, or proving fraud or scienter. Hence, the prospect of 'frivolous' or 'extortionate' litigation increases in direct proportion to the degree to which one moves toward a strict liability regime.

2. Designing a 'Stricter' Liability Approach: A Proposal

For all these reasons, the 'real world' issue becomes whether a second-best substitute can be devised for a strict liability regime that sidesteps or minimizes the foregoing problems. In this article's view, the most direct and practical means to this end would be to convert the gatekeeper into the functional equivalent of an insurer, who would back its auditor's certification with an insurance policy that was capped at a realistic level.[159] As a result, the gatekeeper's liability would be divorced from any showing of fault, but it would also be limited to a level that achieves adequate deterrence without causing the market for gatekeeping services to unravel.

Under this approach, for example, if the corporate client were found liable for $100 million, then the auditor would have to contribute toward that liability up to the amount of its policy. The one mandatory element in this proposal would be a minimum floor on the gatekeeper's insurance policy that would have to equal some adequate multiple of the highest annual revenues received by the gatekeeper from its client over the last several years. For purposes only of illustration, let us assume a multiplier of ten. Now, on the facts of the Enron case, where it has been widely reported that Arthur Andersen received roughly $52 million from Enron in its final year, Andersen's liability would be not less than $520 million (ie $52 million times ten). This is a large number, but it does not approach the roughly $80 billion loss in market capitalization that Enron experienced and for which Andersen could conceivably be held liable under a strict liability regime. In a more typical case where the auditor receives only a $2 million audit fee from the client, the damages would be reduced to only $20 million. Hence, the market for gatekeeping services could easily function under this proposal. The auditor might

[159] Professor Joshua Ronen has offered a somewhat similar idea that does not combine the two roles of auditor and insurer, but does integrate them. Under his proposal, public firms would purchase financial statement insurance from insurers, who would then select the auditors. See Ronen (n 109). Among the problems with this proposal is the danger that the insurer might prefer that the auditor hide, rather than reveal, accounting irregularities if their revelation would trigger its obligation to pay under its policy. Still, Professor Ronen has properly recognized the close connection between auditing and insurance.

also purchase insurance to cover its exposure, but to the extent it passed along this added insurance cost to its clients, it would automatically increase the minimum required floor on its policy under the mandatory 10:1 ratio between minimum liability and direct or indirect revenues from the client.

Some will recognize this proposal as bearing considerable resemblance to Professor Partnoy's modified strict liability proposal.[160] Under his innovative proposal, the client and the gatekeeper would contract for the gatekeeper to bear a minimum percentage of the issuer's losses, possibly subject to a requirement that the gatekeeper must bear some 'specified minimum percentage'.[161] For sake of illustration, assume that the minimum percentage set by Congress in an amendment to the federal securities laws were 5%. If so, on the earlier Enron example, Andersen would be required to pay 5% of Enron's $80 billion loss or $4 billion.

There are essentially three practical differences between these two similar proposals: (1) Professor Partnoy's system is essentially contractual, while this proposal is essentially regulatory; (2) Professor Partnoy uses a percentage of the total damages as his minimum floor, while this proposal uses a multiple of the gatekeeper's highest annual revenues from the client; and (3) while the potential damages, as calculated under Professor Partnoy's proposal, could often bankrupt the gatekeeper, bankruptcy would rarely follow when a multiple of the revenues from the client generated the required minimum floor on the gatekeeper's insurance obligation. Thus, this proposal could actually be supported by the relevant profession, once they recognized that their existing exposure to liability could be even higher. It thus falls (if only barely) within the range of political feasibility.

This proposal's refusal to accept private contracting (in contrast to Professor Partnoy, who relies primarily on contracting and disclosure) is based on three considerations: First, the market for services in some gatekeeping professions (most notably, auditing) is extremely concentrated, and thus conscious parallelism in the pricing behavior of the few actors in the industry becomes likely. Put more simply, if there are only four major auditing firms at present, it becomes unlikely that they would compete vigorously and accept liability significantly above any minimum required threshold. Hence, it is simpler to specify that threshold (but also permit the parties to provide by contract for even greater liability). Second, in a bubble, investors might not care that their gatekeepers were accepting only a minimum liability, and thus the disclosure of the contract between the gatekeeper and the market might have too little impact on the market

[160] See Partnoy (n 150) 540-46; see also S Choi 'Market Lessons for Gatekeepers' (1998) 92 Northwestern U L Rev 916, 951-59. Professor Choi appears to have been the first to suggest that the issuer and the gatekeeper should contract over the share of the gatekeeper's liability for the losses experienced by the issuer's investors.

[161] Partnoy (n 150) 540. Actually, Professor Partnoy does not clearly insist that there be a minimum floor placed on the auditor's liability below which they could not deviate by agreement, but notes that Congress could impose such a minimum percentage, ibid.

to be an adequate deterrent. Third, a contractual approach overlooks that the corporate client may have little incentive to bargain for high liability on the part of the auditor. Not only will higher auditor liability not meaningfully reduce the liability of the client (given the typical relative disparity in their assets), but corporate managers may actually want the auditor to have a low ceiling on its liability in order to make it easier to induce the auditor to acquiesce in risky accounting practices favored by management. Put more simply, if management wants to inflate earnings in order to maximize the value of their stock options, the lower the liability faced by their auditors, the easier it will be for management to convince them to acquiesce in dubious accounting policies.

The key conceptual difference between the two proposals involves this proposal's more explicit adoption of a deterrence framework. Prior proposals for making the auditor an insurer have relied on a tort law rationale, which tries to force the tort feasor to internalize the social costs of its actions by making it pay a higher fee. Neither Professor Partnoy's proposal nor the proposal made here compels the auditor to internalize the full costs of the issuer's fraud, but to the extent that Partnoy's proposal would often lead to higher damages, it should encourage greater precaution and more monitoring. But to that same extent, his proposal would also lead to a greater risk of market failure, either because auditing firms would become insolvent, exit the market, or cease to offer their services to deserving clients. While the relative balance of costs and benefits may seem indeterminate, the real issue is how much additional incentive do auditors need to monitor optimally? Deterrence is excessive to the extent it serves only to shift losses from the issuer to the auditor without reducing the risk of fraud. To the extent that auditor acquiescence in fraud is willful, one can deter it simply by eliminating the expected gain. Under standard deterrence theory, prevention simply requires that the expected punishment cost exceed the expected gain.[162] Professor Partnoy's proposal to use a percentage of the issuer's losses as the minimum floor on contracting does not bear any functional relationship to the expected gain; nor does it increase the penalty to compensate for the limited risk of detection. To the extent, however, that auditor failure is the result of negligence or inadequate precaution, the need for higher penalties becomes clearer, and a focus on the total social loss (rather than simply the expected gain) becomes more justifiable. But even here, we return to a basic dilemma: many aspects of GAAP principles may simply not be 'auditable'.[163] If so, additional deterrence is unjustified because it cannot reduce the overall social loss.

Obviously, this article's proposal of stricter liability with a lower ceiling based on a multiple of the revenues from the client will typically (but not

[162] See generally GS Becker 'Crime and Punishment: An Economic Approach' (1968) 76 J of Political Economy 169.

[163] See Ronen (n 109) 41.

inevitably) result in lesser liability than under the Partnoy proposal.[164] But it still gives the gatekeeper ample incentive to utilize all monitoring controls (including closer monitoring of its own agents) that are reasonably likely to reduce the prospect of fraud or earnings manipulation. Above all, this approach prevents the market for gatekeeping services from unraveling.

How strict need a stricter system of liability be? Here we enter the thicket of political realism. Pure strict liability might be the best rule, but it is probably not politically acceptable to auditors, who represent a powerful political lobby. Nor does it seem defensible to impose a significantly higher standard of liability on the auditor than on its client, the issuer. In this light, the highest standard of liability that might be politically attainable in the case of auditors would be that set forth already for auditors in Section 11 of the Securities Act of 1933, which requires the auditor as an expert to prove as an affirmative defense that the auditor 'had, after reasonable investigation, reasonable grounds to believe and did believe' that its statement were true.[165] In effect, the burden would be shifted to the auditor in all Rule 10b-5 actions to prove its non-negligence and good faith belief in its statements.

3. Implementing the Gatekeeper Role of Attorneys.

The foregoing proposal for 'stricter liability' has been primarily framed with auditors in mind. But should it apply to other gatekeepers, such as, for example, attorneys or securities analysts? Because the economic case for strict liability assumes both that the gatekeeper can prevent misconduct by investing more resources in precaution and that the gatekeeper can pass on its increased costs to the principal, some basic distinctions need to be recognized about gatekeepers. Some are more able than others to prevent and detect misconduct. While the auditor inhabits a relatively precise and rule-bound world, the securities analyst is essentially a prognosticator whose predictions about the future are frequently wrong. Thus, imposing strict liability on the securities analyst, given the analyst's necessarily higher rate of error, may amount to a virtual death sentence for the

[164] To illustrate the difference between the two proposals, consider a very large issuer that experiences a sudden $50 billion decline in its market capitalization as the result of accounting irregularities. Assume further that the issuer's auditor had received only $10 million in fees, and that Professor Partnoy would limit the auditor's exposure to 10% of the total loss (or $5 billion). Thus, there is here a 500:1 ratio between the auditor's projected liability ($5 billion or 10% of the losses) and its own gain ($10 million). This represents overdeterrence – unless one thinks there is less than a 1% chance of detection. In even a minimally efficient market, however, the prospect of detection of accounting irregularities seems far higher than that. In contrast, this article would impose a ceiling on auditor liability on these facts at $100 million (or 10 times its gain).

[165] See section 11(b)(3)(B) of the Securities Act of 1933, 15 USC § 77(k).

analyst. In addition, the analyst cannot pass on its higher exposure to liability to its client in the form of higher fees, because the analyst is not paid by the corporate issuer (but rather by investors through brokerage commissions). If brokerage commissions were increased, investors would simply turn to discount brokers (or others) who did not use securities analysts.

The case of the attorney forces us to focus on other differences. First, functionally, attorneys act only occasionally as gatekeepers, certifying or verifying information for investors, while auditors perform this function primarily (and increasingly exclusively). Second, the role of gatekeeper arguably conflicts with the more typical roles performed by attorneys as either advocates or transaction engineers for their clients. Third, asking attorneys to serve as gatekeepers may dry up the flow of confidential information between attorney and client, thereby jeopardizing the ability of the attorney to serve the client. Based on these premises, the bar (and its academic defenders) have vehemently argued that, if the attorney were compelled to serve as a watchdog, instead of as an advocate or transaction engineer, for the client, the client could no longer depend on the attorney as a zealous advocate or transaction engineer.[166]

Although this debate has generated much heat, little empirical light has been focused on just what could be reasonably expected if attorneys were subjected to a 'noisy withdrawal' standard. Yet, one natural experiment exists that does shed useful light on this question. In 1995, as part of the PSLRA, Congress added Section 10A to the Securities Exchange Act of 1934. This section requires auditors to report to the SEC likely illegal acts that have a material impact on the issuer's financial statement, which an auditor discovers during the course of an audit, unless the issuer takes appropriate remedial action to remedy them.[167] This is the functional equivalent of the noisy withdrawal requirement that the SEC has proposed (but not adopted) for securities attorneys.[168] The existence of this provision raises the obvious question: What has been the experience under it? The short answer is that not much has happened. A 2003 report by the United States General Accounting Office finds that over the period between when Section 10A became effective for fiscal years beginning after 1 January 1996 through 15 May 2003, the SEC has received a grand total of 29 Section 10A reports from auditors.[169] Yet Section 10A's enactment was not resisted by the auditing profes-

[166] For a detailed exposition of this argument that the roles of the attorney and the gatekeeper are essentially inconsistent and that attorneys make poor informational and reputational intermediaries, see JE Fisch and KM Rosen 'Lessons from Enron, How Did Corporate and Securities Law Fail? Is There Role for Lawyers in Preventing Future Enrons?' (2003) 48 Villanova L Rev 1097.

[167] See section 10A ('Audit Requirements') of the Securities Exchange Act of 1934, 15 USC. [78j].

[168] See Securities Exchange Act Release no 34-8186 (29 January 2003).

[169] See US General Accounting Office 'Securities Exchange Act: Review of Reporting Under Section 10A' GAO-03-982R (Washington DC 3 September 2003) 1. The SEC has also

cont. ...

sion, which instead viewed the section as part of a highly desirable political compromise that would secure it litigation protection through the enactment of other provisions of the PSLRA.

From such evidence, it seems a fair inference that attorneys would be even less likely to report misconduct to the SEC under an SEC rule requiring 'noisy withdrawal'. After all, auditors are expected to audit and report damaging information, while such reporting runs counter to the professional culture of attorneys. This conclusion does not mean that attorneys should not be asked to perform a gatekeeping role, but rather that, to be effective, such an obligation must be placed in a context whereby the attorney is playing a clearly defined professional role that the client has invited. Otherwise, the attorney is risking professional disaster and will predictably resist. A serious strategy for converting the attorney into a gatekeeper must also address the tension between the roles of gatekeeper and advocate, possibly by separating the two roles and encouraging firms to employ multiple counsel. That is, the corporation could use different law firms, one to plan and structure a transaction and the other to supervise disclosure. Obviously, this would involve increased costs because duplicative work would be performed. Yet this is essentially what Sarbanes-Oxley did to the accountant, divorcing the roles of auditor and consultant because of the clear conflict of interest. In any event, such a separation need not be legally mandated in the case of the attorney, because it could be left to the corporation to decide if it felt sufficiently threatened by an attorney who was under a legal obligation to perform a gatekeeping function that it wished to hire multiple counsel. Firms would not need to specialize in one or the other role, but ideally a law firm would not serve in both capacities to the same client.

Such a proposal is well in advance of where the SEC is today. To date, the SEC has never articulated any general statement of the attorney's gatekeeper role. Although Section 307 of the Sarbanes-Oxley Act authorizes the SEC to promulgate minimum standards of professional conduct for securities attorneys, the SEC has to this point addressed only the narrow, but sensitive, context of the attorney's obligations when the attorney discovers a material violation of law. Beyond this point, it has made no broader attempt to provide any conceptual overview of the attorney's overall responsibility to investors.[170] Yet the statutory authority to do so seems clearly contained in Section 307. For example, minimum standards of professional conduct could (1) require the attorney to perform reasonable due diligence with respect to the statements made in disclosure documents that the attorney drafts for the corporate client; (2) mandate standards

brought seven enforcement actions over this same interval against auditors for violations of section 10A, ibid. This may also suggest that the SEC is slow to bring enforcement proceedings against professional firms (and would remain similarly reluctant to enforce a 'noisy withdrawal' rule again attorneys).

[170] See Securities Release no 33-8185 (29 January 2003) (adopting final rule establishing standards of professional conduct for attorneys who appear or practice before the Commission).

of independence for attorneys performing certain sensitive tasks incident to securities practice; and (3) subject the attorney to professional discipline for negligence or malpractice, thus giving the SEC a useful enforcement tool in cases where it suspects misconduct but cannot easily prove scienter.

On the premise that securities attorneys should serve as gatekeepers for investors, this article will make three specific proposals. First, the SEC should adopt a limited certification requirement mandating that a securities attorney acknowledge that it has reviewed the non-financial disclosure in publicly filed reports; second, it should establish independence standards for securities attorneys performing certain tasks that require them to be independent of management, such as the conduct of internal corporate investigations for publicly held firms; and third, the SEC should deem negligence by attorneys in the preparation of SEC disclosure documents to amount to unprofessional conduct for which attorneys could be disciplined under the SEC's Rules of Practice (just as auditors can be disciplined today).[171] Uniting these proposals is the idea that the attorney should perform a due diligence investigation of the corporation's non-financial disclosures that roughly corresponds to the auditor's role with respect to financial disclosures.

a. A Negative Assurance Certification

A certification requirement applicable to attorneys can be justified simply on the grounds of consistency. Today, a publicly held corporation's CEO and CFO must certify that each periodic report 'fairly presents in all material respects' the issuer's 'financial condition and results of operations'.[172] Similarly, the securities analyst must also today certify that the analyst truly agrees with his or her research advice to investors.[173] Thus, managers, auditors, and analysts all certify their work, but the corporation's principal counsel does not. Arguably, the attorney should not be able to escape a corresponding obligation, particularly because the auditor takes no responsibility for the textual portion of the disclosure document, which is independent of the financial statements that the auditor certifies. In effect, attorney certification mandates a parallel expert to review the non-financial disclosures of the public corporation, but the attorney as gatekeeper

[171] See rule 102(e)(1)(iv) of the SEC Rules of Practice, 17 CFR § 2001.102(e)(1)(iv) (authorizing SEC to suspend or censure an accountant for 'a single instance of highly unreasonable conduct … [or] … repeated instances of unreasonable conduct'.

[172] See n 141-144 and accompanying text (discussing certification requirements under sections 302 and 906 of Sarbanes-Oxley).

[173] See Securities Act Release no 33-8193 (20 February 2003) (adopting Regulation AC, which requires a research analyst employed by a broker or dealer to certify that the views expressed in the research report accurately reflect his or her personal views).

would not be asked to perform an audit or check facts in the manner that an auditor does.

Specifically, the attorney principally responsible for preparing a document or report filed with the SEC should certify (1) that such attorney believes the statements made in the document or report to be true and correct in all material respects, and (2) that such attorney is not aware of any additional material information whose disclosure is necessary in order to make the statements made, in the light of the circumstances under which they were made, not misleading.[174] The real thrust of this proposal is to require the issuer to subject its principal disclosure documents to the scrutiny of an attorney who would be under a professional obligation to exercise a reasonable level of 'due diligence' in his or her review.[175] Today, there is no barrier to the preparation and filing of such non-financial documents entirely by non-professionals.

At first glance, this proposed certification simply tracks the language of Rule 10b-5. Yet the bar will object that by subjecting the attorney to the requirement that the attorney exercise reasonable care, the attorney is being subjected to unreasonable liability. In truth, however, this proposed obligation would only generalize existing practices in the market because today, in most public underwritten offerings, issuer's counsel does deliver an opinion to the underwriters stating that it is not 'aware' of any material information required to be disclosed that has not been disclosed.[176] SEC rules would therefore simply be requiring for

[174] Issues could arise as to which attorney was principally responsible for preparing a document. The simplest answer to this issue is to require the corporation to disclose the identity of such attorney in the filing and then require that attorney's certification.

[175] An open question, on which this article takes no position, is whether such review should be by an attorney 'independent' of management – a term that additional SEC rules could define.

[176] For a description of this standard opinion in registered public offerings, see R Howe 'The Duties and Liabilities of Attorneys in Rendering Legal Opinions' [1989] Columbia Business L Rev 283, 287. The author of this article, a partner at the New York firm of Sullivan and Cromwell, properly observes that 'such opinions are not really "legal opinions" at all in that they do not state any legal conclusion but only say that the attorney believed certain facts to be true', ibid. Precisely for this reason, such an opinion is more a pledge of the law firm's reputational capital, which the underwriters demand. The counsel giving such opinion does not purport to conclude that all information required to be disclosed has been disclosed (as an auditor might by analogy), but only that it lacks personal knowledge or belief as to any such failure. See also RJ Gilson 'Value Creation by Business Lawyers: Legal Skills and Asset Pricing' (1984) 94 Yale L J 239, 291 (also describing such opinions); RW Painter 'Toward A Market for Lawyer Disclosure Services: In Search of Optimal Whistleblowing Rules' (1991) 63 George Washington L Rev 221, 226-27 and n.19 (discussing judicial interpretation of such opinions). The American Bar Association has characterized this type of opinion as a 'negative assurance' and finds such opinions to be 'unique to securities offerings'. See ABA Comm. on Legal Opinions 'Third-Party Opinion Report, Including the Legal Opinion Accord of the Section of Business Law, American Bar Association' (1991) 47 Business Law 167, 228. Although the ABA considers it generally inappropriate for attorneys to request such 'negative assurance' opinions from other attorneys, the special context of securities offerings is exempted,

cont. ...

1934 Act periodic filings what is already done in the primary market for 1933 Act disclosure documents; the real difference is that in the case of periodic filings under the Securities Exchange Act, there is no analogue to the underwriter to demand such an opinion or certification from the attorney. Thus, SEC action would fill this void. In addition, such a requirement would have a profound symbolic and psychological effect on the bar because it would recognize the attorney's obligations as a gatekeeper. Ideally, the SEC should go even further and require the attorney to certify that the attorney so believed 'after making such inquiry that the attorney reasonably believed appropriate in the circumstances'; this would establish at least a minimal due diligence obligation. To be sure, this is a far cry from the strict liability that the auditor would face, but it is a meaningful enhancement, designed to elicit greater precaution from, and investigation by, attorneys. Indeed, law firms would likely agree to provide such certification only if they could maintain a continuing oversight of the firm; one-time-only certifications would be a service that few firms would dare to provide.

Admittedly, limits need to be recognized on what an attorney can certify. Because the attorney does not audit its client, the attorney should not be asked to certify the accuracy and completeness of all information disclosed in SEC filings; nor should it be asked to investigate the financial statements that the auditor certifies (although the attorney should be required to certify his or her belief that these statements contain no material misrepresentations or omissions).[177] Thus, the proposal made here requires only a negative certification that the attorney had no reason to believe, and did not believe, that the information was materially false or misleading. Legally, such a certification would trigger 'aiding and abetting' liability if the attorney was aware of materially false or misleading information, and it could even trigger criminal liability under various federal statutes. But its primary effect is to recognize that the securities attorney is a gatekeeper for investors.

b. Independence

Auditors, of course, must be independent of their client, and SEC rules have long defined tests for auditor independence. Increasingly, a new literature has warned that attorneys are becoming too economically interconnected with their client to exercise independent judgment, as the result in part of the increasing practice of law firms taking (and even demanding) equity stakes in the client in return for

reflecting the fact that underwriters consider such an assurance to be necessary to them. That the ABA, as the representative of the bar, 'disfavors' such opinions, because of the demands they place on the attorney, probably only underscores the value of such a reform.

177 The attorney thus would not be required to certify that it exercised reasonable care or otherwise investigated the financial statements.

professional services.[178] If some level of independence is necessary for an attorney to function as a gatekeeper, SEC rules of professional conduct could define these limits. To illustrate, a law firm that holds in its portfolio 10% of the corporate client's equity (or, alternatively, equity in the client equal to 10% of its own net asset value) will probably be a poor, or at least a biased, monitor.

In any event, the context that is most sensitive and would most benefit from such rules is that of internal corporate investigations. Often, such investigations are mandated by the SEC, and typically the resulting reports are filed with the SEC. Should the corporation's normal outside counsel perform such an investigation? Or, should SEC rules define the level of independence necessary to conduct such a more sensitive inquiry? Absent SEC action, individual state bar associations will either do nothing (the most likely outcome) or prescribe different and inconsistent standards, thereby creating needless disparities. Uniform standards for corporate internal investigations are desirable and as a practical matter can only come from the SEC. There is no need to offer precise rules here, but only to recognize that professionals are expected to be independent of their clients. Accordingly, the SEC should read Section 307 to grant it authority to define the point at which the attorney is not sufficiently independent of the client to perform certain sensitive tasks.

c. The Due Diligence Obligation

Certification is only a first step. The next logical step would be to mandate due diligence by the attorney in preparing or reviewing SEC filings as a minimum standard of professional conduct. Here, Sarbanes-Oxley changes the picture significantly, because Section 307 of Sarbanes-Oxley authorizes the SEC to establish 'minimum standards of professional conduct for attorneys appearing and practicing before the Commission....' This reference to 'professional conduct' would certainly seem to empower the SEC to adopt rules requiring the attorney both to conduct a minimal due diligence review before the attorney files a document or report with the SEC and to certify its good faith belief in the accuracy of the statements made therein. Indeed, in its existing Rules of Practice, the SEC already holds auditors to precisely such a standard and asserts the power to suspend or disbar them for merely negligent conduct.[179] If this can be done without special statutory authority, then it seems to follow *a fortiori*, after the enact-

[178] See JS Dzienkowski and RJ Peroni 'The Decline in Lawyer Independence: Lawyer Equity Investments in Clients' (2002) 81 Texas L Rev 405; R de Rohan Barondes 'Professionalism Consequences of Law Firm Investments In Clients: An Empirical Assessment' (2002) 39 American Business L J 379.

[179] See 17 CFR § 201.102(e)(iv) (specifying that two forms of 'negligent conduct' – either 'a single instance of highly unreasonable conduct' or 'repeated instances of unreasonable conduct' – could trigger sanctions under Rule 102(e)).

ment of Section 307, that the SEC could require attorneys to take reasonable steps to investigate the accuracy of statements made in documents that they prepare.[180]

The bottom line then is that the SEC is today empowered to adopt rules that could suspend or disbar an attorney for negligence as a form of professional misconduct. Negligence would clearly not support a private cause of action under Rule 10b-5, but it may be the appropriate standard for the imposition of sanctions under Section 307.[181] Such a tradeoff – ie public liability but not private liability for negligence – again seems desirable in that it enhances deterrence without threatening insolvency for law firms.

4. Accessing Counter-Arguments: Can Attorneys Be Gatekeepers?

Any assertion that the SEC should compel the securities attorney to play a greater gatekeeping role inevitably runs into the argument that such a role is either inappropriate for attorneys or will reduce their clients' willingness to confide in them. The first claim that such a role is inappropriate depends largely on one's vantage point. Litigators tend to view the attorney as an advocate for, and protector of, the client – a bulwark between the client and an oppressive state.[182] Securities attorneys are less ready to buy into this rhetoric, however, and do not have the same self- image of themselves. For the most part, they agree that they have at least an ethical responsibility to perform due diligence on documents they draft and file with the SEC. For over a quarter century, prominent securities attorneys have recognized that, as a result, their professional role is closer to that of the auditor than to that of the litigator.[183] The key elements that distinguish the

[180] The attorney would, of course, be entitled to rely on the auditor with respect to financial information certified by the auditor, as in the case of the 'reliance on an expert' defense under Section 11(b)(3)(c) of the Securities Act of 1933. See 15 USC Section 77(k)(b)(3)(c).

[181] Historically, the SEC did once hold attorneys liable for professional negligence in 'aiding and abetting' cases. See *SEC v Spectrum Ltd* 489 F2d 535, 536 (2nd Circuit 1973). This is no longer possible after the Supreme Court mandated a scienter standard in *Hochfelder*, but sanctions for professional misconduct could look to a similar standard.

[182] EA Davis 'The Meaning of Professional Independence' (2003) 103 Columbia L Rev 1281 (arguing that the SEC's up-the-ladder reporting rules inhibit professional independence).

[183] The literature here is enormous, but one brief statement by a securities lawyer of iconic reputation stands out above the field. In 1974, in a famous and much-quoted address, AA Sommer Jr, then an SEC Commissioner, gave an address in which he initially described the securities attorney not as an advocate but rather as 'the field marshal who coordinate[s] the activities of others engaged in the registration process'. See AA Sommer Jr 'The Emerging Responsibilities of the Securities Lawyer, Address to the Banking, Corporation & Business Law Section, N.Y. State Bar Association' (24 January 1974) reprinted in LD Soderquist and T Gabaldon *Securities Regulation* (4th edn Foundation Press Westbury 1999) 617. Then, based on his description of the attorney as more a transaction engineer than an advocate, he offered his normative assessment: 'I would suggest that in securities matters (other than those where

cont. ...

attorney as advocate from the attorney as gatekeeper are: (1) a need for greater independence from the client; (2) a recognition of a duty to the public; and (3) professional skepticism.[184] Exactly these differences need to be recognized by the SEC under Section 307.

The more important counter-argument to imposing gatekeeper obligations on securities attorneys is that attorneys will be unable to communicate as freely with their clients if gatekeeper obligations or 'noisy withdrawal' requirements were imposed. In response to this claim, it is first necessary to recognize that the ultimate goal of the law is to achieve law compliance, not to maximize uninhibited communications between the attorney and the client.[185] The norm of client confidentiality is a means to an end, not the end in itself.

Still, even with this concession, it remains true that lawyers can counsel most effectively when there is open, relatively unconstrained communication between their clients and themselves. Hence, the practical issue becomes whether gatekeeper obligations would necessary chill desirable attorney/client communications. Here, two arguments need to be considered.

First, lawyer/client relationships are less likely to be chilled if corporate clients use the gatekeeping attorney as a specialist, employing one attorney to consult on the transaction and another to review and prepare the disclosures. This may be duplicative, but it is essentially the same duplication that exists between the in-house bookkeeper and the outside auditor. Indeed, because the gatekeeper could prepare the disclosure document, there would not be complete duplication,

advocacy is clearly proper) the attorney will have to function in a manner more akin to that of auditor than to that of the attorney. This means several things. It means that he will have to exercise a measure of independence that is perhaps uncomfortable if he is also the close counselor of management in other matters, often including business decisions. It means he will have to be acutely cognizant of his responsibility to the public who engage in securities transactions that would never have come about were it not for his professional presence. It means that he will have to adopt the healthy skepticism toward the representation of management which a good auditor must adopt. It means that he will have to do the same thing the auditor does when confronted with an intransigent client – resign', ibid 317-319. Although Commissioner Sommer never used the term 'noisy withdrawal' in this speech, the same concept seems to have been, more or less, on his mind, and the elements that he does specifically enunciate – high independence, duty to public investors, professional skepticism – probably are the key elements that distinguish the attorney as advocate from the attorney as gatekeeper.

[184] See Sommer (n 183) 317-319.

[185] Thus, the 'crime/fraud' exception to the attorney/client privilege makes some communications between attorney and client discoverable, even though this result thereby arguably makes clients less ready to confide in their attorneys. The justification for this result, which applies similarly to this context, is that communications so excluded from the privilege are deemed socially undesirable. For the current status of this exception, see *In re Richard Roe Inc* 168 F3d 69 (2nd Circuit 1999). See also DN Zarnow and K Krakaur 'On the Brink of a Brave New World: The Death of Privilege in Corporate Criminal Investigation' (2000) 37 American Criminal L Rev 147 (suggesting that the attorney/client privilege is already highly qualified in this context).

as there is in the case of financial statements. In addition, specialization by attorneys as gatekeepers also mitigates the 'one client practice' problem that challenges all professional service firms, auditors as well as attorneys. A professional with a single dominating client has an incentive to subordinate his own firm's interest in preserving its reputation to his client's demands for acquiescence. But gatekeepers, as specialists, would typically serve multiple clients and hence would be less dominated. Law firms could specialize in this role, or more likely service some clients as gatekeepers and others as transactional engineers.

A second response to the claim that attorney/client communication will be chilled is to focus both on when such communications are most desirable and least desirable. A plausible case can be made that a 'noisy withdrawal' rule threatens primarily the least desirable communications. The starting point for this analysis is the recognition that the typical client knows little law and will almost always want to know if contemplated action is illegal. From this premise, it follows that the corporate official contemplating prospective action will still inquire of counsel whether the course of action under consideration is lawful. Indeed, the more the government pursues white collar criminal prosecutions and punitive regulatory actions in the contemporary post-Enron environment, the more in turn that corporate officers are likely to inquire before they act. When then will communications be most likely to be chilled? The likely answer is that the officer who has already acted may fear inquiring of an attorney if the officer's conduct was lawful – precisely because the officer fears that the attorney may be under an obligation to report unlawful actions to higher authorities or, indirectly, to the SEC. In short, it is the *ex post* inquiry by the client of the attorney that is most likely to be chilled.

If one accepts this premise that *ex ante* communications between counsel and the client are less likely to be chilled than *ex post* communications, several implications follow: First, the impact of imposing gatekeeper obligations on attorneys may be socially desirable. In a well-known article, Professors Kaplow and Shavell have argued that the case for protecting *ex ante* communications between attorneys and clients is far stronger than the case for protecting *ex post* communications.[186] Advice before action leads individuals to comply with the law, they argue, whereas *ex post* advice does not provide a guide for action and may simply allow the defendant to reduce the expected penalty costs, thus encouraging illegality. It is not necessary to fully accept the Kaplow/Shavell analysis to see that its core distinction between *ex ante* and *ex post* advice suggests that we should be more concerned about chilling *ex ante* communications between attorney and client. But this is not what most gatekeeper obligations do; rather, they may induce such communications by making *ex post* advice less possible.

[186] See L Kaplow and S Shavell 'Legal Advice About Information to Present in Litigation: Its Effects and Social Desirability' (1989) 102 Harvard L Rev 565; see also R Posner 'An Economic Approach for the Law of Evidence' (1999) 51 Stanford L Rev 1477, 1531-33.

Second, requiring 'noisy withdrawals' and 'up-the-ladder' reporting also has a deterrent value that is independent of this issue of whether the initial corporate actor will still consult counsel. Few significant actions within a corporation can be taken by a single actor. Decisions made by one person still need to be implemented by others. Thus, even after the initial corporate actor has taken an irrevocable step (and will thereafter be arguably less willing to consult with counsel *ex post*), other corporate actors will need to be contracted and convinced to cooperate with the initial actor. They will have every incentive to consult with counsel because they are still at the *ex ante* stage. In turn, knowledge that others are necessarily likely to learn of the original actor's conduct and to consult with counsel about its legality may deter the original actor. The modern public corporation is embedded with in-house attorneys, and even the possibility that they will report 'up the ladder' should deter some illegal conduct. Hence, even if under some conditions there may be less direct communication between corporate actors and counsel, knowledge that sooner or later counsel is likely to learn *ex post* can still deter corporate actors *ex ante*.

As a result, the principal practical effect that imposing gatekeeper obligations will have on clients is that a client who has been advised by an attorney that contemplated action is unlawful now has greater reason to heed that attorney's advice – again precisely to the extent that the client believes that the attorney may be under a legal obligation to report any misconduct (either inside the corporation or outside). Thus, even if it were true that clients would consult less, this impact could be more than fully offset by the fact that it would become more dangerous to disregard the lawyer's advice. Add to this mix the likelihood that *ex ante* advice will not be chilled, and the net impact is to increase the attorney's leverage over the client by making it more dangerous to ignore the attorney's advice. If law compliance is the goal, such an impact seems socially desirable.

V. Conclusion

The diagnosis of 'gatekeeper failure' made in Part II of this article leads naturally to a multi-part prescription for better law compliance: the law should create, empower, and deter gatekeepers. Deterrence is easy, but it can be overdone. Thus, although this article has favored a shift toward stricter liability, it has coupled this recommendation with a proposed ceiling on liability set at the level necessary to deter the gatekeeper. This proposal may subordinate compensation to deterrence – but only with regard to litigation against gatekeepers, who are seldom in any event in a position to fund full compensation to the investor class.

Empowerment is a trickier question. If we are to reduce accounting and financial reporting irregularities, the optimal strategy must both motivate and empower gatekeepers to insist upon law compliance. In the case of the attorney, the first step toward making the securities attorney a gatekeeper should be to enhance their leverage over their clients in order to enable them to exert greater pressure for law compliance. A mandatory attorney certification standard, enforced by a due diligence obligation, does essentially this by forcing the client to seek the attorney's review. The end goal of these reforms should be to encourage the emergence of a new specialist: the lawyer/gatekeeper, who would practice alongside and not in conflict with the lawyer/advocate and the lawyer/transaction engineer.

Gatekeeper empowerment necessarily requires intruding upon our existing guild-like structure of private self-regulation of the professions. Sarbanes-Oxley already does this in the case of the accounting and analyst professions, but the SEC has not yet compelled the legal profession to recognize its mandatory obligations to the public. Professions, like guilds, will predictably resist any increase in their responsibilities and liabilities to the public, but, as the accounting profession has already found, the professional cannot remain aloof and self-governing once the social cost of gatekeeper failure has become apparent.

Finally, this article does not claim to have answered all problems or designed a complete response to the problem of gatekeeper failure. In particular, a major cause of gatekeeper failure is that, in concentrated markets, competitors do not need to protect their reputations but can accept a more or less equivalent rate of reputational erosion. Because reputations are relative, then, so long as each firm in such a market is confident that its competitors will suffer similar reputational injury, it is free to profit from the slow liquidation of its reputational capital. This process could be a collusive one, or, more likely, it could simply involve a conscious parallelism of action. Still, it reminds us that some notable markets for gatekeeper services are oligopolistic in character, and in such a market gatekeeper failure may become more likely. Assuring real competition then is a significant part of any comprehensive answer.

The Changing World of the CPAs in Japan

HIROSHI ODA

I. The Background to the Reform

In Japan, accountancy as a profession was introduced in 1948 when the Securities and Exchange Law was enacted.[1] A professional body – the Japan Institute of Certified Public Accountants (JICPA) – was founded.[2] As of 1 March 2004, there were 14,826 accountants and 151 accounting firms.[3] Not many changes occurred for half a century, but since the late 1990s the profession has been going through a rather difficult time. This culminated in a major amendment of the Law on CPAs in 2003. This was not necessarily a result of the US Sarbanes-Oxley Act[4] (hereinafter, the SOA); in fact, some reforms preceded the SOA. Japan had its own problems and was addressing them, although in a gradual manner. In a way, one might say that the reform which had already started in Japan was distorted by the SOA.

For many years, the Japanese accounting and audit system was not seen as reflecting the true state of the finances of listed companies. There were instances where the same company prepared financial statements in accordance with both the Japanese standards and the US standards. While the company was in the red under the US standards, it was profit-making under the Japanese standards. Such discrepancies have led to the requirement of a 'legend', a footnote to the audit report, stating that the financial documents have been prepared under the Japanese standards, a practice which started in 1999. In the audit report, which is attached to the English annual report prepared by the Big Five accounting firms, a footnote that the financial statements and the audit report have been prepared in

[1] H Hato *The Amended CPA Law* (Tokyo 2004) 5-12.

[2] <www.jicpa.or.jp> (22 April 2005).

[3] <www.fsa.go.jp> (22 April 2005).

[4] See annex 3 in this volume.

accordance with Japanese accounting standards and audit practices was added. Other countries which were required to attach a legend were Korea and Indonesia; this undermined the credibility of the Japanese system.[5]

In a survey of 3,500 public companies by the Ministry of Economy, Trade and Industry in 2002, 36.7% of the companies prepared the annual report in English. Of the companies which prepared an annual report in English, 6.1% used the US standards, while 0.8% used the IAS. The rest of the companies resorted to the Japanese standards. Of those companies, 52% responded that there was a legend attached to the audit report.[6]

In the first place, this was a problem of accounting standards. Japan has been slow to harmonise accounting standards with international developments. It was only in 2001 that the consolidated accounting system was introduced in company law accounting, although this had been a requirement of the Securities and Exchange Law for some years. The evaluation of assets at current value was also introduced, but there are various exceptions.

In the above-cited survey, although 54.5% of the companies support the recent changes to the accounting standards, 21.1% are of the view that the changes do not suit business practices in Japan, and 38.8% consider that the changes are happening too fast. It is more or less the perception of businesses that the changes in the accounting standards affect company management. More than 54% of the respondents confirmed that the 1999 standards on financial products had some effect.

There is still some resistance against introducing changes to the accounting system. When the chairman of the JICPA was in discussion with the members of the parliament, he was told that the recession was caused by the accounting standards and the audit system![7] In the wake of the financial crisis which began in 1997, the government delayed the changes to the accounting standards in order to avoid further collapse of the banks. There was concern among the bureaucrats and politicians at that time that a full implementation of the accounting reform would affect the banks. Such views still remain. The latest example of resistance relates to the introduction of the impaired accounting system. The 'financial policy project team' of parliamentary members from the ruling political party has urged the Accounting Standard Board of Japan to defer the introduction of the system, and has also proposed that the current value accounting of securities held for the long term should be optional, but this was eventually rejected by the board.[8]

[5] T Inoue 'Commentary on the Amended CPA Law' (2003) 1668 Shôji Hômu 5.

[6] Research Report on the Corporate Accounting System of Japanese Companies, March 2002 by the Ministry of Economy, Trade and Industry (METI). See <www.meti.go.jp> (22 April 2005).

[7] 1670 Shôji Hômu 47.

[8] (2003) 1663 Shôji Hômu 44; (2003) 1666 Shôji Hômu 39.

The necessity for the reform of the CPA system was already recognised in Japan in the 1990s. After all, the last major reform of the CPA Law took place in 1966; since then there have been no major changes to the system.

In 1996, on the eve of the 50th anniversary of the CPA Law, a reform of the accounting system came onto the agenda. There was a proposal for reforms by the JICPA. Already at that time, in the wake of the housing credit institution (*Jusen*) problems and the collapse of regional financial institutions, doubts were raised concerning the reliability of auditing by the CPAs. This concern was shared by the CPAs themselves, and thus proposals were made in order to regain the confidence of the market participants.

The CPA Review Board, which was attached to the Ministry of Finance at that time, took up the JICPA proposals, and after some deliberation it published a ten-point proposal for reform.[9]

The proposals were based upon the perception that in order to galvanise the securities market, truthful disclosure was indispensable, and that this could be achieved by addressing the accounting standards and audit practice. The introduction of a quality control of audits, peer reviews of the US type, and continuous training systems was proposed.

Conspicuously lacking was any reference to measures ensuring the independence of the accountants from the companies they audit, which can be found in the later arguments and in the amended CPA Law. This only became an issue after the financial crisis in 1997, which cast doubt on the capability and independence of the CPAs in performing their role in relation to the failed companies.

It was proposed that information should be provided in the audit report regarding matters which significantly affect the issuer as a going concern. This was a significant step forward from the existing practice.

On the other hand, the goal of the report was to 'remove concerns regarding the CPA audit held by market participants by strengthening *voluntary measures* by the CPAs'. There was little discussion of any strengthening of government supervision over the profession.

The move for reform coincided with the Japanese 'Big Bang' – a major reform of the financial system which was launched in 1996. The Big Bang, which encompassed the banking, securities, and insurance industries, was aimed at the creation of a free and fair financial market open to the global market. This included increased competition between financial institutions (and the gradual dismantling of the barrier between banking and securities businesses), the diversification of the means of corporate finance, and the creation of a fair and transparent market. One underlying idea was the shift from the bank-dominated financial system to a system resorting more to the securities market. This presupposes that investors are provided with accurate information concerning the financial

[9] 'Proposals for the Increased Robustness of Audit by the CPAs', the Report of the CPA Review Board of 24 April 1997.

state of the companies. The improvement of the accounting system was regarded as essential for this purpose. This naturally worked in favour of the reform of the CPA system.

There were also some negative incidents which enhanced the CPA reform. In 1997 a major financial crisis began to unravel. After the collapse of a medium-sized securities company, one of the 19 'city banks' collapsed, followed by the termination of business by Yamaichi Securities. Two long-term credit banks failed the next year and a significant amount of public funds was injected into the banks. The problem was that the banks and securities companies which had failed had all had their accounts audited by CPAs and had been given a 'true and fair' opinion without any qualification before the collapse. There was growing criticism not only of the government and the industry, but also of the CPAs.

Yamaichi Securities, one of the Big Four securities companies, applied for bankruptcy and was declared bankrupt in 1999. The company had concealed losses by shifting them to domestic and overseas 'paper companies'. An independent body set up to investigate the incident after the collapse found that the CPA was also responsible for having failed to detect the problem. Administrators brought an action *vis à vis* the accounting firm, Chuo, for compensation amounting to 6 billion yen. The accountants were accused of neglecting their duty, which resulted in their failure to detect the window-dressing by the management.[10] The parties ultimately settled in 2004. The accounting firm agreed to pay back five years' worth of fees without acknowledging any fault on their part.

The progress of the CPA reform slowed down after 1998. It was only in June 2000 that a sub-committee of the board published an interim report on the 'direction of the reform'.[11] This was an outcome of the discussions of the expanded working group set up in April 1999 and of the board sub-committee since December 1999. Then, in January 2001, the prime minister formally consulted the Financial Systems Council on the review of the CPA system.

The interim report of June 2000 was based upon the premise that in order to increase the credibility of the disclosure of financial information by companies with the aim that companies could be financed smoothly in and outside Japan, it was important to improve the auditing by CPAs and raise its reliability.

For the first time, the independence of the CPAs formally came to the agenda. The problem of the same accountant auditing the same company for a long period of time was raised. While the newly introduced self-regulation (Quality Control Review) of the JICPA mandated the rotation system of ten years, the report proposed seven years, which 'is in line with the international standard'. Another problem which was identified was that of a single CPA who does not belong to an accounting firm auditing a large company. There was no self-regulatory rule on

[10] (1999) 1547 Shôji Hômu 36.

[11] CPA Review Board 'Problems of the Audit System and the Direction of Reform' 29 June 2000.

this matter, but some regulation by law was suggested, namely regarding the auditing of listed companies. The problem of simultaneous provision of auditing and non-auditing service was mentioned, and the creation of a fire wall between these divisions was suggested.

The general tone of the interim report still placed faith in self-regulation by the JICPA. The report endorsed the initiatives of the JICPA in their quality control review. However, the JICPA was urged to introduce a system whereby it could instruct its members to take necessary corrective measures and thus ensure the effectiveness of the quality control review. There was, though, a suggestion that the JICPA should be under an obligation to report the result of the quality control review to the Financial Services Agency (FSA).

By 2002, although more than five years after the launch of the Japanese Big Bang, the securities market in Japan had so far failed to show any sign of recovery, let alone being a driving force for a prosperous economy. Measures comprising the Big Bang were intended to be completed and a free, fair, and global market was to have been created by March 2001, but not all of the measures were implemented as planned, primarily due to the serious state of the economy after the financial crisis.

In 2002, the government reconfirmed its commitment to the structural reform of the securities market in its "Fundamental Policies for the Management of the Economy and Finance and the Structural Reform". This included an 'improvement of the infrastructure to increase the credibility of the securities market among the general public'. This was followed by the Programme for the Promotion of the Reform of the Securities Market published by the FSA in August 2002. It should be noted that this was after the US American enactment of the SOA, which strengthened the independence of the CPA/accounting firms and the supervision of accounting firms in the wake of the Enron/WorldCom saga that began to unravel in late 2001.

The programme, which was sub-titled the "Second Stage" of the structural reform of the securities market, was quite candid in acknowledging that the securities market still lacked dynamism and was insufficient to form the core of the future financial system. It was admitted that the general public did not have sufficient trust in the issuing companies, intermediaries, the market creators, or even the market mechanism itself. (Incidentally, in a survey conducted by the Cabinet Office on the attitude of the general public towards the securities investment, only 12% of the respondents had an experience or intention to invest in the securities market, and 40% of the respondents thought that the securities companies could not be trusted.)[12] Among other problems, the ensurance of the fairness and transparency of the market was focussed in this document. This involved strengthening the supervision of the market and reinforcing the accounting and audit system. The latter included strengthening the supervision of

[12] The Cabinet Office, <www.kantei.go.jp> (21 April 2005).

accounting firms in the light of incidents in the US However, no specifics were given on the mechanism of supervision.

Following this initiative, the Sub-Committee on the CPA System of the Finance Systems Council published its final report in December 2002.[13] The purpose of the CPA reform, as stated in the report, was the consolidation and improvement of the quality of audits by CPAs. The report emphasised that the protection of investors and creditors and the gaining of confidence in the securities market presuppose an audit which guarantees adequate disclosure of financial information and its credibility.

The reform proposed in the report was aimed at the reinforcement of the independence of CPAs more or less in line with the SOA. The strengthening of government control over the CPAs and over the JICPA was also at the core of the changes. In this context, the introduction of a 'monitoring system' by the government over the quality review of the accountants' work, which had been performed by the JICPA as a self-regulatory measure, was also proposed.

The proposed changes included the following points:

- Ensuring the independence of the CPAs and the accounting firms from the client companies;
- Raising the standard of the audit by the accounting firms via effective and appropriate organisation of the audit;
- Continuation of self-regulatory activities by the JICPA to be supplemented by the government;
- Reform of the examination system for CPAs;
- Increase in the number of CPAs (up to 50 thousand by 2022).

In line with this report, a bill for the amendment of the CPA Law was prepared and submitted to the Diet and was adopted on 30 May 2003. The Law took effect in May 2004.

As can be seen from the above developments, the latest amendments to the CPA Law were not necessarily a straight continuation of the reform initiative by the accounting profession which had begun in 1996. Firstly, the original reform proposals were expanded to accommodate problems such as the independence of the CPAs. This resulted from the loss of credibility of the CPAs caused by their conspicuous failures in exposing irregularities when auditing the financial institutions which collapsed during the financial crisis. It should be emphasised that the reform proposals preceded Enron/WorldCom.

Secondly, until 2002 the primary emphasis was on self-regulation by the JICPA rather than government control. In the aftermath of the Enron/WorldCom incidents, the SOA was enacted in the US, and this had a significant impact on the amendments. There was a notable alteration of the policy in the final report by

[13] The Report of the Sub-Committee on the CPA System, Financial Systems Council 'Strengthening of the CPA System' 17 December 2002.

the sub-committee in December 2002 on the independence of the CPAs. It was perceived that 'from a supervisory point of view, it is necessary for the government to play an adequate role in ensuring the fairness, neutrality and effectiveness of self-regulation by the JICPA'. Self-regulatory measures, such as the rules on the rotation of CPAs auditing the same company, were made a statutory requirement.

Thirdly, some new requirements were added, such as the prohibition of simultaneous provision of consulting and auditing services.

Naturally, one may question whether or not the amended CPA Law has gone too far in the direction of the SOA.

II. The Amended CPA Law

1. The Task of CPAs

Unlike most of the laws which serve as the basis for professions such as attorneys, the CPA Law did not have a provision which set out the task of the CPAs. This was always regarded as one of the shortcomings of the CPA Law. The amended Law rectified this situation by introducing the following provision:

> CPAs contribute to the sound development of the national economy by ensuring the fair business activities of companies and other entities and protect investors as well as creditors by securing the credibility of financial documents and other information regarding finance, being independent specialists of audit and accounting.

The protection of creditors, not only investors, was inserted, since the CPAs audit not only companies covered by the Securities and Exchange Law, but also companies which fall within the scope of the Special Measures Law on Audit of Large Companies.

2. Reinforcement of Independence

Independence in this context means independence of the CPAs from the clients. Even without Enron/WorldCom affairs, CPAs have been criticised in a series of window-dressing cases in Japan for overlooking irregularities because of their close links with the client company. The government's intention was to increase the fairness and transparency of the audit and to demonstrate that CPAs are, in substance as well as in appearance, independent from the client companies. In the earlier proposals, this was to be left to the self-regulation of the JICPA. Some requirements concerning the independence of the CPAs were introduced as self-regulatory measures by the JICPA in 1999. The amended Law has made these a statutory requirement.

The content of the amended Law in this respect is similar to that of the SOA. The requirements are:

a. Prohibition of the Simultaneous Provision of Audit and Non-audit Services

There is a potential conflict of interests if a CPA is allowed to provide both services to the same company. This may result in a situation where the CPA audits the outcome of the service which he has provided. The CPA may become dependent on the income from the non-audit business and close his eyes to the irregularities in the accounts. The amended law prohibits a CPA from providing an audit service to a large company to which he provides non-audit service by himself, his spouse, or an entity which he substantially controls and from which he receives continuous remuneration.

The scope of non-audit business is provided by a cabinet order. It is more or less in line with the SOA:

Preparation of accounting books and financial documents;
- Certification and valuation of in-kind contributions;
- Insurance actuary service;
- Outsourcing of internal audits;
- Investment advisory service;
- Securities business;
- Other services involved in the business decisions of the company.

Normally, 'large companies' denote joint stock companies which have 500 million yen or more in capital or 20 billion yen worth of debts.[14] These companies are required to have their accounts audited by a CPA or an accounting firm. There are around 10,000 such companies. However, there was an argument that companies which fall within this category still can be medium-sized companies or unlisted venture businesses which rely on accountants to advise them when preparing their accounts. It was considered impractical to apply the prohibition on the simultaneous provision of audit and non-audit services to these companies. Therefore, by virtue of the Implementation Order of the Law, companies with a capital of less than 10 billion yen and debts of less than 100 billion yen are exempted.[15]

Among matters involving the independence of CPAs from their clients, this had probably been the least-discussed issue in Japan. In recent years, Japanese accounting firms have increasingly become involved in non-audit services such as management consulting and advising on corporate finance matters (for example, M&A). The existence of the problem was acknowledged, as can be seen in the earlier reform proposals, but the problem had been regarded as somewhat remote. As the JICPA president pointed out after the amendments, this was very much an issue which came from the US.[16]

[14] Special Measures Law on the Audit of Large Joint Stock Companies.

[15] Hato (n 1) 108-111.

[16] 1670 Shôji Hômu 43.

The scope of the non-audit services which were to be banned was debated by the JICPA. The JICPA pointed out that the providing of accounting guidance to the client should not be regarded as a non-audit service. It was pointed out that there should be a distinction between full-fledged work and mere guidance.[17]

b. Limitation of the Length of Time for which a CPA can Audit the Same Large Company

A rotation system of CPAs was introduced to prevent close links from being developed over the years between a CPA and the client company. The amended Law prohibits CPAs from auditing the same large company for longer than seven years and also provides for a cooling-off period. The SOA sets the period at five years, but in Japan there was strong resistance from the JICPA, and it was settled at seven years. The parliamentary committee chairman was of the view that the Law should adopt five years like the SOA, while the JICPA insisted that it should be seven years. In fact, the self-regulatory rules dictated ten years. The argument by the JICPA was that five years was too short to get to know the company being audited. The resulting limit is a compromise, but this is to be reviewed by the legislature after seven years with a view to shortening it.[18] the JICPA is of the view that this does not mean that it will necessarily be reduced to five years after the review.[19]

The cooling-off period during which the CPA involved is not allowed to return to audit the company in question is five years in the SOA. There were some arguments against this, it being suggested that even in a one- or two-year interval, the succeeding CPA would be able to find an inappropriate audit, and the predecessor would never be allowed to return to audit the same company. In the end, the period was not specified in the Law. It is determined by the implementation order as two years.

There was an argument also that this system should apply not only to CPAs, but that the accounting firms themselves should rotate; that is, the same accounting firm should not continue auditing the same company for more than a certain period. However, there are few jurisdictions (Italy is one of the rare exceptions) which have gone so far, and this proposal was not accepted. Even in the US, the SOA has not gone this far.[20] Besides, in Japan the top four firms more or less monopolise the auditing of listed companies. Rotating firms may result in difficulties for the client companies.

[17] ibid 43-44.

[18] Inoue (n 5) 27.

[19] ibid 44.

[20] ibid 26.

c. Restriction on the CPA Joining the Client Company

If a CPA audits a company during one financial year, he is not allowed to become a director of that company until the end of the next financial year. The same applies to the CPA who works in an accounting firm and has audited a company as an accountant in charge. This restriction includes those who were CPAs but have ceased to be CPAs.

d. Prohibition of Auditing of Large Companies by a Single CPA

Under the amended Law, CPAs are now under an obligation to work with another CPA or an accounting firm, or to be assisted by another CPA when auditing a large company as defined in the law. In order to maintain the standard of the audit, an organised audit with several CPAs is desirable. If there are several CPAs involved, it is likely to prevent a close link developing with the client.

This was certainly not an SOA-based amendment; it is of Japanese origin. There was an incident of window-dressing involving a listed company in which a small accounting firm was retained and actually assisted the company management in window-dressing. The CPA single-handedly audited the company. The CPA was not only convicted, but also had his registration revoked by the JICPA in 1999 (Mita Industry case).[21] Since then, listing rules have required that a newly listed company should have the account audited by more than two CPAs or an accounting firm. The amended Law has made this official after the amendment, in 2004 a large unlisted company, which is the parent company of a listed company, was found to have been providing false information in its securities report. The company had been audited by a single CPA (not even an accounting firm) for more than 20 years.

3. Strengthening of Supervision by the Government

The amended Law strengthened supervision by the government of the accountants by 'supplementing the limits of self-regulation' under the JICPA. The goal is to ensure the fairness, neutrality, and effectiveness of the audit by the accountants.[22] This expression, 'limits of self-regulation', first appeared in the above-cited 2002 December Report of the Sub-Committee of the Financial Systems Council. Until then, the government did not seem to be particularly dissatisfied with the self-regulation system run by the JICPA. Obviously, the idea of government supervision of the profession has come from the SOA.

[21] ibid 27.

[22] Inoue (n 5) 29.

The agency in charge of supervising the accountants is the Financial Services Agency (FSA; as delegated by the prime minister). This function used to be bestowed on the Ministry of Finance, but as a result of the reform since the late 1990s the function has shifted to the FSA. Under the amendment, the Review Board for Accountants and Audit in place of the previous Review Board for Accountants was set up under the FSA in 2004. This is a collective administrative body which comprises nine part-time commissioners and a chairman. They are appointed by the prime minister with the consent of the Diet. The chairman and the members are guaranteed independence when carrying out their duties. The board has a secretariat. Currently, the chairman is a retired law professor and the members include some academics, the president of the JICPA, and a representative of the Keidanren.

Under the amended Law, the new board continues to exercise the power of disciplining CPAs, but in addition it will exercise supervision of accountants via the 'monitoring' of the quality control review conducted by the JICPA.

The novelties in the amended Law include:

a. Increased Power of Investigation

Previously, the Law granted such a power to the government agency only in cases where there were grounds for disciplinary measures. It was not possible for the agency to enter an office, for example, for the purpose of investigating the internal control system of an accounting firm. Through the amendment, officials of the agency are now empowered to enter the offices of CPAs, foreign CPAs and accounting firms, and other premises related to their business, and to inspect books and documents which are relevant to the business when they consider it necessary and appropriate for the protection of public interest or of investors.

Furthermore, the FSA is now entitled to require the submission of a report or materials of the CPAs, foreign CPAs, and accounting firms when it considers it necessary and appropriate for the protection of public interest or of investors.

b. Quality Control Review and its Monitoring

The JICPA has been conducting a 'quality control review' of the accountants on their internal management and auditing work since 1999 as a self-regulatory measure. At present, around 300 accounting firms and offices are under review by the JIPCA for their management and audit work. If necessary, the JIPCA issues recommendations for improvement.

As a result of the amendments, quality control reviews have become a statutory requirement. The JICPA is now under a statutory obligation to carry out a quality control review of the audit service provided by accountants and report the result to the board on a regular basis or when it is needed. The government is to 'monitor' the quality control review conducted by the JICPA. The object of the monitoring covers the JICPA itself as well as accounting firms and even the client companies. The board is empowered to inspect CPAs, accounting firms, and the JICPA and, if necessary, to recommend that administrative measures be imposed on them.

Before the amendment, although the ultimate power of disciplining accountants belonged to the government, there was an existing system of self-regulation by the JICPA which had been strengthened since the late 1990s. In fact, some of the measures for reinforcing the independence of accountants which were introduced by the amended Law had already been implemented by the JICPA as self-regulatory measures. When the move to tighten government control emerged in the aftermath of the Enron/WorldCom incidents, the JICPA became seriously concerned. It had already introduced the 'quality control review' voluntarily, and a further involvement of the government on this matter seemed to be superfluous. After all, if self-regulatory measures were beginning to work, why should the government be directly involved? Direct supervision by the government or a quasi-governmental body was thought to be against the global trend of respecting self- regulation by professional bodies.[23]

An alternative to direct government control was to set up a new body to take up this function of reviewing accountants. Indeed, there was such a proposal. However, in the US the PCAOB was set up under the SEC, albeit not strictly as a government body, and assumed the supervisory role in a direct manner. The Japanese parallel would be a body attached to the FSA. Thus, the existing Review Board was reorganised into a body overseeing accountants.

In light of the developments in the US, there was a feeling of resignation within the profession that strengthening of direct government involvement was inevitable, if only for the time being. If incidents on the scale of Enron/WorldCom happen in the US and the US government took certain measures, even if Japan presented alternative measures they would not be internationally accepted. A compromise reached was that the quality control review remains the power of the JICPA, but the Review Board will monitor the result of the review. The president of the JICPA had been of the view that the PCAOB type of regulation of the CPAs was excessive in light of the global tendency in the direction of self-regulation. However, he was satisfied in the end that the government had respected the quality control review by the JICPA and had introduced a system of monitoring it instead of direct supervision. This is midway between total self-regulation and direct government supervision and is regarded as a uniquely Japanese approach.[24]

[23] Access FSA no 11-2003, comment by K Hiramatsu <www.fsa.go.jp> (21 April 2005).

[24] Access FSA no 11-2003, comment by A Okuyama 1670 Shôji Hômu 45.

c. Instruction to Take Corrective Measures

In cases where the CPA is in breach of the Law or has failed to comply with an order based upon the Law, the FSA is entitled to give necessary instruction for correcting the situation to the CPA in question. The same applies to accounting firms. This can precede disciplinary measures imposed by the FSA. The failure to comply with the instruction will entail disciplinary action.

4. Introduction of the Designated Partner System

Under the previous system, all partners in an accounting firm had the power of execution of the business; on the other hand, they also bore unlimited liability. However, with the size of accounting firms increasing, this system which was modelled after partnership under English law became unsuitable.

The amended Law introduced the system of designated partners in line with the attorneys' law. Audit firms can now designate partners for the audit service of a specific company who will conduct the audit on behalf of the firm. This partner will bear unlimited liability, while other partners bear only limited liability. It should be noted that this only involves the liability *vis à vis* the client company which has been audited; in relation to a claim by a bona fide third party, all partners still bear unlimited liability.

It should be noted that the US limited liability company system is to be introduced as part of the modernisation of company law in 2005.

III. Measures to Increase the Effectiveness of the Audit by the CPAs

Even prior to the Enron/WorldCom saga and apart from the amendments to the CPA Law, various measures were being taken to strengthen the effectiveness of audits by CPAs.

1. The 'Going Concern' Issue

In the past, there have been instances where, shortly after the CPA gave a certified opinion endorsing the accounts, the company met a sudden death. This also happened with the collapse of financial institutions in the late 1990s. This naturally harmed the credibility of audits by the CPAs. Therefore, an 'early warning system' in the form of comments on the company as a 'going concern' was introduced by the Japan Accounting Standards Board.

In 2002 the audit standards were revised, and accountants are now required to consider 'whether it is appropriate for the company to prepare financial statements upon the premise that the company is to continue as a going concern'.[25] They are under an obligation to check whether there are matters or situations that cast serious doubt on the assumption that the company can continue as a going concern, such as the deterioration of financial indices, the possibility of financial collapse, etc. It should be noted that it is not the CPA's duty to determine whether the company can continue as a going concern or not. The CPA's duty is to ensure that relevant information is properly disclosed by the client company. If there are matters or situations that cast serious doubt on the assumption that the company can continue as a going concern, the CPA is to require the company to disclose the existence of such matters or situations, the substance of the problem, the existence of a doubt as to whether the company will continue as a going concern, details of the measures and plans to address the problems, and whether or not they are reflected on the financial statements. The disclosure can be made as a comment to the financial statements or can be otherwise reflected on the statements.[26]

If it is revealed that such matters or circumstances exist, that there is significant uncertainty whether the problems will be resolved, and that there is serious doubt that the company can continue as a going concern, but nevertheless the matters are properly disclosed in the financial statements, the CPA is to render an opinion endorsing the financial statements without qualification. If the disclosure is insufficient, the CPA is either to endorse the accounts with qualifications (comments) or to render the opinion that the statements are inappropriate.

This system of 'audits on companies as going concerns' was introduced from the US In the past, there was a similar system whereby the CPA was to add a note to the opinion on 'special matters' when the CPA regarded it as particularly necessary. However, CPAs very seldom added such a note, because if the company was listed this may have resulted in the delisting of the company.

The new system came into force in 2003. The JICPA has conducted a survey on its implementation. In the accounting year which ended in March 2003, there were 64 companies about which such special comments had been made by the CPA. In 19 cases the companies' businesses were deteriorating constantly, while in 15 cases the companies' debts exceeded their assets.[27] In the financial year ending in September 2003, 49 companies had such comments. Of these companies, four went bankrupt.[28]

[25] *Kaisei kônin kaikei-shi-hô kaisetsu [Commentary to the New CPA Law]* (Tokyo 2004) 51.

[26] ibid 60-61.

[27] Report by *Zeimu Kenkyû-kai* 25 August 2003.

[28] Report by *Zeimu Kenkyû-kai* 22 December 2003.

CPAs are often criticised for triggering the collapse of companies. The JICPA president at that time stressed that the accountants should not listen to the argument that the survival of the client company is important to society, or that the CPA should not give a negative conclusion since it would harm the local economy. If, as a result of a proper audit, the company fails, this cannot be helped.[29]

2. Stricter Approach by the CPAs

In the past, CPAs tended to be reluctant to confront the client company when they disagreed with the financial statements it had prepared, but this may be changing. In cases where the financial statements prepared by the company are not appropriate and this substantially affects the statements, CPAs will give a negative opinion. If the CPAs are unable to obtain sufficient evidence needed for the audit, they will refrain from giving an opinion. Although the number of cases where the CPA gave a negative opinion has declined since 1998 (naturally, this reflects the state of the economy), the number of cases where the CPA refrained from giving an opinion has more than doubled.[30]

At one major accounting firm, the number of cases in which a panel of experienced accountants decided on cases where the accountants could not reach consensus has doubled as well. Half the cases are related to deferred tax assets, and cases involving the going concern assumptions are also growing in number.

According to a survey conducted by the JICPA in 2003 regarding the audit required by the Commercial Code, in 2002 there were 39 companies regarding which the CPA gave an opinion that the accounts were inappropriate, and regarding 11 companies the CPA declined to give an opinion.[31] The grounds for an opinion of unlawful accounts were:

Insufficient amortisation of fixed assets	41%
Insufficient allowance reserves	24%
Insufficient entry of valuation loss of the inventory, securities, etc	24%
Inappropriate valuation or amortisation of good will	8%

The CPAs declined to give an audit opinion when they were unable to obtain proof of the possibility of debt collection, or of the appropriateness of the valuation of securities for investment (64.7%).

The CPA resigned in 1 out of 11 cases where the CPA refrained from giving an opinion, and in 9 out of 50 cases where a negative opinion had been given.

[29] Okuyama (n 24).

[30] JICPA 'Result of the Survey on the Audit Opinion based upon the Commercial Code' 17 February2004.

[31] ibid.

In the accounting year 2002, the number of declined opinions more than doubled compared to the year before. This is because while the disclosure of the going concern assumption was made mandatory as of accounting year 2003, in 33 cases the company failed to disclose information despite the fact that there was serious doubt as to the assumption that the company was a going concern, and therefore the audit could not proceed.

In 74% of the cases where the CPA gave a negative opinion or refrained from giving an opinion, the auditors of the company expressed the opinion that the CPA's opinion was justifiable. On the other hand, in some cases the company merely reported the negative opinion of the CPA but failed to take any measures, which is clearly in breach of the law.

3. Increasing Tension between CPAs and Clients?

The relationship between the client company and the CPA has become somewhat stressed, primarily due to the increase in audit risks. It has been customary for the same auditing firm to audit the same company for many years.

However, between March 2002 and November 2003, there were 107 companies that were audited on the basis of the Securities and Exchange Law which changed their auditing firm.[32] According to the survey by the JICPA, in 73.3% of such cases the contract was discontinued upon the initiative of the client. The reasons were as follows:

Unification of auditors upon the request of the parent company	54.1%
Problem with the fees	18.9%
Disagreement between the company and the CPA	6.8%
Other reasons	20.2%

In cases where the relationship was discontinued upon the initiative of the accountant, the grounds were:

Increase in the audit risk	55.6%
The opinion or guidance not accepted by the client	11.1%
Unavailability of requested information from the client	7.4%
Other reasons	25.9%

There were 25 cases where the contract was discontinued before the end of the term. There were four cases where the client discontinued the contract due to a disagreement with the CPA, and eight cases where the CPA discontinued due to an increasing risk. Of those companies which changed their CPA during the term,

[32] JICPA 'The Result of the Survey on the Circumstances of the Change of Accountants' 7 April 2004.

four applied for a civil restoration programme, an equivalent of US Bankruptcy Code Chapter 11.

In some cases, after the CPA resigned, the successor CPA was paid lower fees and the time for the audit was reduced. There are some doubts as to whether the governing bodies of the company have properly examined the appropriateness of changing the CPA.

4. Disciplinary Measures Imposed by the JICPA

In the 1990s, even in cases such as the collapse of major banks and securities companies, the CPAs involved were never disciplined for having failed to expose irregularities in the accounts. The JICPA's approach seems to be changing. Disciplinary measures taken by the JICPA are now being published. In 2003, two CPAs were disciplined for allowing a company to leave an irrecoverable claim *vis à vis* a subsidiary without treating it as a loss and for having given a certified opinion.[33] In 2004, an accounting firm and two of its CPAs were disciplined for the failure to detect window-dressing and for giving this company an unqualified certified opinion.[34] In the latter case, the client was a company whose shares were traded over the counter. The company falsified its accounts by entering turnovers which did not exist and then paid dividends. The accounting firm had been shown falsified documents, but since the audit procedure was insufficient it failed to discover the falsification and granted an unqualified 'true and fair' opinion. This was found to be a failure to exercise reasonable care. The firm's membership in JICPA was suspended for two months.

As of July 2004, there were 15 cases of incidents involving the failure to detect window-dressing at the JICPA. However, in some cases the process of disciplinary action has been delayed; the Yamaichi case, for instance, has been pending since 1998.[35]

For its part, the FSA imposes administrative measures based upon the CPA Law. For example, in 2004 the FSA suspended the licenses of two CPAs for discrediting the profession.[36]

[33] (2003) 1673 Shôji Hômu 44.

[34] JICPA Press Release 19 May 2004.

[35] *Nikkei* 3 September 2004.

[36] FSA Press Release 16 April 2004 <www.fsa.go.jp> (21 April 2005).

IV. The Independence of the CPAs' Audit from the FSA – the Resona Bank and the Ashikaga Bank Cases

The amended Law has mainly addressed the independence of CPAs from their client companies. Recent incidents involving some financial institutions shed light on another problem – the independence of the CPAs from the FSA.

In May 2003, Resona Bank, Japan's fifth largest bank, was forced to apply for public funds worth 17 billion USD after its accounting firm (ShinNihon) determined that the bank had failed to meet the BIS capital adequacy ratio of 4%. Resona is a product of the merger of Daiwa Bank and Asahi Bank. The latter was audited by the accounting firm Asahi,[37] while Daiwa was audited by ShinNihon. At first, both firms were jointly auditing Resona, but Asahi withdrew on 30 April. The timing was strange, occurring at a very late stage in the preparation of the financial statements. This was primarily due to a difference regarding the period of allowance of deferred tax assets (DTAs). Asahi was of the view that only three years' worth of DTAs should be considered as capital, while ShinNihon supported Resona in allowing five years' worth of DTAs. Asahi asked Resona to correct the statements but Resona refused, and therefore Asahi resigned.[38]

However, on 15 May ShinNihon informed Resona that it was not going to approve the account. Resona had undergone an FSA inspection which had concluded in April that Resona had cleared the capital adequacy ratio. Despite this, ShinNihon reached the opposite conclusion in May. The FSA had allowed five years' worth of DTAs, while ShinNihon allowed only three years in light of the state of business of the bank. In this sense, the FSA was lagging behind the accountants.[39]

The minister in charge of the FSA had announced earlier that DTAs should be calculated strictly. However, this was not yet reflected in the inspection of the Bank by the FSA.[40] In the meantime, in February 2003 the president of the JICPA issued a statement requiring a strict approach in the audit of major banks intending to tighten control over the counting of DTAs. This has influenced the auditing firms to take a stricter approach. Asahi responded first, and ShinNihon followed after a while. There is a criticism that the change of attitude of the accounting firms upset the stability and foreseeability of accounting, but the president of the JICPA pointed out later that the client in this case had failed to understand the changes in the environment and had continued to calculate DTAs in the same way

[37] Asahi merged with Azsa and became Azsa & Co in 2004.

[38] M Mikami *The Economist* (June 2003) <www.mainichi.co.jp> (21 April 2005).

[39] *Asahi Shinbun* 23 May 2003 (FT Information Ltd – Asia Africa Intelligence Wire); *FT Investor* 20 May 2003.

[40] *Nikkei* 9 December 2003.

as the previous year. Resona sources complained that ShinNihon had previously endorsed the Resona statements, but suddenly changed its position.[41]

In this case, the FSA reportedly tried to influence the CPA's opinion. A note has surfaced that can be interpreted as evidence that the official in charge at the FSA asked the accounting firm to come up with a less rigorous evaluation of the bank's financial standing so that the bank would not need to ask for public funds.[42] A parliamentary commission subsequently heard this case.[43]

Incidentally, in other jurisdictions such changes to accounting methods are regarded as a serious matter which confuses investors. Recently, the UK FSA required the Japanese UFJ Bank, which is also listed in the UK, to explain the changes made to its accounts. In April 2004 the bank announced that they were in the black for the accounting year ending in March 2004. However, in May it announced that it was in the red by 400 billion yen, 'due to the increase in the allowance reserves for bad loans'. UFJ explained this was a result of the adoption of a stricter approach to assets evaluation. There is a possibility that the UK FSA will impose fines.[44]

The Resona case was certainly not the first case where an accounting firm changed its stance at the last moment. Another instance involved Tokyo Sowa Bank, a regional bank in Tokyo. Asahi gave a 'true and fair' opinion on the accounts in April. However, in June, after an inspection by the FSA, the chairman of Asahi visited the bank and asked them to return the certified opinion. An opinion incorporating the result of the FSA inspection was offered in return. The bank collapsed soon afterwards. Asahi is now being sued by the shareholders who relied upon the inaccurate financial statements and purchased shares of the bank.[45]

A more recent incident involved Ashikaga Bank, a regional bank. In this case, which took place after Resona, Ashikaga Bank was found to be insolvent by the FSA inspection. However, before the result of the inspection was published, the auditor, Chuo-Aoyama, reached the opposite conclusion. The bank had announced that the capital adequacy ratio was above 4% in April, but in November it was forced to admit that it was 102 billion yen in the red. The capital adequacy ratio in late September was minus 3.7%.[46] This was because Chuo-Aoyama denied the five years' worth of DTAs as proposed by the bank in late November, ostensibly under pressure from the FSA. Thus, in this case the accounting firm changed its view within six months.

[41] 1670 Shôji Hômu 47.

[42] *Asahi Shinbun* 5 August 2003 (FT Information Ltd – Asia Africa Intelligence Wire).

[43] *FT Investor* 4 June 2003.

[44] *Asahi Shinbun* 1 September 2004.

[45] *Nikkei* 9 December 2003; Y Fujii *Kinyû saisei no gosan [Miscalculation of the Financial Restoration]* (Tokyo 2003) 266-7.

[46] *Nikkei* 29 November 2003.

There were no statements by them regarding the assumption of the bank continuing as a going concern in April.[47] The problem with the Ashikaga Bank is that investors relied on the opinion of the accountants and, before September, had subscribed to the share issue by the bank. Shareholders of the bank are now suing the bank and the accounting firm. They argue that despite the fact that the state of business or the accounting standards did not change in the last six months, the accountants changed their view of insolvency, and that this is against accounting rules and the principle of continuity: 'Although there was strong guidance from the FSA, the audit should have been conducted in a neutral and fair manner.' There was no comment concerning the company as a going concern earlier, and investors were led to believe that there was no concern as to the future of the bank.[48]

The above incidents demonstrate the difficult position of the CPAs. All these incidents involve DTAs, the calculation of which is highly discretionary. Although the minister in charge of Financial Affairs announced in 2003 that there would be a clear-cut rule on this matter, the DTA's audit standards are said to remain rather general. As late as June 2004, a sub-committee of the Financial System Council which had been deliberating on this matter issued a report recommending that rules setting the limit on the entering of the deferred tax payment in the assets should be postponed.[49] This was despite the fact that it acknowledged the necessity of such rules. Without clear-cut rules, naturally, it is difficult for the CPAs to take a strict approach which would be likely to finish the client. Furthermore, with the increased power of the FSA in overseeing the CPAs, there is a likelihood that CPAs will hesitate to take an independent stance from the FSA.

V. Conclusion

The necessity for reform of the accounting system, aimed at increased transparency for investors, has been recognised in Japan for some time. It coincided with the Japanese Big Bang, a major reform intended to create a free, fair, and global financial system. In the late 1990s, the reform proposals became broader in scope following growing criticisms of the profession concerning the CPAs' failure to expose the window-dressing which brought down some securities companies and banks. These proposals largely resorted to self-regulation by the JICPA. The JICPA accordingly introduced various measures to increase the effectiveness of the audits by the CPAs.

[47] *Nikkei* 16 January 2004.

[48] *Nikkei* 28 May 2004.

[49] *Nikkei* 23 June 2004.

However, after the Enron/WorldCom affairs, influenced by the US, the tide seems to have changed. Further reinforcement of the independence of the CPAs from the client companies, and above all broader grounds for interference by the government, were proposed and eventually became law. The amended CPA Law has been significantly influenced by the SOA, although the profession has managed to reach some compromises.

The recent incidents involving the Resona Bank and Ashikaga Bank have cast some doubt on the reliability of the CPAs. However, in cases involving the auditing of financial institutions, maintaining independence from the FSA while being supervised by it at the same time seems to be a rather difficult task. This seems to represent a negative aspect of increased government interference. Furthermore, the matter involved the exercise of wide discretion on the part of the CPAs without the promised clear-cut rules forthcoming from the government. Perhaps it is too harsh to blame the CPAs.

It is questionable whether the reforms which were going on in Japan at the time of the incidents in the US could have realised their intended goal, or whether they were merely a lukewarm attempt to preserve the self-regulation of the profession when an SOA-type law was genuinely needed. Those self-regulatory measures were simply not given much time to be tested and have been surpassed by the SOA-type approach.

Summary of Discussions

Changes of Governance in Europe, Japan, and the US: Discussion Report

HEIKE SCHWEITZER and CHRISTOPH KUMPAN

Traditionally, countries have differed in their fundamental governance structures. The role of the state and the role of markets as mechanisms of economic coordination has always been one of the important dividing lines between different economic systems. The differences in the general institutional set-up of economic governance have formed the background for the development of different corporate governance systems. Based on the difficult experiences with transplanting foreign corporate governance systems into the legal systems of Eastern European countries, there has been a growing awareness that 'institutions matter'. As it strives to understand how corporate governance functions in a given environment and how it can be improved, the discussion needs to transcend the boundaries of corporate governance in its narrow sense to include the broader issue of governance in general and economic governance in particular. This was the thematic starting point of the conference: different corporate governance systems were discussed not as narrow concepts, analyzing the governance structure *within* a firm, but as broad concepts, with a specific emphasis on their systemic elements and conditions. The conference program therefore centered on the relevant players within the institutional set-up of economic governance: corporations, markets, the state, and intermediaries. During the discussions, the interrelations and interactions between these different players and systemic elements were frequently emphasized.

The conference took a dynamic approach to the issue of governance, focusing on current changes in governance structures and mutual influences instead of comparing closed systems. Around the world, the existing systems of corporate governance have come under pressure (see *Hopt/Baum*, Introduction): the process of globalization of trade and the accompanying strengthening of international competition have created external pressures which greatly influence the corporate governance debate in Japan and Europe. In Europe, regional integration has been an additional factor of challenge for traditional governance structures. Universally, technological change and aging are factors which influence economic development and economic governance. In the US, internal pressures for change were created by a series of corporate scandals (such as Enron and WorldCom) that had significant repercussions in the EU and Japan. Other issues that were intensively discussed during the conference were the interaction between reform processes in the US, Europe, and Japan in reaction to these challenges; the tendencies of governance structures to converge; and the developing international dialogue between academics, practitioners, and administrators as an instrument for coordinating persisting differences and processes of change.

I. Governance Systems Between State and Market: Categorization and Evaluation

1. Categorizing Systems of Economic Governance

a. Market Economies vs Corporatist Economies

According to a widely accepted scheme, different systems of economic governance can be distinguished according to the criterion of who determines the allocation of resources. In state economies, the allocation is centrally mandated by the state; in market economies, the individual has the right to decide and those decentralized decisions are coordinated through the market. Corporatist systems have introduced a third layer between the state and the market by endowing social groups with decision- and norm-setting rights.

Based on this classificatory scheme, *Siebert* qualified Germany as a 'restrained market economy' in his presentation. He suggested that among the most important corporatist aspects of the German economy are the institutional set-up of the labor markets, co-determination, and the central position of banks as financing institutions in corporate governance. These corporatist features, he claimed, are at the root of the current high unemployment rates and poor economic growth.

The discussion focused on the normative assumption that a strict market regime is superior to a corporatist regime. *Schmidt* maintained that the German system of co-determination has both economic advantages and disadvantages, and thus the state of technology will determine which side will prevail: co-determination would not be conducive to technological leap-frogging and is hence disadvantageous in a highly innovative environment. *Hopt*, on the other hand, wholly supported *Siebert's* criticism of German corporatism. He also claimed that in spite of its advantages, co-determination could lead to severe conflicts of interest between trade union interests and corporate interests, as the recent case of Bsirske demonstrated.[1] It has also been a hold-up for European integration in the field of corporate law. Corporatism's continued and powerful entrenchment in the current German economic system can be illustrated by the severe delay of the necessary debate on co-determination in Germany. For example, the Baums Commission, entrusted with the task of recommending rules for a German Corporate Governance Codex, has not yet touched on the issue. The German system of co-determination, however, has already come under attack. It is increasingly being challenged by European law, based on the *Centros/Inspire Art* line of ECJ jurisprudence.[2] In order to justify co-determination under these new judgments, two requirements must be fulfilled: the protection of labor interests through worker participation must be a public good legitimately defended by member states; and the impediments to the fundamental freedoms incorporated in the EC Treaty as posed by the current system of co-determination must be necessary to achieve this goal, ie there must not be fewer restrictive means to protect labor interests. *Hopt* doubted whether the second question would be answered in the affirmative by the ECJ.

Coffee noted that corporatist regimes seem to protect managers from the market for corporate control. That might cause a shortfall in managerial responsibility. On the other hand, there might be a trade-off between corporatism and openness to free trade. Systems such as that of the US, which give greater room to the market for corporate control, tend to protect themselves much more strongly against open trade and hence against product market competition than corporatist regimes. Comparing both types of systems, he contended that the differences in the product market competition and the workability of markets for corporate control – both mechanisms of external corporate control – might level each other out. *Coffee* added that the relationship between corporate governance and open trade is still underexplored.

b. Liberal Market Economies vs Coordinated Market Economies

In her presentation, *Pistor* proposed making a distinction between so-called 'Liberal Market Economies' (LMEs) and 'Coordinated Market Economies' (CMEs) instead of using the more traditional terminology of state economies, market economies, and corporatist economies. However, she agreed that the essential criterion for classifying economic systems was the role of the state in the

[1] Bsirske, a worker union leader and a member of the Lufthansa board, was responsible for a strike which affected Lufthansa while he was still a member of the Lufthansa board.

[2] Case C-212/97 *Centros Ltd v Erhvervs- og Selskabsstyrelsen* [1999] ECR I-1459; case C-208/00 *Überseering BV v Nordic Construction Company Baumanagement GmbH* [2002] ECR I-9919; case C-167/01 *Kamer van Koophandel en Fabrieken voor Amsterdam v Inspire Art Ltd* [2003] ECR I-10155.

economy and the allocation of control rights. In order to locate these control rights, she did not focus on specific institutions (such as institutional organization of the labor market or co-determination), but rather analyzed the systemic structure of legal rules. Distinguishing between so-called substantive 'default rules'[3] (rules that allocate the power to determine the meaning and content of an agreement among private parties) and procedural 'default rules' (rules that assign the power of review), she found that all common law countries could be classified as LMEs, whereas all civil law countries could be classified as CMEs. Hence, it seems that the difference between economic systems is not in the institutional set-up of an economy, but in the legal rules of private law.

Pistor's systematization was intensely debated but remained controversial. Several participants questioned the classificatory force of *Pistor's* scheme when applied in practice. Regarding derivative actions – one example chosen by *Pistor* for the purpose of illustrating the CME/LME divide as well as the common law/civil law country divide – *Davies* explained that UK law is closer to German law than to US law. Like German law (which has introduced a 5% threshold as a prerequisite for bringing a suit) but unlike US law (which values derivative suits as an efficient way of enforcing corporate law), UK law is deeply suspicious about the efficiency of derivative suits, fearing suits driven by opportunism instead of by the company's interests. Concerning the policy debate on derivative actions, the German Baums Report[4] and UK papers on derivative actions have taken closely related positions. The German Juristentag[5] has seen some advantages in loosening up the requirements for derivative suits, but has basically supported a continuation of a restrictive policy, seeing real risks in taking the more liberal US route.

Hopt and *Haley* expressed skepticism about the principle of 'good faith' as an illustration of the differences between LMEs and CMEs – or common law and civil law countries. *Pistor* claimed that in LMEs – ie in common law countries – contracts are valid unless they violate procedural rules and/or qualify as 'bad faith', whereas in CMEs – ie in civil law countries – private contracts are governed by a good faith principle which confers residual law-making powers on judges. However, *Hopt* maintained that the good faith/bad faith distinction, being a very fine one, might not lead to significantly different outcomes in many cases. To the extent that it would, the difference in the outcomes could not be explained by the existence of a good faith principle alone, as evidenced by the fact that there is no uniformity in the application of the good faith principle by courts in differ-

[3] *Milhaupt* proposed using the term 'meta-rules' instead of the term 'default rules'.

[4] German Goverment Panel on Corporate Governance, report from July 2001. The full text of the report can be found at <http://www.jura.uni-duesseldorf.de/dozenten/noack/texte/cg/> (12 July 2005). An English translation of the summary can be found at <http://www.shearman.com/documents/government_panel.pdf> (12 July 2005).

[5] German Lawyers Conference.

ent civil law countries. German courts tend to be highly activist (for example, in the area of bank contracts where courts have assumed quasi-legislative functions, but to a certain extent also in the area of corporate law); Swiss courts, on the other hand, are much more cautious about intervening in general business conditions; and French courts are generally reluctant to intervene on the basis of the good faith principle. Even within Germany, courts display different attitudes (eg the German Bundesgerichtshof vs the German Bundesarbeitsgericht). It seems that the willingness of judges to usurp law-making powers does not depend so much on the distinction between CMEs/LMEs, but instead differs significantly from country to country. *Haley* added that both Japan and Germany apply the same theory to the good faith principle, but the outcomes that Japanese courts reach are frequently more like the decisions of US courts.

Making the same point on a more general plane, *Ramseyer* observed that the apparent differences among countries could reflect the different industrial composition of the countries or different urbanization rates rather than any difference between CMEs and LMEs.

Davies also questioned the suggested divide between common law and civil law countries from a historical perspective. After World War II, the UK nationalized large parts of the industry, appointed representatives of worker interest for those industries, and imposed industry-level collective bargaining. Although a different legal structure was chosen, collective bargaining was as binding in the UK during this period as it currently is in Germany. At that time, the UK would have qualified as a CME. Shareholders were too dispersed to exercise control; hence, companies were in reality led by trade unions and management. When Germany introduced its system of co-determination, it was perceived in the UK to be the 'third way' between the UK's 'state socialism' and the market approach of the US Forty years ago, *Davies* concluded, the UK, although it was a common law country, did not fit into the model of a 'liberal market economy'.

Haley suggested that the reason for the greater degree of market orientation and better performance of common law countries might not lie in the structure of the legal rules, but in a greater openness to trade resulting from the fact that most common law countries are historically heavily immigrant countries and at the same time English-speaking countries. *Ramseyer* suggested that in order to find out whether it is really the common law/civil law divide that is at the core of the systemic difference, regressions would have to be run to exclude other potentially relevant factors (such as the degree of urbanization of a given country or its dominant industries).

Ogus, on the other hand, provided some support for *Pistor's* thesis, emphasizing that the role of the judiciary in relation to legislation is a core feature of a legal system and one which differs significantly between common law and civil law countries. Under the French Civil Code, for example, contracts cannot deviate from legislative rules. In England, on the other hand, there was a now largely discredited doctrine which enabled the beneficiaries of legislative interventions to contract out of those rules. As such, legislative rules could be construed as mere 'default rules'.

Milhaupt inquired about the origin of the so-called 'default rules', suggesting that it might be helpful to inspect the legislative process that produced those norms and to look for a story to explain where, in a given legal system, such norms arose and proliferated.

c. Of the Value of Classification and the Comparison of Governance Systems

The debate surrounding the two approaches to the classification of economic governance systems demonstrated some disagreement about the criteria to be used for purposes of classification as well as difficulties in applying them to the idiosyncrasies of any given country. *Coffee* underlined that systems, regardless of the classificatory scheme used, are never 'pure', pointing to the US legal regime of pension funds which he qualified as corporatist. Citing the hybrid nature of most economic systems in existence, some participants expressed doubts about the overall value of such general classificatory endeavors.

The debate also touched on the question of whether one system of corporate governance could be qualified as inherently 'superior' to another. In the past, the corporate governance systems of Japan and Germany, which focus on the corporation as an independent social entity with many stakeholders, have often been said to be better at taking a long-term perspective and to benefit from additional opportunities that were thus opened up to firms. In contrast, the corporate-governance systems of the US and the UK, which look upon shareholders as the owners of the corporation, were considered to be suffering from the detrimental effects of short-termism induced by pressures coming from the stock market. In the nineties, the worldwide stock market boom and the evident successes of market-oriented systems in creating entirely new industries in the information and biotechnology sectors led to a reassessment of such views and a certain ascendancy of market-oriented systems in public political and academic debate. However, most participants remained agnostic on the question of the superiority of any one system (eg *M. Hellwig, Schmidt*). *Rickford* stressed how views on the success of systems have changed over time and reminded the participants of an era when German law was believed to be the most successful model of company law, the secret of its success being that it had more extensive rules (eg in employee participation and group law fields) than other systems. Although all big systems of corporate governance are currently moving in a similar direction toward a transparency-based and market-oriented approach, care should be taken when claiming superiority for any one system. *Grundmann* claimed that even co-determination should not be generally disqualified as disadvantageous, but might, in certain contexts, create confidence and lead to good economic results.

2. Global Changes in Economic Governance: From State to Market

a. Trend Toward Markets in Europe and in Japan

In continental Europe as well as in Japan, significant changes in the systems of economic governance have taken place in recent years. In the European Union, EU law has been applied to attack former barriers to trade and to break up traditional state monopolies. National markets in general and former monopolistic markets in particular have been opened up to trade and competition (*Kirchner*). In the field of corporate governance, a greater degree of outsider control is gradually being introduced into systems that have hitherto been mostly insider-controlled. There is a general trend toward placing more emphasis on competitive markets in today's economies. One example for that general trend is the changing investment pattern of the Deutsche Bank which, under pressure to come up with competitive dividends and earnings – as well as under the pressure of public opinion – is reducing its stakes in various companies. This is a development that can be observed in other banks as well. Another example is the growing readiness of European companies to enlist on stock exchanges. The German 'New Market' ('Neuer Markt') was a promising start. Its failure may have delayed the process by five or six years, but it probably has not stopped it (*Hopt*).

From a long-term historical perspective, this new trend toward markets corrects a countermovement characteristic of the economic development in continental Europe through most of the 20th century which emphasized the role of the state and special social constituencies (corporatism). Several participants observed that at the end of the 19th century, the economies were more open to international trade than at the end of the 20th century – partially due to the then-existing international monetary system which had facilitated investments abroad (*Schmidt*). During the 20th century, a high degree of restrictive state regulation and state support for upholding the corporatist system was supported at times by both trade unions and capitalists who cooperated with the political powers and profited from protection from competition. That was particularly the case in Italy and Germany during the period of fascism (*Ferrarini, Hopt, Schmidt*).

Unsurprisingly, the more recent trend toward markets is not unanimously accepted by society. The fact that banks are pulling out of supervisory boards – which at first sight appears to indicate a trend away from an insider-controlled system to an outsider-controlled, more market-oriented system – might in fact strengthen managerial power if former members of the management rather than shareholder representatives move in (*Schmidt*). An internationalization of boards, desirable in theory, is not (yet) taking place, or if so, rather slowly (*Hopt*). According to *Ferrarini,* it is unclear to what extent capitalists today have a reformatory or conservative role, impeding the transformation of corporatist societies toward a stronger emphasis on markets. There is, he claimed, a persisting antagonism between capital markets and a social democracy.

b. Liberal Trends in Corporate Law: Choice of Governance Structures Replacing Mandatory Law

The trend to liberalize economies is partly reflected in a trend to liberalize corporate law. An example for this is the recent reform of Japanese corporate law, which now allows corporations to choose between different models of board structures (one-tier or two-tier boards). Similar trends can be observed in Europe: both in France and in the Netherlands the law allows companies to choose between a one-tier or two-tier board. Italy lets companies choose between three different varieties of board structures. On the European level, the SE regulation[6] has introduced the concept of choice of board structure as well. The discussion focused on the question of which goals are driving this policy and the importance that can be attributed to it. *Davies* conjectured that, on the EU level, the policy of choice is probably driven by pragmatism: the goal is to get all member states to agree to the SE regulation. On the level of the EU member states, he suggested that the policy of choice might be explained by the goal of enabling companies to more easily raise money on capital markets in different jurisdictions, wherever they might operate. *Ferrarini* explained that in Italy the choice between the traditional Italian board system, an Anglo-American-style unitary board structure, and the German dual board system is not considered useful by companies. Companies rarely choose a system other than the traditional Italian system. One possible explanation is that in practice the transplants work in a rather similar way to the traditional system. The same might be true for Japan, as *Milhaupt* conceded. As it seems there is no real incentive for companies to shift to the 'new committee system', the choice between the two different board systems might not be a very meaningful choice in practice. Maybe, *Milhaupt* suggested, the optional model introduced by Japanese law has a primarily intellectual appeal because it can draw on the Delaware notion of systems competition. *Hopt,* on the other hand, pointed out that when France introduced a choice in its legal system between three different board structures, merely 4% of the public companies actually chose the German board system; but while this was a small number in absolute terms, the companies that adopted the German model belonged to the crucial ones for the economy, ie 20% of the CAC-40 companies. The importance of the French reform is thus greater than is indicated by absolute numbers.

[6] Council Regulation 2157/2001/EC of 8 October 2001 on the Statute for a European Company (SE) [2001] OJ L294/1.

II. Market Regulation as Corollary to Liberalization: Toward a Theory of Regulation

As states withdraw from direct market participation and markets gain renewed importance as mechanisms for coordinating decentralized choices, the regulatory functions of states become central. Liberalizing economies does not translate into deregulation, but frequently leads to re-regulation (and sometimes overregulation), as *Hopt* pointed out. The increased importance of regulation makes it necessary to look for a firm grounding of regulatory practice in regulatory theory.

1. Theoretical Approaches to Regulation

The theoretical debate touched on questions of methodology, in particular on what contributions 'New Institutional Economics' (NIE) could make to a theory of regulation; and it explored the legitimate goals of regulation, focusing on the controversial issue of paternalistic regulation.

a. New Institutional Economics and Its Contribution to a Theory of Regulation

In his presentation, *Kirchner* introduced NIE as a proper concept for analyzing why and when regulatory intervention in a market is justified. NIE rests on the fundament of neoclassical economics but purports to be more realistic in its assumptions (scarcity of resources, methodological individualism, bounded rationality, incomplete information, and positive transaction costs) and not only takes into account the issue of market failure but also deficiencies in the law-making process, deficiencies in public governance structures, and deficiencies in law enforcement. *Ginsburg* criticized the NIE approach as being too open. With such a broad approach, regulation could always be justified. He asked what, using the NIE approach, would be hard evidence for finding that an institution is working well or not. Along similar lines, *Milhaupt* was skeptical about the empirical basis of the NIE approach. *Kirchner* replied that while market failure theory compares well-functioning markets with failing markets and hence tends to take a Nirvana approach, the NIE approach takes existing markets, which are naturally never perfect, as a starting point. *Kirchner* believed that the NIE approach and the welfare economics approach, which underlies traditional market failure theory, are complementary. But he conceded that, within the NIE approach, models for determining which type of governance structure is more effective under real market conditions still need to be developed.

b. Paternalism as a Legitimate Goal of Regulation?

The issue of paternalism as a possible justification for regulatory intervention – an issue not considered in a narrow interpretation of market failure theory – was addressed by *Ogus* in his presentation. *Ogus* proposed a 'rational delegation approach' to paternalism: social psychology literature and, in turn, behavioral law and economics literature have recently emphasized the inherent limitations of individuals in decision-making. Individuals are boundedly rational. In regulatory theory, this requires some deviations from neoclassical economics. Individuals who are aware of their own limitations in decision-making might empower government to make decisions for them in situations where they know their own decisions to be deficient. As possible justifications for paternalistic regulation interpreted in this manner, *Ogus* mentioned the status quo bias, the availability heuristics, excessive discounting of the future, a tendency toward short-term decision-making, selective optimism and control, and social pressure. The potential benefits of 'paternalistic' regulation in curing these deficiencies needs to be compared to the costs of paternalistic intervention. Also, it is necessary to carefully examine alternative instruments of paternalistic intervention. *Spindler* underlined this last point and suggested that a careful analysis of alternative instruments for curing bounded rationality problems frequently leads to non-paternalistic regulation. In many cases, the limitations of individual decision-making could be cured by providing information. In this respect, information and paternalism function as a system of communicating tubes. More recently, German capital market regulation, which had formerly taken a paternalistic approach with respect to futures contracts ('*Börsentermingeschäfte*'), was changed to an informational approach. *Spindler* added that similar questions have arisen in the context of consumer protection law in the field of e-commerce. He was puzzled by the fact that in this context, paternalistic regulation was even developed by market actors themselves. This is the case with eBay: in order to further consumer trust in their auctioning platform and to enhance the marketability of the goods placed there, eBay imposed a vast system of consumer protection regulation through general business conditions for its consumer-to-consumer business. Like *Spindler*, *Grundmann* took the issue of available information to be crucial for determining the need and usefulness of paternalistic regulation. He observed that *Ogus* had taken his examples of possible paternalistic regulations from contract law, but he was skeptical about whether and to what extent such examples could also be found in the area of company law. In company law the informational situation is different in that more information is available, typically more players also know how to use it, and therefore the concept of bounded rationality plays a lesser role.

2. The Regulatory Process in Practice

With a view to specific fields of market regulation, attempts were made to better characterize and comprehend the actual working of the regulatory process as well as to evaluate its potential shortcomings.

a. Allocation of Regulatory Competencies and Regulatory Activism in the EU

For each regulatory task, it is crucial to allocate regulatory competencies. In the EU, there are strong tendencies toward an increase of 'federal' (ie EU) regulatory competencies, although competencies are typically shared rather than completely federal (*Hopt*). *Kirchner* suggested that the shift of regulatory competencies to the EU level could partly be explained by the two-goal approach to regulation within the EU, as opposed to the one-goal approach of the US: whereas US regulation follows only the goal of prudent regulation, EU law also strives for integration (*Kirchner*).

This may also partly explain why the shift of competencies to the EU level has been accompanied by an increase in regulatory activism in the EU: while it has been an important source of deregulation vis-à-vis the member states, the EU produced an enormous amount of regulation itself when competencies shifted to the EU level, as in the field of banking and financial markets (re-regulation) (*Hopt*). Some participants pointed to a danger of overregulation on the EU level – not merely in quantitative terms, but also with regard to content (*Hopt*). In this respect, the scope of regulatory goals pursued by the EU raises particular concerns. The role of social and labor rights is currently increasing in the EU, on a legislative as well as on a jurisprudential level. At present quite a lot of social and labor rights regulation exists on the EU level. And whereas the ECJ emphasized libertarian rights and individual freedom in its first phase of jurisprudence, more recent case law has been characterized by a trend toward emphasizing social and labor rights.

A separate but parallel trend related to the regulatory process in the EU is the partial delegation of regulation to expert groups[7] ('comitology' or 'Lamfalussy' process[8]). This approach has especially been used in the field of financial regulation, where the task to determine the technical content of pertinent regulations within a general framework determined by the Commission, the EU Parliament, and Council was delegated to CESR.[9] The EU Commission monitors the process

[7] See Final Report of the Committee of Wise Men on the Regulation of European Securities Markets of 15 February 2001 at <http://europa.eu.int/comm/internal_market/securities/docs/lamfalussy/ wisemen/final-report-wise-men_en.pdf> (12 July 2005).

[8] Named after the chairman of the Committee of Wise Men.

[9] Committee of European Securities Regulators.

and the EU Parliament is continually informed and able to intervene if necessary.[10] It is this dialogical process which gives legitimacy to the regulation; however, it is not a democratic legitimation. One of the drawbacks of the Lamfalussy process is that it tends to lead toward regulation by expert insiders while excluding the participation and influence of other relevant groups, particularly academia – a trend which mirrors an earlier development in the US (*Hopt*). Academics can hardly cope with the mass and technical detail of new proposals and discussion papers.

A somewhat different account of the regulatory process in the EU was presented by *Ferrarini*. In his view, a delegation 'away' from politics is not characteristic for the regulatory process in the EU, contrary to developments in the US where 'regulation' stands for the delegation of powers from politicians to independent bodies. In the EU, *Ferrarini* claimed, the concept of regulation – to the extent that a clear concept exists at all – is much more politicized. Interest groups and the EU Parliament are almost always present in the regulatory process, even when merely technical questions are decided.

A lively debate arose around the question of to what extent EU financial market regulation is driven by economically legitimate policy goals – namely by the goal to create the necessary framework for a well-functioning capital market, with competitive costs for capital – or by further-reaching policy goals. *Pistor* reproached the EU financial markets regulation for trying to socially engineer markets that do not yet exist. In her view, many regulations do not respond to actual problems, but instead actively attempt to create markets, a policy which she opposed. *Hopt, Grundmann*, and *Rickford* disagreed and held the term 'social engineering' to be unfair. In their view, the EU is trying to foster capital markets, ie to create a framework conducive to their development. In the development of markets, it is frequently difficult to judge which comes first: the market or the market framework. In Germany, for example, economic pressure for the development of a takeover market and the development of a legal framework went hand in hand. Therefore, *Hopt* believed it to be a legitimate policy approach to creating a market-supporting legal framework. *Grundmann* added that the financial market regulations enacted by the EU did not introduce substantive rules but rather disclosure rules. Centralized information rules should not be mistaken for social engineering. They are justified by the specific nature of the informational problems to be solved.

[10] For a more detailed description, see the Final Report of the Committee of Wise Men (n 7).

b. Public Choice Issues in Regulation: The Role of Interest Groups and Other Driving Forces

Following *Macey's* presentation, which demonstrated how recent SEC reforms were influenced by the actions of New York State attorney general Spitzer and *Spindler's* more general theory of crisis-driven vs long-term wave regulation (ie regulation as a response to market failure and long-term regulatory needs), the discussion focused on what factors do and should influence regulation. While there was consensus on the fact that crisis could be an important triggering event for regulatory reform, various participants pointed to the potential pitfalls of crisis-driven regulation. In a democracy, it is typically directed toward the 'political market', ie toward public opinion. This might lead to overreaction or inadequate reaction (*Macey*). Negative, potentially counterproductive side effects of such regulation that are not of equal relevance to public opinion – eg negative effects on foreign investors – are not taken into account. The political market, in that respect, is characterized by market failure (*Kirchner*). On the other hand, crisis can have positive effects on the regulatory process in that it may enable change where legislative inertia has formerly hindered it (*Rickford, Davies*). On a purely descriptive level, a specific dynamic between state-level and federal-level regulation as a reaction to crisis was observed: the crisis in the field of securities regulation in the US led to a shift from the state level to the federal level (Sarbanes-Oxley Act) (*Kirchner*).

On a more general plane, participants stressed that to understand regulatory developments it is necessary to consider public choice issues (eg *Hertig*, *Hopt*, *McCahery, Kirchner*): Which interest groups are (or were) active in the regulatory process? In which phase of the regulatory process were interests groups active – or even could be active? Where are the rents of a given regulation? Who benefits? On a policy level it was held that administrative procedures and policies should be analyzed carefully. The procedures and policies that agencies operate under would have critical importance for the cost of doing business (eg notice periods or the scope for interaction with the agency before a decision is made); but they would also determine which interest groups would be able to gain influence on the activity of a given agency. Policies that increase the cost of interaction with interest groups will decrease the number of interest groups that are able to exercise influence; but well-financed interest groups will overcome those barriers (*Macey* – referring to a so-called 'Regulatory Impact Analysis' as a mechanism to allow interest groups to understand likely outcomes of procedures in their perspectives).

Applied to SEC regulations and the recent reforms in this field, the question arose as to whether the reform process described by *Macey* was evidence of a regulatory capture of the SEC, a theory which *Hopt* disputed. *Macey* agreed that capture might be the wrong word. Instead, one should speak of 'vertical integration' or 'joint policy making', because it is impossible to clearly tell where the SEC process of formulating policies begins and where interest groups still introduce their interests. There was consensus, however, that the constituencies to which SEC regulations referred have changed as an effect of the securities regulation crisis during the last couple of years. Whereas formerly SEC regulation targeted the average shareholders, currently the regulation is focused on activist shareholders and institutional investors (*Hertig, Rickford*). There was no consensus as to whether this shift is good or bad.

Macey related that the SEC, in its regulatory agenda during the last couple of years of reform, reacted to an outsider to the system of securities regulation (Spitzer) who – instead of the SEC – stepped in to uncover serious scandals. In response, the question arose (*Hopt*) of whether this really was evidence of an irremediable and lasting failure of the US system of capital market regulation or merely a sign of a healthy process to remind the SEC of its duties – a process which countered possible tendencies of capture of the agency. The fact that regulatory agencies were sensitive to politically influential outsiders could easily be explained by the fear that Congress might cut their budget if they did not respond to publicly perceived needs. Regulatory agencies compete for budgets just as politicians compete for public approval (*Milhaupt*). Thus, 'competition' by a visible and aggressive state enforcement machine could be an important motivating force for regulators, such as the SEC, to pursue their public interest tasks (*Macey*). *Macey* emphasized, however, that at the same time one of the important characteristics of the rule-making process in the field of securities regulation in the US is currently a self-conscious effort to diminish the scope of regulatory competition. At present, securities regulation is characterized by coordination. Fifteen years ago, stock exchanges all over the US were entrepreneurs in securities-related rule-making, but this is no longer true today. Currently, the New York Stock Exchange has no competitor in rule-making – and the NYSE itself coordinates all its rule-making with the SEC. Similar to the tendency toward price-fixing between competitors in product markets, there is a proclivity toward coordination among regulators in the securities regulation market.

The debate also touched on the question of what motivated Spitzer in pushing his securities regulation reform agenda. As *Kirchner* pointed out, Spitzer was not mainly interested in law-making but in law enforcement; as far as law-making was concerned, he was not interested in state-level corporate law but in federal securities regulation. He conjectured that the reason was the leading position of Delaware in the field of corporate law, leaving little room for Spitzer to influence. With respect to federal law, Spitzer had more options to introduce his own policy agenda via enforcement. *Kirchner* also pointed to a tendency to shift powers in the field of corporate law from the state to the federal level as evidenced by the Sarbanes-Oxley Act.

Turning to the issue of the impact of interest groups on European securities regulation, it was held to be unclear whether interest groups would have a stronger or weaker influence on regulation on an EU level than they previously had on the member state level. Interest groups could exert a strong influence on the European Parliament, as was demonstrated in the context of the takeover directive. Generally, where an EU regulatory agency existed, a strong interest group influence could be expected, as it enabled interest groups to centrally organize themselves. On the other hand, it was not clear what influence interest groups would be able to exert within the comitology process. This process is less transparent than the traditional regulatory process and gives more power to practitioners and experts. It is still open what that means for the influence of interest groups. Where competencies are still shared by the EU and the member states, their influence might lessen since it is more difficult to orchestrate two levels than one (*Hopt*).

One specific feature of lobbying within the European legislative process is the 'lobbying' by member states for their legal system. In this respect, it was noted that the EU financial market law had been strongly influenced by the British model. As leaders in the field of financial market development and financial market regulation, the British had a strong interest in seeing their rules implemented on the EU level. On the other hand, until recently the British were less interested in the field of private law and thus exercised less influence. However, in the field of private law the Germans were very active and thus took the lead in unifying civil law. Therefore, the German influence will probably shape the unification of private law – if it ever takes place (*Baum*).

c. Procedural Issues of Regulation

As the amount of regulation within the EU increases, it is becoming more and more urgent to complement the substantive regulatory approach guiding the decisions about what to regulate and how to regulate it with a well-grounded procedural approach to guide the law-making process and the various inputs needed (such as professional expertise and interest groups). This may necessitate a thorough cost-benefit analysis at the stage of designing regulations and a review of the effects and efficiency of existing regulations and – importantly – clarifying the protection of individual rights and the intensity of judicial review in the application of regulations.

Some of these issues were addressed by *Ginsburg* in his presentation. In the subsequent discussion, *Ginsburg* suggested that there were two fundamentally different ways to regulate. Regulation could be perceived as an internal administrative process, the goal of which was to get the experts and interested parties together to deliberate and decidc. An alternative option is to open the process to the public, to emphasize individual rights implicated in regulation, and to get courts involved in the control of substantive regulation as well as in the application of regulation. The US chose the latter approach. According to *Wymeersch*, protecting individual and human rights in the phase of the application of regulation has also become an important issue within the EU.[11]

[11] The EU Market Abuse Directive contains a specific reference in no 44 of the Reasoning.

The concept of a cost-benefit analysis, which is very common in US administrative and regulatory practice, is also increasingly being adopted by the EU and its member states. In practice, the cost-benefit analysis is a difficult and highly imprecise exercise – more art than science – because before new regulations are enacted, there is often very little empirical data and analysis, even little effort for fact-finding (apart from the dialogue with the affected industry) (*Wymeersch*). *Spindler* mentioned the 'German way' of performing a cost-benefit analysis when drafting new regulations: while the German Parliament is obliged to perform such a cost-benefit analysis, the result of this legal requirement is that, without further inquiry, a sentence is added to each statute that 'this regulation entails no costs'.

Concerning the review of the efficiency of existing regulation, *Kirchner* advocated the concept of sunset regulation: in his opinion, it should be used more frequently in EU law. *Siebert* remained more skeptical, inquiring how sunset regulation outside the field of subsidies – where it could work – should be organized.

d. The Enforcement of Regulations

One of the crucial questions in designing regulations concerns their enforcement. In this regard, questions arose concerning the advantages and disadvantages of private and public enforcement, and possible ways to combine them. Sometimes – as to some extent in the case of SEC securities regulation during the recent series of corporate scandals – regulations fail not because of insufficient substantive quality but because of insufficient enforcement. *Spindler* mentioned that insufficient enforcement of regulations is a recurring problem in German law. He pointed to two mechanisms to force an agency to enforce regulations: the agency could be held liable for damages caused by non-enforcement; and/or NGOs could be endowed with a right to sue the agency, asking the court to require the agency to act.

3. Regulation of Public Undertakings and Sector-Specific Regulation

a. Regulatory Framework for Public Undertakings

In continental Europe, the state has frequently and to a significant extent actively participated in the market through state-owned undertakings ('public undertakings'). Particularly in the important infrastructure sectors (telecommunications, energy, railway, and postal), there has traditionally been no clear separation between public authorities and the system of property ownership. Public undertakings were a widely used means to restrict and regulate competition. As *Mestmäcker* explained in his presentation, EC law respects the existence of public undertakings but requires equal treatment of private and public undertakings under community law. Public undertakings must not be privileged in the competitive process. The influence of public authorities on their undertakings and the ability of these undertakings to disregard economic considerations because of their access to public revenues justify and demand that special rules and obligations be imposed on public undertakings. Such rules mainly exist in the form of state aid rules (Art. 87 et. seq. EC Treaty). The Transparency Directive imposes an additional duty on undertakings with exclusive or special rights (Art. 86 par. 1 EC Treaty) to maintain separate accounts for their different lines of activity in order to impede a cross-subsidization from privileged sectors to competitive activities which would be unlawful under general competition law rules.

The type of problems where public utilities are partly exposed to competition but still operate a vertically integrated natural monopoly network can be illustrated with a view to the energy sector. EC law has introduced the concept of legal unbundling to deal with this problem: the different stages of energy supply have to be organized separately without any regard to the ownership of the assets. *McCahery* doubted that in the end the unbundling philosophy of the EU would translate into lower prices for the consumer. This might explain why unbundling has been delayed in many member states, particularly in the energy field. *Mestmäcker* explained that the idea of the unbundling concept in the electricity field was to restrict monopoly rights to the natural monopoly part – ie to the provision of the physical network – and to enable undistorted competition between energy producers as well as in the distribution of energy by guaranteeing equal access to the network. In order for this concept to work without full vertical disintegration of the network, EU regulations required the network branch of the public utility to behave as if this part was fully divested, and not to take into account the interests of the undertaking as a whole. However, he cautioned that it was doubtful whether such a concept would work without any change in the governance structure.

Rickford asked whether the 'service public' exception in Art. 86 par. 2 of the EC Treaty might, in its application, become a threat to the fundamental freedoms as guaranteed in the EC Treaty, ie whether it was likely that the 'service public' exception would be exploited illegitimately to the national economic advantage. Here, *Mestmäcker* pointed to the role of the ECJ as a guardian of the fundamental freedoms and the inapplicability of national regulation in violation of these freedoms.

Sensui explained in his presentation that Japanese law did not have general state aid rules and provisions similar to Art. 86 EC Treaty which regulate the relationship between public undertakings and the state and impose a general principle of equality of private and public undertakings. However, Japanese law deals with similar problems in a somewhat comparable way through sector-specific regulations and general antimonopoly law.

Answering a question by *Hopt* about US and EU influences causing parallel developments in Germany and Japan in the regulation of public undertakings, *Sensui* explained that Japanese policy is generally responsive to the developments in the EU and the US in this field.

b. Regulation of Bottlenecks: Sector-Specific vs General Regulation, Especially in the Telecommunications and Energy Sectors

As the above-mentioned example of the liberalization of the energy sector illustrates, liberalization will not always be able to eliminate all bottlenecks. Physical networks can remain a natural monopoly or at least an essential facility, access to which is essential for competitors in order to compete in downstream markets.

In his presentation, *Kirchner* advocated general competition law to replace sector-specific regulation in the long run. When opening up former monopolies in the public utilities sectors to competition, a sector-specific ex ante regulation would be needed in order to break up monopolies and open up downstream markets. In this first phase, sector-specific regulation would be superior to general competition law. In the long run, however, strong ex ante regulation of bottlenecks would run the risk of overemphasizing intra-network competition and neglecting inter-network competition. It would be difficult to determine when exactly the switch to general competition law should take place.

In the discussion, *Spindler* pointed out that any kind of sector-specific regulation which concentrated on a specific technology would fail in the medium run, because it would be unable to deal adequately with the dynamic technological evolution. By way of example, he mentioned the regulation of 'voice over IP.' The ITU, as well as national regulators, has been unwilling until now to regulate 'voice over IP' or any type of communication over the Internet. According to *Spindler*, this shows that the technological evolution would frequently be able to destroy monopolies that were connected to a specific technology or distribution channel, like the telecommunications network or the cable network. The possibility of competition through new technologies should caution efforts to regulate. *Kirchner* replied that, when technology changes, the regulatory regime would need to be changed as well. In the EU, this has already been done: the EU introduced the principle of technological neutrality in its new framework regulation. Regulation could be abandoned as soon as a bottleneck disappears (as might happen when communication via the Internet becomes a real substitute).

On the other hand, *M. Hellwig* emphasized that, in the field of electricity, regulation was justified and necessary from an economic perspective because the energy networks were natural monopolies for the foreseeable future. *Kirchner* agreed that in this field, infrastructure-based competition does seem impossible. Still, choices regarding the type of regulatory approach need to be made.

c. Regulatory Agency-Building in the EU

In the EU, the debate about regulation of telecommunications and energy has been accompanied by a debate about whether to assign the regulatory task to member state agencies or whether to create a regulatory agency on the EU level instead. Within the member states, it was debated whether the task of sector-specific regulation should be assigned to the general competition authority or whether sector-specific regulatory agencies should be established. *Kirchner* favored the solution of assigning regulatory authority to the general competition authority. He was skeptical about creating new huge regulatory authorities which might eventually lead to overregulation. In his opinion, assigning the task of sector-specific regulation to the general competition authority was a better way to use scarce resources. It would strengthen the general competition authority instead of creating a new, partially self-interested bureaucracy for 800 enterprises in the energy sector. In its regulatory approach the general competition authority could then connect sector-specific regulation and general competition law, especially via the application of the essential facilities doctrine, which comes close to regulating access to bottlenecks via sector-specific regulation.

Regarding the German decision to refer the regulation of the energy sector to a sector-specific agency, the Regulatory Agency for Telecommunications (RegTP), *Hopt* inquired whether an alternative decision to authorize the Bundeskartellamt (the German general competition authority) might have changed the nature of this competition authority itself, leading it away from its original function.

Rickford drew attention to a similar discussion in the UK about who should become the new regulator in the field of telecommunications. In the UK, the general competition authority also declined to be appointed as the authority for sector-specific regulation – although the telecommunications industry itself favored such a solution: it perhaps expected that the general antitrust authority would take a softer stance on sector-specific regulation. In the end, the task was assigned to a specific body ('OFTEL') designed for the purpose by the Department of Trade and Industry. On a more general level, *Rickford* questioned whether economic regulation should be perceived as a single whole, or whether sector-specific regulation was a separate subject ('a different animal').

The issue of optimal agency-building was also discussed with respect to other fields, specifically a combination of supervisory functions for banking, insurance, and capital markets within one agency (*Hopt, M. Hellwig*). Such a combination seemed to be positive if some operations could be integrated. A huge (combined) agency, however, in which the three divisions work completely separately would not be very sensible. In favor of integration, some people point to the fact that, in certain derivatives markets and markets for asset-backed securities, banks and insurance companies are both present, sometimes as trading partners, sometimes as competitors. Therefore, it is sometimes claimed that their activities in these markets should be subject to the same regulation and supervision, in particular the same capital requirements. Such a claim would make sense if the purpose of the regulation was to protect the markets in question. It does not make sense, however, if the purpose of the regulation is to protect the institutions themselves and their financiers. Because the liabilities of banks and insurance companies, ie demand and savings deposits on the one hand and insurance claims on the other hand, have very different maturity structures and risk structures, there is *prima facie* no reason why the protection of their financiers should call for imposing the same regulatory requirements on both.

III. Corporate Law and Corporate Governance: Structures and Current Legal Developments in the US, Japan, and Europe

1. Corporate Governance Systems Categorized: From Generalizations Toward an Issue-by-Issue Approach

A recurring theme of the discussion was the question of whether and how corporate governance systems could be classified, and whether such a classification would correlate with economic performance.

In his presentation, *Schmidt* proposed making a distinction between insider-controlled and outsider-controlled systems, a distinction which closely correlates to the widely used distinction between bank-based systems and capital market-based systems (for further discussion, see below IV.1).

With a view to Japan, *Ramseyer* opposed the insider-controlled vs outsider-controlled distinction in his presentation, claiming that Japanese corporate governance does not conform to the classification usually associated with it (such as main banking system and cross-shareholding). According to *Ramseyer*, Japanese corporate governance is not systematically different from corporate governance elsewhere. The appearance of a systematically different Japanese corporate governance model was created by a group of Marxists who dominated influential Japanese research institutions in the 1950s and 1960s and strove successfully to establish the picture of the Japanese economy as a different model – not capitalist, but highly successful.

Along similar lines, *Miwa* claimed in his presentation that in Japan, corporate governance has always functioned in a market-oriented manner, that corporations consistently face the discipline of the stock market, and that 'Japan is not so different from the rest of the world'. *Rickford* questioned whether it was really true that capital markets had consistently functioned efficiently in Japan, as *Miwa* suggested, and illustrated his skepticism by depicting his experience with the first mass privatization in the UK in 1984, ie the privatization of British Telecom. The sale of at least 50% of the shares of the company made it necessary to engage in massive international private offering, inter alia in the US and in Japan. When Japanese banks were contacted to help with the offering, they offered to sell 10% of the shares within Japan, and to do so by selling them door-to-door – not via the stock market. *Schmidt* pointed to the fact that financial patterns are very difficult for economists to calculate and expressed his doubts about the allegation that financing patterns in Japan and the US are, and were, the same despite the different institutional set-ups. *Miwa* observed that anecdotes, no matter how many there may be, are still anecdotes. As such, they reflect not the economy itself but rather what people want to hear about the economy. Ever since Marco Polo, he added, there has been strong demand in the West for exotic stories about Japan.

Like *Miwa's* account, *Ramseyer's* description of Japanese corporate governance in the period after World War II was highly controversial. *Haley* pointed to the investigation of the Edwards Commission after World War II that investigated anti-competitive behavior of zaibatsu groups and found that zaibatsu-affiliated banks discriminated against competing companies. He inquired whether there was any indication that since World War II any Japanese bank formerly associated with a zaibatsu group had favored other companies in its keiretsu group or had disfavored competitors in lending. *Ramseyer* replied that the report of the Edwards Commission was completely wrong then and now, prepared within a very short time frame, not based on sufficient data, and written without knowledge of the Japanese language and without access to the necessary documents. *Haley* also inquired about Toyota, which is not affiliated with any keiretsu and does not have a main bank but relies heavily on its own earnings for its financing. According to *Ramseyer,* the Toyota example suggests nothing that is unique for Japan, but is probably based on the desire to maintain control that might be lost through a high degree of debt financing. *Nottage* and *Hertig* inquired how such a wrong image of Japanese corporate governance could survive for such a long period of time. *Ramseyer* replied that there has simply been a market for 'bogus material' – meaning that readers have been willing to buy such research. *Hertig* conjectured that Japanese firms might have been interested in sustaining such 'tales' to scare away foreign firms from entering the Japanese market. *Kanda*, on the other hand, maintained that Japan does have corporate groups; as evidence of this he pointed to the Japanese accounting rules and to the Tokyo Stock Exchange with its special listing rules for subsidiaries (partially owned companies), a group which comprises 50% of all listed companies. The Tokyo Stock Exchange requires that no more than 30% of a company's trade be done within the corporate group. *Baum* drew a parallel between Japanese and German corporate governance, especially to the German 'Hausbanken', and explained that based on the insider-controlled/outsider-controlled distinction, German corporate governance qualifies as insider-controlled. Asked to qualify Japanese corporate governance along these lines, *Ramseyer* felt this to be an impossible task due to the many variations within the Japanese system. With a view to Germany, *M. Hellwig* also emphasized the high degree of variance within the German system: some firms see the Hausbank relationship as important, while others do not; even where it is important, there is – and historically there always has been – a natural tendency of firms to emancipate themselves from dependence on the Hausbank through retained earnings or through the development of additional banking relations. In interpreting survey evidence, one difficulty is that the term 'Hausbank relationship' means different things to different people, and that in 1990 the term probably meant something different than it did in 1960 or 1890.

A different criterion for the classification of corporate governance systems which was repeatedly referred to by participants of the conference was the different types of dominant ownership structures to be empirically observed in different countries, ie the contestability of business from a corporate control perspective (eg *Macey*). A critical issue in comparing corporate governance systems is what percentage of outstanding shares is owned by non-fiduciary non-institutional investors, and what percentage of the GDP would thus be contestable. According to this criterion, the majority of the countries in continental Europe would qualify as non-contestable, eg because of block-shareholding, cross-shareholding, interlocked directors, or golden shares (*Hopt* added the significant number of family companies and diminished contestability). The US and the UK, on the other hand, both qualify as contestable. The validity of this distinction was called into question by *Rickford*, who emphasized the differences between the UK and the US systems of corporate governance when looking at the two countries in more detail.

No consensus was achieved on the issue of how to categorize corporate governance systems. Also, the overall value of such classifications remained controversial. In a comparison between continental Europe and the US, there was consensus that different dominant concepts of corporate governance exist (*Schmidt*), although these concepts may not always be as clear-cut as theory might suggest and may currently be changing. Several participants pointed out that, in reality, different corporate governance systems may co-exist in any given country so that most systems should be classified as hybrids to some extent. This led to the question of whether a general approach of categorizing systems without reference to a more specific context would really be helpful, or whether an issue-by-issue approach would be preferred.

With regard to a possible correlation between the corporate governance system dominant in a country and its economic performance, attention was drawn to potential trade-offs between external and internal mechanisms of efficiency control to which corporations could be subjected. To the extent that firms have to survive in competitive markets, those markets exert a disciplinary function on corporations and subject them to an efficiency constraint. *Coffee* suggested that a trade-off between strong corporate governance principles and openness to trade might possibly exist. For Japan, *Miwa* claimed that markets have always prevented Japanese firms from maintaining systematically inappropriate governance structures and that the institutional framework of an economy and distinctions between different systems of corporate governance do not matter for the economic outcome. Due to its generality, this claim was highly controversial. Several participants proposed making a distinction between sectors and industries subject to strong international competition and 'home industries' that are to some extent protected from competition. Strong product market competition might be able to assure efficient corporate governance in firms, whatever the institutional and legal framework for corporate governance in a given country would be. In contrast, where competition is weaker or lacking, the corporate governance framework might matter. *Kirchner* suggested that if one could find simultaneously lower growth rates of purely domestic industries and governance structures that differ significantly from those in more internationalized industries, it would severely challenge the hypothesis of the lack of importance of the institutional framework.

2. Current Changes in the US

Looking at current legal changes in the US, the conference turned to the Sarbanes-Oxley Act as a reaction to the Enron scandal and other surrounding scandals. The debate focused on whether the Sarbanes-Oxley Act deals adequately with the underlying causes of the scandals and on the effects of the Sarbanes-Oxley Act in the US and in Europe.

As to the causes of the recent series of corporate scandals in the US, *Milhaupt* explained that there are various competing theories. For some, the underlying cause of the corporate scandals is the structure of incentive compensation in the US – an aspect the Sarbanes-Oxley Act does not deal with. For others, the real villain in the recent series of corporate scandals is Alan Greenspan who, through his monetary policy, created a bubble with the series of corporate scandals as typical side effects. If the recent corporate scandals were simply typical bubble behavior, the Sarbanes-Oxley Act would probably not impede similar behavior in the future. *Milhaupt* conceded that the Sarbanes-Oxley Act might, in some respects, refocus attention on important corporate governance standards. Noting, however, the evidence that the compliance costs are substantial, he questioned whether, on balance, the Sarbanes-Oxley Act was worth its costs. *Brown* replied that the costs of compliance with the provisions of the Sarbanes-Oxley Act are catch-up costs. Internal control mechanisms, like those now required by the Sarbanes-Oxley Act, had been legally required since 1977. Because for the last 25 years firms had not complied with the internal control and documentation requirements, as well as with the requirements of certification of financial statements, they need to catch up now, and the initial costs of that may be high. In later phases, compliance with the Sarbanes-Oxley requirements will probably be less costly. The same is true of the audit requirements: in the past, companies pressured auditing companies to perform low-price audits. The result of that was that auditors did not check carefully enough. Reversing this development does not mean that companies are paying too much for audits now. *Pistor* shared the view that from time to time, bubbles had occurred and would always occur – usually in reaction to technological changes and high share price volatility (as in the 1920s and the late 1990s), and that any governance system would collapse under such conditions. However, in the current situation, the Sarbanes-Oxley Act would be a signal indicating 'we want to behave' – a market signal which might not be unimportant. *Hertig* conjectured that even if the face value of the Sarbanes-Oxley Act was not that high, as *Brown* suggested in his presentation, the Sarbanes-Oxley Act would change the behavior of boards in practice. With the Sarbanes-Oxley Act in their back, independent directors would start to ask tough questions. In this respect, the Sarbanes-Oxley Act has a strong psychological influence. *Brown* agreed, adding that the boards had the power to ask tough questions before but had chosen not to use it. The Sarbanes-Oxley Act had not enhanced the power of the board; it had merely strengthened the incentives to use it. He also underlined that the Sarbanes-Oxley Act does not require directors to be perfect; they simply need to exercise good business judgment.

Macey noted another effect of the Sarbanes-Oxley Act, namely that it stopped a movement toward interdisciplinary professional practice (eg mergers between accounting and law firms), for which the big accounting firms had strongly lobbied before. *Davies* replied that in fact, Enron initially chilled the atmosphere concerning interdisciplinary practice. But now in the UK, the issue is already back on the agenda. With respect to interdisciplinary practice, *H.J. Hellwig* noted that the market might sometimes lead to the same result as the Sarbanes-Oxley Act, using the example of law firms that had to separate from their auditing units in order to survive economically. Professional rules applicable to the legal profession bar a law firm from working for a competitor of the company being audited by the auditing department because of the potential conflicts implicated. This might severely hinder a law firm's business. *H.J. Hellwig* also gave an overview of the efforts to liberalize professional regulations in Europe. In a landmark case – the *Wouters* decision[12] – in February 2002, the ECJ held that a prohibition of multidisciplinary partnerships (MDPs) in a Dutch professional regulation issued by the Dutch bar was in line with EU competition law because of the incompatibility of the professional rules applicable to lawyers and auditors: while auditors were not subject to a strict secrecy regulation, such a regulation was a vital element of professional regulation for lawyers. Although a recent study on the liberalization of professional rules advocated opening up MDPs, Commissioner Monti declared that he would not insist on liberalization in situations where there were legitimate dissimilar professional rules – eg with respect to secrecy. In the UK, the issue of multidisciplinary associations was dealt with in the so-called Clementi Review.[13] This review focused on associations between solicitors and barristers, both of whom are subject to similar secrecy rules.

Regarding the impact of the Sarbanes-Oxley Act in Europe, *Pistor* expressed surprise. It was puzzling to see that the Europeans, as a reaction to scandals in the US, tried to signal trust through legislative action. That seemed to be an overreaction to market problems, as it occurred even before such markets had actually developed in Europe. *Davies* disagreed, stating that the scandals in the US had simply been a useful signal for European politicians whose attention had thus

[12] Case C-309/99 *JCJ Wouters and others v Algemene Raad van de Nederlandse Orde van Advocaten* [2002] ECR I-1577.

[13] Review of the Regulatory Framework for Legal Services in England & Wales. The consultation paper from 8 March 2004 can be found at <http://www.legal-services-review.org.uk/content/pubs.htm> (12 July 2005).

been called to already existing problems. For example, in the UK report on reviewing company law,[14] it had already been observed that the existing guarantee of independence of auditors was inadequate. But at that time, no legislative response had followed. After Enron the government listened to those suggestions. The same happened on the European level where the EU Council gave a mandate to move into the field of corporate governance only after the Enron scandal in the US Thus, the impetus to regulate corporate governance in the EU in this respect was a reaction to the Sarbanes-Oxley Act (*Hopt, Rickford*).

Looking at the direct effects of the Sarbanes-Oxley Act on European companies, *Ferrarini* observed that it was difficult for European companies to deal with its provisions. As *Brown* explained in his presentation, the Sarbanes-Oxley Act is deeply rooted in US case law, especially the *Caremark* decision. In Europe, there is no such case law background. *Ferrarini* also pointed to the issue of enforcement: the effectiveness of both private and public enforcement raises questions in Europe, and no true harmonization has taken place in Europe in that respect.

3. Current Changes in Japan

a. Company Law Reform in 2002

Concerning recent changes in the field of corporate governance in Japan, *Milhaupt* discussed three 'foreign legal transplants' in his presentation: the introduction of a duty of loyalty; creation of the position of executive officer; and the introduction of the option to choose a US-style board structure with independent committees. *Milhaupt* analyzed the operation of these three legal transplants as catalysts for corporate law development in Japan, examining the conditions under which such transplants would function successfully in Japan. *Milhaupt* provided particularly detailed evidence of the adoption of the committee system board structure by Japanese companies in the first year in which such an option was available. He offered several hypotheses for why a Japanese firm would find the committee system attractive, but argued that, from a theoretical perspective, the most intuitively appealing – signaling or bonding adherence to good corporate governance practices – was not plausible, because the extremely broad definition of 'outside' director was unlikely to create truly independent committees that would safeguard shareholder interests. Using event studies, *Milhaupt* showed that the stock market did not react to adoption of the committee system, which is consistent with *Milhaupt's* analysis.

[14] See Company Law Review Steering Group 'Modern Company Law for a Competitive Economy: Final Report' URN 01/942 and URN 01/943, to be found at <http://www.dti.gov.uk/cld/final_report/index.htm> (12 July 2005).

The discussion explored the causes and practical effects of this reform. *Macey* alleged that the 2002 company law reform in Japan was driven by the bad state of the Japanese economy and that the law reform measures were initiated by desperate companies. *Oda* characterized this law reform as the first reform 'from below'. He explained that the optional model for governance structures that eventually became law had not been envisioned from the beginning. Instead, the lawmakers were initially looking for a mandatory solution that would have introduced a US-type board structure. But when this solution met resistance – not only from politicians but also from companies – they decided to implement the optional model. *Kirchner* suggested that the Japanese optional model might be explained as an attempt to create a situation in Japan similar to the situation in the EU which had been brought about by recent ECJ case law. With respect to EU law, the ECJ case law expressed doubts about the formerly dominant seat theory and implemented the (historically older) incorporation theory: companies would now be treated according to the law of their incorporation, regardless of their seat, giving them a choice about their structure by letting them choose where to incorporate. In that respect, the Japanese optional model gives Japanese companies a similar choice to that given to European companies by the ECJ jurisprudence.

Concerning the practical importance of the new optional board structure, the participants remained skeptical. *Macey* suggested that the optional model might not be based on a proper policy choice, but might be characterized as a desperate measure to help desperate companies that were suffering from the bad state of the Japanese economy at the time. Nor might the fact that some (though few) companies had adopted the US-like board structure in practice be an indication of its superior efficiency, but simply a type of 'herd' behavior by firms that copied Sony, which took the lead in adopting the new structure. Especially in a company group context, the new committee structure might raise concerns: since representatives of the parent company qualify as 'outside directors', the power in the subsidiary could in effect shift away from the committee to the executive level of the parent.

On a methodological level, the issue of the value of the event studies was raised. *Ramseyer* observed that, whereas event studies might provide significant results in the context of mergers because of the secrecy requirement, which assured that the information did not leak into the market before the public announcement of the transaction, the same may not be true for the change to the committee structure. Thus, one might not expect significant results in event studies in this context. *Milhaupt* accepted this point, although he noted that he did obtain significant results on several individual firms. The event studies were used to supplement, but not replace, the theoretical discussion of the paper. *Milhaupt* noted that in any event, the empirical results – lack of significant market reaction to the announcement of the switch to the committee system – is consistent with his theoretical predictions about the lack of substantive merit in the committee system as adopted in Japan.

In his conclusions, *Milhaupt* observed that other elements of corporate governance might, in practice, be more important for the functioning of Japanese corporate governance than the new optional board structure, particularly the market for corporate control, shareholder activism, and the role of institutional investors.

b. Prospective Company Law Reform in 2005

Tatsuta explained in his presentation that Japanese company law is currently being overhauled again. A new Japanese company law is expected by 2005. The 2005 bill will combine the dispersed company law provisions and will create a comprehensive company law. An important part of the new law is that shareholders will have a choice between different governance structures. Additionally, there will be changes in several other parts of company law, such as the provisions of minimum stated capital.

During the discussion, the question was raised of what was driving the impulses of the current reform efforts. *Milhaupt* inquired as to what interests were served, and whether the reform would largely qualify as a technical cleanup of the Commercial Code without much impact on private corporate governance. *Tatsuta* replied that the cleanup of the Commercial Code was an important purpose, but that the bill would go further – for example, with the intended change in the rules on minimum stated capital. *Hopt* further inquired about the US influence on law-making in Japan via legal literature, comparative law, and economic studies by think tanks, as well as about the influence of academics. *Tatsuta* replied that in the Japanese Legislative Council, both American and German influences on law-making are present.

Baum mentioned an important development within Japanese company law outside the legislative realm. A reform in Japanese company law which dated back to 1950 had introduced shareholder derivative suits. For some 40 or 50 years that law played hardly any role, but that changed suddenly around the year 2000. After a change in the rules concerning the costs of such lawsuits, the number of derivative suits literally exploded. In at least some of these cases, plaintiffs claimed great sums of damages. After another reform of these rules, the number of suits dropped again. *Haley* added that once institutional disincentives to bring derivative suits in the form of high litigation costs were removed, the law stepped in to make derivative action less attractive. Derivative suits would not go well with the strong stakeholder approach of Japanese corporate governance, particularly the emphasis on employees' interests, an interest which would be shared by the state and bureaucracy.

c. Prospective Reform of the Judicial System in Japan

Another reform in Japan is the reform of the judicial system, which is part of a more general law reform intended to decrease regulation (*Rokumoto*). The aim of the reform of the judicial system is to shift power from the government and the bureaucracy to the judiciary, ie a transformation from an ex ante to an ex post control. That reform is a response to the globalization of the economy (*Rokumoto*), because the law in theory and the law in practice have drifted more and more apart. It is also intended to open Japan's lawyer market and to allow foreign lawyers to work in Japan. Moreover, it should help to radically increase the number of lawyers – from 1,000 to 3,000 within 15 years. Additionally, a reform of the law school system is being undertaken based on the US system. However, that reform will not lead to complete transplantation of the US system because Japan will keep its undergraduate legal education.

4. Current Changes in Europe

a. The EU Company Law Action Plan

The EU Company Law Action Plan[15] currently provides the blueprint for envisaged future changes in European company law. The Action Plan covers five areas: corporate governance, raising and maintenance of legal capital, groups of companies, restructuring and new company forms, and other enterprise and foundation forms. The purpose of the proposed actions in these fields is to strengthen shareholders' rights; to simultaneously provide sufficient protection for employees, creditors, and other parties with whom companies deal; and generally to foster efficiency and competitiveness of business. In his presentation, *Hopt* focused on the corporate governance actions proposed in the Action Plan, which will probably provide a major impetus for the harmonization of European company laws. To put the Action Plan into perspective, *Hopt* discussed recent European attempts to harmonize certain fields of company law (various directives, Financial Market Action Plan) and the problems of subsidiarity and regulatory competition within the EU. *Rickford* pointed out that the increasing reliance on disclosure in the Action Plan and in the Winter Report and the proposed adoption of comply-or-explain codes throughout the EU as proposed in the Commissions Directive on accounting followed the Cadbury market enforcement model. But that model had depended for its success in the UK on interventionist institutional investors relying on mandatory legal powers of intervention. These included the

[15] European Commission 'Modernising Company Law and Enhancing Corporate Governance in the European Union – A Plan to Move Forward' COM (2003) 284 final (21 May 2003) (see Annex 1).

powers of a bare majority to dismiss the board without cause, of a 5% minority to requisition a resolution, and of a qualified majority to amend the company articles. These powers operated in conjunction with factual conditions enabling such institutions to exploit the legal powers (very high levels of institutional investment [60-70%] and high levels of concentration of holdings [effective control vested in five to ten institutions]) in the overwhelming majority of listed UK companies. There were also strong formal and informal incentives on institutions to intervene. It was not clear that either the legal powers or the factual conditions on which the Cadbury model depended would be replicated elsewhere in Europe. The history of the Takeover Directive suggested that there would be strong resistance to similar structures of shareholder control. Moreover, even in the UK the Cadbury model had broken down in the key area of controlling board remuneration. Mandatory individual disclosure had always been required. General meeting resolutions on board remuneration policy were now also mandatory. The relevant Commission recommendation proposed mandatory disclosure and the GM resolution approving the policy, but with an important let-out for member states.[16] Moreover, even in the UK the levels and degree of concentration of domestic institutional holdings were falling. It was not clear what could substitute elsewhere in Europe for the enabling conditions in the UK. Directors' liability might be one possibility.

During the discussion, the issue of a possible direct personal liability of directors vis-à-vis investors was controversial. *Spindler* expressed doubts as to whether such direct personal liability vis-à-vis investors was an appropriate policy when other creditors were treated differently. *Hopt* conceded that making directors liable to investors put the latter in a privileged position compared to other creditors. However, the purpose of such a liability was not primarily the protection of a specific group of people (investors), but the protection of markets. Because liability rules could strengthen trust, introducing such a liability would lead in the right direction.

b. Corporate Governance Codes and the Comply-or-Explain Approach: Does It Work?

The increasing role of corporate governance codes in Europe was another topic of the debate. These codes have introduced the so-called 'comply-or-explain' approach into European corporate governance, a mechanism that was successfully used much earlier in US corporate governance. It is based on the belief that

[16] See now Commission Recommendation 2004/913/EC on Fostering and Appropriate Regime for the Remuneration of Directors of Listed Companies [2004] OJ L385/55 art 4.2, which requires a vote by the general meeting on the remuneration policy but allows member states to provide that such a vote shall only be required where shareholders holding 25% or more of the votes at the meeting demand it.

markets can efficiently process information and will punish firms that deviate from the corporate governance codes when such deviations are detrimental to investors ('market discipline'). Whether this mechanism works efficiently in practice was controversial. *Schmidt* pointed out that there are no statistically significant market reactions to non-compliance with the codes, regardless of whether non-compliance is explained or not. Others contended, however, that the fact that the market did not react to certain explanations of deviation from the code did not cast doubt on the comply-or-explain technique itself. Whether the market reacted to information depended on the sensitivity of the market to certain types of information. If the sensitivity is high enough, the market will react. The goal of the comply-or-explain approach is not to have the market react in every case, but to have it react to information which the market considers to be relevant (*Wymeersch*). Moreover, even if such explanations aren't followed by a huge market reaction, there will be a lot of market reaction to litigation facilitated by such disclosure (*Pistor*). The tendency in Europe to take the fact that companies choose not to comply with a code, but rather to explain their deviation from the code as an argument in favor of introducing mandatory regulations, was unanimously criticized by the participants as being in contradiction with the 'comply-or-explain' philosophy (eg *Hopt*).

Spindler raised the question of whether rating agencies and/or auditors should scrutinize and evaluate the quality of a firm's corporate governance (eg compliance with corporate governance codes). *Hopt* maintained that auditors should not evaluate board decisions, but should check whether a company has complied with the rules. *Wymeersch* added that it would cause problems if auditors had to give an opinion about the independence of the boards.

c. External Corporate Governance: The Development of a Market for Corporate Control in the EU

One of the notable recent developments in the EU is the emergence of a 'market for corporate control'. In his presentation, *Grundmann* gave a thorough overview of the new European Takeover Directive.[17] The following discussion focused on the merits and disadvantages of mandatory disclosure of ownership shares in firms, of a mandatory bid rule, and of the duty of neutrality of boards in the context of takeover contests, and it explored the functions and the workability of the market for corporate control in general.

[17] Directive 2004/25/EC of the European Parliament and of the Council of 21 April 2004 on takeover bids [2004] OJ L 142/12.

(1) Disclosure Rules

Some participants questioned the rationality of duties to disclose certain levels of ownership of shares in firms which form the basis of takeover regulation (*Macey*). As they alleged, such disclosures do not help against money laundering, nor do mandatory disclosure rules hinder scandals like Enron: disclosure only works when someone is listening, which was not the case in the Enron situation. While the need for disclosure is questionable, the cost of disclosure is immense because entrepreneurs who are willing to undertake strategic, value-adding investments are likely to be deterred. If a shareholder has to disclose his ownership of shares when it reaches 5%, other investors could free ride on his investment information. Generally, there is no reason to discourage large block holding, since large stockholders have an important stake in the monitoring of a firm.

(2) The Mandatory Bid Rules

The mandatory bid rule introduced into EU takeover law through the takeover directive was heavily debated. *Baum* noted that the aim of the mandatory bid was to shift the ownership of a company, not merely the control over the company. Thus, the aim of the mandatory bid was actually to invalidate the market for corporate control. Where a mandatory bid rule existed, he contended, there could be no 'market for corporate control'. *McCahery* criticized the mandatory bid rule because of its potential to disrupt market equilibriums. He pointed to empirical evidence that 60% of the more recent acquisitions of firms were bad business decisions. One explanation for that could be that it is difficult for European companies to pick the winners when taking over US enterprises. Such informational problems could lead to a considerable rise in transaction costs, making takeovers sometimes too costly. Therefore, takeovers should be optional and not forced via a mandatory bid rule. *Grundmann*, on the other hand, defended the mandatory bid rule as a means to deter bidders who want to loot minority shareholders. In his view, the basic idea of a mandatory bid rule is to force a bidder who believes he can run the company more efficiently to 'take it all' and thus internalize the chances of future profits. Another justification is the principle of equal treatment of present shareholders who should be given their share of the control premium. In a brief historical overview, *Grundmann* explained that in the late 1980s and early 1990s, mandatory bid rules were generally in fashion, although there was significant opposition to such rules in Germany. Today, mandatory bid rules can be found in takeover regulations everywhere in Europe, including Germany, and the debate has shifted to the advantages and disadvantages of defensive measures.

(3) The Duty of Neutrality of Boards in the Context of Takeover Contests

The duty of neutrality of boards in the context of takeover contests was equally controversial.

H.J. Hellwig pointed to the different positions taken by EU and US law in this respect, with EU law tending to take a stricter stance than US law. *Grundmann* explained that the duty of neutrality entails a shift of competences. In his opinion, the question was whether the board of directors or the shareholders meeting should be the ultimate decision-maker. Based on the principal-agent theory, it would be best to let the shareholder meeting decide if the shareholders decided on an informed basis. The real policy question, *Grundmann* maintained, was whether the EU regulation should remain a default rule (as it is now) or become a mandatory rule as it is in the UK. Comparing the duty of neutrality and the duty of loyalty, he held the duty of neutrality to be a preventive tool for avoiding conflicts of interest (before a bid is made). The duty of loyalty, on the other hand, is applied when a conflict of interest would already be present.

(4) The Functions and Workability of Markets for Corporate Control

A significant number of contributions to the debate concerned the function of the market for corporate control as a mechanism to replace bad management, with possible substitutes for this mechanism in environments where the market for corporate control is not fully developed. Thus, *Pistor* stressed that there is an almost equal propensity of the management to be replaced in times of crisis in Japan, Germany, and the US, and that only the methods for bringing about this change differ due to the different cultural backgrounds. *Ferrarini* agreed that there are different ways of changing government, mentioning the example of institutional investors inquiring about the succession plans of the board of directors and trying to get some influence on those decisions. *McCahery* confirmed that there are substitutes for the market for corporate control as a mechanism of external corporate governance. In the Netherlands, neither contestability nor transparency helps in controlling the management. Still, the system in the Netherlands works quickly for replacements, without any 'golden parachutes'. In this respect, the 'old boys' system might work well. *Macey* squared *McCahery's* observations with empirical studies which show that managers are more likely to get sacked where they get negative publicity, and he pondered that it might be easier for mediocre managers to hide in a big economy than in a small one. He added that the private benefits of control, and hence incentives for takeovers, differ significantly between the various jurisdictions.

Macey questioned the workability of the market for corporate control as a control mechanism. Nothing suggests that a robust market for corporate control could have inhibited Enron or any other accounting or financial fraud. Markets for corporate control work only when company shares are undervalued. The shares of Enron, however, were overvalued. Such fraudulent practices severely obstruct the market for corporate control because bidders start to worry about the trustworthiness of the company's numbers. *McCahery* conceded that it is difficult to evaluate the workability of the market for corporate control. Concerning fraud, he pointed to the board as the organ established to prevent fraud.

Grundmann pointed out that the aims of takeover regulation are, in reality, twofold: takeovers can be an advantageous instrument to discipline management, and takeovers sometimes create synergies. *Rickford* called for a genuine open-market approach to takeovers, an approach that allows for genuine contestability of corporate control. According to him, it is impossible to introduce an adequate regulatory regime to compensate for such an open-market approach. Open markets cannot be 'socially engineered' through regulation. He therefore believes the takeover directive to be a failure. *H.J. Hellwig* disagreed. For him, the takeover directive is 'the art of the possible' in a Bismarckian sense. It is merely a first step, but it stands for a pragmatic and flexible approach to rule-making in the EU which currently dominates the law-making process and is overall welcomed.

Regarding takeovers in Europe, *Wymeersch* noted that the rules of the Takeover Directive and the practical problems of takeovers are two separate worlds. In practice, takeovers are frequently blocked by banks – or even, in cases of cross-national takeovers, by the intervention of governments.

(5) Comparative Outlook

Questions similar to those in Europe appear to have emerged in Japan as well. As *Kanda* pointed out, Japanese courts have recently started to deal with the issue of defensive tactics to hostile takeovers. As *Kanda* noted, however, the line of case law is contradictory: of two recently published court decisions, one – from 1 July 2004 – upheld defensive measures, while the other – from a different court – did not.

IV. Intermediaries and Their Regulation

1. Banks as Intermediaries in Insider-Controlled Systems

In any corporate governance system, intermediaries play an important role in generating and processing information and in controlling the actions of corporate actors. Corporate governance systems differ, however, in the design of such intermediary institutions. While in Japan and Germany banks have traditionally been overwhelmingly important as intermediaries, institutional investors such as pension and investment funds play a much more important role in Anglo-Saxon countries. In his presentation, *Schmidt* therefore distinguished between bank-based and market-based – ie insider-controlled or outsider-controlled – corporate governance systems. In an insider-controlled system such as Germany, information is internalized, meaning it is only available to a limited number of internal agents. Typically, the management considers various stakeholder interests to run the company smoothly. In an outsider-controlled system such as the UK, information is available externally; at the same time, management, in running the company, typically considers shareholders' interests only. *Schmidt* found no system to be generally preferable to the other, but maintained that it is imperative to follow a consistent approach. Mixing systems might cause difficulties.

Hopt inquired as to how exactly the two different systems are reflected in the different legal frameworks and what can be inferred from the advantages and disadvantages of each system with regard to the success of different types of enterprises and industries. *Macey* raised the question as to whether the outcome of *Schmidt's* analysis would be different if not only banks but also non-bank lenders were considered. A major drawback of banks is a mismatch within their liquidity structure (assets and liabilities) allowing for a high leverage effect. Therefore, banks would be extremely sensitive to unpredictable liquidity shocks. Continuing on the same point, *M. Hellwig* pointed to the fact that all over the world, over the past three decades, the ability of banks to take on the risks associated with liquidity provision and maturity transformation and to use short-term deposits for long-term lending has been eroded by an intensification of competition for funds. In Germany, this development came later than in other countries, but here, as elsewhere, intermediation margins have been drastically eroded since the admission of money market funds in 1994. The resulting weakening of the financial strength of banks throws doubts on the robustness of bank dominance in finance and governance. *Schmidt* supported that view, adding that German banks have not been very competitive at the deposit stage in the past, especially due to hidden funds. If more interbank lending took place, the banking system would reach its limit and might even cease to function. *Macey* doubted that banks are effectively controlled by depositors. Depositors do not have strong incentives to monitor banks because they are insured through deposit insurance. *Schmidt* disagreed, claiming that banks, due to their specific nature as intermediaries, face punishment from their depositors if they do not monitor borrowers efficiently. *Milhaupt* inquired about more recent changes concerning the role of banks. As the legal barriers between banks and venture capital firms have disappeared and banks have entered new markets, referring only to banks in a traditional sense seems questionable. *Schmidt* conceded that significant changes have taken place. Instead of acting as lenders themselves, banks have more recently become pathfinders for lenders to capital markets. However, these changes and developments have primarily occurred within the US banking system and similar assumptions cannot be made for other countries.

Several participants (*M. Hellwig, Hopt*) criticized *Schmidt's* conception of only two different systems. They also disagreed about the need of preserving consistency of the systems by not mixing their elements. This would not leave much room for piecemeal policy choices (*M. Hellwig*). Legal systems are not as clear-cut in reality as Schmidt assumes, and they can also adapt to new elements to a certain degree (*Hopt*). Moreover, there are examples where one system has gradually switched over into another system (*Hopt*). Along similar lines, *Davies* observed that it is possible to have outsider and insider systems within the same legal system. As an example, he pointed to the fact that the UK and the US generally qualify as outsider systems. Private equity funds, however, display characteristics of an insider-controlled system. Since different systems can coexist, the most interesting endeavor would be the relationship between insider- and outsider-controlled systems within the same legal system. *Schmidt* defended his consistency assumption, interpreting various recent incidents of crisis as an indication of a loss of consistency, leading to a growing instability of the system. He conceded, however, that the future will show whether hybrid systems can work and whether it would even be possible to combine the strengths of outsider- and insider-controlled systems, as in the case of securitization, a hybrid that combines relationships and markets.

Rickford challenged *Schmidt's* analysis as too limited to form a valid theoretical basis for analysis because it covers only two different systems (the US and Germany). There would be more potential for adapting and introducing different elements from other systems. The UK model, for example, differs from the US model because it can be characterized by strong boards and a greater emphasis on 'voice' than on 'exit'. *Schmidt* replied that these differences between the UK and the US models are minor compared to the difference between the German model and the Anglo-Saxon model concerning the function of the board. In Germany the board has the legal obligation to act in the interest of various stakeholders, whereas in the dominant conception of the Anglo-Saxon world, the board is obligated to the shareholders only. The role of the board and certain committees is merely to be advisors for and watchdogs over the management in the interest of the shareholders.

2. Securities Analysts, Auditors, and Rating Agencies as Intermediaries in Market-Based Systems

In outsider-controlled, market-based systems, so-called 'gatekeepers' – securities analysts, auditors, and rating agencies – play an essential role as information intermediaries. This presupposes that they supply investors and potential investors with trustworthy information. On the other hand, each of the gatekeepers has, for different reasons, incentives to provide information to the market that is favorable to the companies. How to deal with these conflicts of interest is one of the core issues in the regulation of gatekeepers. In his presentation, *Coffee* focused on securities analysts and proposed to have them paid by the stock exchanges in order to solve their conflicts of interest.

Spindler pointed to two concepts of regulating securities analysts that are embodied in the EU Market Abuse Directive.[18] Securities analysts have to disclose any conflicts of interest and they have to establish Chinese walls within their firms. In Germany these duties are enforced through liability rules: securities

[18] Directive 2003/6/EC of the European Parliament and of the Council of 28 January 2003 on insider dealing and market manipulation (market abuse) [2003] OJ L96/16.

analysts are liable in the case of a violation of those rules. As *Spindler* noted, in reality the proof of causality between rule violation and damages poses problems.

Much of the discussion focused on whether and how the conflicts of interest problems of rating agencies and auditors could be solved. There was consensus that a uniform solution for all gatekeepers seems impossible. The solution suggested by *Coffee* for securities analysis cannot be transferred to the regulation of rating agencies (*Brown*) because of the differences in the market for analysts and for rating agencies (*Coffee*). While there are many analysts, there are only a few rating agencies. Since competition among rating agencies is lower, competitors have no incentives to be better; they only try not to look worse than the others. *Coffee* suggested that a solution for the conflicts of interest of rating agencies could be to introduce more competition between the rating agencies. Moreover, there has to be a credible threat of litigation in case an agency does not disclose to the market the conflicts of interest that it is aware of. But a public subsidy to rating agencies is not required.

According to *Coffee*, the underlying problem with auditing firms is a conflict-of-interest problem within the audit firm. Audit firms receive a great amount of money from the audited companies for performing non-audit counseling tasks, and are therefore interested in maintaining a good relationship with their client. To deal with this problem, it would be sensible to shorten the period for a lead partner rotation. *Macey* questioned the severity of the conflicts of interest in practice, challenging the numbers on which *Coffee* based his analysis of restatements of financial statements: in 25% of the cases, the restatements were in fact positive in result or contained only technical changes. Also, the statistics *Coffee* used engaged in recounting (eg counting Enron various times because one change affected the statements of several years). *Coffee* replied that the exact numbers do not matter. Most restatements were significantly negative. Looking at Europe, *Ferrarini* wondered why there were so few restatements there. *Coffee* pointed to the higher liability risk in the US compared to Europe. Usually a restatement is initiated by an auditor who is unwilling to certify any longer because of the high risk he has to take to do that.

Regarding policy suggestions, *Macey* agreed with *Coffee* that individual auditor rotation could be a solution because it would leave those auditors less exposed to capture. The competition could then concentrate on client satisfaction. However, the consequences of auditor rotation would be open and the competition between auditors within the auditing firms might entail new problems. There was some agreement that a rotation of *auditing firms* – although in principle the best to resolve the conflict-of-interest issue (*Hopt*) – would not completely solve the problem due to the market structure: since the market of high-class auditors is a highly oligopolistic market (with the 'Big Four'), rotation might lead to a mechanism of market-sharing rather than to real independence. *Macey* also remarked that a comparison of the five auditing firms showed that there are no statistically significant differences in the trustworthiness of these firms, as evidenced by the number of restatements issued by each of those firms. According to those numbers, Andersen (which was Enron's accounting firm) had even done a very good job because it had fewer restatements than other agencies. Referring to the situation in Japan, *Oda* pointed out that initially the CPA law reform in Japan had proposed a firm rotation, but that proposal had been dropped because four (big) auditing firms would not be enough for a meaningful rotation. A rotation of firms, however, has been implemented in Italy together with a rule that forbids simultaneous advisory services when auditing a company (*Ferrarini*). As *Ferrarini* explained, the legislation was intended to reduce the time that an auditor could audit a company from nine to six years. However, it is doubtful whether that will solve the problem because the firm that audits and the firm that advises a company might simply switch positions at the end of the period. Moreover, auditing fees are less attractive than counseling fees. If the auditing business is split from the counseling business, the best people might turn to counseling firms and not to auditing firms (*Hopt*). Such a development has been observed in Japan where accountancy has lost its attraction because of unattractive fees in a highly competitive market (*Oda*).

Rickford suggested that many problems which appear to make it necessary to regulate accountants and securities analysts could be solved by introducing a requirement of shareholder approval for option schemes and remuneration policies, an increasingly widely accepted solution in Europe. *Coffee* remarked that shareholder approval of stock options does exist in the US While increasing shareholder rights might help, abolishing equity compensation would not be the answer, because the real danger is short-term holdings by executives.

V. Changes of Governance: The International Perspective

1. Potential Pitfalls When Comparing Systems

The debate on economic governance issues in general and corporate governance issues in particular has become international today. Comparing different systems and evaluating their importance for economic success is a core ingredient of this debate. There are, however, pitfalls in this task, as was repeatedly observed by participants to the debate. *Rickford* stressed that the work of comparatists frequently focuses on the *legal* differences of systems. Often, however, important distinctions can be found on the factual level. One important difference between the US and the UK system is that the chairman and the CEO of 95% of the UK firms are different persons, whereas in the US they are normally identical. As a second example for illustrating the difficulties of comparisons he pointed to the differences of the board structure. On the one hand, both German and UK boards are usually strong boards. The fact that boards are strong makes the two systems alike in a relevant aspect. On the other hand, strong boards in Germany are stakeholder-oriented, whereas in the UK they are shareholder-oriented. That makes them different.

Macey stressed the importance of knowing at what level of abstraction a comparison is undertaken. On a very high level of abstraction, all systems look similar; on a low level of abstraction, everything looks different. Also, on a low level of abstraction, one frequently finds that different systems can coexist to some extent in each country (*M. Hellwig*). At a higher level of abstraction, there is a danger of overlooking that strategic interdependencies might differ from country to country – sometimes even within the same country (*M. Hellwig*). Along similar lines, *Ramseyer* criticized cross-national comparisons because they are usually based on generalizations. What is really interesting about a country – for example, Japan – is the enormous variety within the country concerning firms, industries, etc. *Haley* emphasized that to effectively compare systems and measure their effectiveness it is necessary to look at the final outcome of the systems instead of merely concentrating on the ingredients.

2. International Trend: The Shift of Powers to the Executive

Despite the aforementioned caveats, the comparative approach has become increasingly important in the era of economic globalization because it helps to find similar solutions to similar problems across countries.

As several participants to the conference observed, globalization and the demand for similar solutions has led to a shift of decision-making powers from the legislative to the executive branch of government (eg *H.J. Hellwig, Macey*). Although the demands of globalization might sometimes justify this shift, there is a risk that the executive branch may use globalization as a pretense to usurp powers. *H.J. Hellwig* mentioned the case of Guantanamo as an example. *Ginsburg* suggested that some harsh legislative measures, such as the Helms-Burton Act,[19] could be interpreted as a consequence of usurpations of legislative powers by the executive. Reactions against the usurpation of powers and intrusions into established legal principles and individual rights by the executive branch could also be expected from NGOs (*H.J. Hellwig*). The role of NGOs in the globalization context remained controversial, however. *Ramseyer* criticized their lack of democratic legitimacy and qualified them as mere interest groups representing elite ideas and interests of rich countries. *H.J. Hellwig,* on the other hand, pointed to the laudable achievements of NGOs in the fight for the protection of the environment (eg the Exxon case).

A shift of powers from the legislative to the executive branch in the context of globalization can also be observed in the EU, where powers have been shifted massively from member states to the EU level. The risk of usurpation associated with this shift can be seen, for example, in some recent cases when the EU Commission foreclosed any policy debates within the EU on matters of securities

[19] Cuban Liberty and Democratic Solidarity Act of 1996, Public Law 104-114, HR 927.

regulation because it had already reached a compromise with the SEC on an international level, a behavior sharply criticized for impeding the democratic process (*Rickford*).

3. Changing Legal Structures in the International Setting: Mechanisms of Change and Practical Examples

a. Mechanisms of Change: Harmonization vs Convergence

International convergence of legal systems and legal rules can be brought about in different ways: through a centralized harmonization of legal rules or through a process of gradual and decentralized convergence.

In the EU, harmonization – or at least partial harmonization – through EU directives has played an important role in creating the Common Market. Law-making powers have gradually shifted from the member states to the EU level. Inherent in the concept of harmonization is a diminished scope for the competition of the various systems of the member states. Harmonization also diminishes the scope for adequate reactions to specific regulatory needs which may still differ between the member states. For example, the right choice between (a) a rather interventionist mandatory regulatory approach, or (b) a more flexible comply-or-explain approach, or (c) pure transparency regulation may depend heavily on the structure of capital markets in a given member state. The structures of the capital markets still differ significantly between the member states, however. Therefore, harmonization may not always be a desirable trend. Rather, harmonization should be very cautiously used as an instrument, with a view to persisting economic, legal, and structural differences between the member states (*Spindler, Rickford, Pistor*). A more decentralized approach to regulation might often be preferable and more effective, also with a view to the danger of a petrification of supranational law which is usually more difficult to change (*Hopt*). *Grundmann* called for a differentiated approach to harmonization: decentralized law-making has the major advantage of creating a variety of (potentially competing) products. On the other hand, centralized information rules might be desirable because they would better solve information problems and would make it easier to process information.

Currently, European regulation is moving away from the concept of full harmonization toward mere convergence of the legal systems, an approach which is much more pragmatic as it aims to get practical solutions at a lower cost and with fewer frictions than full harmonization. *H.J. Hellwig* held this policy to be a laudable example of 'the art of the possible'. Pressures for more harmonization sometimes result from the concept of equivalency which applies, according to EU law, where harmonization has not yet been achieved.

Outside the EU, in international contexts, harmonization is typically not an option. Convergence is sometimes achieved in a completely decentralized manner. Law reforms in the field of economic regulation are prepared on the basis of detailed comparative studies. So-called 'legal transplants' are a common phenomenon (see eg the example of the Japanese board structures or the comply-or-explain approach with respect to corporate governance codes). During the discussion, a controversy arose as to whether the concept of 'legal transplants' was a relevant concept for analyzing legal reform processes. *Macey* stressed that legal transplants are ubiquitous across all legal cultures and asked whether using the concept of 'legal transplants' has any meaningful results when analyzing current company law reforms. *Milhaupt* replied that the reason to care about legal transplants is exactly because they are ubiquitous. Whether legal transplants make legal systems more alike or whether they function differently in different legal environments remains an open question (see above: example of Japanese board structures).

An important way to induce convergence on an international level is the international dialogue. In certain fields, particularly in the field of antitrust, national agencies have started a comprehensive international dialogue in an attempt to discuss and, where necessary, to coordinate their policies. There was a debate at the conference as to whether and to what extent the concept of equivalency – which is important in the context of EU law – could be a useful instrument for the international dialogue (*Hopt, H.J. Hellwig*). The participants agreed that the usefulness of the concept of equivalency in the international setting depends on the issues and the parties involved in the dialogue and their cultural background.

With respect to the normative evaluation of the process of international convergence, there was no consensus. *Schmidt* expressed skepticism with respect to the viability of attempts by the EU to create a new mix between the Anglo-Saxon and the continental European system. Instead, he pleaded for a coherent system, claiming that coherent systems always perform better. *Schmidt's* proposition was challenged by other participants of the conference who, again, emphasized that 'pure' systems do not exist in reality, but that all systems contain elements of other kinds of systems as well, and could hence be called 'hybrid' (see above).

Pressures for an intensified international dialogue and convergence can be created through an aggressive extraterritorial application of national laws: it can force foreign economic actors and thus indirectly foreign countries to accept certain foreign rules. Recently, for example, the SEC has been rather aggressive in its extraterritorial application of the Sarbanes-Oxley Act. *Pistor* expressed surprise about the tepid reaction of the EU to this behavior. A much more outraged response should have been expected.

b. Practical Examples of Internationalization in the Context of Economic Regulation

With respect to certain issues, regulation has truly moved up to an international level, or is about to do so. As an example for internationally concerted actions, the conference discussed Basel II and the debate surrounding standardized international accounting standards.

(1) Basel II

The general goal of the new agreement on banking regulation and supervision that is being proposed by the Basel Committee on Banking Supervision ('Basel II') is to improve the soundness and the stability of the international banking system by inducing banks to strengthen their risk management practices, partly because capital requirements are more precisely calibrated to the banks' risks and partly through market discipline. The disclosure rules contained in the regulatory framework of Basel II are intended to enable markets to react to significant information about the stability of banks (*Wymeersch*). *Spindler* claimed that Basel II might have negative side effects, namely that it could lead to a distortion of the information process between the bank as lender and its clients because the clients would be reluctant to disclose negative information. Even though the new Basel Accord has not yet been signed, the efforts of the Basel Committee to induce banks to securitize their risks and thereby to get them off their books have already been quite successful and may explain why the stock market implosion and the economic slowdown of recent years have not been accompanied by banking crises (*M. Hellwig*). *Wymeersch* confirmed that the worldwide financial stability has increased significantly, even though Basel II has not yet been implemented. Given the finding that, since the mid-nineties, stability in banking has increased, the discussion turned to the question of whether risks have in fact been reduced or whether they have merely been shifted elsewhere. When banks securitize risk, through the sale of asset-backed securities or through interest rate or credit derivatives, insurance companies often provide the counter-party. For interest rate risk, such transactions seem natural because insurance companies' liabilities have different maturities than banks' liabilities. However, one may wonder why insurance companies should be better able to bear credit risks than banks. Basel II concentrated on the banking sector and the desirability of getting risks off the banks' books without considering the implications of this shift for the insurance sector. A comprehensive approach to financial regulation with a view to which institutions are most suited to bear which risks was missing (*M. Hellwig*). The relevance of this criticism was indicated by the fact that, partly through regulatory forbearance, the German life insurance sector in 2003 barely avoided a meltdown due to writedowns on their assets. The situation was somewhat reminiscent of the US savings and loans industry in the early eighties. As of 1981, two-thirds of the US savings industry was effectively insolvent, but through a combination of forbearance and deregulation was allowed to 'gamble for resurrection,' with disastrous consequences for the S&L crisis in the second half of the eighties. Given the impact of market developments since 2000 on life insurance and defined-benefits pension institutions, a repetition of the S&L experience is not out of the question (*M. Hellwig*). *Wymeersch* suggested that in regulating the insurance sector, the accounting rules would play a significant role.

Focusing on procedural aspects, *Wymeersch* noted that the rules of Basel II were developed on the basis of an international dialogue with national institutions, and on several impact studies which were performed to provide a sound economic basis. Although this rule-making process lacked democratic legitimacy, it provided for a different form of legitimacy. As he pointed out, the drafters of Basel II were sensitive to the concerns of national institutions throughout the process. One example of this was that when the German Parliament asked for adjustments of Basel II to better accommodate the interests of small companies, the committee adjusted the rules in that respect.

(2) Accounting Standards

In the field of accounting standards, international convergence might be desirable. However, as *Macey* noted, the collapse of Enron, which took the wind out of the sails of those who had championed US-GAAP as the best accounting system, has not led to a strengthening of efforts for a transatlantic standardization of accounting standards. Rather, for the time being, it has terminated these efforts. The perception that US-GAAP has failed has led to the conclusion in the US that the US rules have to be revised – not to a consideration of foreign or internationally developed solutions (eg the IAS). In this respect, *H.J. Hellwig* disagreed. In his view, the efforts to standardize accounting rules internationally have become stronger. To support his argument he pointed to the memorandum between the European IASB and the US Accounting Standards Board from October 2002.[20] The CESR has been mandated to present recommendations by June 2005 on how convergence of US-GAAP, Canadian GAAP, Japanese GAAP, and the IAS can be achieved. In addition, Japan has started to bring the Japanese GAAP in line with IAS. The EU in turn has promised to take into account some remaining Japanese concerns in this field. *H.J. Hellwig* also expected that Enron and the legislative attempts to deal with its consequences would lead to even more convergence in the field of auditing standards. International convergence in

[20] For the text of the memorandum, see <http://www.iasb.org/docs/press/2002pr15.pdf> and <http://www.fasb.org/news/memorandum.pdf> (both 12 July 2005).

accounting and auditing standards is already foreseen in the proposal of an EU Directive on Auditing, published in March 2004.[21]

VI. Conclusion

Throughout the conference, the discussion showed that the issues at stake in the US, Japan, and Europe are currently quite similar, though the underlying economic and legal structures as well as the solutions to the problems they face can sometimes differ. The participants were aware that these (remaining) differences mattered: they cautioned repeatedly against a precipitate rush for harmonization. Moreover, there was a great awareness of the importance of the overall institutional framework of corporate governance. Most participants argued for a careful analysis of the institutional set-up as a whole when dealing with particular problems. At the same time, there was a broad consensus that an issue-by-issue approach to corporate governance issues was needed in order to cope with today's urgent problems. There appeared to be broad support for combining a macro- and a micro-analysis when dealing with specific issues in the field of corporate governance. How to deal with the unavoidable interaction of still differing systems in the field of corporate governance and economic governance in general was one of the recurring questions during the conference. Whereas some participants warned of 'mixing systems', others appeared to be more optimistic. Generally, the participants agreed that in an era of economic globalization, an international dialogue was necessary on all levels: in the form of close cooperation between agencies, as can currently be observed in the field of competition, but also between academics and practitioners.

[21] European Commission 'Proposal for a Directive on Statutory Audit of Annual Accounts and Consolidated Accounts and Amending Council Directives 78/660/EEC and 83/349/EEC' COM (2004) 177 final (15 March 2004).

Selected Bibliography

Allen F and D Gale 'Comparative Financial Systems' in A Boot and others (eds) *Financial Intermediation* (OUP Oxford 2005, forthcoming)

Allen F and D Gale *Comparing Financial Systems* (MIT Press Cambridge 2000)

Amyx JA *Japan's Financial Crisis: Institutional Rigidity and Reluctant Change* (Princeton University Press 2004)

Amyx JA and P Drysdale (eds) *Japanese Governance: Beyond Japan Inc* (Routledge Curzon London 2003)

Aoki M *Toward a Comparative Institutional Analysis* (Cambridge University Press Cambridge MA 2001)

Aoki M and G Saxonhouse (eds) *Finance, Governance and Competitiveness in Japan* (OUP Oxford 2000)

Armour J and JA McCahery (eds) *After Enron: Improving Corporate Law and Modernising Securities Regulation in Europe and the US* (Hart Publishing Oxford, forthcoming 2005)

Barca F and M Becht *The Control of Corporate Europe* (OUP Oxford 2001)

Basedow J 'Economic Regulation in Market Economies' in J Basedow and others (eds) *Economic Regulation and Competition* (Kluwer Law International The Hague 2002) 1

Basedow J, H Baum, KJ Hopt H Kanda and T Kono (eds) *Economic Regulation and Competition* (Kluwer Law International The Hague 2002)

Basel Committee on Banking Supervision *International Convergence of Capital Measurement and Capital Standards, A Revised Framework* (Bank for International Settlements Basel 2004)

Bäuerle M 'The Retreat of the Welfare State: Challenges to the German Welfare Regime and the Role of Law' (2003) Annual of German and European Law 43

Baum H 'Changes in Ownership, Governance, and Regulation of Stock Exchanges in Germany: Path Dependent Progress and an Unfinished Agenda' (2004) 5 European Business Organization Law Review 677

Baum H (ed) *Japan: Economic Success and Legal System* (de Gruyter Berlin New York 1997)

Baums T and K Scott 'Taking Shareholder Protection Seriously? Corporate Governance in the United States and Germany' University of Frankfurt Working Paper no 119/2003

Bebchuk L and J Fried *Pay without Performance* (Harvard University Press Cambridge 2004)

Bebchuk L and M Roe 'A Theory of Path Dependence in Corporate Governance and Ownership' (1999) 52 Stanford Law Review 127

Becker R and RG Gilson 'Venture Capital and the Structure of Capital Markets: Banks versus Stock markets' (1998) 47 Journal of Financial Economics 243

Becker R and T Hellmann 'The Genesis of Venture Capital: Lessons from the German Experience' in C Keuschnigg and V Kanniainen (eds) *Venture Capital Entrepreneurship, and Public Policy* (MIT Press Cambridge 2004)

Berglöf E and M Burkart 'EU Takeover Policy' (2003) 18 Economic Policy 173

Berkowitz D, K Pistor and JF Richard 'The Transplant Effect' (2003) 51 American Journal of Comparative Law 163

Black B 'Is Corporate Law Trivial?: A Political and Economic Analysis' (1990) 84 Northwestern University Law Review 542

Boot A and others (eds) *Financial Intermediation* (OUP Oxford 2005, forthcoming)

Bratton WW 'Rules, Principles, and the Accounting Crisis in the United States' (2004) 5 European Business Organization Law Review 7

Bratton WW and JA McCahery 'Comparative Corporate Governance and the Theory of the Firm: the Case Against Global Cross Reference' (1999) 38 Columbia Journal of Transnational Law 213

Burkart M, D Gromb and F Panunzi 'Why Higher Takeover Premia Protect Minority Shareholders' (1998) 106 Journal of Political Economy 172

Burrows P 'Analyzing Legal Paternalism' (1995) 15 International Review of Law and Economics 542

Buxbaum M and KJ Hopt *Legal Harmonization and the Business Enterprise – Corporate and Capital Market Law Harmonization Policy in Europe and the USA* (de Gruyter New York 1988)

Camerer C and others 'Regulation for Conservatives: Behavioral Economics and the Case for "Asymmetric Paternalism"' (2003) 151 University of Pennsylvania Law Review 1211

Carney WJ 'The Production of Corporate Law' (1998) 71 Southern California Law Review 715

Chandler III WB and LE Strine Jr 'The New Federalism of the American Corporate Governance System: Preliminary Reflections of Two Residents of One Small State' (2003) 152 University of Pennsylvania Law Review 953

Coffee JC 'A Theory of Corporate Scandals: Why the US and Europe Differ' Columbia Law and Economics Working Paper no 274/2005

Coffee JC 'The Future as History: The Prospects for Global Convergence in Corporate Governance and its Implications' (1999) 93 Northwestern University Law Review 641

Company Law Review Steering Group 'Modern Company Law for a Competitive Economy: Final Report' URN 01/942 and URN 01/943 <http://www.dti.gov.uk/cld/final_report/index.htm> (12 July 2005)

Corporate Governance Committee, Corporate Governance Forum of Japan, *Corporate Governance Principles –A Japanese View* 1998

Correia da Silva LC and others *Dividend Policy and Corporate Governance* (OUP Oxford 2004)

Cunningham LA 'The Sarbanes-Oxley Yawn: Heavy Rhetoric, Light Reform (and It Might Just Work)' (2003) 35 University of Connecticut Law Review 915

Davies PL 'Enron and Corporate Law Reform in the UK and the European Community in Armour' in J Armour and JA McCahery (eds) *After Enron: Improving Corporate Law and Modernising Securities Regulation in Europe and the US* (Hart Publishing Oxford, forthcoming 2005)

Davies PL 'Post-Enron Developments in the United Kingdom' in G Ferrarini and others (eds) *Reforming Company and Takeover Law in Europe* (OUP Oxford 2004) 185

Davies PL *Principles of Modern Company Law* (7th ed Sweet & Maxwell London 2003)

Davis EA 'The Meaning of Professional Independence' (2003) 103 Columbia Law Review 1281

Djankov S, E Glaeser, R La Porta, F Lopez-de-Silanes and A Shleifer 'The New Comparative Economics' (2003) 31 Journal of Comparative Economics 595-619

Dyck A and L Zingales 'Private Benefits of Control: An International Comparison' (2004) 59 Journal of Finance 537

Easterbrook F and D Fischel *The Economic Structure of Corporate Law* (Harvard University Press Harvard 1991)

Ebke W 'Corporate Governance and Auditor Independence' in G Ferrarini and others (eds) *Reforming Company and Takeover Law in Europe* (OUP Oxford 2004)

Edwards V *EC Company Law* (OUP Oxford 1999)

Efendi J, A Srivastava and E Swanson 'Why Do Corporate Managers Misstate Financial Statements: The Role of Option Compensation, Corporate Governance, and Other Factors' <http://ssrn.com/abstract=547922>

Elsas R and JP Krahnen 'Universal Banks and Relationships with Firms' in JP Krahnen and RH Schmidt (eds) *The German Financial System* (OUP Oxford 2004) 197

Enriques L '"Bad Apples, Bad Oranges" A Comment from Old Europe on Post-Enron Corporate Governance Reforms' (2003) 38 Wake Forest Law Review 911

Ferran E 'Company Law Reform in the UK: A Progress Report' (March 2005) ECGI – Law Working Paper No. 27/2005 <http://ssrn.com/abstract=644203>

Ferran E *Building an EU Securities Market* (Cambridge University Press Cambridge 2004)

Ferrarini G (ed) *European Securities Markets: The Investment Services Directive and Beyond* (Kluwer Law International The Hague 1998)

Ferrarini G 'Exchange Governance and Regulation: An Overview' in G Ferrarini (ed) *European Securities Markets: The Investment Services Directive and Beyond* (Kluwer Law International The Hague 1998) 245

Ferrarini G and P Giudici 'Financial Scandals and the Role of Private Enforcement: The Parmalat Case' in J Armour and JA McCahery (eds) *After Enron: Improving Corporate Law and Modernising Securities Regulation in Europe and the US* (Hart Publishing Oxford, forthcoming 2005)

Ferrarini G, KJ Hopt, J Winter and E Wymeersch (eds) *Reforming Company and Takeover Law in Europe* (OUP Oxford 2004)

Ferrarini G, KJ Hopt and E Wymeersch (eds) *Capital Markets in the Age of the Euro – Cross-Border Transactions, Listed Companies and Regulation* (Kluwer Law International The Hague 2002)

Fligstein N *The Architecture of Markets* (Princeton University Press Princeton and Oxford 2001)

Forum Europaeum Group Law 'Corporate Group Law for Europe' (2000) 1 European Business Organization Law Review 165

Freeman J 'Extending Public Law Norms Through Privatization' (2003) 116 Harvard Law Review 1285

Freeman J 'The Private Role in Public Governance' (2000) 75 New York University Law Review 543

Frentrop P *A History of Corporate Governance 1602-2002* (Deminor Brussels et al. 2003)

Gilson R 'Engineering a Venture Capital Market: Lessons from the American Experience' (2003) Stanford Law Review 1067

Gilson R 'Globalization of Corporate Governance: Convergence of Form or Function' (2001) 49 American Journal of Comparative Law 329-357

Gilson R and JN Gordon 'Controlling Shareholders' (2003) 152 University of Pennsylvania Law Review 785-843

Gilson R and CJ Milhaupt 'Choice as Regulatory Reform: The Case of Japanese Corporate Governance' (2004) Columbia Law and Economics Working Paper No. 251; Stanford Law and Economics Olin Working Paper No. 282; ECGI – Law Working Paper No. 22/2004

Ginsburg T and R Kagan (eds) *Institutions and Public Law: Comparative Approaches* (Peter Lang Berlin 2005)

Goergen M and L Renneboog 'Why are the Levels of Control (so) Different in German and UK companies? Evidence from Initial Public Offerings' (2003) 19 Journal of Law, Economics and Organization 141

Gordon JN 'Convergence on Shareholder Capitalism' in CJ Milhaupt (ed) *Global Markets, Domestic Institutions* (Columbia University Press New York 2003) 214

Gordon JN and M Roe (eds) *Convergence and Persistence in Corporate Governance* (Cambridge University Press Cambridge 2004)

Gorton G and FA Schmid 'Capital, Labor, and the Firm: A Study of German Codetermination' (2004) 2 Journal of the European Economic Association 863

Grundmann S 'European Company Law: From Crisis to Boom' (2004) 5 European Business Organization Law Review 601

Grundmann S and F Möslein 'Golden Shares – State Control in Privatised Companies: Comparative Law, European Law and Policy Aspects' (2001) Euredia 02/4, 623

Hackethal A and others 'Corporate Governance in Germany: Transition to a Modern Capital Market-Based System?' (2003) 159 Journal of Institutional and Theoretical Economics 664

Haley JO 'Heisei Renewal or Heisei Transformation: Are Legal Reforms Really Changing Japan?' (2005) 19 ZJapan R/J Japan L vol 10, 5

Haley JO 'Career Employment, Corporate Governance and Japanese Exceptionalism' (2005) <http://law.wustl. edu/Academics/Faculty/Workingpapers/index.html>

Haley JO *Antitrust in Germany and Japan: The First Fifty Years, 1947-1998* (University of Washington Press Seattle 2001)

Hall PA and D Soskice (eds) *Varieties of Capitalism: The Institutional Foundations of Comparative Advantage* (OUP Oxford 2001)

Hamdani A 'Gatekeeper Liability' (2003) 77 Southern California Law Review 53

Hansmann H and R Kraakman 'The End of History for Corporate Law' (2001) 89 Georgetown Law Journal 439

Hellwig MF 'Corporate Governance and the Financing of Investment for Structural Change' in Deutsche Bundesbank (ed) *Investing Today for the World of Tomorrow – Studies on the Investment Process in Europe* (Springer Verlag Berlin Heidelberg New York 2001) 201

Hellwig MF 'On the Economics and Politics of Corporate Finance and Corporate Control' in X Vives (ed) *Corporate Governance* (Cambridge University Press Cambridge 2000) 95

Hellwig, MF 'Banks, Markets, and the Allocation of Risks in an Economy (1998) 154 Journal of Institutional and Theoretical Economics 328

Hertig G and JA McCahery 'Company and Takeover Law Reforms in Europe: Misguided Harmonization Efforts or Regulatory Competition?' (2003) 4 European Business Organization Law Review 179

Higgs D *Review of the role and effectiveness of non-executive directors* DTI, January 2003

High Level Group of Company Law Experts *Report of the High Level Group of Company Law Experts on Issues Related to Takeover Bids 10.1.2002*, reprinted in G Ferrarini et al (eds) *Reforming Company and Takeover Law in Europe* (OUP Oxford 2004) 825

High Level Group of Company Law Experts *Report of the High Level Group of Company Law Experts on a Modern Regulatory Framework for Company Law in Europe 4.11.2002*

Hood C and others *The Government of Risk: Understanding Risk Regulation Regimes* (OUP Oxford 2001)

Hopt KJ 'Modern Company and Capital Market Problems: Improving European Corporate Governance after Enron' (2002) 3 Journal of Corporate Law Studies 221

Hopt KJ 'Common Principles of Corporate Governance in Europe' in BS Markesinis (ed) *The Clifford Chance Millenium Lectures: The Coming Together of the Common Law and. the Civil Law* (Hart Publishing Oxford 2000) 105, also in JA McCahery et al. (eds) *Corporate Governance Regimes, Convergence and Diversity* (OUP Oxford 2002) 175

Hopt KJ and others (eds) *European Corporate Governance in Company Law and Codes* (Report for the European Commission The Hague 2004)

Hopt KJ, H Kanda, M Roe, E Wymeersch and S Prigge (eds) *Comparative Corporate Governance: The State of the Art and Emerging Research* (OUP Oxford 1998)

Hopt KJ and PC Leyens 'Board Models in Europe – Recent Developments of Internal Corporate Governance Structures in Germany, the United Kingdom, France, and Italy' (2004) 1 European Company and Financial Law Review 135

Hopt KJ and K Pistor 'Company Groups in Transition Economies: A Case for Regulatory Intervention?' (2001) 2 European Business Organization Law Review 1

Hopt KJ and E Wymeersch (eds) *Capital Markets and Company Law* (OUP Oxford 2003)

Hopt KJ and E Wymeersch (eds) *Comparative Corporate Governance – Essays and Materials* (de Gruyter Berlin/New York 1997)

Jackson G 'Corporate Governance in Germany and Japan: Liberalization Pressures and Responses' in K Yamamura and W Streeck (eds) *The End of Diversity? Prospects of German and Japanese Capitalism* (Cornell University Press Ithaca 2003)

James H *The End of Globalisation. Lessons from the Great Depression* (Harvard University Press Cambridge 2000)

Jenkinson T and A Ljungqvist 'The Role of Hostile Stakes in German Corporate Governance' (2001) 7 Journal of Corporate Finance 397

Jolis C, C Sunstein and R Thaler 'A Behavioral Approach to Law and Economics' (1998) 50 Stanford Law Review 1471

Kahan M and M Klausner 'Standardization and Innovation in Corporate Contracting (or "The Economics of Boilerplate")' (1997) 83 Virginia Law Review 713

Kanda H 'Trends in Japanese Corporate Governance' in KJ Hopt and E Wymeersch (eds) *Comparative Corporate Governance* (de Gruyter Berlin New York 1997)

Kanda H and CJ Milhaupt 'Legal Transplants: The Director's Fiduciary Duty in Japanese Corporate Law' (2003) 51 American Journal of Comparative Law 887

Kirchner C 'Competition Policy vs. regulation: administration vs. judiciary' in M Neumann and J Weigand (eds) *The International Handbook of Competition* (Edward Elgar Cheltenham 2004)

Kitch EW 'Regulation of the Securities Market' in B Bouckaert and G de Geest (eds) *Encyclopedia of Law and Economics* (Edward Elgar Cheltenham 2000) vol III 821

Kitschelt H and W Streeck (eds) *Germany: Beyond the Stable State* (Frank Cass Publishers London 2003)

Köndgen J 'Ownership and Corporate Governance of Stock Exchanges' (1998) 154 Journal of Institutional and Theoretical Economics 324

Kraakman R, P Davies, H Hansmann, G Hertig, KJ Hopt, H Kanda and EB Rock *The Anatomy of Corporate Law, A Comparative and Functional Approach* (OUP Oxford 2004)

Krahnen JP and RH Schmidt (eds) *The German Financial System* (OUP Oxford 2004)

Kuran T and CR Sunstein 'Availability Cascades and Risk Regulation' (1999) 51 Stanford Law Review 683

La Porta R, F Lopez-de-Silanes, C Pop-Eleches and A Shleifer 'Judicial Checks and Balances' (2004) 112 Journal of Political Economy 445

La Porta R, F Lopez-de-Silanes, A Shleifer and RW Vishny 'Corporate Ownership Around the World' (1999) 54 Journal of Finance 471

La Porta R, F Lopez-de-Silanes, A Shleifer and RW Vishny 'Law and Finance' (1998) 106 Journal of Political Economy 1113

La Porta R, F Lopez-de-Silanes, A Shleifer and RW Vishny 'Legal Determinants of External Finance' (1997) 52 Journal of Finance 1131

Lincoln JR and ML Gerlach *Japan's Network Economy: Structure, Persistence, and Change* (Cambridge University Press Cambridge 2004)

Mahoney P 'The Common Law and Economic Growth: Hayek Might be Right' (2001) 30 Journal of Legal Studies 503

Manow P 'The Uneasy Compromise of Liberalism and Corporatism in Postwar Germany' (Center for German and European Studies Working Paper Berkeley 1999)

Mäntysaari P *Comparative Corporate Governance, Shareholders as a Rule-maker* (Springer Berlin et al. 2005)

McCahery JA, P Moerland, T Raaijmakers and L Renneboog 'The Economics of the Proposed European Takeover Directive' in G Ferrarini and others (eds) *Reforming Company and Takeover Law in Europe* (OUP Oxford 2004) 575

McCahery JA and others (eds) *Corporate Governance Regimes – Convergence and Diversity* (OUP Oxford 2002) 507

Merkt H 'European Company Law Reform: Struggling for a More Liberal Approach' (2004) 1 European Company and Financial Law Review 3

Milhaupt CJ (ed) *Global Markets, Domestic Institutions: Corporate Law and Governance in a New Era of Cross-Border Deals* (Columbia University Press New York 2003)

Milhaupt CJ 'On the (Fleeting) Existence of the Main Bank System and Other Japanese Economic Institutions' (2002) 27 Law and Social Inquiry 425

Milhaupt CJ 'Creative Norm Destruction: The Evolution of Nonlegal Rules in Japanese Corporate Governance' (2001) 149 University of Pennsylvania Law Review 2083

Milhaupt CJ 'A Relational Theory of Japanese Corporate Governance: Contract, Culture and the Rule of Law' (1996) 37 Harvard International Law Review 3

Milhaupt CJ and MD West *Economic Organizations and Corporate Governance in Japan. The Impact of Formal and Informal Rules* (Oxford University Press Oxford 2004)

Miwa Y *State Competence and Economic Growth in Japan* (Routledge Curzon London 2004)

Miwa Y and JM Ramseyer 'Does Relationship Banking Matter? Japanese Bank-Borrower Ties in Good Times and Bad' (2005) 2 J of Empirical Legal Studies 261

Miwa Y and JM Ramseyer 'Capitalist Politicians, Socialist Bureaucrats? Legends of Government Planning from Japan' (2003) 48 Antitrust Bulletin 595

Miwa Y and JM Ramseyer 'The Fable of *Keiretsu*' (2002) 11 Journal of Economics & Management Strategy 169

Miwa Y and JM Ramseyer 'The Myth of the Main Bank: Japan and Comparative Corporate Governance' (2002) 27 Law & Social Inquiry 401

Miwa Y and JM Ramseyer 'The Value of Prominent Directors: Corporate Governance and Bank Access in Transitional Japan, (2002) 31 Journal of Legal Studies 273

Mülbert PO 'Make it or Break It: The Break-Through Rule as a Break-Through for the European Takeover Directive?' in GA Ferrarini and others (eds) *Reforming Company and Takeover Law in Europe* (OUP Oxford 2004) 711

Noack U and D Zetzsche 'Corporate Governance Reform in Germany: The Second Decade' (Center for Business & Corporate Law Research Paper Series no 10 June 2005) 19 (<http://ssrn.com/abstract=646761> (28 June 2005)

Nottage L and L Wolff 'Corporate Governance and Law Reform in Japan: From the Lost Decade to the End of History?' in R Haak and M Pudelko (eds) *Japanese Management: In Search of a New Balance between Continuity and Change* (Palgrave Macmillan New York 2005) forthcoming

Nottage L 'Japanese Corporate Governance at a Crossroads: Variation in "Varieties of Capitalism"' (2001) 27 The North Carolina Journal of International Law & Commercial Regulation 255

OECD Steering Group on Corporate Governance *Survey of Corporate Governance Developments in OECD Countries* (2003)

Ogus A 'Enforcing Regulation: Do We Need the Criminal Law?' in H Sjögren and G Skögh (eds) *New Perspectives on Economic Crime* (Edward Elgar Cheltenham 2004) 42

Ogus A *Regulation: Legal Form and Economic Theory* (Clarendon Press Oxford 1994)

Partnoy F 'Barbarians at the Gatekeepers? A Proposal for a Modified Strict Liability Regime' (2001) 79 Washington University Law Quarterly 491

Perakis E (ed) *Rights of Minority Shareholders* (Bruylant Brussels 2004)

Pistor K, Y Keinan, J Kleinheisterkamp and M West 'The Evolution of Corporate Law (2002) 23 University of Pennsylvania Journal of International Economic Law 791

Pistor K and C Xu 'Incomplete Law' (2003) 35 Journal of International Law and Politics 931

Plessis JJ du and O Sandrock 'The Rise and Fall of Supervisory Codetermination in Germany?' (2005) 16 International Company and Commercial Law Review 67

Prigge S 'A Survey of German Corporate Governance' in KJ Hopt and others (eds) *Comparative Corporate Governance* (OUP Oxford 1998) 943

Rajan RG and L Zingales 'Banks and Markets: The Changing Character of European Finance' in V Gaspar P Hartmann and O Sleijpen (eds) *Second ECB Central European Banking Conference: The Transformation of the European Financial System* (European Central Bank Frankfurt 2003) 124

Rajan RG and L Zingales 'The Great Reversals: The Politics of Financial Development in the 20th Century' (2003) 69 Journal of Financial Economics 5

Rajan RG and L Zingales *Saving Capitalism from the Capitalists* (Random House Business Books London 2003)

Ramseyer JM and M Nakazato *Japanese Law: An Economic Approach* (University of Chicago Press Chicago 1999)

Rickford J 'Fundamentals, Developments and Trends in British Company Law – Some Wider Reflections' (part I) (2004) 4 European and Financial Law Review (vol 1) 391; (part II) (2005) 1 European and Financial Law Review (vol 2) 63

Rickford J 'Codes and Codification of Corporate Governance – The UK Perspective and Europe' Working Paper prepared for the CEPS Roundtable Conference on Corporate Governance Reform in the European Union (2004)

Rieckers O and G Spindler 'Corporate Governance: Legal Aspects' in JP Krahnen and RH Schmidt (eds) *The German Financial System* (OUP Oxford 2004) 350

Roe, MJ *Political Determinants of Corporate Governance: Political Context, Corporate Impact* (OUP Oxford 2003)

Röhl W (ed) *History of Law in Japan Since 1868, Handbook of Oriental Studies* vol 12 (Brill Leiden and Boston 2005)

Rokumoto K 'Law and Culture in Transition' (2001) 49 American Journal of Comparative Law 545

Romano R 'The Sarbanes-Oxley Act and the Making of Quack Corporate Governance' ECGI Finance Working Paper no 52/2004

Romano R 'Empowering Investors: A Market Approach to Securities Regulation' in KJ Hopt and others (eds) *Comparative Corporate Governance: The State of the Art and Emerging Research* (OUP Oxford 1998) 163

Romano R *The Genius of American Corporate Law* (AEI Press Washington DC 1993)

Schaede U *Cooperative Capitalism: Self-Regulation, Trade Association, and the Antimonopoly Law in Japan* (OUP Oxford 2000)

Schmidt RH 'Corporate Governance in Germany: An Economic Perspective' in JP Krahnen and RH Schmidt (eds) *The German Financial System* (OUP Oxford 2004) 386

Schmidt RH and G Spindler 'Path Dependence and Complementarity in Corporate Governance' in J Gordon and M Roe (eds) *Convergence and Persistence in Corporate Governance* (Cambridge University Press Cambridge 2004) 114

Schmidt RH and G Spindler 'Path Dependence, Corporate Governance and Complementarity' (2002) 5 International Finance 311

Schmidt RH and M Tyrell 'What Constitutes a Financial System in General and the German Financial System in Particular?' in JP Krahnen and RH Schmidt (eds) *The German Financial System* (OUP Oxford 2004) 19

Schmidt RH and M Tyrell 'Financial Systems, Corporate Finance and Corporate Governance' (1997) 3 European Financial Management 159

Shiller RJ *Irrational Exuberance* (Princeton University Press Princeton 2001)

Shishido Z 'Reform in Japanese Corporate Law and Corporate Governance: Current Changes in Historical Perspective' (1999) 49 American Journal of Comparative Law 653

Shleifer A *Inefficient Markets* (OUP Oxford 2000)

Shleifer A and R Vishny 'A Survey of Corporate Governance' (1997) 52 Journal of Finance 737

Sidak JG and DF Spulber *Deregulatory Takings and the Regulatory Contract – The Competitive Transformation of Network Industries in the United States* (Cambridge University Press Cambridge 1998)

Siebert H *The German Economy: Beyond the Social Market* (Princeton University Press Princeton 2005)

Smith Report – Financial Reporting Council *Audit Committees: Combined Code Guidance. A report and proposed guidance by an FRC-appointed group chaired by Sir Robert Smith* January 2003

Streeck W and K Yamamura 'Introduction: Convergence or Diversity? Stability and Change in German and Japanese Capitalism' in K Yamamura and W Streeck (eds) *The End of Diversity? Prospects for German and Japanese Capitalism* (Cornell University Press Ithaca 2003) 13

Sunstein CR *Risk and Reason: Safety, Law, and the Environment* (Cambridge University Press Cambridge 2002)

Sunstein CR (ed) *Behavioral Law and Economics* (Cambridge University Press Cambridge 2000)

Sunstein CR 'Behavioral Analysis of Law' (1997) 64 University of Chicago Law Review 1175

Sunstein CR 'Legal Interference with Private Preferences' (1986) 53 University of Chicago Law Review 1129

Teubner G 'Legal Irritants: How Unifying Law ends up in New Divergences' in A Hall and D Soscice (eds) *Varieties of Capitalism* (OUP Oxford 2001)

Vagts D (ed) *Business and Private Organization, International Encyclopedia of Comparative Law* vol XIII (Tuebingen, Dordrecht et al. Mohr Siebeck, Martinus Nijhoff 1972 et s)

Vermeulen EPM *The Evolution of Legal Business Forms in Europe and the United States* (Kluwer Law International The Hague 2003)

Wahlgren P (ed) *Company Law, Scandinavian Studies in Law* vol 45 (Stockholm University Stockholm 2003)

Yamamura K and W Streeck (eds) *The End of Diversity? Prospects for German and Japanese Capitalism* (Cornell University Press Ithaca 2003)

Zamir E 'The Efficiency of Paternalism' (1998) 84 Virginia Law Review 229

Zingales L 'The Costs of Financial Regulation' (Working Paper, available at ssrn.com)

Zürn M and C Joerges (eds) *Law and Governance in Postnational Europe: Compliance Beyond the Nation-State* (Cambridge University Press Cambridge 2005)

Annex 1

Modernising Company Law and Enhancing Corporate Governance in the European Union – A Plan to Move Forward

COMMISSION OF THE EUROPEAN COMMUNITIES

Brussels, 21.5.2003
COM (2003) 284 final

COMMUNICATION FROM THE COMMISSION TO THE COUNCIL AND THE EUROPEAN PARLIAMENT

Modernising Company Law and Enhancing Corporate Governance in the European Union – A Plan to Move Forward

COMMUNICATION FROM THE COMMISSION TO THE COUNCIL AND THE EUROPEAN PARLIAMENT

Modernising Company Law and Enhancing Corporate Governance in the European Union – A Plan to Move Forward

TABLE OF CONTENTS

INTRODUCTION

A dynamic and flexible company law and corporate governance framework is essential for a modern, dynamic, interconnected industrialised society. Essential for millions of investors. Essential for deepening the internal market and building an integrated European capital market. Essential for maximising the benefits of enlargement for all the Member States, new and existing.

Good company law, good corporate governance practices throughout the EU will enhance the real economy:

– An effective approach will foster the global **efficiency and competitiveness of businesses** in the EU. Well managed companies, with strong corporate governance records and sensitive social and environmental performance, outperform their competitors. Europe needs more of them to generate employment and higher long term sustainable growth.

– An effective approach will help to strengthen shareholders rights and third parties protection. In particular, it will contribute to rebuilding European investor confidence in the wake of a wave of recent corporate governance scandals. The livelihood of millions of Europeans, their pensions, their investments are tied up in the proper, responsible performance and governance of listed companies in which they invest.

Scope

This Communication outlines the approach that the Commission intends to follow specifically in the area of **company law and corporate governance.**

Achieving the objectives pursued (fostering efficiency and competitiveness of business, and strengthening shareholders rights and third parties protection) requires a **fully integrated approach**.

Related initiatives, forming part of this integrated approach but not part of this Action Plan, include:

– **The Financial Services Action Plan**[1] **of 1999**, which confirmed the overall objectives which should guide the financial services policy at EU level and set out a framework for an integrated capital market by 2005;

– **The Financial Reporting Strategy**[2] **of 2000**, which seeks to achieve high quality financial reporting through the adoption of a common set of accounting standards and the development of a proper enforcement system, which led to the adoption in 2002 of the Regulation on the application of the international accounting standards;

– **The Communication on Corporate Social Responsibility**[3] **of 2002**, which

[1] Financial Services: Implementing the Framework for financial markets – Action Plan, Communication of the Commission, COM (1999) 232, 11.05.99.

[2] EU Financial Reporting Strategy: the way forward, Communication of the Commission, COM (2000) 359, 13.06.00.

[3] Corporate Social Responsibility: A business contribution to Sustainable Development, Communication of the Commission, COM (2002) 347, 02.07.02. The European Multi-Stakeholder Forum on CSR brings together representative organisations of business, trade-unions and civil society. It will present in 2004 a report about its works to the Commission, which should then make an evaluation of

addresses the social and environmental dimension of business in a global economy and led to the setting

up of a European Multi-Stakeholder Forum with a view to promoting voluntary social and environmental practices of business, linked to their core activities, which go beyond their existing legal obligations;

– The **Communication on Industrial Policy in an Enlarged Europe**[4] of 2002, which addresses the need for EU industry to achieve a more sustainable production structure as a driver of growth and productivity.
– **The Communication on the priorities for the statutory audit in the EU**, which is published together with the present Communication and which covers an EU policy approach aimed at ensuring audit quality and public confidence in the audit profession. It covers issues like the use of ISA's (International Standards on Auditing), public oversight of auditors, and the modernisation of the Eighth Company Law Directive into a comprehensive principles-based approach.

Responding to the High Level Group's report

On 4 November 2002, **a High Level Group of Company Law Experts** appointed by Commissioner Bolkestein in September 2001 and chaired by Jaap Winter presented its Final Report on "A modern regulatory framework for company law in Europe". This report focused on corporate governance in the EU and the modernisation of European Company Law. **The Competitiveness Council** (30 September 2002) invited the Commission to organise an indepth discussion on the forthcoming report and to develop – in co-ordination with Member States – an Action Plan for Company Law, including Corporate Governance, as soon as is feasible, declaring its intention to deal with the Action Plan as a matter of priority. The Ecofin Council has also shown a major interest in this work.
This Communication is the **Commission's response**. It explains why the European regulatory framework for company law and corporate governance needs to be modernised. It defines the key policy objectives which should inspire any future action to be taken at EU level in these areas. It includes an action plan, prioritised, over the short, medium and long term. It indicates which type of regulatory instrument should be used[5], and by when.

Guiding political criteria

In developing this Action Plan, the Commission has paid particular attention to the need for any regulatory response at European level to respect a number of guiding criteria:

– It should fully respect the **subsidiarity and proportionality** principles of the Treaty and the diversity of many different approaches to the same questions in the Member

its results, decide on its future and consider any other appropriate initiative.

4 Industrial Policy in an Enlarged Europe, Communication of the Commission, COM (2002) 714, 11.12.02.

5 When a legislative instrument is considered, this means that the action envisaged requires either the adoption of a new legislative proposal or the modification of one or several existing legislative instruments.

States, while at the same time pursuing clear ambitions (strengthening the single market and enhancing the rights of shareholders and third parties);

– It should be **flexible in application, but firm in the principles**. It should concentrate on priorities; be transparent; and subject to proper due process and consultation;

– It should help **shape international regulatory developments**. The EU must define its own European corporate governance approach, tailored to its own cultural and business traditions. Indeed, this is an opportunity for the Union to strengthen its influence in the world with good, sensible corporate governance rules. Corporate governance is indeed an area where standards are increasingly being set at international level, as evidenced by the recent developments observed in the United States. **The Sarbanes-Oxley Act**, adopted on 30 July 2002 in the wave of a series of scandals, delivered a rapid response. The Act unfortunately creates a series of problems due to its outreach effects on European companies and auditors, and the Commission is engaged in an intense regulatory dialogue with a view to negotiating acceptable solutions with the US authorities (in particular the Securities and Exchange Commission). In many areas, the EU shares the same broad objectives and principles of the Sarbanes-Oxley Act and in some areas robust, equivalent regulatory approaches already exist in the EU. In some other areas, new initiatives are necessary. Earning the right to be recognised as at least "equivalent" alongside other national and international rules is a legitimate and useful end in itself.

1. MODERNISING COMPANY LAW AND ENHANCING CORPORATE GOVERNANCE: THE EU ACQUIS AND THE NEED FOR NEW INITIATIVES

1.1. The EU Company Law Acquis

Historically, most of the initiatives taken at EU level in the area of company law have been based on **Article 44 (2) g (ex 54) of the Treaty** establishing the European Community. This Article, which appears in the Chapter devoted to the right of establishment, requires the European institutions to attain freedom of establishment, *"by co-ordinating to the necessary extent the safeguards which, for the protection of the interests of members and others, are required by Member States of companies or firms within the meaning of the second paragraph of Article 48 (ex 58), with a view to making such safeguards equivalent throughout the Community".*

This Article has been interpreted to include two important grounds for the adoption of EU initiatives in the area of company law:

a) **facilitating freedom of establishment of companies**: the harmonisation of a number of minimum requirements makes it easier for companies to establish themselves in other Member States where the regulatory framework is similar;

b) **guaranteeing legal certainty in intra-Community operations**, where the presence of a number of common safeguards is key for the creation of trust in cross-border economic relationships.

Over the years, the EU institutions have taken a number of initiatives in the area of company law, many leading to **impressive achievements**[6]. Between 1968 (adoption of the First Company Law Directive) and 1989 (adoption of the Twelfth Company Law Directive), nine Directives and one Regulation were adopted. Although the exact situation may differ from one Member State to the other, these European measures have had an **important impact** on national company law. Moreover, their influence was not limited to the types of companies expressly covered in the Directives, because many Member States decided to extend their provisions to other legal forms.

Over the last ten years, the EU company law legislative process has been characterised, in the wake of the Maastricht Treaty of 1992, by more political deference to national law (with a higher number of references to national rules in the legislative proposals). This **more flexible approach** to harmonisation made possible, in particular, the adoption of the European Company Statute (Societas Europaea), in October 2001.

1.2. Reasons for new initiatives at EU level

Now is the right time to give a fresh and ambitious impetus to the EU company law harmonisation process. New initiatives, aiming either at modernising the existing EU company law instruments or at completing the EU framework with a limited number of new, tailored instruments, are needed for the following reasons:

[6] See in Annex 2 the table of existing and proposed European legal instruments in the area of company law.

- **Making the most of the Internal Market**: the growing trend of European companies to operate cross-border in the Internal Market calls for common European company law mechanisms, inter alia, to facilitate freedom of establishment and cross-border restructuring.
- **Integration of capital markets**: dynamic securities markets are vital to Europe's economic future[7]. This requires giving both issuers and investors the opportunity to be far more active on other EU capital markets and to have confidence that the companies they invest in have equivalent corporate governance frameworks. Listed companies want a more coherent, dynamic and responsive European legislative framework.
- **To maximise the benefits of modern technologies** : the rapid development of new information and communication technology (video conferencing, electronic mail and above all the Internet) is affecting the way company information is stored and disseminated[8], as well as the way corporate life is conducted (e.g. virtual general meetings, video-link board meetings, exercise of cross-border voting rights).
- **Enlargement:** the forthcoming enlargement of the EU to 10 new Member States is another gilt-edged reason to revisit the scope of EU company law. The new member countries will increase the diversity of the national regulatory frameworks in the EU, underlying further the importance of a principles-based approach able to maintain a high level of legal certainty in intra-Community operations. In addition to that, initiatives to modernise the EU Acquis will become more urgent than ever to ease the rapid and full transition of these countries to becoming fully competitive modern market economies.
- **Addressing the challenges raised by recent events:** Recent financial scandals have prompted a new, active debate on corporate governance, and the necessary restoration of confidence is one more reason for new initiatives at EU level. Investors, large and small, are demanding more transparency and better information on companies, and are seeking to gain more influence on the way the public companies they own operate. Shareholders own companies, not management - yet far too frequently their rights have been trampled on by shoddy, greedy and occasionally fraudulent corporate behaviour. A new sense of proportion and fairness is necessary.

2. KEY POLICY OBJECTIVES

The Commission considers that future actions at EU level in the area of company law should seek as much as possible to meet the following two policy objectives.

[7] See "Quantification of the Macro-Economic Impact of Integration of EU Financial Markets", Final Report to the European Commission – Directorate-General for the Internal Market by London Economics (in association with PricewaterhouseCoopers and Oxford Economic Forecasting), 12 November 2002, <http://europa.eu.int/comm/internal_market/en/finances/mobil/overview.htm>.

[8] See in this respect the Proposal of June 2002 for a Directive amending the First Company Law Directive, as regards disclosure requirements in respect of certain types of companies, which introduces modern technologies in trade registers. The proposed modifications would allow full advantage to be taken of modern technologies: companies would be able to file their documents and particulars either by paper means or by electronic means, and interested parties would be able to obtain copies by either means.

2.1. Strengthening shareholders rights and third parties protection

Ensuring effective and proportionate protection of shareholders and third parties must be **at the core of any company law policy**. A sound framework for protection of members and third parties, which properly achieves a **high degree of confidence** in business relationships, is a fundamental condition for business efficiency and competitiveness. In particular, an effective regime for the protection of shareholders and their rights, protecting the savings and pensions of millions of people and strengthening the foundations of capital markets for the long term in a context of diversified shareholding within the EU, is essential if companies are to raise capital at the lowest cost.

Maintaining efficient protection of members and third parties will be even more important in the future, in view of the **increasing mobility of companies** within the EU.

To allow European companies to reap the benefits of the unified Internal Market and of the integrating European capital market, ensuring adequate protection of members and third parties should be organised along the following lines:

- The Commission considers firstly that some new tailored initiatives should be taken with a view to enhancing **shareholder rights** and clarifying management responsibilities; and secondly the provisions related to the **protection of creditors** should be modernised with a view to maintaining a high quality framework (e.g. with respect to capital maintenance and alteration).
- A proper **distinction should be made between categories of companies**. A more stringent framework is desirable for listed companies[9] and companies which have publicly raised capital. They should be subject to a certain number of appropriate detailed rules, in particular in the area of disclosure. With respect to other companies, regulatory initiatives should take full account of both their form and size, allowing a more flexible framework for SME's (in the same way as tailored deregulation initiatives have been taken at national level).
- **Modern technologies** can significantly help members and third parties to exercise their rights effectively. At a minimum, company law should enable and encourage as much as possible the use of up-to-date information and communication technologies by companies in their various relationships with members and third parties. The Commission furthermore considers that proper attention must be paid to specific areas where the protection of shareholders and third parties may make it necessary to compel companies to use modern technologies. However, the time has not come yet where the use of modern technologies should be imposed by companies systematically on all members and third parties systematically without the necessary safeguards

[9] The words "listed companies" used in the present Communication cover the companies whose securities are admitted to trading on a regulated market within the meaning of Council Directive 93/22/EEC (OJ L 41, 11.06.1993, p. 27, as last amended by Directive 2000/64/EC of the European Parliament and of the Council (OJ L 290, 17.11.2000, p. 27)) in one or more Member States. The present Action Plan provides where necessary explicit information on the scope of the various actions proposed. In short, the actions presented in the Corporate Governance Section in principle cover listed companies, although some of them are considered to be usefully applicable also to non listed companies. The actions presented in the other sections are generally applicable to all companies, except for the section on pyramids which by nature covers listed companies only.

- The development of a sound economy requires a high degree of confidence in the relationships between the various actors involved, so that the protection of members and third parties will be ensured by a limited number of measures aimed at **combating fraud and abuse** of legal forms. Such measures should be carefully designed, with a view to avoiding that they unduly hinder the development and use of efficient company law structures and systems, which the promotion of efficient and competitive business requires.

2.2. Fostering efficiency and competitiveness of business

Business efficiency and competitiveness, which are crucial components of economic growth and job creation, depend on many factors, one of which is a sound framework of company law. Key to the achievement of this objective is the setting up of a proper balance between actions at EU level and actions at national level. Some company law rules are likely to be best dealt with, and updated, more efficiently at national level, and some competition between national rules may actually be healthy for the efficiency of the single market.

With due respect of the subsidiarity and proportionality principles, business efficiency and competitiveness should be promoted along the following lines:

- EU initiatives in the area of company law should certainly address a number of specific **cross-border issues** (e.g. cross-border merger or transfer of seat, cross-border impediments to the exercise of shareholders rights…), where Community action may be the only way to achieve the pursued objectives.
- In addition to these specific cross-border issues, the necessary attention should be paid to the other initiatives which the promotion of business efficiency and competitiveness requires. As stated above, a certain degree of harmonisation of **defined national issues** reduces legal uncertainties and can thereby significantly enhance business efficiency and competitiveness.
- **Flexibility** should be available to companies as much as possible: where systems are deemed to be equivalent, maximum room should be left open to the freedom of the parties involved.

3. AN EU ACTION PLAN

Achieving the above policy objectives requires a number of initiatives to be taken at EU level in the coming years. The following approach is proposed:

– **Distinguishing the actions in three phases** (short term, medium term, long term), based on clear priorities.
– **Expert consultation** should be an integral part of the preparation of initiatives at EU level in the area of company law and corporate governance. The Commission therefore will regularly seek advice from representatives of Member States, as is the case of the current Group of Company Law National Experts, but also from representatives of the business and the academic sectors, to provide the necessary external input.
– This Communication will be open for public consultation until 31 August 2003. An **open, public consultation** will also be organised where appropriate in the future on the major initiatives following from the Action Plan.
– With respect specifically to corporate governance, a European Corporate Governance Forum will be convened once or twice a year to contribute to co-ordinating the corporate governance efforts of Member States, as is explained in Section 3.1.4. below.

The present Action Plan identifies the nature and the scope of the actions which appear necessary, proposes the type of regulatory instrument which should be used, and establishes clear priorities for the short, medium and long term.

3.1. Corporate Governance

Corporate Governance, which can be defined in many ways, is usually understood as **the system by which companies are directed and controlled**[10]. It is, in the light of the recent corporate scandals, now a major issue globally. Poor corporate governance performance, by some companies, has greatly undermined confidence in capital markets.

Within the EU, Member States have different systems of corporate governance, which reflect their different cultures and the various views about the roles of corporations and the way in which their industry should be financed. Over the last years, corporate governance has been the subject of an increasingly intense debate. **Forty or so corporate governance codes relevant to the European Union have been adopted over the last decade**, at national or international level, with the aim of better protecting the interests of shareholders and/or stakeholders.

[10] Cadbury Report, December 1992. For a more comprehensive definition, see for example the OECD Principles of 1999: "Corporate governance involves a set of relationships between a company's management, its board, its shareholders and other stakeholders. Corporate governance also provides the structure through which the objectives of the company are set, and the means of attaining those objectives and monitoring performance are determined." Corporate governance essentially focuses on the problems that result from the separation of ownership and control, and addresses in particular the principal-agent relationship between shareholders and directors.

Differences in national corporate governance arrangements may create uncertainty and costs for both issuers and investors, which need to be addressed to promote an efficient integration of EU capital markets. As announced in its 1999 Financial Services Action Plan, the Commission launched in 2001 a review of the main corporate governance codes relevant to the EU. The **full comparative study**, prepared for the Commission by Weil, Gotshal & Manges LLP, was finalised in March 2002[11] and concluded **that the EU should not devote time and effort to the development of a European corporate governance code**: the study identified as a more valuable area for the European Commission to focus its efforts on the reduction of legal and regulatory barriers to shareholder engagement in cross-border voting ("participation barriers") as well as the reduction of barriers to shareholders ability to evaluate the governance of companies ("information barriers").

The need for a European code and for additional disclosure of corporate governance practices, as well as a series of additional issues raised by the **Oviedo Council in April 2002** in the wake of the US scandals (the role of non-executive directors and of supervisory boards, management remuneration, management responsibility for financial statements, and auditing practices), were also considered by the **High Level Group of Company Law Experts**. In its Final Report, it confirmed that there is no need for an EU corporate governance code.

In this line of thinking, the Commission observes, firstly, that the main differences between Member States are found in differing company law and securities regulation, as opposed to the corporate governance codes which, according to the March 2002 study, show a remarkable degree of convergence, and, secondly, that the existence of many codes in the EU is not generally perceived as a difficulty by issuers (many issuers continue to be active primarily on their domestic market; when they are active on other markets, they are faced with codes that are pretty similar; and in the rare instances where codes provisions are divergent, the "comply or explain" principle offers a satisfactory solution).

Moreover the Commission considers that:

a) the adoption of a European code would not achieve full information for investors about the key corporate governance rules applicable to companies across Europe, as these rules would still be based on - and part of - national company laws that are in certain respects widely divergent;

b) the adoption of such a code would not contribute significantly to the improvement of corporate governance in the EU, as this code would have either to allow for many different options or confine itself to abstract principles. Trying to harmonise all the elements of a European code would take years and would not be achievable in a reasonable timeframe.

There is nevertheless an active role for the EU to play in corporate governance, because some specific rules and principles need to be agreed at EU level in Directives or Recommendations and a certain co-ordination of corporate governance codes in the EU should be organised to encourage further convergence and the exchange of best practice.

[11] Comparative Study of the Corporate Governance Codes relevant to the European Union and its Member States: <http://europa.eu.int/comm/internal_market/en/company/company/news/corp-gov-codes-rpt_en.htm>.

Therefore at this stage the Commission considers that:

– There is little indication that the development of a European corporate governance code as an additional layer between principles developed at the international level and codes adopted at national level would offer significant added value. In that respect, the Commission notes that corporate governance is now at the forefront of the activities of the OECD, which recently decided to revise its corporate governance principles of 1999 with the aim of adopting a modernised version of these principles in 2004. The Commission is taking an active part in this exercise.

– A self-regulatory market approach, based solely on non-binding recommendations, is clearly not always sufficient to guarantee the adoption of sound corporate governance practices. Only in the presence of a certain number of made-to-measure rules, markets are able to play their disciplining role in an efficient way. In view of the growing integration of European capital markets, **a common approach should be adopted at EU level with respect to a few essential rules and adequate co-ordination of corporate governance codes should be ensured**.

More specifically, the Commission, largely in line with the High Level Group's suggestions, intends to proceed along the following lines[12].

3.1.1. Enhancing Corporate Governance disclosure

Annual Corporate Governance Statement

Listed companies should be required to include in their annual report and accounts a coherent and descriptive statement covering the key elements of their corporate governance structure and practices, which should at least include the following items:

a) the operation of the shareholder meeting and its key powers, and the description of shareholder rights and how they can be exercised;

b) the composition and operation of the board and its committees[13];

c) the shareholders holding major holdings, and their voting and control rights as well as key agreements;

d) the other direct and indirect relationships between these major shareholders and the company;

e) any material transactions with other related parties;

[12] In developing its approach, the Commission has paid particular attention to the following needs: considering where possible a) the use of alternatives to legislation, and b) the preference to be given to disclosure requirements (because they are less intrusive in corporate life, and they can prove to be a highly effective market-led way of rapidly achieving results).

[13] In this respect, it is considered essential for the restoration of public confidence that proper information is given on the way in which the company has organised itself at the highest level to establish and maintain an effective internal control system.

f) the existence and nature of a risk management system;

g) and a reference to a code on corporate governance, designated for use at national level, with which the company complies or in relation to which it explains deviations.

A proposal for a Directive containing the principles applicable to such an annual corporate governance statement, which should appear prominently in the annual documents published by listed companies, is regarded by the Commission as a priority for the short term, so as to rapidly allow market pressures to be better exerted. The definition of these principles will properly take into account the related requirements present in existing (e.g. major holdings[14]) or proposed (e.g. take-over bids) instruments.

Information about the role played by institutional investors

Institutional investors should be obliged:

a) to disclose their investment policy and their policy with respect to the exercise of voting rights in companies in which they invest;

b) to disclose to their beneficial holders at their request how these rights have been used in a particular case.

Such requirements would not only improve the internal governance of institutional investors themselves, but would also enhance participation by institutional investors in the affairs of the companies in which they invest. A requirement for institutional investors to systematically exercise their voting rights is not considered desirable, in view of its potential counterproductive effects (due to a lack of time or resources, institutional investors might simply vote in favour of any proposed resolution to fulfil the requirement).

Institutional investors have an important role to play in the governance of companies in which they invest. Fostering this role will require amendments to a series of existing legal texts (relating to insurance companies, pension funds, mutual and other investment funds, ...), and even more importantly the introduction of such a requirement would deliver its full effects only once the problems related to cross-border voting will have been solved. The Commission therefore intends to take the necessary steps in the medium term.

3.1.2. Strengthening shareholders' rights

Access to information

Shareholders of listed companies should be provided with electronic facilities to access the relevant information in advance of General Meetings. This issue is currently addressed by the Proposal for a Transparency Directive, which essentially enables listed companies to

[14] See Directive 2001/34/EC of the European Parliament and of the Council of 28 May 2001 on the admission of securities to official stock exchange listing and on information to be published on securities (Title IV – Chapter III "Obligations relating to the information to be published when a major holding in a listed company is acquired or disposed of").

use electronic means to inform their shareholders[15] and contains specific provisions guaranteeing a timely access to regulated information when securities are listed in another Member State than the home Member State[16]. The Commission considers this solution as a significant and proportionate first step, which does not preclude the adoption of further measures (which would generally require listed companies to use electronic means to inform their shareholders) in the medium term, if this looks desirable in the light of the implementation of the Transparency Directive (which itself contains a revision clause).

Other shareholders' rights

There is a need for enhancing the exercise of a series of shareholders' rights in listed companies (right to ask questions, to table resolutions, to vote in absentia, to participate in general meetings via electronic means). These facilities should be offered to shareholders across the EU, and specific problems relating to cross-border voting should be solved urgently. The Commission considers that the necessary framework should be developed in a Directive, since an effective exercise of these rights requires a number of legal difficulties to be solved. In view of the important benefits expected from such a framework, the Commission regards the relevant proposal as a priority for the short term.

Shareholder democracy

Strengthening shareholders' rights should be based essentially on a) the provision of comprehensive information on what the various existing rights are and how they can be exercised and b) the development of the facilities necessary to make sure that these existing rights can be effectively exercised. This approach is fully consistent with the OECD Principles of Corporate Governance[17].

The Commission considers that there is a strong medium to long term case for aiming to establish a real shareholder democracy in the EU. The Comparative Study of Corporate Governance Codes relevant to the EU evidenced that corporate governance codes tend to support the one share / one vote principle, although many codes favour some flexibility in this respect. The hardest line is taken by the codes issued by bodies affiliated with investors, which clearly do not support the issuance of shares with reduced or no voting rights. The Commission nevertheless observes that any initiative in this direction, which would give further effect to the principle of proportionality between capital and control advocated by the High Level Group in its First Report on issues related to take-over bids, requires prior study. The Commission therefore intends to undertake a study, in the short to medium term, on the consequences which such an approach would entail.

[15] The home Member State shall allow issuers the use of electronic means for the purposes of conveying information to shareholders, provided such a decision is taken in a general meeting and meets a series of conditions, including the individual consent of the shareholder concerned (See Article 13).

[16] A host Member State may require issuers: a) to publish regulated information on their Internet sites, and b) to alert any interested person, without delay and free of charge, to any new disclosure or any change to regulated information which has already been published (See Article 17).

[17] See the relevant statements, about disclosure (Capital structures and arrangements that enable certain shareholders to obtain a degree of control disproportionate to their equity ownership should be disclosed) and about exercise of rights (shareholders should have the opportunity to participate effectively and vote in general shareholder meetings).

3.1.3. Modernising the board of directors

Board composition

In key areas where executive directors clearly have **conflicts of interests** (i.e. remuneration of directors, and supervision of the audit of the company's accounts), decisions in listed companies should be made exclusively by **non-executive or supervisory directors** who are in the majority independent. With respect to the nomination of directors for appointment by the body competent under national company law, the responsibility for identifying candidates to fill board vacancies should in principle be entrusted to a group composed mainly of executive directors, since executive directors can usefully bring their deep knowledge of the challenges facing the company and of the skills and experience of the human resources grown up within the company. Non-executive directors should, nonetheless, also be included and specific safeguards should be put in place to deal with conflicts of interests when they arise, for example when a decision has to be made on the reappointment of a director.

These requirements should be enforced by Member States at least on a "comply or explain" basis. Certain minimum standards of what cannot be considered to be independent should be established at EU level. With a view to fostering a concrete and active role for non executive or supervisory directors, particular attention will be paid to the issue of the number of mandates that may be held concurrently. Moreover, the impact of interlocking directorships on the independence of directors should be properly addressed in the minimum standards to be established.

The Commission regards these measures as key to the restoration of confidence in the markets, and therefore intends to adopt a Commission Recommendation to this effect in the short term.

Such a Recommendation will define minimum standards applicable to the creation, composition and role of the **nomination, remuneration and audit committees**. In view of the recent accounting scandals, special emphasis will be placed on the audit committee (or equivalent body), with a view to fostering the key role it should play in supervising the audit function, both in its external aspects (selecting the external auditor for appointment by shareholders, monitoring the relationship with the external auditor including non-audit fees if any) and its internal aspects (reviewing the accounting policies, and monitoring the internal audit procedures and the company's risk management system)[18].

The High Level Group further recommended that at least listed companies in the EU should generally have the option between a **one-tier board structure** (with executive and non-executive directors) **and a two-tier board structure** (with managing directors and supervisory directors). The Commission welcomes the idea to offer additional organisational freedom to listed companies, but recognises that the implications of such a proposal should be carefully studied. Much has to be learned in this respect from the adaptation of national law to the Regulation and the Directive on the European Company

[18] In developing the minimum standards applicable to the audit committee, appropriate attention will be paid to a) the access it must have to the relevant information (there might be a scope for specific consideration of the need for greater legal protection for whistleblowers) and b) the extent to which transparency on its activities is desirable.

Statute. The Commission therefore proposes that this recommendation from the High Level Group should be followed up in the medium term.

Directors' remuneration

Shareholders should be able to appreciate fully the relation between the performance of the company and the level of remuneration of directors, both ex ante and ex post, and they should be able to make decisions on the remuneration items linked to the share price. Agreeing with the High Level Group, the Commission considers that an appropriate regulatory regime should be composed of **four key items** (disclosure of remuneration policy in the annual accounts, disclosure of details of remuneration of individual directors in the annual accounts, prior approval by the shareholder meeting of share and share option schemes in which directors participate, proper recognition in the annual accounts of the costs of such schemes for the company).

In order to promote a swift application of such a regime, a Commission Recommendation should be adopted to this effect. The Commission regards this action as key to the restoration of confidence, and intends to adopt such a Recommendation in the short term and to closely monitor its application with a view to identifying whether any further additional rulemaking may be desirable in the medium term.

Directors' responsibilities

With a view to enhancing directors' responsibilities, the **collective responsibility** of all board members for financial and key non financial statements (including the annual corporate governance statement mentioned above in Section 3.1.1.) should be confirmed as a matter of EU law. The Commission considers that such a confirmation in framework provisions constitutes a first step which may be achieved rapidly, and intends to take the necessary initiatives in the short term.

The High Level Group made several other recommendations designed to enhance directors responsibilities : a) introduction of a **special investigation right**, whereby shareholders holding a certain percentage of the share capital should have the right to ask a court or administrative authority to authorise a special investigation into the affairs of the company; b) development of a **wrongful trading rule**, whereby directors would be held personally accountable for the consequences of the company's failure, if it is foreseeable that the company cannot continue to pay its debts and they don't decide either to rescue the company and ensure payment or to put it into liquidation; c) imposition of **directors' disqualification** across the EU as a sanction for misleading financial and non-financial statements and other forms of misconduct by directors. The Commission supports these ideas, whose implementation requires further analysis, and therefore intends to present the relevant proposal for a Directive in the medium term.

3.1.4. Co-ordinating corporate governance efforts of Member States

The Commission shares the view of the High Level Group that **the EU should actively co-ordinate the corporate governance efforts of Member States** through their company laws, securities laws, listing rules, codes, or otherwise. In particular, each Member State should progress towards designating a code of corporate governance, designated for use at national level, as the code with which listed companies subject to their jurisdiction are to comply or in relation to which they are to explain deviations. Co-ordination should not only extend to the making of these national codes, but also to the procedures Member States have in place to monitor and enforce compliance and disclosure. Member States should participate in the co-ordination process set by the EU, but the process itself should be voluntary and nonbinding with a strong involvement of market participants.

The comparative study of codes relevant to the EU concluded one year ago that **these codes show a remarkable degree of convergence**. The Commission nevertheless observes that such a situation may change rapidly: several Member States are currently engaged in important policy initiatives, and the EU will soon be enlarged by 10 new Member States. In addition, standards are increasingly set at the international level and they should be implemented in Member States in a consistent way.

For these reasons, the Commission regards it important to encourage the coordination and convergence of national codes through regular high level meetings of the European Corporate Governance Forum. Participants to such a Forum, which could meet once or twice a year, will comprise representatives from Member States, European regulators (including CESR), issuers and investors, other market participants and academics. Interested MEP's will also be invited to present their views. The Forum will be chaired by the Commission.

3.2.Capital Maintenance and Alteration

The Second Company Law Directive adopted by the Council on 13 December 1976 in respect of the formation of public limited liability companies and the maintenance and alteration of their capital is one of the cornerstones of European company law. It imposes a minimum legal capital to public limited liability companies, and contains a number of detailed provisions aiming at protecting shareholders and creditors, which apply inter alia to the formation stage, to distributions to shareholders, to acquisitions of own shares, to increases in capital and to reductions in capital.

In 1999, a **Report by the Company Law SLIM Group** concluded that the capital maintenance regime organised by the Second Directive could be simplified on a limited number of points, and presented several proposals to this end[19]. From the discussions that followed the presentation of this SLIM Report, it appeared that the implementation of many of these recommendations required further examination.

The High Level Group of Company Law Experts confirmed that most of the SLIM Group proposals were indeed worth implementing and gave some guidance in this respect. In addition, the High Level Group formulated a few additional suggestions aiming at modernising the Second Directive. The Commission considers that a **simplification of the Second Directive** on the basis of these proposals and recommendations would significantly contribute to the promotion of business efficiency and competitiveness without

[19] The topics covered by the SLIM Report were as follows: removal of the requirement for an expert opinion on contributions in kind in defined circumstances, introduction of no par value shares, simplification of the rules applicable to withdrawal of shares, simplification of the rules applicable to acquisition of own shares, reduction of the scope of the prohibition of financial assistance, simplification of the rules applicable to pre-emptive rights.

reducing the protection offered to shareholders and creditors. A proposal to amend the Second Directive along these lines is therefore regarded as a priority for the short term.

The High Level Group further suggested that adequate protection of shareholders and creditors might be achieved, possibly even more effectively, with the introduction at a later stage of an **alternative regime** which would not be based on the concept of legal capital. This alternative regime, whose main lines are briefly outlined by the Group[20], could be offered as an option to Member States who should be able to freely decide to change to the new regime or to retain the Second Directive rules amended as suggested above.

The Commission considers that, before deciding to introduce an alternative regime which would fundamentally depart from the capital maintenance regime currently organised by the Second Directive, further work is needed as to both the exact characteristics of a possible alternative regime and its ability to achieve an effective protection of shareholders and third parties. **A study into the feasibility of an alternative to the capital maintenance regime** will be launched by the Commission in the medium term. The study will have to identify in particular the exact benefits that an alternative regime would offer in comparison with the Second Directive rules amended in the short term.

3.3.Groups & Pyramids

The High Level Group of Company Law Experts pointed out that groups of companies, which today are frequent in most, if not all, Member States, are to be seen as a legitimate way of doing business, but that they may present specific risks for shareholders and creditors in various ways. The Commission, following the Group's recommendation, takes the view that there is no need to revive the draft Ninth Directive on group relations[21] since

[20] Such an alternative regime would notably be based on the requirement for a solvency test before any payment of dividend or other distribution can be made.

[21] A draft "Ninth Company Law Directive on the Conduct of Groups containing a Public Limited Company as a Subsidiary" was circulated by the Commission in December 1984 for consultation. According to its Explanatory Memorandum, the Directive was intended to provide a framework in which groups can be managed on a sound basis whilst ensuring that interests affected by group operations are adequately protected. Such a legal framework, adapted to the special circumstances of groups, was considered to be lacking in the legal system of most Member States.

Apart from its provisions dealing with the notification and disclosure of shareholdings in PLCs, which covered all PLCs, the Directive otherwise applied only when a PLC was the subsidiary of another undertaking (which could itself be a PLC, but could also be a natural person or a legal person).

The main features of the proposal were: a) a definition of a "subsidiary undertaking" which would oblige Member States to provide for "control contracts", b) rules about the disclosure of shareholdings in PLCs, c) detailed rules (Section 4) as to the conduct of a "parent undertaking" towards a PLC subsidiary (including the liability of the parent undertaking for damage to the PLC subsidiary and for its debts), d) detailed rules applicable when the parent undertaking had entered into a "control contract" with a PLC (Section 5), or when it had made a "unilateral declaration instituting a vertical group" (Section 6), which would contain similar safeguards to those prescribed in Section 4 but with important additions (including a rights for the employee representatives on the subsidiary PLC's supervisory body to veto instructions from the parent undertaking).

The consultation on the draft Directive showed that there was very little support for such a comprehensive framework on group law: such an approach was largely unfamiliar to most Member

the enactment of an autonomous body of law specifically dealing with groups does not appear necessary, but that particular problems should be addressed through specific provisions in three areas.

Financial and non financial information

Complete information and disclosure with regard to the group's structure and intragroup relations are a crucial pre-requisite to ensure that the functioning of groups remains compatible with the interests of shareholders and creditors at the different levels. The actual provisions of the Seventh Company Law Directive on consolidated accounts do not sufficiently address these concerns, in that consolidated figures do not reflect the financial situation of the various parts of the group and the degree of dependence of the subsidiaries on the parent company.

The need for better financial and non financial information about groups of companies is already addressed partly by a series of EU measures, whether adopted (application of IAS to consolidated accounts), pending (information to be provided under the proposed Thirteenth Directive), or envisaged (information to be provided in the annual corporate governance statement). The Commission nevertheless observes that the scope of these measures is limited to listed companies. The Commission therefore considers that additional initiatives aiming at improving to the extent necessary the financial and non financial information disclosed by groups are desirable when the parent company is not listed. Since transparency is felt as the most important area of intervention with regard to groups, whether they are listed or not, the Commission regards these additional initiatives as priorities for the short term.

Implementation of a group policy

Member States should be required to provide for a framework rule for groups that allows those concerned with the management of a company belonging to a group to adopt and implement a co-ordinated group policy, provided that the interests of that company's creditors are effectively protected and that there is a fair balance of burdens and advantages over time for that company's shareholders. The Commission sees the introduction of such a rule as an important step towards improved business efficiency and competitiveness, but stresses that appropriate safeguards have to be carefully designed. A proposal for a framework Directive to this effect will therefore be presented in the medium term.

Pyramids

Pyramids, defined by the High Level Group as chains of holding companies with the ultimate control based on a small total investment thanks to the extensive use of minority shareholders, raise a number of problems stemming from their lack of transparency. The Commission notes that the introduction of a requirement to publish an annual corporate governance statement (as suggested in Section 3.1.1. above) would, together with the adoption of the proposed Thirteenth Directive, constitute a first significant improvement in this respect.

States, and the business sector viewed it as too cumbersome and too inflexible. As a consequence, the decision was made not to issue an official proposal.

The Group stressed that pyramidal groups that include listed companies raise particular concerns. It recommended that national authorities should be required not to admit to listing companies belonging to abusive pyramids. The Group defined them as holding companies whose sole or main assets are their shareholding in another listed company, but made an exception for cases where the economic value of such admission is clearly demonstrated, thereby recognising that the definition of what constitutes an abusive pyramid required further consideration. It also suggested that operators of stock indices should properly take into account the free float in determining the respective weight of each company.

The Commission considers it necessary to give further examination to the risk inherent in abusive pyramids. In so doing, the Commission will take account of the need to avoid undue restrictions of companies' freedom to choose their appropriate organisation. The Commission therefore intends to obtain on this issue the expert opinion of the Committee of European Securities Regulators (CESR).

3.4. Corporate restructuring and mobility

The growing integration of the single market leads companies increasingly to do **business across national borders** within the Union. In order to be able to align their structure on their activities, European companies have repeatedly called for the adoption of legal instruments capable of meeting their needs for mergers between companies from different Member States and for transfer of their seat from one Member State to another.

The Commission intends to present in the short term a new proposal for a **Tenth Company Law Directive** on cross-border-mergers[22] as well as a proposal for a **Fourteenth Company Law Directive** on the transfer of the seat from one Member State to another[23]. Both proposals are faced with the task of solving difficulties relating to board structure and employee participation. In this respect, the Commission welcomes the approval in October 2001 of the European Company Statute, which opens up promising prospects for the solution of comparable issues in the Tenth and Fourteenth Directives. In addition to these company law implications of corporate restructuring and mobility, which are covered by the present Communication, attention is paid to their social implications in

[22] Although the laws of some Member States do not prohibit a company from one of those States from absorbing a company from another Member State or from taking part in the formation of a new company by merger with a company registered in another Member State, such an operation may be carried out only with companies from Member States where it is likewise not prohibited by law. The adoption of the European Company Statute offers one solution to these problems (a European Company may be created inter alia by merger of two or more public limited liability companies from different Member States). A proposal for a Tenth Company Law Directive is nevertheless desirable, since a) companies may wish to enter into a cross-border merger without creating a European Company, and b) other types of companies may wish to enter into a cross-border merger.

[23] In the absence of legislation governing the cross-border transfer of seat, such an operation is currently impossible or at least contingent on complicated legal arrangements. This is because Member States laws do not provide the necessary means and, when a transfer is possible by virtue of simultaneously applying national laws, there are frequent conflicts between those laws because of the different connecting criteria applied in the Member States. A legislative effort is needed in this field in order to implement the freedom of establishment in the manner intended by the Treaty.

other Commission initiatives (these social implications are addressed in the Multi-Annual Work Programme of the Social Partners 2003-2005).

The High Level Group made **other recommendations** relating to restructuring transactions, along the following lines: a) some of the requirements currently foreseen by the Third Company Law Directive (mergers of public limited liability companies) and by the Sixth Company Law Directive (division of such companies) should be relaxed in specific cases which make them superfluous; b) Member States should be required to create squeeze-out rights (for majority shareholders) and sell-out rights (for minority shareholders), at least in listed companies, subject to certain thresholds being reached. The introduction of such rights would complement the comparable provisions already contained in the current proposal for a Thirteenth Company Law Directive on take-over bids.

The Commission considers that the simplification of restructuring transactions pursued by the proposed relaxation of some of the requirements currently foreseen by the **Third Directive** and the **Sixth Directive** is desirable in so far as the necessary safeguards are ensured. The Commission notes that this simplification is not perceived by the Group as an immediate priority, and therefore intends to take the necessary initiatives in the medium term.

With respect to the introduction of **squeeze-out rights and sell-out rights**, proposed by the High Level Group in its Restructuring Chapter, the Commission observes that the same objectives are pursued by one of the recommendations made by the SLIM Group about the simplification of the Second Directive, which the High Level Group has endorsed. The Commission therefore intends to consider such an introduction as part of the modernisation of the Second Directive, which the Commission regards as a priority for the short term.

3.5.The European Private Company

The High Level Group noted that the Societas Europaea (SE), adopted in October 2001, may not meet all expectations of the business community, in particular SMEs, and referred to the development, from a private initiative, of a "European Private Company" (EPC) which, as a **new legal form at EU level**, would primarily serve the needs of SMEs which are active in more than one Member State. This concept has received **widespread interest and support** not only from the private sector, but also from the European Economic and Social Committee, and the introduction of such a form is regarded by many as easier to achieve than the European Company Statute.

The Group nevertheless observed that the first priority should be to adopt the **Tenth Directive** on cross-border mergers, which is expected to meet one of the purposes advocated for the EPC. Therefore, and in view of a number of issues which need to be solved (e.g. tax or co-determination issues), the Group recommended that before deciding to submit a formal proposal, the Commission should launch a **feasibility study** in order to clearly identify the practical benefits of – and problems related to – the introduction of an EPC statute.

The Group suggested that such a feasibility study should be launched in the medium term, i.e. after the adoption of the Tenth Directive. The Commission considers that the identification of most of the practical benefits of – and problems related to – the introduction of an EPC statute can be achieved independently from the progress hoped on the Tenth Directive. The Commission will therefore launch a feasibility study **in the short term**, with a view to presenting a proposal for an EPC statute (if the feasibility study confirms the need for such an initiative) in the medium term.

The aim of this feasibility study is to evaluate the advantages and the problems generated by a possible European legal statute for small and medium enterprises in order to facilitate their internationalisation. To this end, the study should conduct an in-depth analysis of the legal, tax and social policy regimes relevant to SMEs in the 25 Member States of the enlarged Union.

3.6. The European Co-operative Society and other EU legal forms of enterprises

The European Council adopted last year a general orientation on the proposal for a Regulation on the **Societas Cooperativa Europaea** (SCE) and proposals of statutes for a **European Association** and a **European Mutual Society** are now examined by the European Parliament and the Council. The Commission observes that a majority of the responses received in the consultation organised by the High Level Group expressed positive views on the usefulness of these statutes.

The Commission intends to **actively support the ongoing legislative process engaged** on these statutes, in response to the explicit desire expressed by the European Parliament for giving significant attention to the development of new European legal forms of enterprises. Adoption by the Council of the Regulation on a European Co-operative Society is hoped for in the near future, while the discussion within the Council of the proposal for a European Association is actively going on. As soon as agreement on this proposal will have been reached, the necessary attention will be devoted to the proposal for a European Mutual Society.

With respect to the possible development of a proposal for a Regulation on a **European Foundation**, before deciding to submit a proposal, the Commission intends to launch a study aiming at assessing in depth the feasibility of such a statute. Such an assessment will have to take account of the lessons to be drawn from the adoption and use of the other European statutes, so that it should best take place in the medium term.

3.7. Enhancing the transparency of national legal forms of enterprises

Increased disclosure requirements for all legal entities with limited liability, are a need which stems from the necessity a) to preserve fair competition[24] and b) to prevent company law from being abused for fraud, terrorism or other criminal activity[25]. The

[24] The First Company Law Directive, which contains essential disclosure requirements (companies must file a series of documents and particulars with a register, and interested parties can obtain a copy thereof), applies only to limited liability companies, and not to a series of alternative forms of enterprise. The creation of a framework for disclosure of basic data on certain other legal entities engaged in economic activities is therefore perceived as a useful tool for trade and competition within the Internal Market.

[25] See in this respect the study "Transparency and Money Laundering: A study of the regulation and its implementation, in the EU Member States, that obstruct anti-money laundering international co-operation (banking/financial and corporate/company regulative fields)", submitted to the Commission in October 2001 by the Transcrime Institute (University of Trento, Italy). This study, commissioned pursuant to conclusion n°58 of the Tampere Special European Council of 1999 and the joint ECOFIN/JAI Council of October 2000, presents recommendations to increase the transparency of limited liability companies as well as other vehicles (as trusts).

Commission is committed to respond to this need, but the scope and nature of this recommendation need to be further examined. In view of the numerous other priorities, the necessary actions will be taken in the medium term.

4. CONCLUSION

The present Communication explains why the European regulatory framework for company law and corporate governance needs to be modernised. It defines the key policy objectives which should inspire any future action to be taken at EU level in these areas. It includes an action plan, prioritised, to plan the various actions which appear necessary over the short, medium and long term. It determines which type of regulatory instrument should be used, and approximately by when.

Further to the conclusions adopted by the Brussels European Council of 20 and 21 March 2003, which requested the adoption of an Action Plan on Company Law and Corporate Governance, the Commission addresses this Communication to the European Parliament and the Council, and transmits it also to the European Economic and Social Committee and the Committee of the Regions.

Comments from all interested parties are invited by 31 August 2003. Comments should be sent to DG MARKT G3, European Commission, B-1049 Brussels (e-mail address: Markt-COMPLAW@cec.eu.int).

The Commission will publish a synthesis of the comments received, and they will be given adequate consideration when implementing the present Action Plan.

ANNEX 1

Modernising Company Law and Enhancing Corporate Governance in the European Union - A Plan to Move Forward		
List of Actions		
SHORT TERM (2003-2005)		
	Description of action	**Preferred type of initiative**[26]
Corporate Governance	Enhanced corporate governance disclosure requirements (including confirmation of collective responsibility of board members for key non financial statements)	Legislative (Directive amending existing legislation)
	Integrated legal framework to facilitate efficient shareholder communication and decision-making (participation to meetings, exercise of voting rights, cross-border voting)	Legislative (Directive)
	Strengthening the role of independent non-executive and supervisory directors	Non legislative (Recommendation)
	Fostering an appropriate regime for directors remuneration	Non legislative (Recommendation)
	Confirming at EU level the collective responsibility of board members for financial statements	Legislative (Directive amending existing legislation)
	Convening a European Corporate Governance Forum to co-ordinate corporate governance efforts of Member States	Non legislative (Commission initiative)
Capital Maintenance	Simplification of the Second Directive, on the basis of the SLIM recommendations as supplemented in the HLG Report (SLIM-Plus)	Legislative (Directive amending existing legislation)

[26] This column gives information about the type of regulatory instrument which should be used:

– When « Directive » is mentioned, this means that the action envisaged requires either the adoption of a new Directive or the modification of one or several existing Directives (in the areas of company law, securities law, financial reporting law…), in accordance with the regulatory powers of the various relevant bodies existing at EU level;

– To the extent possible, the necessary initiatives will be grouped with a view to avoiding a multiplication of legislative initiatives.

Groups of companies	Increased disclosure of group structure and relations, both financial and non financial	Legislative (Directive amending existing legislation)
Restructering	Proposal for a Tenth Directive on cross-border mergers	Legislative Directive
	Proposal for a Fourteenth Directive on cross-border transfer of the seat	Legislative Directive
European Private Company	Feasibility study in order to assess the practical needs for – and problems of – a European Private Company	Non legislative (Study)
EU legal forms	Active process on current proposals (European Association, European Mutual Society)	Legislative (existing proposals)
MEDIUM TERM (2006-2008)		
	Description of action	**Preferred type of initiative**
Corporate Governance	Enhanced disclosure by institutional investors of their investment and voting policies	Legislative Directive
	Choice for all listed companies between the two types (monistic/dualistic of board structure Enhancing the responsibilities of board members (special investigation right, wrongful trading rule, director's disqualification	Legislative Directive Legislative Directive or Directive amending existing legislation
	Examination of the consequences of an approach aiming at achieving a full shareholder democracy (one share/one vote), at least for listed companies	Non legislative (Study)
Capital Maintenance	Review of feasibility of an alternative to the capital maintenance regime	Non legislative (Study)
Groups of companies	Framework rule for groups, allowing the adoption of subsidiary level of a co-ordinated group policy	Legislative Directive
Pyramids	Prohibition of stock exchange listing for abusive pyramids, if appropriate, following further examination and expert input	Legislative (possible Directive amending existing legislation
Restructuring	Simplification of the Third Directive (legal mergers) and Sixth Directive (legal division	Legislative (Directive amending existing legislation

European Private Company	Possible proposal for a Statute for a European Private Company (depending on the outcome of the feasibility study)	Legislative
EU legal forms	Assess the need for the creation of other EU legal forms (e.g. European Foundation)	Non legislative (Study)
Transparency of national legal forms	Introduce basic disclosure rules for all legal entitities with limited liability, subject to further examination	Legislative (Directive or Directive amending existing legislation
LONG TERM (2009 onwards)		
	Description of action	**Preferred type of initiative**
Capital Maintenance	Possible introduction in the Second Company Law Directive of an alternative regime (depending on the outcome of the feasiblity study)	Legislative (Directive amending existing legislation)

ANNEX 2

LIST OF EXISTING AND PROPOSED EUROPEAN COMPANY LAW INSTRUMENTS

Existing European Company Law Instruments	
REGULATIONS	
Title of Act	**Publication Reference**
Council Regulation (EEC) 2137/85 of 25 July 1985 on the European Economic Interest Grouping (EEIG)	[1985] OJ L 199/1
Council Regulation (2001/2157/EC) of 8 October 2001 on the Statute for a European Company SE *supplemented by* Council Directive (2001/86/EC) of 8 October 2001 supplementing the Statute for a European Company with regard to the involvement of employees	[2001] OJ L 294/1 [2001] OJ L 294/22
Regulation (EC) No 1606/2002 of the European Parliament and of the Council of 19 July 2002 on the application of international accounting standards	[2002] OJ L 243/1
DIRECTIVES	
Title of Act	**Publication Reference**
First Council Directive (EEC) 68/151 of 9 March 1968 on co-ordination of safeguards which, for the protection of the interests of members and others, are required by Member States of companies within the meaning of the second paragraph of Article 58 of the Treaty, with a view to making such safeguards equivalent throughout the Community	[1968] OJ L 65/8
Second Council Directive (EEC) 77/91 of 13 December 1976 on coordination of safeguards, which for the protection of the interests of members and others, are required by Member States of companies within the meaning of the second paragraph of Article 58 of the Treaty, in respect of the formation of public limited liability companies and the maintenance and alteration of their capital, with a view to making such safeguards equivalent throughout the Community	[1977] OJ L 26/1
Third Council Directive (EEC) 78/855 of 9 October 1978 based on Article 54(3)(g) of the Treaty concerning mergers of public limited liability companies	[1977] OJ L 295/36

Fourth Council Directive (EEC) 78/660 of 25 July 1978 based on Article 54(3)(g) of the Treaty on the annual accounts of certain types of companies	[1978] OJ L 222/11
Sixth Council Directive (EEC) 82/891 of 17 December 1982 based on Article 54(3)(g) of the Treaty concerning the division of public limited liability companies	[1982] OJ L 378/47
Seventh Council Directive (EEC) 83/349 of 13 June 1983 based on Article 54(3)(g) of the Treaty on consolidated accounts	[1983] OJ L 193/1
Eighth Council Directive (EEC) 84/253 of 10 April 1984 based on Article 54(3)(g) of the Treaty on the approval of persons responsible for carrying out the statutory audits of accounting documents	[1984] OJ L 126/20
Eleventh Council Directive (EEC) 89/666 of 21 December 1989 concerning disclosure requirements in respect of branches opened in a Member State by certain types of company governed by the law of another State	[1989] OJ L 395/96
Twelfth Council Directive (EEC) 89/667 of 21 December 1989 on single-member private limited liability companies	[1989] OJ L 395/40

RECOMMENDATIONS

Title of Act	Publication Reference
Commission Recommendation (2001/256/EC) of 15 November 2000 on quality assurance for the statutory audit in the European Union: minimum requirements	[2001] OJ L 91/91
Commission Recommendation (2001/453/EC) of 30 May 2001 on the recognition, measurement and disclosure of environmental issues in the annual accounts and annual reports of companies	[2001] OJ L 156/33
Commission Recommendation (2002/590/EC) of 16 May 2002 on "Statutory Auditors' Independence in the EU : A Set of Fundamental Principles"	[2002] OJ L 191/22

Proposed European Company Law Instruments	
REGULATIONS	
Title of Act	**Publication Reference**
Amended Proposal for a Council Regulation (EEC) on a statute for a European Association	[1993] OJ C 236/1
Amended Proposal for a Council Regulation (EEC) on a statute for a European Co-operative Society	[1993] OJ C 236/17
Amended Proposal for a Council Regulation (EEC) on a statute for a European Mutual Society	[1993] OJ C 236/40
DIRECTIVES	
Title of Act	**Publication Reference**
Proposal for a Directive of the European Parliament and of the Council amending Council Directive 68/151/EEC, as regards disclosure requirements in respect of certain types of companies : COM (2002) 279	[2002] OJ C 227/377
Proposal for a Directive of the European Parliament and of the Council on take-over bids : COM (2002) 534 final	[2003] OJ C 45 E/1

Annex 2

The Combined Code on Corporate Governance

July 2003

CONTENTS

CODE ON CORPORATE GOVERNANCE

PREAMBLE

1. This Code supersedes and replaces the Combined Code issued by the Hampel Committee on Corporate Governance in June 1998. It derives from a review of the role and effectiveness of non-executive directors by Derek Higgs[1] and a review of audit committees[2] by a group led by Sir Robert Smith.
2. The Financial Services Authority has said that it will replace the 1998 Code that is annexed to the Listing Rules with the revised Code and will seek to make consequential Rule changes. There will be consultation on the necessary Rule changes but not further consultation on the Code provisions themselves.
3. It is intended that the new Code will apply for reporting years beginning on or after 1 November 2003.
4. The Code contains main and supporting principles and provisions. The existing Listing Rules require listed companies to make a disclosure statement in two parts in relation to the Code. In the first part of the statement, the company has to report on how it applies the principles in the Code. In future this will need to cover both main and supporting principles. The form and content of this part of the statement are not prescribed, the intention being that companies should have a free hand to explain their governance policies in the light of the principles, including any special circumstances applying to them which have led to a particular approach. In the second part of the statement the company has either to confirm that it complies with the Code's provisions or – where it does not – to provide an explanation. This 'comply or explain' approach has been in operation for over ten years and the flexibility it offers has been widely welcomed both by company boards and by investors. It is for shareholders and others to evaluate the company's statement
5. While it is expected that listed companies will comply with the Code's provisions most of the time, it is recognised that departure from the provisions of the Code may be justified in particular circumstances. Every company must review each provision carefully and give a considered explanation if it departs from the Code provisions.

---

[1] "Review of the role and effectiveness of non-executive directors", published January 2003.

[2] "Audit Committees Combined Code Guidance", published January 2003.

6. Smaller listed companies, in particular those new to listing, may judge that some of the provisions are disproportionate or less relevant in their case. Some of the provisions do not apply to companies below FTSE 350. Such companies may nonetheless consider that it would be appropriate to adopt the approach in the Code and they are encouraged to consider this. Investment companies typically have a different board structure, which may affect the relevance of particular provisions.
7. Whilst recognising that directors are appointed by shareholders who are the owners of companies, it is important that those concerned with the evaluation of governance should do so with common sense in order to promote partnership and trust, based on mutual understanding. They should pay due regard to companies' individual circumstances and bear in mind in particular the size and complexity of the company and the nature of the risks and challenges it faces. Whilst shareholders have every right to challenge companies' explanations if they are unconvincing, they should not be evaluated in a mechanistic way and departures from the Code should not be automatically treated as breaches. Institutional shareholders and their agents should be careful to respond to the statements from companies in a manner that supports the 'comply or explain' principle. As the principles in Section 2 make clear, institutional shareholders should carefully consider explanations given for departure from the Code and make reasoned judgements in each case. They should put their views to the company and be prepared to enter a dialogue if they do not accept the company's position. Institutional shareholders should be prepared to put such views in writing where appropriate.
8. Nothing in this Code should be taken to override the general requirements of law to treat shareholders equally in access to information.
9. This publication includes guidance on how to comply with particular parts of the Code: first, "Internal Control: Guidance for Directors on the Combined Code"[3], produced by the Turnbull Committee, which relates to Code provisions on internal control (C.2 and part of C.3 in the Code); and, second, "Audit Committees: Combined Code Guidance", produced by the Smith Group, which relates to the provisions on audit committees and auditors (C.3 of the Code). In both cases, the guidance suggests ways of applying the relevant Code principles and of complying with the relevant Code provisions.
10. In addition, this volume also includes suggestions for good practice from the Higgs report.

---

[3] "Internal Control: Guidance for Directors on the Combined Code", published by the Institute of Chartered Accountants in England and Wales in September 1999.

11. The revised Code does not include material in the previous Code on the disclosure of directors' remuneration. This is because "The Directors' Remuneration Report Regulations 2002"[4] are now in force and supersede the earlier Code provisions. These require the directors of a company to prepare a remuneration report. It is important that this report is clear, transparent and understandable to shareholders.

4 The Directors' Remuneration Report Regulations 2002, S.I. no.1986.

CODE OF BEST PRACTICE

SECTION 1 COMPANIES

A. DIRECTORS

A.1 The Board

Main Principle

Every company should be headed by an effective board, which is collectively responsible for the success of the company.

Supporting Principles

The board's role is to provide entrepreneurial leadership of the company within a framework of prudent and effective controls which enables risk to be assessed and managed. The board should set the company's strategic aims, ensure that the necessary financial and human resources are in place for the company to meet its objectives and review management performance. The board should set the company's values and standards and ensure that its obligations to its shareholders and others are understood and met.

All directors must take decisions objectively in the interests of the company.

As part of their role as members of a unitary board, non-executive directors should constructively challenge and help develop proposals on strategy. Non-executive directors should scrutinise the performance of management in meeting agreed goals and objectives and monitor the reporting of performance. They should satisfy themselves on the integrity of financial information and that financial controls and systems of risk management are robust and defensible. They are responsible for determining appropriate levels of remuneration of executive directors and have a prime role in appointing, and where necessary removing, executive directors, and in succession planning.

Code Provisions

A.1.1 The board should meet sufficiently regularly to discharge its duties effectively. There should be a formal schedule of matters specifically reserved for its decision. The annual report should include a statement of how the board operates, including a high level statement of which types of decisions are to be taken by the board and which are to be delegated to management.

A.1.2 The annual report should identify the chairman, the deputy chairman (where there is one), the chief executive, the senior independent director and the chairmen and members of the nomination, audit and remuneration committees. It should also set out the number of meetings of the board and those committees and individual attendance by directors.

A.1.3 The chairman should hold meetings with the non-executive directors without the executives present. Led by the senior independent director, the non-executive directors should meet without the chairman present at least annually to appraise the chairman's performance (as described in A.6.1) and on such other occasions as are deemed appropriate.

A.1.4 Where directors have concerns which cannot be resolved about the running of the company or a proposed action, they should ensure that their concerns are recorded in the board minutes. On resignation, a non-executive director should provide a written statement to the chairman, for circulation to the board, if they have any such concerns.

A.1.5 The company should arrange appropriate insurance cover in respect of legal action against its directors.

A.2 Chairman and chief executive

Main Principle

There should be a clear division of responsibilities at the head of the company between the running of the board and the executive responsibility for the running of the company's business. No one individual should have unfettered powers of decision.

Supporting Principle

The chairman is responsible for leadership of the board, ensuring its effectiveness on all aspects of its role and setting its agenda. The chairman is also responsible for ensuring that the directors receive accurate, timely and clear information. The chairman should ensure effective communication with shareholders. The chairman should also facilitate the effective contribution of non-executive directors in particular and ensure constructive relations between executive and non-executive directors.

Code Provisions

A.2.1 The roles of chairman and chief executive should not be exercised by the same individual. The division of responsibilities between the chairman and chief executive should be clearly established, set out in writing and agreed by the board.

A.2.2[5] The chairman should on appointment meet the independence criteria set out in A.3.1 below. A chief executive should not go on to be chairman of the same company. If exceptionally a board decides that a chief executive should become chairman, the board should consult major shareholders in advance and should set out its reasons to shareholders at the time of the appointment and in the next annual report.

A.3 Board balance and independence

Main Principle

The board should include a balance of executive and non-executive directors (and in particular independent non-executive directors) such that no individual or small group of individuals can dominate the board's decision taking.

Supporting Principles

The board should not be so large as to be unwieldy. The board should be of sufficient size that the balance of skills and experience is appropriate for the requirements of the business and that changes to the board's composition can be managed without undue disruption.

To ensure that power and information are not concentrated in one or two individuals, there should be a strong presence on the board of both executive and non-executive directors.

The value of ensuring that committee membership is refreshed and that undue reliance is not placed on particular individuals should be taken into account in deciding chairmanship and membership of committees.

No one other than the committee chairman and members is entitled to be present at a meeting of the nomination, audit or remuneration committee, but others may attend at the invitation of the committee.

---

[5] Compliance or otherwise with this provision need only be reported for the year in which the appointment is made.

Code provisions

A.3.1 The board should identify in the annual report each non-executive director it considers to be independent[6]. The board should determine whether the director is independent in character and judgement and whether there are relationships or circumstances which are likely to affect, or could appear to affect, the director's judgement. The board should state its reasons if it determines that a director is independent notwithstanding the existence of relationships or circumstances which may appear relevant to its determination, including if the director:

- has been an employee of the company or group within the last five years;
- has, or has had within the last three years, a material business relationship with the company either directly, or as a partner, shareholder, director or senior employee of a body that has such a relationship with the company;
- has received or receives additional remuneration from the company apart from a director's fee, participates in the company's share option or a performance-related pay scheme, or is a member of the company's pension scheme;
- has close family ties with any of the company's advisers, directors or senior employees;
- holds cross-directorships or has significant links with other directors through involvement in other companies or bodies;
- represents a significant shareholder; or
- has served on the board for more than nine years from the date of their first election.

A.3.2 Except for smaller companies[7], at least half the board, excluding the chairman, should comprise non-executive directors determined by the board to be independent. A smaller company should have at least two independent non-executive directors.

A.3.3 The board should appoint one of the independent non-executive directors to be the senior independent director. The senior independent director should be available to shareholders if they have concerns which contact through the normal channels of chairman, chief executive or finance director has failed to resolve or for which such contact is inappropriate.

---

[6] A.2.2 states that the chairman should, on appointment, meet the independence criteria set out in this provision, but thereafter the test of independence is not appropriate in relation to the chairman.

[7] A smaller company is one that is below the FTSE 350 throughout the year immediately prior to the reporting year.

A.4 Appointments to the Board

Main Principle

There should be a formal, rigorous and transparent procedure for the appointment of new directors to the board.

Supporting Principles

Appointments to the board should be made on merit and against objective criteria. Care should be taken to ensure that appointees have enough time available to devote to the job. This is particularly important in the case of chairmanships.

The board should satisfy itself that plans are in place for orderly succession for appointments to the board and to senior management, so as to maintain an appropriate balance of skills and experience within the company and on the board.

Code Provisions

A.4.1 There should be a nomination committee which should lead the process for board appointments and make recommendations to the board. A majority of members of the nomination committee should be independent non-executive directors. The chairman or an independent non-executive director should chair the committee, but the chairman should not chair the nomination committee when it is dealing with the appointment of a successor to the chairmanship. The nomination committee should make available[8] its terms of reference, explaining its role and the authority delegated to it by the board.

A.4.2 The nomination committee should evaluate the balance of skills, knowledge and experience on the board and, in the light of this evaluation, prepare a description of the role and capabilities required for a particular appointment.

A.4.3 For the appointment of a chairman, the nomination committee should prepare a job specification, including an assessment of the time commitment expected, recognising the need for availability in the event of crises. A chairman's other significant commitments should be disclosed to the board before appointment and included in the annual report. Changes to such commitments should be reported to the board as they arise, and included in the next annual report. No individual should be appointed to a second chairmanship of a FTSE 100 company[9].

---

[8] The requirement to make the information available would be met by making it available on request and by including the information on the company's website.

[9] Compliance or otherwise with this provision need only be reported for the year in which the appointment is made.

A.4.4 The terms and conditions of appointment of non-executive directors should be made available for inspection[10]. The letter of appointment should set out the expected time commitment. Non-executive directors should undertake that they will have sufficient time to meet what is expected of them. Their other significant commitments should be disclosed to the board before appointment, with a broad indication of the time involved and the board should be informed of subsequent changes.

A.4.5 The board should not agree to a full time executive director taking on more than one non-executive directorship in a FTSE 100 company nor the chairmanship of such a company.

A.4.6 A separate section of the annual report should describe the work of the nomination committee, including the process it has used in relation to board appointments. An explanation should be given if neither an external search consultancy nor open advertising has been used in the appointment of a chairman or a non-executive director.

A.5 Information and professional development

Main Principle

The board should be supplied in a timely manner with information in a form and of a quality appropriate to enable it to discharge its duties. All directors should receive induction on joining the board and should regularly update and refresh their skills and knowledge.

Supporting Principles

The chairman is responsible for ensuring that the directors receive accurate, timely and clear information. Management has an obligation to provide such information but directors should seek clarification or amplification where necessary.

The chairman should ensure that the directors continually update their skills and the knowledge and familiarity with the company required to fulfil their role both on the board and on board committees. The company should provide the necessary resources for developing and updating its directors' knowledge and capabilities.

Under the direction of the chairman, the company secretary's responsibilities include ensuring good information flows within the board and

[10] The terms and conditions of appointment of non-executive directors should be made available for inspection by any person at the company's registered office during normal business hours and at the AGM (for 15 minutes prior to the meeting and during the meeting).

its committees and between senior management and non-executive directors, as well as facilitating induction and assisting with professional development as required.

The company secretary should be responsible for advising the board through the chairman on all governance matters.

Code Provisions

A.5.1 The chairman should ensure that new directors receive a full, formal and tailored induction on joining the board. As part of this, the company should offer to major shareholders the opportunity to meet a new non-executive director.

A.5.2 The board should ensure that directors, especially non-executive directors, have access to independent professional advice at the company's expense where they judge it necessary to discharge their responsibilities as directors. Committees should be provided with sufficient resources to undertake their duties.

A.5.3 All directors should have access to the advice and services of the company secretary, who is responsible to the board for ensuring that board procedures are complied with. Both the appointment and removal of the company secretary should be a matter for the board as a whole.

A.6 Performance evaluation

Main Principle

The board should undertake a formal and rigorous annual evaluation of its own performance and that of its committees and individual directors.

Supporting Principle

Individual evaluation should aim to show whether each director continues to contribute effectively and to demonstrate commitment to the role (including commitment of time for board and committee meetings and any other duties). The chairman should act on the results of the performance evaluation by recognising the strengths and addressing the weaknesses of the board and, where appropriate, proposing new members be appointed to the board or seeking the resignation of directors.

Code Provision

A.6.1 The board should state in the annual report how performance evaluation of the board, its committees and its individual directors has been conducted. The non-executive directors, led by the senior independent director, should be responsible for performance evaluation of the chairman, taking into account the views of executive directors.

A.7 Re-election

Main Principle

All directors should be submitted for re-election at regular intervals, subject to continued satisfactory performance. The board should ensure planned and progressive refreshing of the board.

Code Provisions

A.7.1 All directors should be subject to election by shareholders at the first annual general meeting after their appointment, and to re-election thereafter at intervals of no more than three years. The names of directors submitted for election or re-election should be accompanied by sufficient biographical details and any other relevant information to enable shareholders to take an informed decision on their election.

A.7.2 Non-executive directors should be appointed for specified terms subject to re-election and to Companies Acts provisions relating to the removal of a director. The board should set out to shareholders in the papers accompanying a resolution to elect a non-executive director why they believe an individual should be elected. The chairman should confirm to shareholders when proposing re-election that, following formal performance evaluation, the individual's performance continues to be effective and to demonstrate commitment to the role. Any term beyond six years (e.g. two three-year terms) for a non-executive director should be subject to particularly rigorous review, and should take into account the need for progressive refreshing of the board. Non-executive directors may serve longer than nine years (e.g. three three-year terms), subject to annual re-election. Serving more than nine years could be relevant to the determination of a non-executive director's independence (as set out in provision A.3.1).

B. REMUNERATION

B.1 The Level and Make-up of Remuneration[11]

Main Principles

Levels of remuneration should be sufficient to attract, retain and motivate directors of the quality required to run the company successfully, but a company should avoid paying more than is necessary for this purpose. A significant proportion of executive directors' remuneration should be structured so as to link rewards to corporate and individual performance.

Supporting Principle

The remuneration committee should judge where to position their company relative to other companies. But they should use such comparisons with caution, in view of the risk of an upward ratchet of remuneration levels with no corresponding improvement in performance. They should also be sensitive to pay and employment conditions elsewhere in the group, especially when determining annual salary increases.

Code Provisions

Remuneration policy

B.1.1 The performance-related elements of remuneration should form a significant proportion of the total remuneration package of executive directors and should be designed to align their interests with those of shareholders and to give these directors keen incentives to perform at the highest levels. In designing schemes of performance-related remuneration, the remuneration committee should follow the provisions in Schedule A to this Code.

B.1.2 Executive share options should not be offered at a discount save as permitted by the relevant provisions of the Listing Rules.

B.1.3 Levels of remuneration for non-executive directors should reflect the time commitment and responsibilities of the role. Remuneration for non-executive directors should not include share options. If, exceptionally, options are granted, shareholder approval should be sought in advance and any shares acquired by exercise of the options should be

---

[11] Views have been sought by the Department of Trade and Industry by 30 September 2003 on whether, and if so how, further measures are required to enable shareholders to ensure that compensation reflects performance when directors' contracts are terminated: See "Rewards for Failure": Directors' Remuneration – Contracts, performance and severance, June 2003.

held until at least one year after the non-executive director leaves the board. Holding of share options could be relevant to the determination of a non-executive director's independence (as set out in provision A.3.1).

B.1.4 Where a company releases an executive director to serve as a non-executive director elsewhere, the remuneration report[12] should include a statement as to whether or not the director will retain such earnings and, if so, what the remuneration is.

Service Contracts and Compensation

B.1.5 The remuneration committee should carefully consider what compensation commitments (including pension contributions and all other elements) their directors' terms of appointment would entail in the event of early termination. The aim should be to avoid rewarding poor performance. They should take a robust line on reducing compensation to reflect departing directors' obligations to mitigate loss.

B.1.6 Notice or contract periods should be set at one year or less. If it is necessary to offer longer notice or contract periods to new directors recruited from outside, such periods should reduce to one year or less after the initial period.

B.2 Procedure

Main Principle

There should be a formal and transparent procedure for developing policy on executive remuneration and for fixing the remuneration packages of individual directors. No director should be involved in deciding his or her own remuneration.

Supporting Principles

The remuneration committee should consult the chairman and/or chief executive about their proposals relating to the remuneration of other executive directors. The remuneration committee should also be responsible for appointing any consultants in respect of executive director remuneration. Where executive directors or senior management are involved in advising or supporting the remuneration committee, care should be taken to recognise and avoid conflicts of interest.

The chairman of the board should ensure that the company maintains contact as required with its principal shareholders about remuneration in the same way as for other matters.

---

[12] As required under the Directors' Remuneration Report Regulations.

Code Provisions

B.2.1 The board should establish a remuneration committee of at least three, or in the case of smaller companies[13] two, members, who should all be independent non-executive directors. The remuneration committee should make available[14] its terms of reference, explaining its role and the authority delegated to it by the board. Where remuneration consultants are appointed, a statement should be made available[15] of whether they have any other connection with the company.

B.2.2 The remuneration committee should have delegated responsibility for setting remuneration for all executive directors and the chairman, including pension rights and any compensation payments. The committee should also recommend and monitor the level and structure of remuneration for senior management. The definition of 'senior management' for this purpose should be determined by the board but should normally include the first layer of management below board level.

B.2.3 The board itself or, where required by the Articles of Association, the shareholders should determine the remuneration of the non-executive directors within the limits set in the Articles of Association. Where permitted by the Articles, the board may however delegate this responsibility to a committee, which might include the chief executive.

B.2.4 Shareholders should be invited specifically to approve all new long-term incentive schemes (as defined in the Listing Rules) and significant changes to existing schemes, save in the circumstances permitted by the Listing Rules.

---

[13] See footnote 7.
[14] See footnote 8.
[15] See footnote 8.

C. ACCOUNTABILITY AND AUDIT

C.1 Financial Reporting

Main Principle

The board should present a balanced and understandable assessment of the company's position and prospects.

Supporting Principle

The board's responsibility to present a balanced and understandable assessment extends to interim and other price-sensitive public reports and reports to regulators as well as to information required to be presented by statutory requirements.

Code Provisions

C.1.1 The directors should explain in the annual report their responsibility for preparing the accounts and there should be a statement by the auditors about their reporting responsibilities.

C.1.2 The directors should report that the business is a going concern, with supporting assumptions or qualifications as necessary.

C.2 Internal Control[16]

Main Principle

The board should maintain a sound system of internal control to safeguard shareholders' investment and the company's assets.

Code Provision

C.2.1 The board should, at least annually, conduct a review of the effectiveness of the group's system of internal controls and should report to shareholders that they have done so. The review should cover all material controls, including financial, operational and compliance controls and risk management systems.

---

[16] The Turnbull guidance suggests means of applying this part of the Code.

C.3 Audit Committee and Auditors[17]

Main Principle

The board should establish formal and transparent arrangements for considering how they should apply the financial reporting and internal control principles and for maintaining an appropriate relationship with the company's auditors.

Code provisions

C.3.1 The board should establish an audit committee of at least three, or in the case of smaller companies[18] two, members, who should all be independent non-executive directors. The board should satisfy itself that at least one member of the audit committee has recent and relevant financial experience.

C.3.2 The main role and responsibilities of the audit committee should be set out in written terms of reference and should include:

- to monitor the integrity of the financial statements of the company, and any formal announcements relating to the company's financial performance, reviewing significant financial reporting judgements contained in them;
- to review the company's internal financial controls and, unless expressly addressed by a separate board risk committee composed of independent directors, or by the board itself, to review the company's internal control and risk management systems;
- to monitor and review the effectiveness of the company's internal audit function;
- to make recommendations to the board, for it to put to the shareholders for their approval in general meeting, in relation to the appointment, re-appointment and removal of the external auditor and to approve the remuneration and terms of engagement of the external auditor;
- to review and monitor the external auditor's independence and objectivity and the effectiveness of the audit process, taking into consideration relevant UK professional and regulatory requirements;
- to develop and implement policy on the engagement of the external auditor to supply non-audit services, taking into account relevant ethical guidance regarding the provision of non-audit services by the external audit firm; and to report to the board, identifying any

---

17 The Smith guidance suggests means of applying this part of the Code.

18 See footnote 7.

matters in respect of which it considers that action or improvement is needed and making recommendations as to the steps to be taken.

C.3.3 The terms of reference of the audit committee, including its role and the authority delegated to it by the board, should be made available.[19] A separate section of the annual report should describe the work of the committee in discharging those responsibilities.

C.3.4 The audit committee should review arrangements by which staff of the company may, in confidence, raise concerns about possible improprieties in matters of financial reporting or other matters. The audit committee's objective should be to ensure that arrangements are in place for the proportionate and independent investigation of such matters and for appropriate follow-up action.

C.3.5 The audit committee should monitor and review the effectiveness of the internal audit activities. Where there is no internal audit function, the audit committee should consider annually whether there is a need for an internal audit function and make a recommendation to the board, and the reasons for the absence of such a function should be explained in the relevant section of the annual report.

C.3.6 The audit committee should have primary responsibility for making a recommendation on the appointment, reappointment and removal of the external auditors. If the board does not accept the audit committee's recommendation, it should include in the annual report, and in any papers recommending appointment or re-appointment, a statement from the audit committee explaining the recommendation and should set out reasons why the board has taken a different position.

C.3.7 The annual report should explain to shareholders how, if the auditor provides non-audit services, auditor objectivity and independence is safeguarded.

---

[19] See footnote 8.

D. RELATIONS WITH SHAREHOLDERS

D.1 Dialogue with Institutional Shareholders

Main Principle

There should be a dialogue with shareholders based on the mutual understanding of objectives. The board as a whole has responsibility for ensuring that a satisfactory dialogue with shareholders takes place.[20]

Supporting Principles

Whilst recognising that most shareholder contact is with the chief executive and finance director, the chairman (and the senior independent director and other directors as appropriate) should maintain sufficient contact with major shareholders to understand their issues and concerns.

The board should keep in touch with shareholder opinion in whatever ways are most practical and efficient.

Code Provisions

D.1.1 The chairman should ensure that the views of shareholders are communicated to the board as a whole. The chairman should discuss governance and strategy with major shareholders. Non-executive directors should be offered the opportunity to attend meetings with major shareholders and should expect to attend them if requested by major shareholders. The senior independent director should attend sufficient meetings with a range of major shareholders to listen to their views in order to help develop a balanced understanding of the issues and concerns of major shareholders.

D.1.2 The board should state in the annual report the steps they have taken to ensure that the members of the board, and in particular the non-executive directors, develop an understanding of the views of major shareholders about their company, for example through direct face-to-face contact, analysts' or brokers' briefings and surveys of shareholder opinion.

D.2 Constructive Use of the AGM

Main Principle

The board should use the AGM to communicate with investors and to encourage their participation.

---

[20] Nothing in these principles or provisions should be taken to override the general requirements of law to treat shareholders equally in access to information.

Code Provisions

D.2.1 The company should count all proxy votes and, except where a poll is called, should indicate the level of proxies lodged on each resolution, and the balance for and against the resolution and the number of abstentions, after it has been dealt with on a show of hands. The company should ensure that votes cast are properly received and recorded.

D.2.2 The company should propose a separate resolution at the AGM on each substantially separate issue and should in particular propose a resolution at the AGM relating to the report and accounts.

D.2.3 The chairman should arrange for the chairmen of the audit, remuneration and nomination committees to be available to answer questions at the AGM and for all directors to attend.

D.2.4 The company should arrange for the Notice of the AGM and related papers to be sent to shareholders at least 20 working days before the meeting.

SECTION 2 INSTITUTIONAL SHAREHOLDERS

E. INSTITUTIONAL SHAREHOLDERS[21]

E.1 Dialogue with companies

Main Principle

Institutional shareholders should enter into a dialogue with companies based on the mutual understanding of objectives.

Supporting Principles

Institutional shareholders should apply the principles set out in the Institutional Shareholders' Committee's "The Responsibilities of Institutional Shareholders and Agents – Statement of Principles"[22], which should be reflected in fund manager contracts.

---

[21] Agents such as investment managers, or voting services, are frequently appointed by institutional shareholders to act on their behalf and these principles should accordingly be read as applying where appropriate to the agents of institutional shareholders.

[22] Available at website: www.investmentuk.org.uk/press/2002/20021021-01.pdf.

E.2 Evaluation of Governance Disclosures

Main Principle

When evaluating companies' governance arrangements, particularly those relating to board structure and composition, institutional shareholders should give due weight to all relevant factors drawn to their attention.

Supporting Principle

Institutional shareholders should consider carefully explanations given for departure from this Code and make reasoned judgements in each case. They should give an explanation to the company, in writing where appropriate, and be prepared to enter a dialogue if they do not accept the company's position. They should avoid a box-ticking approach to assessing a company's corporate governance. They should bear in mind in particular the size and complexity of the company and the nature of the risks and challenges it faces.

E.3 Shareholder Voting

Main Principle

Institutional shareholders have a responsibility to make considered use of their votes.

Supporting Principles

Institutional shareholders should take steps to ensure their voting intentions are being translated into practice.

Institutional shareholders should, on request, make available to their clients information on the proportion of resolutions on which votes were cast and non-discretionary proxies lodged.

Major shareholders should attend AGMs where appropriate and practicable. Companies and registrars should facilitate this.

Schedule A: Provisions on the design of performance related remuneration

1. The remuneration committee should consider whether the directors should be eligible for annual bonuses. If so, performance conditions should be relevant, stretching and designed to enhance shareholder value. Upper limits should be set and disclosed. There may be a case for part payment in shares to be held for a significant period.
2. The remuneration committee should consider whether the directors should be eligible for benefits under long-term incentive schemes. Traditional share option schemes should be weighed against other kinds of long-term incentive scheme. In normal circumstances, shares granted or other forms of deferred remuneration should not vest, and options should not be exercisable, in less than three years. Directors should be encouraged to hold their shares for a further period after vesting or exercise, subject to the need to finance any costs of acquisition and associated tax liabilities.
3. Any new long-term incentive schemes which are proposed should be approved by shareholders and should preferably replace any existing schemes or at least form part of a well considered overall plan, incorporating existing schemes. The total rewards potentially available should not be excessive.
4. Payouts or grants under all incentive schemes, including new grants under existing share option schemes, should be subject to challenging performance criteria reflecting the company's objectives. Consideration should be given to criteria which reflect the company's performance relative to a group of comparator companies in some key variables such as total shareholder return.
5. Grants under executive share option and other long-term incentive schemes should normally be phased rather than awarded in one large block.
6. In general, only basic salary should be pensionable.
7. The remuneration committee should consider the pension consequences and associated costs to the company of basic salary increases and any other changes in pensionable remuneration, especially for directors close to retirement.

Schedule B: Guidance on liability of non-executive directors: care, skill and diligence

1. Although non-executive directors and executive directors have as board members the same legal duties and objectives, the time devoted to the company's affairs is likely to be significantly less for a non-executive director than for an executive director and the detailed knowledge and experience of a company's affairs that could reasonably be expected of a non-executive director will generally be less than for an executive director. These matters may be relevant in assessing the knowledge, skill and experience which may reasonably be expected of a non-executive director and therefore the care, skill and diligence that a non-executive director may be expected to exercise.
2. In this context, the following elements of the Code may also be particularly relevant.
   (i) In order to enable directors to fulfil their duties, the Code states that:
   - The letter of appointment of the director should set out the expected time commitment (Code provision A.4.4); and
   - The board should be supplied in a timely manner with information in a form and of a quality appropriate to enable it to discharge its duties. The chairman is responsible for ensuring that the directors are provided by management with accurate, timely and clear information. (Code principles A.5).

   (ii) Non-executive directors should themselves:
   - Undertake appropriate induction and regularly update and refresh their skills, knowledge and familiarity with the company (Code principle A.5 and provision A.5.1)
   - Seek appropriate clarification or amplification of information and, where necessary, take and follow appropriate professional advice. (Code principle A.5 and provision A.5.2)
   - Where they have concerns about the running of the company or a proposed action, ensure that these are addressed by the board and, to the extent that they are not resolved, ensure that they are recorded in the board minutes (Code provision A.1.4).
   - Give a statement to the board if they have such unresolved concerns on resignation (Code provision A.1.4)
3. It is up to each non-executive director to reach a view as to what is necessary in particular circumstances to comply with the duty of care, skill and diligence they owe as a director to the company. In considering whether or not a person is in breach of that duty, a court would take into account all relevant circumstances. These may include having regard to the above where relevant to the issue of liability of a non-executive director.

Schedule C: Disclosure of corporate governance arrangements

The Listing Rules require a statement to be included in the annual report relating to compliance with the Code, as described in the preamble.

For ease of reference, the specific requirements in the Code for disclosure are set out below:

The annual report should record:

- a statement of how the board operates, including a high level statement of which types of decisions are to be taken by the board and which are to be delegated to management (A.1.1);
- the names of the chairman, the deputy chairman (where there is one), the chief executive, the senior independent director and the chairmen and members of the nomination, audit and remuneration committees (A.1.2);
- the number of meetings of the board and those committees and individual attendance by directors (A.1.2);
- the names of the non-executive directors whom the board determines to be independent, with reasons where necessary (A.3.1);
- the other significant commitments of the chairman and any changes to them during the year (A.4.3);
- how performance evaluation of the board, its committees and its directors has been conducted (A.6.1);
- the steps the board has taken to ensure that members of the board, and in particular the non-executive directors, develop an understanding of the views of major shareholders about their company (D.1.2).

The report should also include:

- a separate section describing the work of the nomination committee, including the process it has used in relation to board appointments and an explanation if neither external search consultancy nor open advertising has been used in the appointment of a chairman or a non-executive director (A.4.6);
- a description of the work of the remuneration committee as required under the Directors' Remuneration Reporting Regulations 2002, and including, where an executive director serves as a non-executive director elsewhere, whether or not the director will retain such earnings and, if so, what the remuneration is (B.1.4);
- an explanation from the directors of their responsibility for preparing the accounts and a statement by the auditors about their reporting responsibilities (C.1.1);

- a statement from the directors that the business is a going concern, with supporting assumptions or qualifications as necessary (C.1.2);
- a report that the board has conducted a review of the effectiveness of the group's system of internal controls (C.2.1);
- a separate section describing the work of the audit committee in discharging its responsibilities (C.3.3);
- where there is no internal audit function, the reasons for the absence of such a function (C.3.5);
- where the board does not accept the audit committee's recommendation on the appointment, reappointment or removal of an external auditor, a statement from the audit committee explaining the recommendation and the reasons why the board has taken a different position (C.3.6); and

an explanation of how, if the auditor provides non-audit services, auditor objectivity and independence is safeguarded (C.3.7).

The following information should be made available (which may be met by making it available on request and placing the information available on the company's website):

- the terms of reference of the nomination, remuneration and audit committees, explaining their role and the authority delegated to them by the board (A.4.1, B.2.1 and C.3.3);
- the terms and conditions of appointment of non-executive directors (A.4.4) (see footnote 10 on page 9); and
- where remuneration consultants are appointed, a statement of whether they have any other connection with the company (B.2.1).

The board should set out to shareholders in the papers accompanying a resolution to elect or re-elect:

- sufficient biographical details to enable shareholders to take an informed decision on their election or re-election (A.7.1).
- why they believe an individual should be elected to a non-executive role (A.7.2).
- on re-election of a non-executive director, confirmation from the chairman that, following formal performance evaluation, the individual's performance continues to be effective and to demonstrate commitment to the role, including commitment of time for board and committee meetings and any other duties (A.7.2).

The board should set out to shareholders in the papers recommending appointment or reappointment of an external auditor:

- if the board does not accept the audit committee's recommendation, a statement from the audit committee explaining the recommendation and from the board setting out reasons why they have taken a different position (C.3.6).

GUIDANCE ON INTERNAL CONTROL (The Turnbull Guidance)

CONTENTS

Note

Principle D.2, provision D.2.1 and provision D.2.2 of the old (1998) Code appear in the new (2003) Code as principle C.2, provision C.2.1 and (in an amended form) provision C.3.5. The Code references in the guidance on internal control should be read accordingly.

INTRODUCTION

Internal control requirements of the Combined Code

1. When the Combined Code of the Committee on Corporate Governance (the Code) was published, the Institute of Chartered Accountants in England & Wales agreed with the London Stock Exchange that it would provide guidance to assist listed companies to implement the requirements in the Code relating to internal control.
2. Principle D.2 of the Code states that 'The board should maintain a sound system of internal control to safeguard shareholders' investment and the company's assets'.
3. Provision D.2.1 states that 'The directors should, at least annually, conduct a review of the effectiveness of the group's system of internal control and should report to shareholders that they have done so. The review should cover all controls, including financial, operational and compliance controls and risk management'.
4. Provision D.2.2 states that 'Companies which do not have an internal audit function should from time to time review the need for one'.
5. Paragraph 12.43A of the London Stock Exchange Listing Rules states that 'in the case of a company incorporated in the United Kingdom, the following additional items must be included in its annual report and accounts:
   (a) a narrative statement of how it has applied the principles set out in Section 1 of the Combined Code, providing explanation which enables its shareholders to evaluate how the principles have been applied;
   (b) a statement as to whether or not it has complied throughout the accounting period with the Code provisions set out in Section 1 of the Combined Code. A company that has not complied with the Code provisions, or complied with only some of the Code provisions or (in the case of provisions whose requirements are of a continuing nature) complied for only part of an accounting period, must specify the Code provisions with which it has not complied, and (where relevant) for what part of the period such non-compliance continued, and give reasons for any non-compliance'.
6. The Preamble to the Code, which is appended to the Listing Rules, makes it clear that there is no prescribed form or content for the statement setting out how the various principles in the Code have been applied. The intention is that companies should have a free hand to

explain their governance policies in the light of the principles, including any special circumstances which have led to them adopting a particular approach.

7. The guidance in this document should be followed by boards of listed companies in:
   - assessing how the company has applied Code principle D.2;
   - implementing the requirements of Code provisions D.2.1 and D.2.2; and
   - reporting on these matters to shareholders in the annual report and accounts.

Objectives of the guidance

8. This guidance is intended to:
   - reflect sound business practice whereby internal control is embedded in the business processes by which a company pursues its objectives;
   - remain relevant over time in the continually evolving business environment; and
   - enable each company to apply it in a manner which takes account of its particular circumstances.

   The guidance requires directors to exercise judgement in reviewing how the company has implemented the requirements of the Code relating to internal control and reporting to shareholders thereon.

9. The guidance is based on the adoption by a company's board of a risk-based approach to establishing a sound system of internal control and reviewing its effectiveness. This should be incorporated by the company within its normal management and governance processes. It should not be treated as a separate exercise undertaken to meet regulatory requirements.

The importance of internal control and risk management

10. A company's system of internal control has a key role in the management of risks that are significant to the fulfilment of its business objectives. A sound system of internal control contributes to safeguarding the shareholders' investment and the company's assets.

11. Internal control (as referred to in paragraph 20) facilitates the effectiveness and efficiency of operations, helps ensure the reliability of internal and external reporting and assists compliance with laws and regulations.
12. Effective financial controls, including the maintenance of proper accounting records, are an important element of internal control. They help ensure that the company is not unnecessarily exposed to avoidable financial risks and that financial information used within the business and for publication is reliable. They also contribute to the safeguarding of assets, including the prevention and detection of fraud.
13. A company's objectives, its internal organisation and the environment in which it operates are continually evolving and, as a result, the risks it faces are continually changing. A sound system of internal control therefore depends on a thorough and regular evaluation of the nature and extent of the risks to which the company is exposed. Since profits are, in part, the reward for successful risk- taking in business, the purpose of internal control is to help manage and control risk appropriately rather than to eliminate it.

Groups of companies

14. Throughout this guidance, where reference is made to 'company' it should be taken, where applicable, as referring to the group of which the reporting company is the parent company. For groups of companies, the review of effectiveness of internal control and the report to the shareholders should be from the perspective of the group as a whole.

The Appendix

15. The Appendix to this document contains questions which boards may wish to consider in applying this guidance.

MAINTAINING A SOUND SYSTEM OF INTERNAL CONTROL

Responsibilities

16. The board of directors is responsible for the company's system of internal control. It should set appropriate policies on internal control and seek regular assurance that will enable it to satisfy itself that the system is functioning effectively. The board must further ensure that the system of internal control is effective in managing risks in the manner which it has approved.
17. In determining its policies with regard to internal control, and thereby assessing what constitutes a sound system of internal control in the particular circumstances of the company, the board's deliberations should include consideration of the following factors:
    - the nature and extent of the risks facing the company;
    - the extent and categories of risk which it regards as acceptable for the company to bear;
    - the likelihood of the risks concerned materialising;
    - the company's ability to reduce the incidence and impact on the business of risks that do materialise; and
    - the costs of operating particular controls relative to the benefit thereby obtained in managing the related risks.
18. It is the role of management to implement board policies on risk and control. In fulfilling its responsibilities, management should identify and evaluate the risks faced by the company for consideration by the board and design, operate and monitor a suitable system of internal control which implements the policies adopted by the board.
19. All employees have some responsibility for internal control as part of their accountability for achieving objectives. They, collectively, should have the necessary knowledge, skills, information and authority to establish, operate and monitor the system of internal control. This will require an understanding of the company, its objectives, the industries and markets in which it operates, and the risks it faces.

Elements of a sound system of internal control

20. An internal control system encompasses the policies, processes, tasks, behaviours and other aspects of a company that, taken together:

- facilitate its effective and efficient operation by enabling it to respond appropriately to significant business, operational, financial, compliance and other risks to achieving the company's objectives. This includes the safeguarding of assets from inappropriate use or from loss and fraud, and ensuring that liabilities are identified and managed;
- help ensure the quality of internal and external reporting. This requires the maintenance of proper records and processes that generate a flow of timely, relevant and reliable information from within and outside the organisation;
- help ensure compliance with applicable laws and regulations, and also with internal policies with respect to the conduct of business.

21. A company's system of internal control will reflect its control environment which encompasses its organisational structure. The system will include:
    - control activities;
    - information and communications processes; and
    - processes for monitoring the continuing effectiveness of the system of internal control.

22. The system of internal control should:
    - be embedded in the operations of the company and form part of its culture;
    - be capable of responding quickly to evolving risks to the business arising from factors within the company and to changes in the business environment; and
    - include procedures for reporting immediately to appropriate levels of management any significant control failings or weaknesses that are identified together with details of corrective action being undertaken.

23. A sound system of internal control reduces, but cannot eliminate, the possibility of poor judgement in decision-making; human error; control processes being deliberately circumvented by employees and others; management overriding controls; and the occurrence of unforeseeable circumstances.

24. A sound system of internal control therefore provides reasonable, but not absolute, assurance that a company will not be hindered in achieving its business objectives, or in the orderly and legitimate conduct of its business, by circumstances which may reasonably be foreseen. A system of internal control cannot, however, provide protection with certainty against a company failing to meet its business objectives or all material errors, losses, fraud, or breaches of laws or regulations.

REVIEWING THE EFFECTIVENESS OF INTERNAL CONTROL

Responsibilities

25. Reviewing the effectiveness of internal control is an essential part of the board's responsibilities. The board will need to form its own view on effectiveness after due and careful enquiry based on the information and assurances provided to it. Management is accountable to the board for monitoring the system of internal control and for providing assurance to the board that it has done so.

26. The role of board committees in the review process, including that of the audit committee, is for the board to decide and will depend upon factors such as the size and composition of the board; the scale, diversity and complexity of the company's operations; and the nature of the significant risks that the company faces. To the extent that designated board committees carry out, on behalf of the board, tasks that are attributed in this guidance document to the board, the results of the relevant committees' work should be reported to, and considered by, the board. The board takes responsibility for the disclosures on internal control in the annual report and accounts.

The process for reviewing effectiveness

27. Effective monitoring on a continuous basis is an essential component of a sound system of internal control. The board cannot, however, rely solely on the embedded monitoring processes within the company to discharge its responsibilities. It should regularly receive and review reports on internal control. In addition, the board should undertake an annual assessment for the purposes of making its public statement on internal control to ensure that it has considered all significant aspects of internal control for the company for the year under review and up to the date of approval of the annual report and accounts.

28. The reference to 'all controls' in Code Provision D.2.1 should not be taken to mean that the effectiveness of every internal control (including controls designed to manage immaterial risks) should be subject to review by the board. Rather it means that, for the purposes of this guidance, internal controls considered by the board should include all types of controls including those of an operational and compliance nature, as well as internal financial controls.

29. The board should define the process to be adopted for its review of the effectiveness of internal control. This should encompass both the scope and frequency of the reports it receives and reviews during the year, and also the process for its annual assessment, such that it will be provided

with sound, appropriately documented, support for its statement on internal control in the company's annual report and accounts.

30. The reports from management to the board should, in relation to the areas covered by them, provide a balanced assessment of the significant risks and the effectiveness of the system of internal control in managing those risks. Any significant control failings or weaknesses identified should be discussed in the reports, including the impact that they have had, could have had, or may have, on the company and the actions being taken to rectify them. It is essential that there be openness of communication by management with the board on matters relating to risk and control.

31. When reviewing reports during the year, the board should:
    - consider what are the significant risks and assess how they have been identified, evaluated and managed;
    - assess the effectiveness of the related system of internal control in managing the significant risks, having regard, in particular, to any significant failings or weaknesses in internal control that have been reported;
    - consider whether necessary actions are being taken promptly to remedy any significant failings or weaknesses; and
    - consider whether the findings indicate a need for more extensive monitoring of the system of internal control.

32. Additionally, the board should undertake an annual assessment for the purpose of making its public statement on internal control. The assessment should consider issues dealt with in reports reviewed by it during the year together with any additional information necessary to ensure that the board has taken account of all significant aspects of internal control for the company for the year under review and up to the date of approval of the annual report and accounts.

33. The board's annual assessment should, in particular, consider:
    - the changes since the last annual assessment in the nature and extent of significant risks, and the company's ability to respond to changes in its business and the external environment;
    - the scope and quality of management's ongoing monitoring of risks and of the system of internal control, and, where applicable, the work of its internal audit function and other providers of assurance;
    - the extent and frequency of the communication of the results of the monitoring to the board (or board committee(s)) which enables it to build up a cumulative assessment of the state of control in the company and the effectiveness with which risk is being managed;

- the incidence of significant control failings or weaknesses that have been identified at any time during the period and the extent to which they have resulted in unforeseen outcomes or contingencies that have had, could have had, or may in the future have, a material impact on the company's financial performance or condition; and
- the effectiveness of the company's public reporting processes.

34. Should the board become aware at any time of a significant failing or weakness in internal control, it should determine how the failing or weakness arose and re-assess the effectiveness of management's ongoing processes for designing, operating and monitoring the system of internal control.

THE BOARD'S STATEMENT ON INTERNAL CONTROL

35. In its narrative statement of how the company has applied Code principle D.2, the board should, as a minimum, disclose that there is an ongoing process for identifying, evaluating and managing the significant risks faced by the company, that it has been in place for the year under review and up to the date of approval of the annual report and accounts, that it is regularly reviewed by the board and accords with the guidance in this document.
36. The board may wish to provide additional information in the annual report and accounts to assist understanding of the company's risk management processes and system of internal control.
37. The disclosures relating to the application of principle D.2 should include an acknowledgement by the board that it is responsible for the company's system of internal control and for reviewing its effectiveness. It should also explain that such a system is designed to manage rather than eliminate the risk of failure to achieve business objectives, and can only provide reasonable and not absolute assurance against material misstatement or loss.
38. In relation to Code provision D.2.1, the board should summarise the process it (where applicable, through its committees) has applied in reviewing the effectiveness of the system of internal control. It should also disclose the process it has applied to deal with material internal control aspects of any significant problems disclosed in the annual report and accounts.
39. Where a board cannot make one or more of the disclosures in paragraphs 35 and 38, it should state this fact and provide an explanation. The Listing Rules require the board to disclose if it has failed to conduct a review of the effectiveness of the company's system of internal control.

40. The board should ensure that its disclosures provide meaningful, high-level information and do not give a misleading impression.

41. Where material joint ventures and associates have not been dealt with as part of the group for the purposes of applying this guidance, this should be disclosed.

INTERNAL AUDIT

42. Provision D.2.2 of the Code states that companies which do not have an internal audit function should from time to time review the need for one.

43. The need for an internal audit function will vary depending on company-specific factors including the scale, diversity and complexity of the company's activities and the number of employees, as well as cost/benefit considerations. Senior management and the board may desire objective assurance and advice on risk and control. An adequately resourced internal audit function (or its equivalent where, for example, a third party is contracted to perform some or all of the work concerned) may provide such assurance and advice. There may be other functions within the company that also provide assurance and advice covering specialist areas such as health and safety, regulatory and legal compliance and environmental issues.

44. In the absence of an internal audit function, management needs to apply other monitoring processes in order to assure itself and the board that the system of internal control is functioning as intended. In these circumstances, the board will need to assess whether such processes provide sufficient and objective assurance.

45. When undertaking its assessment of the need for an internal audit function, the board should also consider whether there are any trends or current factors relevant to the company's activities, markets or other aspects of its external environment, that have increased, or are expected to increase, the risks faced by the company. Such an increase in risk may also arise from internal factors such as organisational restructuring or from changes in reporting processes or underlying information systems. Other matters to be taken into account may include adverse trends evident from the monitoring of internal control systems or an increased incidence of unexpected occurrences.

46. The board of a company that does not have an internal audit function should assess the need for such a function annually having regard to the factors referred to in paragraphs 43 and 45 above. Where there is an internal audit function, the board should annually review its scope of work, authority and resources, again having regard to those factors.

47. If the company does not have an internal audit function and the board has not reviewed the need for one, the Listing Rules require the board to disclose these facts.

APPENDIX

Assessing the effectiveness of the company's risk and control processes

Some questions which the board may wish to consider and discuss with management when regularly reviewing reports on internal control and carrying out its annual assessment are set out below. The questions are not intended to be exhaustive and will need to be tailored to the particular circumstances of the company.

This Appendix should be read in conjunction with the guidance set out in this document.

1. Risk assessment

- Does the company have clear objectives and have they been communicated so as to provide effective direction to employees on risk assessment and control issues? For example, do objectives and related plans include measurable performance targets and indicators?
- Are the significant internal and external operational, financial, compliance and other risks identified and assessed on an ongoing basis? (Significant risks may, for example, include those related to market, credit, liquidity, technological, legal, health, safety and environmental, reputation, and business probity issues.)
- Is there a clear understanding by management and others within the company of what risks are acceptable to the board?

2. Control environment and control activities

- Does the board have clear strategies for dealing with the significant risks that have been identified? Is there a policy on how to manage these risks?
- Do the company's culture, code of conduct, human resource policies and performance reward systems support the business objectives and risk management and internal control system?
- Does senior management demonstrate, through its actions as well as its policies, the necessary commitment to competence, integrity and fostering a climate of trust within the company?
- Are authority, responsibility and accountability defined clearly such that decisions are made and actions taken by the appropriate people? Are the decisions and actions of different parts of the company appropriately co-ordinated?
- Does the company communicate to its employees what is expected of them and the scope of their freedom to act? This may apply to areas

such as customer relations; service levels for both internal and outsourced activities; health, safety and environmental protection; security of tangible and intangible assets; business continuity issues; expenditure matters; accounting; and financial and other reporting.

- Do people in the company (and in its providers of outsourced services) have the knowledge, skills and tools to support the achievement of the company's objectives and to manage effectively risks to their achievement?
- How are processes/controls adjusted to reflect new or changing risks, or operational deficiencies?

3. Information and communication

- Do management and the board receive timely, relevant and reliable reports on progress against business objectives and the related risks that provide them with the information, from inside and outside the company, needed for decision-making and management review purposes? This could include performance reports and indicators of change, together with qualitative information such as on customer satisfaction, employee attitudes etc.
- Are information needs and related information systems reassessed as objectives and related risks change or as reporting deficiencies are identified?
- Are periodic reporting procedures, including half-yearly and annual reporting, effective in communicating a balanced and understandable account of the company's position and prospects?
- Are there established channels of communication for individuals to report suspected breaches of laws or regulations or other improprieties?

4. Monitoring

- Are there ongoing processes embedded within the company's overall business operations, and addressed by senior management, which monitor the effective application of the policies, processes and activities related to internal control and risk management? (Such processes may include control self-assessment, confirmation by personnel of compliance with policies and codes of conduct, internal audit reviews or other management reviews).

- Do these processes monitor the company's ability to re-evaluate risks and adjust controls effectively in response to changes in its objectives, its business, and its external environment?
- Are there effective follow-up procedures to ensure that appropriate change or action occurs in response to changes in risk and control assessments?
- Is there appropriate communication to the board (or board committees) on the effectiveness of the ongoing monitoring processes on risk and control matters? This should include reporting any significant failings or weaknesses on a timely basis.
- Are there specific arrangements for management monitoring and reporting to the board on risk and control matters of particular importance? These could include, for example, actual or suspected fraud and other illegal or irregular acts, or matters that could adversely affect the company's reputation or financial position?

GUIDANCE ON AUDIT COMMITTEES (The Smith Guidance)

CONTENTS

Note

The following guidance is closely based on Sir Robert Smith's proposed guidance published in January 2003 (see footnote 2, page 1), modified for consistency with the final revised Code.

AUDIT COMMITTEES – COMBINED CODE GUIDANCE

1 Introduction

1.1 This guidance is designed to assist company boards in making suitable arrangements for their audit committees, and to assist directors serving on audit committees in carrying out their role.

1.2 The paragraphs in bold are taken from the Combined Code (Section C3). Listed companies that do not comply with those provisions should include an explanation as to why they have not complied in the statement required by the Listing Rules.

1.3 Best practice requires that every board should consider in detail what arrangements for its audit committee are best suited for its particular circumstances. Audit committee arrangements need to be proportionate to the task, and will vary according to the size, complexity and risk profile of the company.

1.4 While all directors have a duty to act in the interests of the company the audit committee has a particular role, acting independently from the executive, to ensure that the interests of shareholders are properly protected in relation to financial reporting and internal control.

1.5 Nothing in the guidance should be interpreted as a departure from the principle of the unitary board. All directors remain equally responsible for the company's affairs as a matter of law. The audit committee, like other committees to which particular responsibilities are delegated (such as the remuneration committee), remains a committee of the board. Any disagreement within the board, including disagreement between the audit committee's members and the rest of the board, should be resolved at board level.

1.6 The Code provides that a separate section of the annual report should describe the work of the committee. This deliberately puts the spotlight on the audit committee and gives it an authority that it might otherwise lack. This is not incompatible with the principle of the unitary board.

1.7 The guidance contains recommendations about the conduct of the audit committee's relationship with the board, with the executive management and with internal and external auditors. However, the most important features of this relationship cannot be drafted as guidance or put into a code of practice: a frank, open working relationship and a high level of mutual respect are essential, particularly between the audit committee chairman and the board chairman, the chief executive and the finance director. The audit committee must be prepared to take a robust stand, and all parties must be prepared to make information freely available to the audit committee, to listen to their views and to talk through the issues openly.

1.8 In particular, the management is under an obligation to ensure the audit committee is kept properly informed, and should take the initiative in supplying information rather than waiting to be asked. The board should make it clear to all directors and staff that they must cooperate with the audit committee and provide it with any information it requires. In addition, executive board members will have regard to their common law duty to provide all directors, including those on the audit committee, with all the information they need to discharge their responsibilities as directors of the company.

1.9 Many of the core functions of audit committees set out in this guidance are expressed in terms of 'oversight', 'assessment' and 'review' of a particular function. It is not the duty of audit committees to carry out functions that properly belong to others, such as the company's management in the preparation of the financial statements or the auditors in the planning or conducting of audits. To do so could undermine the responsibility of management and auditors. Audit committees should, for example, satisfy themselves that there is a proper system and allocation of responsibilities for the day-to-day monitoring of financial controls but they should not seek to do the monitoring themselves.

1.10 However, the high-level oversight function may lead to detailed work. The audit committee must intervene if there are signs that something may be seriously amiss. For example, if the audit committee is uneasy about the explanations of management and auditors about a particular financial reporting policy decision, there may be no alternative but to grapple with the detail and perhaps to seek independent advice.

1.11 Under this guidance, audit committees have wide-ranging, time-consuming and sometimes intensive work to do. Companies need to make the necessary resources available. This includes suitable payment for the members of audit committees themselves. They – and particularly the audit committee chairman – bear a significant responsibility and they need to commit a significant extra amount of time to the job. Companies also need to make provision for induction and training for new audit committee members and continuing training as may be required.

1.12 This guidance applies to all companies to which the Code applies – i.e. UK listed companies. For groups, it will usually be necessary for the audit committee of the parent company to review issues that relate to particular subsidiaries or activities carried on by the group. Consequently, the board of a UK-listed parent company should ensure that there is adequate cooperation within the group (and with internal and external auditors of individual companies within the group) to enable the parent company audit committee to discharge its responsibilities effectively.

2 Establishment and role of the audit committee; membership, procedures and resources

Establishment and role

2.1 The board should establish an audit committee of at least three, or in the case of smaller companies two, members.

2.2 The main role and responsibilities of the audit committee should be set out in written terms of reference and should include:

- to monitor the integrity of the financial statements of the company and any formal announcements relating to the company's financial performance, reviewing significant financial reporting judgements contained in them;
- to review the company's internal financial controls and, unless expressly addressed by a separate board risk committee composed of independent directors or by the board itself, the company's internal control and risk management systems;
- to monitor and review the effectiveness of the company's internal audit function;
- to make recommendations to the board, for it to put to the shareholders for their approval in general meeting, in relation to the appointment of the external auditor and to approve the remuneration and terms of engagement of the external auditor;
- to review and monitor the external auditor's independence and objectivity and the effectiveness of the audit process, taking into consideration relevant UK professional and regulatory requirements;
- to develop and implement policy on the engagement of the external auditor to supply non-audit services, taking into account relevant ethical guidance regarding the provision of non-audit services by the external audit firm;

and to report to the Board, identifying any matters in respect of which it considers that action or improvement is needed, and making recommendations as to the steps to be taken.

Membership and appointment

2.3 All members of the committee should be independent non-executive directors. The board should satisfy itself that at least one member of the audit committee has recent and relevant financial experience.

2.4 The chairman of the company should not be an audit committee member.

2.5 Appointments to the audit committee should be made by the board on the recommendation of the nomination committee (where there is one), in consultation with the audit committee chairman.

2.6 Appointments should be for a period of up to three years, extendable by no more than two additional three-year periods, so long as members continue to be independent.

Meetings of the audit committee

2.7 It is for the audit committee chairman, in consultation with the company secretary, to decide the frequency and timing of its meetings. There should be as many meetings as the audit committee's role and responsibilities require. It is recommended there should be not fewer than three meetings during the year, held to coincide with key dates within the financial reporting and audit cycle[1]. However, most audit committee chairmen will wish to call more frequent meetings.

2.8 No one other than the audit committee's chairman and members is entitled to be present at a meeting of the audit committee. It is for the audit committee to decide if non-members should attend for a particular meeting or a particular agenda item. It is to be expected that the external audit lead partner will be invited regularly to attend meetings as well as the finance director. Others may be invited to attend.

2.9 Sufficient time should be allowed to enable the audit committee to undertake as full a discussion as may be required. A sufficient interval should be allowed between audit committee meetings and main board meetings to allow any work arising from the audit committee meeting to be carried out and reported to the board as appropriate.

2.10 The audit committee should, at least annually, meet the external and internal auditors, without management, to discuss matters relating to its remit and any issues arising from the audit.

---

[1] For example, when the audit plans (internal and external) are available for review and when interim statements, preliminary announcements and the full annual report are near completion.

2.11 Formal meetings of the audit committee are the heart of its work. However, they will rarely be sufficient. It is expected that the audit committee chairman, and to a lesser extent the other members, will wish to keep in touch on a continuing basis with the key people involved in the company's governance, including the board chairman, the chief executive, the finance director, the external audit lead partner and the head of internal audit.

Resources

2.12 The audit committee should be provided with sufficient resources to undertake its duties.

2.13 The audit committee should have access to the services of the company secretariat on all audit committee matters including: assisting the chairman in planning the audit committee's work, drawing up meeting agendas, maintenance of minutes, drafting of material about its activities for the annual report, collection and distribution of information and provision of any necessary practical support.

2.14 The company secretary should ensure that the audit committee receives information and papers in a timely manner to enable full and proper consideration to be given to the issues.

2.15 The board should make funds available to the audit committee to enable it to take independent legal, accounting or other advice when the audit committee reasonably believes it necessary to do so.

Remuneration

2.16 In addition to the remuneration paid to all non-executive directors, each company should consider the further remuneration that should be paid to members of the audit committee to recompense them for the additional responsibilities of membership. Consideration should be given to the time members are required to give to audit committee business, the skills they bring to bear and the onerous duties they take on, as well as the value of their work to the company. The level of remuneration paid to the members of the audit committee should take into account the level of fees paid to other members of the board. The chairman's responsibilities and time demands will generally be heavier than the other members of the audit committee and this should be reflected in his or her remuneration.

Skills, experience and training

2.17 It is desirable that the committee member whom the board considers to have recent and relevant financial experience should have a professional qualification from one of the professional accountancy bodies. The need for a degree of financial literacy among the other members will vary according to the nature of the company, but experience of corporate financial matters will normally be required. The availability of appropriate financial expertise will be particularly important where the company's activities involve specialised financial activities.

2.18 The company should provide an induction programme for new audit committee members. This should cover the role of the audit committee, including its terms of reference and expected time commitment by members; and an overview of the company's business, identifying the main business and financial dynamics and risks. It could also include meeting some of the company staff.

2.19 Training should also be provided to members of the audit committee on an ongoing and timely basis and should include an understanding of the principles of and developments in financial reporting and related company law. In appropriate cases, it may also include, for example, understanding financial statements, applicable accounting standards and recommended practice; the regulatory framework for the company's business; the role of internal and external auditing and risk management.

2.20 The induction programme and ongoing training may take various forms, including attendance at formal courses and conferences, internal company talks and seminars, and briefings by external advisers.

3 Relationship with the board

3.1 The role of the audit committee is for the board to decide and to the extent that the audit committee undertakes tasks on behalf of the board, the results should be reported to, and considered by, the board. In doing so it should identify any matters in respect of which it considers that action or improvement is needed, and make recommendations as to the steps to be taken.

3.2 The terms of reference should be tailored to the particular circumstances of the company.

3.3 The audit committee should review annually its terms of reference and its own effectiveness and recommend any necessary changes to the board.

3.4 The board should review the audit committee's effectiveness annually.

3.5 Where there is disagreement between the audit committee and the board, adequate time should be made available for discussion of the issue with a view to resolving the disagreement. Where any such disagreements cannot be resolved, the audit committee should have the right to report the issue to the shareholders as part of the report on its activities in the annual report.

4 Role and responsibilities

Financial reporting

4.1 The audit committee should review the significant financial reporting issues and judgements made in connection with the preparation of the company's financial statements, interim reports, preliminary announcements and related formal statements.

4.2 It is management's, not the audit committee's, responsibility to prepare complete and accurate financial statements and disclosures in accordance with financial reporting standards and applicable rules and regulations. However the audit committee should consider significant accounting policies, any changes to them and any significant estimates and judgements. The management should inform the audit committee of the methods used to account for significant or unusual transactions where the accounting treatment is open to different approaches. Taking into account the external auditor's view, the audit committee should consider whether the company has adopted appropriate accounting policies and, where necessary, made appropriate estimates and judgements. The audit committee should review the clarity and completeness of disclosures in the financial statements and consider whether the disclosures made are set properly in context.

4.3 Where, following its review, the audit committee is not satisfied with any aspect of the proposed financial reporting by the company, it shall report its views to the board.

4.4 The audit committee should review related information presented with the financial statements, including the operating and financial review, and corporate governance statements relating to the audit and to risk management. Similarly, where board approval is required for other statements containing financial information (for example, summary financial statements, significant financial returns to regulators and release of price sensitive information), whenever practicable (without being inconsistent with any requirement for prompt reporting under the Listing Rules) the audit committee should review such statements first.

Internal controls and risk management systems

4.5 The audit committee should review the company's internal financial controls (that is, the systems established to identify, assess, manage and monitor financial risks); and unless expressly addressed by a separate board risk committee comprised of independent directors or by the board itself, the company's internal control and risk management systems.

4.6 The company's management is responsible for the identification, assessment, management and monitoring of risk, for developing, operating and monitoring the system of internal control and for providing assurance to the board that it has done so. Except where the board or a risk committee is expressly responsible for reviewing the effectiveness of the internal control and risk management systems, the audit committee should receive reports from management on the effectiveness of the systems they have established and the conclusions of any testing carried out by internal and external auditors.

4.7 Except to the extent that this is expressly dealt with by the board or risk committee, the audit committee should review and approve the statements included in the annual report in relation to internal control and the management of risk.

Whistleblowing

4.8 The audit committee should review arrangements by which staff of the company may, in confidence, raise concerns about possible improprieties in matters of financial reporting or other matters. The audit committee's objective should be to ensure that arrangements are in place for the proportionate and independent investigation of such matters and for appropriate follow-up action.

The internal audit process

4.9 The audit committee should monitor and review the effectiveness of the company's internal audit function. Where there is no internal audit function, the audit committee should consider annually whether there is a need for an internal audit function and make a recommendation to the board, and the reasons for the absence of such a function should be explained in the relevant section of the annual report.

4.10 The audit committee should review and approve the internal audit function's remit, having regard to the complementary roles of the internal and external audit functions. The audit committee should ensure that the function has the necessary resources and access to information to enable it to fulfil its mandate, and is equipped to perform in accordance with appropriate professional standards for internal auditors[2].

4.11 The audit committee should approve the appointment or termination of appointment of the head of internal audit.

4.12 In its review of the work of the internal audit function, the audit committee should, inter alia:

- ensure that the internal auditor has direct access to the board chairman and to the audit committee and is accountable to the audit committee;
- review and assess the annual internal audit work plan;
- receive a report on the results of the internal auditors' work on a periodic basis;
- review and monitor management's responsiveness to the internal auditor's findings and recommendations;
- meet with the head of internal audit at least once a year without the presence of management; and
- monitor and assess the role and effectiveness of the internal audit function in the overall context of the company's risk management system.

The external audit process

4.13 The audit committee is the body responsible for overseeing the company's relations with the external auditor.

Appointment

4.14 The audit committee should have primary responsibility for making a recommendation on the appointment, reappointment and removal of the external auditors. If the board does not accept the audit committee's recommendation, it should include in the annual report, and in any papers recommending appointment or reappointment, a statement from the audit committee explaining its recommendation and should set out reasons why the board has taken a different position.

4.15 The audit committee's recommendation to the board should be based on the assessments referred to below. If the audit committee recom-

[2] Further guidance can be found in the Institute of Internal Auditors' Code of Ethics and the International Standards for the Professional Practice of Internal Auditing Standards.

mends considering the selection of possible new appointees as external auditors, it should oversee the selection process.

4.16 The audit committee should assess annually the qualification, expertise and resources, and independence (see below) of the external auditors and the effectiveness of the audit process. The assessment should cover all aspects of the audit service provided by the audit firm, and include obtaining a report on the audit firm's own internal quality control procedures.

4.17 If the external auditor resigns, the audit committee should investigate the issues giving rise to such resignation and consider whether any action is required.

Terms and Remuneration

4.18 The audit committee should approve the terms of engagement and the remuneration to be paid to the external auditor in respect of audit services provided.

4.19 The audit committee should review and agree the engagement letter issued by the external auditor at the start of each audit, ensuring that it has been updated to reflect changes in circumstances arising since the previous year. The scope of the external audit should be reviewed by the audit committee with the auditor. If the audit committee is not satisfied as to its adequacy it should arrange for additional work to be undertaken.

4.20 The audit committee should satisfy itself that the level of fee payable in respect of the audit services provided is appropriate and that an effective audit can be conducted for such a fee.

Independence, including the provision of non-audit services

4.21 The audit committee should have procedures to ensure the independence and objectivity of the external auditor annually, taking into consideration relevant UK professional and regulatory requirements. This assessment should involve a consideration of all relationships between the company and the audit firm (including the provision of non-audit services). The audit committee should consider whether, taken as a whole and having regard to the views, as appropriate, of the external auditor, management and internal audit, those relationships appear to impair the auditor's judgement or independence.

4.22 The audit committee should seek reassurance that the auditors and their staff have no family, financial, employment, investment or business relationship with the company (other than in the normal course of business). The audit committee should seek from the audit firm, on an annual basis, information about policies and processes for maintaining independence and monitoring compliance with relevant requirements, including current requirements regarding the rotation of audit partners and staff.

4.23 The audit committee should agree with the board the company's policy for the employment of former employees of the external auditor, paying particular attention to the policy regarding former employees of the audit firm who were part of the audit team and moved directly to the company. This should be drafted taking into account the relevant ethical guidelines governing the accounting profession. The audit committee should monitor application of the policy, including the number of former employees of the external auditor currently employed in senior positions in the company, and consider whether in the light of this there has been any impairment, or appearance of impairment, of the auditor's judgement or independence in respect of the audit.

4.24 The audit committee should monitor the external audit firm's compliance with applicable United Kingdom ethical guidance relating to the rotation of audit partners, the level of fees that the company pays in proportion to the overall fee income of the firm, office and partner, and other related regulatory requirements.

4.25 The audit committee should develop and recommend to the board the company's policy in relation to the provision of non-audit services by the auditor. The audit committee's objective should be to ensure that the provision of such services does not impair the external auditor's independence or objectivity. In this context, the audit committee should consider:

- whether the skills and experience of the audit firm make it a suitable supplier of the non audit service;
- whether there are safeguards in place to ensure that there is no threat to objectivity and independence in the conduct of the audit resulting from the provision of such services by the external auditor;
- the nature of the non-audit services, the related fee levels and the fee levels individually and in aggregate relative to the audit fee; and
- the criteria which govern the compensation of the individuals performing the audit.

4.26 The audit committee should set and apply a formal policy specifying the types of non-audit work:

- from which the external auditors are excluded;

- for which the external auditors can be engaged without referral to the audit committee; and
- for which a case-by-case decision is necessary.

In addition, the policy may set fee limits generally or for particular classes of work.

4.27 In the third category, if it is not practicable to give approval to individual items in advance, it may be appropriate to give a general pre-approval for certain classes for work, subject to a fee limit determined by the audit committee and ratified by the board. The subsequent provision of any service by the auditor should be ratified at the next meeting of the audit committee.

4.28 In determining the policy, the audit committee should take into account relevant ethical guidance regarding the provision of non-audit services by the external audit firm, and in principle should not agree to the auditor providing a service if, having regard to the ethical guidance, the result is that:

- the external auditor audits its own firm's work;
- the external auditor makes management decisions for the company;
- a mutuality of interest is created; or
- the external auditor is put in the role of advocate for the company.

The audit committee should satisfy itself that any safeguards required by ethical guidance are implemented.

4.29 The annual report should explain to shareholders how, if the auditor provides non-audit services, auditor objectivity and independence is safeguarded.

Annual audit cycle

4.30 At the start of each annual audit cycle, the audit committee should ensure that appropriate plans are in place for the audit.

4.31 The audit committee should consider whether the auditor's overall work plan, including planned levels of materiality, and proposed resources to execute the audit plan appears consistent with the scope of the audit engagement, having regard also to the seniority, expertise and experience of the audit team.

4.32 The audit committee should review, with the external auditors, the findings of their work. In the course of its review, the audit committee should:

- discuss with the external auditor major issues that arose during the course of the audit and have subsequently been resolved and those issues that have been left unresolved;
- review key accounting and audit judgements; and
- review levels of errors identified during the audit, obtaining explanations from management and, where necessary the external auditors, as to why certain errors might remain unadjusted.

4.33 The audit committee should also review the audit representation letters before signature by management and give particular consideration to matters where representation has been requested that relate to non-standard issues[3]. The audit committee should consider whether the information provided is complete and appropriate based on its own knowledge.

4.34 As part of the ongoing monitoring process, the audit committee should review the management letter (or equivalent). The audit committee should review and monitor management's responsiveness to the external auditor's findings and recommendations.

4.35 At the end of the annual audit cycle, the audit committee should assess the effectiveness of the audit process. In the course of doing so, the audit committee should:

- review whether the auditor has met the agreed audit plan and understand the reasons for any changes, including changes in perceived audit risks and the work undertaken by the external auditors to address those risks;
- consider the robustness and perceptiveness of the auditors in their handling of the key accounting and audit judgements identified and in responding to questions from the audit committees, and in their commentary where appropriate on the systems of internal control;
- obtain feedback about the conduct of the audit from key people involved, e.g. the finance director and the head of internal audit; and
- review and monitor the content of the external auditor's management letter, in order to assess whether it is based on a good understanding of the company's business and establish whether recommendations have been acted upon and, if not, the reasons why they have not been acted upon.

---

[3] Further guidance can by found in the Auditing Practices Board's Statement of Auditing Standard 440 "Management Representations".

5 Communication with shareholders

5.1 The terms of reference of the audit committee, including its role and the authority delegated to it by the board, should be made available. A separate section in the annual report should describe the work of the committee in discharging those responsibilities.

5.2 The audit committee section should include, inter alia:

- a summary of the role of the audit committee;
- the names and qualifications of all members of the audit committee during the period;
- the number of audit committee meetings;
- a report on the way the audit committee has discharged its responsibilities; and
- the explanation provided for in paragraph 4.29 above.

5.3 The chairman of the audit committee should be present at the AGM to answer questions, through the chairman of the board, on the report on the audit committee's activities and matters within the scope of audit committee's responsibilities.

SUGGESTIONS FOR GOOD PRACTICE FROM THE HIGGS REPORT

CONTENTS

GUIDANCE ON THE ROLE OF THE CHAIRMAN

The chairman is pivotal in creating the conditions for overall board and individual director effectiveness, both inside and outside the boardroom. Specifically, it is the responsibility of the chairman to:

- run the board and set its agenda. The agenda should take full account of the issues and the concerns of all board members. Agendas should be forward looking and concentrate on strategic matters rather than formulaic approvals of proposals which can be the subject of appropriate delegated powers to management;
- ensure that the members of the board receive accurate, timely and clear information, in particular about the company's performance, to enable the board to take sound decisions, monitor effectively and provide advice to promote the success of the company;
- ensure effective communication with shareholders and ensure that the members of the board develop an understanding of the views of the major investors;
- manage the board to ensure that sufficient time is allowed for discussion of complex or contentious issues, where appropriate arranging for informal meetings beforehand to enable thorough preparation for the board discussion. It is particularly important that non-executive directors have sufficient time to consider critical issues and are not faced with unrealistic deadlines for decision-making;
- take the lead in providing a properly constructed induction programme for new directors that is comprehensive, formal and tailored, facilitated by the company secretary;
- take the lead in identifying and meeting the development needs of individual directors, with the company secretary having a key role in facilitating provision. It is the responsibility of the chairman to address the development needs of the board as a whole with a view to enhancing its overall effectiveness as a team;
- ensure that the performance of individuals and of the board as a whole and its committees is evaluated at least once a year; and
- encourage active engagement by all the members of the board.

The effective chairman:

- upholds the highest standards of integrity and probity;
- sets the agenda, style and tone of board discussions to promote effective decision-making and constructive debate;

- promotes effective relationships and open communication, both inside and outside the boardroom, between non-executive directors and executive team;
- builds an effective and complementary board, initiating change and planning succession in board appointments, subject to board and shareholders' approval;
- promotes the highest standards of corporate governance and seeks compliance with the provisions of the Code wherever possible;
- ensures clear structure for and the effective running of board committees;
- ensures effective implementation of board decisions;
- establishes a close relationship of trust with the chief executive, providing support and advice while respecting executive responsibility; and
- provides coherent leadership of the company, including representing the company and understanding the views of shareholders.

GUIDANCE ON THE ROLE OF THE NON-EXECUTIVE DIRECTOR

As members of the unitary board, all directors are required to:

- Provide entrepreneurial leadership of the company within a framework of prudent and effective controls which enable risk to be assessed and managed;
- Set the company's strategic aims, ensure that the necessary financial and human resources are in place for the company to meet its objectives, and review management performance; and
- Set the company's values and standards and ensure that its obligations to its shareholders and others are understood and met.

In addition to these requirements for all directors, the role of the non-executive director has the following key elements:

- **Strategy.** Non-executive directors should constructively challenge and help develop proposals on strategy.
- **Performance.** Non-executive directors should scrutinise the performance of management in meeting agreed goals and objectives and monitor the reporting of performance.
- **Risk.** Non-executive directors should satisfy themselves on the integrity of financial information and that financial controls and systems of risk management are robust and defensible.
- **People.** Non-executive directors are responsible for determining appropriate levels of remuneration of executive directors, and have a prime role in appointing, and where necessary removing, executive directors and in succession planning.

Non-executive directors should constantly seek to establish and maintain confidence in the conduct of the company. They should be independent in judgement and have an enquiring mind. To be effective, non-executive directors need to build a recognition by executives of their contribution in order to promote openness and trust.

To be effective, non-executive directors need to be well-informed about the company and the external environment in which it operates, with a strong command of issues relevant to the business. A non-executive director should insist on a comprehensive, formal and tailored induction. An effective induction need not be restricted to the boardroom, so consideration should be given to visiting sites and meeting senior and middle management. Once in post, an effective non-executive director should seek continually to develop and refresh their knowledge and skills to ensure that their contribution to the board remains informed and relevant.

Best practice dictates that an effective non-executive director will ensure that information is provided sufficiently in advance of meetings to enable thorough consideration of the issues facing the board. The non-executive should insist that information is sufficient, accurate, clear and timely.

An element of the role of the non-executive director is to understand the views of major investors both directly and through the chairman and the senior independent director.

The effective non-executive director:

- upholds the highest ethical standards of integrity and probity;
- supports executives in their leadership of the business while monitoring their conduct;
- questions intelligently, debates constructively, challenges rigorously and decides dispassionately;
- listens sensitively to the views of others, inside and outside the board;
- gains the trust and respect of other board members; and
- promotes the highest standards of corporate governance and seeks compliance with the provisions of the Code wherever possible.

SUMMARY OF THE PRINCIPAL DUTIES OF THE REMUNERATION COMMITTEE

The Code provides that the remuneration committee should consist exclusively of independent non-executive directors and should comprise at least three or, in the case of smaller companies[1], two such directors.

Duties

The committee should:

- determine and agree with the board the framework or broad policy for the remuneration of the chief executive, the chairman of the company and such other members of the executive management as it is designated to consider[2]. At a minimum, the committee should have delegated responsibility for setting remuneration for all executive directors, the chairman and, to maintain and assure their independence, the company secretary. The remuneration of nonexecutive directors shall be a matter for the chairman and executive members of the board. No director or manager should be involved in any decisions as to their own remuneration;
- determine targets for any performance-related pay schemes operated by the company;
- determine the policy for and scope of pension arrangements for each executive director;
- ensure that contractual terms on termination, and any payments made, are fair to the individual and the company, that failure is not rewarded and that the duty to mitigate loss is fully recognised[3];
- within the terms of the agreed policy, determine the total individual remuneration package of each executive director including, where appropriate, bonuses, incentive payments and share options;
- in determining such packages and arrangements, give due regard to the contents of the Code as well as the UK Listing Authority's Listing Rules and associated guidance;
- be aware of and advise on any major changes in employee benefit structures throughout the company or group;

---

[1] A smaller company is one that is below the FTSE 350 throughout the year immediately prior to the reporting year.

[2] Some companies require the remuneration committee to consider the packages of all executives at or above a specified level such as those reporting to a main board director whilst others require the committee to deal with all packages above a certain figure.

[3] Remuneration committees should consider reviewing and agreeing a standard form of contract for their executive directors, and ensuring that new appointees are offered and accept terms within the previously agreed level.

- agree the policy for authorising claims for expenses from the chief executive and chairman;
- ensure that provisions regarding disclosure of remuneration, including pensions, as set out in the Directors' Remuneration Report Regulations 2002 and the Code, are fulfilled;
- be exclusively responsible for establishing the selection criteria, selecting, appointing and setting the terms of reference for any remuneration consultants who advise the committee;
- report the frequency of, and attendance by members at, remuneration committee meetings in the annual reports; and
- make available the committee's terms of reference. These should set out the committee's delegated responsibilities and be reviewed and, where necessary, updated annually.

This guidance has been compiled with the assistance of ICSA who have kindly agreed to produce updated guidance on their website www.icsa.org.uk in the future.

SUMMARY OF THE PRINCIPAL DUTIES OF THE NOMINATION COMMITTEE

There should be a nomination committee which should lead the process for board appointments and make recommendations to the board.

A majority of members of the committee should be independent non-executive directors. The chairman or an independent non-executive director should chair the committee, but the chairman should not chair the nomination committee when it is dealing with the appointment of a successor to the chairmanship.

Duties

The committee should:

- be responsible for identifying and nominating for the approval of the board, candidates to fill board vacancies as and when they arise;
- before making an appointment, evaluate the balance of skills, knowledge and experience on the board and, in the light of this evaluation, prepare a description of the role and capabilities required for a particular appointment;
- review annually the time required from a non-executive director. Performance evaluation should be used to assess whether the non-executive director is spending enough time to fulfil their duties;
- consider candidates from a wide range of backgrounds and look beyond the "usual suspects";
- give full consideration to succession planning in the course of its work, taking into account the challenges and opportunities facing the company and what skills and expertise are therefore needed on the board in the future;
- regularly review the structure, size and composition (including the skills, knowledge and experience) of the board and make recommendations to the board with regard to any changes;
- keep under review the leadership needs of the organisation, both executive and non-executive, with a view to ensuring the continued ability of the organisation to compete effectively in the marketplace;
- make a statement in the annual report about its activities; the process used for appointments and explain if external advice or open advertising has not been used; the membership of the committee, number of committee meetings and attendance over the course of the year;

- make available its terms of reference explaining clearly its role and the authority delegated to it by the board; and
- ensure that on appointment to the board, non-executive directors receive a formal letter of appointment setting out clearly what is expected of them in terms of time commitment, committee service and involvement outside board meetings.

The committee should make recommendations to the board:

- as regards plans for succession for both executive and non-executive directors;
- as regards the re-appointment of any non-executive director at the conclusion of their specified term of office;
- concerning the re-election by shareholders of any director under the retirement by rotation provisions in the company's articles of association;
- concerning any matters relating to the continuation in office of any director at any time; and
- concerning the appointment of any director to executive or other office other than to the positions of chairman and chief executive, the recommendation for which would be considered at a meeting of the board.

This guidance has been compiled with the assistance of ICSA who have kindly agreed to produce updated guidance on their website www.icsa.org.uk in the future.

PRE-APPOINTMENT DUE DILIGENCE CHECKLIST FOR NEW BOARD MEMBERS

Why?

Before accepting an appointment a prospective non-executive director should undertake their own thorough examination of the company to satisfy themselves that it is an organisation in which they can have faith and in which they will be well suited to working.

The following questions are not intended to be exhaustive, but are intended to be a helpful basis of the pre-appointment due diligence process that all non-executive directors should undertake.

Questions to ask

What is the company's current financial position and what has its financial track record been over the last three years?

What are the key dependencies (e.g. regulatory approvals, key licences, etc)?

What record does the company have on corporate governance issues?

If the company is not performing particularly well is there potential to turn it round and do I have the time, desire and capability to make a positive impact?

What are the exact nature and extent of the company's business activities?

Who are the current executive and non-executive directors, what is their background and their record and how long have they served on the board?

What is the size and structure of the board and board committees and what are the relationships between the chairman and the board, the chief executive and the management team?

Who owns the company i.e. who are the company's main shareholders and how has the profile changed over recent years? What is the company's attitude towards, and relationship with, its shareholders?

Is any material litigation presently being undertaken or threatened, either by the company or against it?

Is the company clear and specific about the qualities, knowledge, skills and experience that it needs to complement the existing board?

What insurance cover is available to directors and what is the company's policy on indemnifying directors?

Do I have the necessary knowledge, skills, experience and time to make a positive contribution to the board of this company?

How closely do I match the job specification and how well will I fulfil the board's expectations?

Is there anything about the nature and extent of the company's business activities that would cause me concern both in terms of risk and any personal ethical considerations?

Am I satisfied that the internal regulation of the company is sound and that I can operate effectively within its stated corporate governance framework?

Am I satisfied that the size, structure and make-up of the board will enable me to make an effective contribution?

Would accepting the non-executive directorship put me in a position of having a conflict of interest?

Sources of information

- Company report and accounts, and/or any listing prospectus, for the recent years.
- Analyst reports.
- Press reports
- Company web site
- Any Corporate Social Responsibility or Environmental Report issued by the company.
- Rating agency reports
- Voting services reports

Published material is unlikely to reveal wrong-doing, however a lack of transparency may be a reason to proceed with caution.

This guidance has been compiled with the assistance of ICSA who have kindly agreed to produce updated guidance on their website www.icsa.org.uk in the future.

SAMPLE LETTER OF NON-EXECUTIVE DIRECTOR APPOINTMENT

On [date], upon the recommendation of the nomination committee, the board of [company] ('the Company') has appointed you as non-executive director. I am writing to set out the terms of your appointment. It is agreed that this is a contract for services and is not a contract of employment.

Appointment

Your appointment will be for an initial term of three years commencing on [date], unless otherwise terminated earlier by and at the discretion of either party upon [one month's] written notice. Continuation of your contract of appointment is contingent on satisfactory performance and re-election at forthcoming AGM's. Non-executive directors are typically expected to serve two three-year terms, although the board may invite you to serve an additional period.

Time commitment

Overall we anticipate a time commitment of [number] days per month after the induction phase. This will include attendance at [monthly] board meetings, the AGM, [one] annual board away day, and [at least one] site visit per year. In addition, you will be expected to devote appropriate preparation time ahead of each meeting.

By accepting this appointment, you have confirmed that you are able to allocate sufficient time to meet the expectations of your role. The agreement of the chairman should be sought before accepting additional commitments that might impact on the time you are able to devote to your role as a non-executive director of the company.

Role

Non-executive directors have the same general legal responsibilities to the company as any other director. The board as a whole is collectively responsible for the success of the company. The board:

- Provides entrepreneurial leadership of the company within a framework of prudent and effective controls which enable risk to be assessed and managed;
- Sets the company's strategic aims, ensures that the necessary financial and human resources are in place for the company to meet its objectives, and reviews management performance; and

- Sets the company's values and standards and ensure that its obligations to its shareholders and others are understood and met.

All directors must take decisions objectively in the interests of the company.

In addition to these requirements of all directors, the role of the non-executive director has the following key elements:

- **Strategy**. Non-executive directors should constructively challenge and help develop proposals on strategy;
- **Performance.** Non-executive directors should scrutinise the performance of management in meeting agreed goals and objectives and monitor the reporting of performance;
- **Risk.** Non-executive directors should satisfy themselves on the integrity of financial information and that financial controls and systems of risk management are robust and defensible; and
- **People.** Non-executive directors are responsible for determining appropriate levels of remuneration of executive directors and have a prime role in appointing, and where necessary removing, executive directors and in succession planning.

Fees

You will be paid a fee of £[amount] gross per annum which will be paid monthly in arrears, [plus [number] ordinary shares of the company per annum, both of] which will be subject to an annual review by the board. The company will reimburse you for all reasonable and properly documented expenses you incur in performing the duties of your office.

Outside interests

It is accepted and acknowledged that you have business interests other than those of the company and have declared any conflicts that are apparent at present. In the event that you become aware of any potential conflicts of interest, these should be disclosed to the chairman and company secretary as soon as apparent.

[The board of the Company have determined you to be independent according to provision A.3.1 of the Code.]

Confidentiality

All information acquired during your appointment is confidential to the

Company and should not be released, either during your appointment or following termination (by whatever means), to third parties without prior clearance from the chairman.

Your attention is also drawn to the requirements under both legislation and regulation as to the disclosure of price sensitive information. Consequently you should avoid making any statements that might risk a breach of these requirements without prior clearance from the chairman or company secretary.

Induction

Immediately after appointment, the Company will provide a comprehensive, formal and tailored induction. This will include the information pack recommended by the Institute of Chartered Secretaries and Administrators (ICSA), available at www.icsa.org.uk. We will also arrange for site visits and meetings with senior and middle management and the Company's auditors. We will also offer to major shareholders the opportunity to meet you.

Review process

The performance of individual directors and the whole board and its committees is evaluated annually. If, in the interim, there are any matters which cause you concern about your role you should discuss them with the chairman as soon as is appropriate.

Insurance

The Company has directors' and officers' liability insurance and it is intended to maintain such cover for the full term of your appointment. The current indemnity limit is £ [amount]; a copy of the policy document is attached.

Independent professional advice

Occasions may arise when you consider that you need professional advice in the furtherance of your duties as a director. Circumstances may occur when it will be appropriate for you to seek advice from independent advisors at the company's expense. A copy of the board's agreed procedure under which directors may obtain such independent advice is attached. The Company will reimburse the full cost of expenditure incurred in accordance with the attached policy.

Committees

This letter refers to your appointment as a non-executive director of the

Company. In the event that you are also asked to serve on one or more of the board committees this will be covered in a separate communication setting out the committee(s)'s terms of reference, any specific responsibilities and any additional fees that may be involved.

This sample appointment letter has been complied with the assistance of ICSA who have kindly agreed to produce updated guidance on their website www.icsa.org.uk in the future.

INDUCTION CHECKLIST

Guidance on Induction

Every company should develop its own comprehensive, formal induction programme that is tailored to the needs of the company and individual non-executive directors. The following guidelines might form the core of an induction programme.

As a general rule, a combination of selected written information together with presentations and activities such as meetings and site visits will help to give a new appointee a balanced and real-life overview of the company. Care should be taken not to overload the new director with too much information. The new non-executive director should be provided with a list of all the induction information that is being made available to them so that they may call up items if required before otherwise provided.

The induction process should:

1. Build an understanding of the **nature of the company**, **its business and the markets in which it operates**. For example, induction should cover:
    - the company's products or services;
    - group structure / subsidiaries /joint ventures;
    - the company's constitution, board procedures and matters reserved for the board;
    - summary details of the company's principal assets, liabilities, significant contracts and major competitors;
    - the company's major risks and risk management strategy;
    - key performance indicators; and
    - regulatory constraints.

2. Build a link with the **company's people** including;
    - meetings with senior management;
    - visits to company sites other than the headquarters, to learn about production or services and meet employees in an informal setting. It is important, not only for the board to get to know the new non-executive director, but also for the non-executive director to build a profile with employees below board level; and
    - participating in board strategy development. 'Awaydays' enable a new non-executive director to begin to build working relationships away from the formal setting of the boardroom.

3. Build an understanding of the **company's main relationships** including meeting with the auditors and developing a knowledge of in particular:
   - who are the major customers;
   - who are the major suppliers; and
   - who are the major shareholders and what is the shareholder relations policy – participation in meetings with shareholders can help give a first hand feel as well as letting shareholders know who the non-executive directors are.

The induction pack

On appointment, or during the weeks immediately following, a new non-executive director should be provided with certain basic information to help ensure their early effective contribution to the company. ICSA has produced, and undertaken to maintain, on their website www.icsa.org a guidance note detailing a full list of such material.

PERFORMANCE EVALUATION GUIDANCE

Guidance on performance evaluation

The Code provides that the board should undertake a formal and rigorous annual evaluation of its own performance and that of its committees and individual directors. Individual evaluation should aim to show whether each director continues to contribute effectively and to demonstrate commitment to the role (including commitment of time for board and committee meetings and any other duties). The chairman should act on the results of the performance evaluation by recognising the strengths and addressing the weaknesses of the board and, where appropriate, proposing new members be appointed to the board or seeking the resignation of directors. The board should state in the annual report how such performance evaluation has been conducted.

It is the responsibility of the chairman to select an effective process and to act on its outcome. The use of an external third party to conduct the evaluation will bring objectivity to the process.

The non-executive directors, led by the senior independent director, should be responsible for performance evaluation of the chairman, taking into account the views of executive directors.

The evaluation process will be used constructively as a mechanism to improve board effectiveness, maximise strengths and tackle weaknesses. The results of board evaluation should be shared with the board as a whole while the results of individual assessments should remain confidential between the chairman and the non-executive director concerned.

The following are some of the questions that should be considered in a performance evaluation. They are, however, by no means definitive or exhaustive and companies will wish to tailor the questions to suit their own needs and circumstances.

The responses to these questions and others should enable boards to assess how they are performing and to identify how certain elements of their performance areas might be improved.

Performance evaluation of the board

- How well has the board performed against any performance objectives that have been set?
- What has been the board's contribution to the testing and development of strategy?

- What has been the board's contribution to ensuring robust and effective risk management?
- Is the composition of the board and its committees appropriate, with the right mix of knowledge and skills to maximise performance in the light of future strategy? Are inside and outside the board relationships working effectively?
- How has the board responded to any problems or crises that have emerged and could or should these have been foreseen?
- Are the matters specifically reserved for the board the right ones?
- How well does the board communicate with the management team, company employees and others? How effectively does it use mechanisms such as the AGM and the annual report?
- Is the board as a whole up to date with latest developments in the regulatory environment and the market?
- How effective are the board's committees? [Specific questions on the performance of each committee should be included such as, for example, their role, their composition and their interaction with the board.]

The processes that help underpin the board's effectiveness should also be evaluated e.g.:

- Is appropriate, timely information of the right length and quality provided to the board and is management responsive to requests for clarification or amplification? Does the board provide helpful feedback to management on its requirements?
- Are sufficient board and committee meetings of appropriate length held to enable proper consideration of issues? Is time used effectively?
- Are board procedures conducive to effective performance and flexible enough to deal with all eventualities?

In addition, there are some specific issues relating to the chairman which should be included as part of an evaluation of the board's performance e.g.:

- Is the chairman demonstrating effective leadership of the board?
- Are relationships and communications with shareholders well managed?
- Are relationships and communications within the board constructive?
- Are the processes for setting the agenda working? Do they enable board members to raise issues and concerns?

- Is the company secretary being used appropriately and to maximum value?

Performance evaluation of the non-executive director

The chairman and other board members should consider the following issues and the individual concerned should also be asked to assess themselves. For each non-executive director:

- How well prepared and informed are they for board meetings and is their meeting attendance satisfactory?
- Do they demonstrate a willingness to devote time and effort to understand the company and its business and a readiness to participate in events outside the boardroom such as site visits?
- What has been the quality and value of their contributions at board meetings?
- What has been their contribution to development of strategy and to risk management?
- How successfully have they brought their knowledge and experience to bear in the consideration of strategy?
- How effectively have they probed to test information and assumptions? Where necessary, how resolute are they in maintaining their own views and resisting pressure from others?
- How effectively and proactively have they followed up their areas of concern?
- How effective and successful are their relationships with fellow board members, the company secretary and senior management? Does their performance and behaviour engender mutual trust and respect within the board?
- How actively and successfully do they refresh their knowledge and skills and are they up to date with:
    - the latest developments in areas such as corporate governance framework and financial reporting?
    - the industry and market conditions?
- How well do they communicate with fellow board members, senior management and others, for example shareholders? Are they able to present their views convincingly yet diplomatically and do they listen and take on board the views of others?

USEFUL WEB LINKS

The Higgs Review (2003), together with full details of the research conducted for the Review and related information:

http://www.dti.gov.uk/cld/non_exec_review

The Cadbury Report (1992), Greenbury Report (1995) and Hampel Report (1998):

http://www.ecgi.org/codes/country_pages/codes_uk.htm

The Smith Report (2003):

http://www.frc.org.uk/publications/content/ACReport.pdf

The Financial Services Authority's Listing Rules (2002) (see in particular paragraph 12.43A):

http://www.fsa.gov.uk/pubs/ukla/

Corporate governance codes in other countries:

http://www.ecgi.org/codes/all_codes.htm

Information on the Company Law Review (2001) and the Company Law White Paper (2002):

http://www.dti.gov.uk/cld/

Copies of guidance produced by the Institute of Chartered Secretaries and Administrators:

http://www.icsa.org.uk

The Institutional Shareholders' Committee's document 'The Responsibilities of Institutional Shareholders and Agents – Statement of Principles' (2002):

http://www.investmentuk.org/press/2002/20021021-01.pdf

The Tyson report on the Recruitment and Development of Non-Executive Directors (2003)

http://www.london.edu/tysonreport/Tyson_Report_June_2003.pdf

The Myners Report on Institutional Investment in the UK (2001):

http://www.hm-treasury.gov.uk/media//843F0/31.pdf

The Directors' Remuneration Report Regulations 2002:

http://www.hmso.gov.uk/si/si2002/20021986.htm

The DTI Consultation document '"Rewards for Failure": Directors' Remuneration – Contracts, Performance and Severance', (2003):

http://www.dti.gov.uk/cld/4864rewards.pdf

The report of the EU High Level Group of Company Law Experts (the "Winter group") (2002):

http://europa.eu.int/comm/internal_market/en/company/company/modern/index. htm

The European Commission's Action Plan for Company Law and Corporate Governance (2003):

http://europa.eu.int/eur-lex/en/com/cnc/2003/com2003_0284en01.pdf

Annex 3

The Sarbanes-Oxley Act

H. R. 3763

One Hundred Seventh Congress of the United States

AT THE SECOND SESSION

Begun and held at the City of Washington on Wednesday, the twenty-third of January, two thousand and two

An Act

To protect investors by improving the accuracy and reliability of corporate disclosures made pursuant to the securities laws, and for other purposes.

Be it enacted by the Senate and House of Representatives of the United States of America in Congress assembled,

SECTION 1. SHORT TITLE; TABLE OF CONTENTS.

(a) SHORT TITLE.—This Act may be cited as the "Sarbanes-Oxley Act of 2002".

(b) TABLE OF CONTENTS.—The table of contents for this Act is as follows:

SEC. 2. DEFINITIONS.

(a) IN GENERAL.—In this Act, the following definitions shall apply:

(1) APPROPRIATE STATE REGULATORY AUTHORITY.—The term "appropriate State regulatory authority" means the State agency or other authority responsible for the licensure or other regulation of the practice of accounting in the State or States having jurisdiction over a registered public

public accounting firm or associated person thereof, with respect to the matter in question.

(2) AUDIT.—The term "audit" means an examination of the financial statements of any issuer by an independent public accounting firm in accordance with the rules of the Board or the Commission (or, for the period preceding the adoption of applicable rules of the Board under section 103, in accordance with then-applicable generally accepted auditing and related standards for such purposes), for the purpose of expressing an opinion on such statements.

(3) AUDIT COMMITTEE.—The term "audit committee" means—

(A) a committee (or equivalent body) established by and amongst the board of directors of an issuer for the purpose of overseeing the accounting and financial reporting processes of the issuer and audits of the financial statements of the issuer; and

(B) if no such committee exists with respect to an issuer, the entire board of directors of the issuer.

(4) AUDIT REPORT.—The term "audit report" means a document or other record—

(A) prepared following an audit performed for purposes of compliance by an issuer with the requirements of the securities laws; and

(B) in which a public accounting firm either—

(i) sets forth the opinion of that firm regarding a financial statement, report, or other document; or

(ii) asserts that no such opinion can be expressed.

(5) BOARD.—The term "Board" means the Public Company Accounting Oversight Board established under section 101.

(6) COMMISSION.—The term "Commission" means the Securities and Exchange Commission.

(7) ISSUER.—The term "issuer" means an issuer (as defined in section 3 of the Securities Exchange Act of 1934 (15 U.S.C. 78c)), the securities of which are registered under section 12 of that Act (15 U.S.C. 78l), or that is required to file reports under section 15(d) (15 U.S.C. 78o(d)), or that files or has filed a registration statement that has not yet become effective under the Securities Act of 1933 (15 U.S.C. 77a et seq.), and that it has not withdrawn.

(8) NON-AUDIT SERVICES.—The term "non-audit services" means any professional services provided to an issuer by a registered public accounting firm, other than those provided to an issuer in connection with an audit or a review of the financial statements of an issuer.

(9) PERSON ASSOCIATED WITH A PUBLIC ACCOUNTING FIRM.—

(A) IN GENERAL.—The terms "person associated with a public accounting firm" (or with a "registered public accounting firm") and "associated person of a public accounting firm" (or of a "registered public accounting firm") mean any individual proprietor, partner, shareholder, principal, accountant, or other professional employee of a public accounting firm, or any other independent contractor or entity that, in connection with the preparation or issuance of any audit report—

(i) shares in the profits of, or receives compensation in any other form from, that firm; or

(ii) participates as agent or otherwise on behalf of such accounting firm in any activity of that firm.

(B) EXEMPTION AUTHORITY.—The Board may, by rule, exempt persons engaged only in ministerial tasks from the definition in subparagraph (A), to the extent that the Board determines that any such exemption is consistent with the purposes of this Act, the public interest, or the protection of investors.

(10) PROFESSIONAL STANDARDS.—The term "professional standards" means—

(A) accounting principles that are—

(i) established by the standard setting body described in section 19(b) of the Securities Act of 1933, as amended by this Act, or prescribed by the Commission under section 19(a) of that Act (15 U.S.C. 17a(s)) or section 13(b) of the Securities Exchange Act of 1934 (15 U.S.C. 78a(m)); and

(ii) relevant to audit reports for particular issuers, or dealt with in the quality control system of a particular registered public accounting firm; and

(B) auditing standards, standards for attestation engagements, quality control policies and procedures, ethical and competency standards, and independence standards (including rules implementing title II) that the Board or the Commission determines—

(i) relate to the preparation or issuance of audit reports for issuers; and

(ii) are established or adopted by the Board under section 103(a), or are promulgated as rules of the Commission.

(11) PUBLIC ACCOUNTING FIRM.—The term "public accounting firm" means—

(A) a proprietorship, partnership, incorporated association, corporation, limited liability company, limited liability partnership, or other legal entity that is engaged in the practice of public accounting or preparing or issuing audit reports; and

(B) to the extent so designated by the rules of the Board, any associated person of any entity described in subparagraph (A).

(12) REGISTERED PUBLIC ACCOUNTING FIRM.—The term "registered public accounting firm" means a public accounting firm registered with the Board in accordance with this Act.

(13) RULES OF THE BOARD.—The term "rules of the Board" means the bylaws and rules of the Board (as submitted to, and approved, modified, or amended by the Commission, in accordance with section 107), and those stated policies, practices, and interpretations of the Board that the Commission, by rule, may deem to be rules of the Board, as necessary or appropriate in the public interest or for the protection of investors.

(14) SECURITY.—The term "security" has the same meaning as in section 3(a) of the Securities Exchange Act of 1934 (15 U.S.C. 78c(a)).

H. R. 3763—5

(15) SECURITIES LAWS.—The term "securities laws" means the provisions of law referred to in section 3(a)(47) of the Securities Exchange Act of 1934 (15 U.S.C. 78c(a)(47)), as amended by this Act, and includes the rules, regulations, and orders issued by the Commission thereunder.

(16) STATE.—The term "State" means any State of the United States, the District of Columbia, Puerto Rico, the Virgin Islands, or any other territory or possession of the United States.

(b) CONFORMING AMENDMENT.—Section 3(a)(47) of the Securities Exchange Act of 1934 (15 U.S.C. 78c(a)(47)) is amended by inserting "the Sarbanes-Oxley Act of 2002," before "the Public".

SEC. 3. COMMISSION RULES AND ENFORCEMENT.

(a) REGULATORY ACTION.—The Commission shall promulgate such rules and regulations, as may be necessary or appropriate in the public interest or for the protection of investors, and in furtherance of this Act.

(b) ENFORCEMENT.—

(1) IN GENERAL.—A violation by any person of this Act, any rule or regulation of the Commission issued under this Act, or any rule of the Board shall be treated for all purposes in the same manner as a violation of the Securities Exchange Act of 1934 (15 U.S.C. 78a et seq.) or the rules and regulations issued thereunder, consistent with the provisions of this Act, and any such person shall be subject to the same penalties, and to the same extent, as for a violation of that Act or such rules or regulations.

(2) INVESTIGATIONS, INJUNCTIONS, AND PROSECUTION OF OFFENSES.—Section 21 of the Securities Exchange Act of 1934 (15 U.S.C. 78u) is amended—

(A) in subsection (a)(1), by inserting "the rules of the Public Company Accounting Oversight Board, of which such person is a registered public accounting firm or a person associated with such a firm," after "is a participant,";

(B) in subsection (d)(1), by inserting "the rules of the Public Company Accounting Oversight Board, of which such person is a registered public accounting firm or a person associated with such a firm," after "is a participant,";

(C) in subsection (e), by inserting "the rules of the Public Company Accounting Oversight Board, of which such person is a registered public accounting firm or a person associated with such a firm," after "is a participant,"; and

(D) in subsection (f), by inserting "or the Public Company Accounting Oversight Board" after "self-regulatory organization" each place that term appears.

(3) CEASE-AND-DESIST PROCEEDINGS.—Section 21C(c)(2) of the Securities Exchange Act of 1934 (15 U.S.C. 78u–3(c)(2)) is amended by inserting "registered public accounting firm (as defined in section 2 of the Sarbanes-Oxley Act of 2002)," after "government securities dealer,".

(4) ENFORCEMENT BY FEDERAL BANKING AGENCIES.—Section 12(i) of the Securities Exchange Act of 1934 (15 U.S.C. 78l(i)) is amended by—

(A) striking "sections 12," each place it appears and inserting "sections 10A(m), 12,"; and

(B) striking "and 16," each place it appears and inserting "and 16 of this Act, and sections 302, 303, 304, 306, 401(b), 404, 406, and 407 of the Sarbanes-Oxley Act of 2002,".

(c) EFFECT ON COMMISSION AUTHORITY.—Nothing in this Act or the rules of the Board shall be construed to impair or limit—

(1) the authority of the Commission to regulate the accounting profession, accounting firms, or persons associated with such firms for purposes of enforcement of the securities laws;

(2) the authority of the Commission to set standards for accounting or auditing practices or auditor independence, derived from other provisions of the securities laws or the rules or regulations thereunder, for purposes of the preparation and issuance of any audit report, or otherwise under applicable law; or

(3) the ability of the Commission to take, on the initiative of the Commission, legal, administrative, or disciplinary action against any registered public accounting firm or any associated person thereof.

TITLE I—PUBLIC COMPANY ACCOUNTING OVERSIGHT BOARD

SEC. 101. ESTABLISHMENT; ADMINISTRATIVE PROVISIONS.

(a) ESTABLISHMENT OF BOARD.—There is established the Public Company Accounting Oversight Board, to oversee the audit of public companies that are subject to the securities laws, and related matters, in order to protect the interests of investors and further the public interest in the preparation of informative, accurate, and independent audit reports for companies the securities of which are sold to, and held by and for, public investors. The Board shall be a body corporate, operate as a nonprofit corporation, and have succession until dissolved by an Act of Congress.

(b) STATUS.—The Board shall not be an agency or establishment of the United States Government, and, except as otherwise provided in this Act, shall be subject to, and have all the powers conferred upon a nonprofit corporation by, the District of Columbia Nonprofit Corporation Act. No member or person employed by, or agent for, the Board shall be deemed to be an officer or employee of or agent for the Federal Government by reason of such service.

(c) DUTIES OF THE BOARD.—The Board shall, subject to action by the Commission under section 107, and once a determination is made by the Commission under subsection (d) of this section—

(1) register public accounting firms that prepare audit reports for issuers, in accordance with section 102;

(2) establish or adopt, or both, by rule, auditing, quality control, ethics, independence, and other standards relating to the preparation of audit reports for issuers, in accordance with section 103;

(3) conduct inspections of registered public accounting firms, in accordance with section 104 and the rules of the Board;

(4) conduct investigations and disciplinary proceedings concerning, and impose appropriate sanctions where justified upon, registered public

accounting firms and associated persons of such firms, in accordance with section 105;

(5) perform such other duties or functions as the Board(or the Commission, by rule or order) determines are necessary or appropriate to promote high professional standards among, and improve the quality of audit services offered by, registered public accounting firms and associated persons thereof, or otherwise to carry out this Act, in order to protect investors, or to further the public interest;

(6) enforce compliance with this Act, the rules of the Board, professional standards, and the securities laws relating to the preparation and issuance of audit reports and the obligations and liabilities of accountants with respect thereto, by registered public accounting firms and associated persons thereof; and

(7) set the budget and manage the operations of the Board and the staff of the Board.

(d) COMMISSION DETERMINATION.—The members of the Board shall take such action (including hiring of staff, proposal of rules, and adoption of initial and transitional auditing and other professional standards) as may be necessary or appropriate to enable the Commission to determine, not later than 270 days after the date of enactment of this Act, that the Board is so organized and has the capacity to carry out the requirements of this title, and to enforce compliance with this title by registered public accounting firms and associated persons thereof. The Commission shall be responsible, prior to the appointment of the Board, for the planning for the establishment and administrative transition to the Board's operation.

(e) BOARD MEMBERSHIP.—

(1) COMPOSITION.—The Board shall have 5 members, appointed from among prominent individuals of integrity and reputation who have a demonstrated commitment to the interests of investors and the public, and an understanding of the responsibilities for and nature of the financial disclosures required of issuers under the securities laws and the obligations of accountants with respect to the preparation and issuance of audit reports with respect to such disclosures.

(2) LIMITATION.—Two members, and only 2 members, of the Board shall be or have been certified public accountants pursuant to the laws of 1 or more States, provided that, if 1 of those 2 members is the chairperson, he or she may not have been a practicing certified public accountant for at least 5 years prior to his or her appointment to the Board.

(3) FULL-TIME INDEPENDENT SERVICE.—Each member of the Board shall serve on a full-time basis, and may not, concurrent with service on the Board, be employed by any other person or engage in any other professional or business activity. No member of the Board may share in any of the profits of, or receive payments from, a public accounting firm (or any other person, as determined by rule of the Commission), other than fixed continuing payments, subject to such conditions as the Commission may impose, under standard arrangements for the retirement of members of public accounting firms.

(4) APPOINTMENT OF BOARD MEMBERS.—

(A) INITIAL BOARD.—Not later than 90 days after the date of enactment of this Act, the Commission, after consultation with the

H. R. 3763—8

Chairman of the Board of Governors of the Federal Reserve System and the Secretary of the Treasury, shall appoint the chairperson and other initial members of the Board, and shall designate a term of service for each.

(B) VACANCIES.—A vacancy on the Board shall not affect the powers of the Board, but shall be filled in the same manner as provided for appointments under this section.

(5) TERM OF SERVICE.—

(A) IN GENERAL.—The term of service of each Board member shall be 5 years, and until a successor is appointed, except that—

(i) the terms of office of the initial Board members(other than the chairperson) shall expire in annual increments, 1 on each of the first 4 anniversaries of the initial date of appointment; and

(ii) any Board member appointed to fill a vacancy occurring before the expiration of the term for which the predecessor was appointed shall be appointed only for the remainder of that term.

(B) TERM LIMITATION.—No person may serve as a member of the Board, or as chairperson of the Board, for more than 2 terms, whether or not such terms of service are consecutive.

(6) REMOVAL FROM OFFICE.—A member of the Board may be removed by the Commission from office, in accordance with section 107(d)(3), for good cause shown before the expiration of the term of that member.

(f) POWERS OF THE BOARD.—In addition to any authority granted to the Board otherwise in this Act, the Board shall have the power, subject to section 107—

(1) to sue and be sued, complain and defend, in its corporate name and through its own counsel, with the approval of the Commission, in any Federal, State, or other court;

(2) to conduct its operations and maintain offices, and to exercise all other rights and powers authorized by this Act, in any State, without regard to any qualification, licensing, or other provision of law in effect in such State (or a political subdivision thereof);

(3) to lease, purchase, accept gifts or donations of or other-wise acquire, improve, use, sell, exchange, or convey, all of or an interest in any property, wherever situated;

(4) to appoint such employees, accountants, attorneys, and other agents as may be necessary or appropriate, and to determine their qualifications, define their duties, and fix their salaries or other compensation (at a level that is comparable to private sector self-regulatory, accounting, technical, supervisory, or other staff or management positions);

(5) to allocate, assess, and collect accounting support fees established pursuant to section 109, for the Board, and other fees and charges imposed under this title; and

(6) to enter into contracts, execute instruments, incur liabilities, and do any and all other acts and things necessary, appropriate, or incidental to the conduct of its operations and the exercise of its obligations, rights, and powers imposed or granted by this title.

H. R. 3763—9

(g) RULES OF THE BOARD.—The rules of the Board shall, subject to the approval of the Commission—

(1) provide for the operation and administration of the Board, the exercise of its authority, and the performance of its responsibilities under this Act;

(2) permit, as the Board determines necessary or appropriate, delegation by the Board of any of its functions to an individual member or employee of the Board, or to a division of the Board, including functions with respect to hearing, determining, ordering, certifying, reporting, or otherwise acting as to any matter, except that—

(A) the Board shall retain a discretionary right to review any action pursuant to any such delegated function, upon its own motion;

(B) a person shall be entitled to a review by the Board with respect to any matter so delegated, and the decision of the Board upon such review shall be deemed to be the action of the Board for all purposes (including appeal or review thereof); and

(C) if the right to exercise a review described in subparagraph (A) is declined, or if no such review is sought within the time stated in the rules of the Board, then the action taken by the holder of such delegation shall for all purposes, including appeal or review thereof, be deemed to be the action of the Board;

(3) establish ethics rules and standards of conduct for Board members and staff, including a bar on practice before the Board (and the Commission, with respect to Board-related matters) of 1 year for former members of the Board, and appropriate periods (not to exceed 1 year) for former staff of the Board; and

(4) provide as otherwise required by this Act.

(h) ANNUAL REPORT TO THE COMMISSION.—The Board shall submit an annual report (including its audited financial statements) to the Commission, and the Commission shall transmit a copy of that report to the Committee on Banking, Housing, and Urban Affairs of the Senate, and the Committee on Financial Services of the House of Representatives, not later than 30 days after the date of receipt of that report by the Commission.

SEC. 102. REGISTRATION WITH THE BOARD.

(a) MANDATORY REGISTRATION.—Beginning 180 days after the date of the determination of the Commission under section 101(d), it shall be unlawful for any person that is not a registered public accounting firm to prepare or issue, or to participate in the preparation or issuance of, any audit report with respect to any issuer.

(b) APPLICATIONS FOR REGISTRATION.—

(1) FORM OF APPLICATION.—A public accounting firm shall use such form as the Board may prescribe, by rule, to apply for registration under this section.

(2) CONTENTS OF APPLICATIONS.—Each public accounting firm shall submit, as part of its application for registration, in such detail as the Board shall specify—

(A) the names of all issuers for which the firm prepared or issued audit reports during the immediately preceding calendar year, and for which the firm expects to prepare or issue audit reports during the current calendar year;

H. R. 3763—10

(B) the annual fees received by the firm from each such issuer for audit services, other accounting services, and non-audit services, respectively;

(C) such other current financial information for the most recently completed fiscal year of the firm as the Board may reasonably request;

(D) a statement of the quality control policies of the firm for its accounting and auditing practices;

(E) a list of all accountants associated with the firm who participate in or contribute to the preparation of audit reports, stating the license or certification number of each such person, as well as the State license numbers of the firm itself;

(F) information relating to criminal, civil, or administrative actions or disciplinary proceedings pending against the firm or any associated person of the firm in connection with any audit report;

(G) copies of any periodic or annual disclosure filed by an issuer with the Commission during the immediately preceding calendar year which discloses accounting disagreements between such issuer and the firm in connection with an audit report furnished or prepared by the firm for such issuer; and

(H) such other information as the rules of the Board or the Commission shall specify as necessary or appropriate in the public interest or for the protection of investors.

(3) CONSENTS.—Each application for registration under this subsection shall include—

(A) a consent executed by the public accounting firm to cooperation in and compliance with any request for testimony or the production of documents made by the Board in the furtherance of its authority and responsibilities under this title (and an agreement to secure and enforce similar consents from each of the associated persons of the public accounting firm as a condition of their continued employment by or other association with such firm); and

(B) a statement that such firm understands and agrees that cooperation and compliance, as described in the consent required by subparagraph (A), and the securing and enforcement of such consents from its associated persons, in accordance with the rules of the Board, shall be a condition to the continuing effectiveness of the registration of the firm with the Board.

(c) ACTION ON APPLICATIONS.—

(1) TIMING.—The Board shall approve a completed application for registration not later than 45 days after the date of receipt of the application, in accordance with the rules of the Board, unless the Board, prior to such date, issues a written notice of disapproval to, or requests more information from, the prospective registrant.

(2) TREATMENT.—A written notice of disapproval of a completed application under paragraph (1) for registration shall be treated as a disciplinary sanction for purposes of sections 105(d) and 107(c).

(d) PERIODIC REPORTS.—Each registered public accounting firm shall submit an annual report to the Board, and may be required to report more frequently, as necessary to update the information contained in its application for registration under this section, and to provide to the Board such additional information as the Board or the Commission may specify, in accordance with subsection (b)(2).

(e) PUBLIC AVAILABILITY.—Registration applications and annual reports required by this subsection, or such portions of such applications or reports as may be designated under rules of the Board, shall be made available for public inspection, subject to rules of the Board or the Commission, and to applicable laws relating to the confidentiality of proprietary, personal, or other information contained in such applications or reports, provided that, in all events, the Board shall protect from public disclosure information reasonably identified by the subject accounting firm as proprietary information.

(f) REGISTRATION AND ANNUAL FEES.—The Board shall assess and collect a registration fee and an annual fee from each registered public accounting firm, in amounts that are sufficient to recover the costs of processing and reviewing applications and annual reports.

SEC. 103. AUDITING, QUALITY CONTROL, AND INDEPENDENCE STANDARDS AND RULES.

(a) AUDITING, QUALITY CONTROL, AND ETHICS STANDARDS.—

(1) IN GENERAL.—The Board shall, by rule, establish, including, to the extent it determines appropriate, through adoption of standards proposed by 1 or more professional groups of accountants designated pursuant to paragraph (3)(A) or advisory groups convened pursuant to paragraph (4), and amend or otherwise modify or alter, such auditing and related attestation standards, such quality control standards, and such ethics standards to be used by registered public accounting firms in the preparation and issuance of audit reports, as required by this Act or the rules of the Commission, or as may be necessary or appropriate in the public interest or for the protection of investors.

(2) RULE REQUIREMENTS.—In carrying out paragraph (1), the Board—

(A) shall include in the auditing standards that it adopts, requirements that each registered public accounting firm shall—

(i) prepare, and maintain for a period of not less than 7 years, audit workpapers, and other information related to any audit report, in sufficient detail to support the conclusions reached in such report;

(ii) provide a concurring or second partner review and approval of such audit report (and other related information), and concurring approval in its issuance, by a qualified person (as prescribed by the Board) associated with the public accounting firm, other than the person in charge of the audit, or by an independent reviewer (as prescribed by the Board); and

(iii) describe in each audit report the scope of the auditor's testing of the internal control structure and procedures of the issuer, required by section 404(b), and present (in such report or in a separate report)—

(I) the findings of the auditor from such testing;

(II) an evaluation of whether such internal control structure and procedures—

(aa) include maintenance of records that in reasonable detail accurately and fairly reflect the transactions and dispositions of the assets of the issuer;

(bb) provide reasonable assurance that transactions are recorded as necessary to permit preparation of financial statements in accordance with generally accepted accounting principles, and that receipts and expenditures of the issuer are being made only in accordance with authorizations of management and directors of the issuer; and

(III) a description, at a minimum, of material weaknesses in such internal controls, and of any material noncompliance found on the basis of such testing.

(B) shall include, in the quality control standards that it adopts with respect to the issuance of audit reports, requirements for every registered public accounting firm relating to—

(i) monitoring of professional ethics and independence from issuers on behalf of which the firm issues audit reports;

(ii) consultation within such firm on accounting and auditing questions;

(iii) supervision of audit work;

(iv) hiring, professional development, and advancement of personnel;

(v) the acceptance and continuation of engagements;

(vi) internal inspection; and

(vii) such other requirements as the Board may prescribe, subject to subsection (a)(1).

(3) AUTHORITY TO ADOPT OTHER STANDARDS.—

(A) IN GENERAL.—In carrying out this subsection, the Board—

(i) may adopt as its rules, subject to the terms of section 107, any portion of any statement of auditing standards or other professional standards that the Board determines satisfy the requirements of paragraph (1), and that were proposed by 1 or more professional groups of accountants that shall be designated or recognized by the Board, by rule, for such purpose, pursuant to this paragraph or 1 or more advisory groups convened pursuant to paragraph (4); and

(ii) notwithstanding clause (i), shall retain full authority to modify, supplement, revise, or subsequently amend, modify, or repeal, in whole or in part, any portion of any statement described in clause (i).

(B) INITIAL AND TRANSITIONAL STANDARDS.—The Board shall adopt standards described in subparagraph (A)(i) as initial or transitional standards, to the extent the Board determines necessary, prior to a determination of the Commission under section 101(d), and such standards shall be separately approved by the time of that determination, without regard to the procedures required by section 107 that otherwise would apply to the approval of rules of the Board.

(4) ADVISORY GROUPS.—The Board shall convene, or authorize its staff to convene, such expert advisory groups as may be appropriate, which may include practicing accountants and other experts, as well as representatives of other interested groups, subject to such rules as the Board may prescribe to prevent conflicts of interest, to make recommendations concerning the content (including proposed drafts) of auditing, quality control, ethics, independence, or other standards required to be established under this section.

(b) INDEPENDENCE STANDARDS AND RULES.—The Board shall establish such rules as may be necessary or appropriate in the public interest or for the protection of investors, to implement, or as authorized under, title II of this Act.

(c) COOPERATION WITH DESIGNATED PROFESSIONAL GROUPS OF ACCOUNTANTS AND ADVISORY GROUPS.—

(1) IN GENERAL.—The Board shall cooperate on an ongoing basis with professional groups of accountants designated under subsection (a)(3)(A) and advisory groups convened under subsection (a)(4) in the examination of the need for changes in any standards subject to its authority under subsection (a), recommend issues for inclusion on the agendas of such designated professional groups of accountants or advisory groups, and take such other steps as it deems appropriate to increase the effectiveness of the standard setting process.

(2) BOARD RESPONSES.—The Board shall respond in a timely fashion to requests from designated professional groups of accountants and advisory groups referred to in paragraph (1) for any changes in standards over which the Board has authority.

(d) EVALUATION OF STANDARD SETTING PROCESS.—The Board shall include in the annual report required by section 101(h) the results of its standard setting responsibilities during the period to which the report relates, including a discussion of the work of the Board with any designated professional groups of accountants and advisory groups described in paragraphs (3)(A) and (4) of subsection (a), and its pending issues agenda for future standard setting projects.

SEC. 104. INSPECTIONS OF REGISTERED PUBLIC ACCOUNTING FIRMS.

(a) IN GENERAL.—The Board shall conduct a continuing program of inspections to assess the degree of compliance of each registered public accounting firm and associated persons of that firm with this Act, the rules of the Board, the rules of the Commission, or professional standards, in connection with its performance of audits, issuance of audit reports, and related matters involving issuers.

(b) INSPECTION FREQUENCY.—

(1) IN GENERAL.—Subject to paragraph (2), inspections required by this section shall be conducted—

(A) annually with respect to each registered public accounting firm that regularly provides audit reports for more than 100 issuers; and

(B) not less frequently than once every 3 years with respect to each registered public accounting firm that regularly provides audit reports for 100 or fewer issuers.

(2) ADJUSTMENTS TO SCHEDULES.—The Board may, by rule, adjust the inspection schedules set under paragraph (1) if the Board finds that different inspection schedules are consistent with the purposes of this Act, the public interest, and the protection of investors. The Board may conduct special inspections at the request of the Commission or upon its own motion.

(c) PROCEDURES.—The Board shall, in each inspection under this section, and in accordance with its rules for such inspections—

(1) identify any act or practice or omission to act by the registered public accounting firm, or by any associated person thereof, revealed by such inspection that may be in violation of this Act, the rules of the Board, the rules of the Commission, the firm's own quality control policies, or professional standards;

(2) report any such act, practice, or omission, if appropriate, to the Commission and each appropriate State regulatory authority; and

(3) begin a formal investigation or take disciplinary action, if appropriate, with respect to any such violation, in accordance with this Act and the rules of the Board.

(d) CONDUCT OF INSPECTIONS.—In conducting an inspection of a registered public accounting firm under this section, the Board shall—

(1) inspect and review selected audit and review engagements of the firm (which may include audit engagements that are the subject of ongoing litigation or other controversy between the firm and 1 or more third parties), performed at various offices and by various associated persons of the firm, as selected by the Board;

(2) evaluate the sufficiency of the quality control system of the firm, and the manner of the documentation and communication of that system by the firm; and

(3) perform such other testing of the audit, supervisory, and quality control procedures of the firm as are necessary or appropriate in light of the purpose of the inspection and the responsibilities of the Board.

(e) RECORD RETENTION.—The rules of the Board may require the retention by registered public accounting firms for inspection purposes of records whose retention is not otherwise required by section 103 or the rules issued thereunder.

(f) PROCEDURES FOR REVIEW.—The rules of the Board shall provide a procedure for the review of and response to a draft inspection report by the registered public accounting firm under inspection. The Board shall take such action with respect to such response as it considers appropriate (including revising the draft report or continuing or supplementing its inspection activities before issuing a final report), but the text of any such response, appropriately redacted to protect information reasonably identified by the accounting firm as confidential, shall be attached to and made part of the inspection report.

(g) REPORT.—A written report of the findings of the Board for each inspection under this section, subject to subsection (h), shall be—

(1) transmitted, in appropriate detail, to the Commission and each appropriate State regulatory authority, accompanied by any letter or comments by the Board or the inspector, and any letter of response from the registered public accounting firm; and

(2) made available in appropriate detail to the public (sub-ject to section 105(b)(5)(A), and to the protection of such confidential and proprietary information as the Board may determine to be appropriate, or as may be required by law), except that no portions of the inspection report that deal with criticisms of or potential defects in the quality control systems of the firm under inspection shall be made public if those criticisms or defects are addressed by the firm, to the satisfaction of the Board, not later than 12 months after the date of the inspection report.

(h) INTERIM COMMISSION REVIEW.—

(1) REVIEWABLE MATTERS.—A registered public accounting firm may seek review by the Commission, pursuant to such rules as the Commission shall promulgate, if the firm—

(A) has provided the Board with a response, pursuant to rules issued by the Board under subsection (f), to the substance of particular items in a draft inspection report, and disagrees with the assessments contained in any final report prepared by the Board following such response; or

(B) disagrees with the determination of the Board that criticisms or defects identified in an inspection report have not been addressed to the satisfaction of the Board within 12 months of the date of the inspection report, for purposes of subsection (g)(2).

(2) TREATMENT OF REVIEW.—Any decision of the Commission with respect to a review under paragraph (1) shall not be reviewable under section 25 of the Securities Exchange Act of 1934 (15 U.S.C. 78y), or deemed to be "final agency action" for purposes of section 704 of title 5, United States Code.

(3) TIMING.—Review under paragraph (1) may be sought during the 30-day period following the date of the event giving rise to the review under subparagraph (A) or (B) of paragraph (1).

SEC. 105. INVESTIGATIONS AND DISCIPLINARY PROCEEDINGS.

(a) IN GENERAL.—The Board shall establish, by rule, subject to the requirements of this section, fair procedures for the investigation and disciplining of registered public accounting firms and associated persons of such firms.

(b) INVESTIGATIONS.—

(1) AUTHORITY.—In accordance with the rules of the Board, the Board may conduct an investigation of any act or practice, or omission to act, by a registered public accounting firm, any associated person of such firm, or both, that may violate any provision of this Act, the rules of the Board, the provisions of the securities laws relating to the preparation and issuance of audit reports and the obligations and liabilities of accountants with respect thereto, including the rules of the Commission issued under this Act, or professional standards, regardless of how the act, practice, or omission is brought to the attention of the Board.

(2) TESTIMONY AND DOCUMENT PRODUCTION.—In addition to such other actions as the Board determines to be necessary or appropriate, the rules of the Board may—

(A) require the testimony of the firm or of any person associated with a registered public accounting firm, with respect to any matter that the Board considers relevant or material to an investigation;

(B) require the production of audit workpapers and any other document or information in the possession of a registered public accounting firm or any associated person thereof, wherever domiciled, that the Board considers relevant or material to the investigation, and may inspect the books and records of such firm or associated person to verify the accuracy of any documents or information supplied;

(C) request the testimony of, and production of any document in the possession of, any other person, including any client of a registered public accounting firm that the Board considers relevant or material to an investigation under this section, with appropriate notice, subject to the needs of the investigation, as permitted under the rules of the Board; and

(D) provide for procedures to seek issuance by the Commission, in a manner established by the Commission, of a subpoena to require the testimony of, and production of any document in the possession of, any person, including any client of a registered public accounting firm, that the Board considers relevant or material to an investigation under this section.

(3) NONCOOPERATION WITH INVESTIGATIONS.—

(A) IN GENERAL.—If a registered public accounting firm or any associated person thereof refuses to testify, produce documents, or otherwise cooperate with the Board in connection with an investigation under this section, the Board may—

(i) suspend or bar such person from being associated with a registered public accounting firm, or require the registered public accounting firm to end such association;

(ii) suspend or revoke the registration of the public accounting firm; and

(iii) invoke such other lesser sanctions as the Board considers appropriate, and as specified by rule of the Board.

(B) PROCEDURE.—Any action taken by the Board under this paragraph shall be subject to the terms of section 107(c).

(4) COORDINATION AND REFERRAL OF INVESTIGATIONS.—

(A) COORDINATION.—The Board shall notify the Commission of any pending Board investigation involving a potential violation of the securities laws, and thereafter coordinate its work with the work of the Commission's Division of Enforcement, as necessary to protect an ongoing Commission investigation.

(B) REFERRAL.—The Board may refer an investigation under this section—

(i) to the Commission;

(ii) to any other Federal functional regulator (as defined in section 509 of the Gramm-Leach-Bliley Act (15 U.S.C. 6809)), in the case of an investigation that concerns an audit report for an institution that is subject to the jurisdiction of such regulator; and

(iii) at the direction of the Commission, to—

(I) the Attorney General of the United States;

(II) the attorney general of 1 or more States; and

(III) the appropriate State regulatory authority.

(5) USE OF DOCUMENTS.—

(A) CONFIDENTIALITY.—Except as provided in subparagraph (B), all documents and information prepared or received by or specifically for the Board, and deliberations of the Board and its employees and agents, in connection with an inspection under section 104 or with an investigation under this section, shall be confidential and privileged as an evidentiary matter (and shall not be subject to civil discovery or other legal process) in any proceeding in any Federal or State court or administrative agency, and shall be exempt from disclosure, in the hands of an agency or establishment of the Federal Government, under the Freedom of Information Act (5 U.S.C. 552a), or otherwise, unless and until presented in connection with a public proceeding or released in accordance with subsection (c).

(B) AVAILABILITY TO GOVERNMENT AGENCIES.—Without the loss of its status as confidential and privileged in the hands of the Board, all information referred to in subparagraph (A) may—

(i) be made available to the Commission; and

(ii) in the discretion of the Board, when determined by the Board to be necessary to accomplish the purposes of this Act or to protect investors, be made available to—

(I) the Attorney General of the United States;

(II) the appropriate Federal functional regulator (as defined in section 509 of the Gramm-Leach-Bliley Act (15 U.S.C. 6809)), other than the Commission, with respect to an audit report for an institution subject to the jurisdiction of such regulator;

(III) State attorneys general in connection with any criminal investigation; and

(IV) any appropriate State regulatory

authority, each of which shall maintain such information as confidential and privileged.

(6) IMMUNITY.—Any employee of the Board engaged in carrying out an investigation under this Act shall be immune from any civil liability arising out of such investigation in the same manner and to the same extent as an employee of the Federal Government in similar circumstances.

(c) DISCIPLINARY PROCEDURES.—

(1) NOTIFICATION; RECORDKEEPING.—The rules of the Board shall provide that in any proceeding by the Board to determine whether a

registered public accounting firm, or an associated person thereof, should be disciplined, the Board shall—

(A) bring specific charges with respect to the firm or associated person;

(B) notify such firm or associated person of, and provide to the firm or associated person an opportunity to defend against, such charges; and

(C) keep a record of the proceedings.

(2) PUBLIC HEARINGS.—Hearings under this section shall not be public, unless otherwise ordered by the Board for good cause shown, with the consent of the parties to such hearing.

(3) SUPPORTING STATEMENT.—A determination by the Board to impose a sanction under this subsection shall be supported by a statement setting forth—

(A) each act or practice in which the registered public accounting firm, or associated person, has engaged (or omitted to engage), or that forms a basis for all or a part of such sanction;

(B) the specific provision of this Act, the securities laws, the rules of the Board, or professional standards which the Board determines has been violated; and

(C) the sanction imposed, including a justification for that sanction.

(4) SANCTIONS.—If the Board finds, based on all of the facts and circumstances, that a registered public accounting firm or associated person thereof has engaged in any act or practice, or omitted to act, in violation of this Act, the rules of the Board, the provisions of the securities laws relating to the preparation and issuance of audit reports and the obligations and liabilities of accountants with respect thereto, including the rules of the Commission issued under this Act, or professional standards, the Board may impose such disciplinary or remedial sanctions as it determines appropriate, subject to applicable limitations under paragraph (5), including—

(A) temporary suspension or permanent revocation of registration under this title;

(B) temporary or permanent suspension or bar of a person from further association with any registered public accounting firm;

(C) temporary or permanent limitation on the activities, functions, or operations of such firm or person (other than in connection with required additional professional education or training);

(D) a civil money penalty for each such violation, in an amount equal to—

(i) not more than $100,000 for a natural person or $2,000,000 for any other person; and

(ii) in any case to which paragraph (5) applies, not more than $750,000 for a natural person or $15,000,000 for any other person;

(E) censure;

(F) required additional professional education or training; or

(G) any other appropriate sanction provided for in the rules of the Board.

H. R. 3763—19

(5) INTENTIONAL OR OTHER KNOWING CONDUCT.—The sanctions and penalties described in subparagraphs (A) through (C) and (D)(ii) of paragraph (4) shall only apply to—

(A) intentional or knowing conduct, including reckless conduct, that results in violation of the applicable statutory, regulatory, or professional standard; or

(B) repeated instances of negligent conduct, each resulting in a violation of the applicable statutory, regulatory, or professional standard.

(6) FAILURE TO SUPERVISE.—

(A) IN GENERAL.—The Board may impose sanctions under this section on a registered accounting firm or upon the supervisory personnel of such firm, if the Board finds that—

(i) the firm has failed reasonably to supervise an associated person, either as required by the rules of the Board relating to auditing or quality control standards, or otherwise, with a view to preventing violations of this Act, the rules of the Board, the provisions of the securities laws relating to the preparation and issuance of audit reports and the obligations and liabilities of accountants with respect thereto, including the rules of the Commission under this Act, or professional standards; and

(ii) such associated person commits a violation of this Act, or any of such rules, laws, or standards.

(B) RULE OF CONSTRUCTION.—No associated person of a registered public accounting firm shall be deemed to have failed reasonably to supervise any other person for purposes of subparagraph (A), if—

(i) there have been established in and for that firm procedures, and a system for applying such procedures, that comply with applicable rules of the Board and that would reasonably be expected to prevent and detect any such violation by such associated person; and

(ii) such person has reasonably discharged the duties and obligations incumbent upon that person by reason of such procedures and system, and had no reasonable cause to believe that such procedures and system were not being complied with.

(7) EFFECT OF SUSPENSION.—

(A) ASSOCIATION WITH A PUBLIC ACCOUNTING FIRM.— It shall be unlawful for any person that is suspended or barred from being associated with a registered public accounting firm under this subsection willfully to become or remain associated with any registered public accounting firm, or for any registered public accounting firm that knew, or, in the exercise of reasonable care should have known, of the suspension or bar, to permit such an association, without the consent of the Board or the Commission.

(B) ASSOCIATION WITH AN ISSUER.—It shall be unlawful for any person that is suspended or barred from being associated with an issuer under his subsection willfully to become or remain associated with any issuer in an accountancy or a financial management capacity, and for any issuer that knew, or in the exercise of reasonable care should have known of such suspension or bar, to permit such an association, without the consent of the Board or the Commission.

(d) REPORTING OF SANCTIONS.—

(1) RECIPIENTS.—If the Board imposes a disciplinary sanction, in accordance with this section, the Board shall report the sanction to—

(A) the Commission;

(B) any appropriate State regulatory authority or any foreign accountancy licensing board with which such firm or person is licensed or certified; and

(C) the public (once any stay on the imposition of such sanction has been lifted).

(2) CONTENTS.—The information reported under paragraph (1) shall include—

(A) the name of the sanctioned person;

(B) a description of the sanction and the basis for its imposition; and

(C) such other information as the Board deems appropriate.

(e) STAY OF SANCTIONS.—

(1) IN GENERAL.—Application to the Commission for review, or the institution by the Commission of review, of any disciplinary action of the Board shall operate as a stay of any such disciplinary action, unless and until the Commission orders (summarily or after notice and opportunity for hearing on the question of a stay, which hearing may consist solely of the submission of affidavits or presentation of oral arguments) that no such stay shall continue to operate.

(2) EXPEDITED PROCEDURES.—The Commission shall establish for appropriate cases an expedited procedure for consideration and determination of the question of the duration of a stay pending review of any disciplinary action of the Board under this subsection.

SEC. 106. FOREIGN PUBLIC ACCOUNTING FIRMS.

(a) APPLICABILITY TO CERTAIN FOREIGN FIRMS.—

(1) IN GENERAL.—Any foreign public accounting firm that prepares or furnishes an audit report with respect to any issuer, shall be subject to this Act and the rules of the Board and the Commission issued under this Act, in the same manner and to the same extent as a public accounting firm that is organized and operates under the laws of the United States or any State, except that registration pursuant to section 102 shall not by itself provide a basis for subjecting such a foreign public accounting firm to the jurisdiction of the Federal or State courts, other than with respect to controversies between such firms and the Board.

(2) BOARD AUTHORITY.—The Board may, by rule, determine that a foreign public accounting firm (or a class of such firms) that does not issue audit reports nonetheless plays such a substantial role in the preparation and furnishing of such reports for particular issuers, that it is necessary or appropriate, in light of the purposes of this Act and in the public interest or for the protection of investors, that such firm (or class of firms) should be

treated as a public accounting firm (or firms) for purposes of registration under, and oversight by the Board in accordance with, this title.

(b) PRODUCTION OF AUDIT WORKPAPERS.—

(1) CONSENT BY FOREIGN FIRMS.—If a foreign public accounting firm issues an opinion or otherwise performs material services upon which a registered public accounting firm relies in issuing all or part of any audit report or any opinion contained in an audit report, that foreign public accounting firm shall be deemed to have consented—

(A) to produce its audit workpapers for the Board or the Commission in connection with any investigation by either body with respect to that audit report; and

(B) to be subject to the jurisdiction of the courts of the United States for purposes of enforcement of any request for production of such workpapers.

(2) CONSENT BY DOMESTIC FIRMS.—A registered public accounting firm that relies upon the opinion of a foreign public accounting firm, as described in paragraph (1), shall be deemed—

(A) to have consented to supplying the audit workpapers of that foreign public accounting firm in response to a request for production by the Board or the Commission; and

(B) to have secured the agreement of that foreign public accounting firm to such production, as a condition of its reliance on the opinion of that foreign public accounting firm.

(c) EXEMPTION AUTHORITY.—The Commission, and the Board, subject to the approval of the Commission, may, by rule, regulation, or order, and as the Commission (or Board) determines necessary or appropriate in the public interest or for the protection of investors, either unconditionally or upon specified terms and conditions exempt any foreign public accounting firm, or any class of such firms, from any provision of this Act or the rules of the Board or the Commission issued under this Act.

(d) DEFINITION.—In this section, the term "foreign public accounting firm" means a public accounting firm that is organized and operates under the laws of a foreign government or political subdivision thereof.

SEC. 107. COMMISSION OVERSIGHT OF THE BOARD.

(a) GENERAL OVERSIGHT RESPONSIBILITY.—The Commission shall have oversight and enforcement authority over the Board, as provided in this Act. The provisions of section 17(a)(1) of the Securities Exchange Act of 1934 (15 U.S.C. 78q(a)(1)), and of section 17(b)(1) of the Securities Exchange Act of 1934 (15 U.S.C. 78q(b)(1)) shall apply to the Board as fully as if the Board were a "registered securities association" for purposes of those sections 17(a)(1) and 17(b)(1).

(b) RULES OF THE BOARD.—

(1) DEFINITION.—In this section, the term "proposed rule" means any proposed rule of the Board, and any modification of any such rule.

(2) PRIOR APPROVAL REQUIRED.—No rule of the Board shall become effective without prior approval of the Commission in accordance with this section, other than as provided in section 103(a)(3)(B) with respect to initial or transitional standards.

(3) APPROVAL CRITERIA.—The Commission shall approve a proposed rule, if it finds that the rule is consistent with the requirements of this Act and the securities laws, or is necessary or appropriate in the public interest or for the protection of investors.

(4) PROPOSED RULE PROCEDURES.—The provisions of paragraphs (1) through (3) of section 19(b) of the Securities Exchange Act of 1934 (15 U.S.C. 78s(b)) shall govern the proposed rules of the Board, as fully as if the Board were a "registered securities association" for purposes of that section 19(b), except that, for purposes of this paragraph—

(A) the phrase "consistent with the requirements of this title and the rules and regulations thereunder applicable to such organization" in section 19(b)(2) of that Act shall be deemed to read "consistent with the requirements of title I of the Sarbanes-Oxley Act of 2002, and the rules and regulations issued thereunder applicable to such organization, or as necessary or appropriate in the public interest or for the protection of investors"; and

(B) the phrase "otherwise in furtherance of the purposes of this title" in section 19(b)(3)(C) of that Act shall be deemed to read "otherwise in furtherance of the purposes of title I of the Sarbanes-Oxley Act of 2002".

(5) COMMISSION AUTHORITY TO AMEND RULES OF THE BOARD.—The provisions of section 19(c) of the Securities Exchange Act of 1934 (15 U.S.C. 78s(c)) shall govern the abrogation, deletion, or addition to portions of the rules of the Board by the Commission as fully as if the Board were a "registered securities association" for purposes of that section 19(c), except that the phrase "to conform its rules to the requirements of this title and the rules and regulations thereunder applicable to such organization, or otherwise in furtherance of the purposes of this title" in section 19(c) of that Act shall, for purposes of this paragraph, be deemed to read "to assure the fair administration of the Public Company Accounting Oversight Board, conform the rules promulgated by that Board to the requirements of title I of the Sarbanes-Oxley Act of 2002, or otherwise further the purposes of that Act, the securities laws, and the rules and regulations thereunder applicable to that Board".

(c) COMMISSION REVIEW OF DISCIPLINARY ACTION TAKEN BY THE BOARD.—

(1) NOTICE OF SANCTION.—The Board shall promptly file notice with the Commission of any final sanction on any registered public accounting firm or on any associated person thereof, in such form and containing such information as the Commission, by rule, may prescribe.

(2) REVIEW OF SANCTIONS.—The provisions of sections 19(d)(2) and 19(e)(1) of the Securities Exchange Act of 1934 (15 U.S.C. 78s (d)(2) and (e)(1)) shall govern the review by the Commission of final disciplinary sanctions imposed by the Board (including sanctions imposed under section 105(b)(3) of this Act for noncooperation in an investigation of the Board), as fully as if the Board were a self-regulatory organization and the Commission were the appropriate regulatory agency for such organization for purposes of those sections 19(d)(2) and 19(e)(1), except that, for purposes of this paragraph—

H. R. 3763—23

(A) section 105(e) of this Act (rather than that section19(d)(2)) shall govern the extent to which application for, or institution by the Commission on its own motion of, review of any disciplinary action of the Board operates as a stay of such action;

(B) references in that section 19(e)(1) to "members" of such an organization shall be deemed to be references to registered public accounting firms;

(C) the phrase "consistent with the purposes of this title" in that section 19(e)(1) shall be deemed to read "consistent with the purposes of this title and title I of the Sarbanes-Oxley Act of 2002";

(D) references to rules of the Municipal Securities Rule-making Board in that section 19(e)(1) shall not apply; and

(E) the reference to section 19(e)(2) of the Securities Exchange Act of 1934 shall refer instead to section 107(c)(3) of this Act.

(3) COMMISSION MODIFICATION AUTHORITY.—The Commission may enhance, modify, cancel, reduce, or require the remission of a sanction imposed by the Board upon a registered public accounting firm or associated person thereof, if the Commission, having due regard for the public interest and the protection of investors, finds, after a proceeding in accordance with this subsection, that the sanction—

(A) is not necessary or appropriate in furtherance oft his Act or the securities laws; or

(B) is excessive, oppressive, inadequate, or otherwise not appropriate to the finding or the basis on which the sanction was imposed.

(d) CENSURE OF THE BOARD; OTHER SANCTIONS.—

(1) RESCISSION OF BOARD AUTHORITY.—The Commission, by rule, consistent with the public interest, the protection of investors, and the other purposes of this Act and the securities laws, may relieve the Board of any responsibility to enforce compliance with any provision of this Act, the securities laws, the rules of the Board, or professional standards.

(2) CENSURE OF THE BOARD; LIMITATIONS.—The Commission may, by order, as it determines necessary or appropriate in the public interest, for the protection of investors, or otherwise in furtherance of the purposes of this Act or the securities laws, censure or impose limitations upon the activities, functions, and operations of the Board, if the Commission finds, on the record, after notice and opportunity for a hearing, that the Board—

(A) has violated or is unable to comply with any provision of this Act, the rules of the Board, or the securities laws; or

(B) without reasonable justification or excuse, has failed to enforce compliance with any such provision or rule, or any professional standard by a registered public accounting firm or an associated person thereof.

(3) CENSURE OF BOARD MEMBERS; REMOVAL FROM OFFICE.—The Commission may, as necessary or appropriate in the public interest, for the protection of investors, or otherwise in furtherance of the purposes of this Act or the securities laws, remove from office or censure any member of

the Board, if the Commission finds, on the record, after notice and opportunity for a hearing, that such member—

(A) has willfully violated any provision of this Act, the rules of the Board, or the securities laws;

(B) has willfully abused the authority of that member; or

(C) without reasonable justification or excuse, has failed to enforce compliance with any such provision or rule, or any professional standard by any registered public accounting firm or any associated person thereof.

SEC. 108. ACCOUNTING STANDARDS.

(a) AMENDMENT TO SECURITIES ACT OF 1933.—Section 19 of the Securities Act of 1933 (15 U.S.C. 77s) is amended—

(1) by redesignating subsections (b) and (c) as subsections (c) and (d), respectively; and

(2) by inserting after subsection (a) the following:"(b) RECOGNITION OF ACCOUNTING STANDARDS.—

"(1) IN GENERAL.—In carrying out its authority under subsection (a) and under section 13(b) of the Securities Exchange Act of 1934, the Commission may recognize, as 'generally accepted' for purposes of the securities laws, any accounting principles established by a standard setting body—

"(A) that—

"(i) is organized as a private entity;

"(ii) has, for administrative and operational pur poses, a board of trustees (or equivalent body) serving in the public interest, the majority of whom are not, concurrent with their service on such board, and have not been during the 2-year period preceding such service, associated persons of any registered public accounting firm;

"(iii) is funded as provided in section 109 of the Sarbanes-Oxley Act of 2002;

"(iv) has adopted procedures to ensure prompt consideration, by majority vote of its members, of changes to accounting principles necessary to reflect emerging accounting issues and changing business practices; and

"(v) considers, in adopting accounting principles, the need to keep standards current in order to reflect changes in the business environment, the extent to which international convergence on high quality accounting standards is necessary or appropriate in the public interest and for the protection of investors; and "(B) that the Commission determines has the capacity

to assist the Commission in fulfilling the requirements of subsection (a) and section 13(b) of the Securities Exchange Act of 1934, because, at a minimum, the standard setting body is capable of improving the accuracy and effectiveness of financial reporting and the protection of investors under the securities laws.

"(2) ANNUAL REPORT.—A standard setting body described in paragraph (1) shall submit an annual report to the Commission and the public, containing audited financial statements of that standard setting body.".

(b) COMMISSION AUTHORITY.—The Commission shall promulgate such rules and regulations to carry out section 19(b) of the Securities Act of 1933, as added by this section, as it deems necessary or appropriate in the public interest or for the protection of investors.

(c) NO EFFECT ON COMMISSION POWERS.—Nothing in this Act, including this section and the amendment made by this section, shall be construed to impair or limit the authority of the Commission to establish accounting principles or standards for purposes of enforcement of the securities laws.

(d) STUDY AND REPORT ON ADOPTING PRINCIPLES-BASED ACCOUNTING.—

(1) STUDY.—

(A) IN GENERAL.—The Commission shall conduct a study on the adoption by the United States financial reporting system of a principles-based accounting system.

(B) STUDY TOPICS.—The study required by subparagraph (A) shall include an examination of—

(i) the extent to which principles-based accounting and financial reporting exists in the United States;

(ii) the length of time required for change from a rules-based to a principles-based financial reporting system;

(iii) the feasibility of and proposed methods by which a principles-based system may be implemented; and

(iv) a thorough economic analysis of the implementation of a principles-based system.

(2) REPORT.—Not later than 1 year after the date of enactment of this Act, the Commission shall submit a report on the results of the study required by paragraph (1) to the Committee on Banking, Housing, and Urban Affairs of the Senate and the Committee on Financial Services of the House of Representatives.

SEC. 109. FUNDING.

(a) IN GENERAL.—The Board, and the standard setting body designated pursuant to section 19(b) of the Securities Act of 1933, as amended by section 108, shall be funded as provided in this section.

(b) ANNUAL BUDGETS.—The Board and the standard setting body referred to in subsection (a) shall each establish a budget for each fiscal year, which shall be reviewed and approved according to their respective internal procedures not less than 1 month prior to the commencement of the fiscal year to which the budget pertains (or at the beginning of the Board's first fiscal year, which may be a short fiscal year). The budget of the Board shall be subject to approval by the Commission. The budget for the first fiscal year of the Board shall be prepared and approved promptly following the appointment of the initial five Board members, to permit action by the Board of the organizational tasks contemplated by section 101(d).

(c) SOURCES AND USES OF FUNDS.—

(1) RECOVERABLE BUDGET EXPENSES.—The budget of the Board (reduced by any registration or annual fees received under section 102(e) for the year preceding the year for which the budget is being computed), and all of the budget of the standard setting body referred to in subsection (a), for each fiscal year of each of those 2 entities, shall be payable from annual accounting support fees, in accordance with subsections (d) and (e). Accounting support fees and other receipts of the Board and of such standard-setting body shall not be considered public monies of the United States.

(2) FUNDS GENERATED FROM THE COLLECTION OF MONETARY PENALTIES.—Subject to the availability in advance in an appropriations Act, and notwithstanding subsection (i), all funds collected by the Board as a result of the assessment of monetary penalties shall be used to fund a merit scholarship program for undergraduate and graduate students enrolled in accredited accounting degree programs, which program is to be administered by the Board or by an entity or agent identified by the Board.

(d) ANNUAL ACCOUNTING SUPPORT FEE FOR THE BOARD.—

(1) ESTABLISHMENT OF FEE.—The Board shall establish, with the approval of the Commission, a reasonable annual accounting support fee (or a formula for the computation thereof), as may be necessary or appropriate to establish and maintain the Board. Such fee may also cover costs incurred in the Board's first fiscal year (which may be a short fiscal year), or may be levied separately with respect to such short fiscal year.

(2) ASSESSMENTS.—The rules of the Board under paragraph (1) shall provide for the equitable allocation, assessment, and collection by the Board (or an agent appointed by the Board) of the fee established under paragraph (1), among issuers, in accordance with subsection (g), allowing for differentiation among classes of issuers, as appropriate.

(e) ANNUAL ACCOUNTING SUPPORT FEE FOR STANDARD SETTING BODY.—The annual accounting support fee for the standard setting body referred to in subsection (a)—

(1) shall be allocated in accordance with subsection (g),and assessed and collected against each issuer, on behalf of the standard setting body, by 1 or more appropriate designated collection agents, as may be necessary or appropriate to pay for the budget and provide for the expenses of that standard setting body, and to provide for an independent, stable source of funding for such body, subject to review by the Commission; and

(2) may differentiate among different classes of issuers.

(f) LIMITATION ON FEE.—The amount of fees collected under this section for a fiscal year on behalf of the Board or the standards setting body, as the case may be, shall not exceed the recoverable budget expenses of the Board or body, respectively (which may include operating, capital, and accrued items), referred to in subsection (c)(1).

(g) ALLOCATION OF ACCOUNTING SUPPORT FEES AMONG ISSUERS.—Any amount due from issuers (or a particular class of issuers) under this section to fund the budget of the Board or the standard setting body referred to in subsection (a) shall be allocated among and payable by each issuer (or each issuer in a particular class as applicable) in an amount equal to the total of such amount, multiplied by a fraction—

(1) the numerator of which is the average monthly equity market capitalization of the issuer for the 12-month period immediately preceding the beginning of the fiscal year to which such budget relates; and

(2) the denominator of which is the average monthly equity market capitalization of all such issuers for such 12-month period.

(h) CONFORMING AMENDMENTS.—Section 13(b)(2) of the Securities Exchange Act of 1934 (15 U.S.C. 78m(b)(2)) is amended—

(1) in subparagraph (A), by striking "and" at the end; and

(2) in subparagraph (B), by striking the period at the end and inserting the following: "; and

"(C) notwithstanding any other provision of law, pay the allocable share of such issuer of a reasonable annual accounting support fee or fees, determined in accordance with section 109 of the Sarbanes-Oxley Act of 2002.".

(i) RULE OF CONSTRUCTION.—Nothing in this section shall be construed to render either the Board, the standard setting body referred to in subsection (a), or both, subject to procedures in Congress to authorize or appropriate public funds, or to prevent such organization from utilizing additional sources of revenue for its activities, such as earnings from publication sales, provided that each additional source of revenue shall not jeopardize, in the judgment of the Commission, the actual and perceived independence of such organization.

(j) START-UP EXPENSES OF THE BOARD.—From the unexpended balances of the appropriations to the Commission for fiscal year 2003, the Secretary of the Treasury is authorized to advance to the Board not to exceed the amount necessary to cover the expenses of the Board during its first fiscal year (which may be a short fiscal year).

TITLE II—AUDITOR INDEPENDENCE

SEC. 201. SERVICES OUTSIDE THE SCOPE OF PRACTICE OF AUDITORS.

(a) PROHIBITED ACTIVITIES.—Section 10A of the Securities Exchange Act of 1934 (15 U.S.C. 78j–1) is amended by adding at the end the following:

"(g) PROHIBITED ACTIVITIES.—Except as provided in subsection (h), it shall be unlawful for a registered public accounting firm (and any associated person of that firm, to the extent determined appropriate by the Commission) that performs for any issuer any audit required by this title or the rules of the Commission under this title or, beginning 180 days after the date of commencement of the operations of the Public Company Accounting Oversight Board established under section 101 of the Sarbanes-Oxley Act of 2002 (in this section referred to as the 'Board'), the rules of the Board, to provide to that issuer, contemporaneously with the audit, any non-audit service, including—

"(1) bookkeeping or other services related to the accounting records or financial statements of the audit client; "

(2) financial information systems design and implementation;

"(3) appraisal or valuation services, fairness opinions, or contribution-in-kind reports;

"(4) actuarial services;

"(5) internal audit outsourcing services;

"(6) management functions or human resources;

"(7) broker or dealer, investment adviser, or investment banking services; "

(8) legal services and expert services unrelated to the audit; and

"(9) any other service that the Board determines, by regulation, is impermissible.

"(h) PREAPPROVAL REQUIRED FOR NON-AUDIT SERVICES.—A registered public accounting firm may engage in any non-audit service, including tax services, that is not described in any of paragraphs (1) through (9) of subsection (g) for an audit client, only if the activity is approved in advance by the audit committee of the issuer, in accordance with subsection (i).".

(b) EXEMPTION AUTHORITY.—The Board may, on a case by case basis, exempt any person, issuer, public accounting firm, or transaction from the prohibition on the provision of services under section 10A(g) of the Securities Exchange Act of 1934 (as added by this section), to the extent that such exemption is necessary or appropriate in the public interest and is consistent with the protection of investors, and subject to review by the Commission in the same manner as for rules of the Board under section 107.

SEC. 202. PREAPPROVAL REQUIREMENTS.

Section 10A of the Securities Exchange Act of 1934 (15 U.S.C. 78j–1), as amended by this Act, is amended by adding at the end the following:

"(i) PREAPPROVAL REQUIREMENTS.—

"(1) IN GENERAL.—

"(A) AUDIT COMMITTEE ACTION.—All auditing services (which may entail providing comfort letters in connection with securities underwritings or statutory audits required for insurance companies for purposes of State law) and non-audit services, other than as provided in subparagraph (B), provided to an issuer by the auditor of the issuer shall be pre-approved by the audit committee of the issuer.

"(B) DE MINIMUS EXCEPTION.—The pre-approval requirement under subparagraph (A) is waived with respect to the provision of non-audit services for an issuer, if—

"(i) the aggregate amount of all such non-audit services provided to the issuer constitutes not more than 5 percent of the total amount of revenues paid by the issuer to its auditor during the fiscal year in which the non-audit services are provided;

"(ii) such services were not recognized by the issuer at the time of the engagement to be non-audit services; and

"(iii) such services are promptly brought to the attention of the audit committee of the issuer and approved prior to the completion of the audit by the audit committee or by 1 or more members of the audit committee who are members of the board of directors to whom authority to grant such approvals has been delegated by the audit committee.

"(2) DISCLOSURE TO INVESTORS.—Approval by an audit committee of an issuer under this subsection of a non-audit service to be performed by the auditor of the issuer shall be disclosed to investors in periodic reports required by section 13(a).

"(3) DELEGATION AUTHORITY.—The audit committee of an issuer may delegate to 1 or more designated members of the audit committee who are independent directors of the board of directors, the authority to grant preapprovals required by this subsection. The decisions of any member to whom authority is delegated under this paragraph to preapprove an activity under this subsection shall be presented to the full audit committee at each of its scheduled meetings.

"(4) APPROVAL OF AUDIT SERVICES FOR OTHER PURPOSES.—In carrying out its duties under subsection (m)(2), if the audit committee of an issuer approves an audit service within the scope of the engagement of the auditor, such audit service shall be deemed to have been pre-approved for purposes of this subsection.".

SEC. 203. AUDIT PARTNER ROTATION.

Section 10A of the Securities Exchange Act of 1934 (15 U.S.C. 78j–1), as amended by this Act, is amended by adding at the end the following:

"(j) AUDIT PARTNER ROTATION.—It shall be unlawful for a registered public accounting firm to provide audit services to an issuer if the lead (or coordinating) audit partner (having primary responsibility for the audit), or the audit partner responsible for reviewing the audit, has performed audit services for that issuer in each of the 5 previous fiscal years of that issuer.".

SEC. 204. AUDITOR REPORTS TO AUDIT COMMITTEES.

Section 10A of the Securities Exchange Act of 1934 (15 U.S.C. 78j–1), as amended by this Act, is amended by adding at the end the following:

"(k) REPORTS TO AUDIT COMMITTEES.—Each registered public accounting firm that performs for any issuer any audit required by this title shall timely report to the audit committee of the issuer—

"(1) all critical accounting policies and practices to be used;

"(2) all alternative treatments of financial information within generally accepted accounting principles that have been discussed with management officials of the issuer, ramifications of the use of such alternative disclosures and treatments, and the treatment preferred by the registered public accounting firm; and

"(3) other material written communications between the registered public accounting firm and the management of the issuer, such as any management letter or schedule of unadjusted differences.".

SEC. 205. CONFORMING AMENDMENTS.

(a) DEFINITIONS.—Section 3(a) of the Securities Exchange Act of 1934 (15 U.S.C. 78c(a)) is amended by adding at the end the following:

"(58) AUDIT COMMITTEE.—The term 'audit committee' means—

"(A) a committee (or equivalent body) established by and amongst the board of directors of an issuer for the purpose of overseeing the accounting and financial reporting processes of the issuer and audits of the financial statements of the issuer; and

"(B) if no such committee exists with respect to an issuer, the entire board of directors of the issuer.

"(59) REGISTERED PUBLIC ACCOUNTING FIRM.—The term 'registered public accounting firm' has the same meaning as in section 2 of the Sarbanes-Oxley Act of 2002.".

(b) AUDITOR REQUIREMENTS.—Section 10A of the Securities Exchange Act of 1934 (15 U.S.C. 78j–1) is amended—

(1) by striking "an independent public accountant" each place that term appears and inserting "a registered public accounting firm";

(2) by striking "the independent public accountant" each place that term appears and inserting "the registered public accounting firm";

(3) in subsection (c), by striking "No independent public accountant" and inserting "No registered public accounting firm"; and

(4) in subsection (b)—

(A) by striking "the accountant" each place that term appears and inserting "the firm";

(B) by striking "such accountant" each place that term appears and inserting "such firm"; and

(C) in paragraph (4), by striking "the accountant's report" and inserting "the report of the firm".

(c) OTHER REFERENCES.—The Securities Exchange Act of 1934 (15 U.S.C. 78a et seq.) is amended—

(1) in section 12(b)(1) (15 U.S.C. 78l(b)(1)), by striking "independent public accountants" each place that term appears and inserting "a registered public accounting firm"; and

(2) in subsections (e) and (i) of section 17 (15 U.S.C. 78q),by striking "an independent public accountant" each place that term appears and inserting "a registered public accounting firm".

(d) CONFORMING AMENDMENT.—Section 10A(f) of the Securities Exchange Act of 1934 (15 U.S.C. 78k(f)) is amended—

(1) by striking "DEFINITION" and inserting "DEFINITIONS"; and

(2) by adding at the end the following: "As used in this section, the term 'issuer' means an issuer (as defined in section 3), the securities of which are registered under section 12, or that is required to file reports pursuant to section 15(d), or that files or has filed a registration statement that has not yet become effective under the Securities Act of 1933 (15 U.S.C. 77a et seq.), and that it has not withdrawn.".

SEC. 206. CONFLICTS OF INTEREST.

Section 10A of the Securities Exchange Act of 1934 (15 U.S.C. 78j–1), as amended by this Act, is amended by adding at the end the following:

"(l) CONFLICTS OF INTEREST.—It shall be unlawful for a registered public accounting firm to perform for an issuer any audit service required by this title, if a chief executive officer, controller, chief financial officer, chief accounting officer, or any person serving in an equivalent position for the issuer, was employed by that registered independent public accounting firm and participated in any capacity in the audit of that issuer during the 1-year period preceding the date of the initiation of the audit.".

SEC. 207. STUDY OF MANDATORY ROTATION OF REGISTERED PUBLIC ACCOUNTING FIRMS.

(a) STUDY AND REVIEW REQUIRED.—The Comptroller General of the United States shall conduct a study and review of the potential effects of requiring the mandatory rotation of registered public accounting firms.

(b) REPORT REQUIRED.—Not later than 1 year after the date of enactment of this Act, the Comptroller General shall submit a report to the Committee on Banking, Housing, and Urban Affairs of the Senate and the Committee on Financial Services of the House of Representatives on the results of the study and review required by this section.

(c) DEFINITION.—For purposes of this section, the term "mandatory rotation" refers to the imposition of a limit on the period of years in which a particular registered public accounting firm may be the auditor of record for a particular issuer.

SEC. 208. COMMISSION AUTHORITY.

(a) COMMISSION REGULATIONS.—Not later than 180 days after the date of enactment of this Act, the Commission shall issue final regulations to carry out each of subsections (g) through (l) of section 10A of the Securities Exchange Act of 1934, as added by this title.

(b) AUDITOR INDEPENDENCE.—It shall be unlawful for any registered public accounting firm (or an associated person thereof, as applicable) to prepare or issue any audit report with respect to any issuer, if the firm or associated person engages in any activity with respect to that issuer prohibited by any of subsections (g) through (l) of section 10A of the Securities Exchange Act of1934, as added by this title, or any rule or regulation of the Commission or of the Board issued thereunder.

SEC. 209. CONSIDERATIONS BY APPROPRIATE STATE REGULATORY AUTHORITIES.

In supervising non-registered public accounting firms and their associated persons, appropriate State regulatory authorities should make an independent determination of the proper standards applicable, particularly taking into consideration the size and nature of the business of the accounting firms they supervise and the size and nature of the business of the clients of those firms. The standards applied by the Board under this Act should not be presumed to be applicable for purposes of this section for small and medium sized non-registered public accounting firms.

TITLE III—CORPORATE RESPONSIBILITY

SEC. 301. PUBLIC COMPANY AUDIT COMMITTEES.

Section 10A of the Securities Exchange Act of 1934 (15 U.S.C. 78f) is amended by adding at the end the following: "(m) STANDARDS RELATING TO AUDIT COMMITTEES.—

"(1) COMMISSION RULES.—

"(A) IN GENERAL.—Effective not later than 270 days after the date of enactment of this subsection, the Commission shall, by rule, direct the national securities exchanges and national securities associations to prohibit the listing of any security of an issuer that is not in compliance with the requirements of any portion of paragraphs (2) through (6).

"(B) OPPORTUNITY TO CURE DEFECTS.—The rules of the Commission under subparagraph (A) shall provide for appropriate procedures for an issuer to have an opportunity to cure any defects that would be the basis for a prohibition under subparagraph (A), before the imposition of such prohibition.

"(2) RESPONSIBILITIES RELATING TO REGISTERED PUBLIC ACCOUNTING FIRMS.—The audit committee of each issuer, in its capacity as a committee of the board of directors, shall be directly responsible for the appointment, compensation, and oversight of the work of any registered public accounting firm employed by that issuer (including resolution of disagreements between management and the auditor regarding financial reporting) for the purpose of preparing or issuing an audit report or related work, and each such registered public accounting firm shall report directly to the audit committee.

"(3) INDEPENDENCE.—

"(A) IN GENERAL.—Each member of the audit committee of the issuer shall be a member of the board of directors of the issuer, and shall otherwise be independent.

"(B) CRITERIA.—In order to be considered to be independent for purposes of this paragraph, a member of an audit committee of an issuer may not, other than in his or her capacity as a member of the audit committee, the board of directors, or any other board committee—

"(i) accept any consulting, advisory, or other compensatory fee from the issuer; or

"(ii) be an affiliated person of the issuer or any subsidiary thereof.

"(C) EXEMPTION AUTHORITY.—The Commission may exempt from the requirements of subparagraph (B) a particular relationship with respect to audit committee members, as the Commission determines appropriate in light of the circumstances.

"(4) COMPLAINTS.—Each audit committee shall establish procedures for—

"(A) the receipt, retention, and treatment of complaints received by the issuer regarding accounting, internal accounting controls, or auditing matters; and

"(B) the confidential, anonymous submission by employees of the issuer of concerns regarding questionable accounting or auditing matters.

"(5) AUTHORITY TO ENGAGE ADVISERS.—Each audit committee shall have the authority to engage independent counsel and other advisers, as it determines necessary to carry out its duties.

"(6) FUNDING.—Each issuer shall provide for appropriate funding, as determined by the audit committee, in its capacity as a committee of the board of directors, for payment of compensation—

"(A) to the registered public accounting firm employed by the issuer for the purpose of rendering or issuing an audit report; and

"(B) to any advisers employed by the audit committee under paragraph (5).".

SEC. 302. CORPORATE RESPONSIBILITY FOR FINANCIAL REPORTS.

(a) REGULATIONS REQUIRED.—The Commission shall, by rule, require, for each company filing periodic reports under section 13(a) or 15(d) of the Securities Exchange Act of 1934 (15 U.S.C. 78m, 78o(d)), that the principal executive officer or officers and the principal financial officer or officers, or persons performing similar functions, certify in each annual or quarterly report filed or submitted under either such section of such Act that—

(1) the signing officer has reviewed the report;

(2) based on the officer's knowledge, the report does not contain any untrue statement of a material fact or omit to state a material fact necessary in order to make the statements made, in light of the circumstances under which such statements were made, not misleading;

(3) based on such officer's knowledge, the financial statements, and other financial information included in the report, fairly present in all material respects the financial condition and results of operations of the issuer as of, and for, the periods presented in the report;

(4) the signing officers—

(A) are responsible for establishing and maintaining internal controls;

(B) have designed such internal controls to ensure that material information relating to the issuer and its consolidated subsidiaries is made known to such officers by others within those entities, particularly during the period in which the periodic reports are being prepared;

(C) have evaluated the effectiveness of the issuer's internal controls as of a date within 90 days prior to the report; and

(D) have presented in the report their conclusions about the effectiveness of their internal controls based on their evaluation as of that date;

(5) the signing officers have disclosed to the issuer's auditors and the audit committee of the board of directors (or persons fulfilling the equivalent function)—

(A) all significant deficiencies in the design or operation of internal controls which could adversely affect the issuer's ability to record, process, summarize, and report financial data and have identified for the issuer's auditors any material weaknesses in internal controls; and

(B) any fraud, whether or not material, that involves management or other employees who have a significant role in the issuer's internal controls; and

(6) the signing officers have indicated in the report whether or not there were significant changes in internal controls or in other factors that could significantly affect internal controls subsequent to the date of their evaluation, including any corrective actions with regard to significant deficiencies and material weaknesses.

(b) FOREIGN REINCORPORATIONS HAVE NO EFFECT.—Nothing in this section 302 shall be interpreted or applied in any way to allow any issuer to lessen the legal force of the statement required under this section 302, by an issuer having reincorporated or having engaged in any other transaction that resulted in the transfer of the corporate domicile or offices of the issuer from inside the United States to outside of the United States.

(c) DEADLINE.—The rules required by subsection (a) shall be effective not later than 30 days after the date of enactment of this Act.

SEC. 303. IMPROPER INFLUENCE ON CONDUCT OF AUDITS.

(a) RULES TO PROHIBIT.—It shall be unlawful, in contravention of such rules or regulations as the Commission shall prescribe as necessary and appropriate in the public interest or for the protection of investors, for any officer or director of an issuer, or any other person acting under the direction thereof, to take any action to fraudulently influence, coerce, manipulate, or mislead any independent public or certified accountant engaged in the performance of an audit of the financial statements of that issuer for the purpose of rendering such financial statements materially misleading.

(b) ENFORCEMENT.—In any civil proceeding, the Commission shall have exclusive authority to enforce this section and any rule or regulation issued under this section.

(c) NO PREEMPTION OF OTHER LAW.—The provisions of subsection (a) shall be in addition to, and shall not supersede or preempt, any other provision of law or any rule or regulation issued thereunder.

(d) DEADLINE FOR RULEMAKING.—The Commission shall—

(1) propose the rules or regulations required by this section, not later than 90 days after the date of enactment of this Act; and

(2) issue final rules or regulations required by this section, not later than 270 days after that date of enactment.

SEC. 304. FORFEITURE OF CERTAIN BONUSES AND PROFITS.

(a) ADDITIONAL COMPENSATION PRIOR TO NONCOMPLIANCE WITH COMMISSION FINANCIAL REPORTING REQUIREMENTS.—If an issuer is required to prepare an accounting restatement due to the material noncompliance of the issuer, as a result of misconduct, with any financial reporting requirement under the securities laws, the chief executive officer and chief financial officer of the issuer shall reimburse the issuer for—

(1) any bonus or other incentive-based or equity-based compensation received by that person from the issuer during the 12-month period following the first public issuance or filing with the Commission (whichever first occurs) of the financial document embodying such financial reporting requirement; and

(2) any profits realized from the sale of securities of the issuer during that 12-month period.

(b) COMMISSION EXEMPTION AUTHORITY.—The Commission may exempt any person from the application of subsection (a), as it deems necessary and appropriate.

SEC. 305. OFFICER AND DIRECTOR BARS AND PENALTIES.

(a) UNFITNESS STANDARD.—

(1) SECURITIES EXCHANGE ACT OF 1934.—Section 21(d)(2) of the Securities Exchange Act of 1934 (15 U.S.C. 78u(d)(2)) is amended by striking "substantial unfitness" and inserting "unfitness".

(2) SECURITIES ACT OF 1933.—Section 20(e) of the Securities Act of 1933 (15 U.S.C. 77t(e)) is amended by striking "substantial unfitness" and inserting "unfitness".

(b) EQUITABLE RELIEF.—Section 21(d) of the Securities Exchange Act of 1934 (15 U.S.C. 78u(d)) is amended by adding at the end the following:

"(5) EQUITABLE RELIEF.—In any action or proceeding brought or instituted by the Commission under any provision of the securities laws, the Commission may seek, and any Federal court may grant, any equitable relief that may be appropriate or necessary for the benefit of investors.".

SEC. 306. INSIDER TRADES DURING PENSION FUND BLACKOUT PERIODS.

(a) PROHIBITION OF INSIDER TRADING DURING PENSION FUND BLACKOUT PERIODS.—

(1) IN GENERAL.—Except to the extent otherwise provided by rule of the Commission pursuant to paragraph (3), it shall be unlawful for any director or executive officer of an issuer of any equity security (other than an exempted security), directly or indirectly, to purchase, sell, or otherwise acquire or transfer any equity security of the issuer (other than an exempted security) during any blackout period with respect to such equity security if such director or officer acquires such equity security in connection with his or her service or employment as a director or executive officer.

(2) REMEDY.—

(A) IN GENERAL.—Any profit realized by a director or executive officer referred to in paragraph (1) from any purchase, sale, or other acquisition or transfer in violation of this subsection shall inure to and be recoverable by the issuer, irrespective of any intention on the part of such director or executive officer in entering into the transaction.

(B) ACTIONS TO RECOVER PROFITS.—An action to recover profits in accordance with this subsection may be instituted at law or in equity in any court of competent jurisdiction by the issuer, or by the owner of any security of the issuer in the name and in behalf of the issuer if the issuer fails or refuses to bring such action within 60 days after the date of request, or fails diligently to prosecute the action thereafter, except that no such suit shall be brought more than 2 years after the date on which such profit was realized.

(3) RULEMAKING AUTHORIZED.—The Commission shall, in consultation with the Secretary of Labor, issue rules to clarify the application of this subsection and to prevent evasion thereof. Such rules shall provide for the application of the requirements of paragraph (1) with respect to entities treated as a single employer with respect to an issuer under section 414(b), (c), (m), or (o) of the Internal Revenue Code of 1986 to the extent necessary to clarify the application of such requirements and to prevent evasion

thereof. Such rules may also provide for appropriate exceptions from the appropriate exceptions from the requirements of this subsection, including exceptions for purchases pursuant to an automatic dividend reinvestment program or purchases or sales made pursuant to an advance election.

(4) BLACKOUT PERIOD.—For purposes of this subsection, the term "blackout period", with respect to the equity securities of any issuer—

(A) means any period of more than 3 consecutive business days during which the ability of not fewer than 50 percent of the participants or beneficiaries under all individual account plans maintained by the issuer to purchase, sell, or otherwise acquire or transfer an interest in any equity of such issuer held in such an individual account plan is temporarily suspended by the issuer or by a fiduciary of the plan; and

(B) does not include, under regulations which shall be prescribed by the Commission—

(i) a regularly scheduled period in which the participants and beneficiaries may not purchase, sell, or otherwise acquire or transfer an interest in any equity of such issuer, if such period is—

(I) incorporated into the individual account plan; and

(II) timely disclosed to employees before becoming participants under the individual account plan or as a subsequent amendment to the plan; or

(ii) any suspension described in subparagraph (A) that is imposed solely in connection with persons becoming participants or beneficiaries, or ceasing to be participants or beneficiaries, in an individual account plan by reason of a corporate merger, acquisition, divestiture, or similar transaction involving the plan or plan sponsor.

(5) INDIVIDUAL ACCOUNT PLAN.—For purposes of this subsection, the term "individual account plan" has the meaning provided in section 3(34) of the Employee Retirement Income Security Act of 1974 (29 U.S.C. 1002(34), except that such term shall not include a one-participant retirement plan (within the meaning of section 101(i)(8)(B) of such Act (29 U.S.C. 1021(i)(8)(B))).

(6) NOTICE TO DIRECTORS, EXECUTIVE OFFICERS, AND THE COMMISSION.—In any case in which a director or executive officer is subject to the requirements of this subsection in connection with a blackout period (as defined in paragraph (4)) with respect to any equity securities, the issuer of such equity securities shall timely notify such director or officer and the Securities and Exchange Commission of such blackout period.

(b) NOTICE REQUIREMENTS TO PARTICIPANTS AND BENEFICIARIES UNDER ERISA.—

(1) IN GENERAL.—Section 101 of the Employee Retirement Income Security Act of 1974 (29 U.S.C. 1021) is amended by redesignating the second subsection (h) as subsection (j), and by inserting after the first subsection (h) the following new subsection:

"(i) NOTICE OF BLACKOUT PERIODS TO PARTICIPANT OR BENEFICIARY UNDER INDIVIDUAL ACCOUNT PLAN.—

"(1) DUTIES OF PLAN ADMINISTRATOR.—In advance of the commencement of any blackout period with respect to an individual account plan, the plan administrator shall notify the plan participants and beneficiaries who are affected by such action in accordance with this subsection.

"(2) NOTICE REQUIREMENTS.—

"(A) IN GENERAL.—The notices described in paragraph (1) shall be written in a manner calculated to be understood by the average plan participant and shall include—

"(i) the reasons for the blackout period,

"(ii) an identification of the investments and other rights affected, "(iii) the expected beginning date and length of the blackout period,

"(iv) in the case of investments affected, a statement that the participant or beneficiary should evaluate the appropriateness of their current investment decisions in light of their inability to direct or diversify assets credited to their accounts during the blackout period, and

"(v) such other matters as the Secretary may require by regulation.

"(B) NOTICE TO PARTICIPANTS AND BENEFICIARIES.—Except as otherwise provided in this subsection, notices described in paragraph (1) shall be furnished to all participants and beneficiaries under the plan to whom the blackout period applies at least 30 days in advance of the blackout period.

"(C) EXCEPTION TO 30-DAY NOTICE REQUIREMENT.—In any case in which—

"(i) a deferral of the blackout period would violate the requirements of subparagraph (A) or (B) of section 404(a)(1), and a fiduciary of the plan reasonably so determines in writing, or

"(ii) the inability to provide the 30-day advance notice is due to events that were unforeseeable or circumstances beyond the reasonable control of the plan administrator, and a fiduciary of the plan reasonably so determines in writing,

subparagraph (B) shall not apply, and the notice shall be furnished to all participants and beneficiaries under the plan to whom the blackout period applies as soon as reasonably possible under the circumstances unless such a notice in advance of the termination of the blackout period is impracticable.

"(D) WRITTEN NOTICE.—The notice required to be provided under this subsection shall be in writing, except that such notice may be in electronic or other form to the extent that such form is reasonably accessible to the recipient.

"(E) NOTICE TO ISSUERS OF EMPLOYER SECURITIES SUBJECT TO BLACKOUT PERIOD.—In the case of any blackout period in connection with an individual account plan, the plan administrator shall provide timely notice of such blackout period to the issuer of any employer securities subject to such blackout period.

"(3) EXCEPTION FOR BLACKOUT PERIODS WITH LIMITED APPLICABILITY.—In any case in which the blackout period applies only to 1 or more participants or beneficiaries in connection with a merger, acquisition, divestiture, or similar transaction involving the plan or plan sponsor and occurs solely in connection with becoming or ceasing to be a participant or beneficiary under the plan by reason of such merger, acquisition, divestiture, or transaction, the requirement of this subsection that the notice be provided to all participants and beneficiaries shall be treated as met if the notice required under paragraph (1) is provided to such participants or beneficiaries to whom the blackout period applies as soon as reasonably practicable.

"(4) CHANGES IN LENGTH OF BLACKOUT PERIOD.—If, following the furnishing of the notice pursuant to this subsection, there is a change in the beginning date or length of the blackout period (specified in such notice pursuant to paragraph (2)(A)(iii)), the administrator shall provide affected participants and beneficiaries notice of the change as soon as reasonably practicable. In relation to the extended blackout period, such notice shall meet the requirements of paragraph (2)(D) and shall specify any material change in the matters referred to in clauses (i) through (v) of paragraph (2)(A).

"(5) REGULATORY EXCEPTIONS.—The Secretary may provide by regulation for additional exceptions to the requirements of this subsection which the Secretary determines are in the interests of participants and beneficiaries.

"(6) GUIDANCE AND MODEL NOTICES.—The Secretary shall issue guidance and model notices which meet the requirements of this subsection.

"(7) BLACKOUT PERIOD.—For purposes of this subsection—

"(A) IN GENERAL.—The term 'blackout period' means, in connection with an individual account plan, any period for which any ability of participants or beneficiaries under the plan, which is otherwise available under the terms of such plan, to direct or diversify assets credited to their accounts, to obtain loans from the plan, or to obtain distributions from the plan is temporarily suspended, limited, or restricted, if such suspension, limitation, or restriction is for any period of more than 3 consecutive business days.

"(B) EXCLUSIONS.—The term 'blackout period' does not include a suspension, limitation, or restriction—

"(i) which occurs by reason of the application of the securities laws (as defined in section 3(a)(47) of the Securities Exchange Act of 1934),

"(ii) which is a change to the plan which provides for a regularly scheduled suspension, limitation, or restriction which is disclosed to participants or beneficiaries through any summary of material modifications, any materials describing specific investment alternatives under the plan, or any changes thereto, or

"(iii) which applies only to 1 or more individuals, each of whom is the participant, an alternate payee as defined in section 206(d)(3)(K)) or any other beneficiary pursuant to a qualified domestic relations order (as defined in section 206(d)(3)(B)(i)).

"(8) INDIVIDUAL ACCOUNT PLAN.—

"(A) IN GENERAL.—For purposes of this subsection, the term 'individual account plan' shall have the meaning provided such term in section 3(34), except that such term shall not include a one-participant retirement plan.

"(B) ONE-PARTICIPANT RETIREMENT PLAN.—For purposes of subparagraph (A), the term 'one-participant retirement plan' means a retirement plan that—

"(i) on the first day of the plan year—

"(I) covered only the employer (and the employer's spouse) and the employer owned the entire business (whether or not incorporated), or

"(II) covered only one or more partners (and their spouses) in a business partnership (including partners in an S or C corporation (as defined in section 1361(a) of the Internal Revenue Code of 1986)),

"(ii) meets the minimum coverage requirements of section 410(b) of the Internal Revenue Code of 1986 (as in effect on the date of the enactment of this paragraph) without being combined with any other plan of the business that covers the employees of the business,

"(iii) does not provide benefits to anyone except the employer (and the employer's spouse) or the partners (and their spouses),

"(iv) does not cover a business that is a member of an affiliated service group, a controlled group of corporations, or a group of businesses under common control, and

"(v) does not cover a business that leases employees.".

(2) ISSUANCE OF INITIAL GUIDANCE AND MODEL NOTICE.— The Secretary of Labor shall issue initial guidance and a model notice pursuant to section 101(i)(6) of the Employee Retirement Income Security Act of 1974 (as added by this subsection) not later than January 1, 2003. Not later than 75 days after the date of the enactment of this Act, the Secretary shall promulgate interim final rules necessary to carry out the amendments made by this subsection.

(3) CIVIL PENALTIES FOR FAILURE TO PROVIDE NOTICE.— Section 502 of such Act (29 U.S.C. 1132) is amended—

(A) in subsection (a)(6), by striking "(5), or (6)" and inserting "(5), (6), or (7)";

(B) by redesignating paragraph (7) of subsection (c)as paragraph (8); and

(C) by inserting after paragraph (6) of subsection (c)the following new paragraph:

"(7) The Secretary may assess a civil penalty against a plan administrator of up to $100 a day from the date of the plan administrator's failure or refusal to provide notice to participants and beneficiaries in accordance with section 101(i). For purposes of this paragraph, each violation with respect to any single participant or beneficiary shall be treated as a separate violation.".

H. R. 3763—40

(3) PLAN AMENDMENTS.—If any amendment made by this subsection requires an amendment to any plan, such plan amendment shall not be required to be made before the first plan year beginning on or after the effective date of this section, if—

(A) during the period after such amendment made by this subsection takes effect and before such first plan year, the plan is operated in good faith compliance with the requirements of such amendment made by this subsection, and

(B) such plan amendment applies retroactively to the period after such amendment made by this subsection takes effect and before such first plan year.

(c) EFFECTIVE DATE.—The provisions of this section (including the amendments made thereby) shall take effect 180 days after the date of the enactment of this Act. Good faith compliance with the requirements of such provisions in advance of the issuance of applicable regulations thereunder shall be treated as compliance with such provisions.

SEC. 307. RULES OF PROFESSIONAL RESPONSIBILITY FOR ATTORNEYS.

Not later than 180 days after the date of enactment of this Act, the Commission shall issue rules, in the public interest and for the protection of investors, setting forth minimum standards of professional conduct for attorneys appearing and practicing before the Commission in any way in the representation of issuers, including a rule—

(1) requiring an attorney to report evidence of a material violation of securities law or breach of fiduciary duty or similar violation by the company or any agent thereof, to the chief legal counsel or the chief executive officer of the company (or the equivalent thereof); and

(2) if the counsel or officer does not appropriately respond to the evidence (adopting, as necessary, appropriate remedial measures or sanctions with respect to the violation), requiring the attorney to report the evidence to the audit committee of the board of directors of the issuer or to another committee of the board of directors comprised solely of directors not employed directly or indirectly by the issuer, or to the board of directors.

SEC. 308. FAIR FUNDS FOR INVESTORS.

(a) CIVIL PENALTIES ADDED TO DISGORGEMENT FUNDS FOR THE RELIEF OF VICTIMS.—If in any judicial or administrative action brought by the Commission under the securities laws (as such term is defined in section 3(a)(47) of the Securities Exchange Act of 1934 (15 U.S.C. 78c(a)(47)) the Commission obtains an order requiring disgorgement against any person for a violation of such laws or the rules or regulations thereunder, or such person agrees in settlement of any such action to such disgorgement, and the Commission also obtains pursuant to such laws a civil penalty against such person, the amount of such civil penalty shall, on the motion or at the direction of the Commission, be added to and become part of the disgorgement fund for the benefit of the victims of such violation.

(b) ACCEPTANCE OF ADDITIONAL DONATIONS.—The Commission is authorized to accept, hold, administer, and utilize gifts, bequests and devises of property, both real and personal, to the United States for a disgorgement fund described in subsection (a). Such gifts, bequests, and devises of money and proceeds from sales of other property received as gifts, bequests, or devises shall be deposited in the disgorgement fund and shall be available for allocation in accordance with subsection (a).

(c) STUDY REQUIRED.—

(1) SUBJECT OF STUDY.—The Commission shall review and analyze—

(A) enforcement actions by the Commission over the five years preceding the date of the enactment of this Act that have included proceedings to obtain civil penalties or disgorgements to identify areas where such proceedings may be utilized to efficiently, effectively, and fairly provide restitution for injured investors; and

(B) other methods to more efficiently, effectively, and fairly provide restitution to injured investors, including methods to improve the collection rates for civil penalties and disgorgements.

(2) REPORT REQUIRED.—The Commission shall report its findings to the Committee on Financial Services of the House of Representatives and the Committee on Banking, Housing, and Urban Affairs of the Senate within 180 days after of the date of the enactment of this Act, and shall use such findings to revise its rules and regulations as necessary. The report shall include a discussion of regulatory or legislative actions that are recommended or that may be necessary to address concerns identified in the study.

(d) CONFORMING AMENDMENTS.—Each of the following provisions is amended by inserting ", except as otherwise provided in section 308 of the Sarbanes-Oxley Act of 2002" after "Treasury of the United States":

(1) Section 21(d)(3)(C)(i) of the Securities Exchange Act of 1934 (15 U.S.C. 78u(d)(3)(C)(i)).

(2) Section 21A(d)(1) of such Act (15 U.S.C. 78u-1(d)(1)).

(3) Section 20(d)(3)(A) of the Securities Act of 1933 (15 U.S.C. 77t(d)(3)(A)).

(4) Section 42(e)(3)(A) of the Investment Company Act of 1940 (15 U.S.C. 80a–41(e)(3)(A)).

(5) Section 209(e)(3)(A) of the Investment Advisers Act of 1940 (15 U.S.C. 80b–9(e)(3)(A)).

(e) DEFINITION.—As used in this section, the term "disgorgement fund" means a fund established in any administrative or judicial proceeding described in subsection (a).

TITLE IV—ENHANCED FINANCIAL DISCLOSURES

SEC. 401. DISCLOSURES IN PERIODIC REPORTS.

(a) DISCLOSURES REQUIRED.—Section 13 of the Securities Exchange Act of 1934 (15 U.S.C. 78m) is amended by adding at the end the following:

"(i) ACCURACY OF FINANCIAL REPORTS.—Each financial report that contains financial statements, and that is required to be prepared in accordance with (or reconciled to) generally accepted accounting principles under this title and filed with the Commission shall reflect all material correcting adjustments that have been identified by a registered public accounting firm in accordance with generally accepted accounting principles and the rules and regulations of the Commission.

"(j) OFF-BALANCE SHEET TRANSACTIONS.—Not later than 180 days after the date of enactment of the Sarbanes-Oxley Act of 2002, the Commission shall issue final rules providing that each annual and quarterly financial report required to be filed with the Commission shall disclose all material off-balance sheet transactions, arrangements, obligations (including contingent obligations), and other relationships of the issuer with unconsolidated entities or other persons, that may have a material current or future effect on financial condition, changes in financial condition, results of operations, liquidity, capital expenditures, capital resources, or significant components of revenues or expenses.".

(b) COMMISSION RULES ON PRO FORMA FIGURES.—Not later than 180 days after the date of enactment of the Sarbanes-Oxley Act of 2002, the Commission shall issue final rules providing that pro forma financial information included in any periodic or other report filed with the Commission pursuant to the securities laws, or in any public disclosure or press or other release, shall be presented in a manner that—

(1) does not contain an untrue statement of a material fact or omit to state a material fact necessary in order to make the pro forma financial information, in light of the circumstances under which it is presented, not misleading; and

(2) reconciles it with the financial condition and results of operations of the issuer under generally accepted accounting principles.

(c) STUDY AND REPORT ON SPECIAL PURPOSE ENTITIES.—

(1) STUDY REQUIRED.—The Commission shall, not later than 1 year after the effective date of adoption of off-balance sheet disclosure rules required by section 13(j) of the Securities Exchange Act of 1934, as added by this section, complete a study of filings by issuers and their disclosures to determine—

(A) the extent of off-balance sheet transactions, including assets, liabilities, leases, losses, and the use of special purpose entities; and

(B) whether generally accepted accounting rules result in financial statements of issuers reflecting the economics of such off-balance sheet transactions to investors in a transparent fashion.

(2) REPORT AND RECOMMENDATIONS.—Not later than 6 months after the date of completion of the study required by paragraph (1), the Commission shall submit a report to the President, the Committee on Banking, Housing, and Urban Affairs of the Senate, and the Committee on Financial Services of the House of Representatives, setting forth—

(A) the amount or an estimate of the amount of off-balance sheet transactions, including assets, liabilities, leases, and losses of, and the use of special purpose entities by, issuers filing periodic reports pursuant to section 13 or 15 of the Securities Exchange Act of 1934;

(B) the extent to which special purpose entities are used to facilitate off-balance sheet transactions;

(C) whether generally accepted accounting principles or the rules of the Commission result in financial statements of issuers reflecting the economics of such transactions to investors in a transparent fashion;

(D) whether generally accepted accounting principles specifically result in the consolidation of special purpose entities sponsored by an issuer in cases in which the issuer has the majority of the risks and rewards of the special purpose entity; and

(E) any recommendations of the Commission for improving the transparency and quality of reporting off-balance sheet transactions in the financial statements and disclosures required to be filed by an issuer with the Commission.

SEC. 402. ENHANCED CONFLICT OF INTEREST PROVISIONS.

(a) PROHIBITION ON PERSONAL LOANS TO EXECUTIVES.—Section 13 of the Securities Exchange Act of 1934 (15 U.S.C. 78m), as amended by this Act, is amended by adding at the end the following:

"(k) PROHIBITION ON PERSONAL LOANS TO EXECUTIVES.—

"(1) IN GENERAL.—It shall be unlawful for any issuer (as defined in section 2 of the Sarbanes-Oxley Act of 2002), directly or indirectly, including through any subsidiary, to extend or maintain credit, to arrange for the extension of credit, or to renew an extension of credit, in the form of a personal loan to or for any director or executive officer (or equivalent thereof) of that issuer. An extension of credit maintained by the issuer on the date of enactment of this subsection shall not be subject to the provisions of this subsection, provided that there is no material modification to any term of any such extension of credit or any renewal of any such extension of credit on or after that date of enactment.

"(2) LIMITATION.—Paragraph (1) does not preclude any home improvement and manufactured home loans (as that term is defined in section 5 of the Home Owners' Loan Act (12 U.S.C. 1464)), consumer credit (as defined in section 103 of the Truth in Lending Act (15 U.S.C. 1602)), or any extension of credit under an open end credit plan (as defined in section 103 of the Truth in Lending Act (15 U.S.C. 1602)), or a charge card (as defined in section 127(c)(4)(e) of the Truth in Lending Act (15 U.S.C. 1637(c)(4)(e)), or any extension of credit by a broker or dealer registered under section 15 of this title to an employee of that broker or dealer to buy, trade, or carry securities, that is permitted under rules or regulations of the Board of Governors of the Federal Reserve System pursuant to section 7 of this title (other than an extension of credit that would be used to purchase the stock of that issuer), that is—

"(A) made or provided in the ordinary course of the consumer credit business of such issuer; "

(B) of a type that is generally made available by such issuer to the public; and

"(C) made by such issuer on market terms, or terms that are no more favorable than those offered by the issuer to the general public for such extensions of credit. "

(3) RULE OF CONSTRUCTION FOR CERTAIN LOANS.—Paragraph (1) does not apply to any loan made or maintained by an insured deposi-

tory institution (as defined in section 3 of the Federal Deposit Insurance Act (12 U.S.C. 1813)), if the loan is subject to the insider lending restrictions of section 22(h) of the Federal Reserve Act (12 U.S.C. 375b).".

SEC. 403. DISCLOSURES OF TRANSACTIONS INVOLVING MANAGEMENT AND PRINCIPAL STOCKHOLDERS.

(a) AMENDMENT.—Section 16 of the Securities Exchange Act of 1934 (15 U.S.C. 78p) is amended by striking the heading of such section and subsection (a) and inserting the following:

"SEC. 16. DIRECTORS, OFFICERS, AND PRINCIPAL STOCKHOLDERS.

"(a) DISCLOSURES REQUIRED.—

"(1) DIRECTORS, OFFICERS, AND PRINCIPAL STOCKHOLDERS REQUIRED TO FILE.—Every person who is directly or indirectly the beneficial owner of more than 10 percent of any class of any equity security (other than an exempted security) which is registered pursuant to section 12, or who is a director or an officer of the issuer of such security, shall file the statements required by this subsection with the Commission (and, if such security is registered on a national securities exchange, also with the exchange).

"(2) TIME OF FILING.—The statements required by this subsection shall be filed—

"(A) at the time of the registration of such security on a national securities exchange or by the effective date of a registration statement filed pursuant to section 12(g);

"(B) within 10 days after he or she becomes such beneficial owner, director, or officer;

"(C) if there has been a change in such ownership, or if such person shall have purchased or sold a security-based swap agreement (as defined in section 206(b) of the Gramm-Leach-Bliley Act (15 U.S.C. 78c note)) involving such equity security, before the end of the second business day following the day on which the subject transaction has been executed, or at such other time as the Commission shall establish, by rule, in any case in which the Commission determines that such 2-day period is not feasible."

(3) CONTENTS OF STATEMENTS.—A statement filed—

"(A) under subparagraph (A) or (B) of paragraph (2) shall contain a statement of the amount of all equity securities of such issuer of which the filing person is the beneficial owner; and "(B) under subparagraph (C) of such paragraph shall indicate ownership by the filing person at the date of filing, any such changes in such ownership, and such purchases and sales of the security-based swap agreements as have occurred since the most recent such filing under such subparagraph.

"(4) ELECTRONIC FILING AND AVAILABILITY.—Beginning not later than 1 year after the date of enactment of the Sarbanes-Oxley Act of 2002—

"(A) a statement filed under subparagraph (C) of paragraph (2) shall be filed electronically;

"(B) the Commission shall provide each such statement on a publicly accessible Internet site not later than the end of the business day following that filing; and

H. R. 3763—45

"(C) the issuer (if the issuer maintains a corporate website) shall provide that statement on that corporate website, not later than the end of the business day following that filing.".

(b) EFFECTIVE DATE.—The amendment made by this section shall be effective 30 days after the date of the enactment of this Act.

SEC. 404. MANAGEMENT ASSESSMENT OF INTERNAL CONTROLS.

(a) RULES REQUIRED.—The Commission shall prescribe rules requiring each annual report required by section 13(a) or 15(d) of the Securities Exchange Act of 1934 (15 U.S.C. 78m or 78o(d)) to contain an internal control report, which shall—

(1) state the responsibility of management for establishing and maintaining an adequate internal control structure and procedures for financial reporting; and

(2) contain an assessment, as of the end of the most recent fiscal year of the issuer, of the effectiveness of the internal control structure and procedures of the issuer for financial reporting.

(b) INTERNAL CONTROL EVALUATION AND REPORTING.—With respect to the internal control assessment required by subsection (a), each registered public accounting firm that prepares or issues the audit report for the issuer shall attest to, and report on, the assessment made by the management of the issuer. An attestation made under this subsection shall be made in accordance with standards for attestation engagements issued or adopted by the Board. Any such attestation shall not be the subject of a separate engagement.

SEC. 405. EXEMPTION.

Nothing in section 401, 402, or 404, the amendments made by those sections, or the rules of the Commission under those sections shall apply to any investment company registered under section 8 of the Investment Company Act of 1940 (15 U.S.C. 80a– 8).

SEC. 406. CODE OF ETHICS FOR SENIOR FINANCIAL OFFICERS.

(a) CODE OF ETHICS DISCLOSURE.—The Commission shall issue rules to require each issuer, together with periodic reports required pursuant to section 13(a) or 15(d) of the Securities Exchange Act of 1934, to disclose whether or not, and if not, the reason therefore, such issuer has adopted a code of ethics for senior financial officers, applicable to its principal financial officer and comptroller or principal accounting officer, or persons performing similar functions.

(b) CHANGES IN CODES OF ETHICS.—The Commission shall revise its regulations concerning matters requiring prompt disclosure on Form 8–K (or any successor thereto) to require the immediate disclosure, by means of the filing of such form, dissemination by the Internet or by other electronic means, by any issuer of any change in or waiver of the code of ethics for senior financial officers.

(c) DEFINITION.—In this section, the term "code of ethics" means such standards as are reasonably necessary to promote—

(1) honest and ethical conduct, including the ethical handling of actual or apparent conflicts of interest between personal and professional relationships;

(2) full, fair, accurate, timely, and understandable disclosure in the periodic reports required to be filed by the issuer; and

(3) compliance with applicable governmental rules and regulations.

(d) DEADLINE FOR RULEMAKING.—The Commission shall—

(1) propose rules to implement this section, not later than90 days after the date of enactment of this Act; and

(2) issue final rules to implement this section, not later than 180 days after that date of enactment.

SEC. 407. DISCLOSURE OF AUDIT COMMITTEE FINANCIAL EXPERT.

(a) RULES DEFINING "FINANCIAL EXPERT".—The Commission shall issue rules, as necessary or appropriate in the public interest and consistent with the protection of investors, to require each issuer, together with periodic reports required pursuant to sections 13(a) and 15(d) of the Securities Exchange Act of 1934, to disclose whether or not, and if not, the reasons therefore, the audit committee of that issuer is comprised of at least 1 member who is a financial expert, as such term is defined by the Commission.

(b) CONSIDERATIONS.—In defining the term "financial expert" for purposes of subsection (a), the Commission shall consider whether a person has, through education and experience as a public accountant or auditor or a principal financial officer, comptroller, or principal accounting officer of an issuer, or from a position involving the performance of similar functions—

(1) an understanding of generally accepted accounting principles and financial statements;

(2) experience in—

(A) the preparation or auditing of financial statements of generally comparable issuers; and

(B) the application of such principles in connection with the accounting for estimates, accruals, and reserves;

(3) experience with internal accounting controls; and

(4) an understanding of audit committee functions.

(c) DEADLINE FOR RULEMAKING.—The Commission shall—

(1) propose rules to implement this section, not later than90 days after the date of enactment of this Act; and

(2) issue final rules to implement this section, not later than 180 days after that date of enactment.

SEC. 408. ENHANCED REVIEW OF PERIODIC DISCLOSURES BY ISSUERS.

(a) REGULAR AND SYSTEMATIC REVIEW.—The Commission shall review disclosures made by issuers reporting under section 13(a) of the Securities Exchange Act of 1934 (including reports filed on Form 10–K), and which have a class of securities listed on a national securities exchange or traded on an automated quotation facility of a national securities association, on a regular and systematic basis for the protection of investors. Such review shall include a review of an issuer's financial statement.

(b) REVIEW CRITERIA.—For purposes of scheduling the reviews required by subsection (a), the Commission shall consider, among other factors—

(1) issuers that have issued material restatements of financial results;

(2) issuers that experience significant volatility in their stock price as

compared to other issuers;

(3) issuers with the largest market capitalization;

(4) emerging companies with disparities in price to earning ratios;

(5) issuers whose operations significantly affect any material sector of the economy; and

(6) any other factors that the Commission may consider relevant.

(c) MINIMUM REVIEW PERIOD.—In no event shall an issuer required to file reports under section 13(a) or 15(d) of the Securities Exchange Act of 1934 be reviewed under this section less frequently than once every 3 years.

SEC. 409. REAL TIME ISSUER DISCLOSURES.

Section 13 of the Securities Exchange Act of 1934 (15 U.S.C. 78m), as amended by this Act, is amended by adding at the end the following:

"(l) REAL TIME ISSUER DISCLOSURES.—Each issuer reporting under section 13(a) or 15(d) shall disclose to the public on a rapid and current basis such additional information concerning material changes in the financial condition or operations of the issuer, in plain English, which may include trend and qualitative information and graphic presentations, as the Commission determines, by rule, is necessary or useful for the protection of investors and in the public interest.".

TITLE V—ANALYST CONFLICTS OF INTEREST

SEC. 501. TREATMENT OF SECURITIES ANALYSTS BY REGISTERED SECURITIES ASSOCIATIONS AND NATIONAL SECURITIES EXCHANGES.

(a) RULES REGARDING SECURITIES ANALYSTS.—The Securities Exchange Act of 1934 (15 U.S.C. 78a et seq.) is amended by inserting after section 15C the following new section:

"SEC. 15D. SECURITIES ANALYSTS AND RESEARCH REPORTS.

"(a) ANALYST PROTECTIONS.—The Commission, or upon the authorization and direction of the Commission, a registered securities association or national securities exchange, shall have adopted, not later than 1 year after the date of enactment of this section, rules reasonably designed to address conflicts of interest that can arise when securities analysts recommend equity securities in research reports and public appearances, in order to improve the objectivity of research and provide investors with more useful and reliable information, including rules designed—

"(1) to foster greater public confidence in securities research, and to protect the objectivity and independence of securities analysts, by—

"(A) restricting the prepublication clearance or approval of research reports by persons employed by the broker or dealer who are engaged in investment banking activities, or persons not directly responsible for investment research, other than legal or compliance staff;

"(B) limiting the supervision and compensatory evaluation of securities analysts to officials employed by the broker or dealer who are not engaged in investment banking activities; and

"(C) requiring that a broker or dealer and persons employed by a broker or dealer who are involved with investment banking activities may not, directly or indirectly, retaliate against or threaten to retaliate against any securities analyst employed by that broker or dealer or its affiliates as a result of an adverse, negative, or otherwise unfavorable research report that may adversely affect the present or prospective investment banking relationship of the broker or dealer with the issuer that is the subject of the research report, except that such rules may not limit the authority of a broker or dealer to discipline a securities analyst for causes other than such research report in accordance with the policies and procedures of the firm;

"(2) to define periods during which brokers or dealers who have participated, or are to participate, in a public offering of securities as underwriters or dealers should not publish or otherwise distribute research reports relating to such securities or to the issuer of such securities;

"(3) to establish structural and institutional safeguards within registered brokers or dealers to assure that securities analysts are separated by appropriate informational partitions within the firm from the review, pressure, or oversight of those whose involvement in investment banking activities might potentially bias their judgment or supervision; and

"(4) to address such other issues as the Commission, or such association or exchange, determines appropriate.

"(b) DISCLOSURE.—The Commission, or upon the authorization and direction of the Commission, a registered securities association or national securities exchange, shall have adopted, not later than 1 year after the date of enactment of this section, rules reasonably designed to require each securities analyst to disclose in public appearances, and each registered broker or dealer to disclose in each research report, as applicable, conflicts of interest that are known or should have been known by the securities analyst or the broker or dealer, to exist at the time of the appearance or the date of distribution of the report, including—

"(1) the extent to which the securities analyst has debt or equity investments in the issuer that is the subject of the appearance or research report;

"(2) whether any compensation has been received by the registered broker or dealer, or any affiliate thereof, including the securities analyst, from the issuer that is the subject of the appearance or research report, subject to such exemptions as the Commission may determine appropriate and necessary to prevent disclosure by virtue of this paragraph of material non-public information regarding specific potential future investment banking transactions of such issuer, as is appropriate in the public interest and consistent with the protection of investors;

"(3) whether an issuer, the securities of which are recommended in the appearance or research report, currently is, or during the 1-year period preceding the date of the appearance or date of distribution of the report has been, a client of the registered broker or dealer, and if so, stating the types of services provided to the issuer;

"(4) whether the securities analyst received compensation with respect to a research report, based upon (among any other factors) the investment banking revenues (either generally or specifically earned from the issuer being analyzed) of the registered broker or dealer; and

"(5) such other disclosures of conflicts of interest that are material to investors, research analysts, or the broker or dealer as the Commission, or such association or exchange, determines appropriate. "(c) DEFINITIONS.—In this section—

"(1) the term 'securities analyst' means any associated person of a registered broker or dealer that is principally responsible for, and any associated person who reports directly or indirectly to a securities analyst in connection with, the preparation of the substance of a research report, whether or not any such person has the job title of 'securities analyst'; and

"(2) the term 'research report' means a written or electronic communication that includes an analysis of equity securities of individual companies or industries, and that provides information reasonably sufficient upon which to base an investment decision.".

(b) ENFORCEMENT.—Section 21B(a) of the Securities Exchange Act of 1934 (15 U.S.C. 78u–2(a)) is amended by inserting "15D," before "15B".

(c) COMMISSION AUTHORITY.—The Commission may promulgate and amend its regulations, or direct a registered securities association or national securities exchange to promulgate and amend its rules, to carry out section 15D of the Securities Exchange Act of 1934, as added by this section, as is necessary for the protection of investors and in the public interest.

TITLE VI—COMMISSION RESOURCES AND AUTHORITY

SEC. 601. AUTHORIZATION OF APPROPRIATIONS.

Section 35 of the Securities Exchange Act of 1934 (15 U.S.C. 78kk) is amended to read as follows:

"SEC. 35. AUTHORIZATION OF APPROPRIATIONS.

"In addition to any other funds authorized to be appropriated to the Commission, there are authorized to be appropriated to carry out the functions, powers, and duties of the Commission, $776,000,000 for fiscal year 2003, of which—

"(1) $102,700,000 shall be available to fund additional com pensation, including salaries and benefits, as authorized in the Investor and Capital Markets Fee Relief Act (Public Law 107–123; 115 Stat. 2390 et seq.);

"(2) $108,400,000 shall be available for information technology, security enhancements, and recovery and mitigation activities in light of the terrorist attacks of September 11, 2001; and

"(3) $98,000,000 shall be available to add not fewer than an additional 200 qualified professionals to provide enhanced oversight of auditors and audit services required by the Federal securities laws, and to improve Commission investigative and disciplinary efforts with respect to such auditors and services, as well as for additional professional support staff necessary to strengthen the programs of the Commission involving Full Disclosure and Prevention and Suppression of Fraud, risk management, industry technology review, compliance, inspections, examinations, market regulation, and investment management.".

SEC. 602. APPEARANCE AND PRACTICE BEFORE THE COMMISSION.

The Securities Exchange Act of 1934 (15 U.S.C. 78a et seq.) is amended by inserting after section 4B the following:

"SEC. 4C. APPEARANCE AND PRACTICE BEFORE THE COMMISSION.

"(a) AUTHORITY TO CENSURE.—The Commission may censure any person, or deny, temporarily or permanently, to any person the privilege of appearing or practicing before the Commission in any way, if that person is found by the Commission, after notice and opportunity for hearing in the matter—

"(1) not to possess the requisite qualifications to represent others;

"(2) to be lacking in character or integrity, or to have engaged in unethical or improper professional conduct; or

"(3) to have willfully violated, or willfully aided and abetted the violation of, any provision of the securities laws or the rules and regulations issued thereunder.

"(b) DEFINITION.—With respect to any registered public accounting firm or associated person, for purposes of this section, the term 'improper professional conduct' means—

"(1) intentional or knowing conduct, including reckless conduct, that results in a violation of applicable professional standards; and

"(2) negligent conduct in the form of—

"(A) a single instance of highly unreasonable conduct that results in a violation of applicable professional standards in circumstances in which the registered public accounting firm or associated person knows, or should know, that heightened scrutiny is warranted; or

"(B) repeated instances of unreasonable conduct, each resulting in a violation of applicable professional standards, that indicate a lack of competence to practice before the Commission.".

SEC. 603. FEDERAL COURT AUTHORITY TO IMPOSE PENNY STOCK BARS.

(a) SECURITIES EXCHANGE ACT OF 1934.—Section 21(d) of the Securities Exchange Act of 1934 (15 U.S.C. 78u(d)), as amended by this Act, is amended by adding at the end the following:

"(6) AUTHORITY OF A COURT TO PROHIBIT PERSONS FROM PARTICIPATING IN AN OFFERING OF PENNY STOCK.—

"(A) IN GENERAL.—In any proceeding under paragraph (1) against any person participating in, or, at the time of the alleged misconduct who was participating in, an offering of penny stock, the court may prohibit that person from participating in an offering of penny stock, conditionally or unconditionally, and permanently or for such period of time as the court shall determine.

"(B) DEFINITION.—For purposes of this paragraph, the term 'person participating in an offering of penny stock' includes any person engaging in activities with a broker, dealer, or issuer for purposes of issuing, trading, or inducing or attempting to induce the purchase or sale of, any penny stock. The Commission may, by rule or regulation, define such term to include other activities, and may, by rule, regulation, or order, exempt any person or class of persons, in whole or in part, conditionally or unconditionally, from inclusion in such term.".

(b) SECURITIES ACT OF 1933.—Section 20 of the Securities Act of 1933 (15 U.S.C. 77t) is amended by adding at the end the following:

"(g) AUTHORITY OF A COURT TO PROHIBIT PERSONS FROM PARTICIPATING IN AN OFFERING OF PENNY STOCK.—

"(1) IN GENERAL.—In any proceeding under subsection (a) against any person participating in, or, at the time of the alleged misconduct, who was participating in, an offering of penny stock, the court may prohibit that person from participating in an offering of penny stock, conditionally or unconditionally, and permanently or for such period of time as the court shall determine.

"(2) DEFINITION.—For purposes of this subsection, the term 'person participating in an offering of penny stock' includes any person engaging in activities with a broker, dealer, or issuer for purposes of issuing, trading, or inducing or attempting to induce the purchase or sale of, any penny stock. The Commission may, by rule or regulation, define such term to include other activities, and may, by rule, regulation, or order, exempt any person or class of persons, in whole or in part, conditionally or unconditionally, from inclusion in such term.".

SEC. 604. QUALIFICATIONS OF ASSOCIATED PERSONS OF BROKERS AND DEALERS.

(a) BROKERS AND DEALERS.—Section 15(b)(4) of the Securities Exchange Act of 1934 (15 U.S.C. 78o) is amended—

(1) by striking subparagraph (F) and inserting the following:

"(F) is subject to any order of the Commission barring or suspending the right of the person to be associated with a broker or dealer;"; and

(2) in subparagraph (G), by striking the period at the end and inserting the following: "; or

"(H) is subject to any final order of a State securities commission (or any agency or officer performing like functions), State authority that supervises or examines banks, savings associations, or credit unions, State insurance commission (or any agency or office performing like functions), an appropriate Federal banking agency (as defined in section 3 of the Federal Deposit Insurance Act (12 U.S.C. 1813(q))), or the National Credit Union Administration, that—

"(i) bars such person from association with an entity regulated by such commission, authority, agency, or officer, or from engaging in the business of securities, insurance, banking, savings association activities, or credit union activities; or

H. R. 3763—52

"(ii) constitutes a final order based on violations of any laws or regulations that prohibit fraudulent, manipulative, or deceptive conduct.".

(b) INVESTMENT ADVISERS.—Section 203(e) of the Investment Advisers Act of 1940 (15 U.S.C. 80b–3(e)) is amended—

(1) by striking paragraph (7) and inserting the following:

"(7) is subject to any order of the Commission barring or suspending the right of the person to be associated with an investment adviser;";

(2) in paragraph (8), by striking the period at the end and inserting"; or"; and

(3) by adding at the end the following:

"(9) is subject to any final order of a State securities commission (or any agency or officer performing like functions), State authority that supervises or examines banks, savings associations, or credit unions, State insurance commission (or any agency or office performing like functions), an appropriate Federal banking agency (as defined in section 3 of the Federal Deposit Insurance Act (12 U.S.C. 1813(q))), or the National Credit Union Administration, that—

"(A) bars such person from association with an entity regulated by such commission, authority, agency, or officer, or from engaging in the business of securities, insurance, banking, savings association activities, or credit union activities; or

"(B) constitutes a final order based on violations of any laws or regulations that prohibit fraudulent, manipulative, or deceptive conduct.".

(c) CONFORMING AMENDMENTS.—

(1) SECURITIES EXCHANGE ACT OF 1934.—The Securities Exchange Act of 1934 (15 U.S.C. 78a et seq.) is amended—

(A) in section 3(a)(39)(F) (15 U.S.C. 78c(a)(39)(F))—

(i) by striking "or (G)" and inserting "(H), or (G)"; and

(ii) by inserting ", or is subject to an order or finding," before "enumerated";

(B) in each of section 15(b)(6)(A)(i) (15 U.S.C. 78o(b)(6)(A)(i)), paragraphs (2) and (4) of section 15B(c) (15 U.S.C. 78o–4(c)), and subparagraphs (A) and (C) of section 15C(c)(1) (15 U.S.C. 78o–5(c)(1))—

(i) by striking "or (G)" each place that term appears and inserting "(H), or (G)"; and

(ii) by striking "or omission" each place that term appears, and inserting ", or is subject to an order or finding,"; and (C) in each of paragraphs (3)(A) and (4)

(C) of section17A(c) (15 U.S.C. 78q–1(c))—

(i) by striking "or (G)" each place that term appears and inserting "(H), or (G)"; and

(ii) by inserting ", or is subject to an order or finding," before "enumerated" each place that term appears.

(2) INVESTMENT ADVISERS ACT OF 1940.—Section 203(f) of the Investment Advisers Act of 1940 (15 U.S.C. 80b–3(f)) is amended—

(A) by striking "or (8)" and inserting "(8), or (9)"; and

(B) by inserting "or (3)" after "paragraph (2)".

TITLE VII—STUDIES AND REPORTS

SEC. 701. GAO STUDY AND REPORT REGARDING CONSOLIDATION OF PUBLIC ACCOUNTING FIRMS.

(a) STUDY REQUIRED.—The Comptroller General of the United States shall conduct a study—

(1) to identify—

(A) the factors that have led to the consolidation of public accounting firms since 1989 and the consequent reduction in the number of firms capable of providing audit services to large national and multi-national business organizations that are subject to the securities laws;

(B) the present and future impact of the condition described in subparagraph (A) on capital formation and securities markets, both domestic and international; and

(C) solutions to any problems identified under subparagraph (B), including ways to increase competition and the number of firms capable of providing audit services to large national and multinational business organizations that are subject to the securities laws;

(2) of the problems, if any, faced by business organizations that have resulted from limited competition among public accounting firms, including—

(A) higher costs;

(B) lower quality of services;

(C) impairment of auditor independence; or

(D) lack of choice; and

(3) whether and to what extent Federal or State regulations impede competition among public accounting firms.

(b) CONSULTATION.—In planning and conducting the study under this section, the Comptroller General shall consult with—

(1) the Commission;

(2) the regulatory agencies that perform functions similar to the Commission within the other member countries of the Group of Seven Industrialized Nations;

(3) the Department of Justice; and

(4) any other public or private sector organization that the Comptroller General considers appropriate.

(c) REPORT REQUIRED.—Not later than 1 year after the date of enactment of this Act, the Comptroller General shall submit a report on the results of the study required by this section to the Committee on Banking, Housing, and Urban Affairs of the Senate and the Committee on Financial Services of the House of Representatives.

SEC. 702. COMMISSION STUDY AND REPORT REGARDING CREDIT RATING AGENCIES.

(a) STUDY REQUIRED.—

(1) IN GENERAL.—The Commission shall conduct a study of the role and function of credit rating agencies in the operation of the securities market.

(2) AREAS OF CONSIDERATION.—The study required by this subsection shall examine—

(A) the role of credit rating agencies in the evaluation of issuers of securities;

(B) the importance of that role to investors and the functioning of the securities markets;

(C) any impediments to the accurate appraisal by credit rating agencies of the financial resources and risks of issuers of securities;

(D) any barriers to entry into the business of acting as a credit rating agency, and any measures needed to remove such barriers;

(E) any measures which may be required to improve the dissemination of information concerning such resources and risks when credit rating agencies announce credit ratings; and

(F) any conflicts of interest in the operation of credit rating agencies and measures to prevent such conflicts or ameliorate the consequences of such conflicts.

(b) REPORT REQUIRED.—The Commission shall submit a report on the study required by subsection (a) to the President, the Committee on Financial Services of the House of Representatives, and the Committee on Banking, Housing, and Urban Affairs of the Senate not later than 180 days after the date of enactment of this Act.

SEC. 703. STUDY AND REPORT ON VIOLATORS AND VIOLATIONS.

(a) STUDY.—The Commission shall conduct a study to determine, based upon information for the period from January 1, 1998, to December 31, 2001—

(1) the number of securities professionals, defined as public accountants, public accounting firms, investment bankers, investment advisers, brokers, dealers, attorneys, and other securities professionals practicing before the Commission—

(A) who have been found to have aided and abetted a violation of the Federal securities laws, including rules or regulations promulgated thereunder (collectively referred to in this section as "Federal securities laws"), but who have not been sanctioned, disciplined, or otherwise penalized as a primary violator in any administrative action or civil proceeding, including in any settlement of such an action or proceeding (referred to in this section as "aiders and abettors"); and

(B) who have been found to have been primary violators of the Federal securities laws;

(2) a description of the Federal securities laws violations committed by aiders and abettors and by primary violators, including—

(A) the specific provision of the Federal securities laws violated;

(B) the specific sanctions and penalties imposed upon such aiders and abettors and primary violators, including the amount of any monetary penalties assessed upon and collected from such persons;

(C) the occurrence of multiple violations by the same person or persons, either as an aider or abettor or as a primary violator; and

(D) whether, as to each such violator, disciplinary sanctions have been imposed, including any censure, suspension, temporary bar, or permanent bar to practice before the Commission; and

(3) the amount of disgorgement, restitution, or any other fines or payments that the Commission has assessed upon and collected from, aiders and abettors and from primary violators.

(b) REPORT.—A report based upon the study conducted pursuant to subsection (a) shall be submitted to the Committee on Banking, Housing, and Urban Affairs of the Senate, and the Committee on Financial Services of the House of Representatives not later than 6 months after the date of enactment of this Act.

SEC. 704. STUDY OF ENFORCEMENT ACTIONS.

(a) STUDY REQUIRED.—The Commission shall review and analyze all enforcement actions by the Commission involving violations of reporting requirements imposed under the securities laws, and restatements of financial statements, over the 5-year period preceding the date of enactment of this Act, to identify areas of reporting that are most susceptible to fraud, inappropriate manipulation, or inappropriate earnings management, such as revenue recognition and the accounting treatment of off-balance sheet special purpose entities.

(b) REPORT REQUIRED.—The Commission shall report its findings to the Committee on Financial Services of the House of Representatives and the Committee on Banking, Housing, and Urban Affairs of the Senate, not later than 180 days after the date of enactment of this Act, and shall use such findings to revise its rules and regulations, as necessary. The report shall include a discussion of regulatory or legislative steps that are recommended or that may be necessary to address concerns identified in the study.

SEC. 705. STUDY OF INVESTMENT BANKS.

(a) GAO STUDY.—The Comptroller General of the United States shall conduct a study on whether investment banks and financial advisers assisted public companies in manipulating their earnings and obfuscating their true financial condition. The study should address the rule of investment banks and financial advisers—

(1) in the collapse of the Enron Corporation, including with respect to the design and implementation of derivatives transactions, transactions involving special purpose vehicles, and other financial arrangements that may have had the effect of altering the company's reported financial statements in ways that obscured the true financial picture of the company;

(2) in the failure of Global Crossing, including with respect to transactions involving swaps of fiberoptic cable capacity, in the designing transactions that may have had the effect of altering the company's reported financial statements in ways that obscured the true financial picture of the company; and

(3) generally, in creating and marketing transactions which may have been designed solely to enable companies to manipulate revenue streams, obtain loans, or move liabilities off balance sheets without altering the economic and business risks faced by the companies or any other mechanism to obscure a company's financial picture.

(b) REPORT.—The Comptroller General shall report to Congress not later than 180 days after the date of enactment of this Act on the results of the study required by this section. The report shall include a discussion of regulatory or legislative steps that are recommended or that may be necessary to address concerns identified in the study.

TITLE VIII—CORPORATE AND CRIMINAL FRAUD ACCOUNTABILITY

SEC. 801. SHORT TITLE.

This title may be cited as the "Corporate and Criminal Fraud Accountability Act of 2002".

SEC. 802. CRIMINAL PENALTIES FOR ALTERING DOCUMENTS.

(a) IN GENERAL.—Chapter 73 of title 18, United States Code, is amended by adding at the end the following:

"§ 1519. Destruction, alteration, or falsification of records in Federal investigations and bankruptcy

"Whoever knowingly alters, destroys, mutilates, conceals, covers up, falsifies, or makes a false entry in any record, document, or tangible object with the intent to impede, obstruct, or influence the investigation or proper administration of any matter within the jurisdiction of any department or agency of the United States or any case filed under title 11, or in relation to or contemplation of any such matter or case, shall be fined under this title, imprisoned not more than 20 years, or both.

"§ 1520. Destruction of corporate audit records

"(a)(1) Any accountant who conducts an audit of an issuer of securities to which section 10A(a) of the Securities Exchange Act of 1934 (15 U.S.C. 78j–1(a)) applies, shall maintain all audit or review workpapers for a period of 5 years from the end of the fiscal period in which the audit or review was concluded.

"(2) The Securities and Exchange Commission shall promulgate, within 180 days, after adequate notice and an opportunity for comment, such rules and regulations, as are reasonably necessary, relating to the retention of relevant records such as workpapers, documents that form the basis of an audit or review, memoranda, correspondence, communications, other documents, and records (including electronic records) which are created, sent, or received in connection with an audit or review and contain conclusions, opinions, analyses, or financial data relating to such an audit or review, which is conducted by any accountant who conducts an audit of an issuer of securities to which section 10A(a) of the Securities Exchange Act of 1934 (15 U.S.C. 78j–1(a)) applies. The Commission may, from time to time, amend or supplement the rules and regulations that it is required to promulgate under this section, after adequate notice and an opportunity for comment, in order to ensure that such rules and regulations adequately comport with the purposes of this section.

"(b) Whoever knowingly and willfully violates subsection (a)(1), or any rule or regulation promulgated by the Securities and Exchange Commission under subsection (a)(2), shall be fined under this title, imprisoned not more than 10 years, or both.

"(c) Nothing in this section shall be deemed to diminish or relieve any person of any other duty or obligation imposed by Federal or State law or regulation to maintain, or refrain from destroying, any document.".

(b) CLERICAL AMENDMENT.—The table of sections at the beginning of chapter 73 of title 18, United States Code, is amended by adding at the end the following new items:

"1519. Destruction, alteration, or falsification of records in Federal investigations and bankruptcy.

"1520. Destruction of corporate audit records.".

SEC. 803. DEBTS NONDISCHARGEABLE IF INCURRED IN VIOLATION OF SECURITIES FRAUD LAWS.

Section 523(a) of title 11, United States Code, is amended—

(1) in paragraph (17), by striking "or" after the semicolon;

(2) in paragraph (18), by striking the period at the end and inserting"; or"; and

(3) by adding at the end, the following:"(19) that—

"(A) is for—

"(i) the violation of any of the Federal securities laws (as that term is defined in section 3(a)(47) of the Securities Exchange Act of 1934), any of the State securities laws, or any regulation or order issued under such Federal or State securities laws; or

"(ii) common law fraud, deceit, or manipulation in connection with the purchase or sale of any security; and "(B) results from—

"(i) any judgment, order, consent order, or decree entered in any Federal or State judicial or administrative proceeding;

"(ii) any settlement agreement entered into by the debtor; or

"(iii) any court or administrative order for any damages, fine, penalty, citation, restitutionary payment, disgorgement payment, attorney fee, cost, or other payment owed by the debtor.".

SEC. 804. STATUTE OF LIMITATIONS FOR SECURITIES FRAUD.

(a) IN GENERAL.—Section 1658 of title 28, United States Code, is amended—

(1) by inserting "(a)" before "Except"; and

(2) by adding at the end the following:

"(b) Notwithstanding subsection (a), a private right of action that involves a claim of fraud, deceit, manipulation, or contrivance in contravention of a regulatory requirement concerning the securities laws, as defined in section 3(a)(47) of the Securities Exchange Act of 1934 (15 U.S.C. 78c(a)(47)), may be brought not later than the earlier of—

"(1) 2 years after the discovery of the facts constituting the violation; or

"(2) 5 years after such violation.".

(b) EFFECTIVE DATE.—The limitations period provided by section 1658(b) of title 28, United States Code, as added by this section, shall apply to all proceedings addressed by this section that are commenced on or after the date of enactment of this Act.

(c) NO CREATION OF ACTIONS.—Nothing in this section shall create a new, private right of action.

SEC. 805. REVIEW OF FEDERAL SENTENCING GUIDELINES FOR OBSTRUCTION OF JUSTICE AND EXTENSIVE CRIMINAL FRAUD.

(a) ENHANCEMENT OF FRAUD AND OBSTRUCTION OF JUSTICE SENTENCES.—Pursuant to section 994 of title 28, United States Code, and in accordance with this section, the United States Sentencing Commission shall review and amend, as appropriate, the Federal Sentencing Guidelines and related policy statements to ensure that—

(1) the base offense level and existing enhancements contained in United States Sentencing Guideline 2J1.2 relating to obstruction of justice are sufficient to deter and punish that activity;

(2) the enhancements and specific offense characteristics relating to obstruction of justice are adequate in cases where—

(A) the destruction, alteration, or fabrication of evidence involves—

(i) a large amount of evidence, a large number of participants, or is otherwise extensive;

(ii) the selection of evidence that is particularly probative or essential to the investigation; or

(iii) more than minimal planning; or

(B) the offense involved abuse of a special skill or a position of trust;

(3) the guideline offense levels and enhancements for violations of section 1519 or 1520 of title 18, United States Code, as added by this title, are sufficient to deter and punish that activity;

(4) a specific offense characteristic enhancing sentencing is provided under United States Sentencing Guideline 2B1.1 (as in effect on the date of enactment of this Act) for a fraud offense that endangers the solvency or financial security of a substantial number of victims; and

(5) the guidelines that apply to organizations in United States Sentencing Guidelines, chapter 8, are sufficient to deter and punish organizational criminal misconduct.

(b) EMERGENCY AUTHORITY AND DEADLINE FOR COMMISSION ACTION.—The United States Sentencing Commission is requested to promulgate the guidelines or amendments provided for under this section as soon as practicable, and in any event not later than 180 days after the date of enactment of this Act, in accordance with the procedures set forth in section 219(a) of the Sentencing Reform Act of 1987, as though the authority under that Act had not expired.

SEC. 806. PROTECTION FOR EMPLOYEES OF PUBLICLY TRADED COMPANIES WHO PROVIDE EVIDENCE OF FRAUD.

(a) IN GENERAL.—Chapter 73 of title 18, United States Code, is amended by inserting after section 1514 the following:

"§ 1514A. Civil action to protect against retaliation in fraud cases

"(a) WHISTLEBLOWER PROTECTION FOR EMPLOYEES OF PUBLICLY TRADED COMPANIES.—No company with a class of securities registered under section 12 of the Securities Exchange Act of 1934 (15 U.S.C. 78l), or that is required to file reports under section 15(d) of the Securities Exchange Act of 1934 (15 U.S.C. 78o(d)), or any other officer, employee contractor, subcontractor, or agent of such company, may discharge, demote, suspend, threaten, harass, or in any other manner discriminate against an employee in the terms and conditions of employment because of any lawful act done by the employee—

"(1) to provide information, cause information to be provided, or otherwise assist in an investigation regarding any conduct which the employee reasonably believes constitutes a violation of section 1341, 1343, 1344, or 1348, any rule or regulation of the Securities and Exchange Commission, or any provision of Federal law relating to fraud against shareholders, when the information or assistance is provided to or the investigation is conducted by—

"(A) a Federal regulatory or law enforcement agency;

"(B) any Member of Congress or any committee of Congress; or

"(C) a person with supervisory authority over the employee (or such other person working for the employer who has the authority to investigate, discover, or terminate misconduct); or

"(2) to file, cause to be filed, testify, participate in, or otherwise assist in a proceeding filed or about to be filed (with any knowledge of the employer) relating to an alleged violation of section 1341, 1343, 1344, or 1348, any rule or regulation of the Securities and Exchange Commission, or any provision of Federal law relating to fraud against shareholders."

(b) ENFORCEMENT ACTION.—

"(1) IN GENERAL.—A person who alleges discharge or other discrimination by any person in violation of subsection (a) may seek relief under subsection (c), by—

"(A) filing a complaint with the Secretary of Labor; or

"(B) if the Secretary has not issued a final decision within 180 days of the filing of the complaint and there is no showing that such delay is due to the bad faith of the claimant, bringing an action at law or equity for de novo review in the appropriate district court of the United States, which shall have jurisdiction over such an action without regard to the amount in controversy."

(2) PROCEDURE.—

"(A) IN GENERAL.—An action under paragraph (1)(A) shall be governed under the rules and procedures set forth in section 42121(b) of title 49, United States Code.

"(B) EXCEPTION.—Notification made under section 42121(b)(1) of title 49, United States Code, shall be made to the person named in the complaint and to the employer.

"(C) BURDENS OF PROOF.—An action brought under paragraph (1)(B) shall be governed by the legal burdens of proof set forth in section 42121(b) of title 49, United States Code.

"(D) STATUTE OF LIMITATIONS.—An action under paragraph (1) shall be commenced not later than 90 days after the date on which the violation occurs.

"(c) REMEDIES.—

"(1) IN GENERAL.—An employee prevailing in any action under subsection (b)(1) shall be entitled to all relief necessary to make the employee whole.

"(2) COMPENSATORY DAMAGES.—Relief for any action under paragraph (1) shall include— "(A) reinstatement with the same seniority status that the employee would have had, but for the discrimination;

"(B) the amount of back pay, with interest; and

"(C) compensation for any special damages sustained as a result of the discrimination, including litigation costs, expert witness fees, and reasonable attorney fees.

"(d) RIGHTS RETAINED BY EMPLOYEE.—Nothing in this section shall be deemed to diminish the rights, privileges, or remedies of any employee under any Federal or State law, or under any collective bargaining agreement.".

(b) CLERICAL AMENDMENT.—The table of sections at the beginning of chapter 73 of title 18, United States Code, is amended by inserting after the item relating to section 1514 the following new item:

"1514A. Civil action to protect against retaliation in fraud cases.".

SEC. 807. CRIMINAL PENALTIES FOR DEFRAUDING SHAREHOLDERS OF PUBLICLY TRADED COMPANIES.

(a) IN GENERAL.—Chapter 63 of title 18, United States Code, is amended by adding at the end the following:

"§ 1348. Securities fraud

"Whoever knowingly executes, or attempts to execute, a scheme or artifice—

"(1) to defraud any person in connection with any security of an issuer with a class of securities registered under section 12 of the Securities Exchange Act of 1934 (15 U.S.C. 78l) or that is required to file reports under section 15(d) of the Securities Exchange Act of 1934 (15 U.S.C. 78o(d)); or

"(2) to obtain, by means of false or fraudulent pretenses, representations, or promises, any money or property in connection with the purchase or sale of any security of an issuer with a class of securities registered under section 12 of the Securities Exchange Act of 1934 (15 U.S.C. 78l) or that is required to file reports under section 15(d) of the Securities Exchange Act of 1934 (15 U.S.C. 78o(d));

shall be fined under this title, or imprisoned not more than 25 years, or both.".

(b) CLERICAL AMENDMENT.—The table of sections at the beginning of chapter 63 of title 18, United States Code, is amended by adding at the end the following new item:

"1348. Securities fraud.".

TITLE IX—WHITE-COLLAR CRIME PENALTY ENHANCEMENTS

SEC. 901. SHORT TITLE.

This title may be cited as the "White-Collar Crime Penalty Enhancement Act of 2002".

SEC. 902. ATTEMPTS AND CONSPIRACIES TO COMMIT CRIMINAL FRAUD OFFENSES.

(a) IN GENERAL.—Chapter 63 of title 18, United States Code, is amended by inserting after section 1348 as added by this Act the following:

"§ 1349. Attempt and conspiracy

"Any person who attempts or conspires to commit any offense under this chapter shall be subject to the same penalties as those prescribed for the offense, the commission of which was the object of the attempt or conspiracy.

(b) CLERICAL AMENDMENT.—The table of sections at the beginning of chapter 63 of title 18, United States Code, is amended by adding at the end the following new item:

"1349. Attempt and conspiracy.".

SEC. 903. CRIMINAL PENALTIES FOR MAIL AND WIRE FRAUD.

(a) MAIL FRAUD.—Section 1341 of title 18, United States Code, is amended by striking "five" and inserting "20".

(b) WIRE FRAUD.—Section 1343 of title 18, United States Code, is amended by striking "five" and inserting "20".

SEC. 904. CRIMINAL PENALTIES FOR VIOLATIONS OF THE EMPLOYEE RETIREMENT INCOME SECURITY ACT OF 1974.

Section 501 of the Employee Retirement Income Security Act of 1974 (29 U.S.C. 1131) is amended—

(1) by striking "$ 5,000" and inserting "$ 100,000";

(2) by striking "one year" and inserting "10 years"; and

(3) by striking "$ 100,000" and inserting "$ 500,000".

SEC. 905. AMENDMENT TO SENTENCING GUIDELINES RELATING TO CERTAIN WHITE-COLLAR OFFENSES.

(a) DIRECTIVE TO THE UNITED STATES SENTENCING COMMISSION.—Pursuant to its authority under section 994(p) of title 18, United States Code, and in accordance with this section, the United States Sentencing Commission shall review and, as appropriate, amend the Federal Sentencing Guidelines and related policy statements to implement the provisions of this Act.

(b) REQUIREMENTS.—In carrying out this section, the Sentencing Commission shall—

(1) ensure that the sentencing guidelines and policy statements reflect the serious nature of the offenses and the penalties set forth in this Act, the growing incidence of serious fraud offenses which are identified above, and the need to modify the sentencing guidelines and policy statements to deter, prevent, and punish such offenses;

(2) consider the extent to which the guidelines and policy statements adequately address whether the guideline offense levels and enhancements for violations of the sections amended by this Act are sufficient to deter and punish such offenses, and specifically, are adequate in view of the statutory increases in penalties contained in this Act;

(3) assure reasonable consistency with other relevant directives and sentencing guidelines;

(4) account for any additional aggravating or mitigating circumstances

H. R. 3763—62

(that might justify exceptions to the generally applicable sentencing ranges;

5) make any necessary conforming changes to the sentencing guidelines; and

(6) assure that the guidelines adequately meet the purposes of sentencing, as set forth in section 3553(a)(2) of title 18, United States Code.

(c) EMERGENCY AUTHORITY AND DEADLINE FOR COMMISSION ACTION.—The United States Sentencing Commission is requested to promulgate the guidelines or amendments provided for under this section as soon as practicable, and in any event not later than 180 days after the date of enactment of this Act, in accordance with the procedures set forth in section 219(a) of the Sentencing Reform Act of 1987, as though the authority under that Act had not expired.

SEC. 906. CORPORATE RESPONSIBILITY FOR FINANCIAL REPORTS.

(a) IN GENERAL.—Chapter 63 of title 18, United States Code, is amended by inserting after section 1349, as created by this Act, the following:

"§ 1350. Failure of corporate officers to certify financial reports

(a) CERTIFICATION OF PERIODIC FINANCIAL REPORTS.—Each periodic report containing financial statements filed by an issuer with the Securities Exchange Commission pursuant to section 13(a) or 15(d) of the Securities Exchange Act of 1934 (15 U.S.C. 78m(a) or 78o(d)) shall be accompanied by a written statement by the chief executive officer and chief financial officer (or equivalent thereof) of the issuer.

"(b) CONTENT.—The statement required under subsection (a) shall certify that the periodic report containing the financial statements fully complies with the requirements of section 13(a) or 15(d) of the Securities Exchange Act pf 1934 (15 U.S.C. 78m or 78o(d)) and that information contained in the periodic report fairly presents, in all material respects, the financial condition and results of operations of the issuer.

"(c) CRIMINAL PENALTIES.—Whoever—

"(1) certifies any statement as set forth in subsections (a) and (b) of this section knowing that the periodic report accompanying the statement does not comport with all the requirements set forth in this section shall be fined not more than $1,000,000 or imprisoned not more than 10 years, or both; or

"(2) willfully certifies any statement as set forth in subsections (a) and (b) of this section knowing that the periodic report accompanying the statement does not comport with all the requirements set forth in this section shall be fined not more than $5,000,000, or imprisoned not more than 20 years, or both.".

(b) CLERICAL AMENDMENT.—The table of sections at the beginning of chapter 63 of title 18, United States Code, is amended by adding at the end the following:

"1350. Failure of corporate officers to certify financial reports.".

TITLE X—CORPORATE TAX RETURNS

SEC. 1001. SENSE OF THE SENATE REGARDING THE SIGNING OF CORPORATE TAX RETURNS BY CHIEF EXECUTIVE OFFICERS.

It is the sense of the Senate that the Federal income tax return of a corporation should be signed by the chief executive officer of such corporation.

TITLE XI—CORPORATE FRAUD ACCOUNTABILITY SEC. 1101. SHORT TITLE.

This title may be cited as the "Corporate Fraud Accountability Act of 2002".

SEC. 1102. TAMPERING WITH A RECORD OR OTHERWISE IMPEDING AN OFFICIAL PROCEEDING.

Section 1512 of title 18, United States Code, is amended—

(1) by redesignating subsections (c) through (i) as sub-sections (d) through (j), respectively; and

(2) by inserting after subsection (b) the following new sub-section:

"(c) Whoever corruptly—

"(1) alters, destroys, mutilates, or conceals a record, document, or other object, or attempts to do so, with the intent to impair the object's integrity or availability for use in an official proceeding; or

"(2) otherwise obstructs, influences, or impedes any official proceeding, or attempts to do so, shall be fined under this title or imprisoned not more than 20 years, or both.".

SEC. 1103. TEMPORARY FREEZE AUTHORITY FOR THE SECURITIES AND EXCHANGE COMMISSION.

(a) IN GENERAL.—Section 21C(c) of the Securities Exchange Act of 1934 (15 U.S.C. 78u–3(c)) is amended by adding at the end the following:

"(3) TEMPORARY FREEZE.—

"(A) IN GENERAL.—

"(i) ISSUANCE OF TEMPORARY ORDER.—Whenever, during the course of a lawful investigation involving possible violations of the Federal securities laws by an issuer of publicly traded securities or any of its directors, officers, partners, controlling persons, agents, or employees, it shall appear to the Commission that it is likely that the issuer will make extraordinary payments (whether compensation or otherwise) to any of the foregoing persons, the Commission may petition a Federal district court for a temporary order requiring the issuer to escrow, subject to court supervision, those payments in an interest-bearing account for 45 days.

"(ii) STANDARD.—A temporary order shall be entered under clause

(i), only after notice and opportunity for a hearing, unless the court determines that notice and hearing prior to entry of the order notice and hearing prior to entry of the order would be impracticable or contrary to the public interest.

"(iii) EFFECTIVE PERIOD.—A temporary order issued under clause (i) shall—

"(I) become effective immediately;

"(II) be served upon the parties subject to it; and

"(III) unless set aside, limited or suspended by a court of competent jurisdiction, shall remain effective and enforceable for 45 days.

"(iv) EXTENSIONS AUTHORIZED.—The effective period of an order under this subparagraph may be extended by the court upon good cause shown for not longer than 45 additional days, provided that the combined period of the order shall not exceed 90 days.

"(B) PROCESS ON DETERMINATION OF VIOLATIONS.—

"(i) VIOLATIONS CHARGED.—If the issuer or other person described in subparagraph (A) is charged with any violation of the Federal securities laws before the expiration of the effective period of a temporary order under subparagraph (A) (including any applicable extension period), the order shall remain in effect, subject to court approval, until the conclusion of any legal proceedings related thereto, and the affected issuer or other person, shall have the right to petition the court for review of the order.

"(ii) VIOLATIONS NOT CHARGED.—If the issuer or other person described in subparagraph (A) is not charged with any violation of the Federal securities laws before the expiration of the effective period of a temporary order under subparagraph (A) (including any applicable extension period), the escrow shall terminate at the expiration of the 45-day effective period (or the expiration of any extension period, as applicable), and the disputed payments (with accrued interest) shall be returned to the issuer or other affected person.".

(b) TECHNICAL AMENDMENT.—Section 21C(c)(2) of the Securities Exchange Act of 1934 (15 U.S.C. 78u–3(c)(2)) is amended by striking "This" and inserting "paragraph (1)".

SEC. 1104. AMENDMENT TO THE FEDERAL SENTENCING GUIDELINES.

(a) REQUEST FOR IMMEDIATE CONSIDERATION BY THE UNITED STATES SENTENCING COMMISSION.—Pursuant to its authority under section 994(p) of title 28, United States Code, and in accordance with this section, the United States Sentencing Commission is requested to—

(1) promptly review the sentencing guidelines applicable to securities and accounting fraud and related offenses;

(2) expeditiously consider the promulgation of new sentencing guidelines or amendments to existing sentencing guidelines to provide an enhancement for officers or directors of publicly traded corporations who commit fraud and related offenses; and

(3) submit to Congress an explanation of actions taken by the Sentencing

Index